A HISTORY
OF THE
MODERN
WORLD

SINCE 1815

Contemporary Europe

WHITE
SEA

Archangel

Dvina R.

L. Onega

adoga

Smolensk

Moscow

RUSSIAN SOVIET FEDERATED
SOCIALIST REPUBLIC

Kuibyshev

Volga R.

Uralsk

Ural R.

KAZAKH S.S.R.

ARAL
SEA

S O V I E T   U N I O N

Kursk

Volgograd
(Stalingrad)

UZBEK S.S.R.

Kiev

Kharkov

Astrakhan

UKRAINIAN S.S.R.

Dnepropetrovsk

Don R.

Rostov

TURKMEN S.S.R.

MOLDAVIAN
S.S.R.

Dnieper R.

SEA OF
AZOV

Grozny

C A S P I A N   S E A

Krasnovodsk

RABIA

Odessa

CRIMEA

C A U C A S I A

GEORGIAN
S.S.R.

Tiflis

AZERBAIJAN
S.S.R.

Baku

AFGHANISTAN

Sevastopol

Batum

ARMENIAN
S.S.R.

BLACK SEA

DOBRUJA

Ardahan

Kars

Yerevan

Varna

Sinop

L. Van

Tabriz

L. Urmia

Teheran

I R A N

Bosporus

Istanbul

Ankara

T   U   R   K   E   Y

Tigris R.

Kirkuk

Isfahan

Dardanelles

Izmir

Adana

Aleppo

Euphrates R.

Baghdad

Antalya

SYRIA

I R A Q

CYPRUS

Beirut

Damascus

Basra

Abadan

Bushire

LEBANON

KUWAIT

P E R S I A N   G U L F

CRETE (Greece)

GOLAN
HEIGHTS

Occupied by Israel

ISRAEL

WEST BANK

UNITED ARAB

Tel Aviv-Jaffa

Amman

BAHRAIN

EMIRATES

OMAN

Jerusalem

Gaza

JORDAN

QATAR

Alexandria

NILE DELTA

El Alamein

Nile R.

Suez Canal

SINAI
PENINSULA

Aqaba

S A U D I   A R A B I A

Cairo

GULF OF SUEZ

GULF OF AQABA

EGYPT

SEVENTH EDITION

A History of the Modern World

Since 1815

R. R. Palmer

Joel Colton

McGraw-Hill, Inc.
New York   St. Louis   San Francisco   Auckland   Bogotá   Caracas   Hamburg
Lisbon   London   Madrid   Mexico   Milan   Montreal   New Delhi   Paris
San Juan   São Paulo   Singapore   Sydney   Tokyo   Toronto

A HISTORY OF THE MODERN WORLD SINCE 1815

1 2 3 4 5 6 7 8 9 0 VNH VNH 9 0 9 8 7 6 5 4 3 2 1

ISBN 0-07-048565-8

This book was set in Times Roman by Monotype Composition Company.
The editors were David Follmer, Niels Aaboe, and Linda Richmond;
the production supervisor was Annette Mayeski.
The cover was designed by Wanda Siedlecka.
The photo editor was Kathy Bendo.
Von Hoffmann Press, Inc., was printer and binder.

Library of Congress Cataloging-in-Publication Data

Palmer, R. R. (Robert Roswell), (date).
    A history of the modern world / R. R. Palmer, Joel Colton. — 7th ed.
        p.   cm.
    Includes bibliographical references and indexes.
    Contents: [1] To 1815 — [2] Since 1815.
    ISBN 0-07-048564-X (v. 1). — ISBN 0-07-048565-8 (v. 2)
    1. History, Modern.   I. Colton, Joel, (date).   II. Title.
D209.P26   1992
909.08—dc20   91-12595

Acknowledgment is hereby made for permission to quote from the following works:

World Population, by A. N. Carr-Saunders. Clarendon Press, Oxford (1936).

British Economic Growth, 1688–1959: Trends and Structure, by Phyllis Deane and W. A. Cole (1962). Reprinted by permission of Cambridge University Press.

"The White Man's Burden" from *The Five Nations* by Rudyard Kipling. Reprinted by permission of The National Trust and Doubleday & Company, Inc.

European Historical Statistics: 1750–1970, by B. R. Mitchell, pp. 316 and 396. Copyright © 1975 by Columbia University Press.

CONTENTS

ILLUSTRATIONS

MAPS AND CHARTS

PREFACE

[*Publisher's Note:* In order to provide an alternative to the hardcover edition, *A History of the Modern World* is being made available in a two-volume paperbound edition. Volume I, *To 1815,* includes chapters I–X; volume II, *Since 1815,* chapters XI–XXIII. The page numbering in these chapters remains the same as in the hardcover text, and the footnotes refer to pages in both volumes.]

ONCE AGAIN we take pleasure in offering a new edition, now the seventh, of a work that continues to be well received. In its content and coverage *A History of the Modern World* remains very much what it was in the sixth edition. Both of us, however, have carefully worked together over the whole volume in another effort to make it more useful and attractive.

The principal new feature is that the period since the end of the Second World War has been completely rearranged and rewritten, and is now presented in three chapters instead of two. The forty-five years since 1945 thus receive as much attention as the similar time spans from Bismarck's unification of Germany to the First World War, or from the American Revolution to the fall of Napoleon. Among other new elements are a new picture essay, a few new maps and tables, some alterations made in response to readers' comments, and various emendations in many places. The bibliography has always been a special feature of the book. It has been brought up to date; and although reviewed and pruned, it remains very extensive, containing perhaps 4,000 titles classified by subject according to the plan of the book as a whole. In general, we have done what we could to make so long and complex a volume more manageable and digestible. The whole structure of chapters, sections and subsections, the frequent cross-references, the chronological tables, and the detailed index are intended for this purpose. A student's Study Guide is also available for those who may wish to use it.

Since its first edition the book has been designed as a history both of Europe and of the "modern world." Emphasis falls on situations and movements of international scope, on what Europeans and their descendants in other continents have done in common, and on the gradual convergence of the European and non-European worlds into a global economy and an interdependent political system. National histories are therefore somewhat subordinated, and in each national history the points of contact with a larger civilization are emphasized. Historic regional differences within Europe, as between western and eastern Europe, are brought out, and the history of the Americas is woven into the story at various points, as are developments of the past two centuries in Asia and Africa. A good deal of institutional history is included. Considerable space is given to the history of ideas, not only in special sections devoted to ideas, but throughout the book in close connection with the account of institutions and events. Social and economic development bulks rather large, as does the impact of wars and revolutions. Since our own age is one in which much depends on political decision, we think of this volume as political history in the broadest sense, in that matters of many kinds, such as religion, economics, social welfare, and international relations, have presented themselves as public questions requiring public action by responsible citizens or governments. It seems to us that many subjects of current research interest, such as women's history, family history, the history of the laboring classes, the history of minorities, or demographic and quantitative studies, are best understood when seen within a wider framework such as this book attempts to provide.

We are again glad to thank all those who have helped with the book over the years, and in particular the half-dozen persons who have acted as consultants for this seventh edition. We are indebted to David Follmer, Niels Aaboe, and Linda Richmond of McGraw-Hill, Inc., our new publisher for this edition. Since they have left the important decisions to us, and all the actual writing is ours, we assume all responsibility for errors, imperfections, questionable judgments, and other possible shortcomings. Esther Howard Palmer and Shirley Baron Colton have contributed in innumerable ways to the newest edition of this history, which can stand as some kind of continuing monument to marriage, friendship, and intellectual collaboration.

R. R. PALMER
JOEL COLTON

A FEW
WORDS ON
GEOGRAPHY

HISTORY IS the experience of human beings in time, but it takes place also in space, on the planet Earth, so that geography always underlies it. It is the business of geography not merely to describe and map the earth and its various areas, but to study the changing relationships between human activities and the surrounding environment.

The earth is over four billion years old. The entire history of mankind since the Middle Stone Age has occupied less than a hundred-thousandth of the time in which the earthly habitat has been developed. Some minerals now put to human use were formed in the earliest ages of the planet, others such as coal and petroleum were not laid down until a few hundred million years ago, but none that are now being consumed in a flicker of geologic time can ever be replaced. Oceans and continents have moved about, changing in size, shape, and location with respect to one another and to the North and South Poles. There was a time when dinosaurs could walk from North America to Europe (as we now call them) on solid land in a warm climate. The continents as we know them became fully distinct less than a hundred million years ago. It is only a few thousand years since the end of the most recent glacial age, which may not be the last. The melting back into the ocean of water frozen over a mile thick in Antarctica and in large parts of North America and Europe produced the coastlines, offshore islands, inland seas, straits, bays, and harbors that we see on a map today, as well as some of the largest river systems and lakes. It is only about three hundred years since the first French explorers saw Niagara Falls, which then looked quite different, because by eating away the underlying rock the falls have receded several hundred feet since that time.

At present, the oceans cover more than two-thirds of the surface of the globe. By no means is all the remaining third suited for occupation by human beings, or indeed by most other animal or vegetable organisms, for much of the land still lies under perpetual ice in Antarctica and Greenland, much is tundra, much is desert, and some is along the windswept ridges of high mountains. Like the oceans, these desolate regions have been important in human history, first in earlier times by acting as barriers. Man, as the anthropologists call him (and her), is now thought to have originated in Africa. He (and she) eventually spread to every continent except Antarctica. In doing so, human groups became isolated from each other for thousands of years, separated by oceans, deserts, or mountains, and so became differentiated into the modern races, though all are derived from the same source and belong to the same species. The same is true of cultures or civilizations over a time period measured in centuries rather than millennia. It is such separation that accounts for the historic cultural differences between Africa, pre-Columbian America, China, India, the Middle East, and Europe. On a smaller scale it explains the differences in languages and dialects.

Separation has also produced differences in flora and fauna, and hence in the plants and animals by which humans live. Wheat became the most usual cereal in the Middle East and Europe, millet and rice in East Asia, sorghum in tropical Africa, maize in pre-Columbian America. The horse, first domesticated in central Asia, was for centuries a mainstay of Europe for muscle power, transportation, and combat, while the less versatile camel was adopted later and more slowly in the Middle East, and America had no beasts of burden except the llama. Not until Europeans began to cross the oceans, taking plants and animals with them, and bringing others back, did these great differences begin to diminish.

The present book is concerned primarily with Europe, and with the last few hundred years. And as a traveler setting out on a journey may obtain a map, study it, and keep its contents as much as possible in mind, so the reader is invited to examine the map of Europe on pages xviii and xix, and keep it in mind while reading the following history. The map shows the topographical features that have remained unchanged in historic times.

Europe is physically separated from Africa by the Mediterranean Sea, which however has been as much a passageway as a barrier. A more effective barrier was created when the Sahara Desert dried up only a few thousand years ago. The physical separation of Europe from Asia has always been less clear; the conventional boundary has long been the Ural Mountains in the Soviet Union, but the Soviet Union recognizes no such distinction. The Urals are in any case low and wide, and it can be argued that Europe is not a continent at all, but a cultural conception arising from felt differences from Asia and Africa. Europe, even with European Russia, contains hardly more than 6 percent of the land surface of the earth. It has about the same area as the United States including Alaska. It is a little larger than Australia, and a little smaller than Antarctica.

If we consider only its physical features Europe is indeed one of several peninsulas jutting off from Asia. It is altogether different, however, from the Arabian and Indian peninsulas, which also extend from the mass of Asia, as shown on the back end papers of the present book. For one thing, the Mediterranean Sea is unique among the world's bodies of water. Closed in by the Strait of Gibraltar, which is only eight miles wide, it is more shielded than the Caribbean or East Asian seas from the open ocean. Hence it has very little tide, and is protected from the most violent ocean storms. Though over two thousand miles long, it is subdivided by islands and peninsulas into lesser seas with an identity of their own, such as the Aegean and Adriatic, and it gives access also to the Black Sea. It is possible to travel for great distances without being far from land, so that navigation developed from early times, and one of the first civilizations appeared on the island of Crete. It is possible also to cross between Europe and Asia at the Bosporus and between Europe and Africa at Gibraltar, so that populations became mixed by early migrations, and various historic empires—Carthaginian, Roman, Byzantine, Arabic, Spanish, Venetian, and Turkish—have used the Mediterranean as an avenue between their component parts. After the Suez Canal was built the Mediterranean became a segment in the "lifeline of empire" for the British Empire in its heyday.

In southern Europe, north of the Mediterranean and running for its whole length, is a series of mountains, produced geologically by the pushing of the gigantic mass of Africa against this smaller Eurasian peninsula. The Pyrenees shut off Spain from the north, as the Alps do Italy; the Balkan Mountains have always been difficult to penetrate; and the only place where one can go at water level from the Mediterranean to the north is by the valley of the Rhone River, so that France, since it came together in the Middle Ages, is the only country that clearly belongs both to the Mediterranean and to northern Europe. North of the mountains is a great plain, with branches in England and Sweden, extending from western France through Germany and Poland into Russia and on into Asia, passing south of the Urals through what is called the Caspian Gate, north of the landlocked Caspian Sea. One might draw a straight line from Amsterdam eastward through the Caspian Gate as far as the borders of western China, and although this line would reach the distance from New York to a point five hundred miles west of San Francisco, one would never in traveling along it be higher above sea level than central Kansas. The continuity of this level plain has at various times opened Europe to Mongol and other invasions, enabled the Russians to move east and create a huge empire, and made Poland a troubled intermediary between Western Europe and what is now the Soviet Union.

The rivers as shown on the map are worth particular attention. Until quite recent times rivers offered an easier means of transportation than any form of carriage by land. The principal rivers also give access to the sea. Most are navigable, especially in the north European plains. With their valleys, whether in level country or confined between mountains, they provided areas where intensive local development could take place. Thus we see that some of the most important older cities of Europe are on rivers—London on the Thames, Paris on the Seine, Vienna and Budapest on the Danube, Warsaw on the Vistula. In northern Europe it was often possible to move goods from one river to another, and then in the eighteenth century to connect them by canals; and the networks of rivers and canals still carry much heavy traffic by barges. The importance of water is shown again by the location of Copenhagen, Stockholm, and Leningrad (formerly St. Petersburg) on the Baltic, which is a kind of inland lake, and of Amsterdam and Lisbon, which grew up after the ocean could be traversed by Europeans.

There are many important geographical conditions that a topographic map cannot show. One is climate, which depends on latitude, ocean currents, and winds that bring or withhold rainfall. In latitude Europe lies as far north as the northern United States and southern Canada, with Madrid and Rome in the latitude of New York, and with Stockholm and Leningrad as far north as the middle of Hudson Bay. All Europe thus is within what is called the temperate zone, somewhat misleadingly, since the temperate zone is by definition the region of pronounced difference between winter and summer. But the parts of Europe that are near the sea have less extreme temperatures than the corresponding northerly regions of America, and the Mediterranean countries have more sunshine and less severe winters than either northern Europe or the northern

WHITE SEA

N. Dvina R.

L. Onega

L. Ladoga

• Leningrad

NORTH RUSSIAN PLAIN

CENTRAL RUSSIAN HIGHLANDS

• Moscow

Volga R.

Oka R.

Kama R.

URAL MOUNTAINS

Tobol R.

Ishim R.

Areas Below Sea Level

0   100   200   300 miles

VOLGA HEIGHTS

Ural R.

BLACK EARTH REGION

KIRGHIZ STEPPE

Syr Darya

Pripet R.

PRIPET
MARSHES

Kiev •

Dnieper R.

Donets R.

Don R.

Volga R.

CASPIAN DEPRESSION

ARAL
SEA

TURANIAN PLAIN

Amu Darya

BLACK

Bug R.

DONETS HEIGHTS

Dniester R.

Pruth R.

CRIMEA

• Odessa

SEA OF
AZOV

CAUCASUS MOUNTAINS

CASPIAN SEA

IANS

NIAN ALPS

• Bucharest

N OF
LLACHIA

Danube R.

N MTS.

Maritsa R.

ODOPE
TS.

Bosporus

• Istanbul

SEA OF
MARMARA

• Ankara

Dardanelles

ASIA MINOR
(ANATOLIAN PENINSULA)

BLACK SEA

ARMENIAN
HIGHLANDS

Araxes R.

L. Van

L. Urmia

ELBURZ MTS.

• Teheran

ZAGROS

MTS.

AEGEAN SEA

hens SEA

DODECANESE I.

Meander R.

TAURUS MOUNTAINS

Kizilirmak

RHODES

CYPRUS

MESOPOTAMIAN PLAINS

Tigris R.

Euphrates R.

• Baghdad

CRETE

SYRIAN

DESERT

PERSIAN GULF

SEA OF GALILEE
Jordan R.

• Jerusalem

DEAD SEA

Alexandria •

NILE DELTA

Suez Canal

Cairo •

Nile R.

GULF
OF SUEZ

SINAI
PENINSULA

GULF OF
AQABA

NEFUD DESERT

United States. Everywhere, however, the winters are cold enough to keep out certain diseases by which warmer countries are afflicted. They have also obliged the inhabitants to expend more effort on clothing, housing, and heating. Warm summers with their growing seasons have produced an annual cycle of agriculture, for which rainfall has been adequate but not excessive. Although the Spanish plateau is arid, and the Mediterranean shores are subject to seasonal variations of rainfall, Europe is the only continent that has no actual desert. Thanks to a combination of causes, including rainfall, ground water, deposits left by retreating glaciers, the character of the underlying rock, and the alternate freezing and thawing, Europe is also for the most part a region of fertile soils. In short, since the end of the Ice Age, or since humans learned how to survive the winters, Europe has been one of the most favored places on the globe for human habitation. In recent times it has been, as shown by the insets of the two maps on pps. II–III and on the back end papers in this book, one of the few large regions, along with China and India, of very high density of population.

Climate itself can change. The Roman ruins in the interior of Morocco and Tunisia remind us that the climate there was once more favorable. Studies of tree rings, fossil plants, and alpine glaciers show that average temperatures were warmer from the end of the Ice Age throughout ancient and medieval times, and then fell during what is called the "little Ice Age" from about 1400 to 1850, when the winters lengthened and the growing season shortened, without drastic consequences for the people, who by that time could simply wear more wool, so that sheep raising and the woolen trade became a main staple of European commerce.

There is no geographical determinism. Climate and the environment not only set limits but provide opportunities for what human beings can do. What happens depends on the application of knowledge and abilities in any particular time and place. A broad river is an obstruction and hence a good boundary under simple conditions; it is less so after bridges connect the two sides. The oceans that long divided mankind became a highway for the Portuguese, Spanish, Dutch, French, and English, and later for others. Distance, which any good map will show by its scale, also varies in its effects according to the means of transportation; it must be remembered that for most of human history neither persons, information, nor commands could travel much more than thirty miles a day, so that localism prevailed, and large organizations, in trade or government, were hard to create and to maintain. For most of its history Europe was in fact made up of a diversity of small local units, pockets of territory each having its own customs, ways of life, and manner of speech, each largely unknown to the others and looking inward upon itself, rather than of the blocks called "Germany" or "France" that we take for granted on a map today. A "foreigner" might come from a thousand miles away or from only ten.

What constitutes a natural resource varies with the state of technology and the possibilities of exchange. The tin of Cornwall at the western tip of Britain became an important resource as long ago as the early Bronze Age, when despite its remoteness it gave rise to some of the first long-distance European trade. Deposits of coal were not massively exploited until the nineteenth century, and petroleum was of no significance, nor even known, until about a century ago. It is a big fact of human history, rather than of geologic history, that some of the world's greatest coal beds happened to be in northwestern Europe and the United States, which could more readily industrialize because they had easy access to abundant fuel, over which they had control, an advantage that was lost as they became more dependent on natural gas and oil. If the future is like the past, it will see a similar conversion of natural materials into natural resources.

The Mediterranean coasts were more wooded three thousand years ago than they are today. It was not only the change of climate that changed their appearance. Many human generations spent in cutting timber, pasturing goats, and planting vines and olives brought about erosion and depletion of the soil. Europe north of the mountains was heavily forested before human intervention. Trees were cut down and burned there as in America centuries later, so that the landscape slowly became an orderly expanse of carefully tended fields, still interrupted by woodlands. The state of agriculture obviously depends on natural conditions. But it depends historically also on the invention and improvement of the plow, the finding of appropriate crops, the rotation of fields to prevent soil exhaustion, and the introduction of livestock from which manure can be obtained as a fertilizer. Socially, agriculture benefits from the existence of stable village communities, and is affected by demographic changes; if a population falls as a result of war or epidemics, some fields will be abandoned and return to "nature"; if population grows, new and less fertile or more distant areas will be brought under cultivation. Nor can agriculture be improved without the building of roads, a division of labor between town and country, and some degree of regional specialization, so that some areas may grow cereals, others raise livestock, and still others be devoted to orchards and vineyards. Basic to agriculture, as to other enterprises, is elementary security. Farming cannot proceed, nor food be stored over the winter, unless the men and women who work the fields can be protected from attack by marauders, brigands, barbarian invaders, warring chiefs, or hostile armies. Such protection, or what might be called the normalcy of peace, was for several centuries imposed by the Roman Empire, in more recent times (barring wars) by the national state, and in between by barons who at least protected the peasants who worked for them, and by kings attempting to pacify their kingdoms.

For maps with exact detail, or extensive coverage, it is best to consult a good historical atlas, of which several are listed in the bibliography at the end of this book. Over fifty maps are included in the present volume, but some are only diagrams rather than true maps; all are intended to supplement the written text, by showing the location and geographical spread of matters under discussion. Many of the maps are mainly designed to show political boundaries at particular dates. Readers in looking at them can use their imagination to fill in the mountains and rivers that these maps cannot show but which can be important for an understanding of the extent of political power. Readers can also, by using their imagination and consulting the scale, convert space into time, remembering that until the invention of the railroad both people and news traveled far more slowly than today, or that at a rate of thirty miles a day it would take three weeks to travel from London to Venice, and at least six weeks for an exchange of letters. In human terms Europe has not been such a small place after all.

PROLOGUE:
A REVOLUTIONARY
HALF-CENTURY

The French Revolution
The Napoleonic Empire
The Peace Settlement of 1814–1815

THE READER will see, if only by looking at the page numbers, that this book is the second half of a larger work. It begins quite abruptly with Europe in the year 1815. It may be asked why a modern history should begin with 1815, and why an account of the modern world seems to be mainly about Europe.

There is no spectacular date to signify the opening of modern times. Yet it is necessary to begin somewhere, and the year 1815 is convenient, because it was in that year that Napoleon Bonaparte was finally defeated at Waterloo, and his attempt at building a European empire was ended. A long period of revolutionary turmoil came to a close in 1815. It had lasted for almost half a century if we count from the American Revolution, which had broken up the old British Empire, temporarily weakened France, and established the United States of America. The new American republic aroused great interest in Europe, for it gave a new meaning and a new force to ideas of constitutional government and of political rights and civil liberties. These ideas were magnified and geographically extended by the French Revolution of 1789. For twenty years, from 1794 to 1814, a renovated France dominated the European continent. The early stages of movements for Latin American independence also began. Looking either to Europe or the Americas, anyone forty years old in 1815 had personal memories of staggering events.

What such a person could not know was, of course, the future, which, as it turned out, was to be a time of extraordinary change. The century from 1815 to 1914, or from the collapse of Napoleon's empire to the First World War, was precisely the period when the modernization of Europe proceeded most rapidly. These hundred years saw the increasing use of power machinery in the Industrial Revolution, the revolution in transportation by the railroad and steamship, the rise of almost instant communications with the telegraph and ocean cables, the development of world markets, modern science, and huge manufacturing and commercial cities. Social classes were restructured; where formerly the difference between aristocrat and commoner had been important, the big difference now was between those who possessed capital and those who depended wholly on their own labor. Politically, the century after 1815 was a time when national consciousness was acutely heightened and various societies were consolidated into national states. Democracy made advances and socialism appeared. The idea of revolution, derived in its modern form from the French Revolution, aroused hopeful expectations in some, and pessimistic fears in others. Meanwhile a vast emigration from Europe built up communities of European type overseas, notably in the United States, whose population rose between 1820 and 1910 from about nine to ninety million. The population of Europe itself more than doubled in these same years, exceeding 400 million at the close of the nineteenth century.

Europe thus created a combination of political and economic power such as had never yet been seen in the world's history. Able now to reach other parts of the earth more speedily and effectively than ever before, Europeans had an overwhelming impact on the ancient cultures of Asia, Africa, and America. The European ascendancy reached its height about the year 1900, with the penetration of China, the transformation of Japan, and the reduction of most of the rest of Asia and of Africa to the status of colonies within a half dozen empires. In the twentieth century the position of Europe has relatively declined, partly because of conflicts within Europe itself, but mainly because the apparatus which had made Europe so dominant can now be found in other parts of the world. Some, like the United States, are essentially offshoots of Europe. Others have neither had nor wanted connections with Europe until recent times. But all peoples in the twentieth century are caught up in a process of modernization or "development," which usually turns out to mean acquiring some of the technical, scientific, and organizational skills first exhibited by Europeans.

The "modern" world consists of a kind of uniform civilization that overlies many traditional cultures. Each region has its own familiar and deeper level of life, Europe and the United States as well as India or Bolivia, but above them all is the interconnected world of science, fast transportation, radio and television, industry and machines, trade and finance, loans and debts, investments and bank accounts. In most countries, as they become modern, there have been pressures for increased democracy, and all modern governments, democratic or not, must seek to arouse the energies and support of their populations. In a modern society old customs loosen, and ancestral religions are questioned. There is a demand for individual liberation, and an expectation of a higher standard of living. Everywhere there is a drive for more equality—between sexes and among races, between high and low incomes, between adherents of different religions, or between different parts of the same country. Movements for social change may be slow and gradual, or revolutionary and catastrophic, but movement of some kind is universal.

Such are a few of the indexes of modernity. Since they appeared first in the history of Europe, or of the European world in the extended sense in which the United States is included, the present book deals mainly with Europe, but gives increasing attention, in the later chapters, to the earth as a whole.

But before beginning at the date 1815, we must look briefly at what went before, and especially at the French Revolution of 1789, in which many of these indexes of modernity were prefigured.

The French Revolution

Unlike the Russian or Chinese revolutions of the twentieth century, the French Revolution ended in a compromise. In 1815 the forces of both the old order and the new era remained very much alive, and the conflict between them continued for generations. In France the Bourbon monarchy was restored in 1814–1815 (having been abolished in 1792), and the European powers that defeated Napoleon were all conservative in that they all opposed revolutionary activity. But the French Revolution had momentous and permanent effects. It had by no means failed, even if its most radical aims were unfulfilled, for it thoroughly transformed the institutions that preceded it, or what was now called the Old Regime. It had shaken Europe, the United States, Canada, Latin America, and the Ottoman Empire, which then spread over the Middle East. It impinged on all of them by the force of its ideals and the sheer weight of its power.

France, at the time of its Revolution, was the leading center of the arts and sciences of Europe. French was the most widely used international language. With 25 million inhabitants in 1789, France had three times as many people as England, and far more than Italy or Spain.[1] There were about as many Germans as Frenchmen, but the Germans could never act together since they lived in a multitude of states within the old and ineffectual Holy Roman Empire. Even Russia, before annexing parts of Poland in the 1790s, was probably no more populous than France. It is hence not surprising that France, revolutionized in the 1790s and then reorganized by Napoleon, exercised an enormous influence that is now hard to imagine.

The Old Regime and the Enlightenment

With the Revolution, the society and government that had existed before it came to be called the Old Regime. The phrase calls up a picture of absolute monarchs and obsequious courtiers, haughty nobles and timid middle classes, luxurious rich and suffering poor, influential archbishops and officious priests, all thrown together in a system of legal privilege and formal rank, with a feudal or seigneurial system of landed property, and a government whose authority rested on tradition, or on dynastic inheritance, or on the teachings of religion. All these things existed in France before 1789, though a closer examination would soon lead to serious qualifications. Louis XVI was indeed an absolute king, legally speaking, in that no one could rightfully oppose his express will or remove him from office. Whether France had any constitution was a debated question; if so, it could be found in no written document, but consisted in a hazy compound of varying customs and disputed rights. The king governed through a bureaucracy of civil servants, who were in fact becoming more professional and more competent in the years before the Revolution. His freedom of action was limited by these bureaucrats, by the legal privileges of the nobility and the church, special arrangements with the great provinces, high courts of law called *parlements,* and the fact that many officials were irremovable because they had property rights in

---

[1] See Appendix III for populations of various countries.

their own offices, which they had purchased or inherited. The Old Regime was thus in a perpetual state of stalemate and confusion. Repeatedly, before 1789, the king was persuaded to support reforms, only to be blocked by these privileged bodies.

The Revolution came from a breakdown of the government, and from mass insurrection following on food shortages which caused desperation among the poor, but when it came it drew on most of the advanced ideas in Europe, or on the thinking of what is called the Enlightenment. The eighteenth century saw a great increase in the number of writers appealing to a general audience, a proliferation of books, periodicals, pamphlets, and reading clubs, and hence the early stages in the formation of a public opinion. Scientific and geographical discoveries produced a new mood. Perhaps the main idea of the Enlightenment was that new forms of knowledge were now available, by which life on earth and in human society could be improved. There was an expectation of "progress"— a new word at the time—a belief that world history, however distressing, yet moved in a desirable direction, and that meanwhile most existing institutions could be deliberately changed for the better by the use of intelligence or "reason." The past was discredited, and the mere fact that a thing was done in a certain way was no argument in its favor. More specifically, the Enlightenment was skeptical of the mysteries of religion, opposed to the authority of the church, and critical of arbitrary and secretive government, which it called despotism. It was shocked by religious intolerance and judicial torture. Chaotic diversity in the laws, unfair taxation, conflicts of jurisdiction, and self-perpetuating local authorities all seemed unreasonable. Many privileges of the nobility now seemed absurd, and it was said in France as in America that people should obtain desirable positions on the basis of talent, not social status. Liberty, equality, the rights of the "citizen" and of the "nation" under a "constitution" were constantly talked about in France for twenty years before 1789. Yet no one foresaw or expected the Revolution, and there was no revolutionary party before the event—again in contrast to the Russian, Chinese, and other later revolutions. Nor was the Enlightenment democratic in a later equalitarian sense. It was mostly an affair of educated persons in the middle and upper classes, including many in the government itself. The collapse of government and popular rebellion gave such persons the opportunity to take action.

What happened was that the French government faced bankruptcy in the 1780s. The trouble arose from both mounting expenses and deficiency of income. Expenses had risen because of French intervention in the American Revolution, for which there was much enthusiasm in France, although the government aided the American insurgents for pragmatic reasons, to check the growing power of England. Government revenues were limited by the fact that much of the wealth of the country was tax-exempt. Legally the French people were divided into three "orders"—Clergy, Nobility, and Third Estate—and freedom from certain kinds of taxation was one of the privileges of the "privileged classes," the Clergy and the Nobility. Since members of these two orders owned a good deal of property, the government was unable to tap the full wealth of the country. Some of the clergy and the nobility were willing to pay more taxes, but only in return for concessions to the church and to the aristocracy that Louis XVI and his ministers were unwilling to grant.

The Revolution of 1789

Louis XVI was obliged to call an election, which, in the absence of other precedents, followed the pattern of the long obsolete Estates General. That is, each Frenchman voted as a member of one of the three "orders." There were less than 100,000 clergy, and no more than 400,000 nobles, in the population of 25,000,000. Yet each order chose its own deputies, who met in three equal houses in May of 1789. A majority in the noble house refused to surrender their corporate identity, while the house of the clergy was internally divided. The Third Estate, in which most of the deputies were lawyers and lesser government officers, with a few merchants and medical doctors, insisted that the three houses should merge into one—making three "orders" into a "nation." It declared itself to be a National Assembly, which it invited members of the other two houses to join. It also claimed the right and duty of writing a constitution. The assembly thus issued a challenge to the king, amounting to an arrogation of sovereign power. The insistence on producing a written constitution, to be accompanied by a declaration of rights, though it flowed from many currents in eighteenth-century thought, was a consequence also of the French enthusiasm for what had been done in the American Revolution. Louis XVI took an ambiguous position; he favored important changes, but supported the noble demand for separate representation, and began to concentrate troops near Paris, with the thought of dissolving the new self-styled National Assembly by force.

The Assembly was saved by the urban rioting and peasant insurrection that broke out in all parts of the country. The summer of 1789 was a time of economic as well as political crisis. Bread prices soared, food was scarce, there was hunger as well as the fear of actual starvation. The king's calling of the Estates General had aroused expectations of relief. As economic distress grew worse, and in the sudden politicizing of opinion, the popular misery was blamed on the stubbornness of the nobility and "aristocrats." Peasants attacked the châteaux of their manor lords, and forced the suspension of payments due on lands which they themselves already owned under "feudal" arrangements. Violence occurred in many provincial towns, where middle-class leaders, taking over from the older authorities, attempted to pacify mobs, provide food supplies, and preserve order. Disturbances in Paris led to an assault on the Bastille, which surrendered to insurrectionists on July 14. Neither the king nor the National Assembly dared to call on the army, for fear that the soldiers might fraternize with the rioters. The king reluctantly recognized the Assembly, which thus faced the task of satisfying the country. Widespread popular revolution had saved the Assembly from extinction, but it expressed the grievances of poor and uneducated men and women with which the Assembly was hardly prepared to deal, and it produced a kind of anarchy throughout the country, as manorial lords and big landowners were intimidated, town councils were ousted, and royal officials abandoned their posts. In these unfavorable circumstances the Assembly proceeded to write a constitution and to reorganize France.

The Constituent Assembly, as it was now called, took two years to complete its constitution. Involved also in legislative and administrative business, operating in a glare of publicity, egged on by militant and vocal activists, and obstructed by counterrevolutionaries who wished to terminate its proceedings, the Assembly worked under very different conditions from those in which the American state constitutions and the federal constitution of the United States had been devised. It did far more than construct a new mechanism of government. It in fact mapped out the outlines of what in later times would sometimes be called bourgeois society, and in any case of the liberal modern state.

It began with promises of a new era. In a memorable session, the night of August 4, 1789, the Assembly decreed the "abolition of feudalism." That is, the peasants were freed of all personal servitudes and of the payments made to lords under the seigneurial system, so that peasants who held land under such "feudal" tenures emerged as small property owners of more modern kind. Tax exemptions, church tithes, and provincial privileges were likewise abolished. A few weeks later the Assembly issued, as a preamble to the coming constitution, its famous Declaration of the Rights of Man and the Citizen. This held that "men are born and remain free and equal in rights," that these rights were "liberty, property, security and resistance to oppression," that sovereign power rested ultimately in the nation, that all public authorities were accountable to the nation, that taxation could only be by public consent, and that citizens must enjoy freedom from arrest and freedom of the press, religion, etc., within certain limits to be set by the law. The Declaration was soon translated into all European languages, and stood as a primary symbol of the Revolution.[2]

The Assembly made Louis XVI into a constitutional monarch, providing a legislature for which about half the adult males were to have an indirect vote. It changed the entire machinery of taxation, public expenditure, fiscal accounting, law courts, and local government. It abolished nobility, and ended the system by which public offices could be bought, sold, and inherited. It did away with trade guilds, internal tariffs, and other barriers to economic freedom within a national market, and began the discussions which resulted in the metric system and decimal currency. Protestants, Catholics, and the non-religious received the same rights. On the principle that citizenship could not depend on race or religion, the Assembly began the process of equalization of rights for Jews and for free blacks. (Slavery itself was abolished in the French colonies in the more radical days of 1794, to be reinstituted under Napoleon.) It took the initial steps in legal codification (to be completed under Napoleon), so that the whole country might have uniform laws instead of the numerous separate regions of historically developed law under the Old Regime. The old provinces such as Brittany and Languedoc disappeared as legal entities. In their place the Assembly divided the country into eighty-three departments, all structurally alike. The idea was to assure equality of taxation, administration, judicial facilities, and public services throughout the national territory. A pattern of standardization and centralization

---

[2] The Rights of Man, reinforced by Thomas Paine's book by that title in 1791, became the watchword of the eighteenth-century revolutions. Almost immediately, Olympe de Gouges in France published her *Rights of Woman* in 1791 and Mary Wollstonecraft in England her *Vindication of the Rights of Woman* in 1792, thus opening up a long argument on the application of the word "man." In English as in French there is only one word for the two meanings. "Man" may mean either any member of the human race, male or female, child or adult (as in German *Mensch* and Latin *homo*), or simply an adult male (as in German *Mann*, Latin *vir*). The former usage will occur from time to time in the present book, and in these contexts the pronouns "he," "him" and "his" are of indeterminate gender. In the French Declaration of the Rights of Man the reference is to the human race in general but it is true that throughout the French Revolution, and in all countries until much later, certain specific rights were restricted to the males, notably in voting, eligibility to office, education, family law, and some aspects of property law.

was thus created (and confirmed by Napoleon) for which France long remained famous.

Late in 1789 the Assembly also confiscated or nationalized all the property of the Catholic church, not only the actual church buildings but also the income-producing properties by which the church and many schools and welfare institutions were endowed. In the following years the revolutionary authorities likewise confiscated the property of émigrés, those who left the country because of hostility to the Revolution. All governments during the French Revolution had a high respect for private property; it was simply argued that the property of the church was not private, having been given by pious donors for public purposes over the centuries; and as for the confiscation of émigré property, it was no different in principle from the confiscation of Loyalist estates during the American Revolution. The nationalized properties represented a substantial proportion of all the rural and urban real estate in France. There was no intention for it to remain in the hands of the state. The purpose was to resell it and to use the proceeds to pay off the royal debt which had precipitated the Revolution, to pay compensation for various abolished rights, to finance the government in the collapse of tax collections, and after 1792 to finance the war. Paper money was issued against the nationalized land. With this paper money the government paid its bills, the paper entered into general circulation, and anyone holding the paper could use it, at face value, to acquire a piece of the new "national domain."

An enormous transfer of property ensued. Anyone who had money, or could obtain credit, might acquire a parcel of land, rural or urban. The whole process was facilitated by inflation, in which the paper money had more value for purchase of land than for buying other commodities. Middle-class persons mainly benefited, but some urban workers were able to buy the homes or shops that they had previously rented, many peasants were able to add to their holdings, and there were even cases of aristocrats who, if they could keep out of trouble, managed to expand their estates. In thus enlarging the number of owners of property, and of a property now freed from the church tithe and feudal restraints, the French Revolution was indeed the bourgeois revolution that Marxists and others have seen in it. But it never became a social revolution in the later sense, being rather a political revolution with great social consequences.

The new constitution, completed in 1791, lasted less than a year. The other measures taken by the Constituent Assembly proved more durable; most of them remained in effect in 1815, entering into the compromise in which the Revolution ended. The more purely constitutional features of the Assembly's work—the powers of the king, the composition of the legislature, the provisions for elections—collapsed in August 1792.

The Radical Phase and After

It is true, as is often said, that the most permanent achievements of the Revolution were already evident (or at least enacted) by 1791. The ensuing radical phase of the Revolution was less successful in its objectives, but it was no mere wild aberration. It was this phase that "saved" the Revolution, that is, prevented the reversal of what was done from 1789 to 1791. It also inspired later generations of revolutionaries who looked back on the "sun of '93," and produced a lasting fear of revolutionary agitation among comfortably situated people, including those who had benefited from the Revolution of '89.

From the beginning, the Revolution generated both radical and reactionary currents. Those most determined to press on with the Revolution, and to silence its enemies, became known as Jacobins. Among its enemies were (secretly) the king himself, various disgruntled nobles and their sympathizers, some of the clergy, ordinary persons alarmed by violence, the émigrés led by Louis XVI's two brothers, and as time passed the foreign powers. The two extremes reinforced each other. The rise of Jacobinism made some moderates despair of the Revolution, while the threat of counterrevolution turned others temporarily into Jacobins. The Assembly ran into a confrontation with the Catholic church. Having deprived the church of its property, and yet believing that religion was good for society, the Assembly subjected the church like everything else to a national reorganization, and undertook to pay salaries to its clergy. The pope and almost all the French bishops disapproved; the bulk of the clergy and the laity were divided. Revolution thus passed into religious schism. Partly for this reason, Louis XVI in June 1791 tried to escape from Paris, so as to put himself at the head of the counterrevolutionary forces. Arrested at Varennes, he was compelled to return. A few radicals murmured that France should now be a republic. Moderates preferred to hold on to a constitutional monarchy even with an unwilling and disloyal king. Their position became difficult with the approach of war, in which Louis XVI was rightly suspected of sympathizing with the foreign powers.

Royalty and aristocracy at the time were in their way international institutions. Kings and nobles had more contacts with each other than with their own peoples, and the "nation" was a revolutionary idea. The pleas of the émigrés were listened to in foreign courts. The French queen, Marie Antoinette, was the sister of the ruler of Austria. With the French king and queen virtually prisoners in their own country, the pressure rose for intervention to protect them. In France a few firebrands preached a kind of world revolution against all kings, although Robespierre and a few other Jacobins opposed it. War between France and Austria began in April 1792.

There were then (and throughout the nineteenth century) five principal states or "great powers" in Europe. France was one of them, as was Great Britain with its colonial empire. Austria, or rather the Austrian monarchy, was another; it included Austria itself, Hungary and Bohemia-Moravia (now Czechoslovakia), and had possessions in north Italy and in what is now Belgium. The kingdom of Prussia, with its capital at Berlin, extended along part of the Baltic coast, and controlled a few detached duchies in western Germany. The fifth great power was the Russian Empire, which reached from the Baltic Sea to the Pacific Ocean. In 1792 Poland was invaded by Russia and Prussia, and by 1795 it disappeared from the map. It remained to be seen what an invasion of France might mean. By 1793 France was at war not only with Austria but with Prussia and Great Britain as well, and also with the Dutch Netherlands, Spain, and the Italian Kingdom of Piedmont (or Sardinia), which adjoined the southeastern corner of France. Since Belgium belonged to Austria, France was now virtually encircled by a league of conservative states intervening against its Revolution.

At first, in the summer of 1792, the French army was in a state of collapse. An Austro-Prussian force, on the point of invasion, issued a manifesto to the city of Paris, threatening it with fearful retribution unless Louis XVI was properly obeyed. Paris responded with a tremendous insurrection on August 10, 1792, in which Louis XVI was deposed, the new constitution scrapped, and a call issued for a newly elected National Convention. One of the first acts of the Convention was to proclaim the French Republic.

For more than a year the Convention, elected from all over the country, was hard pressed by the advanced revolutionary activists of Paris, the "sans-culottes," who had been brought to power by the insurrection of August 10. Members of the Convention were generally of the educated and substantial middle class. The sans-culottes, though a few erratic intellectuals acted as their spokesmen, were generally from the solid working-class world of artisans and shopkeepers. They were not the destitute, the riffraff, or the vagrant and criminal types that they were said to be by their enemies. Given their broad social origins, the two years after August 1792 have been called the "democratic" phase of the French Revolution. One result was to associate, in later times in France and Europe, the idea of democracy with the idea of revolutionary violence and excitement, and so to impede the gradual growth of politically democratic institutions. In any case, this crisis of the Revolution was not democratic in any liberal sense, but a time of revolutionary dictatorship and the Reign of Terror.

The Convention, composed of about 780 members, unanimously found Louis XVI guilty of collusion with the foreign powers, or treason, and a majority voted for his execution in January 1793. The death of the king committed the revolutionaries more firmly than ever to their course. Successful counterrevolution would destroy them; the grisly fate of the regicides who had put to death Charles I of England in 1649 was well remembered. And counterrevolution seemed all too probable in the spring of 1793. The leading French general defected to the Austrians, who began to cross the northern frontier. The British fleet occupied Toulon. In western France and in the great provincial cities there were revolts against Paris. The paper money lost value, prices rose, food was scarce, and the sans-culottes clamored for bread. They denounced big merchants, rich people, aristocrats, moderates, foreigners, and conspirators. They forced the Convention to expel some of its members, the Girondins, so that power passed to a more fierce and energetic group, the Mountain. The Convention set up a Committee of Public Safety which governed for about a year. Its best-known member was Maximilien Robespierre, though he was never a personal dictator, nor was there any leadership cult of the kind that twentieth-century revolutions were to make familiar.

The Revolution reached its climax in the latter half of 1793. A democratic constitution with universal male suffrage was proclaimed, but was suspended for the duration of the war. Price controls and requisitions of food pacified the sans-culottes, and enabled the government to provide for the army. The controls gave offense to the agricultural population, which, however, was relieved at this time of the last vestiges of the old seigneurial payments. Overwhelming numbers remained faithful to the Revolution, so that an army was raised of almost a million men; it was the largest ever seen in Europe, and the first national or citizen army; and it began to win victories against the hired professionals of Prussia and Austria. There were violent antireligious outbursts, churches were pillaged, and a republican calendar replaced the Christian era. Marriage became a civil contract, with divorce allowed. There were long discussions of universal primary education, but little was accomplished. Universities were abolished, to be replaced by special schools of more modern type; the famous engineering school, the Polytechnique, dates from this time. Eminent scientists worked for the government, to assist in producing cannon, muskets, gunpowder, and even military balloons.

Accompanying all this was the Terror, officially proclaimed in September 1793. The Terror, in the strict sense, lasted about a year, until the military emergency was over. Justified as necessary to strengthen the government in time of war, or as a means of promoting a democratic revolution, the Terror also unleashed irrational frenzies of suspicion, private vengefulness, and class hatred. Since the foreign war was compounded by civil war, the repression fell especially heavily on parts of France that were in rebellion against the revolutionary government, and in these areas far more peasants and workers than nobles and aristocrats became its victims. A Law of Suspects threatened not only enemies of the Revolution but even those who showed insufficient enthusiasm for it. Moderation became a fault. Revolutionary courts, open to the public and hence swayed by extremists, acquitted a few but sentenced about 17,000 persons to death. The guillotine, introduced in 1790 as a more humane means of capital punishment, became the usual method of execution. All told, about 40,000 men and women perished in the Terror, including those who died in the prisons, or were summarily dispatched when taken in the field with arms in their hands as rebels. Several hundred thousand were interned in large buildings such as schools, abbeys, and warehouses, but the Terror did not last long enough to develop anything like concentration camps.

Gradually the government, that is, the Committee of Public Safety, got control of the spontaneous lower-class activity of the sans-culottes. Revolutionary initiative became located in the government itself. Robespierre announced the theory of revolutionary dictatorship, intended to be a temporary regime leading to a democratic and constitutional order. He even tried to introduce a new state religion, the cult of the Supreme Being. He was ridiculed for his pains. The Terror mounted in Paris while it subsided elsewhere. The revolutionary leadership fell apart; its members became afraid of each other; and Robespierre was outlawed and put to death by the Convention in July 1794—Thermidor of the Year Two of the Republic.

A few weeks before Thermidor the French army won a great victory in Belgium. Thus began a series of military successes that were to last for twenty years, and would refashion Europe. In France the revolutionary dictatorship was dismantled. The democratic dream evaporated. A new regime, the Directory, under the constitution of 1795, tried to hold the Republic on a middle ground between equalitarian revolution and aristocratic-clerical-royalist reaction. It failed, and gave way to the Consulate, with Napoleon Bonaparte as First Consul. Bonaparte was a sensational young officer in the republican army, who had been promoted to general in 1793, at the height of the Terror, at the age of twenty-four.

As First Consul, from 1799 to 1804, Bonaparte imposed on France his own version of a compromise with the Revolution—to prevent the return both of the Bourbon monarchy and of the extreme or "democratic" revolutionaries, while preserving the main goals of the Constituent Assembly of 1789–1791. He reduced representative institutions to a pretense, censored the press, and stopped all public discussion of politics. He put down the lingering rebellion in western France, and imprisoned, or in a few cases executed, those caught in either republican or royalist conspiracies. To disarm the counterrevolution, as he said, or to desanctify it, he made an agreement with the pope, the "concordat," by which the church surrendered its claims to its former property, so that the new owners were reassured. Émigré bishops returned to France, and Catholic worship was protected by the government against the antireligious harassments of the preceding years. Non-Catholics continued to enjoy the equal rights obtained during the Revolution. New law codes—the civil code (Code Napoleon) and commercial and penal codes—combined the Revolutionary legislation with the jurisprudence of the Old Regime. By efficient management, many reforms projected at the beginning of the Revolution were made to work in practice. Most of the émigrés came back to France and tried to find a place for themselves in the new order. Bonaparte purposely chose as his subordinates both men who had taken part in the Revolution and those who had opposed it. He said that he offered a career open to talents, by which he meant not so much that poor boys should be encouraged to rise, as that even those of high birth must qualify by strict education, practical training, personal ability, and severe competition. Past politics and ancestral rank were supposed to be forgotten. A new elite composed of both bourgeois and aristocrats began to emerge, of the kind that would conduct French affairs throughout the nineteenth century.

Revolutionary and Conservative Forces in Europe

Although it was only in France that a real revolution occurred, complete with massive popular revolt, there were revolutionary currents in other countries, some of them antedating the French Revolution. Old Regime conditions existed even where there were no monarchies. In the republics of Venice and Genoa, as in Switzerland, the Dutch provinces, and the German free cities, there were hereditary patriciates, closed oligarchies, and self-selected ruling groups, as well as unequal taxation, local privileges, exclusive guilds, and confused legal jurisdictions. There were a hundred different tariff zones in Switzerland alone. Protestant as well as Catholic countries had their state churches, and persons outside such churches, though tolerated, had only limited rights. In differing degree, all European countries had been affected by the Enlightenment and by the American Revolution. There was dissatisfaction everywhere; the Dutch staged a revolution against the house of Orange in the 1780s, and the Belgian "democrats," as they explicitly called themselves, rebelled in 1789 against both their Austrian overlords and their own Belgian upper classes.

When war broke out in 1792 there was therefore much sympathy for the French, especially among the middle classes all over Europe. The message of liberty, equality, and fraternity was warmly received. When the French armies began to win victories, and so to move into enemy territory, they found supporters among the Belgians, Dutch, Italians, and Rhineland Germans. Such people generally wanted, not to be dominated by the French, but to use the French for their own purposes against their own Old Regimes. Eventually there was much disillusionment on both sides. Meanwhile, in 1794, the French simply annexed the Austrian Netherlands and bishopric of Liège—what in later times would become the kingdom of Belgium. In the next five years they absorbed the tiny German states west of the Rhine into the French Republic. Combining with the Dutch revolutionaries they set up a Batavian Republic in 1795, and by similar methods, as by-products of the war against Austria, and in conjunction with native supporters, the French established new republics in Italy and Switzerland. Each of these satellite republics had its constitution, declaration of rights, elected legislature, principles of civil equality, and new financial, judicial, and administrative arrangements modeled on the French.

Opposition to the Revolution was similarly international. There were Dutch and Swiss émigrés as well as French, all hoping to return to their former positions in their own countries and all urging the British and Austrians to pursue the war against France with vigor. At the head of the French émigrés was Louis XVI's next oldest brother, who took the title of Louis XVIII in 1795 (the boy "Louis XVII" having died in prison); but not even the conservative European governments recognized him until 1814, and he wandered about Europe for years, residing eventually in Russia, while the other Bourbon brother, the future King Charles X, lived for twenty years in England and Scotland. They engaged in conspiracies that became more futile as the years passed, since most of the French émigrés made their peace with Napoleon after 1800. Spokesmen for the established churches, whether Roman Catholic, Anglican, or Dutch Reformed, generally disliked the Revolution, but even the pope recognized the French Revolution when he signed the concordat with Bonaparte. Prussia turned neutral after 1795, and Spain (though a Bourbon monarchy) even allied itself with regicide France, being more afraid of England. Great Britain, although it had entered the war reluctantly, became the main pillar of conservatism. Its wealth, its landed aristocracy, and its unwritten constitution were admired by partisans of the Old Regime in other countries. The British government, repressing democratic agitation in England and Scotland, carried on the war with its navy and with financial grants to its Continental allies. The counterrevolution won significant victories, as when the British put down the Irish rebellion, abolished the Irish parliament, and joined Ireland with the United Kingdom in 1801, and when Russia, Prussia, and Austria crushed the Polish uprising and divided Poland among themselves in 1795. For a time it seemed that they might at last overwhelm the French Revolution itself, for in 1799 the Austrians drove the French out of Italy, and a Russian army, aiming for France, operated as far west as Switzerland and Holland. The French were again able to defeat them. It was out of this crisis that General Bonaparte emerged as First Consul.

Bonaparte not only reached an apparent reconciliation with the pope, and not only invited back to France those émigrés who would accept him; he also, by his military victories, persuaded the Austrians and the British to make peace. For about a year in 1802 there was no war in Europe. Bonaparte's popularity in France was due to his role as a peacemaker. If only he had stayed out of war, his Consulate might have proved to be a more lasting solution to the problems raised by the Revolution. Such, however, was not to be the case.

The Napoleonic Empire

In 1804 the French Republic was declared to be an Empire, and Bonaparte took the title of Napoleon I, Emperor of the French. Napoleon's personal ambitions were not yet satisfied, but the blame for renewal of hostilities was not altogether one-sided. The other powers were rightly afraid of him, but their own aims were not merely defensive, for they too had their ambitions, the British to obtain colonial and naval supremacy and to keep a balance of power on the Continent; the Russians, Austrians, and Prussians to make territorial acquisitions, and to prevent the resurgence of an independent Poland. For ten years it was Napoleon who prevailed. At its height, in 1810, his "French Empire" included not only France, as enlarged in the 1790s by the incorporation of Belgium and the German left bank of the Rhine, but two long tenacles along the seacoast, annexed as a countermeasure against British maritime influences: one to the north, comprising the Dutch Netherlands and the German North Sea shore; the other to the south, along the Italian coast as far as Rome. His "Grand Empire" included the French Empire proper, and also Spain, a Kingdom of Italy comprising most of north Italy and a Kingdom of Naples in the southern half of the peninsula, along with Switzerland, most of Germany, the nucleus of Poland set up as the Grand Duchy of Warsaw, and much of Croatia and Slovenia under the name of the Illyrian Provinces. At this time, in consequence of repeated Napoleonic victories, Russia, Austria, and Prussia were all technically allied with Napoleon. The Austrians even gave him a daughter of the house of Habsburg as his second wife; she became the mother of his only child. It was only the British, beyond his reach in their island, who consistently refused to recognize or deal with Napoleon in any way.

The powers that defeated Napoleon in 1814–1815 saw in him a symbol of the Revolution. They even called him a Jacobin. He was no revolutionary, but he had a revolutionary impact on Europe. He was a romantic egomaniac in his temperament, and a follower of the classical Enlightenment in his program. He favored almost everything that the Enlightenment had preached, from the subordination of the church to the reform of taxation and the assimilation of Jews. It was as an innovator, organizer, rationalizer, and modernizer that he presented himself to Europe. To the German philosopher Hegel he seemed to be the "World Spirit on horseback," or in other words he represented the progressive forces of Europe in a position of power.

Spread of the Revolution

Under Napoleon some of the changes introduced in France by the Revolution spread to much of the Continent. England remained fixed in its own ways, made even more conservative, and more satisfied in being different from the Continent, by its long struggle against the French Emperor. The new creations in Spain, Poland, and Croatia-Slovenia were too distant, or too unsettled, for the Napoleonic impact to be much felt. It was in Italy and Germany that native reformers for several years were most willing to work with Napoleon.

One change was simply the enlargement of territorial units, that is, of the area within which people could go without passing a frontier, changing money, finding different laws, dealing with unfamiliar officials, or meeting barriers to their trade or professional practice. The units were not yet national. But in north Italy a medley of city-states and duchies was merged into the Kingdom of Italy. In Germany the old Holy Roman Empire, consisting of some three hundred "states," was reorganized into a mere twenty. Most of the free cities disappeared, as did all the church states, where bishops or abbots had been the rulers. Thus Bavaria absorbed the free city of Nuremberg and the bishopric of Bamberg. Various princelings hitherto regarded as sovereign, but who is some cases had no more territory than an English landlord, were likewise "mediatized," becoming subjects of the king of Bavaria, Württemberg, or others, as the case might be. The German rulers who thus expanded their territories were among Napoleon's most ardent supporters. Those of Bavaria, Württemberg, and Saxony, hitherto only electoral princes, were promoted by Napoleon to the rank of "king."

Into these enlarged units the Napoleonic legal codes and administrative apparatus were introduced. Civil equality was a principle of the Code Napoleon; all citizens of the territory, whether noble or nonnoble, were to be treated alike by the state in its judicial and financial operations. Expressing the new law of persons and property, the Code also undermined "feudalism." Seigneurial courts were replaced by local courts maintained by the state and subordinated to appellate and high courts ranged above them. Personal services of peasants to lords were abolished, and payments due to seigneurs were abolished or commuted. Large and small property owners remained, as well as those who owned none at all, but there was no longer one form of property for nobles and an inferior form for others. Property owners paid taxes in proportion to the amount of property that they owned, without regard to social status, and tax collection became more professional and efficient. Church courts were abolished, and persons of all religions received the same civil rights. A new system of local government replaced the quaint peculiarities of old-fashioned towns. Roads were improved, and uniform weights and measures were introduced. Each Napoleonic state also maintained its own army, under the Emperor's supreme command. Napoleon saw in his Grand Army another means of unifying Europe, and in fact, when he invaded Russia in 1812, only a third of his 600,000 soldiers were actually French.

Cosmopolitans for a while were well disposed toward Napoleon. Goethe, a humane man but no democrat, once called him "the expression of all that was reasonable, legitimate, and European in the revolutionary movement." His most irreconcilable enemies were the enemies of the French Revolution. But even in France his supporters gradually turned against him, disillusioned by his repeated wars, his repression of open discussion, and his increasing proclivity to ape the royalty of Europe. In other parts of the Grand Empire there began to be nationalist opposition, most especially in Spain, but also in Italy, the Netherlands, and Germany. In 1789 the "nation" had been a revolutionary conception, with liberal implications, directed against absolute rulers and hereditary privileged classes; the nation was a community of equal citizens capable of determining their own fate. Another kind of national feeling now began to develop, in which national identity meant a sense of difference from other nations, i.e., foreigners. The implications of this kind of nationalism were more conservative, for it stressed historic differences in culture, language, folkways, law, and local customs which the Napoleonic system attempted to override. In this view each nation had a spirit of its own, which the Germans called the *Volksgeist*, and which had to be protected against distortion or corruption by outsiders. One kind of national idea was primarily civic, the other primarily ethnic, and both kinds were to remain important, long after Napoleon's time, for Europe and for the world.

On a practical level, among the European powers, the most persistent adversary of Napoleon was Great Britain. Napoleon seriously planned an invasion of England in 1803, but gave it up. His ships attacked the British fleet, but were worsted at the naval battle of Trafalgar. The British responded by forming coalitions with Austria, Prussia, and Russia, whose armies they helped to finance, and which Napoleon defeated in the battles of Austerlitz, Jena, Friedland, and Wagram, all in central Europe, and all now commemorated in Paris as the names of two streets, a bridge, and a railway station. The contest between Britain and France settled into a trade war, in which each tried to undermine the other's economy by reducing its exports.

There was no military solution until Napoleon, to prevent Russia from trading with Britain, launched an invasion of Russia in 1812. He reached Moscow in September, only to find the city in flames, probably set by the Russians themselves in order to freeze him out of the country. He and his army were obliged to make a hasty and miserable retreat in the dead of winter. In the next year, with Prussia and Austria turning against him, a new alliance defeated him in Germany. The allies pressed on, entered Paris, and obliged him to abdicate. They exiled him to Elba on the Italian coast, in 1814, but he escaped from Elba, rallied surprising support in France, took again to the field, and was defeated again by a British and Prussian army at Waterloo, in Belgium. He was sent this time to the tiny island of St. Helena in the South Atlantic, where he died in 1821.

The Peace Settlement of 1814–1815

The victorious allies believed that they had at last brought an end to the French Revolution and all its work. Yet there was no agreement on what should follow. The allied statesmen had no love for the Bourbon monarchy. In France, after more than twenty years, the Bourbons had been forgotten or remembered with distaste, except by handfuls of royalist true believers. Nevertheless, in the absence of any other acceptable solution, the Bourbon throne was "restored" and Louis XVIII recognized as king. Now a man of sixty, who had spent half his adult life in exile, he was at last prepared to compromise with the Revolution. He issued a constitutional charter, insisting that he did so by his own royal grace and authority, and refusing to accept the principle of national sovereignty; but the charter incorporated most of the great changes which since 1789 had entered into the fabric of French law and society. It also provided for a degree of freedom of speech, political life, and parliamentary government that had been unknown under Napoleon, though politics and voting were confined to a small number of large landowners. As for the allies, they also accepted a Bourbon restoration as most likely to have a stabilizing effect in Europe, since a Bourbon monarchy would be under no pressure to regain the conquests of the Republic and the Empire. It was with Louis XVIII that the allies signed a treaty of peace, by which France was returned to its boundaries of 1791.

To deal with other questions the powers agreed to hold an international congress at Vienna. The recession of the French flood left the future of much of Europe—Belgium, Holland, Germany, Poland, Italy, Spain—fluid and uncertain. There were many other debatable questions. Russia had ambitions against Turkey, and in 1809 had annexed Finland, which it held as an autonomous grand duchy only loosely connected with the tsarist empire. The Spanish empire in America had began to disintegrate during the Napoleonic occupation of Spain. The British were in possession of all the French and Dutch overseas colonies, and of various islands off the coast of Europe.

Both Russia and Great Britain, before consenting to a general conference, specified certain matters that they would decide for themselves as not susceptible to international consideration. The Russians refused to discuss Turkey and the Balkans. They also kept Finland, as well as certain recent conquests in the Caucasus almost unknown to Europe. The British barred all colonial and overseas questions. They simply announced to Europe which of their colonial and insular conquests they would keep and which they would return.

In Europe, the British remained in possession of Malta, the Ionian Islands, and Heligoland. In America, they kept St. Lucia, Trinidad, and Tobago in the West Indies and reasserted their claims to the Pacific Northwest, or Oregon country, to which claims were also made by Russia, Spain, and the United States. Of former French possessions, the British kept the island of Mauritius in the Indian Ocean. Of former Dutch territories, they kept the Cape of Good Hope and Ceylon, but returned the Netherlands Indies. During the Revolutionary and Napoleonic wars in Europe the British had also made extensive conquests in India, bringing much of the upper Ganges valley under their rule. The British emerged, in 1814, as the controlling power in both India and the Indian Ocean. Indeed, of all the colonial empires founded by Europeans in the sixteenth and seventeenth centuries, and whose rivalry had been a recurring cause of war in the eighteenth, only the British now remained as a growing and dynamic system. Only the British in 1814 had a significant navy. With Napoleon defeated, with the Industrial Revolution bringing power machinery to their manufactures, and with no rival left in the contest for overseas dominion, the British embarked on their century of world leadership, which may be said to have lasted from 1814 to 1914.

The Congress of Vienna

The Congress of Vienna assembled in September 1814. Never had such a brilliant gathering been seen. All the states of Europe sent representatives; and many defunct states, such as the formerly sovereign princes and ecclesiastics of the late Holy Roman Empire, sent lobbyists to urge their restoration. But procedure was so arranged that all important matters were decided by the four triumphant Great Powers. Europe was at peace, a treaty having been signed with the late enemy; France also was represented at the Congress by Talleyrand, now minister to Louis XVIII. Castlereagh, Metternich, and the tsar Alexander I spoke for their respective countries, Britain, Austria, and Russia; Prussia was represented by Hardenburg. Aristocrats of the Old Regime, they applied prerevolutionary diplomatic principles to the existing problem. They by no means wished to restore the territorial boundaries obtaining before the wars. They did desire, as they put it, to restore the "liberties of Europe," meaning the freedom of European states from domination by a single power. They thus sought a balance of power, which by an ingenious calculation of forces, with transfer of territory from one government to another, would distribute political power among a number of free and sovereign states. It was hoped that a proper balance would also produce a lasting peace.

There was in fact no long war between Great Powers for a hundred years after the Congress of Vienna, but the Congress made decisions against which the liberal and nationalist movements of the nineteenth century were soon to rebel. From the ruins of Napoleon's Grand Empire it set up the kingdom of the Netherlands (including both the Dutch and the Belgian regions), transferred the German area west of the Rhine to Prussia, revived the kingdom of Piedmont in northwest Italy, and assigned the rest of north Italy (Lombardy and Venetia) to Austria. In central Italy the pope restored himself as temporal ruler of the papal states, and various dukes reclaimed their small duchies. Two Bourbon dynasties, related to the French Bourbons, were restored in the kingdom of Naples (all southern Italy) and in Spain. Opposition to most of those regimes became apparent soon after 1815, except in the Rhineland. The Germans there, who before the French Revolution had lived in a hundred small states, were now willing to accept Prussian rule, and Prussia, formerly an East European state, now for the first time had a firm foothold in Western Europe.

In reconstructing Germany, the Congress made no attempt to put together again the Humpty Dumpty of the Holy Roman Empire. The pleas of the former princelings went unheeded. Except for the transfer of the Rhineland to Prussia, the French and Napoleonic reorganization of Germany was substantially confirmed. The rulers of Bavaria, Württemberg, and Saxony kept the royal crowns that Napoleon had bestowed on them. The German states, now thirty-nine in number, were joined in a loose confederation in which the members remained virtually sovereign. The Congress ignored the yearning of German nationalists for a great unified Fatherland; Metternich especially feared nationalistic agitation; and in any case the nationalists themselves had no practical answer to concrete questions, such as the institutions of government and the frontiers that a united Germany should have.[3] The Congress did declare, somewhat ineffectually, that in each of the German states there should be a representative legislative body.

The assembled diplomats almost came to blows on the question of Poland, or of what was to succeed Napoleon's Grand Duchy of Warsaw. The Russian tsar at this time expressed liberal views, and believed that the partitions of Poland had been a crime; he therefore wished to restore a reunited Poland with himself as its constitutional king. The Prussians were willing to agree, if only they were allowed to annex the kingdom of Saxony. Metternich, speaking for Austria, was alarmed at the possibility of such Russian and Prussian expansion. Castlereagh, speaking for Great Britain, opposed any plan that would bring the power of Russia, by way of Poland, so far into central Europe. Metternich and Castlereagh were on this matter supported by Talleyrand, who shrewdly used this rift between the victors to bring France back into the diplomatic circle as a power in its own

---

[3] The map of Europe in 1815, which appears on the following pages, is often referred to in notes to Chapters 11 through 13, where the reference, however, is to pp. 448–449. Readers of this second half of the larger work should simply convert pp. 448–449 to pp. XL–XLI when wishing to see European boundaries as established in 1815.

Boundary of the German Confederation

0   100   200 miles

KINGDOM OF NORWAY
AND SWEDEN

FINLAND
(Russia, 1808)

Oslo

Stockholm

St. Petersburg

Novgorod

Reval

Riga

Borodir

Smolensk

SCOTLAND

Edinburgh

NORTH SEA

Copenhagen
DENMARK

BALTIC SEA

EAST
PRUSSIA

Danzig

Niemen R.

LITHUANIA

UNITED KINGDOM
OF GREAT BRITAIN AND IRELAND

IRELAND   Dublin

ENGLAND

WALES

SCHLESWIG

HELIGOLAND
(Britain)

HOLSTEIN

Hamburg

Elbe R.

HANOVER

P   R   U   S   S   I   A

Berlin

Vistula R.

Warsaw

KINGDOM OF THE
NETHERLANDS

KINGDOM OF
POLAND
(1815-1831)

Kiev

London

ENGLISH CHANNEL

BELGIUM
(Ind. 1831)

Cologne

Rhine R.

LUX.

HESSE

SAXON
STATES

SAXONY

Breslau

Oder R.

Cracow

GALICIA

UKRAINE

ATLANTIC OCEAN

Rouen

Seine R.

Paris

Metz

LORRAINE

Strasbourg

ALSACE

BADEN

WÜRT-
TEMBERG

BAVARIA

Munich

AUSTRIA

Vienna

Prague

Pressburg

AUSTRIAN EMPIRE

Budapest

HUNGARY

TRANSYLVANIA

Dniester R.

BESSARABIA
(Russia 1812)

MOLDAVIA
(Autonomous 1829)

Odessa

Loire R.

Tours

F   R   A   N   C   E

Berne
SWITZERLAND

TYROL

Lyons

Rhone R.

SAVOY

LOM-
BARDY

Milan

Po R.

VENETIA

PARMA

MODENA

CROATIA

Belgrade

WALLACHIA
(Autonomous 1829)

DOBRUJA

Danube R.

Bordeaux

Toulouse

Marseilles

Nice

PYRENEES

Ebro R.

Toulon

KINGDOM OF SARDINIA

PIEDMONT

Genoa

LUCCA

TUSCANY

PAPAL
STATES

ELBA

BOSNIA

SERBIA
*(Autonomous
1829)*

DALMATIA

ADRIATIC SEA

BULGARIA

Sofia

MONTENEGRO

OTTOMAN

Constantinople

Burgos

PORTUGAL

Madrid

S   P   A   I   N

Tagus R.

Lisbon

Valencia

Barcelona

*CORSICA
(France)*

Rome

Naples

SALONICA

Salonica

AEGEAN SEA

Smyrn

*BALEARIC I.
(Spain)*

SARDINIA

KINGDOM OF THE
TWO SICILIES

IONIAN I.
(Britain)

Athens

RHODES

Seville

Cadiz

Gibraltar *(Britain)*

Palermo

SICILY

GREECE
(Independent 1829)

CRETE

Algiers

MOROCCO

ALGERIA   *(France, 1830)*

TUNIS
(Turkish)

MALTA
(Britain)

MEDITERRANEAN SEA

TRIPOLI

TRIPOLI

EUROPE, 1815

Boundaries are those set by the Congress of Vienna in 1815. In general, a system of five "great powers" prevailed over the Napoleonic Empire. France was reduced to the borders it had had before the Revolutionary-Napoleonic wars. Prussia was firmly installed on both banks of the Rhine, thus obtaining the part of Germany in which industrialization became important fifty years later. South Germany remained as reorganized under Napoleon. Poland was again partitioned as in 1795. The Russian tsar now had not only an enlarged share of Poland but also Finland and Bessarabia. The Austrians added Venetia to what they had held before 1796.

The union of the Dutch and Belgian Netherlands lasted only until 1831, when the kingdom of Belgium was established. Otherwise, the boundaries of 1815 lasted until the Italian war of 1859 which led to the unification of Italy.

right. On January 3, 1815, Castlereagh, Metternich, and Talleyrand signed a secret treaty, pledging themselves to go to war if necessary against Russia and Prussia. So, in the very midst of the peace conference, war again reared its head; and, in the very deliberations of the victors, one party among them allied itself with the vanquished.

No sooner had the news of the secret treaty leaked out than Alexander offered to compromise. He agreed to content himself with a much reduced Polish kingdom. The Congress therefore created a new Poland (called "Congress Poland," which lasted for fifteen years); Alexander became its king, and he gave it a constitution; it comprised much the same area as Napoleon's Grand Duchy, but it reached 250 miles farther west into Europe than had the Russian segment of the third partition of 1795. Some Poles still remained in Prussia and some in the Austrian Empire; Poland was not reunited. With the tsar thus content, Prussia too had to back down. It received only a part of Saxony, the rest remaining to the Saxon king. The addition of both Saxon and Rhenish territories brought the Prussian monarchy into the most advanced parts of Germany. The net effect was to shift the center of gravity of both Russia and Prussia farther west, Russia almost to the Oder River, Prussia to the borders of France.

With the solution of the Polish-Saxon question the main work of the Congress was completed. Other incidental matters were taken up. The Congress initiated international regulation of certain rivers. It issued a declaration against the Atlantic slave trade, which, however, remained ineffective, since the Continental powers were unwilling to grant the British navy the right to make searches at sea, and the British were unwilling to put their naval forces at the disposal of an international body. Committees of the Congress set to work to draft the Final Act.

The work of the Congress was interrupted by Napoleon's return from Elba. After Waterloo, and after Napoleon's second abdication, the allies made a new treaty with France, more severe than the first, since the French seemed to have shown themselves incorrigible in rallying to the Emperor. The new treaty imposed minor changes of the frontiers, an indemnity of 700 million francs, and an army of occupation.

The effect of the Hundred Days, as the episode following Napoleon's return from Elba is called, was to renew the dread of revolution, war, and aggression. Britain, Russia, Austria, and Prussia, after being almost at war with each other in January, again joined forces to get rid of the apparition from Elba, and in November 1815 they solemnly reconfirmed their alliance, adding a provision that no Bonaparte should ever govern France. They agreed also to hold future congresses to review the political situation and enforce the peace. In addition, the tsar Alexander now devised a vague scheme which he called the Holy Alliance, by which all the powers should uphold Christian principles of charity and peace. The Holy Alliance, probably sincerely meant by Alexander as a condemnation of violence, soon came to signify, in the minds of liberals, a kind of unholy alliance of monarchies against liberty and progress.

The Peace of Vienna was the most far-reaching diplomatic agreement before the Peace of Paris which closed the First World War in 1919. It had its strong points and its weak ones. It produced a minimum of resentment in France, for the new French government accepted the new arrangements. It ended almost two centuries of colonial rivalry; for sixty or seventy years no colonial empire seriously challenged the British. Two other causes of friction in the eighteenth century—the control of Poland and the Austro-Prussian rivalry in Germany—were smoothed over for fifty years. A balance of power was restored, that is, a European state system in which a number of sovereign and independent states existed without fear of conquest or domination. Some details of the settlement broke down in 1830, and others in 1848, but not until 1914 was there a war in Europe that lasted longer than a few months, or in which all the Great Powers were involved.

With past issues the peace of 1815 dealt rather effectively; with future issues, not unnaturally, it was less successful. The treaty gave no satisfaction to nationalists and democrats. It was a disappointment to many liberals. The transfer of peoples from government to government, without consultation of their wishes, opened the way under nineteenth-century conditions to a good deal of subsequent trouble. The peacemakers were in fact hostile to both nationalism and democracy, the potent forces of the coming age; they regarded them, with reason, as leading to revolution and war.

Yet the settlement was a compromise. The forces of conservatism, controlling the governments, held down but did not crush those who opposed them. In many places—notably in France, but also in Italy, Germany, the Netherlands, and elsewhere—there were still active middle-aged persons who had favored the French Revolution in their youth, or who had worked for reorganization under Napoleon, or who had become more nationalistic under French domination. There were also many in the rising generation who shared in such sentiments.

A REVOLUTIONARY ERA

The years from the American Revolution through the French Revolution and the empire of Napoleon marked a major turning point for both Europe and much of the rest of the world. The old European colonial systems came to an end with the establishment of the United States, the slave revolt in Haiti and independence of that country, the first steps in the creation of the Spanish-American republics, and the separation of Brazil from Portugal. These were also the years of the Industrial Revolution in Great Britain, metaphorically so called, since industrialization was a gradual and sporadic process not always perceptible to contemporaries.

The changes effected by the American and French Revolutions were mainly in new conceptions of liberty and equality, as reflected in constitutions, law, and personal status. The Americans expressed ideas that were well known in Europe, and so had an influence there. In France the Revolution in some ways only accelerated long continuing trends. It "abolished feudalism," but feudalism had been declining for centuries. It consolidated the modern state by professionalizing its civil service, army, law courts, schools, and tax-collecting machinery, but kings had long worked in these directions. It improved the national trading area by overcoming provincial barriers and introducing uniform law codes, as well as uniform weights and measures in the metric system. Monarchies had made similar efforts. In general, a middle class that had been growing for centuries achieved a victory over older vested interests.

But the Revolution was also innovative. Liberty and the possession of rights were not new in Europe, but hitherto they had depended on one's social class or religion, or on agreements between a ruler and a particular group to which one belonged. Now liberty meant liberty for the individual, not for this or that group. Equality meant equality of civil rights irrespective of social class or religion, and in France even of race. Civil rights included freedom from abuse by government, freedom of speech, religion, and association, and the right to own property. Property itself became more "private," i.e., disentangled from the remnants of lordship. Representative government, which had long meant merely consultation with social estates (such as church, nobility, and towns), now meant a system in which individual voters chose legislators and officials by numerical count for limited terms of office. The word "citizen" became a hallmark of the new era. Where formerly it had meant someone sharing in the liberties of a town, it now meant someone participating in the sovereignty of the nation, which protected individual rights. The most famous document of the era was the French Declaration of the Rights of Man and Citizen of 1789, which proclaimed both national sovereignty and what are now called human and civil rights.

At left, above: Lexington green, near Boston, where "the embattled farmers stood, and fired the shot heard round the world." In the picture, local militia meet a detachment of the British army in the first armed clash of the American Revolution in April 1775.

Below: The battle of Fleurus in Belgium in June 1794. This defeat of the Austrians frustrated intervention against the French Revolution by an alliance of European powers. It opened the way for twenty years of French domination of Europe, first by the French Republic, then by the Napoleonic Empire.

The battle of Fleurus also saw the first use of an aircraft in warfare. The balloon, invented in France a few years before, was one of the scientific innovations that the revolutionary government tried to turn to practical use. In the picture an officer observes the battlefield through a telescope as men on the ground hold the balloon in place. Probably the results were disappointing, since balloons were not thereafter used by either side.

COMMON SENSE;

ADDRESSED TO THE

INHABITANTS

OF

AMERICA,

On the following interesting

SUBJECTS.

I. Of the Origin and Design of Government in general, with concise Remarks on the English Constitution.

II. Of Monarchy and Hereditary Succession.

III. Thoughts on the present State of American Affairs.

IV. Of the present Ability of America, with some miscellaneous Reflections.

Man knows no Master save creating HEAVEN,
Or those whom choice and common good ordain.

THOMSON.

PHILADELPHIA;

Printed, and Sold, by R. BELL, in Third-Street.

MDCCLXXVI.

Thomas Paine, author of both books shown here, took part in both the American and French Revolutions and in the movement for reform of Parliament in Great Britain. Born in England, he arrived in Philadelphia in 1774 with recommendations from Benjamin Franklin, and published his Common Sense *anonymously after armed conflict had begun. Widely read, it helped to persuade Americans to fight for complete independence from Britain.*

RIGHTS OF MAN:

BEING AN

ANSWER TO MR. BURKE's ATTACK

ON THE

FRENCH REVOLUTION.

BY

THOMAS PAINE,

SECRETARY FOR FOREIGN AFFAIRS TO CONGRESS IN THE
AMERICAN WAR, AND
AUTHOR OF THE WORK INTITLED " *COMMON SENSE*."

———————————

LONDON:
PRINTED FOR J. S. JORDAN, No. 166, FLEET-STREET.
MDCCXCI.

Paine returned to England, and when Edmund Burke denounced the French Revolution wrote the Rights of Man *in reply. In it he castigated the British political system while defending the first French constitution of 1789–1791. In danger of arrest in England, he fled to France, where he became an honorary citizen and was elected to the National Convention in 1792. By the end of 1792 more than fifty editions of the* Rights of Man *had appeared in London, Philadelphia, Dublin, and elsewhere, and it had been translated into French, German, and Dutch.*

Convoked for the first time in 175 years, the Estates General of France met in a large hall at Versailles in May 1789. The picture shows Louis XVI seated on his throne, with deputies of the clergy seated at his right (the reader's left), those of the nobility, at his left, and those of the Third Estate, facing him at the other end of the hall. The Third Estate, inviting the others to join it, converted itself into a National Assembly, which took an oath to write a new constitution for France.

At right, above: The three men at an anvil are a noble, a cleric, and a commoner hammering out a new constitution together. The idea at the beginning of the Revolution was for the three estates to "fraternize" in the "nation."

Rioting in Paris, prompted by food shortages, was politicized when Louis XVI assembled troops with the obvious intention of dissolving the National Assembly. The result was the capture of the Bastille, which became a symbol of repression. The National Assembly continued to sit for another two years.

L

tôt tôt tôt
battez chaud
tôt tôt tôt
bon Courage
il faut avoir cœur a l'ouvrage.

LII

Kings fared badly in this revolutionary era, although the main revolutionary thrust was against the "privileged classes"—nobilities, aristocracies, oligarchies, patriciates, hereditary office holders, and the prelates of established churches.

At left, above: Parisians pull down a statue of Louis XIV (1643–1715) three years after the Revolution began. At left, below: a similar incident in New York in 1776, as a statue of King George is pulled down at the beginning of the American Revolution.

With the progress of revolutionary ideas, internal conflict, and foreign war, the French Revolution became more radical and violent. The guillotine, first adopted as a more humane way of inflicting capital punishment, was put to work against enemies of the Revolution. Robespierre himself and four others were denounced as conspirators against liberty. The picture below illustrates their death in July 1794.

The French Revolution (like the American) was financed by paper money. The notes were called assignats because they were "assigned" to, or secured by, real estate confiscated during the Revolution, mostly from the church. Inflation rose rapidly after price controls were abolished late in 1794, and with the continuing war costs and uncertainty as to the government's future. Even notes of denominations as high as 10,000 livres, as shown in the picture, became worthless. The assignats were abolished in 1796, after which France enjoyed a sound currency for many years.

Since the paper money could be used to buy land and buildings on advantageous terms, it served as a mechanism by which a large amount of real property passed into individual private ownership. The more prosperous peasants and middle classes in the towns especially benefited.

As the Republic was unable to stabilize itself it was taken over by a young republican general, Napoleon Bonaparte. In his first years in power he consolidated some of the changes made in the first years of the Revolution; then in 1804 he proclaimed himself Emperor. Repeatedly winning battles against the Austrians, Prussians, and Russians, he developed ever more grandiose ideas of imperial greatness. This painting was executed in 1806 by the famous artist Jacques-Louis David, himself an old revolutionary of 1793, as an idealization of the young republican hero who had crossed the Alps in 1800 to win the battle of Marengo.

Napoleon, having defeated all the powers opposed to him and to the French Revolution—except England—conceived of Paris as the capital of a more modern continent of Europe, to be symbolised by evoking the grandeur of ancient Rome. The following pages show architectural monuments to this vision which still remain among the attractions of Paris.

At left: The Vendôme column, modeled on the second-century column of Trajan in Rome. The bas-reliefs were molded from the bronze of cannon captured at the battle of Austerlitz. Figures of soldiers climb along a spiral ascending the column, as in the column of Trajan. A statue of Napoleon was put at the top. It was taken down in 1814, but a later copy replaced it and still stands.

Below: The church of the Madeleine. Construction had begun in 1764, with the intention of building a church, but by 1800 hardly more than the foundations had been laid. Some then talked of using the structure for a utilitarian purpose, such as a stock exchange, but Napoleon decided to turn it into a Temple of Glory, and as such it was completed in 1810. It became a church after Napoleon's fall in 1814.

The Arch of Triumph was designed and building begun in 1806, but it was not completed until 1836. It is a monument to the Republic as well as to the Empire, with the continuous band of bas-reliefs above the curve of the arch representing 172 battles since Valmy in 1792. The mammoth edifice is located in a great open space, the Etoile (the "star"), first projected by city planners as long ago as Louis XIV. Radiating from this central point are a dozen magnificent avenues, the Champs Elysées to the east and the Avenue de la Grande Armée to the west. The Grand Army was the term used by Napoleon at the height of his power, when his forces included not only French but also Italian, German, and Polish contingents.

The completion of the arch in 1836 signified also the growth of the "Napoleonic legend," when those dissatisfied with the course of events after his fall began to glorify his memory.

A History
of the
Modern
World

SINCE 1815

XI.
REACTION VERSUS PROGRESS, 1815–1848

IN THE PERIOD of some thirty years preceding 1815 two "revolutions" had been taking place. One was the upheaval associated with the French Revolution and the Napoleonic empire. At bottom, it was mainly political, having to do with the organization of government, public power and authority, public finance, taxation, administration, law, individual rights, and the legal position of social classes. The other "revolution," a revolution in a more metaphorical sense, was primarily economic, having to do with the production of wealth, the techniques of manufacture, the exploitation of natural resources, the formation of capital, and the distribution of products to consumers. The political and the economic revolutions, in these years, to a surprising degree, went on independently of each other. Until 1815 the political revolution affected mainly the Continent, while the economic revolution was most active in England. The Continent, while renewing itself politically, remained economically less advanced than England. England, transformed economically, remained conservative in other respects. Hence it has been possible, in the preceding chapters, to deal with the French Revolution and its Napoleonic sequel without attending to the Industrial Revolution, as the economic changes then occurring in England are always called.

It may be (the matter is arguable) that the Industrial Revolution was more

Chapter Emblem: A medal commemorating the Congress of Vienna, showing the victorious rulers of Austria, Russia, and Prussia.

important than the French Revolution or any other. In a telescopic view of world history the two biggest changes experienced by the human race in the past ten thousand years may have been the agricultural or Neolithic revolution which ushered in the first civilizations, and the Industrial Revolution which has ushered in the civilization of the nineteenth and twentieth centuries. However that may be, it proves on closer examination that the economic and the political, the Industrial Revolution (or industrialization) and the other institutions of a society, cannot long be kept apart in an attempt at understanding. The Industrial Revolution occurred first in England, becoming evident about 1780, because of certain political characteristics of English society, because access to world markets had been gained by earlier commercial and naval successes, and because English life offered rewards to the individual for a spirit of risk-taking and innovation. Nor can the effects of political and economic revolution, in England or elsewhere, be kept apart for the years after 1815.

With the defeat of Napoleon and signing of the peace treaty at Vienna in 1815, it seemed that the French Revolution was at last over. European conservatism had triumphed; since it frankly opposed the new "French ideas," it can appropriately be called "reaction." But the processes of industrialization, as they accelerated in England and spread to the Continent, worked against the politically conservative settlement. They greatly enlarged both the business and wage-earning classes, and so made it harder for monarchs and landed aristocrats to maintain their control over public power. Industrial development in the nineteenth century was often called "progress," and progress proved stronger than reaction.

Industrial society arose in England, Western Europe, and the United States, in the nineteenth century, within the system known as capitalism. In the twentieth century, since the Russian Revolution, industrial societies have been created in which capitalism has been vehemently rejected. Industrialism and capitalism are therefore by no means the same. Yet all industrial societies use capital, which is defined as wealth that is not consumed but is used to produce more wealth, or future wealth. An automobile is a consumer's good; the automobile factory is the capital. What distinguishes a capitalist from a noncapitalist society is not the existence of capital, but the kinds of people who control it. The distinctions sometimes become blurred. But in one form of society the control of capital is through "private ownership" or institutions of private property, by which capital is owned by individuals or family trusts, or nowadays by foundations, pension funds, or corporations that are in turn owned by shareholders; in any case not by the state. In such societies, though ownership may be widespread, most capital is controlled by relatively few people, responding to market forces. In the other form of society productive capital in principle belongs to the public, and is in effect "owned" and controlled by the state or its agencies; such societies usually call themselves socialist, because the first socialists rejected the principle of private ownership of the means of production, that is, of capital. In these societies the control of capital, or decisions on saving, investment, and production, are also in the hands of relatively few under some form of central plan.

In Europe the institutions of secure private property had been developed since the Middle Ages, and much that happened in the French Revolution was designed to protect property from the demands of the state. Possession of property was held to be the basis of personal independence and political liberty, and the expectation of keeping future profits inspired, in some, a willingness to commit their capital to new and uncertain ventures. It made possible an entrepreneurial spirit. There had been a commercial capitalism in Europe at least since the sixteenth century.[1] Industrialization in Europe was therefore capitalistic. Countries outside the West-European orbit, and industrializing later, faced a different problem. A country in which little capital had accumulated from the trade and agriculture of previous generations, and which had few capital-owners or enterprising individuals, could hardly industrialize by European methods. If it lacked the European background, in which various political, social, legal, and intellectual features were as important as the economic, it would have to achieve industrialization by other methods. This has usually meant that innovation, planning, decision making, control, and even domination would rest with the state.

So in the short run, within a few years, the Industrial Revolution in Western Europe favored the liberal and modernizing principles proclaimed in the French Revolution. In the middle run, or in half a century, it made Europe overwhelmingly more powerful than other parts of the world, leading to a worldwide European ascendancy in the form of imperialism. In the still longer run, by the twentieth century, it provoked a retaliation, in which other countries tried hastily to industrialize in self-protection, or to improve the condition of their peoples, desperately hoping to catch up with the West while loudly denouncing it as imperialistic and capitalistic. Of these newer industrial societies the Soviet Union and the People's Republic of China would be the most prominent.

52. The Industrial Revolution in Britain

On the whole, from the beginning of history until about 1800, the work of the world was done with hand tools. Since then it has been increasingly done by machines. Before about 1800 power was supplied by human or animal muscle, reinforced by levers or pulleys, and supplemented by the force of running water or moving air. Since then power has been supplied by the human manipulation of more recondite forms of energy found in steam, electricity, the combustion of gases, and most recently within the atom. The process of shifting from hand tools to power machinery is what is meant by the Industrial Revolution. Its beginning cannot be dated exactly. It grew gradually out of the technical practices of earlier times. It is still going on, for in some countries industrialization is barely beginning, and even in the most highly developed it is still making advances. But the first country to be profoundly affected by industrialization was Great Britain, where its effects became manifest in the half-century following 1780.

It seems likely, despite the emphasis placed on revolutionary upheavals by historians, that people are habitually quite conservative. Working people do not put off their old way of life, move to strange and overcrowded towns, or enter the deadly rounds of mine and factory except under strong incentive. Well-to-do people, living in comfort on assured incomes, do not risk their wealth in new and untried ventures except for good reason. The shifting to modern machine

[1] See pp. 120–126.

production requires in any country a certain mobility of people and of wealth. Such mobility may be produced by state planning, as in the industrialization of the Soviet Union. In England a high degree of social mobility existed in the eighteenth century in consequence of a long historical development.

The Agricultural Revolution in Britain

The English Revolution of 1688, confirming the ascendancy of Parliament over the king, meant in economic terms the ascendancy of the more well-to-do property-owning classes.[2] Among these the landowners were by far the most important, though they counted the great London merchants among their allies. For a century and a half, from 1688 to 1832, the British government was substantially in the hands of these landowners—the "squirearchy" or "gentlemen of England." The result was a thorough transformation of farming, an Agricultural Revolution without which the Industrial Revolution could not have occurred.

Many landowners, seeking to increase their money incomes, began experimenting with improved methods of cultivation and stock raising. They made more use of fertilizers (mainly animal manure); they introduced new implements (such as the "drill seeder" and "horse-hoe"); they brought in new crops, such as turnips, and a more scientific system of crop rotation; they attempted to breed larger sheep and fatter cattle. An improving landlord, to introduce such changes successfully, needed full control over his land. He saw a mere barrier to progress in the old village system of open fields, common lands, and semicollective methods of cultivation. Improvement also required an investment of capital, which was impossible so long as the soil was tilled by numerous poor and custom-bound small farmers.

The old common rights of the villagers were part of the common law. Only an act of Parliament could modify or extinguish them. It was the great landowners who controlled Parliament, which therefore passed hundreds of "enclosure acts," authorizing the enclosure, by fences, walls, or hedges, of the old common lands and unfenced open fields. Land thus came under a strict regime of private ownership and individual management. At the same time small owners sold out or were excluded in various ways, the more easily since the larger owners had so much local authority as justices of the peace. Ownership of land in England, more than anywhere else in central or western Europe, became concentrated in the hands of a relatively small class of wealthy landlords, who let it out in large blocks to a relatively small class of substantial farmers. This development, though in progress throughout the eighteenth century, reached its height during the Napoleonic wars.

One result was greatly to raise the productivity of land and of farm labor. Fatter cattle yielded more meat, more assiduous cultivation yielded more cereals. The food supply of England was increased, while a smaller percentage of the population was needed to produce it. Labor was thus released for other pursuits. The greater number of the English country people became wage earners, working as hired men for the farmers and landlords, or spinning or weaving in their cottages for merchants in the towns. The English workingman (and woman) was

[2] See p. 181.

dependent on daily wages long before the coming of the factory and the machine. English working people became mobile; they would go where the jobs were, or where the wages were slightly higher. They also became available, in that fewer of them were needed on the land to produce food. Such conditions hardly obtained except in Great Britain. On the Continent agricultural methods were less productive, and the rural workers were more established on the soil, whether by institutions of serfdom as in eastern Europe or by the possession of property or firm leaseholds as in France.[3]

Industrialism in Britain: Incentives and Inventions

Meanwhile, as the Agricultural Revolution ran its course in the eighteenth century and into the nineteenth, the British had conquered a colonial empire, staked out markets all over the Americas and Europe, built up a huge mercantile marine, and won command of the sea. The British merchant could sell more, if only more could be produced. He had the customers, he had the ships, and moreover he could obtain the capital with which to finance new ideas. The profit motive prompted the search for more rapid methods of production. The old English staple export, woolen cloth, could be marketed indefinitely if only more of it could be woven. The possibilities in cotton cloth were enormous. The taste of Europeans for cottons had been already formed by imports from Asia. By hand methods Europeans could not produce cotton in competition with the East. But the market was endless if cotton could be spun, woven, and printed with less labor, i.e., by machines. Capital was available, mobile, and fluid because of the rise of banking, credit, and stock companies. Funds could be shifted from one enterprise to another. Wealthy landowners and merchants could divert some of their profits to industry. If an invention proved a total loss, as sometimes happened, or if it required years of development before producing any income, still the investment could be afforded. Only a country already wealthy from commerce and agriculture could have been the first to initiate the machine age. England was such a country.

These conditions induced a series of successful inventions in the textile industry. In 1733 a man named John Kay invented the fly shuttle, by which only one person instead of two was needed to operate a loom. The resulting increase in the output of weaving set up a strong demand for yarn. This was met in the 1760s by the invention of the spinning jenny, a kind of mechanized spinning wheel. The new shuttles and jennies were first operated by hand and used by domestic workers in their homes. But in 1769 Richard Arkwright patented the water frame, a device for the multiple spinning of many threads. At first it was operated by water power, but in the 1780s Arkwright introduced the steam engine to drive his spinning machinery. Thus requiring a considerable installation of heavy equipment, he gathered his engines, frames, and workers into large and usually dismal buildings, called "mills" by the English, or "factories" in subsequent American usage. Mechanical spinning now for a time overwhelmed the hand weavers with yarn. This led to the development of the power loom, which became economically practicable shortly after 1800. Weaving as well as

[3] See pp. 125–126.

spinning was therefore done increasingly in factories. These improvements in the finishing process put a heavy strain on the production of raw cotton. An ingenious Connecticut Yankee, Eli Whitney, while acting as a tutor on a plantation in Georgia, in ten days produced a cotton gin, which by speeding up the removal of seeds greatly increased the output of cotton. The gin soon spread through the American South, where the almost decaying plantation economy was abruptly revived, becoming an adjunct to the Industrial Revolution in England. British imports of raw cotton multiplied fivefold in the thirty years following 1790. In value of manufactures, cotton rose from ninth to first place among British industries in the same years. By 1820 it made up almost half of all British exports.

The steam engine, applied to the cotton mills in the 1780s, had for a century been going through a development of its own.[4] Scientific and technical experiments with steam pressures had been fairly common in the seventeenth century, but what gave the economic impetus to invention was the gradual dwindling away of Europe's primeval stocks of timber. The wood shortage became acute in England about 1700, so that it was more difficult to obtain the charcoal needed in smelting iron, and smelters turned increasingly to coal. Deeper coal shafts could not be sunk until someone devised better methods of pumping out water. About 1702 Thomas Newcomen built the first economically significant steam engine, which was soon widely used to drive pumps in the coal mines. It consumed so much fuel in proportion to power delivered that it could generally be used only in the coal fields themselves. In 1763 James Watt, a technician at the University of Glasgow, began to make improvements on Newcomen's engine. He formed a business partnership with Matthew Boulton. Boulton, originally a manufacturer of toys, buttons, and shoe buckles, provided the funds to finance Watt's rather costly experiments, handmade equipment, and slowly germinating ideas. By the 1780s the firm of Boulton and Watt was eminently successful, manufacturing steam engines both for British use and for the export trade.

At first, until further refinements and greater precision could be obtained in the working of iron, the engines were so cumbersome that they could be used as stationary engines only, as in the new spinning mills of Arkwright and others. Soon after 1800 the steam engine was successfully used to propel river boats, notably on the Hudson in 1807, by Robert Fulton, who employed an imported Boulton and Watt engine. Experiments with steam power for land transportation began at the same time. As it was in the coal fields of England a century before that Newcomen's engine had been put to practical uses, so now it was in the coal fields that Watt's engine first became a "locomotive." Well before 1800 the mines had taken to using "rail ways," on which wagons with flanged wheels, drawn by horses, carried coal to canals or to the sea. In the 1820s steam engines were successfully placed on moving vehicles. The first fully satisfactory locomotive was George Stephenson's *Rocket,* which in 1829, on the newly built Liverpool and Manchester Railway, not only reached an impressive speed of sixteen miles per hour but met other more important tests as well. By the 1840s the era of railroad construction was under way in both Europe and the United States.

The Industrial Revolution in Great Britain in its early phase, down to 1830 or 1840, took place principally in the manufacture of textiles, with accompanying

[4] See p. 298.

developments in the exploitation of iron and coal. The early factories were principally textile factories, and indeed mainly cotton mills; for cotton was an entirely new industry to Europe and hence easily mechanized, whereas the long established woolen trade, in which both employers and workers hesitated to abandon their customary ways, was mechanized more slowly. The suddenness of the change must not be exaggerated. It is often said that the Industrial Revolution was not a revolution at all. As late as the 1830s only a small fraction of the British working people were employed in factories. But the factory and the factory system were even then regarded as the coming mode of production, destined to grow and expand, mighty symbols of the irresistible march of progress.

Some Social Consequences of Industrialism in Britain

The Britain that emerged fundamentally unscathed and in fact strengthened from the wars with Napoleon was no longer the "merrie England" of days of yore. The island was becoming crowded with people, as was the lesser island of Ireland. The combined population of Great Britain and Ireland tripled in the century from 1750 to 1850, rising from about 10 million in 1750 to about 30 million in 1850. The growth was distributed very unevenly. Formerly, in England, most people had lived in the south. But the coal and iron, and hence the steam power, lay in the Midlands and the north. Here whole new cities rose seemingly out of nothing. In 1785 it was estimated that in England and Scotland, outside of London, there were only three cities with more than 50,000 people. Seventy years later, the span of one lifetime, there were thirty-one British cities of this size.

Preeminent among them was Manchester in Lancashire, the first and most famous of industrial cities of modern type. Manchester, before the coming of the cotton mills, was a rather large market town. Though very ancient, it had not been significant enough to be recognized as a borough for representation in Parliament. Locally it was organized as a manor. Not until 1845 did the inhabitants extinguish the manorial rights, buying them out at that time from the last lord, Sir Oswald Mosley, for £200,000 or about 1,000,000 dollars. In population Manchester grew from 25,000 in 1772 to 455,000 in 1851. But until 1835 there was no regular procedure in England for the incorporation of cities. Urban organization was more backward than in Prussia or France. Unless inherited from the Middle Ages, a city had no legal existence. It lacked proper officials and adequate tax-raising and lawmaking powers. It was therefore difficult for Manchester, and the other new factory towns, to deal with problems of rapid urbanization, such as provision of police protection, water and sewers, or the disposal of garbage.

The new urban agglomerations were drab places, blackened with the heavy soot of the early coal age, settling alike on the mills and the workers' quarters, which were dark at best, for the climate of the Midlands is not sunny. Housing for workers was hastily built, closely packed, and always in short supply, as in all rapidly growing communities. Whole families lived in single rooms, and family life tended to disintegrate. A police officer in Glasgow observed that there were whole blocks of tenements in the city, each swarming with a thousand ragged children who had first names only, usually nicknames—like animals, as he put it.

The distressing feature of the new factories was that for the most part they required unskilled labor only. Skilled workers found themselves degraded in

BRITAIN BEFORE AND AFTER THE INDUSTRIAL REVOLUTION

In 1700 England, Scotland, and Wales had only one city with a population of more than 100,000. In 1911 they had nearly thirty. The area within the small rectangle in the right-hand panel, roughly the Midlands, is almost exactly the area of Massachusetts.

status. Hand weavers and spinners, thrown out of work by the new machines, either languished in a misery that was the deepest of that of any class in the Industrial Revolution or else went off to a factory to find a job. The factories paid good wages by the standards for unskilled labor at the time. But these standards were very low, too low to allow a man to support his wife and children. This had generally been true for unskilled labor, in England and elsewhere, under earlier economic systems also. In the new factories the work was so mechanical that children as young as six years old were often preferred. Women, too, worked for less and were often more adept at handling a bobbin.

Hours in the factories were long, fourteen a day or occasionally more; and though such hours were familiar to persons who had worked on farms, or at domestic industry in rural households, they were more tedious and oppressive in the more regimented conditions that were necessary in the mills. Holidays were few, except for the unwelcome leisure of unemployment, which was a common scourge, because the short-run ups and downs of business were very erratic during this period of bewildering expansion. A day without work was a day producing nothing to live on, so that even where the daily wage was relatively attractive the worker's real income was chronically insufficient. Workers in the factories, as in the mines, were almost entirely unorganized. They were a mass of recently assembled humanity without traditions or common ties. Each bargained individually with his employer, who, usually a small businessman himself, facing a ferocious competition with others, often in debt for the equipment in his factory, or determined to save money in order to purchase more, held his "wages bill" to the lowest possible figure that he could manage.

The factory owners, the new "cotton lords," were the first industrial capitalists. They were often self-made men, who owed their position to their own intelligence, persistence, and foresight. They lived in comfort without ostentation or luxury, saving from each year's income to build up their factories and their machines. Hard-working themselves, they thought that landed gentlemen were usually idlers and that the poor tended to be lazy. They were usually honest, in a hard and exacting way; they would make money by any means the law allowed, but not beyond it. They were neither brutal nor knowingly hard-hearted. They gave to charitable and philanthropic causes. They believed that they did "the poor" a favor by furnishing them with work and by seeing to it that they worked diligently and productively. Most of them disapproved of public regulation of their business, though a few, driven by competition to expedients that they did not like, such as the employment of small children, would have accepted some regulation that fell on all competitors equally. It was a cotton magnate, the elder Robert Peel, who in 1802 pushed the first Factory Act through Parliament. This act purported to regulate the conditions in which pauper children were employed in the textile mills, but it was a dead letter from the beginning, since it provided no adequate body of factory inspectors. The English at this time, alone among the leading European peoples, had no class of trained, paid, and professional government administrators; nor did they yet want such a class, preferring self-government and local initiative. To have inspectors for one's affairs smacked of Continental bureaucracy. The fact that the older methods of economic regulation were obsolescent, actually unsuited to the new age, had the effect of discrediting the idea of regulation itself. The new industrialists wanted to be let alone. They considered it unnatural to interfere with business and believed that, if allowed to follow their own judgment, they would assure the future prosperity and progress of the country.

Classical Economics: "Laissez Faire"

The industrialists were strengthened in these beliefs by the emerging science of "political economy." In 1776 Adam Smith published his epochal *Wealth of Nations,* which criticized the older mercantilism, with its regulatory and monopolistic practices, and urged, though with moderation, that certain "natural laws" of production and exchange be allowed to work themselves out.[5] Smith was followed by Thomas R. Malthus, David Ricardo, and the so-called Manchester School. Their doctrine was dubbed (by its opponents) laissez faire and in its elaborated form is still called the classical economics. It held, basically, that there is a world of economic relationships autonomous and separable from government or politics. It is the world of the free market, and is regulated within itself by certain "natural laws," such as the law of supply and demand or the law of diminishing returns. All persons should follow their own enlightened self-interest; each knows his own interest better than anyone else; and the sum total of individual interests will add

[5] See pp. 324–325

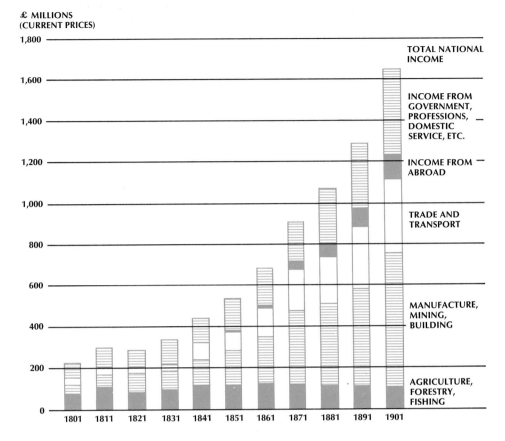

£ MILLIONS
(CURRENT PRICES)

Source: P. Deane and W. A. Cole, *British Economic Growth*
(Cambridge, Eng.: Cambridge University Press, 1962), pp. 166–167.

THE INDUSTRIAL REVOLUTION IN BRITAIN (AS SHOWN BY SOURCES OF INCOME)

Despite uncertainties in such figures several things are apparent. British national income grew about eightfold in the nineteenth century. Incomes derived from agriculture, forestry, and so forth, remained about the same, but sank from one-third to one-sixteenth of all incomes. By 1851 half the national income came from manufacturing, trade, and transportation, and by 1901 three-quarters came from these sources. The category "income from abroad" refers to interest and dividends on loans and investments outside Great Britain, that is, from the export of capital, and this source of income, insignificant in the early years of the century, grew rapidly after the 1850s.

up to the general welfare and liberty of all. Government should do as little as possible; it should confine itself to preserving security of life and property, providing reasonable laws and reliable courts, and so assuring the discharge of private contracts, debts, and obligations. Not only business, but education, charity, and personal matters generally should be left to private initiative. There should be no tariffs; free trade should reign everywhere, for the economic system is worldwide, unaffected by political barriers or national differences. As for workers, according to classical economists before about 1850, they should not expect to make more than a bare minimum living; an "iron law of wages" brings it about that as soon as workers receive more than a subsistence wage they breed more children, who eat up the excess, so that they reduce themselves, and the working class generally, again to a subsistence level. Workers, if discontented, should see the folly of changing the system, for this *is* the system, the natural system—there is no other. Political economy as taught in grim Manchester was not without reason called the "dismal science."

For working people in England the Industrial Revolution was a hard experience. It should be remembered, however, that neither low wages, nor the fourteen-hour day, nor the labor of women and children, nor the ravages of unemployment were anything new. All had existed for centuries, in England and western Europe, as agricultural and commercial capitalism replaced the more self-sufficient economies of the Middle Ages. The factory towns were in some ways better places to live than the rural slums from which many of their people came. Factory routine was psychologically deadening, but the textile mills were in some ways not worse than the domestic sweatshops in which manufacturing processes had previously been carried on. The concentration of working people in city and factory opened the way to improvement in their condition. It made their misery apparent; philanthropic sentiment was gradually aroused among the more fortunate. Gathered in cities, workers obtained more knowledge of the world. Mingling and talking together they developed a sense of solidarity, class interest, and common political aims; and in time they became organized, establishing labor unions by which to obtain a larger share of the national income.

Britain after the fall of Napoleon became the workshop of the world. Though factories using steam power sprang up in France, Belgium, New England, and elsewhere, it was really not until after 1870 that Great Britain faced any industrial competition from abroad. The British had a virtual monopoly in textiles and machine tools. The English Midlands and Scottish Lowlands shipped cotton thread and steam engines to all the world. British capital was exported to all countries, there to call new enterprises into being. London became the world's clearinghouse and financial center. Progressive people in other lands looked to Britain as their model, hoping to learn from its advanced industrial methods, and to imitate its parliamentary political system. Thus more foundations of the nineteenth century were laid.

53.   The Advent of the "Isms"

The combined forces of industrialization and of the French Revolution led after 1815 to the proliferation of doctrines and movements of many sorts. These broke out in a general European revolution in 1848. As for the thirty-three years from 1815 to 1848, there is no better way of grasping their long-run meaning than to reflect on the number of still living "isms" that arose at that time.

So far as is known the word "liberalism" first appeared in the English language in 1819, "radicalism" in 1820, "socialism" in 1832, "conservatism" in 1835. The 1830s first saw "individualism," "constitutionalism," "humanitarianism," and "monarchism." "Nationalism" and "communism" date from the 1840s. Not until the 1850s did the English-speaking world use the word "capitalism" (French *capitalisme* is much older); and not until even later had it heard of "Marxism," though the doctrines of Marx grew out of and reflected the troubled times of the 1840s.

The rapid coinage of new "isms" does not in every case mean that the ideas they conveyed were new. Many of them had their origin in the Enlightenment, if not before. Men had loved liberty before talking of liberalism and been conservative without knowing conservatism as such. The appearance of so many "isms" shows rather that people were making their ideas more systematic. To the "philosophy" of the Enlightenment were now added an intense activism and a partisanship generated during the French Revolution. People were being obliged to reconsider and analyze society as a whole. The social sciences were taking form. An "ism" (excluding such words as "hypnotism" or "favoritism") may be defined as the conscious espousal of a doctrine in competition with other doctrines. Without the "isms" created in the thirty-odd years after the peace of Vienna it is impossible to understand or even talk about the history of the world since that event, so that a brief characterization of some of the most important is in order.[6]

Romanticism

One of the "isms" was not political. It was called "romanticism," a word first used in English in the 1840s to describe a movement then half a century old. Romanticism was primarily a theory of literature and the arts. Its great exponents included Wordsworth, Shelley, and Byron in England, Victor Hugo and Chateaubriand in France, Schiller and the Schlegels and many others in Germany. As a theory of art it raised basic questions on the nature of significant truth, on the importance of various human faculties, on the relation of thought and feeling, on the meaning of the past and of time itself. Representing a new way of sensing all human experience, it affected most thinking on social and public questions.

Possibly the most fundamental romantic attitude was a love of the unclassifiable—of moods or impressions, scenes or stories, sights or sounds or things concretely experienced, personal idiosyncrasies or peculiar customs which the intellect could never classify, box up, explain away, or reduce to an abstract generalization. The romantics, characteristically, insisted on the value of feeling as well as of reason. They were aware of the importance of the subconscious. They were likely to suspect a perfectly lucid idea as somehow superficial. They loved the mysterious, the unknown, the half-seen figures on the far horizon. Hence romanticism contributed to a new interest in strange and distant societies and in strange and distant historical epochs. Where the philosophes of the Enlightenment had deplored the Middle Ages as a time of intellectual error, the romantic generation looked back upon them with respect and even nostalgia, finding in them a fascination, a colorfulness, or a spiritual depth which they missed in their own time. The "Gothic," which rationalists thought barbarous, had a strong appeal for romantics. A Gothic Revival set in in the arts, of which one example was the British Parliament buildings, built in the 1830s.

In medieval art and institutions, as in the art and institutions of every age and

---

[6] For some other "isms" important after 1850, see pp. 519–527.

people, the romantics saw the expression of an inner genius. The idea of original or creative genius was in fact another of the most fundamental romantic beliefs. A genius was a dynamic spirit that no rules could hem in, one that no analysis or classification could ever fully explain. Genius, it was thought, made its own rules and laws. The genius might be that of the individual person, such as the artist, writer, or Napoleon-like mover of the world. It might be the genius or spirit of an age. Or it might be the genius of a people or nation, the *Volksgeist* of Herder, an inherent national character making each people grow in its own distinctive way, which could be known only by a study of its history, and not by ratiocination.[7] Here again romanticism gave a new impetus to study of the past. Politically romantics could be found in all camps, conservative and radical. Let us turn to the more purely political "isms."

Classical Liberalism

The first Liberals, calling themselves by that name (though Napoleon used that word for his own system, as has been seen[8]), arose in Spain among certain opponents of the Napoleonic occupation. The word then passed to France, where it denoted opposition to royalism after the restoration of the Bourbons in 1814. In England many Whigs became increasingly liberal, as did even a few Tories, until the great Liberal party was founded in the 1850s. Nineteenth-century, or "classical," liberalism varied from country to country, but it showed many basic similarities.

Liberals were generally men of the business and professional classes, together with enterprising landowners wishing to improve their estates. They believed in what was modern, enlightened, efficient, reasonable, and fair. They had confidence in man's powers of self-government and self-control. They set a high value on parliamentary or representative government, working through reasonable discussion and legislation, with responsible ministries and an impartial and law-abiding administration. They demanded full publicity for all actions of government, and to assure such publicity they insisted on freedom of the press and free rights of assembly. All these political advantages they thought most likely to be realized under a good constitutional monarchy. Outside of England they favored explicit written constitutions. They were not democrats; they opposed giving every man the vote, fearing the excesses of mob rule or of irrational political action. Only as the nineteenth century progressed did liberals gradually and reluctantly come to accept the idea of universal male suffrage. They subscribed to the doctrines of the rights of man as set forth in the American and French revolutions, but with a clear emphasis on the right of property, and in their economic views they followed the British Manchester School or the French economist J. B. Say. They favored laissez faire, were suspicious of the ability of government to regulate business, wanted to get rid of the guild system where it still existed, and disapproved of attempts on the part of the new industrial laborers to organize unions.

Internationally they advocated freedom of trade, to be accomplished by the

---

[7] See p. 437.
[8] See p. 428.

lowering or abolition of tariffs, so that all countries might exchange their products easily with each other and with industrial England. In this way, they thought, each country would produce what it was most fitted for, and so best increase its wealth and standards of living. From the growth of wealth, production, invention, and scientific progress they believed that the general progress of humanity would ensue. They generally frowned upon the established churches and landed aristocracies as obstacles to advancement. They believed in the spread of tolerance and education. They were also profoundly civilian in attitude, disliking wars, conquerors, army officers, standing armies, and military expenditures. They wanted orderly change by processes of legislation. They shrank before the idea of revolution. Liberals on the Continent were usually admirers of Great Britain.

Radicalism, Republicanism, Socialism

Radicalism, at least as a word, originated in England, where about 1820 the Philosophical Radicals proudly applied the term to themselves. These Radicals in the 1820s included not only the few working-class leaders who were beginning to emerge but also many of the new industrial capitalists, who were still unrepresented in Parliament. They took up where such English "Jacobins" as Thomas Paine had left off a generation earlier, before the long crisis of the French wars had discredited all radicalism as pro-French.[9]

The Philosophical Radicals were a good deal like the French philosophes before the Revolution. They were followers of an elderly sage, Jeremy Bentham, who in prolific writings from 1776 to 1832 undertook to reform the English criminal and civil law, church, Parliament, and constitution. The English Radicals professed to deduce the right form of institutions from the very nature and psychology of man himself. They impatiently waved aside all arguments based on history, usage, or custom. They went to the "roots" of things. ("Radical" is from the Latin word for "root.") They wanted a total reconstruction of laws, courts, prisons, poor relief, municipal organization, rotten boroughs, and fox-hunting clergy. Their demand for the reform of Parliament was vehement and insistent. They detested the Church of England, the peerage, and the squirearchy. Many radicals would just as soon abolish royalty also; not until the long reign of Queen Victoria (1837–1901) did the British monarchy become undeniably popular in all quarters. Above all, radicalism was democratic; it demanded a vote for every adult Englishman. After the Reform Bill of 1832 the industrial capitalists generally turned into liberals, but the working-class leaders remained radical democrats, as will be seen.

On the Continent radicalism was represented by militant republicanism. The years of the First French Republic, which to liberals and conservatives signified horrors associated with the Reign of Terror, were for the republicans years of hope and progress, cut short by forces of reaction. Republicans were a minority even in France; elsewhere, as in Italy and Germany, they were fewer still, though they existed. Mostly the republicans were drawn from intelligentsia such as students and writers, from working-class leaders protesting at social injustice, and from elderly veterans, or the sons and nephews of veterans, to whom the Republic of '93, with its wars and its glory, was a living thing. Because of police

---

[9] See pp. 379, 394.

repression, republicans often joined together in secret societies. They looked with equanimity on the prospect of further revolutionary upheaval, by which they felt that the cause of liberty, equality, and fraternity would be advanced. Strong believers in political equality, they were democrats demanding universal suffrage. They favored parliamentary government but were much less primarily concerned with its successful operation than were the liberals. Most republicans were bitterly anticlerical. Remembering the internecine struggle between the church and the republic during the French Revolution, and still facing the political activity of the Catholic clergy (for republicanism was most common in Catholic countries), they regarded the Catholic church as the implacable enemy of reason and liberty. Opposed to monarchy of any kind, even to constitutional monarchy, intensely hostile to church and aristocracy, conscious heirs of the great French Revolution, organized in national and international secret societies, not averse to overthrowing existing regimes by force, the more militant republicans were considered by most people, including the liberals, to be little better than anarchists.

Republicanism shaded off into socialism. Socialists generally shared the political attitudes of republicanism but added other views besides. The early socialists, those before the Revolution of 1848, were of many kinds, but all had certain ideas in common. All of them regarded the existing economic system as aimless, chaotic, and outrageously unjust. All thought it improper for owners of wealth to have so much economic power—to give or deny work to the worker, to set wages and hours in their own interests, to guide all the labors of society in the interests of private profit. All therefore questioned the value of private enterprise, favoring some degree of communal ownership of productive assets—banks, factories, machines, land, and transportation. All disliked competition as a governing principle and set forth principles of harmony, coordination, organization, or association instead. All flatly and absolutely rejected the laissez faire of the liberals and the political economists. Where the latter thought mainly of increasing production, without much concern over distribution, the early socialists thought mainly of a fairer or more equal distribution of income among all useful members of society. They believed that beyond the civil and legal equality brought in by the French Revolution a further step toward social and economic equality had yet to be taken.

One of the first socialists was also one of the first cotton lords, Robert Owen (1771–1858) of Manchester and the Scottish Lowlands. Appalled at the condition of the millhands, he created a kind of model community for his own employees, paying high wages, reducing hours, sternly correcting vice and drunkenness, building schools and housing and company stores for the cheap sale of workers' necessities. From such paternalistic capitalism in his early years he passed on to a long lifetime spent in crusading for social reforms, in which he was somewhat handicapped, not only by the opposition of industrialists, but by his unpopular radicalism in matters of religion.

Most of the early socialists were Frenchmen, spurred onward by the sense of an uncompleted revolution. One was a nobleman, the Count de Saint-Simon (1760–1825), who had fought in the War of American Independence, accepted the French Revolution, and in his later years wrote many books on social problems. He and his followers, who called themselves not socialists but Saint-Simonians, were among the first clear exponents of a planned society. They advocated the public ownership of industrial equipment and other capital, with control vested in the hands of great captains of industry or social engineers, who should plan vast projects like the digging of a canal at Suez, and in general coordinate the labor and resources of society to productive ends. Of a different type was Charles Fourier (1772–1837), a somewhat doctrinaire thinker who subjected all known institutions to a sweeping condemnation. His positive program took the form of proposing that society be organized in small units which he termed "phalansteries." Each of these he conceived to contain 1,620 persons, each doing the work suited to his natural inclination. Among the practical French no phalanstery was ever successfully organized. A number were established in the United States, still the land of Europe's utopian dream; the best known, since it was operated by literary people, was the Brook Farm "movement" in Massachusetts, which ran through a troubled existence of five years from 1842 to 1847. Robert Owen also, in 1825, had founded an experimental colony in America, at New Harmony, Indiana, on the then remote and unspoiled banks of the Wabash; it, too, lasted only about five years. Such schemes, presupposing the withdrawal of select spirits to live by themselves, really had little to say on the problems of society as a whole in an industrial age.

Politically the most significant form of antediluvian socialism—before the "deluge" of 1848—was the movement stirring among the working classes of France, a compound of revolutionary republicanism and socialism. The politically minded Paris workers had been republican since 1792. For them the Revolution, in the 1820s, 1830s, 1840s, was not finished but only momentarily interrupted. Reduced to political impotence, discriminated against in their rights in the law courts, obliged to carry identity papers signed by their employers, goaded by the pressures of industrialization as it spread to France, they developed a deep hostility to the owning classes of the bourgeoisie. They found a spokesman in the Paris journalist Louis Blanc, editor of the *Revue de progrès* and author of the *Organization of Work* (1839), one of the most constructive of the early socialist writings. He proposed a system of "social workshops," or state-supported manufacturing centers, in which the workers should labor by and for themselves without the intervention of private capitalists. Of this kind of socialism we shall hear more as the story unfolds.

As for "communism," it was at this time an uncertain synonym for socialism. A small group of German revolutionaries, mainly exiles in France, took the name for themselves in the 1840s. They would have been historically forgotten had they not included Karl Marx and Friedrich Engels among their members. Marx and Engels consciously used the word in 1848 to differentiate their variety of socialism from that of such utopians as Saint-Simon, Fourier, and Owen. But the word "communism" went out of general use after 1848, to be revived after the Russian Revolution of 1917, at which time it received a new meaning.

Nationalism: Western Europe

Nationalism, since it arose so largely in reaction against the international Napoleonic system, has already been discussed in the preceding chapter.[10] It was the most pervasive and the least crystallized of the new "isms." In western

[10] See pp. 435–439.

Europe—Britain, France, or Spain—where national unity already existed, nationalism was not a doctrine so much as a latent state of mind, easily aroused when national interests were questioned, but normally taken for granted. Elsewhere—in Italy, Germany, Poland, the Austrian and Turkish empires—where peoples of the same nationality were politically divided or subject to foreign rule, nationalism was becoming a deliberate and conscious program. It was undoubtedly the example of the West, of Great Britain and France, successful and flourishing because they were unified nations, that stimulated the ambitions of other peoples to become unified nations too. The period after 1815 was in Germany a time of rising agitation over the national question, in Italy of the Risorgimento or "resurgence," in eastern Europe of the Slavic Revival.

The movement was led by intellectuals, who often found it necessary to instill in their compatriots the very idea of nationality itself. They seized upon Herder's conception of the *Volksgeist* or national spirit, each applying it to his own people. Usually they began with a cultural nationalism, holding that each people had a language, history, world view, and culture of its own, which must be preserved and perfected. They then usually passed on to a political nationalism, holding that in order to preserve this national culture, and to assure liberty and justice to its individual members, each nation should create for itself a sovereign state. Governing authorities, they held, should be of the same nationality, i.e., language, as those they governed. All persons of the same nationality, i.e., language, should be encompassed within the same state.

Since such ideas could not be fully realized without the overthrow of every government in Europe east of France, thoroughgoing nationalism was inherently revolutionary. Outspoken nationalists were discountenanced or persecuted by the authorities and consequently formed secret societies in large numbers. The Carbonari, organized in Italy in the time of Napoleon, was the best known. There were many others—the *Veri Italiani,* the Apophasimenes, the Sublime and Perfect Masters, etc. In some regions Masonic lodges might serve the same purpose. In many of the societies nationalism was mixed with liberalism, socialism, or revolutionary republicanism in an as yet undifferentiated way. Members were initiated by a complex ritual intended to impress upon them the dire consequences of betraying the society's secrets. They used special grips and passwords and adopted revolutionary names to conceal their identity and baffle the police. They were usually so organized that the ordinary member knew the identity of only a few others, and never of the higher-ups, so that if arrested he could reveal nothing important. The societies kept busy, circulating forbidden literature and generally maintaining a revolutionary ferment. Conservatives dreaded them, but they were not really dangerous to any government that enjoyed the support of its people.

Best known of the nationalist philosophers in western Europe was the Italian Joseph Mazzini (1805–1872), who spent most of his adult life in exile in France and England. In his youth he joined the Carbonari, but in 1831 he founded a society of his own, called Young Italy, and he edited and smuggled into Italy copies of a journal of the same name. Young Italy was soon imitated by other societies of similar aim, such as Young Germany. In 1834 Mazzini organized a filibustering expedition against the kingdom of Sardinia, hoping that all Italy would rise and join him. Undeterred by its total failure, he continued to organize, to conspire, and to write. For Mazzini nationality and revolution were a holy

LANGUAGES OF EUROPE

There are three main European language-families—Germanic, Latin, and Slav. It will be seen that they cover most of Europe. Language areas are shown as they were in the first part of the twentieth century, at which time they had not changed much in over five centuries. The map cannot show local complications which have been a leading source of political trouble—such as the overlapping of adjoining languages, bilingual areas, and the existence of small language "pockets," as of Turkish in the Balkans, Greek in Asia Minor, Yiddish in Poland, or German in scattered parts of eastern Europe. In the extreme northwest is the "Celtic fringe," to which the Breton, Welsh, and Gaelic languages were pushed back in the early Middle Ages. For the area within the diamond-shaped zone no map on the present scale can give a realistic idea; the reader must consult an atlas. In any case, during the Second World War and its aftermath, in Eastern Europe many language pockets were wiped out through exchange, transportation, or destruction of peoples. (See maps, pp. 872–873 and 1039.)

cause in which the most generous and humane qualities were to find expression. He was a moral philosopher, as may be judged from the title of his most widely read book, *The Duties of Man,* in which he placed a pure duty to the nation intermediate between duty to family and duty to God.

To the Germans, divided and frustrated, nationality became almost an obsession. It affected everything from folklore to metaphysics. *Grimm's Fairy Tales,* for example, was first published in 1812. It was the work of the two Grimm brothers, founders of the modern science of comparative linguistics, who traveled about Germany to study the popular dialects and in doing so collected the folk tales that for generations had been current among the common people. They hoped in this way to find the ancient, native, indigenous "spirit" of Germany, deep and unspoiled in the bosom of the *Volk.* The same preoccupation with nationhood revealed itself in the philosophy of Hegel (1770–1831), possibly the most stupendous of all nineteenth-century thinkers.

To Hegel, with the spectacle of the Napoleonic years before him, it was evident that for a people to enjoy freedom, order, or dignity it must possess a potent and independent state. The state, for him, became the institutional embodiment of reason and liberty—the "march of God through the world," as he put it, meaning not an expansion in space through vulgar conquest, but a march through time and through the processes of history. Hegel conceived of reality itself as a process, a development having an inner logic and necessary sequence of its own. He thus broke with the more static and mechanical philosophy of the eighteenth century, with its fixed categories of unchangeable right and wrong. He became a philosopher of unfolding change. The pattern of change he held to be the "dialectic," or irresistible tendency of the mind to proceed by the creation of opposites. A given state of affairs (the "thesis") would in this view inevitably produce the conception of an opposite state of affairs (the "antithesis"), which would equally inevitably be followed by a reconciliation and a fusion of the two (the "synthesis"). Thus it could be thought that the very disunity of Germany, by producing the idea of unity, would inevitably bring about the creation of a German state.

The Hegelian dialectic was soon to be appropriated by Karl Marx to new uses, but meanwhile Hegel's philosophy, with other currents in Germany, made the study of history more philosophically meaningful than it had ever been before. History, the study of time process, seemed to be the very key with which to unlock the true significance of the world. Historical studies were stimulated, and the German universities became centers of historical learning, attracting scholars from many countries. Most eminent of the German historians was Leopold von Ranke (1795–1886), founder of the "scientific" school of historical writing. Ranke, too, though intellectually scrupulous to the last degree, owed much of his incentive to his national feeling. His first youthful work was a study of the *Latin and Teutonic Peoples*; and one of his main ideas, throughout his long life, was that Europe owed its unique greatness to the coexistence and interplay of several distinct nations, which had always resisted the attempts of any one nation to control the whole. By the latter Ranke really meant France—the France of Louis XIV and Napoleon. The Germans, said Ranke in 1830, had a mission from God to develop a culture and a political system entirely different from those of the French. They were destined to "create the pure German state corresponding to the genius of the nation." Whether Western constitutional, parliamentary, and individualist principles were suited to the national character of Germany seemed to Ranke very doubtful.

In economics Friedrich List, in his *National System of Political Economy* (1841), held that political economy as taught in England was suited only to England. It was not an abstract truth but a body of ideas developed in a certain historical stage in a certain country. List thus became a founder of the historical or institutional school of economics. The doctrine of free trade, he said, was designed to make England the world's industrial center by keeping other countries in the status of suppliers of raw material and food. But any country, he held, if it was to be civilized and develop its own national culture, must have cities, factories, industries, and capital of its own. It must therfore put up high tariffs (at least temporarily, in theory) for protection. List, it should be remarked, had developed his ideas during a sojourn in the United States, where Henry Clay's "American system" was in fact a national system of political economy.

Nationalism: Eastern Europe

In eastern Europe the Poles and the Magyars had long been active political nationalists, the Poles wishing to undo the partitions and reestablish their Polish state, the Magyars insisting on autonomy of their kingdom of Hungary within the Habsburg empire.[11] But for the most part nationalism in eastern Europe long remained more cultural than political. Centuries of development had tended to submerge the Czechs, Slovaks, Ruthenians, Romanians, Serbs, Croats, Slovenes—and even the Poles and Magyars in lesser degree. Their upper classes spoke German or French and looked to Vienna or to Paris for their ideas. The native languages had remained peasant languages, and the cultures peasant cultures, barely known to civilized Europeans. It seemed that many of these languages would disappear.[12]

But early in the nineteenth century the process began to reverse itself. Patriots began to demand the preservation of their historic cultures. They collected folk tales and ballads; they studied the languages, composing grammars and dictionaries, often for the first time; and they took to writing books in their mother tongues. They urged their own educated classes to give up "foreign" ways. They wrote histories showing the famous exploits of their several peoples in the Middle Ages. A new nationalism stirred the Magyars; in 1837 a national Hungarian theater was established at Budapest. In what was to become Romania a former Transylvanian peasant youth named George Lazar began as early as 1816 to teach at Bucharest. He lectured in Romanian (to the surprise of the upper classes, who preferred Greek), telling how Romania had a distinguished history back to the Roman emperor Trajan. As for the Greeks, they entertained visions of restoring the medieval Greek empire (known to Westerners as the Byzantine Empire) in which persons of Greek language or Greek Orthodox religion should become the predominant people of the Balkans.

The most far-reaching of the east-European movements was the Slavic Revival. The Slavs included the Russians, Poles, Ukrainians, Byelorussians, and Ruthenians; the Czechs and Slovaks; and the South Slavs, consisting of the Slovenes, Croats, Serbs, and Bulgars. All branches of the Slavs began to come to life. In 1814 the Serb Vuk Karajich published a grammar of his native tongue and a collection of *Popular Songs and Epics of the Serbs*; he worked out a Serbian alphabet, translated the New Testament, and declared that the dialect of Ragusa (now Dubrovnik) should become the literary language of all South Slavs. He was opposed by the Serbian clergy, who preferred to have writing confined to Slavonic, a purely learned language, like Latin; but he found much support outside Serbia, including that of the brothers Grimm. The Czechs had always been a more advanced people than the Serbs, but educated Czechs were usually half Germanized. In 1836 the historian Palacky published the first volume of his *History of Bohemia,* designed to give the Czechs a new pride in their national

[11] On the Poles, see pp. 245–249, 340–341, 436; on the Magyars, pp. 225, 276, 333.
[12] See p. 251.

past. He first wrote his book in German, the common reading language of educated Czechs. But he soon recast it into Czech, significantly reentitling it a *History of the Czech People*. Among Poles the poet and revolutionary Adam Mickiewicz may be mentioned. Arrested by the Russians in 1823 for membership in a secret society, he was soon allowed by the tsarist government to pass into western Europe. From 1840 to 1844 he taught Slavic languages at the Collège de France, using his lecture platform as a rostrum to deliver eloquent pleas for the liberation of all peoples and overthrow of autocracy. He wrote epic poems on Polish historical themes and continued to be active among the revolutionary Polish exiles settled in France.

Russia itself, which Poles and Czechs regarded as very backward, was slower to develop a pronounced national sense. Under Tsar Alexander I a Western or European orientation prevailed, but in Alexander's last years and after his death the doctrines of Slavophilism began to spread. Russian Slavophilism, or the idea that Russia possessed a way of life of its own, different from and not to be corrupted by that of Europe, was simply the application to Russia of the fundamental idea of the *Volksgeist*. Such views in Russia were at least as old as the opposition to the reforms of Peter the Great.[13] In the nationalistic nineteenth century they crystallized more systematically into an "ism," and they tended to merge into Pan-Slavism, which made substantially the same assertions for the Slavic peoples as a whole. But Pan-Slavism, before 1848, was no more than embryonic.

Other "Isms"

Liberalism, radical republicanism, socialism, and nationalism were after 1815 the political forces driving Europe onward toward a future still unknown. Of other "isms" less need be said. Conservatism, too, remained strong. Politically, on the Continent, conservatism upheld the institutions of absolute monarchy, aristocracy, and church and opposed the constitutional and representative government sought by liberals. As a political philosophy, conservatism built upon the ideas of Edmund Burke, who had held that every people must change its institutions by gradual adaptation, and that no people could suddenly realize in the present any freedoms not already well prepared for in the past.[14] This doctrine lacked appeal for those to whom the past had been a series of misfortunes. Conservatism sometimes passed into nationalism, since it stressed the firmness and continuity of national character. But nationalists at this time were more often liberals or republicans. "Monarchism" was conservative and even reactionary. Gone was the enlightened despotism of the last century, when kings had boldly irritated their nobles and defied their churches. After the thunders of the French Revolution aristocracy and monarchy huddled together, and their new watchword was to maintain "the throne and the altar."

Deeper than other "isms," a feeling shared in varying ways by people of all parties, was the profound current of humanitarianism. It consisted in a heightened sense of the reality of cruelty inflicted upon others. Here the thought of the Age

---

[13] See pp. 244–245, 337.
[14] See p. 379.

of Enlightenment suffered no reversal. Torture was gone, and even backward governments showed no inclination to restore it. Conditions in prisons, hospitals, insane asylums, and orphanages improved. People began to be moved by the misery of pauper children, chimney sweeps, women in the mines, and black slaves. Russian serf owners and American slave owners began to show psychological signs of moral doubt. To degrade human beings, use them as work animals, torture them, confine them unjustly, hold them as hostages for others, tear apart their families, and punish their relatives were regarded by Europeans as foreign to true civilization, something distant, "Turkish" or "Asiatic," like the castration of eunuchs, the impressment of janissaries, or the burning of widows. The Christian sense of the inviolability of the human person was now again, in a mundane way, beginning to relieve the sufferings of humanity.

54. The Dike and the Flood: Domestic

It is time now to resume the narrative of political events, broken off at the close of the last chapter with the peace settlement of 1814–1815. The governments that defeated Napoleon wanted to assure themselves above all else that the disturbances of the past twenty-five years would not be renewed. In France the restored Bourbon king, Louis XVIII, aspired to keep his throne for himself and his successors. In Great Britain the Tory governing class hoped to preserve the old England that they had so valiantly saved from the clutches of Bonaparte. In Germany, Austria, Italy, and central Europe the chief aim of Metternich, who for another thirty-three years remained the mastermind of these regions, was to maintain a system in which the prestige of the Habsburg dynasty should be supreme. The aims of the tsar, Alexander, were less clear. He was feared by representatives of the other powers as a dreamer, a self-chosen world savior, a man who said he wanted to bring Christianity into politics, a crowned Jacobin, and even a liberal. It became one of Metternich's chief hopes to convert Alexander to conservatism.

The arrangements made by the victorious powers were in some ways moderate, at least when the provocations they had undergone in the late wars are considered. Partly by the tsar's insistence written constitutions existed after 1814 in France and in Russian or "Congress" Poland. Some of the rulers of south German states allowed a measure of representative government. Even the king of Prussia promised a representative assembly for his kingdom, though the promise was not kept. But it was difficult to maintain any kind of stability. The forces of the political right, the privileged classes (or in France the former privileged classes) denounced all signs of liberalism as dangerous concessions to revolution. Those of the political left—liberals, nationalists, republicans—regarded the newly installed regimes as hopelessly reactionary and inadequate. Statesmen were jittery on the subject of revolution, so that they met every sign of agitation with attempts at repression, which though they might drive agitation temporarily underground really only made it worse by creating additional grievances. A vicious circle was set endlessly revolving.

Reaction after 1815: France, Poland

In France Louis XVIII in 1814 granted an amnesty to the regicides of 1793. But the regicides, like all republicans, found the France of 1814 an uncomfortable place to live in, exposed as they were to the unofficial vengeance of counterrevolutionaries, and in 1815 most of them rallied to Napoleon when he returned from Elba. This exasperated the royalist counterrevolutionaries beyond all measure. A brutal "white terror" broke out. Upper-class youths murdered Bonapartists and republicans, Catholic mobs seized and killed Protestants at Marseilles and Toulouse. The Chamber of Deputies chosen in 1815 (by the tiny electorate of 100,000 well-to-do landowners) proved to be more royalist than the king—*plus royaliste que le roi*. The king himself could not control the mounting frenzy of reaction, which he was sensible enough to realize would only infuriate the revolutionary element still further, as in fact happened. In 1820 a fanatical workingman assassinated the king's nephew, the Duke de Berry. Those who said that all partisans of the French Revolution were criminal extremists seemed to be justified. The reaction deepened, until in 1824 Louis XVIII died and was succeeded by his brother Charles X. Not only was Charles X the father of the recently murdered Duke de Berry, but for over thirty years he had been the acknowledged leader of implacable counterrevolution. As the Count of Artois, youngest brother of Louis XVI, he had been among the first to emigrate in 1789. He was the favorite Bourbon among the most obstinate ex-seigneurs, nobles, and churchmen. Regarding himself as hereditary absolute monarch by the grace of God, he had himself crowned at Reims with all the romantic pomp of ages past, and proceeded to stamp out not only revolutionary republicanism but liberalism and constitutionalism as well.

In Poland, it will be recalled, the Vienna settlement created a constitutional kingdom, with Alexander as king, joined in merely personal union with the Russian empire. The new machinery did not work very well. The Polish constitution provided for an elected diet, a very wide suffrage by the standards of the day, the Napoleonic civil code, freedom of press and religion, and exclusive use of the Polish language. But the Poles discovered that Alexander, though favoring liberty, did not like to have anyone disagree with him. They could make little use of their much touted freedom in any actual legislation. The elected diet could not get along with the viceroy, who was a Russian. In Russia the serf-owning aristocracy viewed Alexander's idea of a constitutional kingdom in Poland with a jaundiced eye. They wanted no experimentation with liberty on the very borders of Russia. The Poles themselves played into the hands of their enemies. For the Poles were nationalist at least as much as they were liberal. They were dissatisfied with the boundaries accorded to Congress Poland. They dreamed of the vast kingdom that had existed before the First Partition and so agitated the interminable question of the Eastern Border, laying claim to huge territories in the Ukraine and Byelorussia.[15] At the University of Vilna professors and students began to join secret societies. Some members of these societies were revolutionaries aiming at driving out Alexander, reuniting with Prussian and Austrian Poland, and reconstituting an independent Polish state. It was in the

---

[15] See map, p. 248.

discovery and breaking up of one such society that Adam Mickiewicz was arrested in 1823. Reaction and repression now struck the University of Vilna.

Reaction after 1815: The German States, Britain

In Germany those who had felt national stirrings during the Wars of Liberation were disillusioned by the peace treaty, which maintained the several German principalities about as Napoleon had left them and purposely united them only in a loose federation, or Bund. National ideas were most common in the numerous universities, where students and professors were more susceptible than most people to the doctrines of an eternal *Volksgeist* and a far-flung *Deutschtum*. National ideas, being a glorification of the German common people, carried with them a kind of democratic opposition to aristocrats, princes, and kings. Students in many of the universities in 1815 formed college clubs, called collectively the *Burschenschaft*, which, as centers of serious political discussion, were to replace the older clubs devoted to drinking and dueling. The *Burschenschaft*, a kind of German youth movement, held a nationwide congress at Wartburg in 1817. Students listened to rousing speeches by patriotic professors, marched about in "Teutonic" costume, and burned a few reactionary books. This undergraduate performance was no immediate threat to any established state, but the nervous governments took alarm. In 1819 a theology student assassinated the German writer Kotzebue, known as an informer in the service of the tsar. The assassin received hundreds of letters of congratulation, and at Nassau the head of the local government barely escaped the same fate at the hands of a pharmacy student.

Metternich now chose to intervene. He had no authority in Germany except in that Austria was a member of the Germanic federation. He regarded all these manifestations of German national spirit, or of any demand for a more solidly unified Germany, as a threat to the favorable position of the Austrian Empire and to the whole balance of Europe. He called a conference of the principal German states at Carlsbad in Bohemia; the frightened conferees adopted certain resolutions, proposed by Metternich, which were soon enacted by the diet of the Bund. These Carlsbad Decrees (1819) dissolved the *Burschenschaft* and the equally nationalistic gymnastic clubs (some of whose members thereupon joined secret societies); and they provided for government officials to be placed in the universities to watch them and for censors to control the contents of books and of the periodical and newspaper press. The Carlsbad Decrees remained in force for many years, and they imposed an effective check on the growth of liberal and nationalist ideas in Germany.

Metternich was unable to persuade the south German rulers to retract the constitutions they had granted. The rulers here, in Bavaria, Württemberg, and elsewhere, found that with representative government they could rally popular support as well as assimilate the numerous new territories that they had obtained from Napoleon. But in general, throughout Germany, after 1820, repression of new or unsettling ideas was the rule. Still more so was this true of the Austrian Empire, which Metternich could more directly control.

Nor did Great Britain escape the dreary rounds of agitation and repression. As elsewhere, radicalism produced reaction, and vice versa. Britain after Waterloo was a country devoted to its old traditions but also afflicted by the most advanced social evils. In 1815, at the close of the wars, the landed classes feared an inrush of imported agricultural products and consequent collapse of farm prices and rentals. The gentry who controlled Parliament enacted a new Corn Law, raising the protective tariff to the point where import of grain became impossible unless prices were very high. Landlords and their farmers benefited, but wage earners found the price of breadstuffs soaring out of reach. At the same time there was a postwar depression in industry. Wages fell and many were thrown out of work. These conditions naturally contributed to the spread of political radicalism, which looked first of all to a drastic reform of the House of Commons, in order that thereafter a radical program of social and economic legislation might be enacted.

A riot broke out in London in December 1816. In the following February the Prince Regent was attacked in his carriage. The goverment suspended habeas corpus and employed *agents provocateurs* to obtain evidence against the agitators. Industrialists of Manchester and the new factory towns, determined to force through the reform of parliamentary representation, took the chance offered by the distress of the working classes to organize mass meetings of protest. At Birmingham a crowd elected a mock member of Parliament. At sprawling Manchester 80,000 people staged an enormous demonstration at St. Peter's Fields in 1819; they demanded universal male suffrage, annual election of the House of Commons, and the repeal of the Corn Laws. Although perfectly orderly they were fired upon by soldiers; 11 persons were killed and about 400 wounded, including 113 women. Radicals called this episode the Peterloo massacre in derisive comparison with the battle of Waterloo. The frightened government thanked the soldiers for their brave upholding of the social order. Parliament rushed through the Six Acts (1819), which outlawed "seditious and blasphemous" literature, put a heavy stamp tax on newspapers, authorized the search of private houses for arms, and rigidly restricted the right of public meeting. A group of revolutionaries thereupon plotted to assassinate the whole cabinet at a dinner; they were caught in Cato Street in London in 1820—whence the name "Cato Street Conspiracy." Five of them were hanged. Meanwhile, for publishing the writings of Thomas Paine, Richard Carlisle spent seven years in prison.

"Our example," wrote the Duke of Wellington to a Continental correspondent in 1819, "will be of value in France and Germany, and it is to be hoped that the world will escape from the general revolution with which we all seem to be threatened."

In summary, reactionary policies entrenched themselves everywhere in the years following the peace. The reaction was due only in part to memories of the French Revolution. It was due even more to the living fear of revolution in the present. This fear, though exaggerated, was no mere hallucination. Sensing the rising flood, the established interests desperately built dikes against it in every country. The same is true of international politics at the time.

55. The Dike and the Flood: International

At the Congress of Vienna the powers agreed to hold meetings in the future to enforce the treaty and take up new issues as they arose. A number of congresses of the Great Powers resulted, which are of significance as an experimental step toward international regulation of the affairs of Europe. The congresses resembled, in a tentative and partial way, the League of Nations that arose after the First World War of 1914–1918, or the United Nations that arose during and after the war of 1939–1945. The powers had also, in 1815, in alarm after the return of Napoleon, subscribed to Alexander I's Holy Alliance, which became the popular term for the collaboration of the European states in the congresses.[16] The Holy Alliance, on the face of it a statement of Christian purpose and international concord, gradually became an alliance for the suppression of revolutionary and even liberal activity, following in that respect the trend of the governments which made it up.

The Congress of Aix-la-Chapelle, 1818

The first general postwar assemblage of the powers took place at the Congress of Aix-la-Chapelle (or Aachen) in 1818. The principal item on the agenda was to withdraw the allied army of occupation from France. The French argued that Louis XVIII would never be popular in France so long as he was supported by a foreign army. The other powers, since they all desired the French to forget the past and accept the Bourbons, withdrew their military forces without disagreement. They arranged also to have private bankers take over the French reparations debt (the 700 million francs imposed by the second Treaty of Paris); the bankers paid the allied governments, and the French in due time paid the bankers. On a few other smaller matters international collective action proved successful.

Tsar Alexander was still the most advanced internationalist of the day. He suggested at Aix-la-Chapelle a kind of permanent European union and even proposed the maintenance of international military forces to safeguard recognized states against changes by violence. Governments if thus reassured against revolution, he argued, would more willingly grant constitutional and liberal reforms. But the others demurred, especially the British foreign minister Lord Castlereagh. The British declared themselves willing to make international commitments against specified contingencies, such as a revival of aggression on the part of France. But they would assume no obligations to act upon indefinite and unforeseeable future events. They reserved the right of independent judgment in foreign policy. Concretely, the congress addressed itself to the problems of the Atlantic slave trade and of the recurring nuisance of the Barbary pirates. It was unanimously agreed that both should be suppressed. To suppress them required naval forces, which only the British possessed in adequate amount, and it meant also that naval captains must be authorized to stop and search vessels at sea. The continental states, always touchy on the subject of British sea power, refused to countenance any such uses of the British fleet. They feared for the freedom of the seas. As for the British, they would not even discuss placing British warships in an international naval pool or putting British squadrons under the authority of an international body. Nothing therefore was done; the slave trade continued, booming illicitly with the endless demand for cotton; and the Barbary pirates were not disposed of until the French occupied and annexed

[16] See p. 451 and map, pp. 448–449.

Algeria some years later. The growth of international institutions was blocked by the separate interests of the sovereign states.

Revolution in Southern Europe: The Congress of Troppau, 1820

Scarcely had the Congress of Aix-la-Chapelle disbanded when revolutionary agitation came to a crisis in southern Europe. It was not that revolutionary or liberal sentiment was stronger here than in the north, in the sense of having more followers, but rather that the governments in question, those of Spain, Naples, and the Ottoman Empire, were inefficient, ignorant, flimsy, and corrupt. Many of the revolutionaries were hardly more than middle-class liberals; indeed, the Spaniards at this time were the first to use the word "liberal" in this modern political sense. Many of them had at first accepted the Napoleonic occupation of Spain as a progressive development, but had then turned against it and proclaimed a new constitution in 1812, modeled on the French revolutionary constitution of 1789–1791.[17] After Napoleon's final defeat they attempted to force the restored Bourbon kings of Spain and Naples to adopt this constitution of 1812.

In 1820 the governments of both Spain and Naples collapsed with remarkable ease before the demonstrations of revolutionaries. The kings of both countries reluctantly took oaths to the Spanish constitution of 1812. But Metternich saw the insurrections as the first symptoms of a revolutionary seizure against which Europe should be quarantined. It was a fact that revolutionary agitation was international, easily leaping across frontiers, because of the operations of secret societies and of political exiles, and because in any case the same ideas had been aroused in all countries by the French Revolution. Metternich considered Italy in particular, since the ejection of Napoleon, to be within the legitimate sphere of influence of the Austrian Empire. He therefore called a meeting of the Great Powers at Troppau, hoping to use the authority of an international congress to put down the revolution in Naples. The governments of Great Britain and France, not eager to play Austria's game, sent only observers to the congress. Metternich's main problem was, as usual, Alexander. What would be the attitude of the liberal tsar, the friend and patron of constitutions, toward the idea of a constitutional monarchy in Naples? At an inn in Troppau Metternich and Alexander met alone, and there held a momentous interview over the teacups. Metternich reviewed the horrors of revolutionism, the unwisdom of granting any concessions lest revolutionaries be encouraged. Alexander was already somewhat disillusioned by the ungrateful feelings of the Poles. He was troubled by rumors of disaffection among officers in his own army. He had always believed that constitutions should be granted by legitimate sovereigns, not extorted from them by revolutionaries, as had happened in Naples. He allowed himself to be persuaded by Metternich. He declared that he had always been wrong, and that Metternich had always been right; and he announced himself ready to follow Metternich's political judgment. The triumph of the Austrian chancellor was complete. The radical tsar now turned reactionary.

Thus fortified, Metternich drew up a document, the protocol of Troppau, for consideration and acceptance by the five Great Powers. It held that all recognized

---

[17] See pp. 373–374, 435.

European states should be protected by collective international action, in the interests of general peace and stability, from internal changes brought about by force. It was a statement of collective security against revolution. Neither France nor Great Britain accepted it. Castlereagh wrote to Metternich that if Austria felt its interests to be threatened in Naples it should intervene in its own name only. It was not the repression of the Neapolitan revolution that the Tories of 1820 objected to, so much as the principle of a binding international collaboration. Metternich could get only Russia and Prussia to endorse his protocol, in addition to Austria. These three, acting as the Congress of Troppau, authorized Metternich to dispatch an Austrian army into Naples. He did so; the Neapolitan revolutionaries were arrested or put to flight; the incompetent and brutal Ferdinand I was restored as "absolute" king; the demon of revolution was seemingly exorcised. Reaction won out. But the Congress of Troppau, ostensibly a Europe-wide international body, had in effect functioned as an antirevolutionary alliance of Austria, Russia, and Prussia. A gap opened between the three Eastern autocracies and the two Western powers—even when the latter consisted of Tories and Bourbons.

Spain and the Near East: The Congress of Verona, 1822

Thousands of revolutionaries and liberals fled from the terror raging in Italy. Many went to Spain, now dreaded by conservatives as the main seat of revolutionary infection. The Near East also seemed about to ignite in conflagration. Alexander Ypsilanti, a Greek who had spent his adult life in the military service of Russia, in 1821 led a band of armed followers from Russia into Romania (still a part of Turkey), hoping that all Greeks and pro-Greeks in the Turkish empire would join him. He expected Russian support, since the penetration of Turkey by the use of Greek Christians had long been a pet project of Russian foreign policy.[18] The possibility of a Turkish empire converted into a "Greek" empire and dependent on Russia was naturally unpleasant to Metternich. To deal with all these matters an international congress met at Verona in 1822.

Alexander, in shifting from liberal to reactionary views, had not changed his belief in the need for concerted international action. Had pure power politics determined his decisions he would doubtless have favored Ypsilanti's Grecophile revolution. But he stood by the principle of international solidarity against revolutionary violence. He refused to support Ypsilanti, who found less enthusiasm for Greek culture among the Romanians and Balkan peoples than he had expected and was soon defeated by the Turks. As for intervention to repress the uprising in Greece itself, the question did not arise, since the Turkish government proved quite able for a time to handle the matter without assistance.

The question of the revolution in Spain was settled by foreign intervention. The Bourbon regime in France had no taste for a Spain in which revolutionaries, republicans, political exiles, and members of secret societies might be harbored. The French government proposed to the Congress of Verona that it be authorized to dispatch an army across the Pyrenees. The Congress welcomed the offer, and despite many dire predictions of ruin, arising from memories of Napoleon's disaster, a French army of 200,000 men moved into Spain in 1823. The campaign

[18] See p. 340.

proved to be a military promenade through a cheering country. Spanish liberals, constitutionalists, or revolutionaries were a helpless minority. The mass of the people saw the invasion as a deliverance from Masons, Carbonari, and heretics and shouted with satisfaction at the restoration of church and king. Ferdinand VII, unscrupulous and narrow-minded, repudiated his constitutional oath and let the vindictive ecclesiastics, grandees, and hidalgos have their way. The revolutionaries were savagely persecuted, exiled, or jailed.

Latin American Independence

The disturbances in Europe had their repercussions in all parts of America. While Great Britain was engaged against Napoleon, the United States fought its inconclusive War of 1812 against the former mother country, and a few years later, after minor military operations, obtained the cession of Florida from Spain. Latin America was affected more positively. The Portuguese royal family, to escape Napoleon, had taken refuge in its Brazilian empire, but when the dynasty was restored at Lisbon one of its members refused to leave Brazil, which remained as an "empire" independent of Portugal until succeeded by a republican regime in 1889.

Spanish America reached over the enormous area from San Francisco to Buenos Aires. Here, too, the thought of the Enlightenment, the news of the American and French Revolutions, the Napoleonic occupation of Spain, and the restoration in 1814 of the Bourbon Ferdinand VII to the Spanish throne all had their effects. The British had been penetrating Spanish America commercially for over a century, and during the Napoleonic wars they had increased their exports to it twentyfold.[19] There were thus business interests in Spanish America that resisted any return to the old Spanish imperial system of trade controls. More fundamental was the resentment, growing up over several generations, felt by the "creoles" for the "peninsulars," the creoles being the whites of Spanish descent born in America, and the peninsulars those born in Spain who were sent out to occupy the highest offices in the empire. In many places most of the people were native Indians or mestizos of mixed Spanish and Indian origin, often living in depressed conditions and far from the capital cities, so that the movement for independence never took on the widespread popular character that it did in the British colonies that became the United States. It was mainly led by creoles who were active in municipal governments in the towns. At times, as when the revolt was against the Napoleonic government in Spain or against the ephemeral liberal regime in Spain in 1820, the movement for independence recruited some very conservative elements among large landowners and high churchmen. But the important leaders, such as Simón Bolívar and José de San Martín, were men who had spent years in Europe and preferred the new constitutional principles, but were in the end frustrated in their aspirations for their own country. The dissensions that long continued to afflict Spanish America were all present within the independence movement itself.

Because of its vast extent, over six thousand miles interrupted by mountain barriers, there could be less unity in the liberation of Spanish America than had

[19] See p. 435.

been possible, however difficult, in the North American rebellion against England. There could be no Continental Congress such as had met in Philadelphia in 1774. Revolts took place separately within the great vice-royalties: New Spain (Mexico), New Granada (Colombia and Venezuela), Peru (including Ecuador and most of Bolivia and Chile), and La Plata (Argentina, with claims over what are now Uruguay and Paraguay).

The first revolts were against Joseph Bonaparte after Napoleon made him king of Spain in 1808. The rebels proclaimed their loyalty to the deposed Ferdinand VII, who, however, when restored in 1814, refused to make any concessions to American demands, so that revolutionary sentiment turned against him also. There followed a series of disconnected struggles between those fighting for independence (with or without much internal change) and combinations of officials, army officers, landowners, and churchmen who remained loyal to the Spanish crown. Bolívar became the liberator of Venezuela and Colombia, San Martín of Argentina and Chile, and both combined in the liberation of Peru. In Mexico, by way of exception, there was a true mass rising of Indians and mestizos, which was put down by the middle- and upper-class leaders, so that independent Mexico entered upon a long period of chronic turmoil. All Spanish America was troubled by disputes over boundaries, federations formed only to dissolve, and attempted conquests and secessions, so that it was only later in the nineteenth century that the map of South and Central America took form as we know it today.

Let us return to the congress of European powers meeting in Verona in 1822. At the very time when a French army suppressed the revolution in Spain the revolutionaries in Spanish America were declaring their independence. At Verona, the tsar Alexander urged the Congress to mediate between Spain and its colonies. This was a euphemistic way of suggesting military intervention in Spanish America, following the principle of the protocol of Troppau. The British objected. Even the Tory government favored revolutions that might break up the Spanish empire into independent states, with which free trade treaties might be negotiated. Without at least benevolent neutrality from the British fleet no armed force could sail to America. The Spanish Americans therefore maintained their independence, thanks in part to the use made by the British of their sea power on this occasion.

The new republics received strong moral support from the United States also. In December 1823 President James Monroe, in a message to Congress, announced the "Monroe Doctrine." It stated that attempts by European powers to return parts of America to colonial status would be viewed as an unfriendly act by the United States. The British foreign minister George Canning (who had just succeeded Castlereagh) had at first proposed a joint statement by Great Britain and the United States against the East European powers on the Spanish American question. President Monroe, at the advice of his secretary of state John Quincy Adams, decided instead to make a unilateral statement in the form of a message to Congress. They intended to aim their "doctrine" at Great Britain as well as the Continental states, since the British, with their command of the sea, were in fact the only power by which the independence of American states could in practice be threatened. Canning, having no such threats in mind, and concerned more with the Congress of Verona, accepted the line taken by the United States. Indeed, he declared with a flourish that he had "called the New World into existence to redress the balance of the Old.'' The Monroe Doctrine, at its inception, was a kind of counterblast to the Metternich doctrine of the protocol of Troppau. Where the latter announced the principle of intervention against revolution, the Monroe Doctrine announced that revolutions in America, if they resulted in regimes recognized by the United States, were outside the pale of attention of European powers. In any case the efficacy of the Monroe Doctrine long depended on the tacit cooperation of the British fleet.

Over three hundred years of European colonial empires in America now came to an end, with few exceptions, in the half-century following the United States declaration of independence. One exception was Canada, where membership in the British empire was voluntary, at least for the English-speaking inhabitants, and where both the English and French Canadians resisted threats of annexation by the United States. The other exceptions were in the West Indies, where Haiti was independent, the smaller islands remained British, French, or Dutch, and the large islands of Cuba and Puerto Rico remained Spanish until the Spanish-American War of 1898.

The End of the Congress System

After the Congress of Verona no more such meetings were held. The attempt at a formal international regulation of European affairs was given up. In the broadest retrospect, the congresses failed to make progress toward an international order because, especially after Alexander's conversion to conservatism, they came to stand for nothing except preservation of the status quo. They made no attempt at accommodation with the new forces that were shaping Europe. It was not the policy of the congresses to forestall revolution by demanding that governments institute reforms. They simply repressed or punished all revolutionary agitation. They propped up governments that could not stand on their own feet.

In any case the congresses never succeeded in subordinating the separate interests of the Great Powers. Perhaps Alexander's repudiation of Ypsilanti was a sacrifice of Russian advantage to international principle; but when the Austrian government intervened to crush the revolution in Naples, and when the French government crushed the revolution in Spain, though in both cases they acted with an international mandate, each was really promoting what it conceived to be its own interests. The interest of Great Britain was to pull away from the system entirely. As defined by Castlereagh and by Canning after him, it was to stand aloof from permanent international commitments, to preserve a free exercise of sea power and foreign policy, and to take a benevolent view toward revolution in other countries. Since France eventually pulled away also, the Holy Alliance ceased to be even ostensibly a European system and became no more than a counterrevolutionary league between the three east-European autocracies. With a majority of the five Great Powers highly illiberal, the cause of liberalism in Europe was advanced by the collapse of the international system. At the same time the collapse of the system opened the way to the uncontrolled nationalism of the sovereign states. ''Things are getting back to a wholesome state again,'' wrote George Canning in 1822. ''Every nation for itself and God for us all!''

Russia: The Decembrist Revolt, 1825

Alexander I, "the man who defeated Napoleon," the ruler who had led his armies from Moscow to Paris, who had frightened the diplomats by the Russian shadow that he threw over the Continent, and who yet in his way had been the great pillar of constitutional liberalism and international order, died in 1825. His death was the signal for revolution in Russia. Officers of the Russian army, during the campaigns of 1812–1815 in Europe, had become acquainted with many unsettling ideas. Secret socities were formed even in the Russian officer corps; their members held all sorts of conflicting ideas, some wanting a constitutional tsardom in Russia, some demanding a republic, some even dreaming of an emancipation of the serfs. When Alexander died it was for a time uncertain which of his two brothers, Constantine or Nicholas, should succeed him. The restless coteries in the army preferred Constantine, who was thought to be more favorable to innovations in the state. In December 1825 they proclaimed Constantine at St. Petersburg, having their soldiers shout "Constantine and Constitution!" The soldiers, it is said, thought that Constitution was Constantine's wife.

But the fact was that Constantine had already renounced his claims in favor of Nicholas, who was the rightful heir. The uprising, known as the Decembrist revolt, was soon put down. Five of the mutinous officers were hanged; many others were condemned to forced labor or interned in Siberia. The Decembrist revolt was the first manifestation of the modern revolutionary movement in Russia—of a revolutionary movement inspired by an ideological program, as distinguished from the elemental mass upheavals of Pugachev or Stephen Razin. But the immediate effect of the Decembrist revolt was to clamp repression upon Russia more firmly. Nicholas I (1825–1855) maintained an unconditional and despotic autocracy.

Ten years after the defeat of Napoleon the new forces issuing from the French Revolution seemed to be routed, and reaction, repression, and political immobility seemed to prevail everywhere in Europe. The dike—a massive dike—seemed to be containing the flood.

56. The Breakthrough of Liberalism in the West: Revolutions of 1830–1832

The dike broke in 1830, nor in western Europe was the stream thereafter stopped. The seepage, indeed, had already begun. By 1825 Spanish America was independent. The British and the French had pulled away from the congress system. The Greek nationalist movement against the Turks had broken out in the early 1820s.

With the defeat of Ypsilanti in 1821 the Greek nationalists turned somewhat away from the idea of a neo-Greek empire and more toward the idea of independence for Greece proper, the islands and peninsulas where Greek was the predominant language. Tsar Nicholas was more willing than Alexander to assist this movement. The governments of Great Britain and France were not inclined to let Russia stand as the only champion of Balkan peoples. Moreover, liberals in the West thought of the embattled Greeks as ancient Athenians fighting the modern oriental despotism of the Turkish empire.

The result was a joint Anglo-French-Russian naval intervention, which destroyed the Turkish fleet at Navarino Bay in 1827. Russia again, as often in the past, sent armies into the Balkans. A Russo-Turkish war and a great Near Eastern crisis followed, in the course of which the rival powers agreed in 1829 to recognize Greece as an independent kingdom. The Balkan states of Serbia, Wallachia, and Moldavia were also recognized as autonomous principalities within the badly shaken Ottoman Empire.[20] From the same crisis Egypt emerged as an autonomous region under Mehemet Ali. Egypt in time became a center of Arabic nationalism, which cut down Ottoman power in the south just as Balkan nationalism did in the north.

France, 1824–1830: The July Revolution, 1830

It was in 1830, and first of all in France, that the wall of reaction really collapsed. Charles X became king in 1824.[21] In the next year the legislative chambers voted an indemnity, in the form of perpetual annuities totaling 30 million francs a year, to those who as émigrés thirty-odd years before had had their property confiscated by the revolutionary state. Catholic clergy began to take over classrooms in the schools. A law pronounced the death penalty for sacrilege committed in church buildings. But the France of the restored Bourbons was still a free country, and against these apparent efforts to revive the Old Regime a strong opposition developed in the newspapers and in the chambers. In March 1830 the Chamber of Deputies, in which the bankers Laffitte and Casimir-Périer led the "leftist" opposition, passed a vote of no confidence in the government. The king, as was his legal right, dissolved the Chamber and called for new elections. The elections repudiated the king's policies. He replied on July 26, 1830, with four ordinances issued on his own authority. One dissolved the newly elected Chamber before it had ever met; another imposed censorship on the press; the third so amended the suffrage as to reduce the voting power of bankers, merchants, and industrialists and to concentrate it in the hands of the old-fashioned aristocracy; the fourth called for a new election on the new basis.

These July Ordinances produced on the very next day the July Revolution. The upper bourgeois class was of course desperate at being thus brazenly ousted from political life. But it was the republicans—the nucleus of revolutionary workers, students, and intelligentsia in Paris—that actually moved. For three days, from July 27 to 29, barricades were thrown up in the city, behind which a swarming populace defied the army and the police. Most of the army refused to fire. Charles X, in no mood to be made captive by a revolution like his long-dead brother Louis XVI, precipitately abdicated and headed for England.

Some of the leaders wished to proclaim a democratic republic. Working people hoped for better conditions of employment. The political liberals, supported by bankers, industrialists, various journalists, and intellectuals, had other aims. They had been satisfied in general with the constitutional charter of 1814; it was only

[20] See maps, pp. 448–449, 660.
[21] See p. 476.

LIBERTY LEADING THE PEOPLE
by Eugène Delacroix (French, 1798–1863)

Delacroix, a founder of the romantic school of painting, painted this picture soon after the July Revolution in Paris in 1830 (see pp. 485–487). It well illustrates the idealistic conception of revolution which prevailed among revolutionaries before 1848, in sharp contrast to the "realistic," "scientific," or "materialistic" conception of revolution that set in after 1848 and was typified by Karl Marx. (See pp. 522–526.) Revolution is shown as a noble and moral act. The figures express determination and courage, but show no sign of hatred or even anger. They are not a class (note how the costume varies from the top hat to the seminude); they are the People, affirming the rights of man. Liberty, holding the tricolor aloft, is a composed and even rational goddess. Romantic though the painter was, he represents the insurgents as realizing an abstract idea—Liberty, or the Republic. It is to this idea that the half-recumbent and presumably wounded figure directs his gaze. Courtesy of the Louvre (Giraudon).

to the policies and personnel of the government that they had objected, and they wished now to continue with constitutional monarchy, somewhat liberalized, and with a king whom they could trust. A solution to the deadlock was found by the elderly Marquis de Lafayette, the aging hero of the American and the French revolutions, who now came forward as symbol of national unity. Lafayette produced the Duke of Orleans on the balcony of the Paris Hôtel de Ville, embraced him before a great concourse of people, and offered him as the answer to France's need. The duke was a collateral relative of the Bourbons; he had also, as a young man, served in the republican army of 1792. The militant republicans accepted him, willing to see what would develop; and the Chamber of Deputies on August 7 offered him the throne, on condition that he observe faithfully the constitutional charter of 1814. He reigned, until 1848, under the title of Louis Philippe.

The regime of Louis Philippe, called the Orléanist, bourgeois, or July Monarchy, was viewed very differently by different groups in France and in Europe. To the other states of Europe and to the clergy and legitimists within France, it seemed shockingly revolutionary. The new king owed his throne to an insurrection, to a bargain made with republicans, and to promises made to a parliament. He called himself not king of France but king of the French, and he flew not the Bourbon lily but the tricolor flag of the Revolution. The latter produced an effect on the established classes not unlike that of the hammer and sickle of a later day. He cultivated a popular manner, wore sober dark clothing (the ancestor of the modern "business suit"), and carried an umbrella. Though in private he worked stubbornly to maintain his royal position, in public he adhered scrupulously to the constitution.

The constitution remained substantially what it had been in 1814. The main political change was one of tone; there would be no more absolutism, with its notion that constitutional guarantees could be abrogated by a reigning prince. Legally the main change was that the Chamber of Peers ceased to be hereditary, to the chagrin of the old nobility, and that the Chamber of Deputies was to be elected by a somewhat enlarged body of voters. Where before 1830 there had been 100,000 voters, there were now about 200,000. The right to vote was still based on the ownership of a considerable quantity of real estate. About one-thirtieth of the adult male population (the top thirtieth in the possession of real property) now elected the Chamber of Deputies. The beneficiaries of the new system were the upper bourgeoisie—the bankers, merchants, and industrialists. The big property owners constituted the *pays légal*, the "legal country," and to them the July Monarchy was the consummation and stopping place of political progress. To others, and especially to the radical democrats, it proved as the years passed to be a disillusionment and an annoyance.

Revolutions of 1830: Belgium, Poland, and Elsewhere

The immediate effect of the three-day Paris revolution of 1830 was to set off a series of similar explosions throughout Europe. These in turn, coming after the collapse of the Bourbons in France, brought the whole peace settlement of 1815 into jeopardy. It will be recalled that the Congress of Vienna had joined Belgium with the Dutch Netherlands to create a strong buffer state against a resurgent France and had also done what it could to prevent direct pressure of Russian power upon central Europe by way of Poland.[22] Both these arrangements were now undone.

The Dutch-Belgian union proved economically beneficial, for Belgian industry complemented the commercial and shipping activity of the Dutch, but politically it worked very poorly, especially since the Dutch king had absolutist and centralizing ideas. The Belgians, though they had never been independent, had always stood stiffly for their local liberties under former Austrian rulers (and Spanish before them); now they did the same against the Dutch. The Catholic Belgians disliked Dutch Protestantism; those Belgians who spoke French (the Walloons) objected to regulations requiring the use of Dutch. About a month after the July Revolution in Paris disturbances broke out in Brussels. The leaders asked only for local Belgian self-government, but when the king took arms against them they went on to proclaim independence. A national assembly met and drafted a constitution.

Nicholas of Russia wished to send troops to stamp out the Belgian uprising. But he could not get his forces safely through Poland. In Poland, too, in 1830, a revolution broke out. The Polish nationalists saw in the fall of the French Bourbons a timely moment for them to strike. They objected also to the appearance of Russian troops bound presumably to suppress freedom in western Europe. One incident led to another, until in January 1831 the Polish diet proclaimed the dethronement of the Polish king (i.e., Nicholas), who thereupon sent in a large army. The Poles, outnumbered and divided among themselves, could put up no successful resistance. They obtained no support from the West. The British government was unsettled by agitation at home. The French government, newly installed under Louis Philippe, had no wish to appear disturbingly revolutionary, and in any case feared the Polish agents who besought its backing as international firebrands and republicans. The Polish revolution was therefore crushed. Congress Poland disappeared; its constitution was abrogated, and it was merged into the Russian empire. Thousands of Poles settled in western Europe, where they became familiar figures in republican circles. In Poland the engines of repression rolled. The tsar's government exiled some thousands to Siberia, began to Russify the Eastern Border, and closed the universities of Warsaw and Vilna. Since meanwhile it was too late for the tsar any longer to contemplate intervention in Belgium, it may be said that the sacrifice of the Poles contributed to the success of the west-European revolution of 1830, as it had to that of the great French Revolution of 1789–1795.[23]

It was true enough, as Nicholas maintained, that an independent Belgium presented great international problems. Belgium for twenty years before 1815 had been part of France. A few Belgians now favored reunion with it, and in France the republican left, which regarded the Vienna treaty as an insult to the French nation, saw an opportunity to win back this first and dearest conquest of the First Republic. In 1831, by a small majority, the Belgian national assembly elected as their king the son of Louis Philippe, who, however, not wishing trouble with the British, forbade his son to accept it. The Belgians thereupon elected Leopold of Saxe-Coburg, a German princeling who had married into the British royal family

---

[22] See pp. 445–447.
[23] See pp. 384–385 and map on p. 248.

and become a British subject. He was in fact the uncle of a twelve-year-old girl who was to be Queen Victoria. The British negotiated with Talleyrand, sent over by the French government (it was his last public service); and the result was a treaty of 1831 (confirmed in 1839) setting up Belgium as a perpetually neutral state, incapable of forming alliances and guaranteed against invasion by all five of the Great Powers. The aim intended by the Treaty of Vienna, to prevent the annexation of Belgium to France, was thus again realized in a new way. Internally Belgium presently settled down to a stable parliamentary system, somewhat more democratic than the July Monarchy in France but fundamentally offering the same type of bourgeois and liberal rule.

Revolutionary disturbances also took place in 1830 in Germany, Italy, Switzerland, Spain, and Portugal. To trace them in any detail is not necessary. In a word, a greater measure of liberalism was established in Switzerland; Spain entered a long period of tortuous parliamentary development confused by civil wars, which arose from a disputed succession to the throne; and in Italy and Germany the 1830 uprisings were quickly put down, showing only the continuance of a radical dissatisfaction still held in check by the authorities. It was in Great Britain that sweeping changes really came.

Reform in Great Britain

The three-day Paris revolution of 1830 had direct repercussions across the Channel. The quick results following on working-class insurrection gave radical leaders in England the idea that threats of violence might be useful. On the other hand, the ease and speed with which the French bourgeoisie gained the upper hand reassured the British middle classes, who concluded that they might unsparingly embarrass the government without courting a mass upheaval.

The Tory regime in England had in fact already begun to loosen up. A group of younger men came forward in the 1820s in the Tory party, notably George Canning, the foreign minister, and Robert Peel, son of one of the first cotton manufacturers.[24] This group was sensitive to the needs of British business and to the doctrines of liberalism.[25] They reduced tariffs and liberalized the old Navigation Acts, permitting British colonies to trade with countries other than Britain. By repealing certain old statutes, they made it lawful for skilled workers to emigrate from England, taking their skills with them to foreign parts, and for manufacturers to export machinery to foreign countries, even though English industrial secrets would thus be given away. By such measures they advanced the liberal conception of a freely exchanging international system; they moved toward freedom of trade. The Liberal Tories also undermined the legal position of the Church of England, forwarding the conception of a secular state, though such was hardly their purpose. They repealed the old laws (which dated from the seventeenth century) forbidding dissenting Protestants to hold public office except through a legal fiction by which they pretended to be Anglicans. They even allowed the Test Act of 1673 to be repealed and Catholic Emancipation to be adopted. Catholics in

[24] See p. 461.
[25] See p. 465.

Great Britain and Ireland received the same rights as others.[26] Capital punishment was abolished for about a hundred offenses. A professional police force was introduced, in place of the old-fashioned and ineffectual local constables. (It is after Robert Peel that London policemen came to be called "bobbies.") The new police were expected to handle protest meetings, angry crowds, or occasional riots without having to call for military assistance.

There were two things that the Liberal Tories could not do. They could not question the Corn Laws, and they could not reform the House of Commons. By the Corn Laws, which set the tariff on imported grain, a tariff raised to new heights in 1815, the gentlemen of England protected their rent rolls; and by the existing structure of the House of Commons they governed the country, expecting the working class and the business interests to look to them as natural leaders.

Never in five hundred years of its history had the Commons been so unrepresentative. No new borough had been created since the Revolution of 1688. The boroughs, or urban centers having the right to elect members of Parliament, were heavily concentrated in southern England. With the Industrial Revolution, population was shifting noticeably to the north. The new factory towns were unrepresented. Of the boroughs, many had decayed over the centuries; some were quite uninhabited, and one was under the waters of the North Sea. In a few boroughs real elections took place, but in some of them it was the town corporation, and in others the owners of certain pieces of real estate, that had the right to name members of Parliament. Each borough was different, carrying over the local liberties of the Middle Ages. Many boroughs were entirely dominated by influential persons called borough-mongers by their critics. As for the rural districts, the "forty-shilling freeholders" chose two members of Parliament for each county, in a convivial assembly much influenced by the gentlefolk. It was estimated about 1820 that less than 500 men, most of them members of the House of Lords, really selected a majority of the House of Commons.

Some two dozen bills to reform the House of Commons had been introduced in the half-century preceding 1830. They had all failed to pass. In 1830, after the Paris revolution, the issue was again raised by the minority party, the Whigs. The Tory prime minister, the Duke of Wellington, the victor of Waterloo and a most extreme conservative, so immoderately defended the existing system that he lost the confidence even of some of his own followers. The existing methods of election in England, he declared, were more perfect than any that human intelligence could contrive at a single stroke. After this outburst a Whig ministry took over the government. It introduced a reform bill. The House of Commons rejected it. The Whig ministry thereupon resigned. The Tories, fearing popular violence, refused to take the responsibility for forming a cabinet. The Whigs resumed office and again introduced their reform bill. This time it passed the Commons but failed in the House of Lords. An angry roar went up over the country. Crowds milled in the London streets, rioters for several days were in control at Bristol, the jail at Derby was sacked, and Nottingham castle burned. Only the passage of the bill, it seemed, could prevent an actual revolution. Using this argument the Whigs got the king to promise to create enough new peers to

---

[26] See pp. 177–178.

change the majority in the House of Lords.[27] The Lords yielded rather than be swamped, and in April 1832 the bill became law.

The Reform Bill of 1832 was a very English measure. It adapted the English or medieval system rather than following new ideas let loose by the French Revolution. On the Continent, where constitutions existed at all (as in France), the idea was that each representative should represent roughly the same number of voters, and that voters should qualify to vote by a flat uniform qualification, usually the payment of a stated amount of property taxes. The British held to the idea that members of the House of Commons represented boroughs and counties, in general without regard to size of population (with exceptions); in other words, no attempt was made to create equal electoral districts. The qualification for voting was enormously simplified, but it still remained rather complex. The franchise, or right to vote, depended on whether one lived in a borough or in a county. It was defined also very largely in terms of rents, because in England, with the high concentration of landownership in the old landowning class, many important people did not own any land at all.

In a borough, under the new law, a man could vote for a member of Parliament if he occupied premises for which he paid £10 annual rental. In a county (a rural area or a small town not considered a borough), a man could vote if he paid £10 annual rental for land held on a long-term sixty-year lease; but he had to pay as high as £50 rental for land occupied on a shorter-term lease in order to be eligible to vote. If he himself owned the land, he could vote if its annual rental value was £2 a year (the old forty-shilling freehold). Thus the vote was nicely distributed according to evidences of economic substance, reliability, and permanence. The total effect on the size of the electorate was to raise the number of voters in the British Isles from about 500,000 to about 813,000. Some persons actually lost their votes, namely, the poorer elements in the handful of old boroughs which had been fairly democratic, like the borough of Westminster in greater London.

The most important thing was not the increased size of the electorate but its redistribution by region and by class. The Reform Bill reallocated the seats in the House of Commons. Fifty-six of the smallest older boroughs were abolished, their inhabitants thereafter voting as residents of their counties. Thirty other small boroughs kept the right to send only one burgess to Parliament instead of the historic two. The 143 seats thus made available were given to the new industrial towns. Here it was the £10-householders who voted, i.e., the middle classes—factory owners and businessmen and their principal employees; doctors, lawyers, brokers, merchants, and newspaper people; relatives and connections of the well-to-do.

The Reform Bill of 1832 was more sweeping than the Whigs would have favored except for their fear of revolution. It was more conservative than the democratic radicals would have accepted, except for their belief that the suffrage might be widened in the future. Whether Great Britain in 1830 was in danger of any real revolution can never be known. In any case a distressed mass of workers was led by an irate manufacturing interest that was unwilling to tolerate any longer its exclusion from political life. Had these elements consented to general violence a real revolution might have occurred. Yet there was no violent revolution in

[27] See note, p. 194.

Britain. The reason probably lies first of all in the existence of the historic institution of Parliament, which, erratic though it was before the Reform Bill, provided the means by which social changes could be legally accomplished and continued, in principle, to enjoy universal respect. Conservatives, driven to the wall, would yield; they could allow a revision of the suffrage because they could expect to remain themselves in public life. Radicals, using enough violence to scare the established interest, did not thereafter face a blank wall; they could expect, once the breach was made, to carry some day a further democratization of Parliament and with it their social and economic program by orderly legislation.

Britain after 1832

But the Reform Bill of 1832 was in its way a revolution. The new business interests, created by industrialization, took their place alongside the old aristocracy in the governing elite of the country. The aristocratic Whigs who had carried the Reform Bill gradually merged with formerly radical industrialists and with a few Liberal Tories to form the Liberal party. The main body of the Tories, joined by a few old Whigs and even a few former radicals, gradually turned into the Conservative party. The two parties alternated in power at short intervals from 1832 to the First World War, this being the classic period in Great Britain of the Liberal-Conservative two-party system.

In 1833 slavery was abolished in the British Empire. In 1834 a new Poor Law was adopted. In 1835 the Municipal Corporations Act, second only to the Reform Bill in basic importance, modernized the local government of English cities; it broke up the old local oligarchies and brought in uniform electoral and administrative machinery, enabling city dwellers to grapple more effectively with the problems of urban life. In 1836 the House of Commons allowed the newspapers to report how its members voted—a long step toward publicity of government proceedings was thus taken. Meanwhile an ecclesiastical commission reviewed the affairs of the Church of England; financial and administrative irregularities were corrected, together with the grosser inequalities between the income of upper and lower clergy, all of which had made the church formerly a kind of closed preserve for the landed gentry.

The Tories, thus assaulted in their immemorial strongholds of local government and the established church, carried a counteroffensive into the strongholds of the new liberal manufacturing class, namely, the factories and the mines. Tories

BIG INVESTMENTS
by Honoré Daumier (French, 1808–1879)

The Revolution of 1830, romanticized by Delacroix, was in fact followed by a period of moneymaking and business ferment (as well as genuine economic development) made famous in the novels of Balzac and the graphic art of Daumier. This lithograph of 1837 shows a financier, with bundles of stock certificates piled beside him, offering to sell shares in factories, foundries, breweries, etc., to a skeptical client. Daumier was a satirist and caricaturist of bourgeois society. Where Rembrandt in the seventeenth century could portray businessmen with a high seriousness (as on p. 165), artists since the 1830s have been generally alienated from such subjects. Courtesy of the Bibliothèque Nationale, Paris.

Grand placement d'actions.

J'ai aujourd'hui de bien bonnes actions à placer, Mr Desrognures, en voulez vous? – C'est selon. Ça avez-vous en actions? – J'ai 3000 actions de fonderies. – Affaire fondue! – 2000 actions des usines. – Usé, usé! – 10,000 actions des brasseries, opérations magnifiques – Que faites les mousser! – J'en ai du recueil des connaissances. – Connu, connu! Enfin, combien cela fait il en bloc? – Un milliard ou deux pas plus. – Un milliard... le papier se mince... cela doit donner ant tires. à 4 sous... ça vaut 30 francs... – Deux milliards pour 30 francs! y pensez-vous mon cher? – Mettez au moins 25 francs! – Pas un liard. – Actions enlevez. Vous faites en marche et si. – Farceur, vous ne dites tous les jours la même chose.

became champions of the industrial workers. Landed gentlemen, of whom the most famous was Lord Ashley, later seventh Earl of Shaftesbury, took the lead in publicizing the social evils of a rapid and indeed ruthless industrialization. They received some support from a few humanitarian industrialists; indeed, the early legislation tended to follow practices already established by the best or strongest business firms. A Factory Act of 1833 forbade the labor of children less than nine years old in the textile mills. It was the first effective piece of legislation on the subject, for it provided for paid inspectors and procedures for enforcement. An act of 1842 initiated significant regulation in the coal mines; the employment underground of women and girls, and of boys under ten, was forbidden.

The greatest victory of the working classes came in 1847 with the Ten Hours Act, which limited the labor of women and children in all industrial establishments to ten hours a day. Thereafter men commonly worked only ten hours also, since the work of men, women, and young people was too closely coordinated for the men to work alone. The great Liberal John Bright, Quaker and cotton magnate, called the Ten Hours Act "a delusion practiced on the working classes." To regulate the hours of labor was contrary to the accepted principles of laissez faire, economic law, the free market, freedom of trade, and individual liberty for employer and worker. Yet the Ten Hours Act stood, and British industry continued to prosper.

Gathering their strength, the Whig-liberal-radical combination established in 1838 an Anti–Corn Law League. Wage earners objected to the Corn Laws because the tariff on grain imports kept up the price of food. Industrial employers objected to them because, in keeping up food prices, they also kept up wages and cost of production in England, thus working to England's disadvantage in the export trade. Defenders of the Corn Laws argued that protection of agriculture was necessary to maintain the natural aristocracy of the country (most land being owned by peers and gentry, as has been seen), but they also sometimes used more widely framed economic arguments, affirming that Britain should preserve a balanced economy as between industry and farming, and avoid becoming too exclusively dependent on imported food. The issue became a straight contest between the industrialists, acting with working-class support, and the aristocratic and predominantly Tory landowning interest. The Anti–Corn Law League, whose headquarters were at Manchester, operated like a modern political party. It had plenty of money, supplied by large donations from manufacturers and small ones from laboring people. It sent lecturers on tour, agitated in the newspapers, and issued a stream of polemical pamphlets and educational books. It held political teas, torchlight processions, and open-air mass meetings. The pressure proved irresistible and received a final impetus from a famine in Ireland. It was a Tory government, headed by Sir Robert Peel, which in 1846 yielded before so vociferous a demand.

The repeal of the Corn Laws in 1846 stands as a symbol of the change that had come over England. It reaffirmed the revolutionary consequences of the Reform Bill of 1832. Industry was now a governing element in the country. Free trade was henceforth the rule. Great Britain, in return for the export of manufactures, became deliberately dependent on imports for its very life. It was committed henceforth to an international and even worldwide economic system. The first to undergo the Industrial Revolution, possessing mechanical power and methods of mass production, the British could produce yarn and cloth, machine tools and railroad equipment, more efficiently and more cheaply than any other people. In Britain, the workshop of the world, people would pour increasingly into mine, factory, and city, live by selling manufactures, coal, shipping, and financial services to the other peoples of the earth, and obtain raw cotton, rare ores, meat, cereals, and thousands of lesser but still vital necessities from the rest of the earth in exchange. The welfare of Britain depended on the maintenance of a freely exchanging worldwide economic system.

It depended also, more than ever, on British control of the sea, which was rarely mentioned by the civilian-minded Anti–Corn Law League, but which, firmly established in the long duel with Napoleon, was now an assumed postulate of economic discussion. No one understood this better than Lord Palmerston, a flamboyant Anglo-Irish Whig aristocrat, who by risky and audacious moves that alarmed his colleagues and threw Queen Victoria into consternation, came forward as the very British bulldog in defense of Britain's name. For example, in 1850 a Moroccan Jew known as Don Pacifico, who was a British subject, got into trouble in Greece because of certain debts owed to him by the Greek government. Though the claim was not above question, Palmerston unloosed the thunders of the British fleet. He sent a squadron to the Piraeus, the port of Athens, and forbade Greek vessels the use of their own harbor until the matter was settled. On another occasion, in 1856, when Chinese authorities arrested a Chinese ship called the *Arrow*, which, though without due right, was flying the British flag, Palmerston again called on the navy, which proceeded to bombard Canton and precipitated the Second Anglo-Chinese War. In other connections, as a good mid–nineteenth-century liberal, Palmerston favored movements for national independence, including that of the Confederate States of America, expecting them to result in the further extension of free trade.

57. Triumph of the West-European Bourgeoisie

In general, the decades following 1830 may be thought of as a kind of golden age of the West-European bourgeoisie, or what in English would be called the upper middle class. In the older meaning, in French, a *bourgeois* had been someone who was not of the nobility but enjoyed an income from business, or a profession, or the ownership of property.[28] After the French Revolution, and even more after 1830, the word took on new meanings, not all of them consistent. Artists, literary people, and old-line aristocrats might disdain the "bourgeois" as a person of uncultivated tastes, supposedly interested only in making money. From another point of view, shared by social theorists and working-class leaders, the bourgeois was someone who could hire others to work for him, either in his business or recreational activities, or as household servants. In a word, the bourgeois was the employer. In any case, the bourgeoisie and the aristocracy tended to become more alike in the nineteenth century in their daily pursuits and style of life, and to draw income from the possession of income-producing property or capital. The bourgeoisie, formerly identified in contrast to the nobility, was now identified in contrast to the working class, that is, those whose whole income depended on daily labor in shops, offices, farms, or factories.

[28] See pp. 121–123, 353, 393.

The reigning liberal doctrine was the "stake in society" theory; those should govern who have something to lose. In the France of the July Monarchy (1830–1848), only about one adult male in thirty had the vote. In the Britain of the first Reform Bill (1832–1867), one man in eight could vote for a member of the House of Commons. In France only the most well-to-do were enfranchised, in Britain virtually the whole middle class, which, however, long supported members of the aristocracy for the highest public positions. In Britain the continuation of the Tory landed interest in politics somewhat blunted the edge of capitalist and managerial rule, resulting in the passage of significant legislation for the protection of industrial labor. In France the aristocratic landed interest, weaker and less public spirited than in England, lost much of its influence by the Revolution of 1830, and less was done to relieve the condition of labor.

The bourgeois age left its mark on Europe in many ways. For one thing, western Europe continued to accumulate capital and build up its industrial plant. National income was constantly rising, but a relatively small share went to the laboring class, and a relatively large share went to owners of capital. This meant that less was spent on consumers' goods—housing, clothing, food, recreation— and that more was saved and available for reinvestment. New stock companies were constantly formed, and the law of corporations was amended, allowing for the extension of corporate enterprise to new fields. The factory system spread from Britain to the Continent and within Britain from the textile industry to other lines of production. The output of iron, a good index to economic advancement in this phase of industrialism, rose about 300 percent in Great Britain between 1830 and 1848 and about 65 percent in France between 1830 and 1845. (All the German states combined, at the latter date, produced about a tenth as much iron as Great Britain, and less than half as much as France.) Railroad building set in in earnest after 1840. In 1840 Samuel Cunard put four steamships into regular transatlantic service. Much capital was exported; as early as 1839 an American estimated that Europeans (mainly British) owned $200,000,000 worth of stocks in American companies. Such investments financed the purchase of British and other goods and helped to rivet together a world economic system, in which western Europe and especially England took the lead, with other regions remaining in a somewhat subordinate status.

The Frustration and Challenge of Labor

The bourgeois age had the effect also of estranging the world of labor. The state in Britain and France was as near as it has ever been to what Karl Marx was soon to call it—a committee of the bourgeois class. Already in France people spoke worriedly of the *prolétaires*, those at the bottom of society, who had nothing to lose. Republicans in France, radical democrats in Britain, felt cheated and imposed upon in the 1830s and 1840s. They had in each country forced through a virtual revolution by their insurrections and demonstrations and then in each country had been left without the vote. Some lost interest in representative institutions. Excluded from government, they were tempted to seek political ends through extragovernmental, which is to say revolutionary or utopian, channels. Social and economic reforms seemed to the average worker far more important, as a final aim, than mere governmental innovations. Workers were told by respected economists that they could not hope to change the system in their own favor. They were tempted, therefore, to destroy the system, to replace it utterly with some new system conceived mainly in the minds of thinkers. They were told by the Manchester School, and by its equivalent in France, that the income of labor was set by ineluctable natural laws, that it was best and indeed necessary for wages to remain low, and that the way to rise in the world was to get out of the laboring class altogether, by becoming the owner of a profitable business and leaving working people about where they were.[29]

The reigning doctrine emphasized the conception of a labor market. The worker sold labor, the employer bought it. The price of labor, or wage, was to be agreed upon by the two individual parties. The price would naturally fluctuate according to changes in supply and demand. When a great deal of a certain kind of labor was required the wage would go up, until new persons moved into the market offering more labor of this type, with the result that something like the old wage would again be established. When no labor was needed none should be bought, and persons who could not sell labor might then subsist for a time by poor relief.

The new Poor Law of 1834 was especially repugnant to the British working class. It corrected crying evils of the old poor laws that had left millions of people in habitual poverty. But the new law did nothing constructive to relieve productive workers suffering from occasional or cyclical unemployment. The new law followed the stern precepts of the dismal science; its main principle was to safeguard the labor market by making relief more unpleasant than any job. It granted relief only to persons willing to enter a workhouse, or poorhouse; and in these establishments the sexes were segregated and life was in other ways made noticeably less attractive than in the outside world. The workers considered the new law an abomination. They called the workhouses "bastilles." They resented the whole conception of a labor market, in which labor was to be bought and sold (or remain unsold) like any other commodity.

In the long run it would be the increase in productivity that would improve the condition of the workers. Meanwhile the friends of the working class offered two means of escape. One was to improve the position of labor in the market. This led to the formation of labor unions for control of the labor supply and collective bargaining with employers. Such unions, illegal in France, were barely legal in Great Britain after 1825, though it was still illegal in both countries to strike. The other means of escape was to repudiate the whole idea of a market economy and of the capitalist system. It was to conceive of a system in which goods were to be produced for use, not for sale; and in which working people should be compensated according to need, not according to the requirements of an employer. This was the basis of most forms of nineteenth-century socialism.[30]

Socialism and Chartism

Socialism spread rapidly among the working classes after 1830. In France it blended with revolutionary republicanism. There was a revival of interest in the great Revolution and the democratic Republic of 1793. Cheap reprints of the

[29] See pp. 461–463, 466.
[30] See pp. 461–463.

writings of Robespierre began to circulate in the working-class quarters of Paris. Robespierre was now seen as a people's hero. The socialist Louis Blanc, for example, who in 1839 published his *Organization of Work,* recommending the formation of "social workshops," also wrote a long history of the French Revolution, in which he pointed out the equalitarian ideals that had inspired the National Convention in 1793. In Britain, as befitted the different background of the country, socialistic ideas blended in with the movement for further parliamentary reform. This was advanced by the working-class group known as the Chartists, from the People's Charter which they drafted in 1838. Between the British Chartists and the French socialists there was considerable coming and going. One Chartist, the Irish-born journalist Bronterre O'Brien, translated a French book on the "conspiracy of Babeuf" of 1796, which itself was a source and inspiration of the rising socialism of France.[31]

Chartism was far more of a mass movement than the French socialism of the day. Only a few Chartists were clearly socialists in their own minds. But all were anticapitalistic. All could agree that the first step must be to win working-class representation in Parliament. The Charter of 1838 consisted of six points. It demanded (1) the annual election of the House of Commons by (2) universal suffrage for all adult males, through (3) a secret ballot and (4) equal electoral districts; and it called for (5) the abolition of property qualifications for membership in the House of Commons, which perpetuated the old idea that Parliament should be composed of gentlemen of independent income, and urged instead (6) the payment of salaries to the elected members of Parliament, in order that people of small means might serve. A convention composed of delegates sent by labor unions, mass meetings, and radical societies all over the country met in London in 1839. "Convention" was an ominous word, with French revolutionary and even terrorist overtones; some members of this British convention regarded it as the body really representing the people, and favored armed violence and a general strike, while others stood only for moral pressure upon Parliament.

A petition bearing over a million signatures, urging acceptance of the Charter, was submitted to the House of Commons. The violent and revolutionary wing, or "physical force" Chartists, precipitated a wave of riots which were effectively quelled by the authorities. In 1842 the petition was again submitted. This time, according to the best estimate, it was signed by 3,317,702 persons. Since the entire population of Great Britain was about 19 million it is clear that the Charter, whatever the exact number of signatures, commanded the explicit adherence of half the adult males of the country. The House of Commons nevertheless rejected the petition by 287 votes to 49. It was feared, with reason, that political democracy would threaten property rights and the whole economic system as they then existed. The Chartist movement gradually died down in the face of firm opposition by the government and the business classes, and was weakened by mutual fears and disagreements among its own supporters. It had not been entirely fruitless; for without popular agitation and the publicizing of working-class grievances, the Mines Act of 1842 and the Ten Hours Act of 1847 might not have been enacted. These measures in turn alleviated the distress of industrial workers and kept alive a degree of confidence in the future of the economic system. Chartism revived

[31] See p. 394.

briefly in 1848, as will be seen in the next chapter; but in general, in the 1840s, British working people turned from political agitation to the forming and strengthening of labor unions, by which they could deal directly with employers without having to appeal to the government. Not until 1867 was the suffrage extended in Great Britain, and it took about eighty years to realize the full program of the Charter of 1838, except for the annual election of Parliament, for which there soon ceased to be any demand.[32]

It is not easy to summarize the history of Europe between 1815 and 1848. Among all the forces set free by the French and Industrial revolutions—liberalism, conservatism, nationalism, republicanism, democracy, socialism—no stabilization had been achieved. No international system had been created; Europe had rather fallen into two camps, composed of a West in which liberal conceptions moved forward, and an East in which three autocratic monarchies held sway. Western Europe favored the principles of nationality; governments in central and eastern Europe still opposed them. The West was growing collectively richer, more liberal, more bourgeois. Middle-class people in Germany, central Europe, and Italy (as well as in Spain and Portugal) did not enjoy the dignities and emoluments that they enjoyed in Great Britain or France. But the West had not solved its social problem; its whole material civilization rested upon a restless and sorely tried working class. Everywhere there was repression, in varying degree, and everywhere apprehension, more in some places than in others; but there was also hope, confidence in the progress of an industrial and scientific society, and faith in the unfinished program of the rights of man. The result was the general Revolution of 1848.

[32] See pp. 609–613, 778.

XII.
REVOLUTION AND THE REIMPOSITION OF ORDER, 1848–1870

FEARS HAUNTING the established classes of Europe for thirty years came true in 1848. Governments collapsed all over the Continent. Remembered horrors appeared again, as in a recurring dream, in much the same sequence as after 1789 only at a much faster rate of speed. Revolutionaries milled in the streets, kings fled, republics were declared, and within four years there was another Napoleon. Soon thereafter came a series of wars.

Never before or since has Europe seen so truly universal an upheaval as in 1848. While the French Revolution of 1789 and the Russian Revolution of 1917 both had immediate international repercussions, in each of these cases a single country took the lead. In 1848 the revolutionary movement broke out spontaneously from native sources from Copenhagen to Palermo and from Paris to Budapest. Contemporaries sometimes attributed the universality of the phenomenon to the machinations of secret societies, and it is true that the faint beginnings of an international revolutionary movement existed before 1848; but the fact is that revolutionary plotters had little influence upon what actually happened, and the nearly simultaneous fall of governments is quite understandable from other causes. Many people in Europe wanted substantially the same things—constitutional government, the independence and unification of national groups, an end to serfdom and manorial restraints where they still existed. With some variation,

Chapter Emblem: A medal showing St. Paul's Church at Frankfurt, then a new building in the neoclassic style, where the German National Assembly met in 1848–1849.

there was a common body of ideas among politically conscious elements of all countries. Some of the powers that the new forces had to combat were themselves international, notably the Catholic church and the far-spreading influence of the Habsburgs, so that resistance to them arose independently in many places. In any case, only the Russian empire and Great Britain escaped the revolutionary contagion of 1848, and the British received a very bad scare.

But the Revolution of 1848, though it shook the whole Continent, lacked basic driving strength. It failed almost as rapidly as it succeeded. Its main consequence, in fact, was to strengthen the more conservative forces that viewed all revolution with alarm. Revolutionary ideals succumbed to military repression. To some extent the governments of the 1850s and 1860s, while hostile to revolution, satisfied some of the aims of 1848, notably in national unification and constitutional government with limited representation, but they did so in a mood of calculated realism, and while reasserting their own authority. The repressed Revolution of 1848 also left a legacy of class fears and class conflict, in which prophets of a new society also became more realistic, as when Karl Marx, branding earlier forms of socialism as "utopian," offered his own views as hard-headed and "scientific."

58. Paris: The Specter of Social Revolution in the West

The July Monarchy in France was a platform of boards built over a volcano. Under it burned the repressed fires of the republicanism put down in 1830, which since 1830 had become steadily more socialistic.[1]

Politics in the July Monarchy became increasingly more unreal. So few interests were represented in the Chamber of Deputies that the most basic issues were seldom debated. Even most of the bourgeois class had no representation. Graft and corruption were more common than they should have been, as economic expansion favored stockjobbing and fraud by business promoters and politicians in combination. A strong movement set in to give the vote to more people instead of to only one man in thirty. Radicals wanted universal suffrage and a republic, but liberals asked only for a broadening of voting rights within the existing constitutional monarchy. The king, Louis Philippe, and his prime minister, Guizot, instead of allying with the latter against the former, resolutely and obtusely opposed any change whatsoever.

The "February" Revolution in France

Reformers, against the king's expressed wishes, planned a great banquet in Paris for February 22, 1848, to be accompanied by demonstrations in the streets. The government on February 21 forbade all such meetings. That night barricades were built in the working-class quarters. These consisted of paving blocks, building stones, or large pieces of furniture thrown together across the narrow streets and intersections of the old city, and constituting a maze within which insurgents prepared to resist the authorities. The government called out the National Guard,

[1] See pp. 485–487, 495–497.

which refused to move. The king now promised electoral reform, but republican firebrands took charge of the semimobilized working-class elements, which held a demonstration outside the house of Guizot. Someone shot at the guards placed around the house; the guards replied, killing twenty persons. The republican organizers put some of the corpses on a torch-lit cart and paraded them through the city, which, armed and barricaded, soon began to swarm in an enormous riot. On February 24 Louis Philippe, like Charles X before him, abdicated and made for England. The February Revolution of 1848, like the July Revolution of 1830, had unseated a monarch in three days.

The constitutional reformers hoped to carry on with Louis Philippe's young grandson as king, but the republicans, now aroused and armed, poured into the Chamber of Deputies and forced the proclamation of the Republic. Republican leaders set up a provisional government of ten men, pending election by all France of a Constituent Assembly. Seven of the ten were "political" republicans, the most notable being the poet Lamartine. Three were "social" republicans, the most notable being Louis Blanc. A huge crowd of workers appeared before the Hôtel de Ville, or city hall, demanding that France adopt the new socialist emblem—the red flag. They were dissuaded by the eloquence of Lamartine, and the tricolor remained the republican standard.

Louis Blanc urged the Provisional Government to push through a bold economic and social program without delay. But since the "social" republicans were in a minority in the Provisional Government (though probably not among Paris republicans generally), Louis Blanc's ideas were very much watered down in the application. He wanted a Ministry of Progress to organize a network of "social workshops," the state-supported and collectivist manufacturing establishments that he had projected in his writings. All that was created was a Labor Commission, with limited powers, and a system of shops significantly entitled "national" rather than "social." The National Workshops, as they are always called in English (though "workshop" suggests something more insignificant than Louis Blanc had in mind), were agreed to by the Provisional Government only as a political concession, and no significant work was ever assigned them, for fear of competition with private enterprise and dislocation of the economic system. Indeed, the man placed in charge of them admitted that his purpose was to prove the fallacies of socialism. Meanwhile the Labor Commission was unable to win public acceptance for the ten-hour day, which the British Parliament had enacted the year before. One action of the Provisional Government, however, had permanent effect, the final abolition of slavery in the French colonies.

The National Workshops became in practice only an extensive project in unemployment relief. Men of all trades, skilled and unskilled, were set to work digging on the roads and fortifications outside of Paris. They were paid two francs a day. The number of legitimate unemployed increased rapidly, for 1847 had been a year of depression and the revolution prevented the return of business confidence. Other needy persons also presented themselves for remuneration, and soon there were too many men for the amount of "work" made available. From 25,000 enrolled in the workshops by the middle of March, the number climbed to 120,000 by mid-June, by which time there were also in Paris another 50,000 whom the bulging workshops could no longer accommodate. In June there were probably almost 200,000 essentially idle but able-bodied men in a city of about a million people.

The Constituent Assembly, elected in April by universal male suffrage throughout France, met on May 4. It immediately replaced the Provisional Government with a temporary executive board of its own. The main body of France, a land of provincial bourgeois and peasant landowners, was not socialist in the least. The new temporary executive board, chosen by the new Constituent Assembly in May, included no "social" republicans. All five of its members, of whom Lamartine was the head, were known as outspoken enemies of Louis Blanc. Blanc and the socialists could no longer expect even the grudging and insincere concessions that they had so far obtained.

The battle lines were now drawn, after only three months of revolution, somewhat as they had been drawn in 1792 after three years.[2] Paris again stood for a degree of revolutionary action in which the rest of the country was not prepared to share. Revolutionary leaders in Paris, in 1848 as in 1792, were unwilling to accept the processes of majority rule or slow parliamentary deliberation. But the crisis in 1848 was more acute than in 1792. A larger proportion of the population were wage earners. Under a system of predominantly merchant capitalism, in which machine industry and factory concentration were only beginning, the workers were tormented by the same evils as the more industrialized working classes of England. Hours were if anything longer, and pay less, in France than in Great Britain; insecurity and unemployment were at least as great; and the feeling that a capitalist economy held no future for the laborer was the same. In addition, where the English worker shrank from the actual violation of Parliament, the French worker saw nothing very sacrilegious in the violation of elected assemblies. Too many regimes in France since 1789, including those preferred by the comfortable classes, had been based on insurrectionary violence for the French workers to feel much compunction over using it for their own ends.

The "June Days" of 1848

On the one hand stood the nationally elected Constituent Assembly. On the other, the National Workshops had mobilized in Paris the most distressed elements of the working class. Tens of thousands had been brought together where they could talk, read journals, listen to speeches, and concert common action. Agitators and organizers naturally made use of the opportunity thus presented to them. Men in the workshops began to feel desperate, to sense that the social republic was slipping from them perhaps forever. On May 15 they attacked the Constituent Assembly, drove its members out of the hall, declared it dissolved, and set up a new provisional government of their own. They announced that a social revolution must follow the purely political revolution of February. But the National Guard, a kind of civilian militia, turned against the insurgents and restored the Constituent Assembly. The Assembly, to root out socialism, prepared to get rid of the National Workshops. It offered those enrolled in them the alternatives of enlistment in the

---

[2] See p. 381–384.

army, transfer to provincial workshops, or being put out of Paris by force. The whole laboring class in the city began to resist. The government proclaimed martial law, the civilian executive board resigned, and all power was given to General Cavaignac and the regular army.

There followed the "Bloody June Days"—June 24 to 26, 1848—three days during which a terrifying class war raged in Paris. Over 20,000 men from the workshops took to arms (more would doubtless have done so had not the government continued to pay wages in the workshops during the insurrection), and they were joined by other unnumbered thousands from the working-class districts of the city. Half or more of Paris became a labyrinth of barricades defended by determined men and equally resolute women. Military methods of the time made it possible for civilians to shoot it out openly with soldiers; small arms were the main weapons, and armies had no armored vehicles or even any very devastating artillery. The soldiers found it a difficult operation, even several generals being killed, but after three days the outcome was in doubt no longer. Ten thousand persons had been killed or wounded. Eleven thousand insurgents were taken prisoner. The Assembly, refusing all clemency, decreed their immediate deportation to the colonies.

The June Days sent a shudder throughout France and Europe. Whether the battle in Paris had been a true class struggle, how large a portion of the laboring class had really participated (it was large in any case), how much they had fought for permanent objectives, and how much over the temporary issue of the workshops—all these are secondary questions. It was widely understood that a class war had in fact broken out. Militant workers were confirmed in a hatred and loathing of the bourgeois class, in a belief that capitalism existed in the last analysis by the callous shooting of laboring men in the streets. People above the laboring class were thrown into a panic. They were sure that they had narrowly escaped a ghastly upheaval. The very ground of civilized living seemed to have quaked. After June 1848, wrote a Frenchwoman of the time, society was "a prey to a feeling of terror incomparable to anything since the invasion of Rome by the barbarians."

Nor were the signs in England much more reassuring. There the Chartist agitation was revived by the February Revolution in Paris.[3] "France is a Republic!" cried the Chartist Ernest Jones; the Chartist petition was again circulated and was soon said to have 6 million signatures. Another Chartist convention met, considered by its leaders to be the forerunner of a Constituent Assembly as in France. The violent minority was the most active; it began to gather arms and to drill. The old Duke of Wellington swore in 70,000 special constables to uphold the social order. Clashes occurred at Liverpool and elsewhere; in London the revolutionary committee laid plans for systematic arson and organized men with pickaxes to break up the pavements for barricades. Meanwhile the petition, weighing 584 pounds, was carried in three cabs to the House of Commons, which estimated that it contained "only" 2 million signatures and again summarily rejected it. The revolutionary menace passed. One of the secret organizers in London proved to be a government spy; he revealed the whole plan at the critical moment, and the revolutionary committee was arrested

[3] See pp. 497–499.

on the day set for insurrection. Most Chartists had in any case refused to support the militants, but the truculent minority of radical workers and journalists had a deeper sense of envenomed class consciousness. The word "proletarian" was imported from France. "Every proletarian," wrote the Chartist editor of *Red Revolution*, "who does not see and feel that he belongs to an enslaved and degraded class is a *fool*."

The specter of social revolution thus hung over western Europe in the summer of 1848. Doubtless it was unreal; in all probability there could have been no successful socialist revolution at the time. But the specter was there, and it spread a sinking fear among all who had something to lose. This fear shaped the whole subsequent course of the Second Republic in France and of the revolutionary movements that had by this time begun in other countries as well.

The Emergence of Louis Napoleon Bonaparte

In France, after the June Days, the Constituent Assembly (keeping General Cavaignac as a virtual dictator) set about drafting a republican constitution. It was decided, in view of the disturbances just passed, to create a strong executive power in the hands of a president to be elected by universal male suffrage. It was decided also to have this president elected immediately, even before the rest of the constitution was finished. Four candidates presented themselves: Lamartine, Cavaignac, Ledru-Rollin—and Louis Napoleon Bonaparte. Lamartine stood for a somewhat vaguely moral and idealistic republic, Cavaignac for a republic of disciplined order, Ledru-Rollin for somewhat chastened "social" ideas. What Bonaparte stood for was not so clear. He was, however, elected by an avalanche of votes in December 1848, receiving over 5,400,000, to only 1,500,000 for Cavaignac, 370,000 for Ledru-Rollin, and a mere 18,000 for Lamartine.

Thus entered upon the European stage the second Napoleon. Born in 1808, Louis Napoleon Bonaparte was the nephew of the great Napoleon. His father, Louis Bonaparte, was at the time of his birth the king of Holland. When Napoleon's own son died in 1832 Louis Napoleon assumed the headship of the Bonaparte family. He resolved to restore the glories of the empire. With a handful of followers he tried to seize power at Strasbourg in 1836 and at Boulogne in 1840, leading what the following century would know as *Putsches*. Both failed ridiculously. Sentenced to life imprisonment in the fortress of Ham, he had escaped from it as recently as 1846 by simply walking off the grounds dressed as a stonemason. He expressed advanced social and political ideas, had probably joined the Carbonari in his youth, and had taken part in the Italian revolutionary uprising of 1830. He wrote two books, one called *Napoleonic Ideas*, claiming that his famous uncle had been misunderstood and checkmated by reactionary forces, and one called the *Extinction of Poverty*, a somewhat anticapitalistic tract like so many others of its time. But he was no friend of "anarchists," and in the spring of 1848, while still a refugee in England, he enrolled as one of Wellington's special constables to oppose the Chartist agitation. He soon returned to France. Compromised neither by the June Days nor by their repression, he was supposed to be a friend of the common people and at the same time a believer in order; and his name was Napoleon Bonaparte.

For twenty years a groundswell had been stirring the popular mind. It is known as the Napoleonic Legend. Peasants put up pictures of the emperor in their cottages, fondly imagining that it had been Napoleon who gave them the free ownership of their land. The completion of the Arch of Triumph in 1836 drove home the memory of imperial glories, and in 1840 the remains of the emperor were brought from St. Helena and majestically interred at the Invalides on the banks of the Seine. All this happened in a country where, government being in the hands of a few, most people had no political experience or political sense except what they had gained in revolution. When millions were suddenly, for the first time in their lives, asked to vote for a president in 1848, the name of Bonaparte was the only one they had ever heard of. "How should I not vote for this gentleman," said an old peasant, "I whose nose was frozen at Moscow?"

So Prince Louis Napoleon became president of the republic, by an overwhelming and indubitable popular mandate, in which an army officer was his only even faintly successful rival. He soon saw the way the wind was blowing. The Constituent Assembly dissolved itself in May 1849 and was replaced by the Legislative Assembly provided for in the new constitution. It was a strange assembly for a republic. It may be recalled that in 1797 the first normal election in the First Republic had produced a royalist majority.[4] Now in the Second Republic, under universal male suffrage, the result was the same. Five hundred of the deputies, or two-thirds, were really monarchists, but they were divided into irreconcilable factions—the Legitimists, who favored the line of Charles X, and the Orléanists, who favored that of Louis Philippe. One-third of the deputies called themselves republicans. Of these, in turn, about 180 were socialists of one kind or another; and only about 70 were political or old-fashioned republicans to whom the main issue was the form of government rather than the form of society itself.

The president and the Assembly at first combined to conjure away the specter of socialism, with which republicanism itself was now clearly associated. An abortive insurrection of June 1849 provided the chance. The Assembly, backed by the president, ousted thirty-three socialist deputies, suppressed public meetings, and imposed controls on the press. In 1850 it went so far as to rescind universal male suffrage, taking the vote away from about a third of the electorate— naturally the poorest and hence most socialistic third. The Falloux Law of 1850 put the schools at all levels of the educational system under supervision of the Catholic clergy; for, as M. Falloux said in the Assembly, "lay teachers have made the principles of social revolution popular in the most distant villages," and it was necessary "to rally around religion to strengthen the foundations of society against those who want to divide up property." The French Republic, now actually an antirepublican government, likewise intervened against the revolutionary republic established by Mazzini in the city of Rome. French military forces were sent to Rome to protect the pope; they remained there twenty years.

To the conservatives Bonaparte knew that he was virtually indispensable. They were so sharply divided between two sets of monarchists—Legitimist and Orléanist—that each would accept any antisocialist regime rather than yield to the other. Bonaparte's problem was to win over the radicals. He did so by urging in 1851 the restoration of universal suffrage, which he had himself helped repeal

[4] See p. 394.

in 1850. He now posed as the people's friend, the one man in public life who trusted the common man. He let it be thought that greedy plutocrats controlled the Assembly and hoodwinked France. He put his lieutenants in as ministers of war and of the interior, thus controlling the army, the bureaucracy, and the police. On December 2, 1851, the anniversary of Austerlitz, he sprang his coup d'état. Placards appeared all over Paris. They declared the Assembly dissolved and the vote for every adult Frenchman reinstated. When members of the Assembly tried to meet, they were attacked, dispersed, or arrested by the soldiers. The country did not submit without fighting. One hundred and fifty persons were killed in Paris, and throughout France probably 100,000 were put under arrest. But on December 20 the voters elected Louis Napoleon president for a term of ten years, by a vote officially stated as 7,439,216 to 646,737. A year later the new Bonaparte proclaimed the empire, with himself as Emperor of the French. Remembering Napoleon's son, he called himself Napoleon III.

How the empire functioned will be seen below. Not only the republic was dead. The republic as republicans understood it, an equalitarian, anticlerical regime with socialist or at least antibourgeois tendencies, had been dead since June 1848. Feeble anyway, it was killed by its reputation for radicalism. Liberalism and constitutionalism were dead also. Bourgeois and property-owning monarchists were greater sticklers for constitutional liberalism than were the republicans or the Bonapartists or than town laborers or rural peasants. But the monarchists, hopelessly divided among themselves, were now pushed aside. For the first time since 1815 France ceased to have any significant parliamentary life.

59. Vienna: The Nationalist Revolution in Central Europe and Italy

The Austrian Empire in 1848

The Austrian Empire of the Habsburgs, with its capital at Vienna, was in 1848 the most populous European state except Russia. Its peoples, living principally in the three major geographical divisions of the empire, Austria, Bohemia, and Hungary, were of about a dozen recognizably different nationalities or language groups—Germans, Czechs, Magyars, Poles, Ruthenians, Slovaks, Serbs, Croats, Slovenes, Dalmatians, Romanians, and Italians.[5] In some parts of the empire the nationalities lived in solid blocks, but in many regions two or more were interlaced together, the language changing from village to village, or even from house to house, in a way quite unknown in western Europe.

Germans, the leading people, occupied all of Austria proper and considerable parts of Bohemia, and were scattered also in small pockets throughout Hungary. The Czechs occupied Bohemia and the adjoining Moravia. The Magyars were the dominant group in the historic kingdom of Hungary, which contained a mixture of nationalities with a considerable number of Slavic peoples. Two of

[5] See maps, pp. 222, 448–449, 470; and pp. 221–223, 275–278, 331–335, 423–425, 447.

the most advanced parts of Italy also belonged to the empire—Venetia, with its capital at Venice, and Lombardy, whose chief city was Milan.

The Czechs, Poles, Ruthenians, Slovaks, Serbs, Croats, Slovenes, and Dalmatians in the empire were all Slavs; i.e., their languages were all related to one another and to the several forms of Russian. Neither the Magyars nor the Romanians were Slavs. The Magyars, as national sentiment grew, prided themselves on the uniqueness of their language in Europe and the Romanians on their linguistic affiliations with the Latin peoples of the West. Romanians, Magyars, and Germans formed a thick belt separating the South Slavs (in later years called Yugoslavs) from those of the north. Germans and Italians within the empire were in continual touch with Germans and Italians outside. The peoples of the empire represented every cultural level known to Europe. Vienna, where the Waltz King Johann Strauss was reigning, recognized no peer except Paris itself. Milan was a great center of trade. Bohemia had long had a textile industry of importance, which was beginning to be mechanized in the 1840s; but 200 miles to the south a Croatian intellectual remarked, about the same time, that the first steam engine he ever saw was in a picture printed on a cotton handkerchief imported from Manchester. In 1848, some denied that any such people as the Ruthenians existed at all. Nor was it clear exactly what groups made up the South Slavs. No such word as Yugoslavia or Czechoslovakia had been invented, and Romania was a term used only by professors.

Thus the empire ruled from Vienna included, according to political frontiers established seventy years later, in 1918, all of Austria, Hungary, and Czechoslovakia, with adjoining portions of Poland, Romania, Yugoslavia, and Italy. But the political authority of Vienna reached far beyond the borders of the empire. Austria since 1815 had been the most influential member of the German confederation, for Prussia in these years was content to look with deference upon the Habsburgs. The influence of Vienna was felt throughout Germany in many ways, as in the enactment and enforcement of the Carlsbad Decrees mentioned in the last chapter.[6] It reached also through the length of Italy. Lombardy and Venetia were part of the Austrian Empire. Tuscany, ostensibly independent, was governed by a Habsburg grand duke. The kingdom of Naples or the Two Sicilies, comprising all Italy south of Rome, was virtually a protectorate of Vienna. The papal states looked politically to Vienna for leadership, at least until 1846, when the College of Cardinals elected a liberal-minded pope, Pius IX—the one contingency upon which Metternich confessed he had failed to reckon. In all Italy there was only one state ruled by a native Italian dynasty and attempting any consistent independence of policy—the kingdom of Sardinia (called also Savoy or Piedmont) tucked away in the northwest corner around Turin. Italy, said Metternich blandly, was only a "geographical expression," a mere regional name. He might have said the same of Poland, or even of Germany, though Germany was tenuously joined in the Bund, or loose confederation, of 1815.

These peoples since the turn of the century had all felt the flutters of the *Volksgeist,* persistent stirrings of a cultural nationalism, and among Germans, Italians, Poles, and Hungarians a good deal of political agitation and liberal reformism had been at work. Metternich, in Vienna, had discouraged such

6 See pp. 476–477.

manifestations for over thirty years, ominously predicting that if allowed to break out they would produce the *bellum omnium contra omnes*—"the war of all against all." As a prophet he was not wholly mistaken, but if it is the business of statesmanship not merely to prophesy events but to control them it cannot be said that the regime of Metternich was very successful. The whole nationalities question was evaded. The fundamental problem of the century, the bringing of peoples into some kind of mutual and moral relationship with their governments— the problem of which nationalism, liberalism, constitutionalism, and democracy were diverse aspects—remained unconsidered by the responsible authorities of central Europe. All that Metternich offered was the idea that a reigning house, with an official bureaucracy, should rule benevolently over peoples with whom it need have no connection and who need have no connection with each other. They were the ideas of the eighteenth century, dating from before the French Revolution and best suited to an agricultural and localistic society.

The March Days

In March 1848, everything collapsed with incredible swiftness. At that time the diet of Hungary had been sitting for some months, considering constitutional reforms and, as usual, debating further means of keeping German influence out of Hungary. Then came news of the February Revolution in Paris. The radical party in the Hungarian diet was aroused. Its leader, Louis Kossuth, on March 3 made an impassioned speech on the virtues of liberty. This speech was immediately printed in German and read in Vienna, where restlessness was also heightened by the news from Paris. On March 13 workingmen and students rose in insurrection in Vienna, manned barricades, fought off soldiers, and invaded the imperial palace. So flabbergasted and terrified was the government that Metternich, to the amazement of Europe, resigned and fled in disguise to England.

The fall of Metternich proved that the Vienna government was entirely disoriented. Revolution swept through the empire and through all Italy and Germany. On March 15 rioting began in Berlin; the king of Prussia promised a constitution. The lesser German governments collapsed in sequence. On the last day of March a Pre-Parliament met to arrange the calling of an all-German national assembly. In Hungary, aroused by Kossuth's national party, the diet on March 15 enacted the March Laws, by which Hungary assumed a position of complete constitutional separatism within the empire, while still recognizing the Habsburg house. The harassed Emperor Ferdinand a few days later granted substantially the same status to Bohemia. At Milan between March 18 and 22 the populace drove out the Austrian garrison. Venice proclaimed itself an independent republic. Tuscany drove out its grand duke and also set up as a republic. The king of Sardinia,[7] Charles Albert (who, stimulated by the Paris revolution, had granted a constitution to his small country on March 4) declared war on Austria on March 23 and invaded Lombardy-Venetia, hoping to bring that area under the house of

---

[7] "Sardinia" was in the northwest corner of the Italian mainland. See the note on p. 194 for an explanation of how this state, with its capital at Turin and its seaport at Genoa, came to be called after the rather desolate island of Sardinia. Of the king and kingdom we must say "Sardinia"; of the dynasty, "Savoy"; the state was often also called "Piedmont."

Savoy. Italian troops streamed up from Tuscany, from Naples (where revolution had broken out as early as January), and even from the papal states (the new pope being in some sympathy with national and liberal aims) to join in an all-Italian war against the seemingly helpless Austrian government.

Thus in the brief span of these phenomenal March Days the whole structure based on Vienna went to pieces. The Austrian Empire had fallen into its main components, Prussia had yielded to revolutionaries, all Germany was preparing to unify itself, and war raged in Italy. Everywhere constitutions had been wildly promised by stupefied governments, constitutional assemblies were meeting, and independent or autonomous nations struggled into existence. Patriots everywhere demanded liberal government and national freedom—written constitutions, representative assemblies, responsible ministries, a more or less extended suffrage, restrictions upon police action, jury trial, civil liberty, freedom of press and assembly. And where it still existed—in Prussia, Galicia, Bohemia, Hungary—serfdom was declared abolished and the peasant masses became legally free from control by their local lords.

The Turning of the Tide after June

The revolution, as in France, surged forward until the month of June, and then began to ebb. For its steady reflux there are many reasons. The old governments had been only stunned in the March Days, not really broken. They merely awaited the opportunity to take back promises extorted by force. The force originally imposed by the revolutionaries could not be sustained. The revolutionary leaders were not really very strong. Middle-class, bourgeois, property-owning, and commercial interests were nowhere nearly as highly developed as in western Europe. The revolutionary leaders were to a large extent writers, editors, professors, and students, men of ideas rather than spokesmen for large positive interests. In Vienna, Milan, and a few other cities the working class was numerous and socialist ideas fairly common; but the workers were not as literate, organized, politically conscious, or irritated as in Paris or Great Britain. They were strong enough, however, to disquiet the middle classes; and especially after the specter of social revolution rose over western Europe, the middle-class and lower-class revolutionaries began to be afraid of each other. The liberated nationalities also began to disagree. The peasants, once emancipated, had no further interest in revolution. Nor were the peasants at this time conscious of nationality; nationalism was primarily a doctrine of the educated middle classes or of the landowning classes in Poland and Hungary. Since the old internationally minded aristocracy furnished the bulk of officers in the armies, and the peasants the bulk of the soldiers, the armies remained almost immune to nationalist aspirations. This attitude of the armies was decisive.

The tide first turned in Prague. The all-German national assembly met at Frankfurt-on-the-Main in May. Representatives from Bohemia had been invited to come to Frankfurt, since many Germans had always lived in Bohemia, and since Bohemia formed part of the confederation of 1815 as it had of the Holy Roman Empire before it. But the idea of belonging to a national German state, a Germany based on the principle that the inhabitants were Germans (which had not been the principle of the Holy Roman Empire or of the confederation of 1815) did not appeal to the Czechs in Bohemia. They refused to go to the all-German congress at Frankfurt. Instead, they called an all-Slav congress of their own. At Prague, in June 1848, this first Pan-Slav assembly met. Most of the delegates were from the Slav communities within the Austrian Empire, but a few came from the Balkans and non-Austrian Poland. Only one Russian was present, the anarchist revolutionary Michael Bakunin. Slavs generally did not at this time look with favor upon Russia, the oppressor of Poles; nor did the tsarist government, under Nicholas I, think well of Pan-Slavism, seeing in it a subversive popular agitation.

The spirit of the Prague congress was that of the Slavic Revival described in the last chapter;[8] the Czech historian Palacky was in fact one of its most active figures. The congress was profoundly anti-German, since the essence of the Slavic Revival was resistance to Germanization. But it was not profoundly anti-Austrian or anti-Habsburg. A few extremists, indeed, maintained that Slavdom should be the basis of political regeneration, and that the world therefore had no place for an Austrian empire. But the great majority at the Prague congress were Austroslavs. Austroslavism held that the many Slavic peoples, pressed on two sides by the population masses of Russians and Germans, needed the Austrian Empire as a political frame within which to develop their own national life. It demanded that the Slavic peoples be admitted as equals with the other nationalities in the Austrian Empire, enjoying local autonomy and constitutional guarantees.

The Germans of Bohemia, the Sudeten Germans, were of course attracted to the Frankfurt Assembly. They were eager to be included in the unified Germany about to be formed. As the Bohemian Czechs would be a minority in a German Germany, so the Bohemian Germans would be a minority in a Czech Bohemia. There was therefore friction among the mixed people of Bohemia and in Prague, a bilingual city.

Victories of the Counterrevolution, June–December

But the Emperor Ferdinand, and the advisers on whom he chose to rely, would have nothing to do with national movements, since they were also liberal, bristling with restrictions upon the powers of the state. All therefore were to be resisted. The first victory of the old government came at Prague. In that city a Czech insurrection broke out on June 12, at the time when the Slav congress was sitting, and was made worse by local animosities between Czechs and Germans. Windischgrätz, the local army commander, bombarded and subdued the city. The Slav congress dispersed. The Habsburg army was in control.

The next victory of the counterrevolution came in north Italy in the following month. Only Lombardy-Venetia, of all parts of the empire, had declared independence from the Habsburgs during the upheavals of March. The diminutive kingdom of Sardinia had lent support and had declared war on Austria. Italians from all over the peninsula had flocked in to fight; and until after the June Days in Paris it seemed not impossible that republican France might intervene, to befriend fellow revolutionaries, as in 1796. But in France no radical or expansionist revolution succeeded. The Italians were left to themselves. Radetsky, the Austrian

[8] See pp. 468–472.

commander in Italy, overwhelmingly defeated the king of Sardinia at Custozza on July 25. The Sardinian king, Charles Albert, retreated into his own country. Lombardy and Venetia were restored with savage vengeance to the Austrian Empire.

The third victory of the counterrevolution came in September and October. The Hungarian radical party of Louis Kossuth was liberal and even democratic in many of its principles, but it was a Magyar nationalist party above all else. Triumphant in the March Days, it completely shook off the German connection. It moved the capital from Pressburg near the Austrian border to Budapest in the center of Hungary. It changed the official language of Hungary from Latin to Magyar. Less than half the people of Hungary were Magyars, and Magyar is an extremely difficult language, quite alien to the Indo-European tongues of Europe. It soon became clear that one must be a Magyar to benefit from the new liberal constitution, and that the Magyars intended to denationalize and Magyarize all others with whom they shared the country. Slovaks, Romanians, Germans, Serbs, and Croats violently resisted, each group determined to keep its own national identity unimpaired. The Croats, who had enjoyed certain Croatian liberties before the Magyar revolution, took the lead under Count Jellachich, the "ban," or provincial governor, of Croatia. In September Jellachich raised a civil war in Hungary, leading a force of Serbo-Croatians, supported by the whole non-Magyar half of the population. Half of Hungary, alarmed by Magyar nationalism, now looked to the Habsburgs and the empire to protect them. Emperor Ferdinand made Jellachich his military commander against the Magyars. Hungary dissolved into the war of all against all.

At Vienna the more clear-sighted revolutionaries, who had led the March rising, now saw that Jellachich's army, if successful against the Magyars, would soon be turned against them. They therefore rose in a second mass insurrection in October 1848. The emperor fled; never had the Viennese revolution gone so far. But it was already too late. The Austrian military leader Windischgrätz brought his intact forces down from Bohemia. He besieged Vienna for five days and forced its surrender on October 31.

With the recapture of Vienna the upholders of the old order took heart. Counterrevolutionary leaders—large estate holders, Catholic clergy, high-ranking army men—decided to clear the way by getting rid of the Emperor Ferdinand, considering that promises made in March by Ferdinand might be more easily repudiated by his successor. Ferdinand abdicated and on December 2, 1848, was succeeded by Francis Joseph, a boy of eighteen, destined to live until 1916 and to end his reign in a crisis even more shattering than that in which he began it.

Final Outburst and Repression, 1849

For a time in the first part of 1849 the revolution in many places seemed to blaze more fiercely than ever. Republican riots broke out in parts of Germany. In Rome someone assassinated the reforming minister of Pius IX. The pope fled from the city, and a radical Roman Republic was proclaimed under three Triumvirs, one of whom was Mazzini, who hastened from England to take part in the republican upheaval. In north Italy Charles Albert of Sardinia again invaded Lombardy. In

Hungary, after the revived Habsburg authorities repudiated the new Magyar constitution, the Magyars, led by the flaming Kossuth, went on to declare absolute independence. But all these manifestations proved short-lived. German republicanism flickered out. Mazzini and his republicans were driven from Rome, and Pius IX was restored, by intevention of the French army.[9] The Sardinian king was again defeated by an Austrian army on March 23, 1849. In Hungary the Magyars put up a terrific resistance, which the imperial army and the anti-Magyar native irregulars could not overcome. The Habsburg authorities now renewed the procedures of the Holy Alliance. The new Emperor Francis Joseph invited the Tsar Nicholas to intervene. Over a hundred thousand Russian troops poured over the mountains into Hungary, soon defeated the Magyars, and laid the prostrate country at the feet of the court of Vienna. This was in August 1849.

The nationalist upheaval of 1848 in central Europe and Italy was now over. The Habsburg authority had been reasserted over Czech nationalists in Prague, Magyars in Hungary, Italian patriots in north Italy, and liberal revolutionists in Vienna itself. Reaction, or antirevolutionism, became the order of the day. Pius IX, the "liberal pope" of 1846, resumed the papal throne, disillusioned in his liberal ideas. The breach between liberalism and Roman Catholicism, which had opened wide in the first French Revolution, was made a yawning chasm by the revolutionary violence of Mazzini's Roman Republic and by the measures taken to repress it. Pius IX now reiterated the anathemas of his predecessors. He codified them in 1864 in the *Syllabus of Errors*, which warned all Catholics, on the authority of the Vatican, against everything that went under the names of liberalism, progress, and civilization. As for the nationalists in Italy, many were disillusioned with the firecracker methods of romantic republicans and inclined to conclude that Italy would be liberated from Austrian influence only by an old-fashioned war between established powers.

In the Austrian Empire, under Prince Schwarzenberg, the emperor's chief minister, the main policy was now to oppose all forms of popular self-expression, with a sophistication, in view of the events of 1848, that Metternich had never known, and with a candid reliance on military force. Constitutionalism was to be rooted out, as well as all forms of nationalism—Slavism, Magyarism, Italianism, and also Germanism, which would draw the sentiments of Austrian Germans from the Habsburg empire to the great kindred body of the German people. The regime came to be called the Bach system, after Alexander Bach, the minister of the interior. Under it, the government was rigidly centralized. Hungary lost the separate rights it had had before 1848. The ideal was to create a perfectly solid and unitary political system. Bach insisted on maintaining the emancipation of the peasants, which had converted the mass of the people from subjects of their landlords into subjects of the state. He drove through a reform of the legal system and law courts, created a free trading area of the whole empire with only a common external tariff, and subsidized and encouraged the building of highways and railroads. The aim, as in France at the same time under Louis Napoleon, was to make people forget liberty in an overwhelming demonstration of administrative efficiency and material progress. But some, at that time, would not forget. A

[9] See p. 506.

liberal said of the Bach system that it consisted of "a standing army of soldiers, a sitting army of officials, a kneeling army of priests, and a creeping army of informers."

60. Frankfurt and Berlin: The Question of a Liberal Germany

The German States

Meanwhile, from May 1848 to May 1849, the Frankfurt Assembly was sitting at the historic city on the Main. It was attempting to bring a unified German state into being, one which should also be liberal and constitutional, assuring civil rights to its citizens and possessing a government responsive to popular will as manifested in free elections and open parliamentary debate. The failure to produce a democratic Germany was long one of the overshadowing facts of modern times.

The convocation of the Frankfurt Assembly was made possible by the collapse of the existing German governments in the March Days of 1848. These governments, the thirty-nine states recognized after the Congress of Vienna, were the main obstacles in the way of unification. The reigning princes and their ministers enjoyed a heightened political stature from political independence. The German states resisted the surrender of sovereignty to a united Germany just as national states in the next century were to resist the surrender of sovereignty to a United Nations. In another way Germany was a miniature of the political world. It consisted of both great and small powers. Its great powers were Prussia and Austria. Austria was the miscellaneous empire described above. Prussia after 1815 included the Rhineland; the central regions around Berlin; West Prussia and Posen (acquired in the partitions of Poland); and historic East Prussia. The former Polish areas were inhabited by a mixture of Germans and Poles.[10] Neither of these great powers could submit to the other or allow the other to dominate its lesser German neighbors. The small German powers, in turn, upheld their own independence in the balance between the two great ones.

This German "dualism," or polarity between Berlin and Vienna, had been somewhat abated under the common menace of the Napoleonic empire. The whole German question had lain dormant, so far as the governments were concerned, nor did it agitate the old aristocracies. In Prussia the Junkers, the owners of great landed estates east of the Elbe, were singularly indifferent to the all-German dream. Their political feeling was not German but Prussian. They were making a good thing of Prussia for themselves and could expect only to lose by absorption into Germany as a whole, for in Germany west of the Elbe the small peasant holding was the basis of society, and there was no landowning element corresponding to the Junkers. The rest of Germany looked upon Prussia as somewhat uncouth and Eastern; but this feeling, too,

---

[10] See maps, pp. 230–231, 448–449; and see pp. 227–229, 246, 447–450.

had been abated in the time of Napoleon, when patriots from all over Germany enlisted in the Prussian service.[11]

Berlin: Failure of the Revolution in Prussia

Prussia was illiberal but not backward. Frederick William III repeatedly evaded his promise to grant a modern constitution. His successor, Frederick William IV, who inherited the throne in 1840, and from whom much was at first hoped by liberals, proved to be a somewhat cloudy and neomedieval romantic, equally determined not to share his authority with his subjects. At the same time the government, administratively speaking, was efficient, progressive, and fair. The universities and elementary school system surpassed those of western Europe. Literacy was higher than in England or France. The government followed in mercantilist traditions of evoking, planning, and supporting economic life.[12] In 1818 it initiated a tariff union, at first with tiny states (or enclaves) wholly enclosed within Prussia. This tariff union, or *Zollverein,* was extended in the following decades to include almost all Germany.

On March 15, 1848, as noted above, rioting and street fighting broke out in Berlin. For a time it seemed as if the army would master the situation. But the king, Frederick William IV, a man of notions and projects, and erratically conscientious, called off the soldiers and allowed his subjects to elect the first all-Prussian legislative assembly. Thus though the army remained intact, and its Junker officers unconvinced, revolution proceeded superficially on its way. The Prussian Assembly proved surprisingly radical, since it was dominated by anti-Junker lower-class extremists from East Prussia. These men were supporting Polish revolutionaries and exiles who sought the restoration of Polish freedom. Their main belief was that the fortress of reaction was tsarist Russia—that the whole structure of Junkerdom, landlordism, serf-owning, and repression of national freedom depended ultimately on the armed might of the tsarist empire. (The subsequent intervention of Russia in Hungary indicated the truth of this diagnosis.) Prussian radicals, like many elsewhere, hoped to smash the Holy Alliance by raising an all-German or even European revolutionary war against Russia, to precipitate which they supported the claims of the Poles.

Meanwhile the radical-dominated Berlin Assembly granted local self-government to the Poles of West Prussia and Posen. But in those areas Germans and Slavs had long lived side by side. The Germans in Posen refused to respect the authority of Polish officials. Prussian army units stationed in Posen supported the German element. As early as April 1848, a month after the "revolution," the army crushed the new pro-Polish institutions set up in Posen by the Berlin Assembly. It was clear where the only real power lay. By the end of 1848, in Prussia as in Austria, the revolution was over. The king again changed his mind; and the old authorities, acting through the army, were again in control.

---

[11] See pp. 439–440.
[12] See pp. 119–120, 232, 335–336.

The Frankfurt Assembly

Meanwhile a similar story was enacted on the larger stage of Germany as a whole. The disabling of the old governments left a power vacuum. A self-appointed committee convoked a Pre-Parliament, which in turn arranged for the election of an all-German assembly. Bypassing the existing sovereignties, voters throughout Germany sent delegates to Frankfurt to create a federated superstate. The strength and weakness of the resulting Frankfurt Assembly originated in this manner of its election. The Assembly represented the moral sentiment of people at large, the liberal and national aspirations of many Germans. It stood for an idea. Politically it represented nothing. The delegates had no power to issue orders or expect compliance. Superficially resembling the National Assembly which met in France in 1789, the German National Assembly at Frankfurt was really in a very different position. There was no preexisting national structure for it to work with. There was no all-German army or civil service for the Assembly to take over. The Frankfurt Assembly, having no power of its own, became dependent on the power of the very sovereign states that it was attempting to supersede.

The Assembly met in May 1848. Its members with a handful of exceptions were not at all revolutionary. They were overwhelmingly professional people—professors, judges, lawyers, government administrators, clergy both Protestant and Catholic, and prominent businessmen. They wanted a liberal, self-governing, federally unified, and "democratic" though not equalitarian Germany. Their outlook was earnest, peaceable, and legalistic; they hoped to succeed by persuasion. Violence was abhorrent to them. They wanted no armed conflict with the existing German states. They wanted no war with Russia. They wanted no general international upheaval of the working classes. The example of the June Days in Paris, and the Chartist agitation in Great Britain, coinciding with the early weeks of the Frankfurt Assembly, increased the dread of that body for radicalism and republicanism in Germany. The tragedy of Germany (and hence of Europe) lies in the fact that this German revolution came too late, at a time when social revolutionaries had already begun to declare war on the bourgeoisie, and the bourgeoisie was already afraid of the common man. It is the common man, not the professor or respectable merchant, who in unsettled times actually seizes firearms and rushes to shout revolutionary utterances in the streets. Without lower-class insurrection not even middle-class revolutions have been successful. The combination effected in France between 1789 and 1794, an unwilling and divergent combination of bourgeois and lower-class revolutionaries, was not and could not be effected in Germany in 1848. One form of revolutionary power—controlled popular turbulence—the Germans of the Frankfurt Assembly would not or could not use. Quite the contrary: when radical riots broke out in Frankfurt itself in September 1848 the Assembly undertook to repress them. Having no force of its own, it appealed to the Prussian army. The Prussian army put down the riots, and thereafter the Assembly met under its protection.

But the most troublesome question facing the Frankfurt Assembly was not social but national. What, after all, was this "Germany" which so far existed only in the mind? Where was the line really to be drawn in space? Did Germany include Austria and Bohemia, which belonged to the Bund of 1815 and had in former days belonged to the Holy Roman Empire?[13] Did it include all Prussia, although eastern Prussia had lain outside the Empire and did not now belong to the Bund? On the side toward Denmark, did it include the duchies of Schleswig and Holstein, which belonged to the Danish king, who was therefore himself, as ruler of Holstein, a member of the 1815 confederation? And if, as poets said, the Fatherland existed wherever the German tongue was spoken, what of the German communities in Hungary and Moravia, or along the upper Baltic and in the city of Riga, or in some of the Swiss cantons and the city of Zurich, or for that matter in Holland, which had left the Holy Roman Empire only two hundred years before—not long as time is measured in Europe.

These last and most soaring speculations, though they had already been launched by a few bold spirits, were put out of mind by the men of the Frankfurt Assembly. The other questions remained. The men at Frankfurt, eager to create a real Germany, naturally could not offer one smaller than the shadow Germany that they so much deplored. Most therefore were Great Germans; they thought that the Germany for which they were writing a constitution should include the Austrian lands, except Hungary. This would mean that the federal crown must be offered to the Habsburgs. Others, at first a minority, were Little Germans; they thought that Austria should be excluded, and that the new Germany should comprise the smaller states and the entire kingdom of Prussia. In that case the king of Prussia would become the federal emperor.

The desire of the Frankfurt Assembly to retain non-German peoples in the new Germany, at a time when these peoples also were feeling national ambitions, was another reason for its fatal dependency upon the Austrian and Prussian armies. The Frankfurt Assembly applauded when Windischgrätz broke the Czech revolution. It expressed its satisfaction when Prussian forces put down the Poles in Posen. On this matter the National Assembly at Frankfurt and the Prussian Assembly at Berlin did not agree. The men of Frankfurt, thinking the Prussian revolutionary assembly too radical and pro-Polish, and wanting no war with Russia, in effect supported the Prussian army and the Junkers against the Berlin revolution, without which the Frankfurt Assembly itself could never have existed.

A still clearer case arose over Schleswig-Holstein. These duchies belonged to the Danish king. Schleswig, the northern of the two, had a mixed population of Danes and Germans. The Germans in Schleswig rebelled in March 1848; and the Danes, who also had a constitutional upheaval at the time, proceeded to incorporate Schleswig integrally into their modernized Danish state. When the Frankfurt Assembly met, it found that the Pre-Parliament had already declared an all-German war upon Denmark in defense of fellow Germans in Schleswig. Having no army of its own, the Frankfurt Assembly invited Prussia to fight the war; and the revolutionary Prussian government in Berlin was at first able to persuade the Prussian generals to initiate a campaign. Great Britain and Russia prepared to intervene to keep control of the mouth of the Baltic out of German hands. The Prussian army simply withdrew from the war. Its officers had no desire to antagonize Russia or to advance the interests of nationalist revolutionaries in Germany. The Frankfurt Assembly, humiliated and helpless, was obliged to accept the armistice concluded by the Prussian generals. Radical socionationalistic

---

[13] See maps, pp. 328, 448–449, 555.

riots broke out against the Junkers, the tsar, and the Frankfurt Assembly; and it was at this time that the Assembly called in Prussian forces for its own protection.

The Failure of the Frankfurt Assembly

By the end of 1848 the debacle was approaching. The nationalists had checkmated each other. Everywhere in central Europe, from Denmark to Naples and from the Rhineland to the Transylvanian forests, the awakening nationalities had failed to respect each other's aspirations, had delighted in each other's defeats, and by quarreling with each other had hastened the return of the old absolutist and nonnational order. At Berlin and at Vienna the counterrevolution, backed by the army, was in the saddle. At this very time, in December, the Frankfurt Assembly at last issued a Declaration of the Rights of the German People. It was a humane and high-minded document, announcing numerous individual rights, civil liberties, and constitutional guarantees, much along the line of the French and American declarations of the eighteenth century, but with one significant difference—the French and Americans spoke of the rights of man, the Germans of the rights of Germans. In April 1849 the Frankfurt Assembly completed its constitution. It was now clear that Austria must be excluded, for the simple reason that the restored Habsburg government refused to come in. The Danubian empire, as already seen, was as profoundly opposed to Germanism as to any other nationalistic movement. The Little Germans in the Assembly therefore had their way. The hereditary headship of a new German empire, a constitutional and federal union of German states minus Austria, was now offered to Frederick William IV, the king of Prussia.

Frederick William was tempted. The Prussian army officers and East-Elbian landlords were not. They had no wish to lose Prussia in Germany. The king himself had his scruples. If he took the proffered crown he would still have to impose himself by force on the lesser states, which the Frankfurt Assembly did not represent and could not bind, and which were in fact still the actual powers in the country. He could also expect trouble with Austria. He did not wish war. Nor was it proper for an heir to the Hohenzollerns to accept a throne circumscribed with constitutional limitations and representing the revolutionary conception of the sovereignty of the people. Declaring that he could not "pick up a crown from the gutter," he turned it down. It would have to be offered freely by his equals, the sovereign princes of Germany.

Thus all the work of the Frankfurt Assembly went for nothing. Most members of the Assembly, having never dreamed of using violence in the first place, concluded that they were beaten and went home. A handful of extremists remained at Frankfurt, promulgated the constitution on their own authority, urged revolutionary outbreaks, and called for elections. Riots broke out in various places. The Prussian army put them down—in Saxony, in Bavaria, in Baden. The same army drove the rump Assembly out of Frankfurt, and that was the end of it.

In summary, Germany in 1848 failed to solve the problem of its unification in a liberal and constitutional way. Liberal nationalism failed, and a less gentle kind of nationalism soon replaced it. The German movement of 1848, like so much else in German history, in the long run contributed to a fateful estrangement between Germany and the West. Thousands of disappointed German liberals and revolutionaries migrated to the United States, which came to know them as the "forty-eighters." They brought to the new country, besides a ripple of revolutionary agitation, a stream of men trained in science, medicine, and music, and of highly skilled craftsmen like silversmiths and engravers.

The Prussian Constitution of 1850

In Prussia itself the ingenious monarch undertook to placate everybody by issuing a constitution of his own, one that should be peculiarly Prussian. It remained in effect from 1850 to 1918. It granted a single parliament for all the miscellaneous regions of Prussia. The parliament met in two chambers. The lower chamber was elected by universal male suffrage, not along the individualist or equalitarian principles of the West, but by a system that in effect divided the population into three estates—the wealthy, the less wealthy, and the general run of the people. Division was made according to payment of taxes. Those few big taxpayers who together contributed a third of the tax returns chose a third of the members of district electoral colleges, which in turn chose deputies to the Prussian lower house. In this way one large property owner had as much voting power as hundreds of working people. Large property in Prussia in 1850 still meant mainly the landed estates of the East-Elbian Junkers, but as time went on it came to include industrial property in the Rhineland also. The Junkers likewise were not harmed by the final liquidation of serfdom. They increased the acreage of their holdings, as after the reforms of Stein;[14] and the former servile agricultural workers turned into free wage earners economically dependent on the great landowners.

For 1850 the Prussian constitution was fairly progressive. If the mass of the people could elect very few deputies under the indirect system described, the mass of the British people, until 1867 or even 1884, could elect no deputies to Parliament at all. But the Prussian constitution remained in force until 1918. By the close of the nineteenth century, with democratic advances making their appearance elsewhere, the electoral system in Prussia, remaining unchanged, came to be reactionary and illiberal, giving the great landowners and industrialists an unusual position of special privilege within the state.

61. The New Toughness of Mind: Realism, Positivism, Marxism

The Revolution of 1848 failed not only in Germany but also in Hungary, in Italy, and in France. The "springtime of peoples," as it was called, was followed by chilling blasts of winter. The dreams of half a century, visions of a humane nationalism, aspirations for liberalism without violence, ideals of a peaceful and democratic republican commonwealth, were all exploded. Everywhere the cry had been for constitutional government, but only in a few small states—Denmark,

[14] See pp. 439-440.

Holland, Belgium, Switzerland, Piedmont—was constitutional liberty more firmly secured by the Revolution of 1848. Everywhere the cry had been for the freedom of nations, to unify national groups or rid them of foreign rule; but nowhere was national liberty more advanced in 1850 than it had been two years before. France obtained universal male suffrage in 1848, and kept it permanently thereafter (except for a brief reversion to a restricted suffrage in 1850–1851); but it did not obtain democracy; it obtained a kind of popular dictatorship under Louis Napoleon Bonaparte. One accomplishment, however, was real enough. The peasantry was emancipated in the German states and the Austrian Empire. Serfdom and manorial restraints were abolished, nor were they reimposed after the failure of the revolution. This was the most fundamental accomplishment of the whole movement. The peasant masses of central Europe were thereafter free to move about, find new jobs, enter a labor market, take part in a money economy, receive and spend wages, migrate to growing cities—or even go to the United States. But the peasants, once freed, showed little concern for constitutional or bourgeois ideas. Peasant emancipation, in fact, strengthened the forces of political counterrevolution.

The most immediate and far-reaching consequence of the 1848 revolutions, or of their failure, was a new toughness of mind. Idealism was discredited. Revolutionaries became less optimistic, conservatives more willing to exercise repression. It was now a point of pride to be realistic, emancipated from illusions, willing to face facts as they were. The future, it was thought, would be determined by present realities rather than by imaginings of what ought to be. Industrialization went forward, with England still far in the lead, but spreading to the Continent and initiating the momentous transformation of Germany. The 1850s were a period of rising prices and wages, thanks in part to the gold rush in California. There was more prosperity than in the 1840s; the propertied classes felt secure, and spokesmen for labor turned from theories of society to the organizing of viable unions, especially in the skilled trades.

Materialism, Realism, Positivism

In basic philosophy the new mental toughness appeared as materialism, holding that everything mental, spiritual, or ideal was an outgrowth of physical or physiological forces. In literature and the arts it was called "realism." Writers and painters broke away from romanticism, which they said colored things out of all relation to the real facts. They attempted to describe and reproduce life as they found it, without intimation of a better or more noble world. More and more people came to trust science, not merely for an understanding of nature, but for insights into the true meaning of man and society. In religion the movement was toward skepticism, renewing the skeptical trend of the eighteenth century, which had been somewhat interrupted during the intervening period of romanticism.[15] It was variously held, not by all but by many, that religion was unscientific and hence not to be taken seriously; or that it was a mere historical growth among peoples in certain stages of development and hence irrelevant to modern

[15] See pp. 314–315, 317–324, 464.

civilization; or that one ought to go to church and lead a decent life, without taking the priest or clergyman too seriously, because religion was necessary to preserve the social order against radicalism and anarchy. To this idea the radical counterpart was of course that religion was a bourgeois i vention to delude the people.

"Positivism" was another term used to describe the new attitude. It originated with the French philosopher Auguste Comte, who had begun to publish his numerous volumes on *Positive Philosophy* as long ago as 1830 and was still writing in the 1850s. He saw human history as a series of three stages, the theological, the metaphysical, and the scientific. The revolutions in France, he thought, both of 1789 and of 1848, suffered from an excess of metaphysical abstractions, empty words, and unverifiable high-flying principles. Those who worked for the improvement of society must adopt a strictly scientific outlook, and Comte produced an elaborate classification of the sciences, of which the highest would be the science of society, for which he coined the word "sociology." This new science would build upon observation of actual facts to develop broad scientific laws of social progress. Comte himself, and his closest disciples, envisaged a final scientific Religion of Humanity, which, stripped of archaic theological and metaphysical concerns, would serve as the basis for a better world of the future. More generally, however, "positivism" came to mean an insistence on verifiable facts, an avoidance of wishful thinking, a questioning of all assumptions, and a dislike of unprovable generalizations. Positivism in a broad sense, both in its demand for observation of facts and testing of ideas, and in its aspiration to be humanly useful, contributed to the growth of the social sciences as a branch of learning.

In politics the new toughness of mind was called by the Germans *Realpolitik*. This simply meant a "politics of reality." In domestic affairs it meant that people should give up utopian dreams, such as had caused the débacle of 1848, and content themselves with the blessings of an orderly, honest, hard-working government. For radicals it meant that people should stop imagining that the new society would result from goodness or the love of justice, and that social reformers must resort to the methods of politics—power and calculation. In international affairs *Realpolitik* meant that governments should not be guided by ideology, or by any system of "natural" enemies or "natural" allies, or by any desire to defend or promote any particular view of the world; but that they should follow their own practical interests, meet facts and situations as they arose, make any alliances that seemed useful, disregard tastes and scruples, and use any practical means to achieve their ends. The same men who, before 1848, had been not ashamed to express pacifist and cosmopolitan hopes now dismissed such ideas as a little softheaded. War, which governments since the overthrow of Napoleon had successfully tried to prevent, was accepted in the 1850s as an obvious means sometimes necessary to achieve a purpose. It was not especially glorious; it was not an end in itself; it was simply one of the tools of the statesman. *Realpolitik* was by no means confined to Germany, despite its German name and despite the fact that the famous German chancellor Bismarck became its most famous practitioner. Two other tough-minded thinkers, each in his own way, were Karl Marx and Louis Napoleon Bonaparte.

Early Marxism

Karl Marx and Friedrich Engels were among the disappointed revolutionaries of 1848. Marx (1818–1883) was the son of a lawyer in the Prussian Rhineland. He studied law and philosophy at several German universities, received a doctoral degree in 1841, and mixed with young German intellectuals for several years. Engels (1820–1893), the son of a well-to-do German textile manufacturer, was sent as a young man to Manchester in England, where his father owned a factory, to learn the business and then manage it. Marx and Engels met in Paris in 1844. There they began a collaboration in thinking and writing that lasted for forty years.

In 1847 they joined the Communist League, a tiny secret group of revolutionaries, mainly Germans in exile in the more liberal Western Europe. The word "communist" then had only a vague and uncertain meaning, and the League, as Engels later recalled, was at first "not actually much more than the German branch of the French secret societies." It agitated like other societies during the Revolution of 1848, and issued a set of "Demands of the Communist Party in Germany," which urged a unified indivisible German republic, democratic suffrage, universal free education, arming of the people, a progressive income tax, limitations upon inheritance, state ownership of banks, railroads, canals, mines, etc., and a degree of large-scale, scientific, collectivized agriculture. It was such obscurely voiced radicalism that alarmed the Frankfurt Assembly. With the triumph of counterrevolution in Germany the Communist League was crushed.

It was for this League that Marx and Engels wrote their *Communist Manifesto,* which was published in January 1848. But there was as yet no Marxism, and Marxism played no role in the Revolution of 1848. As a historical force Marxism set in during the 1870s. Meanwhile, with the failure of the revolution, Engels returned to his factory at Manchester, and Marx also settled in England, spending the rest of his life in London, where, after long labors in the library of the British Museum, he finally produced his huge work called *Capital,* of which the first volume was published in German in 1867. The final two volumes were edited by Engels and published after Marx's death.

Sources and Content of Marxism

Marxism may be said to have had three sources or to have merged three national streams: German philosophy, French revolutionism, and the British Industrial Revolution. As a student in Germany, and for a while thereafter, Marx mingled with a group known as Young Hegelians, who were actually anti-Hegel in that they expected the course of history to lead to a free and democratic society, instead of to the existing Prussian state as Hegel had maintained. They joined with liberals in resisting the repressive measures that prevailed in Germany after the defeat of Napoleon. Like democrats and republicans, they believed that the promise of the French Revolution had not yet been fulfilled, since social and economic equality should follow the civil and legal equality already won.[16] In keeping with the general movement of romanticism, they hoped for a more

[16] See pp. 466–468.

personal emancipation from the trammels of society, government, and religion. In the mid-1840s, elaborating on Hegel, Marx developed the idea of "alienation," a state of mind produced when the human being becomes estranged from the object on which he works, through the historic processes of mechanization, the commercialization of labor, and the ownership of property by others than the workers.

It followed that true freedom was possible only when private property in capital goods was abolished. Some of the writings in which these youthful ideas were worked out in the 1840s were not published until a century later. They then led to a reconsideration of Marxism, in which the early Marx was seen more as a social analyst than as a revolutionary. But they had little impact on the growth of Marxism as a program for revolutionary socialism in the nineteenth century.

Engels, engaged in the Manchester cotton industry, possessed a personal knowledge of the new industrial and factory system in England. He was in touch with some of the most radical Chartists, though he had no confidence in Chartism as a constructive movement. In 1844 he published a revealing book on *The Condition of the Working Classes in England*. He drew from the observation of facts much the same conclusions that Marx drew from philosophical analysis and historical study. The depressed condition of labor was an actual fact.[17] It was a fact that labor received a relatively small portion of the national income, and that much of the product of society was being reinvested in capital goods, which belonged as private property to private persons. Government and parliamentary institutions, also as a matter of fact, were in the hands of the well-to-do in both Great Britain and France. Religion was commonly held to be necessary to keep the lower classes in order. The churches at the time, as a matter of fact, took little interest in problems of the workers. The family, as an institution, was in fact disintegrating among laboring people in the cities, through exploitation of women and children and the overcrowding in inadequate and unsanitary living quarters.

All these facts were seized upon and dramatized in the *Communist Manifesto*, published in January 1848 as a summons to revolution. The outbreak of revolution in France in February, and its rapid spread to other countries, naturally confirmed Marx and Engels in their beliefs. An actual class war that shook Paris in the June Days was taken by them as a manifestation of a universal class struggle, in which the workers or proletariat rose against the owners of capital, the bourgeoisie.

As a call to action, the *Communist Manifesto* was meant to be inflammatory. It went beyond facts to denunciation and exhortation. It said that the worker was deprived of the wealth he had himself created. It called the state a committee of the bourgeoisie for the exploitation of the people. Religion was a drug to keep the worker quietly dreaming upon imaginary heavenly rewards. The worker's family, his wife and children, had been prostituted and brutalized by the bourgeoisie. It seemed to Marx and Engels that the uprooted worker should be loyal to nothing—except his own class. Even country had become meaningless. The proletarian had no country. Workers everywhere had the same problems and faced everywhere the same enemy. Therefore "let the ruling classes tremble at a communist revolution. The proletarians have nothing to lose but their chains.

---

[17] See pp. 459–461, 496–497.

They have a world to win. Workingmen of all countries, unite!'' So closed the *Manifesto*.

But Marx was no mere revolutionary schemer, like the "revolution-makers," as he later scornfully called them. His mature thought was a system for producing revolution, but it showed how revolution would necessarily come by operation of vast and impersonal forces.

It was from English sources that Marx developed much of his economic theory, as expounded at length in *Capital*. From British political economy he adopted the subsistence theory of wages, or Iron Law (which orthodox economists presently abandoned since wages did in fact begin to rise).[18] It held that the average worker could never obtain more than a minimum level of living—of which the corollary, for those who wished to draw it, was that the existing economic system held out no better future for the laboring class as a class. Marx likewise took over from orthodox economists the labor theory of value, holding that the value of any man-made object depended ultimately on the amount of labor put into it—capital being regarded as the stored up labor of former times. Orthodox economists soon discarded the theory that economic value is produced by the input of labor alone. Marx, from the labor theory, developed his doctrine of surplus value. This was very intricate; but "surplus value" meant in effect that workers were being robbed. They received in wages only a fraction of the value of the products which their labor produced. The difference was "expropriated" by the bourgeois capitalists—the private owners of the factories and the machines. And since workers never received in wages the equivalent of what they produced, capitalism was constantly menaced by overproduction, the accumulation of goods that people could not afford to buy. Hence it ran repeatedly into crisis and depressions and was obliged also to be constantly expanding in search of new markets. It was the depression of 1847, according to Marx, that had precipitated the Revolution of 1848; and with every such depression during the rest of his lifetime Marx hoped that the day of the great social revolution was drawing nearer.

What brought all these observations together in a unified and compelling doctrine was the philosophy of dialectical materialism. By dialectic, Marx meant what the German philosopher Hegel had meant,[19] that all things are in movement and in evolution, and that all change comes through the clash of antagonistic elements. The word itself, coming from the Greek, meant originally a way of arriving at a higher conclusion through a series of propositions, as in a logical argument. The implications of the dialectic, for both Hegel and Marx, were that all history, and indeed all reality, is a process of development through time, a single and meaningful unfolding of events, necessary, logical, and deterministic; that every event happens in due sequence for good and sufficient reason (not by chance); and that history could not and cannot happen any differently from the way it has happened and is still happening today. This, it need hardly be said, cannot be demonstrated on any basis of evidence.

Marx differed from Hegel in one vital respect. Whereas Hegel emphasized the primacy of "ideas" in social change, Marx gave emphasis to the primacy of

[18] See pp. 461–462, 623.
[19] See pp. 471–472.

material conditions, or the relations of production, which included technology, inventions, natural resources, and property systems. It is these that create the social world in which people live. It is the relations of production that determine what kind of religions, philosophies, governments, laws, and moral values are accepted. To believe that ideas precede and generate actualities was, according to Marx, the error of Hegel. Hegel had thought, for example, that the mind conceives the idea of freedom, which it then realizes in the Greek city-state, in Christianity, in the French Revolution, and in the kingdom of Prussia. Not at all, according to Marx: the idea of freedom, or any other idea, is generated by the actual economic and social conditions. Conditions are the roots, ideas the trees. Hegel had held the ideas to be the roots and the resulting actual conditions to be the trees. Or as Marx and Engels said, they found Hegel standing on his head and set him on his feet again.

The picture of historical development offered by Marx was somewhat as follows. Material conditions, or the relations of production, give rise to economic classes. Agrarian conditions produce a landholding or feudal class, but with changes in trade routes, money, and productive techniques a new commercial or bourgeois class arises. Each class, feudal and bourgeois, develops an ideology suited to its needs. Prevailing religions, governments, laws, and morals reflect the outlook of these classes. The two classes inevitably clash. Bourgeois revolutions against feudal interests break out—in England in 1642, in France in 1789, in Germany in 1848, though the bourgeois revolution in Germany proved abortive. Meanwhile, as the bourgeois class develops, it inevitably calls another class into being, its dialectical antithesis, the proletariat. The bourgeois is defined as the private owner of capital, the proletarian as the wage worker who possesses nothing but his own hands. The more a country becomes bourgeois, the more it becomes proletarian. The more production is concentrated in factories, the more the revolutionary laboring class is built up. Under competitive conditions the bourgeois tend to devour and absorb each other; ownership of the factories, mines, machines, railroads, etc. (capital) becomes concentrated into very few hands. Others sink into the proletariat. In the end the proletarianized mass simply takes over from the remaining bourgeois. It "expropriates the expropriators," and abolishes the old private property in the means of production. The social revolution is thus accomplished. It is inevitable. A classless society results, because class arises from economic differences which have been done away with. The state and religion, being outgrowths of bourgeois interests, also disappear. For a time, until all vestiges of bourgeois interests have been rooted out, or until the danger of counterrevolution against socialism has been overcome, there will be a "dictatorship of the proletariat." After that the state will "wither away," since there is no longer an exploiting class to require it.

Meanwhile the call is to war. Bourgeois and proletarian are locked in a universal struggle. It is really war, and as in all war all other considerations must be subordinated to it. Periods of social calm are not peace; they are merely interludes between battles. The workers must not be allowed to grow soft or conciliatory, any more than an army should be allowed to forget its primary function of fighting. Workers and labor unions must be kept in a belligerent and revolutionary mood. They must never forget that the employer is their class enemy, and that government, law, morality, and religion are merely so much artillery directed against them. Morals are "bourgeois morals," law is "bourgeois law," government is an instrument of class power, and religion is a form of psychological warfare, a means of providing "opium" for the masses. Workers must not let themselves be fooled; they must learn how to detect the class interest underlying the most exalted institutions and beliefs. In this piece of military intelligence, ferreting out the ways of the enemy, they will be helped by intellectuals especially trained in explaining it to them. Like all fighting forces, the workers need a disciplined solidarity. Individuals must lose themselves in the whole—in their class. It is a betrayal of their class for workers to rise above the proletariat, to "improve themselves," as the bourgeois says. It is dangerous for labor unions merely to obtain better wages or hours by negotiation with employers, for by such little gains the war itself may be forgotten. It is likewise dangerous, and even treasonous, for workers to put faith in democratic machinery or "social legislation," for the state, an engine of repression, can never be made into an instrument of welfare. Law is the will of the stronger (i.e., the stronger class); "right" and "justice" are thin emanations of class interest. We must hold, wrote Marx in 1875, to "the realistic outlook which has cost so much effort to instill into the party, but which has now taken root in it"; and we must not let this outlook be perverted "by means of ideological nonsense about 'right' and other trash common among the democrats and French Socialists."

The Appeal of Marxism: Its Strength and Weaknesses

The original Marxism was a hard doctrine, with both advantages and handicaps in the winning of adherents. One of its advantages was its claim to be scientific. Marx classified earlier and rival forms of socialism[20] as utopian: they rested on moral indignation, and their formula for reforming society was for men to become more just, or for the upper classes to be converted to sympathy for the lower. His own doctrine, Marx insisted, had nothing to do with ethical ideas; it was purely scientific, resting upon the study of actual facts and real processes, and it showed that socialism would be not a miraculous reversal but a historical continuation of what was already taking place. He also considered it utopian and unscientific to describe the future socialist society in any detail. It would be classless, with neither bourgeois nor proletarian; but to lay any specific plans would be idle dreaming. Let the revolution come, and socialism would take care of itself.

Marxism was a strong compound of the scientific, the historical, the metaphysical, and the apocalyptic. But some elements of Marxism stood in the way of its natural propagation. The working people of Europe were not really in the frame of mind of an army in battle. They hesitated to subordinate all else to the distant prospect of a class revolution. They were not exclusively class-people, nor did they behave as such. Enough of religion was still alive in them, and of older natural-law ideas, to inhibit the belief that morality was a class weapon, or right and justice "trash." They had national loyalties to country; they could with difficulty associate themselves emotionally with a world proletariat in an unrelenting struggle against their own neighbors.

---

[20] See pp. 466–468.

The cure for the revolutionism of 1848 proved in time to be the admission of the laboring classes to a fuller membership in society. Wages generally rose after 1850, labor unions were organized, and by 1870 in the principal European countries the workingman very generally had a vote. Through their unions, workers were often able to get better wages and working conditions by direct pressure upon employers. Having the vote, they gradually formed working-class parties, and as they proceeded to act through the state they had less inclination to destroy it. Marx's word for such maneuvers was "opportunism." Opportunism, the tendency of working people to better themselves by dealing with employers and by obtaining legislation through existing government channels, was the most dangerous of all dangers to the Revolution. For in war people do not negotiate or pass laws; they fight. From Marxism the working class absorbed much, including a watchful hostility to employers and a sense of working-class solidarity; but on the whole, as Marxism spread at the close of the nineteenth century it ceased to be really revolutionary.[21] Had the old Europe not gone to pieces in the twentieth-century wars, and had Marxism not been revived by Lenin and transplanted to Russia, it is probable that Marx's ideas would have been domesticated into the general body of European thought, and that much less would be said about them in this book.

62. Bonapartism: The Second French Empire, 1852–1870

We have seen how Louis Napoleon Bonaparte, elected president of the republic in 1848, in 1852 made himself Emperor of the French with the title of Napoleon III.[22] Those willing to fight for the parliamentary and liberal institutions which he crushed were silenced. He became chief of state on a wave of popular acclaim.

Political Institutions of the Second Empire

Napoleon III, like Napoleon I, came to power because of the fear of radicalism in a discredited republic. Otherwise he bore little resemblance to his famous uncle. He was not a professional soldier or a great organizer. When he became president of the republic at the age of forty he had been an adventurer and a conspirator, but he had also written two books on the "social question," and he undoubtedly felt more concern than Napoleon I for the plight of the working classes. Where Napoleon I had been disdainful of public opinion, his nephew recognized it as an opportunity, not a nuisance. Though journalists and intellectuals generally distrusted him, he drew some of them to his side; he tried to placate the Catholic interests; and he appealed to the masses by giving them the vote (however useless), by promises of prosperity, and by pageantry. He understood perfectly that a single leader exerts more magnetism than an elected assembly. And he knew that a Europe still shuddering over the June Days was hoping desperately for order in France.

---

[21] See pp. 622–625.
[22] See pp. 505–507.

He gloried in modern progress. Toward the changes coming over Europe the monarchs of the old school usually showed an attitude of timidity and doubt if not positive opposition. Napoleon III boldly offered himself as the leader in a brave new world. Like his uncle, he announced that he embodied the sovereignty of the people. He said that he had found a solution to the problem of mass democracy. In all the other great Continental states and in Great Britain, in 1852, universal suffrage was thought to be incompatible with intelligent government and economic prosperity. Napoleon III claimed to put them together. Like Marx and other "realists" after 1848 he held that elected parliamentary bodies, far from representing an abstract "people," only accentuated class divisions within a country. He declared that the regime of the restored Bourbons and the July Monarchy had been dominated by special interests, that the Republic of 1848 had first been violent and anarchic, then fallen into the hands of a distrustful assembly that robbed the laboring man of his vote, and that France would find in the empire the permanent, popular, and modern system for which it had been vainly searching since 1789. He affirmed that he stood above classes and would govern equally in the interests of all. In any case, like many others after 1848, he held that forms of government were less important than economic and social realities.

The political institutions of the Second Empire were therefore authoritarian, modeled on those of the Consulate of the first Bonaparte. There was a Council of State, composed of experts who drafted legislation and advised on technical matters. There was an appointive Senate with few significant functions. There was a Legislative Body elected by universal male suffrage. The elections were carefully managed. The government put up an official candidate for each seat whom all officeholders in the district were required to support. Other candidates might offer themselves for election, but there could be no political meetings of any kind, and if the independent candidate put up posters he had to use a different kind of paper from the official candidate. Few ventured in these circumstances to differ with the government.

The Legislative Body had no independent powers of its own. It could not initiate legislation but only consider what was submitted to it by the emperor. It had no control over the budget, for the emperor was legally free to borrow money as he saw fit. It had no power over the army or the foreign office or the making of war and peace. To publish speeches made in the legislative chamber was against the law. Any five members, by requesting a secret session, could exclude the public from the galleries. Parliamentary life sank toward absolute zero.

To captivate public attention and glorify the Napoleonic name the new emperor set up a sumptuous court at the Tuileries. Balked in the ambition to marry into one of the great dynasties, Napoleon III chose as his empress a young Spanish beauty, Eugénie, who was destined to outlive the empire by fifty years, dying in 1920. It was said to be a love match—a sure sign of popularized royalty. The court life of the empire was brilliant and showy beyond anything known at the time in St. Petersburg or Vienna. The note of pageantry was further struck in the embellishment of the city of Paris. Baron Haussmann, one of the most creative of city planners, gave Paris much of the appearance that it has today. He built roomy railway stations with broad approaches, and he constructed a system of boulevards and public squares offering long vistas ending in fine buildings or monuments, as at the Place de l'Opéra. He also modernized the sewers and the water supply. The building program, like the expensive court, had the additional advantage of stimulating business and employment. And the cutting of wide avenues through the crooked streets and congested old houses would permit easier military operations against insurrectionists entrenched behind barricades, should the events of 1848 ever be repeated.

Economic Developments under the Empire

It was as a great social engineer that Napoleon III preferred to be known. In his youth he had tried to read the riddle of modern industrialism, and now, as emperor, he found some of his main backers in former Saint-Simonians, who called him their "socialist emperor." Saint-Simon, it may be recalled, had been among the first to conceive of a centrally planned industrial system.[23] But the Saint-Simonians of the 1850s shared in the new sense of being realistic, and their most signal triumph was the invention of investment banking, by which they hoped to guide economic growth through the concentration of financial resources. They founded a novel kind of banking institution, the *Crédit Mobilier,* which raised funds by selling its shares to the public, and with the funds thus obtained bought stock in such new industrial enterprises as it wished to develop. A land bank, or *Crédit Foncier,* was likewise established to lend funds to landowners for the improvement of agriculture.

The times were exceedingly favorable for expansion, for the discovery of gold in California in 1849, and in Australia soon afterward, together with the newly organized credit facilities, brought a substantial increase in the European money supply, which had a mildly inflationary effect. The steady rise of prices and all money values encouraged company promotion and investment of capital. Railway mileage, increasing everywhere in the Western world, increased in France from 3,000 to 16,000 kilometers in the 1850s. The demand for rolling stock, iron rails, auxiliary equipment, and building materials for stations and freight houses kept the mines and factories busy. The railway network was rationalized, fifty-five small lines in France being merged into six big regional trunks. Iron steamboats replaced wooden sailing ships. Between 1859 and 1869 a French company built the Suez Canal, which it continued to own for almost a century, though the British government after 1875 was the principal stockholder.

Large corporations made their appearance, in railroads and banking first of all. In 1863 the law granted the right of "limited liability," by which a stockholder could not lose more than the par value of the stock, however insolvent or debt-burdened the corporation might become. This encouraged investment by persons of small means, and by capitalists large and small in enterprises of which they knew very little; thus the wealth and savings of the country were more effectively mobilized and put to work. Stocks and shares became more numerous and diversified. The Stock Exchange boomed. Financiers—those whose business was to handle money, credit, and securities—assumed a new eminence in the capitalistic world. A good many people became very rich, richer perhaps than anyone had ever been in France before.

The emperor aspired also to do something for the working class, within the

[23] See p. 467.

limits of the existing system. The land bank was of some use to the more substantial peasants. Jobs were plentiful and wages good, by the ideas of the day, at least until the temporary depression of 1857. The emperor had a plan, as did some of the Saint-Simonians, for organizing forces of workers in military fashion and setting them to clear and develop uncultivated land. Not much was done in this direction. More was accomplished in the humanitarian relief of suffering. Hospitals and asylums were established, and free medicines were distributed. The outlines of a social-service state began somewhat vaguely to appear. Meanwhile the workers were building up unions. All combinations of workers had been prohibited during the French Revolution, and the Le Chapelier Law of 1791 was deemed to be still in force.[24] Gradually the ambiguous legal position of labor unions was clarified. In 1864 it even became legal for organized workers to go on strike. Large labor units, or unions, and large business units, or corporations, were thus legalized at the same time. Napoleon III hardly did enough for labor to rank as a working-class hero, but he did enough to be suspected as "socialistic" by many middle-class people of the day.

Later authoritarian regimes, bent like the Second Empire on a program of economic development, were usually highly protectionist, unwilling to face open competition with the rest of the world. Napoleon III believed in freedom of international trade. He had a project for a tariff union with Belgium, which some Belgians also supported. Belgium was already well industrialized, and a Franco-Belgian union, especially since Belgium had the coal that France lacked, would have formed a trading area of very great strength. But the plan was blocked by private interests in both countries, and strongly opposed by both Great Britain and the German *Zollverein*. The emperor then turned to an all-around reduction of import duties. Since the repeal of the Corn Laws in 1846 the free traders were in power in England.[25] They were eager to abolish trade barriers between Britain and France. Napoleon III, overriding opposition in his Legislative Body, concluded a free trade treaty with Great Britain in 1860. He set aside 40 million francs of government funds to assist French manufacturers in making adjustments to British competition; but this sum was never spent in full, and it has hence been concluded that French industry was able to compete successfully with the more intensively mechanized industry of Britain. The Anglo-French treaty was accompanied by lesser trade agreements with other countries. It looked, in the 1860s, as if Europe might actually be about to enter the promised land of freedom of trade.

Internal Difficulties and War

But by 1860 the empire was running into trouble. It took a few years to overcome the depression of 1857. By his free trade policy the emperor made enemies among industrialists in certain lines. The Catholics objected to his intervention in Italy.[26] After 1860 opposition mounted. The emperor granted more leeway to the Legislative Body. The 1860s are called the decade of the Liberal Empire—all

[24] See p. 375.
[25] See p. 494.
[26] See p. 547.

such terms being relative. How the empire would have fared had purely internal causes been left free scope we shall never know. Louis Napoleon actually ruined himself by war. His empire evaporated on the battlefield in 1870. But he was at war long before that.

"The empire means peace," he had assured his audiences in 1852: *l'empire, c'est la paix*. But war is after all the supreme pageantry (or was then); France was the strongest country of Europe, and the emperor's name was Napoleon. Less than a year and a half after the proclamation of the empire France was at war with a European state for the first time since Waterloo. The enemy was Russia, and the war was the Crimean War. Napoleon III did not alone instigate the Crimean War. Many forces in Europe after 1848 made for war; but Napoleon III was one of these forces. In 1859 the new Napoleon was fighting in Italy, from 1862 to 1867 in Mexico, and in 1870 in France itself, in a war with Prussia which he could easily have avoided. These wars form part of the story of the following chapter.[27]

It is enough to say here that in 1870 the Second Empire went the way of the First, into the limbo of governments tried and discarded by the French. It had lasted eighteen years, exactly as long as the July Monarchy, and longer than any other regime known in France, up to that time, since the fall of the Bastille. Not until the 1920s and 1930s, when dictators sprouted all over Europe, did the world begin to think that Louis Napoleon had been an omen of the future rather than a bizarre reincarnation of the past.

[27] See pp. 547, 557–558; for Mexico, see p. 651.

EARLY
INDUSTRIALISM
AND SOCIAL
CLASSES

Industrialization, as it appeared first in England in the nineteenth century, rested on a combination of coal and iron, of which the steam engine was the most portentous offspring. Steam engines provided power to the textile mills, and when put on wheels they revolutionized transportation. In the factories a new kind of wage-earning working class was assembled. The railway train, powered by steam, running on rails at first made of wood, then of iron, then of steel, carried people and goods at a speed and in a volume never known in the past. It made possible the concentration of population in cities, both gigantic cities such as London, and clusters of smaller cities in which manufacturing processes were carried on. In this urban world, while polite architecture ran through a series of classical, Gothic, Renaissance, and other revivals, more utilitarian structures of a novel kind were built of iron, and then of structural steel. The new habitat provided luxury for a few, comfort for some, and misery for all too many.

Class conflict therefore raged throughout the nineteenth century, but most acutely in the first half. One difficulty was that, though there had long been talk of the progress of science and invention, the actual difficulties of industrialization had been unforeseen. As the first people to undergo the Industrial Revolution, the English had no experience on which to draw. The English imagination dwelt by preference on rural rather than urban themes, especially in the early part of the century, and under the influence of literary romanticism. Government until 1832 was in the hands of a landed aristocracy and country gentry, made conservative in their politics by the French Revolution. Priding themselves on their English liberties, and fearing anything like Continental bureaucracy, the English only gradually endowed their government with adequate powers of regulation, inspection, enforcement, and police.

After 1850 some of the more favorable consequences of modern industry and technology became apparent. While poverty remained chronic, and the working class struggled to better itself, the middle classes grew in numbers and enjoyed new amenities and conveniences. The following pages illustrate the life of social classes in England, and also in France, in this new Age of Iron. The medium here is part of the message, since the nineteenth-century innovations of lithography, photography, and low-cost printing for a wide market are to be observed.

At the left, this piece of popular art (a song-book cover) points up the exciting contrast between new and old. An express train rushes at night, on a high bridge, with the city behind it, through an English countryside illuminated by the moon.

Above: The newly organized London police, in the 1840s, await the arrival of a Chartist procession. Between 1832 and 1848 the Chartists organized mass demonstrations in the vain attempt to democratize the electoral laws and so obtain legislation designed to favor the working classes. The government introduced a more modern and better disciplined police force as a measure of crowd control, and to avoid the kind of chaotic confrontation shown on the following page. The men are in a kind of civilian uniform complete with stovepipe hats.

535

Upper left: The "Peterloo Massacre" of 1819, as caricatured by Cruikshank. A peaceable crowd in St. Peter's Fields, Manchester, was fired upon and dispersed by the yeomanry, a militia of nonprofessional part-time soldiers, mostly rural people out of sympathy with modern cities.

Lower left: These primitive trains, about 1840, are running on wooden rails with "guidance wheels" at an apparently crazy angle to help keep them on the track.

Above: London, or rather one of its poorer quarters, as seen by the French artist Gustave Doré about 1880. The omnipresent railroad is in the background, while in the foreground the mass housing, with the little yards, or rather pens, evokes the atmosphere of a prison.

537

Upper left: A workers' meeting in Paris, as seen by the painter Jean Béraud in 1884. The audience is probably hearing some socialist speeches.

Lower left: The future King Edward VII, then Prince of Wales, with his wife, comfortably installed in box seats, observes the new Bessemer steel-making process at Sheffield in 1875.

Above: The Bon Marché department store in Paris about 1880. The new era is evident in the vast expanse, the proliferation of merchandise, and the presence of affluent women, who have come downtown with their children to shop.

Buildings of cast iron and glass, appearing about 1850, represented the most significant technical innovation in architecture in centuries. The department store on page 539 was of this kind. At the left, above, is the famous Crystal Palace in Hyde Park, London, built to house the Great Exhibition of 1851. The world's fair, or industrial exposition, was another product of the revolution in transportation.

Lower left: The Café de la Rotonde in Paris about 1860. The new French café was designed to be large, airy, open, cosmopolitan, suitable for ladies, and not necessarily alcoholic.

Above: The Eiffel Tower, built for the Paris exposition of 1889, with elevators to carry visitors to the top 984 feet above the ground, long remained the world's highest structure, and still stands as a symbol of nineteenth-century civilization. It was at first criticized as ungainly and vulgarly colossal. A later generation, accustomed to an architecture of concrete slabs and oblong cages, sees its graceful curves and the delicate tracery of its four immense legs.

XIII.
THE CONSOLIDATION OF LARGE NATION-STATES, 1859–1871

O NLY A DOZEN YEARS, from 1859 to 1871, were enough to see the formation of a new German empire, a unified kingdom of Italy, a Dual Monarchy of Austria-Hungary, drastic internal changes in tsarist Russia, the triumph of central authority in the United States, the creation of a united Dominion of Canada, and the modernizing or "Europeanization" of the empire of Japan. All these disparate events reflected profound changes brought in by the railroad, steamship, and telegraph, which made the communication of ideas, exchange of goods, and movement of people over wide areas more frequent and easier than ever before. Politically, all represented the advancing principle of the nation-state.

63. Backgrounds: The Idea of the Nation-State

Before 1860 there were two prominent nation-states—Great Britain and France. Spain, united on the map, was internally so miscellaneous as to belong to a

Chapter Emblem: Medallion to celebrate the Prussian defeat of Austria in 1866, and featuring the King of Prussia, William I, who later became the first German Emperor.

different category. Portugal, Switzerland, the Netherlands, and the Scandinavian countries were nation-states, but small and peripheral. The characteristic political organizations were small states comprising fragments of a nation, such as were strewn across the middle of Europe—Hanover, Baden, Sardinia, Tuscany, or the Two Sicilies—and large sprawling empires made up of all sorts of peoples, distantly ruled from above by dynasties and bureaucracies, such as the Romanov, Habsburg, and Ottoman domains.[1] Except for recent developments in the Americas the same mixture of small nonnational states and of large nonnational empires was to be found in most of the rest of the world.

Since 1860 or 1870 a nation-state system has prevailed. The consolidation of large nations became a model for other peoples large and small. In time, in the following century, other large peoples undertook to establish nation-states in India, Pakistan, Indonesia, Iran, and Nigeria. Small and middle-sized peoples increasingly thought of themselves as nations, entitled to their own sovereignty and independence. Some of these sovereignties that emerged after 1945 comprise fewer people than a large modern city. The idea of the nation-state has served both to bring people together into larger units and to break them apart into smaller ones. In the nineteenth century, outside the disintegrating Ottoman Empire, from which Greece, Serbia, Bulgaria, and Romania became independent, and in which an Arab national movement also began to stir, the national idea served mainly to create larger units in place of small ones. The map of Europe, from 1871 to 1918, was the simplest it has ever been before or since.[2]

About the idea of the nation-state and the movement of nationalism much has been said already in this book. Earlier chapters have described the ferment of national ideas and movements stirred up by the French Revolution and by the Napoleonic domination of Europe, the nationalist agitation and repression of the years after 1815, and the frustration and failure of patriotic aspirations in Germany, Italy, and central Europe in the Revolution of 1848.[3] For many in the nineteenth century, nationalism, the winning of national unity and independence and the creation of the nation-state, became a kind of secular faith.

A nation-state may be thought of as one in which supreme political authority somehow rests upon and represents the will and feeling of its inhabitants. There must be a people, not merely a swarm of human beings. The people must basically will and feel something in common. They must sense that they belong—that they are members of a community, participating somehow in a common life, that the government is their government, and that outsiders are "foreign." The outsiders or foreigners are usually (though not always) those who speak a different language. The nation is usually (though not always) composed of all persons sharing the same speech. A nation may also possess a belief in common descent or racial origin (however mistaken), or a sense of a common history, a common future, a common religion, a common geographical home, or a common external menace. Nations take form in many ways. But all are alike in feeling themselves to be communities, permanent communities in which individual persons, together with

---

[1] See map, pp. 448–449.
[2] See map, pp. 562–563.
[3] See pp. 365, 378–379, 435–441, 468–489, 507–519.

their children and their children's children, are committed to a collective destiny on earth.

In the nineteenth century governments found that they could not effectively rule, or develop the full powers of state, except by enlisting this sense of membership and support among their subjects. The consolidation of large nation-states had two distinguishable phases. Territorially, it meant the union of preexisting smaller states. Morally and psychologically it meant the creation of new ties between government and governed, the admission of new segments of the population to political life, through the creation or extension of liberal and representative institutions. This happened even in Japan and in tsarist Russia. National consolidation in the nineteenth century favored constitutional progress. Although there was considerable variation in the real power of the new political institutions and in the extent of self-government actually realized, parliaments were set up for the new Italy, the new Germany, the new Japan, the new Canada; and the movement in Russia was in the same direction. In Europe, some of the aims which the revolutionists of 1848 had failed to achieve were now realized by the established authorities.

They were realized, however, only in a series of wars. To create an all-German or an all-Italian state, as the revolutions of 1848 had already shown, it was necessary to break the power of Austria, render Russia at least temporarily ineffective, and overthrow or intimidate those German and Italian governments which refused to surrender their sovereignty. In the United States, to maintain national unity as understood by President Lincoln, it was necessary to repress the movement for Southern independence by force of arms. For forty years after 1814 there had been no war between established powers of Europe. Then in 1854 came the Crimean War, in 1859 the Italian War, in 1864 the Danish War, in 1866 the Austro-Prussian War, and in 1870 the Franco-Prussian War. Concurrently the Civil War raged in the United States. After 1871, for forty-three years there was again no war between European powers.

The Crimean War, 1854–1856

Before moving on to the first of the national consolidation movements, the Italian, we must examine the Crimean War which, though seemingly remote and unconnected, helped to make possible the success of the European national movements. Its chief significance in the story of the present chapter is that it seriously weakened both Austria and Russia, the two powers most bent on preserving the peace settlement of 1815 and on preventing national changes. It was also the first war covered by newspaper correspondents, and the first in which women, led by Florence Nightingale, established their position as army nurses.

The pressure of Russia upon Turkey was an old story. Every generation saw its Russo-Turkish war.[4] In the last Russo-Turkish war, to go back no further, that of 1828–1829, the Tsar Nicholas I protected the independence newly won by Greece and annexed the left bank of the mouth of the Danube. Now, in 1853,

---

[4] See pp. 239–240, 339–340, 420, 441, 480, 484–485.

Nicholas again made demands upon the still large but decaying Ottoman Empire, moving in on the two Danubian principalities, Wallachia and Moldavia (later to be known as Romania), with military forces.[5] The dispute this time ostensibly involved the protection of Christians in the Ottoman Empire, including the foreign Christians at Jerusalem and in Palestine. Over these Christians the French also claimed a certain protective jurisdiction. The French had for centuries been the principal Western people in the Near East. They had often furnished money and advisers to the sultan, they carried on a huge volume of trade, they staffed and financed Christian missions, and they were continually talking of building a Suez canal. Napoleon III had especial reason to resent the Tsar Nicholas, who regarded him as a revolutionary adventurer. Napoleon III encouraged the Turkish government to resist Russian claims to protect Christians within Turkey. War between Russia and Turkey broke out late in 1853. In 1854 France joined the side of the Turks, as did Great Britain, whose settled policy was to uphold Turkey and the Near East against penetration by Russia. The two Western powers were soon joined by a small ally, Piedmont, which had no visible interest in the issues in the Near East and entered the war mainly for the purpose of advancing the Italian question.

The British fleet successfully blockaded Russia in both its Baltic and Black Sea outlets. French and British armies invaded Russia itself, landing in the Crimean peninsula, to which all the important fighting was confined. The Austrian Empire had its own reasons not to wish Russia to conquer the Balkans and Constantinople, or to see Britain and France master the situation alone; Austria therefore, though not yet recovered from the upheaval of 1848–1849, mobilized its armed forces at a great effort to itself and occupied Wallachia and Moldavia, which the Russians evacuated under this threat of attack by a new enemy. Tsar Nicholas died in 1855, and his successor Alexander II sued for peace.

A congress of all the great powers made peace at Paris in 1856. By the treaty the powers pledged themselves jointly to maintain the "integrity of the Ottoman Empire." The Russian tide ebbed a little. Russia ceded the left bank of the mouth of the Danube to Moldavia and gave up its claim to the special protection of Christians in the Turkish empire. Moldavia and Wallachia (united as "Romania" in 1858), together with Serbia, were recognized as self-governing principalities under protection of the European powers. It was agreed that Russia should maintain no warships on the Black Sea, and that the Danube should be an international river open to commercial shipping of all nations. At the Congress of Paris all seemed harmonious. There seemed to be such a thing as Europe, undertaking collective obligations, protecting small states, rationally and peaceably conducting its affairs.

But trouble was in the making. Napoleon III needed glory. The Italians wanted some kind of unified Italy. The Prussians, who had done nothing in the Crimean War, and were only tardily invited to the Congress of Paris, feared that their status as a great power might be slipping away. Napoleon III, the Italian nationalists, the Prussians, all stood to gain by change. Change in central Europe and Italy meant a tearing up of the Treaty of Vienna of 1815, long guarded by

---

[5] See maps, pp. 448–449, 660. The historic Moldavia lay west of the Pruth River; the later Moldavian republic in the Soviet Union, east of that river, was formerly called Bessarabia.

Metternich and unsuccessfully challenged by the revolutionaries of 1848. Now, after the Crimean War, the forces opposing change were very weak. It was the Russian and Austrian empires that had stood firmly for the status quo. But these two powers, which had most seriously attempted to uphold the Vienna settlement, could do so no longer. The first proof came in Italy.

64. Cavour and the Italian War of 1859: The Unification of Italy

Italian Nationalism: The Program of Cavour

In Italy there had long been about a dozen sizable states, together with a few very small ones. Several of them had dissolved in the Italian movements that accompanied the wars of the French Revolution. All had been reorganized, first by Napoleon and then by the Congress of Vienna. In the northwest lay the kingdom of Sardinia, more commonly known as Piedmont. Its royal house of Savoy was the only native Italian dynasty in Italy. East of it lay Lombardy, and east of that, Venetia. Since 1814 Lombardy and Venetia belonged to the Austrian Empire. South of Lombardy, in the northwest corner of the "leg" of the peninsula, was the duchy of Tuscany with its capital at Florence. The smaller duchies of Modena, Parma, and Lucca filled the interstices between Tuscany and the northern states. Across the middle of the peninsula were spread the papal states, the hereditary temporal possession of the Roman See. Further south, comprising half of all Italy, lay the large kingdom of Naples or the Two Sicilies, ruled since 1735 by a branch of the Bourbons. The governments of these states were generally content with their separate independence. But the governments were remote from their peoples.

There was a widespread disgust in Italy with the existing authorities, and a growing desire for a liberal national state in which all Italy might be embodied and which might resurrect the Italian grandeur of ancient times and of the Renaissance. This sentiment, the dream of an Italian Risorgimento, or resurgence, had become very heated at the time of the French Revolution and Napoleon, then had been transformed into a moral purpose by the writings of Mazzini.[6] Mazzini, who had invested the cause of Italian unity with almost a holy character, had seen his hopes for a unified republican Italy elevated for a brief moment and then blasted in the general debacle of 1848. In the stormy events of 1848 the papacy had been frightened off by the radical romantic republicanism of Mazzini, Garibaldi, and other firebrands and could no longer be expected to support the cause of Italian nationalism. And in the same events the kingdom of Sardinia had failed in its vow to oust Austria from the Italian peninsula without the aid of any outside great power.[7]

These lessons were not lost on the prime minister of Piedmont (or Sardinia), which was ruled since 1848 as a constitutional monarchy and was now under

[6] See p. 469.
[7] See pp. 509–514, and the note on p. 194.

King Victor Emmanuel. This prime minister after 1852 was Camillo di Cavour, one of the shrewdest political tacticians of that or any age. Cavour was a liberal of Western type. He tried to make Piedmont a model of progress, efficiency, and fair government that other Italians would admire. He worked hard to plant constitutional and parliamentary practices in Piedmont. He favored the building of railroads and docks, the improvement of agriculture, and emancipation of trade. He followed a strongly anticlerical policy, cutting down the number of religious holidays, limiting the right of church bodies to own real estate, abolishing the church courts—all without negotiation with the Holy See. A liberal and constitutional monarchist, a wealthy landowner in his own right, he had no sympathy for the revolutionary and republican nationalism of Mazzini. To him it did not seem that Italy would be united by the methods of conspiracy and secret societies, by hortatory literature smuggled in from political exiles, or by the proclamation of idealistic radical republics, as in 1848, which alarmed the most influential people in the country.[8]

Cavour shared in that new toughness of mind described in the last chapter. He embraced a "politics of reality." He did not approve of republicans but was willing to work with them surreptitiously. He did not idealize war but was willing to make war to unify Italy under the house of Savoy. With unruffled calculation he took Piedmont into the Crimean War, sending troops to Russia, in the hope of winning a place at the peace table and raising the Italian question at the Congress of Paris. It was evident to him that against one great power one must pit another, and that the only way to get Austria out of Italy was to use the French army. It became his master plan deliberately to provoke war with Austria, after having assured himself of French military support.

It was not difficult to persuade Napoleon III to collaborate. The Bonapartes looked upon Italy as their ancestral country, and Napoleon III, in his adventurous youth, had traveled in conspiratorial Italian circles and even participated in an Italian insurrection in 1831. Now, as emperor, in his role of apostle of modernity, he entertained a "doctrine of nationalities" which held the consolidation of nations to be a forward step at the existing stage of history. To fight reactionary Austria for the freedom of Italy would also mollify liberal opinion in France, which in other ways Napoleon was engaged in suppressing. The last note in persuasion was furnished by an Italian republican named Orsini, who in 1858, finding the French emperor too slow to make up his mind, attempted to assassinate him with a bomb. Napoleon III reached a secret agreement with Cavour. In April 1859, Cavour tricked Austria into a declaration of war. The French army poured over the Alps.

There were two battles, Magenta and Solferino, both won by the French and Piedmontese. But Napoleon III was now in a quandary. The Prussians began to mobilize on the Rhine, not wishing France to create an Italian sphere of influence for itself. In Italy, with the defeat of the Austrians, revolutionary agitation broke out all over the peninsula, as it had a decade before—and the French emperor was no patron of popular revolution. The revolutionaries overthrew or denounced the existing governments and clamored for annexation to Piedmont. In France, as elsewhere, the Catholics, fearful that the pope's temporal power would be

---

[8] See pp. 511, 513.

lost, upbraided the emperor for his godless and unnecessary war. The French position was indeed odd, for while the bulk of the French army fought Austria in the north, a detachment of it was still stationed in Rome, sent there in 1849 to protect the pope against Italian republicanism.[9] Napoleon III, in July 1859, at the height of his victories, stupefied Cavour. He made a separate peace with the Austrians.

The Franco-Austrian agreement gave Lombardy to Piedmont but left Venetia within the Austrian Empire. It offered a compromise solution to the Italian question, in the form of a federal union of the existing Italian governments, to be presided over by the pope. This was not what Cavour, or the Piedmontese, or the more fiery Italian patriots wanted. Revolution continued to spread. Tuscany, Modena, Parma, and Romagna drove out their old rulers. They were annexed to Piedmont, after plebiscites or general elections in these regions had shown an overwhelming popular favor for this step. Since Romagna belonged to the papal states the pope excommunicated the organizers of the new Italy. Undeterred, representatives of all north Italy except Venetia met at the Piedmontese capital of Turin in 1860 in the first parliament of the enlarged kingdom. The British government hailed these events with enthusiasm, and Napoleon III also recognized the expanded Piedmontese state, in return for the transfer to France of Nice and Savoy, where plebiscites disclosed enormous majorities for annexation to France.

The Completion of Italian Unity

There were now, in 1860, a north Italian kingdom, the papal states in the middle, and the kingdom of the Two Sicilies still standing in the south. The latter was being undermined by revolutionary agitation, as often in the past.[10] A Piedmontese republican, Giuseppe Garibaldi, brought matters to a head. Somewhat like Lafayette, Garibaldi was a "hero of two worlds," who had fought for the independence of Uruguay, lived in the United States, and been one of the Triumvirs in the short-lived Roman Republic of 1849. He now organized a group of about 1,150 personal followers—"Garibaldi's Thousand," or the Red Shirts— for an armed expedition to the south. Cavour, unable openly to favor such filibustering against a neighboring state, connived at Garibaldi's preparations and departure. Garibaldi landed in Sicily and soon crossed to the mainland. Revolutionists hastened to join him, and the government of the Two Sicilies, backward and corrupt, commanding little loyalty from its population, collapsed before this picturesque intrusion.

[9] See p. 506.
[10] See pp. 479–480, 509–510.

NATION BUILDING, 1859–1867

In eight years from 1859 to 1867 Italy was unified (except for the city of Rome, annexed in 1870), the Habsburg government tried to solve its nationalities problem by creating a Dual Monarchy of Austria-Hungary, the United States affirmed its unity by defeating the Southern secessionist movement, and the Dominion of Canada was formed to include all British North America (with dates shown for accession of provinces) except Newfoundland and Labrador, which were added in 1949. For Germany see the map on p. 555.

UNIFICATION OF ITALY, 1859-1870

PIEDMONT
LOMBARDY
Milan
VENETIA
Turin
Venice
PARMA
MODENA
KINGDOM OF SARDINIA
PAPAL
STATES
Florence
TUSCANY
ROME
SARDINIA
NAPLES
SICILY

FORMATION OF DUAL MONARCHY OF AUSTRIA-HUNGARY, 1867

AUSTRIA
Vienna
Budapest
HUNGARY

FORMATION OF DOMINION OF CANADA, 1867

NORTHWEST TERRITORIES

LABRADOR
1949

NEWFOUND-
LAND
1949

BRITISH
COLUMBIA
1871
ALBERTA
1905
SASKATCHEWAN
1905
MANITOBA
1870
QUEBEC
1867
MARITIME
PROVINCES
1867
ONTARIO
1867
Ottawa

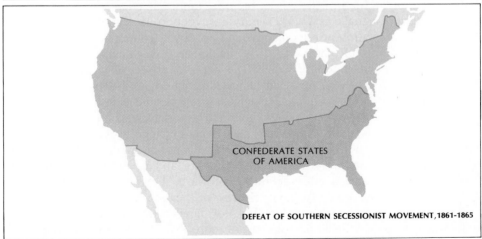

CONFEDERATE STATES
OF AMERICA

DEFEAT OF SOUTHERN SECESSIONIST MOVEMENT, 1861-1865

Garibaldi now prepared to push from Naples up to Rome. Here, of course, he would meet not only the pope but the French army, and the international scandal would reverberate throughout the globe. Cavour decided that so extreme a step must be averted, but that Garibaldi's successes must at the same time be used. Anticipating Garibaldi, a Piedmontese army entered the papal states, carefully avoiding Rome, and proceeded onward into Naples. Garibaldi, though not all his followers, was now ready to accept a monarchy as the best solution to the problem of Italian unification. The chief of the Red Shirts, the one-time foe of kings, consented to ride in an open carriage with Victor Emmanuel through the streets of Naples amid cheering thousands. Plebiscites held in the Two Sicilies showed an almost unanimous willingness to join with Piedmont. In the remainder of the papal states, except for Rome and its environs, plebiscites were held also, with the same result. A parliament representing all Italy except Rome and Venetia met in 1861, and the Kingdom of Italy was formally proclaimed, with Victor Emmanuel II as king "by grace of God and the will of the nation." Venetia was added in 1866, as a prize for Italian aid to Prussia in a war against Austria, and Rome was annexed in 1870 after the withdrawal of French troops in the Franco-Prussian War of 1870.[11]

So Italy was "made," as the phrase of the time expressed it. It had been made by the long high-minded apostolate of Mazzini, the audacity of Garibaldi, the cold policy of Cavour, by war and insurrection, by armed violence endorsed by popular vote.

Persistent Problems after Unification

Very little was settled or ended by unification. Even territorially, the more pronounced nationalists refused to believe that Italian unity was completed. They looked beyond, to regions of mixed population where Italians were numerous or preponderant—to the Trentino, to Trieste, to certain Dalmatian islands, or to Nice and Savoy. They saw in these regions an *Italia irredenta,* "an unredeemed Italy," awaiting in its turn the day of incorporation. "Irredentism" even passed into the English language as a word signifying a vociferous demand, on nationalist grounds, for annexation of regions beyond one's own frontiers.

The occupation of Rome in 1870 by the Italian government opened the rift between church and state still wider. The pope, deprived of territories he had held for a thousand years, renewed his condemnations and chose to remain in lifelong seclusion in the Vatican. His successors followed the same policy until 1929. Hence good Italian patriots were bound to be anticlerical, and good Catholics were bound to look upon the Italian state with unfriendly eyes. The regional differences between northern and southern Italy did not disappear with unification. The north looked upon the agrarian south, the land of priest, landlord, and impoverished peasant, as disgracefully backward. Lawlessness in Sicily and Naples did not disappear with the overthrow of the Bourbons.

The new Italy was parliamentary but not democratic. At first the vote was only given to some 600,000 persons out of more than 20 million. Not until 1913

[11] See pp. 556, 634–636.

was the suffrage significantly broadened. Meanwhile parliamentary life, confined to a few, was somewhat unrealistic and frequently corrupt. With the mass of the population excluded from the vote, the revolutionary agitation continued unabated after the unification. Garibaldi himself, in the 1860s, made two more attempts to seize Rome by violence. In general, the revolutionary movement shifted from the older republican nationalism to the newer forms of Marxian socialism, anarchism, or syndicalism.

But the dream of ages was realized. Italy was one. The period that seemed so shameful to patriots, the long centuries that had elapsed since the Renaissance, were now terminated in the glories of a successful Risorgimento.

65. Bismarck: The Founding of a German Empire

To play upon the divisions among the Germans, keeping them in rivalry with each other and dependent upon outside powers, had been the policy of France ever since the Reformation and of Russia since it began to take part in the affairs of Europe. The pulverization of the Germanic world was in fact a kind of negative prerequisite to the development of modern history as we know it, for without it the economic and cultural leadership of Europe would hardly have become concentrated along the Atlantic seaboard, or a great military empire have arisen in Russia and spread along the Baltic and into Poland.

Gradually, as we have seen, the Germans became dissatisfied with their position. They became nationalistic.[12] Many German thinkers held that Germany was different from the West, destined some day to work out a peculiarly German way of life and political system of its own. To the Slavs the Germans felt immeasurably superior. German philosophy, as shown most clearly in Hegel, took on a certain characteristic tone. It pronounced individualism to be Western; it skipped lightly over individual liberty; it tended to glorify group loyalties, collectivist principles, and the state. It made a great to-do about History, which in the thought of Hegel, and after him Marx, became a vast force almost independent of human beings. History was said to ordain, require, necessitate, condemn, justify, or excuse. What one did not like could be dismissed as a mere historical phase, opening into a quite different and more attractive future. What one wanted, in the present or future, could be described as historically necessary and bound to come.

The German States after 1848

In 1848 a series of revolutions unseated the several governments of Germany. At the Frankfurt Assembly a group composed essentially of private citizens undertook to organize a united Germany by constitutional methods. They failed because they had no power. Hence after 1848 the Germans began to think in terms of power, developing a somewhat extreme admiration for *die Macht*. The men of Frankfurt failed also, perhaps, because they were insufficiently revolutionary.

[12] See pp. 435–441, 471.

The Germans were a sober, orderly, and respectful people. They were still attached emotionally to their several states. What happened in Italy, a revolutionary extermination of all the old governments except that of Piedmont, could not happen in Germany.[13]

After the failure of the 1848 revolution German nationalists and liberals were confused. By 1850 the old states were restored—Austria and Prussia, the kingdoms of Hanover, Saxony, Bavaria, and Württemberg, together with about thirty other states ranging in size down to the free cities of Hamburg and Frankfurt. The loose confederation of 1815, linking all these states together, was restored also.[14] But within this framework great economic and social changes were occurring. Between 1850 and 1870 the output of both coal and iron in Germany multiplied sixfold. In 1850 Germany produced less iron than France, in 1870 more. Germany was overcoming the economic and social lag which had characterized it for 300 years. A *Zollverein,* formed by Prussia in 1834, included almost all Germany outside of Austria and Bohemia and provided a large measure of economic unity. The German cities were growing, bound together by railroad and telegraph, requiring larger supporting areas on which to live. Industrial capitalists and industrial workers were becoming more numerous. With the advantages of unity more obvious than ever, with the ideals of 1848 badly compromised, with an exaggerated respect for the state and for power, and with a habit of accepting the successful event as the "judgment of history," the Germans were ripe for what happened. They did not unify themselves by their own exertions. They fell into the arms of Prussia.

Prussia in the 1860s: Bismarck

Prussia had always been the smallest and most precarious of the great powers. Ruined by Napoleon, it had risen again. It owed its international influence and internal character to its army. Actually it had fought rather fewer wars than other great powers, but, with its army in being, it had followed a program of expansion by conquest or diplomacy. The taking of Silesia in 1740, of parts of Poland in the 1770s and 1790s, of the Rhineland in 1815 by an international bargain were the highlights of Prussian growth.[15] After 1850 those who controlled the destinies of Prussia were apprehensive. Their state had been shaken by revolution. In the Crimean War and at the Congress of Paris they were hardly more than spectators. Italy was unified without any Prussian saying yes or no. It seemed as if the hard-won and still relatively recent position of Prussia might be waning.

Since 1815 the population of Prussia had grown from 11 to 18 million, but the size of the army had not changed. Merely to enforce existing principles of conscription would therefore almost double the army. But this would require increased financial appropriations. After 1850 Prussia had a parliament.[16] It was a parliament, to be sure, dominated by men of wealth; but some of the wealthy Prussians, notably the capital owners of the Rhineland, were liberals who wished

[13] See pp. 469–470.
[14] See pp. 446–447, 518–519 and map, p. 555.
[15] See maps, pp. 230–231.
[16] See p. 519.

the parliament to have control over government policies. These men did not like professional armies and considered the Prussian Junkers, from whom the officer corps was recruited, as their main rivals in the state. The parliament refused the necessary appropriations. The king at this juncture, in 1862, appointed a new chief minister, Otto von Bismarck.

Bismarck was a Junker from old Brandenburg east of the Elbe. He cultivated the gruff manner of an honest country squire, though he was in fact an accomplished man of the world. Intellectually he was far superior to the rather slow-witted landlord class from which he sprang, and for which he often felt an impatient contempt. He shared in many Junker ideas. He advocated, and even felt, a kind of stout Protestant piety. Although he cared for the world's opinion, it never deterred him in his actions; criticism and denunciation left him untouched. He was in fact obstinate. He was not a nationalist. He did not look upon all Germany as his Fatherland. He was a Prussian. His social affinities, as with the Junkers generally, lay to the East with corresponding landowning elements of the Baltic provinces and Russia.[17] The West, including the bulk of Germany, he neither understood nor trusted; it seemed to him revolutionary, turbulent, free-thinking, materialistic. Parliamentary bodies he considered ignorant and irresponsible as organs of government. Individual liberty seemed to him disorderly selfishness. Liberalism, democracy, socialism were repugnant to him. He preferred to stress duty, service, order, and the fear of God. The idea of forming a new German union developed only gradually in his mind and then as an adjunct to the strengthening of Prussia.

Bismarck thus had his predilections, and even his principles. But no principle bound him, no ideology seemed to him an end in itself. He became the classic practitioner of *Realpolitik*. The time came when the Junkers thought him a traitor to his class, when even the king was afraid of him, when he outraged and then mollified the august house of Habsburg, when he made friends with liberals, democrats, and even socialists, and in turn made enemies of them. First he made wars, then he insisted upon peace. Enmities and alliances were to him only matters of passing convenience. The enemy of today might be the friend of tomorrow. Far from planning out a long train of events, then following it step by step to a grand consummation, he seems to have been practical and opportunistic, taking advantage of situations as they emerged and prepared to act in any one of several directions as events might suggest.

In 1862, as minister president, it was his job, or duty, to outface the liberals in the Prussian parliament. For four years, from 1862 to 1866, Bismarck waged this "constitutional struggle." The parliament refused to vote the proposed taxes. The government collected them anyway. The taxpayers paid them without protest—it was the orderly thing to do, and the collectors represented public authority. The limitations of Prussian liberalism, the docility of the population, the respect for officialdom, the belief that the king and his ministers were wiser than the elected deputies, all clearly revealed themselves in this triumph of military policy over the theory of government by consent. The army was enlarged, reorganized, retrained, and reequipped. Bismarck fended off the showers of abuse from the liberal majority in the chamber. The liberals declared that

---

[17] See map, p. 212.

the government's policy was flagrantly unconstitutional. The constitution, said Bismarck, could not have been meant to undermine the state. The government, said the liberals, was itself undermining Prussia, for the rest of Germany hoped to find in Prussia, as Italy had found in Piedmont, a model of political freedom. What the Germans admired in Prussia, replied Bismarck coldly, was not its liberalism but its power. He declared that the Prussian boundaries as set in 1815 were unsound, that Prussia must be prepared to seize favorable opportunities for further growth.[18] And he added one of his most memorable utterances: "Not by speeches and majority votes are the great questions of the day decided—that was the great error of 1848 and 1849—but by blood and iron."

Bismarck's Wars: The North German Confederation, 1867

A favorable opportunity was not long in presenting itself. The Schleswig-Holstein question arose again. We have seen how it had arisen in 1848, and how even the mild men of Frankfurt had insisted, to the point of war, upon the incorporation of the two duchies into their German union.[19] Now in 1863 the story was repeated. The Danes, engaged in a process of national consolidation of their own, wished to make Schleswig an integral part of Denmark. The population of Schleswig was part Dane and part German. The diet of the German confederation, unwilling to see Germans thus annexed outright to Denmark, called for an all-German war upon the Danes, just as the revolutionary Frankfurt Assembly had done. Bismarck had no desire to support or strengthen the existing German confederation. He wanted not an all-German war but a Prussian war. To disguise his aims he acted jointly with Austria. In 1864 Prussia and Austria together went to war with Denmark, which they soon defeated. It was Bismarck's intention to annex both Schleswig and Holstein to Prussia, gaining whatever other advantages might present themselves from future trouble with Austria. He arranged a provisional occupation of Schleswig by Prussia, and of Holstein by Austria. Disputes soon arose over rights of passage, the keeping of internal order, and other problems with which occupying forces are commonly afflicted. While pretending to try to regulate these disputes he allowed them to ripen.

He now proceeded to discredit and isolate Austria. The British government was at the time following a policy of nonintervention in the affairs of the Continent. The Russian empire was in no position for action; it was divided internally by a reform program then at its height; it was in a mood of hostility to Austria, because of events of the Crimean War, and well disposed toward Prussia and Bismarck, because Bismarck in 1863 took care to support it against an uprising of the Poles. To win over the new kingdom of Italy Bismarck held out the lure of Venetia. As for France, Napoleon III was embarrassed by domestic discontents and had his army committed to adventures in Mexico. In addition, Bismarck charmed him at a confidential interview at Biarritz, where vague oral intimations of French expansion were exchanged, and the two men seemed to agree to a needed modernization of the map of Europe. To weaken Austria within Germany, Bismarck presented himself as a democrat. He proposed a reform of the German

[18] See maps, pp. 231, 555.
[19] See p. 518.

The legend of the map reads:

— German Confederation, 1815–1866

Prussia, 1815–1866

Annexed to Prussia, 1866

Joined with Prussia in North German Confederation, 1867

South German States Joined in German Empire, 1871

Alsace-Lorraine, Ceded by France to German Empire, 1871

Austrian Dominions Excluded From German Confederation, 1866, and from German Empire, 1871

Bismarck's German Empire, 1871

0   100   200 miles

THE GERMAN QUESTION, 1815–1871

From 1815 to 1866 there were thirty-nine states in Germany (of which only the largest are shown) joined in the Confederation of 1815. At the Frankfurt Assembly in 1848 (see pp. 516–518) two groups developed: the Great Germans who adhered to the idea of an all-German union, to include the Austrian lands except Hungary; and the Little Germans who were willing to exclude Austria and its empire. Bismarck was a Little German but a Great Prussian. He (1) enlarged Prussia by conquest in 1866, (2) joined Mecklenburg, Saxony, etc., with his enlarged Prussia in a North German Confederation of 1867, (3) combined this in turn with Bavaria, Württemberg, etc., to form the German empire of 1871, (4) conquered Alsace-Lorraine from France, and (5) ejected Austria. The boundaries of Bismarckian Germany remained unchanged until 1918. (See also maps, pp. 230–231, 448–449, 562–563, 728–729.)

confederation, recommending that it have a popular chamber elected by universal male suffrage. He calculated that the mass of the German people were wedded neither to the well-to-do capitalistic liberals, nor to the existing government structures of the German states, nor to the house of Habsburg. He would use "democracy" to undermine all established interests that stood in his way.

Meanwhile the occupying powers continued to quarrel over Schleswig-Holstein. Austria finally raised the matter formally in the German federal diet, one of whose functions was to prevent war between its members. Bismarck declared that the diet had no authority, accused the Austrians of aggression, and ordered the Prussian army to enter Holstein. The Austrians called for federal sanctions in the form of an all-German force to be sent against Prussia. The result was that Prussia, in 1866, was at war not only with Austria but with most of the other German states. The Prussian army soon proved its superiority. Trained to an unprecedented precision, equipped with the new needle-gun, by which the infantryman could deliver five rounds a minute, brought into the zone of combat by an imaginative strategy that made use of the new railroads, commanded by the skill of von Moltke, the Prussian army overthrew the Austrians at the battle of Sadowa (or Königgrätz) and defeated the other German states soon thereafter. The Austro-Prussian, or Seven Weeks' War, was amazing in its brevity. Bismarck hastened to make peace before the other European powers could realize what had happened.

Prussia annexed outright, together with Schleswig-Holstein, the whole kingdom of Hanover, the duchies of Nassau and Hesse-Cassel, and the free city of Frankfurt. Here the old governments simply disappeared before the axe of the "red reactionary." The German federal union disappeared likewise. In its place, in 1867, Bismarck organized a North German Confederation, in which the newly enlarged Prussia joined with twenty-one other states, all of which combined it greatly outweighed. The German states south of the river Main—Austria, Bavaria, Baden, Württemberg, and Hesse-Darmstadt—remained outside the new organization, with no kind of union among themselves. Meanwhile the kingdom of Italy annexed Venetia.

For the North German Confederation Bismarck produced a constitution. The new structure, though a federal one, was much stronger than the now defunct Confederation of 1815. The king of Prussia became its hereditary head. Ministers were responsible to him. There was a parliament with two chambers. The upper chamber, as in the United States, represented the states as such, though not equally. The lower chamber, or Reichstag, was deemed to represent the people and was elected by universal male suffrage. Such flirting with democracy seemed madness to both conservative Junker and liberal bourgeois. It was indeed a bold step, for only France at the time illustrated universal suffrage in Europe on a large scale, and in the France of Napoleon III neither old-fashioned conservatives nor genuine liberals could take much satisfaction. As for Great Britain, where voting rights were extended in this same year, 1867, they were still given to less than half the adult male population. Bismarck sensed in the "masses" an ally of strong government against private interests. He negotiated even with the socialists, who had arisen with the industrialization of the past decade, and who, in Germany at this time, were mainly followers of Ferdinand Lassalle. The Lassallean socialists, unlike the Marxian, believed it theoretically possible to improve working-class conditions through the action of existing governments. To the great annoyance of Marx, then in England (his *Capital* first appeared in 1867), the bulk of the German socialists reached an understanding with Bismarck. In return for a democratic suffrage they agreed to accept the North German Confederation. Bismarck, for his part, by making use of democratic and socialist sentiment, won popular approval for his emerging empire.

The Franco-Prussian War

It was clear that the situation was not yet stable. The small south German states were left floating in empty space; they would sooner or later have to gravitate into some orbit or other, whether Austrian, Prussian, or French. In France there were angry criticisms of Napoleon III's foreign policy. French intervention in Mexico had proved a fiasco.[20] A united Italy had been allowed to rise on France's borders. And now, contrary to all principles of French national interest observed by French governments for hundreds of years, a strong and independent power was being allowed to spread over virtually the whole of Germany. Everywhere people began to feel that war was coming between France and Prussia. Bismarck played on the fears of France felt in the south German states. South Germany, though in former times often a willing satellite to France, was now sufficiently nationalistic to consider such subservience to a foreign people disgraceful. To Bismarck it seemed that a war between Prussia and France would frighten the small south German states into a union with Prussia, leaving only Austria outside—which was what he wanted. To Napoleon III, or at least to some of his advisers, it seemed that such a war, if successful, would restore public approval of the Bonapartist empire. In this inflammable situation the responsible persons of neither country worked for peace.

Meanwhile a revolution in Spain had driven the reigning queen into exile, and a Spanish provisional government invited Prince Leopold of Hohenzollern, the king of Prussia's cousin, to be constitutional king of Spain. To entrench the Prussian royal house in Spain would naturally be distasteful to France. Three times the Hohenzollern family refused the Spanish offer. Bismarck, who could not control such family decisions, but who foresaw the possibility of a usable incident, deviously persuaded the Spanish to issue the invitation still a fourth time. On July 2, 1870, Paris heard that Prince Leopold had accepted. The French ambassador to Prussia, Benedetti, at the direction of his government, met the king of Prussia at the bathing resort of Ems, where he formally demanded that Prince Leopold's acceptance be withdrawn. It was withdrawn on July 12. The French seemed to have their way. Bismarck was disappointed.

The French government went still further. It instructed Benedetti to approach the king again at Ems and demand that at no time in the future would any Hohenzollern ever become a candidate for the Spanish throne. The king politely declined any such commitment and telegraphed a full report of the conversation to Bismarck at Berlin. Bismarck, receiving the telegram, which became famous as the "Ems dispatch," saw a new opportunity, as he put it, to wave a red flag before the Gallic bull. He condensed the Ems telegram for publication, so reducing

[20] See pp. 651–652.

and abridging it that it seemed to newspaper readers as if a curt exchange had occurred at Ems, in which the Prussians believed that their king had been insulted, and the French that their ambassador had been snubbed. In both countries the war party demanded satisfaction. On July 19, 1870, on these trivial grounds, and with the ostensible issue of the Spanish throne already settled, the irresponsible and decaying government of Napoleon III declared war on Prussia.

Again the war was short. Again Bismarck had taken care to isolate his enemy in advance. The British generally felt France to be in the wrong. They had been alarmed by French operations in Mexico, which suggested an ambition to re-create a French American empire. The Italians had long been awaiting the chance to seize Rome; they did so in 1870, when the French withdrew their troops from Rome for use against Prussia. The Russians had been awaiting the chance to upset the clause of the Peace of 1856 which forbade them to keep naval vessels in the Black Sea. They did so in 1870.

The War of 1870, like the others of the time, failed to become a general European struggle. Prussia was supported by the south German states. France had no allies. The French army proved to be technically backward compared with the Prussian. War began on July 19; on September 2, after the battle of Sedan, the principal French army surrendered to the Germans. Napoleon III was himself taken prisoner. On September 4 an insurrection in Paris proclaimed the Third Republic. The Prussian and German forces moved into France and laid siege to the capital. Though the French armies dissolved, Paris refused to capitulate. For four months it was surrounded and besieged.

The German Empire, 1871

With their guns encircling Paris, the German rulers or their representatives assembled at Versailles. The château and gardens of Versailles, since Louis XVI's unceremonious departure in October 1789, had been little more than a vacant monument to a society long since dead. Here, in the most sumptuous room of the palace, the resplendent Hall of Mirrors, where the Sun King had once received the deferential approaches of German princes, Bismarck on January 18, 1871, caused the German Empire to be proclaimed. The king of Prussia received the hereditary title of German emperor. The other German rulers (excepting, to be sure, the ruler of Austria, and those whom Bismarck had himself dethroned) accepted his imperial authority. Ten days later the people of Paris, shivering, hungry, and helpless, opened their gates to the enemy. France had no government with which Bismarck could make peace. It was not at all clear what kind of government the country wanted. Bismarck insisted on the election of a Constituent Assembly by universal suffrage. He demanded that France pay the German Empire a war indemnity of five billion gold francs (then an enormous and unprecedented sum) and cede to it the border region of Alsace and most of Lorraine. Though the Alsatians spoke German, most of them felt themselves to be French, having shared in the general history of France since the seventeenth century. There was strong local protest at the transfer to Germany, and the French never reconciled themselves to this cold-blooded amputation of their frontier. The peace dictated by Bismarck was embodied in the treaty of Frankfurt of May 10, 1871. Thereafter, as will be seen, the French Constituent Assembly gradually proceeded to construct the Third Republic.[21]

The consolidation of Germany transformed the face of Europe. It reversed the dictum not only of the Peace of Vienna but even of the Peace of Westphalia.[22] The German Empire, no sooner born, was the strongest state on the continent of Europe. Rapidly industrialized after 1870, it became more potent still. Bismarck, by consummate astuteness, by exploiting the opportunities offered by a Europe in flux and with no more fighting than that involved in a few weeks in three short wars, had brought about what European statesmen of many nationalities had long said should at all costs be prevented. He outwitted everybody in turn, including the Germans. The united all-German state that issued from the nationalist movement was a Germany conquered by Prussia. Prussia, with its annexations of 1866, embraced almost all Germany north of the Main. Within the empire it had about two-thirds of the area. Before such unanswerable success the Prussian liberals capitulated, and the Prussian parliament passed an "indemnity act"; the gist of it was that Bismarck admitted to a certain high-handedness during the constitutional struggle but that the parliament legalized the disputed tax collections *ex post facto,* agreeing to forgive and forget, in view of the victory over Austria and its consequences. Thus liberalism withered away before nationalism.

The German Empire received substantially the constitution of the North German Confederation. It was a federation of monarchies, each based in theory on divine or hereditary right. At the same time, in the Reichstag elected by universal male suffrage, it rested on a kind of mass appeal and was in a sense democratic. Yet the country's ministers were responsible to the emperor and not to the elected chamber. Moreover, it was the rulers who joined the empire, not the peoples. There were no popular plebiscites as in Italy. Each state kept its own laws, government, and constitution. The people of Prussia, for example, remained for Prussian affairs under the rather illiberal constitution of 1850,[23] while in affairs of the Reich, or empire, they enjoyed an equal vote by universal suffrage. The emperor, who was also the king of Prussia, had legal control over the foreign and military policy of the empire. The German Empire in effect served as a mechanism to magnify the role of Prussia, the Prussian army, and the East-Elbian Prussian aristocracy in world affairs.

66. *The Dual Monarchy of Austria-Hungary*

The Habsburg Empire after 1848

Bismarck united Germany, but he also divided it, for he left about a sixth of the Germans outside his German Empire. These Germans of Austria and Bohemia had now to work out a common future with the dozen other nationalities in the Danubian domain.

The clumsiness of the old Habsburg multinational empire is clear enough, but

---

[21] See pp. 605–607.
[22] See pp. 145–149, and map, pp. 146–147.
[23] See p. 519.

more impressive is its astonishing capacity to live and to survive. Prussia and France, in the 1740s, had tried unsuccessfully to dismember it. Smashed four different times by the French between 1796 and 1809, it outlived this crisis, and after 1815, under Metternich, it guided the counsels of Europe.[24] Broken up in 1848, restored by the intervention of Russia in 1849, dislocated by its effort at mobilization in 1855, attacked by Napoleon III in 1859 and by Bismarck in 1866, it still continued to hold together and disappeared finally only in 1918 in the cataclysm of the First World War.[25] But the events of the 1850s and 1860s greatly altered its character.

The essential question, in a nationalist age, was how the Habsburg government would react to the problems raised by national self-expression. The nationalities did not wish to destroy the empire. Among the Hungarians after 1848–1849, only a handful of extreme radicals dreamed of a Hungary entirely independent. Most of them desired constitutional autonomy for Hungary but were not prepared to sever the link with Vienna. Slav opinion, at the Slav Congress of Prague in 1848, went basically no further than Austroslavism.[26] The peoples of the empire, while increasingly insistent on certain national rights—such as a degree of local self-government, and schools, law courts, and administration in their own language—felt an underlying need for the large political structure which the empire gave.

By Habsburg, in this period, one means primarily Francis Joseph, who as emperor from 1848 to 1916 reigned even longer than his famous contemporary, Queen Victoria. Francis Joseph, like many others, could never shake off his own tradition. His thoughts turned on his house and on its rights. Buffeted unmercifully by the waves of change, he cordially disliked everything liberal, progressive, or modern. He allied himself with the Catholic hierarchy and the Vatican, which also, for decades after 1848, and for understandable reason, set itself bluntly against compromise with the new age. Personally, Francis Joseph was incapable of enlarged views, ambitious projects, bold decisions, or persevering action. And he lived in a pompous dream world, surrounded in the imperial court by great noblemen, high churchmen, and bespangled personages of the army.

Yet the government was not idle; it was, if anything, too fertile in devising new deals and new dispensations. Various expedients were tried after 1849, but none was tried long enough to see if it would work. For several years the ruling idea was centralization—to govern the empire through the German language and with German efficiency, maintaining the abolition of serfdom as accomplished in 1848 (and which required a strong official control over the landlords if it was to work in practice) and favoring the building of railroads and other apparatus of material progress.[27] This Germanic and bureaucratic centralization was distasteful to the non-German nationalities, and especially to the Magyars. It is important to say Magyars, not Hungarians, because the Magyars composed less than half the very mixed population of Hungary within its then existing borders. Nevertheless the Magyars, as the strongest of the non-German groups, and hence the most able to maintain a political system of their own, felt the Germanic

[24] See pp. 275–278, 394–397, 418–422, 424–425, 474–484.
[25] See pp. 507–514, 545, 548, 554–557, 717–718.
[26] See pp. 510–511.
[27] See p. 514.

influence as most oppressive. In the war of 1859 the Magyars sympathized with the Italians.

The Compromise of 1867

In 1867 a compromise was made, known as the *Ausgleich*. It was essentially a bargain between the Germans of Austria-Bohemia and the Magyars of Hungary. It worked to the common disadvantage of the Slavs. Both Germans and Magyars looked upon the Slavs somewhat as many whites in the United States then looked upon blacks, seeing in them a people who had shown no aptitude for civilization except under tutelage. In fact the word "slave" in many languages (German *Sklave*) had originated from the word "Slav." As Count Beust, the Austrian negotiator, put it in 1867, the idea of the Compromise was that each people, Germans and Magyars, should thereafter govern its own barbarians in its own way.

The Compromise created a Dual Monarchy, of a kind unparalleled in Europe. West of the river Leith was the Empire of Austria, east of it the Kingdom of Hungary. The two were now judged exactly equal. Each had its own constitution and its own parliament, to which in each country the governing ministry was henceforth to be responsible. The administrative language of Austria would be German, of Hungary, Magyar. Neither state might intervene in the other's affairs. The two were joined by the fact that the same Habsburg ruler should always be emperor in Austria and king in Hungary. Yet the union was not personal only; for, though there was no common parliament, delegates of the two parliaments were to meet together alternately in Vienna and Budapest, and there was to be a common ministry for finance, foreign affairs, and war. To this common ministry of Austria-Hungary both Austrians and Hungarians were to be appointed.

In effect, the Compromise treated Austria as a kind of German nation-state and Hungary as a Magyar nation-state. It furnished each with parliamentary and constitutional organs, by which the leading nationality was made to feel a sense of participation in government. But the Germans formed less than half the people of Austria, as did the Magyars of Hungary. Austria included the Slovenes, Czechs, Poles, and Ruthenians (and a few Italians); Hungary the Slovaks, the Croats and Serbs, and the Transylvanians, who were essentially Romanians.[28] All these people felt aggrieved.

[28] See maps, pp. 470, 562–563.

EUROPE, 1871

The new features on this map, as compared to the Europe of 1815 (see pp. 448–449), are the existence of a unified German Empire and a unified Kingdom of Italy. The German domain was enlarged by the incorporation of Schleswig (in the neck of the Danish peninsula) and the annexation from France of Alsace and parts of Lorraine, the regions respectively around Strassburg (French Strasbourg) and Metz on the map. From 1871 to 1914 Europe had fewer separate states, fewer land frontiers, and a simpler political geography than at any other time in its history. Except for the voluntary separation of Norway and Sweden in 1905 there were no changes in this period outside the Balkans. (See map, p. 703.)

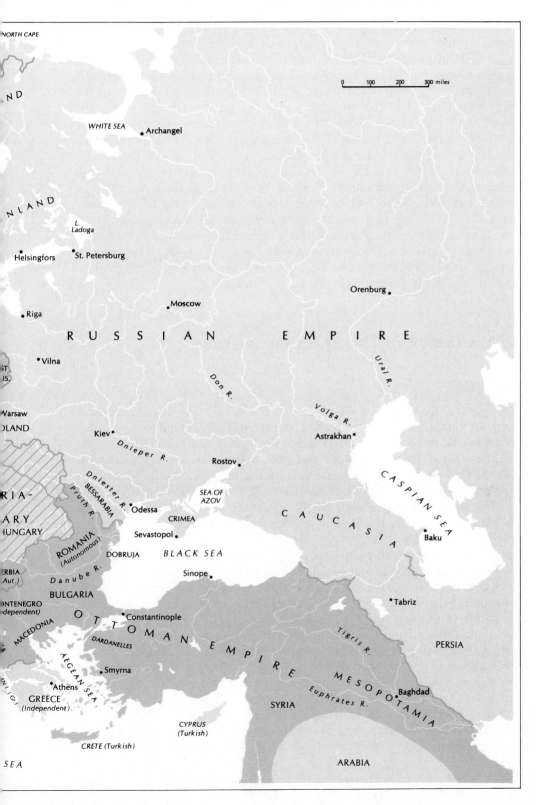

NORTH CAPE

WHITE SEA   • Archangel

L.
Ladoga

• Helsingfors   • St. Petersburg

Orenburg •

• Riga

• Moscow

R U S S I A N   E M P I R E

• Vilna

Ural R.

Warsaw   Kiev •   Don R.   Volga R.

POLAND   Dnieper R.   Astrakhan •

Dniester R.   Rostov •

BESSARABIA   CASPIAN SEA

RIA-   Pruth R.   • Odessa   SEA OF
AZOV

ARY   ROMANIA   CRIMEA   C A U C A S I A

HUNGARY   (Autonomous)   Sevastopol •

DOBRUJA   BLACK SEA   Baku •

ERBIA   Danube R.   Sinope •

Aut.)   BULGARIA   • Tabriz

ONTEGRO   O T T O M A N   E M P I R E   PERSIA

dependent)   Constantinople •

MACEDONIA   Tigris R.

DARDANELLES   M E S O P O T A M I A

AEGEAN   • Smyrna   Baghdad •

SEA

NI (Gr.)   • Athens   SYRIA   Euphrates R.

GREECE
(Independent)

CYPRUS
(Turkish)

CRETE (Turkish)

SEA   ARABIA

0   100   200   300 miles

Both Austria and Hungary, under the Dual Monarchy, were in form constitutional parliamentary states, although the principle of ministerial responsibility was not consistently honored. Neither was democratic. In Austria, after much juggling with voting systems, a true universal male suffrage was instituted in 1907. In Hungary, when the First World War came in 1914, still only a quarter of the adult male population had the vote. Socially, the great reform of 1848, the abolition of serfdom, was not allowed to lead on to upsetting conclusions. The owners of great landed estates, especially in Hungary (but also in parts of the Austrian Empire) remained the unquestionably dominant class. They were surrounded by landless peasants, an agrarian proletariat, composed partly of lower classes of their own nationality, and partly of entire peasant peoples, like the Slovaks and Serbs, who had no educated or wealthy class of their own. National and social questions therefore came together. For some nationalities, and for none more than the Magyars, not only a national but a social and economic ascendancy was at stake. Landlordism became the basic social issue. A landowning class, educated and civilized, faced a peasant mass that was generally ignorant, rude, and left out of the advancing civilization of the day.

67. *Liberalization in Tsarist Russia: Alexander II*

Tsarist Russia after 1856

For Russia also the Crimean War set off a series of changes. The ungainly empire, an "enormous village" as it has been called, stretching from Poland to the Pacific, had proved unable to repel a localized attack by France and Great Britain, into which neither of the Western powers had put anything like its full resources. Alexander II (1855–1881), who became tsar during the war, was no liberal by nature or conviction. But he saw that something drastic must be done. The prestige of western Europe was at its height. There the most successful and even enviable nations were to be found. The reforms in Russia therefore followed, at some distance, the European model.

Imperial Russia was a political organization very difficult to describe. Its own subjects did not know what to make of it. Some, called Westernizers in the mid–nineteenth century, believed Russia destined to become more like Europe. Others, the Slavophiles, believed Russia to be entrusted with a special destiny of its own, which imitation of Europe would only weaken or pervert.

That Russia differed from Europe at least in degree was doubted by nobody. The leading institution was the autocracy of the tsar. This was not exactly the absolutism known in the West. In Russia certain very old European conceptions were missing, such as the idea that spiritual authority is independent of even the mightiest prince or the old feudal idea of reciprocal duties between king and subject.[29] The notion that men have rights, claims for justice at the hands of power, which no one in Europe had ever expressly repudiated, was in Russia a somewhat doctrinaire importation from the West. The tsardom did not rule by

[29] See pp. 16–17, 29. On Russia in the sixteenth and seventeenth centuries, see pp. 234–235.

law; it ran the country by ukase, police action, and the army. The tsars, since Peter and before, had built up their state very largely by importing European technical methods and technical experts, often against strong objection by native Russians of all classes, upon whom the new methods were, when necessary, simply forced. More than any state in Europe, the Russian empire was a machine superimposed upon its people without organic connection—bureaucracy pure and simple. But as the contacts with Europe were joined, many Russians acquired European ideas of a kind in which the autocracy was not interested—ideas of liberty and fraternity, of a just and classless society, of individual personality enriched by humane culture and moral freedom. Many people, with such sentiments, found themselves chronically critical of the government and of Russia itself. The government, massive though it seemed, was afraid of such people. Any idea arising outside of official circles seemed pernicious, and the press and the universities were as a rule severely censored.

A second fundamental institution, which had grown up with the tsardom, was legalized bondage or serfdom. The bulk of the population were serfs dependent upon masters. Russian serfdom was more onerous than that found in east-central Europe until 1848.[30] It resembled the slavery of the Americas in that serfs were "owned"; they could be bought and sold and used in other occupations than agriculture. Some serfs worked the soil, rendering unpaid labor service to the gentry. Others could be used by their owners in factories or mines or rented out for such purposes. Others were more independent, working as artisans or mechanics, and even traveling about or residing in the cities, but from their earnings they had to remit certain fees to the lord, or return home when he called them. The owners had a certain paternalistic responsibility for their serfs, and in the villages the gentry constituted a kind of personal local government. The law, as in the American South, did little or nothing to interfere between gentry and servile mass, so that the serf's day-to-day fortunes depended on the personality or economic circumstances of his owner.

By the mid–nineteenth century both conservative and liberal Russians were agreeing that serfdom must some day end. Serfdom was in any case ceasing to be profitable; some two-thirds of all the privately owned serfs (i.e., those not belonging to the tsar or state) were mortgaged as security for loans at the time of Alexander II's accession. Increasingly serfdom was recognized as a bad system of labor relations, making the muzhiks into illiterate and stolid drudges, without incentive, initiative, self-respect, or pride of workmanship, and also very poor soldiers for the army.

Educated Russians, full of Western ideas, were estranged from the government, from the Orthodox church, which was an arm of the tsar, and from the common people of their own country. They felt ill at ease in a mass of ignorance and obscurantism and a pang of guilt at the virtual slavery on which their own position rested. Hence arose, at about the time under discussion, another distinctive feature of Russian life, the "intelligentsia." In Russia it was thought so exciting to be educated, to have ideas, to subscribe to magazines, or engage in critical conversation that the intelligentsia sensed themselves as a class apart. They were made up of students, university graduates, and persons who had a good deal of

[30] See pp. 237–238, 337–339.

leisure to read. Such people, while not very free to think, were more free to think than to do almost anything else. The Russian intelligentsia tended to sweeping and all-embracing philosophies. They believed that intellectuals should play a large role in society. They formed an exaggerated idea of the direct influence of thinkers upon the course of historical change. Their characteristic attitude was one of opposition. Some, overwhelmed by the mammoth immobility of the tsardom and of serfdom, turned to revolutionary and even terroristic philosophies. This only made the bureaucrats more anxious and fearful, and the government more fitfully repressive.

The Emancipation Act of 1861 and Other Reforms

Alexander II, on becoming tsar, attempted to enlist the support of the liberals among the intelligentsia. He gave permission to travel outside of Russia, eased the controls on the universities, and allowed the censorship to go relatively unenforced. Newspapers and journals were founded, and those written by Russian revolutionaries abroad, like the *Polar Star* of Alexander Herzen in London, penetrated more freely into the country. The result was a great outburst of public opinion, which was agreed at least on one point, the necessity of emancipating the peasants. This was in principle hardly a party question. Alexander's father, Nicholas I, had been a noted reactionary, who abhorred Western liberalism and is memorable for having organized, as the "Third Section" of his chancellory, a system of secret political police until then unparalleled in Europe for its arbitrary and inquisitorial methods. Yet Nicholas I had taken serious measures to alleviate serfdom. Alexander II, basically conservative on Russian affairs, proceeded to set up a special branch of the government to study the question. The government did not wish to throw the whole labor system and economy of the country into chaos, nor to ruin the gentry class without which it could not govern at all. After many discussions, proposals, and memoranda, an imperial ukase of 1861 declared serfdom abolished and the peasants free.

By this great decree the peasants became legally free in the Western sense. They were henceforth subjects of the government, not subjects of their owners. It was hoped that they would be stirred by a new sense of human dignity. As one enthusiastic official put it shortly after emancipation: "The people are erect and transformed; the look, the walk, the speech, everything is changed." The gentry lost their old quasi-manorial jurisdiction over the villages. They could no longer exact forced and unpaid labor or receive fees arising from servitude.

It is important to realize what the Act of Emancipation did and did not do. Roughly (with great differences from region to region) it allocated about half the cultivated land to the gentry and half to the former serfs. The latter had to pay redemption money for the land they received and for the fees which the gentry lost. The Russian aristocracy was far from weakened; in place of a kind of human property largely mortgaged anyway, they now had clear possession of some half the land, they received the redemption money, and were rid of obligations to the peasants.

The peasants, on the other hand, now owned some half the arable land in their own right—a considerable amount by the standards of almost any European country. They did not, however, possess it according to the principles of private property or independent farming that had become prevalent in Europe. The peasant land, when redeemed, became the collective property of the ancient peasant village assembly, or *mir*. The village, as a unit, was responsible to the government for payment of the redemption and for collection of the necessary sums from its individual members. The village assembly, in default of collection, might require forced labor from the defaulter or a member of his family; and it could prevent peasants from moving away from the village, lest those remaining bear the whole burden of payment. It could (as in the past) assign and reassign certain lands to its members for tillage and otherwise supervise cultivation as a joint concern. To keep the village community intact, the government presently forbade the selling or mortgaging of land to persons outside the village. This tended to preserve the peasant society but also to discourage the investment of outside capital, with which equipment might be purchased, and so to retard agricultural improvement and the growth of wealth. Not all peasants within the village unit were equal. As in France before the Revolution, some had the right to work more land than others. Some were only day laborers. Others had rights of inheritance in the soil (for not all land was subject to reassignment by the commune) or rented additional parcels of land belonging to the gentry. These lands they worked by hiring other peasants for wages. These more substantial peasants, as agricultural entrepreneurs, resembled farmers of the type found in France or the United States. None of the Russian peasants, however, after the emancipation, possessed full individual freedom of action. In their movements and obligations, as in their thoughts, they were restricted by their villages as they had once been restricted by their lords.

Alexander II proceeded to overhaul and westernize the legal system of the country. With the disappearance of the lord's jurisdiction over his peasants a new system of local courts was needed in any case, but the opportunity was taken to reform the courts from bottom to top. The arbitrariness of authority and defenselessness of the subject were the inveterate evils. They were greatly mitigated by the edict of 1864. Trials were made public, and private persons received the right to be represented in court by lawyers of their own choosing. All class distinctions in judicial matters were abolished, although in practice peasants continued to be subject to harsh disadvantages. A clear sequence of lower and higher courts was established. Requirements were laid down for the professional training of judges, who henceforth received stated salaries and were protected from administrative pressure. A system of juries on the English model was introduced.

While thus attempting to establish a rule of law, the tsar also moved in the direction of allowing self-government. He hoped to win over the liberals and to shoulder the upper and middle classes with some degree of public responsibility. He created, again by an edict of 1864, a system of provincial and district councils called zemstvos. Elected by various elements, including the peasants, the zemstvos gradually went into operation and took up matters of education, medical relief, public welfare, food supply, and road maintenance in their localities. Their great value was in developing civic sentiment among those who took part in them. Many liberals urged a representative body for all Russia, a Zemsky Sobor or

Duma, which, however, Alexander II refused to concede. After 1864 his policy became more cautious. A rebellion in Poland in 1863 inclined him to take advice from those who favored repression. He began to mollify the vested interests that had been disgruntled by the reforms and to whittle down some of the concessions already granted. But the essence of the reforms remained unaffected.

Revolutionism in Russia

The autocrat who thus undertook to liberalize Russia barely escaped assassination in 1866, had five shots fired at him in 1873, missed death by half an hour in 1880 when his imperial dining room was dynamited, and in 1881 was to be killed by a bomb. The revolutionaries were not pleased with the reforms, which if successful would merely strengthen the existing order. Dissatisfied intelligentsia in the 1860s began to call themselves "nihilists": they believed in "nothing"—except science—and took a cynical view of the reforming tsar and his zemstvos. The peasants, saddled with heavy redemption payments, remained basically unsatisfied, and intellectuals toured the villages fanning this discontent. Revolutionaries developed a mystic conception of the revolutionary role of the Russian masses. They reminded the peasants of the vast rebellions of Stephen Razin and Pugachev, in which they saw a native Russian revolutionary tradition.[31] Socialists, after the failure of socialism in Europe in the Revolution of 1848, came in many cases to believe, as Alexander Herzen wrote, that the true and natural future of socialism lay in Russia, because of the very weakness of capitalism in Russia and the existence of a kind of collectivism already established in the village assemblies or communes.

More radical than Herzen were the anarchist Bakunin and his disciple Nechaiev. In their *People's Justice* these two called for terrorism not only against tsarist officials but against liberals also. As they wrote in the *Catechism of a Revolutionist*, the true revolutionary "is devoured by one purpose, one thought, one passion— the revolution. . . . He has severed every link with the social order and with the entire civilized world. . . . Everything which promotes the success of the revolution is moral, everything which hinders it is immoral." Terrorism (which is really to say assassination) was rejected by many of the revolutionaries, especially by those who in the 1870s took up the scientific socialism of Karl Marx. To Marx it did not seem that frantic violence would advance an inevitable social process. But other groups, recognizing the inspiration of men like Bakunin and Nechaiev, organized secret terroristic societies. One of these, the People's Will, determined to assassinate the tsar. In an autocratic state, they held, there was no other road to justice and freedom.

Alexander II, alarmed by this underground menace, which of course did not escape the attention of the police, again turned for support to the liberals. The liberals, who were themselves threatened by the revolutionaries, had become estranged from the government by its failure to follow through with the reforms of the early 1860s. Now, in 1880, to rally support, the tsar again relaxed the autocratic system. He abolished the dreaded Third Section or secret police set up by his father, allowed the press to discuss most political subjects freely, and

[31] See pp. 238, 337-339.

encouraged the zemstvos to do the same. Further to associate representatives of the public with the government, he proposed, not exactly a parliament, but two nationally elected commissions to sit with the council of state. He signed the edict to this effect on March 13, 1881, and on the same day was assassinated, not by a demented individual acting wildly and alone, but by the joint efforts of the highly trained members of the People's Will.

Alexander III, upon his father's death, abandoned the project for elected commissions and during his whole reign, from 1881 to 1894, reverted to a program of brutal resistance to liberals and revolutionaries alike. The new regime established by peasant emancipation, judicial reform, and the zemstvos was nevertheless allowed to continue. How Russia finally received a parliament in 1905 is explained below in the chapter on the Russian Revolution. At present it is enough to have seen how even tsarist Russia, under Alexander II, shared in a liberal movement that was then at its height. The abolition of serfdom, putting both aristocrat and peasant more fully on a money economy, opened the way for capitalistic development within the empire. And between the two confining walls of autocracy and revolutionism—equally hard and unyielding—European ideas of law, liberty, and humanity inserted themselves in a tentative way.

68. The United States: The American Civil War

The history of Europe, long interconnected with that of the rest of the world, by the early twentieth century became merged with it entirely. Similarly the development of non-European regions, long a collection of separate stories, was to fuse into a single worldwide theme, to which later chapters of this book are largely devoted. It is no great leap at this point to pass to a treatment of areas overseas (as seen from Europe), some of which underwent in the 1860s the same process of national consolidation, or attempted consolidation, already traced in Italy and Germany, Austria, Hungary, and the Russian empire. In particular, foundations were laid for two new "powers" like those of Europe—the United States of America and the Empire of Japan. The huge Dominion of Canada was also established.

Growth of the United States

As in the time of the American Revolution and Napoleon, the history of the United States in the nineteenth century reflected that of the European world of which it formed a part. The most basic fact, besides territorial expansion, was rapid growth. This was so obvious as to lead a French observer in the 1830s, Alexis de Tocqueville, to make a famous prediction: that within a century the United States would have 100 million people and would, along with Russia, be one of the two leading powers of the world. By 1860, with 31 million, the United States was almost as populous as France and more so than Great Britain.

The growth in numbers was due to a prolific birth rate, but also to the arrival of immigrants, who became prolific in their turn. The immigrants—except for an uncounted, because illegal, importation of slaves—came almost entirely from Europe, and before 1860 almost entirely from Great Britain, Ireland, and Germany.

The immigrants did not desire to surrender their native ways. Some brought skills that the new country greatly needed, but immigration also presented a true social problem, obliging peoples to live together without common tradition. On the whole, it appears that the older Americans accepted the reshaping of their country rather calmly, with anti-foreign movements occasionally surfacing but then quickly subsiding. Few concessions were made. English was the language of the public schools, the police, law courts, local government, and public notices and announcements. Usually the immigrant had to know some English to hold a job. On the other hand no one was exactly forced to become "Americanized"—the new arrivals were free to maintain churches, newspapers, and social gatherings in their own tongues. The fact that the English, Scots, and Irish already spoke English, and that the Germans readily learned it, alleviated the language issue. The immigrants did not constitute minorities in the European sense. They were more than willing to embrace American national attitudes as formed in the eighteenth century—the national traditions of republicanism and self-government, of individual liberty, free enterprise, and unbounded opportunity for self-improvement. The old America impressed itself on the new, being somewhat impressed itself in the process. In this sense a new nationality was being consolidated.

The Estrangement of North and South

But at the same time the nation was falling to pieces. North and South became completely estranged. The Industrial Revolution had contrary effects on the two regions. It turned the South into an economic associate of Great Britain. The South became the world's chief producer of raw cotton for the Lancashire mills. The Southerners, living by the export of a cash crop, and producing virtually no manufactures, wished to purchase manufactured goods as cheaply as possible. Hence they favored free trade, especially with Great Britain. In the North, the Industrial Revolution led to the building of factories. Northern factory owners, usually backed by their workers, demanded protection from the inflow of British goods, with which no other country at the time could easily compete. The North therefore favored a high tariff, which the South declared to be ruinous.

More fundamental was the difference in the status of labor. As the demand for raw cotton reached astronomical magnitudes the South fell more deeply under the hereditary curse of the Americas—the slave and plantation system.[32] In the nineteenth century slavery increasingly revolted the moral conscience of the white man's world. It was abolished in the British colonies in 1833, in the French colonies in 1848, and in the Spanish American republics at different dates in the first half of the century. Similarly, serfdom was abolished in the Habsburg possessions in 1848 and in Russia in 1861. The American South could not, and after about 1830 no longer even wished to shake the system off. The South was the Cotton Kingdom whose "peculiar institution" was unfree labor of blacks. Whites were hurt by the system as well as blacks. Few free men could prosper alongside a mass of subservient and virtually uncompensated labor. The incoming Europeans settled overwhelmingly in the North, the South remaining more purely

[32] See p. 261.

"Anglo-Saxon"—except that in its most densely peopled areas some half of the people were of African descent.

In the movement westward, common in North and South, the pressure in the South came mainly from planters wishing to establish new plantations, in the North from persons hoping to set up small farms and from businessmen bent on founding new towns, building railroads, and creating markets. As once France and Great Britain had fought for control beyond the Alleghenies, so now North and South fought for control beyond the Mississippi. In 1846 the United States made war upon Mexico by methods at which Bismarck would not have blushed. The North widely denounced the war as an act of Southern aggression, but was willing enough to take the ensuing conquests, which comprised the region from Texas to the Pacific. The first new state created in this region, California, prohibited slavery. Since 1820 the United States had held together precariously by the "Missouri Compromise," under which new states, as set up in the West, were admitted to the Union in pairs, one "slave" and one "free," so that a rough equality was maintained in the Senate and in the presidential electoral vote. With the creation of California this balance of power was upset in favor of the North, so that in return, by the "compromise of 1850," the North agreed to enforce the laws on runaway slaves to the satisfaction of the South. But the new strictness toward fugitive slaves ran against mounting sentiment in the North. Attempts to arrest blacks in free states and return them to slavery aroused abolitionist sentiment to a higher pitch. The abolitionists, a branch of the humanitarian movement then sweeping the European world, and somewhat resembling the radical democrats who came forward in Europe in 1848, demanded the immediate and total elimination of slavery, without concession, compromise, or compensation for the property interests of the slave owners. Abolitionists denounced the Union itself as the unholy accomplice in a social abomination.

By 1860 a sense of "sectionalism" had developed in the South not different in principle from the nationalism felt by many peoples in Europe. In their proud insistence on states' rights and constitutional liberties, their aristocratic and warlike codes of ethics, their demand for independence from outside influence and for freedom in ruling their own subject people, the Southern whites suggested nothing in Europe so much as the Magyars of the Austrian Empire. They now wondered whether their way of life could be safely maintained within the Union which they had helped to create. They sensed Northerners as outsiders, unsympathetic, foreign, hostile, and the South as potentially an independent and distinct nation. They were aware that within the Union they were increasingly a minority; for where in 1790 North and South had been approximately equal, by 1860 the North had outrun the South in population, mainly because of the stream of migration from Europe. The incipient nationalism of the South was of the type of small nation struggling against the great empire. In the North, nationalism was a sentiment in favor of maintaining the whole existing territory of the United States. Northerners by 1860, with a few exceptions, refused to admit that any state of the Union could withdraw, or secede, for any reason.

In 1860 the new Republican party elected Abraham Lincoln president. It advanced a program of free Western lands for small farmers, a higher tariff, transcontinental railroad building, and economic and capitalistic development on a national scale. The new party's radical wing, to which Lincoln himself did not belong, was vehemently abolitionist and anti-Southern in sentiment. Southern leaders, after the election of Lincoln, brought about the formal withdrawal of their states from the United States of America and the creation of the Confederate States of America reaching from Virginia to Texas. Lincoln ordered the armed forces to defend the territory of the United States, and the resulting Civil War, or war of Southern independence, lasting for four years and involving battles as great as those of Napoleon, was the most harrowing struggle of the nineteenth century with the exception of the Taiping rebellion in China.[33]

European governments, while never recognizing the Confederacy, were partial to the South. The United States stood for principles still considered revolutionary in Europe, so that, while the European working classes generally favored the North, the upper classes were willing enough to see the North American republic end in collapse and failure. In addition, Great Britain and France saw in the breakup of the United States the same advantages that they had formerly seen in the breakup of the Spanish empire.[34] In the Confederate States the British, and the French to a lesser degree, expected to find another free trade country, supplying western Europe with raw materials and buying its manufactures; in short, they saw not a competitor like the North, but a complementary partner to the industry of the Old World. It was likewise during the American Civil War that a French army sent by Napoleon III invaded Mexico to create a puppet empire under an Austrian archduke.[35] Thus the only serious attempt to ignore the Monroe Doctrine, violate the independence of Latin America, and revive European colonialism in the Americas occurred at the time when the United States was in dissolution.

But the North won the war and the Union was upheld. The Mexicans rid themselves of their unwanted emperor. Tsar Alexander II sold Alaska to the United States. The war ended the idea of the Union as a confederation of member states from which members might withdraw at will. In its place triumphed the idea that the United States was a national state, composed not of member states but of a unitary people irrevocably bound together. This doctrine was written explicitly into the Fourteenth Amendment to the Constitution, which pronounced all Americans to be citizens not only of their several states but of the United States and forbade any state to "deprive any person of life, liberty or property without due process of law"—"due process" to be determined by authority of the national government. The new force of central authority was felt first of all in the South. President Lincoln, using his war powers, issued the Emancipation Proclamation in 1863, abolishing slavery in areas engaged in hostilities against the United States. The Thirteenth Amendment in 1865 abolished slavery everywhere in the country. No compensation was paid to the slave owners, who were therefore ruined. The legal authority of the United States was thus used for an annihilation of individual property rights without parallel (outside of modern communism) in the history of the Western world; for neither the nobility in the French Revolution, nor the Russian serf owners in 1861, nor the slave owners of the West Indies in the nineteenth century, nor the owners of businesses

[33] See p. 674.
[34] See pp. 195, 481–483.
[35] See p. 651.

nationalized by twentieth-century socialists in western Europe had to face such a total and overwhelming loss of property values as the slave owners of the American South.

After the Civil War: Reconstruction; Industrial Growth

The assassination of Lincoln in 1865 by a fanatical Southern patriot strengthened those radical Republicans who said that the South must be drastically reformed. With the old Southern upper class completely ruined, Northerners of many types poured into the defeated country. Some came to represent the federal government, some to dabble in local politics, some to make money, and a great many out of democratic and humanitarian impulses, to teach the distressed ex-slaves the elements of reading and writing or of useful trades. Blacks in the South voted, sat in legislatures, occupied public office. This period, called Reconstruction, may be compared to the most advanced phase of the French Revolution, in that "radical republicans" undertook to press liberty and equality upon a recalcitrant country, under conditions of emergency rule and under the auspices of a highly centralized national government with a mobilized army. The Southern whites strenuously objected, and the Northern radicals discredited themselves and gradually lost their zeal. Reconstruction was abandoned in the 1870s, and, by what Europeans would call a counterrevolution, the Southern whites gradually regained control.

The Northern business interests—financiers, bankers, company promoters, railway builders, manufacturers—expanded greatly with the wartime demand for munitions and military provisioning. They received protection by the Morrill tariff of 1861. In the next year, partly as a war measure, the Union Pacific Railroad was incorporated, and in 1869, at a remote spot in Utah, the last spike was driven in the first railroad to span the American continent. The Homestead Act, providing farms to settlers on easy conditions, and the granting of public lands to certain colleges (ever since called "land-grant colleges"), largely for the promotion of agricultural sciences, encouraged the push of population and civilization into the West. Vast tracts of land were given by the government to subsidize railway building. With the destruction of the Southern slaveholders, who before the war had counterbalanced the rising indusrialists, it was now industry and finance that dominated national politics in the increasingly centralized United States. The Fourteenth Amendment, for many years, was mainly interpreted not to protect the civil rights of individual persons, but the property rights of business corporations against restrictive legislation by the states. The shift of political power from the states to the federal government accompanied and protected the shift of economic enterprise from local businesses to far-flung and continent-embracing corporations. As in France under Napoleon III, there was a good deal of corruption, fraud, speculation, and dishonestly or rapaciously acquired wealth; but industry boomed, the cities grew, and the American mass market was created. On Fifth Avenue in New York, and in other Northern cities, rose the pretentious and gaudy mansions of the excessively rich.

In short, the American Civil War, which might have reduced English-speaking America to a scramble of jealously competing minor republics, resulted instead in the economic and political consolidation of a large nation-state, liberal and democratic in its political principles, and committed enthusiastically to private enterprise in its economic system.

69. The Dominion of Canada, 1867

North of the United States, at the time of the Civil War, lay a number of British provinces unconnected with one another, and each in varying degree dependent on Great Britain. The population had originated in three great streams. One part was French, settled in the St. Lawrence valley since the seventeenth century. A second part was made up of descendants of United Empire Loyalists, old seaboard colonists who, remaining faithful to Britain, had fled from the United States during the American Revolution.[36] They were numerous in the Maritime Provinces and in Upper Canada, as Ontario was then called.[37] A third part consisted of recent immigrants from Great Britain, men and women of the working classes who had left the home country to improve themselves in America.

The French firmly resisted assimilation to the English-speaking world around them. Their statute of freedom was the Quebec Act of 1774, which had been denounced as "intolerable" by the aroused inhabitants of the Thirteen Colonies, but which put the French civil law, French language, and French Catholic church under the protection of the British Crown.[38] The French looked with apprehension upon the stream of immigrants, English-speaking and Protestant, which began to flow into Canada about 1780 and thereafter never stopped. There was constant irritation between the two nationalities.

The British government tried various expedients. In 1791 it created two provinces in the St. Lawrence and Great Lakes region—a Lower Canada to remain French, and an Upper Canada to be English. They received the same form of government as that enjoyed by the Thirteen Colonies before their break from the empire. Each colony, that is, had a locally elected assembly with certain powers of taxation and lawmaking, subject to veto by the British authorities, as represented either by the governor or by the London government itself. For many years there was no objection to these arrangements. The War of 1812, in which the United States embarked on the conquest of Canada, aroused a national sentiment among both French and English in that country, together with a willingness to depend politically upon Great Britain for military security. But the internal political differences continued. In Lower Canada the French feared the English-speaking minority. In Upper Canada the old aristocracy of United Empire Loyalists, who had carved the province from the wilderness, hesitated to share control with the new immigrants from Great Britain. Between the provinces there were grievances also, since Lower Canada stood in the way of Upper Canada's outlet to the sea. In 1837 a superficial rebellion broke out in both provinces. It was put down virtually without bloodshed.

[36] See p. 356.
[37] See map, p. 549.
[38] See p. 354.

Lord Durham's Report

In Great Britain at this time the reforming Whigs were busily renovating many ancient English institutions.[39] Some of them had definite views on the administration of colonies. In general, they held that it was not necessary to control a region politically in order to trade with it. This was an aspect of the free trade doctrine, separating economics from politics, business from power. The Whig reformers were rather indifferent to empire, unconcerned with military, naval, or strategic considerations. A few even thought it natural for colonies, when mature, to drop away entirely from the mother country. Whigs, liberals, and radicals all wished to economize on military expenditure, to relieve British taxpayers by cutting down British garrisons overseas.

After the Canadian insurrection of 1837 the Whig government sent out the Earl of Durham as governor. Durham, one of the framers of the parliamentary Reform Bill of 1832, published his views on Canadian affairs in 1839. Durham's Report was long regarded as one of the classic documents in the rise of the British Commonwealth of Nations. He held that in the long run French separatist feeling in Canada should be extinguished and all Canadians brought to feel a common citizenship and national character. He therefore called for the reuniting of the two Canadas into one province. To consolidate this province he proposed an intensive development of railways and canals. In political matters he urged the granting of virtual self-government for Canada and the introduction of the British system of "responsible government," in which the elected assembly should control the executive ministers in the province, the governor becoming a kind of legal and ceremonial figure like the sovereign in Great Britain.

Most of Durham's Report was accepted immediately. Upper and Lower Canada were combined into one province, with the machinery of self-government, in 1840. The British army was withdrawn. The Canadians undertook to maintain their own military establishment, still regarded as necessary, since the era of the famous undefended frontier between Canada and the United States had not yet dawned. The Webster-Ashburton treaty of 1842 put an end to the long dispute over the Maine border. But as late as 1866 the Canadians had to repel armed invaders from the United States, when several hundred Irish Americans, members of the Fenians, an Irish republican secret society, staged an insurrectionary attempt to detach Canada from the British Empire. Local Canadian forces proved sufficient to meet this threat.

The principle of responsible government was established in the late 1840s, the governors of Canada allowing the elected assembly to adopt policies and appoint or remove ministers as it chose. Responsible government, still confined to internal matters, worked satisfactorily from the beginning. But one feature of the new plan, the union of the two Canadas, began to produce friction as the English-speaking immigration continued. The French were afraid of being outnumbered in their own country. Many Canadians therefore turned to the idea of a federation, in which the French and English areas might each conduct its own local affairs, while remaining joined for larger purposes in a central government.

[39] See pp. 489–495.

Founding of the Dominion of Canada

Federalism in Canada was thus partly a decentralizing idea, aimed at satisfying the French element by a redivision into two provinces, and in part a plan for a new centralization or unification, because it contemplated bringing all the provinces of British North America into union with the St. Lawrence and Great Lakes region, to which alone the term Canada had hitherto been applied. While the people of British North America discussed federation the Civil War was disrupting the United States. In the face of this unpleasant example, the Canadians formed a strong union in which all powers were to rest in the central government except those specifically assigned to the provinces. The federal constitution, drafted in Canada by Canadians, was passed through the British Parliament in 1867 as the British North America Act, which constitutionally established the Dominion of Canada. In 1982 the British North America Act was replaced by new arrangements, which explicitly recognized the sovereign independence of Canada and its power to frame a constitution for itself. By the 1980s, however, the French speakers of Quebec had entered more fully into the modern world, and it was again necessary to recognize a special status for Quebec. The western provinces had also matured. The relationship between the central and provincial governments, along with bilingualism, or the equal recognition of the French and English languages, again became serious problems.

By the legislation of 1867 the new dominion received a common federal parliament, in which a ministry responsible to the majority in parliament governed according to British principles of "responsible," or cabinet, government. The original provinces were Quebec and Ontario, formed from the old Canada, plus the maritime provinces of Nova Scotia, New Brunswick, and Prince Edward Island, which joined the dominion in 1867 on the understanding that a railroad would be built to connect them with Quebec City and Montreal. The old Hudson's Bay Company, founded in 1670, transferred its rights of government over the vast Northwest to the dominion in 1869. From these territories the province of Manitoba was created in 1870 and British Columbia in 1871. To link them solidly with the rest of the dominion the Canadian Pacific Railway was completed in 1885. It made possible the development of the prairies, where the provinces of Saskatchewan and Alberta were added in 1905.

The Dominion of Canada, though at first not large in population, possessed from the beginning a significance beyond the mere number of its people. It was the first example of successful devolution, or granting of political liberty, within one of the European colonial empires. It embodied principles which Edmund Burke and Benjamin Franklin had vainly recommended a century before to keep the Thirteen Colonies loyal to Great Britain. The dominion after 1867 moved forward from independence in internal matters to independence in such external affairs as tariffs, diplomacy, and the decisions of war and peace. It thus pioneered in the development of "dominion status," working out precedents later applied in Australia (1901), New Zealand (1907), the Union of South Africa (1910), and in the 1920s, temporarily, in Ireland. By the middle of the twentieth century the same idea, or what may be called the Canadian idea, was even applied to the worldwide problem of colonialism as it affected non-European peoples, notably in India, Pakistan, Sri Lanka, and the former British colonies in Africa, until all these peoples chose to become republics, though still loosely and voluntarily joined together and to Great Britain in a Commonwealth of Nations.

More immediately, in America, the founding of the dominion, a solid band of self-governing territory stretching from ocean to ocean, stabilized the relations between British North America and the United States. The United States regarded its northern borders as final. The withdrawal of British control from Canadian affairs furthered the United States conception of an American continent entirely free from European political influence.

70. Japan and the West

The Japanese, when they allowed the Westerners to discover them, were a highly civilized people living in a complex society. They had many large cities, they enjoyed the contemplation of natural scenery, they went to the theater, and they read novels. With their stylized manners, their fans and their wooden temples, their lacquer work and their painting on screens, their tiny rice fields and their curious and ineffectual firearms, they seemed to Europeans to be the very acme of everything quaint. This feeling is immortalized in *The Mikado* of Gilbert and Sullivan, first performed in 1885. Not long thereafter the idea of Japanese quaintness, like the idea of the Germans as an impractical people given mainly to music and metaphysics, had to be revised. The Europeans, in "opening" Japan, opened up more than they knew.

In 1853, the American Commodore Perry forced his way with a fleet of naval vessels into Yedo Bay, insisted upon landing, and demanded of the Japanese government, somewhat peremptorily, that it engage in commercial relations with the United States and other Western powers. In the next year the Japanese began to comply, and in 1867 an internal revolution took place, of which the most conspicuous consequence was a rapid westernizing of Japanese life and institutions. But if it looked as if the country had been "opened" by Westerners, actually Japan had exploded from within.

Background: Two Centuries of Isolation, 1640–1854

For over two centuries Japan had followed a program of self-imposed isolation. No Japanese was allowed to leave the islands or even to build a ship large enough to navigate the high seas. No foreigner, except for handfuls of Dutch and Chinese, was allowed to enter. Japan remained a sealed book to the West. The contrary is not quite so true, for the Japanese knew rather more about Europe than Europeans did about Japan. The Japanese policy of seclusion was not merely based upon ignorance. Initially, at least, it was based on experience.

The first Europeans—three Portuguese in a Chinese junk—are thought to have arrived in Japan in 1542. For about a century thereafter there was considerable coming and going. The Japanese showed a strong desire to trade with the foreigners, from whom they obtained clocks and maps, learned about printing and shipbuilding, and took over the use of tobacco and potatoes. Thousands also adopted the Christian religion as preached to them by Spanish and Portuguese Jesuits. Japanese traveled to the Dutch Indies and even to Europe. The Japanese in fact proved more receptive to European ideas than other Asian peoples. But shortly after 1600 the government began to drive Christianity underground; in 1624 it expelled the Spaniards, in 1639 the Portuguese, and in 1640 all Europeans except for a few Dutch merchants who were allowed to remain at Nagasaki under strict control. From 1640 to 1854 these few Dutch at Nagasaki were the only channel of communication with the West.[40]

The reasons for self-seclusion, as for its abandonment later, arose from the course of political events in Japan. The history of Japan showed an odd parallel to that of Europe. In Japan, as in Europe, a period of feudal warfare was followed by a period of government absolutism, during which civil peace was kept by a bureaucracy, an obsolescent warrier class was maintained as a privileged element in society, and a commercial class of native merchants grew wealthier, stronger, and more insistent upon its position.

When the first Europeans arrived, the islands were still torn by the wars and rivalries of the numerous clans into which the Japanese were organized. Gradually one clan, the Tokugawa, gained control, taking over the office of "shogun." The shogun was a kind of military head who governed in the name of the emperor, and the hereditary Tokugawa shogunate, founded in 1603, lasted until 1867. The early Tokugawa shoguns concluded from a good deal of evidence that the Europeans in Japan, both merchants and missionaries, were engaging in feudal or interclan politics and even aspiring to dominate Japan by helping Christian or pro-European Japanese to get into power. The first three Tokugawa shoguns, to establish their own dynasty, to pacify and stabilize the country, and to keep Japan free from European penetration, undertook to exterminate Christianity and adopted the rigid policy of nonintercourse with the rest of the world.

Under the Tokugawa Japan enjoyed peace, a long peace, for the first time in centuries. The Tokugawa shoguns completed the detachment of the emperor from politics, building him up as a divine and legendary being, too august and too remote for the hurly-burly of the world. The emperor remained shut in at Kyoto on a modest allowance furnished by the shoguns. The shoguns established their own court and government at Yedo (later called Tokyo); and as Louis XIV brought nobles to Versailles, or Peter the Great forced his uncouth lords to build town houses in St. Petersburg, so the shoguns required the great feudal chieftains and their men-at-arms to reside at least part of the year in Yedo.

The shoguns administered the country through a kind of military bureaucracy or dictatorship. This formidable instrument of state watched over the great lords (called daimyo), who, however, retained a good deal of feudal authority over their subjects in the regions most distant from Yedo. The great lords and their armed retainers (the samurai), having no further fighting to occupy them, turned into a landed aristocracy which spent a good deal of its time in Yedo and other cities. As a leisure class, they developed new tastes and standards of living and hence needed more income, which they obtained by squeezing the peasants, and which they spent by buying from the merchants.

The merchant class greatly expanded by catering to the government and the gentry. Japan in the seventeenth century passed on to a money economy. Many lords fell seriously into debt to the merchants. Many samurai, like lesser nobles

[40] See p. 166.

in France or Poland at the time, were almost ridiculously impoverished, hard-pressed to keep up appearances, with nothing except social status to distinguish them from commoners. The law, as in Europe under the Old Regime, drew a sharp line between classes. Nobles, merchants, and peasants were subject to different taxes and were differently punished for different offenses. What was a crime for a commoner would be excusable for a samurai; or what in a samurai would be a punishable breach of honor would be accepted in a common person. The samurai had the right to carry two swords as a mark of class and could in theory cut down an impudent commoner without arousing further inquiry. In practice the shoguns repressed violence of this kind, but there was much less development of law and justice than in the European monarchies of the Old Regime. Economically the merchants and artisans prospered. By 1723 Yedo was a city with 500,000 people; by 1800 with over 1,000,000, it was larger than London or Paris, and twenty times as large as the largest city in the United States. After 1800 some merchants were able to purchase the rank of samurai for money. The old class lines were beginning to blur.

Though deliberately secluded, the economic and social life of Japan was thus by no means static. The same is true of its intellectual life. Buddhism, the historic religion, lost its hold on many people during the Tokugawa period, so that Japan in its way underwent, like the West, a "secularization" of ideas. As a code of personal conduct there was a new emphasis on Bushido, the "way of the warrior," a kind of nonreligious moral teaching which exalted the samurai virtues of honor and loyalty. With the decline of Buddhism went also a revival of the cult of Shinto, the "way of the gods," the ancient indigenous religion of Japan, which held, among much else, that the emperor was veritably the Son of Heaven. There was much activity in the study and writing of history, arousing, as in Europe, an acute interest in the national past. History, like Shinto, led to a feeling that shoguns were usurpers and that the emperor, obscurely relegated to Kyoto, was the true representative of everything highest and most lasting in the life of Japan.

Meanwhile, through the crack left open at Nagasaki, Western ideas trickled in. The shogun Yoshimune in the mid–eighteenth century permitted the importation of Occidental books, except those relating to Christianity. A few Japanese learned Dutch and began to decipher Dutch books on anatomy, surgery, astronomy, and other subjects. In 1745 a Dutch-Japanese dictionary was completed. For European manufactures also—watches, glassware, velvets, woolens, telescopes, barom-eters—there came to be an eager demand, satisfied as much as possible by the methodical Dutch. Nor were the Japanese wholly uninformed about politics in the West. While the most assiduous Westerner could learn nothing of the internal affairs of Japan, an educated Japanese could, if he wished, arrive at some idea of the French Revolution, or know who was president of the United States.

The Opening of Japan

When Perry in 1853 made his unwanted visit he therefore had many potential allies within Japan. There were nobles, heavily in debt, unable to draw more income from agriculture, willing to embark upon foreign trade and to exploit their property by introducing new enterprises. There were penurious samurai, with no future in the old system, ready and willing to enter upon new careers as army officers or civil officials. There were merchants hoping to add to their business by dealing in Western goods. There were scholars eager to learn more of Western science and medicine. There were patriots fearful that Japan was becoming defenseless against Western guns. Spiritually the country was already adrift from its moorings, already set toward a course of national self-assertion, restlessly susceptible to hazily understood new ideas. Under such pressures, and from downright fear of a bombardment of Yedo by the Americans, which if it would not subdue Japan would at least ruin the declining prestige of the shogunate, the shogun Iesada in 1854 signed a commercial treaty with the United States. Similar treaties were soon signed with the Europeans.

In the following years were sown the seeds of much later misunderstanding between Japan and the West. The whites in those days—European and American—were somewhat trigger-happy in the discharge of naval ordnance against backward peoples. The Japanese, a proud and elaborately civilized nation, soon found that the whites considered them backward. They found, for example, as soon as they learned more of the West by reading and travel, that the treaties they signed in the 1850s were not treaties between equals as understood in the West. These first treaties provided that Japan should maintain a low tariff on imports and not change it except with the consent of the foreign powers. To give outsiders a voice in determining tariff policy was not the custom among sovereign states of the West. The early treaties also provided for extraterritoriality. This meant that Europeans and Americans residing in Japan were not subject to Japanese law but remained under the jurisdiction of their respective homelands as represented by consular officials. Such extraterritorial provisions had long been established in Turkey and were currently taking root in China.[41] Europeans insisted upon them in countries where European principles of property, debt, or security of life and person did not prevail. At the same time, of course, no civilized state ever permitted a foreign power to exercise jurisdiction within its borders. Extraterritoriality was a mark of inferiority, as the Japanese soon discovered.

A strong antiforeign reaction developed after 1854. It was at first led by certain nobles of the western islands, the lords of Choshu and Satsuma, who had never been fully subordinated to the shogun at Yedo, and who now dreamed of overturning the Tokugawa shogunate and leading a national revival with the emperor as its rallying point. Their first idea was to check Western penetration (as two and a half centuries before) by driving the Westerners out. But in 1862 some Englishmen unintentionally violated a small point of Japanese etiquette. One of them was killed. The British government demanded punishment for the offending Japanese, who were followers of the lord of Satsuma. The shogun proved unable to arrange this, and the British navy thereupon itself sailed up and bombarded the capital of Satsuma. In the same year the lord of Choshu, who commanded the straits of Shimonoseki with some ancient artillery, ordered it to fire on passing vessels. The British, French, Dutch, and United States governments immediately protested, and, when the embarrassed shogun proved unable to discipline Choshu, they dispatched an allied naval force to Shimonoseki. The forts and shipping of Choshu were destroyed, and an indemnity of $3,000,000 was imposed. These incidents were remembered in Japan long after they were

[41] See pp. 220, 675.

forgotten in Europe and the United States. It was likewise remembered that the Western powers, discovering that the shogun was not the supreme ruler of the country, sent a naval expedition to Kyoto itself and required the emperor to confirm the treaties signed by the shogun and to reduce import duties, under threat of naval bombardment.

The Meiji Era (1868–1912): The Westernization of Japan

The lords of Choshu and Satsuma now concluded that the only way to deal with the West was to adopt the military and technical equipment of the West itself. They would save Japan for the Japanese by learning the secrets of the Western power. First they forced the resignation of the shogun, whose prestige had long been undermined anyway, and who had now discredited himself first by signing undesirable treaties with the West and then failing to protect the country from outrage. The last shogun abdicated in 1867. The reformers declared the emperor restored to his full authority. It was their intention to use the plenitude of imperial power to consolidate and fortify Japan for its new position in the world. In 1868 a new emperor inherited the throne; his name was Mutsuhito, but according to Japanese custom a name was given to his reign also, which was called Meiji. The Meiji era (1868–1912) was the great era of the westernization of Japan.

Japan turned into a modern national state. Feudalism was abolished, most of the great lords voluntarily surrendering into the emperor's hands their control over samurai and common people. "We abolish the clans and convert them into prefectures," declared one imperial decree. The legal system was reorganized and equality before the law introduced, in the sense that all persons became subject to the same rules regardless of class. In part with the hope of getting rid of extraterritoriality, the reformers recast the criminal law along Western lines, deleting the bizarre and cruel punishments which Europeans considered barbaric. A new army was established, modeled mainly on the Prussian. The samurai in 1871 lost his historic right to carry two swords; he now served as an army officer, not as the retainer of a clannish chief. A navy, modeled on the British, followed somewhat later. Control of money and currency passed to the central government, and a national currency, with decimal units, was adopted. A national postal service began to function and above all a national school system, which soon brought a high rate of literacy to Japan. Buddhism was discouraged, and the property of Buddhist monasteries was confiscated. Shinto was the cult favored by the government. Shinto gave a religious tincture to national sentiment and led to a renewed veneration of the imperial family. In 1889 a constitution was promulgated. It confirmed the civil liberties then common in the West and provided for a parliament in two chambers, but it stressed also the supreme and "eternal" authority of the emperor, to whom the ministers were legally responsible. In practice, in the new Japan, the emperor never actively governed. He remained aloof, as in the past; and political leaders, never fully responsible to the parliament, tended to govern freely in what they conceived to be the interests of the state.

Industrial and financial modernization went along with and even preceded the political revolution. In 1858 the first steamship was purchased from the Dutch. In 1859 Japan placed its first foreign loan, borrowing 5 million yen by a bond issue floated in England. In 1869 the first telegraph connected Yokohama and Tokyo. The first railroad, between the same two cities, was completed in 1872. In 1870 appeared the first spinning machinery. Foreign trade, almost literally zero in 1854, was valued at $200 million a year by the end of the century. The population rose from 33 million in 1872 to 46 million in 1902. The island empire, like Great Britain, became dependent on exports and imports to sustain its dense population at the level of living to which it aspired.

The westernization of Japan still stands as the most remarkable transformation ever undergone by any people in so short a time. It recalls the westernizing of Russia under Peter over a century before, though conducted somewhat less brutally, more rapidly, and with a wider consent among the population. For Japan, as formerly for Russia, the motive was in large measure defense against Western penetration, together with an admiration for Western statecraft and an ambition to become a "power."[42] What the Japanese wanted from the West was primarily science, technology, and organization. They were content enough with the innermost substance of their culture, their moral ideas, their family life, their arts and amusements, their religious conceptions, though even in these they showed an uncommon adaptability. Essentially it was to protect their internal substance, their Japanese culture, that they took over the external apparatus of Western civilization. This apparatus—science, technology, machinery, arms, political and legal organization—was the part of Western civilization for which other peoples generally felt a need, which they hoped to adopt without losing their own spiritual independence, and which therefore, though sometimes rather scornfully dismissed as materialistic, became the common ground for the interdependent worldwide civilization that emerged at the close of the nineteenth century.

In brief, to conclude a long chapter, the world between 1850 and 1870, revolutionized economically by the railroad and steamship, was revolutionized politically by the formation of large and consolidated nation-states. These states at the time all embodied certain liberal and constitutional principles, or at least the machinery of parliamentary and representative government. But the whole earth had also become an arena in which certain mighty beings, called nations or powers, were to act. The Great Powers in 1871 were Great Britain, Germany, France, Austria-Hungary, and Russia. Britain had produced a daughter nation in Canada. Whether Italy was to be called a Great Power was not yet clear. No one knew what Japan would do. All agreed that the United States would one day play a large role in international politics, but the time was not yet.

[42] See pp. 234–245.

XIV.
EUROPEAN
CIVILIZATION,
1871–1914

HALF A CENTURY elapsed between the period of national consolidation described in the last chapter and the outbreak of the First World War in 1914. In this half-century Europe in many ways reached the climax of the modern phase of its civilization, and also exerted its maximum influence upon peoples outside Europe. The present chapter will attempt a description of European civilization in these years, the next chapter an account of the worldwide ascendancy which Europe enjoyed at this time.

For Europe and the European world the years 1871 to 1914 were marked by hitherto unparalleled material and industrial growth, international peace, domestic stability, the advance of constitutional, representative, and democratic government, and continued faith in science, reason, and progress. But in these very years, in politics, economics, and basic thinking there were forces operating to undermine the liberal premises and tenets of this European civilization. Most of the present chapter will be devoted to the continuing triumphs of liberalism, but the signs of its transformation and wane will be pointed out too.

Chapter Emblem: A painting called The Last of England *dated 1852, by Ford Madox Brown, showing two emigrants looking back from their departing ship.*

71. The "Civilized World"

Materialistic and Nonmaterialistic Ideals

With the extension of the nation-state system Europe was politically more divided than ever. Its unity lay in the sharing by all Europeans of a similar way of life and outlook, which existed also in such "European" countries as the United States, Canada, Australia, and New Zealand. Europe and its offshoots constituted the "civilized world." Other regions—mostly in Asia, Africa, and Latin America—were said to be "backward." (They are today referred to as "developing" or "less developed.") Europeans were extremely conscious and inordinately proud of their civilization in the half-century before 1914. They believed it to be the well-deserved outcome of centuries of progress. Feeling themselves to be the most advanced branch of mankind in the important areas of human endeavor, they assumed that all peoples should respect the same social ideals—that so far as they were unwilling or unable to adopt them they were backward, and that so far as they did adopt them they became civilized in their turn.

These ideals of civilization were in part materialistic. If Europeans considered their civilization to be better in 1900 than in 1800, or better in 1900 than the ways of non-Europeans at the same time, it was because they had a higher standard of living, ate and dressed more adequately, slept in softer beds, and had more satisfactory sanitary facilities. It was because they possessed ocean liners, railroads, and streetcars, and after about 1880 telephones and electric lights. But the ideal of civilization was by no means exclusively materialistic. Knowledge as such, correct or truthful knowledge, was held to be a civilized attainment—scientific knowledge of nature, in place of superstition or demonology; geographical knowledge, by which civilized people were aware of the earth as a whole with its general contours and diverse inhabitants. The ideal was also profoundly moral, derived from Christianity, but now secularized and detached from religion. An Englishman, Isaac Taylor, in his *Ultimate Civilization* published in 1860, defined this moral ideal by listing the contrasting "relics of barbarism" which he thought were due to disappear—"Polygamy, Infanticide, Legalized Prostitution, Capricious Divorce, Sanguinary and Immoral Games, Infliction of Torture, Caste and Slavery." The first four of these had been unknown to the approved customs of Europe at least since the coming of Christianity. Torture went out of use about

TRAIN IN THE SNOW
by Claude Monet (French, 1840–1926)
With the Impressionists, and notably with Claude Monet, some of the conventions of Western painting since the Renaissance began to fade. Emphasis shifted from the representation of objects to the perception of them as experienced through the eye. Solid masses melted into the play of light under a variety of atmospheric conditions. The railway age, which developed rapidly in Monet's youth, furnished many subjects to excite his imagination. In this picture the solid iron of the locomotive merges into the indeterminate grays of a dull day in winter. The chill and the low visibility are conveyed as much as the visual images themselves. Courtesy of the Musée Marmottan, Paris (Giraudon). Permission S.P.A.D.E.M. 1970 by French Reproduction Rights, Inc.

1800, even in the illiberal European states, and legalized caste and slavery in the course of the nineteenth century. But there were few non-European peoples, in 1860, among whom two or three of Taylor's "relics" could not be found.

There are certain other indices, more purely quantitative, worked out by sociologists to show the level of advancement of a given society. One of these is the death rate, or number of persons per thousand of population who die each year. In England, France, and Sweden the "true" death rate (or death rate regardless of the proportion of infants and old people, who are most susceptible to death) is known to have fallen from about 25 (per 1,000 per year) before 1850, to 19 in 1914 and 18 in the 1930s. Indeed, before the Second World War, it stood seemingly stabilized at about 18 in all countries of northwestern Europe, the United States, and the British dominions. Death rates in countries not "modern" run over 40 even in favorable times. A closely related index is infant mortality, which fell rapidly after 1870 in all countries affected by medical science. Thus a woman under civilized conditions had to go through pregnancy and childbirth less often to produce the same number of surviving children. Another index is life expectancy, or the number of years of age which a person has an even chance of attaining. In England life expectancy at birth rose from 40 years in the 1840s to 59 in 1933 and 73 in 1980. In India in 1931 it was less than 27 years. It had risen to about 50 in the 1980s. Still another index is the literacy rate, or proportion of persons above a certain age (such as ten) able to read and write. In northwestern Europe by 1900 the literacy rate approached 100. In some countries it still does not rise very far above zero. A further basic index is the productivity of labor, or amount produced by one worker in a given expenditure of time. This is difficult to compute, especially for earlier periods for which statistical data are lacking. In the 1930s, however, the productivity of a farmer in Denmark was over ten times that of a farmer in Albania. All northwestern Europe was above the European average in this respect with the exception of Ireland, whereas Ireland, Spain, Portugal, Italy, and all eastern Europe were below it.

The essence of civilized living doubtless is in the intangibles, in the way in which people use their minds, and in the attitudes they form toward others or toward the conduct and planning of their own lives. The intangibles, however, are not always agreed upon by persons of different culture or ideology. On the quantitative criteria there is less disagreement; all, with few exceptions, wish to lower the death rate, raise the literacy rate, and increase the productivity of human exertion. Even if we apply quantitative or sociological indices alone, we can say that after 1870 there was in fact, and not merely in the opinion of Europeans, a civilized world of which Europe was the center.

The "Zones" of Civilization

Or rather, a certain region of Europe was the center. For there were really two Europes, an inner zone and an outer. A Frenchman writing in the 1920s, describing the two Europes that had risen since 1870, called the inner zone the "Europe of steam," and bounded it by an imaginary line joining Glasgow, Stockholm, Danzig, Trieste, Florence, and Barcelona. It included not only Great Britain but Belgium, Germany, France, northern Italy, and the western portions of the Austrian Empire. Virtually all heavy European industry was located in this zone. Here the railway network was thickest. Here was concentrated the wealth of Europe, in the form both of a high living standard and of accumulations of capital. Here likewise were almost all the laboratories and all the scientific activity of Europe. Here, in the same zone, lay the strength of constitutional and parliamentary government and of liberal, humanitarian, socialist, and reformist movements of many kinds. In this zone the death rate was low, life expectancy high, conditions of health and sanitation at their best, literacy almost universal, productivity of labor very great. To the same zone, for practical purposes, belonged certain regions of European settlement overseas, especially the northeastern part of the United States.

The "outer zone" included most of Ireland, most of the Iberian and Italian peninsulas, and all Europe east of what was then Germany, Bohemia, and Austria proper. The outer zone was agricultural, though the productivity of agriculture, per farm worker or per acre, was far less than in the inner zone. The people were poorer, more illiterate, and more likely to die young. The wealthy were landlords, often absentees. The zone lived increasingly after 1870 by selling grain, livestock, wool, or lumber to the more industrialized inner zone but was too poor to purchase many manufactured products in return. To obtain capital it borrowed in London or Paris. Its social and political philosophies were characteristically imported from Germany and the West. It borrowed engineers and technicians from the first zone to build its bridges and install its telegraph systems and sent its youth to universities in the first zone to study medicine or other professions. Many areas of European settlement overseas, for example in Latin America and the southern part of the United States, may also be thought of as belonging to this outer zone.

Beyond the European world lay a third zone, the immense reaches of Asia and Africa, all "backward" by the standards of Europe, with the exception of the recently Europeanized Japan, and all destined, with the exception of Japan, to become heavily dependent upon Europe in the half-century after 1870. Much of the world's history since 1870 could be written as the story of relations among these three zones; but it is necessary in all human things to guard against formulas that are too simple.

72. Basic Demography: The Increase of the Europeans

European and World Population Growth since 1650

All continents except Africa gained enormously in population in the three centuries following 1650, but it was Europe that grew the most. There is little doubt that the proportion of Europeans in the world's total, including those of European origin in other continents, reached its maximum for all time between 1850 and the Second World War. Estimates are given in the table on p. 588, beginning with 1650.

The causes of the rise in population after 1650 cannot be positively known. Some of them must obviously have operated in Asia as well as Europe. In Europe the organized sovereign states, as established in the seventeenth century, put an

ESTIMATED POPULATION OF THE WORLD BY CONTINENTAL AREAS*

	Millions					
	1650	*1750*	*1850*	*1900*	*1950*	*1990*
Europe	100	150	263	396	532	726
United States and Canada	1	2	26	82	166	278
Australasia-Oceania	2	2	2	6	13	27
Predominantly "European"	103	154	291	484	711	1031
Latin America	12	16	38	74	162	445
Africa	100	106	111	133	217	646
Asia	330	515	822	959	1396	3158
Predominantly "Non-European"	442	637	971	1166	1775	4249
World Total	545	791	1262	1650	2486	5280

	Percentages					
Europe	18.3	19.1	20.8	24.0	21.5	13.8
United States and Canada	.2	.2	2.1	5.0	6.7	5.3
Australasia-Oceania	.4	.2	.2	.3	.5	.5
Predominantly "European"	18.9	19.5	23.1	29.3	28.7	19.6
Latin America	2.2	2.0	3.0	4.5	6.5	8.4
Africa	18.3	13.0	8.8	8.1	8.7	12.2
Asia	60.6	65.0	65.1	58.1	56.1	59.8
Predominantly "Non-European"	81.1	80.5	76.9	70.7	71.3	80.4
World Total	100.0	100.0	100.0	100.0	100.0	100.0

* This table is designed only to show the numbers and proportion of Europeans and persons of European descent in world population over the modern period. It reveals the rapid increase in the proportion of "Europeans" in this sense from 1750 to 1900, and its significant decline in the twentieth century, until by 1990 the proportion is about as it was in 1750. The table is subject to serious reservations. The population of the Soviet Union is divided between Europe and Asia, but millions of Europeans (i.e., Russians) have long lived in the Asian parts of the U.S.S.R. It must be remembered also that the population of the United States has always been of both European and African descent, that the Latin American countries differ widely in their racial composition, and that there are over 4 million persons of European origin in South Africa. In short, the table has nothing to do with race, for there are many whites, notably in the Middle East, who are not European, and many nonwhites in the Americas and elsewhere who participate fully in the kind of civilization derived from Europe.

For world population in the twentieth century, see also p. 1037 below. For particular countries, see Appendix III. SOURCE: For 1650 to 1900, A. N. Carr-Sanders, *World Population* (Oxford: Oxford University Press, 1936); for 1750, 1850 and 1900, John D. Durand, "The Modern Expansion of World Population," in *Proceedings of the American Philosophical Society*, vol. 111 (1967); and for 1950 and 1990 the *United Nations Demographic Yearbook* and *World Population Prospects*, published by the United Nations, New York, 1989.

end to a long period of civil wars, stopping the chronic violence and marauding, with the accompanying insecurity of agriculture and family life, which were more deadly than wars fought between governments. Similarly, the Tokugawa kept peace in Japan, and the Manchu or Ch'ing dynasty brought a long period of order in China. The British rule in India and the Dutch in Java, by curbing famine and violence, allowed populations to mount very rapidly. All such factors, which allowed more people to remain alive longer, also favored the stability of families and the birth and raising of children. Death rates could fall and birth rates could rise from similar causes. The great exception to the swelling rise of population was Africa, where the slave trade removed over 10 million people in three or four centuries, and where slave raiding led to the disruption of African cultures. In the Americas the native Indians were devastated by diseases brought from Europe to which at first they had no immunity.

In Europe, sooner than elsewhere, other causes of growth were at work beyond the maintenance of civil peace. They included liberation from certain endemic afflictions, beginning with the subsiding of bubonic plague in the seventeenth century and the use of vaccination against smallpox in the eighteenth. Agricultural improvement produced more food, notably in England about 1750. The improvement of transportation, by road, canal, and railroad, made localized famine a thing of the past, since food could be moved into areas of temporary shortage. With the Industrial Revolution larger populations could subsist in Europe by importing food from overseas. In the cities of Europe and North America, by 1900, the supply of pure drinking water and facilities for the disposal of garbage and sewage were better than in the past.

Hence population grew for several generations more substantially in Europe and its offshoots than elsewhere. Approximate percentages are given in the table. Asia, by these estimates, increased less than threefold between 1650 and 1900, but Europe increased fourfold, and the total number of Europeans, including the descendants of those who migrated to other continents, multiplied fivefold. The ascendancy of European civilization in the two and a half centuries after 1650, was due in some measure to merely demographic growth. But while in 1900 the proportion of "Europeans" in all continents was approaching a third of the human race, after 1900 this proportion began to fall. In the 1990s it could be projected that "Europeans" would constitute only a tenth of the human beings on the planet in the year 2100.

Stabilization of European Population

Stabilization and relative decline of European population followed from a fall in the birth rate. As early as 1830 the birth rate began noticeably to drop in France, with the result that France, long the most populous European state, was surpassed in population by Germany about 1870, by the British Isles about 1895, and by Italy about 1930. France, once thought to be decadent for this reason, was in fact only the leading country in a population cycle through which the European countries seemed to pass. The birth rate, which had fallen below 30 per 1,000 in France in the 1830s, fell to that level in Sweden in the 1880s, in England in the 1890s, and in Germany, Bohemia, and the Netherlands between 1900 and 1910. After the Second World War there was a temporary rise, but by 1990 the birth rate was only 15 per 1,000 or less in Europe and North America, hardly sufficient to maintain existing population levels. In most of the rest of the world, except China, it was still well over 30.

The reduced birth rate is not a mere dry statistical item, nor does it affect populations merely in the mass. It is one of the indices of modern civilization, first appearing in that inner European zone in which the other indices were also highest, and thence spreading outward in a kind of wave. Concretely, a low birth rate in the nineteenth century meant that families averaged from two to four children, where in former times, or today under conditions not "modern," families are commonly found to consist of ten children or even more. The low birth rate means the small family system, than which few things are more fundamental to modern life. The principal means used to hold down the birth rate, or to limit the family, is the practice of contraception. But the true causes, or reasons why parents wish to limit their families, are deeply embedded in the codes of modern society.

Historical demographers have detected a "European family pattern" as far back as the seventeenth century. It was a pattern in which, in comparison to other societies, Europeans married later, and a larger number never married at all. Late marriage shortened the number of years during which a woman bore children, and enabled young people to acquire skills or accumulate savings (as in tools and household goods) before setting up new families. The effect was a less explosive population growth, and less extreme poverty, than occurred in some other parts of the world. Evidence indicating the practice of contraception can be found in the eighteenth century among the upper classes, by study of the number and spacing of their children. The practice seems to have spread to other social classes during the French Revolution. The Code Napoleon then required that inheritances be divided among all sons and daughters. The French peasants, many of them owners of land, began to limit themselves to two or three children, in order that all children (by inheritance, marriage, and dowries) might remain in as high an economic and social position as their parents. It was thus economic security and the possession of a social standard that led to the reduced birth rate in France.

In the great cities of the nineteenth century, in which standards of life for the working classes often collapsed, the effect might at first be a proliferation of offspring. But life in the city, under crowded conditions of housing, also set a premium on the small family. There were many activities in the city that people with many children could only with difficulty enjoy. After about 1880 child labor became much less frequent among the working classes. When children ceased to earn part of the family income parents tended to have fewer of them. About the same time governments in the advanced countries began to require universal compulsory schooling. The number of years spent in education, and hence in economic dependency upon parents, grew longer and longer, until it became common even for young adults to be still engaged in study. Each child represented many years of expense for its parents. The ever rising idea of what it was necessary to do for one's children, and the desire of parents to give them every possible advantage in a competitive world, were probably the most basic causes of voluntary limitation of the family. Hardly less basic was the desire to lighten the burdens upon mothers. The small family system, together with the decline of infant mortality, since they combined to free women from the interminable bearing and tending of infants, probably did more than anything else to improve the position of civilized women.

But the effects of the small family system upon total population became manifest only slowly. More people lived on into the middle and older age groups, and the fall of the birth rate was gradual, so that in all the leading countries total numbers continued to rise, except in France, which hardly grew between 1900 and 1945. The persistent note was one of superabundant increase. In five generations, between 1800 and 1950, some 200 million "Europeans" grew into 700 million. Since productivity increased even more rapidly, the standard of living for most of these "Europeans" rose in spite of the increase of numbers, and there was no general problem of overpopulation.

Growth of Cities and Urban Life

Where did so many people go? Some stayed in the rural areas where most people had always lived. Rural populations in the "inner zone" became more dense, turning to the more intensive agriculture of truck gardening or dairy farming, leaving products like wool and cereal grains to be raised elsewhere and then imported. But it is estimated that of every seven persons added to the western European population only one stayed on the land. Of the other six, one left Europe altogether and five went to the growing cities.[1]

The nineteenth-century city was mostly the child of the railroad, for with the railroads it became possible for the first time to concentrate manufacturing in large towns, to which bulky goods such as foods and fuel could now be moved in great volume. The growth of cities between 1850 and 1914 was phenomenal. In England two-thirds of the people lived in places of 20,000 or less in 1830; in 1914 two-thirds lived in places of 20,000 or more. Germany, the historic land of archaic towns carried over from the Middle Ages, rivaled England after 1870 in modern industrial urbanization. Whereas in 1840 only London and Paris had a million people, the same could be said by 1914 of Berlin, Vienna, St. Petersburg, and Moscow.[2] Some places, like the English Midlands and the Ruhr valley in Germany, became a mass of contiguous smaller cities, vast urban agglomerations divided only by municipal lines.

The great city set the tone of modern society. City life was impersonal and anonymous; people were uprooted, less tied to home or church than in the country. They lacked the country person's feeling of deference for aristocratic families. They lacked the sense of self-help characteristic of older rural communities. It was in the city that the daily newspaper press, which spread rapidly in the wake of the telegraph after 1850, found its most habitual readers. The so-called yellow or sensational press appeared about 1900. Articulate public opinion was formed in the cities, and city people were on the whole disrespectful of tradition, receptive to new ideas, having in many cases deliberately altered their own lives by moving from the country or from smaller towns. That socialism spread among the industrial masses of European cities is hardly surprising. It is less often realized that some of the more blatant nationalism that arose after 1870 was stimulated by city life, for people felt increasingly detached from all institutions except the state. At the same time city life, by its greater facilities for schooling, reading, and discussion, made for a more alert and informed public opinion of an enlightened kind.

---

[1] See Appendix III for the growth of cities and the map on p. 460 for England.
[2] And, outside Europe, of New York, Chicago, Philadelphia, Rio de Janeiro, Buenos Aires, Calcutta, Tokyo, and Osaka.

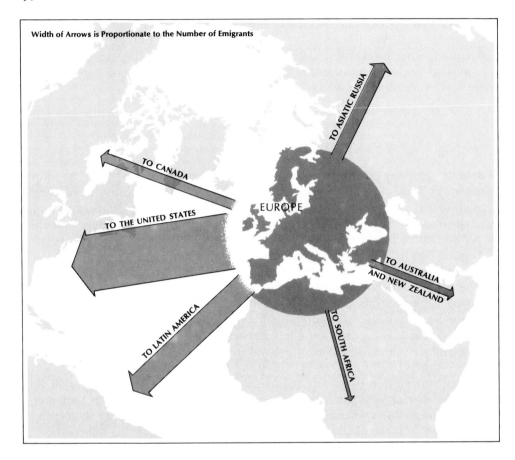

Width of Arrows is Proportionate to the Number of Emigrants

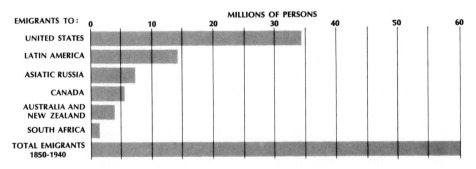

MIGRATION FROM EUROPE, 1850–1940

About 60 million people left Europe in the century preceding the Second World War, distributing themselves as shown in the diagram above. (See figures on p. 593.) About half went to the United States. This huge wave of settlement built up, outside of Europe, populous "European" countries which produced foods and raw materials for Europe and borrowed capital and bought manufactures from Europe, thus helping to support the increasingly dense European population and to build up a worldwide economic system.

Migration from Europe, 1850–1940

During the same period in which cities were growing, almost 60 million people left Europe altogether, of whom possibly a fifth sooner or later returned. The Atlantic Migration—aptly so called, because all crossed the ocean except those who moved from European to Asiatic Russia—towers above all others in magnitude, and possibly also in significance, for it was by this means that earlier colonial offshoots of Europe were transformed into new Europes alongside the old. All parts of Europe contributed, as shown in the table below, which comprises the years from 1850 to 1940. Before 1850 the mass movement had scarcely begun, though at that time over a million immigrants had entered the United States since the close of the Napoleonic wars. After 1940 the character of intercontinental migration was greatly transformed.

It is hard to give satisfactory figures for emigration from Europe. In the statistical sources the English, Scots, Welsh, and Irish are mixed, and until the First World War, that is until 1914, the Poles, Czechs, Yugoslavs, Hungarians, East European Jews, and others were included among emigrants from the Russian, Austro-Hungarian, and German empires. Millions of Jews, Irish, Poles, and many thousands of others are therefore invisible in the figures below, which also include several million Russians who moved from European to Asian parts of what is now the Soviet Union. It must be remembered also that some intercontinental migration did not involve Europeans. For a few years after 1850 black slaves were still brought illegally to the United States and Brazil. Workers went from India to the West Indies and South Africa, and many Chinese settled in the United States and southeast Asia. With these reservations, the following table can be presented for the ninety years preceding the Second World War.

EMIGRATION FROM EUROPE, 1850–1940	
From: British Isles	18,300,000
Italy	10,200,000
Russia	9,000,000
Germany	5,000,000
Spain	4,500,000
Austria-Hungary	4,200,000
Portugal	2,500,000
Sweden	1,200,000
Norway	750,000
Denmark	470,000
Finland	390,000
France	390,000
Switzerland	340,000
Netherlands	210,000
Belgium	150,000
	57,600,000

SOURCE: William Woodruff, *The Impact of Western Man* (New York: St. Martin's Press, 1966), p. 106.

The British and Irish went to the British dominions and the United States. The Italians divided between the United States and Latin America. Spaniards settled overwhelmingly in the Spanish American republics, and the Portuguese in Brazil. The Germans moved overwhelmingly to the United States, though some went to Argentina and Brazil. The new countries received the following influxes of people:

IMMIGRATION INTO VARIOUS COUNTRIES, 1850–1940	
To: United States	32,300,000
Asiatic Russia	7,000,000
Argentina	6,600,000
Brazil	4,700,000
Canada	4,300,000
Australia	2,900,000
New Zealand	650,000
Uruguay	600,000
Cuba	600,000
South Africa	250,000
Mexico	250,000

SOURCE: Woodruff, *Impact*, p. 108.

The extraordinary preponderance of the United States is apparent. At the same time, it is well to rectify the impressions of most Americans on the subject. Almost half the European migration was directed elsewhere than to the United States. Asiatic Russia was second only to the United States in the receipt of new settlers. Germany was by no means a chief source of emigration in this period, especially in proportion to the total national population from which emigrants came. Canada received fewer immigrants than Argentina, and New Zealand was closely followed by Cuba and Uruguay.

The exodus from Europe was due to a remarkable and temporary juxtaposition of causes. One fundamental cause, or precondition, was that before 1914 the new countries welcomed immigration. Hands were wanted to farm the land, build houses, dig in the mines. This was least true of Australia and New Zealand, which preferred to limit themselves to English-speaking settlers, and which also pioneered as social democracies, becoming models, even before 1900, of legislation to protect the working classes. One result was that no inrush of outsiders to compete for jobs at low wages was desired. A similar combination of national preferences and labor protectionism led to laws restricting immigration in the United States in 1921 and 1924. Thereafter immigrants could enter only under quotas, and the quotas were lowest for eastern and southern Europe from which most emigration was then forthcoming.

In Europe there were many conditions propelling emigrants outward. Physically, the steamship made it easier and cheaper to cross the sea, and the railroad helped people to get to the ports as well as to distribute themselves after landing in the new countries. Economically, people in the mass could for the first time afford a long journey. People migrated to improve their material circumstances; but some crests in the wave of emigration coincided with crests in the business cycle in Europe, when jobs in Europe were plentiful and wages at their highest.

Of the opposite case, of actual flight from economic ruin or starvation, the emigration from Ireland after 1846 is the best example. After the revolutions of 1848 a certain number left Europe for political reasons, and, later on, to avoid compulsory military service. The best example of flight from actual persecution is that of the Jews of Russia and Russian Poland, of whom a million and a half moved to the United States in the fifteen years preceding the First World War.

But perhaps most basic in the whole European exodus was the underlying liberalism of the age. Never before (nor since) had people been legally so free to move. Old laws requiring skilled workmen to stay in their own countries were repealed, as in England in 1824.[3] The old semicommunal agricultural villages, with collective rights and obligations, holding the individual to his native group, fell into disuse except in Russia. The disappearance of serfdom allowed the peasant of eastern Europe to change his residence without obtaining a lord's permission.[4] Governments permitted their subjects to emigrate, to take with them their savings of shillings, marks, kronen, or lire, and to change nationality by becoming naturalized in their new homes. The rise of liberty in Europe, as well as the hope of enjoying it in America, made possible the great emigration. For so huge a mass movement the most remarkable fact is that it took place by private initiative and at private expense. Individuals, families, and small local groups (to borrow the metaphor of one authority) detached themselves atom by atom from the mass of Europe, crossed the seas on their own, and reattached themselves atom by atom to the accumulating mass of the New World.

73. The World Economy of the Nineteenth Century

How did the swelling population of Europeans manage to feed itself? How, in fact, did it not merely feed itself but enjoy an incomparably higher standard of living in 1900 than in 1800? By science, industry, transportation, and communications. And by organization—in business, finance, and labor.

The "New Industrial Revolution"

The Industrial Revolution entered upon a new phase. The use of steam power, the growth of the textile and metallurgical industries, and the advent of the railroad had characterized the early part of the century. Now, after 1870, new sources of power were tapped, the already mechanized industries expanded, new industries appeared, and industry spread geographically.

The steam engine itself was refined and improved. By 1914 it still predominated over other power machinery, but electricity with its incomparable advantages came into use. The invention of the internal combustion (or gasoline) engine and the diesel engine gave the world automobiles, airplanes, and submarines in the two decades before 1914; the advent of the automotive and aviation industries made oil one of the most coveted of natural resources. In the new chemical industries industrial research laboratories were replacing the individual inventor.

[3] See p. 489.
[4] See pp. 509–510, 520.

Chemists discovered new fertilizers, and from coal tar alone produced a bewildering array of new products ranging from artificial food flavors to high explosives. With the latter the first great tunnels were built, the Mount Cenis in 1873, the Simplon in 1906—both in the Alps; and great new canals, the Suez in 1869, the Kiel in 1895, the Panama in 1914. Chemistry made possible the production of synthetic fabrics like rayon which revolutionized the textile industry. Electricity transformed all indoor and outdoor lighting. There was a communications revolution too. The telephone appeared in the 1870s. Marconi brought the continents closer together, successfully transmitting wireless signals across the Atlantic in 1901. The moving picture and the radio modestly presented themselves before 1914. Medicine ran a tongue-twisting alphabetical gamut from anesthetics to x-rays; yellow fever was overcome. Vastly improved processes for refining iron ore made possible a great expansion in the production of steel, the key product of the new industrial age; aluminum and other metal alloys were also being produced. Railroad mileage multiplied; the European network, including the Russian, increased from 140,000 miles in 1890 to 213,000 in 1914.

In the new phase of the Industrial Revolution machine industry spread geographically from Britain and Belgium, the only truly industrial countries in 1870, to France, Italy, Russia, Japan, and, most markedly, to Germany and the United States. In Europe industrial production was concentrated in the "inner zone." Three powers alone—Britain, Germany, and France—accounted in 1914 for more than seven-tenths of all European manufactures and produced over four-fifths of all European coal, steel, and machinery. Of the major European powers Germany was now forging ahead. To use steel alone as a criterion, in 1871 Germany was producing annually three-fifths as much steel as Britain; by 1900 it was producing more, and by 1914 it was producing twice as much as Britain—but only half as much as the new industrial giant, the United States. By 1914 American steel output was greater than that of Germany, Britain, and France combined. Britain, the pioneer in mechanization, was being outstripped in both the old world and the new. The three European powers increased their industrial production by about 50 percent in the two decades before 1914, but the United States had a far higher annual growth rate from 1870 to 1913, 4.3 percent as compared to the next leading powers, Germany with 2.9 percent, Britain with 2.2 percent, and France with 1.6 percent.[5] By 1914 the United States had moved ahead of Europe in the mechanization of agriculture, in manufactures, and in coal and steel production, in which it was producing over two-fifths of the world's output. The Americans were pioneering also in assembly-line, conveyor-belt techniques for the mass production of automobiles and all kinds of consumer goods.

Free Trade and the European "Balance of Payments"

It was Britain in the mid–nineteenth century, then the workshop of the world, that had inaugurated the movement toward free trade. It will be recalled that in 1846, by the repeal of the Corn Laws, the British embarked upon a systematic

---

[5] *The New Cambridge Modern History*, Volume XII, rev. ed. (Cambridge: Cambridge University Press, 1968), p. 40.

CLASSIC LANDSCAPE
by Charles Sheeler (American, 1883–1965)

This landscape depicts the River Rouge plant of the Ford Motor Company in 1931, but it also symbolizes what has been called the Second Industrial Revolution, in which electricity, the internal combustion engine, and the automobile were important, and industry spread beyond its original centers in Britain and Western Europe. The picture is "classic" in its clear delineation, its array of familiar mathematical forms, and the universality of its message. The plant seems rational and precise, but the absence of human beings is to be noted; it is as if the machine had a life of its own and could do without human hands. The sharp shadows suggest bright sunshine, despite the smoke pouring from the tall chimney. When the picture was painted no one was alarmed about atmospheric pollution. Courtesy of Mrs. Edsel B. Ford.

free trade policy, deliberately choosing to become dependent upon overseas imports for their food.[6] France adopted free trade in 1860.[7] Other countries soon followed. It is true that by 1880 there was a movement back to protective tariffs, except in Britain, Holland, and Belgium. But the tariffs were impediments rather than barriers, and until 1914 the characteristic of the economic system was the extreme mobility of goods across political frontiers. Politically, Europe was more than ever nationalistic; but economic activity, under generally liberal conditions in which business was supposed to be free from the political state, remained predominantly international and globe-encircling.

Broadly speaking, the great economic accomplishment of Europe before 1914 was to create a system by which the huge imports used by industrial Europe could be acquired and paid for. All European countries except Russia, Austria-Hungary, and the Balkan states imported more than they exported. It was the British again that had led in this direction. Britain had been a predominantly importing country since the close of the eighteenth century. That is to say, despite the expanding export of cotton manufactures and other products of the Industrial Revolution, Britain consumed more goods from abroad than it sent out. Industrialization and urbanization in the nineteenth century confirmed the same situation. Between 1800 and 1900 the value of British exports multiplied eightfold, but the value of imports into Great Britain multiplied tenfold, and in the decade before 1914 the British had an import surplus of about three-quarters of a billion dollars a year. Great Britain and the industrial countries of Europe together (roughly Europe's "inner zone"), at the beginning of the twentieth century, were drawing in an import surplus, measured in dollars, of almost $2 billion every year (the dollar then representing far more goods than it came to represent later). The imports into Europe's inner zone consisted of raw materials for its industries and of food and amenities for its people.

How were the imports paid for? How did Europe enjoy a favorable "balance of payments" despite an unfavorable balance of trade in commodities? Export of European manufactures paid for some imports, and even most, but not all. It was the so-called invisible exports that made up the difference, that is, shipping and insurance services rendered to foreigners, and interest on money lent out or invested, all bringing in foreign exchange. Shipping and insurance were important. An Argentine merchant in Buenos Aires, to ship hides to Germany, might employ a British vessel; he would pay the freight charges in Argentine pesos, which might be credited to the account of the British shipowner in an Argentine bank; the British shipowner would sell the pesos to someone, in England or elsewhere in Europe, who needed them to buy Argentine meat. The far-flung British merchant marine thus earned a considerable amount of the food and raw materials needed by Britain. To insure themselves against risks of every conceivable kind people all over the world turned to Lloyds of London. With the profits drawn from selling insurance the British could buy what they wished. Governments or business enterprises borrowed money in Europe, mainly in England; the interest payments, putting foreign currencies into European and British hands,

[6] See p. 494.
[7] See p. 530.

constituted another invisible export by which an excess of imports could be financed. But the lending of money to foreigners is only part of a larger phenomenon, the export of capital.

The Export of European Capital

The migration of millions of Europeans had the effect of creating new societies, basically European in character, which both purchased manufactures from Europe and produced the food, wool, cotton, and minerals that Europe needed. It could not have had this effect if Europe had exported people only, especially people of such small means as most emigrants were. Europe also exported the capital necessary to get the new settlers and the new worlds into production.

The export of capital meant that an older and wealthier country, instead of using its whole annual income to raise its own standard of living, or to add to its own capital by expanding or improving its houses, factories, machinery, mines, transportation, etc., diverted some of its income to expanding or improving the houses, factories, machinery, mines, and transportation of foreign countries. It meant that British, French, Dutch, Belgian, Swiss, and eventually German investors in the desire to increase their income bought the stocks of foreign business enterprises and the bonds of foreign businesses and governments; or they organized companies of their own to operate in foreign climes; or their banks granted loans to banks in New York or Tokyo, which then lent the funds to local users. Capital arose in Europe to some extent from the savings of quite small people, especially in France, where peasants and modest bourgeois families were notably thrifty. But most capital accumulated from savings by the well-to-do. The owners of a business concern, for example, instead of spending the concern's income by paying higher wages, took a portion of it in profits or dividends, and instead of spending all this on their own living, reinvested part of it in domestic or foreign enterprises. The gap between rich and poor was thus one cause of the rapid accumulation of capital, though the accumulation of capital, in the nineteenth century, produced in turn a steady rise of living standards for the working classes. In a sense, however, the common people of western Europe, by forgoing the better housing, diet, education, or pleasures that a more democratic or consumer-oriented society might have planned for them, made possible the export of capital and hence the financing and building up of other regions of the world.

The British were the chief exporters of capital, followed at some distance by the French, and at the close of the century by the Germans. As early as the 1840s half the annual increase of wealth in Great Britain was going into foreign investments. By 1914 the British had $20 billion in foreign investments, the French about $8.7 billion, the Germans about $6 billion. A quarter of all the wealth owned by the inhabitants of Great Britain consisted in 1914 of holdings outside the country. Almost a sixth of the French national wealth lay in investments outside of France. All three countries had given hostages to fortune, and fortune proved unkind, for in the First World War the British lost about a quarter of their foreign investments, the French about a third, the Germans all.

These huge sums, pouring out from Europe's inner zone for a century before 1914, at first went mainly to finance the Americas and the less affluent regions of

Europe.[8] No country except Great Britain completely built its railways with its own resources. In the United States the railway system was built very largely with capital obtained from England. In central and eastern Europe British companies often constructed the first railways, then sold out to native operating companies or to governments which subsequently ran them. In the Argentine Republic the British not merely financed and built the railways, but long continued to operate and own them. In addition, up to 1914 the British sold about 75 million tons of coal a year to South America to keep the railways going, not to mention items for replacement and upkeep of equipment. Docks, warehouses, mines, plantations, processing and manufacturing establishments all over the world were similarly built up with capital drawn from Europe. European capital also helped emigrants in the new countries to live in a civilized fashion. In the United States, for example, state and local governments very commonly sold their bonds in Europe, to build roads, pave streets, or construct school systems for the westward-moving population. A few of these American bonds proved a partial or total loss to European investors. On the whole, by 1914, the United States had paid back a good deal of its indebtedness. Even so, in 1914, Americans still owed about $4 billion to Europeans—a sum three times as large as the national debt of the United States at the time.

An International Money System: The Gold Standard

The international economy rested upon an international money system, based in turn upon the almost universal acceptance of the gold standard. England had adopted the gold standard in 1816, when the pound sterling was legally defined as the equivalent of 113 grains of fine gold. Western Europe and the United States adopted an exclusively gold standard in the 1870s. A person holding any "civilized" money—pounds, francs, dollars, marks, etc.—could turn it into gold at will, and a person holding gold could turn it into any money. The currencies were like so many different languages all expressing the same thing. All had substantially the same value, and until 1914 the exchange rates between currencies remained highly stable. It was assumed that no civilized country's currency ever "fell"; such things might happen in Turkey or China, or in the French Revolution, but not in the world of practical men, modern progress, and civilized affairs.

The important currencies were all freely exchangeable. A Frenchman, selling silks to a German, and hence receiving German marks, could turn the marks into francs, pounds sterling, or dollars. That is, he was not obliged to buy from Germany or spend his money in Germany but could use the proceeds of his German sale to buy French, British, or American goods or services as he chose. Trade was multilateral. A country needing imports from another country, such as American cotton, did not have to sell to that country to obtain them; it could sell its own goods anywhere and then import according to its needs.

It was the acceptance of the gold standard, and the fact that all important countries possessed a sufficient share of gold to support their currencies, that

---

[8] The penetration of European capital into Asia and Africa, after about 1890, is considered in the following chapter.

Width of Arrow Segments is Proportionate to the Amount of Capital Export

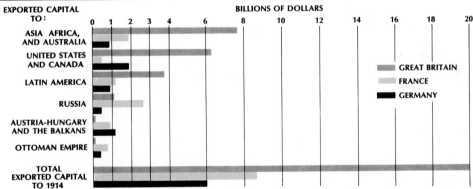

EXPORT OF EUROPEAN CAPITAL TO 1914

In 1914 the British, French, and Germans held upwards of $30 billion in foreign and colonial loans and investments, distributed as shown on the map. Dutch investments, especially in the Netherlands Indies, together with Swiss, Belgian, and Scandinavian holdings, would add several billion dollars more. Proceeds from such investments helped Europeans to pay for the excess of their imports over exports. New and undeveloped countries were built up by capital borrowed from Europe. British capital predominated in the overseas world, while the less advanced regions of eastern Europe and the Near East were financed mainly from Germany and France. Much of the investment shown on this map was lost or expended in the First World War. See pp. 720–725.

made possible so fluid an interchange. At the same time the gold standard had less wholesome effects. It was hard on countries that lacked gold. And it produced a gradual fall of prices, especially between 1870 and 1900, because (until the gold discoveries in South Africa, Australia, and Alaska in the 1890s) the world's production of gold lagged behind the expanding production of industrial and agricultural goods. Persistently declining prices were a hardship to those who habitually worked with borrowed money—many farmers, many businessmen, and debtor nations as a whole. A famous speech of William Jennings Bryan in the United States in 1896, declaring that mankind should not be crucified "upon this cross of gold," expressed a restlessness that was worldwide. But falling prices were an advantage to the wage-earning class, which generally improved its position in these years, and also to the wealthy, the owners and lenders of capital, the bankers and financiers, who so long as prices were falling were repaid in money of more value than that which they had lent.

The center of the global economic and financial system was London. The London banks came forward in consequence of the defeat of Napoleon, the older financial centers in Amsterdam having been ruined in the Revolutionary and Napoleonic wars. It may be recalled also that the victors in 1815 imposed upon France an indemnity of 700 million francs, which in 1818 was taken over by a syndicate of private bankers; the London banks played a leading part in this affair and so developed their connections with many government treasuries.[9] In the Crimean War of 1854–1856, with England at war with Russia, the London banks floated loans for the Russian government—so independent were business and politics at the time. The early adoption of the gold standard in England meant that many people, British and foreign, kept their funds in the form of sterling on deposit in London, where quantities of available capital therefore accumulated.

The banks, too, grew up in the financing of the British export trade, itself borne on the tide of the Industrial Revolution. A small Lancashire manufacturer, for example, might receive an order for a gross of scissors from an unknown merchant in Trieste. He would draw a bill or "sight draft" against the Trieste merchant, and take this bill to a financial institution known as an acceptance house. The acceptance house, which in the course of its business had acquired a microscopic knowledge of the credit of thousands of individuals and firms in all parts of the world, would then "discount" the bill, giving cash to the Lancashire manufacturer and collecting from the Trieste merchant through international banking channels. In this way the bank took a burden off the British manufacturer, and extended short-term credit to foreigners for the purchase of British goods. Many acceptance houses gradually went into the business of long-term foreign lending also. London became the apex of a pyramid which had the world for its base. It was the main center of exchange of currencies, the clearinghouse of the world's debts, the depository from which all the world borrowed, the banker's bank, the insurance man's resort for reinsurance, as well as the world's shipping center and the headquarters of many international corporations.

[9] See pp. 451, 478.

A World Market: Unity, Competition—and Insecurity

Never had the earth been so unified economically, with each region playing its due role in a global specialization. Western Europe, and in 1870 mainly Great Britain, was the world's industrial workshop. Other parts of the earth supplied its many needs. An English economist marveled in 1866 that Britain now had its granaries in Chicago and Odessa, its forests in Canada and the Baltic, its sheep farms in Australia, and its gold and silver mines in California and Peru, while drinking tea brought from China and coffee from East Indian plantations. The same could have been said of most of Europe's "inner zone" by the time of the First World War.

A true world market had been created. Goods, services, money, capital, people moved back and forth almost without regard to national boundaries. Articles were bought and sold at uniform world prices. Dealers in wheat, for example, followed prices in Minneapolis, Liverpool, Buenos Aires, and Danzig as reported by telegraph and cable from day to day. They bought where it was cheapest, and sold where it was dearest. In this way the world's wheat supply was distributed roughly according to need or ability to pay. The worker of Milan, if the Italian crop was poor and prices high, was fed from another source. On the other hand, the Italian wheat grower would in this case feel the pinch of world competition. The world market, while it organized the world into a unified economic system, at the same time brought distant regions into competition for the first time. The producer—whether businessman, factory employee, farmer, or coffee planter—had no secure outlet for his product, as had generally been true in the past. He was in competition not only with the man across the street or down the road, but with the world.

The creation of an integrated world market, the financing and building up of countries outside of Europe, and the consequent feeding and support of Europe's increasing population were the great triumphs of the nineteenth-century system of unregulated capitalism. The system was intricate, with thousands and even millions of individuals and business firms supplying each other's wants without central planning. But it was extremely precarious, and the position of most people in it was exceedingly vulnerable. Region competed against region, and person against person. A fall of grain prices in the American Middle West, besides ruining a few speculators, might oblige the Prussian or Argentine wheat grower to sell at a price at which he could not live. A factory owner might be driven out of business if his competitor successfully undersold him or if a new commodity made his own product obsolete. The worker, hired only when needed by an employer, faced unemployment when business slackened, or the permanent disappearance of his job by the next labor-saving invention. The system went through cycles of boom and depression, the most notable example of the latter being the long depression that set in about 1873 and lasted to about 1893. It rested on expansion and on credit; but sometimes people could not pay their debts, so that credit collapsed, and sometimes expansion failed to keep pace with expectations, and anticipated profits proved to be losses. To combat the essential insecurity of private capitalism, all manner of devices were resorted to. Governments adopted protective tariffs on the one hand and social insurance and welfare legislation on the other; trade unionism and socialist movements grew; business mergers took place. These and other measures, to which we shall return, signalized the gradual decline in the years after 1880 of nineteenth-century unregulated, laissez-faire capitalism.

Changes in Organization: Big Business

A great change came over capitalism itself about 1880 or 1890. Formerly characterized by a very large number of very small units, small businesses run by individuals, partnerships, or small companies, it was increasingly characterized by large and impersonal corporations. The attractions of the "limited liability" corporation as a form of business organization and as a means of encouraging investment arose from laws, enacted by most countries in the nineteenth century, which limited the individual investor's personal loss in the event of a bankruptcy to the amount of his shares of stock in the enterprise. The corporation, in its modern form appearing first with the railroads, became the usual form of organization for industry and commerce. As machinery grew more complicated only a large pool of capital could finance it. And as corporations grew in size and number, relying on the sale of stock and the issue of bonds, the influence of banking and financial circles was enhanced. Financiers, using not so much their own money as the savings of others, had a new power to create or to extinguish, to stimulate, discourage, or combine corporate enterprises in various industries. Industrial capitalism brought finance capitalism with it.[10]

Corporate organization made it possible to concentrate economic processes under unified management. In retail commerce, large department stores appeared about 1890 in the United States and France. In industry, steel offers a good example. Steel became in any case a big business when heavy blast furnaces were introduced. It was not safe for the steel business, or for the blast furnaces, to rely for iron and coal on independent producers who might sell to whomsoever they pleased. The steel works therefore began to operate mines of their own or to buy out or otherwise reduce coal and iron mines to subsidiary status. Some, to assure their markets, began to produce not merely steel but steel manufactures as well—steel ships, railway equipment, naval and military ordnance. Thus entire processes from mining to finished product became concentrated in a "vertical" integration. By "horizontal" integration concerns at the same level combined with each other to reduce competition and to protect themselves against fluctuations in prices and in markets. Some fixed prices, some agreed to restrict production, some divided up markets among themselves. They were called trusts in the United States, cartels in Europe. They were common in many of the new industries at the close of the century, such as chemicals, aluminum, and oil. In steel such combinations produced the great interests of Krupp in Germany, Schneider-Creusot in France, Vickers-Armstrong in Great Britain. It was in the United States that such big business developed furthest, headed by "captains" of industry and "titans" of finance. Andrew Carnegie, by origin a poor Scottish immigrant boy, produced more steel than all England; in 1901 he sold out to an even more colossal organization, the United States Steel Corporation, formed by the financier J. P. Morgan. It was in the United States, too, that concern over monopoly and

[10] See pp. 529–530, 573.

the power of big business in general was felt most strongly; antitrust legislation, beginning with the Sherman Act of 1890, was enacted but never with any substantial effect.

Many of the new combinations were beneficial in making the ups and downs of business less erratic, and so providing more stable prices and more continuous and secure employment. Generally they reduced the costs of production; but whether the savings went into higher profits, higher wages, or lower prices depended on numerous factors. Some trusts were more greedy than others or confronted with only weakly organized or unorganized labor. In any case, for good or ill, decisions rested with management and finance. A new kind of private power had arisen, which its critics like to call "feudal." Since no economic system had ever been so centralized up to that time, never in fact had so few people exercised so much economic power over so many. The middle class, with the rise of great corporations, came typically to consist of salaried employees; the salaried man might spend a lifetime with the same company, and feel toward it, in its disputes with labor or government, a loyalty not unlike that of a lord's retainer in feudal times. The laboring class was less amenable; labor attempted to organize unions capable of dealing with increasingly gigantic employers. It also after about 1880 played an increasingly decisive role in the politics of all advanced nations.

74. The Advance of Democracy: Third French Republic, United Kingdom, German Empire

In the years from 1815 to 1870 European political life had been marked by liberal agitation for constitutional government, representative assemblies, responsible ministries, and guarantees of individual liberties. In the years from 1871 to 1914, even where these liberal objectives were not fully achieved but remained as goals, the most notable political development was the democratic extension of the vote to the working class—the adoption of universal male suffrage, which in turn meant for the first time the creation of mass political parties and the need for political leaders to appeal to a wide electorate. The extension of the suffrage in these years did not take place because of popular agitation as in the days of the Chartists or of the radical reformers in France. Governments for a variety of reasons extended the suffrage on their own. Often democratization took place in a continuing monarchical and aristocratic framework, but almost everywhere by 1914 the machinery at least of democratic self-government was being established. In addition, to counter the growing strength of socialism after 1871, and for humanitarian reasons, governments were also assuming responsibility for the social and economic problems arising from industrialism. The welfare state in its modern form was taking shape.

France: The Establishment of the Third Republic

In France the democratic republic was not easily established, and its troubled early years left deep cleavages within the country. It will be recalled that in

September 1870, when the empire of Napoleon III revealed its helplessness in the Franco-Prussian War, insurrectionaries in Paris, as in 1792 and 1848, again proclaimed the Republic.[11] A provisional government of national defense sought desperately to continue the war, but the cause was hopeless. By January 1871, a bitter siege of Paris came to an end and an armistice was signed. Bismarck, insisting that only a properly constituted government could make peace, permitted the election, by universal male suffrage, of a National Assembly which was to consider his peace terms and draft a constitution for the new French state. When the elections were held in February, it was found, as in 1848 (and, indeed, 1797), that republicanism was so distrusted by the French people as a whole, and most especially in the provinces and rural areas, that a free election brought monarchist elements into power.[12] Republicanism was still thought to be violent—bellicose in its foreign policy, turbulent in its political workings, unfriendly to the church, and socialistic or at least equalitarian in its views of property and private wealth. The new Assembly contained only about 200 republicans out of more than 600 deputies.

But the Paris republicans, who had defended France when Napoleon III failed to do so, who for four months had been besieged, starved, and frozen by the Germans, and who still refused to make peace on the harsh terms imposed by Bismarck and about to be accepted by the Assembly, refused to recognize the latter's authority. A civil war broke out between the National Assembly, now sitting at Versailles, and the city of Paris, where a revolutionary municipal council or "Commune" was set up. Paris, so lately attacked by German soldiers, was now attacked by French.

The Paris Commune, which lasted from March to May 1871, seemed to be another explosion of social revolution. Actually, it was in essence a revival of the Jacobinism of 1793. It was fiercely patriotic and republican, anti-German, opposed to wealthy bourgeois, aristocrats, and clergy, in favor of government controls upon prices, wages, and working conditions, but still not socialist in any sweeping or systematic way. Among its leaders, however, there were a few of the new international revolutionary socialists, who saw in a Jacobin or democratic republic a step toward their new order. Marx in England, and others elsewhere, hopefully read into the Commune the impending doom of the bourgeoisie. This was precisely what more conservative elements feared. To many of the French middle and peasant class, and to people like them all over Europe, it seemed that the "Communards" were wild and savage destroyers of nineteenth-century civilization. The fighting in Paris was atrocious beyond anything known in any preceding French revolution. The Communards, in final desperation, burned a number of public buildings and put to death the archbishop of Paris, whom they held as a hostage. The forces of the National Assembly, when finally triumphant, were determined to root out the inveterate revolutionism of Paris. Some 330,000 persons were denounced, 38,000 arrested, 20,000 put to death, and 7,500 deported to New Caledonia. The Third Republic was born in an atmosphere of class hate and social terror.

The form of government for the new regime still had to be established. The

[11] See p. 558.
[12] See pp. 394, 503, 505.

monarchist majority in the Assembly was itself evenly divided between those who favored a restoration of the Bourbon family and those who favored the Orléanist. In the end, even after they were reconciled, the Bourbon candidate alienated everyone by his stiff insistence on a return to the white flag of the Bourbons. The monarchists checkmated each other. Meanwhile, after extended discussion of various constitutional projects, the Assembly adopted in 1875 not a constitution, but certain constitutive laws. By a margin of one vote, a resolution indirectly amounting to the establishment of a republic was passed. The new laws provided for a president, a parliament in two chambers, and a council of ministers, or cabinet, headed by a premier. The Senate was to be elected by a complicated and indirect system of election, the Chamber of Deputies by universal, direct, male suffrage.

Within two years, in 1877, the role of the president, the ministers, and the parliament was further clarified as a result of an unsuccessful attempt by an early president, Marshal MacMahon, to dismiss a premier of whom he did not approve but who had the backing of the Chamber. MacMahon proceeded to dissolve the Chamber and to hold new elections, but the example of Napoleon III's transformation of the Second Republic into an authoritarian regime was still fresh. The elections vindicated the principle of parliamentary primacy and of the responsibility of the premier and his cabinet to the legislature, a responsibility which in France meant generally but not exclusively to the lower house. The true executive in republican France for a long time was to be the premier and his cabinet, themselves held strictly to account by a majority of the legislature. Unfortunately, that majority, in a parliament where a dozen or so parties were represented, was always difficult to form and could be created only by unstable, temporary, shifting party alliances, coalitions, or blocs. No president, and indeed no premier, could henceforth dissolve the Chamber in order to hold new elections and consult the country as could be done in Britain. Actually, under the Third Republic the substantial machinery of state—ministries, prefectures, law courts, police, army, all under highly centralized control—was carried over virtually untouched as in all upheavals since the time of Napoleon I. France in the nineteenth century, so volatile in appearance, in effect underwent less extensive reorganization than any other leading country in Europe.

Troubles of the Third French Republic

Yet the Third Republic was precarious. The government had changed so often since 1789 that all forms of government seemed to be transitory. Questions which in other countries were party questions became in France questions of "regime"—monarchy versus republic. Many people, especially those influenced by the upper classes, the Catholic clergy, and the professional army officers, continued to feel a positive aversion to the republic. On the other hand, the unmerciful and vindictive repression of the Commune made many middle-class people sympathetic to the republicans. Many turned republican simply because no other form of government established itself, or because it was the form of government that divided the country the least. As republicanism took in wider elements of society, it became less revolutionary and less fearsome. In 1879, for the first time, republicans won control of both houses of the government. In the 1880s their radicalism hardly went further than the founding of a democratic and compulsory school system at government expense and the passage of anticlerical legislation intended to curb church influence in education.

For over a quarter of a century, however, republican energies had to be expended in defense of republican institutions in order to ensure the survival of the regime. An initial crisis arose in 1886–1889, when General Boulanger gathered around him an incongruous following that included not only Bonapartists, monarchists, and aristocrats but also extreme radical republicans, who wished a war of revenge against Germany, and workers disgruntled over their general lot. Boulanger became a popular figure and seemed for a moment about to seize power. But the menace collapsed in a comical failure as the general lost heart at the crucial hour and fled into exile. Meanwhile, in the 1880s and 1890s scandals and revelations of corruption in high republican circles provided ammunition for the antirepublicans. Moreover, the hope that unsympathetic French Catholics would rally to the republic, as urged by French prelates and by Pope Leo XIII in 1892, was shattered by the Dreyfus Affair, which in the late 1890s rocked the country and indeed the world.

In 1894 Captain Dreyfus, a Jewish army officer, was found guilty of treason by a military court and deported to Devil's Island. Evidence accumulated showing his innocence and pointing to the guilt of another officer, a Major Esterhazy, an adventurer known to be riddled with gambling debts. But the army refused to reopen the case, unwilling to admit it had erred; a staff officer, Major Henry, even forged documents to confirm Dreyfus' guilt. Meanwhile anti-Semites, royalists, traditionalists, militarists, and most of the "best" people fought the reopening of the case, deeming it unpatriotic to shake the nation's confidence in the army and wishing also to disgrace the republican regime. The partisans of Dreyfus stubbornly upheld him, both because they believed in justice and because they wished to discredit their adversaries. The country was deeply split. Finally, in 1899, Dreyfus was pardoned, and in 1906, fully exonerated. In the aftermath of the affair the left republicans and socialists revenged themselves by blocking the promotions of antirepublican officers and by anticlerical legislation. In 1905, in a series of laic laws, they "separated" church and state, ending the close relationship established under Napoleon's concordat a century earlier.

The Strength and Weakness of the Republic

The Third Republic, when the First World War came in 1914, a test which it was successfully to meet, had lasted over twice as long as any French regime since 1789. Born unwanted and accidentally, though it still had its opponents, it now commanded the loyalty of the overwhelming mass of the French people. What it had done, since 1871, was to domesticate democratic republicanism in Europe. Republicanism, one of the most militant of revolutionary movements down to 1870, had been shown in France to be compatible with order, law, parliamentary government, economic prosperity, and a mutual tolerance between classes, to the extent at least that they no longer butchered each other in the streets. Industrial workers were in many ways less well off than in England or Germany, but there were fewer of them; and for most people France in these years was a pleasant country, full of painters, writers, scholars, and scientists, full of bankers, bourgeois and well-established farmers, a country living comfortably and unhurriedly on the savings of generations, and one in which, in a close-knit family group, the average man could plan securely for his own and his children's future.

But the very comforts and values of bourgeois France were not those that would equip it for leadership in the modern age of technology and industrial power. Though substantial economic progress was made, the country lagged behind Germany in industrial development; the French entrepreneur showed little inclination to take the business risks needed for industrial growth. Politically, the fragmentation of political parties, itself a democratic reflection of a divided public opinion, and the distrust for historic reasons of a strong executive power led to the rise and fall of numerous short-lived ministries—no fewer than fifty in the years between 1871 and 1914. Ministerial instability was to be a chronic symptom of the Third Republic both before and after 1914; continuity of government policy was, however, generally maintained because of stability in certain key ministries and because of the permanent civil service.

French labor remained a steady source of discontent. Although French workers benefited from some labor legislation in the two decades after 1890, they continued to feel frustrated at the failure to establish a "social republic." Socialist representation in the Chamber grew. However, the most important single party of the republic, the Radicals, or Radical Socialists, were in actuality radical republicans—patriotic, anticlerical, spokesmen for the small shopkeepers and the lesser propertied interests; they drew the line at the advanced social legislation that labor expected from them, and on occasion their leaders even took positive steps to prevent unionization and to suppress strikes. Since some of these Radicals had started out as socialists, the distrust of French workers for all politicians and even for political processes was intensified. But the difficulties of the republic went deeper. The political energies of the republican statesmen had gone into liquidating the past, into curbing the political strength of the monarchists, the church, and the army; by the turn of the century, even before these older issues were fully resolved, the republic was compelled to meet the challenge of labor and to face other domestic and international pressures that were to try it sorely. The Third Republic was to weather the crisis of the First World War but not that of the Second.

The British Constitutional Monarchy

The British constitutional monarchy in the half-century before 1914 was the great exemplar of reasonable, orderly, and peaceable self-government through parliamentary methods. For over sixty years, spanning two-thirds of the nineteenth century, Victoria reigned (1837–1901) and gave her name to a distinguished era of material progress, literary accomplishment, and political stability. The two great parties, Liberal and Conservative, the heirs roughly of the Whigs and Tories, took form in the 1850s, the former producing its great leader in William E. Gladstone, the latter, a series of leaders of whom the most colorful was Benjamin Disraeli.

The advance toward an equalitarian political democracy in Britain was more cautious and slower than in France. The Reform Bill of 1832 had granted the vote to about an eighth of the adult male population. The democratic Chartist agitation of the 1830s and 1840s came to nothing.[13] In 1867, in response to continued demand for a wider suffrage, the Second Reform Bill was passed, Conservatives as well as Liberals outdoing one another in an effort to satisfy the country and to win new political strength for their own party. The bill, adopted under Disraeli's Conservative ministry, extended the suffrage from about 1 million eligible voters to about 2 million, or over a third of the adult males in the United Kingdom, reaching down far enough to include most workers in the cities. Disraeli's colleague Lord Derby called it a "leap in the dark." In 1884, under Liberal auspices, the suffrage was again broadened, this time in the rural areas, adding some 2 million additional voters and enfranchising over three-fourths of all adult males in the country. The suffrage still excluded agricultural workers who did not have a fixed residence, servants living with employers, and such people as unmarried grown sons who lived in the homes of their parents. Not until 1918 did Great Britain adopt universal male suffrage, as generally understood; and at that time women over thirty were given the vote too.

Despite the extension of the suffrage, the leadership of the country at the turn of the century was still in the hands of the upper and wealthier classes. Until 1911 the government paid no salaries to members of the House of Commons, who therefore, in both great parties, were usually gentlemen with private incomes, possessing the same family background and education. An attitude of sportsmanship and good feeling was characteristic of British politics. The two parties alternated in power at regular intervals, each indulgent toward the other, carrying over and developing rather than reversing the policies of its predecessor in office. Both parties sought support where they could find it, the Liberals leaning somewhat more on the industrial and commercial interests, the Conservatives on the landed aristocracy; both sought and succeeded in winning their share of the new working-class vote. It was in these years that both parties, when parliamentary reversals occurred, increasingly appealed to the country in general elections; the traditional crown and cabinet basis of British parliamentary government was being transformed into crown, cabinet, and country.

The Liberals were usually the more willing to pioneer, the first of the four

---

[13] See pp. 497–499, 504.

SUNDAY AFTERNOON ON THE ISLAND OF LA GRANDE JATTE
by Georges Seurat (French, 1859–1891)

This picture of sunny calm, painted in 1886, suggests something of the well-being brought to a great many people by the European civilization of the late nineteenth century. Whether boating, or idly fishing, or quietly sitting and watching, or strolling alone or in pairs or in families with their children, the figures seem to live in a peaceable world which a later age of war, speed, and mechanical amusements has made to seem far away. Technically this is one of the most remarkable pictures ever painted. The artist, an impressionist, created it without the use of lines by filling the canvas with thousands of minute dots of the primary colors, which so blur and mix in the eye as to produce the forms and hues of nature. As a result it seems to be a picture of light itself, with an actual shimmer on the water, an astonishing "grassiness" in the grass, with shadows that seem to be real shadows, and distant figures looking really distant as if seen through the intervening air. Courtesy of The Art Institute of Chicago.

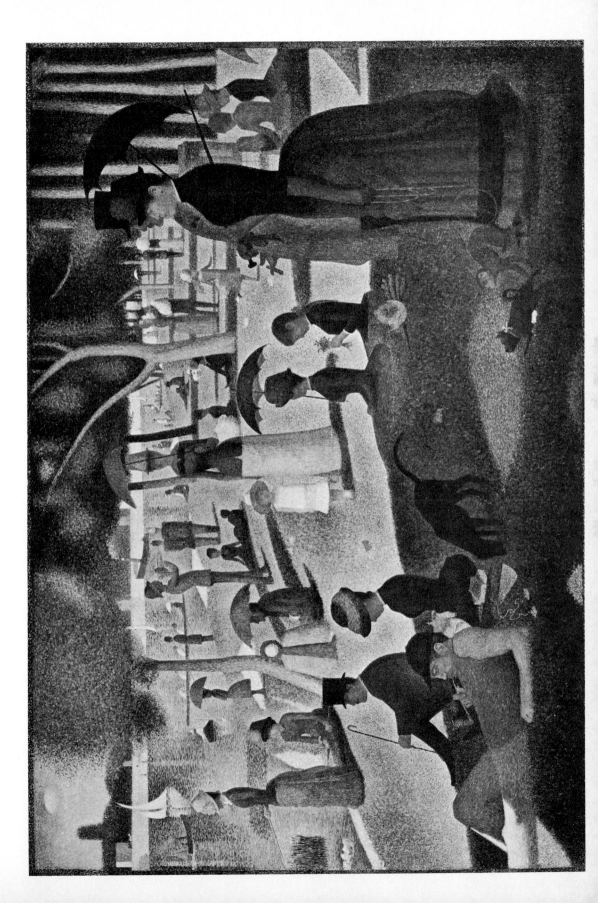

ministries of Gladstone being especially notable in this respect. Gladstone in this first ministry (1868–1874) developed the principle of state-supported public education under the Forster Education Act of 1870, introduced the secret ballot, formally legalized labor unions, promoted competitive examinations for civil service posts, reorganized the upper judiciary, eliminated the purchase and sale of commissions in the army (a form of property in office), and by abolishing religious tests enabled persons not members of the Church of England to graduate from Oxford and Cambridge. The Conservative party, less sensitive to pressure from business interests for a laissez-faire policy in economic matters, and continuing the tradition of early Tory reformers, took the initiative in further labor legislation. Under Disraeli's second ministry (1874–1880), the existing acts regulating public sanitation and conditions in mines and factories were extended and codified, safety measures were enacted to protect sailors, and the first attempt to regulate housing conditions for the poorer classes was initiated. But the Liberals, it must be added, protected the workers' interests too. In Gladstone's second ministry (1880–1885) workers were assured of compensation for injuries not of their own responsibility, and in 1892, before the formation of his fourth ministry (1892–1894), Gladstone campaigned to shorten labor hours and to extend employers' liability in accidents.

British Political Changes after 1900

At the turn of the century important changes were discernible on the British political scene. Labor emerged as an independent political force, the Labour party itself being organized shortly after 1900.[14] The rise of labor had a deep impact upon the Liberal party, and indeed upon liberalism itself. With many persons insisting that protective measures be taken to counteract the poor health, low income, and economic insecurity of the British working people, the Liberals abandoned their traditional position of laissez faire and sponsored a policy of government intervention and social legislation in behalf of working people. The Liberals, though they acted in part for humanitarian reasons, were aware that with the emergence of the Labour party workers who customarily had voted for them might readily transfer their allegiance.

In control of the government from 1906 to 1916, with Herbert Asquith as prime minister and David Lloyd George as chancellor of the exchequer during most of this time, the Liberals put through a spectacular program of social welfare. Sickness, accident, old-age, and a degree of unemployment insurance were adopted, and a moderate minimum wage law was enacted. Labor exchanges, or employment bureaus, were set up over the country. Restrictions on strikes and other trade union activities were removed. To meet the costs of the new program as well as of other government expenditures, Lloyd George's budget of 1909 called for progressive income and inheritance taxes: the wealthier the taxpayer, the higher the rate at which he was taxed. He was in effect advancing the then novel idea of using taxation to modify the extremes of wealth and poverty. It was a "war budget," he said, intended "to wage war against poverty." Its fiscal measures were directed primarily at the landed aristocracy, and it aroused great

[14] See pp. 619–621.

opposition, especially in the House of Lords, where the contest over the budget led to a further constitutional curtailment of the power of the upper house. The Parliament Act of 1911 deprived the Lords of all veto power in money matters and of all but a two-year delaying veto on action of the Commons in other legislation. At this time, too, the government voted to pay salaries to members of the House of Commons, making it possible for workers and others without independent incomes to take seats in Parliament. This last measure was adopted to counteract a court ruling, the Osborne Judgment of 1909, that trade unions could not pay the salaries of workers elected to Parliament.

The Liberal party was embracing a program of positive state intervention in social and economic matters that the older liberalism, nurtured on the doctrines of laissez faire and the Manchester School, would not have accepted. With the Liberals actively seeking the support of labor and altering much in their traditional program, the Conservatives in the twentieth century tended to become the party of industry as well as of landed wealth and to replace the Liberals as the champions of economic liberalism and laissez faire. In the next generation, after the First World War, the Conservatives were to remain one of the two major parties of the country; the Liberals were to be far outstripped by the Labour party.

Meanwhile, despite its gains, labor was not pacified. Real wages showed a tendency to fall after 1900, and great coal and railway strikes broke out in 1911 and 1912. The British capacity to survive crises without violence, while still conspicuous, was being strained. An even more serious threat came from Ireland.

The Irish Question

Britain suffered from one of the worst minorities questions in Europe—the Irish question. After 1801 Britain was known as the United Kingdom of Great Britain and Ireland, Ireland having been incorporated into the United Kingdom as a defensive measure against pro-French sympathies in Ireland during the wars of the French Revolution.[15] The Irish representatives who sat in Parliament were generally obstructionist in their tactics. The Irish had many substantial grievances, among which two were conspicuous. The Irish peasant was defenseless against his landlord, far more so, for example, than the French peasant before 1789; and the Irish people, though predominantly Catholic, were obliged to pay tithes to the established Church of Ireland (an Anglican sister church to the Church of England), which also owned a good deal of the land.

Gladstone, in his first ministry, disestablished the Church of Ireland. He also initiated measures to protect the Irish farm tenant. By 1900, under Conservative auspices, Irish tenants were being assisted by the British government to buy out their landlords—often Englishmen or Anglicized and absentee Irishmen. The Irish also wanted home rule, or a parliament of their own. Gladstone, in trying to give it to them in 1886, split his Liberal party, part of which went along with the Conservatives, not wishing political division of the British Isles. Home rule was finally granted to Ireland in 1914. But the Ulstermen, Presbyterians of north Ireland, objected vehemently to inclusion in an autonomous Ireland, in which they would be outnumbered by the Catholics of the south. The latter, however,

[15] See pp. 350, 395.

insisted with equal vehemence on the inclusion of Ulster, not wishing a political division of Ireland.

The Ulstermen, backed by British Conservatives, started arming and drilling to resist the act of Parliament that authorized home rule. Great Britain, in 1914, was about to see a civil war on its own doorstep. It suffered from something of the insoluble nationalistic disputes that afflicted Austria-Hungary. During the First World War home rule was suspended, and after considerable violence on both sides Catholic Ireland (Eire) received dominion status in 1922, but eventually dissolved all ties with Britain. Ulster remained in the United Kingdom and was dominated by Protestants, so that its Catholic minority remained discontented. No satisfactory solution has yet been found to the "Irish question."

Bismarck and the German Empire, 1871–1890

The German Empire, as put together by Bismarck in 1871 with William I, king of Prussia, as Kaiser, was a federation of monarchies, a union of twenty-five German states, in which the weight of monarchical Prussia, the Prussian army, and the Prussian landed aristocracy was preponderant. It developed neither the strong constitutionalism of England nor the democratic equality that was characteristic of France. To win popular support for his projects, Bismarck exploited existing democratic and socialist sentiment and provided that members of the Reichstag, the lower chamber, be elected by universal male suffrage.[16] Remaining chancellor of the united empire for some twenty years, from 1871 to 1890, he usually tried to have a majority in the Reichstag on his side, but he recognized no dependence on a majority in principle, holding to the doctrine that it was the emperor and his chancellor who were to govern the country. Moreover, in practice, the legislative powers of the lower house were severely restricted, and the upper chamber, representing the princes and not the people, and favored by the government, tended to be more important. Despite the nature of the empire, the Prussian conservatives, the East-Elbian Junker landlords, were at first by no means enthusiastic over Bismarck's unified Germany.[17] They opposed his democratic concessions and were left horrified when in 1872 he undertook to extinguish what was left of their manorial jurisdiction over their peasants.

Bismarck in the 1870s therefore leaned not on the Conservatives but on the National Liberals. With their aid he put through a number of economic and legal measures designed to consolidate the unity of the new empire. Bismarck's first serious conflict developed with the Catholic church. At the very time that he was bent on subordinating all groups within the state to the sovereign power of the new empire, the church had spoken out. In 1864 in the *Syllabus of Errors,* it denounced the encroachment of all governments on educational and church affairs; in 1870 the new dogma of papal infallibility made it incumbent on Catholics to accept unreservedly the pope's pronouncements in matters of faith and morals.[18] To many, the implication was that the new empire could not count on the

---

[16] See pp. 557, 559.
[17] See pp. 514, 552–554.
[18] See p. 634.

undivided loyalty of its Catholic citizens. To defend Catholic interests and those of the south German states where Catholicism predominated, Catholic elements had organized the strong Center party, which now upheld the church pronouncements. In 1871 Bismarck launched the so-called *Kulturkampf,* or "battle for modern civilization." The Liberals joined in eagerly. Like nineteenth-century liberals elsewhere (Gladstone's campaign against Anglican privilege and the French laic laws have just been mentioned), they were strongly anticlerical and disapproved of the influence of organized churches in public and private life. Laws were put through imposing restrictions upon Catholic worship and education, the Jesuits were expelled, and many Catholic bishops throughout Germany were arrested or went into exile. But Bismarck gradually concluded that the anti-Catholic legislation was fruitless, that he had overestimated the danger to the state of organized Catholicism, and that he needed the support of the Center party for other parts of his program.

In 1879, with the support of the Center and Conservative parties but to the dismay of many of his erstwhile Liberal allies, Bismarck abandoned free trade and adopted a protective tariff that provided needed revenues for the government and gave satisfaction both to agricultural and industrial interests. Meanwhile, the country's rapid and spectacular industrial expansion had stimulated the growth of the German working class, and to Bismarck's alarm, socialism was spreading.

The German Social Democratic party had been founded in 1875 by a fusion of Marxian socialists and the reformist followers of Ferdinand Lassalle on an essentially moderate program which Marx had denounced. But even a moderate socialism was mistrusted by Bismarck. He shared in the European horror at the recent Paris Commune, he feared socialism as anarchy, and he knew that socialism was in any case republican, and in that alone a potentially revolutionary movement in an empire of monarchies. Two radical attempts on the emperor's life (in neither case by Social Democrats) provided him with all the excuse he needed. In 1878, having already made peace with the Catholics, he set out to eradicate socialism. Antisocialist laws from 1878 to 1890 prohibited socialist meetings and socialist newspapers. For twelve years socialism was driven underground. But repression was not his only weapon; he turned also to another tactic. Bismarck sought to persuade the workers to place their faith in him and the German Empire rather than in Marx and the prophets of socialism. To that end, in the 1880s, he initiated an extensive program of social legislation. Workers were insured by the state against sickness, accident, and incapacity in old age. "Our democratic friends," said Bismarck, "will pipe in vain when the people see princes concerned with their well-being." In social insurance imperial Germany was, from whatever motives, years ahead of more democratic England, France, and the United States.

Bismarck failed to kill socialism. The number of socialists elected to the Reichstag was greater in 1890 than in 1878—for Bismarck's antisocialist campaign, in deference to the then current standards of civilized government, never suppressed the voter's freedom to vote as he chose. It seems, however, that Bismarck by the later 1880s was more apprehensive than ever of social revolution that would destroy his empire and contemplated some kind of coup d'état in which the Reichstag would be throttled. He never reached this point because in 1890, at the age of seventy-five, he was obliged by the new emperor, William II, to retire.

The German Empire after 1890: William II

William I died in 1888 and was succeeded by his son Frederick III who, incurably ill of cancer, died some three months after his accession. Frederick's son, William II, the last king of Prussia and the last German Kaiser, began his reign (1888–1918) as a young man of twenty-nine, full of startling ideas about his personal power and privileges. He was uncomfortable in the presence of an elder statesman who had made the German Empire, who had been his grandfather's aide and adviser, and whom he regarded partly with veneration and partly as an old fogy. William soon quarreled with Bismarck over continuation of the antisocialist laws and over matters of foreign affairs. When Bismarck forbade his ministers to meet with the emperor on policy matters unless he was present, William resolved that he, and not Bismarck, would rule the empire, and in 1890 he ordered Bismarck to resign, "dropping the pilot," in the celebrated phrase. Under the four chancellors who succeeded Bismarck, it was William who dominated policy.

After 1890 Germany embarked upon what was termed a "new course." In foreign affairs this meant a more aggressive and ambitious colonial, naval, and diplomatic policy, as will appear in the next two chapters. In domestic affairs it meant a more conciliatory attitude toward the masses. The antisocialist laws were dropped, and the system of social security legislation was enlarged and codified. But no democratic adjustment seemed possible. William II believed in the divinely ordained prerogatives of the house of Hohenzollern, and the empire still rested on the power of the federated princes, on the Junkers, the army, and the new industrial magnates. But the Social Democrats, the Progressive party, and other democratic forces were growing in strength. They demanded, for Prussia, a reform of the illiberal constitution of 1850,[19] and for the Reich, real control over the federal chancellor by the majority party in the Reichstag. In the election of 1912 the Social Democrats reached a new high by polling four and a quarter million votes, about one-third of the total, and by electing 110 members to the Reichstag, in which they now formed the largest single party; yet they were excluded from the highest posts of government. Even had war not come in 1914, it is clear that the imperial Germany created by Bismarck was moving toward a constitutional crisis in which political democracy would be the issue.

Developments Elsewhere; General Observations

Of political developments in other European states before 1914, something has already been said in the preceding chapter. Italy had become a constitutional monarchy in the 1860s and completed its unification by the forceful seizure of Rome in 1870.[20] Despite parliamentary forms, Italian political life in substance was characterized by unstable majorities and by opportunistic maneuvering and manipulation by moderate liberal political leaders, who maintained themselves in office for long periods of time by shuffling and reshuffling political coalitions. Deputies, in a form of parliamentary politics that was baptized *trasformismo* (or a kind of "crossing over") moved readily from one party group to another—for

[19] See p. 519.
[20] See pp. 548–550, 558, 636.

favors granted. Giovanni Giolitti, a shrewd tactician who headed several cabinets, governed in this way with only a few interruptions from 1903 to 1914. The liberal leaders were anticlerical, and the quarrel with the papacy over the seizure of the papal territories remained unsettled. The popes refused to recognize the Italian kingdom and forbade Catholics to participate in its affairs or even to vote in elections. Catholics voted nonetheless and in 1907 bishops in each diocese were permitted to relax the ban, as they increasingly did.

Industry had begun to make an appearance in the northern cities like Milan. More as a matter of expediency than out of any democratic impulse, the government moved to extend the franchise to the working classes. The narrow suffrage of 1861 was broadened, first in 1882, and then in 1912, when the new reform increased the number of eligible voters from 3 to 8 million, or virtually universal male suffrage. Because of illiteracy and political inertia not all of the newly enfranchised hastened to exercise their voting privilege. The social problem remained serious, too, despite some modest labor legislation. Poverty and illiteracy, especially in the agrarian south, were grievous problems and radical unrest appeared in the industrial cities. In 1900 Victor Emmanuel's son and successor Humbert was assassinated. The first manifestations of an antiparliamentary ideology, chauvinistic nationalism, and explosive irrationalism appeared in the writings and political activism of literary men like Gabriele d'Annunzio and Filippo Marinetti, the latter publishing in 1909 the manifesto of a violently nihilistic movement he called "futurism." The machinery of political democracy was established in Italy but there could be no assurance about the direction Italian parliamentary democracy was taking.

In the Dual Monarchy of Austria-Hungary, created by the Compromise of 1867, Austria and Hungary were each in form constitutional parliamentary states.[21] In theory, the Emperor-King Francis Joseph ruled through ministries responsible to the legislature in each state. However, in the important sphere of matters affecting the empire as a whole, such as foreign affairs and military questions, there was little parliamentary restraint on the emperor. Here he had virtually final authority; moreover, in all matters he still had broad powers to govern by decree, which he exercised. As in Germany, the tide of socialism was held back both by repressive laws and by social insurance and benevolent legislation. The most serious problem in the empire remained not socialism but agitation by the various subject nationalities, the Czechs and other Slavic peoples. Political democracy took a different course in Austria than in Hungary. In the former, partly as an effort to placate nationalist sentiment, universal male suffrage was introduced in 1907. In the latter it was bitterly and successfully resisted by the Magyars, who saw in it a weapon that could be employed by the Slavs to contest and destroy their preponderance. Austria itself, despite the democratic suffrage, was ruled very much like the German Empire, with the legislature able to debate and criticize but not control policy.

Of other countries it can be said that the political forms of democracy showed signs of advancing everywhere. Universal male suffrage was adopted in Switzerland in 1874, in Belgium in 1893 (though plural voting was still permitted), in the Netherlands in 1896; and in the next few years in Norway and Sweden

[21] See pp. 561–564.

(Norway was peacefully separated in 1905 from Sweden). In southern Europe, besides Italy, universal male suffrage was introduced in Spain, Greece, Bulgaria, Serbia, and after the revolt of 1908, in Turkey. Although both Spain and Portugal were beset by civil wars, constitutional forms were eventually adopted in both countries, universal male suffrage being introduced in Spain in 1890 and a liberal suffrage in Portugal under a republic in 1911. Even tsarist Russia, after the Revolution of 1905, received a Duma, or national parliament, elected on a wide franchise but on an indirect and undemocratic class basis, and with narrow powers.[22] Among states west of the Russian empire, only Hungary and Romania had a highly restricted suffrage on the eve of the First World War. The vote for women progressed more slowly. Women voted before 1914 only in certain western states of the United States, in Australia, New Zealand, Finland, and Norway. Not until after the First World War did female suffrage begin to make significant advances.

The progress of representative and democratic institutions did not mean an end to the rule of monarchs, landed aristocrats, and other minority interests. For one thing, with the exception of France and Switzerland, Europe remained monarchical. Second, despite the growing importance of parliaments, parliamentary control over political life was far from guaranteed; emperors and kings still ruled through their chancellors and prime ministers. Of the major world powers it was mainly in the United States (at least for whites), Britain, and France that democratic and popular control was something of a reality. But the extension of the suffrage, by the relaxation of property qualifications, had a dynamic of its own and was altering the framework of politics everywhere; mass political parties, including socialist parties and confessional, or religious-oriented parties, were replacing the older, narrowly oligarchic political organizations, and support now had to be sought on a wider electoral basis. In almost all Europe, and in many of the outlying areas peopled by European descendants, democracy was advancing, even within the older framework. By 1871, most European nations, with the notable exception of Russia, had already won written constitutions, guarantees of personal freedom, parliamentary and representative institutions, and limitations on absolutism; in the years between 1871 and 1914 the most significant new political factor was the advance of male suffrage.

75. *The Advance of Democracy: Socialism and Labor Unions*

The artisan and laboring classes had never viewed with much pleasure the rise of capitalism or of "bourgeois" liberalism. They had always been doubtful of free competition, unrestrained private enterprise, the Manchester School, laissez faire, the laws of supply and demand, the free market for goods and labor, the idea of an economy independent of states and governments. These were the ideas of middle-class liberals, not of radical democrats. Popular leaders had opposed them in the French Revolution in 1793. The English Chartists had been outspokenly

---

[22] See pp. 744–745.

anticapitalistic, and on the Continent the ideas of socialism had been spreading. In 1848 there was a strong movement among the working classes for a "social" republic, and, though the social revolution failed in 1848, the force of it was enough to terrify the possessing classes and shape the philosophy of Karl Marx.[23] With the advent of the ballot, workers pressed for social legislation and used their political power to gain a greater measure of social democracy.

But in addition, before and after obtaining the ballot, working people resorted to other devices for the improvement of their position. Against the owners of capital, who controlled the giving of jobs, there were two principal lines of action. One was to abolish the capitalists, the other to bargain with them. The former led to socialism, the latter to the formation of labor unions. Socialism, in logic, meant the extinction of the private employer as such.[24] Trade unionism, in logic, meant that the workers had every reason to keep their employers prosperously in business in order that bargaining with them might produce more results. The working-class movement thus contained an internal contradiction which was never completely resolved.

Middle-class and educated people who took up the workers' cause, the "intellectuals" of the movement—Karl Marx, Friedrich Engels, Louis Blanc, Ferdinand Lassalle, and thousands of less famous names—tended more to socialism than to unionism. They thought of society as a whole, they saw the economic system as a system, they thought of the future in long-run terms, and their time scale allowed generously for whole historical epochs to come and go. The actual workers, put to work at an early age, barely educated if at all, with the waking hours of their adult lives spent on manual jobs, were inclined to keep their attention more on unionism than on socialism. To earn a shilling more every week beginning next week, to be spared the nervous strain and physical danger of constant exposure to unprotected machinery, to have fifteen minutes more every day for lunch, were likely to seem more tangible and important than far-reaching but distant plans for a reconstructed society. The worker looked on the intellectual as an outsider, however welcome; the intellectual looked on the worker as shortsighted and timid, however much in need of help.

After the failures of 1848 the socialist and trade union movements diverged for a generation. The 1850s, compared with the hungry '40s, were a time of full employment, rising wages, and increasing prosperity for all classes. Workers set to organizing unions, socialist thinkers to perfecting their doctrines.

The Trade Union Movement and Rise of British Labor

Organizations of wage workers, or labor unions in the modern sense (as distinguished from medieval craft guilds), had long maintained a shadowy and sporadic existence, as in the old French journeymen's associations.[25] But they had always been extralegal, frowned upon or actually prohibited by governments. French revolutionaries in the Le Chapelier Act of 1791, British Tories in the Combination Act of 1799, had been as one in forbidding workers to unite. It was

---

[23] See pp. 495–499, 502–505, 522–526.
[24] See pp. 467–468, 497.
[25] See pp. 374–375, 529–530.

the rise of "bourgeois" liberalism, so insensitive to the worker in most ways, that first gave legal freedom to labor unions. The British unions received a tacit recognition from the Liberal Tories in 1825 and explicit recognition from Gladstone's Liberal ministry in 1871. French unions were recognized by Napoleon III in 1864, then restrained in the reaction caused by the Commune, then fully legalized in 1884. In Germany Bismarck negotiated with labor leaders to find support against the vested interests that stood in his way.

The prosperity of the 1850s favored the formation of unions, for workers can always organize most easily when employers are most in need of their services. The craft union—or union of skilled workers in the same trade, such as carpenters—was at first the typical organization. It was most fully developed in England, where a "new model" unionism was introduced by the Amalgamated Society of Engineers (i.e., machinists) in 1851. It was the policy of the "new model" union officials to take the unions out of politics, to forget the semisocialism of the Chartists, to abandon Robert Owen's grandiose idea of "one big union" for all workers, and to concentrate on advancing the interests of each separate trade. The new leaders proposed to be reasonable with employers, avoid strikes, accumulate union funds, and build up their membership. In this they were very successful; the unions took root; and the two governing parties in England, reassured by the unexpected moderation of working-class spokesmen, combined to give the town worker the vote in 1867.

In the 1880s, and especially with the great London dock strike of 1889, which closed the port of London for the first time since the French Revolution, unions of unskilled workers began to form. Industrial unionism, or the joining in one union of all workers in one industry, such as coal or transportation, regardless of the skill or job of the individual worker, began to take shape at the same time. In some cases the older skilled unionists joined with unskilled laborers who worked beside them. Thus gradually arose, for example, the Transport Workers Union, which half a century later was to give a foreign secretary to the government in the person of Ernest Bevin. By 1900 there were about 2,000,000 union members in Great Britain, compared with only 850,000 in Germany and 250,000 in France.

It was largely because British workers were so far advanced in trade unionism, and so successful in forcing collective bargaining upon their employers, that they were much slower than their Continental counterparts in forming a workers' political party. By the 1880s, when avowed socialists were already sitting in French, Belgian, and German parliaments, the only corresponding persons in Britain were a half-dozen "Lib-Labs," as they were called, laboring men elected on the Liberal ticket. The British Labour party was formed at the turn of the century by the joint efforts of trade union officials and middle-class intellectuals.[26] Where on the Continent the labor unions were often led, and even brought into being, by the socialist political parties, in Britain it was the labor unions that brought into being, and subsequently led, the Labour party. Hence for a long time the Labour party was less socialistic than working-class parties on the Continent. Its origin and rapid growth were due in large measure to a desire to defend the unions as established and respectable institutions. The unions were threatened in their very existence by a ruling of the British courts in 1901, the

[26] See p. 623.

Taff Vale decision, which held a union financially responsible for business losses incurred by an employer during a strike. The shortest and most orderly strike, by exhausting a union's funds, might ruin the union. The year before, steps had been taken to bring together the unions and all other existing labor and socialist organizations into a labor representation committee, in preparation for the elections of 1900; the effort was not very successful and only two of the fifteen labor candidates were returned. But the Taff Vale decision unified all ranks and precipitated the formation of the modern Labour party. In the election of 1906 the new Labour party sent twenty-nine members to Parliament, which thereupon overruled the Taff Vale decision by new legislation. The social legislation put through Parliament by the Liberal party government in the next few years, in good part under pressure from labor, has already been described.[27]

European Socialism after 1850

As for socialism, which had so frightened the middle and upper classes in 1848, it seemed in the 1850s to go into abeyance. Karl Marx, after issuing the *Communist Manifesto* with Engels in 1848, and agitating as a journalist in the German revolution of that year, withdrew to the secure haven offered by England, where, after years of painstaking research, he published the first volume of his *Capital* in 1867. This work, of which the succeeding two volumes were published after his death, gave body, substance, and argument to the principles announced in the *Manifesto*.[28] Marx, during more than thirty years in London, scarcely mixed with the labor leaders then building up the English unions. Hardly known to the English, he associated mainly with political exiles and temporary visitors of numerous nationalities. The first volume of *Capital* was not published in English until 1886.

In 1864 there took place in London the first meeting of the International Working Men's Association, commonly known as the First International. It was sponsored by a heterogeneous group, including the secretary of the British carpenters' union, Robert Applegarth; the aging Italian revolutionary, Mazzini; and Karl Marx. With the union officials absorbed in union business, leadership in the Association gradually passed to Marx, who used it as a means of publicizing the ideas about to appear in his *Capital*. At subsquent annual congresses, at Geneva, Lausanne, Brussels, and Basel, Marx built up his position. He made the Mazzinians unwelcome, and he denounced the German Lassalleans for their willingness to cooperate with Bismarck, arguing that it was not the business of socialists to cooperate with the state but to seize it. His sharpest struggle was with the Russian Bakunin. With his background in tsarist Russia, Bakunin believed the state to be the cause of the common man's afflictions; he was hence an "anarchist," holding that the state should be attacked and abolished. To Marx anarchism was abhorrent; the correct doctrine was that the state—tsarist or bourgeois—was only a product of economic conditions, a tool in the class struggle, a weapon of the propertied interests, so that the true target for revolutionary

[27] See pp. 612–613.
[28] See p. 523.

action must be not the state but the capitalist economic system. Marx drove Bakunin from the International in 1872.

Meanwhile members of the First International watched with great excitement the Paris Commune of 1871, which they hoped might be the opening act of a European working-class upheaval. Members of the International infiltrated the Commune, and the connection between the two, though rather incidental, was one reason why the French provisional government repressed the Commune with such terrified ferocity. But the Commune actually killed the First International. The Commune had been bloody and violent, an armed rebellion against the democratically elected National Assembly of France. Marx praised it as a stage in the international class war. He even saw in it a foretaste of what he was coming to call the "dictatorship of the proletariat." He thus frightened many possible followers away. Certainly British trade unionists, sober and steady men, could have nothing to do with such doings or such doctrines. The First International faded out of existence after 1872.

But in 1875, at the Gotha conference, Marxian and Lassallean socialists effected enough of a union to found the German Social Democratic party, whose growth thereafter, against Bismarck's attempts to stop it, has already been noted. About 1880 socialist parties sprouted up in many countries. In Belgium, highly industrialized, a Belgian Socialist party appeared in 1879. In the industrial regions of France some workers were attracted to Jules Guesde, a self-taught worker, former Communard, and now a rigid Marxist, who held it impossible to emancipate the working class by compromise of any sort; others followed the "possibilist" Dr. Brousse, who thought it possible for workers to arrive at socialism through parliamentary methods; still others supported Jean Jaurès, who eloquently linked social reform to the French revolutionary tradition and the defense of republican institutions. Not until 1905 did the socialist groups in France form a unified Socialist party. In England, in 1881, H. M. Hyndman founded a Social Democratic Federation on the German model and with a Marxist program; it never had more than a handful of members. In 1883 two Russian exiles in Switzerland, Plekhanov and Axelrod, recent converts to Marxism, founded the Russian Social Democratic party, from which the communism of the following century was eventually to be derived. The socialist parties all came together to establish an international league in 1889, known as the Second International, which thereafter met every three years and lasted until 1914.

Revisionist and Revolutionary Socialism, 1880–1914

The new socialist parties of the 1880s were all Marxist in inspiration. Marx died in 1883. Marxism or "scientific socialism," by the force of its social analysis, the mass of Marx's writings over forty years, and an attitude of unyielding hostility to competing socialist doctrines, had become the only widely current form of systematic socialism. Strongest in Germany and France, Marxism was relatively unsuccessful in Italy and Spain, where the working class, less industrialized anyway, more illiterate, unable to place its hopes in the ballot, and habituated to an excitable insurrectionism in the manner of Garibaldi, turned more frequently to the anarchism preached by Bakunin.

Nor was Marxism at all successful in England; workers stood by their trade unions, and middle-class critics of capitalism followed the Fabian Society, established in 1883. The Fabians (so called from the ancient Roman general Fabius Cunctator, the "delayer," or strategist of gradual methods) were very English and very un-Marxist. George Bernard Shaw, H. G. Wells, and Sidney and Beatrice Webb were among early members of the Society. For them socialism was the social and economic counterpart to political democracy, as well as its inevitable outcome. They held that no class conflict was necessary or even existed, that gradual and reasonable and conciliatory measures would in due time bring about a socialist state, and that improvement of local government, or municipal ownership of such things as waterworks and electric lighting, were steps toward this consummation. The Fabians, like the trade union officials, were content with small and immediate satisfactions. They joined with the unions to form the Labour party. At the same time, by patient and detailed researches into economic realities, they provided a mass of practical information on which a legislative program could be based.

The Marxist or Social Democratic parties on the Continent grew very rapidly. Marxism turned into a less revolutionary "parliamentary socialism"—except indeed for the Russian Social Democratic party, since Russia had no parliamentary government. For the growth of socialist parties meant that true workers, and not merely intellectuals, were voting for socialist candidates for the Reichstag, Chamber of Deputies, or whatever the lower house of parliament might be called; and this in turn meant that the psychology and influence of labor unions within the parties were increased. The workers, and their union officials, might in theory consider themselves locked in an enormous struggle with capital; but in practice their aim was to get more for themselves out of their employers' business. They might believe in the internationalism of the workers' interests; but in practice, acting through the parliaments of national states, they would work for orderly legislation benefiting the workers of their own country only—social insurance, factory regulation, minimum wages, or maximum hours. Nor was it possible to deny, by the close of the century, that Marx's anticipations (based initially on conditions of the 1840s) had not come true, at least not yet; the bourgeois was getting richer, but the proletarian was not getting poorer. Real wages—or what the wage earner's income would actually buy, even allowing for the losses due to unemployment—are estimated to have risen about 50 percent in the industrialized countries between 1870 and 1900. The increase was due to the greater productivity of labor through mechanization, the growth of the world economy, the accumulation of capital wealth, and the gradual fall in prices of food and other items that the workers had to buy.

Repeatedly, but in vain, the Second International had to warn its component socialist parties against collaboration with the bourgeoisie. Marxism began in the 1890s to undergo a movement of revisionism, led in France by Jean Jaurès, socialist leader in the Chamber of Deputies, and in Germany by Eduard Bernstein, Social Democratic member of the Reichstag and author in 1898 of *Evolutionary Socialism,* an important tract setting forth the new views. The revisionists held that the class conflict might not be absolutely inevitable, that capitalism might be gradually transformed in the workers' interest, and that now that the workers had not only the vote but a political party of their own, they could obtain their ends through democratic channels, without revolution and without any dictatorship of the proletariat. Most socialists or social democrats followed the revisionists.

This tendency to "opportunism"[29] among Marxists drove the really revolutionary spirits into new directions. Thus there arose revolutionary syndicalism, of which the main intellectual exponent was a Frenchman, Georges Sorel. "Syndicalism" is simply the French word for trade unionism (*syndicat,* a union), and the idea was that the workers' unions might themselves become the supreme authoritative institutions in society, replacing not only property and the market economy, but government itself. The means to this end was to be a stupendous general strike, in which all workers in all industries should simultaneously stop work, thus paralyzing society and forcing acceptance of their will. Syndicalism made most headway where the unions were weakest, as in Italy, Spain, and France, since here the unions had the least to lose and were most in need of sensational doctrines to attract members. Its strongest base was in the French General Confederation of Labor, founded in 1895.

Among orthodox Marxists there was also a revival of Marxist fundamentals in protest against revisionism. In Germany Karl Kautsky arraigned the revisionists as compromisers who betrayed Marxism for petty-bourgeois ends. In 1904 he and other rigorists prevailed upon the Second International to condemn the political behavior of the French socialist Alexandre Millerand who in 1899 had accepted a ministerial post in a French cabinet. Socialists might use parliaments as a forum, the International ruled, but socialists who entered the government itself were unpardonably identifying themselves with the enemy bourgeois state. Not until the First World War did socialists henceforth join the cabinet of any European country. In the Russian Social Democratic party the issue of revisionism came to a head in 1903, at a party congress held in London—for the most prominent Russian Marxists were mainly exiles. Here a group led by Lenin demanded that revisionism be stamped out. Lenin won a majority, at the moment at least, and hence the uncompromising Marxists were called Bolsheviks (from the Russian word for majority), while the revisionist or conciliatory Russian Marxists, those willing to work with bourgeois liberals and democrats, were subsequently known as Mensheviks or the "minority" group.[30] But in 1903 the Russian Marxists were considered very unimportant.

In general, in Europe's "inner zone," by the turn of the century, most people who called themselves Marxists were no longer actively revolutionary. As revolutionary republicanism had quieted down in the Third French Republic, so revolutionary Marxism seemed to have quieted down into the milder doctrines of social democracy. What would have happened except for the coming of war in 1914 cannot be known; possibly social revolutionism would have revived, since real wages no longer generally rose between 1900 and 1914, and considerable restlessness developed in labor circles, punctuated by great strikes. But in 1914 the working class as a whole was in no revolutionary mood. Workers still sought a greater measure of social justice, but the social agitation so feared or hoped for in 1848 had subsided. There seem to have been three principal reasons. Capitalism had worked well enough to raise the workers' living standard above what they

[29] See p. 527.
[30] See p. 739.

could remember of their fathers' or grandfathers'; workers had the vote and so felt that they participated in the state, could expect to benefit from the government, and had little to gain by its overthrow; and third, they had their interests watched over by organized and increasingly powerful unions, by which a larger share in the national income could be demanded and passed on to them.

76. *Science, Philosophy, the Arts, and Religion*

Faith in the powers of natural science has been characteristic of modern society for over three centuries, but never was there a time when this faith spread to so many people, or was held so firmly, so optimistically, and with so few qualms or mental reservations as in the half-century preceding the First World War. Science lay at the bottom of the whole movement of industrialization; and if science became positively popular after about 1870, in that persons ignorant of science came to look upon it as an oracle, it was because it manifested itself to everybody in the new wonders of daily life. Hardly had the world's more civilized regions digested the railroad, the steamship, and the telegraph when a whole series of new inventions already described[31] had begun to unfold itself. In thirty years following 1875 the number of patents tripled in the United States, quadrupled in Germany, and multiplied in all the civilized countries. The scientific and technical advance was as completely international (though confined mainly to the "inner zone") as any movement the world has ever seen. Never had the rush of scientific invention been so fundamentally useful, so helpful to the constructive labors and serious problems of mankind, and in that sense human.

In more basic scientific thinking important changes set in about 1860 or 1870. Up to that time, generally speaking, the underlying ideas had been those set forth by Isaac Newton almost two centuries before.[32] The law of universal gravitation reigned unquestioned, and with it, hardly less so, the geometry of Euclid and a physics that was basically mechanics. The ultimate nature of the universe was thought to be regular, orderly, predictable, and harmonious; it was also timeless, in that the passage of ages brought no change or development. By the end of the epoch considered here, that is, by 1914, the old conceptions had begun to yield on every side.

The Impact of Evolution

In impact upon general thinking the greatest change came in the new emphasis upon biology and the life sciences. Here the great symbolic date is the publication by Charles Darwin of the *Origin of Species* in 1859. Evolution, after Darwin, became the order of the day. Evolutionary philosophies, holding that the way to understand anything was to understand its development, were not new in 1859. Hegel had introduced the evolutionary conception into metaphysics; and he and Marx, into theories of human society.[33] The idea of progress, taken over from

[31] See pp. 595–596
[32] See pp. 297–300.
[33] See pp. 471, 524–525.

the Age of Enlightenment, was a kind of evolutionary philosophy; and the great activity in historical studies, under romantic and nationalistic auspices, had made people think of human affairs in terms of a time process.[34] In the world of nature, the rise of geology after 1800 had opened the way to evolutionary ideas, and venturesome biologists had allowed themselves to speculate on an evolutionary development of living forms. What Darwin did was to stamp evolution with the seal of science, marshaling the evidence for it and offering an explanation of how it worked. In 1871, in his *Descent of Man,* he applied the same hypotheses to human beings.

By evolution, Darwin meant that species are mutable; that no species is created to remain unchanged once and for all; and that all species of living organisms, plant and animal, microscopic or elephantine in dimensions, living or extinct, have developed by successive small changes from other species that went before them. An important corollary was that all life was interrelated and subject to the same laws. Another corollary was that the whole history of living things on earth, generally held by scientists in Darwin's time to be many millions of years, was a unified history unfolding continuously in a single meaningful process of evolution.

Darwin thought that species changed, not by any intelligent or purposeful activity in the organism, but essentially by a kind of chance. Individual organisms, through the play of heredity, inherited slightly different characteristics, some more useful than others in food getting, fighting, or mating; and the organisms that had the most useful characteristics tended to survive, so that their characteristics were passed on to offspring, until the whole species gradually changed. Certain phrases, not all of them invented by Darwin, summed up the theory. There was a "struggle for existence" resulting in the "survival of the fittest" through "natural selection" of the "most favored races"—races meaning not human races but the strains within a species. The struggle for existence referred to the fact that, in nature, more individuals were born in each species than could live out a normal life span; the "fittest" were those individual specimens of a species having the most useful characteristics, such as fleetness in deer or ferocity in tigers; "natural" selection meant that the fittest survived without purpose in themselves or in a Creator; the "favored races" were the strains within a species having good survival powers.

Darwin's ideas precipitated a great outcry. Scientists rushed to defend and churchmen to attack him. The biologist T. H. Huxley became the chief spokesman for Darwin—"Darwin's bulldog." He debated with, among others, the bishop of Oxford. Darwin was denounced, with less than fairness, for saying that men came from monkeys. It was feared that all grounds of human dignity, morality, and religion would collapse. Darwin himself remained complacent on this score. Under civilized conditions, he said, the social and cooperative virtues were useful characteristics assisting in survival, so that "we may expect that virtuous habits will grow stronger, becoming perhaps fixed by inheritance." Much of the outburst against Darwin was somewhat trivial, nor were those who attacked him generally noted for spiritual insight; yet they were not mistaken in sensing a profound danger.

That Darwinism said nothing of God, Providence, or salvation was not surprising; no science ever did. That evolution did not exactly square with the

---

[34] See pp. 315, 326, 437, 471–472.

first chapter of Genesis was disturbing but not fatal; much of the Old Testament was already regarded as symbolic, at least outside certain fundamentalist circles. Even the idea that man and the animals were of one piece was not ruinous; the animal side of human nature had not escaped the notice of theologians. The novel and upsetting effect of evolutionary biology was to change the conception of nature. Nature was no longer a harmony, it was a scene of struggle, "nature red in tooth and claw." Struggle and elimination of the weak were natural, and as means toward evolutionary development they might even be considered good. There were no fixed species or perfected forms, but only an unending flux. Change was everlasting; and everything seemed merely relative to time, place, and environment. There were no norms of good and bad; a good organism was one that survived where others perished; adaptation replaced virtue; outside of it there was nothing "right." The test was, in short, success; the "fit" were the successful; and here Darwinism merged with that toughness of mind, or *Realpolitik,* which came over Europe at the same time from other causes.[35]

Such at least were the implications if one generalized from science, carrying over scientific findings into human affairs, and the prestige of science was so great that this is precisely what many people wished to do. With the popularization of biological evolution, a school known as Social Darwinists actively applied the ideas of the struggle for existence and survival of the fittest to human society. Social Darwinists were found all over Europe and the United States. Their doctrines were put to various uses, to show that some peoples were naturally superior to others, such as whites to blacks, or Nordics to Latins, or Germans to Slavs (or vice versa), or non-Jews to Jews; or that the upper and middle classes, comfortable and contented, deserved these blessings because they had proved themselves "fitter" than the shiftless poor; or that big business in the nature of things had to take over smaller concerns; or that some states, such as the British or German Empire, were bound to rise, or that war was morally a fine thing, proving the virility and survival value of those who fought.

Anthropology and Psychology

The newer life sciences, such as anthropology and psychology, developed very rapidly in the latter part of the nineteenth century. Their effect upon the civilization of the day was not unlike that of Darwinism. Both accepted biological evolution. Both, as the price of being truly scientific, eschewed standards of right and wrong and set themselves to finding out and explaining the mere facts of human behavior.

Anthropology set itself the task of studying the physical and cultural characteristics of all branches of mankind. Physical anthropologists became interested in the several human "races," some of which they considered might be "favored" in the Darwinian sense, that is, superior in inheritance and survival value. It was often concluded, even by scientists at the time, that the whites were the most competent race, and among the whites the Nordics, Teutons, or Germans and Anglo-Saxons. The public, more or less exaggerating such ideas, became more race conscious than Europeans had ever been before. On the other hand the cultural anthropologists, surveying all manner of primitive or complex societies

[35] See pp. 520–521.

with scientific disinterest, seemed sometimes to teach a more deflating doctrine. Scientifically, it seemed, no culture or society was "better" than any other, all being adaptations to an environment, or merely a matter of custom—of the *mores,* as people said in careful distinction from "morals." The effect was again a kind of relativism or skepticism—a negation of values, a belief that right and wrong were matters of social convention, psychological conditioning, mere opinion, or point of view. We are describing, let it be repeated, not the history of science itself but the effects of science upon European civilization at the time.

The impact of anthropology was felt keenly in religion too. Sir James Frazer (1854–1941) in his multivolumed *The Golden Bough* could demonstrate that some of the most sacred practices, rites, and ideas of Christianity were not unique but could be found among primitive societies, and that, moreover, only the thinnest of lines divided magic from religion. Anthropology, like Darwinian evolution, undermined traditional religious beliefs.

Psychology, as a science of human behavior, led to thoroughly upsetting implications about the very nature of man. It was launched in the 1870s as a natural science by the German physiologist Wilhelm Wundt (1832–1920), who developed various new experimental techniques. The Russian Ivan Pavlov (1849–1936) conducted a famous series of experiments in which he "conditioned" dogs to salivate automatically at the ringing of a bell once they had become accustomed over a period of time to associate the sound with the serving of their food. Pavlov's observations were important. They implied that a great part of animal behavior, and presumably human behavior, could be explained on the basis of conditioned responses. In the case of human beings these are responses which humans make automatically by virtue of their earlier environment and training and not through choice or conscious reasoning.

Most significant of all the developments in the study of human behavior was the work of Sigmund Freud (1856–1939) and those influenced by him. Freud, a Viennese physician, founded psychoanalysis at the turn of the century. He came to believe that certain forms of emotional disturbance like hysteria were traceable to earlier forgotten episodes of patients' lives. After first trying various techniques such as hypnosis, which he soon abandoned, he employed free association, or free recall. If patients could be helped to bring these suppressed experiences into conscious recall, the symptoms of illness would often disappear. From these beginnings Freud and his followers explored the role that the unconscious played in all human behavior, he himself stressing the sexual drive. In one of his most famous books, *The Interpretation of Dreams* (1900), he stressed dreams as a key to understanding the unconscious; elsewhere he related his findings to religion, education, art, and literature. Freud and Freudian ideas had great influence on the social and behavioral sciences, and a good deal of the Freudian vocabulary later entered into everyday language and popular culture. In its deepest significance psychoanalysis, by revealing the wide areas of human behavior outside conscious control, suggested that human beings were not essentially rational creatures at all.

The New Physics

The revolution in biology of the nineteenth century, together with the developments in psychology and anthropology, were soon to be matched and surpassed by the revolution in physics. In the late 1890s physics was on the threshold of a revolutionary transformation. Like Newtonian mechanics in the seventeenth century and Darwinian evolution in the nineteenth, the new physics represented one of the great scientific revolutions of all time. There was no single work comparable to Newton's *Principia* or Darwin's *Origin of Species* unless Albert Einstein's theory of relativity, propounded in a series of scientific papers in 1905 and 1916, might be considered as such. Instead there were a series of discoveries and findings, partly mathematical and then increasingly empirical, that threw new light on the nature of matter and energy. In Newtonian physics the atom, the basic unit of all matter, which the Greeks had hypothesized in ancient times, was like a hard, solid, unstructured billiard ball, permanent and unchanging; and matter and energy were separate and distinct. But a series of discoveries from 1896 on profoundly altered this view. In 1896 the French scientist Antoine Henri Becquerel discovered radioactivity, observing that uranium emitted particles or rays of energy. In the years immediately following, from the observations and discoveries of the French scientists Pierre and Marie Curie and the Englishmen J. J. Thomson and Lord Rutherford, there emerged the notion that atoms were not simple but complex, and, moreover, that various radioactive atoms were by nature unstable, releasing energy as they disintegrated. The German physicist Max Planck demonstrated in 1900 that energy was emitted or absorbed in specific and discrete units or bundles, each called a quantum; moreover, energy was not emitted smoothly and continuously as previously thought, nor was it as distinguishable from matter as once supposed. In 1913, the Danish physicist Niels Bohr postulated an atom consisting of a nucleus of protons surrounded by electrically charged units, called electrons, rotating around the nucleus, each in its orbit, like a minuscule solar system.

With radioactivity scientists were being brought back to the idea long rejected, the favored view of the alchemists, that matter was transmutable; in a way undreamed of even by the alchemists, it was convertible into energy. This the German-born Jewish scientific genius Albert Einstein (1879–1955) expressed in a famous formula $e = mc^2$. From his theory of relativity emerged also the profoundly revolutionary notion that time, space, and motion were not absolute in character but were all relative to the observer and the observer's own movement in space. In later years, in 1929 and in 1954, Einstein brought together into one common set of laws, as Newton formerly had done, a unified field theory, an explanation of gravitation, electromagnetism, and subatomic behavior. Difficult as it was to grasp, and a great deal was still the subject of scientific controversy, it modified much that had been taken for granted since Newton. The Newtonian world was being replaced by a four-dimensional world, a kind of space-time continuum; and in mathematics, non-Euclidean geometries were being developed. It turned out, too, that neither cause and effect nor time and space nor Newton's law of universal gravitation meant very much in the subatomic world nor indeed in the cosmos when objects moved with the speed of light. It was impossible, as the German scientist Werner Heisenberg demonstrated a little later, in 1927, by his principle of uncertainty, or indeterminacy, to ascertain simultaneously both the position and the velocity of the individual electron. On these foundations established before the First World War there developed the new science of nuclear physics and the tapping of the atom's energy. The atom was soon discovered to be even more complex than conceived of before 1914, and its potentialities even greater.

Trends in Philosophy and the Arts

The step from pure science to philosophy is a long one, but one that many were prepared to take. Not only was the faith in science widespread but it was widely held that science was the only means of certain knowledge, and that anything unknowable to science must remain unknowable forever—a doctrine called agnosticism, or the acknowledgment of ignorance. Herbert Spencer (1820–1903) in England and Ernst Haeckel (1834–1919) in Germany were widely read popularizers of agnosticism; both also pictured a universe governed by Darwinian evolution. For Spencer especially, all philosophy could be unified, organized, and coordinated through the doctrine of evolution; this doctrine he applied not only to all living things but to sociology, government, and economics as well. The evolution of society, he felt, was toward the increasing freedom of the individual, the role of governments being merely to maintain freedom and justice; they were not to interfere with natural social and economic processes, not to coddle the weak and unfit. Yet, like Darwin himself, Spencer believed that altruism, charity, and good will as individual ethical virtues were themselves useful and laudable products of evolutionary development.

These latter views were not shared by another of the serious writers of the age, also much influenced by evolutionary ideas, the German philosopher Friedrich Nietzsche (1844–1900). More a philosopher of art than of science, and drawing from many intellectual currents of the century, Nietzsche was an unsystematic and unclear thinker to whom it is easy to do less than justice. It is evident, however, that his opinion of mankind was a low one, and that from a background of evolutionary thinking he developed some kind of doctrine of a Superman, a noble being who, in a final triumph of world history, should issue from, lead, dominate, and dazzle the multitude. Qualities of humility, patience, brotherly helpfulness, hope, and love, in short the specifically Christian virtues, Nietzsche described as a slave morality concocted by the weak to disarm the strong. Qualities of courage, love of danger, intellectual excellence, and beauty of character he considered much better. Such views, for better or worse, were actually a new form of classical paganism. Nietzsche was neither much read nor much respected by his contemporaries, who considered him unbalanced or even insane; but he nevertheless expressed with unshrinking frankness many ideas implied in the outlook of his day.

As in the sciences, so in works of creative imagination—pure literature and the fine arts—the changes at the dawn of the twentieth century ushered in the contemporary age. Some writers, like Zola in France or Ibsen in Scandinavia, turned to the portrayal of social problems, producing a realistic literature dealing with industrial strife, strikes, prostitution, divorce, or insanity. Freudian and other views of psychology slowly made themselves felt in works of fiction; the new novels were often more likelike than the old even though they added little to one's faith in human nature. The arts followed the intellectual developments of the age, reflecting, as they do today, attitudes of relativism, irrationalism, social determinism, and interest in the subconscious. On the other hand, never had artist and society been so far apart. The painter Gauguin, an extreme case, fled to the South Seas, went primitive, and reveled in the stark violence of tropical colors. Others became absorbed in technicalities or mere capricious self-expression. Art at its extreme fringe became incomprehensible and the average person was deprived of a means (as old as the cave paintings of the Stone Age) of perceiving, seizing, and enjoying the world about him. After the First World War, and on into the present, the same trends of subjectivism in the arts attracted a wider, if still skeptical audience. People read books without punctuation (or with peculiar punctuation), listened to music called atonal and deliberately composed for effects of discord and dissonance, and studied intently abstract or "nonobjective" paintings and sculpture to which the artists themselves often refused to give titles.

The problem of communication remained serious. The arts suffered from the specialization of the modern world. The artist was not thought of as a collective spokesman or creator of something for common use but as a specialist plying his own trade and pursuing his own concerns. Society itself was divided into busy, self-centered groups, unable to communicate except on superficial matters, and hence in the long run less able to work in common.

The Churches and the Modern Age

Religion, too, was displaced. It was now a long time since almost everyone had looked to religion for guidance. But religion was more threatened after 1860 or 1870 than ever in the past, because never before had science, or philosophies drawing upon science, addressed themselves so directly to the existence of life and of man. Never before had so many of the fundamental premises of traditional religion been questioned or denied. Darwinian evolution had challenged the traditional picture of Creation, and anthropologists had questioned the uniqueness of the most sacred Christian tenets. There developed also the "higher" criticism of the Bible, an effort to apply to the Scriptures the techniques of scholarship long applied to secular documents, to incorporate archeological discoveries, and to reconstruct a naturalistic, historical account of ancient religious times. The movement, going back at least to the seventeenth century,[36] now took on significant proportions and was applied both to the Old Testament and the New. In the case of the Old Testament the patient scrutiny of style and language cast doubt on the validity of certain prophecies; and in the New the inconsistencies of the several Gospel sources were made patent. The German theologian David Friedrich Strauss (1808–1874), one such critical scholar, was the author of a widely discussed *Life of Jesus,* in which many miraculous and supernatural episodes were reverently but firmly explained away as "myth." The sensitive French historian and man of letters Ernest Renan (1823–1892) in a somewhat similar vein wrote on the origins of Christianity and on the life of ancient Israel. The ordinary person's long-established articles of faith were being further undermined. Moreover, the whole tenor of the time, its absorption in material progress, likewise kept people away from church; and the wholesale uprooting, the movement from country to city, often broke religious ties.

[36] See pp. 305–306.

The Protestant churches were less successful than the Catholic in protecting their membership from the disintegrating effects of the age. Church attendance among Protestants became increasingly casual, and the doctrines set forth in sermons seemed increasingly remote. Protestant laymen traditionally trusted their own private judgment and regarded their clergy as their own agents, not as authoritative teachers placed above them. Protestants also had always set special emphasis on the Bible as the source of religious belief; and as doubts accumulated on the literal truth of Biblical narratives there seemed no other source on which to rely.

Protestants tended to divide between modernists and fundamentalists. The fundamentalists, as they were called in the United States, in an effort to defend the literal word of Scripture, were often obliged to deny the most indubitable findings of science. The modernists were willing enough to be scientific and to interpret much of the Bible as allegory, but only with difficulty could they recapture any spirituality or urgent feeling of Christian truth. Most Protestant churches were slow to face the social problems and wholesale injustices produced by the economic system, though a group of "Christian socialists" developed, notably, within the Church of England. And as education and the care of orphans, aged, sick, and insane persons passed to the state, Protestant groups had less to do in the relief of suffering and upbringing of the young. Protestantism, to the regret of many Protestants, became increasingly a customary observance by people whose minds were elsewhere. Not until after the First World War could a strong Protestant revival be discerned, with a reaffirmation of basic doctrines by thinkers like Karl Barth, and a movement on the part of divergent Protestant churches to combine.

The Roman Catholic church proved more resistant to the trends of the age. We have seen how Pope Pius IX (1846–1878), after being driven from Rome by republicans in 1848, gave up his inclinations to liberalism.[37] In 1864, in the

[37] See pp. 512–514.

PAINTING #198 (AUTUMN)
by Vasily Kandinsky (Russian, then in Germany and France, 1866–1944)
What is loosely called modern art dates from the early twentieth century. Where the Impressionists continued to represent objects while losing interest in objective representation, in the next generation many painters gave up the objects themselves, thus launching various nonobjective or "abstract" styles. This *Painting #198* was done in 1914 by Kandinsky, one of the first practitioners of purely abstract painting. Since it is meant to convey color, without reference to physical objects, it does not lend itself to the kind of reproduction here used. Color at this time had a deep and vital meaning for Kandinsky though he later turned to the invention of geometric or linear images as well. For the commonly perceived world of external objects he substituted a universe of his own. "To create a body of artistic work," he said, "is to create a world." Or again, speaking of nature, "it is not enough to see it; we must live it." With such sentiments Kandinsky shared in the antirationalist or vitalistic philosophies of the period. Courtesy of the The Solomon R. Guggenheim Museum. Permission A.D.A.G.P. 1970 by French Reproduction Rights, Inc.

Syllabus of Errors, he denounced as erroneous a long list of widely current ideas, including the faith in rationalism and science, and he vigorously denied that the head of the church "should reconcile and align himself with progress, liberalism, and modern civilization." The *Syllabus* was in form a warning to Catholics, not a matter of dogma incumbent upon them to believe. In dogma, the Immaculate Conception of the Virgin Mary was announced as dogmatic truth in 1854; a century later, in 1950, the bodily assumption of Mary into heaven was proclaimed. Thus the Catholic church reaffirmed in a skeptical age, and against Christian modernists, its faith in the supernatural and miraculous.

Pius IX also convened an ecumenical church council which met at the Vatican in 1870. It was the first such council since the Council of Trent some 300 years before.[38] The Vatican Council proclaimed the dogma of papal infallibility, which holds that the pope, when speaking *ex cathedra* on matters of faith and morals, speaks with a final and supernatural authority that no Catholic may question or reject. The Vatican Council, and the acceptance of papal infallibility by Catholics, was only the climax of centuries of development within the church. In brief, as the world grew more national, Catholicism became more international. As state sovereignty and secularism grew, Catholic clergy looked increasingly to the spiritual powers of Rome for protection against alien forces. Much in the past 300 years had made Catholics distrustful of their own governments or of non-Catholics in their midst—the Protestantism and the state churches of the sixteenth century, the Jansenist movement of the seventeenth, the anticlericalism of enlightened despotism in the eighteenth, the hostility to the church shown by the French Revolution, and by liberalism, republicanism, and socialism in the nineteenth century. By 1870 the net effect was to throw Catholics into the arms of the Holy See. Ultramontanism, the unconditional acceptance of papal jurisdiction, prevailed over the old Gallican and other national tendencies within the church.

[38] See pp. 88–90.

COMPOSITION WITH THE ACE OF CLUBS
by Georges Braque (French, 1882–1963)

This painting, of about the same date as the preceding one by Kandinsky, represents a quite different direction in modern art. It is one of the great works of the Cubist movement. Where the Kandinsky painting presents color without line and seeks to express life and feeling. Braque and the Cubists break up the visual world into lines and planes, in a more analytic and intellectual fashion. Objects recede or disappear, not into an impressionist blur nor a burst of color, but into a carefully contrived and almost mathematical pattern. In the new movement, it made sense to "see" things from more than one direction at a time, as the mind conceives them. Perception is not enough; as Braque once wrote, "the senses deform, but the mind forms." In any case, innovative artists after 1900 turned away from the main concerns of Western painting since the Renaissance: realistic representation of persons, places, or objects; natural color; illusionistic three-dimensional volume; a humanly occupied space with perspectives, horizons, location, and distance as seen by the eye from a single fixed viewpoint. Courtesy of the Musée d'Art Moderne, Paris (Service Photographique). Permission A.D.A.G.P. 1970 by French Reproduction Rights, Inc.

635

In 1870, while the 600 prelates of the Vatican Council were sitting, the new Italian state unceremoniously entered and annexed the city of Rome.[39] The pope's temporal power thus disappeared. It is now widely agreed that with the loss of local temporal interests the spiritual hold of the papacy on Catholics throughout the world has been enhanced. The popes long refused, however, to recognize the loss of Rome; and each pope in turn, from 1870 to 1929, adopted a policy of self-imprisonment in the Vatican grounds. By the Lateran treaty of 1929 the papacy finally recognized the Italian state, and Italy conceded, along with much else, the existence of a Vatican City about a square mile in area, as an independent state not legally within Italy at all. The papacy thus gained that independence from national or secular authority deemed necessary by Catholics to the performance of its role.

Pius IX's successor, Leo XIII (1878–1903), carried on the counteroffensive against irreligion, and instituted a revival of medieval philosophy as represented by Thomas Aquinas.[40] But Leo XIII is chiefly remembered for formulating Catholic social doctrine, especially in the encyclical *Rerum Novarum* ("of modern things") of 1891, to which subsequent pontiffs have adhered, and from which various movements of Catholic socialism are derived. *Rerum Novarum* upheld private property as a natural right, within the limits of justice; but it found fault with capitalism for the poverty, insecurity, and even degradation in which many of the laboring classes were left. It declared that much in socialism was Christian in principle; but it criticized socialism insofar as (like Marxism) it was materialistic and antireligious. The pope therefore recommended that Catholics, if they wished, form socialist parties of their own, and that Catholic workers form labor unions under Catholic auspices. Since the 1830s there had been individual Catholics and Catholic clergy who were socialists, or at least severe critics of the then emerging social order; these were encouraged by the encyclical of 1891, and Catholic (or Christian, as they were often called) socialist parties and labor unions began to appear at the turn of the century. The Roman church thus undertook to free itself from dependency upon capitalism. At the same time it took steps to insure that a future society, if socialist, might be Catholic also.

As for Judaism, the Jews were a small minority, but their condition had always been a kind of barometer reflecting changes in the atmosphere of Europe as a whole. In the nineteenth century the basic trend was toward "emancipation" and "assimilation." Science and secularism had the same dissolving effect upon Orthodox Judaism as upon traditional Christianity. Reform Judaism grew up as the Jewish counterpart to "modernism" in other faiths. Individual Jews increasingly gave up their old distinctive Jewish way of life. In society at large, the prevalence of liberalism allowed them to act as citizens and to enter business or the professions like everybody else. Jews were thus freed from old legal discriminations that had been imposed on them for centuries.

Toward the end of the century two tendencies, counter to assimilation, became evident. One, a cultural and political nationalism, originated with Jews themselves, some of whom feared an assimilation that would lead to a loss of Jewish identity and perhaps even the disappearance of Judaism itself. The other countertendency, or barrier to assimilation, was the rise of anti-Semitism, noticeable in many

[39] See p. 558.
[40] See p. 42.

quarters by 1900. Racist theories, dislike for Jewish competitors in business and the professions, socialist scorn for Jewish capitalists like the Rothschilds, upper-class fears of Jewish revolutionaries and Marxists, together with a growth of ethnic nationalism, which held that France should be purely French and Latin, Germany purely German and Nordic, or Russia purely Russian and Slav, all combined to raise an anti-Semitic hue and cry. In Russia there were actual pogroms, or massacres of Jews. In France the Dreyfus case, dragged out from 1894 to 1906, revealed unsuspected depths of anti-Semitic fury. Many Jews were forced by such hostility into a new sense of Jewish identity. The Hungarian-born Jewish journalist Theodor Herzl was one. Appalled by the turbulence of the Dreyfus affair in civilized France, which he observed firsthand as a reporter for a Vienna newspaper, he founded modern, or political, Zionism when he organized the first international Zionist congress at Basel in 1897. Zionists hoped to establish a Jewish state in Palestine, in which Jews from all the world might find refuge, although there had been no independent Jewish state there since ancient times.

Many Jews, wishing civic assimilation yet despairing of obtaining it, began to sympathize with the Jewish nationlist movement, looking to Zionism and a Jewish renascence as a way to maintain their own dignity. Others insisted that Judaism was a religious faith, not a nationality by itself; that Jews and non-Jews within the same country shared in exactly the same nationality, citizenship, and political and social outlook. Liberals and democrats were of the same opinion. On the integration of Jews into the larger community the traditions of the Enlightenment, the American and French revolutions, the empire of Napoleon I, and the liberalism of the nineteenth century all agreed.

77. *The Waning of Classical Liberalism*

The net effect of the political, economic, and intellectual trends described above was twofold. There was a continued advance of much that was basic to liberalism and at the same time a weakening of the grounds on which liberalism had firmly rested ever since the seventeenth and eighteenth centuries. A third effect might be noted too. Even where the essentials of liberalism persisted, in program and doctrine it underwent important changes; liberalism persisted but the classical type of liberalism was in eclipse.

Classical liberalism, the liberalism in its heyday in the nineteenth century, went back at least as far as John Locke in the seventeenth century and the philosophes of the eighteenth, and found its highest nineteenth-century expression in the writings of men like John Stuart Mill and in the political outlook of men like William Gladstone. Classical liberalism had as its deepest principle the liberty of the individual person.[41] Man, or each specimen of mankind, according to liberals, was or could become a freestanding human being. "Man" meant for them any member of the human race, *homo sapiens,* though in practice, except for a few like Mill, they were thinking of adult males. The very principle of liberalism, however, with its stress on the autonomy of the individual, contributed to the still small but growing movement of women's rights.

[41] See pp. 371, 465.

The individual, in this view, was not simply formed by race, class, church, nation, or state but was ultimately independent of all such things. Individuals did not have such and such ideas because they belonged to such and such a group, but were capable of the free use of reason or of thinking things out independently, apart from their own interests, prejudices, or subconscious drives. And, since this was so, people of different interests could reasonably and profitably discuss their differences, make compromises, and reach solutions by peaceable agreement. It was because they thought all persons potentially reasonable that liberals favored education. They opposed all imposition of force upon the individual, from physical torture to mental indoctrination.

In religion, liberals thought each individual should adopt any faith or no faith as he or she chose, and that churches and clergy should play little or no part in public affairs. In politics, they thought that governments should be constitutional and limited in power, with individuals governing themselves through their chosen representatives, with issues presented, discussed, and decided by the use of intelligence, both by the voters in election campaigns and by elected deputies in parliamentary debate. The will of a majority, or larger number of individuals, was taken as decisive, with the understanding that the minority might become a majority in its turn through individual changes of opinion. At first distrustful of democracy, fearing the excesses of popular rule, and eager to limit political power and the suffrage to the propertied classes, in the course of the nineteenth century liberals had accepted the democratic principle of universal male suffrage. In economics, liberals thought of the whole world as peopled by individuals doing business with one another—buying and selling, borrowing and lending, hiring and firing—without interference from governments and without regard to religion or politics, both of which were thought to impose superficial differences upon the underlying uniformity of mankind. The practical consequences of liberalism were toleration, constitutionalism, laissez faire, free trade, and an international or nonnational economic system. It was thought that all peoples would progress to these same ends.

There never was a time, even in one country, when all liberal ideas were simultaneously triumphant. Pure liberalism has never existed except as a doctrine. Advancing in one way, liberalism would be blocked or reversed in another. On the whole, Europe before 1914 was predominantly liberal. But signs of the wane of liberalism set in clearly about 1880; some, like the changing conceptions of human behavior, have already been mentioned.

The Decline of Nineteenth-Century Liberalism: Economic Trends

The free economy produced many hardships. The worker tossed by the ups and downs of a labor market, the producer tossed by those of a world commodity market, alike clamored for protection against exposure. A severe depression in 1873 sent prices and wages into collapse, and the economy did not fully recover until 1893. European farmers, both small French farm owners and big Junker landlords of East Germany, demanded tariff protection: they could not compete with the American Middle West or the steppes of South Russia, both opened up by rail and steamship, and both of which after 1870 poured their cereals at low prices into Europe. The revival of tariffs and decline of free trade, very marked in Europe about 1880, thus began with the protection of agricultural interests. Industry soon demanded the same favors. In Germany the Junkers and the rising Rhineland industrialists joined forces in 1879 to extort a tariff from Bismarck. The French in 1892 adopted a high tariff to shelter both manufacturing and agricultural interests. The United States, rapidly industrializing, also put up protective tariffs beginning in the 1860s, the earliest of all.

The Industrial Revolution was now definitely at work in other countries than Great Britain. There was an increasing resistance to buying manufactures from England, selling only raw materials and foodstuffs in return. Everywhere there was a revival of the arguments of the German economist Friedrich List, who a half-century before, in his *National System of Political Economy* (1840), had branded free trade as a system mainly advantageous to the British and declared that no country could become strong, independent, or even fully civilized if it remained a semi-rustic supplier of unfinished goods.[42] With Germany, the United States, and Japan manufacturing for export, a nationalist competition for world markets set in, contributing also to the drive for colonies and the phenomena of imperialism described in the next chapter. The new imperialism was another sign of the waning of liberalism, which had been largely indifferent to colonies.

In all these respects the division between politics and economics, postulated by liberals, began to fade. A kind of neomercantilism arose, recalling the attempts of governments in the seventeenth and eighteenth centuries to subordinate economic activity to political ends. A better term is economic nationalism, which became noticeable by 1900. Nations struggled to better themselves by tariffs, by trade rivalries, and by internal regulation, without regard to the effect upon other nations. And for the individual worker or businessman also, in purely economic matters, it now made a great difference to what nation he belonged, by what government he was backed, and under what laws he lived.

It was of course to protect themselves against insecurity and abuse as individuals that workers formed labor unions. It was likewise to protect themselves against the uncertainties of uncontrolled markets that business interests began to merge, to concentrate in large corporations, or to form monopolies, trusts, or cartels. The rise of big business and organized labor undermined the theory and practice of individual competition to which classical liberalism had been attached. Organized labor, socialist parties, universal male suffrage, and a sensitivity to social distress all obliged political leaders to intervene increasingly in economic matters. Factory codes became more detailed and better enforced. Social insurance, initiated by Bismarck, spread to other countries. Governments regulated the purity of foods and drugs. The social service state developed, a state assuming responsibility for the social and economic welfare of the mass of its own subjects. The "new" liberalism, that of the Liberals in England of the David Lloyd George era, of the Republican President Theodore Roosevelt and the Democratic President Woodrow Wilson in the United States, accepted the enlarged role of the government in social and economic matters. Both Theodore Roosevelt and Wilson, and others, sought also to reestablish economic competition by government action against monopolies and trusts. The new liberals were generally less well disposed toward business than toward workers and the

[42] See pp. 471–472.

depressed classes; the improvement of the workers' lot would vindicate the old humanitarian concern of liberalism with the dignity and worth of the individual person. The welfare state, remote as it was from the older liberalism, was the direction taken by the new liberals. Others, liberal and otherwise, viewed with concern the growing power of governments and centralized authority and were apprehensive for individual liberties.

Intellectual and Other Currents

Liberalism, both old and new, was undermined also by many developments in the field of thought described earlier in this chapter—Darwinian evolution, the new psychology, trends in philosophy and the arts. Paradoxically, this great age of science found that man was not a rational animal. Darwinian theory implied that man was merely a high evolved organism whose faculties were merely adaptations to an environment. Psychology seemed to teach that what was called reason was often only rationalization, or a finding of alleged "reasons" to justify material wants or emotional and unconscious needs, and that conscious reflection dominated only a narrow part of human behavior. Ideas themselves were said to be the products of conditioning. There were English ideas or Anglo-Saxon ideas, or bourgeois or progressive or reactionary ideas. In politics, some believed that parties or nations with conflicting interests could never reasonably agree on a program common to both, since neither could ever get beyond the limitations of its own outlook. It became common to dismiss the arguments of an adversary without further thought and without any expectation that thought could overcome difficulties. This insidious "anti-intellectualism" was destructive to liberal principles. If, because of prior conditioning, it was impossible for anyone to change his or her mind, then there was no hope of settling matters by persuasion.

From the view that man was not essentially a rational being, which in itself was only a scientific attempt at a better understanding of human behavior, it was but a short step deliberately to reject reason and to emphasize and cultivate the irrational, to stress the will, intuition, impulse, and emotion, and to place a new value on violence and conflict. A philosophy of "realism," a kind of unrealistic faith in the constructive value of struggle and a tough-minded rejection of ideas and ideals, spread. It was not new. Marxism, since the 1840s, had taught that class war, latent or open, was the motivating power of history. Now Nietzsche rejected the ordinary virtues in favor of courage and daring; and the Social Darwinists glorified the successful and the dominant in all phases of human activity as the "fit" in the perpetual struggle for existence. Other thinkers embraced a frank irrationalism. Georges Sorel, the philosopher of syndicalism, in his *Reflections on Violence* in 1908, declared that violence was good irrespective of the end accomplished (so much did he hate existing society), and that workers should be kept alert in the class war through believing in the "myth" of a future general strike. They should believe in such a strike, with its attendant debacle of bourgeois civilization, even though it was known to be only a "myth." The function of thought, in this philosophy of the social myth, was to keep people agitated and excited and ready for action, not to achieve any correspondence with rational or objective truth. Such ideas passed into the fascism and other activist movements of the twentieth century.

Thus the end of the nineteenth century, the greatest age of peace in Europe's history, abounded in philosophies glorifying struggle. Men who had never heard a shot fired in anger solemnly announced that world history moved forward by violence and antagonism. They said not merely that struggle existed (which would have been a purely factual statement) but that struggle was a positive good through which progress was to be accomplished. The popularity of struggle was due not only to the intellectuals but in part to actual historical events. People remembered that before 1871 certain weighty questions had been settled by force, that the movements of social revolution in 1848 and in the Paris Commune of 1871 had been put down by the military, and that the unity of Italy and Germany, as well as of the United States, had been confirmed by war. In addition, after 1871, all continental European states maintained large standing armies, the largest ever maintained until then in time of peace.

In economic and political matters, even in England, the homeland of liberalism, there were numerous signs between 1900 and 1914 that the older liberalism was on the wane. Joseph Chamberlain led a movement to return to tariff protection (to repeal, so to speak, the repeal of the Corn Laws); it failed at the time, but was strong enough to disorient the Conservative party in 1906. The Liberal party abandoned its traditional laissez-faire policy in sponsoring the labor legislation of the years following 1906. The new Labour party required its members in Parliament to vote as directed by the party, thus initiating a system of party solidarity, eventually copied by others, that hardened the lines of opposition, denied that individuals should freely change sides, and hence reduced the practical significance of parliamentary discussion. The Irish nationalists had long used unparliamentary methods; in 1914, when Parliament at last enacted Irish home rule, the anti-Irish and Conservative interests prepared to resist parliamentary action by force. The suffragettes, as women pioneering for female suffrage were called, despairing of ever getting the men to listen to reason, resorted to amazingly "un-English" and unreasonable arguments. They chained themselves to public buildings, smashed the store fronts in Bond Street, threw acid into mailboxes, and broke porcelains in the British Museum. When arrested they went on hunger strikes, threatening self-starvation, to which the police replied by "forcible feeding" through tubes lowered into their stomachs. And in 1911 and 1912 great railway and coal strikes disclosed the sheer power of organized labor.

Still, it is the persistence of liberalism rather than its wane that should be emphasized at the close of a chapter on European civilization in the half-century before 1914. Tariffs existed, but goods still circulated freely in world trade. Nationalism was heightened, but there was nothing like totalitarianism. Racist ideas were in the air, but they had little political importance. Anti-Semitism was sometimes vocal; but all governments except the Russian protected the rights of Jews, and the years from 1848 to 1914 were in fact the great period of Jewish integration into general society. The laissez-faire state was disappearing, but social legislation continued the humanitarian strain that had always been the essence of liberalism. A few advanced revolutionaries preached social catastrophism, but social democrats and working people were overwhelmingly revisionist, loyal to parliamentary procedures and to their existing states. Doctrinaires exalted the grim beauty of war, but all governments down to 1914 tried to prevent war among the great powers. And there was still a supreme faith in progress.

XV.
EUROPE'S WORLD
SUPREMACY

EuroPEAN CIVILIZATION, as described in the last chapter, spread to the whole earth after about 1870. The large nation-states whose consolidation was described in the chapter before last, and which were now equipped with the overwhelming new powers of science and industry, gained empires for themselves throughout the globe. The history of Europe—as of Asia, Africa, and America—became more involved in the history of the world.

For a while the most active of the imperial nation-states were located in Europe, and the forty years preceding the First World War were the years of Europe's world supremacy. With the rise of the United States the term "Western" came into use, signifying European in an expanded sense. The arrival of Japan made the term "Western" inappropriate for some purposes, and later the industrialization of the Soviet Union created similar verbal difficulties, so that by the mid–twentieth century it was customary to speak of "developed" parts of the earth, alongside which others were seen as "developing" or "less developed." There even came to be a "Third World," which had no geographic identity of its own, but which did not wish to be

Chapter Emblem: A medal commemorating the opening of the Suez Canal in 1869.

identified with either the Western or the Soviet form of modern society. All these terms represented efforts to deal with the same basic reality, namely, a bifurcation between modern and traditional societies, rich countries and poor ones, or between the powerful and the weak.

For the first time in human history, by 1900, it was possible to speak of a world civilization. All countries were drawn into a world economy and a world market. The attributes of modernity, where they existed at all, were much the same everywhere—modern science, modern weapons of warfare, machine industry, fast communications, industrial organization, efficient forms of taxation and law enforcement, and of public hygiene, sanitation, and medicine.

But not all peoples participated in this global evolution on equal terms. It was the Europeans (or "Westerners") who reaped the greatest rewards. Under the impact of modernity both tribal societies and massive old civilizations began to come apart. Scientific ideas changed ways of thinking everywhere, as they had done in Europe. In India, China, or Africa the native industries often suffered, and many people found it harder than ever to subsist even at a low level. The building of railways in China, for example, threw boatmen, carters, and innkeepers out of work. In India, the hand spinners and weavers of cotton could not compete in their own villages with the machine-made products of Lancashire. In parts of Africa, native tribes that had lived by owning herds of cattle, moving from place to place to obtain grazing lands, found white farmers or plantation or mine owners occupying their country and were often forced by the white man's law to give up their migratory habits. Peoples of all races began to produce for export—rubber, raw cotton, jute, petroleum, tin, gold—and hence were exposed to the rise and fall of world prices. A depression tended to become a world depression, dragging all down alike.

Imperialism, or the colonialism of the late nineteenth century, may be briefly defined as the government of one people by another. European imperialism proved to be transitory. It was a phase in the worldwide spread of the industrial and scientific civilization which had originated in Europe's "inner zone."[1] That it was not the last phase became clear as the twentieth century unfolded. The subordinated peoples, forcibly introduced to the West by imperialism, came to feel a need for modernizing and industrializing their own countries and for the aid of Western science, skill, and capital; but they wished to get rid of imperialists, govern themselves, and control the conditions under which modernization and borrowing should take place. In opposition to European empires, subject peoples began to assert ideas learned from Europe—ideas of liberty and democracy, and of an anticapitalism that passed easily into socialism. Many such ideas were derived from the French and American revolutions, or from Marxism, or the whole record of Europe itself.

The present chapter deals only with the imperialist phase of the global transformation. By one of the ironies of history, the imperialist rivalries of the European powers, while representing Europe's world supremacy, also contributed to the disaster of the First World War, and so to the collapse of such supremacy as Europe had enjoyed.

---

[1] See pp. 160, 586–587.

78. *Imperialism: Its Nature and Causes*

European civilization had always shown a tendency to expand. In the Middle Ages Latin Christendom spread by conquest and conversion to include the whole area from Spain to Finland. Then came the age of overseas discoveries and the founding of colonial empires, whose struggles filled the seventeenth and eighteenth centuries, and of which the Europeanization of the Americas was the most far-reaching consequence. At the same time European culture spread among the upper classes of Russia. The defeat of Napoleon left only one of the old colonial empires standing in any strength, namely, the British. For sixty years after 1815 there were no significant colonial rivalries. In many circles there was an indifference to overseas empire. Under principles of free trade, it was thought unnecessary to exercise political influence in areas in which one did business. Actually, in these years, the French moved into Algeria, the British strengthened their Indian empire, the Dutch developed Java and the neighboring islands more intensively, and the Western powers "opened" Japan and began to penetrate China. But there was no overt conflict among Europeans, and no systematic program, doctrine, or "ism."

Rather suddenly, about 1870 or 1880, colonial questions came again to the fore. In the short space of two decades, by 1900, the advanced countries partitioned most of the earth among themselves. A world map by 1900 showed their possessions in some nine or ten colors.

The New Imperialism

The new imperialism differed both economically and politically from the colonialism of earlier times. The older empires had been maritime and mercantile. European traders, in India, Java, or Canton, had simply purchased the wares brought to them by local merchants as produced by local methods. They operated on a kind of cash-and-carry basis. European governments had had no territorial ambitions beyond the protection of way stations and trading centers. To these generalizations America had been an exception. It had neither native states which Europeans respected, nor native industries in which Europeans were interested. Europeans therefore developed territorial claims, and invested capital and brought in their own methods of production and management, especially in the then booming sugar islands of the West Indies.[2]

Under the new imperialism Europeans were by no means content simply to purchase what local merchants provided. They wanted goods of a kind or in a quantity that preindustrial handicraft methods could not supply. They moved into the "backward" countries more thoroughly. They invested capital in them, setting up mines, plantations, docks, warehouses, factories, refineries, railroads, river steamships, and banks. They built offices, homes, hotels, clubs, and cool mountain resorts suitable for white men in the tropics. Taking over the productive life of the country, they transformed large elements of the local population into the wage employees of foreign owners and so introduced the class problems of industrial

---

[2] See pp. 259–262.

Europe in a form accentuated by racial difference. Or they lent money to non-European rulers—the khedive of Egypt, the shah of Persia, the emperor of China—to enable them to hold up their tottering thrones or simply to live with more pleasure and magnificence than they could pay for from their usual revenues. Europeans thus developed a huge financial stake in governments and economic enterprises outside the pale of Western civilization.

To secure these investments, and for other reasons, in contrast to what had happened under the older colonialism, the Europeans now aspired to political and territorial domination. Some areas became outright "colonies," directly governed by white men. Others became "protectorates": here the native chief, sultan, bey, rajah, or prince was maintained and guaranteed against internal upheaval or external conquest. A European "resident" or "commissioner" usually told him what to do. In other regions, as in China or Persia, where no single European state could make good its claims against the others, they arranged to divide the country into "spheres of influence," each European power having advisory privileges and investment and trade opportunities within its own sphere. The sphere of influence was the vaguest of all forms of imperial control; supposedly, it left the country independent.

An enormous differential opened up, about 1875, between the power of European and non-European states. Queen Elizabeth had dealt with the Great Mogul with genuine respect. Even Napoleon had pretended to regard the shah of Persia as an equal. Then came the Industrial Revolution in Europe, iron and steel ships, heavier naval guns, more accurate rifles. Democratic and nationalistic movements produced large and solid European peoples, united in the service of their governments as no "backward" people ever was. Seemingly endless wealth, with modern administration, allowed governments to tax, borrow, and spend almost without limit. The civilized states loomed as enormous power complexes without precedent in the world's history. At the same time it so happened that all the principal non-European empires were in decay. They were receiving a minimum of support from their own subjects. As in the eighteenth century the disintegration of the Mogul empire had enabled the British to take over India,[3] so in the nineteenth century the decrepitude of the sultan of Turkey, the sultan of Zanzibar, the shah of Persia, the emperor of China, and the shogun of Japan made European intervention easy. Only the Japanese were able to revolutionize their government in time to ward off imperialist penetration. Even the Japanese, thanks to early treaties, remained unfree to determine their own tariff policy until after 1900.[4]

So great was the difference in the sheer mechanics of power that usually a mere show of force allowed the whites to impose their will. A garrison of only 75,000 white troops long held India for the British. Numerous sporadic little wars were constantly fought—Afghan wars, Burmese wars, Zulu wars—which passed unnoticed by Europeans in the home country and were no more like true war than the operations of the United States army against the Indians of the western plains. The Spanish-American War of 1898 and the Boer War of 1899 were also wars of colonial type, fought between entirely unequal parties. Often a show of

---

[3] See pp. 278–281, 350–351.
[4] See pp. 579–580.

naval strength was enough. It was the classic age of the punitive or minatory bombardment. We have seen how the American Commodore Perry threatened to bombard Tokyo in 1854.[5] In 1856 the British consul at Canton, to punish acts of violence against Europeans, called upon the local British admiral to bombard that Chinese city. In 1863 the British bombarded Satsuma, and in 1864 an allied force including Americans bombarded Choshu—precipitating revolution in Japan. Similarly, Alexandria was bombarded in 1882 and Zanzibar in 1896. The usual consequence was that the local ruler signed a treaty, reorganized his government, or accepted a European (usually British) adviser.

Incentives and Motives

Behind the aggressiveness lay many pressures. Europeans could not maintain, for themselves in Europe, the style of life to which they had become accustomed, except by bringing the rest of the world within their orbit. But many other needs felt in Europe drove men into distant and savage places. Catholic and Protestant groups sent growing numbers of missionaries to regions increasingly remote and wild. The missionaries sometimes got into trouble with the local people, and some were even killed. Public opinion in the home countries, soon learning of such events by ocean cable, might clamor for political action to suppress such vestiges of barbarism. Similarly, science required scientific expeditions for geographical exploration, or for botanical, zoological, or mineral discoveries, or for astronomical or meteorological observations. Wealthy persons traveled more, now that travel was so easy; they hunted tigers or elephants, or simply went to see the sights. It seemed only reasonable, at the close of the nineteenth century, that all civilized persons wherever they might choose to go should enjoy the security of life and limb and the orderly procedures that only European supervision could provide.

Economically, European life required material goods, many of which only tropical regions could supply. Even the working classes now drank tea or coffee every day. After the American Civil War Europe relied for its cotton increasingly on Africa and the East. Rubber and petroleum became staple needs. The lowly jute, which grew only in India, was used to make burlap, twine, carpets, and the millions of jute bags employed in commerce. The lordly coconut tree had innumerable common uses, which led to its intensive cultivation in the Dutch Indies. Various parts of it could be eaten, or manufactured into bags, brushes, cables, ropes, sails, or doormats or converted into coconut oil, which in turn went into the making of candles, soap, margarine, and many other products.

Industrial countries also attempted to sell their own products, and one of the reasons given by imperialists, in support of imperialism, was the urgent necessity of finding new markets. The industrialization of Germany, the United States, Japan, and other countries, after about 1870, meant that they competed with each other and with Great Britain for foreign trade.[6] The slowly declining price level after 1873 meant that a business firm had to sell more goods to turn over the same amount of money. Competition was more intense. The advanced countries

[5] See pp. 577, 579–581.
[6] See pp. 638–639.

raised tariffs to keep out each other's products. It was therefore argued that each industrial country must develop a colonial empire dependent on itself, an area of "sheltered markets," as the phrase went in England, in which the home country would supply manufactured goods in return for raw materials. The idea was to create a large self-sufficient trading unit, embracing various climates and types of resources, protected if necessary from outside competition by tariffs, guaranteeing a market for all its members and wealth and prosperity for the home country. This phase of imperialism is often called neomercantilism, since it revived in substance the mercantilism of the eighteenth and earlier centuries.[7]

Purely financial considerations also characterized the new imperialism. Money invested in "backward" countries, by the close of the nineteenth century, brought a higher rate of return than if invested in the more civilized ones. For this there were many reasons, including the cheap labor of non-European regions, the heavy and unsatisfied demand for non-European products, and the greater risk of losses in half-unknown areas where European ideas of law and order did not prevail. By 1900 western Europe and the northeastern United States were equipped with their basic industrial apparatus. Their railway networks and first factories were built. Opportunities for investment in these countries became stabilized. At the same time, these countries themselves accumulated capital seeking an outlet. In the mid-century most exported capital was British-owned. By the close of the century more French, German, American, Dutch, Belgian, and Swiss investors were investing or lending outside their own borders. In 1850, most exported capital went to build up Europe, the United States, Canada, Australia, or Argentina—the white man's world. By 1900 more of it was going to the undeveloped regions. This capital was the property of small private savers or of large banking combinations. Investors preferred "civilized" political control over the parts of Asia, Africa, or Latin America in which their railroads, mines, plantations, government loans, or other investments were situated. Hence the profit motive, or desire to invest "surplus" capital, promoted imperialism.

This analysis was put forward by critics like the English socialist J. A. Hobson, who wrote an influential book on imperialism in 1903, and later by Lenin, in his *Imperialism, the Highest Stage of World Capitalism*, written in 1916. They ascribed imperialism primarily to the accumulation of surplus capital and condemned it on socialist grounds. Argued Hobson especially, if more of the national income went to workers as wages, and less of it to capitalists as interest and dividends, or if wealthy people were more heavily taxed and the money used for social welfare, there would be no surplus of capital and no real imperialism. Since the working class, if this were done, would also have more purchasing power, it would be less necessary to look endlessly for new markets outside the country. But the "surplus capital" explanation of imperialism was not entirely convincing. That investors and exporters were instrumental in the rise of imperialism was of course very true. That imperialism arose essentially from the capitalists' pressure to invest abroad was more doubtful. Perhaps even more basic was Europe's need for imports—only by enormous imports could Europe sustain its dense population, complex industry, and high standard of living. It was the demand for such imports—cotton, cocoa, coffee, copper, or copra drawn from the "colonies"—

---

[7] See pp. 119–120, 257–262.

that made investment in the colonies financially profitable. Moreover, non-Europeans themselves often asked for the capital, glad though the European lenders were to lend it at high rates. In 1890 this might mean merely that a shah or sultan wanted to build himself a new palace, but the need of non-Europeans for Western capital was basic, nor was it to decline in later times. Lastly, the imperialism of some countries, notably Russia and Italy, which had little capital and few modern-type capitalists of their own, could not reasonably be attributed to pressure for lucrative foreign investments.

For the British, however, the capitalistic incentive was of great importance. We have seen how the British, in 1914, had $20 billion invested outside of Great Britain, a quarter of all their wealth.[8] About half, or $10 billion, was invested in the British Empire. Only a tenth of French foreign investments was in French colonies. French investment in the colonial world in general, however, including Egypt, Suez, South Africa, and Asia in addition to the French colonies, amounted to about a fifth of all French foreign investments. Only an infinitesimal fraction of German foreign investment in 1914 was in German colonies, which were of slight value. A fifth of German foreign investments, however, was placed in Africa, Asia, and the Ottoman Empire. These sums are enough to suggest the pressures upon the European governments to assert political influence in Africa, Turkey, or China.

In addition, French investors (including small bourgeois and even affluent peasants) had in 1914 a huge stake in the Russian empire. Russia, an imperial power with respect to adjoining countries in the Balkans and Asia, occupied an almost semicolonial status with respect to western Europe. The tsardom in its last twenty years, not unlike the Ottoman sultanate or the Manchu dynasty, was kept going by foreign loans, predominantly French. The French in 1914 had lent over $2 billion to Russia, more than to all colonial regions combined. For these huge outlays the motivation was at least as much political as economic. The French government often urged French banks to buy Russian bonds. The aim was not merely to make a profit for bankers and savers, but to build up and hold together a military ally against Germany.

Politics went along with economics in the whole process of imperialist expansion. National security, both political and economic, was as important an aim as the accumulation of private wealth. So, too, was the growing concern in many quarters over the economic security and welfare of the working classes. The ideas of the British statesman Joseph Chamberlain (1836–1914) illustrated how these motives entered into imperialist thinking.

Chamberlain, father of Neville Chamberlain who was to be prime minister of Britain in the years just prior to the Second World War, began as a Birmingham manufacturer, the type of man who a generation before would have been a staunch free trader and upholder of laissez faire. Discarding the old individualism, he came to believe that the community should and could take better care of its members, and, in particular, that the British community (or empire) could advance the welfare of Britons. As mayor of Birmingham he introduced a kind of municipal socialism, including public ownership of utilities. As colonial secretary from 1895 to 1903, he preached Britain's need for "a great self-sustaining and self-protecting

[8] See p. 599.

empire" in an age of rising international competition—a worldwide British trading area, developed by British capital, which would give a secure source of raw materials and food, markets for exports, and a steady level of profits, wages, and employment.

Chamberlain saw with misgivings the tendencies toward independence in Canada, New Zealand, and the Australian Commonwealth. For these dominions he favored complete self-government, but he hoped that, once assured of virtual independence, they would reknit their ties with each other and with Great Britain. Such a reintegration of the empire he called "imperial federation." Britain and its dominions, in Chamberlain's view, should pool their resources not only for military defense but also for economic well-being. The dominions had already levied tariffs against British manufacturers in order to build up their own. Chamberlain, to favor British exports, urged the dominions to charge a lower duty on British wares than on the same wares coming from foreign countries. In return, he even proposed that Great Britain adopt a protective tariff, so that it might then favor Canadian or Australian goods by imposing on them a lower rate. His plan was to bind the empire together by economic bonds, making it a kind of tariff union, or system of "imperial preference." Since Britain imported mainly meat and cereals from the dominions, Chamberlain was obliged to recommend a tariff even upon these—to "tax the people's food," repudiating the very ark of the covenant of Free Trade upon which the British economy had rested for half a century.[9] The proposal was rejected. Chamberlain died in 1914, his goal unaccomplished. But after the First World War the British Empire, or Commonwealth of Nations, followed closely along the lines he had mapped out.[10]

Whether the economic welfare and security of the European working classes was advanced by imperialism is still debated. It is probable that the worker in western Europe did benefit from imperialism. Socially conservative imperialists were joined in this belief by thinkers of the extreme Left. Marx himself, followed by Lenin, thought that the European worker obtained higher real wages through the inflow of low-priced colonial goods. To Marxists this was unfortunate, for it gave European workers a vested interest in imperialism, made the European proletariat "opportunistic" (i.e., unrevolutionary), and blocked the formation of a true international world proletariat of all races.

Another imperialist argument much heard at the time held that European countries must acquire colonies to which surplus population could migrate without altogether abandoning the native land. It seemed unfortunate, for example, that so many Germans or Italians emigrating to the United States should be lost to the fatherland. This argument was purely specious. No European country after 1870 acquired any colony to which European families in any numbers wished to move. The millions who still left Europe, up to 1914, persisted in heading for the Americas, where in the circumstances no European colony could be founded.[11]

The competitive nature of the European state system introduced other almost exclusively political elements. The European states had to guard their security against each other. They had to keep some kind of balance among themselves,

[9] See pp. 494, 596–599.
[10] See p. 804.
[11] See map, p. 592.

in the overseas world as in Europe. Hence, as in the scramble for Africa, one government often hurriedly annexed territory simply for fear that another might do so first. Or again, colonies came to have an intangible but momentous value in symbolism and prestige. To have colonies was a normal criterion of greatness. It was the sign of having arrived as a Great Power. Britain and France had had colonies for centuries. Therefore the new powers formed in the 1860s—Germany, Italy, Japan, and in a sense the United States—had to have colonies also.

Imperialism as Crusade

Imperialism arose from the commercial, industrial, financial, scientific, political, journalistic, intellectual, religious, and humanitarian impulses of Europe compounded together. It was an outthrust of the whole white man's civilization. It would bring civilization and enlightened living to those who still sat in darkness. Faith in "modern civilization" had become a kind of substitute religion. Imperialism was its crusade.

So the British spoke of the White Man's Burden, the French of their *mission civilisatrice*, the Germans of diffusing *Kultur*, the Americans of the "blessings of Anglo-Saxon protection." Social Darwinism and popular anthropology taught that white races were "fitter" or more gifted than colored.[12] Others argued, more reasonably, that the backwardness of non-Europeans was due to historic and hence temporary causes, but that for a long period in the future the civilized whites must keep a guardianship over their darker protégés. In the psychology of imperialism there was much that was not unworthy. Young men of good family left the pleasant lands of Devonshire or Poitou to spend long and lonely years in hot and savage places, sustained by the thought that they were advancing the work of humanity. It was a good thing to bring clearer ideas of justice to barbaric peoples, to put down slave raiding, torture, and famine, to combat degrading superstitions or fight the diseases of neglect and filth. But these accomplishments, however real, went along all too obviously with self-interest and were expressed with unbearable complacency and gross condescension to the larger part of the human race. As Rudyard Kipling wrote in 1899:

> Take up the White Man's burden—
> Send out the best ye breed—
> Go bind your sons to exile,
> To serve your captives' need;
> To wait in heavy harness,
> On fluttered folk and wild—
> Your new-caught sullen peoples,
> Half devil and half child.

79. The Americas

After the general considerations above, let us examine each of the earth's great regions in turn, and first the Americas, where we must begin our discussion earlier in the century, before the age of the "new imperialism."

---

[12] See pp. 626–628.

In America the breakup of the Spanish and Portuguese empires in the first quarter of the nineteenth century, during and after the Napoleonic wars, left the vast tract from Colorado to Cape Horn very unsettled. Most of the people were Indian or a mixture of Indian and white *(mestizo)*, with clusters here and there of pure European stock, which the nineteenth-century immigration was greatly to increase.[13] Except in inaccessible spots, the Spanish culture and language predominated. In Brazil the culture was Portuguese, and the country, though independent after 1822, remained a monarchy or "empire" until 1889, when it became a republic. In the former Spanish domains the disappearance of royal control left a large number of flaccid and shifting republics, chronically engaged in border disputes with one another. Fortunately for these republics, at the time of independence in the 1820s, European imperialism was at a low ebb. We have seen how the Congress of Verona considered ways of returning them to Spain but was opposed by Great Britain; and how the United States, in 1823, supplemented the British action by announcing the Monroe Doctrine. But it was by the United States that one of the new republics was first threatened from the outside.

The United States and Mexico

Mexico, on becoming independent of Spain, reached almost to the Mississippi and the Rocky Mountains. Hardly was it independent when land seekers from the United States swarmed over its northeastern borders. They brought with them their slaves, to grow the cotton so voraciously demanded in industrial England. The Mexican Republic did not allow slavery. The newcomers proclaimed their own republic, which they called Texas. Agitation developed for annexation to the United States. Mexico objected, but in 1845 the United States annexed Texas. A war followed, in which Mexico lost to the United States not only Texas but the whole region from Texas to the California coast. As is usual in such affairs, the loser preserved a longer memory than the winner. It soon seemed only natural in the United States to possess these regions; in Mexico many decades had to pass before the wound was healed. Mexico had lost half its territory within the first generation of its independence. It was argued at the time that the United States had far better facilities than Mexico for civilizing the region.

The next threat to Mexico came from Europe. Political leaders in Mexico, at a time of internal disorders, contracted large loans in Europe on exorbitant terms, the European leaders rightly estimating Mexican credit to be highly unsound. When the liberal leader Juárez (a pure-blooded Indian, at least racially "non-European") repudiated the loans, the European bondholders demanded satisfaction from their governments. The United States was paralyzed by the Civil War. Great Britain, France, and Spain, which had never recognized the Monroe Doctrine, in 1861 sent combined military forces to Veracruz. The British proposed seizure of the customs houses in Mexican ports, and appropriation of the customs revenues to pay off the debt (an expedient introduced in China three years before); but the French had more ambitious designs. Unknown both to the British,

[13] See pp. 112–114, 481–483.

who wanted only to collect debts, and to the Spanish, who dreamed of setting up a new Bourbon monarchy in Mexico, the Emperor Napoleon III had a secret project for establishing a French satellite state in Mexico, which French capital and exports might subsequently develop.[14] He planned to create a Mexican empire with the Austrian archduke Maximilian as its figurehead emperor. The British and Spanish disapprovingly withdrew their forces. The French army proceeded into the interior. Maximilian reigned for some years, but Napoleon III gradually concluded that conquest of Mexico was impossible, or too expensive. It further appeared, by 1865, that the United States was not going to collapse after all, as expected and even hoped for by the European governing classes. The United States protested strongly to the French government. The French withdrew, Maximilian was captured and shot, and Juárez and the Mexican liberals came back to power.

United States pressure, before 1870, had thus in turn both despoiled and protected the adjoining part of Latin America. This ambivalent situation became characteristic of the New World. As the United States became a great power the Monroe Doctrine became an effective barrier to European territorial ambitions. Latin America never became subject to imperialism as completely as did Asia and Africa. On the other hand, the United States became the imperialist power feared above all others south of the border. It was the *Yanqui* menace, the Colossus of the North.

In the 1870s in the course of its turbulent politics, both natives of Mexico and foreign residents were obliged to pay forced loans to rival leaders. The State Department at Washington demanded that American citizens be reimbursed by the Mexican government. The double standard characteristic of imperialism— one standard for civilized and one for uncivilized states—became clear in the exchange of notes. The Mexican government, now under Porfirio Díaz, attempted to lay down the principle that "foreigners locating in a country accepted the mode of life of the people . . . and participated not only in the benefits of such residence but also in the adversities. Foreigners should enjoy the same guarantees and the same legal protection as natives, but no more." The Mexicans observed that the United States had never recognized the claims of foreigners for losses sustained in its Civil War. The United States, under President Hayes, held on the other hand that citizens of advanced states, operating in more primitive regions, should continue to enjoy the security of property characteristic of their home countries. When on another occasion the United States sent troops to the border, and the Mexicans objected, the secretary of state remarked on "the volatile and childish character of these people and their incapacity to treat a general question with calmness and without prejudice." Mexico retorted that the United States had "disregarded all the rules of international law and practice of civilized nations and treated the Mexicans as savages, as Kaffirs of Africa."

It was, in fact, a principle of international law in the nineteenth century that civilized states might not intervene in each other's affairs but had the right of intervention in "backward" countries. In the dispute of 1877 the United States classified Mexico as backward, "volatile and childish." What the Mexicans

---

[14] See pp. 529–530.

objected to was being treated like "savages and Kaffirs," and not like a civilized nation. They differed on which of the two standards should apply.

United States Imperialism in the 1890s

The 1890s saw a crescendo of imperialism both in Europe and in the United States. In 1895, in a resounding restatement of the Monroe Doctrine, President Cleveland forbade the British to deal directly with Venezuela in a boundary dispute affecting British Guiana. The British were obliged to accept international arbitration. When, however, the adjacent Colombia faced a revolution in the Isthmus of Panama the United States supported the revolutionaries and, consulting nobody, recognized Panama as an independent republic. Here the United States leased and fortified a Canal Zone, over which it long kept control, and proceeded to build the Panama Canal. Panama became in effect what Europeans would call a protectorate of the United States.

Meanwhile what was left of the old Spanish American empire, confined to Cuba and Puerto Rico, was agitated by revolutionary disturbances looking to independence. Sympathies in the United States lay with the revolutionaries. Every sign of the new imperialism showed itself unmistakably. Americans had $50 million invested in Cuba. They bought the bonds issued by Cuban revolutionaries in New York. Cuban sugar, whose production was interfered with by political troubles, was necessary to the famed American standard of living. An orderly and amenable Cuba was vital to American strategic interests in the Caribbean, in the soon to be built canal, and in the Pacific. The barbarity of the Spanish authorities was deplored as an outrage to modern civilization. The newspapers, especially the new "yellow" press, roused the American public to a fury of moral indignation and imperial self-assertion. The climax came when an American warship, the *Maine*, sank under mysterious circumstances in Havana harbor.

The United States easily won the ensuing war with Spain in 1898. Puerto Rico was annexed outright, as were the Philippine Islands on the other side of the world. Cuba was set up as an independent republic, subject to the Platt Amendment, a series of provisions by which the United States obtained the right to oversee Cuba's relations with foreign powers, and to intervene in Cuba in matters of "life, property, individual liberty" and "Cuban independence." Thus the United States obtained another protectorate in the Caribbean. The right of intervention in Cuba was exercised several times in the following two decades, until the growth of Cuban nationalism and subsiding of American imperialism led to abrogation of the Platt Amendment in 1934. Later, after the Second World War, the Philippines formally received independence in 1946 and Puerto Rico became a self-governing commonwealth in 1952.

It was under President Theodore Roosevelt, the peppery "hero of San Juan hill," that the imperial greatness of the United States was most emphatically trumpeted. He announced in 1904 that weakness or misbehavior "which results in a general loosening of the ties of civilized society may . . . require intervention by some civilized nation," and that the Monroe Doctrine might force the United States "to the exercise of an international police power." In the following year

Santo Domingo fell into such financial disorder that European creditors were alarmed. To forestall any pretext for European intervention, the United States sent a financial administrator to Santo Domingo, reformed the economy of the country, and impounded half the customs receipts to pay its debts. Roosevelt declared—in what came to be known as the "Roosevelt Corollary" to the Monroe Doctrine—that, since the United States would not permit European states to intervene in America to collect debts, it must itself assume the duty of intervention to safeguard the investments of the civilized world. The Monroe Doctrine, initially a negative warning to Europe, now stood with the new corollary as a positive notice of supervision of all America by the United States. A quarter of a century of "dollar diplomacy" followed, in which the United States repeatedly intervened, by military or other means, in the Caribbean and Mexico. But the Roosevelt Corollary, like the Platt Amendment, created so much bad feeling in Latin America that the Washington government finally repudiated it.

The story of the Hawaiian Islands was as typical of the new imperialism as any episode in the history of any of the European empires. Known originally to outsiders as the Sandwich Islands, these spots of land long enjoyed isolation in the vastnesses of the mid-Pacific. The growth of navigation in the nineteenth century introduced them to the world. Sailors, whalers, missionaries, and vendors of rum and cloth filled Honolulu by 1840. The native ruler, confused and helpless in the new situation, almost accepted a British protectorate in 1843 and in 1875 did accept a virtual protectorate by the United States, which guaranteed Hawaiian independence against any third party, obtained trading privileges, and acquired Pearl Harbor as a naval base. American capital and management entered the island. They created huge sugar and pineapple industries, entirely dependent on export to, and investment by, the United States. In 1891, when Queen Liliuokalani came to the throne, she tried to check westernization and Americanization. The American interests, endangered by her nativist policies, overthrew the queen and set up an independent republic, which soon sought annexation to the United States. It was the story of Texas reenacted. For several years the issue hung in the balance because of lingering disapproval in the United States for such strong-arm methods. But with Japan revealing imperial designs in 1895, the rush of the other powers into China, the Spanish-American War, acquisition of the Philippines, and plans for the Panama Canal, the United States "accepted its destiny" in the Pacific, and annexed the Hawaiian Republic by joint resolution of Congress in 1898. Hawaii became a state in the American union in 1959.

80. The Dissolution of the Ottoman Empire

The Ottoman Empire in the 1850s

Of all parts of the non European world, the Ottoman, or Turkish, Empire was the nearest to Europe, and with it Europeans had for centuries had close relations. It had for long extended from Hungary and the Balkan peninsula to the south Russian steppes and from Algeria to the Persian Gulf. The empire was not at all like a European state. Immense in extent, it was a congeries of religious communities. Most of its people were Muslim, including both orthodox Muslims and such reform sects as Druses and Wahabis; some were Jews who had always lived in the Near East; many were Christian, principally Greek Orthodox and Armenian, who had also always lived there. The Turks were the ruling class and Islam the dominant religion. Only Muslims, for example, could serve in the army; non-Muslims were known as *raya*, the "flock" or "herd"—they paid the taxes. Persons of different religion lived side by side, each under the laws, courts, and customs of his or her own religious group. Religious officials—patriarchs, bishops, rabbis, imams, ulemas—were responsible to the Turkish government for their own people, over whom therefore they had a great deal of authority.[15]

Western Europeans had their own special rights. Roman Catholic clergy, living mainly in Palestine, looked to the pope in religion and to France for a mundane protector. Western merchants enjoyed the regime of the "capitulations," or special rights granted by the Ottoman government in numerous treaties going back to the sixteenth century. By the capitulations Turkey could not levy a tariff of more than 8 percent on imported goods. Europeans were exempt from most taxes. Cases involving two Europeans, civil or criminal, could be settled only in a court held by a European consul under European law. Disputes between a European and an Ottoman subject were settled in Turkish courts, but in the presence of a European observer.

The Ottoman Empire, in short, completely lacked the European idea of nationalism or national unity. The European idea of sovereignty and a uniform law for all its peoples were also absent, as was the idea of the secular state, or of law and citizenship separated from religion. The empire had fallen behind Europe in scientific, mechanical, material, humanitarian, and administrative achievements.

Turkey was the "sick man of Europe," and its long decline constituted the Eastern Question. Since the loss of Hungary in 1699 the Ottoman Empire had entered on a long process of territorial disintegration. That the empire lasted another two centuries was due to the European balance of power.[16] But by the 1850s the empire was falling away at the edges. Russia had advanced in the Crimea and the Caucasus. Serbia was autonomous, Greece independent, and Romania recognized as a self-governing principality. The French occupied Algeria. A native Arab dynasty, the Sauds, of the Wahabi reform sect, ruled over much of Arabia. A former Turkish governor of Egypt, Mehemet Ali, had established his family as hereditary khedives in the Nile valley.[17] Notwithstanding these changes, the Ottoman Empire in the 1850s was still huge. It encompassed not only the Turkish or Anatolian peninsula (including Armenia and territory south of the Caucasus) but also the central portion of the Balkan peninsula from Constantinople to the Adriatic where many Christians of Slavic nationality lived, Tripoli (Libya) in North Africa, and the islands of Crete and Cyprus. Egypt and Arabia, though autonomous, were still under the nominal suzerainty of the sultan.

The Crimean War of 1854–1856 opened a new phase in Ottoman history as in

[15] See pp. 219–221.

[16] See pp. 221–223, 340, 484–485, and map, p. 660.

[17] See p. 485. The Egyptian ruler, as viceroy under the Ottoman Empire, did not adopt the title of "khedive" until 1867; he was called "sultan" from 1914 to 1922; and thereafter "king" until the overthrow of the monarchy in 1952.

that of Europe.[18] We have seen how this war was followed by the consolidation of great nation-states in Europe, and how even the United States, Canada, and Japan consolidated or modernized themselves at the same time. The Turks tried to do the same between 1856 and 1876.

In the Crimean War the Turks were on the winning side, but the war affected them as it affected Russia, the loser. Exposing their military and political weakness, it pointed up the need of organization. The outcome of the war was taken to prove the superiority of the political system of England and France. It was therefore on Western lines that Turkish reformers wished to remodel. It was not merely that they wished to defend themselves against another of the periodic wars with Russia. They wished also to avoid being periodically saved from Russia by the West, a process which if continued could lead only to French or British control of Turkey.

Attempts at Reform and Revival, 1856–1876

In 1856 the Ottoman government issued the Hatt-i Humayun, the most far-reaching Turkish reform edict of the century. Its purpose was to create an Ottoman national citizenship for all persons in the empire. It abolished the civil authority of religious hierarchs. Equality before the law was guaranteed as was eligibility to public office without regard to religion. The army was opened to Christians and Muslims alike and steps were even taken to include both in nonsegregated military units. The edict announced a reform of taxes, security of property for all, abolition of torture, and reform of prisons. It promised to combat the chronic evils of graft, bribery, and extortion by public officials.

For twenty years there were serious efforts to make the reform decree of 1856 a reality. Western and liberal ideas circulated freely. Newspapers were founded. Writers called for a national Turkish revival, threw off the old Persian style in literature, composed histories of the Ottomans, translated Montesquieu and Rousseau. Foreign loans entered the country. Railroads joined the Black Sea and the Danube. Abdul Aziz (1861–1876), the first sultan to travel to Europe, visited Vienna, London, and the great Paris world's fair of 1867. But powerful resistance developed against such radical changes. Also, the best efforts of the Turkish reformers miscarried. There were too few Turks with skill or experience in the work required. Abdul Aziz took to spending his borrowed money somewhat too freely for purposes of the harem. In 1874 the Ottoman government, having recklessly overborrowed, repudiated half its debt.

A new and more determined reforming minister, Midhat Pasha, goaded by opposition and desperate at the weight of inertia, deposed Abdul Aziz in 1876, deposed the latter's nephew three months later, and set up Adbul Hamid II as sultan. The new sultan at first briskly went along with the reform movement, proclaiming a new constitution in 1876. It declared the Ottoman Empire to be indivisible, and promised personal liberty, freedom of conscience, freedom of education and the press, and parliamentary government. The first Turkish parliament met in 1877. Its members earnestly addressed themselves to reform.

---

[18] See pp. 544–545.

But they reckoned without Abdul Hamid, who in 1877 revealed his true intentions. He got rid of Midhat, packed off the parliament, and threw away the constitution.

Repression after 1876

Abdul Hamid reigned for thirty-three years, from 1876 to 1909. For all this time he lived as a terrified animal, fighting back blindly and ferociously against forces that he could not understand. Once when a consignment of dynamos reached the Turkish customs it was held up by fearful officials, because the contents were declared to make several hundred revolutions per minute. Again, chemistry books for use in the new American college were pronounced seditious, because their chemical symbols might be a secret cipher. The sultan sensed that tampering with the old Ottoman way would lead to ruin. He dreaded any moves to check his own whim or power. He was thrown into a panic by Turkish reformers and westernizers, who became increasingly terroristic in the face of his opposition. Driven away by Abdul Hamid, some tens of thousands of Young Turks, the activists of the reform era before 1876, or their children and successors, lived in exile in Paris, London, or Geneva, plotting their return to Turkey and vengeance upon Abdul the Damned. The sultan was frightened also by agitation among his non-Turkish subjects. Nationalist Armenians, Bulgars, Macedonians, and Cretans defied and taunted the Ottoman authorities, which responded with the Bulgarian massacres of 1876 and the Armenian massacres of 1894. These horrible butcheries of thousands of peasants by Ottoman troops came as a shock to a Europe unused to such violence. Last, and with good reason, Abdul Hamid lived in a creeping fear of the designs of the imperialist European powers upon his dissolving empire.

A thoroughly reformed, consolidated, and modernized Ottoman Empire was the last thing that European governments desired. They might wish for humanitarian reforms in Turkey, for more efficiency and honesty in Turkish government and finance, and even for a Turkish parliamentary system. Such demands were eloquently expressed by liberals like Gladstone in England. But no one wanted what Turkish reformers wanted, a reinvigorated Ottoman Empire that could deal with Europe politically as an equal.

The Russo-Turkish War of 1877–1878: The Congress of Berlin

In Russia, since the time of Catherine II, many had dreamed of installing Russia on the shores of the Bosporus.[19] Constantinople they called Tsarigrad, the Imperial City, which Orthodoxy was to liberate from the infidel. Crusading motives, in a nationalist and imperialist age, reappeared anew in the form of Pan-Slavism.[20] This was now a doctrine preached by leading Russians, including the novelist Dostoevski, the poet Tyutchev, and the publicist Danilevsky. Danilevsky's *Russia and Europe*, published in 1871, predicted a long war between Europe and Russia, to be followed by a grand federation of the East, in which not only Slavs, but Greeks, Hungarians, and parts of Asiatic Turkey would be included under Russian control. This type of Pan-Slavism was favored and patronized by the Russian

[19] See pp. 484, 544–545.
[20] On earlier Pan-Slavism, see pp. 510–511.

government, because it diverted attention from internal and revolutionary troubles. As for the Slav peoples of the Ottoman Empire, they were willing to use Russian Pan-Slavism as a means of combating their Turkish rulers. Insurrection against the Turks broke out in Bosnia in 1875, in Bulgaria in 1876. In 1877 Russia declared war on Turkey. Russia was again on the move against the Ottoman Empire for the sixth time in a hundred years.

The British, who had fought Russia over Turkey in 1854, were prepared to do so again. A number of recent developments added to their apprehension. The Suez Canal was completed in 1869. It was within the territory of the Ottoman Empire. It restored the Near East to its ancient position as a crossroads of world trade. The British also took alarm when Russia, in 1870, in the confusion of the Franco-Prussian War, repudiated a clause in the treaty of 1856 and began to build a fleet on the Black Sea. In 1874 Benjamin Disraeli, a Conservative and an imperialist, became prime minister of Great Britain. By a sudden coup in the following year he was able to buy up, from the almost bankrupt khedive of Egypt, 44 percent of the shares of the Suez Canal Company. In 1876, in a dramatic affirmation of imperial splendor, he had Queen Victoria take the title of empress of India. British commercial and financial interests in India and the Far East were growing, and the Suez Canal, of which the British government was now the principal stockholder, was becoming the "lifeline" of empire. But the Ottoman state, and hence the whole Near East, was now collapsing before the Russians, whose armies advanced rapidly through the Balkans in 1877, reached Constantinople, and forced the Turks to sign a treaty, the treaty of San Stefano. By this treaty Turkey ceded to Russia Batum and Kars on the south side of the Caucasus Mountains, gave full independence to Serbia and Romania, promised reforms in Bosnia, and granted autonomy to a new Bulgarian state, whose boundaries were to be very generously drawn, and which everyone expected to be dominated by Russia. England seethed with a popular clamor for war against Russia. The outcry gave the word "jingoism" to the language:

> We don't want to fight, but by jingo, if we do,
> We've got the men, we've got the ships, we've
> got the money too.

It now appeared that the weakness of Turkey, its inability to fend off foreigners from its borders, would precipitate at least an Anglo-Russian and possibly a general European war. But war was averted by diplomacy. Bismarck assembled a congress of all the European great powers at Berlin. Once again Europe attempted to assert itself as a unity, to restore life to the much-battered Concert of Europe by dealing collectively with the common problem presented by the Eastern Question. The immediate need was to mediate between the Russians and Turks and to placate the British. To prevent any single power from gaining unequal advantage, and to win the acceptance of all powers for the arrangements agreed to, it was deemed necessary to give something to all, or almost all. The congress in effect initiated a partition of the Ottoman domain. It kept peace in Europe at the expense of Turkey. The European balance now both protected and dismembered Turkey at the same time.

The Russians were persuaded at Berlin to give up the treaty of San Stefano that they had imposed on the Turks, but they still obtained Batum and Kars and won independence for the Serbs and Romanians. Montenegro, too, was recognized as an independent state. They compromised on Bulgaria, which was divided into three zones with varying degrees of autonomy, all still nominally within the Ottoman Empire. Austria-Hungary was authorized by the congress to "occupy and administer" Bosnia (but not annex it) in the interests of civilization and in compensation for the spread of Russian influence in the Balkans. To the British (Disraeli boasted he brought home "peace with honor") the Turks ceded Cyprus, a large island not far from the Suez Canal. The French were told that they might expand from Algeria into Tunisia. To the Italians (who counted least) it was more vaguely hinted that some day, somehow, they might expand across the Adriatic into Albania. As Bismarck put it, "the Italians have such a large appetite and such poor teeth." Germany took nothing. Bismarck said he was the "honest broker," with no interest except in European peace.

The treaty of Berlin in 1878 dispelled the immediate threat of war. But it left many continuing problems for later statesmanship to deal with, problems which, because they were not dealt with successfully, became a principal cause of the First World War thirty-six years later. Neither the Balkan nationalists nor the Russian Pan-Slavs were satisfied. The Turks, both reactionaries like Abdul Hamid and the revolutionary Young Turks in exile, were indignant that peace had been made by further dismemberment of their territory. The demonstrated weakness of Turkey was a constant temptation to all concerned. In the years before 1914 German influence grew. Germans and German capital entered Turkey, projecting, and partially completing, a great Berlin to Bagdad railway to be accompanied by the exploitation of Near Eastern resources. The railroad was all but completed before 1914 despite the protests and representations of the Russians, the French, and particularly the British, who saw in it a direct threat to their empire in India.

Egypt and North Africa

For Egypt, technically autonomous within the Ottoman Empire, the 1850s and 1860s were a time of progress in the Western sense as they had been for the empire as a whole. The Egyptian government modernized its administration, court system, and property law, cooperated with the French in building the Suez Canal, encouraged shipping on the Red Sea, and let British and French interests construct railroads. Between 1861 and 1865, while the American South was unable to export raw cotton, the annual export of Egyptian cotton rose from 60 million to 250 million pounds. Egypt more than Turkey was drawn into the world market, and the khedive more than the sultan became a Western type of man. The khedive Ismail built himself a fine new opera house in Cairo, where, in 1871, two years after the opening of the Suez Canal, Verdi's Aïda, written at the khedive's request, was resoundingly performed for the first time.

Such improvements cost a good deal of money, borrowed in England and France. The Egyptian government was soon in financial straits, only temporarily relieved by the sale of Canal shares to Disraeli. By 1879 matters reached the point where Western banking interests forced the abdication of Ismail and his

THE DISSOLUTION OF THE OTTOMAN EMPIRE, 1699–1914

Beginning in 1699, with the loss of Hungary to the House of Austria, the Ottoman Empire entered upon a long process of territorial disintegration which lasted for over two hundred years. Dates shown are those at which territories dropped away. In general, regions lost from 1699 to the fall of Napoleon, 1812–1815, were annexed directly by Austria and Russia. European territories lost in the nineteenth century emerged as independent states, owing to the rise of nationalism and the balance among the great European powers. (See maps, p. 703.) In the Arab world, reaching from Algeria to the Persian Gulf, regions lost before the First World War were absorbed into European colonial empires; those lost in the First World War (1918) were at first mostly assigned to France and Britain as mandates, but after the Second World War emerged as independent Arab states, as did the Republic of Israel (see pp. 943–944). During the First World War Britain, France, Italy, Russia, and Greece took steps to partition Turkey proper, but a Turkish nationalist movement blocked these designs and established a Turkish republic (see pp. 661, 703, 791–792).

replacement by Tewfik, who, with a naïve fascination for the new Western marvels, soon let himself become thoroughly enmeshed by his creditors. This led to nationalistic protests within Egypt, headed by Colonel Arabi. In a pattern repeated in many parts of the colonial world, especially in Manchu China, the nationalists opposed both the foreigners and their own government, charging it with being a mere front for foreign interests. Arabi's movement, an early expression of Arab nationalism, led to riots in Alexandria, where Europeans had to flee aboard British and French shipping in the harbor. A British squadron then unceremoniously bombarded Alexandria. British troops (the French, though invited to take part, refused) disembarked in 1882 at Suez and Alexandria, defeated Arabi, and took Tewfik under their protection. The military intervention of 1882 was said by the British to be temporary, but British troops remained there for a long time, through two world wars and well into the twentieth century, not leaving until 1956.

Egypt became a British protectorate. The British protected the khedive from discontent within his own country, from the claims of the Ottoman Porte, and from the rival attentions of other European powers. The British resident from 1883 to 1907, an exceptionally capable administrator named Evelyn Baring, the first Earl of Cromer, did much to reconstruct the economy of the country, reform its taxation, ease the burdens on the peasants and raise their productivity, while encouraging the growth of raw materials wanted by England and assuring regular payment of interest to British, French, and other holders of Egyptian bonds.

The French strenuously objected when the British stayed on so long in Egypt. It had long been the French who had the greatest investments in the Near East, and Near Easterners who were at all westernized—Egyptian, Syrian, Turkish— overwhelmingly preferred the French language and culture to the English. The French, harboring deep suspicion of British designs in Egypt, compensated themselves by building a North African empire farther west. They developed Algeria, assumed a protectorate over Tunisia, and began to penetrate Morocco. Upon these French advances the British, and soon the Germans, looked with unmitigated disfavor. Rivalry for the spoils of the Ottoman Empire thus created enmity among the Great Powers and constituted a fertile source of the war scares, fears, and diplomatic maneuvers that preceded the First World War. These are related in the following chapter.

The dissolution of the Ottoman Empire became indistinguishable from the whole chronic international crisis before 1914. It is enough to say here, to keep the fate of the Ottoman Empire in focus, that Abdul Hamid's frantic policies came to nothing and that the Young Turks won control of the Ottoman government in 1908. They forced the restoration of the constitution of 1876 and introduced many reforms. In the midst of the revolutionary disturbances of 1908 Bulgaria proclaimed its full independence and Austria annexed Bosnia. In the Turco-Italian War of 1911–1912 Italy took Libya and the Dodecanese Islands from the Turks. In two successive Balkan Wars (1912–1913) Turkey lost nearly all its territory in Europe to Bulgaria, Serbia, Greece, and Albania, the latter becoming an independent state in 1912.[21] Finally, when all Europe became involved in war in 1914, Russia again declared war on Turkey, and the Turks came into the war on the side of Germany, whose political and economic influence in the empire had been steadily growing. During the war, with British aid, the Arabs detached themselves from the empire, becoming eventually independent Arab states. Egypt, too, ended all connections with the empire. In 1923 a Turkish republic was proclaimed. It was confined to Constantinople and the Anatolian peninsula, where

[21] See p. 701, and map, p. 703.

the bulk of the true Turkish people lived. The new republic proceeded to undergo a thorough nationalist and secular revolution.[22]

81. The Partition of Africa

South of Mediterranean Africa lay the Sahara desert, and south of that Black Africa, of which Europeans knew so little that they called it the Dark Continent. Africa is so gigantic that even the part south of the Sahara is almost as large as the whole continent of North America. For centuries Europeans knew only its coasts—the Gold Coast, Ivory Coast, Slave Coast—to which from an inexhaustible interior had come shackled processions of captive slaves, as well as the swelling waters of enormous rivers, like the Nile, Niger, and Congo, whose sources in the dim hinterland were a subject of romantic speculation. The people were black, but diverse both in physique and in culture, and speaking almost a thousand languages. They had learned to work iron as long ago as the third century before Christ, and so only a few centuries later than Europeans. They were adept in many arts, such as bronze sculpture, gold artifacts, weaving, basketry, and the making of ceremonial masks with strikingly symbolic or abstract patterns. Along the northern fringe some had been won to Islam, but mostly they adhered to their traditional religions.

They lived mainly in villages in tribal communities, engaged in agriculture or moving herds of cattle from place to place. But great cities or agglomerations had also arisen, from Timbuktu in the north with its old caravan trade across the Sahara, to the vast complex of buildings at Zimbabwe in the south, which was already in ruins when the Europeans first saw it. There had also been extensive kingdoms whose memory was preserved, in the absence of writing, by specially trained narrators from one generation to the next. But these kingdoms had disappeared or declined. They had been weakened by intertribal wars, or by the slave trade which set Africans against one another to satisfy the demand of outsiders, or by demographic causes that are now hard to trace. Hence Africa, somewhat like the Ottoman Empire and China, met the assault of the Europeans at a time when its powers of resistance were reduced. Before the mid–nineteenth century there were no permanently resident whites south of the Sahara except for a few Arabs who had been on the east coast since the seventh century and the Europeans who had been at the Cape of Good Hope since 1652. In the Union of South Africa, when it was established in 1910, some 1.1 million whites lived along with about 5 million blacks.

The Opening of Africa

Missionaries, explorers, and individual adventurers first opened this world to Europe. The historic pair, Livingstone and Stanley, well illustrate the drift of events. Long before the imperialist age, in 1841, the Scot David Livingstone arrived in southeast Africa as a medical missionary. He gave himself to humanitarian and religious work, with a little occasional trading and much travel and discovery,

---

[22] See pp. 791–793.

but without political or true economic aims. Exploring the Zambesi River, he was the first white man to look upon the Victoria Falls. Fully at home in inner Africa, safe and on friendly terms with its native people, he was quite content to be let alone. But the hectic forces of modern civilization sought him out. Word spread in Europe and America that Dr. Livingstone was lost. The New York *Herald,* to manufacture news, sent the roving journalist H. M. Stanley to find him, which he did in 1871. Livingstone soon died, deeply honored by the Africans among whom he worked. Stanley was a man of the new era. Seeing vast possibilities in Africa, he went to Europe to solicit backers. In 1878 he found a man with the same ideas, who happened to be a king, Leopold II, king of the Belgians.

Leopold, for all his royalty, was at heart a promotor. China, Formosa, the Philippines, and Morocco had in turn attracted his fancy, but it was the central African basin of the Congo that he decided to develop. Stanley was exactly the man he was looking for, and the two founded at Brussels, with a few financiers, an International Congo Association in 1878. It was a purely private enterprise; the Belgian government and people had nothing to do with it. All Africa inland from the coasts was considered to be, like America in the time of Columbus, a *terra nullius*, without government and claimed by nobody, wide open to the first civilized persons who might arrive. Stanley, returning to the Congo in 1882, in a year or two concluded treaties with over 500 chiefs, who in return for a few trinkets or a few yards of cloth put their marks on the mysterious papers and accepted the blue-and-gold flag of the Association.

Since the Dark Continent was still innocent of internal frontiers, no one could tell how much ground the Association might soon cover by these methods. The German explorer Karl Peters, working inland from Zanzibar, was signing treaties with the chiefs of East Africa. The Frenchman Brazza, departing from the west coast and distributing the tricolor in every village, was claiming on the Congo River itself a territory larger than France. The Portuguese aspired to join their ancient colonies of Angola and Mozambique into a trans-African empire, for which they required a generous portion of the interior. Britain supported Portugal. In every case the home governments in Europe were still hesitant over involvement in an Africa of which they knew nothing. But they were pushed on by small organized minorities of colonizing enthusiasts, and they faced the probability that if they missed the moment it would be too late.

Bismarck, who personally thought African colonies an absurdity, but was sensitive to the new pressures, called another conference at Berlin in 1885, this time to submit the African question to international regulation. Most European states, as well as the United States, attended. The Berlin conference attempted to do two things: to set up the territories of the Congo Association as an international state, under international auspices and restrictions; and to draft an international code governing the way in which European powers wishing to acquire African territory should proceed.

The Congo Free State, which in 1885 took the place of the International Congo Association, was not only an international creation but embodied, in principle, what were to be known after the First World War as international mandates or international trusteeships for "backward" peoples. The Berlin conference specified that the new state should have no connection with any power, including Belgium. It delegated the government to Leopold. It drew the boundaries, making the Congo Free State almost as large as the United States east of the Mississippi, and it added certain specific provisions: the Congo River was internationalized, persons of all nationalities should be free to do business in the Congo state, there should be no tariff levied on imports, and the slave trade should be suppressed. Leopold in 1889 reassembled the signatory powers in a second conference, held at Brussels. The Brussels conference took further steps to root out the slave trade, which remained a stubborn though declining evil, because the Muslim world was several generations behind the Christian in abolishing slavery. The Brussels conference also undertook to protect the rights of the local people, correct certain glaring abuses, and reduce the traffic in liquor and firearms.

This attempt at internationalism failed, because Europe had no international machinery by which the hard daily work of executing general agreements could be carried out. Leopold went his own way in the Congo. His determination to make it commercially profitable led him to unconscionable extremes. Europe and America demanded rubber, and the Congo was at the time one of the world's few sources of supply. The Congo people, among the least advanced in Africa, and afflicted by the disease and enervation of a lowland equatorial climate, could be made to tap enough rubber trees only by inhuman severity and compulsion. The trees themselves were destroyed without thought of replacement. Leopold, by ravaging its resources and virtually enslaving its people, was able to draw from the Congo a princely income to be spent in Brussels, but he could never make the enterprise self-supporting. Consumed with debt, he borrowed another 25 million francs from the kingdom of Belgium, agreeing that Belgium should inherit the Congo on his death if the debt was unpaid. In 1908, the reluctant Belgians thus found themselves heirs to some "tropical gardens" to which they had been consistently indifferent. The Free State became the Belgian Congo, and under Belgian administration the worst excesses of Leopold's regime were removed.

The Berlin conference of 1885 had also laid down, for expansion in Africa, certain rules of the game—a European power with holdings on the coast had prior rights in the hinterland; occupation must not be on paper only, through drawing lines on a map, but must consist in real occupation by administrators or troops; and each power must give proper notice to the others as to what territories it considered its own. A wild scramble for "real occupation" quickly followed. In fifteen years the entire continent was parceled out. The sole exceptions were Ethiopia and, technically, Liberia, founded in 1822 as a colony for emancipated American slaves and virtually a protectorate of the United States.

Everywhere a variant of the same process was repeated. First would appear a handful of white men, bringing their inevitable treaties—sometimes printed forms. To get what they wanted, the Europeans commonly had to ascribe powers to the chief which by the customs of the tribe he did not possess—powers to convey sovereignty, sell land, or grant mining concessions. Thus the Africans were baffled at the outset by foreign legal conceptions. Then the Europeans would build up the position of the chief, since they themselves had no influence over the people. This led to the widespread system of "indirect rule," by which colonial authorities acted through the existing chiefs and tribal forms. There were many things that only the chief could arrange, such as security for isolated Europeans, porter services, or gangs of workmen to build roads or railroads.

PRECOLONIAL AFRICA: SITES AND PEOPLES

This map is meant to show Africa before penetration by the Europeans in the nineteenth century. It does not refer to any particular date. Names in brown designate ancient or medieval centers, like the Ghana and Mali empires, which no longer existed in modern times. Even the most extensive African kingdoms had indefinite and shifting boundaries which are hard to indicate on a map. The word "Bantu," as in "Bantu people," refers to a large group of African languages spoken from points north of the Congo to the southern coast. See also map on p. 667.

Labor was the overwhelming problem. For pure slavery Europeans now had an abhorrence, and they abolished it wherever they could. But the African, so long as he lived in his traditional way, did not react like the free wage earner postulated in civilized business and economics. He had little expectation of individual gain and almost no use for money. He worked rather sporadically according to European ideas; work, continuous and laborious work, was in many

African societies left to the women. The result was that Europeans all over Africa resorted to forced labor. For road building, systems like the French *corvée* before the Revolution reappeared. Or the chief would be required to supply a quota of able-bodied men for a certain length of time, and frequently he did so gladly to raise his own importance in the eyes of the whites. More indirect methods were also used. The colonial government might levy a hut tax or a poll tax, payable only in money, to obtain which the native would have to seek a job. Or the new government, once installed, might allocate so much land to Europeans as private property (another foreign conception) that the local tribe could no longer subsist on the lands that remained to it. Or the whole tribe might be moved to a reservation, like Indians in the United States. In any case, while the women tilled the fields or tended the stock at home, the men would move off to take jobs under the whites for infinitesimal pay. The men then lived in "compounds," away from family and tribal kindred; they became demoralized; and the labor they gave, untrained and unwilling, would scarcely have been tolerated in any more civilized community. In these circumstances everything was done to uproot the Africans, and little was done to benefit them.

Conditions improved with the twentieth century, as traditions of enlightened colonial administration were built up. Colonial officials even came to serve as buffers or protectors of the local peoples against the intruding white man's interest. Throughout, it was part of the ethos of imperialism to put down slavery, tribal warfare, superstition, disease, and illiteracy. Slowly a westernized class of Africans grew—chiefs and the sons of chiefs, Catholic priests and Protestant ministers, warehouse clerks and government employees. Young men from Nigeria or Uganda appeared as students at Oxford, the University of Paris, or universities in the United States. Westernized Africans usually resented both exploitation and paternalism. They showed signs of turning nationalistic, like their counterparts in the Ottoman Empire and Asia. If they wanted westernization, it was at a pace and for a purpose of their own. As the twentieth century progressed, nationalism in Africa grew more vocal and more intense.

Friction and Rivalry between the Powers

Meanwhile, in the fifteen years from 1885 to 1900, the Europeans in Africa came dangerously near to open blows. The Portuguese annexed huge domains in Angola and Mozambique. The Italians took over two barren tracts, Italian Somaliland and Eritrea on the Red Sea. They then moved inland, in quest of more imposing possessions, to conquer Ethiopia and the headwaters of the Nile. Some 80,000 Ethiopians, however, slaughtered and routed 20,000 Italians in pitched battle at Adowa in 1896. It was the first time that Africans successfully defended themselves against the whites, and it discouraged invasion of Ethiopia by the Italians (or other Europeans) for forty years. Italy and Portugal, like the Congo Free State and Spain (which retained a few vestiges of former days), were able to enjoy sizable holdings in Africa because of mutual fears among the principal contenders. The principal contenders were Great Britain, France, and Germany. Each preferred to have territory held by a minor power rather than by one of its significant rivals.

The Germans were latecomers in the colonial race, which Bismarck entered with reluctance. By the 1880s all the usual imperialist arguments were heard in

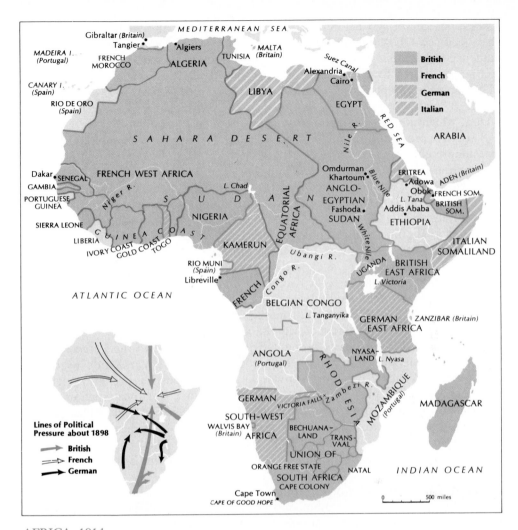

AFRICA, 1914

The map shows the recognized holdings of the Powers in 1914. The inset suggests the directions of political pressure about 1898. These pressures led to the Fashoda crisis in 1898 and the Boer War in 1899. In 1898 the British and German governments held secret discussions on the possible partitioning of the Portuguese colonies, which, however, never came to pass since the British greatly preferred to have the Portuguese colonies remain in the hands of Portugal.

Germany, though most of them, such as the need of new markets, of outlets for emigration, or for the investment of capital, had little or no application in tropical Africa. The Germans established colonies in German East Africa, and in the Cameroons and Togo on the west coast, along with a desert area that came to be called German Southwest Africa. It did not escape the notice of German imperial planners that some day the Congo and the Portuguese colonies might be joined with German East Africa and the Cameroons in a solid German belt across the African heartland. The French controlled most of West Africa, from Algeria across the Sahara and the Sudan to various points on the Guinea coast. They also occupied Obok on the Red Sea, and after the Italian defeat in 1896 their influence in Ethiopia grew. French planners therefore dreamed of a solid French belt across Africa from Dakar to the Gulf of Aden. The French government in 1898 dispatched Captain J. B. Marchand with a small party eastward from Lake Chad, to hoist the tricolor far away on the upper Nile, in the southern part of the Sudan, which no European power as yet "effectively" occupied.

The two presumptive east-and-west belts, German and French, were cut (presumptively) by a north-and-south belt, projected in the British imperial imagination as an "Africa British from the Cape to Cairo." From the Cape of Good Hope Cecil Rhodes pushed northward into what was later called Rhodesia. Kenya and Uganda in the mid continent were already British. In Egypt, a British protectorate since 1882, the British began to support old Egyptian claims to the upper Nile. The first venture proved a disaster, when in 1885 a British officer, "Chinese Gordon," leading an Egyptian force, was killed by aroused Muslims at Khartoum. In the following decade British opinion turned imperialist in earnest. Another British officer, General Kitchener (with a young man named Winston Churchill under his command), again started southward up the Nile and defeated the local Muslims in 1898 at Omdurman. He then pushed on further upstream. At a place called Fashoda he met Marchand.

The ensuing Fashoda crisis brought Britain and France to the verge of war. Already at odds over Egypt and Morocco,[23] the two governments used the encounter at Fashoda to force a showdown. It was a test of strength, not only for their respective plans for all Africa, but for their relative position in all imperialist and international issues. Both at first refused to yield. The British virtually threatened to fight. The French, fearful of their insecurity against Germany in Europe, at last decided not take the risk. They backed down and recalled Marchand from Fashoda. A wave of hatred for the British swept over France.

The British no sooner won this Pyrrhic victory than they became involved in more unpleasantness at the other end of the African continent. In 1890 Cecil Rhodes had become prime minister of the Cape Colony. He was a principal sponsor of the Cape-to-Cairo dream. Two small independent neighboring republics, the Transvaal and the Orange Free State, stood in his way. Their people were Afrikaners—Dutch who had originally settled the Cape in the seventeenth century, then after 1815, when England annexed the Cape of Good Hope, had made the "great trek" to escape from British rule. The Boers, as the English called them, from the Dutch word for "farmer," were simple, obstinate, and old-fashioned. They thought slavery not ungodly and disliked promoters, fortune hunters, foot-loose adventurers, mining-camp people, and other Uitlanders.

The discovery of diamonds and gold in the Transvaal brought the issue to a head. British capital and British people poured in. The Transvaal refused to pass legislation needed by the mining corporations and their employees. In 1895 Rhodes, attempting to precipitate revolution in the Transvaal, sent a party of armed irregulars, under Dr. Jameson, over its borders. This Jameson Raid was a failure, but in Europe a great cry went up against British bullying of a small

[23] See p. 661.

inoffensive republic. The German emperor, William II, dispatched a famous telegram to Paul Kruger, president of the Transvaal, congratulating him on his driving off the invaders "without having to call for the support of friendly powers"—i.e., Germany. Three years later, in 1899, the British Empire went to war with the two small republics. The South African War (Boer War) lasted until 1902; the British sent in 300,000 troops, and to combat an elusive and irregular adversary they felt obliged to ravage the country and intern about 120,000 women and children in concentration camps, where about 20,000 died. But once subdued and brought within the British system the two republics were left with their self-governing institutions. In 1910 the Transvaal, Orange Free State, Cape Colony, and Natal were combined to form the Union of South Africa, which received semi-independent status along the lines of the Dominion of Canada.

The Fashoda crisis and the Boer War, coming in rapid succession, revealed to the British the bottomless depths of their unpopularity in Europe. All European governments and peoples were pro-Boer; only the United States, involved at the time in a similar conquest of the Philippines, showed any sympathy for the British. The British, after the Boer War, began to rethink their international position, as will soon be seen.

As in the case of the Ottoman Empire, rivalry between the Great Powers over the spoils of Africa embittered international relations and helped prepare the way for the First World War. The rivalry over Morocco involving France and Germany entered into the general prewar crisis and will be related in the following chapter. As for Africa as a whole, there was little territorial change after the Boer War, although in 1911 Italy took Libya from the Turks. In 1914 the Germans were excluded from their short-lived empire. Had the Germans won the First World War, the map of Africa would probably have been greatly revised, but since they lost it the only change was to assign the German colonies, under international mandate, to the French and British. With this change, and except for Italy's ephemeral conquest of Ethiopia in 1935, the map of Africa remained what the brief years of partition had made it until the spectacular end of the European empires after the Second World War.[24]

82. Imperialism in Asia: The Dutch, the British, and the Russians

The Dutch East Indies and British India

British India and the Dutch East Indies, in the half-century before the First World War, were the world's ideal colonies. They illustrated the kind of empire that all imperialists would have wished to have, and a glance at them suggests the goal toward which imperialism was logically moving.

Whereas all countries of western Europe showed a surplus of imports, receiving more goods from the rest of the world than they sent out, India and Indonesia invariably, year after year and decade after decade, showed a surplus of exports,

---

[24] See pp. 925–939, and map, p. 926.

sending out far more goods than they took in. This export surplus was the hallmark of the developed colonial area, geared closely into the world market, with low purchasing power for the natives and kept going by foreign investment and management. Both regions, in addition, were so large as to have a good deal of internal business—commerce, insurance, banking, transportation—which never appeared in the statistics for world trade, but which, being dominated by Europeans, added immeasurably to their profits. Both had rich and varied natural resources, tropical in character, so that they never competed with the products of Europe—though India even before 1914 showed tendencies to industrialization. In both regions the people were adept and quick to learn. But they were divided by religion and language, so that, once conquered, they were relatively easy for Europeans to govern. Neither region before the First World War had any self-government at the highest levels. Both were ruled by a civil service, honest and high-minded by its own lights, in which the most illustrious, most influential, and best paying positions were reserved for Europeans. Hence upper-class families in England and the Netherlands valued their empires as fields of opportunity for their sons—somewhat as they had formerly valued an established church. In both India and Indonesia the governments were more or less benevolent despotisms, which, by curbing warfare, plague, and famine, at least allowed the population to grow in numbers. Java, with 5 million people in 1815, had 48 million in 1942. India's population in the same years probably grew from less than 200 million to almost 400 million. Finally, as the last virtue of a perfect colony, no foreign power directly challenged the British in India or the Dutch in their islands.

The Dutch in 1815 occupied little more than the island of Java itself.[25] In the following decades the British moved into Singapore, the Malay peninsula, and north Borneo, and made claims to Sumatra. The French in the 1860s appeared in Indochina. The Germans in the 1880s annexed eastern New Guinea and the Marshall and Solomon islands. Ultimately it was the mutual jealousy of these three that preserved the Dutch position. The Dutch, however, took the initiative themselves. To forestall occupation by other Europeans, and to put down native pirates and find raw materials that the world demanded, the Dutch spread their rule over the whole 3,000-mile extent of the archipelago. They created an empire, in place of the old chain of trading posts concerned only with buying and selling. Revolts were suppressed in 1830, 1849, and 1888; not till the twentieth century was northern Sumatra or the interior of Celebes brought under control. For some decades the Dutch exploited their huge empire by a kind of forced labor, the "culture system," in which the authorities required farmers to deliver, as a kind of tax, stated amounts of stated crops, such as sugar or coffee. After 1870 a freer system was introduced. The Dutch also, as an important matter of policy, favored instruction in the Malay and Javanese languages, not in Dutch. This preserved the native cultures from westernizing disintegration but at the same time meant that Western ideas of nationalism and democracy entered more slowly.

In India, in 1857, the British faced a dangerous rebellion, commonly called the Indian Mutiny, as if it had been a revolt of undisciplined soldiers only. The Indian army, with its sepoys, was the only organization through which Indians could

[25] See p. 166.

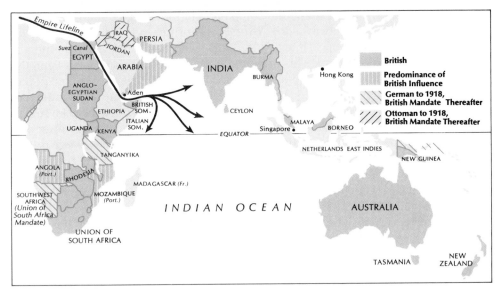

"THE BRITISH LAKE," 1918

This small map shows almost half the surface of the earth. All the most important parts of the British Empire are visible except Canada and the United Kingdom itself. All shores of the Indian Ocean are shown to be British, except for French Madagascar, the politically weak Portuguese, Italian, and Dutch colonies, and the Arabian and Persian coasts, in which British influence was strong. It is easy to see why the Mediterranean and the Suez Canal, leading from Europe into this half-world, were called the lifeline of the British Empire.

exert any collective pressure.[26] The proportion of sepoys in the army was high in 1857 (about five-sixths) because British units had been withdrawn for the Crimean War and for action in China. Many Indians, outside the army, had been restless for decades. Rulers had been conquered and dethroned. Landowners had lost their property and been replaced by new ones more friendly to the British. Religious sentiments were inflamed. The British too obviously regarded Indian beliefs as repulsive; they had outlawed suttee, or widow burning, suppressed the Thugs, a small sect of holy assassins, and one British officer even declared that in ten years the government would abolish caste. The Muslims were agitated by Wahabi fundamentalism. Mysterious propaganda circulated over India. It infiltrated the sepoys, announcing to Muslim soldiers that certain newly issued cartridges were greased with the fat of a pig and to Hindus that the same cartridges were greased with the fat of a cow. Since for Hindus the cow was sacred, and for Muslims to touch pork was profane, much agitation was produced. The sepoys mutinied in the Ganges valley; and with them the other injured interests, including the far-faded Great Mogul and his court, rose against the British.

The British put down the rebellion, aided by the fact that western and southern India took no part in it. But the uprising persuaded the British to a radically new course of policy, pursued basically until the end of the Indian empire almost a

---

[26] On the sepoys see pp. 282–283.

century later. The British East India Company and the Mogul empire were both finally and forever done away with. British authorities ruled directly. But the British concluded that they must rule India with and through the Indians themselves, not against them. This in practice meant a collaboration between the imperial power and the Indian upper classes. The British began to shelter Indian vested interests. They supported the Indian landlords and became more indulgent toward Indian "superstition." Where before 1857, when they conquered an Indian state, they had simply abolished it and incorporated its territories, after the Mutiny they kept the remaining Indian states as protectorates. States existing in 1857, such as Hyderabad and Kashmir and over 200 others, with their galaxy of rajahs and maharajahs, carried on to the end of British rule in 1947. It was largely to provide a fitting summit for this mountain of Indian royalty that Queen Victoria was proclaimed empress of India in 1877.

India had been a considerable manufacturing country by preindustrial standards. Indian merchants had once been important throughout the Indian Ocean, and before 1800 Indian exports to Europe had included many textiles and other finished goods.[27] The native crafts collapsed before modern industrialism reinforced by political power. "India," observed a British expert in 1837, "can never again be a great manufacturing country, but by cultivating her connection with England she may be one of the greatest agricultural countries in the world." Free trade (made possible by military superiority, usually overlooked by the economists) turned Britain into the world's workshop and India into a supplier of raw materials. Indian exports, in the latter part of the nineteenth century, consisted increasingly of raw cotton, tea, jute, oilseeds, indigo, and wheat. The British shipped their manufactures in return. Business in India boomed; India came to have the densest railway network outside of Europe and North America. It is important to note, however, as a commentary on dealing with poor countries, that Britain in 1914 did far more trading with the 6 million people of Australia and New Zealand than with the 315 million impoverished people of India.

The British, in contrast to the Dutch, decided in 1835 to favor instruction in English, not in the native languages. The historian Macaulay, one of the commission to make this recommendation, branded the Indian languages as vehicles of barbarous and unenlightened ideas—a bar to progress. The British also, after the Mutiny, admitted Indians to the civil service and to governors' councils—sparingly indeed, but more than the Dutch in Indonesia. There were also many Indian businessmen. A class of westernized Indians grew up, speaking perfect English, and often educated in England. They demanded more of a role in the affairs of their country. In 1885 the predominantly Hindu Indian National Congress was organized; in 1906, the All-India Muslim League. Muslim separatism, while favored by the British and sometimes even blamed upon them, was natural to India and exploited by some Indian leaders. Nationalism spread. It became increasingly anti-British, and radical nationalism turned also against the Indian princes, capitalists, and businessmen, as accomplices in imperialism, and so took on the color of socialism. In the period of the First World War, under nationalist pressure, the British granted more representation to Indians, especially in provincial affairs, but the movement toward self-rule was never fast enough to overcome the basic anti-British feeling of the Indian peoples.

[27] See pp. 259–262.

Conflict of Russian and British Interests

While no outsider yet threatened the British in India, British statecraft discerned in the northern sky a large cloud which was clearly approaching. The Russian empire had occupied northern Asia since the seventeenth century.[28] About 1850 Russian pressure on inner Asia was resumed. It was a type of imperialism in which neither the demand for markets nor for raw materials, nor for the investment of capital, counted for much. In these matters Russia was itself semicolonial with respect to the West. The Russians had, like the Westerners, a sense of spreading their type of civilization; but Russian expansion was distinctively political in that most of the initiative came from the government. Russia was an icebound empire, craving "warm-water ports." It was a landlocked empire, so that whichever way it turned it moved toward one ocean or another. The ocean was the domain of the Westerners, and in particular the British. In the large picture, Russia pushed by land against the Ottoman Empire, Persia, India, and China, all of which the British (and others) reached by sea. In 1860, on the shores of the Sea of Japan, the Russians founded Vladivostok, the farthest-flung of all Slavic cities, whose name meant Lord of the East. But their advance in the mid-century was mainly in the arid and thinly settled regions of western Asia. The British had already fought two Afghan wars to keep Afghanistan as a no man's land between Russia and India. In 1864 the Russians took Tashkent, in Turkestan. A decade later they touched India itself but were kept away by an Anglo-Russian agreement, which allotted a long tongue of land to Afghanistan and so separated the Indian and Russian empires by twenty miles—the new frontier, in the high Pamirs, on the Roof of the World, was to be sure, scarcely adapted to military operations.

Russian advances in Turkestan, east of the Caspian, increased the pressure on Persia, which had long felt the same pressure west of the Caspian, where cities like Tiflis and Baku, now Russian, had once been Persian. If Tiflis and Turkestan could fall to the Russian empire, there was no reason why Persia should not do so next—except that Persia had a seacoast and so might also be available for occupancy by the British. In 1864 a British company completed the first Persian telegraph as part of the line from Europe to India. Other British investments and interests followed. Oil became important about 1900. In 1890, to bolster the Persian government against Russia, the British granted it a loan—taking the customs in Persian Gulf ports as collateral. In 1900 the Russian government granted the same favor, making its own loan to Persia, and appropriating as security all Persian customs except those of the Gulf. Russian ships appeared in the Persian Gulf in 1900, a demonstration soon countered by a state visit to Persia of the Viceroy of India, Lord Curzon. Clearly Persia was losing control of its own affairs, falling into zones, turning ripe for partition. A Persian nationalist revolution, directed against all foreigners and against the subservient government of the shah, broke out in 1905 and led to the assembly of the first parliament but hardly settled the question of Persian independence. In 1907 the British recognized a Russian "sphere of influence" in northern Persia, the Russians a British sphere in the south.[29]

---

[28] See pp. 235–236.
[29] See pp. 673–674, 698, and map, p. 676.

Imperial ambitions had deepened the hostility between Great Britain and Russia, with disputes over Persia and the Indian borderlands adding fuel to the quarrel they had long waged over the Ottoman Empire. We have seen how the struggle for Africa had at the same time estranged Britain from France and indeed from all Europe.

83. Imperialism in Asia: China and the West

China before Western Penetration

But the biggest bone of imperialist contention was offered by China. On this bone every Great Power without exception tried to bite. The Manchu, or Ch'ing, dynasty (1644–1912) held a suzerainty over the whole area affected by Chinese civilization, from the mouth of the Amur River (as far north as Labrador) to Burma and Indochina (as far south as Panama), and from the ocean westward into Mongolia and Tibet. In the old Chinese view China was the Middle Kingdom, the civilized center of the world surrounded by less enlightened peoples. The Europeans were outlandish barbarians. A few had trickled through to China since the European Middle Ages. But the Chinese people persistently wanted nothing to do with them.

China was moving into an upheaval of its own even before Western influence became of any importance. For 2,000 years the country had seen dynasties come and go in a kind of cycle. The Manchu dynasty in the nineteenth century was clearly nearing its end. It was failing to preserve order or to curb extortion. About 1800 a White Lotus Society revolted and was suppressed. In 1813 a Heavenly Reason Society attempted to seize Peking. In the 1850s a Muslim rebellion set up a temporary independent state in the southwest. Greatest of all the upheavals was the Taiping Rebellion of 1850, in which as many as 20 million people, approximately the population of Great Britain at the time, are thought to have perished. Except that some fragmentary Christian ideas, obtained from missionaries, were expressed by some of the Taipings, the rebellion was due entirely to Chinese causes. The rebels attacked the Manchus, who had come from Manchuria two centuries before, as corrupt foreigners ruling over China. Their grievances were poverty, extortion, rack-renting, and absentee landlords. The Taipings at first set up a state in south China, and their armies were at first disciplined, but the fighting lasted so long that both the Taiping leaders and the Manchu commanders sent against them got out of control, and much of the country sank into chronic banditry and disorder. It was in this period that China's war lords, men controlling armed forces but obeying no government, appeared. The Manchus managed to put down organized Taiping resistance after fourteen years, with some European assistance, led by the British General Gordon, the "Chinese Gordon" who later died at Khartoum. But it is clear that Chinese social confusion, agrarianism, and nationalism (the latter at first only anti-Manchu) antedated the impact of European imperialism.

Into this distracted China the Europeans began to penetrate about 1840. It became their policy to extort concessions from the Manchu empire but at the same time to defend the Manchu empire against internal opposition, as was shown by the exploits of Gordon. This was because they needed some kind of government in China with which they could make treaties, legalizing their claims and binding upon the whole country.

The Opening of China to the West

The modern phase of Chinese relations with the West was inauspiciously opened by the Opium War of 1839–1841. We have already observed how, though Europeans wanted Chinese products, the Chinese had no interest in buying European products in return. Trade therefore was difficult, and the British East India Company had for decades solved the problem of getting Chinese tea for Europe by shipping Indian-grown opium in return, since opium was one available commodity for which a Chinese demand existed.[30] When the Chinese government attempted to control the inflow of opium the British government went to war. Fifteen years later, in 1857, Britain and France combined in a second war upon China to force the Chinese to receive their diplomats and deal with their traders. The Chinese proving contumacious, 17,000 French and British soldiers entered Peking and deliberately burned the emperor's very extensive Summer Palace, an appalling act of vandalism from which soldiers brought back so much loot—vases, tapestries, porcelain, enamels, jades, wood carvings—as to set a fashion in Europe and America for Chinese art.

From the first of these wars arose the treaty of Nanking (1842), from the second the treaties of Tientsin (1857), whose terms were soon duplicated in still other treaties signed by China with other European powers and with the United States. The resulting complex of interlocking agreements imposed certain restrictions on China, or conferred certain rights upon foreigners, which came to be known as the "treaty system." To the British in 1842 the Chinese ceded the island of Hong Kong outright, and somewhat later granted adjoining territories on a long lease. They opened over a dozen cities, including Shanghai and Canton, to Europeans as "treaty ports." In these cities Europeans were allowed to make settlements of their own, immune to all Chinese law. Europeans traveling in the Chinese empire remained subject only to their own governments, and European and American gunboats began to police the Yangtse River. The Chinese likewise paid large war indemnities, though it was they themselves who suffered most of the damages. They agreed to levy no import duty over 5 percent and so became a free trade market for European products. To administer and collect the customs a staff of European experts was introduced. Money from the customs, collected

[30] See pp. 260, 354.

IMPERIALISM IN ASIA, 1840–1914

Boundaries and possessions are as of 1914. During these years the British and Dutch filled out their holdings in India and the East Indies, in each case moving outward from establishments founded long before. The Russians, who had long occupied Siberia, pressed southward in Central Asia, founded Vladivostok in 1860, and penetrated Manchuria at the close of the century. The French built an empire in Indochina, while the United States acquired the Philippines, and the Germans, as latecomers, were confined to miscellaneous parts of the western Pacific. The Japanese won control of Korea and replaced the Russians as the chief outside influence in Manchuria. Meanwhile all obtained special rights and concessions in China. A bid for such concessions by Italy was refused.

0 100 200 300 400 500 miles

ARCTI

Archangel

St. Petersburg

Moscow

R U S S I A N   E M

Tobolsk

Samara

Omsk

Tomsk

TRANS-SIBERIAN RAILRO

Ob R.

Yenisei R.

S I
B I

EUROPE

ASIA

Constantinople

BLACK SEA

MEDITERRANEAN SEA

Astrakhan

CASPIAN
SEA

ARAL
SEA

L. Balkhash

1854

OTTOMAN

Mosul

Baku

1846

1873

1873

1881

1884

1864

Tashkent 1860-65

BOKHARA 1876

EMPIRE

Cairo

Suez Canal

Jerusalem

Baghdad

Basra

Teheran

*RUSSIAN SPHERE,
1907*

Mery
1885

1868

1895

Kashgar

SINKIAN

PERSIA

PERSIAN GULF

Kabul

AFGHAN-
ISTAN

KASHMIR
1846

Indus R.

PUNJAB

T I

HIMALAY

NEPAL

*BRITISH
SPHERE,
1907*

BALUCHISTAN
1883

Delhi

RED
SEA

HEJAZ

ARABIA

Mecca

OMAN

Karachi

INDIA

Cald

Diu
(Portugal)

Bombay

B R I T I S

Ganges

BAY O

A F R I C A

YEMEN

Aden *(Britain, 1839)*

Hyderabad

Yanaor
(France)

Goa
(Portugal)

Madras
Pondicherry
(France)

Karikal *(France*

CEYLON

INDIAN OCEAN

JEHOL

MANCHURIA

GREAT WALL

Kinchow

Mukden

Peking

KOREA

Tientsin   Taku

*GULF OF
CHILI*

Dairen
Port Arthur

*(Lease to
Russia, 1898;
Japan, 1905)*

Chifu

Wei-hai-wei
(Britain, 1898)

Grand Canal

Tsinan

Kiao-chow
(Germany, 1898)   Tsingtao

YELLOW SEA

SHANTUNG

CRITICAL AREA, 1895–1905

0   100   200 miles

CEAN

ALASKA
(Purchased by U.S.A.
from Russia, 1867)

BERING SEA

ALEUTIAN I. (U.S.A., 1867)

KAMCHATKA

Lena R.

Yakutsk

SEA OF
OKHOTSK

SAKHALIN

KURILE I.
(Japan, 1875)

AMUR PROVINCE
1858

KARAFUTO
(Japan, 1905)

E R I A

R E

L. Baikal
Chita

Irkutsk

Amur R.

MANCHURIA

Khabarovsk

MARITIME
PROVINCE
(Russia, 1868)

JAPANESE EMPIRE

Urga

Harbin

Vladivostok
1860

Mukden

SEA OF
JAPAN

OUTER MONGOLIA
(nomous, 1912 Russian Sphere)

INNER MONGOLIA

JEHOL

KOREA
(Japan, 1905, 1910)

Tokyo

Peking

Tientsin

Port Arthur
(Japan, 1905)

PACIFIC OCEAN

Kiao-chow
(Germany, 1898)

Huang Ho

Nanking

Shanghai
(Britain, 1842)

C H I N A   Hankow

Ningpo
1842

EAST
CHINA
SEA

RYUKYU I.

Chungking

Yangtse R.

Foochow

Amoy

MARIANA I.
(Germany, 1899)

lasa

YÜNNAN

KWANGSI
(French Sphere)

Canton
(Britain, 1842)

FORMOSA (Japan, 1895)

PESCADORES (Japan, 1895)

GUAM
(U.S.A., 1898)

TAN

naputra R.

Hong Kong (Britain, 1842)
Macao (Portugal, 1557)

Kwang-chow
(Lease to France, 1898)

HAINAN

CAROLINE I.
(Germany, 1899)

BURMA
(Britain, 1852, 1885)

Hanoi

Manila

PHILIPPINE I.
(U.S.A., 1898, 1899)

NDIA
1852

Rangoon

SIAM

ANNAM

Mekong R.

FRENCH
INDOCHINA
1884, 1907

SOUTH
CHINA
SEA

YAP

GAL   Bangkok

Saigon

PALAU I.

DAMAN I.
Britain)

BRITISH
NORTH BORNEO
1888

NEW GUINEA

KAISER WILHEMSLAND
(Germany, 1884)

SARAWAK
1888

MALAY STATES
(Britain, 1800, 1824)

CELEBES

Singapore
(Britain, 1819)

BORNEO

D U T C H   E A S T   I N D I E S

SUMATRA

(Portugal, 1859)

Batavia

TIMOR   Darwin

JAVA

AUSTRALIA

with a new efficiency, on a swelling volume of imports, went in part to the British and French in payment of the indemnities, but part remained with the Manchu government, which, as noted, the Europeans had no desire to overthrow.

Annexations and Concessions

While China was thus permeated at the center like an aging cheese, by extraterritorial and other insidious privileges for Europeans, whole slabs of it were cut away at the outer rim. The Russians moved down the Amur River, established their Maritime Province, and founded Vladivostok in 1860. The Japanese, now sufficiently westernized to behave like Europeans in such matters, in 1876 recognized the independence of Korea. The British annexed Burma in 1886. The French in 1883 assumed a protectorate over Annam despite Chinese protests; they soon combined five areas—Annam, Cochin China, Tonkin, Laos, and Cambodia—into French Indochina. (The first three were known also as Vietnam, a word not familiar in the West until after the Second World War.) These outlying territories had never, it is true, been integral parts of China proper; but it was with China that they had had their most important political and cultural relations and to the Chinese emperor that they had paid tribute.

Japan, whose modernization has been described already, lost little time in developing an imperialistic urge.[31] An expansionist party already looked to the Chinese mainland and to the south. Japanese imperialism first revealed itself to the rest of the world in 1894, when Japan went to war with China over disputes in Korea. The Japanese soon won, equipped as they were with modern weapons, training, and organization. They obliged the Chinese to sign the treaty of Shimonoseki in 1895, by which China ceded Formosa and the Liaotung peninsula to Japan and recognized Korea as an independent state. The Liaotung was a tongue of land reaching down from Manchuria to the sea; at its tip was Port Arthur. Manchuria was the northeastern part of China itself.

This sudden Japanese triumph precipitated a crisis in the Far East. No one had realized how strong Japan had become. All were astounded that a people

---

[31] See pp. 581–582.

NORTHEAST CHINA AND ADJOINING REGIONS

This area has long been one of the world's trouble zones. Note how Vladivostok is shut off from the ocean by the Japanese islands and Korea, and almost shut off from the mass of Russia by the intervening bulk of Manchuria. Manchuria, which began to be industrialized about 1900, became an object of dispute between China, to which it belonged historically, the Russian empire, to which it had strategic value and offered an access to the open ocean, and the Japanese empire, which found in it an outlet for commercial and military expansion and a buffer against Russia. Manchuria was dominated by the Russians from 1898 to 1905, by the Japanese from 1905 to 1945, and again by the Russians from 1945 to 1950, when they handed over their concessions and privileges to the Chinese Communist government. Korea was dominated by Japan after its victories over China in 1895 and over Russia in 1905. After World War II, Korea was promised independence but was divided at the 38th parallel into a Russian occupation zone and an American zone. After the Korean War (1950–1953, see pp. 879–883) the country remained divided at roughly the same parallel with a Communist regime in the north and a Western-sponsored regime in the south.

who were not "European," i.e., white, should show such aptitude for modern war and diplomacy. It was to be supposed that Japan had designs on Manchuria.

Now it so happened that Russia, not long before, in 1891, had begun to build the Trans-Siberian Railway, whose eastern terminus was to be Vladivostok, the "Lord of the East." Manchuria extended northward in a great hump between central Siberia and Vladivostok. The Russians, whether or not they ever dominated Manchuria themselves, could not allow its domination by another Great Power. It happened also that Germany was at this time looking for a chance to enter the

Spheres of Influence About 1900

Russian

British

German

Far Eastern arena, and that France had formed an alliance with Russia, whose good will it was eager to retain.[32]

Russia, Germany, and France therefore registered an immediate joint demurrer with the Tokyo Foreign Office. They demanded that Japan give up the Liaotung peninsula. The Japanese hesitated; they were indignant, but they yielded. The Liaotung went back to China.

In China many alert people were humiliated at the defeat by the Japanese whom they had despised. The Chinese government, at last facing the inevitable, began madly to plan westernization. Huge loans were obtained from Europe— the customs being pawned as security, following the pattern well established in Turkey, Persia, and Santo Domingo. But the European powers did not wish China to become consolidated too soon. Nor had they forgotten the sudden apparition of Japan. The result was a frantic scramble for further concessions in 1898.

It seemed in 1898 as if the Chinese empire in its turn would be partitioned. The Germans extorted a ninety-nine-year lease on Kiaochow Bay, plus exclusive rights in the Shantung peninsula. The Russians took a lease on the Liaotung peninsula from which they had just excluded Japan; they thus obtained Port Arthur and rights to build railroads in Manchuria to interlock with their Trans-Siberian system. The French took Kwangchow and the British Wei-hai-wei, in addition to confirming their sphere of influence in the Yangtse valley. The Italians demanded a share but were refused. The United States, fearing that all China might soon be parceled out into exclusive spheres, announced its policy of the Open Door. The idea of the Open Door was that China should remain territorially intact and independent, and that powers having special concessions or spheres of influence should maintain the 5 percent Chinese tariff and allow businessmen of all nations to trade without discrimination. The British supported the Open Door, as a means of discouraging actual annexations by Japan or Russia, which, as the only Great Powers adjacent to China, were the only ones that could dispatch real armies into its territory. The Open Door was a program not so much of leaving China to the Chinese, as of assuring that all outsiders should find it literally "open."

If readers will imagine what the United States would be like if foreign warships patrolled the Mississippi as far as St. Louis, if foreigners came and went throughout the country without being under its laws, if New York, New Orleans, and other cities contained foreign settlements outside its jurisdiction, but in which all banking and management were concentrated, if foreigners determined the tariff policy, collected the proceeds, and remitted much of the money to their own governments, if the western part of the city of Washington had been burned (the Summer Palace), Long Island and California annexed to distant empires (Hong Kong and Indochina), and all New England were coveted by two immediate neighbors (Manchuria), if the national authorities were half in collusion with these foreigners and half victimized by them, and if large areas of the country were the prey to bandits, guerrillas, and revolutionary secret societies conspiring against the helpless government and occasionally murdering some of the foreigners— then they can understand how observant Chinese felt at the end of the last century, and why the term "imperialism" came to be held by so many of the world's peoples in abomination.

[32] See pp. 696–698.

One Chinese secret society, its name somewhat literally translated as the Order of Literary Patriotic Harmonious Fists, and so dubbed the Boxers by the amused Westerners, broke out in insurrection in 1899. The Boxers pulled up railway tracks, fell upon Chinese Christians, besieged the foreign legations, and killed about 300 foreigners. The European powers, joined by Japan and the United States, sent a combined international force against the insurgents, who were put down. The victors imposed still more severe controls on the Chinese government and inflicted an indemnity of $330 million. Of this the United States received $24 million, of which, in 1924, it canceled the balance that was still due. On the other hand, as a consequence of the Boxer Rebellion, the Manchu officials strove desperately to strengthen themselves by westernization, while at the same time the revolutionary movement in China, aiming at expulsion of Manchus and foreigners alike, spread rapidly throughout the country, especially in the south, under the leadership of Sun Yat-sen.

84. *The Russo-Japanese War and Its Consequences*

Meanwhile Russia and Japan opposed each other's intrigues in Manchuria and Korea. The Japanese felt a need for supplying their new factories with raw materials and markets on the Asian mainland, for employment for their newly westernized army and navy, and for recognized status as a Great Power in the Western sense. The Russian government needed an atmosphere of crisis and expansion to stifle criticism of tsarism at home; it could not abide the presence of a strong power directly on its East Asian frontier; it could use Manchuria and Korea to strengthen the exposed outpost of Vladivostok, which was somewhat squeezed against the sea and landlocked by Japanese waters. The Russians had obtained a concession from China to build the Chinese Eastern Railway to Vladivostok across the heart of Manchuria. A railway, in Manchuria, implied special zones, railway guards, mining and timber rights, and other auxiliary activities. The Japanese saw the fruits of their successful war of 1895 against China greedily enjoyed by their rival. In 1902 Japan signed a military alliance with Great Britain. We have seen how the British were alarmed by their diplomatic isolation after Fashoda and the Boer War, and how for many years, in the Far East, the Middle East, and the Near East, they had been expecting to have trouble with Russia. The Anglo-Japanese military alliance lasted twenty years.

War broke out in 1904, undeclared, by Japanese naval attack on Russian installations at Port Arthur. Both sides sent large armies into Manchuria. The battle of Mukden, in the number of men engaged, which was 624,000, was the largest battle that human experience had thus far witnessed. Military observers were present from all countries, anxiously trying to learn what the next war in Europe would be like. The Russians sent their Baltic fleet around three continents to the Far East, but to the world's amazement the Russian fleet was met and destroyed at Tsushima Strait by the new and untested navy of Japan. Russian communications by sea were thereby broken, and since the Trans-Siberian Railway was unfinished, and since the Japanese also won the battle of Mukden, Russia was beaten.

At this point the president of the United States, Theodore Roosevelt, stepped upon the scene. With an outpost in the Philippines and growing interest in China, it was to the American advantage to have neither side win too overwhelming a victory in the Far East. The most imperially minded of all American presidents offered his mediation, and plenipotentiaries of the two powers met at Portsmouth, New Hampshire. By the treaty of Portsmouth, in 1905, Japan recovered from Russia what it had won and lost in 1895, namely, Port Arthur and the Liaotung peninsula, a preferred position in Manchuria, which remained nominally Chinese, and a protectorate in Korea, which remained nominally independent, although a few years later in 1910, it was annexed by Japan. Japan also received from Russia the southern half of the island of Sakhalin. Much of what Russia lost to Japan in 1905 was regained forty years later at the end of the Second World War.[33]

The Russo-Japanese War was the first war between Great Powers since 1870. It was the first war fought under conditions of developed industrialism. It was the first actual war between westernized powers to be caused by competition in the exploitation of undeveloped countries. Most significant of all (except for the Ethiopian rout of the Italians), it was the first time that a nonwhite people had defeated a white people in modern times. Asians had shown that they could learn and play, in less than half a century, the game of the Europeans.

The Japanese victory set off long chains of repercussions in at least three different directions. For one thing, the Russian government, frustrated in its foreign policy in East Asia, shifted its attention back to Europe, where it resumed an active role in the affairs of the Balkans. This contributed to a series of international crises in Europe, of which the result was the First World War. Second, the tsarist government was so weakened by the war, both in prestige and in actual military strength, and opinion in Russia was so disgusted at the clumsiness and incompetency with which the war had been handled, that the various underground movements were able to come to the surface, producing the Revolution of 1905. This in turn was a prelude to the great Russian Revolution twelve years later, of which Soviet communism was the outcome. Third, news of Japan's victory over Russia electrified those who heard of it throughout the non-European world. The fact that Japan was itself an imperialist power was overlooked in the excited realization that the Japanese were not white. Only half a century ago the Japanese, too, had been "backward"—defenseless, bombarded, and bulldozed by the Europeans. The moral was clear. Everywhere leaders of subjugated peoples concluded, from the Japanese precedent, that they must bring Western science and industry to their own countries, but that they must do it, as the Japanese had done, by getting rid of control by the Europeans, supervising the process of modernization themselves, and preserving their own native national character. Nationalist revolutions began in Persia in 1905, in Turkey in 1908, in China in 1911. In India and Indonesia many were stirred by the Japanese achievement. In the face of rising agitation, the British admitted an Indian to the Viceroy's executive Council in 1909, and in 1916 the Dutch created a People's Council, to include Indonesian members, in the Indies. The self-assertion of Asians was to grow in intensity after the First World War.

The Japanese victory and Russian defeat can therefore be seen as steps in three mighty developments: the First World War, the Russian Revolution, and the Revolt of Asia. These three together put an end to Europe's world supremacy and almost to European civilization; or at least they so transmuted them as to make the world of the twentieth century far different from that of the nineteenth.

[33] See p. 864.

THE BRITISH IN INDIA

The British presence in India, reaching over three centuries, spanned the whole period from the early trading empires to the latest phases of European imperialism. In the seventeenth century the Indian subcontinent was held together by a Muslim empire whose ruler was known in Europe as the Great Mogul. His revenues, in 1605, were some twenty times greater than those of the King of England. The Europeans were for a long time only handfuls of foreigners operating out of small coastal stations. After 1700 the Mogul authority fell to pieces, leaving a disorganized situation in which the British emerged as the supreme power throughout the country.

India in the nineteenth century represented, in its full form, the European imperialism that by 1900 reached throughout Asia and Africa. Parts of it were ruled by the British directly, parts through the rajahs and maharajahs of Indian states. British power prevented internal warfare and subordinated the conflicts between Hindus and Muslims. Peace generally prevailed except for the great Mutiny, or rebellion, of 1857, which was quickly suppressed. The British introduced their own ideas of law, government, civil service, and education. With food production increased by irrigation and famine relieved by transport of provisions by railroad, population grew very rapidly.

The British invested a great deal of capital in India, in railroads, coal mines, and tea plantations. There was also much development of Indian capital, especially in the new jute, cotton, and steel industries. As the railroad opened the interior to the cheaper products of Lancashire, the old handicraft and village industries were destroyed, to be symbolically revived by Gandhi and his spinning wheel in the 1920s, and in fact replaced by an extensive development of modern manufactures. India moved into the twentieth century as a land of extreme contrasts, of endless villages interrupted by teeming cities, with staggering problems of poverty and over population, yet also as an important industrial country with a heavy involvement in world trade.

The British, throughout their rule in India, lived very much to themselves, occasionally mixing with the Indian upper classes but avoiding intimate or even equal relationships. For many Indians, nevertheless, English became a second language, used both for contacts with the Western world and as a common medium among themselves. A modern Indian upper class, largely English-speaking, grew up with the development of business, government, and the professions. It ultimately took the lead in the national movement against foreign rule. But historic divisions within the country, between Hindu and Muslim, dating back to the Mogul empire and before, brought it about that upon the British withdrawal, in 1947, what had formerly been known as India became the separate states of India and Pakistan. Later Bangladesh was formed by secession from Pakistan.

The gorgeous East, as Milton called it, had been fabled in Europe for its riches since ancient times. Above, right, we see the weighing of the Great Mogul on his birthday, upon which he was to receive an equal weight in gold and jewels. The picture is from an English geography of 1782. As the French Encyclopédie put it at about this time: "The most solemn day of the year was when the emperor was weighed in golden balances in the presence of the people; on that day he received over 50 millions in presents."

At the left is the English factory at Surat, near Bombay, in the early seventeenth century. A "factory" was only a trading center where the agents, or factors, of the East India Company stored their goods.

685

Calcutta, now the largest city in India, is far from being one of the oldest. It was founded by the English East India Company in 1690, and acquired many Western-style buildings in the two following centuries. At the left above is the Old Court House; at the right the early nineteenth-century Government House, with a large British lion astride the neoclassic gate. At the left an English lady is carried in a palanquin, and in both pictures important persons ride by in carriages, surveyed at a distance by some of the plain people of India, one of them with a bullock cart. The two cultures never really merged.

Darjeeling, in the mountains 300 miles north of Calcutta, grew up after 1840 as a cool retreat for Britons in refuge from the Indian heat. At the left is the "big loop" of the Darjeeling Railway, a substantial feat of engineering, by which the imperial rulers were able to make the journey more comfortably. The clouds probably obscure a view of the Himalayas for which Darjeeling is famous.

The railroad also had a transforming impact on India as a whole. By carrying goods it brought the interior into the world market, breaking up old native industries while creating new ones, and by transporting persons it drew together the members of diverse religions, castes, and linguistic groups. A passenger train of 1863 appears above. In its crowded coaches Indians who in former times would have kept scrupulously apart, for fear of pollution, had to rub elbows together, and on long journeys even eat together and breathe the same tainted air. Such proximity, together with the increasing adoption of English, produced a new basis for Indian unity which in the end was to make the British position untenable.

At the right, before the track is laid, a team of elephants hauls the first locomotive into Indore in Central India.

Above left: Queen Victoria is proclaimed Empress of India at Bombay in 1877. The neo-Gothic canopy, built for the occasion, under which an effigy of the queen is enthroned, seems incongruous in the circumstances. It reminds us, together with the more permanent church in the background, that the British maintained their own ways with supreme confidence, making few concessions to the alien culture over which they presided.

In the nineteenth century the traveling Englishwoman became legendary for her indomitability. At the right, two of them go on a jungle picnic. The pith helmets of their escorts, and the bearer carrying the refreshments on his head, may be taken as symbols of the heyday of empire.

The two scenes depicted in the drawings above represent the administration of justice, with a British magistrate at the left, a native magistrate at the right. They seem much alike, and their purpose may be to show how under British rule the Indian judicial system was brought up to British standards of legal procedure.

Many Indians received a thoroughly English education. At the far right is Jawaharlal Nehru at Harrow about 1905. Nehru, born in 1889 of Brahmin parents, his father a wealthy lawyer, was educated at home by English tutors, then sent to Harrow and Cambridge. He joined Gandhi in the independence movement in the 1920s, and served as first prime minister of independent India from 1947 until his death in 1964. British India dug its own grave, or prepared its own successors.

XVI.
THE FIRST
WORLD WAR

SOMEWHERE BEFORE 1914 Europe went off its course. Europeans believed themselves to be heading for a kind of high plateau, full of a benign progress and more abundant civilization, in which the benefits of modern science and invention would be more widely diffused, and even competitive struggle worked out somehow for the best. Instead, Europe stumbled in 1914 into disaster. It is not easy to see exactly where Europe went astray, at what point, that is, the First World War became inevitable, or (since the human mind does not know what is truly inevitable) so overwhelmingly probable that only the most Olympian statesmanship could have avoided it.

85. *The International Anarchy*

After 1870 Europe lived in a repressed fear of itself. The great questions of the mid-century had been settled by force. The German Empire was only the strongest and most obvious of the new structures which armed power had reared. Never had the European states maintained such huge armies in peacetime as at the beginning of the twentieth century. One, two, or even three years of compulsory military service for all young men became the rule. In 1914 each of the Continental

Chapter Emblem: A German medal to celebrate the sinking of the Lusitania in 1915, showing the Cunard Line as a skeleton selling tickets, under an inscription, "Business First."

Great Powers had not only a huge standing army but millions of trained reserves among the civilian population. Few people wanted war; all but a few sensational writers preferred peace in Europe, but many took it for granted that war would come some day. In the last years before 1914 the idea that war was bound to break out sooner or later probably made some statesmen, in some countries, more willing to unleash it.

Rival Alliances: Triple Alliance versus Triple Entente

Political diagnosticians, from Richelieu to Metternich, had long thought that an effective union of Germany would revolutionize the relationships of Europe's peoples. After 1870 their anticipations were more than confirmed. Once united (or almost united), the Germans entered upon their industrial revolution. Manufacturing, finance, shipping, population grew phenomenally. In steel, for example, of which Germany in 1865 produced less than France, by 1900 Germany produced more than France and Great Britain combined. Germans felt that they needed and deserved a "place in the sun," by which they vaguely meant some kind of acknowledged supremacy like that of the British. Neither the British nor the French, the leaders of modern Europe since the seventeenth century, could share wholeheartedly in such German aspirations. The French had the chronic grievance of Alsace and Lorraine, annexed to Germany in 1871. The British as the years passed saw German salesmen appear in their foreign markets, selling goods often at lower prices and by what seemed ungentlemanly methods; they saw Germans turn up as colonial rivals in Africa, the Near East, and the Far East; and they watched other European states gravitate into the Berlin orbit, looking to the mighty German Empire as a friend and protector to secure or advance their interests.

Bismarck after 1871 feared that in another European war his new German Empire might be torn to pieces. He therefore followed, until his retirement in 1890, a policy of peace. We have seen him as the "honest broker" at the Berlin Congress of 1878, helping to adjudicate the Eastern Question, and again offering the facilities of Berlin in 1885 to regulate African affairs.[1] To isolate France, divert it from Europe, and keep it embroiled with Britain, he looked with satisfaction on French colonial expansion. He took no chances, however; in 1879 he formed a military alliance with Austria-Hungary, to which Italy was added in 1882. Thus was formed the Triple Alliance, which lasted until the First World War. Its terms were, briefly, that if any member became involved in war with two or more powers its allies should come to its aid by force of arms. To be on the safe side, Bismarck signed a "reinsurance" treaty with Russia also; since Russia and Austria were enemies (because of the Balkans), to be allied to both at the same time took considerable diplomatic finesse. After Bismarck's retirement his system proved too intricate, or too lacking in candor, for his successors to manage. The Russo-German agreement lapsed. The French, faced by the Triple Alliance, soon seized the opportunity to form their own alliance with Russia, the Franco-Russian Alliance signed in 1894. In its time this was regarded as politically almost impossible. The French Republic stood for everything radical, the Russian

---

[1] See pp. 658, 663–664.

empire for everything reactionary and autocratic. But ideology was thrown to the winds, French capital poured into Russia, and the tsar bared his head to the *Marseillaise*.

The Continent was thus divided by 1894 into two opposed camps, the German-Austrian-Italian against the Franco-Russian. For a time it seemed that this rigid division might soften. Germany, France, and Russia cooperated in the Far Eastern crisis of 1895.[2] All were anti-British at the time of Fashoda and the Boer War. The Kaiser, William II, outlined tempting pictures of a Continental league against the global hegemony of England and her empire.

Much depended on what the British would do. They had long prided themselves on a "splendid isolation," going their own way, disdaining the kind of dependency that alliance with others always brings. Fashoda and the Boer War came as a shock. British relations with France and Russia were very bad. Some in England, including Joseph Chamberlain, therefore thought that a better understanding with Germany was to be sought. Arguments of race, in this race-conscious age, made Englishmen and Germans feel akin.[3] But politically it was hard to cooperate. The Kaiser's Kruger Telegram of 1896 was a studied insult.[4] Then in 1898 the Germans decided to build a navy.

A new kind of "race" now entered the picture, the naval competition between Germany and Great Britain. British sea power for two centuries had been all too successful. The American Admiral Mahan, teaching at the Naval War College, and taking his examples largely from British history, argued that sea power had been the foundation of Britain's greatness, and that in the long run sea power must always choke off and ruin a power operating on the land. Nowhere were Mahan's books read with more interest than in Germany. The German naval program, mounting rapidly after 1898, in a few years became a source of concern to the British, and by 1912 was felt as a positive menace. The Germans insisted that they must have a navy to protect their colonies, secure their foreign trade, and "for the general purposes of their greatness." The British held with equal resolution that England, as a densely populated industrial island, dependent even for food upon imports, must at all costs control the sea in both peace and war. They adhered stubbornly to their traditional policy of maintaining a navy as large as the next two combined. The naval race led both sides to enormous and increasing expenditures. In the British it produced a sense of profound insecurity, driving them as the years passed ever more inescapably into the arms of Russia and France.

Slowly and cautiously the British emerged from their diplomatic isolation. In 1902 they formed a military alliance with Japan against their common enemy, Russia.[5] The decisive break came in 1904, from which may be dated the immediate series of crises issuing in the World War ten years later.

In 1904 the British and French governments agreed to forget Fashoda and the

---

[2] See pp. 679–680.

[3] The will of Cecil Rhodes, who died in 1902, illustrates this point. Rhodes left most of his fortune (£6 million) to establish scholarships at Oxford to be awarded to students in the United States, as an Anglo-Saxon country, the British dominions and colonies, and Germany. The German Rhodes Scholarships were suspended from 1914 to 1930 and again after 1938. The same feeling that Germans were racially akin was common in the United States also; a prominent example of this viewpoint was President Theodore Roosevelt.

[4] See p. 669.

[5] See p. 681.

accumulated bad feeling of the preceding twenty-five years. The French recognized the British occupation of Egypt, and the British recognized the French penetration of Morocco. They also cleared up a few lesser colonial differences and agreed to support each other against protests by third parties. There was no specific alliance; neither side said what it would do in the event of war; it was only a close understanding, an *entente cordiale*. The French immediately tried to reconcile their new friend to their ally, Russia. After defeat by Japan the Russians proved amenable. The British, increasingly uncertain of German aims, proved likewise willing. In 1907 Britain and Russia, the inveterate adversaries, settled their differences in an Anglo-Russian Convention. In Persia, the British recognized a Russian sphere of influence in the north, the Russians a British sphere in the south and east. By 1907 England, France, and Russia were acting together. The older Triple Alliance faced a newer Triple Entente, the latter somewhat the looser, since the British refused to make any formal military commitments.

The Crises in Morocco and the Balkans

The Germans, who already felt encircled by the alliance of France and Russia, naturally watched with concern the drift of England into the Franco-Russian camp. The Entente Cordiale was barely concluded when the German government decided to test it, to find out how strong it really was, or how far the British would really go in support of France. The French, now enjoying British backing, were taking over more police powers, concessions, and loans in Morocco. In March 1905 William II disembarked from a German warship at Tangier, where he made a startling speech in favor of Moroccan independence. To diplomats everywhere this carefully staged performance was a signal: Germany was attempting not primarily to keep France out of Morocco, nor even to reserve Morocco for itself, but to break up the new understanding between France and England. The Germans demanded and obtained an international conference at Algeciras (at which the United States was represented), but the conference, which met in 1906, supported the French claims in Morocco, only Austria voting with Germany. The German government had thus created an incident and been rebuffed. The British, disturbed by German diplomatic tactics, stood by the

ANGLO-GERMAN INDUSTRIAL COMPETITION, 1898 AND 1913

This diagram really shows two things: first, the huge increase in world trade in the last fifteen years before the First World War, shared in by all countries; and second, the fact that German exports grew more rapidly than British. The exports of both countries together, as shown on the diagram, multiplied no less than threefold in these fifteen years. The increase, while due in small part to a slight rise of prices, was mainly due to a real increase in volume of business. If the reader will compare the shaded bands within the large arrows he will see that, for the countries shown, British exports about doubled, but those of Germany multiplied many times. In 1913 total German exports about equaled the British, but German exports to the United States and Russia greatly exceeded the British. Note how the Germans even gained in exports to British India, where the liberalism of British policy freely admitted competitive goods. In merchant marine, though the Germans doubled their tonnage, the British continued to enjoy an overwhelming lead.

French all the more firmly. French and British army and naval officers now began to discuss common plans. Distrust of Germany also inclined the British to bury the hatchet with Russia in the next year. The German attempt to break the Entente simply made it more solid.

In 1911 came a second Morocco crisis. A German gunboat, the *Panther*, arrived at Agadir "to protect German interests." It soon developed that the move was a holdup; the Germans offered to make no further trouble in Morocco if they could have the French Congo. The crisis passed, the Germans obtaining some trifling accessions in Africa. But a member of the British cabinet, David Lloyd George, made a rather inflammatory speech on the German menace.

Meanwhile a series of crises rocked the Balkans. Here at the opening of the twentieth century the situation was very confused. The Ottoman Empire, in an advanced state of dissolution, still held a band of territory from Constantinople westward to the Adriatic.[6] South of this band lay an independent Greece. North of it, on the Black Sea side, lay an autonomous Bulgaria and an independent Romania. In the center and west of the peninsula, north of the Turkish belt, was the small, landlocked independent kingdom of Serbia, adjoined by Bosnia-Herzegovina, which belonged legally to Turkey but had been "occupied and administered" by Austria since 1878. Within the Austro-Hungarian Empire, adjoining Bosnia on the north, lay Croatia and Slovenia.

Serbs, Bosnians, Croats, and Slovenes all spoke basically the same language, the main difference being that Serbs and Bosnians wrote with the eastern or Cyrillic alphabet, the Croats and Slovenes with the western or Roman. With the Slavic Revival and general growth of nationalism these peoples came to feel that they were really one people, for which they took the term South Slavs or Yugoslavs. We have seen how when the Dual Monarchy was formed in 1867, the Slavs of the Habsurg empire were kept subordinate to the German Austrians and to the Magyars.[7] By 1900 the most radical Slav nationalists within the empire had concluded that the Dual Monarchy would never grant them equal status, that it must be broken up, and that all South Slavs should form an independent state of their own. Concretely, this meant that an element of the Austro-Hungarian population, namely, the Croatian and Slovenian nationalists, wished to get out of the empire and join with Serbia across the border. Serbia became the center of South Slav agitation. The Serbs conceived of their small kingdom as the Piedmont of a South Slav Risorgimento, the nucleus around which a new national state could be formed, at the expense of Austria-Hungary.

This brew was brought to a boil in 1908 by two events. First, the Young Turks, whose long agitation against Abdul Hamid has been noted, managed in that year to carry through a revolution.[8] They obliged the sultan to restore the liberal parliamentary constitution of 1876. They showed, too, that they meant to stop the dissolution of the Ottoman Empire, by taking steps to have delegates from Bulgaria and Bosnia sit in the new Ottoman parliament. Second, Russia, its foreign policy in the Far East ruined by the Japanese war, turned

[6] See maps, pp. 470, 660, and 703.
[7] See p. 561.
[8] See p. 657.

actively to the Balkan and Turkish scene. Russia, as always, wanted control at Constantinople. Austria wanted full annexation of Bosnia, the better to discourage Pan-Yugoslav ideas. But if the young Turks really modernized and strengthened the Ottoman Empire, Austria would never get Bosnia nor the Russians Constantinople.

The Russian and Austrian foreign ministers, Isvolsky and Aehrenthal, at a conference at Buchlau in 1908 came to a secret agreement. They would call an international conference, at which Russia would favor Austrian annexation of Bosnia, and Austria would support the opening of the Straits to Russian warships. Austria, without waiting for a conference, proclaimed the annexation of Bosnia without more ado. This infuriated the Serbs, who had marked Bosnia for their own. Meanwhile, that same year, the Bulgarians and the Cretans broke finally with the Ottoman Empire, Bulgaria becoming fully independent, Crete uniting with Greece. Isvolsky was never able to realize his plans for Constantinople. His partners in the Triple Entente, Britain and France, refused to back him; the British in particular were evasive on plans for opening the Straits to the Russian fleet. The projected international conference was never called. In Russia itself public opinion knew nothing of Isvolsky's secret deal. The known fact in Russia was that the Serbs, the little Slav brothers of Russia, had their toes rudely stepped on by the Austrians by the annexation of Bosnia.

This "first Balkan crisis" presently passed. The Russians, weakened by the Japanese war and by recent revolution,[9] accepted the Austrian *fait accompli*. Russia protested but backed down. Austrian influence in the Balkans seemed to be growing. And South Slav nationalism was frustrated and inflamed.

In 1911 Italy declared war on Turkey, from which it soon conquered Tripoli and the Dodecanese Islands. With the Ottomans thus embarrassed, Bulgaria, Serbia, and Greece joined forces in their own war against Turkey, hoping to annex certain Balkan territories to which they believed they had a right. Turkey was soon defeated, but the Bulgarians claimed more of Macedonia than the Serbs would yield, so that the first Balkan war of 1912 was followed in 1913 by a second, in which Serbia, Greece, Romania, and Turkey turned upon and defeated Bulgaria. Albania also, a mountainous region on the Adriatic, mainly Muslim, and known as the wildest place in all Europe, was the subject of angry discord. The Serbs occupied part of it in the two Balkan wars, but the Greeks also claimed a part, and it had also on several occasions been vaguely promised to Italy.[10] Russia supported the Serbian claim. Austria was determined to shut off the Serbs from access to the sea, which they would obtain by annexation of Albanian territory. An agreement of the great powers, to keep the peace, conjured up an independent kingdom of Albania. This confirmed the Austrian policy, kept Serbia from the sea, and aroused vehement outcries in both Serbia and Russia. But Russia again backed down. Serbian expansionism was again frustrated and inflamed.

The third Balkan crisis proved to be the fatal one. It was fatal because two others had gone before it, leaving feelings of exasperation in Austria, desperation in Serbia, and humiliation in Russia.

[9] See pp. 681–682, 741–744.
[10] See pp. 658–659.

The Sarajevo Crisis and the Outbreak of War

On June 28, 1914, a young Bosnian revolutionary, a member of the Serbian secret society called "Union or Death," and commonly known as the Black Hand, acting with the knowledge of certain Serbian officials, assassinated the heir to the Habsburg empire, the Archduke Francis Ferdinand, in the streets of Sarajevo, the Bosnian capital, in the Austrian Empire. The world was shocked at this terrorist outrage and at first sympathized with the protests of the Austrian government. Francis Ferdinand, who would soon have become emperor, was known to favor some kind of transformation of Austria-Hungary, in which a more equal place might be given to the Slavs; but the reformer who makes a system work is the most dangerous of all enemies to the implacable revolutionary, and it is perhaps for this reason that the archduke was killed by the Black Hand.

The Austrian government was determined to make an end to the South Slav separatism that was gnawing its empire to pieces. It decided to crush the independence of Serbia, the nucleus of South Slav agitation, though not to annex it, since there were now thought to be too many Slavs within the empire already. The Austrian government consulted the German to see how far it might go with the support of its ally. The Germans, issuing their famous "blank check," encouraged the Austrians to be firm. The Austrians, thus reassured, dispatched a drastic ultimatum to Serbia, demanding among other things that Austrian officials be permitted to collaborate in investigating and punishing the perpetrators of the assassination. The Serbs counted on Russian support, even to the point of war, judging that Russia could not again yield in a Balkan crisis, for the third time in six years, without losing its influence in the Balkans altogether. The Russians in turn counted on France; and France, terrified at the possibility of being some day caught alone in a war with Germany, and determined to keep Russia as an ally at any cost, in effect gave a blank check to Russia. The Serbs rejected the critical item in the Austrian ultimatum as an infringement on Serbian sovereignty, and Austria thereupon declared war upon Serbia. Russia prepared to defend Serbia and hence to fight Austria. Expecting that Austria would be joined by Germany, Russia rashly mobilized its army on the German as well as the Austrian frontier. Since the power which first mobilized had all the advantages of a rapid offensive, the German government demanded an end to the Russian mobilization on its border and, receiving no answer, declared war on Russia on August 1, 1914. Convinced that France would in any case enter the war on the side of Russia, Germany also declared war on France on August 3.

The German decisions were posited on a reckless hope that Great Britain might not enter the war at all. England was bound by no formal military alliance. Even the French did not know for certain, as late as August 3, whether the British would join them in war. The British clung to scraps of their old proud isolation; they hesitated to make a final choice of sides; and as the foreign secretary, Sir Edward Grey, repeatedly explained, in England only Parliament could declare war, so that the foreign office could make no binding promise of war in advance. It has often been said that, had the German government known as a positive fact that England would fight, the war might not have come. Hence the evasiveness of British policy is made a contributing cause of the war. In reality, the probability that England would fight was so great that to underestimate it, as the Germans

THE BALKANS, 1878 AND 1914

The Ottoman Empire, under the blows of Austria and Russia, had been receding from Europe since 1699 (see map, p. 660). The Congress of Berlin of 1878 undertook to stabilize the situation by recognizing Romania, Serbia, and Montenegro as independent monarchies, and northern Bulgaria as an autonomous principality within the Ottoman Empire. The ambitions of these new states (and of Greece, independent since 1829), together with the discontents of all non-Turkish peoples remaining under Ottoman rule, led to successive altercations culminating in the Balkan wars of 1912–1913. Albania then became independent, and Serbia, Bulgaria, and Greece contiguous. Austrian and Russian pressures meanwhile continued; in 1908 Austria annexed Bosnia, where the South Slav population was related to the Serbs. In Bosnia, at Sarajevo, six years later, the assassination of an Austrian archduke by a South Slav patriot precipitated the First World War.

did, was an act of supreme folly. The British were deeply committed to France, especially through naval agreements. As the German High Seas Fleet grew, the British had been obliged to concentrate naval forces in the North Sea. They had therefore had to withdraw forces from the Mediterranean. In 1914, by agreement with France, the French fleet was concentrated in the Mediterranean, watching over British interests, while the British fleet attended to French interests in the north. The French Channel coast was therefore open to German naval attack, unless the British defended it. Sir Edward Grey accepted this moral obligation, but what swept the British public was the invasion of Belgium. The German plan to crush France quickly was such that it could succeed only by crossing Belgium. When the Belgians protested, the Germans invaded anyway, violating the treaty of 1839 which had guaranteed Belgian neutrality.[11] England declared war on Germany on August 4.

---

[11] See pp. 488–489.

The mere narration of successive crises does not explain why the chief nations of Europe became locked in combat over the murder of an imperial personage within a few days. Among more obvious general causes, the alliance system may be singled out. Europe was divided into two camps. Every incident tended to become a test of strength between the two. A given incident, such as German intervention in Morocco, or the assassination of Francis Ferdinand, could not be settled on its own merits, merely by the parties concerned; however it was dealt with, one of the two camps was deemed to have lost or gained and hence to have lost or gained in influence in other incidents, of perhaps greater purport, that would arise in the future. Each power felt that it must stand by its allies whatever the specific issue. This was because all lived in the fear of war, of some nameless future war in which allies would be necessary. The Germans complained of being "encircled" by France and Russia. They dreaded the day when they might have to face a war on two fronts. Willing to accept even a European-wide war to break their threatened "encirclement" by the Entente powers, they were obliged to hold to their one ally, Austria-Hungary, which was in turn able to sell its support at its own price. The French dreaded a coming conflict with Germany, which in forty years had far surpassed France in population and industrial strength; they were obliged to cling to their ally Russia, which therefore could oblige the French to yield to Russian wishes. As for Russia and Austria, they were both tottering empires. Especially after 1900, the tsarist regime suffered from endemic revolution-ism, and the Habsburg empire from chronic nationalistic agitation. Authorities in both empires became desperate. Like the Serbs, they had little to lose and were therefore reckless. It was Russia that drew France and hence England into war in 1914, and Austria that drew in Germany. Seen in this light, the tragedy of 1914 is that the most backward or politically bankrupt parts of Europe, through the alliance system, dragged the more advanced parts automatically into ruin.

The German Empire, too, faced an internal crisis. The Social Democrats became the largest party in the Reichstag in 1912.[12] Their sentiments for the most part were antimilitarist and antiwar. But the German imperial government recognized no responsibility to a majority in the chamber. Policy was determined by men of the old unreconstructed upper class, in which army and navy interests, now reinforced by the new business interests, were very strong; and even moderates and liberals shared in the ambition to make Germany a world power, the equal of any. The perplexities the ruling groups faced at home, the feeling that their position was being undermined by the Social Democrats, may have made them less unwilling to view war as a way out. And while it is not true that Germany started the war, as its enemies in 1914 popularly believed, it must be granted that its policies had for some years been rather peremptory, arrogant, devious, and obstinate. In a broad sense, the emergence of a consolidated industrial Germany after 1870, making its bid for world-power status relatively late, was a distant and basic cause of the war.

The alliance system was only a symptom of deeper trouble. In a word, the world had an international economy but a national polity. Economically, each European people now required habitual contact with the world as a whole. Each people was to that extent dependent, and insecure. Industrial countries were

[12] See pp. 616–617.

WORLD WAR I

Land fighting in the First World War was mainly confined to the areas shown by the darker horizontal shading. The huge battles on the Western Front, which in expenditure of manpower exceeded those of the Second World War in the West, for four years swayed back and forth over the small area indicated, less than a hundred miles wide.

especially vulnerable, relying as they did on import of raw materials and food, and on export of goods, services, or capital in return. There was, however, no world state to police the worldwide system, assuring participation in the world economy to all nations under all conditions. Each nation had to take care of itself.

Hence came much of the drive for imperialism, in which each Great Power tried to stake out part of the world system for itself. And hence also came the quest for allies and for binding alliances. The alliances, in a world that was in the strict sense anarchic (and seemed likely to remain so), were a means by which each nation attempted to bolster up its security; to assure that it would not be cut off, conquered, or subjected to another's will; to obtain some hope of success in the competitive struggle for use of the world's goods.

86. The Armed Stalemate

The First World War lasted over four years, from 1914 to the end of 1918, the United States entering with effective result in the last year. Germany and its allies were called the Central Powers, while the Entente governments were termed the Allies. The war was appalling in its human costs; on the Western Front, more men were used and killed in the First World War than in the Second.

At first a short war, as in 1870, was universally expected. The German General Staff had its plans ready for a two-front struggle against France and Russia. The disadvantage of fighting on two fronts was offset by the possession of good rail lines, which allowed the rapid shuttling of troops from one front to the other. The German war plan, known as the Schlieffen Plan, rested upon this fact. The idea was first to defeat France by the rapid wheeling motion of a tremendous army through Belgium and then to turn at more leisure against Russia, whose great size and less developed railways would make its deployment much slower.

The War on Land, 1914–1916

On August 3, 1914, the Germans launched 78 infantry divisions in the West. They were opposed by 72 French divisions, 5 British, and 6 Belgian. The Germans swept irresistibly forward. The Schlieffen Plan seemed to be moving like clockwork. The civilian authorities made plans for the conquest and annexation of large parts of Europe. Then a hitch occurred: the Russians were fulfilling the terms of their alliance; the 10 billion francs invested by Frenchmen in Russia now paid their most significant dividend. The Russians pushed two armies into Germany, penetrating into East Prussia. Moltke withdrew forces from the German right wing in France, on August 26, for service in the east. The Germans moved on, but their striking arm was weakened, and their lines of communication were already overextended. Joffre, the French commander, regrouping his forces, with strong support from the relatively small British contingent, and at exactly the right moment, ordered a counterattack. The ensuing battle of the Marne, fought from September 5 to 12, changed the whole character of the war. The Germans were obliged to retreat. The hope of felling France at a single blow was ended. Each side now tried to outflank and destroy the other until the battle lines extended to the sea. The Germans failed to win control of the Channel ports; French and British communications remained uninterrupted. For these reverses the great victories meanwhile won by the Germans in the east, though of gigantic proportions (the battles of Tannenberg and the Masurian Lakes, at which 225,000 Russians were captured), were in the long run small consolation.

In the West the war of movement now settled into a war of position. The armies on the Western Front became almost immobile. The units of horse cavalry—the uhlans, hussars, and lancers that had pranced off to war in high spirits—disappeared from the field. Since aviation was barely beginning, and motor transport was still new (the armies had trucks, but no self-propelled guns, and no tanks until very late in the war), the basic soldier more than ever was the man on foot. The most deadly new weapon was the machine gun, which made it impossible for foot soldiers to advance across open fields without overwhelming artillery preparation. The result was a long stalemate of war in the trenches in which the indispensable infantry sought protection.

In 1915 the Germans and Austro-Hungarians put their main effort into an attempt to knock out Russia. They pressed far into the tsarist empire. The Russian losses were enormous—2 million killed, wounded, or captured in 1915 alone. But at the end of the year the Russian army was still fighting. Meanwhile the British and French, hoping to open up communications with Russia, launched a naval attack on Turkey, aiming at Constantinople by way of the Dardanelles. They poured 450,000 men into the narrow peninsula of Gallipoli, of whom 145,000 were killed or wounded. After almost a year the enterprise was given up as a failure.

In 1916 both sides turned again to northern France in an attempt to break the deadlock. The Allies planned a great offensive along the river Somme, while the Germans prepared one in the neighborhood of Verdun. The Germans attacked Verdun in February. The French commander, Joffre, put in General Pétain to defend it but resisted committing his main reserves, holding them for the coming offensive on the Somme. Pétain and his troops, held to minimum numbers, thus had to take the full weight of the German army. The battle of Verdun lasted six months, it drew the horrified admiration of the world, and it became a legend of determined resistance ("they shall not pass"), until the Germans finally abandoned the attack because they sustained almost as many casualties as the French—330,000 to 350,000—so that their purpose was baffled. While the inferno still raged at Verdun the Allies opened their offensive on the Somme in July. They brought up unheard of amounts of artillery, and the newly raised British army was present in force. The idea was to break through the German line simply by stupendous pressure; on both sides, Allied and German, the art of generalship had sunk to an all-time low. Despite a weeklong artillery bombardment the British lost 60,000 men on the first day of the attack. In a week they had advanced only a mile along a six-mile front. In a month they had advanced only two miles and a half. The battle of the Somme, lasting from July to October, cost the Germans about 500,000 men, the British 400,000, and the French 200,000. Nothing of any value had been gained. It was, indeed, at the Somme that the British first used the tank, an armored vehicle with caterpillar tracks that could crash through barbed wire, lunge over trenches, and smash into machine gun nests; but the tanks were introduced in such small numbers, and with such skepticism on the part of many commanders, that they had no effect on the battle.

The War at Sea

With land armies thus helpless, both sides looked to the sea. The long preponderance of British sea power, and the more recent Anglo-German naval race, would now be tested. The British, with French aid, imposed a strict naval blockade. International law at the time placed goods headed for a country at war into two classes. One class was called "contraband"; it included munitions and certain specified raw materials which might be used in the manufacture of military equipment. The other class, including foodstuffs and raw cotton, was defined as "noncontraband." A country was supposed, by international law, to be able to import noncontraband goods even in wartime. These terms of wartime law had been set forth as recently as 1909 at an international conference held in London. The purpose was to make it impossible for a sea power (that is, the British) to starve out an enemy in wartime, or even to interfere with normal civilian production. The jealousy of Continental Europe for British sea power was an old story.

Such law, if observed, would make the blockade of Germany entirely ineffective, and the Allies did not observe it. To starve out the enemy and ruin his economy was precisely their purpose. Economic warfare took its place alongside armed attack as a military weapon, as in the days of Napoleon.[13] The Allies announced a new international law. The distinction between contraband and noncontraband was gradually abolished. The British navy (aided by the French) proceeded to stop all goods of whatever character destined for Germany or its allies. Neutrals, among whom the Americans, Dutch, and Scandinavians were the ones mainly affected, were not allowed to make for German ports at all.

The United States protested vehemently against these regulations. It defended the rights of neutrals. It reasserted the distinction between contraband and noncontraband, claimed the right to trade with other neutrals, and upheld the "freedom of the seas." Much mutual bad feeling resulted between the American and British governments in 1915 and 1916. But when the United States entered the war it adopted the Allied position, and its navy joined in enforcing exactly the same regulations. International law was in fact changed. In the Second World War the very words "contraband" and "freedom of the seas" were never heard.

The Germans countered with an attempt to blockade England. A few isolated German cruisers were able for some time to destroy British shipping in the several oceans of the world. But the Germans relied mainly on the submarine, against which the British naval power at first seemed helpless. The submarine was an unrefined weapon; a submarine commander could not always tell what kind of ship he was attacking, nor could he remove passengers, confiscate cargo, escort the vessel, or indeed do much except sink it. Citing British abuses of international law in justification, the German government in February 1915 declared the waters surrounding the British Isles to be a war zone, in which Allied vessels would be torpedoed and neutral vessels would be in grave danger. Three months later the liner *Lusitania* was torpedoed off the Irish coast. About 1,200 persons were drowned, of whom 118 were American citizens. The *Lusitania* was a British ship; it carried munitions of war manufactured in the United States for Allied use; and

[13] See pp. 431–434.

the Germans had published ominous warnings in the New York papers that Americans should not take passage upon it. Americans then believed that they should be able to sail safely, on peaceable errands, on the ship of a belligerent power in wartime. The loss of life shocked the country. President Wilson informed the Germans that another such act would be considered "deliberately unfriendly." The Germans, to avoid trouble, refrained for two years from making full use of their submarines. For two years the Allied use of the sea was only partly impeded.

Allied access to the sea was confirmed by the one great naval engagement of the war, the battle of Jutland. The German admirals became restless at seeing their newly built navy skulking behind minefields on the German shores, yet they could not presume to challenge the superior British Grand Fleet, posted watchfully at Scapa Flow. They hoped, however, to decoy smaller formations of British ships, destroy them one by one, and perhaps eventually obtain enough of a naval balance in the North Sea to loosen the British blockade, by which Germany was slowly being strangled. They were themselves, however, trapped into a major engagement in which the British Grand Fleet of 151 ships took them by surprise. After a few hours of furious combat the Germans were able to withdraw into mined waters. They had lost less tonnage and fewer men than the British. They had proved themselves to be dangerously proficient in naval combat. But they had failed to undermine the British preponderance at sea.

Diplomatic Maneuvers and Secret Agreements

With no military solution in sight, both sides looked about for new allies. The Ottoman Empire, fearing Russia, had joined Germany and Austria-Hungary as early as October 1914. Bulgaria, being anti-Serb, had done the same in 1915.

The leading new prospect was Italy, which, though formally a member of the Triple Alliance, had long ago drifted away from it. Both sides solicited the Italian government, which bargained imperturbably with both. The Italian public was divided. Both Catholic and socialist leaders recommended staying at peace, but extreme nationalists saw a chance to obtain their *irredenta*, the border regions in which Italians lived, but which had not been incorporated in the time of Cavour.[14] The Italian government cast its lot with the Allies in the secret treaty of London of 1915. It was agreed that if the Allies won the war Italy would receive (from Austria) the Trentino, the south Tyrol, Istria and the city of Trieste, and some of the Dalmatian Islands. If Britain and France took over Germany's African colonies, Italy should receive territorial increases in Libya and Somaliland. The treaty of London, in short, carried on the most brazen prewar practices of territorial expansionism. It must be remembered that the Allies were desperate. Italy, thus bought, and probably against the will of most Italians, opened up a front against Austria-Hungary in May 1915.

The Allies likewise made plans for a final partition of the Ottoman Empire, which still reached from Constantinople through the Middle East into Arabia and modern Iraq. Britain and France were so dependent on Russia that they gave up their age-old opposition to Russian domination of the Straits. By a secret treaty of 1915 they agreed that, upon an Allied victory, Russia might proceed to the

---

[14] See p. 550.

annexation of Constantinople, along with the whole Bosporus, the Sea of Marmara, and the Dardanelles. By another agreement Mesopotamia was to go to Britain, Syria and southeastern Asia Minor to France, small portions to Italy, and Kurdistan and Armenia to Russia.[15]

Each side tampered with minorities and discontented groups living within the domains of the other. The Germans promised an independent Poland, to embarrass Russia. They stirred up local nationalism in the Ukraine. They raised up a pro-German Flemish movement in Belgium. They persuaded the Ottoman sultan, as caliph, to proclaim a holy war in North Africa, hoping that irate Muslims would drive the British from Egypt and the French from Algeria. This had no success. German agents worked in Ireland, and one Irish nationalist, Sir Roger Casement, landed in Ireland from a German submarine, precipitating the Easter Rebellion of 1916, which was suppressed by the British.

To Americans the most amazing of similar activities was the famous Zimmermann telegram. In 1916 an American military force had crossed the Mexican border in pursuit of bandits, against protests by the Mexican government. Relations between the United States and Germany were also deteriorating. In January 1917 the German state secretary for foreign affairs, Arthur Zimmermann, dispatched a telegram to the German minister at Mexico City, telling him what to say to the Mexican president. He was to say that if the United States went to war with Germany, Germany would form an alliance with Mexico and if possible Japan, enabling Mexico to get back its "lost territories." These latter referred to the region conquered by the United States from Mexico in the 1840s—Texas, New Mexico, and Arizona (California was not mentioned by Zimmermann, who was no doubt somewhat vague on the exact history and location of these Alsace-Lorraines of America). Zimmermann's telegram was intercepted and decoded by the British, and passed on by them to Washington. Printed in the newspapers, it shocked public opinion in the United States.

The Allies were more successful in appealing to nationalist discontent, for the obvious reason that the most active national minorities were within the lands of their enemies. They were able to promise restoration of Alsace-Lorraine to France without difficulty. They promised independence to the Poles, though with some difficulty as long as the Russian monarchy stood. It was easier for them to favor national independence for Czechs, Slovaks, and Yugoslavs, since an Allied victory would dissolve the Austro-Hungarian empire.

Within the Ottoman Empire the British aroused Arab hopes for independence. The British Colonel T. E. Lawrence led an insurrection in the Hejaz against the Turks; and the emir Hussein of Hejaz, with British support, in 1916 took the title of king of the Arabs, with a kingdom reaching from the Red Sea to the Persian Gulf. Zionists saw in the impending Ottoman collapse the opportunity to realize their dream for Palestine.[16] Since Palestine was peopled by Arabs (and had been for over 1,000 years) the Zionist program conflicted with British plans to sponsor Arab nationalism. Nevertheless, in the Balfour note of 1917, the British government promised support for the idea of a "Jewish homeland" in Palestine. For the Armenians these years were especially disastrous. They were a Christian

---

[15] See map on p. 660.
[16] See p. 637, and for Israel pp. 942–945 below.

people living in the eastern part of the Anatolian peninsula where it abuts on Russia, and like other peoples in the Ottoman Empire, including the Turks themselves, they had developed aspirations for a national state of their own, which conflicted with the plans of Turkish reformers to Turkify the empire. It was only twenty years since such clashes had produced the Armenian massacres of 1894 which had horrified Europe. Now in 1915 the Turkish government, as the Russian army threatened its eastern frontier, ordered the deportation of Armenians from the war zone as potential sympathizers with Russia and the Western Allies. Supposedly they were to be resettled in Syria and Palestine. In fact, in the atmosphere of military crisis, political hatred, bureaucratic contempt, and wartime scarcities hundreds of thousands of Armenians perished. It is a fact also that virtually no Armenians remained within what became the Turkish republic a few years later. The surviving Armenians became another of the world's scattered peoples, with no state of their own, except for the small Armenian republic within the Soviet Union.

Meanwhile during the war the British and French easily moved into the German colonies in Africa. The British foreign secretary, Sir Edward Grey, revealed to Colonel House, President Wilson's personal emissary, that the Allies did not intend that Germany should ever get its colonies back.

In China, too, the third important area of imperialist competition, the war accelerated the tendencies of preceding years. The Japanese saw their own opportunity in the self-slaughter of the Europeans. Japan had also been allied to Britain since 1902. In August 1914 Japan declared war on Germany. It soon overran the German concessions in China and the German islands in the Pacific, the Marshalls and Carolines. In January 1915 Japan presented its Twenty-One Demands on China, a secret ultimatum most of which the Chinese were obliged to accept. Japan thereby proceeded to turn Manchuria and north China into an exclusive protectorate.

As for the Germans, their war aims were even more expansionist, and more menacing to existing boundaries in Europe itself. Early in September 1914, when a quick victory seemed within their grasp, Bethmann-Hollweg, who remained chancellor until the summer of 1917, drew up a list of German war aims which stayed unaltered until the end of hostilities. The plans called for an enlarged German Empire dominating all central Europe, and annexations or satellites in both western and eastern Europe. In the east, Lithuania and other parts of the Baltic coast were to become German dependencies, large sections of Poland were to be directly annexed, and the remainder joined with Austrian Galicia to form a German-dominated Polish state. In the west, Belgium was to become a German dependency to provide more direct access to the Atlantic, and French Lorraine with its rich iron ore was to be added to the already German parts of Alsace-Lorraine. Colonial adjustments, including the acquisition of most of central Africa from coast to coast, were also projected. The political map of Europe and of colonial Africa would thus be transformed.

All these developments, especially the Allied negotiations, whether accomplished facts or secret agreements, affecting Europe, Asia, or Africa, became very troublesome later at the peace conference. They continued some of the most unsettling tendencies of European politics before the war. It does not appear that the Allies, until driven by Woodrow Wilson, gave any thought to means of controlling anarchic nationalism or of preventing war in the future. As president of the United States, Wilson for a long time could see little to choose between the warring alliances, though his personal sympathies were with England and France. In 1916 he attempted to mediate, entering into confidential discussions with both sides; but both still hoped to win on their own terms, so that negotiation was fruitless. Wilson judged that most Americans wished to remain uninvolved, and in November 1916 he was reelected to a second term, on the popular cry, "he kept us out of war." Wilson urged a true neutrality of thought and feeling, or a settlement, as he said, that should be a "peace without victory."

As of the end of 1916, it is hard to see how the First World War would have turned out, had not two new sets of forces been brought in.

87. The Collapse of Russia and the Intervention of the United States

The Withdrawal of Russia: Revolution and the Treaty of Brest-Litovsk

The first victim of the First World War, among governments, was the Russian empire. As the Russo-Japanese War had led to the Revolution of 1905 in Russia, so the more ruinous conflict in Europe led to the far greater Revolution of 1917. The story of the Russian Revolution is told in the following chapter. It is enough to say here that war offered a test that the tsarist government could not meet. Bungling, dishonest, and secretive, incapable of supplying the materiel required for modern fighting, driving hordes of peasants into battle in some cases even without rifles, losing men by the millions yet offering no goal to inspire sacrifice, the tsarist regime lost the loyalty of all elements of its people. In March 1917 the troops in St. Petersburg mutinied, while strikes and riots desolated the city. The Duma, or Russian parliament, used the occasion to press its demands for reform. On March 15 Nicholas II abdicated. A Provisional Government took over, made up of liberal noblemen and middle-class leaders, generally democrats and constitutionalists, with at first only one socialist. The Provisional Government remained in office from March to November 1917. Its members, who shared in the liberalism of western Europe, believed that a liberal and parliamentary regime could not succeed in Russia unless the German Empire were defeated. They took steps, therefore, to prosecute the war with a new vigor. In July 1917 an offensive was opened in Galicia, but the demoralized Russian armies again collapsed.

The mass of the Russian people were wearied of a war in which they were asked to suffer so much for so little. Nor did the Russian peasant or workingman feel any enthusiasm for the westernized intellectuals and professional men who manned the Provisional Government. The ordinary Russian, so far as he had any politics, was drawn to one or another of numerous forms of socialism, Marxist and non-Marxist. The Russian Marxist party, the Social Democrats, was divided between Menshevik and Bolshevik factions, the latter being the more extreme. The Bolshevik leaders had for some time lived as exiles in western Europe. Their principal spokesman, V. I. Lenin, with a few others, had spent the war years in Switzerland. In April 1917 the German government offered safe passage to Lenin through Germany to Russia. A railway car full of Bolsheviks, carefully "sealed" to prevent infection of Germany, was thus hauled by a German train to the frontier, whence it passed on to St. Petersburg, or Petrograd, as the city was renamed during the war. The aim of the Germans in this affair, as in the sending of Roger Casement to Ireland in a submarine, was of course to use a kind of psychological warfare against the enemy's home front. It was to promote rebellion against the Provisional Government and thus at last to eliminate Russia.

The position of the Provisional Government became rapidly more untenable, from many causes, until by November 1917 the situation was so confused that Lenin and the Bolsheviks were able to seize power. The Bolsheviks stood for peace with Germany, partly to win popular favor in Russia, and partly because they regarded the war impartially, as a struggle between capitalist and imperialist powers which should be left to exhaust and destroy each other for the benefit of socialism. On December 3, 1917, a peace conference opened between the Bolsheviks and the Germans at Brest-Litovsk. Meanwhile the peoples within the western border of the old Russia—Poles, Ukrainians, Bessarabians, Estonians, Latvians, Finns—with German backing, proclaimed their national independence. The Bolsheviks, since they would not or could not fight, were obliged to sign with Germany a treaty to which they vehemently objected, the treaty of Brest-Litovsk of March 3, 1918. By this treaty they acknowledged the "independence," or at least the loss to Russia, of Poland, the Ukraine, Finland, and the Baltic provinces.

For the Germans the treaty of Brest-Litovsk represented their maximum success during the First World War; it accomplished some of the war aims formulated at the beginning of hostilities. Not only had they neutralized Russia; they also now dominated eastern Europe through puppets placed at the head of the new independent states. They relieved the effects of the naval blockade by drawing considerable quantities of foodstuffs from the Ukraine, though less than they expected. A certain number of German troops remained in the East to preserve the new arrangements. But it was no longer a two-front war. Masses of the German army were shifted from east to west. The High Command, under Hindenburg and Ludendorff since August 1916, prepared to concentrate for a last blow in France to end the war in 1918.

The year 1918 was essentially a race to see whether American aid could reach Europe soon enough, in sufficient amount, to offset the added strength which Germany drew from the collapse of Russia. In March of that year the Germans, beginning with gas attacks and a bombardment by 6,000 artillery pieces, opened a formidable offensive before which the French and British both recoiled. On May 30, 1918, the Germans again stood at the Marne, thirty-seven miles from Paris. At this time there were only two American divisions in action, though the United States had been at war over a year. At this point in the story there are therefore two open questions: how the United States entered the war, and the length of time required for the build-up of its forces overseas.

The United States and the War

We have seen how President Wilson clung persistently to neutrality. The American people were divided. Many had been born in Europe or were the children of immigrants. Those of Irish origin were anti-British; those of German origin were often sympathetic to Germany. On the other hand, since the time of the Spanish-American and Boer Wars, a noticeable current of friendliness to the English had been running, more than ever before in American history. The sale of war materials to the Allies, and the purchase of the bonds of Allied governments, had given certain limited though influential circles a material interest in an Allied victory. The idealism of the country was on the side of England and France, so far as it was not isolationist. An Allied victory would clearly advance the cause of democracy, freedom, and progress far more than a victory of the German Empire. On the other hand, England and France were suspected of somewhat impure motives, and they were allied with the Russian autocracy, the reactionary and brutal tsardom.

The fall of tsarism made a great impression. Democratic and progressive men now came forward even in Russia. No one had ever heard of Lenin or foresaw the Bolshevik Revolution. It seemed in the spring of 1917 that Russia was struggling along the path that England, France, and America had already taken. An ideological barrier had dropped away, and the demand for American intervention to safeguard democracy became more insistent.

The Germans gave up the attempt to keep the United States out. Constricted ever more tightly by the blockade, and failing to get a decision on land, the German government and High Command listened more readily to the submarine experts, who declared that if given a free hand they could force British surrender in six months. It was the chief example in the First World War of the claim that one branch of the service could win the war alone. Civilian and diplomatic members of the government objected, fearing the consequences of war with the United States. They were overruled; it was a good example of the way in which, in Germany, the army and navy had taken the highest policy into their hands. Unrestricted submarine warfare was to be resumed on February 1, 1917. It was foreseen that the United States would declare war, but the German High Command believed that this would make no immediate difference. They estimated in 1917 (correctly) that between the time when the United States entered a European war and the time when it could take part with its own army about a year must intervene. Meanwhile, the planners said, in six months they could force Britain to accept defeat.

On January 31, 1917, the Germans notified Wilson of the resumption of unrestricted submarine attacks. They announced that they would sink on sight all merchant vessels found in a zone around the British Isles or in the Mediterranean. Wilson broke off diplomatic relations and ordered the arming of American freighters. Meanwhile, the publication of the Zimmermann telegram convinced many Americans of German aggressiveness. German secret agents also had been at work in America, fomenting strikes and causing explosions in factories engaged in the manufacture of munitions for the Allies. In February and March several American ships were sunk. Americans regarded all these activities as an interference with their rights as neutrals. Wilson at last concluded that Germany was a menace. Having made his decision, Wilson saw a clear-cut issue between right and wrong, and he obtained a rousing declaration of war from Congress, on April 6, 1917. The United States went to war "to make the world safe for democracy."

At first the German campaign realized and even exceeded the predictions of its sponsors. In February 1917 the Germans sank 540,000 tons of shipping, in March 578,000 tons, in April, as the days grew longer, 874,000 tons. Something akin to terror, with difficulty concealed from the public, seized on the government in London. Britain was reduced to a mere six-weeks' reserve of food. Gradually countermeasures were developed—mine barrages, hydrophones, depth charges, airplane reconnaissance, and most of all the convoy. It was found that a hundred or more freighters together, though all had to steam at the pace of the slowest, could be protected by a sufficient concentration of warships to keep submarines away. The United States navy, which, unlike the army, was of considerable size and ready for combat, supplied enough additional force to the Allies to make convoying and other antisubmarine measures highly effective. By the end of 1917 the submarine was no more than a nuisance. For the Germans the great plan produced the anticipated penalty without the reward—its net result was only to add America to their enemies.

On the Western Front in 1917, while the Americans desperately got themselves ready for the war they had entered, the French and British continued to hold the line. The French, finding in General Nivelle a commander who still believed in the breakthrough, launched an offensive so unsuccessful and so bloody that mutiny spread through the French army. Pétain then replaced Nivelle and restored discipline to the exhausted and disillusioned soldiers, but he had no thought of further attack. "I am waiting for the Americans and the tanks," he said. The British then assumed the main burden. For three months late in 1917 they fought the dismal battle of Passchendaele. They advanced five miles, near Ypres, at a cost of 400,000 men. At the very end of 1917 the British surprised the Germans with a raid by 380 tanks, which penetrated deep into the German lines, but were obliged to withdraw, since no reserve of fresh infantry was at hand to exploit their success. Meanwhile the Austro-Hungarians, strongly reinforced by German troops, overwhelmed the Italians at the disastrous battle of Caporetto. The Central Powers streamed into northern Italy, but the Italians, with British and French reinforcements, were able to hold the line. The net effect of the campaigns of 1917, and of the repulse of the submarine at the same time, was to reemphasize the stalemate in Europe, incline the weary Allies to await the Americans, and give the Americans what they most needed—time.

The Americans made good use of the time given them. Conscription, democratically entitled selective service, was adopted immediately after the declaration of war. The United States army, whose professionals in 1916 numbered only 130,000, performed the mammoth feat of turning over 3.5 million civilians into soldiers. With the navy, the United States came to have over 4 million in its armed services (which may be compared with over 12 million in the Second World War). Aid flowed to the Allies. To the loans already made through private bankers were added some $10 billion lent by the American government itself. The Allies used the money mainly to buy food and munitions in the United States. American farms and factories, which had already prospered by selling to the Allies during the period of neutrality, now broke all records for production. Civilian industry was converted to war uses; radiator factories turned out guns, and piano factories airplane wings. Every possible means was employed to build up ocean shipping, without which neither American supplies nor American armies could reach the theater of war. Available shipping was increased from 1 million to 10 million tons. Civilian consumption was drastically cut. Eight thousand tons of steel were saved in the manufacture of women's corsets, and 75,000 tons of tin in the making of children's toy wagons. Every week people observed meatless Tuesday, and sugar was rationed. Daylight-saving time, invented in Europe during the war, was introduced to save coal. By such means the United States made enormous stocks available for its Allies as well as itself, though for some items, notably airplanes and artillery ammunition, the American armies, when they reached France, drew heavily on British and French manufactures.

The Final Phase of the War

The Germans, as we have seen, victorious in the East, opened a great final offensive in the West in the spring of 1918, hoping to force a decision before American participation turned the balance forever. To oppose it, a unity of command was at last achieved, for the first time, when a French general, Ferdinand Foch, was made commander in chief of all Allied forces in France, with the national commanders subordinate to him, including Pershing for the Americans. In June the Germans first made contact with American troops in significant force, meeting the Second Division at Château-Thierry. The German position was so favorable that civilians in the German government thought it opportune to make a last effort at a compromise peace. The military, headed by Hindenburg and Ludendorff, successfully blocked any such attempts; they preferred to gamble on one final throw. The German armies reached their farthest advance on July 15 along the Marne. There were now nine American divisions in the Allied line. Foch used them to spearhead his counterattack on July 18. The badly overstrained Germans began to falter. Over 250,000 American troops were now landing in France every month. The final Allied offensive which opened in September, with American troops in the Argonne occupying an eastern sector, proved more than the Germans could withstand. The German High Command notified its government that it could not win the war. The German foreign office made peace overtures to President Wilson. An armistice was arranged, and on November 11, 1918, firing ceased on the Western Front.

Since Germany's allies had surrendered during the preceding weeks, the war, or at least the shooting war in western Europe, was now over. The horror it brought to individual lives cannot be told by statistics, which drily report that almost 10 million men had been killed, and 20 million wounded. Each of the European Great Powers (except Italy) lost from 1 million to 2 million in killed alone. The United States, with some 330,000 casualties of all types (of whom 115,000 died) lost in the entire war fewer men than the main combatants had lost in such a single battle as Verdun or Passchendaele.[17] American assistance was

---

[17] Of the 115,000 American deaths only 50,000 represented men killed in battle, the remainder representing mainly deaths by disease. The great influenza epidemic of 1918, which brought death to over 20 million people, civilians and military alike, in all parts of the world, probably accounted for 25,000 deaths in the American army.

decisive in the defeat of Germany. But it came so late, when the others had been struggling for so long, that the mere beginnings of it were enough to turn the scale. On the date of the armistice there were 2 million American soldiers in France, and another 1 million were on the way. But the American army had really been in combat only four months. During the whole year 1918, out of every hundred artillery shells that were fired by the three armies, the French fired 51, the British 43, and the Americans only 6.

88. *The Collapse of the Austrian and German Empires*

The war proved fatal to the German and Austro-Hungarian empires, as to the Russian. The subject Habsburg nationalities, or the "national councils" representing them in the Western capitals, obtained recognition from the Allies, and in October 1918 declared their independence. The last Austrian emperor, Charles I, abdicated on November 12, and on the next day Austria was proclaimed a republic, as was Hungary in the following week. Before any peace conference could convene, the new states of Czechoslovakia, Yugoslavia, an enlarged Romania, a republican Hungary, and a miniature republican Austria were in existence by their own action.

The German Empire stood solid until the closing weeks. Liberals, democrats, and socialists had lately begun to press for peace and democratization. Yet it was the High Command itself that precipitated the debacle. In the last years of the war dictatorial powers had become concentrated in the hands of General Ludendorff, and in September 1918 only he and his closest military associates realized that the German cause was hopeless. On September 29, at supreme headquarters at Spa in Belgium, Ludendorff informed the Kaiser that Germany must ask for peace. He urged that a new government be formed at Berlin, reflecting the majority in the Reichstag, on democratic parliamentary principles.

In calling for immediate peace negotiations, he seems to have had two ideas in mind. First, he might win time to regroup his armies and prepare a new offensive. Or if collapse became unavoidable, then the civilian or democratic elements in Germany would be the ones to sue for peace.

The liberal Prince Max of Baden was found to head a cabinet in which even socialists were included. In October various reforms were enacted, the Bismarckian system was ended, and Germany became a liberal constitutional monarchy. For Ludendorff the changes were not fast enough. What was happening was essentially simple. The German military caste, at the moment of Germany's crisis, was more eager to save the army than to save the empire. The army must never admit surrender; that was an affair for small men in business suits. Emperor, High Command, officers, and aristocrats were unloading frantically upon civilians.

President Wilson unwittingly played into their hands. Speaking now as the chief of the Allied coalition, the one to whom peace overtures were first made, he insisted that the German government must become more democratic. It may be recalled how Bismarck, after defeating France in 1871, demanded a general election in France before making peace.[18] Wilson, unlike Bismarck, really believed

---

[18] See pp. 559, 605.

in democracy; but in a practical way his position was the same. He wanted to be sure that he was dealing with the German people itself, not with a discredited elite. He wanted it to be the real Germany that applied for and accepted the Allied terms. In Germany, as realization of the military disaster spread, many people began to regard the Kaiser as an obstacle to peace. Or they felt that Germany would obtain better terms if it appeared before the Allies as a republic. Even the officer corps, to halt the fighting before the army disintegrated, began to talk of abdication. Sailors mutinied at Kiel on November 3, and councils of workers and soldiers were formed in various cities. The socialists threatened to withdraw from the newly formed cabinet (i.e., go into opposition and end the representative nature of the new government) unless William II abdicated. A general strike, led by minority socialists and syndicalists, began on November 9. "Abdication," Prince Max told the emperor, "is a dreadful thing, but a government without the socialists would be a worse danger for the country." William II abdicated on November 9, and slipped across the frontier into Holland, where despite cries to try him as a "war criminal" he lived quietly until his death in 1941. Germany was proclaimed a republic on the same day. Two days later the war stopped.

The fall of the empire in Germany, with the consequent adoption of the republic, did not arise from any basic discontent, deep revolutionary action, or change of sentiment in the German people. It was an episode of the war. The republic (soon called the Weimar Republic) arose because the victorious enemy demanded it, because the German people craved peace, because they wished to avoid forcible revolution, and because the old German military class, to save its face and its future strength, wished at least temporarily to be excused. When the war ended, the German army was still in France, its discipline and organization still apparently unimpaired. No hostile shot had been fired on German soil. It was said later, by some, that the army had not been defeated, that it had been "stabbed in the back" by a dissolving civilian home front. This was untrue; it was the panic-stricken Ludendorff who first cried for "democracy." But the circumstances in which the German republic originated made its later history, and hence all later history, very troubled.

89. The Economic and Social Impact of the War

Effects on Capitalism: Government-Regulated Economies

European society was forced by the First World War into many basic changes that were to prove more lasting than the war itself. First of all, the war profoundly affected capitalism as previously known. Essential to the older capitalism (or economic liberalism, or free private enterprise) had been the idea that government should leave business alone, or at the most regulate certain general conditions under which businessmen went about their affairs. Before 1914 governments had increasingly come into the economic field. They had put up tariffs, protected national industries, sought for markets or raw materials by imperialist expansion, or passed protective social legislation to benefit the wage-earning classes. During the war all belligerent governments controlled the economic system far more minutely. Indeed, the idea of the "planned economy" was first applied in the First World War. For the first time (with such rare and archaic precedents as the French dictatorship of 1793)[19] the state attempted to direct all the wealth, resources, and moral purpose of society to a single end.

Since no one had expected a long war, no one had made any plans for industrial mobilization. Everything had to be improvised. By 1916 each government had set up a system of boards, bureaus, councils, and commissions to coordinate its war effort. The aim was to see that all manpower was effectively utilized, and that all natural resources within the country, and all that could possibly be imported, were employed where they would do the most good. In the stress of war free competition was found to be wasteful and undirected private enterprise too uncertain and too slow. The profit motive came into disrepute. Those who exploited shortages to make big profits were stigmatized as "profiteers." Production for civilian use, or for mere luxury purposes, was cut to a minimum. Businessmen were not allowed to set up or close down factories as they chose. It was impossible to start a new business without government approval, because the flotation of stocks and bonds was controlled, and raw materials were made available only as the government wished. It was equally impossible to shut down a business engaged in war production; if a factory was inefficient or unprofitable the government kept it going anyway, making up the losses, so that in some cases management came to expect government support. Here too the tests of competition and profitableness were abandoned. The new goal was coordination or "rationalization" of production in the interests of the country as a whole. Labor was discouraged from protesting against hours or wage rates, and the big unions generally agreed to refrain from strikes. For the upper and middle classes it became embarrassing to show their comforts too openly. It was patriotic to eat meagerly and to wear old clothes. War gave a new impetus even to the idea of economic equality, if only to enlist rich and poor alike in a common cause.

Military conscription was the first step in the allocation of manpower. Draft boards told some men to report to the army, granting exemptions to others to work safely in war industries. Given the casualty rates at the front, state determination over individual life could hardly go farther. With the insatiable need for troops, drawing in men originally exempted or at first rejected as physically inadequate, great numbers of women poured into factories and offices, and in Britain even into newly organized women's branches of the armed forces. Women took over many jobs which it had been thought only men could do. Women did not remain in the labor force after the war in such large numbers, most making way for the returning veterans, but the wartime experience in this and the Second World War was part of the process by which the labor force in all countries was enlarged, women's place in society revolutionized, and the lives and outlook of millions of individual women turned outward from the home. It was a process that would be intensified during the Second World War and in the years that followed. During the war governments did not directly force men or women to drop one job and take another. There was no systematic labor conscription except in Germany. But by influencing wage scales, granting draft

---

[19] See pp. 388–390.

exemptions, forcing some industries to expand and others to contract or stand still, and propagandizing the idea that work in an arms factory was patriotic, the state shifted vast numbers of workers to war production. Impressed or "slave" labor was not used in the First World War nor were prisoners of war obliged to give labor service, though there were some abuses of these rules of international law by the Germans, who were possibly the least scrupulous and certainly the most hard pressed.

Governments controlled all foreign trade. It was intolerable to let private citizens ship off the country's resources at their own whim. It was equally intolerable to let them use up foreign exchange by importing unneeded goods, or to drive up prices of necessities by competing with one another. Foreign trade became a state monopoly, in which private firms operated under strict licenses and quotas. The greatest of the exporting countries was the United States, whose annual exports rose from $2 billion to $6 billion between 1914 and 1918. The endless demand for American farm and factory products naturally drove up prices, which, however, were fixed by law in 1917, for the most important items.

As for the European Allies, which even before the war had exported less than they imported, and were now exporting as little as possible, they could make purchases in the United States only by enormous loans from the American government. British and French citizens, under pressure from their own governments, sold off their American stocks and bonds, which were bought up by Americans.[20] The former owners received pounds sterling or francs from their own governments, which in return took and spent the dollars paid by the new American owners. In this way the United States ceased to be a debtor country (owing some $4 billion to Europeans in 1914), and became the world's leading creditor country, to which by 1919 Europeans owed about $10 billion.

The Allies controlled the sea, but they never had enough shipping to meet rising demands, especially with German submarines taking a steady though fluctuating toll. Each government set up a shipping board, to expand shipbuilding at any cost and to assign available shipping space to whatever purposes—troop movements, rubber imports, foodstuffs—the government considered most urgent in view of overall plans. Control and allocation eventually became international under the Interallied Shipping Council, of which the United States was a member after entering the war. In England and France, where all manufactures depended on imports, government control of shipping and hence of imports was itself enough to give control over the whole economy.

Germany, denied access to the sea and also to Russia and western Europe, was obliged to adopt unprecedented measures of self-sufficiency. The oil of Romania and grain of the Ukraine, which became available late in the war, were poor substitutes for the world trade on which Germany had formerly depended. The Germans went with less food than other belligerents. Their government controls became more thorough and more efficient, producing what they called "war socialism." In Walter Rathenau they found a man with the necessary ideas. He was a Jewish industrialist, son of the head of the German electrical trust. One of the first to foresee a long war, he launched a program for the mobilization of raw materials. Early in the war it seemed that Germany might be soon defeated by

[20] See pp. 599–600.

lack of nitrogen, necessary to make explosives. Rathenau sweepingly requisitioned every conceivable natural source, including the very manure from the farmers' barnyards, until German chemists succeeded in extracting nitrogen from the air. The German chemical industry developed many other substitute products, such as synthetic rubber. German production was organized into War Companies, one for each line of industry, with private business firms working under close government supervision.

The other belligerent governments also replaced competition between individual firms and factories with coordination. "Consortiums" of industrialists in France allocated raw materials and government orders within each industry. The War Industries Board did the same in the United States. In Britain, similar methods became so efficient that by 1918, for example, the country produced every two weeks as many shells as in the whole first year of the war and turned out seventy times as much heavy artillery.

Inflation, Industrial Changes, Control of Ideas

No government, even by heavy taxes, could raise all the funds it needed except by printing paper money, selling huge bond issues, or obliging banks to grant it credit. The result, given heavy demand and acute shortages, was rapid inflation of prices. Prices and wages were regulated but were never again so low as before 1914. The hardest hit by this development were those whose money income could not easily be raised—people living on "safe" investments, those drawing annual salaries, professional people, government employees. These classes had been one of the most stabilizing influences in Europe before the war. Everywhere the war threatened their status, prestige, and standard of living. The huge national debts meant higher taxes for years to come. The debt was most serious when it was owed to a foreign country. During the war the Continental Allies borrowed from Britain, and they and the British both borrowed from the United States. They thereby mortgaged their future. To pay the debt, they were bound for years to export more than they imported—or, roughly, to produce more than they consumed. It may be recalled that in 1914 every advanced European country habitually imported more than it exported.[21] That fact, basic to the European standard of life, was now threatened with reversal.

Moreover, with Europe torn by war for four years, the rest of the world speeded up its own industrialization. The productive capacity of the United States increased immensely. The Japanese began to sell in China, in India, in South America the cotton textiles and other civilian goods which these countries for the time being could not obtain from Europe. Argentina and Brazil, unable to get locomotive parts or mining machinery from England, began to manufacture them themselves. In India the Tata family, a group of wealthy Parsees controlling $250 million of native Indian capital, developed numerous manufacturing enterprises, one of which became the largest iron and steel works in the British Empire. With Germany entirely out of the world market, with Britain and France producing desperately for themselves, and with the world's shipping commandeered for war uses, the position of western Europe as the world's workshop was undermined.

[21] See p. 598.

After the war Europe had new competitors. The economic foundations of the nineteenth century had slipped away. The age of European supremacy was in its twilight.

All the belligerent governments during the war attempted to control ideas as they did economic production. Freedom of thought, respected everywhere in Europe for half a century, was discarded. Propaganda and censorship became more effective then any government, however despotic, had ever been able to devise. No one was allowed to sow doubt by raising any basic questions.

It must be remembered that the facts of the prewar crises, as related above, were then largely unknown. People were trapped in a nightmare whose causes they could not comprehend. Each side wildly charged the other with having started the war from pure malevolence. The long attrition, the fruitless fighting, the unchanging battle lines, the appalling casualties were a severe ordeal to morale. Civilians, deprived of their usual liberties, working harder, eating dull food, seeing no victory, had to be kept emotionally at a high pitch. Placards, posters, diplomatic white papers, schoolbooks, public lectures, solemn editorials, and slanted news reports conveyed the message. The new universal literacy, the mass press, the new moving pictures, proved to be ideal media for the direction of popular thinking. Intellectuals and professors advanced complicated reasons, usually historical, for loathing and crushing the enemy. In allied countries the Kaiser was portrayed as a demon, with glaring eyes and abnormally bristling mustaches, bent on the mad project of conquest of the world. In Germany people were taught to dread the day when Cossacks and Senegalese should rape German women and to hate England as the inveterate enemy which inhumanly starved little children with its blockade. Each side convinced itself that all right was on its side and all wrong, wickedness, and barbarity on the other. An inflamed opinion helped to sustain men and women in such a fearsome struggle. But when it came time to make peace the rooted convictions, fixed ideas, profound aversions, hates, and fears became an obstacle to political judgment.

90. The Peace of Paris, 1919

The late ally, Russia, was in the hands of the Bolsheviks, ostracized like a leper colony, and taking no part in international relations. The late German and Austro-Hungarian empires were already defunct, and more or less revolutionary regimes struggled to establish themselves in their places. New republics already existed along the Baltic coast, in Poland, and in the Danube basin but without effective governments or acknowledged frontiers. Europe east of France and Italy was in a state approaching chaos, with revolution on the Russian style threatening. Western Europe was wrenched out of all resemblance to its former self. The Allied blockade of Germany continued. In these circumstances the victors assembled in Paris, in the bleak winter of 1919, to reconstruct the world. During 1919 they signed five treaties, all named after Paris suburbs—St.-Germain with Austria, Trianon with Hungary, Neuilly with Bulgaria, Sèvres with Turkey (1920), and most especially, with Germany the Treaty of Versailles.

The world looked with awe and expectation to one man—the president of the United States. Wilson occupied a lone eminence, enjoyed a universal prestige.

Victors, vanquished, and neutrals admitted that American intervention had decided the conflict. Everywhere people who had been long tried, confused, bereaved, were stirred by Wilson's thrilling language in favor of a higher cause, of a great concert of right in which peace would be forever secure and the world itself at last free. Wilson reached Europe in January 1919, visiting several Allied capitals. He was wildly acclaimed, and almost mobbed, greeted as the man who would lead civilization out of its wasteland.

The Fourteen Points and the Treaty of Versailles

Wilson's views were well known. He had stated them in January 1918 in his Fourteen Points—principles upon which, after victory, peace was to be established. The Fourteen Points demanded an end to secret treaties and secret diplomacy (or in Wilsonian language, "open covenants openly arrived at"); freedom of the seas "alike in peace and in war"; removal of barriers and inequalities in international trade; reduction of armaments by all powers; colonial readjustments; evacuation of occupied territory; self-determination of nationalities and a redrawing of European boundaries along national lines; and, last but not least, an international political organization to prevent war. On the whole, Wilson stood for the fruition of the democratic, liberal, progressive, and nationalistic movements of the century past, for the ideals of the Enlightenment, the French Revolution, and of 1848. As Wilson saw it, and as many believed, the World War should end in a new type of treaty. There was thought to be something sinister about peace conferences of the past, for example, the Congress of Vienna of 1815.[22] The old diplomacy was blamed for leading to war. Lenin in his own way and for his own purposes was saying this in Russia too. It was felt that treaties had too long been wrongly based on a politics of power, or on unprincipled deals and bargains made without regard to the people concerned. Democracy having defeated the Central Powers, people hoped that a new settlement, made in a democratic age, might be reached by general agreement in an atmosphere of mutual confidence. There was a real sense of a new era.

Wilson had had some difficulty, however, in persuading the Allied governments to accept his Fourteen Points. The French demanded a guarantee of German payment for war damages. The British vetoed the freedom of the seas "in peace and war"; it was naval rivalry that had estranged them from Germany, and they had fought the war to preserve British command of the sea. But with these two reservations the Allies expressed their willingness to follow Wilson's lead. The Germans who asked for the armistice believed that peace would be made along the lines of the Fourteen Points with only the two modifications described. The socialists and democrats now trying to rule Germany thought also that, having overthrown the Kaiser and the war lords, they would be treated by the victors with some moderation, and that a new democratic Germany would reemerge into the place in the world which they considered to be due it.

Twenty-seven nations assembled at Paris in January 1919, but the full or plenary sessions were unimportant. Matters were decided by conferences among the Big Four—Wilson himself, Lloyd George for England, Clemenceau for France,

---

[22] See pp. 444–450.

Orlando for Italy. The conjunction of personalities was not a happy one. Wilson was sternly and stubbornly righteous; Lloyd George, a fiery and changeable Welshman; Clemenceau, an aged patriot, the "tiger of France," who had been not exactly young in the War of 1870 (he was born in 1841); Orlando, a passing phenomenon of Italian politics. None of them was especially equipped for the task in hand. Clemenceau was a pronounced nationalist, Lloyd George had always been concerned with domestic reforms, Orlando was by training a professor like Wilson, and Wilson, a former college president, lacked concrete knowledge or intimate feeling for peoples other than his own. However, they democratically represented the governments and peoples of their respective countries, and thus spoke with an authority denied to professional diplomats of the old school.

Wilson first fought a hard battle for a League of Nations, a permanent international body in which all nations, without sacrificing their sovereignty, should meet together to discuss and settle disputes, each promising not to resort to war. Few European statesmen had any confidence in such a League. But they yielded to Wilson, and the covenant of the League of Nations was written into the treaty with Germany. In return, Wilson had to make concessions to Lloyd George, Clemenceau, Orlando, and the Japanese. He was thus obliged to compromise the idealism of the Fourteen Points. Probably compromise and bargaining would have been necessary anyway, for such general principles as national self-determination and colonial readjustment invariably led to differences of opinion in concrete cases. Wilson allowed himself to believe that, if a League of Nations were established and operating, faults in the treaty could later be corrected at leisure by international discussion.

A special kind of disagreement arose over the covenant of the League. Wilson wished to include a clause endorsing religious freedom. The Japanese insisted that it be broadened to condemn racial discrimination as well. The Americans and British were opposed for fear that an international authority might interfere with their immigration practices. In the end both proposals were abandoned.

The great demand of the French at the peace conference was for security against Germany. On this subject the French were almost rabid. The war in the West had been fought almost entirely on their soil. To trim Germany down more nearly to French size, they proposed that the part of Germany west of the Rhine be set up as an independent state under Allied auspices. Wilson and Lloyd George objected, sagely observing that the resulting German resentment would only lead to another war. The French yielded, but only on condition that they obtain their security in another way, namely, by a promise from both Britain and the United States to join them immediately if they were again attacked by the Germans. An Anglo-French-American guarantee treaty, with these provisions, was in fact signed at Paris. France obtained control over the Saar coal mines for fifteen years; during that time, a League commission would administer the Saar territory and in 1935 a plebiscite would be held. Lorraine and Alsace were returned to France. German fortifications and troops were banned from a wide belt in the Rhineland. Allied troops would occupy the Rhineland for fifteen years to assure German compliance with the treaty.

In the east the Allies wished to set up strong buffer states against Bolshevism in Russia. Sympathies with Poland ran very high. Those parts of the former German Empire that were inhabited by Poles, or by mixed populations of Poles and Germans—Posen and West Prussia—were assigned to the new Polish state. This gave Poland a corridor to the sea, but at the same time cut off the bulk of Germany from East Prussia.[23] Danzig, an old German town, became a free city, belonging to no country. Memel also was internationalized; it was soon seized by Lithuania. Upper Silesia, a rich mining country, went to Poland after a disputed plebiscite. In Austria and among the Sudeten Germans of Bohemia, now that there was no longer a Habsburg empire (whose existence had blocked an all-German union in 1848 and in the time of Bismarck),[24] a feeling developed for annexation to the new German republic. But the feeling was unorganized, and in any case the Allies naturally refused to make Germany bigger than it had been in 1914. Austria remained a dwarf republic, and Vienna a former imperial capital cut off from its empire—a head severed from its body, and scarcely more capable of sustaining life. The Bohemian Germans became disgruntled citizens of Czechoslovakia.

Germany lost all its colonies. Wilson and the South African General Smuts, to preserve the principle of internationalism against any imputation of raw conquest, saw to it that the colonies were actually awarded to the League of Nations. The League, in turn, under "mandates," assigned them to various powers for administration. In this way France and Great Britain divided the best of the African colonies; the Belgian Congo received a slight enlargement; and the Union of South Africa took over German Southwest Africa. In the colonial world, Italy got nothing. Japan received the mandate for the German Pacific islands north of the equator, Australia for German New Guinea and the Solomon Islands, New Zealand for German Samoa. The Japanese claimed rights over the German concessions in China. The Chinese at the Paris conference tried to get all special concessions and extraterritorial rights in China abolished.[25] No one listened to such proposals. By a compromise, Japan received about half the former German rights. The Japanese were dissatisfied. The Chinese walked out of the conference.

The Allies took over the German fleet, but the German crews, rather than surrender it, solemnly scuttled it at Scapa Flow. The German army was limited to 100,000. Since the Allies forbade conscription, or the annual training of successive groups of young civilians, the army became exclusively professional, the officer class retained political influence in it, and the means used by the Allies to demilitarize Germany served if anything the contrary purpose. The treaty forbade Germany to have any heavy artillery, aviation, or submarines. Wilson saw his plan for universal disarmament applied to Germany alone.

The French, even before the armistice, had stipulated that Germany must pay for war damages. The other Allies made the same demand. Wilson, at the conference, was stupefied at the size of the bills presented. The Belgians suggested, for their own share, a sum larger than the entire wealth of all Belgium according to officially published Belgian statistics. The French and British proposed to charge Germany with the entire expenses, including war pensions, incurred by them during the war. Wilson observed that "total" reparation, while not strictly unjust, was absolutely impossible, and even Clemenceau noted that

[23] See maps, p. 248, panel 4, and 728–729.
[24] See pp. 514–518, 551–557.
[25] See pp. 675–680.

"to ask for over a trillion francs would lead to nothing practical." The insistence on enormous reparations was in fact largely emotional. No one knew or considered how Germany would pay, though all dimly realized that such sums could only be made up by German exports, which would then compete with the Allies' own economic interests. The Germans, to avoid worse, even offered to repair physical damages in Belgium and France, but were brusquely refused on the ground that the Belgians and French would thereby lose jobs and business. No total at all was set for reparations in the treaty; it was made clear that the sum would be very large, but it was left for a future commission to determine. The Allies, maddened by the war, and themselves loaded with fantastic debts to the United States, had no desire in the matter of reparations to listen to economic reason and regarded the reparations as simply another means of righting a wrong and of putting off the dangers of a German revival. As a first payment on the reparations account the treaty required Germany to surrender most of its merchant marine, make coal deliveries, and give up all property owned by German private citizens abroad. This last proviso ended Germany's prewar career as an exporter of capital.

It was with the specific purpose of justifying the reparations that the famous "war guilt" clause was written into the treaty. By this clause Germany explicitly "accepted the responsibility" for all loss and damage resulting from the war "imposed upon them (the Allies) by the aggression of Germany and her allies." The Germans themselves felt no such responsibility as they were now obliged formally to accept. They considered their honor as a people to be impugned. The "war guilt" clause gave a ready opening to agitators in Germany and made even moderate Germans regard the treaty as something to be escaped from as a matter of self-respect.

The Treaty of Versailles was completed in three months. The absence of the Russians, the decision not to give the Germans a hearing, and the willingness of Wilson to make concessions in return for obtaining the League of Nations, made it possible to dispose of intricate matters with considerable facility. The Germans, when presented with the completed document in May 1919, refused to sign. The Allies threatened a renewal of hostilities. A government crisis ensued in Berlin. No German wished to damn himself, his party, or his principles, in German eyes, by putting his name to a document which all Germans regarded as outrageous. A combination drawn from the Social Democratic and Catholic parties finally consented to shoulder the hateful burden. Two abashed and virtually unknown representatives appeared at the Hall of Mirrors at Versailles, and signed the treaty for Germany in the presence of a large concourse of Allied dignitaries.

The other treaties drafted by the Paris conference, in conjunction with the Versailles treaty, laid out a new map for eastern Europe and registered the recession of the Russian, Austrian, and Turkish empires. Seven new independent states now existed: Finland, Estonia, Latvia, Lithuania, Poland, Czechoslovakia, and Yugoslavia. Romania was enlarged by adding areas formerly Hungarian and Russian; Greece was enlarged at the expense of Turkey. Austria and Hungary were now small states, and there was no connection between them. The Ottoman Empire presently disappeared: Turkey emerged as a republic confined to Constantinople and Asia Minor, Syria and Lebanon went to France as mandates of the League of Nations, Palestine and Iraq to Great Britain on the same basis.[26] The belt of states from Finland to Romania was regarded as a *cordon sanitaire* (sanitary zone) to prevent the infection of Europe by communism. The creation of Yugoslavia realized the aims of the South Slav or Pan-Serb movement which had set off the fatal crisis of 1914. The fact, however, that Italy received Trieste and some of the Dalmatian Islands (in keeping with the secret treaty of 1915) left the more ambitious Yugoslavs discontented.

Significance of the Paris Peace Settlement

The most general principle of the Paris settlement was to recognize the right of national self-determination, at least in Europe. Each people or nation, as defined by language, was in principle set up with its own sovereign and independent national state. Nationalism triumphed in the belief that it went along naturally with liberalism and democracy. It must be added that the peacemakers at Paris had little choice in this matter, for the new states had already declared their independence. Since in eastern Europe the nationalities were in many places intermixed, and since the peacemakers did not contemplate the actual movement and exchange of populations to sort them out, each new state found alien minorities living within its borders or could claim that people of its own kind still lived in neighboring states under foreign rule. There were Hungarians in Czechoslovakia, Ruthenians in Poland, Poles in Lithuania, Bulgars in Romania— to cite only a few examples. Hence minority problems and irredentism troubled eastern Europe, as they had before 1914. Eventually it was the complaint of Germans in Czechoslovakia that they were an oppressed minority, together with the irredentist demand of Germany to join these outlying Germans to the Fatherland, that produced the Munich crisis preceding the Second World War.[27]

The Treaty of Versailles was designed to put an end to the German menace.

---

[26] The secret treaty of 1916 (p. 709) promising the Straits to Russia lapsed with the Revolution, neither the Bolsheviks nor the Allies recognizing an agreement made with the tsarist government.

[27] See pp. 840–842.

EUROPE, 1923

The map shows European boundaries between the two World Wars, after the Peace of Versailles and certain other agreements. Comparison with the language map (p. 470) will suggest how the principle of nationality was recognized. Germany returned Alsace-Lorraine to France and lost the region around Danzig (the "Polish corridor") to Poland— essentially the area taken by Prussia in the First Partition of 1772 (see map, p. 230.) In place of the Austro-Hungarian empire we find the "succession states," Austria, Hungary, Czechoslovakia, Yugoslavia, and Romania. Austria-Hungary also lost Trieste and some of the Dalmatian Islands to Italy. Poland regained its independence, and Finland and the three Baltic states, Estonia, Latvia, and Lithuania, emerged from the tsarist empire. Most of Ireland became a "free state" in the British Commonwealth of Nations, only Ulster remaining in the United Kingdom.

These boundaries lasted until 1938, when, as the Second World War approached, the Germans annexed Austria and the Sudeten part of Czechoslovakia.

ARCTIC OCEAN

0   100   200   300 miles

Reykjavik •   ICELAND
                (Denmark)   Narvik •

                                                                    NORWAY

FAEROE I.
(Denmark)   SWEDEN

ORKNEY I.   Oslo •
SCAPA FLOW
                                                                    Stockholm •
                        • Edinburgh
            ULSTER   NORTH SEA   DENMARK
    IRISH   • Copenhagen   BALTIC
    FREE STATE   GREAT BRITAIN
    Dublin •   • Liverpool   Danzig •
ATLANTIC OCEAN   Hamburg   POLISH
                                                          • Bremen   CORRIDOR
                        NETHERLANDS
            London •   Amsterdam • Rhine GERMANY   • Berlin
                                        WEIMAR REPUBLIC
                        Brussels • RUHR   Weimar •   • Dresden
                        BELGIUM   • Cologne
                        LUX. • • Frankfurt   • Prague
                                                     CZECHOSL
            Paris • Metz SAAR   Stuttgart
    Versailles •   • Strasbourg •   • Vienna
                        Munich •   Budap
    FRANCE   SWITZERLAND   AUSTRIA   HU
            Geneva • Locarno •
    Bordeaux •   Trent •   Trieste •
                                              • Fiume
    Bilbao •   YUG
                                                     • Zara
    Marseilles •   • Florence   ADRIATIC   (Italy)
                    CORSICA   SEA
PORTUGAL   Madrid • (France)
            • Barcelona   Rome • ITALY
Lisbon • SPAIN
                                    Naples •
    • Seville   BALEARIC I.
Cadiz •   (Spain)
Tangier • Gibraltar (Britain)   SARDINIA
    SPANISH
    MOROCCO   Algiers •   SICILY
                                              MALTA (Brita
MOROCCO   ALGERIA   TUNISIA   MEDITERRANEA
(France)   (France)   (France)

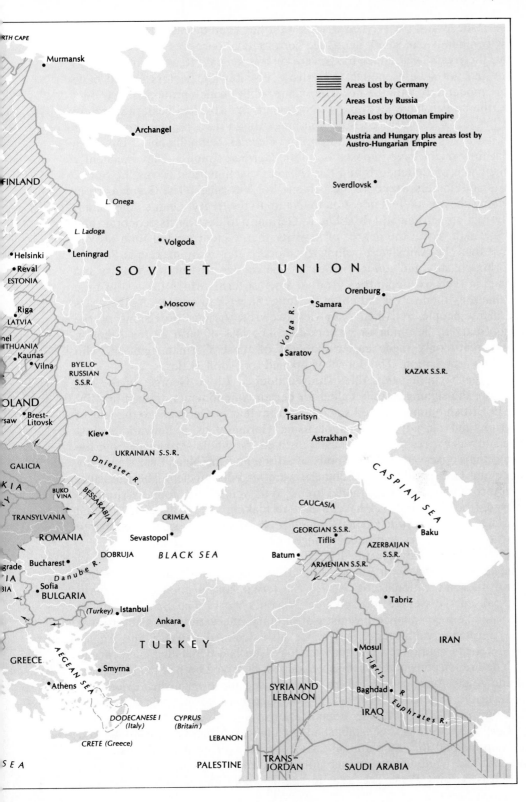

Areas Lost by Germany
Areas Lost by Russia
Areas Lost by Ottoman Empire
Austria and Hungary plus areas lost by Austro-Hungarian Empire

RTH CAPE

Murmansk

Archangel

FINLAND

L. Onega

L. Ladoga

Helsinki
Reval
ESTONIA

Riga
LATVIA

nel
THUANIA
Kaunas
Vilna

BYELO-
RUSSIAN
S.S.R.

OLAND
rsaw
Brest-
Litovsk

Kiev

UKRAINIAN S.S.R.

Dniester R.

GALICIA

KIA

BUKO
VINA

BESSARABIA

TRANSYLVANIA

ROMANIA

grade
Bucharest

DOBRUJA

Danube R.

IA
BIA
Sofia
BULGARIA

CRIMEA

Sevastopol

BLACK SEA

(Turkey) Istanbul

Ankara

TURKEY

GREECE

Athens

AEGEAN SEA

Smyrna

DODECANESE I
(Italy)

CYPRUS
(Britain)

CRETE (Greece)

SEA

PALESTINE

LEBANON

TRANS-
JORDAN

SYRIA AND
LEBANON

IRAQ

Baghdad

Mosul

Tigris R.

Euphrates R.

IRAN

Tabriz

SAUDI ARABIA

SOVIET   UNION

Sverdlovsk

Volgoda

Leningrad

Moscow

Volga R.

Samara

Orenburg

Saratov

KAZAK S.S.R.

Tsaritsyn

Astrakhan

CAUCASIA

GEORGIAN S.S.R.
Tiflis

Batum

ARMENIAN S.S.R.

AZERBAIJAN
S.S.R.

CASPIAN SEA

Baku

It was not a successful treaty. The wisdom of it has been discussed without end, but a few comments can safely be made. For practical purposes, with respect to Germany, the treaty was either too severe or too lenient. It was too severe to conciliate and not severe enough to destroy. Possibly the victors should have dealt more moderately with the new German republic, which professed their own ideals, as the monarchical victors over Napoleon, in 1814, had dealt moderately with the France of the restored Bourbons, regarding it as a regime akin to their own. As it was, the Allies imposed upon the German Republic about the same terms that they might have imposed upon the German Empire. They innocently played the game of Ludendorff and the German reactionaries; it was the Social Democrats and liberals who bore the "shame" of Versailles. The Germans from the beginning showed no real intention to live up to the treaty. On the other hand, the treaty was not sufficiently disabling to Germany to destroy its economic and political strength. Even the degree of severity that it incorporated soon proved to be more than the Allies were willing to enforce. The treaty makers at Paris in 1919, working hastily and still in the heat of war, under pressure from press and propaganda in their own countries, drafted a set of terms which the test of time showed that they themselves did not in the long run wish to impose. As the years passed, many people in Allied countries declared various provisions of the Versailles treaty to be unfair or unworkable. The loss of faith by the Allies in their own treaty only made easier the task of those German agitators who demanded its repudiation. The door was opened for Adolf Hitler.

Even at the beginning the Allies showed doubts. Lloyd George, in the last weeks before the signing, tardily called for certain amendments, though in vain; for in 1919 British opinion shifted somewhat from fear of Germany to the fear of Bolshevism, and already the idea of using Germany as a bulwark against communism was expressed. The Italians disliked the whole settlement from the beginning; they observed that the spoils of Africa and the Near East went only to France and Great Britain. The Chinese were also dissatisfied. The Russians, when they reentered the international arena some years later, found a situation that they did not like and had had no part in making. They objected to being faced with a *cordon sanitaire* from Finland to Romania and soon remembered that most of this territory had once belonged to the Russian empire.

The United States never ratified the Treaty of Versailles at all. A wave of isolationism and disgust with Europe spread over the country; and this feeling, together with some rational criticism of the terms, and a good deal of party politics, caused the Senate to repudiate Wilson's work. The Senate likewise refused to make any advance promises of military intervention in a future war between Germany and France, and hence also declined to ratify the Anglo-French-American guarantee treaty on which Wilson had persuaded Clemenceau to rely. The French considered themselves duped, deprived both of the Rhineland and of the Anglo-American guarantee. They raised more anguished cries over their insecurity. This led them to try to hold Germany down while it was still weak, in turn raising many further complications.

The League of Nations was established at Geneva. Its mere existence marked a great step beyond the international anarchy before 1914. Wilson's vision did not die. But the United States never joined; Germany was not admitted until 1926, or Russia until 1934. The League could handle and dispatch only such business as the Great Powers were willing to allow. It was associated with a west-European ascendancy that no longer corresponded to the facts of the world situation. Its covenant was part of the Versailles treaty, and many people in many countries, on both sides in the late war, saw in it, not so much a system for international adjudication, as a means for maintaining a new status quo in favor of Britain and France.

The First World War dealt a last blow to the ancient institutions of monarchy and aristocratic feudalism. Thrones toppled in Turkey, in Russia, in Austria-Hungary, in the German Empire and the individual German states; and with the kings went the courtly retainers and all the social preeminence and special advantage of the old landed aristocracies. The war was indeed a victory for democracy, though a bitter one. It carried further a process as old as the French and American revolutions. But for the basic problems of modern civilization, industrialism and nationalism, economic security and international stability, it gave no answer.

XVII.
THE RUSSIAN
REVOLUTION
AND THE
SOVIET UNION

No LESS POWERFUL than the First World War as a force shaping the twentieth century has been the revolution in Russia, of which the decisive step was the seizure of power by the Bolshevik party in November 1917. The Russian Revolution of 1917 can be compared in its magnitude only with the French Revolution of 1789. Both originated in deep-lying and distant causes, and both made their repercussions felt in many countries for many years. The present chapter will set forth the revolutionary process in Russia over half a century. We shall begin with the old regime before 1900, pass through the two revolutions of 1905 and 1917, and survey the Union of Soviet Socialist Republics down to 1939, at which time a new order had been consolidated under Joseph Stalin, a form of "planned economy" realized, and the last of the original revolutionaries, or Old Bolsheviks, either silenced or put to death.

The comparison of the Russian Revolution to the French is enlightening in many ways. Both were movements of liberation, the one against "feudalism" and "despotism," the other against "capitalism" and "imperialism." Neither was a strictly national movement dealing with merely domestic troubles; both addressed their message to all the world. Both attracted followers in all countries. Both aroused a strong reaction on the part of those whose view of life was endangered. And both showed the same pattern of revolutionary politics: a

Chapter Emblem: One of a series of bronze medals issued by the Leningrad mint in honor of Lenin and the Russian Revolution of 1917.

relative unity of opinion so long as the problem was to overthrow the old regime, followed by disunity and conflict over the founding of the new, so that one set of revolutionaries eliminated others, until a small, organized, and determined minority (Jacobin democrats in 1793, Bolshevik communists in 1918) suppressed all opposition in order to defend or advance the revolutionary cause; and in short order (within a matter of months in France, years in Russia), many of the most intensely revolutionary leaders were themselves suppressed or liquidated.

The differences are equally deserving of notice. Relatively speaking, or compared in general civilization with other European countries, Russia in 1900 was in the rear, and France in 1780 in many ways in the lead. The main strength of the French Revolution lay in the middle classes, who soon managed to prevail over more extreme pressures. In the Russian Revolution middle-class people were also active, especially at first, but they proved unable to cope with mass discontents, and succumbed to a more radical party which appealed to workers and peasants. In France, so to speak, the revolution just "happened," in that ordinary people from many walks of life unexpectedly found themselves in a revolutionary situation, and even the Jacobin dictatorship was improvised by individuals who had spent their lives thinking of other things. In Russia professional revolutionaries worked for the revolution long in advance, and the dictatorship of the Bolsheviks realized the plans and preparations of twenty years. In France the revolution was followed by a reaction in which émigrés returned, dispossessed classes reappeared in politics, and even the Bourbons were restored. The French Revolution was followed by a century of uneasy compromise. The Russian Revolution effectively wiped out its opposition; few émigrés returned; no Romanovs regained their throne. The Russian Revolution was in this sense more immediately successful. But in the long run the differences reemerged. By 1990 the ideas proclaimed in Russia in 1917 had failed to give satisfaction even in the Soviet Union, while those proclaimed in France in 1789 were widely accepted, such as representative constitutional government, with equal civil rights under national sovereignty and legal safeguards for persons and property.

The repercussions of the Russian Revolution were the more far-reaching because of the very ambivalence of Russia itself. Since the days of Peter the Great and before, it had always faced toward both Europe and Asia. It was European, yet it was also outside Europe, and even opposed to it. If about 1900 it was the least developed of the major European countries, it was at the same time the most developed, industrialized, or modernized part of the non-European world. Its revolution could win sympathy on the left in Europe because it reinforced the old European socialist objections to capitalism. It aroused the interests of submerged peoples in other continents because it also denounced imperialism (i.e., the possession of colonies by Europeans), affirming that imperialism was merely the "highest stage" of capitalism, and that both must be overthrown together. The Soviet Union, once established, came to occupy an intermediate position between the West and the colonial world (or what later came to be called the Third World). In the West it could long be feared or admired as the last word in social revolution. In the colonial, or formerly colonial, world it suggested new beginnings, a new way to become modern without being capitalistic or European, a step in a worldwide rebellion against European supremacy. The Russian Revolution thus not only produced communism and hence fascism in Europe, but added strength to the revolt of Asia, as explained in the following chapters.

Although professional revolutionaries worked for revolution in Russia, they did not "cause" it. Lenin and the Bolsheviks did not bring about the Russian Revolution. They captured it after it had begun. They boarded the ship in midstream. The Russian Revolution, like all great revolutions, originated in a totality of previous history and in the prolonged dissatisfaction of many kinds of people.

91. Backgrounds

Russia after 1881: Reaction and Progress

We have seen in earlier chapters how the tsarist autocracy arose, how it ruled as a machine superimposed upon its subjects, how the upper class became westernized while the masses sank further into serfdom, and how an intelligentsia developed, divorced both from the work of government and the activities of the people.[1] It has been explained in Chapter XIII how Alexander II freed the serfs in 1861 and created provincial and district councils or zemstvos, elected mainly by landowners, which attended to such matters as roads, schools, and hospitals.[2]

In 1881 Alexander II was assassinated by members of the People's Will. His son, Alexander III (1881–1894), tried to stamp out revolutionism and to silence even peaceable criticism of the government. Revolutionaries and terrorists were driven into exile. The People's Will as an organized group became extinct. Jews were subjected to pogroms, by far the worst of any (until then) in modern times. For the first time the empire adopted a program of systematic Russification. Poles, Ukrainians, Lithuanians, the peoples of the Caucasus, the scattered German communities, the Muslim groups in central Asia, all faced the prospect of forcible assimilation to the Great Russian culture. The philosopher and chief official of this movement was Pobiedonostsev, procurator of the Holy Synod, or layman head, under the tsar, of the Russian Orthodox Church. Pobiedonostsev saw in the West something alien and doomed. Drawing on such old enemies of the French Revolution as Edmund Burke, he attacked Western rationalism and liberalism in his writings, declared that Slavs had a peculiar national character of their own, and dreamed of turning Holy Russia into a kind of churchly community, in which a disciplined clergy should protect the faithful from the insidious influence of the West.

This is not, however what happened. In the closing decades of the nineteenth century Russia became more than ever before a part of European civilization. Almost overnight it presented Europe with great works of literature and music that Europeans could appreciate. The Russian novel became known throughout the Western world. All could read the novels of Tolstoy (1828–1910) without a

---

[1] See pp. 234–245, 336–342, 564–569.
[2] See p. 567.

feeling of strangeness; and if the characters of Turgenev (1818–1883) and of Dostoevski (1821–1881) behaved more queerly, the authors themselves were obviously within the great European cultural family. The melodies of Tchaikovsky (1840–1893) and of Rimsky-Korsakov (1844–1908) became very familiar throughout Europe and America; if they sometimes seemed hauntingly wild, distant, or sad, they still betrayed no more than the usual amount of national idiosyncrasy. Russians also contributed to the sciences, notably chemistry. They were considered to be especially talented in the more abstruse intellectual exercises, such as higher mathematics, physics, or chess.

Russia also, from the 1880s, began to pass through the Industrial Revolution and take its place as an integral part of the world economic system. European capital entered the country, financing railways, mines, and factories (as well as government and the army) until by 1914 Europeans had about the same amount invested in Russia as in the United States, some four billion dollars in each case.[3] In 1897, under the reforming ministry of Count Witte, Russia adopted the gold standard, making its currency readily convertible with all others. In the quarter-century between 1888 and 1913 the Russian railway mileage more than doubled, the miles of telegraph wires multiplied fivefold, the number of post offices trebled, and the number of letters carried by the mails multiplied seven times. Although still industrially undeveloped by Western standards, without, for example, any machine tool industry or chemical plants, Russia was industrializing rapidly. Exports rose in value from 400 million rubles in 1880 to 1.6 billion in 1913. Imports, though smaller, grew more rapidly, quintupling in the same period. They consisted of such items as tea and coffee and of the machines and industrial goods made in western Europe. For a long time after the Revolution, the Soviet Union conducted less foreign trade than did the Russian empire on the eve of the First World War. The Soviet regime, to keep control over its own economic system, tried to depend as little as possible on outside markets and sources of supply.

Industrialization, in Russia as in all countries, brought an increase both of the business and of the wage-earning classes, or, in socialist terminology, of the bourgeoisie and of the proletariat. Though growing, they were still not numerous by standards of the West. Factory workers, laboring for eleven or more hours a day, for low wages under hard conditions, were in somewhat the same position as in England or France before 1850.[4] Unions were illegal, and strikes prohibited. Nevertheless, great strikes in the 1890s called attention to the misery of the new industrial workers. There was one distinctive feature to the Russian proletariat. Russian industry was heavily concentrated; half of Russia's industrial workers were employed in factories employing over 500 persons. It was easier for workers under such circumstances to be organized economically and at the proper time to be mobilized politically. As for the Russian business and capitalist class, it was relatively the weaker because of several features in the situation. Ownership of much of Russia's new industrial plant was in foreign hands. Much was owned by the tsarist government itself; Russia already had the largest state-operated economic system in the world. Moreover, in Russia (unlike the United States at

[3] See pp. 599–600, 648.
[4] See pp. 459–461, 492–499, 501–505.

the time) the government itself was a heavy borrower from Europe; hence it was less dependent financially on its own people and more able to maintain an absolutist regime.

Nevertheless, the rising business and professional classes, reinforced by enterprising landowners, were strong enough to form a liberal segment of public opinion, which emerged in 1905 as the Constitutional Democratic party (or "Cadets"). Many of those who were active in the provincial zemstvos also became Constitutional Democrats. They were liberals, progressives, or constitutionalists in the Western sense, thinking less about the troubles of factory workers and peasants than about the need for a nationally elected parliament to control the policies of state.

Russia remained predominantly agricultural. Its huge exports were mainly farm and forest products. The peasants formed four-fifths of the population. Free from their former lords since 1861, they lived in their village communes or *mirs*.[5] In most communes much of the land was divided and redivided among peasant households by agreement of the village community, nor could anyone leave without communal permission. The peasants still carried a considerable burden. Until 1906 they paid redemption money arising from the Emancipation of 1861, and even after that other forms of onerous payments. They also paid high taxes, for the government defrayed the interest on its foreign loans from taxes raised at home. The constantly rising export of cereals (also used to pay off debts contracted by Russia in the West) tended to keep food from the farmer's table; many peasants raised the best wheat for sale and ate black bread themselves. The farm population, in short (as in other countries in similar stages of their development), bore a considerable share of the costs of industrialization.

Under such pressures, and because of their crude methods of cultivation, the peasants were forever demanding more land. "Land hunger" was felt both by individual families and by the *mirs*. The Emancipation had turned over roughly half the land to peasant ownership, individual and collective; and in the following half-century the peasants added to their share by buying from nonpeasant owners. The *mirs* were by no means obsolescent. They were in fact flourishing; they acquired far more land by purchase than did individual buyers, and perhaps half or more of the peasants valued communal security above the uncertain pleasures of private property. The exceptions were the minority of more enterprising and wealthier peasants, later called the kulaks. Such a one was Leon Trotsky's father, who, a hard-working, plain, and illiterate man, owned or leased the equivalent of a square mile of land, employed scores of field hands at harvest time, and permanently maintained a large domestic staff. That such a "big farmer" could afford so many employees suggests the poverty in which the bulk of the peasants lived. Not all of the well-to-do peasants were as affluent as Trotsky's father, but the big farmers stood out conspicuously from the mass, by whom they were not liked.

The Emergence of Revolutionary Parties

The peasants were the ancient source of revolutionary disturbance in Russia. Fables about Pugachev and Stephen Razin circulated in peasant legend.[6] After

[5] See pp. 566–567.
[6] See pp. 238, 337–339.

the Emancipation the peasants continued to believe that they had some kind of rights in *all* the land of former estates on which they had formerly been serfs— not merely in the portion that had been allotted to peasant possession. They demanded (and obtained) credit from the government to buy from the big landowners or former masters. Their land hunger could not be appeased. They remained jealous of the landed aristocrat's very existence. In Russia, as elsewhere in Europe, and unlike the United States, the rural population was divided into two sharply distinct classes, on the one hand the peasants of all types, who worked the soil, and on the other the gentry who resided upon it. The two never intermarried. They differed not merely economically but in speech, dress, and manners, and even in the looks of their faces and hands. But in the last three decades of the nineteenth century the Russian peasants were notably quiet, insurrectionism seemingly having subsided.

The other traditional source of revolutionary disturbance lay among the intelligentsia.[7] In the conditions in which the Russian empire had grown up, many of the best and purest spirits were attracted to violence. Revolutionary intelligentsia (as distinguished from those who were simply liberal or progressive) yearned for a catastrophic overthrow of the tsardom. Since the days of the Decembrists[8] they had formed secret organizations, comprising a few hundreds or thousands of members, engaged in outwitting the tsarist police, by whom they were bafflingly interpenetrated. At a Bolshevik party congress held in 1913, out of twenty-two delegates present, no less than five, unknown to the others, were government spies.

The revolutionary intelligentsia, since there was normally little that they could do, spent their time in vehement discussion and interminable refinement of doctrine. By 1890 the terrorism and nihilism of the 1870s were somewhat passé. The great question was where these willing officers of a revolutionary movement could find an army. Disputation turned upon such topics as whether the peasants or the new factory workers were the true revolutionary class, whether the peasants were potentially proletarian or incurably petty bourgeois, whether Russia was bound to experience the same historical process as the West, or whether it was different; and, specifically, whether Russia had to go through capitalism or might simply skip the capitalist stage in reaching the socialist society.

Most of the revolutionary intelligentsia were "populists." Some had once belonged to the now broken People's Will. Some continued to approve of terrorism and assassination as morally necessary in an autocratic country. They generally had a mystical faith in the vast inchoate might of the Russian people, and since most Russians were peasants, the populists were interested in peasant problems and peasant welfare. They believed that a great native revolutionary tradition existed in Russia, of which the peasant rebellion of Pugachev, in 1773, was the chief example.[9] The populists admired the Russian communal village or *mir*, in which they saw the European socialist idea of a "commune" represented. They read and respected Marx and Engels (indeed, a populist first translated the *Communist Manifesto* into Russian); but they did not believe that an urban

---

[7] See pp. 565–566.
[8] See p. 484.
[9] See pp. 337–339.

proletariat was the only true revolutionary class. They did not believe that capitalism, by creating such a proletariat, had inevitably and logically to precede socialism. They said that, in Russia, the horrors of capitalism could be skipped. They addressed themselves to the plight of the farmer and the evils of landlordism, favored strengthening the *mir* and equalizing the shares of all peasants in it, and, since they did not have to wait for the prior triumph of capitalism in Russia, they thought that revolution might come quite soon. This populist sentiment crystallized in the founding in 1901 of the Social Revolutionary party.

Two populists, Plekhanov and Axelrod, fleeing to Switzerland in the 1870s, there became converted to Marxism. In 1883 they founded in exile the organization from which the Russian Social Democratic or Marxist party was to grow. A few Marxists began to declare themselves (though not publicly) in Russia itself. When the youthful Lenin met his future wife Krupskaya in 1894, she already belonged to a circle of argumentative Marxists. The fact that the peasants in the 1890s were disappointingly quiescent, while machine industry, factory labor, and strikes were developing rapidly, turned many of the revolutionary intelligentsia, though only a minority, from populism to Marxism. To Plekhanov and Axelrod were added, as young leaders, Lenin (1870–1924), Trotsky (1879–1940), Stalin (1879–1953), and others.

Of these it was Lenin who, after Marx, was to be claimed by communism as a father. Lenin was a short almost rotund man, with a bounding quickness and intense, penetrating gaze. High cheekbones and somewhat slanting eyes showed an Asiatic strain on the paternal side; Russian friends at first said that he looked "like a Kalmuck." His hair receded in early youth, leaving a massive forehead, behind which a restless mind was inexhaustibly at work. Even in his twenties he was called the Old One. He was of upper-middle-class origin, son of an inspector of schools who rose in the civilian bureaucracy to a rank equivalent to major general. His boyhood was comfortable and even happy, until the age of seventeen, when his elder brother, a student at St. Petersburg, became somewhat incidentally involved in a plot to assassinate Alexander III, for which he was put to death by order of the tsar himself. Because of the blot on the family record it became impossible for Lenin to continue with his law studies. He soon joined the ranks of professional revolutionaries, having no other occupation and living precariously from the party funds, which came mainly from the donations of well-to-do sympathizers.

Arrested as a revolutionary, he spent three years of exile in Siberia. Here the tsarist government treated educated political prisoners with an indulgence not later shown by the Soviet regime. Lenin and most of the others lived in cottages of their own or boarded with local residents. No labor was required of them. They borrowed books from Europe; met and visited with one another; debated, played chess, went hunting, meditated, and wrote. They chafed, however, at being cut off from the mainstream of Russian political life back home. Lenin, his term over, proceeded in 1900 to western Europe, where except for short secret trips to Russia he remained until 1917. His intellectual vigor, irresistible drive, and shrewdness as a tactician soon made him a force in the party. Genius has been called the faculty for everlasting concentration upon one thing. Lenin, said his one-time close associate Axelrod, "for twenty-four hours of the day is taken up with the revolution, has no thoughts but thoughts of revolution, and even in his sleep dreams of nothing but revolution.''

In 1898 the Marxists in Russia, spurred on by émigrés, founded the Social Democratic Labor party. They were not more revolutionary than the larger group of Social Revolutionaries. They simply had a different conception of the revolution. First of all, as good Marxists, they were more inclined to see the revolution as an international movement, part of the dialectical process of world history in which all countries were involved. Russia for them was no different from other countries except that it was less advanced. They expected the world revolution to break out first in western Europe. They particularly admired the German Social Democratic party, the largest and most flourishing of all the parties that acknowledged the fatherhood of Marx.[10]

If the Social Democrats were more oriented to Europe than the Social Revolutionaries, it was because so many of their spokesmen lived there in exile. They tended to think that Russia must develop capitalism, an industrialist proletariat, and the modern form of class struggle before there could be any revolution. Seeing in the urban proletariat the true revolutionary class, they looked upon all peasantry with suspicion, ridiculed the *mir*, and abhorred the Social Revolutionaries. Like Marx himself, the Russian Marxists disapproved of sporadic terrorism and assassination. For this reason, and because their doctrine seemed somewhat academic and their revolution rather conditional and far in th future, the Marxists were for a time actually favored by the tsarist police, wh regarded them as less dangerous than the Social Revolutionaries.

Split in the Social Democrats: Bolsheviks and Mensheviks

The Russian Marxists held a second party congress in Brussels and London in 1903, attended by émigrés like Lenin and delegates from the underground in Russia, and by Social Democrats and members of lesser organizations. The purpose of the congress was to unify all Russian Marxism, but in fact it split it forever. The two resulting factions called themselves Bolshevik, or majority, and Menshevik, or minority. Lenin was the main author of the split and hence the founder of Bolshevism. Although he obtained his majority after one participating organization, the Jewish Bund, had seceded in indignation, and by calling for surprise votes on tactical issues, and although after 1903 it was usually the Mensheviks who had the majority, Lenin clung proudly and stubbornly to the term Bolshevism, with its favorable connotation of a majority in his support. For a number of years after 1903 the Social Democrats remained at least formally a single Marxist party, but they were irreconcilably divided into two wings. In 1912 the Bolshevik wing organized itself as a separate party.

Bolshevism, or Leninism, originally differed from Menshevism mainly on matters of organization and tactics. Russian Marxists referred to each other as ''hards'' and ''softs.'' The ''hards'' were attracted to Lenin, the ''softs'' repelled by him. Lenin believed that the party should be a small revolutionary elite, a hard core of reliable and zealous workers. Those who wished a larger and more

[10] See pp. 615–616, 622–623.

open party, with membership for mere sympathizers, became Mensheviks. Lenin insisted upon a strongly centralized party, without autonomy for national or other component groups. He demanded strong authority at the top, by which the central committee would determine the doctrine (or "party line") and control personnel at all levels of the organization. The Mensheviks favored a greater degree of influence by the membership as a whole. Lenin thought that the party would strengthen itself by purges, expelling all who developed deviations of opinion. The Mensheviks favored covering up or bridging over all but the most fundamental disagreements. The Mensheviks came to recommend cooperation with liberals, progressives, and bourgeois democrats. Lenin regarded such cooperation as purely tactical and temporary, never concealing that in the end the Bolsheviks must impose their views through a dictatorship of the proletariat. The Mensheviks, in short, came to resemble the Marxists of western Europe, so far as that was possible under Russian conditions.[11] Lenin stood for the rigid reaffirmation of Marxian fundamentals—dialectical materialism and irreconcilable class struggle.

If we ask what Leninism added to the original Marxism,[12] the answer is not easy to find. Lenin accepted Marx's governing ideas: that capitalism exploited the workers, that it necessarily produced and preceded socialism, that history was logically predetermined, that class struggle was the law of society, that existing forms of religion, government, philosophy, and morals were weapons of the ruling class. He did, however, develop and transform into a first-rank element of Marxism certain theories of "imperialism" and of the "uneven development of capitalism" that had been propounded in only general terms by Marx and Engels. In the Marxist-Leninist view, "imperialism" was exclusively a product of monopoly capitalism, that is, capitalism in its big business, "highest," and "final" stage, which develops differently and at different times in each country. Monopoly capitalism is bent on exporting surplus capital and investing it in underdeveloped areas for greater profits.[13] The unceasing drive for colonies and markets in a world already almost completely partitioned leads inevitably to international "imperialist" wars for the "redistribution" of colonies, as well as to intensified national colonial struggles for independence; both provide new revolutionary opportunities for the proletariat.

In other respects, Lenin roundly denounced all who attempted to "add" anything to the fundamental principles of Marx. Nothing infuriated him so much as revisionist efforts to tone down the class struggle, or hints that Marxism might in the last analysis perhaps find room for some kind of religion. As he wrote in 1908: "From the philosophy of Marxism, cast of one piece of steel, it is impossible to expunge a single basic premise, a single essential part, without deviating from objective truth, without falling into the arms of bourgeois-reactionary falsehood." Lenin was a convert. He discovered Marxism; he did not invent it. He found in it a theory of revolution which he accepted without reservation as scientific and on which he was more outspokenly dogmatic even than Marx himself. His powers of mind, which were very great, were spent in demonstrating how the unfolding events of the twentieth century confirmed the analysis of the master.

But it was by his powers of will that Lenin was most distinguished, and if

[11] See pp. 622–623.
[12] See pp. 522–526.
[13] See pp. 647–648.

Leninism contributed little to Marxism as a theory it contributed a great deal to it as a movement. Lenin was an activist. He was the supreme agitator, a field commander in the class war, who could dash off a polemical pamphlet, dominate a party congress, or address throngs of workingmen with equal ease. Beside him, Marx and Engels seem almost to be mere recluses or sociologists. Marx and Engels had preferred to believe that the dictatorship of the proletariat, when it came, would represent the wishes of the great majority in a society in which most people had become proletarians. Lenin more frankly foresaw the possibility that the proletarian dictatorship might represent the conscious wishes of a small vanguard and might have to impose itself on great masses by an unshrinking use of force.

Above all, Lenin developed Marx's idea of the role of the party. He drew on the rich experience of pre-Marxist revolutionaries in Russia—the mysterious use of false names, invisible ink, secret ciphers, forged passports, and hidden rendezvous—the whole conspiratorial wonderland which, when it existed to a lesser degree in the West before 1848, drew Marx's scorn and laughter. Lenin's conception of the party was basically Marx's, reinforced by his own experience as a Russian. The party was an organization in which intellectuals provided leadership and understanding for workers, who could not see for themselves. For trade unionism, concerned only with the day-to-day demands of workers, Lenin had even less patience than Marx. "The unconscious growth of the labor movement," he wrote, "takes the form of trade unionism, and trade unionism signifies the mental enslavement of the workers to the bourgeoisie." The task of intellectuals in the party, the elite, or experts, was to make the trade unions and the workers class-conscious and hence revolutionary. Armed with "objective" knowledge, known to be correct, the party leadership naturally could not listen to the subjective opinions of others—the passing ideas of laborers, of peasants, of mistaken party subordinates, or of other parties pretending to know more than Marx himself. The idea that intellectuals supply the brains and workers the brawn, that an elite leads while the toilers meekly follow, is understandable enough in view of the Russian background, which had created on the one hand a painfully self-conscious intelligentsia, and on the other a repressed working class and peasantry deprived of all opportunity for political experience of their own. It was one of the most distinctive traits of Leninism and one of the most foreign to the democratic movement of the West.

Leninism accomplished the marriage of Russian revolutionary traditions with the Western doctrine of Marxism. It was an improbable marriage, whose momentous offspring was to be communism. But at the time, when Bolshevism first appeared in 1903, it had little or no effect. A real revolution broke out in Russia in 1905. It took the revolutionary émigrés almost entirely by surprise.

92. The Revolution of 1905

Background and Revolutionary Events

The almost simultaneous founding at the turn of the century of the Constitutional Democratic, Social Revolutionary, and Social Democratic parties was clearly a sign of mounting discontent. None of these was as yet a party in the Western sense, organized to get candidates elected to office, for there were no elections in Russia above the provincial zemstvo level. All three parties were propaganda agencies, made up of leaders without followers, intellectuals who followed various lines of thought. All, even those who became Constitutional Democrats, were watched by the police and obliged to do most of their work underground. At the same time, after 1900, there were signs of growing popular unrest. Peasants were trespassing on lands of the gentry and even rising in local insurrections against landlords and tax collectors. Factory workers sporadically refused to work. But with these popular movements none of the new parties had formed any solid links.

The government refused to make concessions of any kind. The tsar, Nicholas II, who had mounted the throne in 1894, was a man of narrow outlook. To the Little Father all criticism seemed merely childish. Tutored in his youth by Pobiedonostsev,[14] he regarded all ideas questioning autocracy, Orthodoxy, and Great Russian nationalism as un-Russian. That persons in the government should be controlled by interests outside the government—the mildest liberalism or most orderly democracy—seemed to the tsar, the tsarina, and the leading officials to be a monstrous aberration. Autocracy, for them, was the best and only, as it was the God-given, form of government for Russia.

The chief minister, Plehve, and the circles at court, hoped that a short successful war with Japan would create more attachment to the government. The war went so badly that its effect was the reverse.[15] Critics of the regime (except for the handful of the most internationalist Marxists) were sufficiently patriotic to be ashamed at the ease with which Russia was defeated by an upstart and Asian power. As after the Crimean War, there was a general feeling that the government had exposed its incompetence to all the world. Liberals believed that its secret methods, its immunity to criticism or control, had made it sluggish, torpid, obstinate, and inefficient, unable either to win a war or to lead the economic modernization that was taking place in Russia. But there was little that the liberals could do.

The police had recently allowed a priest, Father Gapon, to go among the St. Petersburg factory workers and organize them, hoping thus to counter the propaganda of revolutionaries. Father Gapon took up their grievances in all seriousness. They believed, as simple peasants only recently transplanted to the city, that if only they could reach the ear of the Little Father, the august being high above all hard capitalists and stony officials, he would hear their complaints with shocked surprise and rectify the evils that afflicted Russia. They drew up a petition, asking for an eight-hour day, a minimum daily wage of one ruble (fifty cents), a repudiaton of bungling bureaucrats, and a democratically elected Constituent Assembly to introduce representative government into the empire. Unarmed, peaceable, respectful, singing "God save the Tsar," a crowd of 200,000—men, women, and children—gathered before the tsar's Winter Palace one Sunday in January 1905. But the tsar was not in the city, and his officials

[14] See p. 734.
[15] See pp. 681–682.

were afraid. Troops marched up and shot down the demonstrators in cold blood, killing several hundred.

"Bloody Sunday" in St. Petersburg snapped the moral bond upon which all stable government rests. The horrified workers saw that the tsar was not their friend. The autocracy stood revealed as the force behind the hated officials, the tax collectors, the landlords, and the owners of the industrial plants. A wave of political strikes broke out. Social Democrats (more Mensheviks than Bolsheviks) appeared from the underground or from exile to give revolutionary direction to these movements. Councils or "soviets" of workers were formed in Moscow and St. Petersburg. The peasants, too, in many parts of the country spontaneously began to erupt, overrunning the lands of the gentry, burning manor houses and doing violence to their owners. Social revolutionaries naturally tried to take this movement in charge. The liberal Constitutional Democrats, professors, engineers, business people, lawyers, leaders in the provincial zemstvos founded forty years before, tried also to seize leadership or at least use the crisis to force the government's hand. All agreed on one demand—that there should be more democratic representation in the government.

The tsar yielded grudgingly and as little as possible. In March 1905 he promised to call to office men "enjoying the confidence of the nation." In August (after the ruinous battle of Tsushima) he agreed to call a kind of Estates General, for which peasants, landowners, and city people should vote as separate classes. Still the revolution raged unchecked. The St. Petersburg Soviet, or workers' council, led mainly by Mensheviks (Lenin had not yet reached Russia), declared a great general strike in October. Railroads stopped, banks closed, newspapers ceased to appear, and even lawyers refused to go to their offices. The strike spread to other cities and to the peasants. With the government paralyzed, the tsar issued his October Manifesto. It promised a constitution, civil liberties, and a Duma to be elected by all classes alike, with powers to enact laws and control the administration.

The tsar and his advisers intended to divide the opposition by releasing the October Manifesto, and in this they succeeded. The Constitutional Democrats, with a Duma promised, allowed themselves to hope that social problems could henceforth be dealt with by parliamentary methods. Liberals were now afraid of revolutionaries, industrialists feared the strength shown by labor in the general strike, and landowners demanded a restoration of order among the peasants. Aroused peasants and workers were not yet satisfied: the former still wanted more land and less taxation, the latter a shorter working day and a living wage. The several branches of revolutionary intellectuals worked upon the continuing popular agitation, hoping to carry matters forward until the tsarist monarchy was abolished and a socialist republic established with themselves at its head. They believed also (and correctly) that the October Manifesto was in any case a deception, which the tsar would refuse to adhere to as soon as revolutionary pressure was removed. The soviets continued to seethe, local strikes went on, and there were mutinies among soldiers at Kronstadt and sailors in the Black Sea fleet.

But the government was able to maintain itself. With the middle-class liberals now inactive or demanding order, the authorities arrested the members of the St.

Petersburg Soviet. Peace was hastily made with Japan, and reliable troop units were recalled from the Far East. The revolutionary leaders fled back to Europe, or again went underground, or were caught and sent to prison or to Siberia; executions were carried out in the countryside.

The Results of 1905: The Duma

The chief apparent result of the Revolution of 1905 was to make Russia, at least ostensibly, into a parliamentary type of state, like the rest of Europe. The promised Duma was convoked. For ten years, from 1906 to 1916, Russia had at least the superficial attributes of a semiconstitutional monarchy.

But Nicholas II soon showed that he did not intend to yield much. He drew the teeth of the new Duma before the creature could even be born, by announcing in advance, in 1906, that it would have no power over foreign policy, the budget, or government personnel. His attitude toward constitutional monarchy continued until 1917 to be entirely negative; the one thing that tsarism would not allow was any real participation in government by the public. Within this "public" the two extreme fringes were equally impervious to liberal constitutionalism. On the right, stubborn upholders of pure autocracy and the Orthodox church organized the Black Hundreds, terrorizing the peasantry and urging them to boycott the Duma. On the left, in 1906, the Social Revolutionaries and both the Bolshevik and Menshevik wings of the Social Democrats likewise refused to recognize the Duma, urged workers to boycott it, and refused to put up any candidates for election.

The short-lived first Duma was elected in 1906 by a system of indirect and unequal voting, in which peasants and workers voted as separate classes, and with proportionately far less representation than was granted to the landlords. In the absence of socialist candidates, workers and peasants voted for all sorts of people, including the liberal Constitutional Democrats (the "Cadets"), who obtained a sweeping majority. The Cadets, when the Duma met, found themselves still fighting for the bare principle of constitutional government. They demanded true universal male suffrage and the responsibility of ministers to a parliamentary majority. The tsar's response was to dismiss the Duma after two months. The Cadets fled to Viborg in autonomous Finland, which the tsarist police generally let alone. It is significant that these constitutional liberals and democrats, in council at Viborg, again appealed for a general strike and nonpayment of taxes—that is, for mass revolution. But real revolutions are not easy to start, and nothing happened.

A second Duma was elected in 1907, with the government trying to control the elections through suppression of party meetings and newspapers, but since Social Revolutionaries and Mensheviks now consented to take part, some eighty-three socialists were elected. The Cadets, becoming fearful of the revolutionary left, concluded that constitutional progress must be gradual and showed a willingness to cooperate with the government. But the Duma came to an abrupt end when the government denounced and arrested some fifty socialists as revolutionaries bent only on destruction. A third Duma, elected after an electoral change that gave increased representation to the landed propertied class and guaranteed a conservative majority, managed to hold several sessions between

1907 and 1912, as did a fourth Duma from 1912 to 1916. The deputies, by following the lead of the government, by addressing themselves only to concrete issues, by losing themselves in committee work, and by avoiding the basic question of where supreme power lay, kept precariously alive a modicum of parliamentary institutions in the tsarist empire.

The Stolypin Reforms

Some officials believed that the way to checkmate the revolutionaries, and strengthen the hold of the monarchy, was for the government, while keeping all controls in its own hands, to attract the support of reasonable and moderate people by a program of reforms. One of these was Peter Stolypin, whom the tsar retained as his principal minister from 1906 to 1911. It was Stolypin who dissolved the first two Dumas. But it was not his policy merely to stand still. His aim was to build up the propertied classes as friends of the state. He believed, perhaps rightly, that a state actively supported by widespread private property had little to fear from doctrinaire intellectuals, conspirators, and émigrés. He therefore favored and broadened the powers of the provincial zemstvos, in which the larger landowners took part in administering local affairs. For the peasantry he put through legislation more sweeping than any since the Emancipation.

Seeing in the *mir* the source of communal agrarian restlessness, Stolypin hoped to replace this ancient institution with a regime of private individual property. He abolished what was left of the redemption payments for which the *mirs* had been collectively responsible.[16] He allowed each peasant to sell his share of the communal rights and to leave the commune at will. He authorized peasants to buy land freely from the communes, from each other, or from the gentry. He thus favored the rise of the class of "big farmers," the later kulaks, who obtained control of large tracts, worked them with hired help, and produced cash crops for the market. At the same time, by allowing peasants to sell out and leave the *mir* (it would generally be the worst farmers or most improvident persons who did so), he hastened the formation of a migratory wage-earning class, which would either seek work from the big farmers or go off to take jobs in the city. The creation of a mobile labor force, and of a food supply raised by big farmers for the market, would thus advance the industrialization of Russia.

The Stolypin policy was successful. Between 1907 and 1916, 6.2 million families out of 16 million who were eligible applied for legal separation from the *mir*. There was no mistaking the trend toward individual property and independent farming. But the results of the Stolypin program must not be exaggerated. The *mir* was far from broken. A vast majority of peasants were still involved in the old system of common rights and communal restrictions. The land shortage was still acute in the agricultural areas where yields were highest. Land hunger and poverty continued in the countryside. There were kulaks, to be sure, to be resented and envied, but the largest landed proprietors were still the gentry. About 30,000 landlords owned nearly 200 million acres of land, and another 200 million acres made up other large landed estates.

Stolypin was not left long to carry on his program. The tsar gave him only an

---

[16] See pp. 566–567.

unwilling support. Reactionary circles disliked his tampering ways and his Western orientation. Social Revolutionaries naturally cried out against dissolution of the communes. Even Marxists, who should in theory have applauded the advance of capitalism in Russia, feared that Stolypin's reforms might do away with agrarian discontent. "I do not expect to live to see the revolution," said Lenin in these years. Stolypin was shot dead while attending the theater in Kiev, in the presence of the tsar and tsarina, in 1911. The assassin, a member of the terrorist wing of the Social Revolutionaries, is thought also to have been a secret agent of the reactionary tsarist police. It may be added that Stolypin's predecessor, Plehve, and about a dozen other high officials within the past few years had similarly died at the hands of assassins.

But all in all, violent and half barbaric though it still was, the Russian empire on the eve of the First World War was moving in a Western direction. Its industries were growing, its railways expanding, its exports almost half as great in value as those of the United States. It had a parliament, if not a parliamentary government. Private property and individualist capitalism were spreading to new layers of the people. There was a guarded freedom of the press, illustrated, for example, by the legal and open establishment of the Bolshevik party paper, *Pravda*, in St. Petersburg in 1912. It is not possible to say how far this development might have gone, for it was menaced on both the right and the left by obstinate and obscurantist reactionaries upholding the absolute tsardom and by revolutionaries whom nothing but the end of tsardom and wholesale transformation of society could appease. But both extremes were discouraged. The desperation of extreme reactionaries in the government, the feeling that they might in any case soon lose their position, perhaps made them the more willing to precipitate a European war by armed support of Serbian nationalists. As for the revolutionary parties, and especially the Bolsheviks, they were losing in membership on the eve of the war, their leaders lived year after year in exile, dreaming of the great days of 1905 which stubbornly failed to repeat themselves and sometimes pessimistically admitting, as Lenin did, that there might be no revolution in their time.

93. The Revolution of 1917

End of the Tsardom: The Revolution of March 1917

War again put the tsarist regime to a test that it could not meet. In this war, more total than any had ever been, willing cooperation between government and people was indispensable to success. This essential prerequisite the tsarist empire did not have. National minorities, Poles, Ukrainians, the peoples of the Caucasus, Jews, and others, were disaffected. As for the socialists, who in every other European parliament voted for funds to finance the war, the dozen otherwise disunited socialists in the Duma refused to do so and were promptly jailed.[17] The ordinary worker and peasant marched off with the army, but without the sense

[17] See p. 772.

of personal conviction felt by common people in Germany and the West. More decisive was the attitude of the middle class. Because they patriotically wished Russia to win, the glaring mismanagement of the government was the more intolerable to them. The disasters with which the war opened in 1914, at Tannenberg and the Masurian Lakes, were followed by the advance of the Central Powers into Russia in 1915, at the cost of 2 million Russian soldiers killed, wounded, or captured.[18]

At the war's outbreak middle-class people, as in all countries, offered their assistance to the government.[19] The provincial zemstvos formed a union of all zemstvos in the empire to facilitate the mobilization of agriculture and industry. Business groups at Petrograd (St. Petersburg lost its Germanic name at this time) formed a Commercial and Industrial Committee to get the factories into maximum production. The government distrusted these signs of public activity arising outside official circles. On the other hand, organized in this way, middle-class people became conscious of their own strength and more critical of the bureaucracy. Rumors spread that some officials in the war ministry itself were pro-German, reactionaries who feared the liberalism of England and France, with which Russia was allied.

Life at court was bizarre even for Russia. The tsarina Alexandra, German by origin, looked upon all Russians outside her own circle with contempt, incited her husband to play the proud and pitiless autocrat, and took advice from a self-appointed holy man, the mysterious Rasputin. She was convinced that Rasputin possessed supernatural and prophetic powers, because he had apparently cured her young son, the tsarevitch, of hemophilia. Rasputin, by his influence over her, had a voice in appointments to high office. All who wished an audience with the imperial pair had to go through him. Patriotic and enlightened persons of all classes vainly protested. In these circumstances, and given the military defeats, the union of zemstvos and other such war-born bodies complained not merely of faults of administration but of fundamental conditions in the state. The government responded by holding them at arm's length. The tsarist regime, caught in a total war, was afraid of the help offered by its own people.

During the war, in September 1915, the Duma was suspended. It was known that reactionaries—inspired by the tsarina, Rasputin, and other sinister forces—expected that a victory in the war would make it possible to kill liberalism and constitutionalism in Russia. The war thus revived all the basic political issues that had been latent since the Revolution of 1905. The union of zemstvos demanded the assembly of the Duma. The Duma reassembled in November 1916 and, conservative though it had always been, expressed loud indignation at the way affairs were conducted. Among all elements of the population, dissatisfaction with the course of the war and with the government's ineptitude mounted. In December Rasputin was assassinated by nobles at the court. The tsar began to consider repression and again adjourned the Duma. Machine guns were issued to the police. Members of the Duma, and of the new extragovernmental bodies, concluded that the situation could be saved only by force. It is when moderate persons, normally concerned with their own business, come to such conclusions

[18] See p. 707.
[19] See pp. 718–721.

that revolution becomes a political possibility. The shift of moderates and liberals, their need of a coup d'état to save themselves from reactionaries, likewise raised the long failing prospects of the minority of professional revolutionaries.

Again it was the workers of Petrograd who precipitated the crisis. Food had become scarce, as in all the belligerent countries. But the tsarist administration was too clumsy and too demoralized by graft to institute the controls that had become usual elsewhere, such as maximum prices and ration cards. It was the poorest who felt the food shortage most keenly. On March 8, 1917, food riots broke out, which soon developed, doubtless with the help of revolutionary intellectuals, into political insurrection. Crowds shouted, "Down with the tsar!" Troops within the city refused to fire on the insurgents; mutiny and insubordination spread from unit to unit. Within a few days a Soviet of Workers' and Soldiers' Deputies, on the model of 1905, had been organized in Petrograd.

Middle-class leaders, with the government now helpless, demanded dismissal of the ministry and formation of a new one commanding the confidence of a majority of the Duma. The tsar retaliated by disbanding the Duma. The Duma set up an executive committee to take charge until the situation clarified. There were now two new authorities in the city: one, the Duma committee, essentially moderate, constitutionalist, and relatively legal; the other, the Petrograd Soviet, representing revolutionary forces arising by spontaneous upsurge from below. The Petrograd Soviet (or workers' "council") was to play in 1917 a role like that of the Paris Commune of 1792, constantly pushing the supposedly higher and more nationwide authority to the left. The Soviet became the public auditorium and administrative center of the working-class upheaval. Since it was generally socialist in its outlook, all the factions of doctrinaire socialists—Social Revolutionaries, Mensheviks, Bolsheviks—tried to win it over and utilize it for their own ends.

The Duma committee, under pressure from the Petrograd Soviet, on March 14 set up a Provisional Government under Prince Lvov. The Duma liberals, as a concession to the Soviet, admitted one socialist to the new government, Alexander Kerensky, a moderate, legal-minded Social Revolutionary, and they furthermore consented to demand the abdication of Nicholas II. The tsar was then at the front. He tried to return to his palace near Petrograd, but the imperial train was stopped and turned back by troops. The army, fatefully, was taking the side of the Revolution. The very generals in the field, unable to vouch for the loyalty of their men, advised abdication. Nicholas yielded; his brother the grand duke declined to succeed him; and on March 17, 1917, Russia became a republic.

The Bolshevik Revolution: November 1917

The Provisional Government, following the best precedents of European revolutions, called for elections by universal male suffrage to a Constituent Assembly, which was to meet late in the year and prepare a constitution for the new regime. It tried also to continue the war against Germany. In July an offensive was mounted but the demoralized armies were quickly routed. Pending final decision by the Constituent Assembly, the Provisional Government promised wholesale redistribution of land to the peasants but took no action. Meanwhile, the peasants, driven by the old land hunger, were already overrunning the rural districts, burning and looting. At the front the armies melted away; many high officers refused to serve the republic, and masses of peasant soldiers simply turned their backs and went home, unwilling to be absent while land was being handed out. The Petrograd Soviet, opposing the Provisional Government, called for speedy termination of the war. Fearing reactionary officers, it issued on March 14 its Order No. 1, entrusting command within the army to committees elected by both officers and soldiers. Discipline collapsed.

The Revolution was thus already well advanced when Lenin and the other Bolsheviks arrived in Petrograd in the middle of April.[20] They immediately took sides with the Petrograd Soviet against the Provisional Government, and with similar soviets that had sprung up in other parts of the country. In July an armed uprising of soldiers and sailors, which the Bolshevik central committee disapproved of as premature, was put down. The Bolsheviks were blamed, and Lenin had to flee to Finland. But as a bid for popular support the Provisional Government named the socialist Kerensky as its head in place of Prince Lvov in an uneasy coalition of moderate socialists and liberals. Kerensky's middle position was next threatened from the right. The newly appointed military commander, General Kornilov, dispatched a force of cavalry to restore order. Not only conservatives but liberals wished him success in the hope that he would suppress the soviets. Kornilov's movement was defeated, but with the aid of the Bolsheviks, who rallied with other socialists, and of revolutionary-minded soldiers in the city who offered armed resistance. Radicals denounced liberals as accomplices in Kornilov's attempt at counterrevolution, and both camps blamed Kerensky for having allowed the plot to be hatched under his government. Both liberals and moderate socialists abandoned Kerensky, and he had to form a government of uncertain political support. Meanwhile the food shortage worsened, with transport disarranged and the farm population in turmoil, so that workers in the city listened more willingly to the most extreme speakers.

The Bolsheviks adapted their program to what the most aroused elements in a revolutionary people seemed to want. Lenin concentrated on four points: first, immediate peace with the Central Powers; second, redistribution of land to the peasants; third, transfer of factories, mines, and other industrial plants from the capitalists to committees of workers in each plant; and, fourth, recognition of the soviets as the supreme power instead of the Provisional Government. Lenin, though a rigid dogmatist on abstract questions, was a flexible and bold tactician and his program in 1917 was dictated more by the immediate situation in Russia than by considerations of theoretical Marxism. What was needed was to win over soldiers, peasants, and workers by promising them "peace, land, and bread." With this program, and by infiltration and parliamentary stratagems, as well as by their accuracy as political prophets—predicting the Kornilov counterrevolution and "unmasking" the trend of middle-way liberals to support it—the Bolsheviks won a majority in the Petrograd Soviet and in soviets all over the country.

Lenin thereupon raised the cry, "All power to the Soviets!" to crush Kerensky and forestall the coming Constituent Assembly. Kerensky, to broaden the base on which he stood, and unable to wait for the Constituent Assembly, convoked a kind of preparliament representing all parties, labor unions, and zemstvos.

[20] See pp. 713, 737–741.

Lenin and the Bolsheviks boycotted his preparliament. Instead they called an all-Russian Congress of Soviets.

Lenin now judged that the hour had come for the seizure of power. The Bolsheviks themselves were divided, many like Zino iev and Kamenev opposing the move, but Lenin was backed by Trotsky, Stalin, and a majority of the party Central Committee. Troops garrisoned in Petrograd voted to support the soviets, which the Bolsheviks now controlled. On the night of November 6–7, 1917, the Bolsheviks took over telephone exchanges, railway stations, and electric power plants in the city. A warship turned its guns on the Winter Palace, where Kerensky's government sat. The latter could find almost no one to defend it. The hastily assembled Congress of Soviets pronounced the Provisional Government defunct and named in its place a Council of People's Commissars, of which Lenin became the head. Trotsky was named commissar for foreign affairs, Stalin commissar for nationalities. Kerensky fled, eventually arriving in the United States, where he lived until 1970.

At the Congress of Soviets Lenin introduced two resolutions. One called upon the belligerent governments to negotiate a "just democratic peace," without annexations and without indemnities; the second "abolished all landlord property" immediately and without compensation. Although determined to establish a proletarian dictatorship, the Bolsheviks knew the importance of the Russian peasants. The millions of acres belonging to the large estates that were now expropriated provided a base of support for the new regime without which it could hardly have survived.

Thus was accomplished the Bolshevik or November Revolution.[21] But the long awaited Constituent Assembly remained to be dealt with. It met in January 1918. Thirty-six million persons had voted for it. Of these, 9 million had voted for Bolshevik deputies, showing that the Bolshevik program, launched less than a year before by a small band of émigrés, had a widespread mass appeal. But almost 21 million had voted for Kerensky's party, the agrarian, populist, peasant-oriented Social Revolutionaries. However, said Lenin, "to hand over power to the Constituent Assembly would again be compromising with the malignant bourgeoisie." The Assembly was broken up on the second day of its sessions; armed sailors dispatched by the people's commissars simply surrounded it. The dissolution of the Constituent Assembly was a frank repudiation of majority rule in favor of "class rule"—to be exercised for the proletariat by the Bolsheviks. The dictatorship of the proletariat was now established. Two months later, in March 1918, the Bolsheviks renamed themselves the Communist party.

The New Regime: The Civil War, 1918–1922

In these same months, the Communists, or Bolsheviks, signed the peace of Brest-Litovsk with Germany, surrendering to Germany control over the Baltic provinces, Poland, and the Ukraine.[22] The conquests of two centuries were thus abandoned; not since the days of Peter the Great had the Russian frontier been so far from

---

[21] Also known as the October Revolution, since according to the Julian calendar, used in Russia until 1918, the events described took place in October.
[22] See p. 713.

central Europe. To Lenin it made no difference. He was convinced that the events that he had just mastered in Russia were the prelude to a general upheaval; that the war, still raging in the west, would bring all Europe to the inevitable proletarian or Marxist revolution; that Imperial Germany was therefore doomed; and that Poles, Ukrainians, and others would soon emerge, like the Germans themselves, as free socialist peoples. In any case, it was largely by promising peace that Lenin had won enough backing to overthrow Kerensky, who on this deep popular demand had delayed too long, waiting for England and France to release Russia from its treaty obligations as an ally. But real peace did not come, for the country sank immediately into civil war.

Not only old tsarist reactionaries, and not only liberals, bourgeois, zemstvo members, and Constitutional Democrats, but all types of anti-Leninist socialists as well, Mensheviks and Social Revolutionaries, scattered in all directions to organize resistance against the regime of soviets and people's commissars, and they obtained aid from the Western Allies. Both sides competed for the support of the peasants.

As for the new regime, the oldest of its institutions was the party, founded as a wing of the Social Democrats in 1903; the next oldest were the soviets, dating from 1905 and 1917; and then came the Council of People's Commissars set up on the day of the coup d'état. The first institution founded under the new order was a political police, an Extraordinary All-Russian Commission of Struggle Against Counterrevolution, Speculation, and Sabotage, commonly known from its Russian initials as the Cheka and in later years, without basic change of methods or purpose, under such successive names as the OGPU, the NKVD, the MVD, and the KGB. It was established on December 7, 1917. In January 1918 the Red Army was founded, with Leon Trotsky as war commissar and virtually its creator. In July a constitution was promulgated.

In social policy the Bolsheviks at first adopted no long-range plans, contenting themselves with a mixture of principle and expediency known as "war communism." They nationalized some of the largest industrial enterprises but left the bulk under the control of workers' committees. The pressing problem was to find food, which had ceased to move through any normal channels. The peasants, very much as in the French Revolution under similar conditions—worthless money, insecure property titles, unruly hired hands, armed marauding, and a doubtful future—were producing less food than usual, consuming it themselves, or hoarding it on their own farms. The response of the government and city workers was also much as in 1793. The new government levied requisitions, required the peasants to make stated "deliveries," and invited labor unions to send armed detachments into the country to procure food by force. Since it was naturally the big farmers who had the surplus, they came into disrepute as starvers of the people. Class war broke out, rabid, ferocious, and elemental, between farmers who feared that their very subsistence as well as their property would be taken away, and city people, often supported by hungry agricultural laborers, who were driven to desperation by famine. Many peasants, especially the larger farmers, therefore rallied to anti-Bolshevik political leaders.

Centers of resistance developed on every side. In the Don valley a small force assembled under Generals Kornilov and Denikin, with many army officers, gentry landowners, and expropriated business people taking part in it. The Social

Revolutionaries gathered followers on the middle Volga. In the spring of 1918 Georgia, Armenia, and Azerbaijan in the Caucasus, all proclaimed their independence. At Omsk a disaffected group proclaimed the independence of Siberia. As a military organization the most significant was a force of some 45,000 Czechs, who had deserted or been captured from the Austro-Hungarian armies and had then been organized as a Czech Legion to fight on the side of Russia and the Allies. After the November Revolution and the peace of Brest-Litovsk, these Czechs decided to leave Russia by way of the Trans-Siberian Railroad, return to Europe by sea, and resume fighting on the Western Front. When Bolshevik officials undertook to disarm them they allied with the Social Revolutionaries on the Volga.

The Allied governments believed that Bolshevism was a temporary madness that with a little effort could be stopped. They wished above all to bring Russia back into the war against Germany. So long as the war in Europe lasted, they could not reach Russia by the Black or Baltic Sea. A small Allied force took Murmansk and Archangel in the north. But for Allied military intervention the best opening was in the Far East, through Vladivostok. The Japanese, who had declined military aid to their Allies in any other theater, received this proposal with enthusiasm, seeing in the ruin of the Russian empire a rare opportunity to develop their sphere of influence in East Asia. It was agreed that an interallied military force should land at Vladivostok, cross Siberia, join with the Czechs, break up Bolshevism, and fall upon the Germans in eastern Europe. For this ambitious scheme Britain and France could supply no soldiers, engaged as they were on the Western Front; the force turned out to be American and Japanese, or rather almost purely Japanese, since Japan contributed 72,000 men and the United States only 8,000. They landed at Vladivostok in August 1918.

The civil war lasted until 1920, or even later in some places. It became a confused melee in which the Bolsheviks struggled against Russian opponents, independence-minded nationalities, and foreign intervention. The Red Army fought in the Ukraine first against the Germans, and then against the French, who occupied Odessa as soon as the war ended in Europe. It reconquered the Ukraine, Armenia, Georgia, and Azerbaijan, which had declared their independence; put to flight a hundred thousand "Whites," as the counterrevolution-aries were called, under Wrangel in the south; and fought off Admiral Kolchak, who in Siberia proclaimed himself ruler of all Russia. In 1920, the Bolsheviks carried on a war with the new republic of Poland, which was scarcely organized when it set out to recover the huge Ukrainian and Byelorussian territories that had been Polish before 1772.[23] British, French, and American troops remained at Archangel until the end of 1919, the Japanese at Vladivostok until the end of 1922.

But the anti-Bolshevik forces could never unite. The anti-Communist Russians represented every hue of the political spectrum from unregenerate tsarists to left-wing Social Revolutionaries. Many of the rightist anti-Bolsheviks openly antagonized the peasants by proceeding to restore expropriated landed estates in areas they occupied; many engaged in vindictive reprisals in a kind of "white terror." The Allies themselves could not agree; the French sent troops to the

[23] See map, p. 248.

Ukraine and gave aid to the Poles, but the British and Americans wanted to be rid of all military entanglements as soon as the armistice with Germany was signed. Leon Trotsky, on the other hand, forged in the crucible of the civil wars the hard and solid metal of the Red Army, recruiting it, organizing it, restoring its discipline, equipping it as best he could, assigning political commissars to watch it, and assuring that trustworthy officers occupied its high command. The Bolsheviks could denounce the foreign intervention and appeal to national patriotism; and they could win peasant support by the distribution of land. By 1922 the Bolsheviks, or Communists, had established themselves up to the frontiers of the former tsarist empire in every direction except on the European side. There the band of Baltic states—Finland, Estonia, Latvia, and Lithuania— remained independent; Romania had acquired Bessarabia, the new Romanian frontier reaching now almost to Odessa; and Poland, as a result of the war of 1920, retained a frontier farther east than the Allies themselves had intended. Russia had lost thousands of square miles of territory and buffer areas acquired over the centuries by the tsars.[24] They remained lost until the Second World War. But peace was won and the regime stood.

It was during these civil wars that the Red Terror broke out in Russia. Like the famous Terror in France in 1793, it was in part a response to civil and foreign war. Before the Bolshevik Terror, the old Jacobin Terror paled. They differed as the cruelty and violence endemic in the old Russia differed from the more humane or law-abiding habits of western Europe. Thousands were shot merely as hostages (a practice unknown to Europe for some centuries); and other thousands without even the summary formalities of revolutionary tribunals. The Cheka was the most formidable political police that had yet appeared. The Bolshevik Terror was aimed at the physical extermination of all who opposed the new regime. A bourgeois class background would go far to confirm the guilt of the person charged with conspiring against the Soviet state. As a chief of the Cheka said: "The first questions you should put to the accused person are, To what class does he belong, what is his origin, what was his education, and what is his profession? These should determine the fate of the accused. This is the essence of the Red Terror." But a working-class background for a man or a woman made little difference. In 1918 a young woman named Fanny Kaplan shot at Lenin and wounded him. She deposed that she had favored the Constituent Assembly, that her parents had emigrated to America in 1911, that she had six working-class brothers and sisters; and she admitted that she had intended to kill Lenin. She was of course executed, as were others in Petrograd. When the sailors at Kronstadt, who were among the first adherents of the Bolsheviks, rose in 1921, objecting to domination of the soviets by the party (threatening a kind of leftist renewal of the revolution, like the Hébertists who had opposed Robespierre), they were branded as petty-bourgeois and shot down by the thousands. The Terror struck at the revolutionists themselves quite as much as it did the bourgeoisie; it was to continue to do so long after the Revolution was secure.

The Terror succeeded in its purpose. Together with the victories of the Red Army, it established the new regime. Those "bourgeois" who survived took on the protective coloration of "toilers." No bourgeois as such presumed to take

---

[24] See p. 726 and map on pp. 728–729.

part in the politics of Russia. Mensheviks and other socialists fleeing to Europe told appalling stories of the human toll taken by Lenin. Horrified European socialists repudiated communism as an atrocious, Byzantine, Asiatic perversion of Marxism. But, at whatever cost, Lenin and his followers were now able to start building the socialist society as they understood it.

94. The Union of Soviet Socialist Republics

Government: The Nationalities and Federalism

With the end of the civil wars and foreign intervention, and with the termination of the war with Poland, it became possible in 1922 to establish the Union of Soviet Socialist Republics. Its first members were four in number: The Russian Soviet Federated Socialist Republic (which extended to Siberia and the Pacific), the Ukrainian Soviet Socialist Republic, the Byelorussian (or White Russian, i.e., ethnic White Russian) Soviet Socialist Republic, and the Transcaucasian Soviet Federated Socialist Republic (which united the reconquered Caucasus republics of Georgia, Armenia, and Azerbaijan).[25] In the new Union, which geographically replaced the old Russian empire, the name Russia was not officially used. The

---

[25] The original Russian and Transcaucasian federated republics were subsequently reorganized to create additional republics so that there were eleven in number. Out of the Transcaucasian republic emerged the Georgian, Armenian, and Azerbaijan Soviet Socialist Republics; out of the Russian S.F.S.R. were created five republics in central Asia: the Uzbek, Turkmen, Tadzhik, Kazakh, and Kirghiz S.S.R.'s. After the outbreak of the Second World War the U.S.S.R. occupied and sovietized adjoining territory and created five additional soviet republics (one of them, the Karelo-Finnish, lost that status in 1956). For the fifteen soviet republics the population figures for 1940 and 1989 were as follows:

	1940	1989
Russian S.F.S.R.	109,000,000	147,000,000
Ukrainian S.S.R.	40,000,000	51,700,000
Byelorussian (White Russian) S.S.R.	10,000,000	10,200,000
Armenian S.S.R.	1,250,000	3,300,000
Georgian S.S.R.	3,500,000	5,500,000
Azerbaijan S.S.R.	3,200,000	7,000,000
Uzbek S.S.R.	6,300,000	19,900,000
Turkmen S.S.R.	1,200,000	3,500,000
Tadzhik S.S.R.	1,500,000	5,100,000
Kazakh S.S.R.	6,100,000	16,500,000
Kirghiz S.S.R.	1,500,000	4,300,000
ADDED IN 1940:		
Karelo-Finnish S.S.R.	500,000	——
Moldavian S.S.R.	2,500,000	4,300,000
Lithuanian S.S.R.	2,900,000	3,700,000
Latvian S.S.R.	2,000,000	2,700,000
Estonian S.S.R.	1,100,000	1,600,000
TOTAL U.S.S.R.	192,550,000	286,300,000

It will be seen that the Russian and the other two Slavic republics (the Ukrainian and the Byelorussian) have grown in half a century by scarcely one-third, while the others (except the three Baltic republics) have more than doubled in population. Though the Russians remain by far the most numerous, the trend has been toward a greater weight for the Asian (and Islamic) elements in the Soviet Union. See also below, p. 1006.

guiding conception was a blend of the national and the international: to recognize nationality by granting autonomy to national groups, while holding these groups together in a higher union and allowing new groups to enter regardless of historic frontiers. In 1922 the expectation of world revolution was still alive. The constitution, formally adopted in 1924, pronounced the founding of the U.S.S.R. to be "a decisive step by way of uniting the workers of all countries into one World Soviet Socialist Republic." It made the Union, in principle, fluid and expansible, declared that any member republic might secede (none to this date has peacefully) and that newly formed soviet socialist republics might join (none ever did voluntarily). When after the outbreak of the Second World War the U.S.S.R. occupied contiguous territories (once part of the tsarist empire)— the three Baltic states, Estonia, Latvia, and Lithuania, after two decades of independence; Bessarabia, detached from Romania; and Karelia, taken from Finland after the Russo-Finnish War—these territories were added to the U.S.S.R. in 1940 as soviet socialist republics. Bessarabia became the Moldavian S.S.R., and Karelia temporarily, from 1940 to 1956, had the status of a Karelo-Finnish S.S.R.

The federal principle in the U.S.S.R. was designed to answer the problem of nationalism. The tsardom, in its last decades, had tried to deal with this problem by systematic Russification. The nationalities had resisted, and nationalist discontent had been one of the forces fatally weakening the empire. Nationalism, or the demand that national groups should have their own political sovereignty, had not only broken up the Austro-Hungarian empire but "Balkanized" central and eastern Europe. This might have happened after 1917 in Russia except for the fact that the Red Army during the civil wars occupied large parts of the tsarist empire which had broken away and declared their independence. As it turned out, in 1922 the U.S.S.R. occupied a sixth of the world's land area and was adjoined on the west by a Europe which in one twenty-seventh of the world's land surface contained twenty-seven independent states.

A hundred languages were spoken in the Soviet Union, and fifty distinct nationalities were recognized within its borders. Many of these were extremely small, splinter groups or isolated communities left by the ebb and flow of humanity in inner Asia over thousands of years. All recognized nationalities received a cultural autonomy, or the right to use their own language, have their own schools, wear their own dress, and follow their own folkways without interference. Indeed, the Soviet authorities favored the growth of cultural nationalism. Some fifty languages were reduced to writing for the first time, and the new regime encouraged the singing of national songs, performance of dances, and collection of folklore. Administratively the nationalities were put on various levels, with varying degrees of separate identity according to their size and importance. The most important were the soviet republics themselves. Within the soviet republics were autonomous republics, autonomous regions, and cultural districts, all having some representation in the upper legislative house, the Soviet of Nationalities, created by the constitution of 1936. But in practice the Russian S.F.S.R., with over half the population and three-fourths of the territory of the Union, predominated over the others. When to the Russian were added the Ukrainian (or Little Russian) and the Byelorussian republics, whose people were not very different from the Great Russians, the overwhelmingly Russian and Slavic character of the Union was marked. Moreover all political and economic rights were severely limited by the concentration of authority in the hands of the central government. There was little substance in the formal claim that each constituent republic was sovereign and had the right to conduct its own foreign affairs (like the British Dominions), on the basis of which the Soviets demanded sixteen (and received three) votes in the assembly of the United Nations when that body was formed in 1945. During the Second World War there was evidence that separatism had not wholly died down, remaining especially alive in the Ukraine, and several autonomous areas were officially dissolved for separatist acitivites or even for collusion with the German invaders. Grievances persisted, and by the late 1980s there were openly voiced discontents and secessionist pressures in every one of the fifteen constituent republics. It became problematic whether the Soviets could prevent the disintegration of the multinational state that they had inherited from the tsars.

Government: State and Party

Government in the Union, and in each component republic, followed a pattern worked out during the Revolution and written into the constitutions of 1924 and 1936. In theory, a principle of parallelism was adopted. On the one hand was the state; on the other, paralleling the state but technically not part of it, was the party. But the close interlocking relationship between the two made the parallelism virtually meaningless.

On the side of the state, the distinctive institution was the council or soviet. Here elections took place, and authority proceeded from the bottom upward to the top. Under the constitution of 1924 only "toilers" had the right to vote. Surviving bourgeois, private traders, "persons using the labor of others to make a profit," as well as priests, were excluded from the suffrage. An indirect system of elections prevailed. In each village and town the voters chose a local soviet; the local soviet elected delegates to a provincial soviet, which in turn sent delegates to a soviet of the republic; the soviets of these republics sent delegates to a Union-wide Congress of Soviets, the supreme law-enacting body of the country. Soviets at all levels chose executive officials; the Congress of Soviets chose the Council of People's Commissars, or ministry.

In the constitution of 1936 a more direct democratic procedure was introduced. Voters henceforth directly elected members of the higher soviets, a secret ballot was adopted, and no class was any longer denied the vote. A bicameral parliament was created, a Supreme Soviet, with an upper chamber, the Soviet of Nationalities, and a lower chamber, the Soviet of the Union, in which there was one representative for every 300,000 persons. On the state side, as set forth in the constitution of 1936, the government embodied many seemingly democratic features.

Yet alongside the state, at all levels and in all localities, was the party. Only one party was allowed, the Communist, though nonparty members might be elected to the soviets or to other official positions. In the party, authority began at the top and proceeded downward. At its apex stood the Central Committee, whose membership varied from about seventy in the 1930s to more than double that in later years. Within the Central Committee a powerful Politburo,[26] or political bureau, of about a dozen members dominated discussions of policy and personnel. An even more powerful general secretary, the office that Stalin virtually fashioned, dominated the entire structure and apparatus with authority over appointments and assignments at all levels. Although a party congress was held every few years, and issues debated, ultimately the congress simply registered policies already laid out by the higher bodies. Thus power and authority flowed downward and outward, as in an army, or as in a highly centralized government agency or large private corporation in the West, except that the party was not subject to any outside control. Discipline was likewise enforced in ways not used in liberal countries, the fearsome machinery of the secret police being available for use against party members as well as those outside.

The number of party members, men and women, which could not have been more than 70,000 at the time of the Revolution, rose to about 2 million by 1930, 3 million by 1940, and to 19 million in the late 1980s. The Leninist ideal of a highly disciplined party, made up of faithful and zealous workers who willingly carried out orders, the ideal on which the Bolsheviks had separated from the Mensheviks in 1903, continued to characterize the communist party in the Soviet Union. Old Bolsheviks, those who had been members in the lean years before 1917, long continued to occupy the seats in the Politburo and other important party positions. A party of 2 million members, though small in contrast to the population of the U.S.S.R., still represented an enormous growth for the party itself, in which for each old member (who had joined before 1917) there were thousands of new ones. To preserve party unity under the new conditions strict uniformity was enforced. Members intensively studied the principles of Marxism-Leninism, embraced dialectical materialism as a philosophy and even a kind of religion, learned to take orders without question or compunction and to give authoritative leadership to the mass of nonparty members among whom they worked. The base of the party structure consisted of small nuclei or cells. In each factory, in each mine, in each office, in each class at the universities and technical schools, in each labor union, in each at least of the larger villages, one, two, or a dozen of the local people (factory workers, miners, office workers, students, etc., as the case might be) belonged to the party and imparted party views and party momentum to the whole.

The function of the party, in Marxist terms, was to carry out the dictatorship of the proletariat. It was to lead the people as a whole to the realization of socialism and, in day-to-day affairs, to coordinate the ponderous mechanism of government and make it work. Party members were present at all levels of the government. Throughout the whole structure, the party decided what the state should do.

The party in the U.S.S.R., by the 1930s, functioned as a tightly knit, highly disciplined leadership group. Those who joined it were willing to work hard, devote themselves to party matters day and night, absorb and communicate the party policy (or "line"), go where they were sent, attend meetings, speak up, perceive and explain the significance of small passing events for the Soviet Union or the world revolution, and master intricate technical details of farming,

---

[26] For a few years, from 1952 to 1966, it was called the Presidium.

THE UNION OF SOVIET SOCIALIST REPUBLICS

The U.S.S.R. is over 5,000 miles long and covers one-sixth of the land area of the globe, including 42 percent of Europe and 43 percent of Asia, though the conventional distinction between Europe and Asia is not officially recognized in the Soviet Union. It is the only state that immediately adjoins so many important political regions—Europe in the west, the Middle East in the south, China along a long frontier, Japan across a narrow sea, and the United States on the side toward Alaska and the Aleutian Islands. The Union has fifteen member republics, of which the Russian is by far the largest. Most of it lies farther north than Lake Superior, but around Tashkent, in the latitude of New York and Chicago, cotton and citrus fruits are grown by irrigation. The diversion of rivers for this purpose, however, has led to the spread of deserts and the gradual drying up of the Aral Sea.

manufacturing, or the care of machinery, so that others would look to them willingly for advice. The party was a specially trained elite whose members were in constant touch with each other. It was the thin stream of lifeblood which, by circulating through all the diverse tissues of the U.S.S.R.—the multitudinous republics, soviets, bureaus, army, industrial, and other enterprises owned under socialism by the state—kept the whole complex body unified, organic, functioning, and alive.

If the party was a leadership group, the corollary was that more than ninety-five out of a hundred persons were condemned to be followers, and while it is perhaps true (as apologists for the system have said) that under any system true leadership is exercised by a tiny fraction of people, the difference between Communist and non-Communist in the U.S.S.R. became a clear matter of social status. As the years passed, many Communists in the U.S.S.R. were less the revolutionary firebrand type than the successful and efficient man or woman in any social system. They represented the satisfied, not the dissatisfied. They enjoyed material privileges, such as access to the best jobs, better housing, special food coupons, automobiles, or priorities on trains. They developed a bourgeois concern for the advantages of their own children. They became a new vested interest. Within the party, members had to be not so much leaders as followers. A homogeneous and monolithic organization had to present a solid front to the far more numerous but unorganized outsiders. Within the party, from time to time, a great deal of difference of opinion and open discussion was tolerated (indeed, since there was only one party all political questions were intraparty disputes), but in the end the entire membership had to conform. The party favored a certain fertility of mind in inventing ways to get things done, but it did not favor, and in fact repressed, originality, boldness, risk-taking, or freedom of thought or action. The dangers of stagnation in such a system became apparent within the Soviet Union itself in later times.

The New Economic Policy, 1921–1927

By 1920 "war communism," as we have seen, had hopelessly antagonized the peasants, who, it was estimated, were cultivating only 62 percent as much land as in 1914.[27] This fact, together with a severe drought and the breakdown of transportation, produced great famine. Millions of people died. The ravages of eight years, of the World War, the Revolution, the civil wars, the Terror, had left the country in ruins, its productive facilities thrown back by decades as compared with 1914. The rising of the Kronstadt sailors in 1921 revealed profound disillusionment in the revolutionary ranks themselves. Lenin concluded that socialization had advanced too fast. He openly advocated a compromise with capitalism, a strategic retreat. The New Economic Policy, or NEP, adopted in 1921, lasted until 1927. Most of the decade of the 1920s saw a relaxation of tempo (and of terror) for most people in the U.S.S.R.

Under the NEP, while the state controlled the "commanding heights" of the economy, maintaining state ownership of the basic productive industries, it allowed a great deal of private trading for private profit. The basic problem was

---

[27] See pp. 750–752.

to restore trade between town and country. The peasants would produce nothing beyond the needs of their own subsistence unless they could exchange their surplus for city-made wares such as clothing or tools. The city people had to be fed from the country if they were to turn out factory products or even continue to live in the city. Under the NEP, peasants were allowed to sell their farm products freely. Middlemen were allowed to buy and sell farm products and manufactured articles at will, to whom they pleased, at market prices, and at a profit to themselves. The NEP therefore favored the big individualist farmer or kulak. Indeed, rural changes initiated before 1914 were still at work;[28] peasant families consolidated millions of acres as private property in 1922, 1923, and 1924. Correspondingly, other peasants became "proletarians," wage-earning hired hands. The NEP also favored the sprouting of a new-rich commercial class, neobourgeois who ate expensive dinners in the restaurants of Moscow, and whose very existence seemed to explode the dream of a classless society. Under the NEP the worst damages of war and revolution were repaired. But there was no real progress, for in 1928 Russia was producing only about as much grain, raw cotton, cattle, coal, and oil as in 1913, and far less than it presumably would have produced (given the rate of growth before 1913) had there been no revolution.

Stalin and Trotsky

Lenin died in 1924 prematurely at the age of fifty-four after a series of paralyzing strokes that left him incapacitated in the last two years of his life. His embalmed remains were put permanently on view in the Kremlin; Petrograd was renamed Leningrad; a leader cult was built up around his name and image. The party presented him as a deified equal of Marx himself, and it became necessary for all schools of communist thought to claim unflinching fidelity to the Leninist tradition. Actually, in his own lifetime, the Old Bolsheviks had never regarded Lenin as infallible. They had often differed with him and with each other. As he lay dying, and after his death, his old companions and contemporaries, carrying on the feuding habits of the émigré days, fought with each other for control of the party in Lenin's name. They disputed over Lenin's intentions. Had he secretly thought of the NEP as a permanent policy, as Bukharin maintained? If not, how would he have modified it, and, most especially, how soon? Quietly, behind the scenes, as general secretary of the party, without much attention to broader problems, a hitherto relatively modest member named Joseph Stalin, whom Lenin had warned against, was drawing all the strings of party control into his own hands. More openly and vociferously Leon Trotsky, who as war commissar in the critical years had been only less conspicuous than Lenin himself, raised the basic issues of the whole nature and future of the movement.

Trotsky, in 1925 and 1926, inveighed against the lassitude that had descended upon socialism.[29] The NEP with its tolerance of bourgeois and kulaks excited his contempt. He developed his doctrine of "permanent revolution," an incessant

---

[28] See pp. 745–746.
[29] For communists, though not for socialists, the terms "communism" and "socialism" were almost interchangeable, since Russian Communists regarded their own system as true socialism and all other socialism as opportunistic, reactionary, or false. Communism has also been defined, in the U.S.S.R., as a future state of society toward which socialism, i.e., Soviet socialism, is the intermediate stage.

drive for proletarian objectives on all fronts in all parts of the world. He stood forth as the exponent of world revolution, which many in the party were beginning to discard in favor of first building socialism in one country. He denounced the tendency to bureaucratic ossification in the party and urged a new movement of the masses to give it life. He called for more forceful development of industry and for the collectivization of agriculture, which had figured in Communist manifestos ever since 1848.[30] Above all, he demanded immediate adoption of an overall plan, a central control and operation of the whole economic life of the country.

Trotsky failed to carry the party with him. He was charged with leftist deviationism, machinations against the Central Committee, and inciting to public discussion of issues outside the party. Stalin wove his web. At a party congress in 1927, 95 percent of the delegates dutifully voted for Stalin and the Central Committee and fewer than 5 percent for Trotsky. Trotsky was first exiled to Siberia, then banished from the U.S.S.R.; he lived first in Turkey, then France, then Mexico, writing and propagandizing for the "permanent revolution," stigmatizing developments in the U.S.S.R. as "Stalinism," a monstrous betrayal of Marxism-Leninism, organizing an underground against Stalin as he had done in former days against the tsar. He was murdered in Mexico in 1940 under mysterious circumstances, presumably by a Soviet agent or sympathizer. Not until the late 1980s was anyone in the U.S.S.R. permitted to talk or write about him and his contributions to the Revolution.

95. Stalin: The Five-Year Plans and the Purges

Economic Planning

Hardly had Trotsky been expelled when Stalin and the party appropriated certain fragments of his program. In 1928 the party launched the First Five-Year Plan, aimed at rapid industrialization and the collectivization of agriculture. "Planning," or the central planning of a country's whole economic life by government officials, was to become the distinctive feature of Soviet economics and the one that, for a time, was to have the greatest influence on the rest of the world.

In retrospect, it seems strange that the Communists waited ten years before adopting a plan. The truth seems to be that the Bolsheviks had only confused ideas of what to do after their seizure of power. Marxism for the most part gave only general hints. Marxism was primarily an analysis of existing or bourgeois society. It was also a theory of class war. But to portray any details of a future society, or specify what should be done after the class war had been won by the proletariat, was according to Marx and Engels sheer utopian fantasy. The bourgeoisie, to be sure, would be destroyed; there would be "social ownership of the means of production," and no "exploitation of man by man"; everyone would work, and there would be neither leisure class nor unemployment. This was not much to go on in the operation of a modern industrial system.

[30] See pp. 522–523.

One great constructive idea had been mapped out, most clearly by Engels. *Within* each private enterprise, Engels had observed, harmony and order reigned; it was only *between* private enterprises that capitalism was chaotic. In the individual factory, he noted, the various departments did not compete with each other; the shipping department did not purchase from the production department at prices fluctuating according to daily changes in supply and demand; the output of all departments was planned and coordinated by management. In a larger way, the great capitalist mergers and trusts, controlling many factories, prevented blind competition between them, assigned specific quotas to each, anticipated, coordinated, and stabilized the work of each plant and each person by an overall policy. With the growth of large corporate enterprise, observed Engels, the area of economic life under free competition was constantly reduced, and the area brought under rational planning was constantly enlarged. The obvious next step, according to Engels and other socialists, was to treat *all* the economic life of a country as a single factory with many departments, or a single enormous monopoly with many members, under one unified, far-seeing management.

During the First World War the governments of belligerent countries had in fact adopted such centralized controls.[31] They had done so not because they were socialistic, but because in time of war people were willing to subordinate their usual liberties to a single overwhelming and undisputed social purpose—victory. The "planned society" therefore made its first actual (though incomplete) appearance in the First World War. It was partly from socialist doctrine as exemplified by Engels, partly from experience of the war, and in even larger measure from the irresistible pressure to meet the continuing chronic problems of the country by raising its productive level that Stalin and the party in Russia gradually developed the idea of a plan. The war experience was especially valuable for the lessons it gave on technical questions of economic planning, such as the kind of bureaus to set up, the kind of forecasts to make, and the kind of statistics to collect.

In the U.S.S.R. it was decided to plan for five years into the future, beginning with 1928. The aim of the plan was to strengthen and enrich the country, make it militarily and industrially self-sufficient, lay the groundwork for a true workers' society, and overcome the Russian reputation for backwardness. As Stalin said in a speech in 1929: "We are becoming a country of metal, a country of automobiles, a country of tractors. And when we have put the U.S.S.R. in a motor car and the *muzhik* in a tractor . . . we shall see which countries may then be 'classified' as backward and which as advanced."

The First Five-Year Plan was declared fulfilled in 1932, and a Second Five-Year Plan was launched, lasting until 1937. The Third, inaugurated in 1938, was interrupted by the war with Germany in 1941. New plans were introduced after 1945.[32]

The First Five-Year Plan (like its successors) listed the economic goals to be achieved. It was administered by an agency called the Gosplan. Within the frame of general policy set by the party, the Gosplan determined how much of every article the country should produce, how much of the national effort should go

[31] See pp. 718–721.
[32] See pp. 906–908.

into the formation of capital, and how much into producing articles for daily consumption, what wages all classes of workers should receive, and at what prices all goods should be exchanged. Because all decisions were made at the top, it was as much a command economy as a planned economy. At the bottom level, in the individual factory, the local management drew up its "requirements," or estimates of what it would need, in raw material, machinery, trained workers, plant facilities, and fuel, if it was to deliver the planned quantity of its product at a stated date. These estimates were passed up the planning ladder (or, thousands of such estimates up thousands of ladders) until they reached the Gosplan, which, balancing them against each other and against other needs as seen at the top, determined how much steel, coal, etc., should be produced, and in what qualities and grades; how many workers should be trained in technical schools and in what particular skills; how many machines should be manufactured and how many spare parts; how many new freight cars should be constructed and which lines of railway track needed repair; and how, where, when, and to whom the steel, coal, technicians, machines, and rolling stock should be made available. The plan, in short, undertook to control, by conscious management, the flow of resources and work force which under free capitalism was regulated by shifts in demand and supply, and through changes in prices, wage levels, profits, interest rates, or rent.

The system was exceedingly intricate. It was not easy to have the right number of ball bearings, for example, arrive at the right place at the right time, in exact correspondence to the amounts of other materials or to the number of workers waiting to use them. Sometimes there was overproduction, sometimes underproduction. The plan was often amended as it was applied in action. Countless reports, checkups, and exchanges of information were necessary. A huge class of bureaucrats came into existence to handle the paperwork. The plan achieved some of its goals, exceeded a few, and failed in some. The criterion for fulfillment was almost always quantitative.

The primary objective of the First Five-Year Plan was to build up the heavy industry, or capital wealth, of the U.S.S.R. The aim was to industrialize without the use of foreign loans.[33] Russia in 1928 was still chiefly an agricultural country. The world offered hardly any case of a country shifting from agriculture to industry without borrowing capital from abroad. Britain, the original home of the Industrial Revolution, was the best example, although even there, in the eighteenth century, a great deal of capital invested in England was owned by the Dutch. An agricultural country could industrialize from its own resources only by drawing upon agriculture itself. An agricultural revolution had been prerequisite to an industrial revolution in England.[34] By enclosure of land, the squeezing out of small independent farmers, and the introduction of scientific cultivation, under the auspices of a growing class of wealthy landowners, England had both increased its production of food and released many of the rural population to find employment

---

[33] The Bolsheviks had repudiated the entire debt of the tsarist empire. Their credit in capitalist countries was therefore not good, so that, in addition to fearing dependence upon foreign lenders, they were in any case for a long time unable to borrow large sums.

[34] See pp. 456–457.

in industry. The First Five-Year Plan called for a similar agricultural revolution in Russia, without benefit to landlords and under the auspices of the state.

The Collectivization of Agriculture

The plan, as originally conceived, called for the collectivization of only one-fifth of the farm population, but Stalin suddenly revised the plan in the winter of 1929 to include the immediate collectivization of the greater part of the peasantry. The plan set up collective farms, averaging a few thousand acres apiece, which were considered to be the property not of the state but of the peasants collectively who resided on them. (A few state-operated collective farms were also established, as models for the others.) Individual peasants were to pool their privately owned fields and livestock in these collectives. Those peasants who possessed fields or stock in considerable amount, the prosperous peasants or kulaks, resisted surrendering them to the new collectives. The kulaks were therefore liquidated as a class. Zealous detachments of Communists from the cities used violence; poor peasants turned upon rich ones; hundreds of thousands of kulaks and their families were killed and many more transported to labor camps in remote parts of the Soviet Union. The trend that had gone on since Stolypin and indeed since the Emancipation, building up a class of property-owning, labor-hiring, and "bourgeois" peasants, was now abruptly reversed. Collectivization was intended to convert the peasantry into a class more nearly resembling the proletariat of Marxian doctrine, a class of people who as individuals owned no capital and employed no labor, and so would better fit into a proletarian, or socialist, state. The year 1929, not 1917, was the great revolutionary year for most people in Russia.

Collectivization was accomplished at the cost of village class war in which the most capable farmers perished, and at the cost also of a wholesale destruction of livestock. The big farmers slaughtered their horses, cattle, pigs, and poultry rather than give them up. Even middling and small farmers did the same, caring nothing about animals that were no longer their own. The ruinous loss of animals was the worst unforeseen calamity of the First Five-Year Plan. The agricultural disorders led to a deadly famine in southeast Russia in 1932 that cost millions of lives. Despite the famine Stalin refused to cut back on cereal and other food exports because they were needed to pay for industrial imports under the Five-Year Plan.

By introducing thousand-acre units in place of very small ones, collectivization made it possible to apply capital to the soil. Formerly the average peasant had been far too poor to buy a tractor and his fields too tiny and dispersed for him to use one, so that only a few rare kulaks had employed any machinery. In the course of the First Five-Year Plan hundreds of Machine Tractor Stations were organized throughout the country. Each, in its region, maintained a force of tractors, harvesting combines, expert agronomists, etc., which were dispatched from one collective farm to another by local arrangement. The application of capital was intended to increase the output per peasant. It was also much easier administratively for higher authorities to control the agricultural surplus (products not consumed by the village itself) from a single collective farm than from numerous small and unorganized peasants. Each collective was assigned a quota.

Members of the collective could sell in a free market any products they raised beyond this quota; but meanwhile the government knew the quantity of agricultural produce it could count on, either to feed the cities and other regions that did not produce their own food, or for export in the world market to pay for imports of machinery from the West. By 1939 all but a negligible fraction of the peasantry was collectivized. But collectivization failed to increase agricultural output, and agriculture remained a troubled sector of the economy. Collectivization made possible, however, the success of industrialization by augmenting the supply of industrial workers. Since the villages needed less labor, 20 million people moved from country to city between the years 1926 and 1939 and were available for jobs in the new industries.

It was the peasants who bore the burden of collectivization. Not only had they been subjected to violence and expropriation, but the new collectives threw the peasants back into something like the *mir*, condemning them to the rounds of communal living, robbing them of the chance to make any decisions of their own. The incentive to improve the land they worked, and to pass on those improvements to their heirs, was gone. By obliging peasants to make "deliveries" below market prices, it even revived some features of the type of serfdom and forced labor that had prevailed a century before over most of eastern Europe.[35] On the other hand, although the collectives varied widely in their degree of prosperity, it is probable that by 1939 a great many of the rural people were better housed and better fed than they had been before the Revolution. But millions had not survived the ordeal of collectivization, and the whole experience undermined the morale of those who had.

The Growth of Industry

While the agricultural base was being revolutionized, industrialization went rapidly forward. At first there was considerable dependence on the capitalist countries. Engineers and other technicians from western Europe and the United States took service in the Soviet Union. Much machinery was imported. But the worldwide depression that set in about 1931, bringing a catastrophic fall of agricultural prices, made foreign-made machines more costly in terms of the cereals that were the chief Soviet export. The international situation also deteriorated. While the U.S.S.R. always considered the whole outside world hostile to it, both Japan and Germany in the 1930s showed overt hostility. From the beginning the Five-Year Plans had as one of their objectives the military self-sufficiency of the country. The Second Five-Year Plan, launched in 1933, though in some ways less ambitious than the first, showed an even greater determination to cut down imports and achieve national self-sufficiency, especially in the heavy industry basic to war production.

No ten years in the history of any Western country ever showed such a rate of industrial growth as the decade of the first two plans in the Soviet Union. In Great Britain industrialization had been gradual; in Germany and the United States it had been more rapid, and in each country there had been decades in which output of coal or iron doubled; but in the U.S.S.R., from 1928 to 1938,

[35] See pp. 509–510, 566–567.

production of iron and steel expanded four times and that of coal three and a half times. In 1938 the U.S.S.R. was the world's largest producer of farm tractors and railway locomotives. Four-fifths of all its industrial output came from plants built in the preceding ten years. Two plants alone, at the new cities of Magnitogorsk in the Urals and Stalinsk 1,000 miles farther east, produced as much iron and steel as the whole Russian empire in 1914. In 1939 the U.S.S.R., as measured by purely quantitative standards, was surpassed in gross industrial output only by the United States and Germany.

The plans called for a marked development of industry east of the Urals, and so brought a modernization of life for the first time to inner Asia, in a way comparable only to the movement of machine industry into the once underdeveloped Great Lakes region of the American Middle West. Pittsburghs, Clevelands, and Detroits rose in the old Turkestan (now divided into the five Asian Soviet socialist republics) and in Siberia. Copper mines were opened in the Urals and around Lake Balkhash, lead mines in eastern Asia and in the Altai Mountains. New grain-producing regions were developed in Siberia and in the Kazakh S.S.R., whence grain was shipped westward to Russia proper, or southward to the Uzbek S.S.R., which was devoted mainly to cotton. Tashkent, the Uzbek capital, formerly a remote town of bazaars and caravans, grew to be a city of over half a million, a center of cotton culture, copper mining, and electrical industries, connected with the north by the newly built Turksib Railway. The Kuznetsk basin, in the south, 2,000 miles inland from every ocean, was found to possess coal deposits of high grade. Kuznetsk coal and the iron ores of the Urals became complementary, though separated by a thousand miles, somewhat like Pennsylvania coal and Minnesota iron in the United States. The opening of all these new areas, requiring the movement of food to the Uzbek S.S.R. in exchange for cotton, or of Ural iron to the new Kuznetsk cities, demanded a revolution in transportation. The railroads in 1938 carried five times as much freight as in 1913.

These astounding developments were enough to change the relative economic strength of the world's peoples with respect to one another. It was significant that inner Asia was for the first time turning industrial. It was significant, too, that although the U.S.S.R. had less foreign trade than had the Russian empire, it carried on more trade than the old Russia with its Asian neighbors, with which it formed new and close connections. In part because of these developments in Asia, the Russia that went to war with Germany in 1941 proved to be a different antagonist from the Russia of 1914. Industrialization in the Urals and in Asia enabled the U.S.S.R. (with a good deal of Allied assistance) to survive the German occupation and destruction of the older industrial areas in the Don valley. The new "socialist fatherland" proved able to absorb terrible losses and strike back. A great deal of the increased industrial output had gone to equip and modernize the Red Army.

At the same time, the degree of industrialization of the U.S.S.R. can easily be exaggerated. It was phenomenal because it started from so little. Qualitatively, by Western criteria, standards of production were low. Many of the hastily constructed new plants were shoddy and suffered from rapid depreciation. In efficiency, as shown by output per worker employed, the U.S.S.R. continued to lag behind the West. In intensity of modernization, as shown by output of certain items in proportion to the whole population, it also lagged. Per capita of its huge population, in 1937, the U.S.S.R. produced less coal, electricity, cottons, woolens, leather shoes, or soap than did the United States, Britain, Germany, France, or even Japan, and less iron and steel than any of them except Japan. Production of paper is revealing because paper is used in so many "civilized" activities— in books, newspapers, magazines, schools, correspondence, placards, maps, pictures, charts, business and government records, and household articles and amenities. Where the United States about 1937 produced 103 pounds of paper per person, Germany and Great Britain each 92, France 51, and Japan 17, the U.S.S.R. produced only 11.

Social Costs and Social Effects of the Plans

Industrialization in Russia demanded a huge and continuing sacrifice on the part of the people. It was not merely that kulaks lost their lives, or that millions of others, whose exact numbers have never been known, were found to be enemies of the system and sent off to correctional labor camps. All were required to accept a program of austerity and self-denial, going without the better food, housing, and other consumers' goods that might have been produced, in order that the capital wealth and heavy industry of the country might be built up. As much as a third of the national income was reinvested in industry every year— twice as much as in the England of 1914, though probably not more than in the England of 1840. The plan required hard work and low wages. People were told to look to the future, to the time when, the basic industries having been built, better housing, better food, better clothing, and more leisure would follow. Morale was sustained by propaganda. One of the chief functions of party members was to explain why sacrifices were necessary. In the late 1930s life began to ease; food rationing was abolished in 1935, and a few more products of light industry, such as dishes and fountain pens, began to appear in Soviet retail stores. Living standards were at least up to those of 1927 with prospects brighter for raising them. But the need for war preparations, as the world again approached chaos, again drove back the vision of the Promised Land.

Socialism, as realized in the plans, did away with some of the evils of unrestrained free enterprise. There was no acknowledged unemployment. There was no cycle of boom and depression. There was less misuse of women and children than in the early days of industrialism in the West. There was a minimum below which no one was supposed to fall. On the other hand, there was no economic equality. Marxism, indeed, had never seen complete equality of income as a principal objective. While there was no handful of very rich people, as in the West (where the income of the very rich usually came from inherited property), the differences in income were nevertheless great. High government officials, managers, engineers, and favored artists and intellectuals received the highest rewards. People with large incomes, by buying government bonds or accumulating personal possessions, could build up precarious little fortunes for themselves and their children. They could not, however, under socialism, own any industrial capital, i.e., buy shares of stock or other equities. There was, of course, no stock exchange.

Competition persisted. In 1935 a miner named Stakhanov greatly increased his

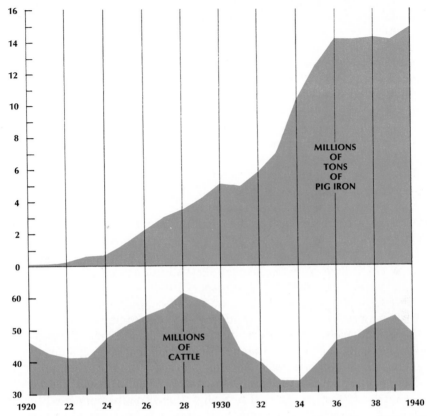

Source: B. R. Mitchell, *European Historical Statistics* (New York: Columbia University Press, 1975), pp. 316, 396.

PIG IRON AND CATTLE IN THE SOVIET UNION, 1920–1940

If pig iron is taken as a measure of industrial activity and number of cattle as a similar indication for agriculture, the chart reveals clearly what happened in the twenty years after the Revolution—an enormous build-up of heavy industry at the expense of food supplies. Iron mines and forges, in the disorganization of the Revolution and civil war, were producing almost nothing in 1920. By the late 1920s, output of pig iron regained the pre-Revolutionary level, but the great upsurge came with the Second Five-Year Plan. By 1940 Russia produced more pig iron than Germany, and far more than Britain or France. Numbers of cattle grew in the 1920s, but fell catastrophically during the collectivization of agriculture after 1929, and by 1940 hardly exceeded the figure for 1920.

daily output of coal by devising improvements in his methods of work. He also greatly increased his wages, since Soviet workers were paid at piece rates. His example proved contagious; workers all over the country began to break records of all kinds. The government publicized their achievements, called them Stakhanovites and "labor heroes," and pronounced the movement to be "a new and higher stage of socialist competition." In labor circles in the United States such straining to increase output would be called a speed-up, and piecework wages had long been anathema to the organized labor of all countries. Nor was management free from competitive pressure. A factory manager who failed to show the net income (or "profit") upon which the plan counted, or who failed to meet his quota of output, might lose not only his job but his social status—or even his life. Poor management was often construed as sabotage. Insufficient use of the workers and resources allocated to a factory was considered a betrayal of Soviet society and a waste of the property of the nation. The press, not otherwise free, freely denounced whole industries or individual executives for failures to meet the plan.

Foreign observers often found the distinctive feature of the new system to lie in this kind of competition or emulation, or in a feeling that everybody was busily toiling and struggling to create a socialist fatherland. Workers in the 1930s, it seemed, had a real belief that the new industrial wonders were their own. It became a national pastime to watch the mounting statistics, the fulfilling of quotas or "targets." Newspaper readers read no comic strips; they read eagerly about the latest doings (or misdoings) on the economic front.

Solidarity was purchased at the price of totalitarianism.[36] The government supervised everything. There was no room for skepticism, independence of thought, or any criticism that weakened the will to achieve. As in tsarist times, no one could leave the country without special permission, which was given far more rarely than before 1914. There was, of course, only one party. There were no free labor unions, no free press, no freedom of association, and at best only an irritable tolerance for religion. Soviet Jews had many complaints. Art, literature, and even science became vehicles of political propoganda. Dialectical materialism was the official philosophy. Conformity was the ideal, and the very passion for solidarity made for fear and suspicion of all who might go astray. As for the number of people sacrificed to Stalin's Juggernaut—liquidated bourgeois, liquidated peasants, purged party members, disaffected persons sentenced to long terms in labor camps—a precise figure is difficult to arrive at, but it certainly reached many millions over the years, which many suspected at the time, and which a later generation of Soviet leaders confirmed.

The Purge Trials of the 1930s

In 1936 socialism was judged to have proved so successful that a new constitution for the U.S.S.R. was proclaimed. It enumerated, as rights of Soviet citizens, not merely the usual civil liberties of Western democracy but the rights to steady employment, rest, leisure, economic security, and a comfortable old age. All forms of racism were condemned. It reorganized the Soviet republics and granted equal and direct universal suffrage, as explained above.[37] The constitution of 1936 was favorably commented upon in the West, where it was hoped that the Russian Revolution, like former revolutions, had at last turned into more peaceable and quiet channels. It was nonetheless apparent that the Communist party remained the sole governing group in the country, that Stalin was tightening his dictatorship, and that the party was racked by internal troubles.

It was natural that the rapid changes of the 1930s should provide divergences of opinion among the party leaders. Because open disagreement with Stalin's

[36] On totalitarianism, see pp. 828–832.
[37] See p. 756.

policies was not possible, many may have turned to conspiracy. A moderate group, led by Bukharin, had urged more gradual methods in collectivizing the peasants and greater latitude for small private business, as in the days of the NEP. On the left, the mastermind was the exiled Trotsky. Whether there were conspiracies or not, Stalin acted preemptorily. As early as 1933 the party underwent a drastic purge, in which a third of its members were expelled. Even the faithful were appalled at Stalin's growing ruthlessness. Serge Kirov, an old friend and revolutionary companion of Stalin since 1909, head of the Leningrad party apparatus, and member of the Politburo since 1930, showed signs of leading the disaffected. In 1934 he was assassinated in his office, very probably by a police agent of Stalin's. Stalin used the assassination to strike out at his opponents, imagined or real, by a revival of terror, immediately executing over a hundred persons, and launching the extraordinary purges of the next four years.

A series of sensational trials took place. In 1936 sixteen Old Bolsheviks were brought to trial. Some, like Zinoviev and Kamenev, had been expelled from the party in 1927 for supporting Trotsky and subsequently, after the proper recantations, had been readmitted. Now they were charged with the murder of Kirov, with plotting the murder of Stalin, and with having organized, in 1932, under Trotsky's inspiration, a secret group to disorganize and terrorize the Central Committee. To the amazement of the world, all the accused made full confession to the charges in open court. All blamed themselves as unworthy and erring reprobates. All were put to death. In 1937, after similar trials, seventeen other Old Bolsheviks met the same fate or received long prison sentences. In 1938 Bukharin and others, denounced as "rightists," were charged with wanting to restore bourgeois capitalism and were executed. The same confessions and self-accusations followed in almost every case, with no other verifiable evidence adduced. How these confessions were obtained in open court from hardened revolutionaries apparently in full possession of their faculties and bearing no sign of physical harm mystified the outside world. Only later did it become clear that psychological torture had broken the will of those accused, and that threats against their families (or promises to spare them) had played a part. In addition to these public trials there were other arrests, private inquisitions, and executions. In 1937, in a secret court martial, Marshal Tukhachevski and seven other top generals were accused of Trotskyism and conspiring with the Germans and Japanese, and were summarily shot. The purges embraced the highest levels of the party, government, military, intellectual, and scientific circles, and reached down to the lesser echelons as well. In later years the KGB itself disclosed that in the years 1930–1953 (the year of Stalin's death) 3,778,334 persons had been tried and sentenced for "counterrevolutionary" activity and crimes against the state, most of them in the Great Terror of 1934–1938, and that 786,098 were executed; unknown others died in the prison camps to which they were sent. The innocence of many of Stalin's victims was officially confirmed and their reputations posthumously restored.

By these purges Stalin's dictatorship was reinforced. It may be that a real danger of renewed revolution was averted. Had the tsarist government dealt as summarily with Bolsheviks as Bolsheviks dealt with one another there could have been no November Revolution. Above all, Stalin rid himself by the purges of all possible rivals for his own position. He disposed of the embarrassment of having colleagues about him who could remember the old days, who could quote Lenin as a former friend, or belittle the reality of 1937 by recalling the dreams of 1917. After 1938 there were virtually no Old Bolsheviks left. The aging but still explosive professional revolutionaries were now dead. A younger group, products of the new order, practical, constructive, impatient of "agitators," and acquiescing in Stalin's dictatorship, were operating what was now an established system.

96. *The International Impact of Communism, 1919–1939*

Socialism and the First World War

Marxism had always been international in its outlook. To Marx, and the early Marxists, existing states (like other institutions) owed their character to the class struggle. They were no more than committees of the bourgeoisie to govern the proletariat, destined to be dismantled and pass away in the course of inevitable historic processes. After Marx's death, as Marxist parties grew in numbers, and as states of western Europe became more democratic, most people who called themselves Marxists accepted the national state, seeing in it a means by which the workers' lot could be gradually improved. This view was part of the movement of "revisionism," or what more rigorous Marxists called "opportunism."[38] In the First World War national loyalty proved its strength. The socialist parties in the Reichstag, the French Chamber, and other parliamentary bodies voted for war credits without hesitation. Socialist workers reported for mobilization like everyone else. In Germany socialists said that the reactionary Russian tsardom must be resisted; in France, that the Germans menaced the entire French nation. In general, all political parties, including the socialists, declared a moratorium on party politics during the war.

Small minorities of socialists in every country, however, refused to accept the war. Marxian socialism had long taught that workers of all nations were bound by the supreme loyalty of class, that their real enemies were the capitalists of their own countries, that international wars were capitalist and "imperialist" quarrels, and that class struggle was the only kind of warfare that the proletarian should accept. These socialists denounced the action of the socialist majorities as a sellout to capitalism and imperialism. They met in international conferences with each other and with socialists from the neutral countries. Active among them were Lenin and other Russian Social Democrats then in Switzerland. "The only task for socialists," wrote Lenin in 1914, "is to convert the war of peoples into a civil war." The minority or antiwar socialists met at the small Swiss town of Zimmerwald in 1915, where they drew up a "Zimmerwald program," calling for immediate peace without annexations or indemnities. This had no effect on most socialists in the belligerent countries. The Zimmerwald group itself soon began to split. Most Zimmerwalders regarded peace, or the repudiation of the

---

[38] See pp. 526–527, 622–625.

war, as their aim. But a "Zimmerwald Left" began to develop, inspired mainly by Lenin and the Russian émigrés. This faction made its aim not peace but revolution. It hoped that the war would go on until it caused social revolution in the belligerent countries.

Then in April 1917, with the German imperial government arranging their trip and wishing them *bon voyage*, Lenin and the other Bolsheviks went back to Russia and accomplished the November Revolution. Lenin, until his death in 1924, believed that the Russian Revolution was only a local phase of a world revolution—of *the* revolution of strict Marxian doctrine. Russia, for him, was the theater of currently most active operations in the international class war. Because he expected proletarian upheaval in Germany, Poland, the Danube valley, and the Baltic regions, he accepted without compunction the treaty of Brest-Litovsk. He took no pride in Russia; he was no patriot or "social-chauvinist," to use his own term. In the founding of the U.S.S.R. in 1922 he saw a nucleus around which other and greater soviet republics of any nationality might coalesce. "Soviet republics in countries with a higher degree of civilization," he wrote, "whose proletariat has greater social weight and influence, have every prospect of outstripping Russia as soon as they start upon the road of proletarian dictatorship."

The First World War was in fact followed by attempted revolutions in Germany and eastern Europe. With the German and Austro-Hungarian empires wrecked, socialists and liberals of all descriptions strove to establish new regimes. Among socialists the old differences persisted, between socialists or social democrats favoring gradual, nonviolent, and parliamentary methods, and a more extreme group which saw in postwar disintegration a chance to realize the international proletarian revolution. The first group looked upon the Bolshevik Revolution with horror. The second looked upon it with admiration. The first group included not only trade union officials and practical socialist politicians, but such prewar giants of Marxian exegesis as Karl Kautsky and Eduard Bernstein. Even Kautsky, who had upheld pure Marxism against the revisionism of Bernstein, could not stomach the methods of Lenin. The mass of European socialists, with their fiercest leaders removed, were to remain characterized by relative moderation. Marxist in principle, they were in fact more than ever wedded to gradual, peaceable, and parliamentary methods.

In the second group, the sifted residue of uncompromising Leninist neo-Marxists, who accepted the Bolshevik Revolution, were Karl Liebknecht and Rosa Luxemburg. Organizing the Spartacist movement.[39] in Germany, they attempted, in January 1919, to overthrow the majority socialist government in Germany, as Lenin had overthrown the Provisional Government in Russia in November 1917. In the second group also was Béla Kun, who had turned Bolshevik during a sojourn in Russia, and who set up and maintained a soviet regime in Hungary for several months in 1919.

Lenin and the Bolsheviks, though absorbed in their own revolution, gave all possible aid to the fringe of left socialists of Europe. They sent large sums of money to Germany, to Sweden, to Italy. When the Bolshevik Radek was arrested in Berlin he was said to have a plan for proletarian revolution in all central Europe

[39] See p. 783 and note.

in his possession. The party considered sending Russian troops to Hungary to support Béla Kun. But the chief instrument of world revolution, created in March 1919, was the Third or Communist International.

The Founding of the Third International

The Second International, which since its foundation in 1889 had met every two or three years until 1914, held its first postwar meeting at Berne in 1919.[40] It represented socialist parties and labor organizations of all countries. The Berne meeting was stormy, for a small minority vehemently demanded "revolution as in Russia, socialization of property as in Russia, application of Marxism as in Russia." Overruled at Berne, they repaired to Moscow and there founded a new International in conjunction with the Russian Communist party, and with Lenin and the Russians dominating it completely. It was Lenin's hope, by founding a new International of his own, to discredit moderate socialism and to claim for the Communists the true line of succession from the First International of Karl Marx. The First International, he declared, had laid the foundations for proletarian struggle, the Second had broadened it, the Third "took over the work of the Second International, cut off its opportunistic, social-chauvinist, bourgeois and petty-bourgeois rubbish, and began to carry into effect the dictatorship of the proletariat."

The first congress of the Third International in 1919 was somewhat haphazard, but at the second, in 1920, the extreme left parties of thirty-seven countries were represented. The Russian party was supposedly only one component. Actually, it supplied most of the personnel and most of the funds; the Bolshevik Zinoviev was its first president, remaining in this office until his disgrace as a Trotskyist in 1927. The Third or Communist International—the Comintern—was in part a spontaneous rallying of Marxists from all countries who accepted the Bolshevik Revolution as the true fruition of Marxism and so were willing to follow the Russian lead; but, even more, it was the creation and weapon of the Bolsheviks themselves, by which to discredit and isolate the moderate socialists and bring about world revolution. Of all enemies the Communists hated the socialists most, reserving for them even choicer epithets than they bestowed upon capitalists and imperialists, because Communists and socialists were competing for the same thing, the leadership of the world's working class.

Parties adhering to the Comintern were obliged to drop the old name "socialist" and call themselves Communist. They were obliged to accept strong international centralization. Where the Second International had been a loose federation, and its congresses hardly more than forums, the Third International put strong powers in the hands of its Executive Committee, whose orders the Communist parties of all countries had to obey. Since there was a kind of interlocking directorate by which members of the Central Committee of the party in Russia sat also as members of the Executive Committee of the Third International, the top Communists in Russia had, in the Comintern, an "apparatus" by which they could produce desired effects in many countries—the use of party members to

[40] See pp. 622–624.

penetrate labor unions, foment strikes, propagandize ideas, or interfere in elections.

The second congress of the International, in 1920, endorsed a program of Twenty-One Points, written by Lenin. These included the requirements that each national party must call itself Communist, repudiate "reformist" socialism, propagandize labor unions and get Communists into the important union offices, infiltrate the army, impose an iron discipline upon members, require submission to the orders of the international Executive, use both legal channels and secret underground methods, and expel promptly any member not hewing to the party line. Making no pretense of respect for parliamentary democracy, the second congress ruled that "the only question can be that of utilizing bourgeois state institutions for their own destruction." As for the labor movement, Lenin wrote that "the struggle against the Gomperses, the Jouhaux, the Hendersons[41] . . . who represent an *absolutely similar* social and political type as our Mensheviks . . . must be waged without mercy to the end." The Comintern was not an assemblage of humanitarians engaged in welfare work; it was a weapon for revolution, organized by revolutionaries who knew what revolution was.

For several years the U.S.S.R., using the Comintern or more conventional diplomatic channels, promoted world revolution as best it could. Communists from many countries went to Russia for indoctrination. Native-born or Russian agents proceeded to the Dutch Indies, to China, to Europe, to America. Until 1927 the Chinese revolutionists welcomed assistance from Moscow; the Russian Borodin became an adviser in their affairs. In 1924, in England, publication of the "Zinoviev letter," in which, at least allegedly, the Comintern urged British workers to provoke revolution, led to a great electoral victory for the Conservative party. The Bolshevik menace, real and imagined, produced everywhere a strong reaction. It was basic to the rise of fascism described in the following chapters.

In 1927, with the suppression of Trotskyism and world revolutionism in Russia, and with the concentration under Stalin on a program of building socialism in one country, the Comintern moderated its activities. In 1935, as fascist dictators became noisily bellicose and threatened the Soviet Union, the U.S.S.R. through the Comintern instructed all Communist parties, each in its own country, to enter into coalitions with socialists and advanced liberals in what were called "popular fronts," to combat fascism and reaction and so support the national defense of their own countries. During the Second World War (in 1943), as a gesture of good will to Great Britain and the United States, the U.S.S.R. abolished the Comintern entirely. It reappeared for a few years from 1947 to 1956 under a new name, the Communist Information Bureau or Cominform, and was then disbanded.[42]

It was not through the Comintern that the U.S.S.R. exerted its greatest influence on the world in the years after 1917. It exerted its influence by the massive fact of its very existence. By 1939 it was clear that a new type of economic system had appeared. Before 1917 no one in Europe or Asia had thought

---

[41] Samuel Gompers (1850–1924), began as a cigar maker, president of the American Federation of Labor, 1886–1924; Léon Jouhaux (1879–1954), began as a factory worker, secretary general of the French General Confederation of Labor, 1909–1947, resigned in 1947 to found a new labor organization in opposition to communism; Arthur Henderson (1863–1935), began as an iron-molder's apprentice, chairman of the Parliamentary Labour Party, 1908–1910, 1914–1917, Member of Parliament, 1903–1931, Secretary of State for Foreign Affairs, 1929–1931.

[42] For the U.S.S.R. and for international communism after 1945, see pp. 903–918.

that anything was to be learned from Russia. Twenty years later even critics of the U.S.S.R. feared that it might represent the wave of the future. Its sheer power was soon demonstrated in the Second World War. Marxism was no longer merely a theory; there was an actual society, embracing a sixth of the globe, which called itself Marxist.

In every country those who were most critical of capitalist institutions compared them unfavorably to those of the Soviet Union. Most of those who in the 1930s hoped to profit from the Soviet experience were not actually communist. Some believed that something like Soviet results might be obtained without the use of Soviet methods, which were dismissed as typically Russian, a deplorable heritage from the Byzantine Empire and the tsars. With the appearance of Communism and Communist parties, socialism and socialist ideas seemed in contrast to be middling and respectable. Everywhere in the 1930s the idea of "planning" began to find favor. Workers obtained more security against the fluctuations of capitalism. The so-called backward peoples, especially in Asia, were particularly impressed by the achievement of the U.S.S.R., which had shown how a traditional society could modernize without falling under the influence of foreign capital or foreign guidance.

For a long time the Communist party in the Soviet Union presented itself as the leader of world revolution and tried to exert control over Communist parties in all other countries. This became increasingly difficult. Over the years the U.S.S.R. pursued diplomatic and military policies, and engaged in acts of aggression and territorial expansion, such as the tsarist state might have done. By the late 1980s the U.S.S.R. was no longer an innovative, or some would say, a viable society. Its economic system was in a shambles; the component republics demanded autonomy or independence. The revelation from within the Soviet Union itself of the persecution and deaths of millions of innocent victims, along with the restiveness of its own nationalities, undermined its role as leader of oppressed peoples elsewhere. European Communist parties proclaimed their independence from Moscow and a new form of communism emerged in the People's Republic of China. Yet all Communist parties, including the Chinese, derived from Marxism and the Russian Revolution of 1917, once hailed as the first great victory over capitalism and imperialism.

XVIII.
THE
APPARENT
VICTORY OF
DEMOCRACY

WE HAVE FOLLOWED events in the Soviet Union to about the year 1939 but have left the story of Europe and the rest of the world at the signing of the peace treaties of 1919. We must deal now with the period of just twenty years that elapsed betweeen the formal close of the First World War in 1919 and the outbreak of the Second World War in 1939. In these twenty years the world made a dizzy passage from confidence to disillusionment and from hope to fear. It went through a few years of superficial prosperity, abruptly followed by unparalleled economic disaster. For a time, in the 1920s, democracy seemed to be advancing almost everywhere; then, in the 1930s, dictatorship began to spread. Let us first examine the apparent triumphs of democracy in the 1920s, turn next to the devastating worldwide effects of the Great Depression that began in1929, and then, in the following chapter, trace the painful decade of the 1930s.

97. *The Advance of Democracy After 1919*

The first years following the war were troubled. Even the victors faced serious difficulties in reconversion from war to peace. Veterans demobilized from the huge armies found themselves unemployed and psychologically restless. Farms and factories geared to maximum production during the war faced a sudden disappearance of markets. They produced more than could now be sold, so that the war was followed by a sharp postwar depression, which, however, had run its course by 1922. Basically, the economic position even of the victors was

Chapter Emblem: A medal struck in honor of the Peace of Versailles, 1919.

seriously damaged, for the war had disjointed the world of 1914, in which industrial western Europe had lived by exchange with eastern Europe and with overseas countries.

Gains of Democracy and Social Democracy

The war, President Wilson had said, was fought to make the world safe for democracy. Political democracy now made advances everywhere. The new states that emerged from the war all adopted written constitutions and universal suffrage. Democracy made advances even in countries that had long been in large measure democratic. Great Britain dropped the last barriers to universal male suffrage in 1918. The most conspicuous innovation was the growing enfranchisement of women. In 1918 female suffrage with certain restrictions was adopted in Great Britain; in 1928 the restrictions were dropped and the vote was granted on an equal basis with men. In 1920, through an amendment to the constitution, female suffrage became general in the United States. Women voted also in Germany and in most of the new states of Europe. In the Soviet Union women received the vote on an equal basis with men after the Revolution in 1917.

In most European countries the successors of the old prewar socialists gained in strength. With the left wings of the old socialists generally seceding, calling themselves Communists, and affiliated with each other and with Moscow in the Communist International, the European socialists or social democrats were preponderantly a party of peaceable or revisionist Marxism, entirely willing to carry on the class conflict by parliamentary and legislative methods. Labor unions, with new self-confidence gained from the role they had played in the war, grew in membership, prestige, and importance.

Social legislation which before the war would have seemed radical was now enacted in many places. An eight-hour legal working day became common, and government-sponsored insurance programs against sickness, accident, and old age were either adopted or extended; an act of 1930, in France, insured almost 10 million workers. An air of progressive democracy pervaded Europe and the European world. The social service, or welfare, state, already under way in the late nineteenth century, was becoming more firmly established.

Only in Italy in the early postwar years, of the states that might have been expected to continue their prewar democratic gains, did democracy receive a sharp setback. Italy had been a parliamentary state since 1861 and had introduced a democratic suffrage in the elections of 1913. In 1919 the Italians held their second elections under universal male suffrage. But Italian democracy soon abruptly ended. In 1922 an agitator named Benito Mussolini, leading a movement which he called Fascism (thereby adding a new word to the world's political vocabulary), killed off the Italian parliament and founded his Fascist regime.[1] Lenin had already founded the first single-party state; Mussolini became the first of the dictators of postwar Europe outside the Soviet Union. Fascist Italy, in the 1920s, was the chief exception in what seemed to be a rising tide of democracy.

[1] See pp. 549, 818–822.

The New States of Central and East-Central Europe

In central and east-central Europe—in Germany, in the territory of the former Austro-Hungarian empire, and in the western fringe of former tsarist Russia—new states and new governments struggled to establish themselves. The new states included, besides republican Germany, the four successor states to the Habsburg empire—Austria, Hungary, Czechoslovakia, and Yugoslavia; and the five states that had broken away from the Russian empire—Poland, Finland, Estonia, Latvia, and Lithuania.[2] The other small states in eastern Europe, Romania, Bulgaria, Greece, and Albania, had already been independent before 1914; their boundaries underwent some modification and their governments considerable reorganization after the war. Turkey, the successor to the Ottoman Empire, is considered elsewhere.[3]

The new states were to a large extent accidents of the war. Nowhere, except possibly in Poland, did they represent a deeply felt, long-maturing, or widespread revolutionary sentiment. Only an infinitesimal number of Germans in 1914 would have voted for a republic. Even among the nationalities of Austria-Hungary in 1914 few persons would have chosen the complete breakup of the Habsburg empire. The republicans, moderate socialists, agrarians, or nationalists who now found themselves in power had to improvise governments for which there had been little preparation. They had to contend with reactionaries, monarchists, and members of the old aristocracy. They had also to deal with the real revolutionaries, who, inspired by Lenin's success, hoped to bring about the dictatorship of the proletariat. A communist revolt broke out in Germany in 1919 but was quickly suppressed; soviet regimes were actually set up but soon crushed in Hungary and in the German state of Bavaria; and as late as 1923 there was a communist uprising in the German state of Saxony.

The new states all embodied the principle of national self-determination, which held that each nationality should enjoy political sovereignty—one nation, one government. But people in this region were and always had been locally intermixed.[4] Each of the new states therefore included minority nationalities; for, with the exception of an exchange of populations between Greece and Turkey, arranged in 1923, there was no thought of the actual physical removal of "alien" groups. Poland and Czechoslovakia were the most composite of the new states. Each of these two possessed, in particular, among its several minorities, a considerable population of disaffected Germans.

Nevertheless, despite economic and nationalist troubles, the new states and governments attempted at the outset to make themselves democratic. Except for the German republic they were all relatively small. All the newly created states were republics except Yugoslavia, which was under the older Serbian dynasty. Hungary started out in 1918 as a republic, but the attempt of Béla Kun to found a Hungarian Soviet Republic in 1919 brought back the counterrevolutionaries who restored the Habsburg monarchy in principle, though they were prevented by foreign pressure from restoring the king in person. Hungary emerged in 1920

[2] See map, pp. 728–729.
[3] See pp. 791–793.
[4] See map, p. 470.

as a monarchy with a perennially vacant throne, under a kind of dictatorship exercised by Admiral Horthy. All smaller states of Europe, including Hungary, possessed at least the external apparatus of democracy until the 1930s; that is, they had constitutions, parliaments, elections, and a diversity of political parties. If civil liberty was sometimes violated, the right to civil liberty was not denied; and if the elections were sometimes rigged, they were at least in principle supposed to be free.

Economic Problems of Eastern Europe; Land Reform

Eastern Europe for centuries had been an agrarian region of large landed estates, which supported on the one hand a wealthy landowning aristocracy of almost feudal outlook, and on the other an impoverished mass of agricultural workers with little or no property of their own. The landed aristocracy had been the chief support of the Austro-Hungarian empire and an important pillar of the old order in the tsarist empire and in eastern Prussia. The mass of the rural population, through all this region, had been free from serfdom, or released from subjection to manorial landlords, only since the middle of the preceding century.[5] The middle class of business and professional men was small except in Austria and Bohemia, the western portion of Czechoslovakia. In general, the whole region was conscious of lagging behind western Europe, not only in industry, factories, railroads, and great cities, but also in literacy, schooling, reading habits, health, death rates, length of life, and material standard of living.[6]

The new states set out to modernize themselves, generally on the model of the West. They introduced democratic and constitutional ideas. They put up protective tariffs, behind which they tried to develop factories and industries of their own. But the new national boundaries created difficulties. Where Europe in 1913 had had 6,000 miles of frontiers, after the war it had almost 10,000, and all the increase was in eastern Europe. Goods circulated much less easily. Protected industries in the old agricultural regions produced inefficiently and at high cost. Old and

---

[5] See pp. 513, 520, and map, p. 212.
[6] See pp. 585–586.

established industries, in Austria, Czechoslovakia, and western Poland, cut off by the new frontiers and new tariffs from their former markets, fell upon hard times. The working class of Vienna lived in misery, because Vienna, a city of 2 million persons, formerly the capital of an empire of 50 million, was now the capital of a republic of 6 million. In Czechoslovakia the German minority living in the Sudetenland complained that in hard times the German businesspeople and workers, because of government policies, always suffered more than their Czech counterparts. Economically, the carving up of eastern Europe into a dozen independent states was self-defeating.

The greatest of reforms undertaken by the new east-European states was the reform of landownership. Although it far from solved basic economic problems in the area, it did have substantial effect on the pattern of land distribution. The whole traditional agrarian base of society was overturned. The work of the revolutions of 1848, which, in the Habsburg lands, had liberated the peasants but left them landless, was now carried a step further. The example of the Russian Revolution gave a powerful stimulus, for in Russia in 1917 peasants had driven off landlords, and communists won a hearing among discontented and propertyless peasants from Finland to the Balkans. Not until 1929, it should be recalled, did the Soviet Union embark on the collectivization of agriculture; until then, communism appeared to favor the small individual farmer. But it may be said with equal truth that the model for agrarian reform lay in the West, especially in France, the historic land of the small peasant proprietor.

Land reform worked out differently in different countries. In the Baltic states the big properties belonged almost entirely to German families, the "Baltic barons," descendants of the medieval Teutonic Knights.[7] In Estonia, Latvia, and Lithuania the nationalist dislike for Germans made it easier to liquidate landlords. Small farms here became the rule. In Czechoslovakia over half the arable land was transferred from large to small owners; here again, the fact that many great landowners had been German, in some cases since the days of the Thirty Years' War,[8] made the operation more palatable, though it inflamed the German minority in Bohemia. In Romania and Yugoslavia the breakup of large estates, though considerable, was less thorough. In Finland, Bulgaria, and Greece the issue hardly arose, since small landownership was already common. Land reform had least success in Poland and Hungary, where the landed magnates were exceptionally strong and well rooted.

After the land reforms, political parties of peasants or small landholders became the chief democratic force within the various states on the western border of Russia. Often they inclined to socialism, especially since capitalism was associated in their minds with foreign investors and outsiders. On the other hand, the great landowners, the former aristocrats of the prewar empires, whether already expropriated or merely threatened with expropriation, were confirmed in a reactionary outlook. The land reforms did not solve basic economic problems. The new small farms were very small, frequently no more than ten acres. The peasant owners lacked capital, agricultural skill, and knowledge of the market. Farm productivity did not rise. In place of old differences between landlord and

[7] See p. 79 and map, p. 44.
[8] See pp. 141–142, 224.

tenant there developed new differences between the more comfortable peasants and the proletarian hired hands. The continuance of relative poverty, the obstinacy of reactionary upper classes, the new stresses and strains among the peasants themselves, the economic distortions produced by numerous tariff walls, and the lack of any sustained tradition of self-government all helped to frustrate the democratic experiments launched in the 1920s.

98. *The German Republic and the Spirit of Locarno*

The keystone of Europe was Germany. Germany, too, had its revolution in 1918. But it was a revolution without revolutionaries, a negative revolution caused more by the disappearance of the old than by any vehement arrival of the new. The emperor and the High Command of the army, in the last weeks of the war, had bowed out of the picture, leaving it to others to face defeat and humiliation.[9] For a time, after November 1918, the men in charge of affairs were mainly Social Democrats. The Social Democrats were Marxists, but their Marxism was the tamed, toned down, and revisionist Marxism that had prevailed for twenty years before the advent of Lenin. They were trade union officials and party managers. They could look back, in 1918, on decades spent in developing labor organizations and building up the Social Democratic party, which in 1912 had become the largest single party in the Reichstag.[10] Now, in 1918, they were a cautious and prudent group, essentially conservative, more anxious to preserve what they had already achieved than to launch audacious new social experiments. Before 1917 the Social Democrats considered themselves well to the left. But the Bolshevik Revolution in Russia, and the emergence of a pro-Bolshevik or communist element in Germany, put the Social Democrats in the middle. The middle is an awkward spot, especially in disturbed times; the Communists regarded the Social Democrats as reactionaries, despicable traitors to the working-class movement; whereas the true reactionaries, recruited from old monarchists, army officers, Junker landowners, and big business groups, saw in social democracy, or professed to see in it, a dangerous flirtation with Bolshevism.

The middle group in Germany, the Social Democrats reinforced by the Catholic Center party and others, was more afraid of the left than of the right. They were appalled, in 1918 and 1919, by the stories brought out of Russia, not merely by fugitive bourgeois or tsarist aristocrats, but by refugee Social Democrats, Mensheviks, and anti-Leninist Bolsheviks, many of whom the socialists had long known and trusted in the Second International. In January 1919 the Spartacists,[11] led by Karl Liebknecht and Rosa Luxemburg, attempted to bring about a proletarian revolution in Germany, like that in Russia. Lenin and the Russian Bolsheviks aided them. For a time, there seemed to be a possibility that Germany might go communist, that the Spartacists might succeed in imposing a dictatorship of the proletariat. But the Social Democratic Provisional Government crushed the Spartacist uprising, turning for that purpose to demobilized army officers and

---

[9] See pp. 717–718.
[10] See pp. 615–616, 622–625.
[11] So named from Spartacus, a Roman slave who led a slave revolt in south Italy in 72 B.C.

volunteer vigilantes recruited from the disbanding army. The Spartacist leaders Liebknecht and Luxemburg were arrested and shot while in police custody. The events of "Spartacus Week" widened a chasm between Social Democrats and Communists, not bridged even in Hitler's concentration camps.

Shortly after, elections were held for a National Constituent Assembly. No single party received a majority, but the Social Democrats were the leading party. A coalition of Social Democrats, Center party, and liberal democrats dominated the Assembly. After several months of deliberations at the city of Weimar, in July 1919, a constitution was adopted establishing a democratic republic. The Weimar Republic (as the regime in Germany from 1919 to the advent of Hitler in 1933 is called) was soon threatened ominously from the right. In 1920 a group of disaffected army officers staged a *Putsch*, or armed revolt, put the republican government to flight, and attempted to place a puppet of their own, one Dr. Kapp, at the head of the state. The Berlin workers, by turning off public utilities, stopped the Kapp *Putsch* and saved the republic. But the Weimar government never took sufficiently firm measures to put down private armed bands led by reactionary or outspokenly antidemocratic agitators. One of these was soon to be Adolf Hitler, who as early as 1923 staged an abortive revolt in Munich.[12] Nor, being democratic and liberal, did it ever deny the rights of election to the Reichstag, and of free speech in the Reichstag and in public, either to communists or to antidemocratic reactionaries.

The Weimar Republic was in principle highly democratic. The constitution embodied all the devices then favored by the most advanced democrats, not only universal suffrage, including the vote for women, but proportional representation and the initiative, referendum, and recall. But except for the legal eight-hour day and a few other such safeguards to the workers' welfare (and traditional demands of organized labor) the republic of which the Social Democrats were the main architects in its formative years was remote from anything socialistic. No industries were nationalized. No property changed hands. No land laws or agrarian reforms were undertaken, as in the new states of eastern Europe; the East-Elbian Junkers remained untouched in their landed estates. There was almost no confiscation even of the property of the former kaiser and other ruling dynasties of Bismarck's federal empire. The very statues of emperors, kings, princes, and grand dukes were left standing in the streets and squares. Officials, civil servants, police agents, professors, schoolteachers of old imperial Germany remained at their respective duties. The army, though limited by the Versailles treaty to 100,000 men, remained the old army in miniature, with all its essential organs intact, and lacking only in mass. The soldiers were peasant youths enlisted for long terms and soon formed to German and Prussian military traditions. In the officer corps the old professional and aristocratic influences remained strong.

Never had there been a revolution so mild, so reasonable, so tolerant. There was no terror, no fanaticism, no stirring faith, no expropriation, no émigrés. There had in truth been no revolution at all, in the sense in which England, France, the United States, Russia, and other countries, either recently or in the more distant past, had experienced revolutions.

---

[12] See p. 824.

The German Democracy and Versailles

The supreme question, for Europe and the world, was how Germany would adjust to the postwar conditions. How would the Germans accept the new internal regime of democracy? How would they accept the new German frontiers and other provisions of the Treaty of Versailles? These two questions were unfortunately interconnected. The Weimar Republic and the Treaty of Versailles were both products of the defeat of Germany in the war. There were many in Germany who favored democracy, notably the numerous Social Democrats, and many more possibly could have been won over to it, given time and favorable conditions. But no one, not even the Social Democrats, accepted the Treaty of Versailles or the new German frontiers as either just or final. If "democracy" in Germany meant the perpetual acceptance of the treaty without amendment, or if it meant economic distress or hardship which could either reasonably or unreasonably be explained as consequences of the treaty, then "democracy" would lose such appeal as it had for the Germans.

The German republicans, we have seen, protested against the Versailles treaty before signing, and signed only under pressure.[13] The Allies continued the wartime naval blockade after the armistice; this confirmed, in German eyes, the argument that the Treaty of Versailles was a *Diktat*, a dictated peace, Carthaginian, ruthless, and vengeful. The "war guilt" clause, while it perhaps on the one hand satisfied a peculiar Anglo-American sense of morality, on the other hand offended a peculiar German sense of honor. Neither the reparations demanded of them, nor the new frontiers, were accepted by the Germans as settled. Reparations they regarded as a perpetual mortgage on their future. They generally expected, some day, to revise their eastern frontier, recover at least the Polish corridor, and merge with German-speaking Austria.

The French lived in terror of the day when Germany would recover. Their plans for their own security, and for the collective security of Europe against a German revival, had been disappointed. They had been unable to detach the Rhineland from Germany. The United States Senate had refused to ratify the treaty, signed at Paris by Wilson, by which the United States was to guarantee France against German invasion in the future.[14] Both Britain and the United States showed a tendency to isolation, to pull away from the Continent, to get back to "normalcy," to work mainly for a restored trade in which a strong Germany would be a large customer. The League of Nations, of which the United States was not a member, and in which every member nation had a veto, offered little assurance of safety to a people so placed as the French. The French began to form alliances, against a potentially resurgent Germany, with Poland, Czechoslovakia, and other east-European states. They insisted also on German payment of reparations. The amount of reparations, left unstated in the treaty, was fixed by a Reparations Commission in 1921 at 132 billion gold marks. This sum, the equivalent of $35 billion, was soon pronounced by various Western economists to be more than Germany could possibly contrive to pay.

[13] See p. 726.
[14] See pp. 723–724, 731.

The Weimar government in these circumstances looked to the Soviet Union, which had been no party to the Versailles treaty and claimed no reparations. The Soviet government meanwhile, concluding from the failure of proletarian revolution in Germany and Hungary that the time was not ripe for the sovietizing of Europe, prepared to enter into normal diplomatic relations with established governments. Germany and the Soviet Union, despite ideological repugnance, thus signed the treaty of Rapallo in 1922. In the following years the Soviet Union obtained needed manufactures from Germany, and German factories and workers were kept busy by orders from the Soviets. The German army dispatched officers and technicians to give instruction to the Red Army. Obliged by the Treaty of Versailles to restrict its activities, the German army was in fact able, through its work in Russia, and through a number of subterfuges at home, to maintain a high standard of training, planning, technical knowledge, and familiarity with new weapons and equipment. The good understanding between Germany and Russia naturally caused apprehension in the West.

Reparations, the Great Inflation of 1923, Recovery

The French, blocked in the attempt to collect reparations, and assisted by the Belgians, in 1923 sent units of the French army to occupy the industrial sites of the Ruhr valley. The Germans responded by general strikes and passive resistance. To sustain the workers the Weimar government paid them benefits, grinding paper money off the printing presses for this purpose. Germany, like other belligerent countries, had suffered from inflation during and after the war; neither the imperial government nor the Weimar statesmen had been willing to impose heavier taxes to offset it. But what now swept Germany was different from ordinary inflation. It was of catastrophic and utterly ruinous proportions. Paper money became literally worthless. By the end of 1923 it took over 4 trillion paper marks to equal a dollar.

This inflation brought far more of a social revolution than the fall of the Hohenzollern empire had ever done. Debtors paid off debts in worthless money. Creditors received baskets full of meaningless paper. Salaries even when raised lagged behind the soaring cost of living. Annuities, pensions, proceeds of insurance policies, savings accounts in the banks, income from bonds and mortgages— every form of revenue which had been arranged for at some time in the past, and which often represented the economy, foresight, and personal planning of many years—now turned to nothing. The middle class was pauperized and demoralized. Middle-class people were now materially in much the position of workers and proletarians. Their whole view of life, however, made it impossible for them to identify themselves with the laboring class or to accept its Marxist or socialist ideologies. They had lost faith in society itself, in the future, in the old burgher codes of self-reliance and rational planning of their own lives in an understandable world. A kind of moral void was created, with nothing for them to believe in, hope for, or respect.

The inflation, however, by wiping out all outstanding indebtedness within the country, made it possible, once the losses were written off and accepted, to start up economic production afresh. The United States was persuaded to play a reluctant role. The United States, in these years, demanded payment of the huge

war debts owed to it by the Allies.[15] The Allies—Britain, France, Belgium—
insisted that they could not pay debts to the United States unless they collected
reparations from Germany. In 1924 the Dawes Plan, named for the American
Charles G. Dawes, was instituted in Germany to assure the flow of reparations.
By the Dawes Plan the French evacuated the Ruhr, the reparations payments
were cut down, and arrangements made for the German republic to borrow
abroad. A good deal of American private capital was invested in Germany in the
following years, both in German government bonds and in German industrial
enterprises. Gradually, so at least it seemed, Germany was put on its feet. For
four or five years the Weimar Republic even enjoyed a bustling prosperity, and
there was a good deal of new construction in roads, housing, factories, and ocean
liners. But the prosperity rested in good measure on foreign loans, and the Great
Depression that began in 1929 reopened all the old questions.

The Spirit of Locarno

These years of economic prosperity were years also of relative international calm.
No issue, in truth, was dealt with fundamentally. The universal German hatred
for the Treaty of Versailles elicited no concessions from the Allies. Conceivably,
had the Allies been willing at this time to amend the treaty by international
agreement, they might have taken wind from the sails of nationalistic rabble-
rousers in Germany and so spared themselves much later grief. It may be,
however, that no possible concession would have sufficed. The great problem
was to prevent a German overthrow of the treaty structure by violence, especially
in eastern Europe where the Germans regarded the new frontiers as basically
subject to reconsideration. After the Ruhr incident, and adoption of the Dawes
Plan, a group of moderate and peace-loving men shaped the foreign policy of the
principal countries—Gustav Stresemann in Germany, Édouard Herriot and
Aristide Briand in France, Ramsay MacDonald in England.

The charter of the League of Nations provided for international sanctions
against potential aggressors. Like the system of congresses after the Peace of
Vienna, the League was supposed to assure peaceable compliance with the peace
treaties, or their modification without resort to force.[16] No one expected the
League, by any authority of its own, to prevent war between Great Powers, but
the League achieved various minor pacifications in the 1920s, and in any case its
headquarters at Geneva offered a convenient meeting place in which statesmen
could talk.

As a further assurance against war, in 1925 at Locarno, the European powers
signed a number of treaties. These marked the highest point in international good
will reached between the two World Wars. Germany signed a treaty with France
and Belgium guaranteeing their respective frontiers unconditionally. It signed
arbitration treaties with Poland and Czechoslovakia—not guaranteeing these
frontiers as they stood, but undertaking to attempt changes in them only by
international discussion, agreement, or arbitration. France signed treaties with
Poland and Czechoslovakia promising military aid if they were attacked by

[15] See pp. 721–722, 725–726.
[16] See pp. 477–481, 482.

Germany. France thus fortified its policy of balancing German power in the East by its own diplomatic alliances and by supporting the Little Entente, as the alliance of Czechoslovakia, Yugoslavia, and Romania was called. Great Britain "guaranteed"—i.e., promised military aid in the event of violation—the frontiers of Belgium and France against Germany. It did not give an equivalent guarantee with respect to Czechoslovakia or Poland. The British took the view that their own security would be threatened by German expansion westward, but not by German expansion to the east. It was on the borders of Czechoslovakia and Poland, fourteen years later, that the Second World War began. Had Britain gone along with France in 1925 in guaranteeing these two countries, then stuck to the guarantee, the Second World War might possibly have been prevented. On the other hand, no war ever depends on any single decision; it is the accumulation of many decisions that matters.

In 1925 people talked with relief of the "spirit of Locarno." In 1928 international harmony was again strengthened when the French foreign minister Briand and the United States Secretary of State Frank B. Kellogg arranged for the Pact of Paris. Ultimately signed by sixty-five nations, it condemned recourse to war for the solution of international controversies. Although no measures of enforcement were provided and a number of reservations were added before certain countries signed, the Pact solemnly affirmed the will of the nations to renounce war as an instrument of national policy.

In the mid-1920s the outlook was indeed full of hope. At Locarno, Germany had of its own volition (and not by the *Diktat* of Versailles) accepted its borders both east and west, to the extent of abjuring violence and unilateral action even in the east. In 1926 Germany joined the League of Nations. Germany was a going concern as a democratic republic. Democracy seemed to work, as well as could be expected, in most of the new states of eastern Europe, and Communist Russia itself had halted its postwar revolutionary offensive. The world was again prosperous, or seemed to be so. World production was at or above the prewar level. In 1925 the world's production of raw materials, it was estimated, was 17 percent greater than in 1913. World trade, by 1929, measured in hard money—gold—had almost doubled since 1913. The war and the postwar troubles were remembered as a nightmare escaped from. It seemed that, after all, the world had been made safe for democracy.

But complacency was shattered by the great world depression, by the growth of a malignant nationalism in Germany, due in part to the depression, and by the assertion of a new militancy in Japan, which also was not unrelated to the depression. But let us turn first to the postwar years in Asia.

99. The Revolt of Asia

Resentments in Asia

The peoples of Asia had never been satisfied with the position in which the great European expansion of the nineteenth century had placed them.[17] Increasingly

[17] See pp. 642–650, 669–681.

they condemned everything associated with "imperialism." In this respect there was little difference between countries actually governed by Europeans as parts of European empires in the nineteenth century, such as British India, the Netherlands Indies, French Indochina (or the American Philippines), and countries that remained nominally independent under their own government, such as China, Persia, and the Ottoman Empire. In the former, as political consciousness awakened, there was objection to the monopoly of Europeans in the important offices of government. In the latter, there was objection to the special rights and privileges enjoyed by Europeans, the widespread impounding of customs revenues to pay foreign debts, the capitulations in Turkey, the extraterritorial rights in China, the spheres of influence in Persia which divided the country between British and Russians.

By imperialism, in either case, aroused Asians meant a system whereby the affairs of their own country were conducted, its resources exploited, its people employed, for the benefit of foreigners, Europeans, or white people. They meant the system of absentee capitalism, by which the plantations, docks, or factories before their eyes, and on which they themselves labored, were the property of owners thousands of miles away whose main interest in them was a regular flow of profits. They meant the constant threat that an alien civilization would disintegrate and eat away their own ancient cultures. They meant the nuisance of having to speak a European language, or the calamity of having to fight in wars originated by Europeans. And they meant the airs of superiority assumed by whites, the race consciousness exhibited by all Westerners, though perhaps most of all the British and Americans, the color line that was everywhere drawn, the attitudes varying between contempt and condescension, the relation of native "boy" and European "sahib." Imperialism to them signified the gentlemen's clubs in Calcutta to which no Indian was ever admitted, the hotels in Shanghai from which Chinese were carefully kept out, the park benches in various cities on which no "native" could ever sit. In deeper psychology, as well as in economics and in politics, the revolt of self-conscious Asians was a rebellion against social inferiority and humiliation.

The revolt against the West was generally ambivalent or two-sided. It was a revolt against Western supremacy, but at the same time, in most cases, those who revolted meant to learn from and imitate the West, in order that, by taking over Western science, industry, organization, and other sources of Western power, they might preserve their own identity and emerge as the West's equals.

The crisis in Asia had broken out with the Russo-Japanese War, when an Asian people, in 1905, defeated a great European power for the first time.[18] In 1906 revolution began in Persia, leading to the assembly of the first majlis, or parliament. In 1908 the Young Turks staged a successful revolution in Constantinople and summoned a parliamentary assembly to represent all regions then in the Ottoman Empire. In 1911 the revolutionists in China, led by Sun Yat-sen, overthrew the Manchu dynasty and proclaimed the Chinese Republic. In each case the rebels charged their old monarchs—shah, sultan, emperor—with subservience to Western imperialists. In each case they summoned national assemblies on the prevailing democratic model of Europe, and they proposed to revive, modernize, and

[18] See pp. 681–682.

westernize their countries to the degree necessary to avoid domination by the West.

First World War and Russian Revolution

In the First World War almost all the Asian peoples were somehow involved. The Ottoman Empire, allied with Germany, immediately repudiated all the capitulations, or special legal rights of Europeans. Persia attempted to remain neutral and to get rid of the partition made in 1907 between British and Russian spheres, but it became a battleground of British, Russian, and Turkish forces. China, which joined the Allies, attempted at the peace conference to have the extraterritorial rights in China abolished. We have seen how this request of the Chinese Republic was refused, and how the Allies, instead, transferred many of the prewar German concessions to the Japanese.[19] The dependent regions of Asia, the Dutch, French, and British possessions, were stimulated economically by the war.[20] The Netherlands Indies, though remaining neutral, increased its output of foodstuffs, oil, and raw materials. India developed its steel industry and textile manufactures and contributed over a million soldiers, combat and service troops, to the British cause. All the dependent regions were stirred by Woodrow Wilson's call to make the world safe for democracy.

The home governments made concessions. They were naturally afraid to go too far; they insisted that their subject peoples were not yet capable of self-government. They had huge investments at stake, and the whole world economy depended on the continuing flow of raw materials from tropical and subtropical countries. But they did compromise. In 1916 the Dutch created a legislative assembly to advise the governor general of the Indies; half its members were Indonesians. In 1917 the British agreed to a measure of self-government in India; an Indian legislative assembly was set up with 140 members, of whom 100 were elected, and in the provinces of British India the number of elected representatives and of local Indian officials was increased. The French in 1922 provided for a somewhat similar assembly in Indochina. Thus all three imperial powers, at about the same time, began to experiment with consultative bodies whose membership was partly elective, partly appointive, and partly non-European, partly European. The United States introduced an elected assembly in the Philippine Islands in 1916.

The Russian Revolution added a new stimulus to unrest in Asia. The Bolsheviks denounced not only capitalism but also imperialism. In Marxist-Leninist ideology imperialism was an aspect of capitalism.[21] Colonial peoples also tended to identify the two, not so much for Marxist reasons as because modern capitalism was a foreign or "imperialist" phenomenon in colonial countries, where the ownership and the management of large enterprises were both foreign. Nationalism in Asia, the movement for independence or for more equality with the West, thus easily shaded off into socialism and the denunciation of capitalistic exploitation. The Bolsheviks were quick to see the advantages for themselves in this situation. As

---

[19] See p. 725.
[20] See p. 721.
[21] See p. 740.

it became clear that the world revolution, as expected by Lenin, would not soon come to pass in Europe, the Russian communists turned to Asia as the theater in which world capitalism might be attacked by a great flanking movement. In September 1920 a "congress of oppressed Eastern peoples" assembled at Baku, on the coast of the Caspian Sea. Zinoviev, head of the Communist International, called for war upon "the wild beasts of British capitalism." Not much was accomplished at the conference. But a few extremists from Asian countries in the following years sojourned in Moscow, and a few communists dispatched from Moscow stirred up the discontents which existed, quite without Russian instigation, all over Asia.

The postwar situation in Asia was thus extremely fluid. People who were not communists hailed communism as a liberating force. Anti-Westerners declared that their countries must westernize. Nationalism overshadowed all other isms. In the Indian National Congress rich Indian capitalists consorted with socialist leaders, with whom they were held together in relative harmony so long as the common enemy was the British.

The Turkish Revolution: Kemal Atatürk

The most immediately successful of the revolutionary movements was the one in Turkey. The Young Turks at first, in 1908, had meant to prevent the further dissolution of the Ottoman Empire.[22] This proved to be impossible. In the Balkan wars of 1912–1913 the Ottoman power was almost totally excluded from the Balkan peninsula. In the World War, in which the Turks were on the losing side, the Arabs with a great deal of British assistance broke away. After the war, in 1921, the Greeks invaded the Anatolian peninsula. They dreamed of a Great Greece embracing both sides of the Aegean. Europeans still regarded Turkey as the sick man of Europe, the Ottoman state as doomed to extinction, and the Turkish people as barbarous and incompetent. The Allies had agreed in 1915 to partition Turkey; and after the war the Western powers favored the Greek invasion. Italian and French forces occupied parts of Anatolia, and Italians, French, and British undertook to take Constantinople from Turkish rule, though its disposition remained uncertain. (It had been promised to Russia in 1915, before the Bolshevik Revolution.[23]) In these circumstances a powerful army officer named Mustapha Kemal rallied Turkish national resistance. Within two years, and with aid from the Soviet Union, the Turks drove the Greeks and the Western Allies away. They affirmed their hold on the Anatolian peninsula, and on both shores of the Straits, including Constantinople, which was renamed Istanbul.[24]

The Nationalists, under the energetic drive of Mustapha Kemal, now put through a sweeping revolution. They abolished the sultanate and the caliphate, since the sultan had somewhat compromised himself with foreigners, and was also, as caliph or commander of the faithful, a religious functionary for all Islam and hence a conservative influence. The Turkish Republic was promulgated in 1923.

[22] See p. 657, and maps, pp. 660, 703.
[23] See pp. 709–710.
[24] See map, p. 660.

Where the Ottoman Empire had been a composite organization made up of diverse religious communities, among which the Muslims were the ruling group, the Turkish Republic was conceived as a national state in which the "people," i.e., the Turkish people, were sovereign. Universal suffrage was introduced, along with a parliament, a ministry, and a president with strong powers. Non-Turks in Asia Minor now became "foreign" in a way they had not been before. We have seen the fate of the Armenians during the First World War.[25] The other large non-Turkish and Christian people were the Greeks. After the war about 1.4 million Greeks either fled or were officially transported from Asia Minor to Greece, and, in exchange, some 400,000 Turks residing in northern Greece were transported to Turkey. The exchange of populations caused great hardship, it uprooted most of the Greek element that had lived in Asia Minor since 1000 B.C., and it overwhelmed the impoverished Greek kingdom by obliging it suddenly to absorb a mass of destitute refugees, who were a quarter as numerous as the population of Greece itself. But it enabled the Turkish Republic to acquire a relatively homogeneous population, ending minority disputes between Greece and Turkey until Cyprus posed new problems after the Second World War.

For the first time in any Muslim country the spheres of government and religion were sharply distinguished. The Turkish Republic affirmed the total separation of church and state. It declared religion to be a private belief, and it tolerated all religions. Government was reorganized on secular and nonreligious principles stemming from the French Revolution. The law of the Koran was thrust aside. The new law was modeled on the Swiss Code, the most recently codified European legislation, itself derived from the Code Napoleon.

Mustapha Kemal urged women to put aside the veil, to come out of the harem, to vote, and to occupy public office. He made polygamy a crime. Men he required by law to discard the fez. He fought against the fez as Peter the Great had fought against the beard, and for the same reason, seeing in it the symbol of conservative and backward habits. The hat, "headgear of civilization," correspondingly became the symbol of progress. The people shifted to Western dress. The Western alphabet became mandatory; literate Turks had to learn to read again, and illiteracy was reduced. The Western calendar and the metric system were adopted. Turks were required to assume hereditary family surnames, like Westerners; Kemal himself took the name Atatürk, or Great Turk. The capital was moved from Istanbul to Ankara. The republic put up a high tariff. In 1933 it adopted a five-year plan for economic development. The Turks, having shaken off foreign influence, were determined not to become again dependent on Western capital or capitalism. The five-year plan provided for mines, railroads, and factories, mainly under government ownership. At the same time, while willing to accept Russian aid against the Western powers, the republic had no patience with communism, which it suppressed. The Turks wanted a modern Turkey—by and for the Turks.

Persia experienced a similar revolution, somewhat less drastic. In 1921 Reza Khan, an army officer, overthrew the older ruling dynasty and in 1925 became shah. The old concessions, capitulations, and spheres were done away with, and the Persian government renegotiated its oil contracts, asserting more control over

---

[25] See pp. 710–711. On the multinational character of the Ottoman Empire see pp. 219–220 and 654–656.

foreign corporations and receiving a larger return from them in taxes and royalties. In 1935, to emphasize its break with the past, Persia took the name of Iran.

The National Movement in India: Gandhi and Nehru

India at the close of the First World War was on the verge of revolution against British rule.[26] Discontented Indians looked for leadership to Mohandas K. Gandhi, the Mahatma, or Holy One, who in the following decades, though hardly typical of modern Asia, attained a worldwide eminence as the champion of subjected peoples. Gandhi had been educated in England in the 1890s and had practiced law in South Africa, where he became aware of racial discrimination as a worldwide problem. In India, after 1919, he led a movement for self-government, for economic and spiritual independence from Great Britain, and for greater tolerance within India itself both between Hindus and Muslims and between upper-caste Hindus and the depressed outcastes and untouchables. The weapons he favored were those of the spirit only; he preached nonviolence, passive resistance, civil disobedience, and the boycott. He took to self-imposed fasts and hunger strikes to cope with his British jailers and later with the Indians themselves. He and his most loyal followers, as the troubles mounted, refused to be elected or take part in the partially representative institutions that the British cautiously introduced and also boycotted the British economic position in India, by refusing to buy or use goods imported from England. The latter touched the British in a sensitive spot. Before the World War half of all exports of British cotton cloth had gone to India. By 1932 this proportion fell to a quarter. Gandhi turned against all industrialism, even the mechanized industry that was growing up in India itself. He put aside Western costume, took to using a spinning wheel and living on goat's milk, urged Indian peasants to revive their old handicrafts, and appeared on solemn occasions clad in no more than a homespun loincloth. By the high level of his principles Gandhi made himself an inspiration to many groups that differed on more mundane matters. Even in the West he was regarded as one of the great religious teachers of all time.

India was very much divided within, and the British maintained that because of these divisions the ending of British rule would precipitate anarchy. There were Hindus and Muslims, between whom clashes and terrorist outrages were chronic. (Gandhi was himself murdered in 1948 by an anti-Muslim Hindu fanatic.) There were the hundreds of oriental potentates of the native states. There were Indian capitalists, like the Tata family, and growing masses of proletarians produced by Indian industrialization.[27] There were the higher castes and the outcastes, and there were hundreds of millions of peasants living in a poverty unimaginable in the West. In politics, there were those who demanded full independence, boycotted the British, and spent years in jail, as did Gandhi and his more practical-minded but devoted follower, Jawaharlal Nehru; and there were the moderates who believed that they might best advance the welfare of India by accepting government office, cooperating with the British, and working for dominion status within the British Empire. Marxism exerted a strong appeal,

---

[26] See pp. 669–672, 682.
[27] See p. 721.

not indeed on the spiritual and pacific Gandhi, but on Nehru and even many of the less radical leaders. In the 1920s the Soviet Union stood in their eyes for the overthrow of imperialism; in the 1930s it pointed the way by its adoption of five-year plans. For a people wishing to raise itself by its own bootstraps, to move from poverty to industrial strength and higher living standards without loss of time, and without dependence on foreign capital and capitalism, the Soviet Union with its economic planning seemed to offer a more appropriate model and more practical lessons than the rich democracies of the West, with their centuries of gradual progress behind them.

The twenty years between world wars were years of repeated disturbance, of rioting and repression, of sporadic violence despite the exhortations of Gandhi, of conferences and round tables, reforms and promises of reform, with a drift in the 1930s toward more participation of Indians in the affairs of the Indian empire. Independence was not won until after the Second World War; with it took place a partition of the Indian subcontinent into two new nations, a predominantly Hindu India and a predominantly Muslim Pakistan.[28]

In the Netherlands Indies, where the nationalist movement was less developed than in India,[29] the interwar years were more quiet. A serious rebellion, in which communists took part, broke out in 1922 but was suppressed by the Dutch. The peoples of the archipelago were almost as diverse as those of India. Only the Dutch empire had brought them politically together. Opposition to the Dutch gave them a common program. In 1937 the legislative council petitioned for the grant of dominion status. But not until after the Second World War and the failure of a military effort to repress the nationalists did the Dutch concede independence.[30]

The Chinese Revolution: The Three People's Principles

The Chinese Revolution had opened in 1911 with the overthrow of the Manchu dynasty, which itself had belatedly begun to introduce westernizing reforms. The Chinese Republic was proclaimed, but the first immediate result was the establishment in Peking of a military dictatorship exercised by General Yüan Shih-kai, who had been a close adviser to the Manchus and who, until his death in 1916, never ceased to cast covetous eyes on the now empty imperial throne itself. In the south the veteran revolutionary Dr. Sun Yat-sen reorganized the Kuomintang (National People's, or Nationalist party), successor to the prerevolutionary network of underground societies of which he had been the chief architect. Sun, elected the first president of the republic by a revolutionary provisional assembly, resigned within a few months in favor of General Yüan, who he mistakenly believed would unite the country under a parliamentary regime. Subsequently, in the confusion that followed the struggle for power in Peking after Yüan's death in 1916, Sun was proclaimed president of a rival government in the south at Canton, which exercised a nominal power over the

[28] See pp. 920–922.
[29] See pp. 669–670.
[30] See p. 923.

southern provinces. Not until 1928 could any government have any basis for claiming actual rule over China—and even then, there were important exceptions. For most of these years the country was virtually in the hands of contending war lords, each of whom pocketed the customary taxes in his own locality, maintained his own army, and recognized no superior authority.

It was Sun Yat-sen who best expressed the ideas of the Chinese Revolution. Born in 1867 and educated under American influence in the Hawaiian Islands, he had received a medical degree at Hong Kong, had traveled extensively about the world, studied Western ideas, lectured to Chinese audiences in America, collected money for his conspiracies against the Manchus, and had returned from Europe to take part in the revolution. Shortly before his death in 1925 Sun gathered the lectures which he had been expounding for years into a book, *The Three People's Principles*. The book sheds much light on the revolt of China, and of all Asia, against the supremacy of the West.

The three people's principles, according to Sun Yat-sen, were democracy, nationalism, and livelihood. Livelihood meant social welfare and economic reform—a more equitable distribution of wealth and land, a gradual end to poverty and unjust economic exploitation. By nationalism Dr. Sun meant that the Chinese who had always lived mainly in the clan and family had now to learn the importance of the nation and the state. They were in fact a great nation, he thought, the world's most cultured, and had once prevailed from the mouth of the Amur to the East Indies. But they had never been cohesive. The Chinese had been "a sheet of loose sand"; they must now "break down individual liberty and become pressed together into an unyielding body like the firm rock which is formed by the addition of cement to sand."

By democracy Sun Yat-sen meant the sovereignty of the people. Like Rousseau, he gave little attention to voting, elections, or parliamentary processes. He believed that while the people were sovereign, the able should govern. Government should be conducted by experts, a principle he criticized the West for neglecting. Dr. Sun felt a warm sympathy for Lenin. Yet he was by no means a doctrinaire Marxist. Marxism he thought inapplicable to China, arguing that the Chinese must take Marxism as they took all other Western ideas, avoiding slavish imitation, using, adapting, amending, rejecting as they saw fit. China had no native capitalism in any Marxist or Western sense. The "capitalists" in China, he said, were owners of land, especially in the cities, such as Shanghai, where the coming of Westerners had raised land values to dizzy heights. Hence if China could get rid of imperialism it would take a long step toward getting rid of capitalism also; it could begin to equalize landowning and confiscate unearned rents. Since China, he observed, had no true capitalists the state itself must undertake capitalist and industrial development. This would require loans of foreign capital and the services of foreign managers and technicians, adding another reason why the Chinese state, to maintain control, must be strong.

With Sun Yat-sen, in short, democracy easily shaded off into a theory of benevolent and constructive dictatorship. Marxism, communism, socialism, "livelihood," the planned society, welfare economics, and antiforeign and anti-imperialist sentiment were all mixed together—in some ways as the ideas of the Chinese Communists would later be.

The first aim of Sun Yat-sen and of the revolutionists in China was to shake off the "treaty system" that had bound China to outside interests since 1842.[31] In this respect the Paris peace conference had been disappointing; the Chinese not only failed to obtain the abolition of Western privileges and extraterritorial rights but could not block the retention by Japan of many of the former German concessions that the Japanese had taken over during the war.[32] Widespread student and worker demonstrations directed against the Western powers took place on May 4, 1919. The May Fourth movement heightened the antiforeign consciousness.

As the Western powers proved obdurate, Sun and the Kuomintang turned to Russia. They declared the Russian and Chinese revolutions to be two aspects of the same worldwide movement of liberation. The Chinese Communist party, organized in 1921, became allied with the Kuomintang in 1923. The latter accepted Russian communist advisers, notably the veteran revolutionist Borodin, whom Sun Yat-sen had known years before in the United States.[33] The Soviet Union, following its strategy of outflanking world capitalism by penetrating Asia, sent military equipment, army instructors, and party organizers into China. It also surrendered the Russian concessions and extraterritorial rights acquired in China by the tsars. The Chinese policy of friendliness to Russia began to produce the hoped for effects; the British, to draw China from Russia, gave up a few of their lesser concessions at Hankow and other cities.

China: Nationalists and Communists

The Kuomintang, its armies reorganized and strengthened, now displayed a fresh vitality and after 1924 launched a military and political offensive, planned by the ever active Russian advisers, supported by the Chinese Communists, and headed by Chiang Kai-shek, who succeeded to the leadership of the Kuomintang upon Sun's death in 1925. Chiang's main objectives were to compel the independent war lords and the regime still holding office in Peking to accept the authority of a single Nationalist government. By the end of 1928 Chiang's armies had swept northward, occupied Peking, and transferred the seat of government to Nanking. Chiang now exercised at least nominal control over most of China, although effective control was still limited by the recalcitrance of many provincial war lords. The outside powers, acknowledging the accomplishments of the Kuomintang, extended diplomatic recognition to the Nanking government and conceded its right to organize and run the country's tariff and customs affairs. They also partially surrendered their extraterritorial privileges and pledged to abolish them completely in the near future.

In 1927, while a measure of national unity was being forged in the country, an open break occurred between the Kuomintang and its left wing. In the course of the northern military campaign, and particularly in the seizure of Nanking, popular disturbance and excesses, including the killing of a number of foreigners, had

[31] See pp. 678–681.
[32] See p. 725.
[33] See p. 775.

taken place, allegedly fomented by the Communists. These radical disturbances frightened and alienated the wealthier and more conservative element in the Kuomintang and so jeopardized Chiang's chief source of financial assistance for his government and army. Chiang himself, also, had never apparently considered the alliance with either the Communists or the Russians as anything more than one of convenience. Chiang took decisive action, purging Communists and Russian advisers from the Kuomintang, and executing many. Borodin and others fled to Moscow, and a Communist-led uprising in Canton was forcefully suppressed. A number of armed Communist groups fled to the safety of the mountain regions in the south and joined other guerrilla contingents. In that way the Chinese Red Army was formed; among its leaders were Mao Tse-tung, a former librarian, teacher, newspaper editor, and union organizer, who had been one of the founding members of the party, and Chu Teh, who had held high rank in the Kuomintang armies.

Chiang, with the renewed financial and moral support of the Kuomintang bankers, resumed the northern offensive whose success by 1928 has been described. But the original revolutionary impulse of the Kuomintang was now very much dissipated. Made up of men who feared social upheaval and who often regarded their own maintenance in power as their chief problem, it exercised a kind of one-party dictatorship over most of China under Chiang's leadership. Chiang himself recognized mounting popular dissatisfaction with the reluctance or inability of the Kuomintang to initiate reforms, but he was still busy consolidating the regime and after 1931 he had to contend with Japanese aggression. During these years he conceived a deadly hatred for Communists and those who actively agitated for revolutionary reform.

The Communists, operating now in southeast China, fed on popular discontent and drew support from the poor peasantry by a systematic policy of expropriation and distribution of large landed estates as well as by intensive propaganda. They succeeded in fighting off Chiang's armies and even in winning over part of his troops. Organizing a network of local soviets, in 1931 they proclaimed a Chinese Soviet Republic in the southeast. When the Nationalist armies succeeded in dislodging them, the Communists, under Mao's leadership, undertook in 1934–1935 an amazing 6,000-mile march over near-insuperable terrain to north-central Yenan, closer, it was said, to Soviet supply lines. About 90,000 began the Long March, of which only half survived. They entrenched themselves again, fought off the Nationalist armies, and built up a strong popular following among the rural masses. With the Japanese invasion of north China well under way they abandoned their revolutionary offensive and pressed Chiang to end the civil war and to create a united front against the Japanese aggressor. Chiang reluctantly consented, so that by 1937 an alliance was formed between the Kuomintang and the Communists; the Chinese Red Army was placed under Nationalist control; a united China would face the Japanese. But the uneasy alliance between Kuomintang and Communists was not to last even until the defeat of Japan in the Second World War. Kuomintang and Communists would soon engage in a deadly struggle for power.[34]

[34] See pp. 914–918.

Japan: Militarism and Aggression

The Nationalist movement in China caused apprehension in Japan, whose rise as a modern power has already been traced.[35] The Japanese, at least since the Sino-Japanese War of 1895, had looked upon the huge disintegrating area of China as a field for expansion of their own interests, in this scarcely differing from Europeans, except that they were closer to the scene. During the World War they had presented their Twenty-One Demands on China, taken over the German concessions in Shantung, and sent troops into eastern Siberia.[36] During the war the industrialization of Japan proceeded apace; Japan captured many markets while the Europeans were locked in the struggle; and after the war the Japanese remained one of the chief suppliers of textiles for the rest of Asia. The Japanese could produce at lower prices than the Europeans, prices at which the penniless masses of Asia were more able to buy. Densely packed in their mountainous islands, they sustained their standard of living by importing raw materials and selling manufactures. But the Chinese Nationalists hoped to erect a protective tariff; it was for this reason, among others, that they denounced the treaty system, which for almost a century had bound China to international free trade. The Chinese, like the Turks, hoped to industrialize and westernize their own country behind a high tariff wall, which would shut out Japanese manufactures as well as others.

During the 1920s the civilian, liberal, Western-oriented element in Japan remained in control of the government. In 1925 universal male suffrage was adopted. It was still the fashion in Europe and America to view the Japanese with sympathetic approval, as the most progressive of all non-Europeans, the one Asian people who had ably learned to play its part in the advancing worldwide civilization. But there was another facet to Japan. The constitution of 1889 and parliamentary operations were but a façade that concealed political realities. Only in Japan of all modern countries did a constitutional law prescribe that the war and navy ministers must be active generals or admirals. The diet itself had sharply restricted powers. Ministers governed in the name of the supreme and sacred authority of the emperor, to whom they were alone responsible. Economically, the government's sponsorship of industrial growth had resulted in a tremendous concentration of economic power in the hands of four family trusts known collectively as the Zaibatsu. The business interests and the civilian political leaders all looked to an expanding empire and growing markets, but the most restless group in Japan drew its strength from the nationalist revival which, even before the "opening" of Japan in 1854, had cultivated Shinto, emperor worship, and the way of the warrior as a new and modern way of life.[37] This element was recruited in large part from the old clansmen and samurai, whom the "abolition of feudalism" had uprooted from their accustomed ways, and who in many cases found no outlet for their energies in the new regime. Many of these men now served as officers in the army. Often they regarded the West as decadent. They dreamed of the day when Japan would dominate all East Asia.

[35] See pp. 577–582.
[36] See pp. 711, 725, 752–753.
[37] See pp. 579, 581.

About 1927 this group began to hold ministries in the Japanese government and to turn Japanese policy into increasingly aggressive and militaristic attitudes toward China. In 1931 Japanese army units stationed in southern Manchuria (where the Japanese had been since defeat of the Russians in 1905), alleging the mysterious murder of a Japanese officer at Mukden, seized Chinese arsenals and spread northward over all Manchuria. In 1932, charging the Chinese with economic warfare against Japan (Chinese boycotts were in fact damaging the Japanese export trade), the Japanese landed 70,000 troops at Shanghai. They soon withdrew, preferring to concentrate at this stage on the occupation of the northern part of China. They declared Manchuria to be an independent state under an emperor they themselves selected (the last Chinese emperor, the "boy-emperor" Pu Yi, deposed in 1911), and renamed the state Manchukuo.

After the Manchurian invasion the Chinese appealed to the League of Nations. The League sent a commission of inquiry, which, under Lord Lytton, found Japan at fault for disturbing the peace. Japan defiantly withdrew from the League. The small powers in the League generally cried for military sanctions, but the Great Powers, knowing that they would be the ones to bear the burden of military intervention against Japan, and in any case inclined to see no threat to their own immediate security, refused to take any stronger measures, so that, in effect, the Japanese remained in occupation of Manchuria and northeast China. With the Japanese conquest of Manchuria one tributary of the coming torrent had begun to flow. But the world at this time was also stunned by economic depression. Each government was preoccupied with its own internal social problems.

100. The Great Depression: Collapse of the World Economy

The capitalist economic system was a delicate and interlocking mechanism, in which any disturbance was rapidly transmitted with accelerating impact through all the parts.[38] For many basic commodities prices were determined by the free play of supply and demand in a worldwide market. There was much regional division of labor; large areas lived by producing a few specialized articles for sale to the world as a whole. A great deal of production, both local and international, especially in the 1920s, was financed by credit, which is to say by promises of repayment in the future. The system rested upon mutual confidence and mutual exchange—on the belief of the lender, creditor, or investor that he would get his money back, on the belief of the borrower that he could pay his debts, on the ability of farms and factories to market their products at prices high enough to bring a net return, so that farmers and factory people might purchase the output of other factories and farms, and so on round and round in countless circles of mutual interdependence, and throughout the world as a whole.

The Prosperity of the 1920s and Its Weaknesses

The five years after 1924 were a period of prosperity, in that there was a good deal of international trade, building, and development of new industries. The

[38] See pp. 595–604, 718–722.

automobile, for example, still an oddity in 1914, became an article of mass production after the war; and its widespread use increased the demand for oil, steel, rubber, and electrical equipment, caused the building or rebuilding of tens of thousands of miles of roads, and created whole new secondary occupations for thousands as truckdrivers, garage mechanics, or filling-station attendants. Similarly the mass popularity of radios and moving pictures had repercussions in all directions. The ensuing expansion was most phenomenal in the United States, but almost all countries enjoyed it in greater or lesser degree. "Prosperity" became a mystic term, and some thought that it would last indefinitely, that the secret of human plenty and of progress had been found, and that science and invention were at last realizing the hopes of ages.

But there were weaknesses in this prosperity, various imperfections in this or that gear or valve of the mechanism, flaws which, under stress, were to bring the whole intricate structure to a halt. The expansion was largely financed by credit, or borrowing. Laboring people received less than a balanced share; wages lagged behind profits and dividends, so that mass purchasing power, even when inflated by installment buying (another form of credit), could not absorb the vast output that it was technically possible to produce. And throughout the world the whole decade of the 1920s was a time of chronic agricultural depression, so that farmers could neither pay their debts nor purchase manufactures to the degree required for the smooth functioning of the system.

Military operations in the First World War had reduced wheat fields under cultivation in Europe by a fifth. The world price of wheat went up, and farmers in the United States, Canada, and elsewhere increased their acreage. Often, to acquire land at high prices, they assumed mortgages which in later years they were unable to repay. After the war Europe restored its own wheat production, and eastern Europe reentered the world market. Agriculture was increasingly mechanized. Where, in the nineteenth century, one man could cut ten times as much grain with a single horse-drawn reaper as with a scythe, and where, before 1914, he could cut fifty times as much with a combined reaper and binder, he could again increase his output fivefold after the war, by using a tractor-drawn harvester-thresher combine. At the same time dry farming opened up new land, and agronomic science increased the yield per acre. The result of all these numerous developments was a superabundant output of wheat. But the demand for wheat was what economists call "inelastic." By and large, within the area of the Western world, people already ate as much bread as they wanted and would buy no more; and the undernourished masses of Asia, who in pure theory could have consumed the excess, could not pay even low costs of production or transportation. The world price of wheat fell incredibly. In 1930 a bushel of wheat, in terms of gold, sold for the lowest price in four hundred years.

Wheat growers in all continents were faced with ruin. Growers of many other crops faced the same dismal prospect. Cotton and corn, coffee and cocoa all collapsed. Brazilian and African planters were caught by overproduction and falling prices. In Java, where not only had the acreage in sugar been extended, but the unit yield of sugar from the cane had multiplied ten times under scientific cultivation over the past century, the bottom dropped out of prices in the world market. There were indeed other and more profitable forms of agricultural production—for example, in oranges and eggs, of which world consumption was steadily growing. But the coffee planter could not shift to eggs, nor the Iowa farmer to oranges. Not to mention the requirements of climate, the ordinary farmer or peasant lacked the capital, the special knowledge, or the access to refrigerated transportation that these newer branches of agriculture demanded. For the one thing that the average farmer or peasant knew how to do—grow wheat and other cereals—the new wonderful world of science and machinery had too little place.

The acute phase of the Great Depression, which began in 1929, was made worse by this chronic background of agricultural distress, since there was no reserve of purchasing power on the farms. The farmer's plight became even worse when the city people, struck by depression in industry, cut down their expenditures for food. Agricultural depression, rather than industrial depression, was at the bottom of widespread troubles in the interwar years throughout eastern Europe and the colonial world.

The Crash of 1929 and the Spread of Economic Crisis

The depression, in the strict sense, began as a stock market and financial crisis. Prices of stocks had been pushed upward by years of continuing expansion and high dividends. At the beginning of 1929 prices on the European stock exchanges began to weaken. But the real crisis, or turning point, came with the crash on the New York Stock Exchange in October 1929. Here values had been driven to fantastic heights by excessive speculation. Not only professional speculators, but quite ordinary people, in the United States, as an easy way to make a good deal of money, bought stock with borrowed funds. Sometimes, trading on "margin," they "owned" five or ten times as much stock as the amount of their own money put into it; the rest they borrowed from brokers, and the brokers borrowed from banks, the purchased stock in each case serving as collateral. With money so easy to obtain, people pushed up stock prices by bidding against each other and enjoyed huge fortunes on paper; but if prices fell, even a little, the hapless owners would be obliged to sell their stock to pay off the money they had borrowed. Hence the weakening of values on the New York Stock Exchange set off uncontrollable tidal waves of selling, which drove stock prices down irresistibly and disastrously. In a month stock values dropped by 40 percent, and in three years, from 1929 to 1932, the average value of fifty industrial stocks traded on the New York Stock Exchange dropped from 252 to 61. In these same three years 5,000 American banks closed their doors.

The crisis passed from finance to industry, and from the United States to the rest of the world. The export of American capital came to an end. Americans not only ceased to invest in Europe but sold the foreign securities that they had. This pulled the foundations from under the postwar revival of Germany and hence indirectly of much of Europe. Americans, their incomes falling, ceased to buy foreign goods; from Belgium to Borneo people saw their American markets slip away, and prices tumbled. In 1931 the failure of a leading Vienna bank, the *Creditanstalt*, sent a wave of shivers, bankruptcies, and business calamities over Europe. Everywhere business firms and private people could not collect what was owed them, or even draw on money that they thought they had in the bank. They could not buy, and so the factories could not sell. Factories slowed down or closed entirely. Between 1929 and 1932, the latter year representing the depth of the depression, world production is estimated to have declined by 38 percent, and the world's international trade fell by two-thirds. In the United States the national income fell from $85 billion to $37 billion.

Unemployment, a chronic disease ever since the war, assumed the proportion of pestilence. In 1932 there were 30 million unemployed persons statistically reported in the world; and this figure did not include the further millions who could find work only for a few hours in the week, or the masses in Asia or Africa for whom no statistics were to be had. The worker's wages were gone, the farmer's income now touched bottom; and the decline of mass purchasing power forced more idleness of machinery and more unemployment. People in the prime of life spent years out of work. Young people could not find jobs or establish themselves in an occupation. Skills and talents of older people grew rusty. Millions were reduced to living, and supporting their families, on the pittances of charity, doles, or relief. Great modern cities saw an outburst of sidewalk art, in which, at busy street corners, jobless able-bodied men drew pictures on the pavement with colored chalk, in the hope of attracting a few sixpence or dimes. People were crushed in spirit by a feeling of uselessness; months and years of fruitless job hunting left them demoralized, bored, discouraged, embittered, frustrated, and resentful. Never had there been such waste, not merely of machinery which now stood still, but of the trained and disciplined labor force on which all modern societies were built. And people chronically out of work naturally turned to new and disturbing political ideas.

Reactions to the Crisis

Optimists at the time, of whom President Herbert Hoover in the United States was one, declared that this depression, though a severe one, was basically only another periodic low point in the business cycle, or alternation of expansion and contraction, which had ebbed and flowed in the Western world for over a century. Prosperity, they blithely said, was "just around the corner." Others felt that the crisis represented the breakdown of the whole system of capitalism and free private enterprise. These people, in many cases, looked for signs of the future in the planned economy then being introduced in the U.S.S.R. There was something in both views. After 1932, in part for purely cyclical reasons—because the depression cut down indebtedness and reduced the costs of doing business—it again became possible to produce and sell. World steel production, for example, which had stood at 121 million tons in 1929, and then collapsed to 50 million in 1932, by 1936 again reached 122 million. To a considerable degree, to be sure, revival was due to rearmament. On the other hand, the Great Depression did put an end to the old economic system in the old sense. Even if such a stricken economy had internal powers of full recuperation after a few years, people would not stand for such terrifying insecurity in their personal lives. The horrors of mass unemployment were long remembered.

All governments took steps to provide work and incomes for their people. All, in one way or another, strove to free themselves from dependency on the uncertainties of the world market. The interlocking world economy collapsed both from the depression itself and from the measures adopted to cure it. The most marked economic consequence of the depression was a strong movement toward economic nationalism—toward greater self-sufficiency within the sphere which each government could hope to control.

The internationalism of money, the gold standard, and the free convertibility of currencies one into the other were gradually abandoned. Countries specializing in agricultural exports were among the first to be pinched. Agricultural prices were so low that even a large quantity of exports failed to produce enough foreign currency to pay for needed imports; hence the exporting country's currency fell in value. The currencies of Argentina, Uruguay, Chile, Australia, and New Zealand all depreciated in 1929 and 1930. Then came the turn of the industrial countries. England, as the depression went on, could not sell enough exports to pay for imports. It had to pay for imports in part by sending gold out of the country; thus the gold reserve supporting the pound sterling declined, and people who had pounds sterling began to convert their pounds into dollars or other currencies for which they thought the gold basis was more secure. This was known, in the poetic language of economics, as the "flight from the pound." In 1931 Great Britain went off the gold standard, which is to say that it devaluated the pound. But after Britain devaluated, some twenty-odd other countries, to protect their own exports and their own industries, did the same. Hence somewhat the same relative position reappeared. Even the United States, which possessed most of the world's gold supply, abjured the gold standard and devalued the dollar in 1934. The purpose was mainly to help American farmers, for with dollars cheaper in terms of foreign currencies, foreigners could afford to buy more American agricultural products. But it became harder for foreigners to sell to the United States.

Hence the depression, adding its effects to those of the World War and postwar inflation, led to chaos in the international monetary exchanges. Governments manipulated their currencies to uphold their sagging exports. Or they imposed exchange controls: they required that foreigners from whom their own people purchased, and to whom they thus gave their own currency, should use this currency to buy from them in return. Trade, which had been multilateral, became increasingly bilateral. That is, where a Brazilian importer of steel, for example, had formerly bought steel wherever he wished, at such price or of such quality as he preferred, he now had to obtain steel, often regardless of price or precise quality, from a country to which Brazil had sold enough of its own products to make payment possible. Sometimes, notably in the relations between Germany and east-European countries in the 1930s, bilateralism degenerated into actual barter. The Germans would exchange a certain number of cameras with Yugoslavia in return for a certain number of pigs. In such cases the very conception of a market disappeared.

Currency control was one means of keeping one's own factories from idleness, by holding or capturing export markets in time of depression. Another way of keeping one's own factories going (or farms, or mines, or quarries) was to shut out competitive imports by the old device of protective tariffs. The United States, hit by depression in 1929, enacted the unprecedentedly high Hawley-Smoot tariff in 1930. Other countries, equally or more distressed, now could sell less to America and hence buy less American goods. Other countries likewise raised their own tariffs, in the desperate hope of reserving national markets for their own people. Even Great Britain, citadel of free trade in the nineteenth century, turned to protectionism. It also revived and adopted Joseph Chamberlain's old idea of an imperial tariff union, when in 1932, by the Ottawa agreements, Britain and the British dominions adopted a policy of having lower tariffs against one another than against the world outside.[39]

Even tariffs were not always enough. Quotas or quantitative restrictions were adopted in many states. By this system a government said in effect not merely that goods brought into the country must pay a high tariff duty, but that above a certain amount no goods could be brought in at all. Increasingly both importers and exporters worked under government licenses, in order that a country's entire foreign trade could be centrally planned and managed. Such methods approached those of the Soviet Union, which asserted a government monopoly of all foreign trade, exported only in order to finance imports, and determined, without the bother of tariffs, the exact quantity of imported commodities that it would take.

Thus the world economy disintegrated into fiercely competing national economic systems. In the oceanic wreckage of the Great Depression, each state tried to create an island of economic security for its own people. Some efforts were made to break down the rising barriers. An International Monetary and Economic Conference, meeting in London in 1933, attempted to open the clogged channels of world trade; it ended in failure, as did attempts to stablilize the exchange rates of various currencies. Soon thereafter, the wartime Allies defaulted on their debt payments to the United States.[40] Legislation in Congress then denied them the right to float bonds, or obtain new loans, in the American securities market. American actions thus reinforced economic nationalism. The era that had opened with Woodrow Wilson's dream of international economic cooperation was ending with an unprecedented intensification of economic rivalry and national self-centeredness; it was only one of the promises of the postwar world to be blasted by the Great Depression.

[39] See p. 649.
[40] See pp. 720, 725–726, 782.

XIX.
DEMOCRACY
AND
DICTATORSHIP

Ｉｎ THE 1920s, people in a general way believed that the twentieth century was realizing all those goals summed up in the idea of progress; in the 1930s, they began to fear that "progress" was a phantom, to speak the word self-consciously with mental quotation marks, and to be content if only they could prevent a relapse into positive barbarization and a new world war.

The Great Depression ushered in the nightmare of the 1930s. Everywhere the demand was for security. Each nation tried to live economically, so far as possible, within itself. Each regulated, controlled, guided, planned, and tried to rescue its own economic system, attempting to be as little influenced as possible by the unpredictable behavior of other countries, or by the free rise and fall of prices in an uncontrolled world market. Within each country the same search for security encouraged the advancement of the welfare state and social democracy. Where democratic institutions were strong and resilient, governments took steps to protect individuals against the ravages of unemployment and destitution, and to help guard against future catastrophes. On the other hand, where democratic governments were not well established or taken for granted, which was the case in many countries after the First World War, dictatorship spread alarmingly in the 1930s with the coming of the depression. Democracy was said to be suited only to wealthy or prosperous countries. Unemployed people generally cared far more for economic help, or for promises of economic help, than for any theory of how persons wielding public power should be selected. The cry was for a leader, someone who would act, make decisions, assume responsibilities, get results, inspire confidence, and restore national pride. The Great Depression

Chapter Emblem: A postage stamp featuring Hitler and Mussolini, and reading "Two Peoples, One War," for use in Italian East Africa about 1940.

opened the way for unscrupulous and ambitious political adventurers, for dictators like Adolf Hitler in Germany, whose solution to all problems, economic, political, and international, it turned out, was war.

101. *The United States: Depression and New Deal*

Profound changes took place in the United States, where the stock market crash of 1929 had precipitated the great economic collapse. In 1932 national income had dropped to less than half of what it had been in 1929; 12 million to 14 million were unemployed. The Republican President Herbert Hoover, elected in 1928 at the floodtide of prosperity, was identified in the public mind with the hard times. Hoover viewed with disfavor any large-scale government intervention, convinced that the business cycle that had brought the depression would in turn bring prosperity, and that once business confidence was restored recovery would begin. His administration did act, proposing for the world economy a one-year suspension of payments on all intergovernmental debts and at home giving financial assistance to banks and railroads, expanding credit facilities, and helping to save the mortgages of some farmers and small home owners. But Hoover would not go further; he opposed immediate direct federal relief to the jobless; veterans seeking payment of their wartime bonuses to tide them over the bad times were ejected from Washington; unemployment, business failures, and farm foreclosures continued. In the election of 1932 the millions of unemployed workers, disheartened urban lower middle classes, and distressed farmers swept the Republican administration from office and elected the first Democratic president since Woodrow Wilson. The new president was Franklin Delano Roosevelt. The combination of recovery, relief, and reform legislation that he inaugurated is known as the New Deal.

The new president embarked on a program of improvisation and experimentation, but with such dispatch and vigor as to generate at once an electric enthusiasm. Within a short time an impressive array of legislation was put through Congress. The program of assistance to farmers, small home owners, and industry initiated under the Hoover administration was expanded so that it was no longer recognizable.

THE ASSEMBLY LINE
by Diego Rivera (Mexican, 1886–1957)
Not all twentieth-century artists have been attracted to pure abstraction or exploration of the unconscious. Among others, social activists and revolutionaries have continued to engage in narrative painting and realistic representation. Diego Rivera was one of the great painters of the Mexican Revolution. Regarded as the greatest living muralist and known also for his Marxist opinions, he was commissioned in 1931 by The Detroit Institute of Arts to decorate the walls of a large new hall. The fragment reproduced here shows part of the assembly line in an automobile plant, with workers of various races working speedily and as a team, while "bourgeois" visitors in the background somewhat stupidly watch and marvel. It was the machine age that Rivera meant to portray, rendering it with a mixture of realism and artistic heightening, and a sense of automatism, movement, and power. Courtesy of The Detroit Institute of Arts.

The government provided financial assistance for the relief of the unemployed and sponsored a broad public works program to absorb the jobless, first by loans to the states for the construction of housing, roads, bridges, and schools, later by a direct federal works program. To meet the financial crisis, the banks were temporarily closed and then reopened under stricter supervision. The dollar was taken off the gold standard and devalued, principally to help the farmers compete in foreign markets. In agriculture the government gave subsidies to farmers who agreed to curtail farm production, even subsidizing the destruction of crops and livestock, so that ruinous surpluses which had been one cause of the agricultural distress might be eliminated. It was a paradox, to be sure, for the government to reduce acreage and destroy agricultural products while city populations were in want. But the administration was endeavoring not only to cope with the immediate situation but to meet the deep-seated agricultural crisis that antedated the depression. Subsequently, farmers received subsidies for devoting part of their land to soil-conserving crops. A Civilian Conservation Corps promoted conservation and reforestation, and relieved unemployment by giving jobs to almost 3 million young people. For industry a National Recovery Administration (the NRA) for a time encouraged business firms to set up voluntary "codes of fair competition," which helped to regulate prices and production.

All these measures were designed to set the ailing capitalist system on its feet again by creating purchasing power and stimulating industrial activity. The major innovation was government spending, or "deficit financing." Although never following any consistent economic philosophy, the New Deal policies indirectly reflected the theories of the British economist John Maynard Keynes. In his earlier writings and in his most famous book, *The General Theory of Employment, Interest, and Money*, published in 1936, he argued that if private investment funds were idle, government funds must be employed to encourage economic activity and to increase purchasing power until such time as private funds flowed again. In order to get money into circulation and to "prime the pump" of industrial production, the government undertook a huge borrowing and spending program. Unorthodox as "deficit financing" was, it seemed to many at the time the only direct and rapid method of preventing economic collapse in a capitalist system. In all these recovery and reform activities the federal government assumed a role that it had hitherto played only in wartime. Alphabetical agencies proliferated; the federal payroll grew; the government debt more than doubled between 1932 and 1940.

From the beginning, some longer-range reform measures were adopted in addition to the recovery measures. To prevent overspeculation and the recurrence of a crash such as that of 1929, a Securities and Exchange Commission was created to regulate the issuance of stock and to supervise the operations of the stock exchange. Bank deposits were guaranteed by federal insurance so that depositors would not lose their lifetime savings. A Tennessee Valley Authority served as a pilot program in flood control, regional economic development, and cheap public power production.

After 1935 the focus shifted to regulation and reform. Sound economic recovery had not been achieved; there were still at least 5 million persons who could not find jobs in private industry. Businessmen who at first had been responsive to the government's leadership now resisted the government's regulation of finance and industry. The Supreme Court declared the NRA and other New Deal measures unconstitutional.

The major New Deal reforms after 1935 were designed to improve the condition of labor and to moderate economic insecurity. A broad national Social Security Act in 1935 provided for unemployment, old-age, and disability insurance. Here the United States was a latecomer. Germany, Britain, and other European countries had had such legislation since before the First World War. A Fair Labor Standards Act established forty hours as a maximum normal workweek and set a minimum hourly wage; child labor was abolished. A third measure, the National Labor Relations (or Wagner) Act, virtually transformed the American industrial scene. For the first time the federal government and the law were solidly aligned on the side of the unions. The new act guaranteed the right of workers to set up and bargain through unions of their choice, outlawed company unions, and prohibited employers from interfering with union organizing or discriminating against union members. Under its aegis the older American Federation of Labor (AFL) was revitalized and a new vigorous Congress of Industrial Organizations (CIO) came into being, which organized workers on an industrywide basis and reached down to unskilled workers in such industries as automobile, steel, textile, maritime, and rubber. Millions never before organized, including women and black workers, became part of powerful labor unions with expanding treasuries. Total union membership rose from about 4 million in 1929 to 9 million by 1940. Militant and conscious of its new strength but hardly touched by revolutionary ideology, American labor chose not to create a third party but to operate within the traditional two-party system.

Other reforms included a tax revision bill, which arranged for steeply graduated income taxes, levies on corporate profits, and the plugging of various corporate tax-evasion loopholes. The New Deal later tried also to reverse the trend toward the concentration of economic power, which it had itself stimulated under the NRA, by an investigation into monopoly and monopoly practices, and a trust-busting campaign. A program of slum clearance and low-cost housing made a start toward providing adequate housing. Aid was given to the tenant farmer and the sharecropper. All this was undertaken to help those whom the president described in 1937 as "one-third of a nation ill-nourished, ill-clad, ill-housed." If the New Deal did not feed, clothe, and house them, or strike at the deeper roots of American poverty, urban decay, and racial discrimination, as many later argued, it at least demonstrated that the national community cared, and it showed the enormous potential for government action along all those fronts.

Government spending and renewed confidence in the soundness of the country's institutions created a slow, gradual, and partial recovery. In mid-1937, however, a recession occurred, i.e., business activity slid backward, when government spending slowed down; the recession did not end until 1938 when government spending was resumed. National income reached $71 billion by 1939, double what it had been at the depth of the depression but still short of 1929. Despite substantial progress, business activity did not regain the high-water mark of June 1929. Resistance from the business community itself may have played a part. The rising public debt, antibusiness pronouncements by the government, heavier corporate and income taxes, and the many concessions to labor undoubtedly frightened off business investments and led to what was called a "sit-down strike'' of capital. Some claimed that wage rates had risen too sharply, adding to production costs and therefore discouraging business expansion. The New Deal did much to help economic recovery, but it did not end the depression. Complete recovery, the elimination of unemployment, the full use (and expansion) of the nation's productive capacity had to wait upon the huge war expenditures, by which Depression spending was to be dwarfed. By 1938 or so the New Deal was over; the administration turned its attention from domestic reform to the gathering storm in Europe and the Far East.

The changes were substantial under what some called the "Roosevelt Revolution.'' Enlarging the role of the federal government as no previous administration had done, the New Deal transformed the noninterventionist state into a social service or welfare state. The government imposed controls on business, entered business itself (as in the TVA), used its powers to redistribute wealth, and introduced a broad social security system. Labor's power and political influence grew. The responsibility of public authority for the social and economic welfare of the people was clearly established. When the Republican party later returned to power, it opposed in principle the further growth of the welfare state and the expanding role of the federal government, but it retained the New Deal reforms, a tacit admission that the New Deal had not intended to destroy capitalism but to revive it.

The New Deal, however, engendered violent feelings, which lingered on. Roosevelt, himself of patrician and well-to-do background, denounced the "economic royalists''; in turn he was called a "traitor to his class.'' When the Supreme Court declared New Deal measures unconstitutional, he made plans to reorganize and enlarge the court, which aroused more political hostility. Despite vociferous opposition, in the election of 1936 Roosevelt won all but two states, and he was subsequently reelected in 1940 and 1944 (during the wartime emergency, to be sure, and with increasingly smaller majorities) for an unprecedented third and fourth term. A constitutional amendment, adopted in 1951, limited a president to two terms.

Roosevelt's opponents, at the time and later, argued that the New Deal had created an enormous regulatory bureaucracy, expensive and cumbersome, a threat to the freedom and self-reliance of the citizenry. But others contended that despite its waste and inconsistencies, unorthodox financial policies, enlargement of the executive power, and expansion of the bureaucracy, it represented a bold and humanitarian way of meeting the great crisis; it preserved and reaffirmed American faith in its democratic system—at a time when democracy was succumbing elsewhere.

102. Trials and Adjustments of Democracy in Britain and France

British Politics: The 1920s and the Depression

Britain, like the United States, even in the troubles of the depression, remained firmly attached to representative institutions and democratic principles. The Great

Depression aggravated and intensified Britain's older economic difficulties. More dependent on overseas markets than any other people, the British until 1914 had managed to hold their lead, exporting industrial products and capital, selling insurance and other services, and importing foodstuffs. But in the years before 1914 the British were increasingly losing their markets because of the emergence of other economically aggressive industrial nations, the growth of tariff barriers, the development of indigenous textile and other industries in India and elsewhere in the East, the competition of new textile products with British cottons and woolens, and the substitution of new sources of fuel for British coal. The losses were accelerated by the economic disruption of the First World War, the disappearance of many overseas investments, and the postwar disorganization and impoverishment of markets. The rise in tariffs after the war and the customs barriers raised in the new small states of Europe also hurt British exports. After 1918 Britain lived in a world no longer dependent on, or eager for, its manufactures. Britain's very historical primacy as the pioneer industrial country was also a handicap. Both labor and management had become adjusted to older conditions, and the more recently industrialized countries had less antiquated techniques and machinery.

The net result of all this was that in the interwar years, even in times of relative prosperity for the rest of the world, Britain was in depression and suffered severely from unemployment. The unemployment insurance adopted in 1911 was called heavily into play. By 1921 over 2 million unemployed were receiving benefit payments, contemptuously called the "dole" by those who disliked it. Unemployment insurance, an expanded old-age pension system, medical aid, government-subsidized housing, and other social welfare measures helped to relieve economic distress and to prevent any drastic decline in the living standards of British workers. The welfare state was well under way in Britain before the Labour party took office after the Second World War.

The labor unions made a strenuous effort to retain wage gains and other concessions won in wartime. Industry, hard-pressed itself, resisted. This situation reached a climax in 1926 in the coal-mining industry, which was in a particularly bad plight; government subsidies had not helped and even conservative investigators had recommended some form of amalgamation and public management. A strike by the coal miners led to a "general strike" supported by the other British unions; about half of the 6 million organized workers in Britain left their jobs as a token of sympathy and solidarity. But the government declared a state of emergency and made use of army and navy personnel and middle-class volunteers to take over essential services. The strike ended in failure, and even in a setback for the trade unions, which were put under stricter control by the Trades Disputes Act of 1927, a measure that declared all general or sympathy strikes illegal and even forbade the unions from raising money for political purposes.

After the election of 1922, the Labour party displaced the Liberal party as the second of the two great parties of the country and faced the Conservatives as the official opposition.[1] The Labour party could more consistently and more actively champion both labor legislation and bolder measures to deal with Britain's troubled economic state. The Labour party, moreover, which had been no more

[1] See pp. 612–613, 619–621, 640–641.

than a loose federation of trade union and socialist organizations before the war, tightened its organizational structure and, bridging the gap between the trade unionists and the socialists, committed itself in 1918 to a program of socialism. But it was a program of gradualist, democratic socialism operating through customary British parliamentary procedures and hence able to gain the good will of large sections of the middle classes.

Twice, in 1924 and in 1929, Labour governed the country with Ramsay MacDonald as prime minister, in each case as a coalition government. In 1924 Labour proved its moderation. It did no more than extend unemployment relief and inaugurate housing and public works projects; indeed it acted firmly in the face of strikes that broke out. But it aroused opposition when it gave diplomatic recognition to the Soviet Union and pledged a loan to the Soviets for the purchase of British goods. Meanwhile newspapers published the so-called Red (or Zinoviev) letter purporting to be secret instructions for British Labour groups from the head of the Communist International urging preparations for a Communist uprising in Britain.[2] The document's authenticity has never been established, but the Conservatives successfully exploited it and won the election of 1924.

In the election of May 1929, however, Labour's representation almost doubled, and the Conservative representation dropped proportionately. MacDonald again became prime minister. Thus the Wall Street crash and the worldwide depression came while the Labour party government was in office. The effects of the depression were quickly felt. Unemployment, which had hovered about the 1 million mark in 1929, soon approached the 3 million figure. The government expended large sums to supplement the unemployment insurance payments. Gold flowed out of the country, tax receipts declined, the public debt grew. Alarmed by the mounting deficit, MacDonald made plans to introduce a severe retrenchment policy, even to the extent of reducing the "dole" payments. The Labour party was outraged; some of the Labour ministers in his cabinet refused to support him. He was read out of the party, along with those ministers who had gone along with him. MacDonald thereupon formed an all-party coalition cabinet known as the National government, which in an election of 1931 won an overwhelming victory, but it was the Conservative members of the coalition who took a majority of the seats in Parliament.

The new government represented an effort to maintain national unity in the face of economic emergency. Not a single seat in Parliament in the next election in 1931 went to either the Communists or to a British Fascist party organized by Sir Oswald Mosley; in 1935 the Communists won one seat.

The National government coped with the depression chiefly along retrenchment lines, under Ramsay MacDonald from 1931 to 1935, Stanley Baldwin to 1937, and Neville Chamberlain after 1937. In addition to retrenchment and budget balancing, the government encouraged industry to reorganize and rationalize production by providing low-interest loans. Mainly, the government concentrated on the kind of economic nationalist measures that have already been described.[3] As in the United States, despite some recovery from the depths of the depression, none of the steps taken brought full recovery or full employment. Unemployment persisted until military conscription and an expanded armament program absorbed the jobless. The Labour party, partially recovering its strength in the election of 1935, denounced the timid expedients of the Conservatives, whom it held responsible for the apathy and gloom gripping the country.

Britain and the Commonwealth: Imperial Relations

To the older British Empire—India, the crown colonies, protectorates, and spheres of influence—the postwar settlement added a number of League of Nations mandates. British rule in its various forms extended to almost 500 million people, a fourth of the earth's population and land surface. It was principally in Ireland, Egypt, India, and Palestine that the British faced complex imperial problems after the First World War. In Palestine, where the British exercised a League of Nations mandate, Arabs and Jews fought with each other and with Britain. In Egypt, in 1922, Britain, although retaining the right to station some troops there, formally ended the protectorate it had established forty years earlier; but many questions, especially the status of the Sudan, remained unresolved. In India the agitation for national independence, as we have seen, grew more intense. In these areas nothing resembling a solution was arrived at until after the Second World War. In Ireland the independence movement managed to establish a separate republic.

The Irish question had disoriented English politics for forty years.[4] Irish home rule, authorized by Parliament in 1914, was deferred for the duration of the war. Irish nationalists, during the war, accepted German support and rose in rebellion in 1916. After the war, in 1919 and 1920, the Irish Nationalist or Sinn Fein party fought a small but savage war of independence against the British forces known as "Black and Tans." The British blocked independence, but in 1922 recognized the Irish Free State, granting it dominion status. The Protestant majority in Ulster, the northern counties where Presbyterians of Scottish origin had lived for three centuries, preferred to remain outside the Free State and continued to be part of the United Kingdom of Great Britain and Northern Ireland, to the vehement dissatisfaction of the Irish republicans. In 1937 a new constitution for the Irish Free State affirmed the full sovereignty of Ireland (or Eire, as it was for a time called), the country remaining, however, in the British Commonwealth of Nations. Politics remained unsettled, for the Irish agitated for the annexation of Ulster, conducted tariff wars with a Britain from which they were now cut off, strove to revive Gaelic in place of the English language, and fell into disputes in which Irish moderates were pitted against Irish extremists, the latter perpetrating an occasional assassination, or other outrage, to further their cause. The last formal ties with the British Commonwealth were severed in 1949, when the Republic of Ireland was proclaimed. The Irish continued to claim jurisdiction over Ulster and to support the cause of the Irish Catholic minority there.

As for the dominions, the political status of these areas of white settlement overseas was now more clearly defined than ever before. The dominions— Canada, Australia, New Zealand, and the Union of South Africa—had long pursued their own policies, even levying tariffs against British goods. They had

---

[4] See pp. 613–614, 641, 710; for developments after 1945, see p. 889.

all joined loyally with Great Britain in the First World War, but all were stirred by a nationalism of their own and desired their independence to be regularized and promulgated to the world. An imperial conference of 1926 defined ''dominion status,'' which was corroborated by the Statute of Westminster of 1931. The dominions became legally equal with each other and with Great Britain. No act passed by the British Parliament could apply to a dominion save by the dominion's own consent. Despite independent policies in economic matters and even in foreign affairs, the bonds between the dominions and Britain were firm; the support of the dominions in the Second World War was to be vital in Britain's survival. After the war the Commonwealth became a larger and even more flexible institution.

France: The 1920s and the Coming of the Depression

When the depression came to France, agitation of fascist type made more headway than in Britain or the United States. Earlier, in the 1920s, France was preoccupied with recovery from the physical destruction of the war, the instability of public finances, and the fear of a resurgent Germany. Immediately after 1919, and for most of the 1920s, the government was run by coalitions of parties of the conservative right, i.e., parties supported by business and financial interests, well disposed toward the army and church, and interested in economy and stability in domestic affairs. For about two years, from 1924 to 1926, the Radical Socialists were in control; this party of the moderate left, whose leader was Edouard Herriot, served as spokesman for the lower classes, the small businessmen and farmers; it advocated progressive social legislation so long as increased taxes were not necessary. Despite its name, a carryover from an earlier era, it was firmly committed to private enterprise and private property; it was staunch in its defense of individual liberties and was fervently anticlerical; sometimes, it seemed, its anticlericalism was a substitute for any more positive program.

Although the Radical Socialists cooperated in parliamentary elections with the Socialists, the other major party of the left, the two parties differed too profoundly on economic policies to preserve stable coalitions. In the 1920s the Socialists, led by Léon Blum, were still recovering from the secession of the more orthodox Marxists who had formed a French Communist party. Both left and right in France shaded off into antidemocratic groups that were hostile to the parliamentary republic. These included the Communists on the left, who sat in parliament and took part in elections; and on the extreme right, royalists of the *Action Française* and other antirepublican organizations, which operated principally outside the Chamber as militant and noisy pressure groups.

The outstanding figure of the moderate conservative right was Raymond Poincaré; it was he who sent troops into the Ruhr in 1923, when the Germans failed to pay reparations; and it was he who now ''saved'' the franc. The reparations question was extremely important for French finances. The country had undertaken a large-scale reconstruction program to repair the wartime devastation of northern and eastern France, and had counted upon the defeated enemy to pay. When German reparations were not paid as anticipated, the public debt mounted, a balanced budget became impossible, and the franc declined precipitously. The huge war expenditures, heavy loss of foreign investments, notably in Russia, and an outmoded taxation program which invited widespread evasion added to French difficulties. After 1926, when the financial crisis reached a climax, a "national union" ministry under Poincaré inaugurated new taxes, tightened tax collection somewhat, cut down drastically on government expenditures in order to balance the budget, and eventually stabilized the franc—at about one-fifth of its prewar value. The internal debt was thus in effect largely repudiated, to the despair of many bondholders, but the threat of a runaway inflation, like that of the Weimar Republic, was avoided. From 1926 to 1929 the country prospered. New factories, replacing those destroyed in the war, were modern and up to date. The index of industrial production rose; tourists flocked in. As in many other countries, workers did not share proportionately in the prosperity of the 1920s. The unions received a sharp setback when, immediately following the war, a series of strikes of major proportions ended in failure; the unions were also divided between a Communist and non-Communist national confederation; collective bargaining in the country was virtually unknown. The workers were not mollified by a social insurance program adopted by a reluctant parliament, which went into effect in 1930.

The Great Depression came later to France and was less severe than in the United States or Germany. Trade declined. Unemployment and part-time employment increased; at the worst period, in 1935, close to 1 million workers were unemployed; perhaps half of those employed worked part-time. Industrial production, which in 1930 was 40 percent above the prewar level, sank by 1932 back to the 1913 figure. The government displayed the usual pattern of unstable, shifting, short-lived ministries; in 1933 five ministries rapidly succeeded one another (there were some forty all told in the twenty interwar years). The cabinets formed after 1932 followed a policy of retrenchment and economy, and clung to the gold standard. Meanwhile, in Germany Adolf Hitler had become chancellor in 1933; France's domestic difficulties were intensified by mounting international tension.

Depression Ferment and the Popular Front

In the uneasy years of the depression, the latent hostility to the republic came to the surface. Fascist-type "leagues" appeared in open imitation of Italian and German fascist organizations, many obtaining funds from wealthy industrialists; the older *Action Française* and right-wing veterans' associations like Colonel de le Rocque's *Croix de Feu* were also active. The same elements that had been antirepublican, antidemocratic, or monarchist since the French Revolution and which had rallied behind Boulanger and denounced Dreyfus[5] now grew more strident in their attacks on the parliamentary republic.

In 1934 it seemed for a moment that the opportunity awaited by the antirepublican elements had come. A political and financial scandal of the kind familiar in prewar French public life shook the country. A financial manipulator and adventurer with excellent political connections, Stavisky by name, induced the municipal authorities at Bayonne to launch a flotation of worthless bonds. Faced with exposure, he fled and apparently committed suicide; the sensationalist press

[5] See pp. 607–608.

encouraged the rumor that he had been shot by the police to prevent the implication of high-ranking politicians. A clamor went up accusing the government of involvement in the financial scandal. Where elsewhere such an affair would have called only for turning the incumbents out of office, in France it supplied ammunition for those who demanded the end of the republic itself, which was equated with corruption and venality.

The agitation reached a climax in the riots of February 1934. A mob of fascist tendency assembled in the Place de la Concorde, threatened the Chamber, and battled with the police; several were killed and hundreds injured. French liberals and democrats, organized labor, and socialists were outraged by the threat to the republic. The Communists, hostile to the fascist groups, were unfriendly to the government too, but soon, guided by the Comintern, they sensed the danger to the Soviet Union in the event of a French fascist triumph and joined with the antifascists. As elsewhere, in the 1930s the Communists emerged from their sectarian revolutionary isolation, became intensely patriotic, and widened their prestige, influence, and appeal. An impressive labor-sponsored general strike was held a week after the riots. Shortly thereafter, liberals, socialists, and communists drew together in a political coalition that came to be known as the Popular Front, of the kind that was being organized, or advocated, in many countries in the 1930s. It campaigned on a pledge to defend the republic against fascism, to take measures against the depression, and to introduce labor reforms. In the spring of 1936 it won a decisive victory at the polls. The French Socialists for the first time in their history became the leading party in the Chamber; their chief, Léon Blum, long a spokesman for democratic and reformist socialism, became premier of a coalition cabinet of Socialists and Radical Socialists; the Communists, who had increased their representation in the Chamber from 10 to 72 seats, did not join the cabinet but pledged their support.

The Popular Front and After

Blum's Popular Front ministry, although it lasted little more than a year, put through a program of far-reaching legislation. In part, this was due to the Popular Front election program, in part to unforeseen events, for the tremendous enthusiasm generated by the victory led to a spontaneous nationwide wave of "sit-down strikes," which did not subside until Blum pledged a number of immediate reforms.

Parliament in short order passed laws providing for a forty-hour week, vacations with pay, and a collective bargaining law. As in the case of the Wagner Act in the United States, the encouragement given to collective bargaining led to the nationwide signing of collective contracts for the first time in the country's history and to enormous growth in trade union membership, from about 1 million to 5 million in a year's time. Labor's strength grew also when the Communist and non-Communist labor confederations reunited. Other legislation was important too. Steps were taken to nationalize the armaments and aviation industry; the fascist armed leagues were, at least in theory, dissolved; the Bank of France was reorganized and placed under government control to break the power of the "two hundred families." Machinery was established for the arbitration of labor disputes. Aid was given to farmers through price fixing and government purchases of wheat.

As in the United States all these measures aimed at both recovery and reform; Blum spoke openly of his program as a "French New Deal." But French conservatives, and the quasi-fascists to their right, cried revolution; they uttered dark predictions that a French Lenin would follow Blum. They did not conceal their sullen resentment at what had come to pass: the fate of Catholic France in the hands of a leftist, a Socialist, and a Jew. Even salvation by a warrior from outside the country, one who had demonstrated his anti-Bolshevism, would be preferable. They envied the protection given to established interests by Mussolini, and there were those who even muttered "better Hitler than Léon Blum."

The Popular Front reforms, long overdue though they were, came to France at a time when the sands were rapidly running out. While France had a forty-hour week, German arms plants were operating at full capacity. In the shadow of Nazi remilitarization a rearmament program had to be undertaken at the very same time as reform; even moderates argued that the country could not afford both. Opposition from many quarters hindered success. French employers balked at cooperating in the new reforms and tried to pass on rising production costs to the consumer. Labor was disgruntled at the price rises that canceled out its wage gains. Both employers and labor applied the forty-hour week in such a manner that plants were shut down for two days a week instead of operating in shifts, as the law had intended. Nothing could check the flight of gold from the country. Industrial production hardly rose; even in 1938, when it had shown substantial recovery in other countries, it was only 5 percent higher in France than at the depth of the depression. In July 1936 the Spanish Civil War had broken out. The Communists attacked the Blum government for refusing aid to the hard-pressed Spanish Popular Front government across the Pyrenees; Blum, following the lead of Britain and fearing involvement, resisted. In 1937, after a year in office, the Blum government was overthrown by the Senate, which refused to grant it emergency financial powers. The Popular Front coalition rapidly disintegrated. By mid-1938 the Radical Socialists had abandoned their allies on the left, and under Edouard Daladier formed a conservative ministry, whose attention was increasingly occupied by the international crisis. Little remained of the Popular Front, or indeed of the strength of labor, which declined rapidly and exhausted itself further by an unsuccessful general strike in 1938 in protest against nullification of the forty-hour week. For the French worker, 1936 had gone the way of other "great years"; the comfortable classes had been thrown into panic by the social turmoil; internal division and class hatreds had grown sharper. Yet the French democracy, the Third Republic itself, had been successfully preserved and its domestic enemies repulsed, at least for a time.

Western Europe and the Depression

Britain and France, and indeed all western Europe, Europe's "inner zone," never fully recovered from the Great Depression before the Second World War came. When economic expansion later resumed after the war, the interwar years seemed like a deep trough in Europe's economic history. Western Europe barely maintained its old inherited equipment in the depression and was unable to utilize even its existing machinery to capacity. Moreover, as the events of 1929 had clearly shown, Europe's economic dependence on the United States was pronounced, and the U.S.S.R. was becoming an industrial giant. The economic destiny of Europeans in the 1930s was very much in doubt.

There were other signs of decline. The birth rate in western Europe in the 1930s declined to its lowest recorded levels as young people postponed marriage and married people limited the size of their families because of economic and psychological stresses. Birth rates did not run significantly higher than death rates, the population stagnating and growing older. There was a scarcity of men of middle age because of the casualties of the First World War. Politically neither British nor French democratic political leaders were able to cope successfully with the economic dilemmas of the depression era. Nor could the Socialists, who found neither Marxian economics nor class struggle ideas helpful but failed to renew or reinvigorate their own doctrines in any significant way.

103. *Italian Fascism*

Though they shade into each other imperceptibly, it is possible to distinguish dictatorship from totalitarianism. Dictatorship, an old phenomenon in history, has commonly been regarded as a mere expedient, designed for emergencies and believed to be temporary; at most, it is a theory of government. Totalitarianism, as it arose after the First World War, was not merely a theory of government but a theory of life and of human nature. It claimed to be no expedient but a permanent form of society and civilization, and so far as it appealed to emergency for justification, it regarded life itself as an everlasting emergency. Let us first review the pertinent events in Italy and Germany and then return to the idea of totalitarianism.

The belief widely held in the 1920s that democracy was generally advancing was not deeply disturbed by the failure of Russia or Turkey or China to develop effective parliaments or liberal institutions. These were backward countries, in the throes of revolution; some day, when conditions quieted down, it could be supposed, they would move forward to democracy as known in the West. The first jarring exception to the apparent victory of democracy was furnished by Italy, a country that was an integral part of civilized Europe, one that since 1861 had accepted parliamentary liberalism, but where, in 1922, Benito Mussolini seized control of the government and proclaimed *Fascismo*.

Mussolini, born in 1883, the son of a blacksmith, was a fiery and pugnacious character, who before the war had followed the career of professional revolutionary, left-wing socialist, and radical journalist. He had read and digested such works as Sorel's *Reflections on Violence* and Nietzsche's writings.[6] During the war he turned intensely nationalist, clamored for intervention on the side of the Allies, and demanded the conquest from Austria of *Italia irredenta*, the "unredeemed" Italian lands to the north and across the Adriatic. In the war he rose to the rank of corporal. In March 1919 he organized, mainly from demobilized and restless ex-soldiers, his first fighting band, or *fascio di combattimento*. *Fascio* meant a bunch or bundle, as of sticks; it called to mind the Latin *fasces*, or

---

[6] See pp. 630, 640.

bundle of rods, carried by the lictors in ancient Rome as a symbol of state power—for Mussolini loved to conjure up ancient glories.

In 1919 Italian glories were dim. Italy had entered the war on the side of the Allies quite frankly for territorial and colonial spoils; the secret treaty of London in 1915 promised the Italians certain Austrian lands and a share in German and Turkish possessions. During the war Italian arms did not especially shine; Italian troops were routed at Caporetto in 1917. Yet Italy lost over 600,000 lives in the war, and the Italian delegates came to the peace conference confident that their sacrifices would be recognized and their territorial aspirations satisfied. They were rapidly disappointed. Wilson refused to honor the provisions of the London secret treaty and other demands of the Italians. Britain and France displayed no eagerness to side with Italy. The Italians received some of the Austrian territories promised to them, but they were given no part of the former German or Turkish possessions as mandates.

After the war Italy, like other countries, suffered from the burden of wartime debt and from acute postwar depression and unemployment. Social unrest spread. In the countryside land seizures took place, not in any significant proportions but enough to spread concern among landowners; tenant farmers refused to pay rents; peasants burned crops and destroyed livestock. In the cities great strikes broke out in heavy industry and in transportation. Some of the strikes turned into sit-down strikes, the workers refusing to leave the plants; demands were raised even for worker control of the factories. Moderate socialist and labor leaders disavowed all such extremism, but left-wing socialists who, as elsewhere, had turned communist and joined the Third International, fanned the existing discontents. Meanwhile, armed bands of young men, most prominent of whom were the Blackshirts or Fascists, brawled with Communists and ordinary workers in the streets. By the late summer of 1920 the strikes and the agrarian unrest had subsided, although violence in the streets persisted.

During the months of turmoil the government refrained from any bold action. The Italian parliamentary system in the prewar years had never functioned impressively nor commanded widespread esteem; now respect for parliament and the weak, shifting, coalition ministries sank even lower. In 1919 the first postwar election was held, under a law that added proportional representation to the universal male suffrage introduced in 1913. The Socialists and a new Catholic Popular, or Christian Socialist, party made an impressive showing. In 1921, in the wake of the postwar disturbances, new elections were held. Liberals and democrats, moderate socialists, and the Catholic Popular party were all returned in large numbers. Mussolini's Fascist movement won 35 of the 500-odd seats. Despite this less than impressive showing (the best ever made by the Fascists in a free election), the Fascist ranks were swelling, in the backwash, as it were, of the postwar unrest.

Mussolini and the Fascists at first went along with the radical tide; they did not disapprove the factory seizures; they inveighed against plutocracy and war profiteers and called for a high levy on capital and profits. But Mussolini, never one to sacrifice opportunity for principles or doctrine, soon came forward with his Fascists as the upholders of national law and order, and hence property; he now pledged battle "against the forces dissolving victory and nation." Although the social agitation subsided, burning itself out on its own, and there had never been any real threat of a Soviet-style revolution, the propertied classes had gone through a great fright; they found comfort in the Fascist movement and were willing to lend it financial support. Patriots and nationalists of all classes rallied to it, as well as the lower middle class, pinched by economic inflation and, as elsewhere, unable to find protection or solace in labor unions or socialist movements. The black-shirted upholders of national order proceeded methodically to administer beatings (and doses of castor oil) to Communists and alleged Communists, to Socialists and Christian Socialists, and to ordinary persons who did not support them; nor did they refrain from arson and murder. Vigilante squadrons, the *squadristi*, broke up strikes, demolished labor union headquarters, and drove from office duly elected Socialist and Communist mayors and town officials. Mussolini reinforced his claim as paladin of law, authority, and order by declaring his loyalty to king and church; a few years earlier he had been a rabid republican and anticlerical.

In October 1922 the "March on Rome" took place. The Blackshirts mobilized for a threatened coup and began to converge from various directions on the capital; Mussolini remained at a safe distance in Milan. The liberal-democratic coalition cabinet had viewed the events of the past two years with disapproval but at the same time with satisfaction that the Blackshirts were serving a useful national purpose by suppressing troublemakers on the left. Now they made belated but ineffectual gestures to save the situation by an effort to have martial law declared; the king refused to approve. The cabinet resigned and Mussolini was named premier. It was all quite legal, or almost so. Indeed Italy was still in form a constitutional and parliamentary government. Mussolini headed only a coalition ministry and received from parliament no more than a year's grant of full emergency powers to restore order and introduce reforms.

But soon it was clear in whose hands power rested. Before the expiration of his emergency powers Mussolini forced through parliament a law providing that any party securing the largest number of votes in an election should automatically receive two-thirds of the seats in the legislature. This was Mussolini's solution to the instability of coalitions and blocs in parliamentary governments like those of Italy and France (and indeed of most other Continental democracies), where a single party hardly ever enjoyed a majority. The two-thirds law was not even necessary. In the 1924 elections, although seven opposition slates appeared, the Fascists, aided by government control of the electoral machinery and the use of *squadristi*, received well over three-fifths of the total vote.

After the elections of 1924 the highly respected Socialist deputy Matteotti publicly exposed hundreds of cases of armed Fascist violence, and of fraud and chicanery. He was murdered by Fascists. There was widespread indignation in the country, and the press clamored for Mussolini's resignation. The opposition parties even seceded from the Chamber, wanting to have nothing to do with such a government. Mussolini, not directly involved in the assassination, expressed a willingness to punish the perpetrators, but he eventually took full responsibility, and moved to consolidate his dictatorship. Within a few years he reduced the Italian parliament to a nonentity, put the press under censorship, destroyed the labor unions, deprived labor of the right to strike, and abolished all political parties except the Fascist party.

Fascism in the 1920s was an innovation which the rest of the world was slow to understand. In his more flamboyant moments Mussolini strutted, stuck out his jaw, and glared ferociously; he jumped through flaming hoops to show his virility and had his chief subordinates do likewise; to the outside world this seemed an odd way of demonstrating fitness for public office. He denounced democracy as historically outmoded and declared that it accentuated class struggle, split people into countless minority parties, and led to selfishness, futility, evasion, and empty talk. In place of democracy he preached the need of vigorous action, under a strong leader; he himself took the title of Leader, or *Duce*. He denounced liberalism, free trade, laissez faire, and capitalism, along with Marxism, material-ism, socialism, and class consciousness, which he said were the evil offspring of liberal and capitalistic society. In their place he preached national solidarity and state management of economic affairs, under the same Leader's farseeing and audacious vision. And in fact Mussolini seemed to bring a kind of efficiency; as the saying went, he at least made the trains run on time.

Mussolini introduced, at least in theory, the syndical, or corporative state. This had been discussed in both left- and right-wing circles for many years. Left-wing syndicalism, especially before the First World War, looked to revolutionary labor unions to expropriate the owners of industry and then to assume the direction of political and economic life. A more conservative syndicalism was endorsed and encouraged by the Catholic church, with which, as has been noted in a previous chapter, Mussolini made his peace with the signing of the Lateran accord in 1929.[7] The conservative type looked nostalgically toward a revival of the medieval guilds, or "corporations," in which master and journeymen, employer and employees, had labored side by side in a supposedly golden age of social peace.

The Fascist corporative system really resembled neither, because in it the hand of the state was writ large, something that none of the older corporative doctrines had anticipated. It went through a number of complicated stages, but as it finally emerged in the 1930s, it provided for the division of all economic life into twenty-two major areas, for each of which a "corporation" was established. In each corporation representatives of the Fascist-organized labor groups, the employers, and the government determined working conditions, wages, prices, and industrial policies; and in a national council these representatives were supposed jointly to devise plans for Italy's economic self-sufficiency. In each case the role of government was decisive and the whole structure was under the jurisdiction of the minister of corporations. As a final step, these corporative economic chambers were integrated into the government proper so that in 1938 the old Chamber of Deputies was superseded by a Chamber of Fasces and Corporations representing the corporations and the Fascist party, its members selected by the government and not subject to popular ratification.

None of this was democratic, but this was an improvement over democracy, the Fascists asserted. A legislature in an advanced economic society, they said, should be an economic parliament; it should represent not political parties and geographical constituencies but economic occupations. Organization along such lines would do away with the anarchy and class conflict engendered by free capitalism, which only sap the strength of the national state. Real authority in

[7] See p. 636.

any event rested with the government—the Head of the Government, who settled most matters by decree. In point of fact, social unrest and class conflict were "ended," not by the corporative system as such, but by the prohibition of strikes and lockouts and the abolition of independent labor unions. The corporative system represented the most extreme form of state control over economic life within a framework of private enterprise and a relatively capitalistic economy, that is, one in which ownership continued to rest in private hands. It was the Fascist answer to Western-style democracy and to Soviet proletarian dictatorship. Fascism, said Mussolini, is the "dictatorship of the state over many classes cooperating."

When the depression struck, none of Italy's economic controls availed very much. Mussolini was eager to lay upon the world depression the blame for Italy's continuing economic ills. He turned to a vigorous program of public works and to increasing economic self-sufficiency. A "battle of wheat" was launched to increase food production; progress was made in reclaiming swamp areas in central Italy and in developing hydroelectric power as a substitute for the coal that Italy lacked. Throughout the Fascist era no fundamental reform took place in the position of the peasants. The existing structure of society, which in Italy meant social extremes of wealth and poverty, remained unaltered. Fascism failed to provide either the economic security or the material well-being for which it had demanded the sacrifice of individual freedom. But it undeniably substituted a widespread psychological exhilaration, a feeling that Italy was undergoing a heroic national revival; and after 1935 to support that feeling Mussolini turned increasingly to military and imperialist adventures.

Fascism came to be regarded in other countries as a possible alternative to democratic or parliamentary government, as an actual corrective to troubles whose reality no one could deny. All communists hated it, and so did all socialists, labor leaders, moderate leftists, and idealistic liberals. Wealthier or established people, because of fear of Bolshevism, made more allowances in its favor. In east-European countries, often highly nationalistic, or influenced by disgruntled landowners, or simply unused to settling questions by majority vote, Fascism made a considerable appeal. In the Latin countries, in Spain, Portugal, and France, Mussolini's corporative state found champions and admirers. Sometimes, in Europe and elsewhere, intellectuals spun refined, sophisticated theories about the new order of discipline and authority, forgetting how Mussolini himself with unusual candor had written, "Fascism was not the nursling of a doctrine worked out beforehand with detailed elaboration; it was born of the need for action."

104. Totalitarianism: Germany's Third Reich

The Rise of Adolf Hitler

It was in Germany that Mussolini found his aptest pupil. Born in Austria in 1889, Adolf Hitler did little before the war. He was not an intellectual, like the prewar journalist Mussolini. He was never a socialist, but he fell into a restless and somewhat ignorant type of radicalism. Son of an Austrian customs official, he lost his father at fourteen and his mother a few years later. He dropped out of high school at sixteen and at nineteen came to the great metropolis of Vienna as an art student but was never accepted into the academy to which he sought admission. When the small inheritance left by his parents ran out and a government grant for orphan students ended, he drifted into various menial jobs, occasionally selling a few of his postcard and poster paintings but mainly eking out a marginal existence with hardly any friends, money, or livelihood. The young Hitler did not like what he saw in Vienna: neither the trappings of the Habsburg court, nor the noblemen of eastern Europe who rode by in their carriages, nor the mixed nationalities of the Danubian empire, nor the Vienna worker's attachment to international Marxism, nor above all the Jews, who thanks to a century of liberal influences had become assimilated to the German culture and now occupied many distinguished positions in business, law, medicine, and journalism in the city. He became exceedingly race conscious, like many others in many countries at the time;[8] the youthful Hitler took a special satisfaction in thinking of himself as a pure German of the good old German stock. He became violently anti-Semitic, and he also disliked aristocracy, capitalism, socialism, cosmopolitanism, internationalism, and "hybridization."

His aversion to Austria led him in 1913 to move to Munich, capital of the South German state of Bavaria. Once again he drifted without livelihood except by occasionally selling a few of his watercolors. When the war broke out, he volunteered for the Germany army. He was a good soldier, serving as a dispatch runner to the front line, and at one point was the victim of a gas attack that temporarily blinded him and injured his vocal cords. Although he rose in rank only to the rough equivalent of corporal, he received important military decorations for his services. For Hitler, as for Mussolini and others, the war was a thrilling, noble, and liberating experience. The average individual, in modern society, led a pretty dull existence. Peace, for many, was a drab routine from which war was an exciting emancipation. Human atoms, floating in an impersonal and unfriendly world, they were stirred by the nationalism which the war aroused into a sense of belonging to, believing in, fighting for something greater than themselves, but which was yet their own. When peace returned, they felt a moral letdown.

When the war ended, Hitler remained for a time on active duty and was transferred to Munich. Bavaria in 1919 was a principal focus of the Communist offensive in central Europe; a Bavarian Soviet Republic even existed for about three weeks until crushed by the federal government in Berlin. The Communist threat made Bavaria a busy center for anticommunist, antisocialist, antirepublican, and antidemocratic agitation of all kinds, and the seat of a disgruntled illiberalism. It swarmed with secret societies and paramilitary organizations led by discontented army officers or others who fitted with difficulty into the new Weimar democracy. Hitler, working with the army's political instruction program which had been created to combat socialist and democratic propaganda among the demobilized veterans and workers and to keep alive a patriotic and military spirit, joined at the army's behest a tiny party called the German Workers' party and soon became its leader. Early in 1920 he proclaimed its 25-point program, the party now calling itself the National Socialist German Workers' party. Thus were born the Nazis,

---

[8] See pp. 627–628, 636–637, 650, 697, 788–790.

so called from the German way of pronouncing the first two syllables of *National*. Now demobilized, Hitler was fully launched on a career of radical politics.

In earlier pages we have noted the beginnings of the Weimar Republic and the burdens it was compelled to bear from the start—the Versailles peace, reparations, the catastrophic inflation of 1923.[9] Something has been said also of the failure of the republicans to inaugurate the kind of deep social changes that might have democratized the political and social structure of German society and thereby strengthened republican forces. For five years after the war, violence remained sporadic in Germany. Communist agitation continued; but more dangerous, because they attracted more sympathy among the Germans, were the maneuvers of monarchist and antirepublican organizations, which maintained armed bands and threatened uprisings like the Kapp *Putsch* of 1920.[10] (One such private "army" was the Brownshirts or Storm Troopers maintained by the Nazis.) Such bands even resorted to assassination. Thus Walter Rathenau was murdered in 1922; he had organized German production during the war, and in 1922 he was foreign minister, but he had democratic and internationalist inclinations—and was a Jew. Another victim was Matthias Erzberger, a leading moderate politician of the Catholic Center party—he had helped "betray" the army by signing the armistice.

In 1923, when reparations payments were not forthcoming, the French army occupied the Ruhr. A clamor of national indignation swept over Germany. Hitler and the National Socialists, who since 1919 had obtained a considerable following, denounced the Weimar government for shameful submission to the French. They judged the moment opportune for seizing power, and at the end of 1923, in imitation of Mussolini's march on Rome the year before, the Brownshirts staged the "beer hall *Putsch*" in Munich. Hitler jumped on the platform, fired a revolver at the ceiling, and shouted that the "national revolution has broken out." But the police suppressed the disturbance, and Hitler was sentenced to five years in prison. He was released in less than a year; the Weimar democracy dealt mildly with its enemies. In prison he wrote his book, *Mein Kampf (My Struggle)*, a turbid stream of personal recollection, racism, nationalism, collectivism, theories of history, Jew baiting, and political comment. *Mein Kampf* sold widely. The book and the publicity that had accompanied the five-week trial converted Hitler into a political figure of national prominence. The former soldier was not alone in his ideas; no less a person than General Ludendorff, who had distinguished himself in the war,[11] and after the war became one of the most grotesquely unbalanced of the old officer class, gave his warm support to Hitler and even took part in the beer hall *Putsch*.

Beginning in 1924, with the French out of the Ruhr, reparations adjusted, a new and stable currency adopted, and loans from foreign countries, mainly the United States, Germany began to enjoy an amazing economic revival. National Socialism lost its appeal; the party lost members, Hitler was regarded as a charlatan and his followers as a lunatic fringe. All seemed quiet. Then came the Great Depression in 1929. Adolf Hitler, who might have faded out of history, was

[9] See pp. 717–718, 783–787.
[10] See p. 784.
[11] See p. 717.

made by the circumstances attending the depression in Germany into a figure of Napoleonic proportions.

No country suffered more than Germany from the worldwide economic collapse. Foreign loans abruptly ceased or were recalled. Factories ground to a halt. There were 6 million unemployed. The middle class had not really recovered from the great inflation of 1923;[12] when struck again, after so brief a respite, they lost all faith in the economic system and in its future. The Communist vote steadily mounted; the great middling masses, who saw in communism their own death warrant, and who are extremely numerous in any highly developed society, looked about desperately for someone to save them from Bolshevism. The depression also stirred up the universal German loathing for the Treaty of Versailles. Many Germans explained the ruin of Germany by the postwar treatment it had received from the Allies—the constriction of its frontiers, the loss of its colonies, markets, shipping, and foreign investments, the colossal demand for reparations, the occupation of the Ruhr, the inflation, and much else.

Any people in such a trap would have been bewildered and resentful. But the way out chosen by the Germans was perhaps a product of deeper attitudes formed by German experience in the past centuries. Democracy—the agreement to obtain and accept majority verdicts, to discuss and compromise, to adjust conflicting interests without wholly satisfying or wholly crushing either side—was hard enough to maintain in any country in a true crisis. In Germany democracy was itself an innovation, which had yet to prove its value, which could easily be called un-German, an artificial and imported doctrine, or even a foreign system foisted upon Germany by the victors in the late war.

Hitler inflamed all such feelings by his propaganda. He denounced the Treaty of Versailles as a national humiliation. He denounced the Weimar democracy for producing class struggle, division, weakness, and wordy futility. He called for "true" democracy in a vast and vital stirring of the people, or *Volk*, behind a Leader who was a man of action. He declared that Germans, pure Germans, must rely only on themselves. He inveighed against Marxists, Bolsheviks, communists, and socialists, throwing them all together in a deliberate beclouding of the issues; but he claimed to favor the right kind of socialism for the little man, i.e., the doctrine of the National Socialist German Workers' party. He ranted against unearned incomes, war profits, the power of the great trusts and chain stores, land speculators, interest slavery, and unfair taxes. Above all, he denounced the Jews. Jews, like others, were found in all political camps. To the left, Jewish capitalists were anathema. To the right, Jewish revolutionaries were a horror. In anti-Semitism Hitler found a lowest common denominator upon which to appeal to all parties and classes. At the same time the Jews were a small minority (only 600,000 in all Germany), so that in an age of mass politics it was safe enough to attack them.

In the election of 1930 the Nazis won 107 seats in the Reichstag; in 1928 they had won only 12; their popular vote went up from 800,000 to 6.5 million. The Communist representation rose from 54 to 77. By July 1932 the Nazis more than doubled their popular vote, won 230 seats, and were now by far the largest single party though because of the multiplicity of parties they fell well short of a majority.

[12] See pp. 786–787.

In another election, in November 1932, the Nazis, though still well out in front, showed some loss of strength, losing 2 million votes, and dropping to 196 seats. The Communist vote had risen progressively to a peak of 100 in November 1932.

After the relative setback of November 1932 Hitler feared that his movement was passing. But certain conservative, nationalist, and antirepublican elements— old aristocrats, Junker landowners, army officers, Rhineland steel magnates, and other industrialists—had conceived the idea that Hitler could be useful to them. From such sources, which supported other reactionary causes as well, came a portion of Nazi funds. This influential group, mainly from the small Nationalist party, imagined that they would be able to control Hitler and hence control the wave of mass discontent of which in such large measure he had made himself the leader; they were little disturbed by his anticapitalist program.

After Bruening's resignation in June 1932, Franz von Papen headed a Nationalist cabinet with the backing of the influential army leader General Kurt von Schleicher. In December 1932 Schleicher forced Papen's downfall and succeeded him. When he, too, was compelled to resign a month later, both men, intriguing separately, prevailed upon President Hindenburg to name Hitler chancellor of a coalition cabinet. On January 30, 1933, by entirely legal means, Adolf Hitler became chancellor of the German Republic; other positions in the new cabinet were occupied by the Nationalists, with whom the Nazis were to share power. But to share power was not their aim. Hitler called for another election. A week before election day the Reichstag building caught fire. The Nazis, without any real evidence, blamed it on the Communists. They frightened the population with a Red scare, suspended freedom of speech and press, and set loose the Brownshirts to bully the voters. Even so, in the election, the Nazis won only 44 percent of the vote; with their Nationalist allies, they had 52 percent. Hitler, trumpeting a national emergency, was voted dictatorial powers by a pliant Reichstag from which the Communist deputies had been excluded. The Nazi revolution now began.

The Nazi State

Hitler called his new order the Third Reich. He declared that, following on the First Reich, or Holy Roman Empire, and the Second Reich, or empire founded by Bismarck, the Third Reich carried on the process of true German history, of which, he said, it was the organic outgrowth and natural culmination. The Third Reich, he prophesied, would last a thousand years.

Like Mussolini, Hitler took the title of Leader, or, in German, the *Führer*. He claimed to represent the absolute sovereignty of the German people. Jews were considered un-German. Democracy, parliamentarianism, and liberalism were stigmatized as "Western" and together with communism labeled as "Jewish." The new "racial science" classified Jews as non-Aryans[13] and included as Jewish anyone who had one Jewish grandparent. Almost at once Jews were driven from public office, the civil service, teaching, and other professions. The Nuremberg laws of 1935 deprived Jews of all citizenship rights and forbade intermarriage or even sexual relations between Jews and non-Jews. On November 9, 1938,

---

[13] See note, p. 11.

Kristallnacht, the "night of broken glass," the anti-Semitism of Nazi Germany turned to fierce violence. When a seventeen-year-old Polish-Jewish student, distraught by the mistreatment of his parents, shot and killed a German diplomatic official in the German Embassy in Paris, Nazi storm troopers in a savage orgy of vandalism, looting, and incendiarism smashed Jewish shops, businesses, and synagogues in German cities, beat up thousands of Jews, and rounded up 30,000 to be sent to concentration camps. Party and government leaders moved in to control the storm troopers and to use anti-Semitism for their own purposes. The government levied a billion-mark fine on the Jewish community for provoking the assault and collected the insurance payments for the shattered glass and other property damage. Jews who in the wake of these events belatedly tried to flee the country discovered that neither they nor their families could readily find places of refuge; the doors in Europe and the United States were for the most part closed to them. The events of 1938 in Germany still resembled an older-style pogrom, but they foreshadowed the state-organized systematic destruction, in the Holocaust, of six million East European (and German) Jews in the grisly death camps.[14]

The new totalitarian order was thought of as absolutely solid, or monolithic, like one huge single slab of rock in which no particle had any separate structure. Germany ceased to be federal; all the old states such as Prussia and Bavaria were abolished. All political parties except the National Socialists were destroyed. The Nazi party was itself violently purged on the night of June 30, 1934, when many of the old Brownshirt leaders, those who represented the more social revolutionary wing of the movement, were accused of plotting against Hitler and were summarily shot. A secret political police, the Gestapo (*Geheime Staatspolizei*), together with People's Courts, and a system of permanent concentration camps in which thousands were detained without trial or sentence, suppressed all ideas at variance with the Leader's. Law itself was defined as the will of the German people operating in the interests of the Nazi state. Churches, both Protestant and Catholic, were "coordinated" with the new regime; their clergy were forbidden to criticize its activities, international religious ties were discouraged, and efforts were made to keep children out of religious schools. The government encouraged anti-Christian pagan movements, in worship of the old Teutonic gods, but nothing was sponsored so much as worship of Nazism and its *Führer*. A Nazi Youth Movement, and schools and universities, indoctrinated the rising generation in the new concepts. The total, all-encompassing repression thwarted the efforts of a few dedicated Germans to develop a broad resistance movement.

Labor unions also were "coordinated"; they were replaced by a National Labor Front. Strikes were forbidden. Under the "leadership principle" employers were set up as small-scale *Führers* in their factories and industries and given extensive control, subject to close government supervision. An extensive public works program was launched, reforestation and swamp drainage projects were organized, housing and superhighways were built. A vast rearmament program absorbed the unemployed and within a short time unemployment disappeared. Even under Nazi statistics labor's share in the national income was reduced, but workers had jobs; and an organization called Strength Through Joy attended to

[14] See p. 859 and map, p. 858.

the needs of people with small incomes, providing entertainment, vacations, and travel for many who could never otherwise afford them.

The government assumed increasing controls over industry, while leaving ownership in private hands. In 1936 it adopted a Four-Year Plan of economic development. All countries after the Great Depression tended to economic nationalism, but Nazi Germany set up the goal of autarchy and self-sufficiency—absolute independence from foreign trade. German chemists developed artificial rubber, plastics, synthetic textiles, and many other substitute products to enable the country to do without raw materials imported from overseas. Germany took advantage of its position as the chief market on which east Europeans were dependent. Mixing political threats with ordinary business, the Nazis bartered for Polish wheat, Hungarian lumber, or Romanian oil, often giving in return such articles as it was convenient for Germany to dispose of, rather than those that the east Europeans wanted.

For Europe as a whole one of the basic economic problems, especially after the World War, was that while the Continent was economically a unit dependent on exchange between diverse regions, politically it was cut to pieces by tariff restrictions, currency differences, and hothouse industries artificially nurtured by nationalist ambition. The Nazis claimed to have a solution for this problem in a network of bilateral trade agreements assuring all neighboring peoples an outlet for their products. But it was a solution in which Germans were to be the most industrial, most advanced, most powerful, and most wealthy, and other Europeans relegated to permanently inferior status. And what could not be accomplished under trade agreements and economic penetration could be accomplished by conquest and war. Within a few years after 1933, although the regime had its share of bureaucratic confusion and personal rivalries, the Nazi revolution had turned Germany into a huge disciplined war machine, its internal foes liquidated or silenced, its mesmerized masses roaring their approval in giant demonstrations, ready to follow the Führer in storming new Valkyrian heights. "Today Germany," went an ominous phrase, "tomorrow the whole world."

Totalitarianism: Some Origins and Consequences

Totalitarianism was a many-sided thing. It had appeared first with the Bolshevik Revolution, for in the denial of individual liberty the Soviet regime did not differ from the most extreme anti-Soviet totalitarianism as manifested in Germany. (Although Mussolini was the first to use the term "totalitarian," and advance it as an ideology, the Fascist regime that he established was probably not sufficiently all-encompassing to merit that term.) There were at first important differences in principle. Theoretically, the proletarian dictatorship was temporary; it did not glorify the individual Leader-Hero; and it was not nationalistic, for it rested on a principle of worldwide class struggle in all nations alike. It adopted a democratic-sounding constitution and paid at least lip service to individual rights. Its constitution officially condemned racism, and it did not deliberately and consciously cultivate an ethics of war and violence. But as time passed, Soviet totalitarianism became harder to distinguish from others. The Soviet dictatorship and one-party state seemed as permanent as any political system; the hollowness of the constitution and the guarantee of individual rights became more apparent; a cult developed around the person of Stalin; and the emphasis became more nationalistic, falling less on the workers of the world and more on the glories of the Soviet Fatherland.

Totalitarianism, as distinct from mere dictatorship, though it appeared rather suddenly after the First World War, was no historic freak. It was an outgrowth of a good deal of development in the past. The state was an institution that had continuously acquired new powers ever since the Middle Ages; step by step, since feudal times, it had assumed jurisdiction over law courts and men at arms, imposed taxes, regulated churches, guided economic policy, operated school systems, and devised schemes of public welfare. The First World War had continued and advanced the process.[15] The twentieth-century totalitarian state, mammoth and monolithic, claiming an absolute domination over every department of life, now carried this old development of state sovereignty to a new extreme. For centuries, for example, the state had clashed with the church. The twentieth-century dictators did the same. In addition, however, they were in most cases not merely anticlerical but explicitly anti-Christian, offering, or rather imposing, a "total" philosophy of life.

This new philosophy drew heavily upon a historic nationalism which it greatly exaggerated. It derived in part from the organic theory of society, which held that society (or the nation or state) was a kind of living organism within which the individual person was but a single cell. Individuals, in this theory, had no independent existence; they received life itself, and all their ideas, from the society, people, nation, or culture into which they were born and by which they were nurtured. In Marxism, the absolute subordination of individuals to their class came to much the same thing. Individuals were a microscopic cell, meaningless outside the social body. They were but clay to be molded by the imprint of their groups. It made little sense, given such theories, to speak of the individual's "reason" or "freedom," or to allow individuals to have their own opinions (which were formed for them by environment), or to count up individual opinions to obtain a merely numerical majority. Valid ideas were those of the group as a whole, of the people or nation (or, in Marxism, the class) as a solid block. Even science was a product of specific societies; there was a "Nazi science" which was bound to differ in its conclusions from democratic bourgeois, Western, or "Jewish" science; and for the Soviets there was a Soviet science, consistent with dialectical materialism, and better equipped to see the truth than the decadent bourgeois, capitalistic, or "fascist" science of the non-Soviet world. All art, too—music, painting, poetry, fiction, architecture, sculpture—was good art insofar as it expressed the society or nationality in which it appeared.

The avowed philosophy of totalitarian regimes (like much modern thought) was subjective. Whether an idea was held to be true depended on whose idea it was. Ideas of truth, or beauty, or right were not supposed to correspond to any outer or objective reality; they had only to correspond to the inner nature, interests, or point of view of the people, nation, society, or class that entertained such ideas. The older concepts of reason, natural law, natural right, and the

---

[15] See pp. 718–722.

ultimate alikeness of all mankind, or of a common path of all mankind in one course of progress, disappeared.[16]

The totalitarian regimes did not simply declare, as a dry finding of social science, that peoples' ideas were shaped by environment. They set about shaping them actively. Propaganda became a principal branch of government. Propaganda was hardly new, but in the past, and still in the democratic countries, it had been a piecemeal affair, urging the public to accept this or that political party, or to buy this or that brand of coffee. Now, like all else, it became "total." Propaganda was monopolized by the state, and it demanded faith in a whole view of life and in every detail of this coordinated whole. Formerly the control of books and newpapers had been mainly negative; under Napoleon or Metternich, for example, censors had forbidden statements on particular subjects, events, or persons. Now, in totalitarian countries, control of the press became frighteningly positive. The government manufactured thought. It manipulated opinion. It rewrote history. Writers were required to present whole ideologies, and books, newspapers, magazines, and the radio diffused an endless and overwhelming cloud of words. Loudspeakers blared in the streets, gigantic blown-up photographs of the Leader looked down in public places. The propaganda experts were sometimes fanatics, but often they were cynics like Dr. Goebbels in Germany, too intelligent to be duped by the rubbish with which they duped their country.

The very idea of truth evaporated. No norm of human utterance remained except political expediency—the wishes and self-interest of those in power. No one could learn anything except what the government wanted people to know. No one could escape the omnipresent official doctrine, the insidious penetration of the very recesses of the mind by ideas planted by outsiders for their own purposes. People came to accept, and even to believe, the most extravagant statements when they were endlessly repeated, year after year. Barred from all independent sources of information, having no means by which any official allegation could be tested, the peoples of totalitarian countries became increasingly in fact, and not merely in sociological theory, incapable of the use of reason.

Racism, more characteristic of Nazi Germany than of totalitarianism in general, was a further exaggeration, or degradation, of older ideas of nationalism and national solidarity. It defined the nation in a tribal sense, as a biological entity, a group of persons possessing the same physical ancestry and the same or similar physical characteristics. Anti-Semitism was the most venomous form of racism in Europe. While a latent hostility to Jews had always been present in the Christian world, modern anti-Semitism had little to do with Christianity. It arose in part from the fact that, in the nineteenth century, with the general removal of religious disabilities, the Jews entered into general society and many of them achieved positions of prominence, and especially so in Germany, so that from the point of view of any individual non-Jew they could be represented as dangerous competitors in business or the professions. But most of all, anti-Semitism was inflamed by propagandists who wished people to feel their supposed racial purity more keenly or to forget the deeper problems of society, including poverty, unemployment, and economic inequities.

For totalitarianism was an escape from the realities of class conflict. It was a

[16] See pp. 308–309, 312, 315, 325–327, 371–372, 473–474, 584, 637.

way of pretending that differences between rich and poor were of minor importance. Typically, a totalitarian regime came into power by stirring up class fears, then remained in power, and represented itself as indispensable, by declaring that it had settled the class problem. Thus Mussolini, Hitler, and certain lesser dictators, before seizing office, pointed alarmingly to the dark menace of Bolshevism; and, once in power, declared that all classes stood shoulder to shoulder in slablike solidarity behind the Leader. Nor were events in Russia (or in China after the Second World War) altogether different. The Bolsheviks in 1917, armed with the ideas of Karl Marx, aroused the workers against capitalists, landlords, middle-class people, and rich peasants; then, once in power and after extensive liquidations, they declared that the classless society had arrived, that no true social classes any longer existed, and that all citizens stood solidly behind a regime from which, they said, all good citizens benefited equally. Only the democracies admitted that they suffered from internal class problems, from maladjustments between rich and poor or between favored and unfavored groups in society.

The dictatorships blamed their troubles on forces outside the country. They accused dissatisfied persons of conspiring with foreigners or refugees—with being the tools of Trotskyism, imperialism, or international Jewry. Or they talked of the struggle between rich nations and poor nations, the "have" and the "have not" countries, and thus transformed the problem of poverty into an international struggle. In the distinction between "have" and "have-not" countries there was, of course, more than a grain of truth; in more old-fashioned language some countries (in fact the European democracies, as well as the United States and the British dominions of the 1930s) had "progressed" farther than others. It is probable that any propaganda is more effective if partly true. But when the totalitarians blamed their troubles on other countries and transformed the conflict between "have" and "have not" into a struggle between nations, they gave the impression that war might be a solution for social ills.

Violence, the acceptance and even glorification of violence, was indeed the characteristic most clearly distinguishing the totalitarian from the democratic systems. We have seen how a cult of violence, or belief that struggle was beneficial, had arisen before the First World War.[17] The war itself habituated people to violence and direct action. Lenin and his followers showed how a small group could seize the helm of state under revolutionary or chaotic conditions. Mussolini in 1922 taught the same lesson, with further refinements; for the Italy in which he seized power was not at war, and it was merely the threat or possibility of revolution, not revolution itself, that provided him with his opportunity. In the 1920s, for the first time since the seventeenth century, some of the most civilized parts of Europe, in time of peace, saw private armies marching about the country, bands of uniformed and organized ruffians, Blackshirts or Brownshirts, who manhandled, abused, and even killed law-abiding citizens with inpunity. Nor would anyone in the 1920s have believed that, by the 1930s, Europe would see the reintroduction of torture.

The very ethics of totalitarianism was violent and neopagan. It borrowed from Nietzsche and other prewar theoreticians, who, safe and civilized, had declared

---

[17] See pp. 640–641.

that men should live dangerously, avoid the flabby weakness of too much thought, throw themselves with red-blooded vigor into a life of action. The new regimes all instituted youth movements. They appealed to a kind of juvenile idealism, in which young people believed that by joining some kind of squad, donning some kind of uniform, and getting into the fresh air they contributed to a great moral resurgence of their country. Young men were taught to value their bodies but not their minds, to be tough and hard, and to regard mass gymnastics as patriotic demonstrations. Young women were taught to breed large families without complaint, to be content in the kitchen, and to look with awe upon their virile mates. The body cult flourished while the mind decayed. Especially in National Socialism the ideal was to turn the German people into a race of splendid animals, pink-cheeked, Nordic, and upstanding. Contrariwise, euthanasia was adopted for the insane and was proposed for the aged. Later, in the Second World War, when the Nazis overran eastern Europe, they committed Jews to the gas chambers, destroying some 6 million human beings by the most scientific methods. Animals were animals; one bred the kind one wanted and killed the kind one did not.

The Spread of Dictatorship

The trend toward dictatorship spread in Europe in the 1930s. By 1938 only ten out of twenty-seven European countries remained democratic, in the sense that different political parties honestly competed for office and that citizens within generous limits thought and acted as they pleased. They were Great Britain and France; Holland, Belgium, and Switzerland; Czechoslovakia and Finland; and the three Scandinavian countries.

The promise of the early 1920s that constitutional and democratic government would flourish was thwarted. The weakness or absence of a parliamentary or democratic tradition, low education and literacy standards, the hostility of reactionary elements, the fear of Bolshevism, and the dissatisfaction of existing national minorities, all coupled with the economic strains resulting from the Great Depression, contributed to the collapse of the new representative institutions. Apart from the avowedly totalitarian or fascist regimes of Germany and Italy, the new dictatorships and authoritarian systems generally rested on a combination of personal and military power, but several reflected or absorbed some of the ideological features of a generic fascism. In Portugal, Salazar inaugurated a clerical-corporative dictatorship in 1932 that lasted for over four decades. In Austria, Dollfuss fused various right-wing political and military elements into a clerical-fascist "Christian" dictatorship which violently suppressed the Socialists and sought in vain to counter the German threat. In Spain General Franco came to power (after a bloody civil war to be described). In many respects the dictatorships of Latin America under a diversity of caudillos and military juntas, in both origin and character, resembled the European military dictatorships.

The authoritarian regimes were alike in repressing individual liberties, banning opposition parties, and abolishing or nullifying parliamentary institutions. Many borrowed features of fascism, establishing a corporative state, outlawing independent labor organizations, and forbidding strikes; many, like Hungary, Romania, and Poland, instituted anti-Semitic legislation. None went so far in the total coordination of all political, economic, intellectual, and biological activities in a revolutionary mass-based dictatorship as did Hitler's Third Reich.

The acceptance and glorification of violence, it has been noted, was the feature most clearly distinguishing the totalitarian from the democratic systems. War in the Nazi and Fascist ethics was a noble thing, and the love of peace a sign of decadence. (The Soviet regime by its own theory regarded war with non-Soviet powers as inevitable some day, but did not preach it as a positive moral good.) The exaltation of war and struggle, the need for maintaining national solidarity, the habit of blaming foreign countries for social troubles, together with the considerable armaments programs on which the dictatorships embarked, plus the personal ambition and egotistical mania of individual dictators, made the decade of the 1930s a time not only of domestic reaction but of recurrent international crises, of which the last, in 1939, led to war.

XX.
THE
SECOND
WORLD WAR

PEACE IN THE ABSTRACT, the peace that is the mere absence of war, does not exist in international relations. Peace is never found apart from certain conditions; it means peaceable acceptance of given conditions, or peaceable and orderly transformation of conditions by negotiation and agreement. The conditions, in the 1930s, were basically those laid down by the Paris peace conference of 1919—the states recognized, the frontiers drawn, the terms agreed to, at the close of the First World War. In the 1930s neither Germany, Italy, Japan, nor the U.S.S.R. was content with these conditions; they were "revisionist" or dissatisfied powers; and the first three were willing to undertake war itself to make a change. Great Britain, France, and the United States were satisfied powers, expecting no benefit from change in the conditions; but on the other hand they had lost faith in the conditions and were unwilling to risk war for the sake of upholding them. They had made a treaty in 1919 which a dozen years later they were unwilling to enforce. They stood idly by, as long as they could, while the dissatisfied powers tore to pieces the states recognized, the frontiers drawn, and the terms agreed to at the Peace of Paris. From the Japanese invasion of Manchuria in 1931 to the outbreak of European war in 1939, force was used by those who wished to upset international order, but never by those who wished to maintain it.

Chapter Emblem: A pocket watch stopped when the atomic bomb was dropped on Hiroshima, Japan, in 1945.

105. The Weakness of the Democracies: Again to War

The Pacifism and Disunity of the West

While dictators stormed, the Western democracies were swayed by a profound pacifism, which may be defined as an insistence on peace regardless of consequences. Many people now believed, especially in England and the United States, that the First World War had been a mistake, that little or nothing had been gained by it, that they had been deluded by wartime propaganda, that wars were really started by armaments manufacturers, that Germany had not really caused the war of 1914, that the Treaty of Versailles was too hard on the Germans, that vigorous peoples like the Germans or Italians needed room for expansion, that democracy was after all not suited to all nations, that it took two to make a quarrel, and that there need be no war if one side resolutely refused to be provoked—a whole system of pacific and tolerant ideas in which there was perhaps the usual mixture of truth and misunderstanding.

The pacifism of the West had other roots, most evident in France. About 1.4 million Frenchmen had died in World War I; half of all French males between the ages of 20 and 32 in 1914 had been killed. To the French it was inconceivable that such a holocaust should be repeated. French strategy was therefore defensive and sparing of manpower. If war came, the French expected to fight it mainly in the elaborate fortifications, called the Maginot Line, which they built on their eastern frontier facing Germany, from the Swiss to the Belgian border; to its north the Ardennes forest was to be a barrier to any invader. During the depression France was torn by internal class conflict and by fascist and quasi-fascist agitation.[1] Many French of the right, historically unsympathetic to the republic and seeing, or claiming to see, in such movements as the Popular Front the threat of social revolution, did not conceal their admiration for Mussolini or even for Hitler. Abandoning their traditional role as ardent nationalists, they would do nothing to oppose the dictators. On the other hand, many on the left looked with sympathy upon the Soviet Union. France was ideologically too divided in the 1930s to possess any firm foreign policy, and all elements took false comfort from the supposed impregnability of the French Chinese Wall.

A similar situation, in lesser degree, prevailed in Great Britain and the United States. The loss and bloodshed of the First World War were remembered. It was well known that another world war would be even more horrible; there was an unspeakable dread of the bombing of cities. Typical of the time was a resolution adopted by students at Oxford in 1933 that they would never take up arms for their country under any conditions; peace movements appeared among American college students too. The pull between left and right was felt in England and America. In the 1930s, when any international action seemed to favor either the U.S.S.R. on the one hand, or Hitler and Mussolini on the other, it was hard to establish any foreign policy on a firm basis of national unity. In Britain some members of the upper classes were overtly sympathetic to the fascist dictators

---

[1] See pp. 815–817.

or saw in them a bulwark against communism. The government itself tried to be noncommittal; it believed that some means of satisfying or appeasing the more legitimate demands of the dictators might be found. Neville Chamberlain, prime minister after 1937, became the principal architect of the appeasement policy.

The United States government, despite President Roosevelt's repeated denunciation of the aggressors, followed in practice a policy of rigid isolation. Neutrality legislation, enacted by a strong isolationist bloc in Congress in the years 1935 to 1937, forbade loans, export of munitions, and use of American shipping facilities to any belligerent once the president had recognized a state of war in a given area. Many believed that the United States had been drawn into the First World War by such economic involvement. From this American neutrality legislation the aggressors of the 1930s derived great benefit, but not the victims of aggression.

As for the rulers of the U.S.S.R., they were revisionist and dissatisfied in that they did not accept the new frontiers of eastern Europe nor the territorial losses incurred by Russia in the First World War. They resented the *cordon sanitaire* created in 1919 against the spread of Bolshevism, the ring of small states on their borders from Finland to Romania, which were almost without exception vehemently anti-Soviet. They had no fondness for the international status quo nor had they abandoned their long-range revolutionary objectives. But, as Communists and as Russians, they were obsessed by fear of attack and invasion. Their Marxist doctrine taught the inherent hostility of the entire capitalist world; the intervention of the Western Allies in the Revolution and civil wars confirmed their Marxist theory. And long before the Bolshevik Revolution, in the days of Napoleon and earlier, the fertile Russian plains had tempted ambitious conquerors. Resentful and suspicious of the outside world, in the 1930s the men in the Kremlin were alarmed primarily by Germany. Hitler, in *Mein Kampf* and elsewhere, had declared that he meant to obliterate Bolshevism and subordinate large stretches of eastern Europe to Germany.

The Soviets became interested in collective security, in international action against aggression. In 1934 they joined the League of Nations. They instructed Communist parties to work with socialists and liberals in popular fronts.[2] They offered assistance in checking fascist aggressors, signing mutual assistance pacts with France and Czechoslovakia in 1935. But many people fled from the Soviet embrace with a shudder. They distrusted Soviet motives, or they were convinced that the purges and trials of the 1930s had left the Soviets weak and undependable as allies, or they felt that the fascist dictators might be diverted eastward against the Soviets and so spare the Western democracies. Here again, though the Soviet Union was ostensibly willing, no effective coaliton against aggression could be formed.

The March of Nazi and Fascist Aggression

Adolf Hitler perceived these weaknesses with uncanny genius. Determined to wreck the whole treaty system, which most Germans, to be sure, found humiliating, he employed tactics of gradual encroachment that played on the hopes and fears of the democratic peoples. He inspired in them alternating tremors

[2] See p. 775.

of apprehension and sighs of relief. He would rage and rant, arouse the fear of war, take just a little, declare that it was all he wanted, let the former Allies naïvely hope that he was now satisfied and that peace was secure; then rage again, take a little more, and proceed through the same cycle.

Each year he precipitated some kind of emergency, and each time the French and British saw no alternative except to let him have his way. In 1933, soon after seizing power, he took Germany out of the League and out of the Disarmament Conference then taking place. He successfully wooed Poland, long France's ally, and in 1934 the two countries signed a nonaggression treaty. That same year the Nazis of Austria attempted a *Putsch*, assassinated the Austrian chancellor, Dollfuss, and demanded the union of Austria with Germany. The Western powers did nothing. It was Mussolini who acted. Not desiring to see Germany installed at the Brenner Pass, he mobilized large Italian forces on the frontier, discouraged Hitler from intervening openly in Austria, and so preserved the independence of Austria for four more years. In January 1935 a plebiscite was conducted in the Saar by the League of Nations as stipulated under the Versailles treaty. Amidst intense Nazi agitation, the Saar voted for reunion with the Reich. Two months later, in March 1935, Hitler dramatically repudiated those clauses in the Versailles treaty intended to keep Germany disarmed; he now openly built up the German armed forces. France, England, and Italy protested such arbitrary and one-sided denunciation of an international treaty but did nothing about it. Indeed, Great Britain entered into a naval agreement with Germany, to the consternation of the French.

On March 7, 1936, using as his justification the new Franco-Soviet pact, Hitler repudiated the Locarno agreements[3] and reoccupied the Rhineland; i.e., he sent German troops into the German territory west of the Rhine, which by the Treaty of Versailles was supposed to be a demilitarized zone. There was talk in the French government of action, and at this time Hitler might have been checked, for German military strength was still weak and the German army was prepared to withdraw, or at least consult, at signs of resistance. But the French government was divided and unwilling to act without Britain; and the British would not risk war to keep German troops from occupying German soil. The next year, 1937, was a quiet one, but Nazi agitation flared up in Danzig, which the Treaty of Versailles had set up as a free city. In March 1938 German forces moved into Austria, and the union of Austria and Germany, the *Anschluss*, was at last consummated. In September 1938 came the turn of Czechoslovakia and the Munich crisis. To understand it we must first pick up other threads in the story.

Mussolini, too, had his ambitions and required sensational foreign triumphs to magnetize the Italian people. Since 1919 the Italians had been dissatisfied with the peace arrangements. They had received nothing of the former Turkish territories and German colonies that had been liberally parceled out, as mandates, to Great Britain, France, Belgium, Japan, South Africa, Australia, and New Zealand.[4] They had never forgotten the humiliating defeat of Italian forces by Abyssinia at Adowa in 1896.[5] Ethiopia, as Abyssinia was now called, remained

[3] See p. 788.
[4] See p. 725.
[5] See p. 666.

the only part of black Africa (with the exception of Liberia) that was still independent.

In 1935 Italy went to war with Ethiopia. The League of Nations, of which Ethiopia was a member, pronounced the Italian action an unwarranted aggression and imposed sanctions on Italy, by which members of the League were to refrain from selling Italy either arms or raw materials—oil was excepted. The British even gathered large naval forces in the Mediterranean in a show of strength. In France, however, there was considerable sympathy for Mussolini in important quarters, and in England there was the fear that if sanctions became too effective, by refusal of oil or by closure of the Suez Canal, Italy might be provoked into a general war. Mussolini was thus able to defeat Ethiopia in 1936 and to combine it with Italian Somaliland and Eritrea in an Italian East African empire. The Ethiopian Emperor Haile Selassie made futile pleas for further action at Geneva. The League of Nations again failed, as in the case of the occupation of Manchuria by Japan, to provide machinery for disciplinary action against a wayward Great Power.[6]

The Spanish Civil War, 1936–1939

Hardly had the Ethiopian crisis been disposed of, to the entire satisfaction of the aggressor, when an even more serious crisis broke out in Spain. In 1931, after a decade of political disturbance, a rather mild revolution had driven out Alfonso XIII, of the Bourbon family, and brought about the establishment of a democratic Spanish Republic. Old hostilities within the country came to a head. The new republican government undertook a program of social and economic reform. To combat the old entrenched power of the church, anticlerical legislation was enacted: church and state were separated, the Jesuit order dissolved and its property confiscated, and the schools removed from clerical control. The old movement for Catalan independence was somewhat mollified by the grant of considerable local autonomy. To placate the peasantry the government began to break up some of the larger landed estates and to redistribute the land. The government's program was never pushed vigorously enough to satisfy extremist elements, who manifested their dissatisfaction in strikes and uprisings, particularly in industrial Barcelona, the Catalan capital, and the mining areas of the Asturias, but it was radical enough to antagonize the great property owners and the churchmen. After 1933 the government fell into the hands of rightist and conservative parties, who ruled through ineffective and unpopular ministries. An insurrection of the miners in the Asturias was put down with much brutality. Agitation for Catalan independence was repressed.

In February 1936 new elections were held. All groups of the left—republicans, socialists, syndicalists, anarchists, communists—joined in a Popular Front against monarchists, clericals, army officers, other adherents of the old regime, and Falangists, or Spanish fascists. The left won a victory at the polls, and pressed forward with a reform program. In July 1936, a group of military men led an insurrection against the republican government; General Francisco Franco emerged as leader. The parties of the left united in resistance and the whole

[6] See p. 799.

country fell into civil war. It was the most devastating war in all Spanish history; over 600,000 human beings lost their lives, and it was accompanied by extreme cruelties on both sides. For nearly three years the republican or loyalist forces held their own before finally succumbing to the insurgents led by Franco, who in March 1939 established an authoritarian, fascist-type rule over the exhausted country.

Spain provided a rehearsal for the greater struggle soon to come. The republican government could legitimately have looked forward to the purchase of arms abroad to suppress the rebellion, but Britain and France were resolved not to let the war expand into a general conflict. They forbade the shipment of war materials to the republican government; even the French Popular Front government put obstacles in the way of aid to the hard-pressed Spanish Popular Front. The United States extended its neutrality legislation to cover civil wars and placed an embargo on the export of arms to Spain. At British and French instigation twenty-seven nations, including all the major European powers, agreed not to intervene or take sides. But the nonintervention policy proved a fiasco. Germany, Italy, and the Soviet Union intervened anyway. The former two supported Franco and denounced the republicans as the tools of Bolshevism, while the U.S.S.R. supported the republic, reinforced the growing strength of the Spanish Communists, and stigmatized the rebels under Franco as the agents of international fascism. Germans, Italians, and Russians sent military equipment to Spain, testing their tanks and planes in battle. The fascist bombings of Guernica, Madrid, and Barcelona horrified the democratic world. The Germans and Italians sent troops (the Italians over 50,000); the Soviets if only for geographical reasons did not send troops but sent technicians and political advisers. Thousands of volunteers of leftist or liberal sympathy, from the United States and Europe, went to Spain to serve with the republican forces. Spain became the battlefield of contending ideologies. The Spanish Civil War split the world into fascist and antifascist camps.

As in the case of Ethiopia, the war in Spain helped bring Germany and Italy together. Mussolini had at first, like others, feared the revival of a militant Germany. He had outfaced Hitler when the latter threatened to absorb Austria in 1934. The Ethiopian war, Italian ambitions in Africa, and a clamorous Italian demand for ascendancy in the Mediterranean, the *mare nostrum* of the ancient Romans, estranged Italy from France and Britain. In 1936, soon after the outbreak of the Spanish Civil War, Mussolini and Hitler came to an understanding, which they called the Rome-Berlin Axis—the diplomatic axis around which they hoped the world might turn. That year Japan signed with Germany an Anti-Comintern Pact, soon ratified by Italy too; ostensibly an agreement to oppose communism, it was actually the foundation for a diplomatic alliance. Each, thus furnished with allies, was able to push its demands with more success. In 1938 Mussolini accepted what he had denied to Hitler in 1934—the German absorption of Austria.

Meanwhile, in 1937, Japan, using as a pretext the firing upon Japanese troops at the Marco Polo Bridge near Peking, launched a brutal full-scale invasion of China and within a short time controlled most of the country. The Chinese could fight on only from the hinterland. The League again ineffectually condemned Japan. The United States refrained from applying its neutrality legislation since no war was officially declared. This made possible the extension of loans to

China, the victim of aggression, but also made possible the purchase by the Japanese of vitally needed scrap iron, steel, oil, and machinery from American industry. The Japanese profited from the tensions in the Western world, which in 1938 were rapidly mounting.

The Munich Crisis: Climax of Appeasement

By annexing Austria in March 1938 Hitler added about 6 million Germans to the Reich. Another 3 million Germans lived in Czechoslovakia.[7] All those who were adults in 1938 had been born under the Habsburg empire. They had never, since 1918, been content with their new position as a minority in a Slavic state and had long complained about various forms of subtle discrimination. There were Polish, Ruthenian, and Hungarian minorities also, and since even the Slovaks had a strong sense of separate identity, there was in actuality no preponderant national majority of any kind. The fact that Czechoslovakia had one of the most enlightened minorities policies in Europe, enjoyed the highest living standard east of Germany, and was the only country in central Europe in 1938 that was still democratic only demonstrated the difficulty of maintaining a multinational state even under the most favorable of conditions.

Czechoslovakia was strategically the keystone of Europe. It had a firm alliance with France, which had repeatedly guaranteed to defend it against German attack, and an alliance with the Soviet Union, which was contingent on the functioning of the French alliance. With Romania and Yugoslavia it formed the Little Entente, upon which France relied to maintain the existing boundaries in that part of Europe. It had a well-trained army, important munitions industries, and strong fortifications against Germany, which, however, were located in precisely the Sudeten border area where the population was almost all German. When Hitler annexed Austria—since Vienna is further east than Prague—he enclosed Czechoslovakia in a vise. From the German point of view it could now be said that Bohemia-Moravia, which was almost a third German anyway, formed a bulge protruding into the German Reich.

The Sudeten Germans of Czechoslovakia, whether Nazis or not, fell under the influence of agitators whose aim was less to relieve their grievances than to promote National Socialism. Hitler fomented their demands for union with Germany. In May 1938 rumors of an imminent German invasion caused the Czechs to mobilize; Russia, France, and England issued warnings. Hitler, not actually intending to invade at that time, was forced to issue assurances but was nevertheless determined to smash the Czechs in the autumn. France and England were appalled by their narrow escape from war. The French were nervous and acquiesced in the leadership of Britain, which in the following months strove to avoid any firm stand that might precipitate war. The Czechs, under pressure from Britain and France, accepted British mediation on the Sudeten issue and in the summer of 1938 offered wide concessions to the Sudeten Germans amounting to regional autonomy, but this was not enough to satisfy Hitler, who loudly proclaimed that the plight of the Germans in Czechoslovakia was intolerable and must be corrected. The Soviets urged a firm stand, but the Western powers had

[7] See pp. 725, 727–730, 779–783, and maps, pp. 470 and 728–729.

little confidence in Soviet military strength and, given the Soviet geographical situation, their ability to render assistance to Czechoslovakia; moreover, they feared that firmness might mean war. They could not be sure whether Hitler was bluffing. He might, if opposed, back down; but it seemed equally likely, or indeed more so, that he was entirely willing to fight. The Western powers discounted intelligence reports of a military-civilian plot to unseat Hitler if, in the event of Western resistance, war broke out over Czechoslovakia.

As the crisis grew in September 1938, the British prime minister, Neville Chamberlain, who had never flown in his life before, flew to Germany twice to sound out Hitler on his terms. The second time Hitler raised his demands so that even the British and French could not accept them. Mobilization began; war seemed imminent. Suddenly, in the midst of the unbearable tension, Hitler invited Chamberlain and Edouard Daladier, the French premier, to a four-power conference at Munich, to be attended by his ally, Mussolini. The Soviet Union and Czechoslovakia itself were excluded. At Munich Chamberlain and Daladier accepted Hitler's terms and then put enormous pressure on the Czech government to yield—to sign its own death warrant. France, urged on by England in an appeasement course that it was only too willing to follow, repudiated its treaty obligation to protect Czechoslovakia, ignored the Soviets who reaffirmed their willingness to aid the Czechs if the French acted, and abandoned its whole system of a Little Entente in the East. The Munich agreement permitted Germany to annex the adjoining fringe of Bohemia in which the majority of the people were Germans. This fringe contained the mountainous approaches and the fortifications, so that its loss left Czechoslovakia militarily defenseless. After promises to guarantee the integrity of what remained of Czechoslovakia, the conference disbanded. Chamberlain and Daladier were welcomed home with cheers. Chamberlain reported that he had brought "peace in our time." Again the democracies sighed with relief, hoped that Hitler had made his last demand, and told themselves that, with wise concessions, there need be no war.

The Munich crisis, with its death sentence to Czechoslovakia, revealed the helpless weakness into which the Western democracies had fallen by 1938. It may be that there was, in fact, little that the French and British could do, at Munich, to save Czechoslovakia. Their countries lagged behind Germany in military preparedness. They were impressed by the might of the German army and air force. Bolder leaders than Daladier and Chamberlain, knowing the state of their own armed forces, would have declined to risk a quarrel. They loved peace and would buy it at a high price, not daring to believe that they were dealing with a blackmailer whose price would always be raised. They suffered, too, from another moral uncertainty; by the very principle of national self-determination, accepted by the victors after the First World War, Germany could argue that it had a right to all that it had hitherto demanded. Hitler, in sending German troops into the German Rhineland, in annexing Austria, stirring up Danzig, incorporating the Bohemian Germans, had only asserted the right of the German people to have a sovereign German state. Moreover, if Hitler could be diverted eastward, enmeshed in a war with Russia, then communism and fascism might destroy each other—so one might hope. Possibly it was one of Hitler's motives, in the Munich crisis, to isolate Russia from the West and the West from Russia. If so, he succeeded well enough.

In the weeks following Munich the international commission set up to arrange the new boundaries worked further injustices on Czechoslovakia, dispensing even with the plebiscites which had been agreed to for disputed areas. Meanwhile the Poles and Hungarians brought forth their demands on the hapless Czechs. The Poles seized the Teschen district; and Hungary, under a German and Italian award, took 7,500 square miles of Slovakia. France and Britain were not consulted and did not seriously protest.

End of Appeasement

The final disillusionment came in March 1939. Hitler marched into Bohemia-Moravia, the really Czech part of Czechoslovakia, which he transformed into a German protectorate. Exploiting Slovak nationalism, he declared Slovakia "independent." Czechoslovakia, merely trimmed down at Munich, now disappeared from the map. Having promised to take only a bite, Hitler swallowed the whole. He then seized Memel from Lithuania and raised demands for Danzig and the Polish Corridor. A horrible realization now spread in France and Britain. It was clear that Hitler's most solemn guarantees were worthless, that his designs were not limited to Germans, but reached out to all eastern Europe and beyond, that he was essentially insatiable, that he could not be appeased. In April 1939 his partner in aggression, Mussolini, took over Albania.

The Western powers now began to make preparations for a military stand. Britain, changing its East European policy at the eleventh hour, gave a guarantee to Poland, and followed that with guarantees to Romania and Greece. That spring and summer the British tried to form an anti-German alliance with the U.S.S.R. But Poland and the Baltic states were unwilling to allow Soviet armies within their borders, even for the purpose of defending themselves against the Germans. The Anglo-French negotiators refused to put pressure on them. Since the Poles, in 1920, had conquered more territory than the Allies had meant them to have,[8] pushing their eastern border well into Byelorussia, almost to Minsk, the Anglo-French scruples seemed to the Soviets unnecessarily delicate. They did not wish the Germans to launch an attack on them from a point as far east as Minsk. They may have thought also that what the French and British really wanted was for the Soviet Union to take the brunt of the Nazi attack. They considered it an affront that the British sent lesser officials as negotiators to Moscow when the prime minister himself had three times flown personally to deal with Hitler. Having quietly undertaken negotiations earlier that spring, the Soviets, on August 23, 1939, openly signed a treaty of nonaggression and friendship with Hitlerite Germany. In a protocol kept secret at the time, it was agreed that in any future territorial rearrangement the Soviet Union and Germany would divide Poland between them, that the Soviet Union would enjoy a preponderant influence in the Baltic states and have its claim to Bessarabia, lost to Romania in 1918, recognized. In return the Soviets pledged to stay out of any war between Germany and Poland, or between Germany and the Western democracies.

The Nazi-Soviet Pact stupefied the world. Communism and Nazism, supposed to be ideological opposites, had come together. A generation more versed in

[8] See p. 752, and map, p. 248.

ideology than in power politics was dumbfounded. The pact was recognized as the signal for war; all last minute negotiations failed. The Germans invaded Poland on September 1. On September 3 Great Britain and France declared war on Germany. The second European war in a generation, soon to be a world war, began.

106. The Years of Axis Triumph

Nazi Europe, 1939–1940: Poland and the Fall of France

The Second World War opened with an assault on Poland. German forces totaling over 1 million men, spearheaded by armored divisions and supported by the massed air power of the *Luftwaffe*, rapidly overran western Poland and subdued the ill-equipped Polish armies. The outcome of the campaign, a spectacular example of *Blitzkrieg*, or lightning warfare, was clear within the first few days; organized resistance ended within a month. The Germans set about to integrate their Polish conquest into the Reich.

Simultaneously, the Soviet Union, acting under the secret clauses of the Nazi-Soviet Pact, moved into the eastern half of Poland two weeks after the German invasion; the territory occupied was roughly equivalent to that lost to Poland in 1920. The Soviets proceeded also to establish fortified bases in the Baltic states—Estonia, Latvia, and Lithuania. Finland resisted Soviet demands. It refused to cede border territories sought by the Russians or to yield military rights within their country. The Soviets insisted; Leningrad, the second major city of the U.S.S.R., lay only twenty miles from the Finnish frontier. When negotiations foundered, the Soviets attacked in November 1939. Finnish resistance was valiant and at first effective, but the small country was no match for the U.S.S.R. Western democratic sympathies were with the Finns; the British and French sent equipment and supplies and planned an expeditionary force. The Soviet Union was expelled from the League of Nations for the act of aggression—the only power ever to be expelled. By March 1940 the fighting was over. Finland had to yield somewhat more territory to the U.S.S.R. than originally demanded but retained its independence.

Meanwhile all was deceptively quiet in the West. The pattern of 1914, when the Germans reached the Marne in the first month of hostilities, failed to repeat itself. The French sat behind their Maginot Line; the British had few troops; the Germans did not stir from behind their Siegfried Line, or West Wall, in the Rhineland. Hardly any air action took place. It was called the "phony war." The Western democracies rejected Hitler's peace overtures after the conquest of Poland but clung to their peacetime outlook. The hope still lingered that somehow a real clash might even yet be averted. During this same strange winter, a cold and bitter one, the Germans put their forces through special training, whose purpose became apparent in the spring.

On April 9, 1940, the Germans suddenly attacked and overran Norway, ostensibly because the British were laying mines in Norwegian waters in an endeavor to cut off German sources of Swedish iron ore. Denmark, too, was overrun, and an Allied expeditionary force with inadequate air strength had to withdraw. Then on May 10, the Germans delivered their main blow, striking at the Netherlands, Belgium, Luxembourg, and France itself. Nothing could stand against the German armored divisions and dive bombers. The Nazi use of massed tanks, though already demonstrated in Poland, took the French and British by surprise. Strategically, the Allies expected the main advance to be in central Belgium, as in 1914, and indeed as in the original German plan, which had been altered only a few months earlier. Hence the French and British sent into Belgium the best-equipped troops they had. But the Germans delivered their main armored thrust, seven divisions, through Luxembourg and the Ardennes forest, long considered by the French General Staff impassable to tanks. In France, skirting the northwestern end of the Maginot Line, which had never been extended to the sea, the German armored divisions crossed the Meuse, drove deep into northern France against confused and ineffective resistance and, racing westward toward the Channel ports, cut off the Allied armies in Belgium. The Dutch, fearful of further air attack on their crowded cities, capitulated. The Belgian king sued for an armistice, and a large part of the French armies surrendered. The British fell back upon Dunkirk and could hope only to salvage their broken forces before the trap closed completely. Fortunately Hitler had halted the advance of his overextended armored divisions. In the week ending June 4 an epic evacuation of over 330,000 British and French troops was successfully executed from the beaches of Dunkirk, under air cover, with the help of all kinds of British vessels, manned in part by civilian volunteers, even though the precious equipment of the shattered army was all but totally abandoned.

In June the German forces drove relentlessly southward. Paris itself was occupied on June 13, Verdun two days later; by June 22 France sued for peace and an armistice was signed.

France, obsessed by a defensive military psychology at the outset of the war, its armies unprepared for mechanized warfare, its government divided, its people split into hostile and suspicious factions, had fallen into the hands of an openly defeatist group of leaders. The fall of France left the world aghast. Everyone knew that France was no longer its former self, but it had still been considered a Great Power, and its collapse in one month seemed inconceivable. Some French, fleeing to England, established a Free French movement under General Charles de Gaulle; others formed a resistance movement in France. The British made the bitter decision to destroy a part of the French fleet anchored in the Algerian harbor of Oran to prevent its falling into enemy hands.

France itself under the terms of the armistice was occupied in its northern two-thirds by the Germans. The Third Republic, its capital now at Vichy in the unoccupied southern third, was transformed by vote of a confused and stunned parliament into an authoritarian regime headed by the eighty-four-year-old Marshal Pétain and the cynical and unscrupulous Pierre Laval. The republic was dead; the very slogan *Liberty, Equality, Fraternity* was banned from official use. Pétain, Laval, and others, claiming that they were acting to shield France from further suffering, proceeded to collaborate with the Nazis and to integrate Vichy France into the "new order" in Europe.[9] The French people had hard choices to make.

[9] See maps, pp. 850–851 and 892–893.

Some chose to cooperate with the collaborators and the victorious Germans; others chose in a variety of ways to resist; most went about their daily lives waiting out the trying times until the fortunes of war might change.

Mussolini attacked France in June 1940, as soon as it was clear that Hitler had defeated it. Shortly thereafter, he invaded Greece and moved against the British in Africa. The *Duce* tied his own destinies, for good or ill, to those of the *Führer*. Since the Germans were emphatically the senior partner in this combination, since they were on good terms with Franco in Spain, and since the U.S.S.R. was benevolently neutral, they now dominated the European continent. History seemed to repeat itself, in the distant and unreal way in which it ever repeats. The Germans controlled almost exactly the same geographical area as Napoleon. Organizing a new "continental system," they made plans to govern, exploit, and coordinate the resources, industry, and labor of Europe. Not having planned for a long war, and only belatedly mobilizing their resources for a sustained military effort, they intensified the exploitation of their conquered subjects. They impressed millions, prisoners of war or civilians, as slave labor, to work under close control in the German war industries. They garrisoned Europe with their soldiers, creating what they called *Festung Europa,* the Fortress of Europe. In every country they found sympathizers, collaborators, or "quislings"—the prototype was Vidkun Quisling, who had organized a Norwegian Fascist party in 1933 and was Norwegian premier from 1942 to 1945. Once Hitler was at war with the Soviet Union, some Europeans joined Hitler in the crusade against Bolshevism; 500,000 non-Germans fought in the divisions of the Waffen SS.

The Battle of Britain and American Aid

In 1940, as in 1807, only Great Britain remained at war with the conqueror of Europe. After Dunkirk the British awaited the worst, momentarily expecting invasion. Winston Churchill, who replaced Chamberlain as prime minister in May 1940 during the military debacle, rose to the summit of leadership in adversity. To Parliament and the British people he promised nothing but "blood, toil, tears, and sweat." He pledged implacable war against "a monstrous tyranny, never surpassed in the dark, lamentable catalogue of human crime." To the American democracy across the Atlantic he appealed "Give us the tools, and we will finish the job." The United States began to respond.

Since 1939, and even before, the American government had been anything but neutral. Opinion was excitedly divided. One group, called isolationist, opposed involvement in the European war, believing that Europe was hopeless, or that the United States could not save it, or that the Germans would win anyway before America could act, or that Hitler, even if victorious in Europe, constituted no danger to the United States. Another group, the interventionists, urged immediate aid to the Allies, believing that Hitler was a menace, that fascism must be destroyed, or that the Nazis, if they subjugated all Europe, would soon tamper with the Latin American republics. President Roosevelt was an interventionist, convinced that American security was endangered; he tried to unite national opinion by declaring that the United States might openly assist the Allies without itself fighting, by using "measures short of war."

The neutrality legislation of the mid-1930s was amended in November 1939, when the ban on the sale of arms was repealed. Roosevelt described Britain as "the spearhead of resistance to world conquest"; the United States was to be "the great arsenal of democracy." Both were fighting for a world, he said, in which the Four Freedoms were to be secure—freedom of speech, freedom of worship, freedom from want, and freedom from fear. In June 1940, immediately after Dunkirk, the United States sent a small initial shipment of arms to Britain. A few months later the United States gave the British fifty overage destroyers in return for the right to maintain American bases in Newfoundland, the Bermudas, and the British Caribbean islands. In 1941 it adopted Lend-Lease, a policy of providing arms, raw materials, and food to powers at war with the Axis. At the same time, in 1940 and 1941, the United States introduced conscription, built up its army and air force, and projected a two-ocean navy. Plans for joint hemisphere defense were developed with the Latin American republics. To protect its shipping it secured bases in Greenland and Iceland and convoyed Allied shipping as far as Iceland. In October 1941 German submarines sank an American destroyer. It is likely that the Germans, as in 1917, would have eventually provoked war with the United States to stop the flow of aid to their enemies even had war not come from another quarter.

After the fall of France, the Germans stood poised for an invasion of Britain. But they had not calculated on such rapid and easy successes in Europe, they had no immediately practical plan for an invasion, and they needed to win control of the air before a sea invasion could take place. Moreover, there was always the hope, in Hitler's mind at least, that the British might sue for peace, or even become an ally of Germany. The air assault on Britain began that summer and reached its climax in the autumn of 1940. Never until then had any bombing been so severe. But the Germans were unable to win control over the air in the battle of Britain. Gradually the British Royal Air Force fought off the bombers with more success; new radar devices helped detect the approach of enemy planes, as did a remarkable British intelligence operation called Ultra, by which the British (with the help of the Poles) early in the war broke the code of an important German communications device, called Enigma, used for military conversations at the highest level. This crucial intelligence operation was not revealed until many years after the war's end. Although Coventry was wiped out, the life and industry of other cities badly disrupted, and thousands of people killed, 20,000 in London alone, still the productive activity of the country carried on. Nor, contrary to the predictions of air power theorists, did the bombings break the morale of the civilian population.

In the winter of 1940–1941 the Germans began to shift their weight to the east. Hitler set aside the planned invasion of Britain, for which he seems never to have had much enthusiasm anyway. He had already decided, like Napoleon before him, that before committing his resources to an invasion of England he must dispose of the U.S.S.R., a project much closer to his heart.

The Nazi Invasion of Russia: The Russian Front, 1941–1942

The Nazi-Soviet Pact of 1939 which had precipitated the war, like the alliance between Napoleon and Alexander I, was never a warm or harmonious understanding. Both parties probably entered it mainly to gain time. The Soviets gained space as well, pushing their borders westward. Stalin, incredibly, seems to have convinced himself that he could remain uninvolved in the war going on. But he and the Nazis soon began to dispute over eastern Europe. The Soviets, with the Nazis preoccupied by the war, hoped to win complete control over the Baltic and to gain influence in the Balkans as well. They had already occupied eastern Poland and the three Baltic states and won territory from Finland. In June 1940, to the chagrin of the Germans, they quietly sovietized and converted the three Baltic states into member republics of the U.S.S.R. The old German landowning class, the famous "Baltic barons," who had lived there for centuries, were uprooted and were returned to German soil. At the same time, the Soviets seized from Romania the Bessarabian province that they had lost in the First World War and incorporated it, too, as a Soviet republic. The Russians were expanding toward the Balkans, another area of historic Russian interest, and seemed bent on winning control over eastern Europe.

This the Germans viewed with dismay. They wished to reserve eastern Europe for themselves as a counterpart to industrial Germany. Hitler moved to bring the Balkans under German control. By early 1941 he blackmailed or, by territorial concessions, cajoled Romania, Bulgaria, and Hungary into joining the Axis; they became Axis lesser partners and were occupied by German troops; Yugoslavia also was occupied despite resistance by the army and population. Greece, too, was subjugated, the Germans coming to the rescue of Mussolini's hard-pressed troops. Hitler thus barred Soviet expansion in the Balkans and made the Balkan states part of the Nazi new order. The Balkan campaigns delayed his plans, but now, to crush the Soviets, and to gain the wheat harvests of the Ukraine and the oil wells of the Caucasus, the core of the Eurasian "heartland," Hitler struck, and on June 22, 1941, invaded the U.S.S.R. Stalin, ignoring warnings he had received, was caught completely by surprise and momentarily seemed incapable of mounting any kind of defense.

The German army threw 3 million men into Russia along a vast 2,000-mile front. The Russians gave way. One swift moving battle melted into another. By the autumn of 1941 the Germans had overrun Byelorussia and most of the Ukraine. In the north, Leningrad was in a state of siege; in the south, the Germans had entered the Crimean peninsula and were besieging Sebastopol. And toward the center of the vast front, the Germans stood, exhausted, but apparently victorious, within twenty-five miles of Moscow. But the overconfident German forces had not calculated on the stubbornness of Soviet resistance as Stalin recovered from his initial shock, replaced some of his military commanders, and rallied the country to the defense of the Russian motherland. Nor were the Germans prepared to fight in an early and extraordinarily bitter Russian winter, which suddenly descended upon them. A counteroffensive, launched by the Red Army that winter, saved Moscow. Hitler, disgusted and impatient with his subordinates, took over direct command of military operations; he shifted the main attack to the south and began a great offensive in the summer of 1942 directed toward the oil fields of the Caucasus. Sebastopol soon fell; the siege of Stalingrad began. After the failure to take Moscow, Hitler, aware now that the war would not be brief, took steps to mobilize the German economy on a full wartime basis. Germany had been ready for war in 1939 as no other major power had been, but without preparation in depth for a protracted conflict. In the early months of 1942 Hitler found in Albert Speer an organizing genius who, despite all kinds of obstacles from party leaders and government functionaries, coordinated labor and resources in the next two years and tripled armaments production.

1942, the Year of Dismay: Russia, North Africa, the Pacific

A year after the invasion, in the fateful summer of 1942, the German line reached from beleaguered Leningrad in the north, past the western outskirts of Moscow, past Stalingrad on the Volga southward to the Caucasus Mountains; the Germans were within a hundred miles of the Caspian Sea. But the Russians had traded space for time. Though the industrial Don basin and the food-producing Ukraine were overrun, the deliveries of Caucasus oil rendered hazardous and uncertain, the Russians continued to fight; industries were shifted to the new Ural and Siberian cities; and neither the Soviet economy nor the Soviet government was yet struck in a vital spot. A ''scorched earth'' policy, in which the retreating Russians destroyed crops and livestock, and guerrilla units wrecked industrial and transportation facilities, guaranteed that Russian resources would not fall into the hands of the advancing conqueror.

Simultaneously, late in 1942 the Axis also moved forward in North Africa. Here the desert campaigns started in September 1940 with an Italian eastward offensive from Libya, which succeeded in crossing over into Egypt. The stakes were high—control over Suez and the Mediterranean. At the height of the battle of Britain, Churchill made the decision to send troops and supplies, much needed at home, to North Africa. A British counteroffensive against vastly superior numbers swept the Italians out of Egypt and by early 1941 the British moved deep into Libya. Shortly thereafter the British overran Ethiopia and ended Mussolini's short-lived East African empire. But in North Africa fortunes were fickle. A German elite force, the Afrika Korps under General Rommel, in the spring of 1941 attacked in Libya and drove the British back to the Egyptian frontier. A few months later, once more on the offensive, the British advanced into Libya. Again fortunes shifted. By mid-1942 Rommel had repulsed the British and penetrated Egypt. The British took up a stand at El Alamein, seventy miles from Alexandria, their backs to the Suez Canal. Here they held the Germans.

But it seemed in 1942 that the Axis armies, breaking through the Soviet Caucasus and across the isthmus of Suez in North Africa, might enclose the whole Mediterranean and Middle East in a gigantic vise, and even, moving farther east, make contact with their allies the Japanese, who were at this time penetrating into the Indian Ocean. For the Pacific situation in the latter half of 1941 had also exploded. It was Japan that finally drew the United States into war.

The Japanese, in 1941, had conducted a war against China for ten years. With the war raging in Europe, Japanese expansionists saw a propitious moment to assert themselves throughout east Asia. In 1940 they cemented their alliance with Germany and Italy in a new three-power pact; the following year they concluded a neutrality treaty with the Soviet Union. From the Vichy French the Japanese obtained a number of military bases and other concessions in Indochina. The United States belatedly placed an embargo on the export of such materials as scrap iron and steel to Japan. Hesitating to precipitate any all-out drive of the Japanese toward the Dutch East Indies and elsewhere, the United States still sought some definition of Japanese ambitions in southeast Asia. The new Japanese prime minister, General Hideki Tojo, a staunch champion of the Axis, publicly proclaimed that the influence of Britain and the United States was to be totally eliminated from Asia, but he agreed to send representatives to Washington for negotiations.

At the very time that the Japanese representatives in Washington were carrying on conversations with the Americans, on December 7, 1941, without warning, the Japanese launched a heavy air raid on the American naval base at Pearl Harbor in Hawaii and began to invade the Philippines. Simultaneously, they launched attacks on Guam, Midway, Hong Kong, and Malaya. The Americans were caught off guard at Pearl Harbor; close to 2,500 were killed, the fleet was crippled, and the temporary disablement of the American naval forces allowed the Japanese to roam at will in the western Pacific. The United States and Great Britain declared war on Japan on December 8. Three days later Germany and Italy declared war on the United States, as did the Axis puppet states.

The Japanese, working overland through Malaya, two months later captured Singapore, a British naval base long famous for its supposed impregnability, the veritable Gibraltar of the East. The sinking by air of the British battleship *Prince of Wales*, a feat often pronounced by naval experts to be impossible, added to the general consternation. In 1942 the Japanese conquered the Philippines, Malaya, and the Netherlands Indies. They invaded New Guinea and threatened Australia; they moved into the Aleutians. They streamed into the Indian Ocean, occupied Burma, and seemed about to invade India. Everywhere they found ready collaborators among enemies of European imperialism. They held up the idea of a Greater East Asia Co-Prosperity Sphere under Japanese leadership, in which the one clear element was that the European whites should be ejected. Meanwhile, as noted, the Germans stood at the Caucasus and almost at the Nile. And in the Atlantic, even to the shores of the United States and the American republics, German submarines were sinking Allied ships at a disastrous rate. The Mediterranean was unusable. For the Soviet-Western alliance, 1942 was the year of dismay. Despite Allied naval and air victories in the Pacific, the late summer and autumn of 1942 was the worst period of the war. Few realized, wrote the United States Chief of Staff General George C. Marshall some years later, how "close to complete domination of the world" were Germany and Japan and "how thin the thread of Allied survival had been stretched." That Germany and Japan had no plans to concert their strategy and operations was no small factor in the eventual Allied victory.

EUROPE, 1942

The map shows Europe at the height of Axis military successes during World War II, just before the Soviet victory at Stalingrad and the Western invasion of North Africa. Austria, the Sudetenland, Bohemia-Moravia, Poland, and Alsace-Lorraine were all joined to Hitler's Reich. The Atlantic Coast from southern France to northern Norway was under German military occupation, as was much of Russia almost to the Caspian Sea. Southern Europe from Vichy France to Romania was also occupied or allied. See also the map on pp. 856–857.

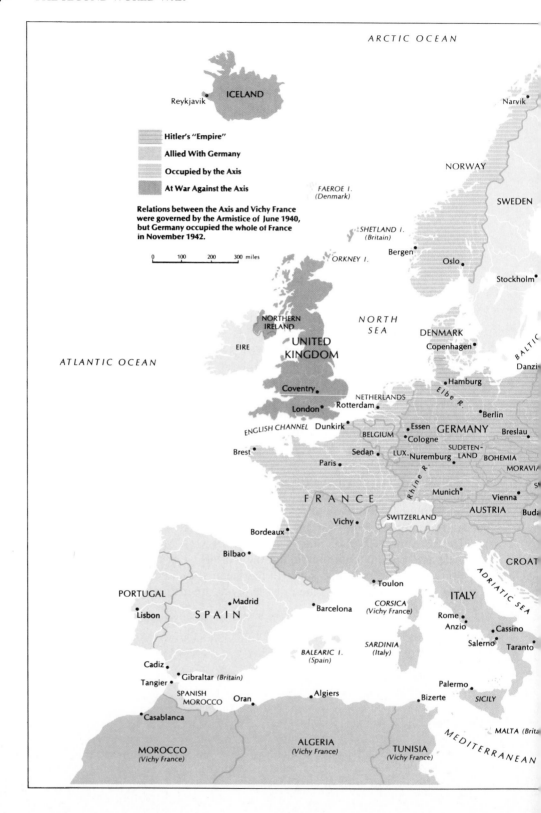

ARCTIC OCEAN

ICELAND

Reykjavik

Narvik

Hitler's "Empire"

Allied With Germany

Occupied by the Axis

At War Against the Axis

Relations between the Axis and Vichy France
were governed by the Armistice of June 1940,
but Germany occupied the whole of France
in November 1942.

0   100   200   300 miles

FAEROE I.
(Denmark)

NORWAY

SWEDEN

Bergen

Oslo

Stockholm

SHETLAND I.
(Britain)

ORKNEY I.

NORTH
SEA

DENMARK

Copenhagen

BALTIC

Danzi

ATLANTIC OCEAN

NORTHERN
IRELAND

UNITED
KINGDOM

EIRE

Coventry

London

Hamburg

Elbe R.

Berlin

Breslau

NETHERLANDS

Rotterdam

Essen   GERMANY

ENGLISH CHANNEL   Dunkirk

BELGIUM

Cologne

SUDETEN-
LAND   BOHEMIA

Brest

Sedan

LUX. Nuremburg

MORAVIA

Paris

Rhine R.

Munich

Vienna

S

FRANCE

SWITZERLAND

AUSTRIA   Buda

Vichy

Bordeaux

Bilbao

CROAT

Toulon

ADRIATIC SEA

PORTUGAL

Madrid

SPAIN

Barcelona

CORSICA
(Vichy France)

ITALY

Rome

Anzio

Cassino

Salerno

Taranto

Lisbon

SARDINIA
(Italy)

BALEARIC I.
(Spain)

Cadiz

Gibraltar (Britain)

Tangier

SPANISH
MOROCCO

Oran

Algiers

Palermo

Bizerte   SICILY

Casablanca

MOROCCO
(Vichy France)

ALGERIA
(Vichy France)

TUNISIA
(Vichy France)

MALTA (Brita

MEDITERRANEAN

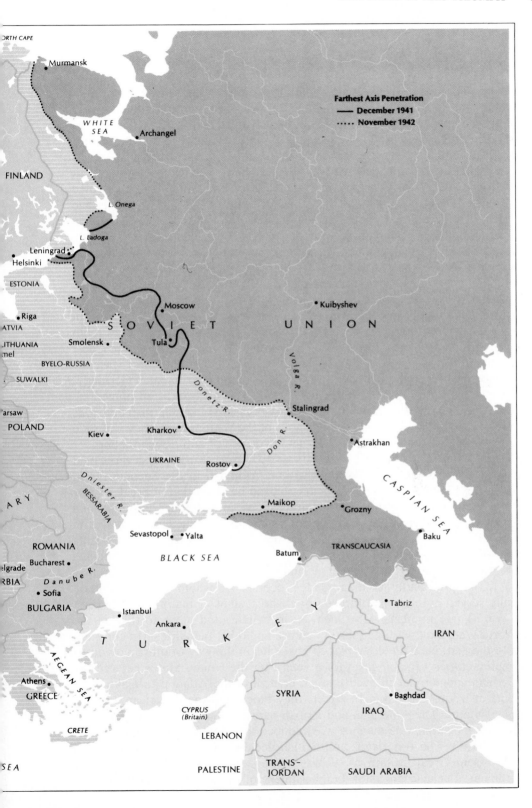

Farthest Axis Penetration
—— December 1941
···· November 1942

107. The Western–Soviet Victory

Plans and Preparations, 1942–1943

By January 1942 twenty-six nations, including the three Great Powers—Britain, the United States, and the U.S.S.R.—and representing every continent, were aligned against the Axis, a combination to which President Roosevelt gave the name the United Nations. Each pledged to use all its resources to defeat the Axis and never to make a separate peace. The Grand Alliance against the Axis aggressors, which could not be created in the 1930s, had at last been consummated.

The two Atlantic democracies, the United States and Great Britain, pooled their resources under a Combined Chiefs of Staff. Never had any two sovereign states formed so intimate a coalition. In contrast with the First World War an overall strategy was in effect from an early date. It was decided that Germany was the main enemy, against which it was necessary to concentrate first. For the time being the Pacific war was relegated to the background. Australia became the chief base for operations against the Japanese. The American navy and air force soon brought Japanese southward expansion to a halt and frustrated Japanese efforts to cut off supply lines to Australia; naval and air victories were won in the spring of 1942 in the battle of the Coral Sea and at Midway, the only relief to the overall gloom of that period. In the summer American forces landed at Guadalcanal in the Solomon Islands. A long ordeal of "island hopping" began.

In Europe the first point of concentration was an air bombardment of Germany. The Soviet Union, dissatisfied, called for a true "second front," an immediate invasion by ground forces that would relieve the pressure of the German divisions that were devastating their country. Suspicious of the West as ever, they regarded the failure to establish a second front as new evidence of anti-Soviet feeling.

But neither the United States nor Britain, in 1942, was ready to undertake land action by a direct assault on *Festung Europa*. Although in the Second World War, as in the First, more than two years elapsed between the outbreak of war in Europe and the intervention of the United States, and although in the second war American military preparations began much sooner, the United States in 1942 was still involved in the cumbersome processes of mobilization, converting industry to the production of war materials for itself and its Allies, imposing controls on its economy to prevent a runaway inflation, and giving military training to its profoundly civilian-minded people, of whom over 12 million eventually served in the armed forces—over three times as many as in the First World War. Large numbers of women, as in Britain, and more so than in the First World War, took wartime jobs in defense and other industries. (In contrast, almost to the end, Nazi ideology placed obstacles in the way of utilizing women in German factories.) In any case, for a year after the United States entered the war, German submarines enjoyed enough control of the Atlantic to make large shipments of troops too risky. In effect, they blockaded the American army in the United States. The American and British navies gradually won the battle of the Atlantic; the submarine menace was reduced to tolerable proportions by the first part of 1943. The Americans and British decided to begin the assault upon Germany, from Great Britain as a base, with a massive and prolonged air bombardment. Because precision bombardment of factories and other military targets proved difficult either by day or by night, the air assaults became area bombings; German cities were bombed mercilessly and civilians were the largest casualties. In Hamburg in 1943 fires raged on and destroyed most of the city after several days of incessant bombing. Since not everything could be shipped across the Atlantic at the same time, and since the United States and Britain were engaged in war with Japan as well, land invasion had to be deferred until 1944. The embattled Russians questioned whether the Western Allies ever really meant to face the German army at all.

The Turning of the Tide, 1942–1943: Stalingrad, North Africa, Sicily

Meanwhile, at the end of 1942 the tide had begun to turn. In November an Anglo-American force under the command of General Dwight D. Eisenhower effected a surprise invasion of Algeria and Morocco in an amphibious operation of unprecedented proportions. The Allies, failing to win the cooperation of the French in North Africa as they had hoped to do, turned to the Vichy French political leader Admiral Darlan in a calculated act of expediency that brought protest in many quarters. Darlan assisted the Allies in assuming control but was soon assassinated. In the competition that developed in the succeeding months for leadership of the French liberation committee, newly established in Algiers, General de Gaulle, though virtually ignored by President Roosevelt, easily pushed aside all rivals and moved forward with plans for France's revival.

On the Continent, after the North African landings, the Germans took over control of unoccupied France as well; they were frustrated, however, in the effort to seize the remainder of the French fleet when French crews scuttled their ships at Toulon. In North Africa the invading forces fought their way eastward into Tunisia. Meanwhile British forces under General Montgomery, having held the Germans at El Alamein in June 1942, had already launched their third (and final) counteroffensive in October, even before the invasion; they now pushed the Germans westward from Egypt until a large German force was crushed between the two Allied armies and destroyed in Tunisia. By May 1943 Africa was cleared of Axis forces. Mussolini's dream of an African empire had been thwarted; the Mediterranean was open; the threat to Egypt and the Suez Canal was ended.

At the same time it became clear, in the winter of 1942–1943, that the Germans had suffered a catastrophic reversal in the Soviet Union in the titanic battle of Stalingrad. In August 1942 massive German forces, an army of over a quarter million, began an all-out assault on Stalingrad, the vital key to all transport on the lower Volga; by September they had penetrated the city itself. Stalin ordered his namesake city held at all costs; Russian soldiery and the civilian population took a desperate stand. Hitler, still gambling on one big victory, was as obstinate in ordering the city taken. After weeks of fighting the Germans occupied most of the city when suddenly a great Red Army counterattack, led by General Zhukov, trapped the German army, and took a terrible toll; fewer than 100,000 were left to surrender in February 1943. The Soviets followed up their victory with a new counteroffensive, a great westward drive that regained for them what they had initially lost in the first year of the war. After Stalingrad, despite some setbacks, the Soviet Union was on the offensive for the remainder of the war. Stalingrad (or Volgograd as it was later renamed) was a turning point not only in the history of the war but in the history of central and eastern Europe as well.

American equipment meanwhile all through 1943 arrived in the Soviet Union in prodigious quantities. The terms of Lend-Lease were liberally extended to the Soviets; a stream of American vehicles, clothing, food, and supplies of all kinds made its way laboriously to the U.S.S.R. through the Arctic Ocean and through the Persian Gulf. Machinery and equipment were sent for the Soviet arms plants, which were themselves tremendously increasing their output. Anglo-American bombing meanwhile was cutting into German airplane production at home. The Allied contribution to the Soviet war effort was indispensable, but Russian human losses were tremendous. The Soviet Union lost more men in the battle of Stalingrad than the United States lost in combat during the entire war in all theaters combined.

With contemporary American successes in the Solomon Islands at the end of 1942 and the slow throttling of German submarines in the Atlantic, the beginning of the year 1943 brought new hope for the Allies in all quarters. In a spectacular campaign in July–August 1943, the British, Canadians, and Americans conquered the island of Sicily. Mussolini fell; the twenty-one-year-old Fascist regime came to an end. Mussolini set up an "Italian Social Republic" in the north, but it was no more than a German puppet government. (Some months later, in April 1945, the *Duce*, as he attempted to flee the country, was seized, shot, and strung up like a slaughtered pig by anti-Fascist Italians.) When the new Italian government under Marshal Badoglio, in August 1943, tried to make peace, the German army occupied Italy. The Allies, having crossed to the Italian mainland from Sicily, attacked from the south. In October the Badoglio government declared war on Germany, and Italy was recognized by the Allies as a "cobelligerent." But the Germans stubbornly blocked the advance of the Allies to Rome despite new Allied landings and beachheads. The Italian campaign turned into a long and disheartening stalemate because the Western Allies, concentrating troops in Britain for the approaching cross-Channel invasion, could never spare enough for the Italian front.

The Allied Offensive, 1944–1945: Europe and the Pacific

Festung Europa, especially along its western approaches, the coasts of Holland, Belgium, and France, bristled with every kind of fortification that German scientific and military ingenuity could devise. A seaborne attack upon Europe was an operation of wholly unprecedented kind. It differed from the earlier amphibious attacks on Algeria, Sicily, or the Pacific islands in that the defender in Europe, in the very part of Europe where the road and railway network was thickest, could immediately rush overwhelming reserves to the spot attacked— except insofar as feinting tactics kept him uncertain, air power destroyed his transport, or the Russians held the bulk of his forces in the East. Precise and elaborate plans had been worked out. Ten thousand aircraft were to provide aerial protection, scores of warships were to bombard the coast, 4,000 ships were to carry the invading troops and their supplies across the Channel, artificial harbors were to be created where none existed.

The invasion of Europe began before dawn on June 6, 1944. The spot selected was the coast of Normandy directly across the Channel from England; false intelligence reports, planted by the Allies, led the Germans to expect the main thrust at Calais. An unparalleled combination of forces, British, Canadian, and American, land, sea, and air, backed up by huge accumulations of supplies and troops assembled in Great Britain, and the whole under the unified command of General Eisenhower, assaulted the French coast, established a beachhead, and maintained a front. The Allies poured in their strength, over 130,000 men the first day, 1 million within a month. The Germans were at first thrown back more easily than had been expected. By August Paris was liberated, by September the Allies crossed the frontier of Germany itself. In France, Italy, and Belgium the Resistance movements, which had grown up in secret during the years of German occupation, came into the open and drove out Germans and pro-German collaborators. In Germany itself no widespread or deeply rooted Resistance movement ever developed, but a small group of Germans, military and civilian, formed an underground. On July 20, 1944, after the failure of earlier efforts, it attempted to assassinate Hitler by exploding a bomb at his military headquarters in East Prussia; Hitler was only injured and took a fearsome revenge on the conspirators.

In August, in another amphibious operation, the Allies landed on the French Mediterranean coast and swept up from southern France to join the Allied forces advancing against stiffening resistance. At one point, momentarily, the Allied offensive suffered a serious reversal. A sudden German drive under Hitler's direct personal orders in December 1944, unleashed under radio silence to thwart Allied intelligence, was launched against thinly held American lines on the Belgian sector in the Ardennes, created a "bulge" in the advancing armies, and caused heavy losses and confusion. But the Allies rallied, and Hitler used up his armored reserves in the effort. Neither the Ardennes counteroffensive nor the new destructive weapons rained on Britain, jet-propelled flying bombs and rockets, opening up the missile age, availed the Germans. All this time the American and British kept up their massive air bombardments, killing over 50,000 civilians in the fire-bombing of Dresden in February 1945. On the ground they pushed on and smashed through the heavily fortified Siegfried Line. The last natural obstacle, the Rhine, was crossed when in March 1945 American forces by a stroke of luck discovered an undestroyed bridge at Remagen; they poured troops over it and established a bridgehead—the first troops to cross the Rhine in combat since the armies of Napoleon. The main crossing, under the British, subsequently took place farther to the north. Soon the Allies were accepting wholesale surrenders in the Ruhr valley.

Meanwhile in 1944 the Russian armies swept the Germans from the Ukraine, Byelorussia, the Baltic states, and eastern Poland. By August they reached the suburbs of Warsaw. The Polish underground rose against the Germans but the Soviets, determined that Poland not be liberated by noncommunist Polish leadership, refused to permit aid to the rising, and it was crushed, with a heavy loss of Polish lives. The Polish martyrdom was severe. Earlier, the mass graves of 12,000 Polish army officers were found in the Katyn Forest, the evidence indicating, despite Soviet denials, that they were the victims of the retreating Russian armies after the German invasion began. The Russians, their lines overextended, and checked for several months by German strength in Poland, pushed southward into Romania and Bulgaria; both countries changed sides and

WORLD WAR II

These two maps show the global character of the war and the central position of the United States with respect to the European and Pacific theaters. The numbered legends summarize the successive stages of the war in both the Eastern and Western hemispheres. In 1942, with the Germans reaching as far east as Egypt and Stalingrad, and the Japanese as far west as Burma, the great danger to the Soviet-Western alliance was that these two might join forces, dominate southern Asia, control the oil resources of the Persian Gulf, and stop the flow of Western supplies to the Soviet Union from this direction. The almost

The following labels appear on the map:

INDIA
TIBET
SINKIANG
MONGOLIA
SOVIET UNION
5. Soviet Union Enters the War August 8, 1945
ALASKA
CANADA
Seattle
UNITED STATES
San Francisco
BERING SEA
CHINA
MANCHUKUO
Peiping
Vladivostok
KARAFUTO
SAKHALIN
ATTU ALEUTIANS
Dutch Harbor
KISKA
BAY OF BENGAL
BURMA
Chungking
Shanghai
KOREA
Hiroshima
JAPAN
2. Greatest Japanese Expansion, June 1942
THAILAND
Canton
Hong Kong
Nagasaki
Tokyo
6. Atomic Bombs Dropped on Hiroshima and Nagasaki August 1945
Japan Surrenders September 2, 1945
1. Japan Attacks Pearl Harbor December 7, 1941
INDO-CHINA
FORMOSA
OKINAWA
4. U.S. Forces Reoccupy the Philippines October 1944
Manila
PHILIPPINE I.
IWO JIMA
MIDWAY
HAWAIIAN I. (U.S.A.)
Pearl Harbor
Singapore
SUMATRA
LEYTE
MARIANA I.
SAIPAN
GUAM
TINIAN
WAKE
PACIFIC   OCEAN
BORNEO
YAP
PALAU
CAROLINE I.
ENIWETOK
JAVA
CELEBES
TRUK
KWAJALEIN
MARSHALL I.
Hollandia
HOWLAND I. (U.S.A.)
INDIAN OCEAN
NEW GUINEA
Port Moresby
SOLOMON I.
GILBERT I.
GUADALCANAL
3. U.S. Forces Land on Guadalcanal August 7, 1942
CORAL SEA
NEW HEBRIDES (Britain & France)
TUTUILA (U.S.A.)
FIJI I. (Britain)
AUSTRALIA
Sydney
NEW ZEALAND

Supply Lines
Allied Land or Naval Attacks
Allied Air Thrusts
Soviet Thrusts into Manchuria and Korea

Japanese Empire 1940
Occupied by Japan, June 1942
At War Against Japan, August 7, 1945

simultaneous Soviet-Western successes, late in 1942, at Stalingrad and El Alamein, and in the invasion of Morocco-Algeria and of Guadalcanal, proved to be the turning point of the war. In 1943 the German submarine campaign in the Atlantic was defeated, so that American troops and supplies could move more freely to Europe. The invasion of Normandy in June 1944, with continuing Soviet pressure from the east, brought about German surrender in May 1945. Meanwhile, in the Pacific, American occupation of the islands and reoccupation of the Philippines prepared the way for the surrender of Japan, consummated by two atomic bombs in August 1945.

declared war against Germany. Early in 1945 the Soviets, reopening their offensive, forced their way into East Prussia and Silesia and by February reached the Oder, forty miles from Berlin, where Zhukov paused to regroup his forces. In March and April Russian forces occupied Budapest and Vienna.

The final drive on Germany began. Hitler moved troops from the collapsing western front to reinforce the stand on the Oder and to protect his capital. In April the Americans reached the Elbe, about sixty miles from Berlin, with hardly any obstacles before them; but here they halted, by decision of General Eisenhower. The Americans, whose supply lines were already overextended,

Percentage of Jewish Population Annihilated

- 83-90
- 65-77
- 50-60
- 11-26

Figures Indicate Number of Jews Killed under Nazi Racial Policies (In Thousands)

THE HOLOCAUST

The map shows what the Nazis called their Final Solution, that is, their program of destroying the Jews and Judaism. Before the Second World War most European Jews lived in Poland and the adjoining parts of the Soviet Union which the Germans occupied during the war, so that most of the deaths occurred in these areas. The map shows both the number killed in each country and the percentage of its Jewish population that were victims of this deliberate genocide. The numbers add up to about 6 million men, women, and children, or an estimated two-thirds of the Jewish population of Europe as a whole. Although word of this annihilation policy reached the outside world through the Vatican and other sources, the Allied leaders at first disbelieved the reports, and then, giving priority to their military objectives, did nothing to stop the systematic slaughter.

wanted a clear line of demarcation from the Russians; they also believed it necessary to divert forces southward against a possible German last stand in the Alps. But mainly the decision was made as a gesture of good will toward the Russians, who were to be permitted to take Berlin as compensation for the heavy sacrifice in the common cause, and to preserve the Western-Soviet coalition until final victory. Similarly, the American troops that moved southward were held back from taking Prague and the Soviets were permitted to take the Czech capital too. At the end of the war the Soviets were in control of all the major capitals of central and eastern Europe.

The Western Allies and the Soviets offered no terms to Hitler, nor to any Germans. They demanded unconditional surrender, and the Germans fought on in the very streets of Berlin. On the last day of April Hitler perished by his own hand in the ruins of his capital after denouncing some of his closest party subordinates as traitors. Admiral Doenitz, designated by Hitler as his successor, went through the formalities of surrender on May 8, 1945. Since fighting had already ceased on the Italian front a few days earlier, the war in Europe was over.

Meanwhile a generation reared to mistrust the fabricated atrocity tales of the First World War painfully, and belatedly, became aware of the real German horrors of the Second—hostages rounded up and shot in reprisal for resistance; whole villages like Lidice in Czechoslovakia or Oradour-sur-Glane in France razed to the ground and their inhabitants slain or deported; concentration camps like Dachau and Buchenwald, where the prisoners were given minimal rations and worked to death, and where Allied troops found only pitifully emaciated survivors; above all, the mass death camps with gas chambers and crematory ovens at Auschwitz (where at its peak 12,000 victims a day were gassed to death), Treblinka, Belzéc, Sobibor, and others, where "inferior" peoples could be systematically liquidated. In the areas of Nazi domination in Eastern Europe, the Nazis first used special mobile units to gas "undesirables," but as the war went on they transported millions of men, women, and children in cattle cars to these mass death camps where they were put to death. By far the largest proportion killed were almost 6 million Jews, but Poles, Russians, other Slavic peoples, Gypsies, and others were slain as well. For the Jews in what came to be known as the Holocaust, the annihilation policy, decided upon at a high-level Nazi meeting at Wannsee in January 1942, was to be the "Final Solution" to the "Jewish problem" which Hitler had agitated, with maniacal fury, for so many years. Genocide, the planned, systematic effort to destroy a whole people, was the greatest of the Nazi sins against humanity.

In the Pacific, against Japan, operations had dragged on for three years, hampered by the strategic decision to concentrate against Germany first. Slowly, from points in the Solomon Islands, the easternmost fringe of the Indonesian archipelago, American forces, at first very small, worked their way in a northwesterly direction toward faraway Japan. They had to fight in turn for Guadalcanal, for New Guinea, for the reconquest of the Philippines. They had to fight for the Japanese islands and atolls in the mid-Pacific (taken by Japan from the Germans after the First World War and converted into powerful naval bases), the Gilbert Islands, the Marshalls, the Carolines, the Marianas. In October 1944 they won a great naval victory at the battle of Leyte Gulf. Finally, in one of the war's greatest and final battles, they won the island of Okinawa, only 300 miles from Japan itself. Okinawa was captured just as the Germans collapsed in Europe. From the new Allied bases that had been won, from Saipan, from Iwo Jima, from Okinawa, and from aircraft carriers a heavy bombing offensive was launched against Japan, such as had devastated Germany in the preceding two years, shattering Japanese industry, destroying the remnants of the Japanese navy, and compelling the Japanese government to give serious thought to suing for peace. The Allied leaders refused to believe that Japanese defenses were ready to crumble or that the Japanese were ready to negotiate. The American army prepared to shift combat troops from the European theater to the Far East. The stage was being set for a full-scale invasion of Japan itself.

Then, on August 6, 1945, an American aircraft dropped an atomic bomb, built in the United States in utmost secrecy by European refugee and American scientists, on the city of Hiroshima, with a population of 200,000 people. The city was destroyed in this single explosion, and 78,000 lives were lost; thousands of others were injured or suffered the long-term effects of radiation. Two days later, the Soviet Union, which had pledged to enter the conflict in the East within three months after the surrender of Germany, declared war on Japan and invaded Manchuria. On August 9 a second atomic bomb struck Nagasaki and killed tens of thousands more. The Japanese made peace at once. On September 2, 1945, the formal surrender was signed. The emperor was permitted to remain as head of state, but the Japanese islands were placed under the rule of a United States army of occupation.

The Second World War of the twentieth century was over, the greatest conflict in human history. The same cold impersonal statistics that had recorded 10 million killed in the First World War now reported 15 million military deaths and (unlike the First World War) at least that many civilian fatalities. Soviet military deaths were estimated at over 7 million (and total deaths at 20 million), German at 3.5 million, Chinese at 2.2 million, Japanese at 1.3 million; British and Commonwealth losses were about 350,000, American about 300,000, French about 200,000. The military death figures would have been greater except that one of every two soldiers seriously wounded was saved by new sulfa and penicillin drugs and by blood plasma transfusions. None of these statistics could be more than approximate and no one could begin to estimate the complete toll of human lives lost in the war, directly or indirectly, from the Allied and Axis bombings, the Nazi mass slayings, the Nazi and Soviet deportation policies, and the postwar famines and epidemics. Some estimates place the total at 50 to 60 million men, women, and children, but at such figures the human mind retreats and human sensitivities are dulled. It is enough to say that peace had come.

108. The Foundations of the Peace

Whereas the First World War had been concluded by a peace conference a few months after the close of hostilities, the Second World War ended in no such clear-cut settlement. Nothing like the Treaty of Versailles of 1919 followed the defeat of Germany in 1945. The terms of peace, as they gradually developed, left no such single symbol of humiliation as the Versailles treaty had represented.

THE SURVIVOR
by George Grosz (German, then American, 1893–1959)

George Grosz, born in Germany, came to the United States in 1932 to avoid the Nazis. He painted this powerful picture in 1945 at the close of the Second World War. It suggests what is meant by the collapse of civilization. The hideous figure crawling out of the wreckage, according to the artist's own explanation, is insane with fear. He is starving, filthy, abandoned, and alone. In his teeth he desperately clasps a knife, which he will use to fight another terrified survivor, should he meet one, or to hunt for and cut up food. Note the symbolism of a broken swastika in the arrangement of the man's body and the debris. The picture is of course meant to be repulsive, to show the depths to which humanity can be degraded, and so shock people into constructive action. Courtesy of Mrs. Marc J. Sandler.

The peace terms emerged episodically, at first during a series of conferences among the Allied nations during the war, and then in a series of de facto arrangements in the years after 1945.

The foundations of a peaceable postwar world were being laid, it was thought, at a number of meetings where the strategy of the war itself was being planned. In August 1941 Roosevelt and Churchill met at sea off the coast of Newfoundland and drew up the Atlantic Charter. There were meetings in 1943 at Casablanca, at Cairo, and at Teheran (close enough to the Soviet Union for Stalin to participate); and in the final phase of the war, in February 1945, at Yalta, and in July 1945, at Potsdam, in the environs of shattered Berlin.

The Atlantic Charter, issued jointly by Roosevelt and Churchill at their first meeting, resembled in spirit the Fourteen Points of Woodrow Wilson. It pledged that sovereign rights and self-government would be restored to all who had been forcibly deprived of them, that all nations would have equal access to world trade and world resources, that all peoples would work together to achieve improved living standards and economic security. The postwar peace, it promised, would assure people of all lands freedom from fear and want, and end force and aggression in international affairs. Here, and in the Four Freedoms enunciated by President Roosevelt, the ideological basis of the peace was proclaimed. At the 1943 conferences, and through other consultations, the Allies endeavored to concert their military plans. At Casablanca, in January 1943, they resolved to accept nothing less than the "unconditional surrender" of the Axis powers. This vague formula, adopted somewhat cavalierly at American initiative, and without much thought to possible political implications, was intended mainly to prevent a recurrence of anything like the ambiguity surrounding the armistice of 1918.[10] Though much criticized in later years (and not fully applied in the case of Japan), it is doubtful whether the decision had any bearing on the outcome of events. German resistance was stubbornly prolonged because of Hitler's fierce obstinacy and the loyalty of the German military, not because the Allies did not offer suitable peace terms.

At Teheran, in December 1943, Roosevelt and Churchill met with Stalin for the first of two wartime meetings. They discussed the postwar occupation and demilitarization of Germany, laid plans for a postwar international organization, and debated strategy for winning the war. Throughout the war Roosevelt, unwilling to disturb the unity of the Western-Soviet coalition in the global struggle in which America was engaged, followed a policy of postponing controversial territorial and political decisions until victory was assured. Churchill was more apprehensive. Steeped in traditional balance-of-power politics, he sensed that without prior diplomatic bargaining and political arrangements, the victory over the Nazis would leave Russia dominant over all central and eastern Europe. At Teheran he proposed operations in the Mediterranean and an invasion through the Balkans, for political reasons but mainly out of concern for the casualties that a cross-Channel invasion would involve. But Roosevelt persuaded him otherwise. It was agreed that a landing in France would take place in the spring of 1944; thus the major second front that Stalin had been promised would finally be opened. Stalin pledged that he would launch a simultaneous offensive on the eastern front.

[10] See p. 723.

The strategy that would win the war in the next eighteen months was decided upon at Teheran, but that strategy, without political agreements, all but guaranteed the Soviet domination of eastern Europe. Later, in October 1944, as the Russian armies advanced westward, Churchill visited Stalin and sketched out a demarcation of spheres of influence for the Western powers and the Soviets in the Balkan states (a Soviet preponderance in Romania and Bulgaria, a Western preponderance in Greece, and an even division of influence in Hungary and Yugoslavia). Soviet control over the Baltic states had virtually been conceded by the British earlier. But Roosevelt would not agree to any such arrangement, which he considered old-fashioned and a dangerous revival of the worst features of pre-1914 diplomacy.

Soon, however, political decisions had to be made. The two conferences that arrived at the most important political decisions were the meetings at Yalta and at Potsdam in 1945. The Yalta meeting in February 1945 took place when the Allies were close to final victory—closer, events disclosed, than anyone at the time realized. The three Allied statesmen met at an old tsarist Crimean summer resort on the Black Sea, toasted their common triumphs, and, as at Teheran, took the measure of each other. Roosevelt thought of himself as a mediator between Churchill and Stalin where European issues were involved. He took pains to avoid giving Stalin the impression that he and Churchill were in any sense united against him; in point of fact, Roosevelt was suspicious of Churchill's devotion to empire and colonial ties, which he considered anachronistic for the postwar world. Despite differences, the Big Three reached agreements, at least formally, on Poland and eastern Europe, the future of Germany, the war in the Far East, and the projected postwar international organization, the United Nations.

The discussion of Poland and eastern Europe raised the most serious difficulties. Stalin's armies, having driven the Nazi forces to within forty miles of Berlin, were in control of Poland and almost all eastern and central Europe. The Russians remembered these areas as anti-Soviet, and Poland particularly as the perpetrator of aggression against Soviet territory in 1920, and as the ancient corridor of attack upon Russia. Stalin had already taken steps to establish a "friendly" government in Poland, i.e., a government subservient to the Soviets. Neither Roosevelt nor Churchill had fought the war against the Nazis to leave the Soviet Union the undisputed master of central and eastern Europe and in a position to impose a totalitarian political system on all this vast area. At Yalta, Roosevelt and Churchill extracted from Stalin a number of promises for the areas he controlled. In accordance with the Atlantic Charter, the liberated states were to be permitted provisional governments "broadly representative of all democratic elements in the population," i.e., not consisting merely, as in the case of the provisional government of Poland already established, of authorities subservient to the Soviets. They pressed Stalin to pledge also the "earliest possible establishment through free elections of governments responsive to the will of the people." The pledge was a verbal concession that cost the Soviet leader little; he rejected the suggestion of international supervision over the elections. The Declaration on Liberated Europe, promising sovereign rights of self-determination, provided a false sense of agreement.

A number of territorial changes were also accepted, pending final settlement at a postwar peace conference. It was agreed that the Russian-Polish, or eastern, boundary of Poland should be set roughly at the so-called Curzon line, the frontier contemplated by the Allies in 1919 before the Poles conquered territory to their east. The Poles were to be compensated, in the north and west, at the expense of Germany.[11] On this and on other matters relating to Germany there was a large area of accord; the three were united in their hatred of German Nazism and militarism. Germany was to be disarmed and divided into four occupation zones under the administration of the Big Three powers and France—the latter at the insistence of Churchill. There was vague talk, at Yalta and earlier, of dismembering Germany, of undoing the work of Bismarck, but the difficulties of such an undertaking were understood and the proposal was eventually discarded. Also discarded, as impracticable, was the Morgenthau plan, seriously considered as late as 1944, which was designed to transform industrial Germany back into an eighteenth-century pastoral and agricultural economy. The Americans and British rejected as excessive the Soviet proposals for reparations, a sum of $20 billion to be paid in kind, half to the Soviets. It was agreed, however, that reparations would go to those countries that had borne the main burdens of the war and suffered the heaviest losses. The Soviet Union was to receive half of whatever total sum was set.

To the satisfaction of everyone, the participants agreed on plans for a postwar international organization, to be called the United Nations. Roosevelt believed it essential to win the Soviets over to the idea of an international organization. He was convinced that the Great Powers, cooperating within the framework of the United Nations, and acting as international police, could preserve the future peace and security of the world. No less than Stalin or Churchill, he emphasized the importance of the Great Powers in the new organization, although he accepted a dignified role for the smaller nations as well. All agreed that each of the Great Powers, the permanent members of the new organization's Security Council, would have a veto power on important decisions. The Soviets pressed for sixteen votes in the General Assembly of the new organization, arguing that their constitution gave sovereign rights to each of their constituent republics and that the British dominions would each have a seat. In the interests of harmony, at Churchill's behest, they were given three seats.

Critical agreements were reached on East Asia. Here political and military decisions were inextricably linked. The Soviets had remained neutral in the Pacific war despite their historic interests in the Far East. Given the magnitude of the war effort on the European front, no one had pressed them to enter the Pacific war earlier. It was agreed to wait at least until the Germans were on the verge of defeat. At Yalta, Stalin agreed to enter the war against Japan, but Soviet "public opinion," he averred, would demand compensation. The U.S.S.R. would enter the war against Japan "two to three months" after Germany had surrendered. In return, the Soviets were to have restored to them territories and rights that tsarist Russia had lost to Japan forty years before in the Russo-Japanese war of 1904–1905,[12] with the addition of the Kurile Islands, which had never been Russian before. The concessions were the price to be paid for Soviet assistance against

[11] See maps, pp. 248 and 893.
[12] See pp. 681–682 and map, p. 679.

the Japanese, considered indispensable for the final defeat of Japan. What really exasperated so many in later years was that the Soviet Union's entry into the war, as pledged, was not of any military consequence; it came two days after the Hiroshima bomb had been dropped and at a time when the Japanese were in a desperate state, near collapse and surrender, even without the dropping of the atomic bomb. The concessions in the Far East need not have been made. Even without the Yalta agreement, nothing perhaps except outright force could have deterred Stalin from moving into Manchuria after the Japanese collapse (and thereby contributing to the eventual Chinese Communist victory over the Chinese Nationalists), or indeed from controlling central and eastern Europe as he wished. The Yalta agreement, however, lent an aura of respectability to Soviet expansion.

Roosevelt made concessions at Yalta because he believed he needed Soviet support in the last phase of the war against Japan and because he wished to preserve the Western-Soviet coalition until final victory was guaranteed. He believed also that wartime cooperation would produce postwar harmony. Churchill, less sanguine about the future and about "diplomacy by friendship," would have preferred a franker definition of spheres of influence. Such ideas were ruled out as the thinking of a bygone era. Yet the spirit of the Atlantic Charter, so closely identified with the American president, the pledge of sovereign self-determination of all peoples, was already being contravened.

At Potsdam, in July 1945, after the German collapse, the Big Three met again. A new American president, Harry S Truman, represented the United States; President Roosevelt had died in April, on the eve of final victory. Churchill, in the midst of the conference, was replaced by a new British prime minister, Clement Attlee, after the Labour party's victory at the polls. Stalin still represented the Soviet Union. By now, disagreements between the Western Allies and the Soviets had deepened, not only over Soviet control in Poland, eastern Europe, and the Balkans, but over German reparations and other matters. Yet the Western leaders were still prepared to make concessions in the hope of establishing harmonious relations. Agreements were announced on the postwar treatment of Germany, on German disarmament, demilitarization, "denazification," and the punishment of war criminals. It was agreed that each power might take reparations in kind from its occupation zone and that the Russians would get substantial additional deliveries from the Western zones so that the original $10 billion Soviet demand was virtually met. Pending the final peace treaty, German territory east of the Oder-Neisse rivers was committed to Polish administration. The details of this decision had earlier been postponed; now the Polish-German boundary was set at the western Neisse, even further west than originally envisaged. Poland thus extended its territorial boundaries about a hundred miles westward as compensation for Russian westward expansion at Polish expense. German East Prussia was divided between the Soviet Union in the north and Poland in the south. Königsberg, founded by the Teutonic Knights, for centuries the ducal seat of Prussian dukes and the coronation city of Prussian kings, became the Russian city of Kaliningrad. The ancient German cities of Stettin and Breslau became the Polish cities of Szczecin and Wroclaw. Danzig became Gdansk. The de facto administration of these areas hardened into permanent rule. The transfer of the German population in these eastern areas was supposed to be effected in an orderly and humane fashion; but millions of Germans were driven from their homes or fled within a few months. For them (and for the Germans who were expelled from Czechoslovakia) it was the final consummation of the war that Hitler had unleashed.

The Potsdam participants agreed that peace treaties would be signed as soon as possible with the former German satellite states; the task of preparing them was entrusted to a council of foreign ministers representing the United States, Britain, France, the Soviet Union, and China. In the months that followed, the widening chasm between the Soviets and the West manifested itself in stormy meetings in London, Paris, and New York, as well as in a peace conference held in Paris in 1946, at which were represented the twenty-one states that had contributed substantial military forces to the defeat of the Axis powers. In February 1947, treaties were signed with Italy, Romania, Hungary, Bulgaria, and Finland. All these states paid reparations and agreed to certain territorial adjustments. In 1951 a peace treaty was signed with Japan, but not by the Soviets, who made their own peace in 1956. The years went by but no final peace treaty was signed with Germany, a Germany divided into two. For the wartime Western-Soviet coalition had fallen apart, shattering the dreams and aspirations of those who had fought the Second World War to a resounding triumph over one kind of aggression and totalitarianism, and then found themselves confronted with a new age of crisis.

XXI.
THE POSTWAR ERA:
THE AGE OF THE
SUPERPOWERS

A CATACLYSM, according to Webster's dictionary, is "any violent change involving sudden and extensive alterations of the earth's surface; hence, any upheaval, especially a social or political one." A cataclysm in nature, as we may imagine it, is a time when volcanoes erupt, earthquakes rumble, old mountain systems are broken down, new peaks and ranges thrust themselves upward, the very coastlines assume new shapes, living creatures flee from destruction, old forms of life become extinct, and new forms of life, at first unnoticed, enter upon careers in which they are later to flourish.

The human world has been in the grip of such a cataclysm since 1914. The First World War, the collapse of the old European dynasties, the Russian Revolution, the Great Depression, the Nazi dictatorship, the Second World War, the nuclear bomb, the rise of Communist China, the end of the European colonial empires in Asia and Africa—all are part of the changes that have altered the coastlines of modern human society, and for which "cataclysm" is not too strong a word.

It is difficult to do justice to the complexities of contemporary history and to keep current with the onrushing events of our own times. The chapters that follow can only sketch the most memorable developments of the postwar era and the contemporary age.

Chapter Emblem: The United Nations emblem, showing a wreath enclosing the earth as seen from above the north pole.

109. The Cold War: The Opening Decade, 1945–1955

Certain problems that had confronted mankind for over a century became even more complex and more urgent in the second half of the twentieth century. Three can be singled out: science, the organization of industrial society, and national sovereignty.

The atomic bomb dramatized the problem of science. The world shuddered at the instantaneous destruction of Hiroshima. The postwar contest to produce more sophisticated nuclear weapons spurred the realization that a third world war would be unimaginably more awful, and even unthinkable. Human beings possessed the means to annihilate not only civilization but even human existence on the planet, a thought especially shocking to a world that set one of its highest values on scientific progress.

The problem of science was not new. Science, and its partner, invention, had for a long time transformed both industry and war. It had conquered many of the dread plagues and diseases of the world. People had long known that science could be applied either constructively or destructively. It was the magnitude of destructive possibilities that now made thoughtful people worry over the problem. The accumulation of scientific knowledge, instead of heightening the quality of human life, took on the ghastly distortions of a nightmare. Scientists themselves, after the first atomic explosion, affirmed the need for a moral regeneration. They insisted that science was neutral, free from blame for the horrors of Hiroshima and Nagasaki, that the trouble lay not with science but the uses to which scientific knowledge was put.

The problem of organizing industrial society was also unresolved. There were in theory two opposite social poles. At one, best represented by the U.S.S.R., all capital was owned by the state and supplied to workers as needed, and all interchange was carefully planned by public authorities in advance. At the other pole, best demonstrated by the United States, capital was owned by private persons, who chose the channels of investment and hence determined the availability of jobs, and interchange took place through the mechanism of the market. Neither the "socialist" nor the "capitalist" system was pure in practice, and mixed economies became the rule in many countries. The chief drawback in the Soviet system was its lack of freedom, in the American its lack of economic stability. For a long time Americans expended a good deal more effort trying to correct the lack of security than the Soviets did to correct the lack of freedom.

Another question hinged on the unity and diversity of the modern world. Was the modern world really "one world," or was it not? It was one world in the sense that there was a close-knit, interdependent economy, that political events and environmental changes affected the whole globe, and that world cultures interacted as never before. But it was far from homogeneous. All admired the steam turbine and stood in awe of nuclear fission, but beyond the material level schemes of values diverged. No people wished to be subordinated to another, or to a higher body, or to lose its way of life in a uniform world civilization. Here lay the root of the problem of national independence and of its corollary, world organization.

After the Second World War, as after the First, an international organization was set up to prevent war in the future.[1] A conference of all anti-Axis powers, held at San Francisco in 1945, established the United Nations and drew up its Charter. The new organization was designed to maintain international peace and security and encourage cooperation in solving international social, economic, and cultural problems. Of its numerous agencies, two were central. The General Assembly was a deliberative body in which all member states, however small, were considered equal. The Security Council, whose primary responsibility was to preserve peace, consisted of fifteen members: the five Great Powers, who were permanent members, and ten rotating members chosen by the Assembly for two-year terms. Apart from the two superpowers, the United States and the U.S.S.R., it was not easy to define the Great Powers in 1945, but the permanent seats were assigned to the United States, the Soviet Union, Great Britain, France, and China.[2]

Each permanent member had a veto power. Thus the Security Council could act on important matters only if the Great Powers were unanimous. Although widely criticized, the veto was considered necessary. In major crises the agreement of the Great Powers would be needed to maintain world peace. The U.S.S.R. demanded the veto most frankly (and used it most freely), but the United States, too, would not have joined without this safeguard. Many remembered that the old League was weak because the United States had never joined, and the Soviet Union had been admitted only belatedly. In the following years even small countries refused to abide by judgments of the United Nations. No nation, large or small, was willing to forgo its independence or submerge itself in a world state with authority to put down violence, as any national state could do within its own borders.

The United Nations had fifty-one original members. Its headquarters was located in New York. The Charter provided for the admission of new members, including the former Axis countries and their satellites, and also wartime neutrals, so that it could be truly international. From 1947 to 1955 a few additional states were admitted; in 1955 sixteen additional nations; and in the next two decades, after decolonization, the organization expanded to over three times its original number.

The United Nations failed to fulfill the role projected for it in the postwar era. The Security Council was powerless to intervene in matters affecting relations between the United States and the U.S.S.R. The United Nations remained one of the few arenas where the Americans and Soviets could meet and debate, but it could not prevent the two superpowers from drifting further and further apart. On the other hand the UN from the beginning helped mediate regional disputes and played a role in peacekeeping missions. The office of the secretary general grew in importance. With the expansion of the UN to include the nations of the Third World—a term devised to describe the "developing" countries, mostly former colonial countries, not directly aligned with either the Western or Soviet camp—the General Assembly became

---

[1] See pp. 724, 730–731, 864.

[2] Nationalist China (the Republic of China, or Taiwan) occupied the seat until 1971, even though the People's Republic of China (Communist China) governed the Chinese mainland after 1949.

a forum for debate in which the developing nations, critical of the wealthier West, gave voice to their social and economic grievances.

The Cold War: Origins and Nature

The Second World War, in effect, left only two Great Powers still standing in any strength, the United States and the Soviet Union. The United States emerged physically unscathed from the war, its economy stronger than ever before. Although it quickly demobilized, it alone possessed the atomic bomb. The Soviet Union had been devastated by the war, in which over 20 million of its population had perished, but it was still a formidable military power, with 4 million soldiers under arms and in control of populations and territories in central and eastern Europe well beyond its pre-1939 boundaries. It became common to speak of the two as superpowers—continental land giants, possessing enormous resources, overshadowing all other states, including the powers of Western Europe long dominant in the modern centuries. The characteristic of a two-state system is that each power knows in advance who its only dangerous enemy can be. In such a situation a diplomatic equilibrium is more difficult. Measures taken by either power for its security are seen as aggression or as provocations to the other, and each exaggerates the other's strength. After the war the United States and the U.S.S.R. fell into this unhappy dual relationship. It was compounded by deep-seated ideological tensions between capitalist democracy and Marxist-Leninist communism dating back to the Bolshevik Revolution of 1917. A diplomatic and ideological clash of interests set in that came to be known as the "Cold War," so called because the antagonisms and rivalries, intense though they were, fell short of open or direct hostilities between the two powers.

It was not possible for anyone (even in the U.S.S.R.) to know what Stalin, who dictated all decisions, or his lieutenants in the Kremlin really believed or intended at the end of the Second World War. Probably, as Marxist-Leninists, they considered a clash between the U.S.S.R. and the Western capitalist powers as inevitable at some point in the future. Probably they were disturbed by the economic strength of American capitalism, which sought free markets in Eastern Europe and elsewhere, and by the American monopoly of the atomic bomb. Undoubtedly they saw an opportunity to consolidate their hold over the territories gained during the war (or regained, since some of these had been lost at the end of the First World War[3]), and to create a favorable outer buffer zone for Soviet national security. Undoubtedly they also saw in the aftermath of the Second World War, as of the First, an opportunity to promote the international Marxist revolution (even if Stalin was wary about Communist movements, as in Yugoslavia or China, over which he did not have full control). Whether the Soviets were acting to protect their national security, fulfill old Russian territorial ambitions, or promote communism on a world scale, President Truman and his advisers, and a great majority of the American people, became convinced that the Soviets were bent not only on consolidating their grip on Eastern Europe but were embarking on a worldwide Communist offensive, which it was the responsibility of the United States, as the only power in the West able to act effectively, to

---

[3] See pp. 713, 727, and map, pp. 728–729.

contain. Before long the Americans came to ascribe all ferment and unrest on the globe to initiatives launched by the Kremlin.

In Europe at the close of hostilities, Soviet armies occupied Eastern Europe and Germany as far west as the Elbe River. American, British, and French armies held the remainder of Germany, most of Austria, and all of Italy.[4] During the war, the power, or powers, liberating an area exercised political authority. In that way in the sweep of the Red Army the Soviets came to control much of Central and Eastern Europe; 100 million people passed under their domination. On the other hand, the United States excluded the Soviets from any active role in its occupation of Italy (and, in Asia, of Japan). For the Soviets, occupation meant full control over the political, economic, and social institutions of a country and the right to shape them in the Soviet image. The Western powers, on the other hand, had hoped for pluralist and democratic societies, open to Western trade and influence. During the war the Americans and British had conceded Soviet predominance in Eastern Europe, but they now resented the transformation of Poland and other East European countries into Soviet-dominated Communist states, even if for Stalin it was the only way to guarantee "friendly regimes" on his borders. From Potsdam on, Truman denounced the Soviets for violating their pledge of free elections for the East-European states and for failing to cooperate in the joint occupation of Germany. To the Americans Soviet consolidation of control over Eastern Europe seemed like the first step in a plan for unlimited expansion in Europe and elsewhere, not unlike the Nazi and Fascist aggression of the 1930s, to which Truman, resolved not to repeat the lessons of appeasement, frequently compared it. Stalin may have been more a Russian nationalist than an ideologue committed to worldwide Communist revolution, but his stubbornness, paranoia about Western capitalist encirclement, and lack of concern for world public opinion, made it difficult for the West to deal with him or to distinguish between what might have been legitimate Soviet security needs and expansionist missionary zeal. In time Americans, too, became obsessed with a missionary zeal of their own.

Soviet actions fed the belief that Stalin's ambitions transcended Eastern Europe. In Asia, as agreed at Yalta, the Soviets had declared war on Japan in August 1945, after the end of the war in Europe, and moved into Manchuria, where they were well positioned to help the Chinese Communists. In Korea, once the Japanese were defeated, the Soviets by agreement occupied the northern part of the country down to the thirty-eighth parallel, but also took steps to consolidate their occupation zone into a Communist government. The Americans, British, and Soviets had jointly occupied Iran during the war to forestall a Nazi takeover. The Soviets refused to evacuate their troops at the stipulated time, pressed for oil concessions (such as the British and the Americans enjoyed), and lent aid to separatists in the north. The Soviets also pressed for a trusteeship over the former Italian colonies in North Africa on the southern coast of the Mediterranean, within easy reach of the Suez Canal, and they massed troops on the Turkish border, pressing for joint control over the Black Sea straits in order to guarantee naval access to the Mediterranean through the Dardanelles—an old tsarist goal. The British, as the guardians of the Mediterranean and Middle East, attempted

---

[4] See pp. 855–859, 864–866.

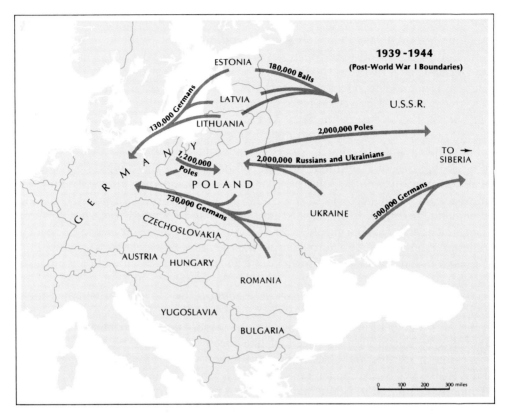

DEPORTATION AND RESETTLEMENT, 1939–1950

The age-old distribution of nationalities in Central and Eastern Europe was radically transformed between 1939 and 1950. Not only were about 6 million Jews put to death, with over 300,000 of the survivors emigrating to Israel by 1950, but millions of Germans, Poles, and others were forcibly uprooted.

The first stage, shown in the left-hand panel, began with the Nazi-Soviet Pact of 1939, after which the Germans occupied western Poland, while the Russians annexed eastern Poland and the three Baltic republics. Western Poland received Poles expelled from Germany, while in eastern Poland about 2 million Poles were deported to Siberia, being replaced by about the same number of Russians and Ukrainians. Many Estonians, Latvians, and Lithuanians were moved to other parts of the Soviet Union. Germans who had lived in Eastern Europe for centuries were displaced. Thousands "returned" to Germany from the Baltic republics and from places in Romania and elsewhere where they had long formed German enclaves. The "Volga Germans" and others in south Russia were sent to Siberia.

to bolster the Turkish defenses. And in Greece, in a bitter civil war which raged from 1946 to 1949, Communist guerrilla forces, emerging from the Resistance and enjoying wide popular support, battled the British-supported royalist, or nationalist, army. Stalin, as if recognizing his wartime commitment to Churchill that Greece should lie in the Western sphere of influence, lent little aid, but Tito's independent Communist regime in Yugoslavia helped the Communist guerrillas. The Communist pressures on Turkey, Greece, and Iran aroused deep concerns

1945 - 1950
(Post-World War II Boundaries)

ESTONIAN S.S.R.
300,000 Balts
300,000 Balts
300,000 Balts
LATVIAN S.S.R.
LITHUANIAN S.S.R.
BYELORUSSIAN S.S.R.
RUSSIAN F.S.S.R.
2,300,000 Russians and Ukrainians
EAST GERMANY
11,600,000 Germans
GERMANY
POLAND
WEST GERMANY 3,500,000 Germans
4,500,000 Poles
UKRAINIAN S.S.R.
1,800,000 Ukrainians, Krim Tartars, Kalmucks, etc.
TO SIBERIA
CZECHOSLOVAKIA
500,000 Germans
AUSTRIA
HUNGARY
MOLDAVIAN S.S.R.
ROMANIA
YUGOSLAVIA
BULGARIA

320,000 Jews to Israel (1945-1950 only)
120,000 from Poland
91,000 from Romania
37,000 from Bulgaria
33,000 from Turkey
22,000 from Czechoslovakia
17,000 from Hungary

0   100   200   300 miles

A second stage (right-hand panel) came with the Soviet victory and the collapse of Hitler's Reich. The German-Polish frontier was now moved westward to the Oder River. Millions of Germans from east of the Oder, along with more millions from the Sudeten regions of Czechoslovakia and a continuing stream from Hungary and Romania, were thrown back into what remained of Germany, most of them fleeing to the Western zone, but some to what was the Soviet zone in 1945. Poles streamed into what had been Germany east of the Oder; others came into Poland from the Ukraine. Russians moved into what had been eastern Poland and the Baltic states. Ukrainians and various non-Russian minorities were sent to Siberia. Some Balts escaped to the West (including the United States); others were redistributed to various places in the Soviet Union.

There was a considerable resettlement also of Hungarians, Slovaks, and Finns. The most conspicuous changes, however, in addition to the virtual disappearance of East European Jewry, were the expulsion of the Germans from Eastern Europe and a westward movement of Poles and Russians. (Source: *Westermanns Atlas zur Weltgeschichte*.)

in the West about Soviet strategic designs on the eastern Mediterranean and on the precious oil reserves of the Middle East.

One of the casualties of the tense atmosphere was a plan for international supervision of atomic weapons. The United States knew that it was only a matter of time before the Soviets (and other nations) could build the atomic bomb, since the scientific basis for it was known. At the moment the British alone shared the secret. Under the Baruch Plan introduced into the United Nations in 1946, the United States proposed that atomic energy be controlled by an international authority and that its use be limited to peaceful purposes. Such an international body would have had the right to send inspectors into any country to check violations and enforce sanctions, not subject to a veto in the Security Council. The Soviets objected and would not forgo their veto. The idea that foreigners might freely examine their society was repugnant to them. They questioned the good faith of the United States, which alone possessed atomic bombs which it would not destroy (or halt further testing and production) until the proposed international authority was in operation. To be sure, large segments of American public opinion also favored national rather than international control. Some Americans were even hesitant to continue the wartime partnership with the British. They, in turn, fearful of an American relapse into isolationism, undertook to become a nuclear power on their own. The Baruch Plan foundered on mutual suspicion and mistrust. The Soviets proceeded with their own atomic research and technology, which yielded results even sooner than expected: by 1949 the Soviets were a nuclear power. The nuclear armaments race, universally dreaded, began.

The atmosphere hardened all through 1946 and 1947. The American policy of containment, as formulated by Dean Acheson, George F. Kennan, and others in the State Department, postulated that the Russians would expand wherever a power vacuum existed. Because the Soviets had no precise timetable for conquest, the West should show both patience and firmness; with time Soviet society itself might change. Meanwhile the West needed to maintain its military strength and use economic and other counterpressures to resist the Soviets. Containment became the cornerstone of American policy, but it came to be interpreted in more rigorously military terms than some of its proponents had intended and it was accompanied by a tendency to blame all global restlessness on a monolithic Soviet-controlled communism. Meanwhile Churchill, even before the Soviets had fully completed the transformation of Eastern Europe into Communist satellites, made an eloquent speech in March 1946 in which he described the "iron curtain" that had descended separating Eastern and Western Europe—"from Stettin in the Baltic to Trieste in the Adriatic." That spring the United States turned down a long-pending Soviet request for a reconstruction loan, Lend-Lease having ended with the war, and also cut off reparations deliveries to the Soviets from the American occupation zone of Germany.

Early in 1947 Great Britain, forced to reassess its priorities because of financial difficulties, and to cut back on its commitments in the Mediterranean, informed Washington that it could no longer aid the anti-Communist forces in Greece or support Turkey in its resistance to Soviet pressures. The United States quickly moved to fill the vacuum. Truman not only agreed to provide the necessary assistance in the Mediterranean but formulated in March 1947 in the Truman Doctrine a broad national policy to contain communism everywhere—"to assist free peoples who are resisting attempted subjugation by armed minorities or by outside pressures." The Truman Doctrine committed the United States to unprecedented global responsibilities. Some advisers believed that the policy was too broad, that American national interests were not clearly enough defined, and that the United States was committing itself to a global enterprise that could overstrain its resources. The Marshall Plan, designed to hasten European economic recovery and hence check Communist expansion, as we shall see, was also announced that spring.[5]

During this time the American national security state took shape. A National Security Council was created in 1947 to advise the president on security matters and a Central Intelligence Agency to coordinate the gathering of intelligence. The CIA soon received authorization to conduct covert operations as well. The authority of the executive branch to conduct foreign policy grew. In 1948, the United States adopted its first peacetime military draft.

The Soviets meanwhile denounced the American capitalist and imperialist "warmongers." With the United States arming Greece and Turkey, American carriers able to sail the length of the Mediterranean or lie off the coast of Murmansk, American air bases established in the Middle East, the Americans in occupation of Japan, Okinawa, and South Korea, and the Americans possessing the atomic bomb, the Soviets felt threatened and encircled. Soviet suspicions, dating from Western intervention in the Russian Revolution and civil war in 1918; their exclusion from the Munich Pact; the delay in opening up a second front in the Second World War; the cessation of Lend-Lease at the end of the war; the rejection of the postwar loan; and other sources of friction, became inflamed.[6] In 1947 the Soviets, in order to exert closer control over all Communist parties, reestablished the old Communist International, or Comintern, abandoned in 1943 as a gesture of wartime cooperation and goodwill, renaming it, innocuously enough, the Communist Information Bureau, or Cominform. In 1947 the Soviets replaced coalition governments in central and eastern Europe, in which the Communists had shared power, with regimes completely dominated by Communist parties. In Czechoslovakia, where President Benes's democratic coalition was seen by many as a possible bridge between East and West, the Czech Communist party, faced with defeat in a forthcoming election, seized power in February 1948. A grave crisis now arose over Berlin.

Germany: The Berlin Blockade and the Airlift of 1948–1949

The key to the rebuilding of Europe, and the strongest area of Soviet-Western contention, was Germany, divided by agreement into four zones and occupied by the wartime Allies. The Ruhr, in the Western zone, was still Europe's industrial heartland. During the war the Allies had agreed to joint Allied policies for a defeated Germany, even though each of the four powers was to occupy a separate zone. Berlin also was divided into four separate Allied sectors, but with joint administration for the city as a whole. All had agreed that Germany should pay reparations, both in capital equipment and current production, especially to the Soviet Union, which had suffered most from German military power, and that limits should be placed on German productive capacity.

At the war's end, the Americans quickly came to favor the economic reconstruction of Germany as necessary for European recovery and for the

[5] See pp. 883–884.
[6] See pp. 752, 840–842, 852–853.

reduction of European dependence on American financial aid. The Soviets, on the other hand, were determined to use German resources to repair the devastation in the Soviet Union. They removed large amounts of food and machinery, stripping entire plants in their eastern zone. The refusal of the Western Allies to permit the dismantling of factories in their zones and their insistence that the Soviets take their share of current production only from the Soviet zone fueled strong Soviet resentment. By May 1946 joint administration of occupied Germany had all but broken down. Early in 1947 the United States and Britain united their two zones (which they called "Bizonia"); the French, overcoming their initial reluctance to see a revived Germany, soon merged its zone as well. The Western powers encouraged the reconstruction of governments in the individual states and the naming of delegates to a constituent assembly to set up a federal republic. The Soviets, in their zone, took steps to establish a Communist-dominated government. Two Germanys were emerging.

In June 1948 the Western powers, recognizing the need for drastic currency reform to speed West German economic revival, suddenly revoked the old worthless currency and at a one-to-ten ratio issued a new German mark, the Deutsche mark. The Soviets, who had not been consulted, objected to this as a violation of the wartime agreement to treat Germany as a single economic unit and in retaliation cut off all road and rail access to Berlin, which lay one hundred miles deep within the Soviet zone. The blockade was a sharp challenge and test of will. If the West abandoned Berlin, it could lose authority in all Europe, and open the way for Soviet westward expansion. Aware that they could not resort to military measures against the much stronger Soviet ground forces, the Allies responded to the blockade with a massive air lift. For close to a year, American and Western aircraft flew in thousands of tons of food and other supplies to the occupation forces and to the 3 million inhabitants of West Berlin. The Soviets harassed the planes but avoided direct confrontation, and finally, in May 1949, lifted the blockade.

Each side proceeded with the formation of a German government. The Federal Republic of Germany, its capital in Bonn, came into existence in September 1949, the German Democratic Republic, its capital in the eastern sector of Berlin, one month later. There were now two Germanys.[7] The division of Europe had further hardened.

The Atlantic Alliance

In 1948 Britain, France, Belgium, the Netherlands, and Luxembourg had formed a West European Union for collective self-defense. In 1949 the United States took the lead in creating a larger military alliance and collective security system. The United States, Canada, and ten European nations met in Washington, signed the Atlantic Pact, and agreed to military arrangements for the joint defense of Western Europe. It was a military alliance of unlimited duration and broad scope: "an armed attack against one or more" was to be considered "an attack against all." By it the United States formally committed itself to the security of Western

---

[7] See map, p. 893.

Europe and agreed to supply funds and equipment for European rearmament. It was the first military alliance of this kind in American history.

Out of the treaty developed the North Atlantic Treaty Organization (NATO) with a network of military arrangements and chain of command under an American general. Because West Germany remained the most vulnerable target for Soviet aggression, large numbers of American troops (eventually over 300,000) were stationed there as the nucleus of the NATO armed forces. With overwhelming Soviet superiority in ground forces, the NATO defense strategy was based not on ground troops alone but on American air power, which would provide a nuclear umbrella for Western Europe as well. The treaty was a solemn affirmation of American determination not to abandon the Continent. In later years the West Europeans became restive with American leadership, or alternatively feared an American decoupling from Europe, but NATO remained Western Europe's shield against Soviet aggression. The Truman Doctrine, the Marshall Plan, and the Atlantic alliance were the three prongs of the American and Western response to a potential Soviet bid for global supremacy, of which Western Europe would be the principal prize.

Meanwhile the West European countries were making impressive economic progress and cooperating with each other in economic and other ways. In a few short years after the devastating war Western Europe had reconstructed itself politically, recovered economically, and was rearming. The Soviets could not be expected to view the revival and growing unity of Western Europe with equanimity. American financial and military assistance to Western Europe, the Atlantic alliance, the containment policy, all defensive in Western eyes, were hostile acts from the Soviet perspective. The Soviet Union drew its six satellite or client states, variously styled people's republics or people's democracies, closer to it. It formalized economic ties by creating in 1949 a Council for Mutual Economic Aid (or Comecon), and a few years later consummated the existing network of military alliances in the Warsaw Pact of 1955. The Soviets augmented their existing armor and air power and continued their nuclear research.

By 1949 Stalin's postwar expansion effort seemed contained and Truman could claim success for his policies. The Soviets had dropped their demands on Turkey and departed from Iran. Quasi-insurrectionary strikes launched by Communist parties in Western Europe had failed, as did a Communist bid for power in Italy in the elections of 1948, in which the Vatican and the United States strongly supported the anti-Communist camp. Marshal Tito in 1948 successfully defied the Cominform and Yugoslavia went its separate Communist way. In Greece the American- and British-backed Greek royalists triumphed in 1949 against the Communist guerrillas. The Soviet blockade of Berlin had failed to drive the West from the city.

The rivalry over Europe ended in stalemate. The Soviet threat to Western Europe diminished. The continent remained divided into a Western and Eastern Europe, Germany into two Germanys, Berlin into West and East Berlin. (The term Central Europe tended to drop from use.) After the failure of the Soviet blockade of Berlin, there was no further overt conflict in Europe. Despite renewed threats to Berlin, each side recognized the strength and security concerns of the other. But any thoughts that the world might settle into peace, no matter how uneasy, were shattered in June 1950. The Western-Soviet struggle shifted to Asia.

The Revival of Japan

In Asia events also moved rapidly in the early postwar years. In China the Chinese Communists triumphed over the Nationalists and proclaimed the People's Republic of China in 1949. In Japan the United States used its military occupation from 1945 to 1952 to foster democratic institutions and revive the Japanese economy.

Rejecting Soviet demands for a share in the occupation of Japan, the United States, with British and French approval, lodged full authority in General Douglas MacArthur, the supreme commander of the occupation forces. In good part in response to Cold War tensions the American occupation encouraged reconstruction, and the Japanese, in the wake of their disastrous defeat, cooperated fully with the occupation authorities. A new constitution in 1946 ended divine-right rule, transferred sovereignty from the emperor to the people, established machinery for parliamentary government, gave women the vote, and encouraged local self-government. The constitution forever renounced war and the threat or use of force as a means of settling international disputes; the small Japanese armed forces were restricted to defense purposes. The Americans abandoned earlier plans to dismantle industries and transfer them as reparations to Asian nations that had been the victims of Japanese conquest. Although trials of Japanese war criminals were held, there were no extensive purges.

Efforts at social and economic reform under the occupation were less sweeping than originally planned. The large family holdings in heavy industry and banking were dissolved, but within a short time new forms of economic concentration replaced them. Labor unions were reinstituted but their powers were curtailed. The occupation inaugurated a program of land redistribution, with a limit on large landholdings, but many peasants lacked the means to purchase the land offered them. Although a moderate socialist party emerged, and militant activists in later years frequently demonstrated their discontent, political control remained in the hands of conservatives drawn from the upper social classes. By the end of the occupation the Liberal Democratic party, a conservative political grouping, dominated the government.

The conservative-led political consensus that emerged had a strong commitment to economic recovery and growth. Like Western Europe, Japan, too, rose from the ashes. In 1945 it had been prostrate, a fourth of its housing destroyed, agricultural and industrial output reduced to half its prewar level, its shipping and financial reserves gone. Under the occupation and with American help the economy revived and expanded; by 1954 its gross national product reached prewar levels. Labor self-discipline and social patterns of deference and loyalty kept industrial unrest to a minimum. Close cooperation between government and business encouraged savings, investment, research, and economic growth. The very need to rebuild the economy from the bottom up proved to be an advantage. Beginning in the early 1950s the economy grew at an amazing rate of nearly 10 percent each year, manufacturing output at 14 percent a year. Despite the forced repatriation of millions of Japanese from Manchuria, Korea, and other parts of Asia, and the addition of large numbers of rural workers to the labor force, Japan still had a labor shortage. The response to it was an intense level of automation. Japan became a pioneer in advanced high technology and came to depend on technology and productivity to sustain its growth. Its consumer products soon entered the world economy, its exports eventually rivaling those of the Americans and the Europeans. Because a large military establishment was forbidden, expenditures that might have gone into the military, as in the past, were now plowed into investment. By the 1950s Japan was once again a major economic power, a bastion of social stability, and a major new element in the global economy. For the Soviets the revival of Japan under American auspices, which they saw as a counterweight to Soviet influence, and as a bulwark against revolution in Asia, was still another threat.

Containment in Asia: The Korean War

In June 1950 the Korean War broke out. The Western Allies and the Soviet Union had agreed that Korea, once an object of imperialist rivalry between Japan and tsarist Russia, but under Japanese rule since 1910, would become free and independent after Japan's defeat. At the war's end the United States, for reasons of military expediency, proposed that Soviet troops temporarily occupy the northern part of the country down to the thirty-eighth parallel and United States troops the southern half. But postwar negotiations on the unification of the country foundered. The U.S.S.R. established a satellite government in its occupation zone under the Communist leader Kim Il Sung and built up North Korean military strength. The United States developed its own client state in the south and lent economic and military assistance. In 1947 a UN commission sought to sponsor nationwide elections, but the Soviet Union would not permit supervision of elections in the north. The elections in the south in May 1948 resulted in the presidency of Syngman Rhee, who, despite superficial forms of democracy, governed repressively. Anti-Communism in Asia and elsewhere did not necessarily equate with democratic government. After the elections the United States withdrew its occupation forces but continued military and economic support. The Soviet Union also removed its occupation forces but left behind a well-trained and well-equipped North Korean army. Despite the original intention, there were now two Koreas.

By 1950 the situation in East Asia, as we have seen, had altered dramatically. First, Japan had revived. The United States through its postwar occupation had created a stable Japan, friendly to the West, and with a prospering economy. Secondly, the Chinese Communists, with only limited and grudging Soviet support, had triumphed over the Nationalists in the long civil war, and in October 1949 had proclaimed the Chinese People's Republic. Although relations between the Chinese Communists and the Soviets were neither warm nor cordial, the two countries, out of mutual concern over the revival of Japan and the deepening American influence in East Asia, drew together in a mutual defense pact in February 1950. The U.S.S.R. campaigned to have the People's Republic of China replace Nationalist China in the United Nations. When the effort failed, the Soviets in protest boycotted the Security Council meetings.

Although border skirmishes between North and South Korea had been frequent, the full-scale North Korean invasion of the south came as a surprise. To the West it was an open act of military aggression, the first clear-cut act of military aggression of the Cold War. Because of the boldness of their initiative and their superior forces, the North Koreans expected a quick victory. They gambled that the United States would not intervene and that the outside world would lodge no more than a moral protest. Only a few months earlier the American Secretary of State Dean Acheson, although one of the architects of containment, had somewhat narrowly defined the defense perimeter vital to American interests in East Asia as including Japan and the Philippines but had failed to include South Korea, perhaps omitting it because it was so clearly known to be an American client state.

The precise inspiration for the invasion remained unclear. North Korea, concerned over South Korea's avowed ambition to unite the country on pro-Western terms, may have taken the initiative on its own. The invasion seems to have surprised the Soviets who, as noted, were boycotting the Security Council at the time and hence unable to exercise their veto when the Americans persuaded the Security Council to condemn the invasion and authorize military countermeasures. The Chinese, recovering from their civil war, barely established in power, and still facing a challenge from the Nationalists in Taiwan, could scarcely have helped initiate it. Although Stalin may not have incited the North Korean attack, the sweeping initial North Korean successes offered the Soviets an opportunity to profit from the fast-moving events and to check the growing American influence in Japan and East Asia. The Soviets quietly furnished military aid to North Korea and denounced the United States for intervening in Asian affairs—on the very doorsteps of the U.S.S.R. and of the People's Republic of China.

For the American government, and for most Americans, it was difficult, even impossible, to believe that the attack had not been engineered in Moscow, or that the North Koreans were capable of independent action. The assumption was that the Soviets, probing in Asia for weak spots, as they had elsewhere, had found one and now must be halted. Korea, like Berlin, became another test of American and Western will. Truman, already concerned about the "loss of China" (the formula used at the time for the Chinese Communist victory) saw it as a test, as he said, of the "free world's commitment to liberty." The attack challenged the entire system of collective security and containment constructed to stem the tide of Soviet communism. The Soviets had passed "beyond the use of subversion" to "armed invasion and war." Korea, he said, would be "the Greece of the Far East." The Americans quickly prevailed on the Security Council to condemn North Korea as an aggressor and to take military action. Without asking for an American declaration of war because it was a "police action," Truman ordered American combat troops to Korea and called for air strikes above the thirty-eighth parallel. General MacArthur, the wartime hero of the Pacific, who had successfully presided over the occupation of Japan, was named commander of the UN forces.

In the early fighting that summer the American-led United Nations forces were driven south and forced to retreat to the very water's edge, but in September MacArthur made a remarkable amphibious landing on the western side of the peninsula, drove the North Koreans back above the thirty-eighth parallel, and rapidly moved north toward the Yalu River, the boundary between Korea and the Manchurian province of the People's Republic of China. In late October, Chinese soldiers suddenly appeared in large numbers and drove back the advancing

UN armies. Within two weeks Chinese troops drove the UN forces back below the thirty-eighth parallel. It was an entirely new war. The People's Republic of China was committed. The European allies, gratified at first by the American show of determination, grew worried that the war could escalate into a global, possibly nuclear, conflict.

Meanwhile the battle lines seesawed. MacArthur forced the Chinese and North Korean troops to retreat, again crossed the thirty-eighth parallel, and demanded unconditional surrender. He proposed to blockade the Chinese coast, bomb Chinese cities, encourage the Chinese Nationalists to attack the Chinese mainland, and even seal off Korea from Manchuria by a field of radioactive waste. Truman, however, recognized that MacArthur's actions could lead to full-scale war with China, Soviet intervention, and even world war, and without the full support of the European allies. When the general publicly flouted his authority, he relieved him of his command and replaced him.

In July 1951 a cease-fire agreement brought large-scale fighting to a halt, but armistice negotiations dragged on, deadlocked over the repatriation of North Korean prisoners who did not wish to return home. In July 1953 under General Eisenhower's presidency, an armistice was signed, the line of partition drawn roughly where the fighting had begun three years earlier, at the thirty-eighth parallel, with provision for a demilitarized buffer zone. The partition hardened into a long-term division. North Korea became a Communist state and a full-fledged ally of the Soviet Union. South Korea, unable to achieve political democracy under Syngman Rhee or his successors, nonetheless became a dynamic capitalist economy, far outstripping North Korea in economic strength. In later years pressures emerged for the reunification of the country or at the least for closer relations between the two regimes. Militants blamed the artificial division of their country on the Cold War and on the superpowers, and on the Americans more than anyone else. Four decades later, over 40,000 American troops remained stationed in South Korea.

The United States spent over $15 billion on the war. Because it could not supply all its military needs on its own, the war vastly stimulated the economic growth of Western Europe and Japan, and also quickened the pressures for German rearmament. Fifteen countries supported the United States and participated in the fighting, but it was largely an American military operation, the United States furnishing half the ground forces and close to all the naval and air power. The Americans suffered over 34,000 battle deaths in the undeclared war, three-fifths as many as in the First World War; the American wounded were estimated at over 100,000. The South Koreans suffered over 1 million casualties in dead, wounded, and missing, the North Koreans and the Chinese an equal number. The Soviets had fought by proxy.

In American eyes a flagrant act of aggression had been checked. In Western Europe, despite the anxiety over MacArthur's recklessness, the show of American firmness was reassuring. As seen in the Communist world, however, and indeed in many of the nonaligned countries in Asia like India or Indonesia, the great capitalist power, the United States, had been prevented from reasserting Western imperialist supremacy in the East. In its efforts to create regional security pacts in Asia, the United States found little enthusiasm among the larger non-Communist Asian powers, who disliked communism but also distrusted the West. Although the United States had been the least involved of all the Great Powers in nineteenth-century territorial imperialism in Asia, its new leadership of the Western world made it a symbol of Western oppression, buttressed by the suspicion that its free-world rhetoric masked the drive to open world markets for American capitalism—an image assiduously cultivated by the Soviets and, even more aggressively, by the Chinese Communists.

On the other hand, the success in checking the North Korean act of aggression by force of arms reinforced the American belief that military strength and decisiveness could check Communist expansion anywhere; containment would be global. The Korean War inaugurated an era of deep American involvement in Asia and served as prelude to an even longer and more costly conflict, the war in Vietnam in the following decade.[8] In late 1952 the United States successfully tested its first thermonuclear or hydrogen bomb, hundreds of times more powerful than the atomic bomb used at Hiroshima; the Soviets shortly thereafter, in 1953, did the same.

The Korean War had its repercussions in Europe. Even though there were still misgivings in France and in other parts of Europe over a revival of German military strength, the Americans pressed for West German rearmament. When a French proposal for a European Defense Community (with a "European" army, in which the Germans would serve as "European" soldiers) failed to pass the French legislature in 1954, West Germany was authorized to create an army of its own under the overall command of NATO. Concern over a resurgent German militarism by now was receding. The West German constitution guaranteed civilian control over the military; a strong antimilitarist movement had emerged in the country itself. By agreement, however, Germany was prohibited from manufacturing nuclear weapons or materials for chemical or biological warfare. In 1955 the Federal Republic of Germany became a full member of NATO.

The Korean War hastened a peace treaty with Japan. In the peace treaty signed in 1951 in San Francisco by fifty nations, but without Soviet participation, no general reparations were exacted, but individual countries were to work out their own reparations agreements. In a separate security pact the United States retained military rights in Japan and occupied nearby islands, where, it was agreed, the United States would remain as long as necessary for peace and security. A year later the American occupation of Japan itself formally ended. The Soviets made no move to return the Kurile Islands, which they had occupied at the end of the Second World War. The United States meanwhile signed security pacts with Australia, New Zealand, and the Philippines and tightened its global commitments.

The decades that followed the troubled international relations of the early Cold War brought new confrontations and crises—over Berlin, Cuba, Vietnam, the Middle East, Afghanistan, to name only the most important—and above all, a mounting nuclear arms race between the two superpowers and the stockpiling of the most formidable weaponry ever assembled. But before continuing with the Cold War, we must examine in this and the following chapter many other developments of these years—the remarkable economic recovery and political reconstruction of Western Europe, the reshaping of the

[8] See pp. 975–980.

global economy, the world of the Communist countries, and the emergence of new nations from the old Western colonial empires. Let us first turn to Western Europe.

110. *Western Europe: Economic Reconstruction*

The Second World War left Europe in a worse state of disorder than the First. Physical destruction was incomparably greater. The war had ruined one of the world's chief industrial areas and brought its economic system to collapse. Even when the worst local devastation was repaired, suffering and distress persisted. With problems of transportation and exchange unresolved, Western Europe was cut off from the areas with which it had carried on trade. It had long lived on imports, for which it could no longer pay. During the war the West Europeans, and especially the British, had used up their overseas investments and lost a good share of the shipping services they had once provided. Overseas countries had built up their own industries and needed those of Europe less, and the United States had taken over markets once in European hands.

At the same time, Western Europe was not to be written off; its population exceeded that of either of the superpowers and even in ruins, despite the wartime strategic bombing, it still possessed one of the world's leading industrial plants and the skills needed to rehabilitate and run them. The Europeans did not wish to be rescued by either of the superpowers. Most rejected communism as a form of slavery. Yet dependence on the benefactions of the United States they feared as a gamble. Memories of the stock-market crash of 1929, the economic collapse of Europe after the withdrawal of American capital, and the Great Depression bred skepticism about dependence on American capitalism. But between the two superpowers the Soviets had more to gain by chaos in Western Europe, and the United States more to gain by its rebuilding.

The Marshall Plan and European Recovery

For the non-Communist world, the single most important factor in the early postwar years was the productivity of the American economic system. The American economy had expanded enormously during the war. At the war's end the United States accounted for two-thirds of the world's industrial production and held two-thirds of the world's gold. Its gross national product was two and a half times higher than in 1939, its exports three times greater, and despite predictions about postwar economic collapse, its economy continued to grow rapidly.

When Lend-Lease ended after the war, the United States sent billions of dollars worth of goods to Western Europe to relieve distress and made loans to individual states, especially to Britain. The Europeans quickly set about to salvage their industrial plant, less severely devastated, it turned out, than originally thought, and to rebuild their economies. Within two years, by 1947, the nations of Western Europe were approaching their prewar levels of production. But American aid was still desperately needed to continue the purchase of food, fuel, raw materials, and industrial parts essential to full economic recovery and expansion. By the spring of 1947 recovery appeared at risk. The poorest harvest in a century was feared. With Cold War tensions mounting, Communist parties in France and Italy, which had earlier cooperated in postwar reconstruction, began launching strikes. Even if the Soviet Union was not actively promoting revolutionism in Western Europe, understanding perhaps that the West would not tolerate overt revolution there, the Americans were concerned about European stability. American economic aid so far had been improvised and piecemeal. But in June 1947, on the basis of confidential American reports of continuing distress and threats to stability, Secretary of State George C. Marshall used the occasion of his Harvard commencement address to invite the Europeans to cooperate in drawing up blueprints for a broad program of reconstruction, for which the United States would provide the financial support. The plan, formulated in humanitarian terms, was "directed not against country or doctrine, but against hunger, poverty, desperation, and chaos." To reinforce its nonpolitical character, the United States extended the invitation to all European governments, including the Soviet Union and the East European states. The Soviet Union, as some of the plan's sponsors may have suspected, rejected the proposal and summarily withdrew from the initial planning conference in Paris. It forbade the participation of its East European satellites, some of which had evinced interest, recognizing that involvement would subject their economies to outside scrutiny and perhaps draw them into the Western economic orbit. It denounced the plan as "a new venture in American imperialism."

The West-European countries responded with alacrity. Under the Marshall Plan, or European Recovery Program, as it was enacted by Congress, American aid was coordinated with each country's needs and with joint European priorities in order to maximize the benefits. The Office for European Economic Cooperation (OEEC) in Paris, with which the Americans worked closely, identified projects, coordinated the planning, and allocated the funds.

The Marshall Plan had a profound psychological and economic effect on the European economies and the results exceeded the boldest anticipations of its American sponsors. The West Europeans utilized their technical and managerial skills to improve transportation facilities, modernize their infrastructure, and vastly expand their productive capacity. They reduced trade barriers among themselves and facilitated trade by setting up a payments union. Hard currency, now available for needed imports, limited financial pressures and reduced the need for further austerity, sacrifice, and hardship. The Marshall Plan accelerated the recovery already under way, made recovery smoother than it would have been, and encouraged the economic cooperation of the European countries with each other. The United States used its economic resources to help revive its competitors, but the program also served American interests by restoring a world market, of which the United States would be one of the chief beneficiaries. By creating markets for American exports, it helped fuel the postwar boom in the United States economy. The Americans thus satisfied their humanitarian impulse, served their economic needs, and reduced the drift of Europeans into the Communist camp. At the same time the Marshall Plan sharpened the division between the Soviet bloc and the West.

Economic Growth in Western Europe

For West Germany the currency reform of 1948, which precipitated the Berlin blockade, ignited an amazing economic revival and expansion, the *Wirtschafts-wunder*, or "economic miracle." Marshall Plan funds were at first administered by the Western occupation authorities, but once the Federal Republic of Germany was established, it joined the other European nations in the Office of European Economic Cooperation. Like the other European countries, West Germany benefited from the Korean War and the demand for goods that the Americans could not satisfy. By 1950 West Germany exceeded prewar German production levels before embarking on a spectacular economic boom. By 1958 it was the leading industrial country of Western Europe. Not only West Germany but France, Italy, and other West European countries experienced an "economic miracle" also. For two and a half decades, from 1948 to 1974 (when a worldwide recession set in), the Western European economies grew at unprecedented and uninterrupted rates of growth. The West Europeans basked in prosperity and rising living standards. Europeans would later speak of the "silver fifties" and the "golden sixties," the French (counting from 1944) of the "thirty glorious years." Although Britain's economy, burdened by older industries and the loss of overseas markets, lagged behind, it too grew faster than at any time in the interwar years. Japan, as earlier noted, from the 1950s on also embarked on a phenomenal economic expansion.

The prosperity of Western Europe derived from a competitive free market and private enterprise economy, but was accompanied everywhere by extensive economic planning, systematic government intervention, and a network of social services to help cope with the instability of competitive capitalism and the business cycle. No one anywhere wished to repeat the hard times and suffering of the Great Depression. Keynes's theories, first formulated in the 1930s but without many adherents at that time,[9] took hold in the postwar era and dominated government policy in the 1950s and 1960s even when conservative governments were in control. Governments kept their economies under close surveillance and used their fiscal and monetary powers to promote investment, production, and employment and to control inflation. They took "countercyclical" measures, that is, at signs of decline in the business cycle they increased government expenditures in order to keep demand high. Full employment was accepted as a goal. Improved statistical techniques and economic forecasting, although scarcely precision instruments, made economic planning and "fine tuning" feasible. Planning took the form of guidance and direction, not coercion, and differed markedly from the rigid, detailed, and doctrinaire centralized planning of the Soviet bloc.

In Britain, France, and Italy (less so in West Germany, which had lived through heavy state control under the Nazis), the postwar governments also nationalized a number of the key sectors of the economy to bring them under government control. But even in these mixed economies, the private capitalist sector represented the major share of economic activity. In all Western Europe economic growth became a central objective, virtually an obsession. Governments and

---

[9] See pp. 799–804 and 808.

people came to expect growth rates far exceeding those of the past. It was as if Western Europe was catching up, compensating for the lost time of the interwar years and the Second World War, and for the economic stagnation of a generation.

When the sustained economic growth of the next two decades led to a labor shortage, West Germany and other countries invited foreign workers to join their labor force. Spaniards, Portuguese, Italians from southern Italy, Turks, Greeks, Yugoslavs were invited in as "guest workers." Four and a half million arrived in the Federal Republic of Germany alone, over half of them Turks, who did not return home but formed large unassimilated enclaves, following their Muslim faith, in West Berlin and other cities. After the collapse of the European empires, immigrants from the former European colonies in Asia, Africa, and the Caribbean also arrived in Western Europe in large numbers. From the 1950s on a steady stream of immigrants came to Britain from India, Pakistan, the West Indies, and Africa. France drew large numbers from its former North African colonies, especially Algeria. The Netherlands became home for many Indonesians. Political refugees also arrived in Europe from Vietnam and other parts of Asia. The new Europeans were of different cultures, religion, and racial composition. Mosques became a not uncommon sight in European cities. The influx of guest workers and immigrants by the millions created difficulties later in the less affluent times after 1974. The presence of the new Europeans led to friction, often overtly racial, testing the flexibility and tolerance of a European society becoming increasingly multiethnic and multicultural.

With a postwar baby boom and an influx of at least 13 million immigrants and refugees the population of Western Europe grew by 25 percent between 1945 and 1970. But by the 1960s the birth rate of the West Europeans leveled off and the West European population began to decline.

In these same postwar years the contemporary welfare state grew, going well beyond its pre-1914 origins or its expansion in the interwar years. The postwar governments gave a high priority to social objectives, to what the French Resistance charter had called "a more just social order:" the right to a suitable job; government compensation in the event of unemployment or disability; social security in old age; free or subsidized health care; and the redistribution of wealth and income through progressive taxation. The protection of the contemporary welfare state was intended to be universal, not confined, as in earlier times, to the poor and disadvantaged. Its social objectives could be achieved in the 1950s and 1960s because of a salutary interplay of government, management, and labor; all shared in the consensus about investment and growth. Only later, in the 1980s, did the argument gather strength that all these entitlements had become excessive, and an impediment to economic growth.

111. Western Europe: Political Reconstruction

Western Europe also faced overwhelming challenges of political reconstruction at the end of the war. Britain was economically exhausted and in the process of liquidating its empire. France, recovering from the collapse of 1940, the occupation, and the divisiveness of collaboration, faced colonial wars. Italy had to renew its political life after two decades of fascism. Germany, after the Nazi rout, was divided and under military occupation. Nevertheless political reconstruction went forward. Britain resumed its role as the world's oldest parliamentary democracy; France and Italy adopted new constitutions; out of the Western zone of occupied Germany the Federal Republic of Germany emerged in 1949.

The smaller states of Western Europe also resumed democratic processes. Only Spain and Portugal remained for a time under dictatorships until those dictatorships also came to an end in the mid-1970s. The memories of dictatorship receded. The suffrage was broadened. Women finally received the vote in France and Italy immediately after the war, in Switzerland in 1971. In a suffrage reform that went almost unnoticed, the legal voting age in most countries was quietly reduced to eighteen in the 1970s.

In the early postwar years a renovating spirit swept Western Europe. The memories of 1914–1918, the economic dislocations of the 1920s, the miseries of the Great Depression of the 1930s, the sacrifices of the Second World War, haunted everyone. The wartime Resistance movements, demanding an end to the aggressive nationalism and militarism that cost Europe so much travail, called for a federal union of Europe to prevent future wars. The Resistance proclamations emphasized economic and social rights as well as political freedom. Liberal democracy was important but not sufficient; postwar governments were asked to provide protection against the insecurities of old age, disability, unemployment, ill health.

The earliest elections confirmed the strength of the Resistance spirit, but before long politics reverted to older ways. The welfare state idea persisted, as did the impulse for an integrated Europe, but politics became more pragmatic and less ideological. Socialists, following the Scandinavian model, became social-democratic reformists, accepting capitalism but insisting that they could manage capitalist economies more effectively than liberals, centrists, or conservatives. In France and Italy the presence of large Communist parties, with strong attachments to the Soviet Union in the early postwar years, complicated matters. In West Germany, Italy, and to a lesser extent in France, the Christian Democrats, drawing inspiration from religious and ethical precepts, played a key role in shaping the new regimes. They accepted the welfare state but backed away from the egalitarianism of the socialists and, over time, became increasingly representative of conservative and business interests.

Great Britain: Labour and Conservative

In Great Britain, the first elections in ten years unseated Winston Churchill and the Conservative-led wartime coalition and voted in a Labour government in July 1945. For the first time in its history Labour had a majority of its own.[10] Governing from 1945 to 1951, with Clement Attlee as prime minister, it set the course of British life for years to come. It was a Labour government that accepted the liquidation of the British empire in India.

Once the center of high capitalism, Britain became the world's chief exemplar

[10] See pp. 619–621, 811–812.

of parliamentary socialism and the modern welfare state. On the premise that the country's basic industries could not be left to the unplanned anarchy of capitalism and unregulated competition, the Labour government nationalized the Bank of England, the coal mines, electricity and gas, iron and steel, and other parts of the economy. Because four-fifths of industry remained in private hands, what emerged was a mixed economy. At the same time Labour greatly expanded and revamped the social insurance program inherited from the Liberal reforms of 1906–1914.[11] All parties had committed themselves during the war to an extension of these welfare services. The Beveridge Report of 1942 had sketched a program to guarantee "full employment in a free society" and social security for all "from the cradle to the grave." Labour now extended insurance coverage for unemployment, old age, and other contingencies, inaugurated a comprehensive national health service, and sharply increased income and inheritance taxes.

In the elections of 1951 Labour lost its majority in Parliament. The Conservatives returned to office and governed uninterruptedly for the next thirteen years under a succession of prime ministers, but after 1964 the two parties alternated in office.[12] The shifting electoral fortunes stemmed from division within the country over the welfare state introduced by Labour, dissatisfaction with the performance of the economy, and frustration at Britain's diminished global status.

During their years in office, the Conservatives restored some nationalized industries to private control and modified the national health insurance program, but did little else to dismantle the welfare state. Both parties recognized, however, that the social reforms of the welfare state could be absorbed only if the economy prospered. But the country faced nagging economic problems. After the Second World War Britain was much weaker than after the First.[13] The liquidation of its investments to pay for the war, the loss of export markets, and its reduced income from shipping and other services adversely affected its balance of payments, and undermined the pound. With American financial aid, an intensified export drive, an austerity program that reduced imports, and curtailment of military and imperial commitments, the British economy and trade position improved and the country experienced a modest prosperity. But the British failed to rebuild their obsolescent capital equipment and infrastructure as effectively as their West European neighbors across the Channel.

British industry was outstripped even in its own domestic market. Its economy grew more slowly than that of Western Europe and Japan. When out of power, Labour argued that the Conservatives lacked economic dynamism and were responsible for the lagging economy. But Labour in office did no better and was forced to devalue the pound and extend austerity measures. When inflation set in during the late 1960s, and intensified in the 1970s, the trade unions demanded wage increases to match rising prices. Strikes and prolonged work stoppages troubled the economy and divided British society. Until the late 1970s, when a

---

[11] See pp. 612–613.

[12] The prime ministers in the years 1945–1990 were: Clement R. Attlee (Labour), 1945–1951; Sir Winston Churchill (Conservative), 1951–1955; Sir Anthony Eden (Conservative), 1955–1957; Harold MacMillan (Conservative), 1957–1963; Sir Alec Frederick Douglas-Home (Conservative), 1963–1964; Harold Wilson (Labour), 1964–1970; Edward Heath (Conservative), 1970–1974; Harold Wilson (Labour), 1974–1976; James Callaghan (Labour), 1976–1979; and Margaret Thatcher (Conservative), 1979–1990.

[13] See pp. 810–811.

new era opened,[14] the question was whether Labour or the Conservatives could better manage British decline, not how they could overcome it.

Meanwhile troubles in Northern Ireland persisted. After the partition in 1922, the six counties of Northern Ireland, predominantly Protestant, had remained part of the United Kingdom. The Catholic minority, about one-third the population, protested militantly that they were victims of political and economic discrimination, and pressed for annexation to the Republic of Ireland. Open violence broke out in 1969, inflamed by the Irish Republican Army on the one hand and Protestant extremists on the other. In the years that followed, over 2,500 persons lost their lives, and no compromise was in sight.

The French Republic: Fourth and Fifth

After the liberation of France General Charles de Gaulle, the very incarnation of the Resistance, became provisional president. Because no one wished to return to the Third Republic after its ignominious collapse in 1940, nor to the stalemate society of the interwar years, elections were held for a Constituent Assembly. With the parties of the right discredited by their role in Vichy, the left emerged enhanced in strength and prestige. The Communists, the Socialists, and the Popular Republic Movement (or MRP), a Catholic progressive party akin to Christian Democrats elsewhere on the Continent, formed the provisional government. The left parties pressed for a systematic purge of collaborators, despite the difficulties in determining levels of guilt. The purge, which had begun as soon as the army reached French soil, initially took the form of angry drumhead trials and executions. Gradually, the process was brought under more orderly judicial procedures. Even so, the trials of Pétain and Laval were impassioned showpieces; the country had suffered too much to let collaboration go unavenged.

The Fourth Republic in its machinery of government differed in only a few details from the Third.[15] Once again the presidency was only ceremonial and the premier and cabinet were responsible to an all-powerful legislature. De Gaulle made no secret of his dislike for the constitution being prepared in 1946, the return of party rivalries, and the domination of the legislature, all of which interfered with his vision of a strong France ready to resume a leadership role in world affairs. He resigned in protest in December 1946. The three parties continued their tripartite coalition under Socialist leadership until the Communists, reflecting the heightened tensions of the Cold War, fomented a series of strikes and were expelled from the cabinet in May 1947.

Parliamentary division and ministerial instability grew more serious. The Socialists and the MRP formed unstable coalitions with each other and with the reviving smaller parties. Periodically de Gaulle returned to the political scene, heading a movement called the "Rally of the French People," which he described as "above parties." Except for the brief reform ministry of Pierre Mendès-France in 1954–1955, governmental ineffectiveness in the midst of domestic and foreign crises filled the public with cynicism, hostility, and indifference.

Yet despite its record of political instability—25 cabinets succeeding one

[14] See pp. 985–987.
[15] See pp. 605–609, 814–817.

another from 1946 to 1958—the Fourth Republic enacted a significant body of legislation. The provisional government nationalized several key industries. As in Britain, a mixed economy emerged. The existing social security legislation was expanded. A farsighted economic plan, drawn up by Jean Monnet, who later played a large role in the creation of the European Economic Community,[16] enlarged and modernized the country's economic base and paved the way for industrial expansion. A flexible form of economic planning, inspired by Monnet, in which government, management, and labor played mutually reinforcing roles, became an accepted part of French economic life. By 1952 production levels were one and a half times those of 1938, and industrial output was growing at an annual rate of over 5 percent. From 1946 to 1966 production tripled whereas in the half-century from 1889 to 1940 it had merely doubled. Meanwhile Monnet and the MRP premier, Robert Schuman, took the lead in promoting European economic integration in the 1950s and in tightening ties with the other West-European countries. The country also displayed a demographic vitality for a time that confounded earlier pessimists.[17]

What finally brought down the Fourth Republic was the strain of trying to preserve the old French colonial empire. France alone, of all the major powers, was almost continuously at war for close to fifteen years. It could envy the lot of the losers in the Second World War, Germany, Italy, and Japan, with no restless colonies to subdue. France fought relentlessly to preserve its empire. The constitution of 1946 provided representation in Paris for the colonies, but the limited reforms did not satisfy nationalists pressing for independence. From 1946 to 1954 the French forces unsuccessfully fought in Indochina until they finally had to withdraw. Within a matter of months, the Algerian war broke out. That war drained the resources, morale, and self-esteem of the French even more. The *colons*, as the European settlers in Algeria were called, and army leaders adamantly opposed French withdrawal and staged an insurrectionary coup in Algiers in May 1958. When civil war threatened, the country turned to the one man it believed could save the situation—Charles de Gaulle, then living quietly in self-imposed retirement. The army leaders, the settlers in Algeria, and the parties of the right were convinced, given his solicitude for the army and French national pride, that he would keep Algeria French. De Gaulle accepted the summons. In June 1958 the National Assembly invested him as premier, giving him emergency powers for six months and the authority to prepare a new constitution.

In that way the Fifth Republic was born. In the autumn of 1958 the new constitution was overwhelmingly accepted in a popular referendum, and de Gaulle was elected president. The presidency, as de Gaulle had long urged, became the fulcrum of power in the Fifth Republic. The president was the final authority in foreign affairs and national defense. The president named the prime minister (as the premier was now called), and had the right to dissolve the National Assembly, call for new elections, submit important questions to popular referendums, and assume emergency powers, all of which de Gaulle did in his eleven years in office.

[16] See pp. 900–902.
[17] See pp. 589–590, 818.

Political instability disappeared; in the first eleven years of the Fifth Republic there were only three cabinets.

De Gaulle settled the Algerian crisis in his own way. Sensitive to the revolution sweeping the colonial world, he step by step evolved a policy of independence for Algeria, which the country approved in a referendum in July 1962. Even earlier he granted independence to all of the French colonies in sub-Saharan Africa.[18] With peace, governmental stability, and economic prosperity, the French reconciled themselves to the loss of empire and took pride in their heightened importance on the world scene under de Gaulle. France became the world's fifth industrial power, behind only the United States, the U.S.S.R., West Germany, and Japan. In 1960 France became the fourth nation, along with the United States, the U.S.S.R., and Britain, to develop a nuclear capacity. De Gaulle even created an independent nuclear strike force. Soon France became Western Europe's largest producer of nuclear energy for peacetime energy needs.

After the settlement of the Algerian crisis, de Gaulle built a kind of plebiscitary democracy by direct appeals to the electorate. Although civil liberties were preserved and free speech and free elections maintained, the old democratic ferment disappeared. The older political parties were paralyzed or impotent; skilled technicians ran the affairs of state; and de Gaulle, an uncrowned republican monarch, presided as arbiter over the nation's destinies.

The nation grew restless. A reorganized Socialist party took the lead in uniting the left and reaching out to the middle classes. The country also became impatient with de Gaulle's extravagant posturing in world affairs. Suddenly, in May 1968, grievances in the overcrowded universities sparked a revolt that led to demonstrations by hundreds of thousands of students and then brought 10 million workers out on strike, paralyzing the economy and threatening the regime itself. De Gaulle survived the revolt but only after assuring himself of army support. Holding out the threat of communism and chaos, he won an overwhelming majority for his party in new elections. The country seemed to forget the outburst. Educational changes were introduced, but the economic disruption of the spring hurt the economy. In 1969 de Gaulle chose to make a referendum on a series of constitutional and regional reforms a vote of confidence in himself. When it lost by a small margin, he resigned and retired to his country estate, where he died a year later, an august, heroic, austere, and often exasperating figure, whose exploits in war and peace assured him a lasting place in France's history. The stability of the Fifth Republic was one of his greatest accomplishments.

The Federal Republic of Germany

To communicate to the German people and to the entire world the enormity of the Nazi crimes, the four wartime Allies convened an international trial in 1945–1946 at Nuremberg. Hitler, Himmler, and Goebbels were already dead, but twenty-two other Nazi leaders and the major Nazi organizations were indicted for crimes against peace, i.e., plotting and waging a war of aggression; war crimes, which were defined as violations of the accepted laws and conventions of warfare;

---

[18] See pp. 917–918, 933.

and crimes against humanity, i.e., acts of mass murder and genocide. The evidence of evil deeds, massive and incontrovertible, was set down for posterity in many volumes of recorded testimony. Despite the high moral purpose of the trials and an honest effort to establish fair judicial procedures for the accused, some critics at the time and later questioned their appropriateness, especially the decision to try the leaders of a defeated sovereign nation for planning and waging war, and to indict an agency like the General Staff. Some questioned the propriety of the Soviet Union, which had itself contributed to the outbreak of the war, shared in the partition of Poland, and incorporated the Baltic states into its borders, sitting in judgment on the Nazis. Others dismissed the trials as victors' justice. Yet the Nuremberg trials contributed in their way to reinforcing international standards of civilized behavior. The court condemned twelve of the defendants to execution and eleven were hanged, Goering escaping execution by taking poison in his prison cell. Seven received prison terms of varying length, including life sentences; three were acquitted. The last of the Nuremberg prisoners, Rudolf Hess, serving a life sentence, died in Spandau prison in 1987.

On a lesser scale a "denazification" program, carried out by the four occupation authorities, each in its own way, and later by German courts under Allied supervision, produced mixed results. Because so many technically trained and professional Germans had been members of Nazi organizations, it became difficult to exclude them from public life if the normal processes of government were to resume, which the Americans were eager to see. Some individuals guilty of the more heinous crimes associated with the Third Reich and who had fled the country were still being apprehended and tried several decades after the war's end, by the Germans themselves or in French or Israeli courts.

Divided Germany (and divided Berlin) became a central arena of the Cold War. There was no intention initially of keeping Germany divided, but the sharp differences between the Western powers and the Soviets led to the creation of two German states. The German Democratic Republic became a Communist state, one of the most dependable client states of the Soviet Union. The Federal

GERMANY AND ITS BORDERS, 1919–1990

The upper panel shows the boundaries established after the Treaty of Versailles. Note the free city of Danzig and the Polish Corridor; for these and other areas lost in the First World War see also the map on pp. 728–729. In the middle panel we see the borders at the height of the Second World War in 1942. The Reich proper had then annexed (1) Luxembourg, (2) Alsace and Lorraine from France, (3) Carniola from Yugoslavia, (4) Austria, (5) the Sudeten regions and a Bohemian-Moravian protectorate from Czechoslovakia, (6) the free city of Danzig, and (7) Poland, which was renamed the "General Government." Beyond the borders of the Reich, the Germans occupied France, Belgium, the Netherlands, Denmark, and Norway, and in Eastern Europe had set up controls over the former Baltic states, Byelorussia, and the Ukraine. The lower panel shows Germany after Hitler's defeat. All conquests have been lost, and Poland now reaches westward almost to Berlin. A communist East Germany (the German Democratic Republic) and a democratic West Germany (the Federal Republic of Germany) grew out of the zones occupied respectively by the Soviets and the West. After the fall of the Communist regime the two Germanys were reunited in 1990.

THE WEIMAR REPUBLIC

HITLER'S
GROSSDEUTSCHES REICH

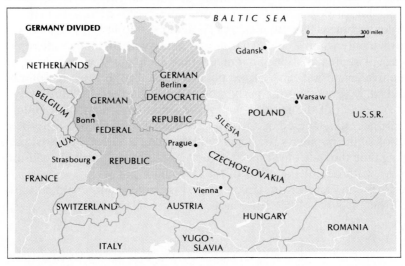

GERMANY DIVIDED

Republic of Germany became a prosperous parliamentary democracy, fully integrated into the Western political, economic, and military structure.

The German *Wirtschaftswunder*, or "economic miracle," has already been mentioned. By 1950 industrial production surpassed the level of all prewar Germany and within a few years the Federal Republic of Germany with its dynamic export economy became the leading industrial country of Western Europe. The chaos and ruin of 1945, when Hitler's total defeat brought the collapse of organized government, the loss of territory, and widespread suffering, were all but forgotten.

The West German government, even while shaping overall economic policies, encouraged private industry and a capitalist, competitive economy, but also provided broad social services so that it was accurate to refer to a "social market economy." The guaranteed benefits came to exceed those of most other major industrial Western countries. The Federal Republic also pioneered in bringing labor and capital together; a "codetermination" law gave workers seats on the boards of directors of larger firms. The labor unions accepted a role as social partners in the expanding economy, moderating their wage demands to avoid aggravating inflationary pressures.

With the support of the Western occupying powers, who had first encouraged the establishment of independent governments in each state (or *Land*) in West Germany, a constitutional convention representing the ten German states met in 1948–1949 in the quiet Rhineland city of Bonn, which became the federal capital, wrote a Basic Law (or *Grundgesetz*), and officially established the Federal Republic of Germany. The Basic Law, designedly not called a constitution, was to be temporary, valid only until at some future date the two parts of Germany could be reunited. An extensive bill of rights was one of the most prominent features of the Basic Law. Power was decentralized under a federal system, with considerable authority delegated to the states. The founders deliberately set out to avoid the weaknesses of the Weimar Republic.[19] The president, elected indirectly and not by popular vote, was a ceremonial figure with limited political power; a president of stature could, however, as the years revealed, exercise considerable moral authority. The head of government, or real executive, was the chancellor, responsible, along with the cabinet, to the majority in the popularly elected lower house, the Bundestag. To avoid instability, a chancellor could be overthrown only when a new majority was ready with an immediate replacement. Proportional representation guaranteed that each party would be apportioned seats equivalent to its share of the popular vote, but to prevent splinter parties and political fragmentation, a party received seats in the legislature only if it won at least 5 percent of the national vote. The Christian Democratic Union and the Social Democrats emerged as the chief parties and shared between them a large proportion of the popular vote. The Free Democrats, a liberal centrist party, were for a long time the only small party in the legislature and formed coalitions, when necessary, with one or the other of the two major parties.

The Christian Democratic Union (CDU) governed uninterruptedly for twenty years, from 1949 to 1969. In reaction to the Nazi barbarism, it sought to

---

[19] See pp. 785–786, 824.

infuse politics with a moral idealism and ethical purpose. Not a confessional party, it appealed to both Protestants and Catholics, now almost equally represented in the country, and received strong support from the business community and large segments of the middle classes. The dominating figure in the party and government in the early years was the Christian Democratic leader, Konrad Adenauer, who had begun his career in the pre-1914 imperial era. A patriarchal, strong-willed personality, his ambition was to regain for Germany a position of dignity and international respect. He became chancellor in 1949 at the age of seventy-three (with only a slim majority) and governed for fourteen years. Opponents criticized *der Alte* ("the old man") for creating a "chancellor's democracy," but he provided the resolute leadership, stability, and continuity that made possible the remarkable economic expansion of the early 1950s and the regaining of West German sovereignty. His economics minister, Ludwig Erhard, succeeded him as chancellor in 1963. Elections held every four years confirmed the Christian Democrats as the leading party. Adenauer successfully integrated the Federal Republic of Germany into the emerging political, economic, and military structures of Western Europe. He strengthened ties with France, cooperated in the movement for European economic integration, and won the support and confidence of the United States and the other Western powers. The major opposition party, the Social Democrats, heirs to the Social Democratic party founded in the 1870s,[20] criticized him for his close identification with the United States and the West, and for ignoring the issue of national reunification. Dropping its Marxist ideology at a key party congress in 1959, it broadened its appeal to the middle classes and younger voters.

In 1965 the Social Democrats, who by now had softened their neutralist stand in foreign affairs, joined the Christian Democrats and the Free Democrats in a "grand coalition." Willy Brandt, for many years the popular Social Democratic mayor of West Berlin, as foreign minister launched his "Eastern policy," or *Ostpolitik*, a policy which without abandoning ties to the West encouraged building bridges to the Soviet Union and Eastern Europe, including East Germany. In 1969, he received the support of the Free Democrats and became chancellor of a new coalition, ending the twenty-year rule of the Christian Democrats. Brandt negotiated important treaties with the Soviet Union and Poland in 1970, formally conceding the German frontier at the Oder-Neisse boundary. His government officially recognized the German Democratic Republic, and promoted closer economic ties with it and Eastern Europe. A spy scandal cut short his chancellorship in 1974 and his Social Democratic colleague Helmut Schmidt took over.

Within a decade after the disastrous military defeat that had left a shattered and divided country, the Federal Republic of Germany was a major economic and political power, a coveted ally of the West in the Cold War, an equal member of the North Atlantic Treaty Organization. In time a new generation appeared that felt little responsibility for the crimes of the Nazis. Inflammatory issues faded, material progress seemed triumphant over ideology, and democracy seemed assured.

[20] See pp. 615–616.

The Italian Republic

During the bitter struggle to oust the German armies from the Italian peninsula after the fall of Mussolini in 1943, the Italian political parties, repressed for over two decades, sprang to life. All supported the provisional governments in the task of postwar reconstruction and committed themselves to social and moral renewal. In 1946, even though the king had abdicated in favor of his son, the country voted by a narrow margin to abolish the Savoy monarchy, never very distinguished, and now tarnished by its cooperation with the Fascist regime.[21] A constitution for the new Italian Republic established a ceremonial presidency, cabinet government, and legislative supremacy. Proportional representation guaranteed equitable representation for all political parties, large and small, no one paying much attention to the question of coherent majorities.

The Christian Democrats became the dominant party. More than a successor to the old Catholic Popular party,[22] it appealed to all classes and sectors of Italian society, successfully blending support for democratic political principles, a moderately regulated free-enterprise economy, and the labor tenets of social Catholicism. Although the party maintained its independence of the Church, it remained close to the hierarchy. In Alcide De Gasperi, who had survived the Fascist years as a librarian in the Vatican, it found an effective leader. For seven formative years from 1946 to 1953 he presided over a series of coalition governments, which made possible postwar economic reconstruction and expansion. In the Cold War he kept Italy firmly in the Western camp. The Communist party successfully publicized its role in the Resistance, capitalized on the cooperation of the country's elites with Fascism, and exploited existing grievances to become the second leading party in the country, which it long remained. As in France, the Communists at first held seats in the cabinet and cooperated in economic reconstruction. But when they fomented politically inspired strikes in 1947, De Gasperi dismissed them from his ministry. In 1948, as noted earlier, the United States, intervening openly for the first time in its history to influence a European election, threw its weight behind the Christian Democrats to thwart the Communist campaign. The Christian Democrats for the first and only time won an absolute majority in the legislature. The Communists, despite their continuing parliamentary strength and support from a third to a fourth of the electorate, remained excluded from the cabinet.

After De Gasperi's disappearance from the political scene in 1953, the Christian Democrats governed under a succession of short-lived coalition cabinets formed with small centrist parties, notably the Republicans and the Liberals. It became difficult to form stable parliamentary coalitions and durable cabinets; the average life of a cabinet was seven months. Over the years, the Christian Democrats became faction-ridden and less interested in reform than in patronage. Abandoning their initial idealism, they catered to propertied and conservative interests. In the early 1960s the Socialists, who had by now dissociated themselves from the Communists, for a time became part of the governing coalition, but this "opening to the left" by the Christian Democrats did not alter political rigidities. Although

[21] See pp. 818–822.
[22] See pp. 617, 819.

prospering economically, the country grew impatient with the uninterrupted tenure of the Christian Democrats.

The Communists gained further strength in the 1960s. They weakened their ties with Moscow, renounced such tenets of Marxist-Leninist orthodoxy as the dictatorship of the proletariat, and tempered their assault on religion. Architects of what came to be known as "Eurocommunism," they declared that each nation, without deferring to Moscow, must find its own way to a new society through parliamentary democracy and national consensus. The Italian Communists condemned the Soviet military intervention in Eastern Europe and elsewhere (soon to be described) and, ironically, accepted Italian membership in NATO. The strongest Communist party in the Western world, the Italian party counted 1.8 million members at its peak in the mid-1970s, winning the support of 35 percent of the electorate, controlling a powerful labor union confederation, and governing in many major cities, including Rome, with Communist mayors and municipal councils. But when it pressed for seats in the national government, the Christian Democrats rejected the proposal. With the emergence of a revived Socialist party on the national and municipal levels, Communist strength later eroded.

The unstable political scene did not interfere with unprecedented economic growth and prosperity. The industrial triangle of Genoa, Milan, and Turin in northern Italy provided the nucleus for recovery and expansion. A prosperous mixed economy emerged. By 1949 industrial production reached 1939 levels. From 1953 on, Italy's rate of industrial growth rivaled that of West Germany and France. Unlike other countries of Western Europe, Italy could count on its own reservoir of available labor from the underdeveloped Italian South, which even in times of advancing prosperity remained the country's unresolved trouble area. Italy was transformed from the primarily agricultural country it had been before the Second World War into one of the world's half-dozen leading industrial nations.

In the late 1960s the economic scene became clouded. Italian products became less competitive, a trade deficit developed, inflation set in, and the lira weakened. Because austerity measures were required, the government retrenched on social needs. In the autumn of 1969 labor discontent burst out in a wave of strikes that subsided only after substantial wage increases, which further accelerated inflation and ushered in a period of economic uncertainties in the 1970s.[23]

Despite political instability and social turbulence, the Italian Republic showed flexibility and resilience, a capacity to improvise and compromise, an ability to absorb a large Communist party into its parliamentary democracy, and a commitment to honor civil rights and individual freedoms. Fascism seemed forgotten, like a bad dream of the interwar years, a hiatus in history. An economic revolution had elevated living standards for most, if not all, Italians.

112. *Reshaping the Global Economy*

Even before the close of hostilities the United States, with British support, had developed a bold initiative to reshape the postwar world economy. Determined

[23] See pp. 984–985.

to avoid the economic nationalism, trade restrictions, bilateralism, and currency instability of the interwar years, the planners hoped to restore the free flow of multilateral trade and the stable currencies of the pre-1914 era.[24] In July 1944 the United States convened an international conference of forty-four nations at Bretton Woods in New Hampshire. The participants pledged to reduce trade barriers and work for stable currencies in the postwar world.

The first effort after the war to establish a formal international trade organization to oversee world commerce foundered. Attempts to curtail or abolish preferential systems, trade restrictions, and protectionism met with resistance. Even Britain refused to commit itself to ending its "imperial preferences" arrangements. But an alternative strategy proved more successful. The United States had already negotiated trade agreements with a number of countries to reduce tariffs on a reciprocal basis, each agreement including a "most-favored nation" clause whereby a concession to one country was extended to all. These piecemeal arrangements led in 1947 to a broader commitment, the General Agreement on Tariffs and Trade (GATT), subscribed to by twenty-three nations initially, which became the foundation of postwar global commerce. GATT laid down rules to prevent discrimination in international trade, set up administrative procedures for handling complaints, and provided a framework for continuing negotiations. Lengthy bargaining sessions, or "rounds," designed to lower tariffs and remove nontariff barriers, became a prominent feature of the economic landscape. By 1990 ninety-seven countries were participating. GATT was only a partial substitute for a formal international trade organization, but it contributed to the vast expansion of world trade in the 1950s and 1960s. Even when more competitive trade rivalries from the 1960s on threatened a revival of protectionism it kept alive the need for negotiation and compromise.

The "world economy" in the postwar years meant the world's non-Communist or free-market economies. The strategic centers were North America and Western Europe, soon joined by Japan, which doubled its share of world trade between 1951 and 1960 and continued to increase its share. Integrated into this world economy were Latin America, Asia, the Middle East, Australasia, and Africa, so that it was truly an economy of global dimensions. The Soviet Union played no part in any of the postwar trade negotiations and restricted its commerce principally to the East European bloc, tying the satellites closely to it. Not until the late 1960s did the Soviet Union and the East European countries develop significant trade and financial relations with the West; not until the late 1980s did they seek integration into the global economy.

Currency Stability: Toward the "Gold-Dollar" Standard

If the liberalization of trade was the first goal of the wartime Bretton Woods conference, the second objective was stabilization of the world's currencies. The chaos of the interwar years when nation after nation abandoned the gold standard and competed in currency devaluations to gain trade advantages haunted

---

[24] For the "global economy" of the nineteenth century, see pp. 595–604 and 643, and for its changing character after 1914, see pp. 718–722 and 799–804. For a "global economy" in the eighteenth century, see also pp. 257–264. The theme is noted at the beginning of this book, pp. 9–10.

everyone.[25] The Bretton Woods conference sought to restore the equivalent of the pre-1914 gold standard, which under British leadership had provided fixed exchange rates and the ready convertibility of all currencies into gold (or into British pounds sterling, then considered the equivalent of gold itself). Currency stabilization, however, turned out to be more difficult than anticipated. The plan for sterling to serve as a reserve currency alongside the dollar proved impossible because of British financial weakness. Britain, the world's second largest creditor nation in 1939, became one of the world's largest debtor nations after the war, its currency in chronic difficulties. Meanwhile huge American trade and dollar surpluses made it impossible for nations with dollar shortages to convert their currencies at fixed exchange rates into dollars (the dollar having been set at $35 per ounce of gold). Not until the end of 1958, by which time Western Europe and Japan had expanded their trade and doubled their dollar reserves, was convertibility possible. For a few years thereafter, each major currency had a par value in gold and in dollars. For that same short time the American dollar, like the British pound before 1914, was accepted as the equivalent of gold itself. But the postwar economic scene changed rapidly; the era of the "gold-dollar standard," as we shall see, proved short-lived.

Meanwhile two agencies projected at Bretton Woods and established after the war helped in international financial settlements. The International Monetary Fund (IMF) provided loans for temporary balance of payments difficulties to help reduce the need for currency devaluations. The International Bank for Reconstruction and Development (or World Bank) made long-term loans to governments for economic development or guaranteed the loans made by private bankers. Both agencies played a larger role in later years than in the immediate postwar era. Both were located in Washington, their major funding provided by the United States. The economic center of gravity for the West, like the political and the military, lay on the American side of the Atlantic.

European Integration: The Common Market and the European Community

As Western Europe expanded economically, it also drew closer together. There had long been proposals for a European federation, but it was the wartime Resistance movements that reinforced the idea that Europe's future lay in unity. The Cold War, the Marshall Plan, and cooperative European recovery efforts further promoted the desire for unity. A number of European leaders pressed for the creation of a "United States of Europe." In 1948 delegates representing the parliaments of ten countries met in Strasbourg to establish a Council of Europe with the hope that it might become a legislative body for a federated Europe. The British, interested in cooperation but not integration, opposed any form of supranational authority. Although the Council of Europe grew in membership over the years and continued to support the idea of federation, it never became an important political force.

European integration took an entirely different path. In 1948 the three small

[25] See pp. 802–804.

countries, Belgium, the Netherlands, and Luxembourg, created a customs union, called Benelux, which provided the benefits of a sizable free trade area. At the same time Jean Monnet, a visionary but intensely practical French economist and administrator, at an early date recognized that the first steps to unity had to be along economic lines. Political leaders like Schuman in France, Paul-Henri Spaak in Belgium, Adenauer in West Germany, and De Gasperi in Italy responded warmly to proposals for economic integration. In 1952, under a plan designed by Monnet, six West European countries, France, West Germany, Italy, and the three Benelux nations, placed their coal and steel industries under a form of supranational authority, establishing the European Coal and Steel Community (ECSC) with headquarters in Luxembourg. Initially the plan was designed to allay anxiety about the revival of German heavy industry and guarantee access for all to the coal and steel resources of the Ruhr, but it went much further. The participating nations not only agreed to eliminate import duties and quotas on coal and steel but placed production under a common High Authority with extensive decision-making powers. A council of ministers represented the six governments, but the High Authority carried out major administrative functions.

Monnet was the first president of the ECSC, which in the years that followed integrated West European heavy industry, modernized production, provided new kinds of institutional machinery for cooperation among the member states, and paved the way for additional economic integration that would extend beyond a single sector of the West European economy. In a momentous second step, the same six nations, on March 25, 1957, signed the Treaty of Rome, creating a large free trade area or customs union, the European Economic Community (EEC) or Common Market, its headquarters in Brussels, with the explicit goal of moving toward full economic and even political integration. The treaty called for the elimination of tariff barriers among the six nations, the development of a common tariff with respect to the outside world, the harmonization of social and economic policies, and the free movement of capital and labor. The last provision made it possible for migrant, or "guest" workers to move back and forth without impediment to meet the labor needs of the expanding economies. Under a second treaty the six countries also agreed to coordinate their nonmilitary atomic research and technology in a European Atomic Community (Euratom). The European Economic Community (and Euratom) took over much of the institutional machinery of the ECSC.

The European Economic Community, or Common Market, in operation in 1958, embracing six nations and 175 million people, quickly became one of the thriving economic aggregates of the expanding world economy. By 1968, even earlier than anticipated, the last internal tariff was dropped and trade among the six nations grew at a rate double that of trade with outside countries. The EEC represented the six nations in negotiations with GATT. Its influence spread to the former European colonies, with which it worked out preferential trade arrangements. A value-added tax imposed by each member-country at the point of production eliminated the need for indirect taxes; a portion of that tax and of the external tariffs gave the Community independent revenues. Through the Common Market, Western Europe set about to recapture a key role in the new configuration of global affairs; without it, Europe would be dwarfed by the superpowers. It helped absorb a revived West Germany into Europe and ended the internecine rivalries that had exhausted the Continent in the first half of the twentieth century.

In 1967 the three "communities," the European Coal and Steel Community, the European Economic Community, and Euratom consolidated themselves into what was designated the European Community. The three high commissions became the European Commission and the common assemblies became the European Parliament, meeting in Strasbourg. Walter Hallstein, the West German president of the European Commission, described himself as "the first European prime minister." The members of the European Parliament took seats by party affiliation and not by nation. In 1979, for the first time, they were not chosen by their respective governments but were elected by a European-wide electorate. The European Parliament enjoyed only limited legislative authority; but, like the European Commission, it kept alive the idea of unity. Final decision making still rested with the council of ministers, whose decisions on fundamental matters had to be unanimous.

At the beginning Great Britain refrained from joining the Common Market. Britain's economic ties to the Commonwealth, its dependence on low-priced food imports, and its unwillingness to accept any supranational authority persuaded both the Labour and Conservative parties to refrain from joining. As an alternative, Britain helped create in 1960 a more limited customs union of seven states, a European Free Trade Association (EFTA), in which Norway, Sweden, Denmark, Austria, Switzerland, and Portugal joined with Britain in reducing tariff barriers but which had no larger ambitions for economic or political integration. For a time EFTA seemed to be a rival to the Common Market, but the sense of competition between them eased and trade between the two trading blocs grew. Britain, its own economy lagging behind that of the West Europeans, eventually sought membership in the Common Market in 1963, but its request was twice vetoed by President de Gaulle, who was wary of Britain's special relationship with the United States and saw Britain as a rival to his own country for leadership on the Continent. Not until after he passed from the political scene in 1969 was Britain admitted and the Community enlarged.[26]

If the years 1958–1968 showed remarkable gains in economic integration, the advance toward political unity was slower. De Gaulle understood the contribution of the Common Market to the prosperity of Western Europe as well as the importance of a strong Western Europe as a counterpoise to the two "hegemonic superpowers," but he firmly opposed political or supranational authority for the Community. Europe had to be a Europe of sovereign states, a "Europe des patries." The council of ministers retained its importance. The more dedicated Europeanists were disappointed. Yet the supranational economic and political machinery of the Community, the day-to-day cooperation of the European civil servants or bureaucrats (inevitably called "Eurocrats") in Luxembourg, Brussels, and Strasbourg, and the close consultation on common interests were favorable signs for unity, even apart from the military and defense ties that brought the Western Europeans together in NATO. French-German friendship, cemented by de Gaulle and Adenauer, and reinforced by their successors, remained the linchpin of cooperation within the Community. The likelihood of political union, a "United

[26] See p. 990.

States of Europe" remained remote. The Europeans showed no haste to surrender their national sovereignty and independence, but the European Community created a strong sense of common destiny, a shared faith in democratic institutions and market economies, and a concern for human rights and social needs. The European Community not only contributed immeasurably to the economic and political strength of Western Europe but helped restore it to a larger role in world affairs.

Western Europe once again played a central role in the world's economy, accounting in the 1960s for one-fourth of all imports and one-fifth of all exports; for a time its exports equalled those of the United States and Japan combined. One-third of the largest multinational corporations, that is, corporations which set up subsidiaries outside their own country for manufacturing or sales, were European. London, Frankfurt, and Paris again became important financial centers. In 1971 West European steel production surpassed that of the United States. European (and Japanese) automobiles cut sharply into American domestic and foreign markets. Self-sufficient in food, Western Europe became the world's largest exporter of dairy products, even though 10 million people left the farms for the cities in the 1950s and 1960s. The Federal Republic of Germany enjoyed a gross national product second only to that of the United States and the U.S.S.R., even though it had only one-fourth the population of each; it accounted for one-third of the Common Market gross national product. Although the United States still led Western Europe in per capita income, the gap was narrowing. Western Europe and Japan were whittling away at the American economic lead in production and trade and bringing to a close the era of the dollar's supremacy.

End of the Gold-Dollar Standard, 1971

New trading patterns created new monetary problems. The growth of the West European economies, especially that of the Federal Republic of Germany, and of the Japanese economy led to an explosive expansion in the 1960s of West European and Japanese exports, which competed successfully in the American domestic market and in markets throughout the world. Because American exports no longer exceeded its imports, the American trade balance shifted unfavorably. By 1970 the American trade deficit with Western Europe rose to over $10 billion a year. Continuing American military expenditures abroad as well as corporate investment in Western Europe and in the developing countries accelerated the outflow of American capital. Not only the balance of trade but the total balance of payments shifted unfavorably. The United States spent more abroad than it earned abroad. The postwar dollar shortage in other countries gave way to a "dollar glut." Western Europe accumulated large dollar reserves (or "Euro-dollars"), some $50 billion by 1971; oil-rich Arab states held "petrodollars." The number of dollars held abroad exceeded American gold reserves.

The shift in the American economic position undermined confidence in a dollar which many now viewed as overvalued. The Americans argued that they had faithfully kept the dollar pegged to its gold value to preserve international stability. De Gaulle, ever resentful of American political and economic hegemony, demanded an end to the gold-dollar standard and a return to gold itself. In 1965 France, claiming its right under the existing system, redeemed hundreds of millions of its dollar holdings for gold. Even though other central banks in Europe and Japan did not follow suit, private investors speculated against the dollar. American gold and foreign currency reserves dropped precipitously. The image of the dollar as an unassailable citadel of strength in the postwar era faded.

In 1971 President Nixon unilaterally suspended gold convertibility and devalued the dollar; a second devaluation followed in 1973. The monetary system projected at Bretton Woods came to an end. The world monetary system entered a new era. Despite many proposals, there was no formal reform of the system. Instead, on a day-to-day basis, and with mixed success, the world's major currencies were allowed to "float," that is, to fluctuate daily against each other and against the dollar. Gold itself fluctuated freely and official gold prices were abolished. Because the leading central banks made periodic adjustments in the exchange rates, it was really an era of "managed floating." Although the American dollar remained the world's principal reserve currency, the West German mark, the Swiss franc, and the Japanese yen took their place beside the dollar as key currencies. The new arrangements more accurately reflected the redistribution of economic power.

The breakdown of the postwar monetary arrangements did not affect the world's currencies as seriously as might have been expected. Currencies did not collapse because they were no longer exchangeable for gold, but fluctuations in the major currencies remained unsettling. The West European countries (without Britain) established a European Monetary System to keep currency variations within narrower limits, but it too developed problems. The world continued to grope its way toward new monetary arrangements, relying mainly on close international consultation and rapid exchange of information. The major players were learning to "manage" exchange rates but still had much to learn. Some looked to a modified Bretton Woods system, with predictable if not fixed exchange rates; others to a strengthened International Monetary Fund, or other international agency. In the interdependent global economy everyone knew that cooperation and partnership were essential.

113. The Communist World: The U.S.S.R. and Eastern Europe

Stalinism in the Postwar Years

In March 1953 Russia's twentieth-century Peter the Great died. Stalin had a massive impact during his close to thirty years in power. He was responsible for industrialization, the rallying of the country in the Great Patriotic War, the expansion of the nation's borders, the consolidation of Communist regimes in Eastern Europe, and the emergence of the Soviet Union as a nuclear superpower.[27] But the human costs of the Stalinist transformation of the country were staggering. Millions fell victim to his forced collectivization of the countryside and the ensuing famine, and additional millions to his purges. Western and Soviet scholars alike have estimated the total figure of Stalin's victims at least as high as 20 million.

[27] See pp. 762–772, 855–858, 870–875, 882.

Because the civil war and war communism earlier, under Lenin, also cost millions of lives the Bolshevik Revolution must be counted among the costliest experiments in social engineering in all history.

The Stalinist terror continued during the war. Entire ethnic groups like the Crimean Tatars and the Volga Germans, suspected of collaboration with the Nazis, were forcibly moved east to Siberia. Mass deportations took place from the three Baltic republics formally annexed in 1940.[28] At the war's end, returning Soviet soldiers who had been prisoners of war and civilian deportees forced to work for the Nazis in Europe were sent off to labor camps because their exposure to the West made them suspect. The network of forced labor camps grew in size. Ideological restrictions tightened. Stalin's personal suspicions, growing sharper with the passage of the years, filled even his closest associates with dismay. The unbridled authority of the NKVD (later the KGB), the secret political police that did Stalin's bidding, continued in power, gaining ascendancy over the party itself. In later years, in a freer atmosphere, the country debated whether Stalin's dictatorship represented a logical outgrowth of the Bolshevik Revolution itself and of many of Lenin's policies, or was an aberration.

Controls over intellectual life in the postwar years took on a vehemently nationalistic and xenophobic tone; deviations from Stalin's "line" in economics, music, genetics, history, and linguistics were forbidden. An officially inspired anti-Semitism, thinly disguised as anti-Zionism emerged; Jewish intellectuals were accused of being "rootless cosmopolitans." Party purges and massive arrests continued into the last years of Stalin's life. The political police meanwhile fabricated conspiracies to justify the terror. In the fictitious "doctors' plot," officially announced in early 1953, a score of Jewish doctors were arrested for plotting to poison Stalin and other Kremlin leaders; one month after Stalin died, his successors withdrew the charges and freed the imprisoned doctors.

Khruschev: The Abortive Effort at Reform

After Stalin's death the party leaders were resolved to exercise collective control, determined that no single leader should again dominate party and government. To thwart a coup by Lavrenti Beria, who had headed the secret police since 1939, the new leaders quickly arrested and executed him. In the struggle for power, authority gradually shifted to Nikita S. Khruschev. Outwardly jovial and ebullient, Khruschev was a tough and hardened realist who had enforced Stalin's purges in the Ukraine as provincial secretary and had been a member of the Central Committee since 1934 and of the Politburo since 1939. But he was shrewd enough to recognize the need for change.

In part to win allies against conservatives in the party who were opposed to change, Khruschev encouraged a greater measure of cultural and intellectual freedom—a "thaw." He put restraints on the still formidable powers of the political police. He surprised many with his attack on Stalin himself. In a speech to the twentieth party congress in 1956, he officially revealed or corroborated the "crimes of the Stalin era," making partial but nonetheless startling disclosures of the Stalinist terror and confirming the worst speculations of Western critics

---

[28] See map, pp. 872–873.

over the years. Stalin had been personally responsible for the purges and executions of the 1930s and millions of victims had been innocent of the charges against them; his most intimate colleagues had lived in fear for their lives. Khruschev also revealed Stalin's initial loss of nerve and ineptitude at the time of the German invasion in June 1941.

The attack on Stalin undermined faith in a regime which had permitted these evils. Khruschev's speech immediately unloosed a reaction in the East European satellites. Open rebellion broke out in Hungary. The other party leaders were uneasy at Khruschev's liberalizing reforms; his flamboyant personality made them also fear a new "cult of personality."

The "thaw" was never systematic or thorough. In 1958 Boris Pasternak was forbidden to accept the Nobel Prize in literature because his novel, *Dr. Zhivago*, by stressing individual freedom, implicitly condemned the oppressiveness of Soviet society. But in 1962 Alexander Solzhenitsyn was permitted to publish his *One Day in the Life of Ivan Denisovich*, a depiction of human suffering in the world of the forced labor camps. Khruschev continued his de-Stalinization campaign. Cities named in Stalin's honor were renamed; Stalingrad, the most famous, became Volgograd. Stalin's body was removed from the mausoleum on Red Square, where it lay next to Lenin's, and buried outside the Kremlin Wall.

For the economy Khruschev pressed decentralization. He attempted to loosen tight central economic controls by creating regional economic councils. He offered factory managers greater autonomy and incentives for efficiency and profitability. Meanwhile the country successfully tested the hydrogen bomb, launched Sputnik, and built its first intercontinental ballistic missiles. The Soviet economy was second only to that of the United States in gross national product. Within a decade, Khruschev boasted in the 1960s, the Soviet economy would surpass the American. The stress on heavy industry and on military expenditures meant, of course, continuing privation for the ordinary citizen and the emphasis on quantitative production concealed deep flaws in the system as a whole.

Khruschev's most ambitious effort lay in agriculture, the weakest sector of the economy ever since Stalin's forced collectivization. He sought to bring under cultivation the "virgin lands" of Soviet Central Asia, in Kazakhstan and elsewhere, but crop failures thwarted the experiment. His reforms did little to alter the bureaucratized system of collective and state farms inherited from Stalin or inspire the collective farmers to increase their crops. For the party itself he unsuccessfully sought fixed terms of office for important party posts. Few of his reforms were acceptable to the government and party bureaucrats, the *apparatchki,* who saw their privileged positions threatened and who mustered opposition to his "hare-brained" schemes.

Khruschev pursued an erratic and truculent foreign policy. Proclaiming that war was not inevitable with the United States and other capitalist countries, he spoke of "peaceful coexistence," and relations for a time improved, as we shall see. But in 1960 he scuttled a summit meeting with Allied leaders and in 1962 overreached himself in the Cuban missile crisis.[29] He also clashed openly with Communist China. His boastfulness and recklessness, his retreat in Cuba, the failure of his agricultural and other economic policies, his attempt to tamper with

[29] See pp. 974–975.

the party itself led to his downfall. In 1964 he was ousted from all of his offices. He lived quietly in Moscow until his death in 1971. In the post-Stalin era, a reformer did not necessarily have to fear for his life, but there were clear limits to the reforms the party and bureaucracy would tolerate.

The Brezhnev Era

In replacing Khruschev in 1964, the party again attempted unsuccesssfully to separate the top government and party posts and to stress collective leadership. Leonid I. Brezhnev, who became party secretary, soon eclipsed all other colleagues. A tough-minded, colorless, and dour political personality, Brezhnev dominated the party and government for close to eighteen years. He repressed dissent at home and in Eastern Europe. The "thaw," incomplete as it was, ended. Physically incapacitated at the close of his tenure but still clinging to power, Brezhnev died in office in 1982. During his rule, he increased the country's military and naval strength but he also renewed efforts at détente with the West. The superficial stability of the Brezhnev years concealed social tensions and serious economic failures.

Yet the Brezhnev years began with a promise of reform. The party reversed some of Khruschev's policies but moved forward with others. While phasing out his regional economic councils, it tried to provide incentives for higher productivity in industry and agriculture. But the reforms, never far-reaching, aroused the opposition of the ever wary party and government bureaucracy, and were abandoned within a relatively short time.

A Troubled Economy and Society

Centralized planning for the economy, inaugurated by Stalin in 1928,[30] resumed after the war under the Fourth Five Year Plan (1946–1950) and subsequent plans. Wartime devastation was repaired and the economy grew impressively, even if not as rapidly as outsiders at the time were given to believe. Gross national product increased at a respectable annual rate. By the 1970s the Soviet Union was the world's leading producer of coal, steel, pig iron, cement, cotton, natural gas, and oil. It built defense industries and pioneered in space technology, and was one of the two nuclear superpowers of the world. Whereas in 1950 Soviet gross national product was only 30 percent of the American, in 1975 it was 60 percent. The Soviet Union appeared to be developing into a modern industrial society; many hoped that industrialization would lead it toward a more democratic society as well. But there were deep flaws in the system.

Rigid controls, concentration of expenditures and skills on heavy industry and armaments, and overall planning that virtually ignored consumer needs, all features of the Soviet economy since the 1930s, prevented any real advance in living standards. Conditions improved, to be sure, after 1950, and Soviet citizens enjoyed job security and a network of social services. Per capita consumption tripled; people were better clothed and ate a more varied diet; more refrigerators, more washing machines, and television sets were available in the 1970s than

---

[30] See pp. 762–770.

before. But consumer products were of shoddy quality; many items, including food, remained scarce; store shelves were empty; people spent long hours waiting in queues. Urban housing needs remained especially urgent. The intense demand for consumer goods encouraged a thriving black market and an underground economy.

All these problems were openly acknowledged, but efforts to remedy the situation would have required loosening party and governmental controls. Many years after the Revolution, despite industrialization and military strength that made it one of the world's two military superpowers, the Soviet citizen could purchase only two-fifths the goods and services that an American could, and living standards were below those of several of the satellite states in Eastern Europe.

The U.S.S.R. lagged in newer industrial technology. After the war it had restored its old factories, coal mines, steel mills, shipyards, and railroad network, but with the older technology of the 1930s. It was this obsolescent economy that expanded after the war at a time when the West, Japan, and other parts of East Asia were using computers, electronics, and automation. Only in military and space technology could the Soviets still marshal talents and resources for impressive projects. Otherwise central planning stifled initiative and entrepreneurship. From the late 1960s on, the U.S.S.R. encouraged foreign capital and Western industrial technology, but after 1974 the socialist countries, too, were caught up in the global economic recession. At the outset of the 1980s the Soviet economic growth rate dropped to 2 percent, then virtually to zero. The infrastructure fell into decay. The Soviet Union ranked as a formidable military and nuclear superpower but not as a modern industrial society. Official production targets were met at the sacrifice of quality. Support for improved technology, efficient management, and productivity, all spurred in open market economies by competition, lagged.

Agriculture persisted as the weakest part of the economy. Despite large investments in the 1970s, double those of the previous decade, and the creation of an artificial fertilizer industry, output did not increase. The much vaunted mechanization of the collective farms proved to be an illusion. Farm machinery was often poorly utilized and spare parts were unavailable. Poor roads made it difficult to transport farm products to markets or to processing plants. Meanwhile, in the 1970s, 15 million farm workers left the farms for the cities in search of better opportunities. Because the government decided to increase meat production, grain needs for livestock tripled between 1960 and 1980, adding further to the strain on agriculture. There were poor harvests as well. By 1980 domestic production of grain had fallen so far below government targets that for the next six years the government ceased publishing production figures. What began in the 1960s as the need to import grain intermittently became a permanent practice after 1972, with the United States one of the chief suppliers. The imports consumed foreign exchange that might otherwise have been available to purchase industrial machinery.

The Brezhnev regime refused to face the flawed economy realistically. Bribery, embezzlement of state funds, and corruption became widespread. For the average citizen life remained bleak. There was a sharp increase in drunkenness and absenteeism. Economic tinkering alone could not reverse the trend, but the entrenched party and government bureaucracy, the *nomenklatura,* the dignitaries in the party and government named to their posts by the party, rejected any reforms that might reduce their authority. An aging party and government elite controlled the country. From 1966 to 1985 three-fourths of the party's Central Committee were regularly and dutifully reelected. From 1975 on, when Brezhnev suffered a stroke, a small clique around him made the important decisions. When he became further incapitated in the next few years, the same sycophantic circle continued to project the image of the strong leader, shielding him, inflating his merits, showering him with decorations and medals, and building up a cult of adulation.

On the cultural front, a hard line prevailed. De-Stalinization ended. The regime clamped down on dissidents who, encouraged by the earlier relaxation of controls, pressed for greater freedom. Yet in spite of repression, the dissident movement grew. Never large in numbers, the dissidents represented the scientific and cultural leaders of the country—the intelligentsia. Underground journals appeared; privately-printed manuscripts (called *samizdat*) circulated secretly; scientists and other intellectuals signed open petitions of protest. Some fled abroad and others were expelled from the country. Solzhenitsyn was exiled for allowing the publication abroad of his book, *The Gulag Archipelago*, which described the network of forced labor camps in even more brutal detail than his earlier work. The nuclear physicist, Andrei Sakharov, for speaking up against the return to Stalinism, was removed from his work in Moscow and banished from the capital. Soviet Jews, chafing at the restrictions on their cultural and religious freedom, attempted to emigrate, and in the peak year 1979 over 50,000 left the country; but the rules soon changed, and in the early 1980s emigration was sharply reduced. The Brezhnev coterie also kept an iron grip on the East European satellites, as we shall see, and in 1979 the Soviets sent troops into Afghanistan to prop up a faltering Marxist regime, involving the country in what became a nine-year military misadventure.[31]

At great cost to an already strained economy, the Brezhnev regime directed vast expenditures into a defense program designed to achieve parity with the United States in strategic arms and to build a modern navy. The United States in turn responded with its own build-up and the arms race escalated. In other ways the regime made efforts to relax tensions with the West. The Soviets joined in the European Economic and Security Conference at Helsinki in 1975 and signed the Helsinki accords, pledging peace, cooperation, and respect for human rights. Strategic arms limitation talks with the United States resulted in the signing of a treaty in 1979. But the brief period of détente soon ended and in the early 1980s the Cold War entered a more intense phase.[32]

When Brezhnev died in 1982, the cult of Brezhnev disappeared overnight. There had been little enthusiasm for him or for the small circle that surrounded him. The Brezhnev years, it was widely acknowledged, had led to stagnation, an unwillingness to address the growing problems of the economy, repression in Eastern Europe, and an unpopular war in Afghanistan. Although the country no

[31] See pp. 992–993.
[32] See pp. 996–997.

longer had the Stalinist terror to fear, repression and abuse of authority continued in the party-dominated police state.

Brezhnev's Successors: Andropov and Chernenko

In choosing Yuri V. Andropov as Brezhnev's immediate successor in 1982, the party leadership conceded the need for change. Although Andropov had headed the state security police for fifteen years, he had curbed some of its arbitrary powers. As head of the KGB, he had been in a unique position to appreciate the true state of Soviet society and the economy. He brought economists and other specialists to Moscow to assist him. Publicly he inveighed against the corruption of party and government officials, dismissed some of the old guard, and pledged incentives and rewards for farm and factory workers. Andropov might have changed matters, but for a good part of his brief fifteen-month tenure he was incapacitated by illness and died in office. The Politburo, determined to avoid further change, chose as his successor Konstantin U. Chernenko, who had been a close associate of Brezhnev. Ironically, he, too, was aging and ill at the time of his selection. He took no new initiatives. The party and country seemed to be marking time while economic problems worsened, the war dragged on in Afghanistan, and the arms race continued. By the end of 1984 Chernenko, terminally ill, made no further public appearances and died in March 1985. His successor was to open a new era in Soviet history.[33]

Eastern Europe: The Decades of Dictatorship

Although nothing like the Russian Revolution of 1917[34] erupted in Europe after the Second World War, communism made dramatic advances in Central and Eastern Europe, not through popular revolution but through the Red Army's military presence and the support given to local Communist leaders. The revolutionary flare-ups in Europe after the First World War had flickered out,[35] but with the Second World War eleven European states and 100 million Europeans fell under Communist-style governments. The areas considered in 1919 to be a protective buffer against Bolshevism were now under Communist domination. An "iron curtain," as Churchill said, had descended, roughly along the old Elbe-Trieste line, sharpening the centuries-old divergencies in the development of Western and Eastern Europe.[36]

In 1939, even before the U.S.S.R. was at war, the three Baltic states Estonia, Latvia, and Lithuania came under Soviet control under the terms of the Nazi-Soviet pact, and in 1940 they were incorporated into the U.S.S.R. as Soviet socialist republics. Later in the sweep of military operations during the last months of the war Poland, Hungary, Romania, Bulgaria, and Czechoslovakia fell into the orbit of Soviet influence. In all these states, which the West came to

[33] See pp. 1002–1008.
[34] See pp. 722, 746–754.
[35] See p. 779.
[36] See pp. 125–126, 210–249, 585–586, 781–783, and map, p. 212.

call satellites, Communist-dominated coalition governments took control. East Germany, initially part of the joint Allied occupation of Germany, was shaped into a sixth Soviet satellite as the German Democratic Republic. Yugoslavia and Albania, liberated by their own partisan leaders rather than by the Red Army, were governed by Communist regimes but with looser ties to the Soviet Union and soon broke with the Soviets. Despite its defeat in the Soviet-Finnish War in 1940, Finland escaped Communist domination. Accepting its wartime territorial losses, it maintained its independence by a cautious neutrality in foreign policy and a discreetly correct relationship with the Soviets. Austria, after a decade of joint occupation by the four Allied powers, gained independence as a neutral state in 1955.

Consolidation of Communist Control

The Soviets consolidated control in Eastern Europe in stages. In Poland, Bulgaria, Romania, and Hungary, Soviet military occupation made it possible for local Communist leaders, many trained in Moscow and returning from exile, to dominate left coalition governments. In Bulgaria, Communist domination was complete from the beginning. In the case of Poland, Western pressure at Yalta and Potsdam forced the Soviets to give representation to the government-in-exile in London; the leader of the agrarian party returned to Poland to serve for a time as deputy premier. In the early coalition governments, the Communists shared power but held the key ministries of interior, propaganda, and justice, and controlled the police, the army, and the courts. Individuals alleged to have been "fascist" or to have collaborated with the Nazis were barred from public life and from voting; the loose definition of "fascist" and "reactionary" barred many who were only anti-Communist. In the first elections, in Poland and elsewhere, purges and disfranchisement made a mockery of Stalin's pledge at Yalta to hold free and unfettered elections in Eastern Europe. Protests by the United States and Great Britain only hardened the Soviet position.

The new regimes confiscated and redistributed large estates and put uncultivated land to use, so that 3 million peasant families acquired about 6 million acres of land; the agrarian reforms were the final blow to the landed aristocracy that had once ruled in Eastern Europe.[37] They also nationalized the economy. As they struggled with postwar reconstruction, the new regimes, as noted earlier, lent a sympathetic ear to the American invitation in 1947 to accept Marshall Plan aid. But Stalin was not disposed to permit the East European countries to drift into the Western economic orbit, nor did he view favorably the growing pressure for free elections in which the Communists could lose their hold. After the summer of 1947, wherever non-Communists were still strong, the Communists ousted their political rivals and banned or reduced to impotence all other political parties. In Czechoslovakia, as we have seen, the coalition government lasted longer than elsewhere but fell victim to a Communist coup in February 1948.

With the Communists in control, the leaders of the opposition political parties were forced into flight, imprisoned, or in other ways silenced. The new regimes, most notably in Poland and Hungary, clashed also with the Catholic Church;

high-ranking prelates were denounced, brought to public trial and imprisoned, and church property confiscated. The Communist leaders themselves soon became Stalin's victims. From 1949 to 1953, reflecting the repression in the Soviet Union in Stalin's last years, purges, arrests, trials, confessions, and executions occurred in the highest ranks of each party. Leaders were accused of nationalist deviations and of conspiring with Tito, the independent-minded Communist leader of Yugoslavia.

After the consolidation of Communist power in the new "people's democracies" steps were taken to collectivize agriculture, with uneven results. In Bulgaria, the most docile of the satellites, over half the arable land was collectivized, but in Hungary only about a third. In Poland, where resistance was strongest, collectivization was halted after a short time, and most of the land remained in private possession. The collectivization process delayed the postwar recovery of Eastern Europe. Agriculture in the people's republics, as in the Soviet Union, remained the weakest part of the economy. Peasants diligently cultivated the land permitted them individually but worked reluctantly on the large collectives.

Under Soviet-style centrally planned economies and five-year plans, the East European countries industrialized. Poland and Hungary, agricultural before the war, became industrial states; Czechoslovakia and East Germany, already industrial, expanded their manufacturing base. But as a result of the emphasis on heavy industry to the neglect of consumer goods, and pressures to complement the economy of the Soviet Union, industrialization brought only slow improvement in East European living standards.

The Soviets formalized their economic relationship with East Europe through the Council for Mutual Economic Assistance (COMECON), established in 1949 in reaction to the integration of Western Europe accompanying the Marshall Plan, but it never worked as cooperation among equals. The Soviets provided low-cost raw materials and oil and offered a large market for East European goods, regardless of their quality, but much of the economic cooperation principally benefited the Soviet Union. The Warsaw Pact, signed in 1955, brought the six East European countries together into a mutual defense alliance. Large numbers of Soviet troops remained stationed in Eastern Europe, mainly in East Germany.

In the early postwar years, Yugoslavia, freed from the Nazis largely by its own partisan armies, made a remarkable show of resistance to the Soviets. The Yugoslav Communist leader, Marshal Tito, loosened centralized controls over the economy, abandoned the collectivization of agriculture, pursued an independent foreign policy, and openly defied Moscow. The Soviet leadership denounced him but after Stalin's death sought to woo him back to the fold. The first major Communist figure to declare his independence of Moscow, Tito established a model that other Communist leaders and parties would later follow.

Ferment and Repression in East Germany, Poland, and Hungary, 1953–1956

The changes in the Soviet Union after Stalin's death directly affected the Soviet satellites. The East Europeans chafed at land collectivization, forced industrialization, austere living standards, subservience to the Soviet Union, and harsh rule by Stalinist-type leaders who remained in power for years after Stalin's death. An initial outburst, riots in East Berlin in June 1953, was quickly suppressed. The ferment rose to the surface after Khrushchev denounced the brutal character of the Stalin dictatorship and, in an attempt to win back Yugoslavia, made the official concession that "different roads to socialism" were possible. That concession and his "de-Stalinization" speech in 1956 opened a Pandora's box; destroying Stalin's infallibility destroyed Soviet infallibility as well.

In 1956, open revolt broke out in Poland and Hungary, led by the East European Communist party leaders themselves. In Poland, where national sentiment and religious attachments ran deep, pressures for internal freedom and for independence from Moscow led to riots and demonstrations. The unrest brought to power the Communist leader Wladyslaw Gomulka, who had at one time been discredited and even imprisoned for his nationalist deviationism. Gomulka relaxed political and economic controls, halted collectivization of the farms, improved relations with the Catholic church, and took steps to loosen the bonds to Moscow. The country as a whole saw him as an alternative to direct Soviet control. Khruschev threatened military action, but then backed down. For a few years, Gomulka curbed police terror and created a freer atmosphere, but the reform era was short-lived.[38]

In Hungary, in 1956, events took a tragic turn. When news of Gomulka's success in Poland reached Budapest, demonstrations broke out; young rioters even toppled a statue of Stalin. The reform-minded Communist leader Imre Nagy, who had earlier been driven from the premiership in 1955 for his efforts at liberalization, returned to power. His reform program and release of political prisoners ignited pressures for democratization, parliamentary government, and the severance of ties to Moscow. The Soviets took alarm. They forced the party leadership to remove Nagy from power and to replace him with Janos Kadar, a leader more subservient to Moscow, who accepted Soviet intervention. Khruschev dispatched troops, tanks, and artillery to suppress the "counterrevolution," as the Soviets termed it, and forcefully reestablished Communist rule. Severe reprisals followed. Nagy himself was imprisoned, then tried and hanged, and his body thrown into a mass grave. In the wake of the repression, 200,000 Hungarians fled into exile, mainly to the United States, more than at any time since the crushing of the European revolutions of 1848–1849.[39] The Soviet tanks in Budapest destroyed any remaining illusions about the benevolence and liberalism of Stalin's successors and shook the Communist faithful in Western Europe and elsewhere.

The 1960s: The "Prague Spring"

Despite the failure of the Hungarian uprising, the longing for liberalization and independence refused to be suppressed. In Hungary, once the regime was preserved, even Kadar, who remained in power for the next three decades, created a freer cultural and intellectual atmosphere and loosened economic controls. In Poland the church retained a powerful hold on the population, an

[38] See pp. 972, 1009.
[39] See pp. 512–513, 519.

unofficial culture flourished, and agitation grew in the cities and countryside. In Romania, Nicolae Ceausescu took over as party leader in 1964 and ruled through a harsh personal dictatorship; yet the Romanian leader asserted his independence of the Soviets in foreign affairs and resisted pressures for tighter economic integration into the Soviet economy.

In Czechoslovakia in the 1960s the internal reforms went furthest and posed the most direct challenge to the Soviets. The reform movement climaxed in 1968 when Alexander Dubcek, who spoke openly of "communism with a human face," emerged as party and government leader. Dubcek curbed police repression, permitted freedom of the press, democratized the government, and legalized non-Communist political organizations. Compatriots and outsiders alike hailed the "Prague spring." For Brezhnev, who had displaced Khruschev in 1964, and the Soviet leadership, such far-reaching reforms represented a threat to the Soviet grip on Eastern Europe. In August 1968 they ended the "Prague spring." Brezhnev dispatched 250,000 troops, including token Polish, Hungarian, Bulgarian, and East German contingents to crush the incipient revolution. The hapless Czechs, stunned and infuriated, were forced to restore Communist party control, remove Dubcek, reimpose censorship, and curb democratization. Reprisals followed and the new leadership imposed severe dictatorial controls. Once again the Soviets had crushed a "counterrevolution." The Soviets served notice that under the "Brezhnev Doctrine" (as it came to be called) they reserved the right to intervene if a socialist regime was threatened anywhere. They served notice also of the limits to which they would tolerate freedom and independence in central and eastern Europe. The events in Prague in 1968, even more than the suppression of the 1956 Hungarian uprising, alienated the Communist faithful in many parts of the world.

In the Era of Détente

By the 1960s, despite the continuing political repression, a rural, agrarian Eastern Europe was being shaped into an urban, industrial society. Consumer goods were scarce but in greater supply, and in the case of East Germany, Czechoslovakia, and Hungary, more abundant than in the Soviet Union itself. Hungary pioneered in introducing elements of a market economy and in encouraging a consumer society—"goulash communism," it was called. The German Democratic Republic, although small in population, with no more than 17 million people, emerged as one of the world's ten leading industrial powers. Poland's economy grew, in spite of many strains and scarcities. In the 1960s and early 1970s, the satellites all enjoyed moderate rates of economic growth, but mainly in the old-line industries. In the 1970s, the East European countries sought and obtained private investment capital and advanced technology from the West, linking themselves to the world economy. All of the states, including the Soviet Union, traded with countries outside the Soviet sphere, borrowed capital, and encouraged tourism. The value of trade between the Soviet bloc and the outside world increased fourfold. But the East European states, especially Poland, became heavily indebted to the West and the prospects of a continuing expansion of trade faded with the onset of the world economic slowdown in 1974.[40] Export markets shrank and the East Europeans found it difficult to meet even the interest payments on their debts. From the mid-1970s on, Eastern Europe, like the Soviet Union, entered a period of retrenchment, economic stagnation, and deteriorating living conditions.

114. The Communist World: The People's Republic of China

The Civil War

The proclamation in October 1949 of the People's Republic of China by the Chinese Communists, the final episode in the long civil war between the Nationalists and the Communists, was among the most momentous of events shaping the postwar world.

The civil war had gone on intermittently since 1927.[41] An uneasy alliance, formed in 1937 to fight the Japanese, barely survived the war years. The People's Liberation (or Red) Army, although nominally under the command of Chiang Kai-shek and the Kuomintang, waged its own guerrilla warfare against the Japanese. The Nationalists, cut off by the Japanese from the urban centers of eastern China, suffered from chaotic economic conditions and uncontrolled inflation. Chiang's regime became increasingly corrupt, authoritarian, and repressive.

The victory over Japan in 1945 set the stage for renewed civil war. Nationalist troops, with United States aid, returned to eastern China. The Communists, moving out from their guerrilla bases, poured into the northern provinces and made contact with the Russians in Manchuria. They rejected the demand that they surrender the northern provinces, disband their army, and accept Nationalist political control. An American-sponsored truce temporarily halted hostilities, but when the U.S.S.R. withdrew from Manchuria in the spring of 1946 (after removing Manchurian industrial assets as reparations), Nationalists and Communists clashed over control of the border province. The Communists, for their part, were quite willing to plunge the country into civil war to achieve their ends; the Nationalists were bent on repressing all opposition, even non-Communist.

In the fighting from 1946 to 1949, the Nationalists, despite substantial financial and material support from the United States, lost ground steadily. By the autumn of 1949 the Communists had routed the Kuomintang armies. Chiang withdrew his shattered forces to the island of Taiwan (and to the lesser islands of Matsu and Quemoy) where he established a small but soon prospering Republic of China; until 1971 it continued to occupy the seat set aside for China in the United Nations.

[40] See p. 984.
[41] See pp. 796–797, 864.

The New Regime

For the next twenty-seven years, until his death in 1976, Mao Zedong, as uncontested head of the party, guided the destinies of the new state, officially named the People's Republic of China. For the first time since the Revolution of 1911, and indeed for generations before that, a unified central government controlled China, able to direct and mobilize the most populous nation in the world. Although the Chinese Communists were a small hardened group of successful Marxist-Leninist revolutionaries, they were not completely alien to the Chinese cultural tradition. They continued a long pattern of imperial bureaucratic government that stretched back three to four thousand years. Moreover, they articulated a widespread hostility to Western imperialism, which had all but carved their country to pieces in the nineteenth century,[42] and they inherited an ancient tradition of Chinese preeminence in the East Asian world. With traditional ways of life disrupted by decades of revolution, civil struggle, and the war against Japan, the Communists provided a surrogate for older Confucian values and set China on a modern path.

The Chinese Communists leaned heavily on Soviet experience. The party controlled each level of government and manipulated all organs of information and indoctrination. In the first few years, revolutionary excesses were committed and by Mao's own estimate, some 700,000 "counterrevolutionaries" lost their lives and countless others were sent to labor camps. In 1956, in a burst of enthusiasm for greater diversity and toleration, Mao proclaimed: "let a hundred flowers bloom, let a hundred schools of thought contend." But as soon as critics came forward, he quickly instituted a new period of repression that sent thousands, labeled "rightists," to forced labor camps.

The new regime mobilized the nation in order to rebuild the war-devastated economy and to transform the country into an industrial power. It nationalized the economy; eliminating the old landlord class in the countryside, it established agricultural cooperatives as a preliminary to collectivization. The country's initial Five-Year Plan, launched in 1953, concentrated on heavy industry and, with Soviet economic and technical assistance, recorded considerable success. Not all targets were reached, especially not in agriculture. The same floods and droughts that had troubled China for centuries refused to obey government decrees.

Impatient with the slow progress, Mao launched a radical plan in 1957, heralded as the "Great Leap Forward," designed to speed up economic change and quickly transform the country's industry and agriculture. The existing cooperatives were amalgamated into larger and more comprehensive collectivized units, or "people's communes." Planned as self-sufficient entities, tightly organized in military fashion in a hierarchy of production brigades, the communes became responsible for the mechanization of the farms along with the development of local rural industry. Communal kitchens, nurseries, and boarding schools left women freer to work on an equal basis in the fields and factories.

The "Great Leap Forward" turned into a disaster. Despite the image Mao had cultivated as the champion of the peasantry, he met immediate resistance from

---

[42] See pp. 674–681.

the countryside. The persistent opposition of the peasants and crop failures in the next two years brought a disastrous famine, which took millions of lives. The government retreated. Moderates came forward within the party to curb Mao's excessive zeal. Although the land remained collectivized, the more rigid and utopian aspects of the communal experiment were suspended. Farmers were even permitted to sell or barter a portion of their crops.

In contrast the industrial sector continued to grow. In the years before the Communist regime, annual steel production had never reached 1 million tons; by 1960 it exceeded 18 million. By 1960 China ranked among the top ten powers in the world in industrial output and had created an industrial base for further expansion. The government also marshaled the country's scientific and technological talents and successfully tested an atomic bomb in 1964 and a hydrogen bomb in 1967, and orbited space satellites in the 1970s.

The regime transformed life in many ways. Road, rail, and air transport physically unified the country. Impressive strides were made in public sanitation and public health, which received a high national priority. Labor gangs systematically drained and filled snail-infested canals, curbing the spread of diseases like schistosomiasis. The government made progress in overcoming illiteracy. It reformed and simplified the written Chinese language, and moved toward a single spoken tongue. It also adopted a new transliteration system for Chinese names spelled in the Roman alphabet.[43] Women, encouraged to reject traditional virtues of obedience and deference, received legal equality with men and could count on new opportunities. Old abuses like child marriage and concubinage were outlawed. More profoundly than the Russian, the Chinese Revolution refashioned the habits and ethos of a gigantic population, reaching remote villages and hamlets untouched for centuries. Within a generation an agrarian, semifeudal country was developing into a modern industrial society.

Suddenly, beginning in 1966, the country was convulsed by the Cultural Revolution, unleashed by Mao himself and his close associates. Fearful that the Revolution would not survive him, and that its purity was endangered, he called for a purge of the highest ranks of government and party, and for the removal of all those who had allegedly succumbed to bureaucratic routine or lacked the zeal to push on with the social revolution. He mobilized millions of students and other young people as Red Guards, or armed shock troops, to press the Maoist revolutionary cause. Converging on Beijing and other cities, they denounced bourgeois ways, attacked the vestiges of Western imperialist culture, and brutally harassed and humiliated government and party officials as well as cultural and educational leaders. When fanatical mobs threatened to tear the country apart, army leaders intervened with Mao and received his authorization to restore order.

The revolutionary turbulence continued, even if not at the same peak. Because Mao proclaimed the virtues of the land, white collar workers, students, professors, and party officials were forcibly sent off to the countryside to labor in the fields. The economy and the entire educational system broke down. By the time the

---

[43] The Pinyin (or phonetic) system, which more closely approximates Mandarin Chinese pronunciation, replaced the older Wade-Giles spelling in 1979. Mao Tse-tung is rendered as Mao Zedong, Peking as Beijing, Chou En-lai as Zhou Enlai, Teng Hsiao-p'ing as Deng Xiaoping, etc. For some older names like Sun Yat-sen or Chiang Kai-shek the original spellings are often retained; the older spellings for all names have been retained throughout the earlier pages of this book.

worst of the disturbances were over in 1969, hundreds of thousands of lives had been lost. Three million persons had been sent to labor camps or to work in the fields. Thousands of high-ranking officials in the government and party, including two-thirds of the party's central committee, had been purged. The impact of the Cultural Revolution lingered on and an authoritarian pall settled over the country.

The pragmatic and moderate Zhou Enlai, who had faithfully served Mao for many years as premier and foreign minister, and who might have been his successor, died early in 1976. A few months later, Mao died, long ailing and in his eighties. The Great Helmsman was widely mourned as the towering father of the Revolution for over half a century, and as one of the giant figures in the history of China. He had forged a revolutionary party and a revolutionary army, led the Long March,[44] fought the Japanese, defeated the Nationalists, and presided over a revolution that had unified, revitalized, and modernized the country. His theoretical teachings on the struggle against imperialism and on the vanguard role of the peasantry, and his practical successes in guerrilla warfare, influenced revolutionaries all over the world. His most famous precept, that "political power grows out of the barrel of a gun," reinforced revolutionary zeal everywhere. His homilies, published in a little red book called *The Living Thoughts of Chairman Mao*, were widely quoted and assiduously studied. Mao's revolution had brought equality for the peasants, technological progress, unity, and pride. But his radical experiments and the uncontrolled violence he had unleashed were costly. His successors tempered their praise for Mao, lauding his monumental achievements as a revolutionary leader, but criticizing him for his "grave blunders."

Foreign Affairs

The emergence of China as a second major Communist power undermined the ideological leadership of the Soviet Union. Although the Soviets had not always wholeheartedly supported the Chinese Communists in their civil war with the Kuomintang, once the Communist regime was established the U.S.S.R. surrendered to China the concessions it had acquired in Manchuria under the Yalta agreement.[45] For a time relations remained cool but correct, although Mao always resented being treated as a junior partner. In the 1950s the Chinese received military aid, capital loans, and technical assistance from the Soviets. The Korean War, in which Chinese troops fought the Americans as alien intruders who threatened their very borders, drew them close for a time to the Soviet Union. Western observers were convinced that a monolithic world communist movement existed. The Chinese Communists meanwhile bitterly resented American support for the regime in Taiwan and the continuing American effort to bar the People's Republic of China from the United Nations.

Although professing peace, China itself pursued an aggressive foreign policy. In 1950, pressing old Chinese claims of suzerainty and in the guise of liberating the country from clerical, i.e., Buddhist, despotism, China occupied Tibet and forcibly maintained its rule there over the years. Monasteries were closed; the Dalai Lama, the country's ruler was forced into exile; and large numbers of

[44] See p. 797.
[45] See p. 864.

Chinese arrived as settlers. In 1962 China clashed also with India, formerly one of its staunchest champions, in border disputes along India's northeastern frontier.

In the 1960s relations with the Soviet Union became strained. The two states hurled polemics at each other in their rivalry for ideological leadership and for control of the lands of inner Asia into which Russia had expanded in the age of the tsars. Mao accused Khruschev of pusillanimous behavior in the Cuban missile crisis of 1962. In 1972 the two countries clashed in armed conflict along the Ussuri River over border territory that divided Manchuria and Russia's maritime provinces, and they continued to confront one another with large armies in other border areas. While both countries supported North Vietnam in the Vietnam War, after the war China opposed the Soviet-backed intervention by Vietnam in Cambodia. Not until the 1980s was there a rapprochement and a promise of troop reductions along their borders.

With time relations with the United States improved. In 1971, when American objections were withdrawn, the People's Republic of China finally replaced Nationalist China in the United Nations and took a permanent seat on the Security Council. The following year the American president, Richard Nixon, paid a dramatic visit to China and was welcomed by Mao. Diplomatic channels opened up and relations were normalized. The Chinese People's Republic, despite domestic problems, was emerging as one of the great potential centers of global power. And in 1976 it was about to embark on an impressive new era of modernization under Mao's successor.

XXII.
EMPIRES INTO NATIONS: ASIA, AFRICA, THE MIDDLE EAST

OF ALL THE GREAT POLITICAL CHANGES in the history of the modern world, affecting hundreds of millions of people, nothing was more revolutionary, more dramatic, or more sudden than the end of the European overseas colonial empires. The German and Turkish empires disappeared with military defeat in the First World War, the Italian and the Japanese in the Second. But in 1945 the British, the French, the Dutch, the Belgians, and the Portuguese still governed large parts of the world's population.

Wartime ideology during the Second World War had reinforced nationalist agitation for independence and freedom. It was difficult to wage war in the name of self-determination and democracy, often with the colonial countries as allies, without strengthening the idea of freedom among subject peoples. After the war the Europeans learned that they could rule only at prohibitive military cost, and in blatant contradiction to their own professed ideals of self-government. Within two decades after 1945 the major European empires disappeared. In some instances the colonial powers, bowing to the pressures of nationalist agitation for independence, liquidated their colonial holdings without armed struggle, as in the British withdrawal from the Indian subcontinent in 1947. In others the European powers withdrew only after protracted bloody wars, as in the case of the Dutch in Indonesia, the French in Indochina and Algeria, and the Portuguese in Angola and Mozambique. The United States also played a part in the transformation; it gave independence to the Philippines, granted Puerto Rico commonwealth status, took in Alaska and Hawaii as equal members of the federal union, and surrendered its privileges in the Panama Canal Zone.

Chapter Emblem: The official symbol for the World Population Year, 1974.

The end of the colonial empires and the emergence of the new nations must count among the most far-reaching consequences of the two World Wars, and especially of the Second. But many of the new nations were nations only in a limited sense. They were sovereign and independent territorial entities, having definite boundaries, internationally recognized, and with seats in the United Nations, but many of them lacked the internal coherence and shared experience of nation-states in the older sense of the word.[1] Nor did nationhood for the most part bring democracy, civil rights, the rule of law, or even civilian predominance over the military.

115. End of the European Empires in Asia

End of the British Empire

The end in 1947 of British rule in India, the largest and most populous of all colonial areas ruled by Europeans, was epoch-making. The Indian National Congress, founded in 1885, grew in strength in the interwar years under the political and moral leadership of Gandhi and Nehru. The Congress party leaders, educated and affluent, demanded independence but wished also to avoid social revolution in the giant country. Along with the British-trained Indian civil service, they were well prepared to carry on the functions of an independent state.[2]

During the Second World War India supported the British, but at the same time Gandhi, Nehru, and the Congress party stepped up a "quit India" campaign. To retain Indian support in the war effort and to counter Japanese anti-Western propaganda, the British pledged independence. But the Muslim League, also founded before the First World War, claimed to speak, under Muhammad Ali Jinnah's leadership, for millions of Muslims unwilling to live in an India dominated by the Hindus and the Congress party, and insisted on its own national state, rooted in Islam. The Congress leadership pressed for a unified, secular India, with freedom of worship for all religions.

To end the impasse the British decided to partition the subcontinent. In 1947 they granted independence, as dominions, to two states: India, predominantly Hindu, with a population at that time of 350 million, which in 1950 formally became the Republic of India, and Pakistan, mainly Muslim, with a population of 75 million, which came to call itself the Islamic Republic of Pakistan. Because of the Muslim demographic concentration in the old empire, Pakistan was established in two disconnected parts, West and East Pakistan, separated by a thousand miles of Indian territory. Sixty million Muslims were left in India, which helped keep India a multireligious, secular state, as Gandhi and Nehru had desired.

Independence brought with it terrible communal riots between the Hindu and Muslim communities costing an estimated 1 million lives; 12 million Hindus and Muslims were caught up in turbulent mass expulsions and migrations. Gandhi was himself assassinated in 1948 by a Hindu fanatic, who resented his appeals

[1] See p. 543.
[2] See pp. 669–672, 793–794.

for reconciliation. Only after the uglier features of the communal warfare subsided, could the tasks of governing begin.

Nehru, who governed India as prime minister from 1947 until his death in 1964, set the country firmly on the course of parliamentary democracy, even though the Congress party remained the dominant political organization. The new government wrestled with the country's enormous problems of poverty, overpopulation, and linguistic, ethnic, and religious diversity. India remained on its democratic course except for a brief lapse in 1975–1977, when Nehru's daughter Indira Gandhi (unrelated to the founder of Indian nationalism), while prime minister, flouted constitutional government and was driven from office by an aroused opposition. A few years later, she returned to office and governed constitutionally until her assassination in 1984 by Sikh soldiers of her own bodyguard sympathetic to a Sikh secessionist movement in the Punjab. Her son, Rajiv Gandhi, who took office as a symbol of unity, governed, somewhat ineptly, for the next five years until the Congress party itself was ousted from office in national elections in 1989, after over forty years in power.

Nehru, who believed that economic planning and government controls were necessary for an underdeveloped country like India with its vast and heterogeneous population, laid the foundations for a moderate, flexible socialism and a mixed economy. The country made impressive progress. A modern industrial India took shape and it came to be ranked as the eighth largest industrial nation of the world. In 1974 India demonstrated its scientific and technological prowess when it developed a nuclear bomb. Agricultural production rose, so that by the late 1970s the country was exporting grain and other agricultural products; between 1965 and 1983 it tripled its wheat harvest. When in the 1980s economic growth slowed down, the government, without abandoning the nationalized sector, moved toward a market economy and encouraged additional private investment.

India remained a land of contradictions. Poverty persisted. Rising consumer standards barely affected nine-tenths of the population, and per capita income in the early 1990s was still no more than $250 a year. The masses of the population in village India remained impoverished, illiteracy remained high, and the caste system persisted. The cities were congested and slum-ridden. The most serious problem was population growth. Population more than doubled in the first forty years after independence and threatened to outstrip economic advances. Demographers predicted that India, with over 850 million people in 1990 and an annual growth rate of over 2 percent, could overtake China as the world's most populous nation. Sporadic government efforts to promote birth control were ineffective.

In the postcolonial era, India was unique. Constitutional government and parliamentary democracy succeeded as nowhere else among the new nations. Although beset by ethnic and other antagonisms, it did not abandon its democratic processes. In foreign affairs Nehru's policy of neutralism and nonalignment in the Cold War, clearly articulated at the Bandung conference of emergent Asian and African nations in 1955, found a responsive chord in many parts of the Third World. Although Nehru initially championed the People's Republic of China and its right to pursue its own path of social development, he opposed the Chinese occupation of Tibet in 1950; moreover, open fighting broke out between India and China in 1962 over border disputes. India quarreled with Pakistan and twice went to war over the border territory of Kashmir, which remained in dispute even in later years, and over the emergence of Bangladesh. It intervened with troops in Sri Lanka (as Ceylon came to be called in 1972) to mediate ethnic violence in its small island neighbor to the south, which had also received independence, in 1948, from Britain.

In Pakistan the independence leader, Jinnah, died shortly after independence and his successor was assassinated. Despite efforts to establish a parliamentary democracy, the country succumbed to military dictatorship within a decade. Authoritarian governments pressed forward with agricultural reform and industrialization, and an industrial Pakistan also took shape. Its awkward territorial arrangement did not last. In East Pakistan, carved out of the old state of Bengal, more than half the population lived in a crowded area one-sixth the size of West Pakistan, where the federal government was located. In 1971 political and social resentments exploded into secession and civil war. When the leaders of East Pakistan proclaimed a new state of Bangladesh (or ''Bengali nation''), the Pakistani government dispatched a large army to suppress the rebellion and killed hundreds of thousands in the unequal civil war. The secession would have failed except that India massively intervened, defeated the Pakistani army, and compelled the recognition of Bangladesh. It was one of the few secessionist movements that succeeded in the postcolonial world. The Indian subcontinent was now divided into three large nations. Bangladesh remained impoverished, one of the poorest and most densely populated nations in the world, with a rapidly growing population of over 110 million in 1990, subject not only to natural disasters like floods, drought, and famine but to political violence, assassinations, and military coups.

In Pakistan, civilian rule was briefly restored under the presidency of Ali Bhutto, but in 1977 General Zia took power and imprisoned and executed the president. Only after Zia's death in an airplane crash in 1988, were democratic elections held. Benazir Bhutto, the Western-educated daughter of the former president, returned from exile, won the election, and became the first woman to become prime minister of an Islamic nation, with the high promise of liberalization and modernization. But fundamentalist and military pressures brought her downfall within two years. The continuing quarrel with India over Kashmir was especially worrisome because both countries had a nuclear capacity.

Burma (which in 1989 renamed itself Myanmar) became independent in 1948 and followed a course of its own. From the outset the military exercised a parallel power with the authorities established by the democratic constitution. The country embarked on the ''Burmese road to socialism,'' nationalizing all industry and agriculture and virtually cutting itself off from the outside world. The result was isolation, poverty, and continued civil war. Not until the late 1980s did a democratic movement sweep the country, try to end the ''constitutional dictatorship,'' and press for a transition to democracy.

To the south, in the Malayan peninsula, the British united its various dependencies after the war but independence was delayed for a decade because of tensions among the Malays, ethnic Chinese, Indians, and others, as well as by a mostly Chinese-led Communist insurgency which the British stubbornly fought for years. In 1957 Britain granted independence to Malaya, which shortly thereafter joined with Singapore and other small former British dependencies to form the Federation of Malaysia. Singapore withdrew from the federation in 1965 to become a small thriving island nation on its own. Malaysia remained troubled by ethnic antagonisms but nonetheless developed a prospering economy.

The New Commonwealth

The British empire in Asia was gone, but most of its former members in Asia (as well as in Africa, the Caribbean, and the Pacific), even after becoming independent, retained a voluntary association with the Commonwealth of Nations, as the British Commonwealth was now called. The adherence of the newly independent states made the Commonwealth an even more flexible institution than it had been.[3] It grew into an association of close to fifty independent communities which accepted the British sovereign as symbolic head of the Commonwealth and agreed to consult, though not necessarily act in concert, on matters of common concern. Although the new members of the Commonwealth lacked the ties that bound Australians, New Zealanders, and Canadians to Britain in the old "white" Commonwealth, the new Commonwealth helped to transmit Western technology, political institutions, and economic aid to parts of the world as far flung as the British empire had once been, and promoted Western and non-Western interaction. Not all the former members of the British empire joined or stayed in the Commonwealth. Burma from the beginning chose to remain outside, and as the years went by, the Commonwealth lost Ireland in 1949, South Africa in 1969, and Pakistan in 1975.

The Dutch Empire: Indonesia

Another great empire in the East, the Netherlands Indies,[4] also came to an end, but not without bloodshed. As elsewhere in Asia, the Japanese during the war exploited anti-Western sentiments and even found nationalist leaders to use as collaborators in their occupation, but at the same time a broad resistance movement emerged in which the Communists played a major role. Once the Japanese were ousted at the war's end, and before the Dutch could return, the Indonesian nationalist leader Sukarno (Indonesians use only their family name in public life) proclaimed the country's independence. When the Dutch returned, they fought the nationalist movement intermittently but stubbornly for four years, until in 1949 they formally ceded independence.

Sukarno, who retained power over the next two decades, governed dictatorially under a policy variously called "guided democracy" and "Indonesian socialism," which brought little improvement to the country. For a time he managed to control the large Indonesian Communist party, which, backed by the People's Republic of China, grew in numbers and influence and in 1965 attempted a coup. An army leader, General Suharto, suppressed the rebellion, ousted Sukarno, and permitted the slaughter by Islamic fundamentalists of thousands of Communists and others accused of leftist sympathies. Suharto retained power over the years under a system of controlled elections, moved the country closer to the West,

---

[3] See pp. 813–814.
[4] See pp. 669–670.

encouraged foreign investment, and with considerable success promoted economic modernization.

Here too, rapid population growth imposed continuing pressure on the economy. In the four decades after independence the population doubled to an estimated 190 million, the fifth most populous country in the world. In Indonesia, as in Malaysia, Singapore, Taiwan, and other parts of Asia, there was often no absolute repression, but no genuine democracy either. Under authoritarian regimes, the ruler or dominant ruling group coopted all political parties under the umbrella of national unity, and discouraged militant opposition or open dissent.

End of the French Colonial Empire: Indochina

The French colonial empire also fell apart, here, too, not without a struggle. The first of France's postwar colonial wars was fought over Indochina. When France offered autonomy to the states of Indochina at the end of the Second World War within a continuing French federation, Cambodia and Laos accepted, but Vietnam (as Cochin-China, Tonkin, and Annam had jointly come to be called) demanded full independence. Open warfare broke out in 1946. French armies and Communist-led Vietnamese forces fought each other for the next seven and a half years.

The Communist leader Ho Chi Minh, who headed the independence movement in Vietnam, had spent many earlier years in London, Paris (where he helped found the French Communist party in 1920), and Moscow. Returning to Vietnam in 1941 to organize guerrilla warfare against the Japanese, he proclaimed at the war's end an independent republic of Vietnam with Hanoi as its capital. The returning French, willing to concede autonomy but not independence, tried at first to reassert control over the country by using an ineffectual former emperor of Annam as a puppet. When negotiations failed and fighting began at the end of 1946, Ho used his guerrilla armies against the French. Because the Communists led the independence movement, the French could claim that they were fighting to stem the tide of world communism, not to preserve nineteenth-century colonial privileges. Yet communism in Asia was often linked to nationalism, anticolonialism and anti-Westernism, and genuine popular discontent.

The United States, anticolonial but ready to champion anti-Communist causes in the Cold War, aided the French financially, but President Eisenhower refrained from open military intervention. The war meanwhile severely drained French morale and resources. In the spring of 1954 an international conference of the major powers met in Geneva to arrange, among other matters, a settlement in French Indochina. At the very time that the conference met, the French army, after a long, costly siege, suffered a severe defeat at the battle of Dien Bien Phu. The conference, with French acquiescence, recognized the independence of Vietnam, as well as of Cambodia and Laos. The colonial empire in French Indochina thus came to an end. Under the agreement, Vietnam was provisionally partitioned at the seventeenth parallel into a northern and southern sector until elections could be held for the entire country. Neither Ho nor the Western-backed regime in the south was satisfied with this decision and the settlement of 1954 was short-lived. A civil war of ever-increasing intensity broke out, in which the

United States from the early 1960s on became deeply involved. That story is recounted elsewhere.[5]

The Americans and the Philippines

The Americans, too, shared in the liquidation of colonial empires in Asia. The United States, which had granted self-governing commonwealth status to the Philippines in 1934 as a first step, granted full independence in 1946. The Philippines retained close economic and military ties with the United States. A succession of repressive governments did little to help the lot of the impoverished peasants, curb the power of the landholding elite, or suppress political disorder. For over twenty years Ferdinand Marcos, elected president in 1965, governed virtually as a dictator, with American acquiescence. The assassination in 1983 of an opposition leader, Benigno Aquino, sparked a widespread opposition movement that, in 1986, forced Marcos into exile. His successor, Corazón Aquino, widow of the martyred opposition leader, faced continuing opposition and revolutionary pressures from the right and the left but restored democracy and civil rights, and slowly inaugurated land and other reforms.

116. The African Revolution

Africa is a large continent, considerably larger than North and Central America combined. With an estimated population of 220 million in 1950 and 650 million in the early 1990s, it has one of the fastest growing populations in the world. North Africa, stretching from Morocco to Egypt, Muslim and Arab, belongs also to the Mediterranean world and, even more, to the Islamic Middle East in racial composition, culture, geography, and history. South of the Sahara is black Africa, where Islam, Christianity, and various traditional African animist faiths are found. An ethnic and linguistic map of black Africa would reveal hundreds of different ethnic concentrations and over 100 major (and many more minor) languages, but a great many Africans, since the colonial era, also speak English or French. In some areas there has been substantial settlement by Europeans, most notably at the southern end of the continent.

Politically, in 1945, and even in 1950, the map of Africa was scarcely different from what it had been in 1914. All of Africa was European-governed with the three exceptions of Egypt, Liberia, and Ethiopia (which had regained its independence from Italy during the war).[6] Yet by the early 1960s, most of Africa was independent or close to achieving independence. By 1980, when Zimbabwe (formerly British Southern Rhodesia) became independent, there were fifty-one independent sovereign states in Africa; in 1990, with the independence of Namibia (once German Southwest Africa), there were fifty-two. They made up close to a third of the membership of the United Nations. The new states differed from the older European nations in many ways. Because African geographical boundaries

[5] See pp. 975–979.
[6] See pp. 662–669, 813, 837, 853.

had been drawn, often arbitrarily, by the European colonial powers, the new
states contained within their borders diverse ethnic and linguistic groups, many
antagonistic to each other, and related peoples were often distributed over two
or more of the new countries. The African states had less of a unified national
heritage than older nations in Europe and elsewhere. Once the African states
obtained independence, they rapidly assumed the full panoply of national
sovereignty but faced the need to weld their disparate peoples into nationhood.

CONTEMPORARY AFRICA

This map should be compared with those for Precolonial Africa (p. 665) and for Africa
in 1914 at the height of European colonialism (p. 667). The first of the new states (except
Libya) was Ghana, the former British Gold Coast, which became independent in 1957
and took its name from a medieval African kingdom that had been located further north.
The following decades saw the independence of Algeria and of numerous republics in
black Africa in place of the French, British, Belgian, and Portuguese colonial empires.

French North Africa: The French-Algerian War

The decision by the wartime Allies in 1951 to grant independence to the former Italian colony of Libya, along with agitation for the British to end the vestiges of their control in Egypt, galvanized all of French North Africa into action. (More will be said of Libya and Egypt in our discussion of the Middle East.) Arab nationalist leaders in Morocco, Tunisia, and Algeria—the Maghreb, as these Arab states of northwest Africa are called—now mounted a vigorous campaign for independence. Morocco and Tunisia were not outright colonies but protectorates under their traditional rulers, the Moroccan sultan and the Tunisian bey.[7] After the failure of various concessions and maneuvers, the French in 1956 granted independence to the two countries. The Moroccan sultan became king, with the trappings of a constitutional monarchy, but the monarchy supervised both spiritual and temporal life and allowed little dissent or dilution of its authoritarian powers. Tunisia became a republic and was governed by its first president, Habib Bourguiba, under a one-party regime for thirty years. In both countries modernization and pressures for liberalization continued, often against counterpressures from traditionalists.

Algeria, a French colony since the 1830s, the French considered an integral part of France. It was represented in the French legislature like any constituency of metropolitan France, except that the vote for its representatives was heavily weighted in favor of the European settlers and to the disadvantage of the Arab majority. Of the 9 million inhabitants, at least 1 million were European settlers, or *colons,* mostly French who, like the family of the French writer Albert Camus, had lived there for generations. Since the Europeans controlled the economy and owned most of the land and industry, they feared for their political and economic privileges if Algeria were cut loose from France and governed by an Arab majority smarting from years of unequal treatment. At a moment when France and the French army had barely recovered from the disastrous rout in Indochina, revolt broke out in the autumn of 1954.

The French-Algerian war lasted seven and a half years, involving 500,000 French troops at its peak, and costing close to a million lives. The Algerian Liberation Front received aid and support from Egypt and other sympathetic Arab states. Torture and cruelty were common on both sides; the violence spread to Paris as extremist Algerians attacked moderates. The French were confronted with a choice of losing Algeria or of continuing to bear the military, financial, and moral strain of a divisive colonial war. In the midst of a cabinet crisis in Paris, an insurrection in May 1958, led by die-hard settlers and army leaders in Algiers, brought General Charles de Gaulle to power,[8] who, the army leaders were convinced, would press on with the war. But de Gaulle soon spoke of autonomy and self-determination for the Algerians once a truce had been arranged, and in 1961 he won the backing of the French electorate for full independence. Army leaders rebelled, and some of his closest former associates helped form a secret army of terrorists, who bombed and killed, and even attempted his assassination, but in 1962 French rule ended. After independence there was a

[7] See pp. 661, 698–700.
[8] See p. 890.

mass exodus of Europeans from Algeria, but most of the French and Algerians were grateful that de Gaulle had ended the ordeal. The French accepted the loss of Algeria, and soon other parts of their empire, and with a prospering economy turned their attention to other matters. Algeria came to be governed by a military-supported one-party dictatorship. Yielding to mass pressure which mounted in the 1980s, the National Liberation Front, the governing party, finally agreed to multiparty elections, which in 1990 resulted in a substantial victory for Islamic fundamentalists opposed to the secular regime.

Oil revenues for a time provided a measure of prosperity, but when oil revenues dropped, unemployment and debt mounted. Over 2 million Algerians migrated in search of jobs, mainly to France. Relations with France after independence grew friendly. The French provided technical assistance for the joint exploration of Algerian oil and natural gas resources. The presence of large numbers of Algerians in Paris and other French cities created friction, but the bitterness of the French-Algerian war itself faded.

End of British Rule: West Africa

In North Africa, as in Asia, nationalist agitation for independence, already under way in the interwar years,[9] might have been expected. In Africa south of the Sahara the movement for liberation was never as far advanced and the pace of independence after the Second World War was breathtaking. Here black populations lived in colonial empires carved out by the Europeans either in the colonial age that had opened in the fifteenth century or in the brief decade and a half after 1885 of European imperialist competition.[10]

Independence movements, barely in existence earlier, now made their presence felt. In their colonies the British first resisted the mounting nationalist pressures, imprisoning or exiling nationalist leaders, but then yielded. Compelled earlier to dissolve their Indian empire, and to cut military and imperial commitments, they gave way in Africa too. They first provided broader African representation in the colonial legislative assemblies, then granted autonomy and independence to the colonies as dominions, and in short order the dominions became independent republics.

The Gold Coast (Ghana) became the first British colony to achieve independence. The British initially resisted a militant civil disobedience movement led by the British- and American-educated Kwame Nkrumah. When they conceded self-government, they freed the imprisoned Nkrumah, and he became prime minister. In 1957 the British granted the colony dominion status, and in 1960 it became an independent republic. Nkrumah was elected president. With independence, the country shed a name identified with centuries of imperialist exploitation and called itself Ghana, recalling an African kingdom somewhat to the north, which had flourished from the sixth century to the eleventh century in the European Middle Ages. The immensely popular Nkrumah gathered extensive power into his own hands, banned opposition parties, and governed for close to

---

[9] For Asia see pp. 788–799.
[10] See pp. 107–114, 662–669.

ten years as a dictator. In Africa (and in Asia) the charismatic nationalist leaders upon whom the colonial countries relied in their struggle for independence often turned into personal dictators once independence was won, and the party of the independence movement often became the sole legal party. In 1966 Nkrumah's arbitrary rule, unbridled public and private extravagances, and cult of personality led to his overthrow by military leaders; a series of other coups followed. In 1979, a junior officer, Flight Lieutenant Jerry Rawlings, after an unsuccessful effort to restore civilian government, reimposed a military dictatorship, which continued to govern the country for many years.

Nkrumah introduced, and his successors continued, "African socialism," placing the economy under rigorous state control. In these new forms of socialism in Asia, Africa, and the Middle East, the state ran the economy, but ruling elites retained power and wealth and the bureaucracy expanded. There was little of the egalitarianism promised by earlier socialism. Once prosperous with abundant natural resources, the world's largest producer of cocoa and the source of a tenth of the world's gold, the Ghanaian economy steadily declined in the years after independence and the country became heavily dependent on foreign loans. In the mid-1980s, as elsewhere, the emphasis on state socialism waned. The government liquidated a large number of state enterprises, sold them to private investors, and encouraged a profit incentive in industry and agriculture. With financial assistance from the World Bank and with market-oriented reforms, economic growth slowly resumed, but there was little change in the authoritarian political system.

Nigeria was the largest British-governed territory in Africa and the most populous country in all Africa (in 1990 it had a population close to 120 million). It encompassed over 200 ethnic groups, the largest of which were the Hausa and Fulani in the north, Islamic in religion, and the Yoruba and Ibo, mainly Christian, in the south. As pressures for independence increased, as many as 15 of the larger ethnic groups sought independence as individual sovereign states. The British gave the country dominion status in 1960, and in 1963 it became a republic. To cope with the ethnic diversity, the constitution established three large geographical regions and twenty-one separate states. The Nigerian federal republic, with its democratic machinery, multiple political parties, and guarantees of civil rights, was for a time a model for the rest of the continent.

But the Northern Region came to dominate the country, regional and ethnic dissatisfactions erupted, and military coups thwarted the experiment in constitutional democracy. The educated and skilled Ibos, economically advanced and politically ambitious, saw themselves deprived of an appropriate national role. Although their population was mainly concentrated in the south and east, they filled white collar, civil service, and technical jobs throughout the country. The Ibos themselves initiated a military coup in 1966, but a Hausa-led military takeover almost immediately followed and became the signal for a slaughter of Ibos. Large numbers fled to the east, where in 1967 they proclaimed an independent state of Biafra. A terrible civil war to prevent the secession lasted for two and half years, from 1967 to 1970, and resulted in a million deaths, many of them children who died from starvation in the blockaded area before the rebellion ended. After the war, the federal government pursued a policy of reconciliation, helped reintegrate the Ibos into national life, and sought to overcome regional and religious differences.

For a few years the Nigerian military leaders helped restore constitutional government and permitted open elections, but in the face of renewed political instability and economic difficulties they reimposed military control. Even so, the military leaders who took power in 1985, in the sixth military coup since independence, pledged to restore democratic government. More than elsewhere in sub-Saharan Africa, Nigeria clung to a commitment to constitutionalism despite continuing ethnic, regional, and religious tensions.

For a time, in the 1970s, Nigeria had a booming economy, based on its large oil resources, discovered and exploited in the 1950s, which made it the world's sixth largest oil producer. People flocked to the urban areas from the countryside and from neighboring states like Ghana to take part in the boom. Lagos, the Nigerian capital, quadrupled in size. But in the mid-1980s, when the world market experienced an oil glut, petroleum prices plummeted. The oil wealth had not stimulated broader economic development; the country had become dependent on food imports and suffered from inflation and debt.

End of British Rule: East Africa

In East Africa, especially in Kenya, the independence movement encountered greater obstacles. In Kenya a minority of white settlers, who owned the rich plantation areas, stubbornly resisted the independence movement headed by Jomo Kenyatta. The nationalists responded with violence and acts of terrorism in the 1950s, highlighted by the armed revolt of a terrorist organization, the Mau Mau. Kenyatta was imprisoned and then exiled. But pressures for independence grew. After a decade of rising tension, the British increased African representation in the colonial government, brought Kenyatta back from exile, and in 1963 granted Kenya independence. Most of the British planters left the country. Until his death in 1978 Kenyatta dominated the country's political life, presenting a facade of parliamentary government, but permitting only one legal party and imprisoning ethnic and political opponents. His successor, Daniel arap Moi, continued to govern under the same kind of authoritarian one-party regime, rejecting pressures for liberalization.

In 1961 the British granted independence to Tanganyika, where they exercised a UN trusteeship over what had been, in 1914, the major part of German East Africa, and to Zanzibar, a British island protectorate since 1890. The two states united in 1964 to form Tanzania.

Here, too, the nationalist leader came to dominate the government after independence. Julius Nyerere allowed only one party, and relinquished power to a successor only after twenty-five years in office. By promoting literacy and establishing Swahili as the official language of public life, he helped unite the country's ethnic and linguistic groups more effectively than elsewhere on the continent. His economic policies were less successful. Also a champion of "African socialism," he nationalized much of the economy, including agriculture. He drew close to the Soviet Union and to China, and for a time Tanzania served as a bridgehead for Chinese Communist influence on the continent. Here, too, in the mid-1980s with a new generation emerging, the government denationalized many state industries, sought to end overly rigid planning and controls, and restored collective farms to family cultivation.

Uganda, a third state in East Africa, which Winston Churchill once described as the "pearl of Africa," had a promising beginning in 1962 as a parliamentary republic, but then became the sad scene for over twenty years of continuing turmoil and butchery. At independence, several kingdoms and ethnic groups were incorporated into the new nation-state with autonomy under a federal system, but in 1966 the prime minister Milton Obote took over as dictator and in a push for instant nationhood summarily abolished all of the old kingdoms such as Buganda as obstacles to national unity. After five years of disorder, during which Obote promoted his fellow northerners to leading positions, a flamboyant, ruthless military officer, Idi Amin, once the country's heavyweight boxing champion, seized power and for the next eight years brutalized the country, shocking Africa and the world with executions, massacres, and torture in some of which he personally participated. Over 300,000 individuals lost their lives; whole ethnic groups were singled out for destruction. A once prosperous agricultural economy with thriving coffee, tea, and cotton exports, lay in ruins. Professionals and intellectuals fled. Asians, mostly Indian, who had been deeply involved in the country's commerce and industry, were expelled. When in 1979 Amin seemed likely to invade Tanzania over disputed border territory, a Tanzanian army with the backing of other African states invaded Uganda, overthrew the dictator, established military rule, and oversaw elections in which Obote returned to power.

But after the withdrawal of the Tanzanian army, Obote crushed internal opposition with a repression reminiscent of his predecessor; additional tens of thousands lost their lives or fled into exile, and authority collapsed. Even when five years later a military coup overthrew Obote, chaos continued. Then, in 1986, a new military leader, Yoweri Museveni, moved to end what he deplored as the "massive hemorrhage" of Ugandan lives, set about to restore constitutional government, and with international assistance took the first steps to rehabilitate the devastated country. Economic production in Uganda in 1989 was one-fifth what it had been at the time of independence, but the restoration of political stability and internal security made economic growth once again possible. There were many obstacles to recovery, including the epidemic spread of AIDS, which, from the mid-1980s on, even more than in other parts of Africa, was ravaging the country.

Southern Africa

In Southern Rhodesia and even more so in South Africa, a white minority held out the longest against sharing or yielding power. In other parts of southern Africa the British peacefully gave independence to Zambia and Malawi, under black majority governments, in 1964 (and to Botswana two years later). In Southern Rhodesia the British tried to negotiate political rights for the black majority before granting independence, but the small self-assertive white community resisted, and in 1965 proclaimed the country's independence from Britain. After fifteen years of international pressures, the recalcitrant white leaders yielded and in 1980 Southern Rhodesia became the state of Zimbabwe, with a black majority government. The independence leader Robert Mugabe soon dominated the political scene, combining the posts of president and prime minister, and taking steps to create a one-party state.

In the extreme south of the continent, in what had become the Union of South Africa in 1910,[11] the situation remained tense. Here the whites, though a minority, were far more numerous than elsewhere in Africa south of the Sahara, and had lived there for a much longer time. About half the whites, the Afrikaners, were descendants of Dutch Calvinist immigrants from as far back as the founding of Cape Town in 1652, and of French Huguenot refugees; the other half represented immigration from Great Britain since the 1820s. The two halves did not easily mix. The Afrikaners, during their long isolation from Europe, developed a new language of their own, Afrikaans, derived mainly from Dutch, and they retained unpleasant memories of British expansion, especially of the "Boer" war and the concentration camps of 1899–1902. In the 1980s about 5 million whites, themselves divided, lived uneasily with 25 million blacks and 3 million mixed peoples and Asians, who were treated as nonwhites. The whites were numerous enough to constitute an established outpost of European civilization and to develop the most advanced economy of the continent, but they were greatly outnumbered, and fearful of losing their dominant status.

In 1948 an Afrikaner Nationalist party came to power. Enforcing existing measures of racial segregation already on the books, it established a strict and sweeping policy of "apartheid" (the Afrikaans word for "segregation"). It excluded blacks from political life and imposed blatant forms of discrimination, not only in public accommodations and transportation but extending even to private social activities. Its major gesture, autonomous homelands for various tribal groupings ("bantustans"), of which four of a projected ten were set up, found little favor. Opponents of apartheid, black and white, were silenced by imprisonment and even torture. The nationalist leader Nelson Mandela, arrested in 1963 and sentenced to life imprisonment, remained a prisoner for 27 years until freed in 1990, when he resumed his leadership role in the continuing struggle. The regime, increasingly isolated from the international community, severed all ties in 1961 with Britain and the Commonwealth nations, which were critical of its racial policies, and that same year proclaimed itself the Republic of South Africa. The black leadership in the African National Congress, whose history went back to 1912, grew more militant and turned to armed struggle to gain its ends. Strikes, riots, and demonstrations became common. The armed repression of the demonstrators at Sharpeville, in the Transvaal, in 1960 and at Soweto, a black suburb of Johannesburg, in 1976 were among the most tragic clashes. In the 1980s the government assumed emergency police powers and imposed press censorship to prevent the publicity attendant upon the repeated episodes of violence.

The government's efforts to introduce modest reforms—like abandoning the "pass system," or identity cards, for work and residence for blacks—were met by hardened opposition. The refusal of South Africa to end its racial policies brought pressure from the other states of Africa and from the outside world. The United States, which had its own history of racial oppression and had gone through a civil rights revolution of its own in the 1950s and 1960s, with its own

---

[11] See pp. 668–669.

martyred black heroes like Martin Luther King, Jr., joined with others in imposing economic sanctions and encouraging corporate withdrawal of investments. At the end of the 1980s a reform-minded South African president, F. W. de Klerk, took the first steps toward easing segregation and sharing political power, both desperately needed to avoid a deepening of the crisis.

South Africa also refused to surrender the League of Nations mandate it exercised since 1920 over what had once been German Southwest Africa, or even transform it into a United Nations trusteeship, which it saw as preparation for independence under a black majority government. In 1966 the United Nations declared the South African mandate ended, renamed the area Namibia, and called for its immediate independence. South Africa resisted and independence forces began a guerrilla war. The war ended in 1988 when all parties agreed to a phased withdrawal under international supervision and to Namibia's independence, which in 1990 was officially recognized.

The French Sub-Saharan Empire

The French, largely as a result of the bloody war in Algeria, dissolved their vast colonial empire in sub-Saharan Africa peacefully. After the Second World War they had hoped that a French-educated and assimilated African elite would maintain its ties to France in a loosely organized French Union. They gave the African colonies representation in the French parliament and promised self-governing institutions. But control remained centralized in Paris and by the mid-1950s the African colonies, inspired by nationalist movements elsewhere, pressed for independence. De Gaulle, still facing the Algerian crisis, recognized the inexorable pressure for independence and offered the black sub-Saharan colonies their freedom. By 1960 all fifteen colonies had chosen independence. Many, however, retained a close association with France for economic aid and cultural cooperation. France remained a strong presence among the francophone nations (and indeed the strongest presence of all the Western countries on the African continent as a whole), training the armies of the new states, lending financial assistance, and taking a leading role in economic development. On almost a dozen occasions after 1960 the French intervened with military forces, small in number but mobile and well-equipped. In 1979 they helped overthrow a brutal dictator who had seized power in the Central African Republic in 1966 and proclaimed himself emperor. In Chad, they intervened when rebels in the north backed by Libya threatened to overthrow the government. The French organized the African Financial Community, helped stabilize the African currency, and became the largest donor of aid to the continent. While some African leaders criticized the French presence as neocolonialism, many welcomed it and viewed it more as a partnership than an intrusion. As elsewhere in Africa, the promise of democratic government in the former French colonies turned for the most part into civilian

[12] The francophone, or French-speaking, sub-Saharan African states are Benin (until 1975 called Dahomey), Cameroon, the Central African Republic, Chad, the Congo Republic, Gabon, Guinea, Ivory Coast, Madagascar (or Malagasy Republic), Mali, Mauritania, Niger, Senegal, Togo, and Burkina Faso (until 1984 Upper Volta). A sixteenth state, Djibouti, received independence in 1977. Morocco, Algeria, and Tunisia, in North Africa, are also part of francophone Africa, as is Zaire, once the Belgian Congo.

or military dictatorships, with varying degrees of repression. Senegal was a rare exception.

The Belgian Congo: Zaire

The Belgian Congo was a byword for European imperialist exploitation in the late nineteenth century.[13] The most abusive features were remedied before 1914, but political control remained concentrated in Brussels and little was done to prepare the large colony (it was eighty times the size of Belgium) for self-government. Agitation for independence intensified when the French Congo and other French African colonies won their freedom. Faced with the pressures for independence, the Belgian government, which had once proposed a transition period of thirty years, decided against gradualism and in 1960 announced its withdrawal in six months' time. The two leading nationalist leaders, Joseph Kasavabu and Patrice Lumumba, were at odds with one another, innumerable ethnic and regional antagonisms were present, and no one was prepared to carry out the responsibilities of government. The army mutinied, the soldiers turning against their European officers; unrestrained violence broke out against those European whites who had not fled; and the southeastern copper-producing province of Shaba (then called Katanga), under still a third nationalist leader, Moise Tshombe, seceded. Belgian paratroopers, hastily flown back, and a United Nations international police force attempted to restore order. When the leftist leader Lumumba was assassinated in 1961, the troubled situation became even more dangerous because of a threatened Soviet-Western confrontation. The Soviet Union charged the Europeans and their American supporters with deliberately creating the chaos so that the Europeans might return, and threatened intervention to defend the new state.

Two and a half years later, in 1963, the Shaba secession ended. But the government continued to battle leftist rebels with Belgian and American help. In 1965, Colonel Joseph Désiré Mobutu ended the anarchy with a personal dictatorship. He nationalized the large mining enterprises and most of the rest of the economy. To symbolize the new era, he Africanized all geographical and personal names. Because Christian names were dropped, he himself took the name Mobutu Sese Seko. In 1971 the Belgian Congo became Zaire, as did the famous river. Leopoldville, the capital, and Stanleyville, the second largest city, both carrying names reminiscent of European imperialism, became Kinshasa and Kisangani; Lake Albert became Lake Mobutu.

Zaire, the third largest country in size in Africa (second only to the Sudan and Algeria), its cities widely separated and with poor, overgrown roads, had vast copper, diamond, cobalt and other mineral resources, but its potential riches remained underdeveloped. The nationalized mines were poorly managed, and falling copper prices in the 1980s further hurt the economy. Food had to be imported and the country fell heavily into debt while corruption became an open scandal under a repressive regime. Only when the dictator himself imposed austerity measures in the late 1980s did the economy show signs of reviving.

Belgium had governed the Congo directly, but it had also administered, under

---

[13] See pp. 662–664.

a League mandate and a United Nations trusteeship, two small territories which before 1914 had been parts of German East Africa, and which now, in 1962, became the independent states of Rwanda and Burundi. It was in Burundi that one of the most violent of the many ethnic explosions of postindependence Africa occurred. A small minority of the population, the Tutsi (or Watutsi), physically distinguished by their extraordinarily tall stature (some were seven feet tall) had since the last century dominated and repressed the Hutu majority, who comprised 85 percent of the population. In 1972 the Hutu leaders, after an earlier attempted coup had failed, led a rebellion which began with the slaying of hundreds of Tutsi. The Tutsi crushed the uprising and took a fearsome revenge, massacring tens of thousands of Hutu, and seemingly were bent on their total destruction. The worst of the internecine warfare faded by the mid-1970s, but ethnic tensions continued. In Rwanda, in contrast, the Hutu gained control of the country immediately after independence and forced large numbers of Tutsi to flee.

End of the Portuguese Colonial Empire

Of all the colonial powers Portugal, under an authoritarian dictatorship itself until 1974, clung longest to its colonies, symbols of grandeur from the days of Vasco da Gama's explorations and the early age of European expansion.[14] To retain Angola, on the southwestern African coast, and Mozambique, on the southeastern, both at one time flourishing centers of the slave trade and under Portuguese rule for over 400 years, the Portuguese dictatorship stubbornly fought a colonial revolt which broke out in 1961 and lasted thirteen years. In the course of the fighting disaffected elements in the Portuguese army, radicalized by the prolonged colonial war, turned against the regime and overthrew it in 1974 in a bloodless coup. The following year Portugal granted independence to Angola, Mozambique, and its other small African colonies, Cape Verde, São Tomé and Principe, and Guinea-Bissau. Hundreds of thousands of Portuguese fled, mainly to South Africa.

In Angola independence touched off a struggle for power by competing nationalist groups in which outside powers intervened, the Soviet Union and Cuba on the one side, the United States and South Africa on the other. The Soviet Union supported an avowedly Marxist faction with weapons and advisers. Fidel Castro, who, as we shall see, projected himself as a Marxist defender of oppressed colonial peoples everywhere, dispatched 50,000 troops. The leftist group, which won out, proclaimed a "people's republic" in 1976 and consolidated power, but fighting continued with rebels who had the support of the United States and South Africa. The war dragged on for fourteen years, ruined the country, and cost hundreds of thousands of lives. Not until the late 1980s did the outside powers agree to withdraw and enable the difficult task of reconciliation to begin.

Mozambique, exhausted by the decade of guerrilla war against Portugal, also established a "people's republic." The government was soon engaged in a continuing civil war with a militant rightist group. The war against Portugal, the rightist insurgency, and drought and famine cost over half a million lives in the

[14] See pp. 107–109.

small country and displaced one and a half million others. Although Angola and Mozambique remained under Marxist governments, they abandoned their ideological rigidity in the late 1980s and sought desperately needed economic aid from the West.

Ethiopia, Somalia, Sudan

Ethiopia, Eritrea, and Somalia, on the Horn of Africa, in the easternmost part of the continent, were all once part of Italian East Africa. In Ethiopia, once the Italians were defeated in 1941, Haile Selassie was restored as emperor.[15] In 1962 Ethiopia annexed Eritrea, to its north, which unsuccessfully sought independence of its own and launched an armed rebellion that continued for decades. In 1973 a leftist military coup deposed Haile Selassie, established a Marxist and vehemently anti-Western regime, nationalized much of the economy, and became a client state of the Soviet Union.

Ethiopia faced not only continuing guerrilla war with Eritrea but also irredentist pressure from its eastern neighbor, Somalia, which received recognition as an independent state in 1960. Shortly after independence, an army coup brought a leftist military dictatorship to power, which was also Soviet-backed. But when Somalia in 1977 moved to annex the Ogaden region of Ethiopia (where Somalis had long made their home), the Soviets, forced to choose, supported Ethiopia. It was Soviet military aid (and 17,000 Cuban troops airlifted from Angola) that made possible an Ethiopian victory over Somalia. In 1984 Ethiopia proclaimed itself a "people's democratic republic," with one legal party, the "Workers' Party of Ethiopia," and established an authoritarian state socialism. The country meanwhile suffered from drought and famine in which tens of thousands starved to death and thousands of refugees fled to neighboring countries, many to Somalia. The international community was shocked when shipments of food and supplies to alleviate the suffering were blocked or diverted to prevent their reaching the rebellious north. The Soviets finally lost interest in helping Ethiopia suppress the Eritrean rebellion, and in keeping Ethiopia as a client state, and the country sought reconciliation with the West. After 1985 the Horn of Africa was no longer entangled in Cold War rivalries but continued to suffer from natural catastrophes and political unrest.

West of Ethiopia is Sudan, the largest country in Africa, which became independent in 1956, when joint Anglo-Egyptian rule ended. On the eve of independence it fell into deadly civil war. The black population in the southern provinces, some of whom were Christian and others followers of traditional African animist faiths, rose in rebellion against the Arab northerners in control of the government, whom they saw as bent on imposing Islamic law on the country. By 1972 the government had put down the rebellion, but it had lasted seventeen years and cost over a million and a half lives. The government granted autonomy to the south, but its periodic efforts in later years to extend Islamic law provoked new restlessness.

Sudan, a victim itself of the drought and famine that struck Ethiopia in the 1980s, had to absorb a half million refugees from Ethiopia. The rebellions, civil

---

[15] See pp. 837–838, 853.

wars, national wars, famine, and drought, from which Ethiopia, Somalia, and Sudan suffered in the postwar years, displaced a human flood of some 2 million refugees. The casualties of war and famine were in the millions.

The African Revolution

For Africa one age came to a close after the Second World War and a new era opened. Only a map of contemporary Africa can communicate the vast political transformation that had occurred.[16] The unfinished item on the political agenda for the African revolution remained the extension of democratic rights to the black majority in South Africa.

Independence provided a deep source of self-esteem. The word *uhuru*, or freedom, rang through the continent in the heady days of decolonization. Léopold Sedar Senghor, the poet-president of the formerly French colony of Senegal, gave voice to the idea of *négritude*, a powerful, far-reaching black self-consciousness, a pride in ancient cultural roots and modern achievements, which struck a responsive chord in Americans of African descent, whose ancestors had been brought in chains from some of the very lands, like Senegal, that were now modern sovereign states. Black Africa exulted when the Nigerian playwright, poet, and novelist Wole Soyinka, who blended Yoruba and Western traditions in his writings, received the Nobel Prize for literature in 1986.

The African revolution brought an end to Western colonialism and ushered in a new era of independence and national sovereignty, but it did not bring with it democratic government, civil and human rights, the resolution of ethnic and regional antagonisms, or a meaningful improvement in the quality of human lives. Ethnic hatreds, civil wars, regional conflict, and brutal internal repression, took a toll in the millions. Africans killed Africans in the years of independence, mainly in civil wars within the borders of the new states. Ethnic loyalties still transcended national loyalty. Natural disasters and old and new diseases (like AIDS, which had a devastating impact on the continent) added to the death toll. African refugees made up 4 million of the world's 14.5 million refugees in the early 1990s.

Most of the new states began their political careers after independence with constitutions, elected parliaments, independent judiciaries, and guarantees of civil liberties. But under the pressure of ethnic conflict, economic burdens, and political instability, the machinery of constitutional government quickly became submerged under dictatorship, generally military. In country after country, generals, admirals, colonels, majors, captains, even a flight lieutenant in Ghana and a master sergeant in Liberia, pushed aside the civilian rulers. The warrior caste became the new rulers, often a law unto themselves, tyrannizing the population. Nigeria, alone, which at least made sporadic efforts to preserve constitutional government and a federal system for its multi-ethnic state, counted six military coups in the years from 1966 to 1985. At the very outset, charismatic independence leaders, like Nkrumah in Ghana, Kenyatta in Kenya, and Nyerere in Tanzania, transformed themselves into virtual dictators under varying degrees of authoritarianism; some became "presidents for life." Of over 150 African heads of state in the first three decades of independence, only six voluntarily relinquished their offices. In Zambia

[16] See map, p. 926.

and in the Ivory Coast, leaders like Kenneth Kaunda and Félix Houphouet-Boigny governed under a milder authoritarianism, but mainly the dictatorships, military, or civilian with military backing, were repressive and tyrannical and brooked no opposition or dissent. There were only a few examples of free elections, multiparty systems, political pluralism, and freedom from censorship. Of forty-six black-governed sub-Saharan states, only Botswana, Senegal, Gambia, Mauritius, and newly independent Namibia allowed relatively free and unpressured multiparty elections. Some African leaders argued that strong central governments were needed, not multiparty democratic systems, to counter the separatist ethnic and regional forces, cope with economic underdevelopment, and provide the cohesiveness for national unity. Others considered democracy an alien concept, an importation from the West, difficult to nurture in societies with high illiteracy, a small middle class, and different cultural patterns, including a political tradition of lifetime tenure for tribal chieftains and of governing by consensus. Many Africans rejected such arguments and maintained that, like other peoples of the world, they should choose and control their rulers, and one day would do so. In earlier years the West, too, had experienced turbulent periods of nation-building, had looked to absolute and hereditary monarchy as a source of stability, and had contributed its share of bloodshed and warfare to history.

Many of the African states for a time were professedly Marxist. They spoke of "African socialism" and styled their regimes "people's democratic republics." In Mozambique the main avenues were named for Lenin and Mao Zedong; the flag of the People's Republic of the Congo (formerly the French Congo) displayed a hammer and sickle. They turned away from free enterprise, which they identified with the profit-making, exploitation, and racial humiliation of Western colonialism. They looked to the state to oversee the new economies to guarantee rapid development; they nationalized their foreign and domestic enterprises and they collectivized agriculture. In this vision, public ownership would better promote the welfare of the people and provide the promise of a more egalitarian society. In the years of the Cold War many of these states received technical and military assistance from the Soviet Union, the East European Communist regimes (especially East Germany), and the People's Republic of China. But state control often led to bureaucracy, widespread corruption, and economic stagnation. At the close of the 1980s, a movement seemed to be under way, from one end of Africa to another, even under leftist regimes, to encourage the private economic sector, release entrepreneurial energies, and provide incentives for production. There were signs, too, of a relaxation of dictatorial regimes, a willingness to permit dissent, and even opposition parties and contested elections.

Africa had one of the highest population growth rates in the world, many states growing at rates close to 4 percent and expected to double in numbers by the first decade of the new century. Sub-Saharan Africa's population of over 500 million in 1990 was expected to triple in the next forty years. Family planning services to facilitate birth control were inadequate. It was common for African women to bear seven children, in part because infant mortality rates were high and children were seen as providing security in old age or in case of disability. Uncontrolled population growth threatened to outstrip economic advances.

The catalogue of disaster and suffering in the first generation of independence was grim: civil war, ethnic slaughter, regional wars, drought, floods, and famine;

the frustration of democratic hopes, the emergence of brutalizing dictatorships and of military tyrannies; economic stagnation; disease and malnutrition; a flood of refugees from wars, persecution, and natural catastrophes; a population growing faster than food production; and a crushing accumulation of external debt. In the early 1990s Africa had the slowest economic growth of any part of the world; in the 1980s its output grew at only 0.4 percent annually. Once self-sufficient in food, after 1964 it became a net importer of food. In any list of the world's poorest nations, Ethiopia, Mozambique, Mali, Niger, Chad, and other African countries were at or close to the bottom. Meanwhile African expenditures on arms exceeded the international assistance received for economic development. The African revolution had far to go before the quality of life could improve. Yet in spite of the painfully slow progress, Africans felt a sense of control over their own destiny. They did not necessarily wish to be recast in the Western democratic image, or destroy their natural environment in the interests of economic development; they knew that material progress did not by itself make for a humane society. Nonetheless sustainable economic growth was prerequisite to survival and to the improvement of human life, as were political and social stability, and peace.

117. *Ferment in the Middle East*

In the Islamic, or Muslim, world, Arab and non-Arab, the older age of imperialism also ended and a powerful sense of identity swept through it. The huge wealth pouring in from oil resources strengthened pressures for modernization but also reinforced Islamic pride in its cultural heritage. The Islamic world was determined to share in Western material advances on its own terms. Meanwhile religious and cultural barriers slowed the pace of modernization. An elitist organization of society, opposition to the full assimilation of women, and widespread illiteracy presented powerful obstacles. The pace of transformation was uneven and the more than forty Islamic countries differed vastly from each other, but everywhere older life styles were undermined by new wealth, industry, modern forms of urbanization, and Western technology and culture at the same time that Islamic self-consciousness intensified.

The principal non-Arab Muslim states were Pakistan, Bangladesh, Indonesia, Malaysia, Iran, Afghanistan, and Turkey. In Turkey, state and religion had been separate since the secularizing reforms of Kemal Ataturk.[17] Something has been said about many of these countries in previous pages. The Arab states stretched from the Atlantic coast of North Africa to the Persian Gulf, from Morocco to Iraq. In Saudi Arabia and elsewhere Islam was the official state religion. Millions of Muslims lived also in many other parts of the world: in India, the Soviet Union, Nigeria, other African countries, and increasingly in recent times in Western Europe. In the Middle East, Arab and non-Arab, lay an important part of the world's petroleum reserves on which the economic activity of the industrial world vitally depended. The region became one of the world's most troubled areas.

[17] See pp. 791–793.

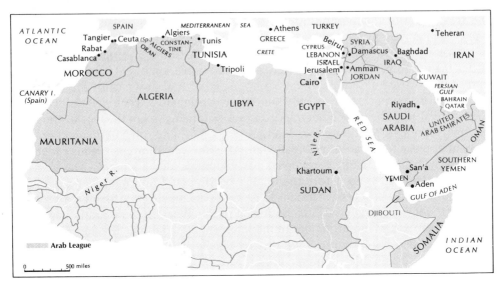

THE ARAB WORLD

The Arabic language zone is one of the most extensive in the world, reaching from the Atlantic Ocean to the Persian Gulf. In 1945 the Arab states formed a League, which has come to have twenty-two members, including the Palestine Liberation Organization. The League has proved to be rather loose, with much disagreement among its members, except for their attitude toward an Israeli state in the midst of an otherwise predominantly Arab world.

The Arab states emerged from the Ottoman Empire during and after the First World War to become British and French League of Nations mandates.[18] Egypt became nominally independent in 1922 and Iraq in 1932, although the British retained treaty rights in each until after 1945. Syria, Lebanon, Jordan, Saudi Arabia, and Yemen all became independent during or after the Second World War, when the British and French ended their mandates. In 1945 the seven states formed an Arab League. In the decades that followed, newly independent Arab states in Africa, like Algeria, and in the Arabian peninsula, like Kuwait, joined so that it grew to have twenty-two members. The unity of the Arab world was more superficial than real; divisive rivalries persisted. The pan-Arabism advocated by Egypt's Colonel Nasser in the 1950s and Libya's Colonel Qadaffi in the 1980s failed to rally much support. What united Arabs after the Second War was a common opposition to the state of Israel, which itself emerged as a new state in 1948.

The Arab opposition to Israel reflected anti-Westernism. From the beginning the Arab states viewed Israel as a Western-backed intrusion into their land. The result was a series of continuing tensions which brought wider international forces into play and made the Middle East one of the most unsettled and most turbulent parts of the world.

[18] See pp. 661, 710, 725, 813, and maps, pp. 660 and above.

The Emergence of Israel

Zionism, the commitment to establish (or reestablish) a Jewish homeland had developed in the late nineteenth century in response to European anti-Semitism. Before 1914 a small number of Jewish pioneers from Eastern Europe made their way to Palestine, then part of the Ottoman Empire. During the First World War the British, by the Balfour Declaration of 1917, voiced support for a Jewish homeland in Palestine[19] but in other ways supported emergent Arab nationalism. After the demise of the Ottoman Empire, the British received a League of Nations mandate for Palestine. From 1919 on Jewish settlers arrived in larger numbers, and in the 1930s, after the triumph of Nazism in Germany, Jewish immigration swelled. To placate the Arabs, who opposed the influx, and all proposals for partition, the British placed a limit on Jewish immigration.

The whole question poignantly reemerged at the end of the Second World War when the homeless survivors of the Nazi Holocaust, which had all but wiped out the European Jews, sought out Palestine as a place of refuge and were turned away by the British in deference to Arab protests. The Arabs objected to the surrender, or partition, of their land because of Europe's persecution of the Jews. Britain, failing to work out a compromise, terminated its mandate and turned the matter over to the United Nations, which in 1947 divided Palestine into a Jewish and an Arab zone, and placed the city of Jerusalem under international control. The Arab states rejected the partition. In May 1948 the Zionist leaders, who had made preparations for independence and could count on strong American support, proclaimed the Republic of Israel. Syria, Lebanon, Jordan, Egypt, and Iraq refused to recognize the new state and went to war. The Arab armies invaded, but the Israelis (as the citizens of the new republic called themselves) won. At the cease-fire in 1949 Israel increased its original territory by about half and established its capital in West Jerusalem. But Jordan during the war annexed central Palestine, including the west bank of the Jordan River, and assumed control of East Jerusalem, from which it barred Jewish worshipers. Tensions remained high.

The Arab states, unwilling to negotiate peace or recognize the existence of Israel, refused to absorb the half-million Palestinian refugees who had been dispossessed. To many Arabs Israel was a new form of Western expansion into the Middle East. The Israelis, on the other hand, saw themselves as creating a Jewish homeland so that persecuted Jews would never again be without a refuge. Jewish immigrants from anywhere in the diaspora were automatically entitled to citizenship. The Israelis also saw themselves as building a bridgehead for Western scientific, technological, and democratic advances in an economically underdeveloped area where democracy had made little headway.

In the decades after independence Israel under a parliamentary government succeeded in building a modern, Western-style, urban, industrial, and democratic society with a large role for labor unions and cooperatives and extensive social services. They produced and exported not only foodstuffs and other consumer goods but high technology products and military hardware. Through ingeniously engineered irrigation schemes, they reclaimed vast stretches of the Negev desert,

[19] See pp. 636–637, 710.

where they grew citrus fruits and other crops. For close to three decades, they enjoyed one of the world's highest economic growth rates. In later years Israel received many immigrants from Asia and Africa with widely disparate backgrounds. The economy began to falter because of heavy defense burdens, but also from large social service expenditures insisted on by the powerful labor interests. Although a secular state, orthodox religious leaders (as in many of the Muslim countries) exercised influence out of proportion to their numbers and insisted on sabbatarian rules and on clerical authority in such matters as marriage and divorce. At great financial strain, the Israelis developed powerful modern military forces and air power, on which they depended for survival. Four more Arab-Israeli wars were fought after 1948–1949: in 1956, the war in the Sinai; in 1967, the Six-Day War; in 1973, the Yom Kippur War; and in 1982, the war in Lebanon. The Middle East became a theater of the Cold War as well. The United States supported Israel. The U.S.S.R., which had originally supported Israel also, reversed itself and for many years backed and armed the Arab states, a change that caused concern to the United States, which was determined to prevent the expansion of Soviet influence in the Middle East.

The Arab-Israeli Wars after Independence

At first Egypt took the lead in the *jehad*, or holy war, against Israel. In 1956 the Egyptian leader Colonel Nasser announced that the Suez Canal would be nationalized and placed under Egyptian control. The British, supported by the French and Israelis, retaliated with military intervention. The Soviet Union backed Nasser, as did the emergent states of Asia and Africa, which looked upon Egypt as resisting an old-fashioned imperialist invasion. When the United States refused to support the military action, Britain, France, and Israel to their chagrin were compelled to withdraw. The Egyptians agreed to operate the canal on an impartial basis, but continued to bar Israeli shipping. Meanwhile the Syrians mounted border raids.

In 1967 Egypt's move to close the Gulf of Aqaba threatened to strangle the

ISRAEL AND ADJOINING REGIONS

"Palestine" is the term by which Europeans long designated a small region of mixed population, but predominantly Arab, which belonged to the Ottoman Empire until the First World War. European Jews, with the Zionist movement, began to migrate to it in the nineteenth century. In 1922 the League of Nations "mandated" it to the British, who tried to restrict Jewish immigration in an attempt to satisfy the Arabs. After the death of millions of Jews during the Second World War the Zionist idea of an independent Jewish state won increasing numbers of adherents. In 1947 the United Nations proposed a partition between Jewish and Arab states, with Jerusalem as a separate zone. The Arabs rejected the plan, and in the Arab-Israeli war of 1948 the Israelis won recognition of wider boundaries than those first proposed. The Arab states still refused recognition of Israel. In the Six-Day War of 1967 the Israelis occupied additional territory as shown in the lower lefthand panel. In 1973, in the "Yom Kippur" war, Egypt and Syria attacked Israel, but Israel defeated them and continued to occupy the Sinai except that in the peace negotiations that followed Egypt was allowed to regain the east bank of the Suez Canal, and a United Nations demilitarized zone was set up between the two adversaries. In 1982 Israel returned the Sinai to Egypt, but retained the small area known as the Gaza Strip.

Israeli economy and Israel retaliated in a preemptive strike. In six days of hostilities, the Israelis defeated the Egyptian, Syrian, and Jordanian armies, captured vast amounts of equipment, mostly of Soviet origin, and occupied extensive territories. Israel took over the west bank of the Jordan river and East Jerusalem from Jordan, the Golan Heights from Syria, and the Sinai peninsula and the Gaza Strip from Egypt. It now governed a territory four times its original size; over 1 million additional Arabs came under Israeli rule. The Arab states, smarting under the humiliating defeat, refused to sign a peace treaty and still refused even to recognize Israel's existence.

After the 1967 war, Nasser's successor Anwar al-Sadat projected himself as leader of the Arab crusade against Israel. In October 1973 Egyptian forces surprised the Israelis by attacking on the Jewish holy day Yom Kippur, establishing a bridgehead on the Sinai peninsula. Syria simultaneously attacked in the north. Recovering from the surprise attack, Israel first defeated the Syrian forces, then crossed the Suez Canal and trapped the Egyptian forces.

With the Israelis near victory and in control of additional Arab territory, the Arab countries supporting Egypt and Syria dramatically introduced a new strategic weapon, an embargo on oil shipments. They sought to pressure the United States and Western Europe into demanding Israeli withdrawal from all Arab territories occupied since 1967, including the newly conquered ones. Although the embargo was lifted a few months later in early 1974, the oil-producing nations had meanwhile quadrupled the price of oil. The embargo and the rise in oil prices had consequences far beyond the conflict in the Middle East.[20] The war ended with an American-mediated settlement. Israel withdrew its forces from the west bank of the Suez canal, but continued to occupy most of the Sinai Peninsula.

Recognizing the impasse, Sadat broke the united Arab front against Israel and encouraged friendlier relations with Israel. The other Arab states, Syria in the lead, rejected any settlement and pressed for Israeli withdrawal from all occupied Arab territories. In 1975 the Arab states persuaded the UN General Assembly, in which the formerly colonial states of Asia and Africa now held a majority, to adopt a resolution condemning Zionism as a form of racism—even though Zionism had originated as a defense against anti-Semitism and Israel as a response to the Nazi Holocaust.

It was evident that unless a settlement were reached new and even deadlier conflicts would explode. To be agreed upon was the disposition of the territories occupied by Israel since 1967, the demand of the Palestinian Arabs for an independent national state, and the recognition and guarantee of Israel's legitimacy and security. In 1979, at American initiative, Egypt and Israel signed a peace treaty, under which Israel withdrew from the Sinai Peninsula, retaining only the Gaza Strip, and was guaranteed the free use of the Suez Canal. Outraged, the other Arab states expelled Egypt from the Arab League. Sadat himself was later assassinated by fundamentalist Egyptian army officers. Syria, Libya, and Iraq took the lead in rejecting any wider settlement.

The Palestinian Arabs added a highly volatile element. They grew increasingly militant, conducting guerrilla warfare operations against Israel and engaging in violent terrorist activities in many parts of the world to call attention to their cause. In 1964, under the leadership of Yasir Arafat, they organized the Palestine Liberation Organization (PLO), which became a full member of the Arab League and received official recognition from many quarters as a government-in-exile for the Palestinian Arabs. Refusing to recognize the legitimacy of Israel, the PLO professed to speak for the 1.5 million Palestinians under Israeli rule, demanded the evacuation of all territories occupied by Israel since 1967, and called for the establishment of a Palestinian state on the west bank of the Jordan River and the Gaza Strip.

Israel itself became more intransigent. In 1977 a conservative, nationalist party, backed by orthodox religious groups, replaced the Labor party, which had

[20] See pp. 982–984.

governed since independence. Even though the conservative leader Menachem Begin signed the peace treaty with Egypt, the new leadership encouraged Israelis to make permanent settlements in the occupied west bank of the Jordan River (for which Begin even used the old Biblical names of Judea and Samaria) and the Gaza Strip, and rejected negotiations with the Palestinian Arabs. In 1980 the government unified the Israeli capital by formally annexing East Jerusalem, which it had occupied since 1967. It also reacted aggressively to a new threat from within Lebanon, its northern neighbor.

Turmoil in Lebanon

In 1975 a long-simmering civil war broke out in Lebanon that brought bloodshed, turmoil, and anarchy. When the French gave up their League of Nations mandate over Lebanon in 1944, it was arranged that power would be shared among the diverse Christian and Muslim religious communities, but with political advantages for the Christians, then the majority of the population. Over the years many Christians emigrated and the Muslims grew to form the majority. The Muslim sects, aroused by Arab nationalism, took up the cause of the Palestinian Arabs. When the Christian-dominated government attempted to suppress extremist Muslim groups, a civil war erupted, which quickly became complicated by outside intervention. The Palestine Liberation Organization, expelled from Syria for fomenting unrest, settled in Beirut and systematically organized guerrilla incursions into Israel. Muslim armed forces of various Islamic sects fought the Lebanese army and the Christian militia, and with each other. In the chaos in Beirut and elsewhere, the authority of the government collapsed. Syria intervened to restore peace, but with little success. Israel, to counter the repeated PLO guerrilla raids, crossed the Lebanese border and set up a buffer area in southern Lebanon. But the raids did not end. In 1982 the Israelis launched a full scale invasion, reached Beirut, and forced the ouster of the PLO forces.

Lebanon's travail did not end, nor did the Israeli intervention halt new guerrilla raids. Continuing civil war among warring militias reduced Beirut to shambles. Syria, Iran, and Iraq armed and trained extremist militants, who kidnapped and held hostage American and European civilians. Syria and Iraq each armed separate militias. A multinational peacekeeping force in 1983 failed to restore order and was compelled to withdraw after terrorist bomb explosions killed American and French soldiers. Syria's 40,000 troops soon controlled almost three-fourths the country's territory.

In 1988 Christians and Muslims in Lebanon, in the hope of restoring peace, agreed to readjust the existing political arrangements to provide greater representation for the Muslims. Because the attempted settlement did not call for the withdrawal of the Syrian forces, many Lebanese denounced it and the fighting continued. Israel was still threatened by the chaos in Lebanon and by the threat of Syrian expansion. Many, even within the Arab world, feared the territorial ambitions and aspirations for pan-Arab leadership of the Syrian ruler, Hafaz al-Assad, who had governed his own country dictatorially since 1971, was an implacable foe of Israel, and had spoken openly of "a greater Syria." Many remembered that in the old Ottoman Empire the two countries of the Levant had been governed for centuries as a single unit and had been divided only under the

French mandate. Lebanon's agonies seemed to defy solution. In a war that had already gone on for fifteen years an estimated 150,000 had died in the small, once prosperous, country of three and a half million; other thousands had fled.

Israel and the Occupied Territories

Over 800,000 Palestinian Arabs lived in the West Bank and Gaza Strip, occupied by Israel since the 1967 war. At the end of 1987 nationalist agitation by young Palestinians flared up into what became a sustained uprising—the *intifada*, as it was called in Arabic. The Israeli military met the stone-throwing, fire-bombing, and civil disobedience with armed repression which cost hundreds of lives. The ferocity of the repression divided the country, hurt the economy, and threatened to undermine the Israeli democracy. The PLO exploited the popular explosion to press for recognition of an independent Palestinian state. The Israelis, although willing to consider elections in the occupied territories, adamantly rejected a role for the PLO.

The larger issue of Arab-Israeli relations remained unsettled. With the waning of the Cold War, the Arab states recognized in the late 1980s that they could no longer count on Soviet support. The United States and other countries continued efforts to mediate a settlement. Any genuine settlement seemingly had to revolve around the formula "territory for peace": Israel to give up some or all of the territory occupied since 1967 in return for Arab recognition of Israel's legitimacy and existence. The status of the Palestinians would have to be resolved in favor of some form of self-government. Israel's insecurity, despite American support, lay rooted in the fact that its small population lived in a hostile Middle East. Many Israelis had no desire to govern large numbers of Arabs but feared that surrender of the occupied territories would open the path to the destruction of their state.

Libya

Libya added to the explosiveness in the Middle East. Once part of Italian East Africa, it received independence in 1951 by a decision of the United Nations. The discovery of oil in 1958 transformed the country of only 4 million into a leading petroleum producer. In 1969 Colonel Qadaffi ousted the existing monarchy and established a dictatorship that blended Islamic orthodoxy, Arab nationalism, and a self-styled state socialism. Using his country's oil wealth for political purposes, he projected himself as a spokesman for pan-Arabism and aspired to a large role in African affairs as well.

Libya became headquarters for terrorist activities on behalf of the Palestinians—bomb explosions in European airports, the hijacking of commercial airliners and ships, and the taking of hostages. Matters reached such a pass that in 1986, in retaliation for the bombing of a West Berlin discotheque crowded with American military personnel, the United States sent aircraft to bomb military installations in Tripoli. Libya remained one of the most vehemently anti-Western of the Arab states.

Revolution in Iran

Where change occurred rapidly in the Middle East, in Arab and non-Arab countries, traditionalists resented modernization. They especially opposed secularism and the disruption of older religious and cultural institutions as a Western subversion of their society. Scarcely anyone, however, could have anticipated the fierce anti-Westernism of the fundamentalist Islamic revolution that erupted in 1979, not in an Arab state but in Iran. Iran was a Shiite state—nine-tenths of the Islamic world adhered to the Sunni branch of Islam[21]—but Shiite revolutionary leaders in Iran sought to foment fundamentalist revivalism everywhere in the Muslim world.

Over the centuries Persia (or Iran, as it was renamed in 1935) had a long history of foreign domination. At the opening of the twentieth century, like the Ottoman Empire, it was too weak to resist foreign control. Britain and tsarist Russia, coveting the country's newly discovered oil resources, partitioned it into spheres of influence.[22] After the First World War the British made an effort to consolidate control, but in 1921 an army officer Reza Khan seized power, made himself hereditary ruler, or shah, in 1925, and embarked on a program of modernization, abolishing extraterritorial rights for foreigners and curtailing the powers of the *mullahs*, the Islamic clergy. During the Second World War, when his machinations brought him uncomfortably close to the Axis, the British and Russians occupied the country and in 1941 forced him to abdicate in favor of his son. After the war, American influence became paramount and the young shah, Muhammad Reza, identified himself with the West. When a reform prime minister Muhammad Mossadegh and an assertive parliament moved to nationalize the oil industry in the 1950s, the shah, with American and British support, blocked the effort. In the 1960s, with oil wealth, he embarked upon an extensive industrial and educational development program, broke up estates controlled by the clergy and feudal landowners, sent students in large numbers to study abroad, and with American aid reorganized the armed forces. At the same time he presided over a repressive, authoritarian regime, crushing opposition from traditionalist clerical leaders, moderates, and leftists alike. The United States, pleased with the economic and military modernization of its anti-Soviet ally in a strategic part of the world, ignored the swelling tides of resentment within the country. In 1978 opposition forces coalesced and strikes and riots broke out. The shah invoked martial law, but was forced to flee in January 1979.

In February the aged leader of the religious community, the Ayatollah Ruhollah Khomeini, returned from Paris. For fifteen years he had lived in exile, denouncing the shah's pro-Western and anticlerical regime. Within a matter of days he assumed leadership of the revolution and proclaimed an "Islamic republic." His Revolutionary Guards quickly defeated the shah's troops. Supreme control rested with the ayatollah and his council of religious

---

[21] The schism originated in an armed struggle over the succession to Muhammad after the prophet's death in 632, in which the Shiite faction supported Ali, Muhammad's son-in-law, and the Sunni favored another line of succession. The schism became permanent. There are differences in doctrine and ritual as well between the two branches. The Shiite form of Islam became the state religion in Persia (Iran) in the sixteenth century: elsewhere there are many minority Shiite communities.

[22] See p. 698.

associates, appointed to guarantee the fidelity of the new regime to Islam and assure control of the revolution through a network of mosques throughout the land. The revolutionary authorities restored traditional Islamic ways of life. Women were ordered to wear veils and head scarves and the traditional long black dress, the *chador*. All music was banned from radio and television; the Islamic prohibition on alcohol was strictly enforced. Islamic law, interpreted by the clerics, took precedence over secular law. Revolutionary justice, in the form of drumhead trials and public execution for religious, moral, or political offenses, took the lives of thousands. The ayatollah's theocracy pushed aside the Westernized leaders, even those who had welcomed the overthrow of the shah. The first president was forced to flee into exile, the foreign minister executed. Industry was nationalized, and tight state control imposed over the economy. In the chaos, oil production and revenues fell. Militants, among them young men and women students at the universities, were aroused to frenzied heights by the ayatollah's fervid denunciations of the West.

The anti-Western fury turned against the United States, which was excoriated as "the great Satan." When in the autumn of 1979 the United States admitted the exiled and ailing shah to its shores, Revolutionary Guards and student militants seized the American Embassy in Teheran in November 1979 in retaliation and held fifty American hostages for close to fifteen months, insisting upon the return of the shah and his wealth to Iran. The failure of an ill-conceived American air rescue added to the American humiliation.

The War Between Iran and Iraq

Iran made no secret of its desire to establish its leadership in the Muslim world, non-Arab and Arab, and to project its theocracy as a model for others. In 1980 war broke out with Iraq, its Arab neighbor to the west. The ayatollah had denounced Iraq both for persecuting its Shiite community and for abandoning Islamic principles. Iraq, also rich in oil, was a nationalistic Arab state, but under an authoritarian, military-backed secular regime. Saddam Hussein, even before he became president in 1979, for many years ruled the country ruthlessly, suppressing all dissent and summarily executing political opponents. He headed the Arab Baath Socialist party, a component of a pan-Arab movement dedicated to Arab revival—the word "Baath" means "renaissance." (A rival branch of the movement ruled in Syria.) As part of the regime's socialist program, it had nationalized oil production and used the revenues to modernize the economy and the military. But ideology was less important to Hussein than the consolidation of political power at home and the use of military power for nationalist ends abroad.

The war itself erupted over a long-smoldering border dispute between the two states over a waterway that served as a vital outlet for Iraq to the Persian Gulf. It had once been awarded to Iraq by an international commission but had fallen under Iran's control. Iraq, seizing an opportunity to exploit the revolutionary turmoil in Iran, and gambling on a quick victory, bombed Iranian oil fields in September 1980, invaded Iran, and occupied the disputed territory. Iran rallied after the initial invasion, expelled the Iraqi forces from its borders in 1982, and pushed deep into Iraq, hoping to overthrow Hussein and his hated regime. When

Iraq stiffened its defenses, Iran dispatched assault waves of young conscripts, many scarcely in their teens, with small gains at huge human costs. (In one of the rare instances in the years since the First World War, poison gas was used on the battlefield by both sides. Iraq used it as well against its Kurdish minority, accused of collaborating with Iran.) Both sides rained missiles on each other's cities.

As the war dragged on, it assumed a larger international dimension. The land war became a tanker war in the Persian Gulf, involving Saudi Arabia, Kuwait, and other Arab Gulf states that were dependent on trade with the West and were unsympathetic to Iran's Shiite fundamentalism. Both Iran and Iraq attacked

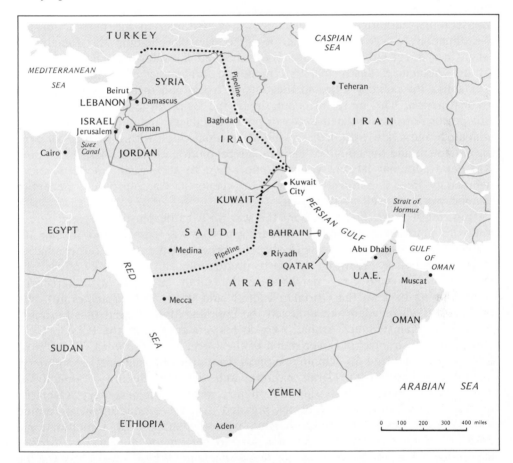

THE PERSIAN GULF AND THE MIDDLE EAST

The industrialized world of Europe, Japan, and North America is heavily dependent on oil imported from this region. The Third World, except where oil is produced locally, is also vulnerable. The oil is exported both by sea from the Persian Gulf and by pipeline to the Red Sea and Mediterranean, from which it must be transported by sea to the consuming countries to provide heating oil, motor fuel, and electric light and power. To protect the flow of this vital commodity the consuming countries sent naval forces to the Gulf during the Iran-Iraq war of 1980–1988 and resorted to full-scale military intervention in 1991. See pp. 994, 1042.

neutral shipping in the Persian Gulf to prevent arms shipments. When the attacks threatened the flow of oil through the Persian Gulf, the United States stepped up its naval presence, with support from the British and French. The Western presence kept oil shipments flowing and reinforced the continuing strategic objective of preserving Western influence in the Gulf.

By 1987 it was clear that the Iranian counteroffensive had failed. In August 1988 Iran accepted a cease-fire. The war had gone on for eight years, and cost over a million lives. At the end of the war the Iranian economy was in chaos, its armed forces exhausted and depleted. The ayatollah's appeal had gone unheeded by other Muslim states and had alienated the Arab Gulf states. But the ayatollah still retained a dedicated following in Iran and still sought to assert his authority in the Islamic world. His call to the faithful for the assassination of a writer, Salman Rushdie, for blaspheming the founder of Islam in a novel published in the West shocked the international community. After Khomeini's death in 1989 moderate pragmatic elements sought to reestablish the country's ties to the outside world and to undertake economic reconstruction. The more stringent dress and behavior codes were relaxed. But power remained divided between political leaders, many of them Western-educated, and a new ayatollah serving as spiritual guide with a strong following in parliament and the country. The Iranian revolution raised the larger question whether traditional Islamic values could adapt to secularism, modernization, democracy, and a pluralist society. The events in Iran unsettled the entire Islamic world as well as the West.

Iraq, for its part, emerged from the war with battle-seasoned armed forces but with a troubled economy. Saddam Hussein was resolved to recoup his country's economic fortunes. Unable to persuade the other oil producing states, particularly Kuwait, to curb production and raise oil prices, he denounced his small Arab neighbor to the south, pressed vague territorial claims (going back to the Ottoman Empire and the British protectorate), and in August 1990 invaded and annexed the emirate. Many feared that he might move next against Saudi Arabia, expand his influence over the Persian Gulf, and acquire a stranglehold over much of the world's oil resources. The United States took the lead in winning support from the international community, including several of the Arab nations, and the UN Security Council for economic sanctions against Iraq and military measures if necessary. Over the next few months the United States pursued a massive build-up of its armed forces in the deserts of Saudi Arabia, with the support of a multinational coalition. Soon the objective became less to defend the area against further aggression than to force Iraq to leave Kuwait. When Iraq refused, the Americans and their allies unleashed a crushing air attack and followed this with a ground assault, which within a few days forced Iraq's withdrawal from Kuwait. How to maintain stability in this vital area of the Middle East with its many rivalries and competing interests remained a critical concern for the states of the Persian Gulf, the Arab nations, Israel, and the international community.[23]

[23] See pp. 982–983, 1042.

118. *The Developing World: Expectations and Frustrations*

The End of Empire

At the beginning of the twentieth century, or even in 1945, the sweeping nature and extent of the colonial revolution was unanticipated. At best the colonial world was expected to evolve slowly toward self-government. The rapid and complete dissolution of the colonial empires was astounding. The age of imperialism, to be sure, had been accompanied by exploitation, brutality, and degradation, and it left a permanent scar on subject peoples all over the globe. Yet it was also the instrument whereby many of the scientific, material, intellectual, and humanitarian advances of the West spread to the rest of the world. The West no longer dominated these areas politically, but Western culture, technology, and institutions remained important. Industry, science, secularization, social mobility, the idea of individual freedom affected remote parts of the world. The new values and institutions created dislocations and tensions, transforming the landscape of the non-Western world. In some places, as in the Islamic reaction in Iran, there was an explosion of resentment at the Western intrusion, but mostly there was hope that some amalgam could be forged of modernization, secularism, and traditional values.

In few parts of the formerly colonial world did Western-style democracy prevail along with independence. Not until the 1980s did pressures for political and economic liberalization begin to gather in the former colonial world—in parts of Asia, Africa, and the Middle East, as well as in Latin America. Neither by their own efforts nor by internationally assisted development programs were levels of agricultural and industrial production raised, illiteracy and disease overcome, and living standards elevated, as had been hoped. Independence, the end of imperialism, brought a new sense of dignity but did not automatically bring freedom, self-government, human rights, and the improvement of the human condition.

The Third World

In the years after the Second World War, the term "Third World" was used to describe the less economically advanced, or developing, nations of Asia, Africa, and Latin America. The term was coined originally to distinguish the "developing world" from the two "industrial worlds"—the Western bloc of nations (including Japan) and the Communist bloc led by the Soviet Union. Although the original meaning was being eroded by the disintegration of the Soviet bloc in the late 1980s, the term seemed destined to survive. Most of the Third World nations were until recently colonial countries. Latin America was included even though independence there dated back to the nineteenth century.

After the Second World War the United States took the lead in promoting the economic and social advancement of the developing countries, assisting them with money and technical aid. Other industrial countries, once recovered from the war, committed small but significant shares of their annual gross national product to development assistance. International agencies emerged to provide additional funding and expertise. With Western science and technology available and with economic planning by their governments, the Third World countries looked forward to modernization, economic growth, and social progress. Central planning, nationalized economies, and government controls held the attraction of accomplishing these ends more rapidly than private capitalism. Nehru's moderate socialism and economic planning in India was one model. Others turned to the Soviet or Chinese examples and received development assistance from those sources.

In the postwar decades projects were financed for improving agriculture, building industry, and combatting disease and illiteracy. The 1960s were known as the "development decade." President Kennedy spoke of raising the "banner of hope" for the poor and hungry. Dams and wells, irrigation schemes, hydroelectric projects, factories and processing mills, and education at all levels were all part of the program. Industrialization was expected to end or reduce dependence on imports. In agriculture, the Green Revolution enabled farmers to use innovative strategies for planting and harvesting. The initial results of development were gratifying. Many parts of the Third World experienced significant progress, achieving targets of 5 to 6 percent growth annually; per capita income rose; infant mortality rates fell. It seemed possible to speak of a revolution of rising expectations.

But advances were still slow and the Third World states found little change in their relative position. Despite measurable progress, they did not share proportionately in the industrial world's tremendous postwar economic expansion, in the course of which per capita income in the wealthiest nations had tripled. The gap between richer and poorer nations widened, rather than narrowed. Using the United Nations and other organizations as a forum for their economic grievances, the Third World nations in the late 1960s argued for a reshaping of the international economy—a "New International Economic Order"—to give them greater access to the investment funds, capital goods, and technology of the West and to shift international financing from Western-dominated agencies like the World Bank. They resented also the multinational corporations, which while introducing Western capital and technology, kept economic decision making in private hands in their own countries. In the tensions of the Cold War the developing countries formed a bloc of nonaligned states, which grew from twenty-five in 1961 to over one hundred in the 1980s—"nonaligned" but always more critical of the wealthier West than of the Soviet Union. Since the formerly colonial world was situated mainly in the southern parts of the two hemispheres, the confrontation also assumed the configuration of a "north-south" contest.

In the recession that began in 1974[24] the developing countries experienced not only a decline in international trade, falling commodity prices, and a slowdown in economic growth but a shrinkage of international assistance funds. After the recession, they staggered under heavy debts incurred during the optimistic years of expanding world trade and rising commodity prices. Oil-producing countries, to give one example, had overcommitted themselves to the rise in oil prices.

[24] See pp. 982–984.

RICH COUNTRIES AND POOR COUNTRIES*

	Gross National Product per Capita		
	1968	1978	1988
Japan	$1,440	$7,020	$21,050
United States	4,440	10,100	19,870
European Community	2,020	6,790	14,200
Kuwait	3,650	15,240	13,670
Saudi Arabia	500	7,720	6,200
Latin America and Caribbean	490	1,460	1,860
China	90	220	340
India	100	190	340
Sub-Saharan Africa	120	400	330

* The table shows the extreme difference between high-income and low-income countries over a period of twenty years, from data assembled and analyzed by the World Bank and converted into United States dollars. The extraordinary growth of Japan is apparent, as is the rapid rise of two oil-producing states in the Persian Gulf. The poverty of the "south," the southern parts of the continents, is also clear. Economic well-being in sub-Saharan Africa has declined.

The figures are averages, and like all averages must be approached with caution. As averages per inhabitant they tell nothing about differences of income *within* each area. The figure for Kuwait is high partly because its population is so small, and figures for China and India are low partly because of their enormous populations. The average for the European Community is lowered by membership of relatively poor countries such as Greece, Portugal, and Ireland. Comparable figures have not been available to the World Bank for the U.S.S.R., nor for Iran and Iraq among the oil-producing states of the Persian Gulf.

SOURCE: The World Bank, *World Tables, 1989–1990.*

Third World debt, principally to private commercial banks, soared, one-third of it owed by the Latin American countries, Brazil, Mexico, Venezuela, and Argentina.

After four decades of the development experience, both the Third World countries and the industrial countries were reassessing the mixed results. Despite advances in some countries, per capita income in the poorest countries had scarcely risen. Almost everywhere the agricultural sector had received a lower priority than the industrial. Agricultural production, even when it increased, failed to keep up with often explosive population growth. To earn foreign exchange, governments had encouraged export crops and neglected food production. In general, an agricultural economy was thought to be a sign of inferiority. The Third World countries were anxious to build their own industries and end dependence on others, but their products were often not competitive either at home or in the world market. Much of the economic aid and capital investment was channeled to industrial projects in the capitals or other large cities, sometimes to nonproductive and extravagant showpieces; little went to help the rural poor, who sank into ever deepening poverty. Millions meanwhile had fled the countryside for the presumed attractions of city life, only to face joblessness, live in congested shantytowns and slums, and breathe polluted air.

In the rush for development, government control frequently led to clumsy bureaucracies and often to extravagance and corruption (not entirely unknown in private-enterprise economies either). In many instances governments used development funds to boost prestige and pride, rather than to improve the lives of their people. In later years, in the 1980s, they began to look to the West, to

Japan, and to the newly industrialized smaller countries of Asia for models. Even in India, which experienced substantial economic improvement, per capita income (because of population growth) rose only from $150 to $250 in the years 1950 to 1990; in South Korea during those years it increased from $350 to $2,900. There was no disagreement about the important role for government in stimulating economic development, but its presence in the Third World countries was out of proportion to the results.

Continuing Problems

In the 1980s economic growth even regressed. Forty-three developing countries finished the decade with lower per capita income. The percentage of the world's population living in poverty, slowly declining in earlier decades, rose. Because of population growth, the numbers of the impoverished were far larger than before. An estimated 1.2 billion human beings, one-fourth the world's population, lived in absolute poverty, in sub-Saharan Africa, Asia, Latin America, and the Middle East. Hundreds of millions suffered from tropical diseases and malnutrition.

The Third World, of course, was not homogeneous. The People's Republic of China (often not included at all as part of the Third World) continued to industrialize and modernize in its own way. The newly industrialized countries in East Asia like Taiwan, Singapore, South Korea, and Hong Kong—the "little tigers"—built powerful export economies and left the Third World behind them. India turned into an exporter of grain and a nuclear power. Countries like Nigeria, Mexico, and the states of the Middle East were rich in oil resources but fell victim to the violent gyrations of world oil prices. Although some nations like India, Indonesia, Malaysia, Argentina, and Brazil were building modern economies, they faced crushing problems of population growth. Pakistan, Egypt, and Peru, trying to develop their economies, were so beset with growing populations that they could scarcely feed their people or foresee much economic improvement in the near future. At the very bottom of any economic scale were a number of sub-Saharan African states, as well as Bangladesh in South Asia, which together formed a kind of "Fourth World," an impoverished group of hundreds of millions of people. In parts of sub-Saharan Africa, of every 1,000 infants, over 170 died before reaching their first birthday. In Malawi life expectancy at birth was forty-four for a male child, slightly higher for a female. In Kenya life expectancy at birth was about fifty-one, in India about fifty-six—a higher figure, to be sure, than for the European or American middle or upper classes only a century ago, but no match for the life expectancy at birth of well over seventy in industrially advanced countries.

The distribution of wealth—a problem in the wealthier countries as well—was particularly acute in the nations where there were fewer goods and services to distribute, and where they were often distributed with gross inequity between an elite cultivating Western standards of luxury and the impoverished masses. The rising expectations and hopeful visions for the Third World of the early postwar decades were turning into ever-deeper frustrations. In point of fact there was no Third World. There were only two worlds, one relatively rich, one poor.

THE MODERN WORLD IN VARIED SETTINGS

Evidences of modernity have spread by the late twentieth century to all parts of the world. Among them are airplanes and oil derricks, computer technology and carbonated soft drinks, such as may be seen in different continents in the following pages.

There is a new global uniformity in certain aspects of civilization. It is no longer a matter of Westernization, as used to be said of what happened in Japan and Russia, nor of the Americanization of the world that has sometimes been pointed to with alarm. It is a process in which Europeans and Americans have been instrumental, but which arises from the effects of modern science, engineering, medicine, transportation, television, and almost instantaneous communications. It seems that human beings of all cultures and races may develop an aptitude to pursue these activities, and that they have wants that such activities can supply.

But as modern civilization becomes more widespread it must adapt to a variety of traditional cultural settings, which must in turn adapt to it. Cultures interpenetrate each other. Older ones are eroded not only in Asia and Africa but in the West itself, where practices that have characterized Europe at least since the Renaissance—in painting, sculpture, architecture, literature, religion, personal values, child rearing, and family life—have increasingly been called into question. Some may resist modernization by reaffirming their own identity, and so may feel a new attachment to their own background, especially in religion. Accepting the interdependence of a world civilization, they strive not only for political but for cultural and spiritual independence.

To operate an airline, or any other appurtenance of modern civilization, requires a high degree of accuracy, division of labor, and the synchronization of the efforts of many persons who must perform certain actions at a given time. These in turn presuppose the objectivity of knowledge and rationality of behavior, and an acceptance of discipline, foresight, organization, and management. But these very qualities generate their opposite. It is a paradox that new philosophies of subjectivity and irrationalism, revolts against form, and demands for free self-expression have also been thought of as signs of modernity in the twentieth century. Organization restricts liberty, yet is necessary to modern life. It is not easy to adapt to the social environment created to improve the human condition. The paradox is as old as Rousseau, yet is felt increasingly every day.

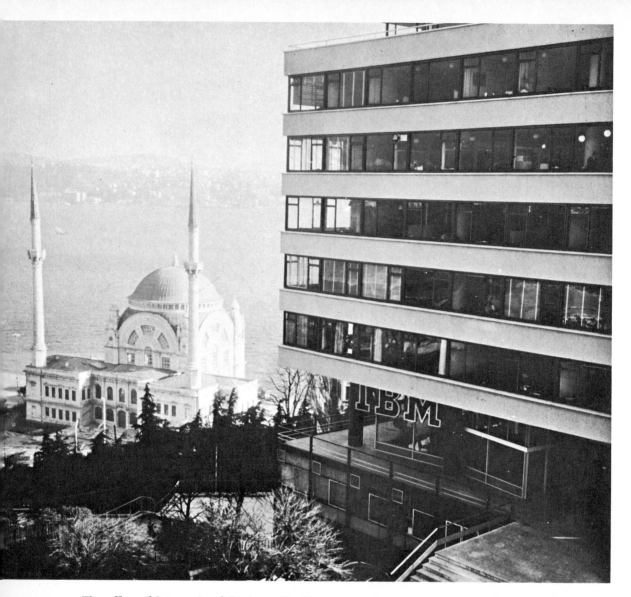

The office of International Business Machines seems in strange company alongside the mosque in Istanbul, Turkey, but it would seem no more so alongside a Gothic church in Europe. Here there is the additional juxtaposition of East and West.

Nigeria, the most populous state in black Africa, has become one of the most important producers and exporters of crude oil. Here is an oil derrick in the swampy area of the delta of the Niger river. As other countries become dependent on Nigeria for energy, so Nigeria becomes vulnerable to fluctuations in the demand for oil.

The older centers of industrial production in Europe, North America, and Japan all feel the pressure from newer competitors. Here Brazilian workers assemble a Volkswagen in São Paulo.

Right: Pope John Paul II upholds the traditional values of Roman Catholic Christianity by using the most advanced technology in his frequent travels. He is shown here arriving in Warsaw.

Below: At Jiddah on the Red Sea, now a city with high-rise apartments, automobiles, and parking problems, a group of Muslims engage in one of the daily prayers prescribed by Islam. They may be on their way to Mecca, only a few miles away.

959

The assumptions underlying Western art since the Renaissance have perhaps been abandoned most fully in sculpture. The statue which celebrated a great individual or an allegorical figure from the fifteenth century through the nineteenth has become even more rare than the realistic portrait painting; it might even be thought ludicrous today.

Henry Moore, at the left, born in England in 1898, was one of the leading sculptors of the twentieth century. He is shown in a room with his collection of plaster maquettes, the working models for the finished products over his long career. As early as 1920, breaking with European traditions of sculpture, he became interested in the art of pre-Columbian America, black Africa, and archaic or preclassical Greece. The models on these shelves reveal influences of this kind. In the quest for a new accent, for boldness of line or emphatic abstraction, the modern and the primitive come together.

961

Above: Ayatollah Khomeini's revolution in Iran brought out violent anti-Western demonstrations. Depicted here is a group of Iranian women, wearing the chador to assert their traditional Islamic values, which they mean to enforce with these modern and imported weapons.

Left: One effect of modern medicine and public hygiene has been a huge growth of population. At New Delhi in India a large sign, promoting a government campaign for family planning, poses a question: Do you want joy and comfort with two children, or destitution with four?

Above: Life goes on as this Chinese boy enjoys a Western beverage while sitting on the Great Wall of China. Most of the present wall dates from the seventeenth century, but some parts were built two thousand years ago to protect Chinese culture from the barbarians of that day.

Right: Two youths work on a computer problem at Ibadan University in Nigeria. Their costumes reflect their own time and place, but the young man at the right shows a concentration and perplexity that are universal. The multiplication of universities, with their attendant problems, is a sign of modernization in all countries.

Some modern improvements have been introduced sooner in Japan than in Europe or America. Here a super-express passes Mount Fuji on the way from Tokyo to Osaka. Initiated in 1964, these trains achieved a speed of over 150 miles an hour. Since then, very high-speed trains with a special roadbed have been built also in France.

Right: These apartments in the South Bronx in New York City, built at the beginning of the present century, have proved less durable than most human constructions. The decay is not in the masonry of the buildings but in economic and social conditions.

Below: This pyramid at Giza, near Cairo, was built about 2500 B.C., some two thousand years before the introduction of the camel into Egypt and more than four thousand before the motor car. It will outlast "modern times."

XXIII.
THE
CONTEMPORARY
AGE: A WORLD
TRANSFORMED

BY THE LATE 1950s the immediate postwar era had slipped into the past. Western Europe and Japan had rebuilt themselves with American aid, the Soviet Union had completed its postwar reconstruction, and regions of the world that had formerly belonged to colonial empires, and China as well, were asserting their independence. Yet the underlying conflict remained. The Cold War continued to manifest itself in an arms race punctuated but not halted by arms agreements, and by intervention of the superpowers in various parts of the globe, where each attempted to prevent the other from gaining an advantage.

As the years passed the phenomenon of "bipolarity," or the predominance of the United States and the Soviet Union, began to fade. It showed signs of being transformed into a situation recalling that of the nineteenth century, when a half-dozen merely "great" but not "super" powers had dealt with one another politically, and a kind of global economy had existed, allowing for much international freedom of trade and movement of capital. The sharp ideological

Chapter Emblem: The earth as seen from a satellite 22,300 miles away, transmitting a photograph to a station in North Carolina.

antagonism between the Communist and the non-Communist world likewise lost its edge. With the rise of Japan it became impossible to identify industrial and financial might with the West. And no one could foresee the sudden revolutionary changes in the late 1980s, when the demand for democracy, on the Western model, swept over Eastern Europe, the Soviet Union, and even China. Nor could anyone in the 1990s predict the future. In looking to the future it is possible to anticipate, consider probabilities, make preparations, and study the long-range trends of the past, but it is impossible to foretell the coming shape of world affairs.

119. The Cold War: Confrontation and Détente, 1955–1975

The Soviet leaders who succeeded Stalin after 1953 seemed at times more conciliatory, and willing to acknowledge the need for arms control and cooperation in the nuclear age. An alternative of peaceful coexistence and competing world systems promised to open up and there were even recognizable periods of détente, or formal relaxation of tensions. But dangerous confrontations recurred, the nuclear arms build-up assumed unprecedented forms and dimensions, and relations seesawed over the next several decades between conciliation and crisis.

By 1955 the Cold War had stabilized. In Asia the Korean War was over. In Europe the North Atlantic Treaty Organization, strengthened by the West German armed forces, faced the Warsaw Pact nations. The iron curtain still divided Europe, but the threat of direct military confrontation receded. The Western powers and the Soviet Union were able to agree in 1955 on a treaty with Austria, ending the joint Allied occupation and leaving Austria independent and neutral. Nikita S. Khruschev had emerged as the dominant Soviet leader. Sharp-tongued, volatile, boastful, he announced that the Soviets would abandon their revolutionary principles only "when shrimp learn to whistle" and pledged that the Soviets would "bury" Western capitalism, but at the same time he rejected the inevitability of war and emphasized the "possibility and necessity of peaceful coexistence." President Eisenhower, in office from 1953 to 1961, continued the American policy of containment and the American military build-up. Eisenhower's secretary of state, John Foster Dulles, who saw the Cold War in almost apocalyptic terms as a Manichean contest between good and evil, urged a "rollback" of Soviet power. Despite his rhetoric, and despite active American military support for anti-Communist forces in Central America, Asia, and elsewhere, American policy remained limited to containment. NATO meanwhile adopted a policy of "massive retaliation," that is, a resort to nuclear arms were it to be necessary in the event of Soviet aggression.

In 1955 Eisenhower, along with the British and French, met at Geneva with Soviet leaders in a friendlier atmosphere than any since the Second World War. Although no agreements were reached, the American president could speak of "a new spirit of conciliation and cooperation." But tensions mounted over Berlin. The Soviets, incensed that East Germans were fleeing in large numbers to West

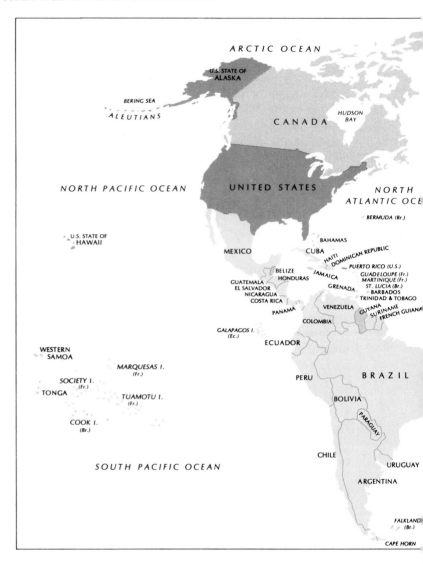

Berlin and then to West Germany, demanded that the Western powers end their occupation of West Berlin, but backed down when Eisenhower forcefully rejected the ultimatum. In 1959 Khruschev visited President Eisenhower at his weekend retreat in Camp David, spoke of peaceful coexistence, and even of mutual disarmament. Another summit conference was arranged for Paris. The superpowers seemed to recognize their common interests in preserving stability and peace. But by then Khruschev, under attack at home, and from Mao in China, for being

THE CONTEMPORARY WORLD

On a small political map of the contemporary world the most readily visible changes, as compared to a map of the world before the Second World War, are the breakup of the European colonial empires in Asia and Africa, the emergence of several new states in Asia and of some fifty independent republics in Africa, the peripheral expansion of the Soviet Union, and the appearance of the People's Republic of China.

too conciliatory toward the West, produced evidence, irrefutable to be sure, of American reconnaissance flights over Soviet territory and broke up the conference. By the summer of 1960 the "spirit of Geneva" and the "spirit of Camp David" had faded. When Khruschev spoke before the United Nations, he boasted of Soviet arms production and vehemently denounced the United States. Crises over Berlin and elsewhere were far from settled.

The United States, unwavering in its resolve to maintain its defense of Western

Europe, accepted Soviet hegemony east of the iron curtain. As we have seen, the Americans protested but did not intervene when in 1953 the Soviets put down antigovernment riots in East Berlin, or when in 1956 the Soviets exerted pressure on Poland to curb its reform movement, or when the Soviets, even more dramatically, sent troops and tanks that year to crush the Hungarian revolt, or later, in 1968, the Czech revolt. The United States offered little more than moral encouragement.[1] At the same time one part of the world after another was being brought into the American strategic defense system. In the Suez crisis (which broke out simultaneously with the troubles in Hungary) the United States deterred Britain, France, and Israel from pressing military action against Egypt,[2] at least in part because it might have encouraged Soviet intervention on the other side. The three countries were frustrated, but the Soviets were kept out. The "Eisenhower Doctrine," which asserted American primacy in the defense of the Middle East, pledged assistance to any government in that region requiring protection against "international Communism." Under that policy, Eisenhower dispatched marines to Jordan and Lebanon in 1958 when their pro-Western governments were threatened. In the Western Hemisphere the United States rallied the Latin American republics to resist domination or control of any American state by the "international Communist movement." American foreign policy in the Cold War remained firmly based on the premise that all unrest was Soviet-inspired.

The nuclear arms race continued. In October 1957 the Soviets, to the world's astonishment, demonstrated their prowess in the new era of rocket technology when they successfully launched *Sputnik*, the first artificial satellite to orbit in outer space. A few months later the United States launched its own space satellite, *Explorer I*. The space age had opened. The military implications of space rocketry quickly became apparent. The same principles of propulsion could launch armed missiles over long distances. In 1958 the Soviets developed the first intercontinental ballistic missile (or ICBM, as it came to be called), capable of delivering nuclear warheads to North America and elsewhere thousands of miles away. The United States developed its own intercontinental ballistic missiles and proceeded to build up an arsenal of nuclear weapons far larger than that of the Soviets. A new kind of arms race, based on "mutual deterrence," was emerging; it was now useless to speak of "massive retaliation." An uneasiness spread in Western Europe that the United States might not so readily defend Western Europe now that American cities were vulnerable to nuclear destruction. Charles de Gaulle, the French president, gave voice to these and other misgivings in the 1960s and called for a more independent role for the West Europeans. Rejecting the rigid patterns of the Cold War and viewing postwar international affairs more as a struggle between Great Powers than as a conflict of ideologies, he called for a return to a more traditional recognition of spheres of national interest and for a reunification of Europe—"from the Atlantic to the Urals." He declined to follow the American lead in foreign policy in Europe or elsewhere. Although he kept France in the Atlantic alliance, in a gesture of independence he withdrew France from the integrated NATO military command in 1966 and pressured NATO into moving

[1] See p. 912.
[2] See p. 942.

its headquarters from French soil. His aspirations for a leadership role for France created uneasiness among many Europeans, but he nevertheless articulated a widespread European discontent with American hegemony in world affairs.

The Kennedy Years, 1961–1963

The gravest direct Soviet-American confrontation came during the Kennedy presidency. President Kennedy heightened the rhetoric of the Cold War. The country "had to pay any price, bear any burden, meet any hardship, support any friend or oppose any foe in order to assure the success and survival of liberty." He accused his Republican predecessor of allowing the Soviets to move ahead in the missile race and took steps to close the "missile gap." Humiliated by Soviet successes in space, he pledged that the Americans would reach the moon before the end of the decade, and encouraged large expenditures on space exploration. The defense budget increased dramatically, as did missile production. Under the policy of "flexible response," the United States and its NATO allies were prepared to meet aggression with conventional weapons before resorting to nuclear arms. At the same time Kennedy increased foreign aid to the developing countries and sponsored the Peace Corps, which took young Americans to Latin America, Asia, and Africa to aid in social and economic development programs designed to improve life and reduce the attractions of communism. For Latin America, which resented the large sums that had gone to Europe, he organized the Alliance for Progress to encourage investment and growth, but economic development remained slow there, for the most part, and democracy difficult to achieve.

In Cuba Kennedy inherited an explosive situation. During the 1950s a zealous young law-school graduate, Fidel Castro, had effectively organized guerrilla warfare against the reactionary but pro-Western dictatorship of Fulgencio Batista, and in 1958 forced him into exile. Many in the United States and elsewhere regarded Castro as a progressive revolutionary favorably disposed to democracy and committed to much-needed change in a country where a dictatorship supported by American business interests had long kept the population impoverished. But Castro was no simple reformer. He inaugurated a sweeping agrarian program, expropriated large American corporate holdings, and imprisoned or executed political opponents. Thousands of Cubans fled to the United States, mostly to Miami. Although he had originally kept his movement aloof from the Cuban Communist party, he now joined ranks with the Communists in order to broaden his political base. When Eisenhower, alarmed by Castro's leftist regime and the threat of communism in the Western Hemisphere, imposed a strict embargo on imports from Cuba, Castro moved closer to the Soviet Union. Within a short time, four-fifths of Cuban trade was with the Soviet Union and Eastern Europe. The United States broke off diplomatic relations and the CIA secretly trained a small group of Cuban refugees for an armed invasion of the island, confident that the invaders could easily topple the Castro regime.

Kennedy inherited the plans for the invasion and, without seriously reassessing the Castro threat, resolved to go forward with them and end the Communist menace ninety miles from the American mainland. The invasion at the Bay of Pigs on April 17, 1961, turned into a fiasco; most of the 1,500 invaders were captured. Castro now inflated his revolutionary rhetoric, openly projected himself as a Marxist-Leninist, took steps to transform Cuba into a socialist state, reaffirmed the country's ties as a client state of the Soviet Union, and championed the cause of international revolution everywhere. The United States tightened its embargo.

At a Kennedy-Khruschev meeting in Vienna that year, the Soviet leader delivered a new ultimatum for the powers to leave Berlin. Kennedy, smarting over the Bay of Pigs defeat, reaffirmed the Western resolve to remain in Berlin, asked Congress to expand the military forces, inaugurated a civil defense program, and made plans for fall-out shelters in the event of nuclear war. The Atlantic alliance backed him. The immediate crisis passed. But in the summer of 1961 the Soviets, still bent on checking the exodus from East Berlin (over 3 million East Germans had already fled), constructed the Berlin Wall, a twenty-eight-mile-long rampart of concrete and barbed wire, with armed sentry stations. The Wall stood as a grim physical reminder of the Cold War; East Germans who braved the barrier met their deaths. Khruschev also ended a three-year moratorium on nuclear testing; both sides resumed tests, both underground and in the atmosphere.

The Cuban Missile Crisis of 1962

The most dangerous confrontation did not occur in Berlin, but in Cuba where, in the fall of 1962, Khruschev showed an unanticipated recklessness. Announcing his intention to defend Cuba against a second American invasion (plans for which existed), he dispatched Soviet soldiers and technicians to the island to construct missile sites that would have brought the American mainland within easy target range. For the United States to allow this Soviet intrusion into America's own backyard was unthinkable; moreover, it could inalterably change the nuclear balance between the two superpowers. During thirteen tense days in October President Kennedy and his advisers resolved not to take any precipitous military action but to stand firm, fully aware that the showdown could lead to nuclear war. Kennedy imposed a blockade (or "quarantine") of the island, forbidding further deliveries of arms and supplies. The launching of any nuclear missile from Cuba, he made clear, would lead to a "full retaliatory response upon the Soviet Union." At the height of the emergency American planes carrying nuclear bombs were airborne. Although Khruschev blustered that the blockade was illegal, the Soviet leader backed down; on October 24 two Soviet ships and their submarine escort turned back. In one note Khruschev agreed to remove the missile sites in return for an American pledge not to invade Cuba. In a second note, more aggressive in tone, he demanded the removal of American missile sites in Turkey. Kennedy shrewdly replied only to the first message, but privately let it be known that the United States would eventually remove its missiles in Turkey. By October 28, the most ominous crisis of the postwar world, an eyeball-to-eyeball confrontation that had brought the superpowers to the brink of nuclear war, was over.

Khruschev had lost face, weakening him still further at home; in 1964 he was ousted from power. China, which was assuming the role of spokesman for the Third World, ridiculed Khruschev's capitulation. Even though tensions once again eased, and the Soviets would never again show such recklessness, the Cuban crisis had a direct effect on the arms race. Both the Soviet Union and the

United States moved to expand their nuclear arsenal, and the Soviets under Khruschev's successors were determined to achieve nuclear parity.

The United States and the Vietnam War

The scene now shifted to Southeast Asia, already caught up in the Cold War and the American effort to contain Communist expansion. In Vietnam, as we have seen, Communists and non-Communists had together fought against the Japanese in the Second World War and then from 1946 to 1954 waged a successful struggle for independence against the French, in which the Vietnamese Communist leader, Ho Chi Minh, played a leading role.[3] The international conference at Geneva in 1954 after the French withdrawal formally recognized the independence of Vietnam, Laos, and Cambodia, all parts of former French Indochina. But in Vietnam the coalition which had waged the war against the French had fallen apart and Communists and anti-Communists who called themselves nationalists, confronted each other. Neither the Communists under Ho Chi Minh, dominant in the north, nor the nationalists in the south wanted a divided country. On a provisional basis the Geneva conference partitioned Vietnam at the seventeenth parallel until peace could be restored, elections held, and the country unified. Ho Chi Minh presided over North Vietnam with its capital at Hanoi, north of the seventeenth parallel; in the south Ngo Dinh Diem governed an American-backed anti-Communist regime, with Saigon as its capital. The partition divided the population into roughly equal halves of 20 million people each, but with little relationship to historic or ethnic realities.

The Western-backed Diem regime in South Vietnam, realizing that the Communists had acquired a large popular following in the struggle against the Japanese and French, refused to participate in the elections scheduled for 1956 and proclaimed itself an independent republic, which Ho's Democratic Republic of Vietnam in the north refused to recognize. Meanwhile some ten thousand Communist guerrilla soldiers (the Viet Cong, or Vietnam Communists), who had remained in the south after the main armies withdrew under the Geneva agreement, began to harass the American-backed South Vietnam regime. Skilled in insurgent warfare, the Viet Cong won support by distributing land to the peasants and by denouncing South Vietnam as a puppet of the West. The Viet Cong guerrillas were soon reinforced by regular North Vietnam troops infiltrating the south. A National Liberation Front projected itself as a revolutionary government for the south, of which the Viet Cong remained the military arm. The U.S.S.R. gave generous military and economic aid to North Vietnam, which found its way to the Communist combat forces in the south. The Chinese Communists, not unhappy to see a divided Vietnam, a country with which they had long had differences, played a more restrained role. South Vietnam, hard pressed despite technical advice and assistance from the United States, appealed for more and more American aid.

The United States, from President Eisenhower on, saw a need to fill the vacuum created by the French withdrawal and to check Communist expansion in Indochina. In order to prevent the other states in Southeast Asia from toppling

---

[3] See p. 924.

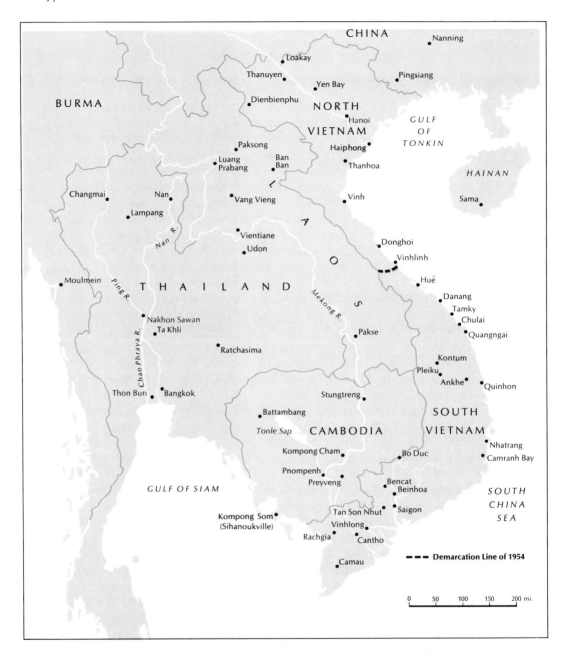

one by one—"like a tumbling row of dominoes," in Eisenhower's phrase, Eisenhower sent aid and military advisers. Kennedy further bolstered the Diem regime with additional military advisers, financial backing, and arms. The United States acted on the premise that the war was not a civil war among the Vietnamese but a war between two independent states, one anti-Communist and therefore to be supported, and the other Communist, receiving aid and support from the Soviet Union. Vietnam was simply part of the global struggle between communism and democracy. In time the Saigon regime's authoritarian practices, ineptitude,

VIETNAM AND ITS NEIGHBORS

French Indochina, for about sixty years before World War II, comprised the old Asian territories of Cambodia, Laos, and Vietnam, though the French called northern Vietnam Tonkin and southern Vietnam Annam. Shaken by Japanese invasion in World War II, the French proved unable after a long struggle to resist the Vietnamese movement for independence that drew strength also from Communist affiliations. When the French withdrew in 1954, an international agreement (the Geneva Accords) provided for partition of Vietnam until unity could be restored. Since the north was now Communist, the United States undertook to strengthen South Vietnam by favoring reforms and by measures of economic and military assistance. This involvement grew in the 1960s into a large-scale though undeclared war, in which the United States intervened with over half a million troops. Hostilities ended in 1975 with Communist regimes established in Vietnam, Laos, and Cambodia.

corruption, and acts of coercion against its large Buddhist population became increasingly embarrassing to its American sponsors.

American involvement deepened and spanned the administration of five presidents, from Eisenhower to Gerald Ford. Under Eisenhower a few hundred military advisers were present, and military and economic aid began; as early as 1959 two military advisers were killed in an attack north of Saigon. In 1961, under Kennedy, additional military advisers and American support troops arrived; a year later 4,000 military personnel were on hand, and the first battle deaths were reported. The Kennedy administration, through the CIA, intervened directly in South Vietnam politics; the Americans first propped up and then in 1963 helped to overthrow the increasingly repressive government of Diem, in the course of which Diem and his brother were murdered.

After Kennedy's tragic assassination in November 1963, and the succession of Lyndon B. Johnson to the presidency, American intervention to achieve a military victory in Vietnam reached a climax. In 1964, on the alleged ground that North Vietnam torpedo boats in the Gulf of Tonkin had attacked United States destroyers, Johnson ordered immediate air strikes against North Vietnam and secured support for a joint congressional resolution empowering him to take "all necessary measures" to defend the United States and its ally. The Gulf of Tonkin resolution was the only explicit congressional sanction for the deepening American involvement. After 1965 heavy air raids on supply bases in the north and on Communist-controlled areas in the south became an almost daily occurrence. American bombers attacked as far north as Hanoi. To root out the elusive Viet Cong in the countryside American soldiers conducted "search and destroy" missions among the hapless villagers, and American planes dropped incendiary materials and chemicals, burning whole villages, defoliating hundreds of thousands of acres of land, and turning the survivors into homeless refugees. The bombing raids, the commitment of American ground troops, and the casualties mounted. In 1966 there were close to 200,000 American troops in Vietnam; by 1969 at the maximum there were 543,400. Token forces, besides the South Vietnam army, participated from other countries, from Thailand, the Philippines, Australia, and New Zealand, but it was an American war. In the massive bombings from 1965 to 1968 more tons of explosives were dropped than against all the Axis powers in the Second World War, but at no point were nuclear weapons used.

The large-scale American military intervention was unable to overcome the persistence of the North Vietnamese, aided by the Soviet Union, which never directly intervened with combat troops but lent assistance of other kinds. Exaggerated military reports to Washington about the "pacification" of the countryside and about the number of enemy casualties (or "body counts") were confounded by the Communists' Tet, or New Year's, offensive at the opening of 1968, which although unsuccessful, only fortified American resolve to continue the war. To many, however, it was clear that a settlement had to be sought.

From the beginning America's allies in Western Europe were critical of the American involvement and, even more so, of the deepening intervention. De Gaulle, a moralizer when it suited his purposes, called it "detestable" for "a great nation to ravage a small one." At home the war became a root cause of disorders and protests on college campuses and in the cities. A wide array of public opinion turned against the war. Some opponents raised larger issues. They questioned whether the United States, despite its enormous strength, should assume the responsibility, or even had the capability, to police the world against Communist aggression; whether the American presence in Vietnam was an unwanted foreign presence reminiscent of Western intrusion in the age of imperialism; whether the South Vietnamese regime could be stabilized and democratized to make the sacrifices worthwhile; and whether the air raids and continued hostilities might not end in the utter destruction of the hapless country. Critics with a knowledge of Asian history argued that the Vietnamese had a long record of independence and that even a Vietnam united under the Communists would not lead to subordination to the Soviets, or to China.

The need to win the war became an obsession with President Johnson. Like his predecessors, he was convinced that it was in America's vital interest to contain communism in Southeast Asia; otherwise the Communists would be "in Hawaii and next they will be in San Francisco." He, too, refused to repeat the lessons of appeasement of the 1930s. Above all, he could not see himself presiding over the first war lost by the United States. But with victory remote, and with resentment against the war rising, he decided not to seek reelection in 1968 and announced a halt to the bombing in the north so that peace negotiations could go forward. By November 1968 all bombing ceased—for a time. The Hanoi government and the National Liberation Front opened preliminary peace talks in Paris with the United States and South Vietnam even though the fighting went on. Johnson's successor, President Nixon, pledged an early end to the war, promised to shift to South Vietnam the major responsibility for its own defense, and began to withdraw troops. Yet the United States in the next three years in some ways became even more deeply involved. In response to stalemated peace talks in Paris and continuing Communist advances, Nixon ordered the resumption of heavy air attacks and widened the war by an "incursion" into Cambodia to cut off North Vietnam supply lines. The war spread to Laos as well.

Demonstrations mounted in the United States at the widening of the unpopular war. At the end of 1972 North Vietnam was subjected to even heavier bombing. Meanwhile Nixon's national security adviser and later secretary of state, Henry Kissinger, encouraged the bombings and military pressure but held secret talks with the North Vietnam representatives and finally brought about a cease-fire agreement in January 1973. The agreement ended direct military involvement for the United States and concluded the longest war—like the Korean, an undeclared one—the country had ever fought. Over eight years elapsed from the arrival of the first Marine contingent in 1965 to the withdrawal of the last troops at the end of March 1973, or twelve years, if the involvement is dated from 1961.

Even though American troops were withdrawn, hostilities between North Vietnam and South Vietnam continued as each sought additional territory before a final settlement was reached. Both sides violated the cease-fire, and fighting resumed on a major scale in 1973. Although the United States remained committed to the defense of South Vietnam, Congress refused additional expenditures for military aid. North Vietnam dominated the fighting. Corruption and demoralization in South Vietnam grew worse; army desertions mounted. Nevertheless, the end came as a surprise. At the close of 1974, the North Vietnamese captured key cities in the southern provinces. The government of South Vietnam lost heart and ordered withdrawal to the coast; a planned retreat degenerated into rout. The North Vietnamese, with complete victory in their grasp, poured thousands of troops south across the demilitarized zone. Swarms of refugees fleeing south added to the confusion. By April 1975 North Vietnam's armies controlled three-fourths of South Vietnam, and Saigon fell.

North Vietnamese troops entered Saigon, and renamed the capital Ho Chi Minh City in honor of the Communist leader who had died in 1969. After thirty years of almost uninterrupted fighting, first against the French and then in the civil war between north and south in which the United States had massively intervened, peace had finally come, and with it total Communist victory. Reunification and reorganization of the country along Communist lines proceeded quickly. The new regime launched a ''political reeducation'' campaign, national-ized property, and forcibly moved large numbers of the population from the cities to the countryside. Thousands, mostly ethnic Chinese, tried to flee in makeshift, overcrowded boats, many perishing in the attempt or discovering that the countries which they reached would not offer them a haven. The term ''boat people'' for the unfortunate refugees became part of the world's political lexicon.

In the wake of North Vietnam's victory, Cambodia and Laos also fell under Communist control. Thirty years after the end of the Second World War, all that had once been French Indochina was in Communist hands, and a reunified Vietnam emerged as an important military power in Southeast Asia.

The Vietnam War was costly; about one and a quarter million Vietnamese were estimated to have died in the fighting. For the United States the war was a searing experience. Battle and battle-related deaths exceeded 58,000, a greater death toll than in the Korean War.[4] From 1960 to 1975 the hostilities cost the United States over $140 billion. The impact of these expenditures was heightened by the failure to place taxes on a wartime basis, contributing to the inflation that

[4] Department of Defense figures show:

	Battle Deaths	Other Deaths	Wounded	Total Deaths
World War I (1917–1918)	53,402	63,114	204,002	116,516
World War II (1941–1945)	291,557	113,842	670,846	405,399
Korean War (1950–1953)	33,629	20,617	103,284	54,246
Vietnam War (1965?–1973)	47,382	10,753	153,303	58,135

later set in. The political and moral costs were enormous. The war also created a mistrust of presidential power—of an "imperial presidency." Congress adopted legislation in 1973 intended to curb and control presidential initiatives that could lead to future episodes like Vietnam. The deadly bombings, the reports of enemy casualties, the gruesome war scenes visible in the first war reported in detail on television, the revelation of atrocities and war crimes committed by American troops (as at My Lai in 1968, first covered up and then made the subject of a public inquiry and trial), the disclosure of widespread drug addiction among American soldiers, the sensitivity of veterans that their sacrifices in the unpopular war were unappreciated, were all deeply disturbing. America's giant industrial and military power had failed to bring victory. Technological superiority in armaments and air power proved inadequate against an enemy skilled in insurgent warfare and imbued with a revolutionary zeal.

The travail of Southeast Asia did not end. During the Vietnam War the North Vietnamese had infiltrated border areas of Cambodia and helped arm Communist insurgents, the Khmer Rouge, who, after five years of civil war, overthrew the government in 1975. The ruthless Pol Pot, the leader of the Cambodian Communists, subjected Cambodia (or Kampuchea, as it was renamed) to brutal dictatorship and grisly terror; an unknown number, perhaps 2 to 3 million, died in the small country from 1975 to 1978 as a result of mass executions, forced labor, and famine.

But the Khmer Rouge turned out to be more pro-Chinese than suited the Vietnamese. In 1979 Vietnam, backing a dissident group of Communist rebels, and invading with large numbers of troops, overthrew the Pol Pot regime. In retaliation, China invaded the border provinces of Vietnam, but soon withdrew. The Soviet Union throughout these events supported Vietnam. International pressure for the withdrawal of Vietnam from Cambodia was without effect until in the late 1980s the Soviets themselves encouraged the withdrawal, but instability still threatened. Ancient rivalries between China and Vietnam, and between Vietnam and Cambodia, and tensions between the Soviet Union and China prolonged the agonies of Southeast Asia. There was no monolithic communism in this part of the globe.

Brezhnev in the 1970s: Détente, the Helsinki Conference of 1975

After Khruschev's fall from power in 1964 the more phlegmatic Leonid I. Brezhnev emerged as the dominant Soviet leader and headed both party and state for the next eighteen years, building the country's military and naval strength even at a disregard for the costs to the economy. Brezhnev avoided direct confrontation and saw political and economic advantages in a relaxation of tensions and arms negotiations. The open rift with China made détente with the West even more important. No direct confrontation even approximating the Cuban missile crisis occurred. On the other hand, the two superpowers vied with each other for influence in the Middle East and other strategic areas of the world and the Soviets consolidated their hold on Eastern Europe. Brezhnev told his compatriots that détente did not "in the slightest abolish, nor can it alter, the laws of the class struggle," and he defined détente as "a way to create more favorable conditions" for advancing the Communist cause.

The Soviet grip on Eastern Europe grew tighter. When, in 1968, liberalizing reforms in Czechoslovakia threatened the one-party state, Brezhnev, as we have seen, ruthlessly crushed the "Prague spring." In what came to be known as the "Brezhnev Doctrine" the Soviets proclaimed the right to intervene in the name of "proletarian internationalism" in any socialist country to protect socialism against "internal or external forces" and prevent the "restoration of a capitalist regime." It was a kind of mirror image of the Truman Doctrine. Czechoslovakia returned to a tight dictatorship ruled by party bosses with close ties to Moscow. The United States did no more than protest the armed intervention in Czechslovakia; once again it would not challenge events behind the iron curtain. But the invasion of Czechoslovakia undermined Soviet leadership among Western Communist parties, which openly denounced the brutal intervention.

When President Nixon took office in 1969, despite the ongoing war in Vietnam he sought to introduce greater flexibility into the American policy of containment and to pursue a policy of more systematic détente. Under Kissinger's influence he came to believe, not unlike de Gaulle, that in foreign policy national self-interest for any country counted more than ideology. The United States would be unable to curb Soviet expansionism altogether but it could offer economic concessions and other inducements for cooperation and peace. Under the Nixon-Kissinger policy the United States linked Western technology, trade, and investment to Soviet cooperation in international affairs and to a softening of Soviet policies at home and in its client states in Eastern Europe. The economic inducements were important because the Soviet Union's economic difficulties were aggravated by its growing arms burden. Khruschev's earlier boast of surpassing the West economically had proved hollow. The Soviets badly needed Western technology, Western investment credits, and because of its persistent agricultural crises, Western grain. In the new atmosphere American and West European private bankers made large loans to the East European nations, which benefited even more than the Soviets from détente. The two Germanys moved closer together in economic relations, recognized each other diplomatically, and were admitted to the United Nations in 1973 as two separate sovereign states.

The Nixon-Kissinger policies developed out of a reassessment of global realities. Unlike the bipolar situation in 1945 when there were only two superpowers, there were now five existing or emergent power centers: the United States, the U.S.S.R., Western Europe, Japan, and the People's Republic of China. In addition, the Third World countries, despite their heterogeneity, were also an important presence. Meanwhile the world's most populous nation, China, even if it was still isolated and in the throes of its Maoist Cultural Revolution, required special attention. The United States moved to normalize relations. Nixon, who had built his domestic political career on anti-Communism, visited Beijing in 1972 and opened up diplomatic and economic relations. It was at this time, in 1973, that the United States supported the entry of the People's Republic of China into the United Nations and the transfer to it of the permanent seat on the Security Council occupied by Taiwan.

The American opening to China increased pressure on the Soviets to pursue détente. At the same time the Soviet arms build-up under Brezhnev meant that the Soviets were approaching nuclear parity. Both sides were interested in negotiating arms limitations. The Strategic Arms Limitation (or SALT) talks begun under President Johnson were resumed. In 1972 Nixon visited Moscow. He and the Soviet leaders reaffirmed the goal of "peaceful coexistence" and signed the SALT I treaty. Each nation agreed to reduce its antimissile defense system to make it possible to work toward equality in offensive weapons. They agreed also to hold stipulated offensive weapons to a fixed ceiling for a period of five years. The treaty did not halt the arms race but it reduced fears on both sides of a preemptive strike, and promised continued negotiations. After Nixon resigned from the presidency in 1974 after the Watergate scandal, détente continued under President Ford, his successor and former vice president.

Détente offered an opportunity to settle or phase out some unresolved issues of the Second World War. In 1975, in what resembled a peace conference for Europe, three decades after the Second World War had ended, thirty-five nations—the sixteen members of NATO, the seven Warsaw Pact states, and twelve European countries not formally members of either alliance—met at Helsinki in a Conference on Security and Cooperation in Europe, and pledged themselves to work for permanent peace in Europe, economic and cultural cooperation, and the protection of human rights. The Helsinki Final Act, as the agreement was called, although not a formal treaty, ratified the de facto European territorial boundaries set up after the Second World War, including the Oder-Neisse boundary between West Germany and Poland. For the surveillance of human rights "Helsinki watch committees" were established. The U.S.S.R. seemed to consider the commitment to human rights a small price to pay in exchange for the economic and other benefits of détente. It expected to keep strict limits on dissent within its own country and in the East European states. It failed to see how much Helsinki would encourage dissenters to defy repression. The Helsinki conference was the high point of this era of détente; not long thereafter Soviet-Western relations took another downward turn. But before we examine it, we must turn to the changes in the world's economy, to which the Soviet Union and the Eastern bloc were now more closely tied than ever before.

120. Recession and Recovery: The Global Economy

Interdependence is a form of dependency, and the expansion of the global economy after the Second World War made each country vulnerable to events in distant places. In 1974, after two and a half decades of spectacular growth,[5] the Western economic boom wound down abruptly. Signs of economic slowdown and inflationary pressures had already been visible in the late 1960s and recession might have occurred in any event, but it was the oil embargo growing out of the third Arab-Israeli War in the autumn of 1973 that precipitated the crisis.[6]

Oil had replaced coal as a major source of energy in Europe by the 1960s. Readily available at low prices, the oil came primarily from the vast reserves of the Middle East and was transported easily and economically by tanker through

[5] See pp. 885–886.
[6] See pp. 942–944.

the Persian Gulf and Suez Canal. The major international oil companies, mostly American, controlled prices and production, and the oil was paid for in dollars. The entire Western global economy as well as the Japanese had come to depend on cheap oil. In 1960, fourteen of the oil exporting countries in the Middle East, Africa, and Latin America formed the Organization of Petroleum Exporting Countries (or OPEC) to curb the monopoly concessions enjoyed by foreign companies and to assume a larger share of authority over production and prices. Within OPEC the Arab states of the Middle East were the most assertive. The oil issue turned intensely political in October 1973 when the Arab oil-producing states embargoed the shipment of oil to states accused of supporting Israel. That winter the OPEC cartel cut back production and quadrupled oil prices. Panic spread in Western Europe and Japan, and in the United States, which needed foreign oil to supplement its domestic resources. Never had an essential commodity risen in price so rapidly; never did the whole Western industrial complex seem so vulnerable. The oil shortage and the price escalation, coming on the heels of the international monetary difficulties of 1971–1973 described earlier, sharply increased balance of payment deficits for all oil-importing countries, undermined currencies, and accelerated an inflationary spiral already under way. Not only did the oil crisis interrupt the spectacular growth of the West European economies, it also revealed the weaknesses in European unity. Apprehensive over their oil supplies, some European states scrambled to negotiate individual agreements with the Arab states.

The immediate panic caused by the oil embargo passed, but prices remained at a higher level than ever before. Later in the decade, in 1979, a second oil crisis occurred when Iran, in the midst of its revolution, halted oil exports and the OPEC cartel once again doubled prices. In the 1980s the Iran-Iraq War further cut off oil supplies and threatened the free movement of tankers through the Persian Gulf, prompting the United States and other Western countries to take naval action. Still, for a time, the oil cartel seemed less cohesive and intimidating than originally feared. Additional energy resources also became available. After the discovery of oil in the North Sea, Britain and Norway became exporters of oil. The Netherlands and other countries turned to natural gas, France to nuclear energy. Many countries initiated energy conservation measures. When prices declined in the 1980s, because of falling demand, oil-producing countries like Nigeria and Mexico found themselves deeply in debt because they had geared their economies to the sale of high-priced oil. The decline in oil revenues led to restlessness in the Arab states. The Persian Gulf crisis precipitated by Iraq's invasion of Kuwait in August 1990, and the American and international response, demonstrated the critical role that oil still played in international affairs.

The Recession: Stagnation and Inflation

The recession that began in 1974 was the most severe since the 1930s, although it never approximated the depths of the Great Depression.[7] What set it apart from previous economic declines was the accompanying inflation, triggered by the oil crisis, which raced on in major industrial countries at double-digit annual figures.

---

[7] See pp. 799–804.

In some European countries the annual rate of inflation rose to over 20 percent; it reached 27 percent in Britain in 1975. For a time economic growth came to a standstill in Western Europe. By the late 1970s the recession was worldwide. Bankruptcies shook several countries; production declined; economic growth halted or slowed. In the twenty-four non-Communist industrial countries the number of jobless was estimated at 15 million in 1975 and over 32 million in 1983. Over 10 percent of the American and West European labor force was unemployed. American factories operated at only two-thirds their capacity.

The economic troubles were cushioned for the unemployed in industrial countries. Labor unions were still strong, although declining in membership and influence, and welfare benefits more advanced than they had been in the 1930s. Unemployed automobile workers in Essen, Turin, or Detroit could count on severance pay, trade union benefits, and government unemployment compensation far beyond the welfare payments and dole of earlier generations. These benefits not only reduced human suffering but prevented an even greater decline in consumer purchasing power. The recession aggravated the problem of "structural unemployment." Because of automation, high technology, and the dwindling importance of many older, less efficient industries, like coal mining, shipbuilding, and textiles (and other so-called "smokestack" or "sunset" industries), many workers would never return to their old jobs or use their old skills again. Even after prosperity returned, some cities in the American Midwest and northern England remained depressed and blighted.

The combination of stagnation and inflation (dubbed "stagflation" by journalists) created unprecedented problems for governments attempting to cope with the recession. Keynesian theory,[8] which had gained a wide following after 1945, called for government spending and deficit financing in slow times to buoy demand and keep employment stable. With inflation rampant, such measures became questionable. The dilemma centered on whether curbing inflation or reducing unemployment should claim the highest priority. Efforts to fight inflation by tight money and high interest rates would discourage investment, aggravate the business slowdown, and swell the ranks of the unemployed. Government spending to prime the pump or lowered interest rates to facilitate private borrowing fed inflation. With the American economy in difficulties, the Western industrial countries looked to West Germany and its powerful economy and trade surplus to take the lead in expanding investment and production. West Germany, however, mindful of the hyperinflation of the 1920s,[9] set its highest priority on controlling inflation; it kept interest rates high and rejected expansionist policies. Other countries adopted the same stance. By the early 1980s inflation was brought under control in Western Europe, but with levels of unemployment unheard of in the early postwar decades.

Monetarism came to replace Keynesianism in many influential circles. Tight control over the amount of money in circulation and high interest rates were the tools used to control inflation. Faith in Keynesianism, and even in government spending for social purposes, the hallmark of twentieth-century progressive liberalism and the welfare state, was seriously shaken. From 1950 to the mid

[8] See pp. 808 and 885.
[9] See pp. 786–787.

1970s, the percentage of gross national product expended on social measures in the industrial countries had more than doubled. Margaret Thatcher, who became the British prime minister in 1979, led the campaign against the welfare state and was joined by Ronald Reagan, the American president from 1981 to 1989. They challenged the welfare state as costly, wasteful, paternalistic, and bureaucratic, and as undermining individual responsibility and initiative. Nationalized industries, where they existed, came under attack. Public spending for social measures was curbed (but high expenditures maintained for national defense) and private enterprise encouraged by tax reductions, deregulation, and curtailment of trade union power. In this view it was the supply side of the equation, not the demand, that required stimulation; the results would trickle down to the population as a whole, with a safety net in place for the truly disadvantaged. The return of prosperity in the 1980s reinforced confidence in the free market economy—despite the vicissitudes of the business cycle. The conservative position seemed confirmed by a worldwide movement toward market economies and away from centralized planning, which in its rigidly Marxist form in the Soviet Union and elsewhere had manifestly failed. The defenders of progressive liberalism and the welfare state continued to argue that social democracy was a logical counterpart to political democracy in an industrial world and that free-market economies had to be supplemented by a social concern for one's citizens. The welfare state seemed destined to survive, but in modified form.

Recession, Recovery, and Political Change in Western Europe

Britain was especially hard hit by the recession. Of all the industrial nations, it suffered the highest rate of inflation. Unemployment rose and the pound dropped to the lowest point in its history. To avert collapse, the country depended on foreign loans. The trade unions, which controlled the Labour party, refused to accept the necessary sacrifices that both parties felt necessary and disruptive strikes in coal and transportation in 1978–1979 weakened and exasperated the country. Radical factions in the Labour party pressed for increased natonalization, and for a more neutral foreign policy. In 1979, alienated by the confusion and collapse of moral authority, for which it placed the blame mainly on Labour, the electorate returned the Conservatives to office. Margaret Thatcher, the first woman prime minister in any major Western country, headed a government resolved to change matters. She immediately initiated a policy of deflation, cutting government expenditures, curbing imports, resisting trade union wage demands, and encouraging investment, productivity, and economic growth. Inflation declined dramatically, but unemployment rose higher than at any time since 1931. The Thatcher government seemed headed for trouble until Argentina invaded the disputed Falkland (Malvina) Islands off the coast of South America in 1982. The prime minister stirred old patriotic and imperial memories when she dispatched a small armada 8,000 miles and thwarted the attempted takeover. The Conservatives won a sweeping parliamentary majority in 1983, and again four years later.

In time Thatcher's philosophy of society and government emerged even more decisively. Private enterprise, if free and unencumbered, could create wealth that would benefit the people more than the government-supported welfare state, which drained the economy and diverted resources. She returned to private enterprise over one-third the nationalized industries, provided tax and other incentives to business, and curbed the power of the unions to call strikes or to block technological innovation. But she also made it possible for ordinary working-class families living in public housing ("council houses," the British called them) to purchase their homes. Her announced goal was a "property-owning democracy," a "people's capitalism."

For a time in the 1980s the Thatcher policies were successful. Britain could point to the highest economic growth rate of all the European countries, rising productivity, low inflation, a stronger pound, a higher standard of living for most people, widened home ownership, and buoyant self-confidence. Unemployment, however, remained high; fiscal retrenchment hurt education, especially the universities; and pockets of deep depression persisted, especially in the north of England and in Scotland and Wales where traditional industries like coal mining and shipbuilding were in difficulties. The south and southeast enjoyed a bustling prosperity, especially in the high technology industries around London and Cambridge. London reinforced its position as a world financial center and the United Kingdom became once again a leading creditor nation. Decades of economic decline and demoralization seemed to have been reversed. The opposition was disunited and in disarray. In the elections of 1987, Labour's popular vote dropped to its lowest point since 1918, and union membership declined. But when the economy took a downturn shortly afterwards, Thatcher introduced a number of fiscal measures that brought to a head a variety of accumulated resentments and led, in 1990, to her fall from leadership in the Conservative party and her replacement as prime minister. Labour meanwhile, under new moderate leadership, challenged the Conservatives, arguing that the Thatcher era had favored the rich and appealed to those who wanted a more equitable society. The impact, however, of the Thatcher years was decisive. No longer were the British satisfied with "managed decline."

In France, by contrast, politics in the 1980s at first took a leftward turn. The austerity program adopted to combat inflation was unpopular, and the government's aloofness, elitism, and seeming unconcern with social issues under de Gaulle's successors in the 1970s helped the Socialist-led opposition grow in strength. In 1981 François Mitterrand achieved the goal he had set for himself and the Socialist party. A moderate Socialist, whose socialism owed more to the liberal idealism of the wartime Resistance than to Marxism, he revitalized the Socialist party, persuaded it to drop its class-struggle rhetoric, relegated the Communists to a subordinate place on the left, and successfully reached out to all those who chafed at the social insensitivities of the Gaullists and conservatives. Not only did he win the presidency, but his Socialist party triumphantly gained an unprecedented absolute majority in the National Assembly.

Inspired in part by the Popular Front reforms of 1936 and by those of the early postwar years,[10] he at once introduced labor reforms, reducing the work week and adding a fifth week of annual paid vacations. Following up on the nationalizations of 1945, he nationalized the remaining large banks as well as several leading industrial corporations. One of the few European leaders still faithful to Keynesian precepts,

[10] See pp. 815–817, 885, 889–890.

Mitterrand expected government pump priming and labor reforms to raise purchasing power, stimulate the economy, and thus absorb the costs of the expanded welfare state. But increased labor costs made French products less competitive internationally and private investment dried up. The country faced slower economic growth, a mounting trade deficit, rising inflation, unemployment, and a weakening franc. Within two years Mitterrand changed course. He halted further nationalization and reforms, and called for retrenchment and austerity to cope with inflation, and changed the emphasis to modernization. Cutting off subsidies to the decaying sectors, he shifted support to the high technology sectors of the economy. The new policies encouraged economic growth even if unemployment remained high. Many of his leftist followers were disenchanted and frustrated by the turn of events. But many in the country were gratified that he had placed national interests above sectarianism. Politics in France held the promise of being less polarized than in the past.

In assuming the leadership of the left, Mitterrand had isolated the Communists and dramatically reduced their electoral strength. Without a dynamic Communist competitor, the French Socialists could now act more like socialists and social democrats elsewhere, campaigning for moderate reform, accepting alternation in office with centrist or conservative parties, counting on middle-class support, and content to help manage capitalist economies. The Socialists retained a residue of idealism, egalitarianism, and concern for the quality of life—a rose in a clenched fist remained the symbol of the party. But the Socialists, like the conservatives, became mostly concerned with building a strong economy, from which everyone, including the working class, would benefit.

Wherever Socialist parties took office in Western Europe in the 1980s in the wake of the recession, they followed a similar pattern. In Italy the long tenure of the Christian Democrats, who had formed forty consecutive cabinets since 1945, was finally interrupted in 1981, and a Socialist coalition headed by Bettino Craxi governed from 1983 to 1987 for an unprecedented four years. In Spain, in 1982, the Socialist Felipe Gonzalez, formed the first government of the left in the post-Franco constitutional monarchy since the Spanish Civil War.[11] In Portugal, after the turbulence of the 1974 revolution, a Socialist and a Social Democratic party competed with each other, each believing in moderate reform. In Greece the Socialist Andreas Papandreaou, who had returned from political exile when the "regime of the colonels" ended, headed a Socialist government from 1981 to 1989. Modernization, economic growth, and market economies overshadowed, if they did not entirely replace, older ideologies.

In West Germany the Social Democratic government of Helmut Schmidt moved to control inflation, its chief worry, through policies of retrenchment and fiscal conservatism, but the industrial slowdown brought unemployment to a country which for years had known only labor scarcity. Even after recovery, unemployment persisted at about 8 percent. The doors once open to guest workers closed tight; bonuses were offered to those who would return home; a small fringe party alarmingly exploited antiforeign sentiment, as in Britain and France. The Christian Democrats in 1982 regained the support of the Free Democrats and returned to office with Helmut Kohl as chancellor.

[11] See pp. 838–839.

Economic growth resumed, although at more modest rates, and the mark remained one of the world's strongest currencies.

Recovering from the recession, the German Federal Republic remained the most productive nation in Western Europe, its gross national product was exceeded only by the two superpowers and Japan, and it accounted for a third of the combined output of the European Community. With a population less than one-quarter the American, and a territory no larger than the state of Oregon, its gross national product was one-third that of the United States in the 1980s, and its volume of foreign trade nearly equal. Its economy suffered from some structural weaknesses, including the decay of older traditional industries, unemployment, a decline in venture capital, rigidities imposed by labor, and the growing predisposition of a consumer society to prize leisure and security. But the Federal Republic had a powerful economy, a stable parliamentary democracy, a minimum of social friction, a more pluralistic, tolerant, and egalitarian society than Germany had ever previously known. A vigorous new populist, grass roots movement, the Greens, drew the country's attention to environmental and ecological issues and in 1983 won the 5 percent vote needed for parliamentary representation.

Although there was no crisis of regime or challenge to the constitutional system, some critics attacked West German society for its materialism and self-centeredness. Others questioned whether the Federal Republic, although a remarkably stable regime, was capable of arousing deeply felt emotional or patriotic attachments while Germany remained divided. But the prospects for reunification of the two Germanys in the 1980s seemed remote—it would remain "one nation and two states," in Willy Brandt's phrase. The transformation of Eastern Europe in 1989 upset many predictions, as we shall see.

The American Economy

The United States recovered from the recession sooner than the Europeans. The American economy had its ups and downs after 1973, suffered its severest decline and most serious inflation from 1978 to 1982, then recovered and embarked again on an extended period of expansion over the next seven or eight years. In the 1980s unemployment dropped below the "acceptable" figure of 6 percent and the labor force as a whole grew, although many of the newly employed were in lower-paid service industries. In Western Europe, even after recovery, there were still 18 million unemployed as late as 1990. Japan's economic slowdown was never as serious as elsewhere and the country soon resumed its upward climb. The American recovery helped to promote world recovery. From 1982 on, the world economy and world trade were growing, but at rates lower than in the earlier postwar decades.

The economic primacy of the United States accentuated some of its own economic problems. The oil crisis of the 1970s had reinforced the strength of the dollar and, with recovery, the dollar rose steadily in value from 1981 to 1985. Meanwhile American exports faced strong competition from Western Europe and Japan, and beginning in the 1980s from the newly industrialized small states in the Pacific like Singapore, South Korea, Taiwan, and Hong Kong, where labor costs were low and newer, highly mechanized plants provided a competitive edge. The strong dollar made it even more difficult for the United States to sell abroad and aggravated its already heavy trade deficit. With the cooperation of other major industrial countries, the United States brought down the high value of the dollar in 1985. Over the next three years the dollar lost almost 50 percent of its value in relation to foreign currencies, declining to its lowest level since 1945. Japanese, West Europeans, Canadians, Arabs, and others found it easier to buy into American corporations, banks, brokerage houses, and real estate. By the late 1980s foreign holdings of American assets totaled $1 trillion. Meanwhile the Japanese economy reached such giant dimensions that corporations like the Fujita Bank and the Toyota Corporation were valued at five to ten times the market value of the largest American companies. The Nomura Securities Corporation of Tokyo became the largest brokerage firm in the world. Not one of the world's ten largest banks was American. From 1985 on, for the first time since 1914, the United States was a debtor nation. Foreign interests owned more assets in the United States than Americans owned abroad, which meant a steady outflow of interest, dividends, and rents. Even when American exports expanded, imports remained high and the country still showed an unfavorable trade balance. Moreover, the annual budget deficit mounted and the national debt soared: at the end of the 1980s, it exceeded $2.5 trillion. Foreign capital financed the American debt and profited from the interest on the loans.

Even in prosperous times, there was widespread concern in the United States over the budget, trade, and balance-of-payments deficits, the heavy burden of defense expenditures, the foreign acquisition of American assets, and the fluctuations of the dollar. There was concern also over inadequate savings and investment in a consumer-oriented society, a relative decline in productivity, a lag in industrial research and development, and the shortcomings of American education for an increasingly competitive global economy. Deep pockets of poverty also persisted within the country. Some wondered whether the United States, still the premier economic and military power, might lose its primacy because of economic weaknesses—as Spain, France, and Britain had in the modern centuries. The prospects that opened up in the mid 1980s of an end to the Cold War, and of relief from the burden of arms expenditures, brought some reassurances to the United States. But the growing strength of Japan, the Pacific basin countries, and the reorganized European Community, the economic potential of a reunited Germany, and international uncertainties could further erode its economic leadership.

The Financial World

The world's stock exchanges and financial markets were centered in New York City. Deregulation in the 1980s brought with it a sharp increase in financial acquisitions, mergers, and takeovers. Computerized trading, considered superior to human judgment, contributed to market volatility, as did new forms of trading in "options" and "futures." As in the 1920s, the lines between speculation and investment (in the banking world as well) became blurred. In October 1987, a tremor ran through the United States and world markets when stocks on the New York Stock Exchange declined sharply, losing close to one-fourth their value and conjuring up memories of the October 1929 crash and the ensuing Great

Depression.[12] The market recovered and the 1987 crash did not, as feared, have serious repercussions on the American and world economy. The episode did make clear the interdependence of the world's financial markets. The reverberations of the 1987 shock in New York were felt instantly in London, Frankfurt, Tokyo, Hong Kong, Singapore, Taipei, Sidney, and elsewhere. The financial markets, like the currency markets, were decentralized but more interwoven than ever before. With telecommunications and other advanced technology, even if New York remained the center, a single financial market operated around the world and around the clock, sensitive to changes anywhere.

The sense of mutual interdependence in the global economy came to be widely shared. The United States, Western Europe, and Japan recognized that the prosperity of each depended on the smooth functioning of the world economy. The heads of state of the seven largest non-Communist industrial powers (the "Group of Seven"—the United States, Britain, France, the Federal Republic of Germany, Italy, Canada, and Japan) met from the 1970s on in annual economic summits to consult on the state of the economy. The leading central banks cooperated in efforts to stabilize interest and exchange rates. The Organization for Economic Cooperation and Development (OECD) brought together the twenty-four leading non-Communist industrial nations of the world, and GATT continued its "rounds" of negotiations to reduce tariffs. The integration of the Soviet Union and Eastern Europe into the world economy, initiated in the 1970s in the initial period of détente, and further encouraged after 1985, provided new opportunities for international cooperation. The developing Third World nations, however, remained on the periphery, their heavy debt and slow economic growth a continuing problem.

The Enlarged European Community: Problems and Opportunities

After de Gaulle's passing from the political scene in 1969, the way opened up for enlarging the six-nation European Community.[13] In 1973 Britain, Denmark, and Ireland were admitted; the six became nine. In the next decade, with the admission of Greece in 1981 and Spain and Portugal in 1985, the nine became twelve.

But the Community expanded just as the economic recession struck in 1974. The growth and the greater diversity in membership created new tensions. The British opposed additional supranational authority for the Community or even closer economic integration. They objected also to the common agricultural policy which the Community had worked out in 1968 to encourage greater efficiency. Countries like France and Italy received large subsidies for their farmers, whose agricultural and dairy products were kept from the open market and stored at great expense to keep prices high. Britain, a large food importer, complained of paying a disproportionate share of the EC budget without receiving commensurate benefits. The admission of the less industrially advanced southern Mediterranean states introduced serious regional differences. Despite the original promise and accomplishments of the Community as a whole, the free trading area was still far

---

[12] See pp. 801–804.
[13] See pp. 900–902.

from complete. Countries still placed quotas on agricultural imports; France kept out Italian wines. Burdensome administrative regulations at the borders persisted.

Except for a limited circle of Europeanists, the enthusiasm for political unification had dimmed. With enlargement and greater diversity, the Community became more intergovernmental and less supranational. It was the national governments themselves that had to cope with the economic slowdown and monetary instability. In 1973 the governmental leaders even began meeting on a regular basis, the presidency rotating among the member states. The first elections to the European Parliament in 1979, noted earlier, were more symbolic than substantial, nor did the Parliament's influence as a legislature grow significantly. Yet even if the more ambitious dreams of a United States of Europe went unrealized, the Community, for all its problems, remained an important and vibrant institution.

Toward a "Single Europe": 1992

Even during the prosperous 1960s, the European economy did not maintain its growth in all areas. The world itself had entered a new phase of the Industrial Revolution, a "postindustrial" stage in which automation and other forms of advanced or high technology dominated production. Progress was no longer measured in coal and steel or in ships and textiles but in nuclear reactors, microelectronics, telecommunications, computers, and space technology. More workers were employed in the service sectors than in the older basic industries. The service, or tertiary, sector grew faster than agriculture or industry. In the new technology, the Europeans found themselves outdistanced by the Americans and the Japanese. American multinational corporations controlled most of the high technology industries in Europe—before the Japanese arrived to compete. Trade competition from Japan and the new industrial countries of the Pacific basin increased. The recession hit Europe hard and made it more difficult to promote research and development. Western Europe lagged behind other parts of the world. In the 1970s and on into the 1980s journalists spoke of "Euro-sclerosis" and "Europessimism."

New approaches were advanced to invigorate the European Community. Although internal tariffs had disappeared, nontariff obstacles still impeded the flow of trade. Nationally dictated, and therefore varying, standards of production and quality prevailed. In 1986, the twelve member-nations moved toward creating a "single Europe." They agreed to establish common production standards, eliminate paperwork at border crossings, remove impediments to the flow of capital, seek uniformity in tax rates, recognize each other's professional and commercial licensing, work toward a unified currency and central banking system, honor a common charter of labor rights, and create a truly integrated "single Europe," a "Europe without borders"—all to be accomplished by the close of 1992. The Community already represented a domestic market of 325 million people (a third larger than that of the United States), and was the largest trading bloc in the global economy, accounting for 40 percent of all international trade. If it succeeded in achieving true integration, it could enlarge investment, develop high technology, increase productivity, end the lagging rate of growth, and reduce unemployment, still distressingly high. It could compete with the Americans, the

Japanese, and the dynamic small Pacific countries. There was always the danger that the Community, too, might set up protectionist barriers, increasing the threat of global protectionism. So great was the potential of the new Community that outside corporations, mainly from North America and Japan, hastened to establish subsidiaries and make investments within its borders.

The concern surfaced that the advanced industrial nations might divide into large regional trading blocs—an American-led North American bloc, a Japanese-led Pacific bloc, and the new European Community—and that competitive barriers might block the free international trade that had contributed so much to prosperity. The world's economic interdependence had to be respected universally if world commerce were to flourish.

121. *The Cold War Rekindled*

Under President Jimmy Carter, who took office in 1977, détente took a downward turn. More than any American president since Woodrow Wilson, Carter sought to infuse American foreign policy with moral idealism; human rights, he said, must be "the soul of our foreign policy." Détente with the Soviet Union was more closely linked than before to respect for human rights; economic aid would be forthcoming only if the Soviets permitted freedom to dissenters, the right of emigration for Soviet Jews and others, and an end to coercion in Poland. The Soviets did not take kindly to these public pressures. Both sides meanwhile reinforced their military and nuclear strength.

Carter, however, encouraged the strategic arms talks and after tortuous negotiations, a SALT II treaty was signed in January 1979. Both countries agreed to parity in the total number of strategic, or long-range, nuclear missiles. Although the number of missiles remained high and nothing prevented the development of new sophisticated weapons, the agreement might have been another breakthrough in achieving a balance of strategic power. But before it could be ratified by the Senate, the Soviet Union brandishing the "Brezhnev Doctrine,"[14] moved troops into the neighboring state of Afghanistan in December 1979 in order to bolster a weak pro-Soviet leftist regime that it believed threatened from within. It was the first Soviet military intervention of this kind outside Eastern Europe. Carter not only condemned the act as invasion and aggression but denounced it as a new phase of expansion by the Soviets threatening the entire Middle East—"a steppingstone in their possible control over much of the world's oil supplies." He warned in January 1980 that "an attempt by any outside force to gain control of the Persian Gulf region will be regarded as an assault on the vital interests of the United States" and would be repulsed "by any means necessary, including military force." He withdrew the SALT II treaty from the Senate, embargoed sales of grain and high technology to the Soviets, approved aid to the Afghan insurgents in rebellion against the leftist government, sent arms to Pakistan for the use of the rebels, increased the military budget, set up procedures at home for a renewal of the draft, and called for a boycott of the 1980 Olympic Games scheduled for Moscow. The Soviet invasion of Afghanistan, he informed

---

[14] See pp. 913, 981.

the U.S.S.R., was the most serious threat to world peace since 1945. The European allies were taken aback. Some argued that the Afghanistan episode was a regional matter, that the Soviet Union was acting to prevent instability on its borders, and that détente should continue. Unwilling to disturb the commercial relations with the Soviets and Eastern Europe made possible by détente, they refused to support the economic embargo which, among other consequences, would have interfered with the completion of a Soviet natural gas pipeline to Western Europe. As it happened, Afghanistan turned out to be the U.S.S.R.'s Vietnam; 100,000 troops fought for over eight and a half years before withdrawing ignominiously in 1989. Like the Americans in Vietnam, the Soviets were unable to use their overwhelming military power to defeat the Muslim guerrillas who, armed with American weapons, fought fierce battles from their mountain strongholds.

At the very time of the Soviet intervention in Afghanistan the United States itself became preoccupied with the Iran hostage crisis.[15] The crisis was a heavy blow to American prestige. To add to Carter's humiliation, the hostages were freed only a few hours before the inauguration of his Republican successor, Ronald Reagan, as president in January 1981.

The Reagan Years: From Revived Cold War to New Détente

There was no doubt of the new president's commitment to a hard line in the Cold War. The Soviet Union, Reagan proclaimed, represented "the forces of evil in the modern world" and was "an evil empire" with "dark purposes." After the humiliation of the hostage crisis, he pledged to restore America's lost prestige. During the 1970s, the Soviet Union, despite the strain on its economy, had built up its military strength, modernized its conventional fighting forces, created a powerful navy, and achieved nuclear parity. Although there was evidence that the United States had kept up in the arms race, Reagan was convinced that the United States had fallen behind. He doubled defense appropriations, sponsored the largest peacetime military spending in the nation's history, and took a confrontational stand against communism everywhere. In Afghanistan, he stepped up arms shipments to the Muslim guerrillas and to Pakistan, which was backing the rebels. Against the Communist government in Poland he applied economic sanctions when, under pressure from the Soviets, as we shall see, it imposed martial law in 1981 in a desperate effort to suppress the Solidarity trade union movement.[16] He reinforced the embargo on the sale of high technology to the Soviets and to Eastern Europe; the embargo on grain sales was dropped because of opposition from American farmers.

In Central America and the Caribbean, Reagan accused the Soviets of using Castro's Cuba and the leftist Sandinista regime in Nicaragua as proxies to spread communism in the Western Hemisphere. The United States armed anti-Communist opponents of the regime in Nicaragua and reinforced anti-Communist regimes in neighboring states to the point where congressional critics feared that events in Central America could lead to a new Vietnam.

[15] See p. 948.
[16] See p. 1010.

In 1983 American forces invaded the small Caribbean island of Grenada to overthrow a leftist government which was permitting the Cubans to build an airport of possible military use.

Even more than his predecessors, Reagan and his advisers believed it necessary to support repressive authoritarian regimes so long as they were anti-Communist on the theory that one day such regimes might be liberalized, whereas Communist governments would transform their societies in an irreversible way. Critics argued that the revolutionary movements in Central America and elsewhere sprang not from the Cold War but from old systems of privilege and exploitation, and they insisted that military solutions, Cold War rhetoric, and support to repressive regimes were not the appropriate response.

In Libya, the administration demonstrated the American capacity for unilateral military action when it bombed military installations in Tripoli in retaliation for what it was convinced were Libyan-sponsored terrorist activities.[17] The European allies, alarmed by the president's belligerency, opposed the operation and refused to permit air passage to the American bombers. In Lebanon, in the throes of its confused and bloody civil war,[18] the United States rejected the proposal for a United Nations peacekeeping force (in which the U.S.S.R. would have participated) in favor of a multinational peacekeeping force. In 1982 the American fleet bombarded the Lebanon coast and landed marines; in retaliation, terrorists blew up the United States Embassy and in a bomb explosion of the American command center killed 265 marines. The United States and the other members of the peacekeeping force withdrew.

In the war between Iran and Iraq that broke out in 1980,[19] in the course of which attacks by both belligerents on tankers in the Persian Gulf threatened the flow of oil from the Arab Gulf states, the United States, once again to keep the Soviets out, rejected the proposal for a United Nations naval force to assure navigation. Instead, it escorted a selected number of tankers on its own under the protection of the American flag; there were some armed clashes and loss of lives, but the oil deliveries went through.

Nuclear Arms Control

No nuclear weapons were used in any of these conflicts in the years after 1945, yet over every crisis hung the ultimate threat of a nuclear clash. We have seen how the earliest negotiations on nuclear disarmament, at a time when the United States alone possessed the atomic bomb, were broken off in 1947, how in 1949 the Soviets successfully tested their first atomic bomb, ending the American monopoly, and how the United States in 1952 and the Soviet Union shortly thereafter developed the hydrogen or thermonuclear bomb, which by its chain reaction had vastly more destructive capacity than the mere 20,000 tons of TNT of the Hiroshima bomb.[20] By the 1960s both superpowers were building strategic long range missiles, i.e., intercontinental ballistic missiles, capable of delivering

[17] See p. 946.
[18] See pp. 945–946.
[19] See pp. 948–950.
[20] See p. 860.

their nuclear warheads accurately and swiftly thousands of miles away to targets in each other's homeland; they could be launched from land (from stationary or mobile sites), from sea (from ships or submarines), or from bombers in the air. The world had entered a new age of military technology. Guided missiles were the key strategic weapons of the modern age. Because of their immense destructive power, the nuclear weapons could not be used without unleashing unspeakable damage. Nuclear arms were built not for use but for deterrence.

Because nuclear testing threatened to poison the earth's atmosphere, and perhaps even damage the genetic endowment of present and future generations, controls were imperative. In 1963 the United States and the U.S.S.R. initiated a partial test-ban treaty, which banned testing in the atmosphere, water, and outer space, and permitted only underground testing. Not all nations subscribed to the treaty, nor did the controls prevent additional nations from acquiring a nuclear capacity. France in 1960 followed Britain in becoming a fourth nuclear power, China in 1964 became a fifth, and India in 1974 a sixth. (By 1990 Pakistan, Israel, and South Africa were among countries that had achieved or were on the threshold of achieving nuclear capability.) A nonproliferation treaty was proposed by the superpowers and ratified by the UN General Assembly in 1968, but it lacked binding force and was ignored by countries bent on developing nuclear power. The danger persisted that terrorist organizations might also divert nuclear materials for their political purposes.

So long as the peaceful use of nuclear energy was encouraged, it was difficult to prevent proliferation. Nations purchasing nuclear power plants from industrial countries, ostensibly for peaceful purposes, could reprocess the plutonium from the spent fuel and build nuclear bombs, as India did. The search for alternative energy sources in the 1970s to replace oil stimulated many nations to build nuclear power plants that could easily be diverted to nonpeaceful purposes. Accidents at nuclear power plants at Three Mile Island, Pennsylvania, in 1979, and at Chernobyl in the Soviet Union in 1986 did not deter the building of nuclear power plants but underscored the need for safer construction. From Chernobyl, radioactive materials in the atmosphere traveled as far as Western Europe.

From the 1960s on debate continued in the United States about the "missile gap," about the comparative numbers of the American and Soviet missile systems deployed on land and sea and in the air, and about the vulnerability to attack of the American land-based systems. By the 1970s, with the Soviet missile build-up after the Cuban crisis of 1962, the two superpowers had achieved a rough parity. Although both recognized superiority as a self-defeating goal, nothing restrained them from a continuing strategic arms build-up. Strategists on each side supported the build-up. Using advanced computer systems, they calculated the potential casualties in a nuclear exchange between the superpowers in millions of deaths (or "megadeaths") and evaluated the effects of deterrents and counter deterrents, and of "first strikes" and "counter strikes" on each nation's ability to wage and survive nuclear war. The balance of power was spoken of as a "balance of terror;" experts referred to "mutually assured destruction" (the acronym for which, ironically, was MAD). Deterrence became the widely accepted formula. Each side amassed huge stockpiles of arms, capable of destroying each other many times over, in what was described as "overkill." The two countries were also under continuing pressure to modernize their systems competitively. When the Soviets developed defense systems, that is, antiballistic missiles, which undermined deterrence, the American response had been to build its own defense systems and more powerful offensive weapons—like the MIRV (a "multiple independently targeted reentry vehicle"), a delivery system carrying up to ten nuclear warheads, each independently guided to separate targets, each warhead many times more powerful than the Hiroshima bomb. The Russians countered with their own multiwarhead systems—all leading to an even higher level of armaments and greater uncertainty. Each side had satellite reconnaissance systems but for a time neither could determine the number of warheads on the other side and hence know with accuracy the other's capability. After the first SALT treaty, signed in 1972,[21] each side developed new weapons outside the classes that were limited. The United States developed cruise missiles, designed to fly low to the ground and hence protected from defense systems; the Soviets, supersonic bombers. SALT II, signed in 1979 but (as we have seen) never ratified, produced tentative agreement on equality in the total number of strategic long-range weapons and on multiple warheads. But protracted discussions continued. Each side had its triad of land-based, sea-based, and air-launched missiles.

At the opening of the 1990s each superpower had about 25,000 nuclear weapons, of which 11,000 on each side were strategic, i.e., long-range, or intercontinental. Together the two arsenals exceeded 500,000 megatons (millions of tons) of explosive power, dwarfing the total explosive power used in all previous wars. If only a small number of these nuclear arms reached their targets, the two countries could destroy each other's major cities and countryside and kill millions in the attack and in the radioactive effects, which would spread to neighboring areas. In the "nuclear winter" that might follow, some feared for human survival. There was always the dread possibility also of accident, miscalculation, or failure of communication. So deliberately suspended over the human race was the nuclear sword of Damocles that a direct communication link, or "hot line," was installed between the Kremlin and the White House in 1963, soon after the Cuban missile crisis, and in the following decades modernized and improved. It was designed to prevent the accidental outbreak of a nuclear war because of political misunderstanding, human error, or mechanical slipup; direct communication between the tribal chieftains was necessary in the nuclear age. No more than a twenty-minute warning might be available.

The debate over security in the Cold War went beyond that of the defense strategists. Many pointed to the danger, the paradox, and even the immorality of building vast nuclear arsenals to prevent nuclear war; some (in the West) even urged unilateral disarmament. Others argued that without a high level of armaments a nation could be subject to nuclear blackmail. They maintained that the nuclear balance between the two opposing camps, and the principle of deterrence, had protected the peace. Everyone, to be sure, recognized the need to reduce the political tensions and insecurity that fed the arms competition. Yet in the rekindled Cold War tensions of the early 1980s there seemed to be no solution to the impasse. Reluctantly, the world had to reconcile itself to the existing "balance of terror," except for piecemeal negotiations on arms limitations. The unexpected changes in the Soviet Union and in the Soviet bloc after 1985

[21] See p. 982.

transformed American-Soviet relations, ended the Cold War as the world had known it since 1945, and called for a reassessment of defense needs and strategies in a new era.

122. *China Under Deng*

After Mao's passing in 1976 moderates and radicals competed for leadership.[22] Mao's widow Jiang Qing, one of the firebrands of the Cultural Revolution, together with a small group of Maoist radicals, sought to exploit the weakness in the leadership in order to win control and purge the moderates, but the attempt failed and she and three associates were arrested and imprisoned. From behind the scenes Deng Xiaoping, the leader of the moderates, emerged to become the most powerful figure in the country. Deng was a veteran party leader who had fallen out of favor with Mao in 1956–1957, was purged and humiliated in 1967 during the Cultural Revolution for having taken the "capitalist road," and purged for a third time in 1976 by the Maoists. To counteract the Maoist cult of personality Deng declined to accept the leading post in either government or party, but instead placed his protégés in top positions.

Deng's Reforms

By late 1978 Deng won the party over to a sweeping reform program, designed to curb the radical and utopian phases of the Revolution, put aside Marxist ideology and class struggle, and focus on economic growth. The moderates proposed "modernization" in agriculture, industry, science and technology, and defense. Deng thoroughly transformed the central economic planning, nationalized industry, and collectivized agriculture inherited from Mao—and indirectly from the Soviets. Because the country was still "in the primary stage of socialism," he sanctioned capitalist practices, encouraging private enterprise, production for profit, and a competitive marketplace. For state-owned industries he demanded profitability and accountability. It would be "a marriage," he said, "between a planned and a market economy." He began by dismantling the collectivized farms and communes, which had proved disastrous for agriculture, restoring the land to individual farmers and their families to cultivate. He opened the country to foreign investment, welcoming Western science, technology, and management techniques. Although heavy industry was not neglected, a new emphasis was placed on consumer goods; factories that once manufactured military hardware now produced refrigerators, washing machines, bicycles, and motorcycles.

Deng's "socialist market economy" transformed the country. The most striking success was in the countryside. Farmers sold a significant portion of their product on the open market. Within a decade output doubled; food became available for the cities, and even for export. In other parts of the economy retail outlets, repair shops, and other small businesses were in private hands. Special economic enclaves were established along the southern coast to encourage foreign enterprise, much of it from Hong Kong. Foreign capital flowed in; a stock exchange was

[22] See p. 917.

introduced. The results were impressive. Gross national product, which had never increased by more than 2 or 3 percent annually under Mao, grew at an average 9 percent annually and more than doubled in the 1980s. Many of the new entrepreneurs (and even some farmers) became wealthy. The big cities took on the aspect of a consumer society. Temporary joblessness was tempered by the welfare state network of social services—"the iron rice bowl." The country enjoyed an unprecedented rise in living standards. The People's Liberation Army was reduced in size, but modernized and made more professional; the government bureaucracy was trimmed down. State-owned industries still accounted for the major share of production, but the growing private sector represented the most vibrant part of the economy.

Even if China remained a one-party state, a "people's democratic dictatorship" in the official phrase, and individual human rights were often flouted, a more open and relaxed cultural and intellectual atmosphere prevailed. People tuned in on radio and television programs from the outside world. Students traveled and studied abroad. Many Western books (including this one, in its 1978 edition) were translated into the Chinese language. At no time since the Communist revolution were the people so free to absorb ideas from the outside world. Foreign tourists flocked in to admire the new China, which built hotels and other accommodations for them. What earlier patriots and reformers like Sun Yat-sen had dreamed of, and what Mao had failed to achieve because of his revolutionary excesses, Deng seemed to be accomplishing. Ideology was taking a back seat to material advance, to the idea of a "rich and strong China."

Deng also wished to provide an orderly succession. He dislodged veterans of the older generation (many, like him, survivors of the Long March[23]) who clung to older Maoist ways, resisted Western political and economic ideas, and tried to block reform. The old guard retained a network of influence, but younger leaders emerged. The country deferred to Deng as a central authority figure, but he seemingly used his vast powers without presumption or arrogance.

As the decade progressed, however, it became clear that Deng's reform program, for all its accomplishments, had serious imperfections. The rapid economic growth fueled inflation (a 20 to 30 percent annual rate in the late 1980s), threatening to wipe out the rise in living standards. Because of the emphasis on consumer goods, the needs of the economic infrastructure were neglected. In the effort to decentralize, the provincial governments won greater independence and a larger control over revenues. And despite its avowals, the government could not bring itself to liquidate its unprofitable state-owned industries, one-fifth of which operated at a loss. An erratic system of price controls encouraged a black market. Even agricultural production slowed down. The consumer society bred extravagance, conspicuous consumption, and wastefulness. Corruption became widespread because government and party leaders were closely tied to business enterprises, government and private. The idealistic voiced dissatisfaction with growing inequalities and inequities in the socialist society. In response to the cumulative problems a retrenchment program in 1988 called for a pause in further reform.

With time and vigilance the economic difficulties in the transitional economy

[23] See p. 797.

might have been overcome. What brought Deng's memorable decade of reform to a close was the refusal to permit political reform and democratization to accompany the economic reforms. According to Deng and others in the party, the country, for all its advances, was unprepared for democracy, which would only breed chaos and confusion, as it had in the Cultural Revolution, and interfere with the order and stability needed for economic growth and modernization. Further, nothing could be permitted to weaken the stewardship of the party, the heir to the old imperial dynasties, over the country's destiny. Yet in the freer atmosphere that Deng had encouraged, many of the country's intellectual leaders, and younger people destined to be its future leaders, pressed for a loosening of the party's political controls, a freer press, and the right to criticize the widespread corruption and other shortcomings of the system. The beginnings of political liberalization in socialist societies in the Soviet Union and in Eastern Europe and democratic advances elsewhere in the world reinforced the restlessness in China. When at the end of 1986, Hu Yaobang, general secretary of the party and at the time the 82-year-old Deng's designated successor, encouraged the belief that greater political freedom might be permitted, students took to the streets to show their support. When Hu vacillated in suppressing the demonstrations, he was summarily dismissed.

The Democracy Movement

Two years later the democratic ferment came to a head. Hu's death in April 1989 set off a series of student demonstrations in the huge central square in Beijing called Tiananmen, or Gate of Heavenly Peace. The demonstrators, honoring Hu as a champion of political reform, demanded democratization. Students from other parts of the country arrived to join what came to be called the democracy movement and ordinary citizens lent their support. The demonstrations mounted in intensity. At one point a mock statue of the Goddess of Liberty (its name and Phrygian cap recalling both the American and French Revolutions) appeared. Student demonstrators resorted to a hunger strike. For seven weeks the demonstrators brought the capital and other parts of the country to a standstill. At the height of the ferment a million people may have been massed in and around Tiananmen Square. For a time the party seemed likely to accede to the more moderate demands. Zhao Ziyang, who had succeeded Hu as party leader, pressed for conciliation. But Deng, who took the side of the hard-liners, would not tolerate a recurrence of anarchy and turmoil nor permit the continuing embarrassment and humiliation of the party and government. When the government imposed martial law, a human wall of students and sympathizers prevented the soldiers from entering the square. Although their numbers had somewhat declined, the students refused to abandon the square. In the predawn hours of Sunday, June 4, the army moved in with tanks, trucks, and armored cars and opened fire, with hundreds of victims. Perhaps no government could have tolerated the defiance of law and order and loss of prestige, but even modest concessions, patience, or the exhaustion of the demonstrators might have brought the demonstrations to a peaceful end. The army and the Deng regime, inexcusably, now had the people's blood on their hands. Deng's enormous popularity plummeted.

In the repressive atmosphere that followed, Deng and the party attributed the "counterrevolutionary" rebellion to a "Western-inspired conspiracy." For his conciliatory stance, Zhao was dismissed from all his posts. The new party and government leaders, echoing Deng, alleged that counterrevolutionaries "had attempted to install capitalism in China and make it dependent on certain foreign countries." While the nation still urgently needed Western technology and foreign investment, and wished to continue with its "socialist market economy," the party would henceforth supervise the private sector closely, reinforce Marxist ideology and political education, and determine the pace and timetable of change.

Forty years after its founding in 1949 the People's Republic of China could look back upon a quarter-century of revolutionary transformation and turmoil under Mao, a brief interlude before Deng, and a decade under Deng of economic progress, stability, openness to the West, and a freer intellectual atmosphere—until the yearning for greater freedom led to the massive demonstrations in the spring of 1989 and their repression. In the euphoria of the Deng years, many forgot the intense suspicion of the West that Deng shared with Mao, derived from the years when a weak China had lain open to exploitation.[24]

In the distant past Confucian scholars, trained to enter the emperor's service, accepted the right of the emperor to rule autocratically but reserved the right to criticize harsh or incompetent rule. A ruler governed not by force alone, but by moral example, virtue, and rectitude—or risked losing the "mandate of Heaven." The democracy movement brought into question the right of the party to rule in the old way, especially when authoritarianism was itself in decline in other parts of the Communist world. The democracy movement demonstrated how deeply liberal values—or "bourgeois liberalism," as it was denounced—had penetrated China and how powerful were the pressures for political change. Continuing economic modernization, even under authoritarian control, could still lead to political liberalization. Fortunes were fickle in China, as Deng's own career demonstrated; Zhao or other moderates might reemerge. After the passing of Deng and his aged contemporaries, a new generation would come to power.

Population Growth

On a less dramatic front (beneath the surface of mere "events," as some historians would say), the pressure of the expanding population on the economy remained serious. Not irrelevantly, the character for "population" in the Chinese language depicts a mouth. For a time, of all the larger developing countries China was the most successful in coping with population growth. Through a system involving central direction and local control, a one-child-per-family rule (with stiff penalties for violations), massive education programs, social pressures, and outright coercion, the birth rate significantly slowed down, which in China's case affected global demography as well. But in the unstable decade of the Cultural Revolution from 1966 to 1976 family planning services suffered a setback and the birth rate rose. The years of relative prosperity under Deng made it difficult to enforce the one-child rule because some affluent families, both in the cities and countryside, were willing to risk large fines for having more than one child. Nor were contraceptive devices always the most modern or most efficient.

[24] See pp. 674–681, 915.

In 1982 the Chinese population, one-fifth the world's total, passed the billion mark and in the early 1990s the population was growing at the rate of 15 million annually, not at the targeted rate of 11.5 million. By 2050 the population could reach 1.5 billion. The need to feed, clothe, and house this immense population would continue to make enormous demands on the economy, no matter how modernized. Meanwhile China entered the 1990s under a tightened authoritarian and Marxist regime—in sharp contrast to the changes taking place elsewhere.

123. *Crisis and Transformation in the Soviet Union*

The world was astonished in the 1980s to see some of the basic structures of Soviet communism, as developed since the Russian Revolution, begin to come apart. It is not easy to explain how someone as seemingly unorthodox as Mikhail S. Gorbachev could have risen to supreme power from within the Soviet system except that the country was in dire straits and that the party leadership itself was desperate. As a young man Gorbachev had taken a law degree in Moscow and then additional training at the agricultural institute in Stavropol, his home city in southwestern Russia. After work as an agricultural researcher, he shifted to a full-time party assignment in the region and came to the attention of Andropov and other party leaders in Moscow. He was appointed to the party secretariat in Moscow in 1978, with special responsibility for agriculture. The new post afforded him an inside view of the country's deep-seated economic troubles. In 1980 he became a member of the Politburo and by 1984 he was directing the party's secretariat. After the disheartening experience of an incapacitated Brezhnev clinging to power and of his two successors dying in office at a time when the country was mired in difficulties,[25] the Politburo in March 1985 seems to have decided that it was time for change. At 54, Gorbachev was by far its youngest member. Gromyko, too closely identified with the Stalin years to be chosen as general secretary himself, ultimately endorsed Gorbachev and is said to have reassured those with doubts: "He has a nice smile but he has iron teeth."

Gorbachev at once demonstrated a dynamism and vigor absent from the leadership for years. His first task was to convince the party and country of the need for fundamental economic restructuring—*perestroika* he called it—if economic stagnation was to be overcome. *Perestroika* meant a drastic modification of the centrally planned, command economy inherited from Stalin and carried forward with only minor changes since. The older system, however well it had earlier served the industrialization of the country, the test of the Second World War, or postwar reconstruction, was ill-suited for the contemporary industrial (and postindustrial) world which demanded advanced technology and new skills. Industry and agriculture cried out for independence in order to release creative energies, provide incentives for productivity, raise quality levels, and satisfy consumer needs. Gorbachev's proposed remedies were decentralization, self-management for industry and agriculture, an end to the rigidities imposed by the *apparat*, or party and government bureaucracy, and incentives for productivity. He moved cautiously, believing that exhortation and a sense of urgency would

[25] See p. 909.

bring results, but his appeals and initial moderate reforms clashed with the vested interests of the entrenched bureaucrats.

For his reforms to succeed, Gorbachev needed the support of the country, which he hoped to win through political change. Thus his call for *glasnost*, or "openness," which he closely linked to economic reform. (The two Russian words *perestroika* and *glasnost* quickly entered the world's political vocabulary.) By *glasnost* he meant the right to voice the need for change, the freedom to criticize the existing system, the necessity even to reexamine past mistakes and wrongdoings. Even if *glasnost* originally had a more limited objective, it took on a dynamic of its own. It led to a totally unprecedented opening up of Soviet society, a freer press, and an end to the decades of totalitarian control over political, cultural, and intellectual life. The ferment that had been choked off after Khruschev's "thaw" was reborn. The press, publications, theater, and political discourse opened up as at no time since 1917. Books and plays written in the 1960s or earlier but not permitted publication or performance made their appearance, including Pasternak's *Dr. Zhivago* (and eventually even Solzhenitsyn's *Gulag Archipelago*). Gorbachev permitted the physicist Sakharov, a leading dissenter, to return to Moscow from exile and allowed him to take an active part in political life. Soviet Jews, who at one point had been refused permission to leave the country, were permitted to emigrate in large numbers. The atmosphere changed profoundly. People were freer and less fearful. The legal codes were revised to enhance civil liberties, protect freedom of expression, and prevent police abuses. The KGB itself came under public and legislative scrutiny. The practice of committing political opponents to psychiatric hospitals halted. Gorbachev even spoke of freedom of conscience and tolerance for religion, negotiating a rapprochement with the Orthodox Church and visiting the Vatican. He also endorsed freedom for the arts, stifled by years of uniformity and conformity.

In 1987, on the occasion of the seventieth anniversary of the Bolshevik Revolution, Gorbachev spoke openly of "Stalin's enormous and unforgivable crimes." The courts rehabilitated Stalin's political opponents and victims; leaders like Bukharin, Zinoviev, Kamenev, and Radek (though not yet Trotsky) were restored to their places in history.[26] A monument to Stalin's victims was planned while the press openly discussed the total number of his victims, clearly in the millions. New history textbooks were prepared, as well as a revised history of the party. Gorbachev told the country that there should be "no forgotten names or blanks in history or literature."

Despite his wide-ranging strictures, Gorbachev did not challenge the role of the Communist party as the directing agent of Soviet society, but he set in motion forces that were leading to the end of the party's monopoly on power. Remembering how Khruschev had been dislodged after only a few years,[27] he set out, much in the style of a Western politician, to mobilize a wide popular base for himself. Reform could not be imposed from above. Regional and local Soviets should exercise authority, as Lenin had wished. The people, he said, needed more than a "good tsar." Constitutional reforms in 1988 created a new national

[26] See pp. 770–772.
[27] See pp. 905–906, 974–975.

legislature. Multicandidate elections replaced the older one-party slate of nominees. What began as a technocratic vision of a more efficient economy was setting the country on the way to a profound transformation of Soviet life and society.

In the freer atmosphere the government released information suppressed for years, even of nuclear accidents before Chernobyl. At sessions of party meetings and of the new legislature the public heard for the first time outspoken critiques of Soviet society: descriptions of poverty, corruption, crime, alcoholism, and drugs; of shortcomings in medicine, health, and housing; of environmental decay. Tens of millions lived at or below the poverty line, perhaps one-fifth the population. Despite its much vaunted health care system, the country ranked fiftieth internationally in infant mortality, with an average in 1985 of 26 deaths per 1,000 births. (In the United States, by no means a shining example itself, the rate was 10.6 per thousand.) The Soviet Union was the only industrial country in which life expectancy was regressing; it ranked thirty-second. Because of inadequate housing there was intense pressure to limit families, but with modern contraceptive measures unavailable, abortion was the common procedure; one and a half abortions took place for every live birth. Statistics on the poor grain harvests were revealed, as were the huge budgetary deficits resulting from defense costs and the subsidization of inefficient state enterprises.

Within a few years Gorbachev came to recognize that the country's economic problems were more intractable than he had thought, that *perestroika* was not far-reaching enough. In 1988 new regulations stipulated that state-owned enterprises would be held to strict "accountability" and "profitability" and the state subsidies would be phased out. Gosplan, the central planning agency in Moscow,[28] was separated from the daily operations of the state enterprises. Bureaucratic agencies in Moscow and in each of the fifteen republics were reduced in size or eliminated. For the first time since Lenin's NEP, when Lenin had liberalized the economy in the early 1920s,[29] individuals were encouraged to start up businesses on their own or form cooperatives, and even hire workers. Later reforms even abandoned the hallowed phrase, the "collective ownership of the means of production." Private enterprise and the huge state industries were to be integrated into a market-based economy, linked to the outside world. Foreign capital for trade and investment and joint ventures with foreign firms were welcomed. Soviet managers were encouraged to travel abroad to learn advanced (sometimes elementary) business and accounting practices. Even as state ownership shrank, the economy was to remain a socialist economy—a "socialist market economy" or, in a later phrase, a "regulated market economy." But the new reforms only created confusion and yielded no benefits to the consumer; impatience grew.

Gorbachev's initial reforms in agriculture also required reassessment. In 1985 he had accepted the existing system of state and collective farms, even if allowing them greater discretion to run their affairs. But nearly half the country's 50,000 state and collective farms continued to show a loss, or a bare profit, and required large subsidies, and production did not rise. Four years later Gorbachev launched a more extensive agrarian policy foreshadowing the end of the sixty years of

---

[28] See pp. 762–768.
[29] See p. 760–761.

collectivized agriculture imposed by Stalin. Farmers and farm families could now work with state and collective farms on a share-crop basis, or farm their own land. Moreover, farmers could henceforth lease land on a lifetime basis, and even bequeath to their children the right to till the same land. But the state remained the legal owner of the land—unlike China, where Deng had at the very beginning of his reforms dismantled the collective farms and returned the land outright to the farmers. Despite the encouragement to small independent farming, the agricultural reforms fell far short of satisfying the long demoralized rural population or providing incentives for increased production.

Political changes initiated in 1988–1989 clearly loosened the monopoly grip of the party. The new legislature differed sharply from the older Supreme Soviet, which had been elected on the basis of a single slate and had met methodically over the years only to rubber-stamp legislation prepared for it. Although one-third of the seats remained reserved for the party and its affiliates, multicandidate, openly contested elections were held in March 1989, the first since November 1917.[30] Voters elected a Congress of People's Deputies, with 2,250 seats, which in turn chose a smaller standing legislative body, a new Supreme Soviet with 542 members. A president was to hold office for a five-year term. The legislature was empowered to initiate legislation of all kinds and freely debate issues. In 1990 Gorbachev persuaded the legislature to create a presidency with broad executive powers, partly on the American and partly on the French model, with authority to act in domestic emergencies and foreign affairs. Opposition parties, although not legally sanctioned, were forming across the land. They were emerging in the central legislature and, even more so, in the legislatures of the restless component republics. National, regional, and local elections dealt a continuing blow to old-guard party leaders, who in large numbers were repudiated at the polls.

Gorbachev had brought about stunning changes, unprecedented in the years since the Revolution. If his initial impulse had been only to restructure and revitalize the economy, his reforms had taken on a momentum of their own, and democratic values were becoming ends in their own right. The superiority of the state over the party was being affirmed. The elected representatives of the people were exercising independent authority. Gorbachev seemed to govern from a constitutionally secure position. His reforms appeared irreversible, barring an extralegal eventuality. Although he had concentrated enormous power in his own hands, he seemed initially to use his vast power with moderation in order to restructure and democratize Soviet society. Western political leaders in the Great Depression had sought to save capitalism by reforming it.[31] Gorbachev was bent on saving the Communist system by reform. Meanwhile his attitudes toward the West and toward the transformation of Eastern Europe, as we shall see, were no less staggering. What remained unclear was whether after all these accomplishments he could maintain a secure position and move decisively to a complete overhaul of the ailing system.

Yet from the beginning the country was divided, disoriented, dissatisfied. It was torn between the old guard who resisted the Gorbachev changes and reformers who believed that he had not gone far enough either politically or economically

[30] See pp. 748–750.
[31] See pp. 806–817.

to undo the past and meet the country's needs. As time went by, praise for his policies gave way to trenchant criticism—for the continuing dismal economic record, for his indecisive, sometimes contradictory, steps in building a market economy, for his reluctance to relax agricultural controls more completely, for the armed repression of ethnic unrest, for rejecting the demands of the constituent republics that they be given freedom from central control, and for the role still exercised by the party. Gorbachev seemed to shrink from a market-oriented competitive economy, for all its promise of higher productivity. He may have feared the painful short-term dislocations and political unrest that would inevitably follow, or he was still committed to preserving what he could of the old system and continued to rely on old guard party advisers.

Meanwhile the relaxation of totalitarian controls had released smoldering ethnic and political tensions within the country. Azerbaijanis and Armenians fought each other over disputed territory; violence flared up in Georgia and elsewhere. Every one of the fifteen federated constituent republics raised demands for freedom from central control and for self-government, some even for sovereignty and independence. The largest republic, the Russian Soviet Federated Socialist Republic, with half the nation's population, elected as its president the most vocal of Gorbachev's opponents and pressed for autonomy. Secessionist pressures went further in the three Baltic republics, incorporated since 1940 into the U.S.S.R. Estonians, Latvians, and Lithuanians remembered their twenty years of independence between the two world wars and how they had fallen victim to the Nazi-Soviet pact of 1939. With democratization they were able to challenge Soviet control and demanded independence. In 1990 Lithuania became the first Soviet republic to proclaim secession, to which Gorbachev responded with a combination of diplomatic maneuvering, delaying tactics, economic pressures, and then outright military force. That military measures might also be used elsewhere disturbed even the closest supporters of Gorbachev.

The Soviet leader accepted the idea of a federation council to advise on all matters relating to the republics, but beyond that he drew the line. It was unlikely that Gorbachev, the party, or the country's military leaders would permit the dissolution of the Soviet Union without a struggle. And it had to be added that *glasnost* not only opened the way to greater freedom of expression, it also made possible the reemergence of older forms of intolerance, bigotry, and anti-Semitism in the search for scapegoats. Like Khruschev before him Gorbachev, too, had opened a Pandora's box. He had unleashed forces that he seemingly could not control.

Ideology and World Affairs

In the new era, Communist ideology and the view of world affairs that had helped to create and prolong the Cold War of the post-1945 years were also transformed. Gorbachev repudiated ideological struggle. He cited the progress of science and technology as requiring "a different road to the future." In an interdependent globe besieged by nuclear, ecological, and economic dangers, the highest concern must be "universal human interests" and the "universal human idea." Since Marx and Lenin had taught their followers to reject "universal" ideals as a smoke screen for class rule and oppression, the turnabout was startling.

NATIONALITIES IN THE SOVIET UNION ABOUT 1990

Member Republics	Population	Percentage within Each Republic of		
		Major Nationality	Russians	Others
Slavic				
RSFSR	147,000,000	82%	—	18% — of about 30 nationalities
Ukraine	51,700,000	73	22%	5 — mainly Byelorussians
Byelorussia	10,200,000	78	13	9 — mainly Poles, Ukrainians
Baltic				
Lithuania	3,700,000	80	9	11 — mainly Poles
Latvia	2,700,000	52	34	14 — mainly Ukrainians
Estonia	1,600,000	62	30	8 — mainly Ukrainians
Moldavian	4,300,000	64	13	23 — mainly Ukrainians
Caucasian				
Georgia	5,500,000	70	6	24 — mainly Armenians, Azerbaijanis
Armenia	3,300,000	93	2	5 — mainly Kurds, Azerbaijanis
Azerbaijan	7,000,000	83	6	11 — mainly Armenians
Central Asian				
Uzbek	19,900,000	71	8	21 — mainly Tadzhiks, Kazakhs
Kazakh	16,500,000	40	38	22 — mainly Ukrainians
Tadzhik	5,100,000	62	8	30 — mainly Uzbeks
Kirghiz	4,300,000	52	22	26 — mainly Uzbeks, Ukrainians
Turkmen	3,500,000	72	10	18 — mainly Uzbeks, Kazakhs
Total U.S.S.R.	286,300,000			

NATIONALITIES IN THE SOVIET UNION

Fifteen national republics constituted the Soviet Union in the early 1990s. Since the individual's nationality is officially designated and counted in the census, each republic is known to have a mixed population. The term "Major Nationality" in the table means the nationality from which the republic takes its name.

Many nationalities are quite dispersed. Each republic, in varying degree, if it were to become independent would still have internal minorities and might lose valuable workers by emigration. The Russians in particular are spread throughout the Union in governmental, managerial, technical, and professional positions. About half the population of the U.S.S.R. is Russian, and seventy percent is Slavic. All the nationalities have an interest in independence, either because they are historically rooted where they have been for centuries, as in the larger republics or the Baltic and Caucasian republics, or because of their Islamic religion in Azerbaijan and Central Asia. More rapid growth of the Muslim population in Central Asia is reducing the proportion of Russians in these areas.

The U.S.S.R. is a pluralistic society, but not in the same sense as the United States. The mixed ethnicity of the United States has arisen from immigration since colonial times (in which the former slave trade must be included), while in the U.S.S.R. it has arisen mainly from conquest and annexation. This generalization should be qualified by the fact that for centuries there has been much migration within the present borders of the U.S.S.R., and that the United States has also engaged in conquest and annexation, as in the case of the American Indians and the annexations from Mexico in the 1840s. The great difference is that in the United States the ethnic groups have tended generally to merge into an English-language mainstream, while in the U.S.S.R. they have strongly resisted Russification under both the tsarist empire and the Soviet Union.

For population changes since 1940 see p. 754.

Source: Soviet census of 1989; Office of Population Research, Princeton University

Gorbachev demolished the image of the Soviet Union as a military threat and promoter of world revolution. He became a familiar and popular figure in Western capitals as a negotiator, diplomat, statesman, and often Western-style politician. He followed his conciliatory words with deeds, removing troops and weapons from Eastern Europe, negotiating nuclear arms reduction agreements with the United States, ending the Soviet war in Afghanistan, and helping to resolve world regional conflicts in Namibia, Angola, Cambodia, and elsewhere. And he accepted, even encouraged, reforms in Eastern Europe, perhaps not foreseeing how far they would go and how they would bring to an end, in 1989, the Soviet grip on all Eastern Europe. He spoke up for human rights, paid tribute to the standards embodied in the Helsinki accords, and called for a "common European home" for Western and Eastern Europe. The Cold War of the post-1945 years, which had been brought on, or at least intensified, by Soviet revolutionary ideology and expansionism—which in turn led to the American containment policy and counter crusade—gave promise of ending, even if other kinds of tensions could be expected to continue. For Gorbachev, détente and arms reduction were essential to relieve an intolerable burden on the Soviet economy; détente went hand in hand with domestic reform.

The Reagan-Gorbachev Breakthrough

In the early 1980s Soviet–United States relations had reached their lowest point since the Cuban missile crisis. Then within a few years the climate changed abruptly, to the point where after 1985 a new kind of détente set in, more genuine and holding out higher expectations than at any time in four decades.

Early in the Reagan administration, during the Brezhnev era, discussions resumed on strategic arms limitations (now called START), but in an atmosphere of mistrust, suspicion, strain, and continuing arms build-up. Especially disturbing was the deployment in Eastern Europe in the late 1970s, in the Brezhnev era, of new Soviet intermediate-range nuclear missiles, i.e., missiles capable of reaching targets within a radius of 600 to 3,000 miles. Together with its European allies the United States made plans to reinforce existing defenses in Western Europe with equally modern American missiles, while simultaneously pressing the Soviets to reduce or remove their missiles. The construction of the missile sites touched off popular demonstrations in Western Europe in opposition, but the West European governments remained firm in their support. In Reagan's first term of office he did not meet at all with the incapacitated Brezhnev or with either of the two ailing Soviet leaders who in quick succession followed him. But in 1985 after the emergence of Gorbachev, who saw the need to reduce the strain on the troubled Soviet economy, the possibilities for arms limitation opened up. Unlike his predecessors, Gorbachev seemed to view détente not as an alternate way of pursuing revolutionary goals but as essential to avoiding catastrophe in the nuclear age. Reagan, convinced that the United States had rebuilt its own military strength, held four summit meetings with Gorbachev over the next two and a half years.

At their third meeting, in Washington, in December 1987, the two leaders, in a remarkable agreement, consented to remove the land-based intermediate-range missiles each had installed in Europe. Gorbachev agreed also to reduce the number of short-range land-based nuclear missiles, that is, those with a range of 300 to 600 miles. The Soviets were willing to destroy over four times as many missiles as the United States. Even more unprecedented was the willingness to permit the United States to verify the destruction of the weapons—the on-site verification which had long been a stumbling block to arms reduction. Finally, the two leaders agreed, in principle, that the next step would be to discuss the reduction of strategic, or long-range, missiles.

In the summit meetings in Washington and then in Moscow, the two leaders had closer contact with each other's people than ever before. Gorbachev mingled with throngs in crowded Washington streets. Reagan, in Moscow, in the shadow of Lenin's tomb, spoke openly about the Soviet repression of dissidents, the refusal to permit Jews to emigrate, religious repression, and the war in Afghanistan. Gorbachev in his turn committed his country to the withdrawal of Soviet troops from Afghanistan—a "bleeding wound" he called it. The Soviets were eager to cut their commitments and to abandon their adversarial stance all over the globe. Meanwhile Gorbachev was lending encouragement to the vast changes taking place in Eastern Europe which would transform the Cold War pattern of international relations. In 1990 Gorbachev and President George Bush, Reagan's successor, could jointly hail the end of the Cold War.

124. *The Revolutions of 1989 in Central and Eastern Europe*

In the mid-1980s central and eastern Europe remained under Stalinist-type party bosses, some in office for over thirty years, impervious to pressure for reform.[32] But cracks and fissures had begun to appear. The years of détente had already opened up the East European states to Western loans and investments and to closer contacts with the West. East European dissidents called for a recognition of the human rights guaranteed by the Helsinki agreement, to which the Soviet Union and the East European bloc had subscribed. They wrote about ending their party-state dictatorships and the restoration one day of a "civil society."

As in the Soviet Union itself, East Europeans began to discuss the shortcomings of their centrally planned economies. Excessive centralization and bureaucratic control stifled initiative and productivity; large subsidies were spent to maintain inefficient state-run monopolies, unchallenged by competition. A scarcity of investment capital interfered with the growth of new industries; the older plants and the infrastructure of the countries were decaying. Only in Hungary were decentralizing reforms and tentative steps toward a market economy being tried. Since the 1970s the East European economies had stagnated. It was openly admitted that large numbers lived in poverty. In East Germany, the showcase for achievements under central planning, economic growth had slowed and consumer goods were scarce. Even if state-run planned economies were to continue, many argued for greater latitude for free market competition, incentives for entrepreneurs and workers, and the encouragement of joint ventures with the outside capitalist world.

---

[32] See pp. 909–914.

Meanwhile the East European countries had to cope with the billions of dollars of debt incurred to Western banks in the 1970s, of which Poland owed close to half. To pay the interest alone on these huge sums and also control inflation demanded even greater austerity and reduced living standards.

Poland: The Example of the Solidarity Movement

In the 1970s and 1980s pressures for economic reform, and political liberalization appeared almost everywhere, but nowhere as much as in Poland. Gomulka, who governed Poland for fourteen years after 1956, had disappointed the reformers.[33] In part because of continuing economic difficulties, he reintroduced repressive measures, used troops to put down strikes, persecuted church leaders, and in 1968 even permitted an anti-Semitic campaign against the small number of Jews still remaining in Poland. In 1970, after riots over food prices, the party replaced him with the reform-minded Edmund Gierek, who embarked on an ambitious economic development program, financed by heavy borrowing from the West. The initial results were promising, but to meet its debt obligations, the country had to expand its exports at the expense of domestic consumption. With the shrinkage of Western markets, heavy interest burdens, and glaring inefficiencies in the central planning system itself, economic conditions steadily worsened.

In 1980 the rise in food prices led to widespread strikes, which began in the Lenin shipyards in Gdansk and spread rapidly. The freer atmosphere that Gierek had permitted made it possible for workers to organize trade unions outside the official structure and then to create an aggressive independent trade union federation called Solidarity, the first of its kind in any Communist country. The movement found a militant leader and national symbol of protest in Lech Walesa. When the swelling movement demanded legal authorization, the government yielded. Before long Solidarity claimed a national membership of 10 million industrial and agricultural workers, and enjoyed wide popular support and church backing. There were calls for free elections and a role for Solidarity in the government. The Soviets, still in the Brezhnev era, once again saw a socialist regime threatened. They put heavy pressure on the Polish government and party to curb Solidarity, oust Gierek, and install the steely General Jaruzelski as party leader and premier. When strikes and demonstrations continued, raising the possibility of open Soviet military intervention, Jaruzelski in 1981–1982 imposed martial law, imprisoned Walesa and other labor leaders, and banned Solidarity.

Once the power of Solidarity was curbed and the Soviet threat of intervention reduced, Jaruzelski himself took a different tack. Recognizing the impossibility of meeting the country's desperate economic problems with a sullen labor force, he released Walesa and other labor leaders, ended martial law in 1984, and attempted a reform program of his own. International efforts also contributed to liberalization in Poland. Pope John Paul II, the first Polish pope ever to head the Roman Catholic church, inspired huge demonstrations for freedom during his visits. Lech Walesa was honored with a Nobel Peace Prize in 1983. The United States had imposed economic sanctions when martial law was declared.

Although Solidarity remained outlawed, Jaruzelski's economic measures,

---

[33] See p. 912.

modeled on the Hungarian reforms, provided some opportunities for private enterprise and incentives for economic productivity. But the reforms failed to improve the economy, satisfy the popular restiveness, or mollify the widespread resentment at the dictatorship. Labor militancy, economic discontent, religious feelings, and pressure by intellectual leaders continued to build up to create a national resistance. From 1985 on, Gorbachev's reform program in the Soviet Union added further inspiration. His example and the knowledge that the Soviets would not intervene to check liberalization in Eastern Europe—that the Brezhnev Doctrine was dead—encouraged the movement for reform within the Polish party itself.

Early in 1989 General Jaruzelski and the party leadership, faced with continuing unrest, not only gave Solidarity legal status but promised parliamentary elections in which Solidarity and other groups could put forward candidates even though the Communist party was to be guaranteed a fixed number of seats. The government restored freedom of worship and legalized the status of the church. The first open elections in Poland in over forty years, in June, gave Solidarity a landslide victory in all the contested seats. A coalition cabinet in which the Communists were a minority, the first since the early postwar years, took office. The Polish Communist party, itself eager to discard the past, quickly transformed itself into a Western-type socialist party, but large numbers drifted away in any event. The party-state dictatorship ended without bloodshed. The dike in Eastern Europe was first breached in Poland. It fell to the new coalition government to manage the severely troubled economy. The new government resolved to restructure the economy all at once along free market lines. Despite economic uncertainties, and political divisions among those who had brought about the revolution, Poland in the 1990s moved toward a market economy and parliamentary democracy, in charge of its own destiny.

Hungary: Reform into Revolution

In Hungary the attempt at reform in 1956, initiated by the Communist party leadership itself, had been brusquely interrupted when the Soviets intervened with troops and tanks to suppress the "counterrevolution." Imre Nagy, the party leader, and other leaders of the revolt were hanged.[34] For the next thirty-two years, the hard-line Janos Kadar ran the country. But even under Kadar the party, without relinquishing its monopoly on political control, moved away from the rigidities of a centrally planned command economy, encouraged a degree of private enterprise, turned to the West for capital investment, and relaxed its hold on the country. For a time the economy expanded and standards of living rose, but the limited economic reforms accomplished no fundamental change. The economy stagnated in the early 1980s while discontent spread. After 1985, in the wake of Gorbachev's reforms in the Soviet Union, some modeled on the Hungarian example itself, a new impetus for reform emerged in the country and party.

In 1988 the party, anxious to encourage change and still maintain power, eased Kadar out of office. Early the next year the new leadership, in a momentous step, agreed to permit opposition parties and multiparty elections, and began to

[34] See p. 912.

dismantle much of the older party-state apparatus, including the security police. To expunge the past it even dissolved the party itself and reconstituted it along democratic socialist lines. A wide range of opposition groups came forward. Reform, initiated by the party, had turned into revolution, and without bloodshed. The new leaders redefined the 1956 uprising as a progressive people's movement and formally condemned those who had invited Soviet intervention. Nagy's body was exhumed from a mass grave and given a hero's reburial. Whatever the problems that loomed ahead, the country had swept aside the humiliation of 1956, reasserted its national independence, restored self-government and civic freedom, and opened the way to a market-oriented economy and a pluralist democracy.

The developments in Hungary precipitated even more dramatic events. The new Hungary, looking westward, symbolically demolished a portion of the barbed-wire barrier on its Austrian border. A few months later, in September 1989, when large numbers of East Germans vacationing in Hungary obtained permission from the West German embassy in Budapest to emigrate to the West, Hungary opened its border with Austria and allowed the Germans to exit. For the first time since 1961 East Germans found a way to leave their country. Hungary opened up a floodgate for even more dramatic changes in Eastern Europe.

The German Democratic Republic: A "Gentle" Revolution

With Gorbachev's positive attitude toward reform, it was understandable that the pace of change in Eastern Europe would have accelerated, but neither he nor anyone else could have anticipated the dimensions it was taking. In the spring of 1989 there still appeared to be little chance for a Communist sharing of power, let alone a revolutionary transformation, in the four hard-line dictatorships, the German Democratic Republic, Czechoslovakia, Bulgaria, and Romania.

In the German Democratic Republic Erich Honecker, in power since 1961, stubbornly attempted to hold the line. Although the country boasted the strongest economy and highest per capita income in Eastern Europe, its citizens enjoyed far fewer amenities than the West Germans. The Berlin Wall built in 1961 barred their exodus to the West. Even though Honecker after 1970 accepted closer economic and political relations with West Germany, he remained adamant against relaxing political or economic controls at home.

But the East Germans followed avidly the Gorbachev reforms and the rush of events in Poland and Hungary. When in the autumn of 1989 Hungary opened the way for them to leave, thousands seized the opportunity. Honecker, gambling that if his compatriots were free to travel they might not choose to emigrate, announced a relaxation on travel restrictions. But the trickle soon became a flood. The East Germans, many of them skilled workers and professionals, were fleeing the repression and drabness of East Germany for the Federal Republic of Germany, where as Germans they were entitled by law to receive citizenship and assistance in finding homes and jobs. By the end of 1989, 350,000 of East Germany's population of 17 million had fled and at least that many more emigrated in the early months of 1990.

As demonstrations against the government mounted, Gorbachev made clear that Honecker could not expect the Soviet troops stationed in East Germany to save the regime and warned against the use of force to prevent reform. In Leipzig, over 100,000 demonstrators, assembling first in churches, marched in solemn procession with lighted candles, calling for the resignation of the party and government leaders and for an end to the police state. The party forced Honecker's resignation.

The new leadership pleaded for an end to the flight to the West, promised free elections, and announced the right of free and unrestricted travel. On November 9, 1989, the government opened the Berlin Wall, the hated symbol of confinement. East Berliners could cross over freely to West Berlin, make purchases, and return home. Nonetheless, the exodus to West Germany continued. By now even the freedom of movement, the end of censorship, parliamentary supervision over the state security police, and the pledge of free elections did not suffice. With the public disclosure of abuses, corruption, and luxurious living by Honecker and the party elite while ordinary people had suffered over the years, the entire party structure came crashing down. The Politburo and Central Committee resigned, Honecker and other leaders were arrested on charges of corruption and embezzlement, and younger reformers assumed control. The party reconstituted itself as the Party of Democratic Socialism. Within a few months its membership dropped from 2.4 million to 890,000. Delegates from a wide variety of opposition groups, exultant over their "gentle" revolution and the collapse of the party-state dictatorship, met with reform-minded representatives of the former Communist party to oversee the transition to a new constitutional regime.

Once the German Democratic Republic was no longer a Communist state, pressure for reunification began to build in both Germanys. In many quarters the prospect of a reunified Germany of close to 80 million people, the most populous country of Europe outside the Soviet Union, possessing one of the world's most powerful economies, stirred grim ghosts of the past. The "German question" resurfaced.[35] The entire postwar settlement was at issue. Since no final peace treaty had ever been signed, reunification required the approval of the four major Allied powers of the Second World War. There was hesitation, but no one, more than 40 years after the end of the war, could deny the German people the right of self-determination. Moreover, the Federal Republic of Germany had demonstrated its commitment to democracy and to economic and political cooperation with the West. There was confidence that a reunified Germany could integrate East Germany and still remain part of Western Europe and the European Community. Despite the unspeakable crimes of the Nazi era, it was unreasonable to insist upon unalterable traits of national character or blame the Nazi atrocities forever on the generations that followed.

Reunification moved forward swiftly in 1990. The four Allied powers gave their approval and relinquished their occupation rights. Germany confirmed the cession of territories in the east to the U.S.S.R. and Poland and pledged the inviolability of the German-Polish border.[36] The two states merged their economies and the West German mark became the common currency. On October 3, 1990, after 45 years of division, all preliminaries completed, their economies and their legal and political systems unified, the two states formally merged to become an enlarged Federal Republic of Germany, its capital in Berlin. In the first nationwide

[35] See pp. 516–517, 550–559, and maps on pp. 555 and 893.
[36] See pp. 863, 872, 982, and maps on pp. 248 and 873.

elections, Chancellor Helmut Kohl and his Christian Democrats, who had played a key role in all the stages of reunification, won a sweeping victory at the polls.

Czechoslovakia: " '89 is '68 Upside Down"

The same revolutionary spirit erupted in Czechoslovakia in 1989. After Soviet and Warsaw Pact military forces had ruthlessly crushed the "Prague spring" in 1968, hard liners had taken over.[37] In the 1980s they disapproved of Gorbachev's reforms in the Soviet Union and stifled dissent at home. But the dissidents quietly grew in numbers and influence. Charter '77, an organization of intellectuals formed after the Helsinki agreement,[38] became a rallying point for the struggle against the dictatorship. The country followed with intense interest the disintegration of Communist power in Poland, Hungary, and East Germany. When demonstrations broke out in the autumn of 1989, the government responded by arresting the dissident leaders. In October, demonstrators gathering in Wenceslas Square in Prague to commemorate the seventy-first anniversary of the founding of the Czechoslovak republic and to honor the memory of Thomas Masaryk, its first president, called for the release of the imprisoned dissidents—and for the resignation of the government. The reform movement gained momentum when the Soviet Union and other Warsaw Pact nations voted to apologize for the military invasion of August 1968. In November mass protests spread. The opposition coalesced in a loose coalition headed by the Civic Forum, which looked for leadership and inspiration to the dissident playwright Vaclav Havel, an outspoken opponent of the regime, who for long periods had been interned.

The demonstrations grew in intensity. Some 350,000 demonstrators in Prague on November 24 furiously demanded an end to the party-state dictatorship; a general strike threatened to bring the country to a standstill. The government and party leaders all at once resigned. Alexander Dubcek, the hero of 1968, dramatically appeared on a balcony alongside a new reform-minded Communist prime minister, who appointed opposition leaders to his cabinet, pledged a free press and free elections, dissolved the secret police, and even abolished the compulsory teaching of Marxism-Leninism in the universities. The party's forty-one year monopoly on power ended. Havel, only recently in prison, became provisional president; no one since Masaryk had been so popular. The opposition was strong enough to insist on a cabinet in which the Communists were a minority. Gorbachev took steps to withdraw the 75,000 Soviet troops stationed in the country since 1968. Someone exultantly observed: " '89 is '68 upside down." The people had wrested control without bloodshed—in a "velvet" revolution—and set the country on the road to democracy.

Of all the nations in the Eastern bloc Czechoslovakia had the strongest democratic tradition. Despite ethnic tensions from the beginning, it had experienced genuine parliamentary democracy in the interwar years and was the last of the East European states to succumb to Communist dictatorship after the Second World War. Even though its economy was one of the strongest of the Eastern bloc, it lagged far behind the West and required vast infusions of capital

---

[37] See p. 981.
[38] See p. 982.

to modernize and replace its older technology. Under the new regime it, too, moved toward a market-oriented economy and a pluralist democracy—the "civil society" that Havel and others had sought. Czechoslovakia, formed in 1918 out of the demise of the Habsburg empire, sacrificed to Hitler in the Munich Pact of 1938, victim of a Communist coup in 1948 and of Soviet military intervention in 1968, had known its share of travail.[39] Ahead lay harsh new economic rigors and renewed ethnic problems, but exciting prospects as well.

Bulgaria: A Palace Revolution

Even Bulgaria, the most docile of the Soviet client states, where the party held tight rein, fell to the revolutionary contagion in 1989. Word of the upheavals in central and eastern Europe led to mass demonstrations in Sofia that autumn demanding an end to the dictatorship. Pressure from within the party forced the resignation of Todor Zhivkov, the party leader who had run the country since 1954. His foreign minister took over, pledged parliamentary elections, economic reforms, and an end to the party's monopoly on power. Opposition groups emerged, fragmented yet strong enough to pressure the new government into curbing the power of the security police. Zhivkov himself was arrested on charges of corruption and mismanagement.

The revolution in Bulgaria may have been a palace coup within the party, but it, too, arose in response to deep mass resentments and ended the party-state dictatorship. In a country that had known little freedom even in the pre-Communist years, the question was whether the reform-minded Communists (who renamed themselves Socialists) could work together with the opposition in making the transition to parliamentary democracy.

Romania: The Showdown with Ceausescu

Everywhere the end of the Communist dictatorships in Eastern Europe had come without bloodshed. But in Romania events took a violent turn. At first it seemed as though the winds of change would not reach Bucharest. Since 1965, for twenty-four years, the dictator Nicolae Ceausescu had held firm control over party and government, building a cult of personality around himself and using his wife and other family members to help him govern. He remained isolated in a rigid autocracy with a large private security force, which he favored over the regular army. He had long concentrated on transforming a backward agrarian society into a modern industrial society regardless of the human cost. For his modernization program he borrowed heavily from the West, but was determined to remain independent of the outside world. The country regularly paid the interest on its debt, despite the sacrifices this meant for an already suffering and deprived population. All dissent, even grumbling, was kept under tight surveillance and control. What was distinctive about Ceausescu was his early break from Moscow control and his independent position in foreign and military affairs despite nominal membership in the Warsaw Pact. Unlike the other members of the Eastern bloc, he supported Israel in the Arab-Israeli wars and refused to join in the invasion

---

[39] See pp. 779, 840–841, 912–913.

of Czechoslovakia in 1968. His independent foreign policy brought favorable treatment from the West despite revulsion at his harsh tyranny and unconcealed megalomania.

Throughout the revolutionary autumn of 1989 Ceausescu ignored the upheavals in central and eastern Europe. But in December protest riots broke out in the provinces. When the military refused the government's orders to fire on the demonstrators, the dictator's security forces took over, killing hundreds, and word of the brutality spread. When Ceausescu attempted to address an official rally outside the presidential palace, he was met, incredibly, on two successive days with interruptions and heckling. The security forces attempted to suppress the demonstrators, but on the second day the angry crowds forced the dictator to flee the capital.

For days a battle raged in Bucharest between the dictator's security forces and the regular army units until the security forces were routed. Ceausescu and his wife were apprehended in the provinces, given a hasty military trial, and on Christmas day executed by a firing squad, soldiers drawing lots for the honor. A National Salvation Front, consisting of former members of the Ceausescu regime and of emergent opposition groups, came forward to lead the revolt, restore order, and dismantle the police state. Although former Communists were prominent in the new regime, and the strength of the opposition parties was still unclear, the party's sole authority had been abolished and one of the most repressive dictatorships of the Eastern bloc had come to an ignominious end.

The Revolutions of 1989

The extraordinary and amazing events of 1989, occurring in the bicentennial year of the great French Revolution, in many ways echoed the European revolutions of 1789 and 1848, as well as the American Revolution of 1776.[40] In a sense there was no actual revolution in 1989 because the old regimes simply collapsed and were replaced without violence. But the upheaval was revolutionary in that it demolished existing authority and brought on abrupt and radical change. It could remain peaceful because it faced no strong internal opposition and no threat of foreign intervention. It reasserted the ideals proclaimed in 1776, 1789, and 1848. Human rights meant the old "rights of man," and democracy meant representative and constitutional government, honestly contested elections, and guarantees against repression by the state. With the revolutions of 1989 Eastern Europe rejoined the West.

Without Gorbachev's liberalization in the Soviet Union and the inspiration of Solidarity's successful struggle in Poland, the revolutionary changes in central and eastern Europe in 1989 could not have taken place as they did. With a suddenness that took even the closest observers by surprise, smoldering resentments came to a head all at once. Gorbachev, committed to curtailing economic and military obligations in Eastern Europe for the sake of the Soviet economy, accepted the end of the Communist regimes imposed forty years earlier in the wake of the Second World War. Neither he nor others could have foreseen that the reforms would mean the dissolution of the Communist parties, the end of the

---

[40] See pp. 351–360, 365–378, 500–519.

Warsaw Pact, or the reunification of Germany. The Soviets surrendered an empire, much as the Western powers had surrendered their colonial empires a few decades earlier.[41]

The groundwork for change had been prepared by the close economic ties and other contacts with the West in the years of détente, the Helsinki agreement, the stubborn challenge of Solidarity, and the unwavering courage of the dissidents. But it was Gorbachev's clear signal that the Soviets would not intervene outside their own borders that made the stupendous chain of events possible, toppling one regime after another, closing one era and opening another. The dramatic flight of the East Germans symbolized the desire of all Eastern Europe to escape from behind the iron curtain.

The masses of people demonstrating in central and eastern Europe voiced common grievances. They gathered in throngs, first in the thousands, then in the hundreds of thousands, in the cobbled squares of the capitals and provincial cities and articulated long repressed resentments. They demanded free elections, an end to the Communist party's monopoly of power, and a restoration of political and civil rights and human dignity. Refusing to settle for partial concessions from above, they insisted on a full voice in their own destiny—the right to speak their minds, publish their thoughts, read an uncensored press, form political parties, live without a secret police, vote for candidates of their own choosing, and join with other citizens in a free society. They had too long been the pawns of omnipotent party-state regimes, for which totalitarian was not too strong a word, which had self-righteously demanded sacrifices and subservience in the name of an ultimate utopia. They objected to the centrally planned bureaucratic command economies, which had deprived them of decent living standards. They envied the immeasurably more prosperous economies of the United States, Western Europe, and elsewhere (despite their economic recessions and other problems). The official formula, that they enjoyed the rights and privileges of an egalitarian "socialist" society, had turned out to conceal political repression, economic stagnation, and social immobility. For many, the public revelation of the privileges and luxuries enjoyed by the party elite was the final shock.

The revolution, except in Romania, was carried out for the most part by placards and candles, not by rifles. The revolutionists, armed only with a moral cause, would have found it difficult to prevail if any of the governments in question had chosen to unleash the army and the police. The repression at Tiananmen Square in China in 1989 could have been repeated in Eastern Europe.[42] But the ruling elites, without Soviet support to bolster them, yielded; they simply lost the will to govern under what was for them, too, an alien system.

The revolution occurred less by explosion than by implosion. In country after country, the Communist parties crumbled, redesigning themselves along democratic socialist and social democratic lines. They repudiated Lenin's "democratic centralism,"[43] which had become a cover for dictatorial control. Even with these changes the party membership deserted in the hundreds of thousands. The opposition came forward as discussion groups or "forums," scarcely political

---

[41] See pp. 919–939.
[42] See p. 999.
[43] For Lenin's conception of the party see pp. 739–741.

parties, but eager to fill the vacuum. Journalists, playwrights, artists, poets, teachers, students—the intelligentsia, as they were still called—played a large role, as they had in the dissident movement. Heroes of the struggle were honored, like Nagy, the leader of the 1956 revolt in Hungary, who had paid with his life. It was a time for apologies. The Warsaw Pact nations apologized for the invasion of Czechoslovakia in 1968. The Czechoslovak president apologized for the expulsion of the Sudeten Germans at the end of the Second World War.[44] The German Democratic Republic (as the Federal Republic had years earlier) belatedly accepted its share of responsibility for the victims of the Holocaust. The Soviet Union conceded that the invasion of Afghanistan in 1979 was illegal, that the secret clauses of the German-Soviet pact of 1939 had led to the annexation of the Baltic republics, and that the Soviet government had massacred thousands of Polish officers in the Katyn Forest in 1940.[45] The world of the Eastern bloc had indeed turned upside down.

In the rapid succession of events, in the spread of the revolutionary contagion, even in the role of the intellectual leaders, the upheaval of 1989 was most reminiscent of 1848, when the system in central and eastern Europe maintained by Metternich for thirty-three years suddenly came to a revolutionary end.[46] In 1989 also, the dike broke and the flood of revolutionary change swept in. But the parallel should not be pressed too far. In 1848–1849 the armies of the reactionary dynasties, and especially of the Russian tsar, intervened to crush the revolutionists and delayed for many years the achievement of their goals. Yet it was justifiable in 1989 to recall the "springtime of nations" in 1848 and to see the end of one historic era and the opening of another.

A Time of Transition

The countries of central and eastern Europe entered a period of transition, the outlines of which were still vague. The inchoate opposition movements that brought down the dictatorships had to transform themselves into coherent political parties in order to assume their proper role in the emergent parliamentary democracies. The centrally planned economies had to be transformed into market economies. The fading out of state subsidies and price controls in order to free competitive private enterprise and raise production levels would inevitably in the short run lead to bankruptcies, inflation, unemployment, and instability. Economic conditions might worsen, even with infusions of Western aid, before improving.

The market economy could take many forms. The state had always played a large role in central and eastern Europe. It was unlikely that the new regimes would turn to any laissez-faire model of private enterprise, more likely that they would turn to mixed economies, with a large role for private enterprise and with an elaborate protective net of social services. Marginal as socialism was in American life, democratic socialism still had an appeal in Europe. The Soviet dictatorships had tarnished the image of socialism, but its egalitarian message, tied to respect for democracy and individual rights, as propounded by the British

[44] See p. 873.
[45] See pp. 842–843, 855, 992–993.
[46] See p. 509.

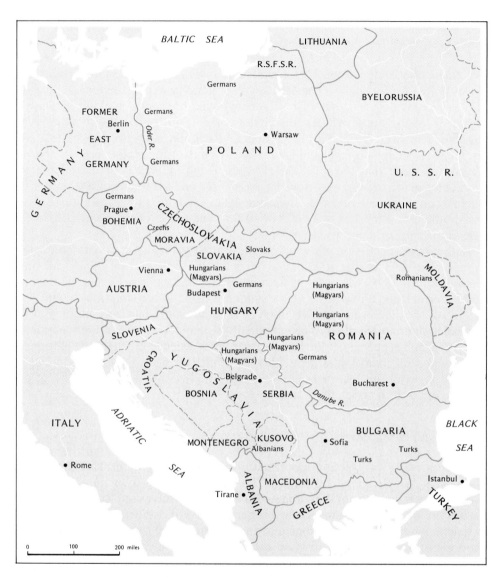

Labour party, the French Socialist party, and the German and Scandinavian Social Democratic parties, retained its attraction for many.[47]

Other explosive issues confronted central and eastern Europe. After the Second World War the population was distributed more homogeneously than ever before, but sizable minorities still remained within many national borders, as the accompanying map shows. Ethnic differences, repressed during the decades of Soviet rule, now surfaced openly. Irredentist pressures could emerge to redeem lost lands and reestablish ethnic ties. Anti-Semitism, held in check, or at least controlled officially, over the last four decades, as in the Soviet Union, might reappear if once again scapegoats were needed for frustrations and hardships. Should political and economic tensions or ethnic frictions mount, new forms of

[47] See pp. 621–624, 887, 986–988.

NATIONALITIES IN CENTRAL AND EASTERN EUROPE

Democratization and economic renewal in these countries are made more difficult by the persistence of ethnic differences. Poland and Hungary are now the most homogeneous within their present boundaries, with about 95 percent of the people of Poland actually Polish, and of Hungary, Hungarian. But in Poland and Hungary, as in Czechoslovakia and Romania, there still remain Germans who have lived there for centuries. About 3 million Hungarians are in regions that were formerly part of the Kingdom of Hungary but are now parts of Romania, Yugoslavia, and Czechoslovakia. The word "Moldavia" once meant northern Romania, but is applied now to the Moldavian Soviet Socialist Republic in the Soviet Union, where most of the people speak the Romanian language. About a million Turks have been in Bulgaria since the Ottoman Empire, as have the Albanians in Yugoslavia. There are about 2 million Muslims in southern Yugoslavia, most of them Slavs converted to Islam in Ottoman times. Serbs, Croats, and Slovenes are uncomfortable with one another in Yugoslavia, and in Czechoslovakia the Slovaks have long had grievances against the Czechs. Handfuls of Jews in these countries have survived the Holocaust. There are also many Gypsies, also victims of Nazi persecution, most numerously in Romania. For the shifting boundaries and movements of people that have resulted in this ethnic diversity see maps on pp. 248, 470, 660, 728–729, and 872–873. For numbers of national minorities in these countries today see the *Statesman's Yearbook* for 1989–1990.

authoritarian dictatorships could make their appearance even if they would not be Marxist-Leninist regimes.

Marxist-Leninist ideology as the undergirding for one-party dictatorships still persisted in the People's Republic of China, the most populous country in the world, and in the smaller states of North Korea, Vietnam, and Cuba. But anti-Communist ferment was stirring in other areas where leftist governments prevailed. Yugoslavia, Communist but long independent of the Soviets, was moving away from its older political and economic system, as was Albania. In Western Europe, in France, Italy, Spain, and Portugal, once strong Communist parties were reexamining their faith and adapting to changed circumstances. Marxism, born in the mid–nineteenth century in response to the instability and inequities of capitalism, would survive as a tool of criticism and analysis for scholars, but it seemed destined to limited appeal as a political philosophy, at least in the distorted form the Russian Revolution had given it.[48] Even proletarian internationalism lost much of its appeal because it had resulted in Soviet hegemony. The revolutions of 1989 heralded a return to the political processes and rights inherent in the liberalism of the West. It once again made possible democratic and pluralist societies, in which the citizens themselves through responsible governments had a new opportunity to work out their political and economic destinies.

125. *Intellectual and Social Currents*

Much of twentieth-century culture had its origins in the years from 1871 to 1914,[49] but since those years science, philosophy, the arts, and religion have crossed

[48] See pp. 740–741, 749.
[49] See pp. 625–637.

new frontiers or taken new directions. Even to single out a few of these developments will suggest the vast changes in the contemporary era.

The Advance of Science and Technology

Although science and technology expanded rapidly in the half-century before the First World War, the pace quickened in the following years. Scientific discovery advanced more rapidly in the years after 1919 than in all previous human history. For one thing, more scientists were at work. At the opening of the twentieth century, about 15,000 scientists were exploring scientific problems; in the latter half of the century, over a half-million scientists were engaged in research, more than in all previous centuries combined. Over 85 percent of all scientists who had ever lived were at work in our own age.

The average person experienced the triumphs of science most dramatically in medicine and public health. Nothing in previous medical discovery could equal the contributions of sulfa drugs, antibiotics, cortisone, and other substances used to combat formerly crippling or deadly diseases, including pneumonia and tuberculosis; hormones, adrenalin, and insulin were also available to promote health or relieve suffering. Vaccines combated a number of dread diseases, including, after 1955, poliomyelitis; by 1975 smallpox had been eradicated worldwide. Remarkable accomplishments in surgery included the transplanting of vital organs. Apart from the advances in medical science, people benefited from modern technology in ways too familiar to need recounting. For entertainment, radio and the motion picture were available and, after the Second World War, television. Washing machines, freezers, frozen foods, and microwave ovens lightened household duties. After 1947 airplanes could fly faster than the speed of sound; giant airships could traverse huge distances in a few hours; tourist travel to distant parts of the earth became commonplace. A world of computers, electronics, robotics, rocketry, and space technology opened, and the world seemed on the threshold of a new industrial age based on nuclear power.

It was a shattering experience when the new fatal disease AIDS (Acquired Immunity Deficiency Syndrome) appeared in the early 1980s and threatened to assume global epidemic proportions. The first case was reported in the United States in mid 1981, but the disease seems to have originated earlier and elsewhere. Although statistics were difficult to track, it was estimated that millions were infected globally. Although many were confident that medical science would devise a vaccine or other method of treatment or prevention, and that information and education on sexual practices and drug use would help check its spread, uncertainty and anguish increased as time went by without a cure. In its potential for disaster some ominously likened it to the Black Death of the fourteenth century.[50]

Nuclear Physics

In pure, or theoretical, science the transformation of physics in the twentieth century could be compared only to the scientific revolution of the sixteenth and

[50] See p. 48.

seventeenth centuries. Early in the twentieth century scientists had discovered the natural radioactivity of certain elements, physicists like Max Planck and Albert Einstein had developed quantum physics and relativity theory, and Einstein had propounded his now famous theory for the conversion of mass into energy.[51] After 1919 a series of discoveries led to a deeper understanding of the atom. The cyclotron, developed in 1932 at Cambridge University, made it possible to penetrate or "bombard" the nucleus of the atom at high speed. The nucleus, scientists learned, consisted not only of protons but of other particles like neutrons as well. In 1938 two German chemists Otto Hahn and Fritz Strassman discovered that when they bombarded the atomic nucleus of the heavy radioactive element uranium with neutrons it became unstable and split into two, which meant that energy trapped within the atom could be released. Other scientists, including Lise Meitner, a German-Jewish scientist who had been forced to flee to Sweden, further expanded upon these findings. In 1939 Nils Bohr, a Danish physicist, brought word of these developments to American scientists.

The implications of this breakthrough in theoretical science were clear. If the atoms in a large amount of uranium were split in a chain reaction, enormous amounts of energy would be released. In the troubled atmosphere of 1939 the possibility arose of its use for military purposes. When the war came, scientists in the United States, including Einstein, who had fled the Nazis in 1934, prevailed upon the American government to explore its military use before the Germans succeeded in doing so. In 1942 American and British scientists and European refugee scientists like the Italian Enrico Fermi brought about the first sustained nuclear chain reaction. This in turn led to the secret preparation of the atomic bomb at Los Alamos, its testing at Alamagordo in the New Mexican desert on July 16, 1945, and its use by the United States against Japan at Hiroshima and Nagasaki in August 1945. The bomb tested at Alamagordo and the bombs dropped on Japan heralded the atomic age.

After the war even more staggering technical developments followed. The hydrogen or thermonuclear bomb was built independently by the Americans and by the Soviets in 1952–1953; it involved nuclear fusion, or the joining together of hydrogen and other light elements at great heat, using the atomic or fission bomb as a detonator with a stupendous chain reaction. Such thermonuclear fusion is believed to be responsible for the energy of the sun itself.

The first use of nuclear energy was for military purposes, but it held constructive peacetime potential; a tiny grain of uranium (or plutonium, another radioactive element) could produce power equal to almost 3 tons of coal. In the early 1990s over 15 percent of the world's electricity was generated by nuclear power plants; in a country like France over 65 percent. At the same time the awesome explosive powers unleashed by the scientists and the dangers of radioactivity were alarming. Accidents in nuclear power plants, as occurred in the Soviet Union in the Urals in 1957, at Three Mile Island in Pennsylvania in 1979, and at Chernobyl in the U.S.S.R. in 1986, threatened the surrounding population and environs with the release of radioactive gases; nor could nuclear meltdowns be ruled out. Popular opposition to the building of nuclear power plants grew, as did concern over their proper design.

[51] See pp. 294–298, 628–630.

In military affairs a true nuclear clash of arms could mean apocalypse. Scientists who had prepared the first atomic bomb believed it to be so awesome a weapon as to make its future use unthinkable and in that way bar future major wars. In part they were correct; a balance of terror emerged so that for over forty-five years, since August 1945, no nuclear weapon has been used in warfare. But nuclear bombs became part of the world's arsenal, an ever present threat to human life on the planet and to the planet itself. The nuclear powers possessed missiles armed with warheads in the thousands, each of which represented power equal to the explosive force used in all previous warfare since the invention of gunpowder.

In later years scientists used linear accelerators like the cyclotron and even more powerful colliders and supercolliders as atom smashers to explore the nature of the atom and the behavior of its subatomic particles. Building upon the work of Einstein and others, the theoretical physicists searched for an overarching theory that would explain the interrelationship of gravity, electromagnetism, and nuclear force, all of which were to be found in the subatomic world and in the cosmos as a whole.

Implications of Science and Technology

As in the case of nuclear physics, science in the contemporary age was closely allied with technology and the organized effort to exploit new scientific findings. Government and industry subsidized most scientific research. Laboratory equipment was expensive, and complex investigation required large-scale collaborative efforts; the solitary scientific investigator (and inventor) was disappearing. The subsidization of research for national purposes raised the fear that scientific discoveries might serve political and not human goals.

Science had always affected the way people thought about themselves and their universe. The Copernican revolution had removed the earth from its central position in the scheme of things; Darwinian evolution had demonstated that *Homo sapiens* was biologically a species that had evolved and survived.[52] The philosophical implications of twentieth-century physics were only vaguely understood, yet they reinforced theories of relativism in all spheres. Ironically, at the very time that the average person was awed by the capabilities of science, scientists themselves recognized that they had no magic key to the nature of things. Generally they claimed no more than the ability to determine, or guess at, relationships, which in the world of the atom (as in the cosmos itself) were mysterious and uncertain.

Some questioned scientific and technological advance and asked whether modern technology had grown beyond human control. Ecologists pointed to the wastage and spoliation of natural resources and the threat to the environment. In another way the life-preserving features of medicine and public health could result in overpopulation and in perhaps unmanageable pressure upon the limited resources of the globe. The techniques developed to save or prolong human life also raised ethical and legal questions, including new definitions of life and death, and the rights in such matters of patients, families, hospitals, and physicians.

[52] See p. 626.

Questions arose over test-tube fertilization and other forms of artificial conception made possible in the late 1970s. Some, who condemned modern technology, extolled the virtues of a prescientific and preindustrial age; others called for sharper awareness of present and future dangers. No longer was the idea of progress equated with the advance of science and technology.

Meanwhile, in the quest to understand nature the old divisions between the sciences broke down and new sciences appeared. Biochemistry, cell and molecular biology, biophysics, astrophysics, geophysics, and other subdisciplines arose, and all made intensive use of mathematics. In biology genetics made important advances. While physicists discovered new atomic particles, biochemists isolated the organic substance found in the genes and chromosomes of all living cells, the chemical carriers of all hereditary characteristics. When scientists and biotechnologists discovered the genetic "code" and synthesized the basic substance of heredity, it became possible by splicing genes to alter the characteristics of microorganisms and of plant and animal species, with staggering implications.

The other life sciences and social sciences also grew in importance. Psychological exploration of human behavior, as well as the treatment of mental and emotional disorders through psychiatry and psychoanalysis, expanded rapidly. Freud, who had first developed his theories of psychoanalysis before 1914, became more widely known in the 1920s.[53] His emphasis on the human sex drive and sexual repression was much modified. Many students of human behavior rejected him and argued that his contributions were not universally or scientifically valid but reflected the values of pre-1914, middle-class, male-dominated Viennese society. New schools emerged with different interpretations and techniques, but the search, initiated by Freud, for the unconscious sources of individual and collective human conduct remained a hallmark of contemporary thought and culture.

Anthropologists and other social scientists increasingly stressed the relativism of all culture. They denied notions of cultural superiority or hierarchies of cultural values, or even that there were objective criteria of historical progress. If Western society, they noted, made notable progress in science and technology, other cultures accomplished more in self-discipline, individual integrity, and human happiness. The very adjective "primitive," as opposed to "civilized," tended to disappear, and a new cultural humanism emerged that recognized and esteemed values distinct from the Western tradition.

Space Exploration

Among the most dramatic developments in science and technology in the second half of the twentieth century was space exploration. In the 1950s the Soviets and the Americans competed with each other as part of the Cold War; each made important advances in rocket research. Even before 1914 the significance of rocketry had been grasped by pioneers in aerodynamics, and toward the end of the Second World War the Germans first used rockets in warfare.[54] Both the U.S. and the U.S.S.R. now mastered multistage rocket launching. The Soviets opened

[53] See p. 628.
[54] See p. 855.

the space age when in 1957 they launched *Sputnik*, the world's first artificial satellite, and then in 1961 sent the first human in orbital flight around the earth. In 1961 and 1962 the Americans sent their own astronauts into space. In the 1960s both countries launched unmanned automated spaceships to probe and explore the moon and then the planets of the solar system and their satellites. Early in the 1960s President Kennedy pledged that Americans would land on the moon before the end of the decade. In 1969 three American astronauts, as planned in Project Apollo, made the quarter-million-mile journey to the moon while millions over the globe watched on television. In the next three years the Americans made five additional trips to the moon. The automated robot spaceships, launched in the 1960s on long journeys to explore the planets of the solar system, were highly successful. The American spaceships approached or orbited the planets and soft-landed instrument packages, which over a period of years sent back a rich harvest of data, providing more knowledge than ever before possessed about the nature and origins of the planets, and about the earth itself. The later space probes explored the more distant planets. *Voyager 2*, launched in 1977, traveling close to 4.5 billion miles over twelve years' time, reached the outermost planets before flying into interstellar space. In 1990 the United States launched a powerful space telescope, capable of seeing far into other galaxies.

The Soviets also conducted impressive space probes, to the moon, to Mars, and to Halley's Comet, whose behavior had been predicted in the seventeenth century,[55] and which once again returned close enough for observation in 1986. The Soviets also built a permanent space station and set records in testing human endurance in weightless space.

As time went on, Cold War rivalries played less of a role in space exploration, but military objectives were never completely absent. The U.S. and the U.S.S.R., and later other countries, launched spy satellites for reconnaissance and information-gathering. The United States began research in the 1980s into an enormously costly strategic defense initiative that would deploy laser-like weapons in outer-space (hence called "star wars") to thwart nuclear missile attacks.

But by the 1980s space enterprise showed promise of international cooperation, and was no longer confined to the military superpowers. France, China, Japan, and other countries became spacefaring nations, planning and launching satellites and space probes of their own. The European Space Agency carried out its own operations. A cooperative multinational human expedition to Mars sometime in the twenty-first century was discussed. On the other hand, the need for human expeditions came under serious scrutiny. Dismayed by a number of serious space accidents and impressed by the accomplishments of the robot spaceships, many contended that unmanned space flights could accomplish more, at less cost, and at less risk to human life. Others objected to the enormous expense of space exploration when acute social needs remained unfulfilled. But its champions defended it as part of the continuing human effort to cross new frontiers, expand horizons, and explore the unknown. The twentieth century might be remembered, apart from the destructiveness of its wars, as the century in which humans first set foot on the moon and with robot spaceships, devised and guided by human intelligence, explored the planets.

[55] See p. 301.

Philosophy: Existentialism in the Postwar Years

A loosely organized body of ideas called "existentialism" grappled in the early postwar years with the human predicament. The existentialists formed no one school of thought and held no coherent body of principles. There were Christian and atheist existentialists. Yet all held some beliefs and attitudes in common. All reflected a troubled civilization, a world disturbed by war and oppression, a civilization of material progress and moral uncertainty in which the individual could be crushed by the very triumphs of science and technology.

Existentialist thought owed a debt to Pascal, Nietzsche, and others who had underscored the tragic element in human existence and the limitations on the power of human reason.[56] More directly it owed a debt to Søren Kierkegaard, the Danish religious philosopher, whose writings became better known when translated into German in 1909. But it was French writers, and especially Jean-Paul Sartre, who after the Second World War developed existentialist thought in literature and philosophy in a form that for a time gave it a wide popular following. In a hostile world, the existentialists contended, human beings had to make choices and commitments on their own. They were "condemned to be free," wrote Sartre, and were alone responsible for their choices. The authentic existentialist could not be contemplative only but had to be committed to belief and action, even though aware that human action could not change the world. Albert Camus, influenced by the existentialists, drew upon the myth of Sisyphus, who was condemned to roll his stone uphill even though it rolled back down again, his very humanity growing out of courage and perseverance at a hopeless and absurd task. Existentialism emphasized the anguish of human existence, the frailty of human reason, the fragility of human institutions, and the need to reassert and redefine human freedom. Although its popular following waned, existentialism never completely disappeared from contemporary thought in philosophy or religion.

Philosophy: Logic and Language; Semiotics and Literary Criticism; History

Professional philosophy in the twentieth century seemed to contribute less to an understanding of contemporary problems than in the past. Always concerned with the origins and nature of knowledge, it had also shared an interest in metaphysics and ethics. In the twentieth century it became highly analytical. In the formal study of logic, symbolic logic substituted mathematical symbols for language. On the eve of the First World War Bertrand Russell and Alfred North Whitehead explored logic and mathematics in their monumental *Principia Mathematica*. In the 1920s an influential group of philosophers and mathematicians in Vienna, among them Ludwig Wittgenstein, sought to introduce the methodology and precision of mathematics into the study of philosophy as a whole, in what they called logical positivism. They rejected the ambiguities of language used in traditional speculation on morals and values, turning away from the nondemonstrable—i.e., "God, death, what is higher,'' in Wittgenstein's phrase. The Vienna group disintegrated in the 1930s but the influence of logical positivism remained important. Most of the professional philosophers continued to emphasize scientific rigor and linguistic analysis. A smaller number, responsive to contemporary ethical concerns, devoted themselves to unresolved human and social dilemmas.

In philosophy, as in literary studies, the study of semiotics emerged in which all writing and speech were treated as a system of signs. The relationship of words to things, in all languages, its disciples emphasized, was arbitrary and conventional, not natural. The new study had its greatest influence not in professional philosophy, where it played a role too, but in literary criticism. The inspiration in literature derived from a number of French writers, but fundamentally from the pre-1914 philologist Ferdinand de Saussure, whose lectures were posthumously published on the eve of the First World War. His theories were expanded upon and applied after 1945 by Roland Barthes, Michel Foucault, Jacques Derrida, and other scholars of various disciplines and nationalities.

Like Saussure, they focused upon the wide gap between language and reality. All writers used the same words, they said, but used them in different ways in accordance with their own experiences and background. It was for the reader to examine and analyze (or "deconstruct") a given body of writing (or "text") with no concern for past efforts at interpretation. The work of the critic was said to be as much a creative enterprise as literary creation itself. Deconstruction, which won its largest following in the United States, made it possible, its proponents claimed, to reveal the class, racial, ethnocentric, or sexual orientation of a work and its author. It also contested older, rigid, hierarchical standards of literary quality, blurred distinctions between elite and popular culture, and loosened up and broadened the organized canon of writings studied in literature, history, law, religion, and other disciplines. Its opponents saw it as abandoning traditional literary history and undermining the objective values and standards that had long held a place in literary studies.

The writing of history also underwent a profound change. A group of French historical scholars (called the *Annales* school, from a journal with which they were associated) became increasingly influential after the Second World War. They focused on long-term elements in historical change such as population, economy, climate, and natural resources, relegated politics to a lesser role, and avoided the traditional narrative of "events." They studied also the lives of ordinary people in the past and tried to reconstruct the collective outlook of social classes. The newer social history in France, England, and the United States also paid special attention to the inarticulate and illiterate, and all those with strong oral traditions, such as the American slaves in the antebellum south, the English working classes, the peoples of Africa, reconstructing their culture and lives even when sources were understandably scarce. Another new emphasis simultaneously opened up on the historical study of women from antiquity to the present, leading, among other results, to the reassessment of some historical eras. A variety of themes were also newly explored historically: marriage, divorce, the family, childhood, sexuality, even insanity and death through the ages. For their part, many traditional historians, who had not been wholly insensitive to these concerns, deepened their own narratives under the influence of the newer history.

The Creative Arts

The revolution against older traditions in the creative arts continued. Ever since the Renaissance, visual artists had followed certain norms of representation and space perspective. But much of modern, or contemporary, art prided itself on being nonobjective; it rejected the idea of imitating or reconstructing nature, or mirroring it with realism or photographic fidelity. The artistic revolution inaugurated before 1914,[57] picked up in intensity in the interwar years and after 1945. It seemed to mirror the political turbulence of the times and the disillusionment with rationalism and optimism. It reflected the influence of Freudian and other schools of psychology and the emphasis on the unconscious and irrational, as well as the relativity of the new physics and its uncertainties about the nature of matter, space, and time.

Artists continued the pre-1914 experimentation in color, form, and use of materials, but went well beyond, seeing the world around them in new ways. The Spanish artist Pablo Picasso systematically distorted and deformed in order to convey his image of human and nonhuman figures. Some artists expressed themselves through geometric form; others left reality behind and worked out of their own subconscious. The results were fascinating but frequently baffling. After the Second World War, the United States took over from France the leadership role in the visual arts. American artists developed schools of abstract art that included improvisation and automation in which the unconscious was also said to dictate the artist's work. Additional, even broader, experimentation continued.

Contemporary art resulted in original and striking expressions of form and color, but the conscious subjectivism widened still further the gap between artist and public. The artist, painter, and sculptor (and the poet, musician, playwright, and novelist, who were also rejecting the older conventions) were conveying their own vision of the world, not an objective reality that could easily be understood by others. Perhaps the greatest innovation was that the public, baffled as it was by much of contemporary art, came to accept the avant-garde as normal, even if on occasion it rebelled against it. Democratic societies accepted the need for artistic experimentation and innovation, which had been frowned upon or banned as degenerate or socially dangerous in totalitarian societies like Nazi Germany or (until it became a more open society in the mid 1980s) the Soviet Union. Representational art, of course, never completely disappeared anywhere, and many artists reaffirmed it, contributing to a growing pluralism in contemporary art.

The focus on subjectivism and the unconscious was reflected in literature too. The reconstruction of lost time and the unfolding of the individual's innermost experience through a stream of consciousness and flood of memories appeared first in the work of Marcel Proust and James Joyce before and shortly after the First World War. After 1945, not only writers but cinematographers experimented with probing the unconscious in evocative but mystifying ways. All of this was in contrast to the entertainment provided through the mass media, especially movies and television, and hardly touched the average citizen.

Sometime in the early 1970s the phenomenon of postmodernism emerged in

[57] See illustrations, with captions, on pp. 632–635, 780, 861, 1029, 1040.

architecture, literature, and other art forms. Architects rejected the severe plastic and glass of the modern building style and made modifications, often mixing the new and the old. In all areas the postmoderns borrowed from the past, not systematically but haphazardly. Unlike the modernists of an earlier era, they did not openly reject or rebel against the commercialization and materialism of contemporary culture but embraced it and at times with humor and wit projected it in new ways. The American architect Robert Venturi and his collaborators wrote a book called *Learning from Las Vegas* (1972). Composers introduced street noises (and silences) into their music. Repetition, as in the commercial world of packaging, marketing, and television advertising, was adopted as technique. The artist Andy Warhol created pictures in that manner of Coca-Cola bottles and of the film star Marilyn Monroe. In fiction the postmoderns mingled actual events and fantasy. A play by Harold Pinter or Samuel Beckett was very different from a play by Shakespeare, Molière, or Ibsen. The postmoderns also rejected traditional ideas of structure, seeing no need in literature or art for a beginning, a middle, and an end. It was too soon to tell whether postmodernism was only the current phase of the modernist rebellion against traditionalism, or a sequel to it with new messages.

Religion in the Contemporary World

Religion was in flux in the contemporary world. With the continuing inroads of secularism, the challenges of science, and the post-1945 advances of communism in Eastern Europe, China, and elsewhere, organized religion suffered many setbacks. But the churches survived Marxist regimes and despite setbacks the traditional religions retained their vitality.

Statistics on religious affiliation are never exact, but some figures in the closing decade of the twentieth century were clear. Islam, with over 900 million adherents, was the fastest growing faith; it made large inroads in postcolonial Africa. In Asia, in addition to over 600 million Muslims, there were 685 million Hindus and 310 million Buddhists. Christianity, if all branches are added together, remained the largest religion, counting 1.7 billion adherents, of which more than half were Roman Catholic, a fourth Protestant, and a fourth Eastern Orthodox. The ecumenical movement in Christianity, the organized effort to unite the many branches of Protestantism, and eventually all Christianity, which began in the nineteenth century, made headway after the Second World War. A World Council of Churches was founded in 1948. When in the 1960s the Roman Catholic church

TWINNED COLUMN
by Antoine Pevsner (Russian, then French, 1886–1962)
Antoine Pevsner, like Kandinsky and Chagall (see pp. 633 and 635), left his native Russia after the Soviet regime began to disapprove of "modern" art. The picture here shows one of his sculptures, a bronze piece about forty inches high, constructed in 1947. The symmetry and the column recall the classical tradition, but the work also conveys the scientific and technological interests of the twentieth century. Pevsner's sculptural space is not the familiar medium in which human beings live and move, but a more abstract space, known to mathematics, quite apart from man's peculiarities of size and physical senses. Courtesy of the Solomon R. Guggenheim Museum.

abandoned its insistence on a privileged position in Christianity, it too encouraged ecumenicism. The Christian churches moved toward a closer dialogue with non-Christian world faiths as well. In Judaism, the older trend to secularism persisted, but more striking was the growth in all branches of the religion.

As in the nineteenth century, tensions between modernism (in its religious sense) and fundamentalism continued.[58] For the most part the Protestant churches reconciled their traditional teachings with science and scholarship, minimized the supernatural and dogmatic aspects of their faith, and sought to adapt the teachings of the gospel to the social needs of the contemporary world. But the two world wars and the troubled century dealt a blow to modernism and to the inherent optimism of the social gospel. In the 1920s, not only did fundamentalism revive, but a sophisticated intellectual reaction set in among Protestant theologians that emphasized revealed religion and elements of faith. The Swiss theologian Karl Barth in his writings from 1919 to the 1960s endeavored to lead Protestantism back to the root principles of the Reformation. There was much interest in Kierkegaard, the nineteenth-century Danish theologian who, like Luther himself, had resolved his own deep anguish by a personal commitment to religious experience. After the Second World War, as a result of the work of Barth, Paul Tillich, and others, a powerful movement in Protestantism reasserted its dependence on revealed religion and denied that human reason could ever properly judge divine revelation. Some church writers, unable to explain the wrenching experience of the war and the Holocaust, spoke of "post-Auschwitz theology" and alluded to "God's removal from history." On the whole, modernism, an acceptance of contemporary science and scholarship, and a willingness to become involved with the challenge of modern times remained characteristic of liberal Protestantism.

The Roman Catholic Church

The Roman Catholic church seemed to be in one of its great historic phases in the second half of the century. Although the church no longer actively suppressed modernism, the Vatican reaffirmed dogmatic training in the seminaries and the catechism for the instruction of the laity. In 1950 Pius XII, who headed the church during the war and for fourteen years after, proclaimed the dogma of the Assumption, the literal, or bodily, taking-up of the Virgin Mary into heaven, the only new Roman Catholic dogma to be proclaimed in the twentieth century.

Pius XII was succeeded in 1959 by John XXIII. Although elected at the age of 77, and reigning for only four and a half years until his death in 1963, John proved to be one of the most innovative popes of modern times. Above all, he worked to bring the church and its teachings into greater harmony with the contemporary world. His powerful encyclicals gave a global emphasis to the older social teachings of the church and called upon the wealthier nations to share their resources with the less favored in the developing world. In one encyclical, *Pacem in Terris* (1963), the first ever addressed to Catholics and non-Catholics alike, he appealed for peace and a worldwide concern for human rights. A believer in ecumenicism, he opened dialogues with other faiths. Among other reforms he

---

[58] See pp. 631–636.

enlarged the College of Cardinals in order to increase its non-Italian representation. In 1962, in a momentous step, ignoring the advice of his own theologians, he convened the Second Vatican Council, the first such council since 1870, and as it turned out, the most important church council since the sixteenth-century Council of Trent.[59] Vatican II reshaped contemporary Catholicism. The bishops and prelates assembled from all over the world rejected the draft reports prepared by the Vatican theologians and substituted their own reforms.

John did not live to see the Council's labors completed. His successor, Paul VI, shared John's social concerns and encouraged ecumenicism, but he was more conservative in other ways. The Council nonetheless moved forward with its reforms and completed its work in 1965. Accepting the principle of religious pluralism, it abandoned its older insistence on a Catholic monopoly on religious truth. It affirmed the principle of collegiality, an old view that had gone into eclipse in the modern centuries, that the pope must share his authority with the prelates of the church, thus affirming the authority of the national churches on substantive matters. It revised the liturgy and various church practices. The Mass, henceforth, would be said in vernacular tongues instead of in Latin, the practice since the eighth century. The Council relaxed restrictions on dress for priests and nuns. It gave the laity a larger role in religious practices. In one historic declaration, the Council explicitly absolved the Jewish people from the charge of deicide that had inflamed anti-Semitism over the ages. John XXIII's goal—the revitalization and updating of church teachings and practices—was amply fulfilled by the Council. There were limitations, to be sure. Celibacy for the clergy remained unmodified; nor was the ordination of women as priests sanctioned. Paul VI, meanwhile, upheld papal supremacy and took a conservative stance on moral issues, especially on birth control.

After Paul VI's death in 1978 (and after a successor died after only 34 days in office), John Paul II, the archbishop of Cracow, became the new head of the church, the first Polish pope ever elected, and the first non-Italian pontiff in over 450 years. He became a widely admired but controversial pope. Robust, earthy, energetic, versatile in languages, and magnetic in personality, he had a keen sense of pageantry and papal majesty. Not only did he encourage the Christian ecumenical movement, he reached out to non-Christians as well, traveling widely in Asia and Africa. With the Soviet Union and the countries of Eastern Europe he entered into diplomatic negotiations to improve the status of the church, even while condemning atheism and the persecution of believers. As we have seen, he contributed much to the revolutionary transformation of his own country and Eastern Europe in the 1980s.

On global, social, and economic issues, John Paul II spoke with warmth and eloquence. He condemned racism of all kinds, listing apartheid, anti-Semitism, tribal conflicts, injustices to aboriginal peoples, and the discrimination, xenophobia, and racial hatred encountered by Third World immigrants in Western Europe, notably in Britain, France, and Germany.

Although on many social issues John Paul took a progressive stance, in matters of church doctrine and governance he unequivocally favored orthodoxy and papal supremacy, and a narrow interpretation of sexual morality, disappointing many

[59] See pp. 88–90, 634.

who believed that the Second Vatican Council had opened a new era of collegiality and liberalization in all areas. He appointed conservative archbishops and bishops, silenced dissenting theologians, and curbed the growing assertiveness of national churches. In Latin America he put an end to "liberation theology," curtailing the activities of priests who wished to enlist their religious faith in the struggle against class oppression and exploitation. He would not countenance marriage for the clergy, the ordination of women as priests, rights of divorce (or of remarriage for the divorced), or homosexuality. His authoritarian stance on controversial issues engendered protest against the "new Roman centralism," the failure to modernize the church more thoroughly, and the unwillingness to respect the spirit of shared authority promised by the Council. His defenders argued that in upholding tradition, he was restoring a balance upset by overly rapid change in the church.

Other Developments

Judaism, the third important faith of the Western world, was haunted in the years after 1945 by the traumatic experience of the Holocaust.[60] Of the world's 18 million Jews, one-third lived in the United States. Jews everywhere, and especially in the United States, and not only Zionists, lent moral and financial support to the state of Israel, although many were troubled by Israeli militancy and intransigence, especially in its occupied territories, and by the role in domestic Israeli politics of ultraorthodox religious groups that refused to accept a secular state. Support for Israel was reinforced by the hostility of several of the Arab states and the Palestine Liberation Organization. Anti-Zionism, not only in the Arab world but elsewhere as well, at times served as a thin screen for anti-Semitism. In the Soviet Union, Jews insistent on practising their faith met harassment and persecution and, when they were permitted, emigrated in large numbers.

The major non-Western religions, Islam, Hinduism, and Buddhism, also made efforts to adjust millennia-old doctrines to the secular tendencies of the contemporary age, or in some instances adamantly refused. Iran was a dramatic example of resistance to accommodation. Some Eastern religions attracted adherents in the West: Islam among African Americans, Buddhist meditative teachings and practices among students, intellectuals, and others. The large numbers of African and Asian immigrants to Western Europe, and of Asian immigrants to the United States, brought their religious faiths with them.

In many parts of the world, fundamentalism was on the rise. It took a dim view of the secular changes of modern times. As a result of the separation of church and state, organized religions in much of the world could no longer enforce religious views with state power. Fundamentalists of all persuasions called for an unswerving adherence to sacred texts regardless of changing times and circumstances, or the evolution of religious doctrine. To a greater or lesser degree they were identified with a messianic and charismatic leadership, a close identity of religious and political values, a strict moral code interpreted and enforced by religious leaders, and the mobilization of mass following to accomplish their ends.

[60] See p. 859 and map, p. 858.

Even if popular frenzy or the adulation of a religious leader like the Ayatollah Khomeini nowhere reached the heights that they did in Iran from 1979 to 1989, a fundamentalist religious fervor emerged in many separate parts of the globe. The separatism of the fundamentalists ran counter to the blending of religions and cultures in the contemporary age.

Activism: The Youth Rebellion

In the second half of the twentieth century young people seemed to acquire a collective identity that historically youth did not possess earlier. It was possible to speak of a youth market, a youth culture, youth movements. In part the phenomenon was demographic in origin, the result of the baby boom, the extraordinary number of births in the decade and a half after the Second World War. A large cohort grew up in a rapidly changing world.

In the 1960s a youth activism made a startling appearance, sparked by a widespread student rebellion. A generation came to college age and attended institutions of higher learning in larger numbers than ever before. It was a generation that knew nothing firsthand of the Great Depression, the turbulence of the 1930s, or the Second World War. It grew up in an era of global change and scientific breakthroughs, to which their elders were no certain guides. The young people took for granted the scientific, technological, and other accomplishments of their world and concentrated on its deficiencies—the flagrant contradictions of wealth and poverty within nations and among nations, racial injustices, discrimination, colonialism, the impersonal quality of mechanized society and bureaucratized institutions (including colleges and universities), the violence that destroyed human beings in continuing wars, and always the threat of nuclear destruction. The rebelliousness extended beyond the traditional generation gap; it was directed at all established society.

The revolt burst forth in the late 1960s in widely separate parts of the world. The Cultural Revolution in China,[61] although in an entirely different context, was not unrelated, and indirectly inspired it. At the peak of the movement in 1967–1968 students demonstrated and rioted on campuses and battled police all over the world; American, Canadian, Mexican, West German, French, Italian, and Spanish universities were heavily involved. France was at the center of the storm. There demonstrations reached near-revolutionary dimensions in the spring of 1968 and threatened to overthrow the regime when 10 million workers also went out on strike, partly in sympathy and partly for their own grievances. But the ultramilitancy of the students alienated many, and the government restored order. Such initial grievances as inadequate physical facilities in the overcrowded universities and impersonal and remote instructon were almost forgotten in the upheavals in Paris and elsewhere. Some of the earliest and largest demonstrations took place in the United States, sparked by the struggle for civil rights for American blacks and heightened by resistance to American involvement in the unpopular Vietnam War. The assassinations in 1968 of the dedicated black leader of the civil rights movement, Martin Luther King, Jr., and of Robert Kennedy, brother of the slain president, fueled further anger in the ranks of the young.

[61] See p. 916.

The rebelling students made heroes of the sworn foes of the established order: Fidel Castro and his martyred lieutenant Che Guevara, Ho Chi Minh, Mao Zedong, militant American black leaders, the heralds of the colonial revolution such as Frantz Fanon (the West Indian author of *The Wretched of the Earth*), and others. They read the neo-Marxist philosopher Herbert Marcuse, who warned that the very tolerance of bourgeois society was a trap to prevent true protest against injustice; they learned from him that the industrial working class, coopted by the existing system, was no longer a revolutionary force. A New Left dismissed older revolutionaries in the Soviet Union as timid bureaucrats unaware that the revolution had entered a new phase, and that leadership would come from Maoist China and the Third World. They attacked modern materialism, affluence, and conformity, and the power structure of contemporary society. Many believed in confrontation and action for the sake of action, recalling an older anarchism and nihilism. They called on each other to destroy in order to purify.

The rebellion in its mass phase faded by 1970. In the United States it helped bring the Vietnam War to an end. Only a small number of extremists continued a kind of urban guerrilla war through underground terrorist organizations. Mostly, the rebels of 1968 moved on to places in established society. While many people shuddered at the attack on traditional institutions and orderly processes, others were shaken out of their complacency about social and racial inequities. Efforts were made subsequently in France, West Germany, and elsewhere to reform university administration and to provide more adequate teaching facilities. The youth movement, even after it subsided, had a continuing effect on all age groups in loosening older standards of language, dress, and sexual relationships.

The Women's Liberation Movement

The feminist, or women's liberation, movement was another, but more enduring, manifestation of contemporary social ferment. From the time of the French Revolution a few thinkers in France and England had raised the question of equal rights for women.[62] The modern movement had its origin in the United States in the mid–nineteenth century when Elizabeth Cady Stanton and a small group of associates in 1848 proclaimed a declaration of independence for women, demanding the right to vote, equal compensation for work, legal equality, and expanded educational opportunities. The movement spread abroad. In Britain, later in the century, it was taken up by the suffragettes. The right to vote was won in a few American states and in a few smaller countries before the First World War, in many more nations after 1918, and in almost all other countries after 1945.[63] But other objectives went unrealized.

The militant contemporary phase began in the United States in the mid 1960s, a sequel to the civil rights movement on behalf of the American black population. The women's liberation movement, inspired by Simone de Beauvoir's *The Second Sex*, published in France in 1949, and Betty Friedan's *The Feminine Mystique*, which appeared in the United States in 1963, contended that women, half or more of the human race, had been and continued to be oppressed by a male-dominated

---

[62] See p. 372.
[63] See pp. 617–618, 641, 778, 887.

society and that they were not permitted access to positions of authority, leadership, and power. Although some of the more blatant forms of legal discrimination in such matters as property rights, for example, had been or were being removed, feminists demanded an end to all barriers to equality.

The argument for equal rights was most meaningful in the advanced industrial countries. Elsewhere, in the poorer, less developed nations women had to overcome centuries-old neglect, abject repression, abuse, and disregard of the most elementary human rights. The United Nations, from the time of its founding in 1945, committed itself to equal political, economic, and educational rights for women. But in Africa, Asia, and Latin America adult illiteracy rates a generation later were still significantly higher for women than for men and were declining more slowly. Opportunities for higher education were also more circumscribed. In the developing areas, where a majority of the world's women lived, equal rights for women also hinged upon economic development and social advances for the entire population. It had to be noted that discrimination was not confined to capitalist societies. Despite Communist promises, the advance to equality, or even to equality of opportunity, in the Soviet Union and in the People's Republic of China was disappointing.

Some women, more so than in the past, when authority resided only with reigning women sovereigns, held positions of the highest authority in their countries at various times in the years after 1945. Among them were Indira Gandhi in India, Golda Meir in Israel, Margaret Thatcher in Britain, Corazón Aquino in the Philippines, Benazir Bhutto in Pakistan, and other women presidents or prime ministers in such widely differing countries as Sri Lanka, Malta, Yugoslavia, Portugal, Norway, Iceland, Nicaragua, and Ireland. In Bangladesh and in Japan women led opposition parties.

Meanwhile the development of advanced contraceptive technology, especially the birth control pill in the early 1960s, provided a new biological freedom for women. Changing social patterns tolerating sexual freedom and new forms of relationships also contributed to social liberation. In the last decades of the twentieth century women were filling a higher share of places in higher education and in professional schools than ever before. As more women became part of the labor force at all levels, the demand arose not only for equal compensation for equal work, still far from realized, but also for equal pay for comparable work, that is, for jobs traditionally reserved for women. Working women in all societies pressed for shared responsibilities of household duties and parental obligations. Although there were disagreements in and outside the women's liberation movement on the methods and tempo of change, wide agreement existed on the need to utilize fully all of society's human resources in every part of the globe. If that could be accomplished, it would count among the most memorable of the revolutionary changes of the contemporary era.

126. A New Era

The changes in the Soviet Union after 1985 and in central and eastern Europe in 1989 swept away the foundations on which international relations had rested since the Second World War. A new era opened. The Cold War resulted from Soviet expansion, real and perceived, and the American-led effort to contain that expansion. For both sides it had assumed the aspect of a global ideological crusade. The build-up of military force, backed by unprecedented nuclear power, created a balance of terror that in its way prevented an all out war, which neither side could have won in any conventional sense. The Cold War never resulted in a direct clash of arms between the superpowers but took the form of repeated crisis and confrontation, as in Berlin or Cuba. Where wars were waged, one or the other superpower fought by proxy—in Korea, Vietnam, Central America, the Middle East, Africa, Afghanistan, and elsewhere. Nuclear arms were never used but they were ever present. The world escaped nuclear catastrophe in the four and a half decades after 1945.

In the early 1990s the superpowers were still heavily armed. The British and French retained their nuclear arsenals. The Soviets had large conventional forces and nuclear parity with the United States. But there was a new spirit, a changed reality, and a transformed atmosphere. The Soviet Union had surrendered its East European satellites without a struggle, the Warsaw Pact had disintegrated, and both sides were receptive to arms limitations and troop reductions. Economic weakness and political uncertainties made the threat of Soviet aggression improbable. The political division between Western and Eastern Europe, frozen for over four decades, had disappeared. The prospects opened up of "a common European home," in Gorbachev's phrase.

The commitments of the United States and Canada to Europe remained firm. Although the North Atlantic Treaty Organization would assume a different form and function, North America and Europe intended to retain their close ties in an Atlantic Community. It was in their common interest to see a reunited Germany anchored in institutions like the European Community and to reaffirm the security and cooperation provisions of Helsinki. A strong Germany, committed to democratic processes, did not necessarily have to represent a threat to its neighbors, or to the world.

The West Europeans used the years after 1945 to bury old national antagonisms, integrate a democratic Federal Republic of Germany into the European Community, and grow closer together. But while peace was preserved in Europe, millions perished in wars, rebellions, and civil strife in the Middle East, Africa, Asia, and Latin America. Many of these conflicts were unrelated to the Cold War. The superpowers did not always control world events. Nor would the passing of the Cold War bring an end to regional conflict. The Middle East remained an explosive area, as the crisis in the Persian Gulf in 1990–1991 demonstrated, and so did other parts of the globe. The developing countries were spending large sums on weapons, some of them concentrating on nuclear arms, missiles, and chemical warfare. Meanwhile the economic plight of the poorer nations had deteriorated in the 1980s. They were in urgent need of development assistance, which after the experience of the past might now be used more effectively in helping their impoverished people. They needed relief also from their heavy debt burdens. The hope for democratic advances in many of these countries, if they were to materialize, also held the promise of a new era.

The bipolarity of the early postwar years was yielding to a multipolar system in which the United States, despite its many problems, could still claim political, economic, and military primacy. But it could become, at some future date, only first among equals. The European Community and Japan could be expected to play a large role on the world stage of the future; in the case of Japan, perhaps even a role commensurate with its economic strength. The People's Republic of China, if it were to regain political stability, would assume a role of importance. Regional blocs in the Middle East or in the Pacific rim, and emergent powers like India, would surely carry political weight. The developing nations would demand to be integrated into the world polity. New alignments, new balances of power, and new economic rivalries could be expected to emerge.

The Population Explosion

Of all the developments in the post-1945 years one of the most spectacular was the world's population growth. As a result of major medical discoveries, improved health and sanitation measures, and more efficient methods of food production and distribution, death rates declined dramatically after 1945, but without a counterbalancing reduction in births. The number of human beings grew so rapidly, and at so fast a rate, that demographers spoke of a population explosion. It took humanity several millions of years to reach the one billion mark, sometime about 1830. In 1950 the world's population was 2.5 billion; in 1960, 3 billion; in 1975, 4 billion; and only twelve years later, in 1987, 5 billion. An increase of 90 to 100 million annually was projected for the 1990s, so that a 6 billion figure was rapidly approaching. The time required to add a billion people to the world's population was growing shorter and shorter.

The global growth rate peaked in 1970 and then declined somewhat, in part because birth rates dropped for a time in China. But the annual increases for the world remained staggering and in 1989 the growth rate of 1.7 percent showed signs of rising. Demographers pushed well into the twenty-first century the time and estimated figure at which stabilization might be achieved; many debated the maximum numbers that the earth's resources could sustain.

The impact of the fall in death rates on population was exemplified in India, where the death rate in 1990 was half what it was in 1950 and the population rose from 350 million to over 850 million. Adding 16 million people annually, India's population could exceed one billion by the end of the twentieth century. If China maintained its slower growth rate, India could surpass China as the world's most populous nation. Nigeria, with its high 3.3 percent annual growth rate, might well end up in third place behind India and China.

Population increase was largely a phenomenon of the developing countries in Africa, the Middle East, Asia, and Latin America, where three-fourths the world's population lived, and where birth rates were highest. In North America and in Europe in contrast, population was scarcely growing. Industrialization, urban life, and social pressures for smaller families had begun to slow long-term birth rates ever since the late nineteenth century.[64] By 1985 fertility rates in Europe were below the replacement level of two births per couple. Europe had experienced a baby boom in the years after the Second World War, reaching a postwar peak in 1965, but from that point on, in the wake of changing patterns of social and sexual relationships and the availability of modern contraceptive devices, the

[64] See pp. 590–591.

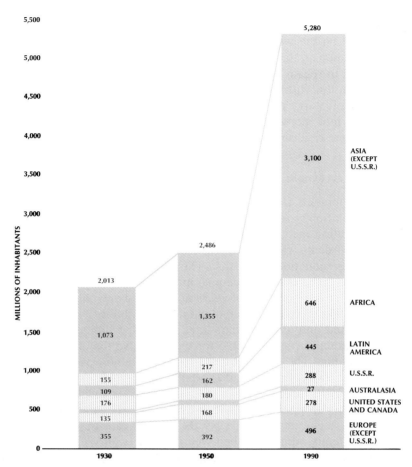

THE POPULATION EXPLOSION

In the late 1980s the world's population passed the 5 billion mark. It had doubled in less than half a century, and more than doubled in Asia, Africa, and Latin America. It was projected to exceed 6 billion by the year 2000. Growth was most rapid in the poorer countries, where it contributed to chronic social unrest and political instability. The wealthier or "developed" part of the world, including Japan and other parts of East Asia, had a slower growth rate, but in 1990 it comprised only about a quarter of the world's population.

Comparison may be made with the table on page 588, where the categories are somewhat different, being designed to show the rise and decline in the proportion of "Europeans" in the global total. But the table shows no doubling of world population in any half-century from 1650 to 1950, so that the recent increase is truly an "explosion." Such a rate of increase cannot continue indefinitely; the question is whether it can be slowed down before the earth's resources are overstrained.

Source: *United Nations Demographic Yearbook*.

replacement level fell. By 1985, in a number of European countries there were fewer births annually than deaths, most notably in the Federal Republic of Germany and Italy; population decline was also under way in the United Kingdom, Denmark, and other European countries. In the U.S.S.R. (in its European areas) and in central and eastern Europe, where economic privation and housing shortages had contributed to low birth rates, decline was also evident. Measured against the dramatic increase in global figures, Europe's population decline translated into an ever shrinking share of the world's population. Elsewhere the explosive growth threatened to cancel economic advances and leave hundreds of millions in poverty and want. Many religious and cultural barriers to family planning remained before the world could slow its population growth.

The Threat of Environmental Degradation

As grave a threat as the global population explosion was for the world's resources, the planet faced other dangers. From 1950 to 1990 global economic production grew fivefold, consuming coal, oil, natural gas, and a variety of chemicals in the process. Industrial countries emitted quantities of toxic gases into the atmosphere, eroding the protective ozone layer that shielded the earth from excessive heat and radiation. The result, likened to the effect of a greenhouse, threatened a warming of the earth's climate, with potentially alarming consequences for the world's food production. Industrial pollution also caused the acid rain that laid waste to forests, lakes, and rivers. Severe environmental damage in the U.S.S.R. and in the East European nations confirmed that pollution was not confined to any single socioeconomic system; economic planners there had pressed development with no regard for the ecological consequences.

As in the industrial world, developing nations also paid little attention to their environment. Under the pressure of expanding population and rapid urbanization, they slashed and burned tropical forests for ranching, other commercial purposes, and resettlement. Arable acreage declined. In the four decades from 1950 to 1990, the world lost one-fifth of its topsoil and one-fifth of its tropical rain forests. Nowhere was this as striking as in Latin America and Africa. The destruction of the Amazon Forest in Brazil dramatized the extent of the damage. In Africa, intensive cultivation and overgrazing turned arable and pasture land into desert.

The developing countries, with much good cause, blamed the world's environmental woes on the industrially advanced nations, but they too, were reluctant to impose restraints. In the 1980s a newly sensitized world began to speak of sustainable growth rates, growth that could be maintained without destruction of the world's natural habitat. The necessary sacrifices, to be sure, would be relatively greater for the Third World countries because they were still in the early stages of development. Alternative forms of energy, some as old as the sun and the wind, others new, like nuclear energy (although expensive and still dangerous in some respects), were under consideration. As awareness of the ecological danger to the planet grew, grass-roots environmental organizations multiplied, attracted political attention, and in a number of countries turned into "Green" political parties. For the long-range questions of unprecedented population increase and the continuing deterioration of the environment no easy solutions were in sight.

One World: The Fate of Humanity

The worst of all eventualities for the world would still be global war. A world in which nations still possessed awesome nuclear arms and in which biological and chemical weapons proliferated remained endangered. In 1945 the victors in the Second World War had founded the United Nations as an instrument for preserving peace.[65] But for over forty years it remained in the shadows as the United States and the U.S.S.R. waged their Cold War. On some occasions, when the vital interests of the superpowers were not directly involved, it managed a peacekeeping function. In the Korean War it played a role only because the Soviet Union was absenting itself from the Council and could not exercise its veto, but in the great crises of the Cold War—the Berlin blockade, the Cuban missile crisis, the Vietnam War, the Soviet interventions in Eastern Europe, and the invasion of Afghanistan—it had little impact.

The composition of the United Nations changed markedly from the time of its inception. The 51 original members tripled and grew to 157 in the early 1980s and to 159 by 1990. When even very small former colonies achieved independence, as in the case of the Caribbean or Pacific island dependencies, many of these new nations had populations no larger than a small American or European city. St. Christopher and Nevis, once a British colony in the Caribbean, admitted to the UN in 1983, had a population of 40,000. The eighty smallest members of the United Nations together represented less than 10 percent of the earth's population. Each member, however, voted in the UN General Assembly in full equality with the larger nations. For much of the time the General Assembly served as a forum for discussion of grievances against the wealthier nations and exacerbated rather than alleviated tensions.

Many of the social and economic issues raised were real, however, and a number of the UN's smaller agencies played a positive role in grappling with them. With the decline of Soviet influence and the move toward Western-style market-oriented economies and more open regimes, many developing nations showed signs of tempering their strident anti-Westernism. They were anxious, however, that their enormous needs not be swept aside or ignored because of other priorities..

It was to the Security Council, and especially its five permanent members, that the UN founders had assigned the responsibility for maintaining peace. As the Cold War ended, it was possible that the Security Council would return to

---

[65] See pp. 868–869.

the role originally intended for it and play a stabilizing role in world affairs. In the late 1980s it helped mediate a cease-fire in the Iraq-Iran war, oversaw Namibia's move toward internal peace and independence, encouraged regional peace agreements in Central America, and mediated conflicts in Cambodia, Sudan, and Ethiopia. Whether it could resolve other tensions and disputes remained to be seen.

In August 1990 the UN faced its first great crisis of the new era when Iraq invaded, overran, and annexed its Arab neighbor, Kuwait.[66] At American initiative, the Security Council with the unanimous agreement of its five permanent members—the United States, the U.S.S.R., the People's Republic of China, Britain, and France—acted to uphold the collective security provisions of the Charter. The Council condemned Iraq's act of aggression, imposed economic sanctions, and endorsed military intervention. President Bush took the lead in creating a multinational coalition. The United States assembled a formidable military force in the Middle East, including over a half-million American troops, and early in 1991 unleashed a massive air assault on Iraq that forced it to withdraw from Kuwait with scarcely any ground fighting. The end of the Cold War had not brought peace to the world, but it made possible cooperation and joint action by the major powers, and widened the opportunities for the peacekeeping role of the Security Council. The hope revived that in the "new world order," as Bush described it, the international community and the UN could function more effectively in disputes in the Middle East and elsewhere.

Even if the UN were to assume a larger role in world affairs, there was still little hope that it could accomplish all the goals once held out for it. To save succeeding generations from the scourge of war; to advance human rights; to promote equality for men and women; to protect the freedom of nations, large and small; to promote social progress and raise living standards; to work for peace and security—these were still the contemporary world's loftiest objectives. But the world's nations, large and small, were not yet ready to transcend their national interests. A federation of the world's peoples and a parliament for humankind remained remote.

All the problems of the contemporary age—war and peace, the social implications of science and technology, the rivalry between nations, the quest within nations for freedom, equality, and economic well-being—were all aspects of one overriding problem, the fate of humanity, and of each generation of humanity. How could human beings, regardless of sex, color, creed, or nationality—beings said by some to be made in the image of God, by others to have a natural right to liberty and happiness, by still others to have the freedom to create meaning in a meaningless universe—live out their lives, fulfill their destiny, and pass on their heritage to future generations?

These concluding chapters began with the image of a cataclysm. The analogy is still pertinent. A cataclysm, as already observed, is not a time of downfall only. Mountains crumble, but others are thrust up. Lands vanish, but others rise from the sea. So it is with the political and social cataclysm of our times. Old landmarks

[66] See map, p. 949.

are worn down. Colonial empires pass away; new nations arise in their place. Subjugated countries regain their freedom. Rigid ideologies are undermined. The ascendancy of Europe, the West, and the white race closes; they learn to negotiate with others, not to rule them. Everywhere there is a fluidity in social relationships. Women and minorities struggle for an equal place in society. The gap between rich and poor among nations, and often within nations, widens. Never has war been so potentially destructive. The menace of a nuclear war which would blight much of civilization, perhaps destroy it, wanes but does not disappear. Uncontrolled economic growth threatens the environment and population growth presses on natural resources. New interventions are needed to sustain the earth's expanding billions. But there is a growing global recognition of all these concerns. To close this book on a note of placidity would indeed be inappropriate, but so, too, would it be to close it on a note of doom.

APPENDIXES, BIBLIOGRAPHY, AND INDEX

APPENDIX I: CHRONOLOGICAL TABLES

TABLE ONE: TO 1517

EUROPE AS A WHOLE: POLITICAL AND SOCIAL	EUROPE AS A WHOLE: THOUGHT AND LETTERS	BRITISH ISLES
	500–300 B.C. Classical Greek civilization: Plato, Aristotle	
146 B.C. Greeks conquered by Roman Republic		
31 B.C. Roman Empire		
306–337 Emperor Constantine: toleration of Christianity	1st century B.C.–1st century A.D. Classical Roman civilization: Cicero, Vergil	43–410 Roman Empire in Britain
5th century: Germanic invasions	426 Saint Augustine's *City of God*	
476 Roman Empire in West ends		596 Conversion of Anglo-Saxons
7th century: spread of Islam		
800 Coronation of Charlemagne		871–899 Alfred the Great
9th century: Norse and Magyar invasions		
1054 Schism of West and East: Roman Catholic church and Orthodox Eastern church	1033–1109 Anselm	1066 Norman conquest
1073–1085 Pope Gregory VII	1079–1142 Abelard	
1095–1099 First Crusade	12th century: coming of Arabic and Greek science	12th century: development of the monarchy in England
12th century: rise of towns		
1147–1221 Crusades: Second–Fifth	12th–13th century: universities, scholasticism	
1198–1216 Pope Innocent III		
	1215 Fourth Lateran Council	1215 Magna Carta
13th century: rise of parliaments	1267–1273 Thomas Aquinas' *Summa Theologica*	
1294–1303 Pope Boniface VIII		1295 Model Parliament

WESTERN EUROPE	CENTRAL EUROPE	EASTERN EUROPE
		6th–4th century B.C. Greek city-states
		356–323 B.C. Alexander the Great
		4th–1st century B.C. Hellenistic Age
31 B.C.–476 Roman Empire	31 B.C.–476 Roman Empire in western and southern Germany	31 B.C.–1453 Roman Empire in East
		330 Constantinople founded (formerly Byzantium)
496 Conversion of Franks		395–1453 Eastern Roman (Byzantine) Empire
	568 Founding of Venice	
711 Muslims in Spain		
732 Muslim defeat at Tours		
768–814 Charlemagne	768–814 Charlemagne	
987–1792 Capetian monarchy in France	*962–1806 Holy Roman Empire*	
		10th century: conversion of Swedes, Poles, Hungarians to Rome; Russians to Constantinople
	1056–1106 Emperor Henry IV	
		1001–1918 Kingdom of Hungary
	1075–1122 Investiture struggle	1054 Schism of East and West: Orthodox Eastern church
12th century: development of the monarchy in France		
		12th century: Teutonic Knights in Prussia
1208 Albigensian Crusade	13th century: failure of the Empire to organize Germany and Italy	
		13th century: conversion of East Baltic peoples to Rome
1309–1378 Babylonian Captivity: papacy in Avignon		
		1236 Tartars in Russia
	1356 Golden Bull	
		1389 Turks in Balkan Peninsula

EUROPE AS A WHOLE: POLITICAL AND SOCIAL	EUROPE AS A WHOLE: THOUGHT AND LETTERS	BRITISH ISLES
1348–1350 Black Death	1328–1384 John Wycliffe	1337–1453 Hundred Years' War
1378–1417 Schism of the West: papacy in Rome and Avignon		
1414–1418 Council of Constance	1415 Death of John Huss	1381 Wat Tyler's rebellion
1453 Roman Empire in East ends	15th century: Italian Renaissance	1455–1485 Wars of the Roses
	1452–1519 Leonardo da Vinci	
	1454–1455 Printing; Gutenberg Bible	
1492 Discovery of America	1466–1536 Erasmus	*1485–1603 The Tudors*
1498 Portuguese reach India	1513 Machiavelli's *The Prince*	1485–1509 Henry VII
1517 Protestant Reformation begins	1517 Luther's 95 Theses	1509–1547 Henry VIII

TABLE TWO: 1517–1618

EUROPE AS A WHOLE: POLITICAL AND SOCIAL	EUROPE AS A WHOLE: THOUGHT AND LETTERS	BRITISH ISLES
1517 Protestant Reformation begins	1517 Luther's 95 Theses	1509–1547 Henry VIII
1519–1648 Habsburg supremacy		
1519–1556 Charles V		
1519–1522 Magellan circumnavigates globe		1521 Henry VIII's *Defense of Seven Sacraments*
1529 Turks besiege Vienna		
	1530 Loyola's *Spiritual Exercises*	
1531 First stock exchange at Antwerp	1534 Luther's German Bible	1534 Act of Supremacy
	1536 Calvin's *Institutes of the Christian Religion*	1536–1539 Dissolution of monasteries
		1539 Six Articles
1540 Founding of Jesuits	1543 Copernicus' *Revolutions of Heavenly Orbs* and Vesalius' *Structure of the Human Body*	1547–1553 Edward VI
1541–1564 Calvin at Geneva		
1545–1563 Council of Trent		
	1550–1650 Golden age of Spanish literature	1553–1558 Mary I
1555 Peace of Augsburg		
1556–1598 Philip II of Spain		1558–1603 Elizabeth I
		1559 Knox and the Reformation in Scotland
	1561–1626 Francis Bacon	

WESTERN EUROPE	CENTRAL EUROPE	EASTERN EUROPE
1337–1453 Hundred Years' War		
1378–1417 Schism in church: papacy in Rome and Avignon		
	1420–1431 Hussite Wars	
1412–1431 Joan of Arc	*1438–1918 Habsburg Emperors*	
		1453 Turks take Constantinople; end of Byzantine Empire
1461–1489 Louis XI of France		
1479–1516 Ferdinand and Isabella of Spain		
1494 French invasion of Italy		1480 Ivan the Great ends Tartar control over Russia
1515–1547 Francis I of France	1519–1556 Charles V	

WESTERN EUROPE	CENTRAL EUROPE	EASTERN EUROPE
1515–1547 Francis I of France	1519–1556 Charles V Emperor	
1516 Concordat of Bologna		1520–1566 Suleiman the Magnificent
	1521 Luther banned	
	1526 Charles V at war with Turks	1526 Turks occupy Hungary
	1529 Turks besiege Vienna	
		1533–1584 Ivan the Terrible, first Tsar of Russia
1536 Franco-Turkish alliance against Charles V		1535 First French capitulations in Turkey
1547–1559 Henry II of France	1546–1547 Schmalkaldic War	
		1553 English in White Sea
1556–1598 Philip II of Spain	1555 Peace of Augsburg	
	1556–1564 Ferdinand I	
1559–1589 Weakness of monarchy in France		
1562–1598 Wars of Religion in France		

EUROPE AS A WHOLE: POLITICAL AND SOCIAL	EUROPE AS A WHOLE: THOUGHT AND LETTERS	BRITISH ISLES
		1563 The 39 Articles
	1564–1642 Galileo 1564–1616 Shakespeare	
		1569 Norfolk's rebellion
1571 Defeat of Turks at Lepanto		
	1576 Bodin's *Republic* 1580 Montaigne's *Essays* 1582 Gregorian calendar	1577 Alliance with Nether- lands
1588 Spanish Armada		1588 Spanish Armada
	1596–1650 Descartes	
		1603–1714 The Stuarts 1603–1625 James I
1607 English found Virginia 1608 French found Quebec		
1609 Spanish found Santa Fé 1612 Dutch found New York	1611 King James' Bible	

TABLE THREE: 1618–1714

EUROPE AS A WHOLE: POLITICAL AND SOCIAL	EUROPE AS A WHOLE: THOUGHT AND LETTERS	BRITISH ISLES
	1561–1626 Francis Bacon 1564–1642 Galileo 1596–1650 Descartes	*1603–1714 The Stuarts* 1603–1625 James I
1618–1648 Thirty Years' War		
17th century: English, French, Dutch in America; Dutch in South Africa and Indonesia	1623–1662 Pascal 17th century: flowering of English, French, and Dutch literature	1625–1649 Charles I
1619 First African slaves in Virginia	1625 Grotius' *Law of War and Peace*	1637 Ship money case
		1640–1660 Long Parliament
1648 Peace of Westphalia	1642–1727 Isaac Newton	1642–1648 Puritan Revolution and Civil War 1649 Execution of Charles I
1650 World population estimate: 500 million		1649–1658 Rule of Cromwell 1649–1653 Commonwealth 1653–1660 Protectorate 1660 Restoration
1661–1715 Age of Louis XIV	1660s Beginnings of scientific societies	1660–1685 Charles II
		1670s Rise of Whigs and Tories 1673 Test Act

WESTERN EUROPE	CENTRAL EUROPE	EASTERN EUROPE
	1564–1576 Maximilian II	
1566 Netherlands revolt begins		
1572 Massacre of St. Bartholomew		1571 Defeat of Turks at Lepanto
1574–1589 Henry III of France	1576–1612 Rudolf II	1574 Turks take Tunis
1589–1792 Bourbons in France		
1589–1610 Henry IV of France		1604–1613 Russia: Time of Troubles
1598 Edict of Nantes		
	1608 Protestant Union	
	1609 Catholic League	
1610–1643 Louis XIII of France	1612–1619 Matthias	*1613–1917 Romanovs in Russia*
	1618 Thirty Years' War begins	1613–1645 Michael Romanov, Tsar

WESTERN EUROPE	CENTRAL EUROPE	EASTERN EUROPE
1610–1643 Louis XIII of France	1618–1648 Thirty Years' War	*1613–1917 Romanovs in Russia*
	1619 Emperor Ferdinand II	1613–1645 Tsar Michael Romanov
	1620 Battle of White Mountain	
1624–1642 Richelieu	1629 Edict of Restitution	17th century: spread of serfdom in Russia and Eastern Europe
1629 Peace of Alais		
1635 France in Thirty Years' War		
1642–1661 Mazarin	1640–1688 Frederick William, Great Elector of Brandenburg	
1643–1715 Louis XIV of France		
1648 Peace of Westphalia	1648 Peace of Westphalia	
1652–1674 Three Anglo-Dutch Wars		
1659 Peace of Pyrenees	17th and 18th centuries: decline in German states	
1665–1700 Charles II of Spain		1667 Russian church reforms: Old Believers
1667–1668 Louis XIV's War of Devolution		1670 Revolt of Stephen Razin in Russia
1672–1678 Louis XIV's Dutch war		
		1682–1725 Peter the Great

EUROPE AS A WHOLE: POLITICAL AND SOCIAL	EUROPE AS A WHOLE: THOUGHT AND LETTERS	BRITISH ISLES
1683 Turks threaten Vienna		
		1685–1688 James II
	1687 Newton's *Principia*	
		1688 "Glorious Revolution"
1689–1697 War of League of Augsburg		1688–1702 William and Mary
	1690 Locke's *Treatises on Government; Human Understanding*	
	1697 Bayle's *Dictionary*	
1701–1714 War of Spanish Succession		1702–1714 Anne
		1707 Union of England and Scotland: United Kingdom of Great Britain
1713–1714 Treaties of Utrecht and Rastadt		

TABLE FOUR: 1714–1815

EUROPE AS A WHOLE: POLITICAL AND SOCIAL	EUROPE AS A WHOLE: THOUGHT AND LETTERS	BRITISH ISLES
1713–1714 Treaties of Utrecht and Rastadt	18th century: Age of Enlightenment	
		1714–1837 Hanoverians
		1714–1727 George I
		1720 South Sea Bubble
		1721 Walpole's ministry
1740–1789 Enlightened despotism in Europe	1740–1789 Enlightenment at its peak	1727–1760 George II
		1739 War of Jenkins' Ear
1740–1763 British-French colonial wars: America, India	1740–1760 Voltaire at his height	
1740–1748 War of Austrian Succession	1748 Montesquieu's *Spirit of Laws*	
1750 World population estimate: 700 million		1745 Jacobite Rebellion
1756 Diplomatic Revolution	1751–1768 French *Encyclopedia*	
		1760–1820 George III
1756–1763 Seven Years' War	1761 Rousseau's *Social Contract*	
1763 Treaties of Paris and Hubertusburg: British supremacy in Canada and India		1769 Watt's steam engine
		1769 Arkwright's waterframe

WESTERN EUROPE	CENTRAL EUROPE	EASTERN EUROPE
	1683 Turks threaten Vienna	1683 Turks threaten Vienna
1685 Revocation of Edict of Nantes		1683–1718 Habsburg victories over Turks
1689–1697 War of League of Augsburg	1697–1733 Augustus of Saxony King of Poland	1697–1718 Charles XII of Sweden
		1699 Austro-Turkish Peace of Karlowitz
1700–1931 Bourbons in Spain		
1700–1746 Philip V of Spain		
1701–1714 War of Spanish Succession	*1701–1918 Hohenzollern kings in Prussia*	
	1701–1713 Frederick I of Prussia	1709 Battle of Poltava

WESTERN EUROPE	CENTRAL EUROPE	EASTERN EUROPE
	1711–1740 Charles VI of Austria	1682–1725 Peter the Great
1715–1774 Louis XV of France	1713–1740 Frederick William I of Prussia	
1715–1723 Regency in France	1713–1740 Austria: Pragmatic Sanction	
1720 Mississippi Bubble		1721 Russo-Swedish Treaty of Nystadt
18th century: culmination of "Old Regime" in France	1740–1786 Frederick II of Prussia	1733–1738 War of Polish Succession
	1740–1780 Maria Theresa of Austria	1739 Austro-Turkish Peace of Belgrade
	1740–1745 Silesian Wars	
	1756 Habsburg-Bourbon Alliance	
	1756–1763 Seven Years' War	
		1762–1796 Catherine II of Russia
		1768–1774 Russo-Turkish War

EUROPE AS A WHOLE: POLITICAL AND SOCIAL	EUROPE AS A WHOLE: THOUGHT AND LETTERS	BRITISH ISLES
1776 American Declaration of Independence 1776–1783 War of American Independence	1776 Adam Smith's *Wealth of Nations*	1776 American Revolution
1789 French Revolution begins	1784 Herder's *Philosophy of History of Mankind* 1790 Burke's *Reflections on the French Revolution* 1790s Spread of French revolutionary ideas Beginnings of romanticism	1782–1806 Ministries of William Pitt the Younger
1792–1815 Revolutionary and Napoleonic wars		
1792–1797 War of First Coalition		1793–1814 War with France
1798–1801 War of Second Coalition		1798 Rebellion of Ireland 1801 Union of Great Britain and Ireland 1802–1803 Peace of Amiens
1803–1805 War of Third Coalition		
1804–1814 "Grand Empire" 1806–1812 Continental System	1804–1811 Napoleonic codes	
1809–1811 Napoleon at height 1812 Invasion of Russia, and retreat 1812 U.S.-British War 1813 Battle of Leipzig 1814–1815 Congress of Vienna 1815 Waterloo		1808–1814 Peninsular War in Spain 1814 Alliance of Chaumont

TABLE FIVE: 1815–1871*

WORLD AS A WHOLE	EUROPE AS A WHOLE	BRITISH ISLES
		1760–1820 George III 1760–1830 Beginnings of modern industry
1806–1825 Latin American countries win independence	1814–1815 Congress of Vienna 1814–1848 Influence of Metternich	1807 British slave trade ended 1815 Corn Laws: higher taxes on grain imports
	1818 Congress of Aix-la-Chapelle	
	1820 Congress of Troppau 1822 Congress of Verona	1819 Repression: Peterloo massacre, Six Acts

* Note change in column headings.

WESTERN EUROPE	CENTRAL EUROPE	EASTERN EUROPE
		1772 First Partition of Poland
1774–1793 Louis XVI of France		1773–1774 Pugachev Rebellion
		1774 Russo-Turkish Treaty of Kuchuk Kainarji
1778 French-American Alliance	1780–1790 Joseph II of Austria	
1789 French Revolution begins	1780s Cultural revival of Germany	1787–1792 Russo-Turkish War
1792 First French Republic established		1793 Second Partition of Poland
		1795 Third Partition of Poland
1793–1794 The Terror	1797 Treaty of Campo Formio	1796–1801 Paul I of Russia
1795–1799 Directory		
1799 Bonaparte's coup	1798–1814 French predominance	
1799–1804 Consulate		
		1801–1825 Alexander I of Russia
1804–1814 Napoleon I: The Empire		
1807 Peace of Tilsit	1806 End of Holy Roman Empire	1806–1812 Russo-Turkish War
	1806 Confederation of the Rhine	1807 Franco-Russian Alliance
		1812 Napoleon's invasion of Russia
1814 Restoration of Bourbons	1813–1814 German War of Liberation: Leipzig	
1815 Hundred Days; Waterloo		

WESTERN EUROPE	CENTRAL EUROPE	EASTERN EUROPE
		1801–1825 Alexander I of Russia
1814–1830 Restoration: Bourbons in France	1814–1848 Influence of Metternich	
1814–1824 Louis XVIII of France		
	1819 Carlsbad Decrees	

WORLD AS A WHOLE	EUROPE AS A WHOLE	BRITISH ISLES
1823 Monroe Doctrine		
	1830 Revolutions	
		1832 First Reform Bill
1839–1842 First Anglo-Chinese (Opium) War		1833 Slavery abolished
		1837–1901 Victoria: the Victorian Age
		1838–1848 Chartism
		1842 Mines Act
1842–1858 "Treaty System" established in China		1846 Repeal of Corn Laws
		1847 Ten Hours Act
	1848 Revolutions; Marx and Engels' *Communist Manifesto*	
1850 World population estimate: 1.2 billion		1850–1873 Golden age of British capitalism: free trade
1850–1864 Taiping Rebellion in China		
1854–1868 Japan opened to West	1854–1856 Crimean War	
1857–1858 Indian Mutiny: Sepoy Rebellion		
1859 Darwin's *Origin of Species*	1859 Austro-Italian War	
1860 Russians found Vladivostok		
1861–1865 American Civil War		
1863–1867 French in Mexico		
	1864–1876 First International	
	1866 Austro-Prussian War	
1867 Dominion of Canada	1867 Marx's *Capital*	1867 Extension of suffrage
1868 Meiji Restoration in Japan		1868–1874 Gladstone's first ministry
1870 Vatican Council I	1870–1871 Franco-Prussian War	
	1871–1918 German Empire	

TABLE SIX: 1871–1919

WORLD AS A WHOLE	EUROPE AS A WHOLE	BRITISH ISLES
1871 Darwin's *Descent of Man*		
		1874–1880 Disraeli's ministry
	1878 Congress of Berlin	
	1879 Dual Alliance: Germany, Austria	

WESTERN EUROPE	CENTRAL EUROPE	EASTERN EUROPE
1824–1830 Charles X of France		
		1825 Decembrist revolt in Russia
1830 Revolution in France and Belgium	1830 Revolutionary flurries	1825–1855 Nicholas I of Russia
		1828–1829 Russo-Turkish War
1830–1848 July Monarchy in France: Louis Philippe		1829 Independence of Greece
		1830 Revolution in Poland fails
1848 Revolution: Second French Republic	1848 Revolution: Frankfurt Assembly	
1852 Napoleon III: Second French Empire	1848–1916 Francis Joseph of Austria	
		1853 Russo-Turkish War
		1854–1856 Crimean War
		1855–1881 Alexander II of Russia
		1858 Formation of Romania
	1859–1870 Unification of Italy	
1860 Free trade with England		
1860–1870 Liberal empire		1861 Emancipation of Russian serfs
	1862–1871 Bismarck: minister in Prussia	
	1866–1871 Unification of Germany	
	1867 Dual Monarchy in Austria-Hungary	
1870–1871 Franco-Prussian War; fall of Napoleon III		
1870–1940 Third Republic in France	*1871–1918 Hohenzollerns in Germany*	1870s Populism and Nihilism in Russia

WESTERN EUROPE	CENTRAL EUROPE	EASTERN EUROPE
1870–1940 Third Republic in France	1871–1918 German Empire	
1871 Paris Commune	1871–1890 Bismarck chancellor	1877 Russo-Turkish War
		1878 Autonomy of Bulgaria; independence of Serbia

WORLD AS A WHOLE	EUROPE AS A WHOLE	BRITISH ISLES
1880–1914 Height of imperialism	1880s Socialist parties founded: revisionism 1882 Triple Alliance: Germany, Austria, Italy	1880–1886 Gladstone's ministries
1883–1893 French in Indochina		1884 Extension of suffrage
1885 Berlin Conference on Africa 1885–1898 Partition of Africa		
1893 New Zealand: vote to women	1889 Second International	1892–1894 Gladstone's fourth ministry
1894 Sino-Japanese War 1895–1898 Western imperialism in China 1898 Spanish-American War 1899–1902 Boer War 1900 Freud's *Interpretation of Dreams* 1900 World population estimate: 1.6 billion 1902 Anglo-Japanese Alliance 1902 Australia: vote to women	1894 Franco-Russian Alliance	1899–1902 Boer War 1900–1906 Labour party formed 1903–1914 Women's suffrage movement
1904–1905 Russo-Japanese War 1905 Einstein's relativity theory	1904 Anglo-French Entente 1905 Morocco crisis	
1907 Anglo-Russian division of Persia	1907 Triple Entente: Britain, France, Russia 1908 Bosnian crisis	1906–1911 Liberal party: social legislation, parliamentary reform
1911 Chinese Revolution	1911 Agadir crisis 1912–1913 Balkan crises	
1914 Assassination of Francis Ferdinand 1914–1918 First World War	1914–1918 First World War	1914 Ulster crisis 1914–1918 First World War 1916 Battle of Jutland 1916–1922 Irish troubles
1917 United States enters war 1917 Russian Revolution 1919 Peace of Paris	1919 Peace of Paris	

TABLE SEVEN: 1919–1945

WORLD AS A WHOLE	EUROPE AS A WHOLE	BRITISH ISLES
		1918 Limited suffrage for women
1919 Peace of Paris	1919 Peace of Paris 1919 Parliamentary regimes in new states	
1920 U.S.: vote to women		

WESTERN EUROPE	CENTRAL EUROPE	EASTERN EUROPE
		1881 Assassination of Alexander II
	1888–1918 William II of Germany	
1894–1906 Dreyfus affair in France		1894–1917 Nicholas II, Tsar
1901–1905 Laic laws: separation of church and state in France	1898–1914 German naval race with England	
1900 Growth of democracy: male suffrage in Netherlands 1896, vote to women in Norway 1913	1900ff. Growth of democracy: male suffrage in Austria 1907, etc.	
		1903 Russian Social Democrats: Bolshevik-Menshevik split
		1904–1905 Russo-Japanese War
		1905 Revolution in Russia
		1906 Finland: vote to women
		1908 Bosnian crisis
		1908 Young Turk Revolution
		1912–1913 Balkan Wars
1914 Battle of Marne	1914 Assassination of Francis Ferdinand	1914 Battle of Tannenberg
1916 Verdun and the Somme		1917 Russia: fall of tsardom; Bolshevik Revolution
1918 Armistice	1918 Fall of German, Austro-Hungarian, and Ottoman empires	

WESTERN EUROPE	CENTRAL EUROPE	EASTERN EUROPE
		1918–1920 Russian Civil War
1919 Paris Peace Conference	1919 Treaty of Versailles	1919–1923 Greek-Turkish War
	1919–1933 Weimar Republic	
		1920–1943 Third International

WORLD AS A WHOLE	EUROPE AS A WHOLE	BRITISH ISLES
1922–1929 Prosperity decade	1922–1943 Fascism in Italy: Mussolini	1922 Irish Free State; British Northern Ireland
	1923 Turkish Republic 1923 Ruhr crisis	
	1925 Locarno Pact	1924 First Labour government
		1926 General Strike 1926 Statute of Westminster: independence of Dominions 1928 Full suffrage for women
1929 Stock market crash; Great Depression begins		1929–1931 Second Labour Government: MacDonald resignation
1930 World population estimate: 2 billion 1931–1932 Manchurian crisis 1931–1945 Japanese in China	1930s Great Depression 1930s Decline of democracy: rise of dictators	1931–1940 National Government 1931 Britain leaves gold standard 1932 Britain adopts tariffs; imperial preferences
1933–1945 F. D. Roosevelt's presidency 1933 Failure of World Economic Conference	1933–1945 Hitler in Germany; Third Reich 1933–1938 Germany rearms, remilitarizes Rhineland, annexes Austria	
1935–1936 Ethiopian crisis 1936–1939 Spanish Civil War	1936–1938 Popular Fronts: France, Spain 1936–1939 Spanish Civil War	1936 Keynes' *General Theory of Employment, Interest, and Money* 1936 Edward VIII abdicates; George VI
	1937 Rome-Berlin-Tokyo Axis	
1938 Munich crisis 1939–1945 Second World War 1940–1942 Axis victories	1938 Munich crisis 1939 Nazi-Soviet Pact 1939–1945 Second World War 1940–1945 German domination of Europe: racist policies: concentration camps, the Holocaust	1938 Chamberlain: Munich Conference 1939–1945 Britain at war 1940 Churchill replaces Chamberlain 1940 Battle of Britain
1941 Atlantic Charter 1941 U.S.S.R., U.S. enter war 1944–1945 Allies liberate Europe, Asia 1945 Yalta and Potsdam conferences 1945 U.S. drops atomic bombs: Hiroshima, Nagasaki 1945 United Nations established	1945 Death of Hitler and of Mussolini	1945 Labour election victory

WESTERN EUROPE	CENTRAL EUROPE	EASTERN EUROPE
		1920–1921 Russo-Polish War
	1922–1943 Fascism in Italy: Mussolini	1921–1928 NEP in Russia
		1922 U.S.S.R. established as federation
		1922 Russo-German treaty of Rapallo
	1923 French occupy Ruhr	
	1923 German currency crisis	1924 Death of Lenin
	1924 Dawes Plan	1924–1953 Stalin in power
		1927 Expulsion of Trotsky
1928–1974 Dictatorship in Portugal: Salazar		1928–1933 First Five-Year Plan; collectivization of agriculture
1930s Great Depression	1930s Great Depression	
1931 Spanish Republic		
1934 Stavisky riots in Paris	1933–1945 Germany: Third Reich, Hitler	1934 U.S.S.R. joins League of Nations
1936–1939 Spanish Civil War	1934 First Austrian crisis	
1936–1937 Popular Front government in France	1936 Germany remilitarizes Rhineland	1936 New Soviet constitution
		1936–1938 Soviet purges and trials
	1938 Germany annexes Austria	
	1938 Munich: Sudeten territory to Germany	
	1939 Germany annexes Czechoslovakia	1939 Nazi-Soviet Pact
1939 Spain: Franco dictatorship established	1939 Nazi-Soviet Pact	1939 Germany invades Poland
1940 Fall of France	1940–1944 Germany dominates Europe	1939–1940 Russo-Finnish War
		1939–1940 Soviets absorb Baltic states
1940–1944 German occupation of Western Europe		1941 Germany invades Russia
		1942–1943 Battle of Stalingrad
	1943 Allies invade Italy; fall of Mussolini	1943–1945 Russian offensives
1944–1945 Allies liberate Western Europe	1944–1945 Allied and Russian offensives	

TABLE EIGHT: 1945–1959*

WORLD AS A WHOLE	ASIA	AFRICA
1945 United Nations established: 51 members 1945 Death of Roosevelt 1945 Cold War begins	1945 Arab League formed: 7 states	1945 Colonial empires continue; only four independent African states
	1945–1946 Occupation of Japan; new constitution	
1945–1953 U.S.: Truman presidency		
	1946–1954 French war in Indochina	
1947 Truman Doctrine; Marshall Plan 1947 General Agreement on Tariffs and Trade (GATT) 1947–1949 End of British and Dutch empires in Asia 1948 UN: Declaration of Human Rights 1949 U.S.S.R. tests atomic bomb 1949 Communist triumph in China: People's Republic of China 1949 North Atlantic Treaty Organization (NATO) 1950 World population estimate: 2.5 billion; beginning of population explosion	1947 India and Pakistan independent 1947–1964 India: Nehru prime minister 1948 Assassination of Gandhi 1948 Burma independent 1948 Israel established 1948 First Arab-Israeli war 1949 People's Republic of China established: Mao Zedong 1949 Dutch leave Indonesia	1948 South Africa: Nationalist party enforces apartheid
1950–1953 Korean War	1950–1953 Korean War 1950s Japan: regains sovereignty; economic expansion 1950 China occupies Tibet	
1951 Japanese peace treaty		1951 Libya independent
1952 U.S. tests hydrogen bomb		1952 Egypt: monarchy ousted; Nasser
1953 U.S.S.R. tests hydrogen bomb 1953 Genetics: DNA double-helix structure discovered 1953–1961 U.S.: Eisenhower presidency		
	1954 French leave Indochina; Vietnam partitioned: North and South Vietnam	1954–1962 French-Algerian War

* Note change in column headings.

WESTERN EUROPE	CENTRAL EUROPE	EASTERN EUROPE
1945–1946 Cold War: Europe divided	1945 Allied occupation of Germany: four zones	1945–1948 Communist satellites established
1945–1946 Woman suffrage in France, Italy, Belgium, etc.	1945 Italian elections: Christian Democratic coalitions begin	1946–1950 Soviet Fourth Five-Year Plan
1945–1951 Britain: Labour Government		
1945–1958 Fourth French Republic	1946 Italy: monarchy ends; Italian Republic	
1946 France: Monnet Plan	1946 Nuremberg trials	
	1946–1953 Italy: De Gasperi premier	
	1947 Peace treaties with Italy, Hungary, etc.	1947–1956 Cominform
1948–1952 Marshall Plan: European Recovery Plan	1948–1949 Berlin blockade and airlift	1948 Communist takeover in Czechoslovakia
	1948 Italian elections: Communist setback	1948–1955 Yugoslavia splits with U.S.S.R.: Tito
1949 Council of Europe	1949 German Federal Republic (West Germany); German Democratic Republic (East Germany)	1949 Council of Mutual Economic Assistance
1949 North Atlantic Treaty Organization (NATO)		
1950s West European economic expansion	1949–1963 West Germany: Adenauer chancellor; economic expansion	1949 U.S.S.R. tests atomic bomb
1951 European Coal and Steel Community (ECSC)		1951–1955 Soviet Fifth Five-Year Plan
1951–1964 British Conservatives in office		
1952 Britain: Elizabeth II succeeds George VI	1952 Allied occupation of West Germany ends	
1952 Britain tests atomic bomb		
	1953 East Berlin uprising	1953 Death of Stalin
		1953 Soviets test hydrogen bomb
		1953–1955 Malenkov premier; emergence of Khrushchev
1954 West German rearmament		
1954 French defeat in Indochina; war in Algeria begins		

WORLD AS A WHOLE	ASIA	AFRICA
	1955 Bandung Afro-Asian conference	
1956 Suez Canal crisis	1956 Suez crisis: second Arab-Israeli war	1956 Suez crisis: Britain, France, Israel vs. Egypt
		1956 Morocco, Tunisia independent
		1956–1972 Sudan independent: civil war
1957 U.S.S.R. launches space satellite: Sputnik		1957 Gold Coast (Ghana) gains independence: Nkrumah presidency, dictatorship
1957–1962 End of British, French, Belgian colonial empires in Africa		1957–1962 British colonies gain independence: Ghana, Nigeria, Kenya, Uganda, etc.
1958–1963 Pope John XXIII: reforms in Catholic church	1958–1960 China: Great Leap Forward; famine	1958 French colonies win self-government; French Community formed
	1958–1961 Syria, Egypt form United Arab Republic; union disolved	1958–1961 Egypt and Syria form short-lived United Arab Republic
1959 Cuban revolution: Castro		

TABLE NINE: 1960–1975

WORLD AS A WHOLE	ASIA	AFRICA
1960 World population estimate: 3 billion		
1960–1962 Belgian Congo: civil war		1960–1962 Belgians leave Congo (Zaire): civil war
1960s U.S., U.S.S.R.: nuclear arms build-up	1960s North-South Vietnam War	1960 French colonies fully independent: Gabon, Senegal, Mali, etc.
1960s U.S.: civil rights movement; women's liberation movement		
1961–1973 U.S. involvement in Vietnam War		
1961–1963 U.S.: Kennedy presidency		
1961 U.S.S.R. and U.S. space flights; Soviets launch first man in space		1961 South Africa leaves Commonwealth: white minority government
		1961–1975 Portuguese colonies: war for independence
1962 U.S.-Soviet Cuban missile crisis	1962 Chinese-Soviet rift	1962 Algeria independent
1962 Chinese-Soviet rift		
1962–1965 Vatican Council II: reforms in Catholic church	1962 Chinese-Indian border war	

WESTERN EUROPE	CENTRAL EUROPE	EASTERN EUROPE
1955 West Germany in NATO	1955 Austrian peace treaty	1955 Warsaw Pact
		1956 Khrushchev denounces Stalin's crimes
		1956 Polish, Hungarian risings crushed
1957 Rome treaties: European Economic Community (EEC, or Common Market): 6 members	1957 Rome treaties: European Economic Community (EEC)	1957 U.S.S.R. launches Sputnik
		1958 U.S.S.R. deploys first intercontinental ballistic missile
1958 Fifth French Republic: de Gaulle first president		1958–1964 Khrushchev in power
1959 British form European Free Trade Association		

WESTERN EUROPE	CENTRAL EUROPE	EASTERN EUROPE
1960 Belgium withdraws from Congo		
1960 France becomes fourth nuclear power		
1960s Spain: industrialization		1960s Liberalization in Soviet satellites
		1960s Industrialization in German Democratic Republic, Poland, Hungary, etc.
	1961 Berlin Wall built	1961 U.S.S.R. launches first man in space
		1961 Soviets test 50-megaton nuclear bomb
1962 French leave Algeria		1962–1963 Chinese Communists split with U.S.S.R.

WORLD AS A WHOLE	ASIA	AFRICA
1963–1978 Pope Paul VI		1963 Organization of African Unity formed: 32 states
1963 Partial nuclear test ban agreement		
1963 U.S.: President Kennedy assassinated		
1963–1969 U.S.: Johnson presidency		
1964 U.S.: Civil Rights Act	1964 Death of Nehru	
1964–1965 Vietnam War: U.S. involvement deepens	1964 Vietnam War: U.S. commits air and ground forces	
	1964 China tests atomic bomb; becomes fifth nuclear power	
	1964 Palestine Liberation Organization (PLO) formed	
1965 United Nations: 110 members		1965 Rhodesia: white minority government proclaims independence from Britain
	1966 Indonesia: Sukarno ousted; Suharto	1966 UN supports Namibia (formerly South African mandate) in independence struggle
	1966–1969 Chinese Cultural Revolution	
	1966–1977 Indira Gandhi: first ministry	1966 Nkrumah overthrown in Ghana
	1967 Arab-Israeli war: Six Day War	1967–1970 Nigeria suppresses Biafra secession
1968 Student demonstrations: U.S., France, Mexico, Japan, etc.	1968 Chinese-Soviet border clashes in Manchuria	1960s– Newly independent states: civil wars, dictatorships, etc.
1968 U.S.: assassinations of Martin Luther King, Jr., R. F. Kennedy		
1968 Vietnam War continues; peace talks in Paris		
1969–1974 U.S.: Nixon presidency; détente diplomacy		
1969 American astronauts land on moon	1969 Vietnam: death of Ho Chi Minh	
1970s American and Soviet space explorations, manned and unmanned		
1970s East-West détente		
1970s Voting age lowered to 18: U.S., Britain, France, etc.		
1971 People's Republic of China in UN; replaces Taiwan	1971 Bangladesh: secession from Pakistan	1971–1979 Uganda: repressive regime of Idi Amin
1972 U.S.-Soviet Strategic Arms Limitation Treaty (SALT I)		
1973 U.S. troops leave Vietnam		

WESTERN EUROPE	CENTRAL EUROPE	EASTERN EUROPE
1963 EEC: de Gaulle vetoes British entry	1963–1968 West Germany: Erhard succeeds Adenauer; Christian Democratic coalition continues	
1964–1970 Britain: Labour in office		1964 Khrushchev ousted 1964–1982 Brezhnev in power: military and naval build-up
1965 France: de Gaulle reelected president		
1967 European Community (EC): reorganization 1968 France: near-revolutionary student and labor demonstrations	1967–1974 Greece: military dictatorship	1968 Soviets invade Czecho-slovakia; end liberal Czech regime; Brehznev Doctrine
1969 France: de Gaulle resigns presidency 1969– Northern Ireland: Catholic-Protestant clashes 1970s Voting age lowered to 18: Britain, France, West Germany, Italy, etc. 1970–1974 Britain: Conserva-tives in office	1969–1974 West Germany: Brandt chancellor; Social Democratic government; closer relations with Eastern Europe	1970s East-West détente: political, economic ties with West
1973 Britain, Denmark, Ireland join EC: 9 members	1973 German Federal Republic admitted to UN	1973 German Democratic Republic admitted to UN

WORLD AS A WHOLE	ASIA	AFRICA
1973 Chile: military coup ousts leftist government		
1973–1974 Arab oil embargo		1973–1974 Ethiopia: drought and famine; Haile Selassie ousted
1974–1982 World economic recession	1974 Turkish invasion of Cyprus	
1974 U.S.: Nixon resigns; Ford presidency		
1974 India becomes sixth nuclear power		
1975 End of Vietnam War	1975 End of Vietnam War: Communist victories in Vietnam, Laos, Cambodia	1975 End of Portuguese rule in Angola, Mozambique, etc.
1975 End of last European (Portuguese) empire in Africa		
1975 Helsinki Conference on European Security and Cooperation: peak of détente	1975–1979 Cambodia: Khmer Rouge dictatorship under Pol Pot	

TABLE TEN: 1975–

WORLD AS A WHOLE	ASIA	AFRICA
1975 Helsinki Conference on European Security and Cooperation	1975 Civil war in Lebanon begins	1975– Civil war in Angola: foreign intervention
1977 Nuclear nonproliferation treaty signed	1976 China: death of Mao	1977–1978 Somalia and Ethiopia at war
1977–1981 U.S.: Carter presidency	1978– China under Deng: modernization and reform	
1978– Pope John Paul II		
1979 Soviets invade Afghanistan	1979 Camp David accords: Israel-Egypt peace treaty	
1979 Cold War renewed	1979–1988 Soviets at war in Afghanistan	
1979 SALT II treaty (not ratified by U.S. Senate)	1979–¡1988 Vietnam invades, occupies Cambodia	
1980 U.S. embargo on U.S.S.R.	1980–1984 India: Indira Gandhi second ministry	1980s Debt problems; slow economic development, rapid population growth
1980–1981 U.S. hostage crisis in Iran	1980–1988 Iran-Iraq war	1980s Zimbabwe (Rhodesia) independent: black majority government
1981–1989 U.S.: Reagan presidency	1981 Egypt: assassination of Anwar al-Sadat	
1981– New disease AIDS appears		
	1982 Israel invades Lebanon; ousts PLO	
	1982 Arab League: 22 members	
1983 U.S. invades Grenada	1984 Assassination of Indira Gandhi	1984 South Africa: pressures to end apartheid; emergency rule

WESTERN EUROPE	CENTRAL EUROPE	EASTERN EUROPE
		1970s Economic difficulties; rising debt
1974–1982 Economic recession	1974–1982 Economic recession	
	1974–1982 Schmidt Social Democratic chancellor	
1974 Portugal: revolution; end of dictatorship		
1975 Spain: death of Franco; constitutional monarchy under Juan Carlos I		
1975 Helsinki Accords	1975 Helsinki Accords	1975 Helsinki Accords

WESTERN EUROPE	CENTRAL EUROPE	EASTERN EUROPE
1975 Helsinki Accords	1975 Helsinki Accords	1975 Helsinki Accords
1979 EC: Greece 10th member		1979 Soviets invade Afghanistan; détente ends
1979 EC: elections for European Parliament		
1979– British Conservatives in office: Thatcher prime minister; curbs welfare state		
1980s European demonstrations against nuclear missile sites		1980s East European governments: mounting debt problems
		1980 Yugoslavia: death of Tito
		1980–1981 Poland: strikes and unrest; rise of Solidarity; martial law
1981– France: Mitterrand Socialist president	1981 Italy: break in Christian Democratic governments after 40 cabinets	1981–1985 Soviet Eleventh Five-Year Plan; economic slowdown
1982 Britain thwarts Argentine takeover of Falklands	1982– West Germany: Kohl heads Christian Democratic government	1982 Death of Brezhnev; successors: Andropov, Chernenko die in office
1982 Spain joins NATO: 16th member	1983–1987 Italy: Craxi Socialist premier	

WORLD AS A WHOLE	ASIA	AFRICA
		1984 Ethiopia: extended drought and famine
1985 Scientists report threat to ozone layer of earth		
1985 U.S.S.R.: Gorbachev in office; efforts to end Cold War	1986 Philippines: Marcos dictatorship overthrown	1986 U.S. bombs Libya in retaliation for terrorist activities
		1986 Uganda: end of 15 years of civil war
1987 Stock market collapse; recovery	1987– Israel: Palestinian uprising begins	
1987–1988 Cold War wanes: Reagan-Gorbachev meetings; intermediate range nuclear missiles eliminated in Europe		
1987–1988 U.S. protects oil tankers in Persian Gulf during Iran-Iraq war	1988 Iran-Iraq war ends	
1989– U.S.: Bush presidency	1989 Burma (renamed Myanmar): democratic stirrings	
1989 U.S. invades Panama	1989 Vietnam ends occupation of Cambodia	1989 South Africa: de Klerk president; reforms
1989 Revolutions in Eastern Europe: end of Communist regimes; Berlin Wall falls	1989 China suppresses democracy movement	1989 Civil war in Angola ends
		1989 Civil war in Namibia ends; South Africa, Cuba, Angola withdraw
1989 Chile: first free elections since 1970		
1990 German reunification		1990 Namibia independent
1990 World population over 5 billion		1990 52 independent states in Africa
1990 UN membership: 159		
1990 Voyager 2 travels 3.7 billion miles in outer space		
1990–1991 Persian Gulf crisis and war; U.S. and allies force Iraq to leave Kuwait	1990–1991 Iraq annexes Kuwait; Arab states join U.S.-led coalition; force Iraq's withdrawal	

WESTERN EUROPE	CENTRAL EUROPE	EASTERN EUROPE
1985 Spain and Portugal join EC: 12 members		1985– Gorbachev Soviet leader: political, economic, constitutional reforms
		1986 Chernobyl nuclear plant disaster
1987 Britain: Conservatives reelected; Thatcher third term		1987–1988 Gorbachev-Reagan arms negotiations
1988– France: Mitterrand reelected president		1988–1989 Soviets withdraw from Afghanistan
	1989 Hungary opens way for East Germans to leave for West Germany	1989 Soviets hold multi-candidate elections; other political reforms
1989 Britain, France, U.S., U.S.S.R. agree to German unification	1989 Fall of Berlin Wall 1989 Fall of Communist regime in East Germany	1989 Revolutions: end of Communist regimes in Poland, Hungary, Czechoslovakia, East Germany, Bulgaria, Romania
1990 Britain: Thatcher leaves office	1990 West Germany and East Germany formally merge: Federal Republic of Germany	1990– East European regimes: free elections, market economies 1990– U.S.S.R.: secessionist pressures from Baltic and other Soviet republics; mounting economic problems 1991 Warsaw Pact dissolved
1992 EC: full economic integration projected		

APPENDIX II:
RULERS AND REGIMES
In Principal European Countries since 1500

Habsburg Line

MAXIMILIAN I	1493–1519
CHARLES V	1519–1556
FERDINAND I	1556–1564
MAXIMILIAN II	1564–1576
RUDOLPH II	1576–1612
MATTHIAS	1612–1619
FERDINAND II	1619–1637
FERDINAND III	1637–1657
LEOPOLD I	1658–1705
JOSEPH I	1705–1711
CHARLES VI	1711–1740

Charles VI was succeeded by a daughter, Maria Theresa, who as a woman could not be elected Holy Roman Emperor. French influence in 1742 secured the election of

Bavarian Line

CHARLES VII	1742–1745

On Charles VII's death the Habsburg control of the Emperorship was resumed.

Lorraine Line

FRANCIS I	1745–1765

(husband of Maria Theresa)

Habsburg-Lorraine Line

JOSEPH II	1765–1790

(son of Francis I and Maria Theresa)

LEOPOLD II	1790–1792
FRANCIS II	1792–1806

The Holy Roman Empire became extinct in 1806.

The rulers of Austria from 1438 to 1740, and at least titular kings of Hungary from 1526 to 1740, were the same as the Holy Roman Emperors. After 1740:

Habsburg Line (through female heir)

MARIA THERESA	1740–1780
JOSEPH II	1780–1790
LEOPOLD II	1790–1792
FRANCIS II	1792–1835

In 1804 Francis II took the title of Emperor, as Francis I of the Austrian Empire. Austria was declared an "empire" because Napoleon proclaimed France an empire in that year, and because the demise of the Holy Roman Empire could be foreseen.

FERDINAND I	1835–1848
FRANCIS JOSEPH	1848–1916
CHARLES I	1916–1918

The Austrian Empire became extinct in 1918.

Tudor Line

Kings of England and Ireland

HENRY VII	1485–1509
HENRY VIII	1509–1547
EDWARD VI	1547–1553
MARY I	1553–1558
ELIZABETH I	1558–1603

In 1603 James VI of Scotland, a great-great-grandson of Henry VII, succeeded to the English Throne.

Stuart Line

Kings of England and Ireland, and of Scotland

JAMES I	1603–1625
CHARLES I	1625–1649

Republican Interregnum

The Commonwealth   1649–1653
The Protectorate
OLIVER CROMWELL   1653–1658
Lord Protector
RICHARD CROMWELL   1658–1660

Restored Stuart Line

CHARLES II   1660–1685
JAMES II   1685–1688

In 1688 James II was forced out of the country, but Parliament kept the crown in a female branch of the Stuart family, calling in Mary, the daughter of James II, and her husband William III of the Netherlands.

WILLIAM III   1689–1702,
AND MARY II   1689–1694
ANNE   1702–1714

In 1707, through the Union of England and Scotland, the royal title became King (or Queen) of Great Britain and Ireland. The Stuart family having no direct Protestant heirs, the throne passed in 1714 to the German George I, Elector of Hanover, a great-grandson of James I.

Hanoverian Line

Kings of Great Britain and Ireland
GEORGE I   1714–1727
GEORGE II   1727–1760
GEORGE III   1760–1820
GEORGE IV   1820–1830
WILLIAM IV   1830–1837

William IV having no heirs, the British throne passed in 1837 to Victoria, a granddaughter of Geroge III. Though the British family has continued in direct descent from George I, it has dropped the Hanoverian designation and is now known as the House of Windsor. From 1877 to 1947 the British rulers bore the additional title of Emperor (or Empress) of India.

VICTORIA   1837–1901
EDWARD VII   1901–1910
GEORGE V   1910–1936
EDWARD VIII   1936
GEORGE VI   1936–1952
ELIZABETH II   1952–

FRANCE

Valois Line

LOUIS XI   1461–1483
CHARLES VIII   1483–1498
LOUIS XII   1498–1515
FRANCIS I   1515–1547
HENRY II   1547–1559
FRANCIS II   1559–1560
CHARLES IX   1560–1574
HENRY III   1574–1589

In 1589 the Valois line became extinct, and the throne passed to Henry of Bourbon, a remote descendant of French kings of the fourteenth century.

Bourbon Line

HENRY IV   1589–1610
LOUIS XIII   1610–1643
LOUIS XIV   1643–1715
LOUIS XV   1715–1774
LOUIS XVI   1774–1792

The Republic

Convention   1792–1795
Directory   1795–1799
Consulate   1799–1804

The Empire

NAPOLEON I   1804–1814
Emperor of the French
and King of Italy

Restored Bourbon Line

LOUIS XVIII   1814–1824

(Royalists count a Louis XVII, 1793–1795, and date the reign of Louis XVIII from 1795.)

CHARLES X   1824–1830

The Revolution of 1830 gave the throne to the Duke of Orleans, descendant of Louis XIII.

Orleans Line

LOUIS-PHILIPPE   1830–1848

The Second Republic

1848–1852

The Second Empire

NAPOLEON III   1852–1870
Emperor of the French

The Third Republic

1870–1940

Vichy Regime

1940–1944

Provisional Government

1944–1946

The Fourth Republic

1946–1958

The Fifth Republic

1958–

PRUSSIA (AND GERMANY)

A continuous Hohenzollern line ruled until 1918.

Electors of Brandenburg and Dukes of Prussia

GEORGE WILLIAM   1619–1640
FREDERICK WILLIAM   1640–1688
the "Great Elector"
FREDERICK III   1688–1713

In 1701 Frederick III was permitted by the Holy Roman Emperor to entitle himself King in Prussia, as Frederick I.

Kings of Prussia

FREDERICK I	1701–1713
FREDERICK WILLIAM I	1713–1740
FREDERICK II, the "Great"	1740–1786
FREDERICK WILLIAM II	1786–1797
FREDERICK WILLIAM III	1797–1840
FREDERICK WILLIAM IV	1840–1861
WILLIAM I	1861–1888

In 1871 William I took the title of German Emperor.

German Emperors

WILLIAM I	1871–1888
FREDERICK III	1888
WILLIAM II	1888–1918

The German Empire became extinct in 1918. It was succeeded by the

Weimar Republic

1919–1933

(an unofficial title for what was still called the Deutsches Reich, a phrase not easy to translate accurately)

The Third Reich

1933–1945

(an unofficial title for the Deutsches Reich under Adolf Hitler)
Allied Military Government in 1945 was followed by

German Federal Republic (West Germany)

1949–1990

German Democratic Republic (East Germany)

1949–1990

The two Germanys were united in 1990 as German Federal Republic

1990–

SARDINIA (AND ITALY)

In 1720 Victor Amadeus II, Duke of Savoy, took the title of King of Sardinia, having acquired the island of that name.

Kings of Sardinia

VICTOR AMADEUS II	1720–1730
CHARLES EMMANUEL III	1730–1773
VICTOR AMADEUS III	1773–1796
CHARLES EMMANUEL IV	1796–1802
VICTOR EMMANUEL I	1802–1821
CHARLES FELIX	1821–1831
CHARLES ALBERT	1831–1849
VICTOR EMMANUEL II	1849–1878

In 1861 Victor Emmanuel II took the title of King of Italy.

Kings of Italy

VICTOR EMMANUEL II	1861–1878
HUMBERT I	1878–1900

VICTOR EMMANUEL III   1900–1946
HUMBERT II   1946

In 1936 Victor Emmanuel III took the title of Emperor of Ethiopia, which became meaningless with British occupation of Ethiopia in 1941. In 1946 the Kingdom of Italy became extinct and was succeeded by the

Italian Republic

1946–

SPAIN

FERDINAND AND ISABELLA   1479–1504/1516

Isabella died in 1504, but Ferdinand lived until 1516, whereupon the Spanish thrones were inherited by their grandson Charles, who became Charles V of the Holy Roman Empire, but was known in Spain as Charles I.

Habsburg Line

CHARLES I   1516–1556
PHILIP II   1556–1598
PHILIP III   1598–1621
PHILIP IV   1621–1665
CHARLES II   1665–1700

With Charles II the Spanish Habsburg line became extinct, and the throne passed to the French Bourbon grandson of Louis XIV of France and great-grandson of Philip IV of Spain.

Bourbon Line

PHILIP V   1700–1746
FERDINAND VI   1746–1759
CHARLES III   1759–1788
CHARLES IV   1788–1808

Bonaparte Line

JOSEPH   1808–1813
(brother of Napoleon)

Restored Bourbon Line

FERDINAND VII   1813–1833
ISABELLA II   1833–1868

In 1868 Isabella abdicated; after a regency, and a brief reign by Amadeus I (Savoy), 1871–1873, there was a short-lived First Republic, 1873–1874, succeeded by

ALFONSO XII   1874–1885
ALFONSO XIII   1885–1931

In 1931 a republican revolution unseated Alfonso XIII.

Second Spanish Republic

1931–1936

Spanish Civil War

1936–1939

Regime of General Francisco Franco

1939–1975

Upon the death of Franco the Bourbon family was restored.

JUAN CARLOS I   1975–

RUSSIA (AND U.S.S.R.)

Grand Dukes of Moscow

IVAN III, the "Great"   1462–1505
BASIL III   1505–1533
IVAN IV, the "Terrible"   1533–1584

In 1547 Ivan IV took the title of Tsar of Russia.

Tsars of Russia

IVAN IV, the "Terrible"   1547–1584
THEODORE I   1584–1598
BORIS GODUNOV   1598–1605

Time of Troubles

1604–1613

Romanov Line

MICHAEL   1613–1645
ALEXIS   1645–1676
THEODORE II   1676–1682
IVAN V AND PETER I   1682–1689
PETER I, the "Great"   1689–1725
CATHERINE I   1725–1727
PETER II   1727–1730
ANNA   1730–1740
IVAN VI   1740–1741
ELIZABETH   1741–1762
PETER III   1762

Catherine II, the "Great"	1762–1796
Paul	1796–1801
Alexander I	1801–1825
Nicholas I	1825–1855
Alexander II	1855–1881
Alexander III	1881–1894
Nicholas II	1894–1917

In 1917 the tsardom became extinct.

Provisional Government

1917

Communist Revolution

1917

Union of Soviet Socialist Republics

1922–

APPENDIX III: HISTORICAL POPULATIONS OF VARIOUS COUNTRIES AND CITIES

Figures for dates before the nineteenth century arise from estimates, in some cases subject to a wide margin of error. Those for the nineteenth and twentieth centuries generally reflect census returns, at dates within a few years before or after the round date indicated. For cities, the figures for 1950 and 1990 refer to metropolitan areas without regard to municipal boundaries. Estimates for cities for earlier dates are conveniently assembled in Tertius Chandler and Gerald Fox, *3000 Years of Urban Growth* (New York, 1974) and in Jan de Vries, *Urbanization, 1500–1800* (Cambridge, Mass., 1984).

The rapid growth of European cities in the nineteenth century was made possible by the railroad and was a sign of industrial progress. More recently the population of the largest European and North American cities has stabilized or even declined. The largest cities are now often found in the less economically developed countries, where urban growth arises more from rural poverty and economic underdevelopment than from industrialization.

For countries, the use of the table is mainly for rough comparisons. It shows, for example, that France was about five times as populous as England in the Middle Ages, and was still more populous than all the German states at the time of the French Revolution, or that Spain declined under the Habsburgs in the seventeenth century, and that Ireland lost population after the famine and ensuing emigration. All countries except Ireland grew rapidly in population in the nineteenth century. For Russia, the figures from 1750 to 1950 reflect territorial expansion as well as internal growth. All figures for China are very uncertain, though unquestionably very large. The projected populations of countries for the year 2000 are from *World Population Prospects* (United Nations, New York, 1989).

For 1950 and 1990 the figures for Ireland include both the Republic of Ireland and Northern Ireland, and "Germany" includes the former East and West Germany. In 1990 the Irish Republic was about twice as populous as its northern neighbor, and West Germany was almost four times as populous as East Germany, with which it was reunited in that year.

CITIES in thousands

	LONDON	MANCHESTER	PARIS	MARSEILLES
14th Century	50	3 –	200	
15th Century				
16th Century	200			
17th Century	575	15 –	450	50 +
18th Century	750		500	90
1800	865	77	600	111
1850	2681	303	1422	195
1900	6581	544	3670	491
1950	8346	2421	4823	655
1990	9400	2580	8707	1110

	FLORENCE	BERLIN	VIENNA	PRAGUE
14th Century	50 +			
15th Century	60	10 –	20	25 +
16th Century	65	12	40 +	40 +
17th Century	75	20	100	40 +
18th Century	75	100	220	75
1800	84	172	247	75
1850	114	500	444	206
1900	206	2712	1675	382
1950	374	3337	1766	922
1990	426	3092	1481	1194

	TOKYO	HONG KONG	JAKARTA	CALCUTTA
1900	1440	284	116	1125
1950	6277	2360	3200	2610
1990	11906	5500	6503	9194

AMSTERDAM	ANTWERP	LISBON	MADRID	ROME
	5	20 +	5 −	30 −
20 −	35			50 −
35	100	100	60	100
100 +	50	73	80	130
150	50	120	120	150
201	62	180	160	153
224	88	240	281	175
511	277	356	540	463
838	584	790	1618	1652
1016	478	808	3183	2815

WARSAW	BUDAPEST	STOCKHOLM	ST. PETERSBURG LENINGRAD	MOSCOW
70		60	100	
100	54 +	76	220	250
150	178	93	485	365
700	732	301	1150	1000
804	1571	744	3182	4847
1649	2089	663	4948	8815

CAIRO	LAGOS	RIO DE JANEIRO	MEXICO CITY	NEW YORK
570	42	750	345	3400
2100	230	2413	2233	12911
6052	1061	5090	14750	18054

COUNTRIES in millions

	ENGLAND AND WALES	SCOTLAND	IRELAND	FRANCE
1300	3.5			15.0
1500	2.8	.8	1.0	16.0
1700	5.5	1.2	2.8	19.0
1800	8.9	1.6	5.2	27.0
1850	17.9	2.9	6.5	34.2
1900	32.5	4.5	4.5	38.5
1950	43.0	5.0	4.3	41.8
1990	50.1	5.4	4.9	56.2
2000 projected	50.6	5.5	5.0	58.2

	SWEDEN	POLAND	RUSSIA U.S.S.R.	CHINA
1300		1.3		
1500		2.5		
1700	1.6	2.8	12	150
1800	2.3	4.3	30	300
1850	3.5	6.0	62	400
1900	5.1	28.3	104	
1950	7.0	24.8	180	547
1990	8.3	38.4	286	1,135
2000 projected	8.3	40.4	307	1,289

	BRAZIL	MEXICO	CANADA	U.S.A.
1800		6.0	.4	5.3
1850			2.4	23.2
1900	20.0	13.6	5.4	76.0
1950	52.6	25.7	14.0	152.0
1990	150.3	88.6	26.5	250.1
2000 projected	179.5	107.2	27.6	266.2

BELGIUM	NETHERLANDS	GERMANY	SPAIN	ITALY
.7	.4	7.0		8.0
1.4	1.0	12.0	6.8	10.5
1.6	1.8	15.0	7.5	13.3
3.0	2.0	25.0	10.5	17.2
4.3	3.1	33.8		24.3
6.7	5.1	56.3	19.1	33.6
8.6	10.1	68.3	27.9	46.8
9.9	14.8	77.1	39.3	57.3
10.0	15.2	76.4	40.8	57.9

JAPAN	INDIA PAKISTAN BANGLADESH	INDONESIA	EGYPT	NIGERIA
			2.5	
30.0			5.0	
45.0	294.0	36.0	10.0	
83.2	356.9	60.4	20.0	23.2
123.4	1,092.7	180.5	54.1	113.0
129.1	1,355.6	208.3	66.7	159.1

BIBLIOGRAPHY

The following reading lists are intended for the convenience of students, teachers, and general readers. Although professional students of history may also find them useful, no attempt has been made to provide comprehensive coverage of any areas or topics, or to include specialized monographs. The aim throughout has been to call attention to the most reliable works, to which the reader may turn for additional bibliographical guidance. Classification follows the plan of chapters in the present book. For reasons of space, untranslated works in foreign languages are excluded, as are general textbooks, articles in periodicals, and (with a few exceptions) primary source materials.

Many of the titles are now or will be available in paperback; up-to-date listings may be found in the *Paperback Book Guide for Colleges*. An asterisk in the reading lists below indicates current availability in a paperback edition.

Introduction

Guides and Reference Works

There are literally hundreds of thousands of books on historical subjects, and it is difficult to find titles and authors on any particular topic. One useful but outdated bibliographical tool is the American Historical Association's *Guide to Historical Literature* (1931); rev., 1961). Currently being revised, it is scheduled for publication in 1995; new technology, it is hoped, will facilitate future updating. To keep up with the outpouring of historical books, it is helpful to read the book reviews and listings of new books in the *American Historical Review*, the *Journal of Modern History* and other periodicals.

Chronological listings of events and dates may be found in W. L. Langer, *An Encyclopedia of World History: Ancient, Medieval, and Modern, Chronologically Arranged* (rev., 1972, but not kept current); G. S. Freeman-Grenville, *Chronology of World History* (1978); and S. H. Steinberg, *Historical Tables, 58 B.C.–A.D. 1985* (rev. by J. Paxton, 1987). No attempt can be made here to describe the many multivolume encyclopedias such as the *Encyclopaedia Britannica* (now in its controversial 15th ed., 1974, which was itself revised in 1983). Convenient one-volume reference tools are the *Random House Encyclopedia* (rev., 1990), the *Concise Columbia Encyclopedia* (rev., 1989), and the *Cambridge Encyclopedia* (1990).

Among historical atlases that place European history in its world setting, G. Barraclough (ed.), the (London) *Times Atlas of World History* (1978), is the most impressive. Also useful are the *Rand McNally Atlas of World History** (1957, 1983), the *New Oxford Atlas* (1975), Hammond's *Historical Atlas of the World* (rev., 1985), and

the series of *Penguin Historical Atlases* (many eds.).

The *New Cambridge Modern History* (14 vols., 1957–1979) has superseded the older series (14 vols., 1902–1912). The volumes, which will be referred to in the chapters below, contain valuable contributions by specialists from all over the world but often fail to provide a synthesis for the period covered. Volume 13 (1979), edited by P. Burke, is a welcome collection of thematic essays, and Volume 14 (1975), edited by H. C. Darby and H. Fullard, is an atlas. The volumes in the *Oxford History of Modern Europe*, of which several have been published to date, provide histories of individual nations. An American series, *The Rise of Modern Europe* (20 vols., 1936–1985), known as the "Langer series" for its general editor, W. L. Langer, provides three to four volumes for each of the modern centuries and will be described in the chapters that follow. The multivolume collaborative UNESCO *History of Mankind* (1963 ff.) has suffered from the need to arrive at political consensus on subjects covered. There are a variety of other series, too many to list here, under the auspices of commercial publishers.

Histories in Special Areas

For European economic history, a valuable collaborative work is C. M. Cipolla (ed.), *The Fontana Economic History of Europe** (6 vols., 1972–1976), with chapters contributed by an international roster of experts. A useful, one-volume synthesis is S. B. Clough and R. T. Rapp, *European Economic History* (rev., 1975), and on a broader scale, R. Cameron, *A Concise Economic History of the World: From Paleolithic Times to the Present* (1989). Of special interest is C. P.

Kindleberger, *A Financial History of Western Europe** (1984). On economic thought, one may read R. L. Heilbroner, *The Worldly Philosophers** (1953); E. Whittaker, *Schools and Streams of Economic Thought* (1960); E. Heimann, *History of Economic Doctrines* (1964); and H. W. Spiegel, *The Growth of Economic Thought* (rev., 1983).

On rural and agrarian history, the best introduction is D. B. Grigg, *The Agricultural Systems of the World: An Evolutionary Approach** (1974), which may be supplemented by B. H. S. van Bath, *The Agrarian History of Western Europe, 500–1850* (trans. from Dutch, 1963).

Geographical influences on history are discussed in D. C. Whittlesey, *Environmental Foundations of European History* (1949); E. A. Freeman and J. B. Bury, *The Historical Georgraphy of Europe* (1974); N. J. G. Pounds, *An Historical Geography of Europe* (3 vols., 1973–1985), ranging from 450 B.C. to 1914; and the essays in E. Genovese and L. Hochberg (eds.), *Geographic Perspectives in History* (1989). J. G. Simmons, *Changing the Face of the Earth: Culture, Environment, and History** (1989), traces the human impact on the planet over the centuries, and E. Le Roy Ladurie examines an important subject in *Times of Feast, Times of Famine: A History of Climate Since the Year 1000* (trans. 1971).

Although historians are examining intellectual and cultural history in new ways, for the history of ideas one still reads with profit B. Russell, *A History of Philosophy* (1945); J. H. Randall, Jr., *Making of the Modern Mind** (1926, 1976); and the same author's later work, *The Career of Philosophy* (2 vols., 1962–1965). An impressive comprehensive survey of formal philosophy is F. C. Copleston, *A History of Philosophy* (9 vols., 1946–1975). An admirable synthesis for the history of ideas in the modern period is F. L. Baumer, *Modern European Thought: Continuity and Change in Ideas, 1600–1950* (1977). Other useful introductions are C. Brinton, *Ideas and Men: The Story of Western Thought* (1950, 1963), published for the modern period as *The Shaping of the Modern Mind** (1953); and R. N. Stromberg's two volumes: *An Intellectual History of Modern Europe* (rev., 1975), and *European Intellectual History since 1789* (rev., 1986).

On political thought, R. Berki, *The History of Political Thought** (1977), is an illuminating, brief introduction, and Q. Skinner, *The Foundations of Modern Political Thought* (2 vols., 1978), a masterful account for the early modern centuries. G. H. Sabine, *A History of Political Theory* (1937; rev. by T. L. Thorson, 1984), remains a valuable survey. On the need to examine political ideas and political vocabulary in the context of their times, one should read J. G. A. Pocock, *Politics, Language, and Time: Essays on Political Thought and History* (1971).

For demography the reader may turn to D. V. Glass and C. Eversley, *Population in History: Essays in Historical Demography* (1965); E. A. Wrigley, *Population and History** (1969); C. M. Cipolla, *Economic History of World Population** (1974); and T. McKeown, *The Modern Rise of Population* (1977). The pioneering study of A. M. Carr-Saunders, *World Population: Past Growth and Future Trends* (1936), still merits reading. A work of extraordinary scope with broad implications for future demographic research is E. A. Wrigley and R. Schofield, *The Population History of England, 1541–1871: A Reconstruction* (1981). To keep up with current trends, one should consult the *United Nations Demographic Yearbook* and other periodical literature.

T. Chandler and G. Fox provide statistical data and other information on the historical growth of the world's cities in *3000 Years of Urban Growth* (1974). A comprehensive history of cities from ancient times to the present in all parts of the globe is P. Bairock, *Cities and Economic Development* (1988), while the history of European urbanization in all its aspects is recounted in P. M. Hohenberg and L. H. Lees, *The Making of Urban Europe, 1000–1950* (1985). B. R. Mitchell, *European Historical Statistics, 1750–1979** (rev., 1980) is valuable for population, trade, and other social and economic topics.

For the impact of famines, disease, and the movements of peoples, one may read W. H. McNeill, *Plagues and Peoples* (1976); the same author's *The Human Condition: An Ecological and Historical Review* (1981); and T. McKeown, *The Origins of Human Disease* (1988). On famine and food, one may read E. P. Prentice, *Hunger and History: The Influence of Hunger on Human History* (1939); R. N. Salaman, *The History and Social Influence of the Potato** (1949; ed. and rev. by J. G. Hawkes, 1985); E. Forster and R. Forster (eds.), *European Diet from Preindustrial to Modern Times* (1975); R. P. Multhauf, *Neptune's Gift: A*

History of Common Salt (1978); and the essays in R. I. Rotberg and T. K. Rabb (eds.), *Hunger and History: The Impact of Changing Food Production and Consumption Patterns on Society** (1985). An appetite for culinary history may be whetted by S. Mennell, *All Manners of Food, Eating and Taste in England and France from the Middle Ages to the Present** (1987).

Books on military history treating war as a social and human phenomenon include the older J. U. Nef, *War and Human Progress: An Essay on the Rise of Industrial Civilization* (1950, 1965); A. Vagts, *A History of Militarism: Romance and Realities of a Profession** (1937); and Q. Wright, *A Study of War* (2 vols., 1942; 1 vol. abr., 1965). To these may be added T. Ropp, *War in the Modern World** (rev., 1962); M. Howard, *War in European History* (1976); and R. A. Preston, S. F. Wise, and A. Roland, *Men in Arms: A History of Warfare and Its Interrelationship with Western Society* (rev., 1991). Two superb surveys ranging from earliest times to the present are: A. Jones, *The Art of War in the Western World** (1989), and R. L. O'Connell, *Of Arms and Men: A History of War, Weapons, and Aggression** (1990). J. Keegan, *The Face of Battle** (1977), and his other books are works of distinction. The importance of technology is stressed in B. and F. Brodie, *From Crossbow to H-Bomb* (rev., 1973); W. H. McNeill, *The Pursuit of Power: Technology, Armed Force, and Society Since A.D 1000** (1982); and M. van Creveld, *Technology and War: From 2000 B.C. to the Present* (1988). Other informative books include: P. Contamine, *War in the Middle Ages** (trans. 1986); A. Corvisier, *Armies and Societies in Europe, 1494–1789* (trans. 1979); G. Best, *Humanity in Warfare* (1980); and S. Mansfield, *The Gestalts of War: An Inquiry into its Origins and Meanings as a Social Institution* (1982). For strategy and the nature of command one turns to P. Paret (ed.), *Makers of Modern Strategy: From Machiavelli to the Nuclear Age* (1986); J. Keegan, *The Mask of Command* (1987); and M. van Creveld, *Command in War** (1985).

Three very different books deserve special mention here: W. H. McNeill, *The Rise of the West: A History of the Human Community** (1963), a notable effort to recount the human experience in a global setting; E. R. Wolf, *Europe and the People Without History** (1983), by an anthropologist, which helps to understand Western history as it was seen by societies in Asia, Africa, and the Americas; and P. F. Kennedy, *The Rise and Fall of the Great Powers** (1987), which examines the political and economic fortunes of each nation that at one time played the leading role in world affairs over the modern centuries.

New Directions in Historical Writing

Several collections of essays provide insights into contemporary trends in historical writing, among them: M. Kammen (ed.), *The Past Before Us: Contemporary Historical Writing in the United States** (1980), prepared under the auspices of the American Historical Association; C. F. Delzell (ed.), *The Future of History* (1977); G. G. Iggers and H. T. Parker (eds.), *International Handbook of Historical Studies: Contemporary Research and Theory* (1979); and T. K. Rabb and R. I. Rotberg (eds.), *The New History: The 1980s and Beyond** (1982).

In recent years, stimulated by the *Annales* school of historical writing in France (the name derived from the French periodical *Annales: Societies, Economies, Civilisations*) and by newer kinds of working-class history in England, in which E. P. Thompson, *The Making of the English Working Class* (1963), was a pioneer, historians have concerned themselves increasingly with a newer social history distinct from older interests in the history of social classes and labor and laboring conditions. They have been examining such subjects as the history of the family and of women; sexuality and marriage; the daily lives and outlook (or *mentalité*) of the urban and rural poor; and popular culture—all studied as history "from the bottom up." Many such works are listed below in the appropriate chapters. An introduction to the new social history is provided in O. Zung (ed.), *Reliving the Past: The Worlds of Social History* (1985); P. Burke, *Popular Culture in Early Modern Europe** (1978); S. Easton and others, *Disorder and Discipline: Popular Culture from 1550 to the Present* (1988); and C. Mukerjee and M. Schudson (eds.), *Rethinking Popular Culture** (1990).

The history of the family and related subjects have been studied (with divergent conclusions) in P. Ariès, *Centuries of Childhood: A Social History of Family Life** (trans. 1962), a pioneering work; E. Shorter, *The Making of the Modern Family* (1975), whose conclusions have been widely criticized; L. Stone, *The Family, Sex, and Marriage in England, 1500–1800** (1977; abr. 1979), a remarkable study; R. Trumbach, *The Rise of the Egalitarian Family* (1978); and M. Mitterauer and R. Sieder, *The European Family: Patriarchy to Partnership, 1400 to the Present* (1982). Related studies include J. R. Gillis, *Youth and History: Tradition and Change in European Age Relations, 1770 to the Present* (rev., 1981); L. A. Pollock, *Forgotten Children: Parent-Child Relationships from 1500 to 1900** (1984); L. Stone, *Road to Divorce: England, 1530–1987* (1990); and R. Phillips, *Putting Asunder: A History of Divorce in Western Society* (1988).

An example of the diversity of the new social history is the series edited by P. Ariès and G. Duby, *A History of Private Life* (6 vols.; trans. 1987–1989), with specialists editing and contributing to each volume. The volumes range from Rome to the contemporary era and provide information on the intimate details of life in the private domain, including, of course, changing definitions of privacy. Other subjects related to the newer social history are studied in P. Ariès, *Western Attitudes Toward Death: From the Middle Ages to the Present* (trans. 1976), and in various books by M. Foucault, including *Madness and Civilization: A History of Insanity in the Age of Reason* (trans. 1965), *Discipline and Punish: The Birth of the Prison* (trans. 1979), and *A History of Sexuality* (2 vols.; trans. 1978, 1986).

Although the *Annales* historians have contributed a good deal to the newer social history, they have also been important for their emphasis, often quantitative and interdisciplinary, on long-term factors that influence the course of historical change, such as geography, environment, resources, climate, population, diet, and disease, which in their view often merit closer attention than "events." Here F. Braudel, *The Mediterranean and the Mediterranean World in the Age of Philip II* (2 vols., 1949; trans. 1972–1974), and other books to be described in later chapters were pioneering works.

The *Annales* writers and others may be examined in T. Stoianovich, *French Historical Method: The Annales Paradigm* (1976); P. Burke, *The French Historical Revolution: The Annales School, 1929–1989** (1990); and G. C. Iggers, *New Directions in European Historiography* (1975). A co-founder of *Annales* who died in the Resistance during the Second World War is studied with care in

C. Fink, *Marc Bloch: A Life in History* (1989). Some of the reflections of the *Annales* school on historical method are to be found in M. Bloch, *The Historian's Craft** (trans. 1953); M. Foucault, *The Order of Things: An Archaeology of the Human Sciences* (trans. 1970); F. Braudel, *On History* (trans. 1980); E. Le Roy Ladurie, *The Territory of the Historian** (trans. 1979), and *The Mind and Method of the Historian* (trans. 1981); F. Furet, *In the Workshop of History** (trans. 1984); and J. Le Goff and P. Nora (eds.), *Constructing the Past: Essays in Historical Methodology* (1985).

History of Women

There has been considerable attention in recent decades, most noticeably in the United States, to the history of women. Many of the writings call for reassessments of various historical eras. These contributions may be sampled in R. Bridenthal, C. Koonz, and S. Stuard (eds.), *Becoming Visible: Women in European History** (rev., 1987), with essays from ancient times to the twentieth century; M. J. Boxer and J. H. Quataert (eds.), *Connecting Spheres: Women in the Western World, 1500 to the Present** (1986), case studies with informative overview chapters; B. S. Anderson and J. P. Zinsser, *A History of Their Own: Women in Europe from Prehistory to the Present** (2 vols., 1988), thematically organized; and B. G. Smith, *Changing Lives: Women in European History since 1700** (1989), a pioneer narrative account. Three documentary histories available are J. C. Fout and E. Reimer (eds.), *European Women: A Documentary History, 1789–1945* (1980); J. O'Faolain and L. Martines (eds.), *Not in God's Image: Women in History from the Greeks to the Victorians* (1973); E. O. Hillerstein, L. P. Hume, and K. M. Offen (eds.), *Victorian Women: Women's Lives in England, France, and the United States** (1981); and S. G. Bell and K. M. Offen (eds.), *Women, the Family, and Freedom: The Debate in Documents** (2 vols., 1983). J. B. Elstain, *Public Man, Private Woman: Women in Social and Political Thought* (1981), is illuminating on political thinkers and their treatment of the subject of women from Aristotle on. Two vividly written books by A. Fraser, but in the older style of restricting women's history to women of the upper classes, are *The Weaker Vessel* (1985), and *The Warrior*

Queens (1989), the latter on women since ancient times who led their nations in war.

An important monograph is J. W. Scott and L. A. Tilly, *Women, Work, and Family* (1978), focusing on French and English women in the modern centuries. Two informative studies are S. G. Bell, *Women: From the Greeks to the French Revolution** (1980), and P. Stock, *Better Than Rubies: A History of Women's Education* (1978), from the Renaissance to the present. Three provocative, analytical books, stressing gender issues as central to historical understanding, are J. Kelly, *Women, History, and Theory: The Essays of Joan Kelly** (1984, published posthumously); G. Lerner, *The Creation of Patriarchy** (1986); and J. W. Scott, *Gender and the Politics of History* (1988).

Historiography, Philosophy of History, Historical Method

A comprehensive introduction to the history of historical writing is E. Breisach, *Historiography: Ancient, Medieval, and Modern** (1983). One will also wish to read A. D. Momigliano, *Studies in Historiography* (1966); H. Butterfield, *The Origins of History* (1949; rev., 1981); and Butterfield's other writings, of which several have been collected in *Herbert Butterfield on History* (1984). A good anthology is F. Stern (ed.), *The Varieties of History: From Voltaire to the Present** (rev., 1973).

There are many volumes on the philosophy of history written by professional students of philosophy, and sometimes not directly attuned to the needs and interests of practicing historians. Two convenient introductions are the anthologies edited by H. Meyerhoff (ed.), *The Philosophy of History in Our Time** (1959), and P. Gardiner (ed.), *Theories of History* (1959). The best scholarly introduction is R. E. Atkinson, *Knowledge and Explanation in History: An Introduction to the Philosophy of History** (1978). Also informative are W. H. Dray's two books: *Philosophy of History** (1964), and *On History and Philosophers of History* (1989); and W. H. Walsh, *An Introduction to the Philosophy of History** (1976). Other recommended studies are R. Aron, *Introduction to the Philosophy of History* (1948, trans. 1961); R. G. Collingwood, *The Idea of History** (1946); A. C. Danto, *Analytical Philosophy of History* (1965); and M. Mandelbaum, *The Anatomy of Historical Knowl-*

edge (1977). Two rewarding volumes are P. Munz, *The Shapes of Time: A New Look at the Philosophy of History* (1977); and L. Krieger, *Time's Reasons: Philosophies of History Old and New* (1989).

On the relationship of history to other disciplines and its own distinctive role one may turn to such varied explorations as: A. L. Rowse, *The Use of History** (1946), the first volume in the English *Teach Yourself History* series, a series written for the general reader; C. Gustavson's two books: *A Preface to History** (1955) and *The Mansion of History** (1975); E. H. Carr, *What Is History?* (1962); A. Nevins, *The Gateway to History* (rev., 1962); G. L. Elton, *The Practice of History* (1967); H. S. Hughes, *History as Art and Science** (1957); S. Kent, *Writing History* (rev., 1967); L. Gottschalk, *Understanding History* (rev., 1969); and A. Marwick, *The Nature of History** (rev., 1989). There is much practical information interestingly presented in J. Barzun and H. F. Graff, *The Modern Researcher** (rev., 1985).

Psychological dimensions to the writing of history may be examined in S. Friedländer, *History and Psychoanalysis** (trans. 1978); P. Loewenberg, *Decoding the Past: The Psychohistorical Approach** (1983); and P. Gay, *Freud for Historians** (1985). For an introduction to the quantitative analysis of historical data one may turn to W. D. Aydelotte and others, *The Dimensions of Quantitative Research in History* (1972), and R. Floud, *An Introduction to Quantitative Methods for Historians** (rev., 1979). Of special interest also is R. G. Hawks, *Economics for Historians** (1980).

The writing of biography may be examined in J. A. Garraty, *The Nature of Biography* (1957); P. M. Kendall, *The Art of Biography* (1965); C. D. Bowen, *Biography: The Craft and the Calling* (1968); M. Pachter, *Telling Lives* (1979); and D. Beales, *History and Biography** (1981). New ways of tapping neglected sources are examined in P. Thompson, *The Voice of the Past: Oral History* (1978) and D. Henige, *Oral Historiography** (1982); and a valuable medium is explored in P. Sorlin, *The Film in History: Restaging the Past* (1980).

Challenging reassessments of cultural and intellectual history, borrowing from philosophy, anthropology, and literary criticism, which may remain elusive for many readers, may be sampled in L. Hunt (ed.), *The New Cultural History** (1989); D. LaCapra, *Rethinking Intellectual History: Texts, Contexts, Language** (1983); D. LaCapra and S. L. Kaplan (eds.), *Modern European Intellectual History: Reappraisals and New Perspectives** (1982); and H. White, *The Content of the Form: Narrative Discourse and Historical Representation* (1987).

Books critical of newer trends in historical writing include J. Barzun, *Clio and the Doctors: Psychohistory, Quantohistory, and History* (1974); J. H. Hexter, *On Historians: Reappraisals of Some of the Makers of Modern History* (1979); T. W. Hamerow, *Reflections on History and Historians* (1987); and G. Himmelfarb, *The New History and the Old* (1987). Two probing accounts of the historical profession in the United States, with insights into past and present historiographical debates are P. Novick, *That Noble Dream: The "Objectivity Question" and the American Historical Profession** (1988) and J. Higham, *History: Professional Scholarship in America** (rev., 1988).

Among thoughtful reflections by American and British historians who have themselves made notable contributions to the writing of history, the following may be suggested: G. S. R. Kitson Clark, *The Critical Historian* (1967); C. V. Wedgwood, *The Sense of the Past* (1960); J. H. Plumb, *The Death of the Past* (1970); B. Lewis, *History Remembered, Recovered, Invented* (1975); F. Gilbert, *History: Choice and Commitment* (1977); W. H. McNeill, *Mythistory and Other Essays* (1986); C. Vann Woodward, *Thinking Back: The Perils of Writing History** (1986), and *The Future of the Past* (1989); L. Stone, *The Past and the Present* (1981), and the *Past and the Present Revisited** (1988); D. Cannadine, *The Pleasures of the Past* (1989); and W. J. Bouwsma, *A Usable Past** (1990).

Finally, there are numerous anthologies, historical readings, collections of source materials, and problems series in historical interpretation, of which publishers generally keep readers and teachers well informed. A few titles in these categories will be cited at the end of each chapter.

XI.   Reaction Versus Progress, 1815–1848

The resettling of European institutions after the French Revolution and Napoleon in many ways marked the opening of a new historical era. There are numerous general, national, and topical histories, accordingly, that take their starting point around 1815.

Nineteenth-Century Europe

Helpful guides to all aspects of nineteenth-century history include M. S. Anderson, *The Ascendancy of Europe, 1815–1914** (rev., 1986); T. S. Hamerow, *The Birth of a New Europe: State and Society in the Nineteenth Century* (1983); and R. Gildea, *Barricades and Borders: Europe, 1800–1914** (1987). There are informative chapters also in C. Morazé (ed.), *The Nineteenth Century, 1775 to 1905* (1977), Vol. V of the UNESCO History of Mankind. Valuable for its tables, charts, and maps is N. J. G. Pounds, *An Historical Geography of Europe, 1800–1914** (1985), and a useful reference tool is G. A. Kertesz (ed.), *Documents in the Political History of the European Continent, 1815–1939* (1969).

For an introduction to selected aspects of the social history of the age, there are two volumes by J. R. Gillis, *The Development of European Society, 1770–1870* (1977), and *Youth and History . . . 1770 to the Present** (rev., 1981), cited earlier; P. Stearns, *European Society in Upheaval: Social History Since 1800* (1967); and the essays in R. J. Besucha (ed.), *Modern European Social History** (1972). A major work in social and cultural history spanning the nineteenth century to 1914 is P. Gay, *The Bourgeois Experience: Victoria to Freud*, of which two of the projected five volumes have appeared: Vol. I, *Education of the Senses** (1984) and Vol. II, *The Tender Passion** (1986); both are far-reaching explorations of middle class sexuality and morality. The fourth volume of the History of Private Life series also takes in these years: M. Perrot (ed.), *From the French Revolution to the Great War* (1987). C. Morazé develops an important theme in *The Triumph of the Middle Classes** (trans. 1966), which should be supplemented by P. M. Pilbeam, *The Middle Classes in Europe, 1789–1914: France, Germany, Italy, and Russia** (1990). For rural change in the late eighteenth and nineteenth centuries, there is an important study by J. Blum, *The End of the Old Order in Rural Europe** (1978). For religion one may read H. Vidler, *The Church in the Age of Revolution: 1789 to the Present Day* (1961), and H. McLeod, *Religion and the People of Western Europe, 1789–1970* (1981). For the history of women, in addition to general works already cited, there are available P. Branca, *Women in Europe Since 1750* (1978); P. S. Robertson, *An Experience of Women: Patterns and Change in Nineteenth-Century Europe* (1982); and the essays in S. Delamont and L. Duffin (eds.), *The Nineteenth-Century Woman: Her Cultural and Physical World* (1978).

Europe, 1815–1848

General guides to the era of reconstruction and reorientation after 1815 include F. B. Artz, *Reaction and Revolution, 1814–1832** (1934), and W. L. Langer, *Political and Social Upheaval, 1832–1852** (1969), both in the Langer series; and G. de Bertier de Sauvigny, *Metternich and His Times* (trans. 1967). There are valuable sections by specialists in Vol. IX of the New Cambridge Modern History, C. W. Crawley (ed.), *War and Peace in an Age of Upheaval, 1793–1830* (1965), and for this and the following two chapters in Vol. X, J. P. T. Bury (ed.), *The Zenith of European Power, 1830–1870* (1960), with an overview for each volume by the editor. E. J. Hobsbawm has written one of his stimulating books on this era, *The Age of Revolution: Europe, 1789–1848** (1962), already cited, the first of a trilogy on the nineteenth century. For the papacy in the revolutionary ferment of the age, one may read E. E. Y. Hales, *Revolution and Papacy, 1769–1846* (1960), and O. Chadwick, *The Popes and European Revolution* (1981).

Industrial Revolution

Authoritative treatment is found in the final three volumes of the collaborative Cambridge Economic History of Europe, Vols. VI–VIII (1965–1988), which examine economic history during and since the Industrial Revolution. D. S. Landes' important contribution to Vol. VI has been published separately in expanded form as *The Unbound Prometheus: Technological Change and Industrial Development in Western Europe from 1750 to the Present** (1969). Other informative accounts are C. M. Cipolla (ed.), *The Emergence of Industrial Societies* (1973), Vols. III and IV of the Fontana Economic History of Europe; T. Kemp, *Industrialization in Nineteenth Century Europe* (rev., 1985); A. S. Milward and S. B. Saul, *The Economic Development of Continental Europe, 1780–1870* (1973); W. O. Hender-

son, *The Industrialization of Europe* (1973); S. Pollard, *Peaceful Conquest: The Industrialization of Europe, 1760–1970** (1981); and C. Trebilcock, *The Industrialization of the Continental Powers, 1780–1914** (1981). There are also thoughtful essays in P. Mathias and J. A. Davis (eds.), *The First Industrial Revolutions* (1990). The social and political implications behind the growth of an industrial civilization are examined in J. McManners, *European History: Men, Machines, and Freedom** (1967); and the process of modernization in E. A. Wrigley, *People, Cities, and Wealth: The Transformation of Traditional Society** (1987). On a special subject, as a contribution to an understanding of modernization, D. S. Landes has written *Revolution in Time: Clocks and the Making of the Modern World** (1983).

The complexities surrounding the emergence of industrialism in England are examined in numerous books. Brief informative accounts include T. S. Ashton, *The Industrial Revolution 1760–1830** (1948); G. N. Clark, *The Idea of the Industrial Revolution* (1953); W. M. Flynn, *Origins of the Industrial Revolution* (1966); P. Deane, *The First Industrial Revolution** (rev., 1979); and the essays in R. M. Hartwell (ed.), *The Causes of the Industrial Revolution in England* (1967). A classic account, P. Mantoux, *The Industrial Revolution in the Eighteenth Century* (1906; rev. and trans. 1928; reissued 1983 with forewords by T. S. Ashton and J. K. Galbraith), although modified by subsequent research, may still be read with profit. Recent literature ties economic growth and industrialization more closely to the early modern centuries, sees no clearly defined, straight path to industrial development, and notes that the economic surge in growth in these years even went unnoticed. Two books, among others, offering such interpretations are M. Berg, *The Age of Manufactures, 1700–1820: Industry, Innovation, and Work in Britain** (1985), and E. A. Wrigley, *Continuity, Chance, and Change: The Character of the Industrial Revolution in England* (1988). For general guidance one may also read P. Mathias, *The First Industrial Nation: An Economic History of Britain, 1700–1914* (rev., 1983). S. Pollard and C. Holmes have edited a helpful volume of documents, *The Process of Industrialization, 1750–1870* (1968), and a useful reference tool is B. R. Mitchell, *British Historical Statistics* (1988).

Insights into the nineteenth-century manufacturers are provided in A. Howe, *The*

Cotton Masters, 1830–1860 (1984); F. Crouzet, *The First Industrialists: The Problem of Origins* (1985); L. Davidoff and C. Hall, *Family Fortunes: Men and Women of the English Middle Class, 1780–1850** (1987); and R. S. Fitton, *The Arkwrights: Spinners of Fortune* (1989). A challenging sociological study is N. J. Smelser, *Social Change in the Industrial Revolution: An Application of Theory to the British Cotton Industry* (1959). Changes in British agriculture and the nature of the enclosure movement may be studied in D. B. Grigg, *English Agriculture: An Historical Perspective* (1989), and J. A. Yelling, *Common Field and Enclosure in England 1450–1850* (1977); and the general impact of social and economic change in the countryside is studied broadly in K. D. M. Snell, *Annals of the Labouring Poor: Social Change and Agrarian England 1660–1900** (1985).

Social Consequences of Industrialism

There is a large and controversial literature on the effects of industrial change on the British working classes. F. Engels, *The Condition of the Working Class in England* (1844, many reprintings), and A. Toynbee, *Lectures on the Industrial Revolution in England* (1884, reprinted 1969), were classic descriptions of such exploitation, while J. L. and B. Hammond in several vehement books such as *The Town Labourer, 1760–1832: The New Civilization** (1919), *The Age of the Chartists** (1930), and other works also argued the economic abuse of the common people. The economic histories of J. H. Clapham, *An Economic History of Modern Britain* (3 vols., 1926–1938), and the works of others provided a less bleak view, as do J. T. Ward, *The Factory System, 1830–1855* (1962), M. I. Thomis, *Responses to Industrialization: The British Experience 1780–1850** (1976), and other writers. An extremist viewpoint minimizing the evil effects of early industrialism is set forth in a collection of essays edited by F. A. von Hayek, *Capitalism and the Historians** (1954). The debate took a new turn with books such as P. Laslett, *The World We Have Lost: England Before the Industrial Age** (1965), cited earlier, which somewhat overemphasizes the stability of the early modern centuries, and E. P. Thompson, *The Making of the English Working Class** (1963), which reinforces the picture of a militant working-class culture emerging to resist industrial society. At the same time E. J. Hobsbawm sharpened the debate with considerable empirical data in *Industry and Empire: An Economic History of Britain Since 1750* (1968), and sought to demonstrate in detail that the older picture of exploitation was indeed more accurate. For a contemporary synthesis the reader may turn to two books by J. Rule: *The Experience of Labour in Eighteenth-Century English Industry* (1984) and *The Labouring Classes in Early Industrial England, 1750–1850** (1986).

Two representative studies of labor conditions in this age are E. Gauldie, *Cruel Habitations: A History of Working Class Housing, 1780–1918* (1973), and K. Williams, *From Pauperism to Poverty* (1981), on the poor laws. E. R. Pike, *Human Documents of the Industrial Revolution in Britain** (reissued 1988), depicts working-class experiences; as do D. Vincent, *Bread, Knowledge and Freedom: A Study of Nineteenth-Century Working Class Autobiography* (1981); I. Pinchbeck, *Women Workers and the Industrial Revolution, 1750–1850* (1930; reissued 1969); and the relevant sections of I. Pinchbeck and M. Hewitt, *Children in English Society* (2 vols., 1969–1973). In a very different vein G. Himmelfarb, *The Idea of Poverty: England in the Early Industrial Age* (1954), examining the literature of these years, demonstrates the complexities involved in defining poverty and social responsibilities.

For protest movements of the age, D. G. Wright, *Popular Radicalism: The Working Class Experience, 1780–1880** (1988) is helpful as a summary. Some specific studies would include M. I. Thomas, *The Luddites: Machine-Breaking in Regency England* (1979); R. J. White, *Waterloo to Peterloo* (1957); D. Rend, *Peterloo: The Massacre and Its Background* (1958); E. J. Hobsbawm and G. Rudé, *Captain Swing* (1969), a study of the rural poor and agrarian unrest; and J. Knott, *Popular Opposition to the 1834 Poor Law* (1986). On an important subject there is G. Rudé, *Criminal and Victim: Crime and Society in Early Nineteenth-Century England* (1985), which may be supplemented by M. Ignatieff, *A Just Measure of Pain: The Penitentiary and the Industrial Revolution, 1750–1850* (1979). For the Chartists older studies have been superseded by J. T. Ward, *Chartism* (1973); D. Jones, *Chartism and the Chartists* (1975); and D. Thompson, *The Chartists: Popular Politics in the Industrial*

Revolution (1984). Two Chartist leaders are vividly portrayed in J. Epstein, *The Lion of Freedom: Feargus O'Connor and the Chartist Movement, 1832–1842* (1982), and J. Wiener, *William Lovett** (1989). The creation in England and Ireland of a modern police system more to suppress popular protest than to control crime is studied in detail in S. H. Palmer, *Police and Protest in England and Ireland, 1780–1850* (1988).

Reforms and social policy are examined in S. G. Checkland, *British Public Policy, 1776–1939: An Economic, Social, and Political Perspective** (1985). Factory reform is discussed in M. W. Thomas, *The Early Factory Legislation* (1948), and J. T. Ward, *The Factory System, 1830–1955* (1962). For the pressures to repeal the tariffs on grain, one may read N. McCord, *The Anti-Corn-Law League, 1838–1846* (1958); and B. Hilton, *Corn, Cash, Commerce: The Economic Policies of the Tory Governments, 1815–1830* (1978). On the Reform Bill of 1832, an outstanding study is M. Brock, *The Great Reform Act** (1973). An informative brief account of pressures for reform in these years is J. R. Dinwiddy, *From Luddism to the First Reform Bill: Reform in England, 1810–1832** (1985), in the British Historical Association series.

The antislavery movement as part of this age of protest is studied in several books. The history of slavery as an institution is explored in three books by D. B. Davis, *The Problem of Slavery in Western Culture* (1966); *Slavery and Human Progress* (1984); and for these years, *The Problem of Slavery in the Age of Revolution, 1770–1823** (1975), cited in Chapter X. Full scale accounts of the role of slavery in the Atlantic world, going far beyond the pioneer work of E. Williams, *Capitalism and Slavery* (1944), are available in R. Blackburn, *The Overthrow of Colonial Slavery* (1989), a comprehensive and moving account, and D. Eltis, *Economic Growth and the Ending of the Transatlantic Slave Trade* (1988), an equally impressive work. How the British in response to secular and religious reformers and populist pressures abolished the slave trade in 1807 and slavery as a colonial institution in 1833, even though it ran counter to their economic self-interest, is studied in R. Anstey, *The Atlantic Slave Trade and British Abolition, 1760–1810* (1975); and in two books by S. Drescher, *Econocide: British Slavery in the Era of Abolition* (1977), and *Capitalism and Anti-Slavery: British Mobilization in Comparative Perspective* (1988), focusing on activist pressures in England that set it apart from other countries.

For general accounts of Britain in the years after 1815 moving on into the early Victorian age that opened in 1837, one still reads with profit E. L. Woodward, *The Age of Reform, 1815–1848* (1938), but the most informative synthesis is now N. Gash, *Aristocracy and People: Britain, 1815–1865** (New History of England series, 1979). Other helpful books are A. Wood, *Nineteenth-Century Britain, 1815–1914* (1960); D. Thomson, *England in the Nineteenth Century* (rev., 1964); A. Briggs, *The Age of Improvement, 1783–1867** (rev., 1979), and his many other books; and D. Marshall, *Industrial England, 1776–1861* (1973). Of special importance is H. Perkin, *The Origins of Modern English Society, 1780–1880** (1969; reissued 1985).

There are many biographies of the political leaders and reformers of the age. Among them are G. M. Trevelyan, *Lord Grey of the Reform Bill* (1920; reissued 1929); N. Gash's outstanding study of Peel: *Mr. Secretary Peel* and *Sir Robert Peel** (2 vols.; rev., 1985); C. R. Fay, *Huskisson and His Age* (1951); C. Driver, *Tory Radical: The Life of Richard Oastler* (1946); G. F. A. Best, *Shaftesbury* (1964); and J. Pollock, *Wilberforce* (1978). G. M. Trevelyan's older biography of John Bright (1913) may be compared with K. Robbins, *John Bright* (1979); and G. D. H. Cole's study of William Cobbett (1924) with G. Spater, *William Cobbett: The Poor Man's Friend* (2 vols., 1982). How Richard Cobden dominated the values, ambitions, and strategies of middle-class radicalism emerges from N. C. Edsall, *Richard Cobden: Independent Radical* (1986), and W. Hinde, *Richard Cobden: A Victorian Outsider* (1987). Radical social criticism is also studied in W. Stafford, *Socialism, Radicalism, and Nostalgia, 1775–1830** (1986). There is a biography of Robert Owen by G. D. H. Cole (1930) and studies of Owen by F. Podmore (1924) and M. Cole (1953). For women in the era one may turn to J. H. Murray, *Strongminded Women and Other Lost Voices from Nineteenth-Century England** (1982).

France, 1815–1848

As a sequel to the volumes on the Revolution, an eight-volume series on the history of France from 1815 to the twentieth century, published by Seuil as the *Nouvelle Histoire de la France Contemporaine*, has become available in translation as The Cambridge History of Modern France. The first volume, A. Jardin and A.-J. Tudesq, *Restoration and Reaction, 1815–1848** (1973; trans. 1983) is mostly a political narrative. A brief overview of these years is provided in W. Fortescue, *Revolution and Counter-Revolution in France, 1815–1852** (1988), and a helpful work of reference is E. L. Newman (ed.), *Historical Dictionary of France from the 1815 Revolution to the Second Empire* (2 vols., 1987). Among accounts that begin in this era and go on into the nineteenth century are R. Magraw, *France, 1815–1914: The Bourgeois Century** (1983); J. P. T. Bury, *France, 1814–1940** (rev., 1986); and R. Price, *A Social History of Nineteenth-Century France** (1988). For economic developments one may turn to F. Caron, *An Economic History of Modern France* (trans. 1979); two books by R. Price, *The Economic Modernization of France* (1975), and *An Economic History of Modern France, 1730–1914* (1981); R. E. Cameron, *France and the Economic Development of Europe, 1800–1914* (1961); and P. O. Brien and C. Keyder, *Economic Growth in Britain and France, 1780–1914* (1978). On a special subject J. N. Moody, *French Education Since Napoleon* (1978) is rewarding.

For the years 1815–1830 G. de Bertier de Sauvigny, *The Bourbon Restoration* (trans. 1966) remains valuable, while P. Mansel, *The Court of France 1789–1830* (1988) demonstrates how Louis XVIII and Charles X continued the pre-Revolutionary monarchy. D. Higgs, *Nobles and Nineteenth-Century France: The Practice of Inegalitarianism* (1987) refutes the assumption that the nobility lost its identity after 1789. Conservative ideas and activities are examined in P. Spencer, *Politics of Belief in Nineteenth-Century France* (1954); P. N. Stearns, *Priest and Revolutionary: Lamennais and the Dilemma of French Catholicism* (1967); D. Porch, *Army and Revolution: France, 1815–1848* (1974); and R. Rémond, *The Right Wing in France: From 1815 to de Gaulle* (trans. 1966), useful for this period on into the twentieth century. A. Dansette, *The Religious History of Modern France* (2 vols.; trans. 1961), may be supplemented by two other broad-range studies: R. Gibson, *A Social History of French Catholicism, 1789–1914* (1989), and N. Ravitch, *The Catholic Church and the French Nation, 1685–*

1985 (1990). Of special interest is A. B. Spitzer, *The French Generation of 1820* (1987).

The July Monarchy

For the revolutionary events of 1830 one may read D. H. Pinkney, *The French Revolution of 1830* (1972), and C. H. Church, *Europe in 1830: Revolution and Political Change* (1893), which places the revolution in its European-wide setting. For Louis Philippe's reign, H. A. C. Collingham, *The July Monarchy: A Political History of France 1830–1848** (1988), is a detailed political and diplomatic account, while D. H. Pinkney, *Decisive Years in France, 1840–1847* (1986) persuasively presents these years of the July monarchy as a watershed in French social and economic development. Labor and popular stirrings are ably studied in R. J. Bezucha, *The Lyon Uprising of 1834: Social and Political Conflict in the Early July Monarchy* (1974), and in E. Berenson, *Populist Religion and Left-Wing Politics in France, 1830–1852* (1984).

An impressive study in cultural and social history focusing on the importance of the Revolution in the political culture and lives of the people is M. Agulhon, *The Republic in the Village: The People of the Var from the French Revolution to the Second Republic* (1971; trans. 1982). Newer approaches to social history are found also in W. H. Sewell, Jr., *The Language of Labor from the Old Regime to 1848** (1980) and W. M. Reddy, *The Rise of Market Culture: The Textile Trade and French Society, 1750–1900** (1984), as much a study in cultural anthropology as economic history. P. N. Stearns explores class relationships in *Paths to Authority: The Middle Class and the Industrial Labor Force in France, 1820–1848* (1978). Two outstanding studies in urban history are J. M. Merriman, *The Red City: Limoges and the French Nineteenth Century** (1985), and W. H. Sewell, Jr., *Structure and Mobility: The Men and Women of Marseille, 1820–1870* (1985). L. S. Kramer, *Threshold of a New World: Intellectuals and the Exile Experience in Paris, 1830–1848* (1988) conveys the cultural vitality of the capital as it appeared to exiles like Marx and others. An older study of importance is L. Chevalier, *Laboring Classes and Dangerous Classes in Paris During the First Half of the Nineteenth Century* (trans. 1973).

For women in this age one may read B. G. Smith, *Ladies of the Leisure Class: The Bourgeoises of Northern France in the Nineteenth Century** (1982), and C. G. Moses, *French Feminism in the Nineteenth Century** (1984). An informative comparative study is T. McBride, *The Domestic Revolution: The Modernization of Household Service in England and France, 1820–1920* (1976). An insightful monograph illuminating aspects of early industrialization and the role of women is G. L. Gullickson, *The Spinners and Weavers of Auffay: Rural Industry and the Sexual Division of Labor in a French Village, 1750–1850* (1986), and the impact of rapid change on children is explored in C. Heywood, *Childhood in Nineteenth-Century France: Work, Health, and Education among the Classes Populaires* (1988). A special subject is explored in P. O'Brien, *The Promise of Punishment: Prisons in Nineteenth-Century France* (1981), and G. Wright, *Between the Guillotine and Liberty: Two Centuries of the Crime Problem in France** (1983).

Biographical Accounts

On Thiers, a historian-statesman of this era, one may read J. P. T. Bury and R. P. Tombs, *Thiers, 1797–1877: A Political Life* (1986). For a second statesman and historian, D. Johnson, *Guizot: Aspects of French History, 1787–1874* (1963), illuminates his life and much else. On Charles X one may read V. D. Beach, *Charles X of France: His Life and Times* (1971), and for Louis Philippe, T. Howarth, *Citizen-King* (1961).

Germany, 1815–1848

J. J. Sheehan, *German History, 1770–1866** (1990), cited in Chapter VIII, is invaluable for these years, and also insightful is W. Carr, *A History of Germany, 1815–1985** (rev., 1987). A third book, A. Ramm, *Germany, 1789–1919: A Political History*, is especially helpful on political thought. Two important inquiries into the failure of German liberal democracy to triumph before time ran out in 1914 are J. J. Sheehan, *German Liberalism in the Nineteenth Century** (1978), and J. L. Snell and H. A. Schmitt, *The Democratic Movement in Germany, 1789–1914* (1976). L. Krieger, *The German Idea of Freedom: History of a Political Tradition* (1957), traces the concept with much subtlety from the eighteenth century onward. Other illuminating books are H. Kohn, *The Mind of Germany: The Education of a Nation* (1960), and K. Epstein, *The Genesis of German Conservatism** (1975), cited earlier. There are several thoughtful essays on these years in L. E. Jones and K. H. Jarausch (eds.), *In Search of a Liberal Germany: German Liberalism from 1789 to the Present* (1990). Three books offering additional insights into politics, economics, and national stirrings in these years are T. S. Hamerow, *Restoration, Revolution, and Reaction: Economics and Politics in Germany, 1815–1871** (1958); R. H. Thomas, *Liberalism, Nationalism and the German Intellectuals, 1822–1847* (1952); and M. Kitchen, *The Political Economy of Germany, 1815–1914* (1978). A special subject is explored in W. Laqueur, *Young Germany: A History of the German Youth Movement* (1962). The role of German women in society is examined in two collaborative volumes: R.-E.B. Joeres and M. J. Maynes (eds.), *German Women in the Eighteenth and Nineteenth Centuries: A Social and Literary History* (1986), and J. C. Fout (ed.), *German Women in the Nineteenth Century: A Social History** (1986).

Austria, Poland, Greece, Spain, Italy, and Other Countries

On the Habsburg monarchy after 1815, the best study is C. A. Macartney, *The Habsburg Empire, 1790–1918* (1969), a masterful survey with full treatment of all the nationalities. Recommended also are A. Wandruszka, *The House of Habsburg* (trans. 1964); R. A. Kann, *A History of the Habsburg Empire, 1526–1918** (1974), both cited earlier; and A. Steed, *The Decline and Fall of the Habsburg Empire 1815–1918** (1989). A. J. P. Taylor, *The Habsburg Monarchy, 1809–1918** (rev., 1949), B. Jelavich, *The Habsburg Empire in European Affairs, 1814–1918** (1969), and F. R. Bridge, *The Habsburg Monarchy Among the Great Powers, 1815–1918* (1991), emphasize foreign affairs. For economic history one turns to D. F. Good, *The Economic Rise of the Habsburg Empire 1750–1914* (1984), cited in Chapter VIII. All aspects of Austrian history on into the twentieth century are ably treated in B. Jelavich, *Modern Austria: Empire and Republic, 1815–1986** (1987).

For Europe from the Baltic to the Aegean, R. Okey, *Eastern Europe, 1740–1985** (rev., 1987), covers these years. Valuable for the Ottoman Empire here and in subsequent chapters are M. S. Anderson, *The Eastern Question, 1774–1923* (1966), and M. E. Yapp, *The Making of the Modern Near East, 1792–1923** (1988). For Russia, among many histories that begin with Alexander I, there are H. Seton-Watson, *The Russian Empire, 1801–1917** (Oxford History of Modern Europe, 1967) and J. N. Westwood, *Endurance and Endeavor: Russian History, 1812–1986* (rev., 1987). A major study of Alexander's successor is W. B. Lincoln, *Nicholas I: Emperor and Autocrat of All the Russias* (1978). For developments in Russia in these years, one may consult A. G. Mazour, *The First Russian Revolution, 1825: The Decembrist Movement** (1937, 1961); M. Zetling, *The Decembrists* (1985); and M. Raeff, *The Decembrist Movement* (1966), a narrative with documents. For Poland, one turns to the second volume of N. Davies, *A History of Poland: God's Playground* (2 vols., 1981), which begins in 1795; his briefer *Heart of Europe: A Short History of Poland** (1986); and P. Wandycz, *The Lands of Partitioned Poland 1795–1918** (1974), all cited earlier. R. F. Leslie, *Polish Politics and the Revolution of 1830* (1956), is a key monograph for these years, and there are chapters by specialists for the later years in the volume edited by Leslie, *The History of Poland Since 1863* (1980).

For the Balkans, informative volumes are R. L. Wolff, *The Balkans in Our Time** (rev., 1978), and B. Jelavich, *History of the Balkans* (2 vols., 1983), the first volume on the eighteenth and nineteenth centuries, the second on the twentieth. Two brief informative surveys are L. S. Stavrianos, *The Balkans Since 1815** (1965), and B. and C. Jelavich, *The Balkans* (1965); and Serbian history is studied in detail in M. B. Petrovich, *A History of Modern Serbia, 1804–1918* (2 vols., 1976). For Greece, a balanced and authoritative study is R. Clogg, *A Short History of Modern Greece** (rev., 1986). Stirrings in this period are described in C. M. Woodhouse, *The Greek War of Independence* (1952); D. Howarth, *The Greek Adventure* (1976); and in two volumes (one of essays, the other of documents) edited by R. Clogg: *The Struggle for Greek Independence* (1973) and *The Movement for Greek Independence, 1770–1821* (1976).

For the Risorgimento in Italy and the ferment and frustrations of the movement for unification, the best general accounts are D. Beales, *The Risorgimento and the Unification of Italy* (1971); H. Hearder, *Italy in the Age of the Risorgimento, 1790–1870** (1983); and S. Woolf, *A History of Italy, 1700–1860: The Social Constraints of Political Change** (rev., 1986). These histories may be supplemented by G. T. Romani, *The Neapolitan Revolution of 1820–1821* (1950); C. M. Lovett, *The Democratic Movement in Italy, 1830–1876* (1982); and additional books cited in the following two chapters.

For Belgium and the Dutch Netherlands in these and subsequent years, a discerning account by an eminent Dutch historian is E. H. Kossman, *The Low Countries, 1780–1940* (Oxford History of Modern Europe, 1978). The emerging importance of Belgium in international affairs is traced in J. E. Helmreich, *Belgium and Europe: A Study of Small-Power Diplomacy* (1976). For Spain, a masterful, balanced, and comprehensive account is R. Carr, *Spain, 1808–1975* (Oxford History of Modern Europe; rev., 1982), cited in Chapter X. Books on the colonial revolt in Latin America will be cited later.

Nineteenth-Century Thought

One still profits from a remarkable older study, J. T. Merz, *A History of European Thought in the Nineteenth Century* (4 vols., 1896–1914). Two overall surveys carrying social and other thought forward to the twentieth century are G. L. Mosse, *The Culture of Western Europe: The Nineteenth and Twentieth Centuries* (rev., 1988), and R. N. Stromberg, *European Intellectual History Since 1789** (rev., 1986). Useful anthologies are E. C. Black, *The Posture of Europe, 1815–1940: Readings in European Intellectual History** (1964), and E. Weber (ed.), *Paths to the Present: European Thought from Romanticism to Existentialism** (1960). For the interplay of ideas and politics, one may read D. C. Somervell, *English Thought in the Nineteenth Century** (1929; reissued 1950); and J. Bowle, *Politics and Opinion in the Nineteenth Century** (1954). Provocative general books include G. O. Griffith, *Interpreters of Man: A Review of Secular and Religious Thought from Hegel to Barth* (1943); P. Roubiczek, *The Misrepresentation of Man: Studies in European Thought in the Nineteenth Century* (1947); and M. Peckham, *Beyond the Tragic Vision: The Quest for Identity in the Nineteenth Century** (1962). Political and other meanings of romanticism are examined in J.

Barzun, *Classic, Romantic, and Modern** (rev., 1961); in the same author's *Berlioz and the Romantic Century** (1950; reissued 1982); and in D. O. Evans, *Social Romanticism in France, 1830–1848* (1951).

On the nature of ideology, the best introduction is D. McLellan, *Ideology** (1986). Also helpful are G. Rudé, *Ideology and Popular Protest** (1980); and for political alignments, D. Caute, *The Left in Europe Since 1789** (1966), and H. Rogger and E. Weber (eds.), *The European Right: A Historical Profile** (1965).

On historians and their contributions to nineteenth-century views of life, one may read A. Mitzman, *Michelet, Historian: Rebirth and Romanticism in Nineteenth Century Europe* (1990); L. Krieger, *Ranke, The Meaning of History* (1977); J. Clive, *Macaulay* (1973, 1987); J. Hamburger, *Macaulay and the Whig Tradition* (1976); G. C. Iggers, *The German Conception of History: From Herder to the Present* (1968); M. Mandelbaum, *History, Man, and Reason: A Study of Nineteenth-Century Thought* (1971); and H. White, *Metahistory: The Historical Imagination in Nineteenth-Century Europe* (1973), a provocative but complex book. On Hegel one may read B. T. Wilkins, *Hegel's Philosophy of History* (1975); L. Dickey, *Hegel: Religion, Economics, and the Politics of Spirit, 1770–1807* (1987); and J. E. Toews, *Hegelianism: The Path Toward Dialectical Humanism 1805–1841** (1985).

The "Isms": Nationalism, Liberalism, Conservatism, Socialism

The vast literature on nationalism, including the many older studies by C. J. H. Hayes and H. Kohn, may be approached through L. L. Snyder, *Varieties of Nationalism: A Comparative Study* (1976), a convenient introduction; B. C. Shafer, *Faces of Nationalism: New Realities and Old Myths* (1972); and several books by A. D. S. Smith including *Theories of Nationalism** (rev., 1983), and *The Ethnic Origins of Nations** (1986). K. W. Deutsch, *Nationalism and Social Communication** (1953) remains important. R. Bendix, *Kings or People: Power and the Mandate to Rule* (1978), is a bold large-scale effort to examine the transition to modern conceptions of legitimacy in government. H. Seton-Watson, *Nations and States: An Enquiry into the Origins of Nations and the Politics of Nationalism* (1977),

another large-scale investigation, examines nationalism on a global scale. Of special importance are the studies undertaken by C. Tilly into national development in *The Formation of National States in Western Europe* (1975), cited in Chapter I, and *Coercion, Capital, and European States, 990–1990* (1990).

For the origins, meaning, and evolution of classical liberalism a good introduction is, J. Gray, *Liberalism** (1986), which may be read along with A. Arblaster, *The Rise and Decline of Western Liberalism** (1986). An influential earlier account, H. J. Laski, *The Rise of European Liberalism** (1936), and others have seen the history of liberalism as the gradual taming in later times of a seventeenth-century revolutionary doctrine. Two useful anthologies are A. Bullock and M. Shock (eds.), *The Liberal Tradition** (1957), and D. Sidorsky (ed.), *The Liberal Tradition in European Thought** (1970).

Among books on the leading exemplar of classical liberalism, one may read R. J. Halliday, *John Stuart Mill* (1976), a brief introductory account; G. Himmelfarb, *On Liberty and Liberalism: The Case of John Stuart Mill* (1974); B. Semmel, *John Stuart Mill and the Pursuit of Virtue* (1984); D. F. Thompson, *John Stuart Mill and Representative Government* (1976); and the vehemently critical M. Cowling, *Mill and Liberalism* (rev., 1990). In an area where Mill and his wife pioneered, A. Rossi has edited John Stuart and Harriet Taylor Mill, *Essays on Sex Equality* (1970). Mill and others are studied in S. R. Letwin, *The Pursuit of Certainty: David Hume, Jeremy Bentham, John Stuart Mill, Beatrice Webb* (1963); and Bentham in a biography by M. Mack (1963) and a brief study by J. Dinwiddy (1989). For the persistence of conservatism one may read P. Viereck, *Conservatism Revisited: The Revolt Against Revolt, 1815–1949** (1949; reissued 1965); J. Weiss, *Conservatism in Europe, 1770–1945: Traditionalism, Reaction, and Counter-Revolution* (1977); and R. A. Nisbet, *Conservatism: Dream and Reality** (1986).

Three good starting places for the study of the socialist and revolutionary tradition are F. E. Manuel, *The Prophets of Paris: Turgot, Condorcet, Saint-Simon, Fourier, Comte** (1962), which stresses the link between Enlightenment ideas and nineteenth-century social thought; J. L. Talmon, *Political Messianism: The Romantic Phase* (1960); and J. H. Billington, *Fire in the*

Minds of Men: Origins of the Revolutionary Faith (1980), which in colorful detail focuses on the more conspiratorial revolutionaries. F. E. and F. P. Manuel masterfully trace an important theme in *Utopian Thought in the Western World** (1979), which may be supplemented with K. Kumar, *Utopia and Anti-Utopia in Modern Times* (1987).

The best one-volume introduction to the origins and evolution of socialism is A. S. Lindemann, *A History of European Socialism** (1983). Informative also are N. I. MacKenzie, *Socialism: A Short History* (1949); L. Derfler, *Socialism Since Marx: A Century of the European Left** (1973); and W. Lerner, *A History of Socialism and Communism in Modern Times: Theorists, Activists, and Humanists** (1982). G. Lichtheim, *The Origins of Socialism* (1969), *A Short History of Socialism** (1970), and his other writings are especially stimulating. Two large-scale comprehensive studies, stressing the interaction of individuals, movements, and ideas, are G. D. H. Cole, *A History of Socialist Thought* (4 vols., 1953–1956), covering the years 1789 to 1939, and C. Landauer and others, *European Socialism: A History of Ideas and Movements from the Industrial Revolution to Hitler's Seizure of Power* (2 vols., 1960). E. H. Carr, *Studies in Revolution* (1950), is a series of incisive essays on earlier and later socialists. A key utopian socialist is studied in J. F. Beecher, *Charles Fourier: The Visionary and His World* (1987), and a second, who attracted a wide following, in F. E. Manuel, *The New World of Henri Saint-Simon* (1956), G. G. Iggers, *The Cult of Authority: The Political Cult of the Saint-Simonians* (1958), and R. B. Carlisle, *The Proffered Crown: Saint Simonianism and the Doctrine of Hope* (1987). On the link between socialism and women activists, one may read M. J. Boxer and J. H. Quataert (eds.), *Socialist Women: European Socialist Feminism in the Nineteenth and Early Twentieth Centuries** (1978), and other books to be cited in Chapter XIV. A. Fried and R. Sanders, *Socialist Thought: A Documentary History** (1964), and I. Howe (ed.), *Essential Works of Socialism** (1976) are handy anthologies.

Economic Thought

For the development of economic ideas, one may also turn to the histories of economic doctrine and thought mentioned in the introductory section. An innovative and rewarding book is M. Berg, *The Machinery Question and the Making of Political Economy, 1815–1848* (1980). J. K. Galbraith, *The Age of Uncertainty* (1977), is a sprightly series of essays on economic thinkers from Adam Smith to the present, and R. Heilbroner, *The Worldly Philosophers** (1953), is useful on the economic liberals. For Adam Smith's moral and economic ideas, one may read D. A. Riesman, *Adam Smith's Sociological Economics* (1976); D. Winch, *Adam Smith's Politics: An Essay in Historiographic Revision** (1978); and D. McNally, *Political Economy and the Rise of Capitalism: A Reinterpretation* (1990). For Malthus, a biographical account, stronger for his life than his intellectual contributions, is P. James, *Population Malthus: His Life and Times* (1979).

International Affairs After the Congress of Vienna

For diplomacy and international affairs, F. R. Bridge and R. Bullen, *The Great Powers and the European States System, 1815–1914** (1980), is a comprehensive survey beginning with these years. Books on the Congress of Vienna have been cited at the end of Chapter X. For the post-Napoleonic era the reader may turn to H. G. Schenk, *The Aftermath of the Napoleonic Wars: The Concert of Europe—An Experiment* (1947); E. V. Gulick, *Europe's Classical Balance of Power** (1955); and P. W. Schroeder, *Metternich's Diplomacy at Its Zenith, 1820–1823* (1962), an especially valuable study. H. Kissinger, *A World Restored: Metternich, Castlereagh and the Problems of Peace, 1812–1822* (1957), already cited, discusses balance-of-power politics and ideology before the author became a practitioner of the art. I. C. Nichols, Jr., analyzes the congress system in action in *The European Pentarchy and the Congress of Verona, 1822* (1971).

British foreign affairs and diplomatic history in general in the post-Napoleonic era may also be followed through three outstanding books by C. K. Webster: *The Foreign Policy of Castlereagh, 1815–1822* (1925), *Palmerston, Metternich, and the European System, 1830–1841* (1934), and *The Foreign Policy of Palmerston* (2 vols., 1951). Other accounts of political leaders and events include C. J. Bartlett, *Castlereagh* (1967); J. Derry, *Castlereagh* (1976);

W. Hinde, *George Canning* (1989); D. Southgate, *'The Most English Minister': The Policies and Politics of Palmerston* (1966); and K. Bourne, *Palmerston: The Early Years* (1982), with a second volume projected. C. Howard, *Britain and the Casus Belli, 1822–1902* (1974), focuses on British foreign ministers throughout the nineteenth century.

The involvement of the European powers and the United States in Latin America is studied in C. K. Webster, *Britain and the Independence of Latin America, 1812–1830* (1944); A. P. Whitaker, *The United States and the Independence of Latin America, 1800–1830* (1941); D. Perkins, *A History of the Monroe Doctrine* (1941; reissued 1963); and B. Perkins, *Castlereagh and Adams* (1965), the third volume of his longer study. A special perspective is provided in J. J. Johnson, *A Hemisphere Apart: The Foundations of United States Policy Toward Latin America* (1990), which focuses on the years 1815–1830. For all aspects of the colonial revolutions one may turn to J. Lynch, *The Spanish American Revolutions, 1808–1821* (rev., 1986), and to the appropriate chapters in Vol. III of L. Bethell (ed.), *The Cambridge History of Latin America* (1988), both cited earlier. Two biographical introductions to the subject are J. B. Trend, *Bolivar and the Independence of Spanish America** (Teach Yourself History series, 1948), and J. Kinsbrunner, *Bernardo O'Higgins** (1968). How Spain responded to its colonies is recounted in M. P. Costeloe, *Imperial Spain and the Spanish American Revolutions, 1810–1840* (1986).

*Problems and Readings**

P. N. Stearns (ed.), *A Century for Debate: Problems in the Interpretation of European History, 1789–1914* (1969), and G. Rudé, *Debate on Europe* (1972), summarize the historiographical debate on several issues. Specialized pamphlets include G. A. Cahill (ed.), *The Great Reform Bill of 1832: Liberal or Conservative?* (1969); J. M. Merriman (ed.), *1830 in France* (1976); J. B. Halsted (ed.), *Romanticism: Definition, Explanation, and Evaluation* (1965); H. F. Schwarz (ed.), *Metternich: The "Coachman of Europe": Statesman or Evil Genius?* (1962); M. Walker (ed.), *Metternich's Europe, 1815–1848* (1986); and E. E. Kraehe, *The Metternich Controversy* (1971).

Social and economic themes are explored in P. A. M. Taylor (ed.), *The Industrial Revolution in Britain: Triumph or Disaster?* (rev., 1970); A. J. Taylor, (ed.), *The Standard of Living in Britain in the Industrial Revolution* (1975); M. L. McDougall (ed.), *The Working Class in Modern Europe* (1975); A. Lees and L. Lees (eds.), *The Urbanization of European Society in the Nineteenth Century* (1976); and A. Esler (ed.), *The Youth Revolution: Conflict of Generations in Modern History* (1974). Many pamphlets of essays and readings in the Anvil series are useful: H. Kohn, *Nationalism: Its Meaning and History* (1955); P. Viereck, *Conservatism: From John Adams to Churchill* (1956); J. S. Schapiro, *Liberalism: Its Meaning and History* (1958); the same author's *Movements of Social Dissent in Modern Europe* (1962); J. H. Stewart, *The Restoration Era in France, 1814–1830* (1968); and P. Beik, *Louis Philippe and the July Monarchy* (1965). On Latin American subjects, two titles in the same series are R. A. Humphreys and J. Lynch, *The Origins of the Latin American Revolutions, 1808–1826* (1967), and J. J. Johnson, *Simón Bolívar and Spanish-American Independence, 1783–1830* (1968).

XII. Revolution and the Reimposition of Order 1848–1870

The best synthesis for the background, the events, and the aftermath of the revolutions of 1848 is W. L. Langer, *Political and Social Upheaval, 1832–1852** (1969), in the series that the author edited. Other informative studies include P. S. Robertson, *Revolutions of 1848: A Social History** (1952); P. N. Stearns, *1848: The Revolutionary Tide in Europe** (1974); J. Sigman, *1848: The Romantic and Democratic Revolutions in Europe* (trans. 1973); and the brief G. Fasel, *Europe in Upheaval: The Revolutions of 1848** (1970). As a sequel to an earlier volume for the years 1789 to 1848, E. J. Hobsbawm continues his provocative analysis in *The Age of Capital, 1848–1875** (1976), adding a global dimension to the account, and useful for this and the chapters that follow. An outstanding attempt to view the period 1848–1918 as a whole from the point of view of international affairs is A. J. P. Taylor, *The Struggle for Mastery in Europe,*

1848–1918 (Oxford History of Modern Europe, 1954).

Revolutions in Various Countries

FRANCE. General histories include G. Duveau, *The Making of a Revolution** (trans. 1968), a vivid account; F. A. De Luna, *France Under Cavaignac* (1969); and R. Price, *The French Second Republic: A Social History* (1972). Informative also are the essays edited by R. Price, *Revolution and Reaction: 1848 and the Second French Republic* (1976). M. Agulhon, *The Republican Experiment, 1848–1852** (1983), Vol. II of the Cambridge History of Modern France, subtly examines the assumptions behind formal political positions and highlights republican and revolutionary symbolism.

Studies offering insights into popular militancy and the reactions engendered include P. H. Amann, *Revolutions and Mass Democracy: The Paris Club Movement in 1848* (1976); M. Traugott, *The Armies of the Poor: Determinants of Working Class Participation in the Parisian Insurrection of 1848* (1985); J. W. Merriman, *The Agony of the Republic: The Repression of the Left in Revolutionary France, 1848–1851* (1978); and T. W. Margadant, *French Peasants in Revolt: The Insurrection of 1851* (1979), a study of the provincial response.

HABSBURG LANDS. For Austria one may read J. Redlich, *Emperor Francis Joseph of Austria* (1929), an absorbing biography; J. Blum, *Noble Landowners and Agriculture in Austria, 1815–1848: The Origins of the Peasant Emancipation of 1848* (1948); A. Schwarzenberg, *Prince Felix zu Schwarzenberg: Prime Minister of Austria, 1848–1852* (1947); and R. J. Rath, *The Viennese Revolution of 1848* (1957).

For the other parts of the empire in revolt one may read B. K. Kiraly, *Ferenc Deák* (1975); I. Deak, *The Lawful Revolution: Louis Kossuth and the Hungarians, 1848–1849* (1979), a vivid account, demonstrating Kossuth's strengths and shortcomings; and S. Z. Pech, *The Czech Revolution of 1848* (1969). The end of the revolution is described in A. Sked, *The Survival of the Habsburg Empire: Radetsky, the Imperial Army, and the Class War, 1848* (1979), and in I. W. Roberts, *Nicholas I and the Russian Intervention in Hungary* (1991).

ITALY. Books on the Risorgimento have been cited in Chapter XI; others on unification will be described in the chapter that follows. Studies relevant to the events of 1848 are G. M. Trevelyan, *Garibaldi's Defense of the Roman Republic, 1848–1849* (1907; reissued 1949); the same author's *Manin and the Venetian Revolution of 1848* (1923); and P. Ginsborg, *Daniele Manin and the Venetian Revolution of 1848–49* (1979). Informative also are K. R. Greenfield, *Economics and Liberalism in the Risorgimento: Nationalism in Lombardy, 1814–1848* (1934); A. J. P. Taylor, *The Italian Problem in European Diplomacy, 1847–1849* (1934); and two books by E. E. Y. Hales: *Pio Nono [Pius IX]: European Politics and Religion in the Nineteenth Century* (1954) and *Revolution and Papacy, 1769–1846* (1960).

GERMANY AND THE FRANKFURT ASSEMBLY. Informative studies include V. Valentin, *1848: Chapters of German History* (trans. 1940); L. B. Namier, *1848: The Revolution of the Intellectuals** (1946), sharply critical of the Frankfurt Assembly; and E. Eyck, *The Frankfurt Parliament, 1848–1849* (1968), a detailed account of the assembly itself.

ENGLAND AND IRELAND. The influence of the events in France and elsewhere on the Continent and the government's confrontation with both Chartism and Irish nationalism are recounted in J. Saville, *1848: The British State and the Chartist Movement** (1987). A special subject is graphically treated in C. B. Woodham-Smith, *The Great Hunger: Ireland 1845–1849* (1962).

Marx and Marxism

D. McLellan, *Karl Marx: His Life and Thought** (1973), is an outstanding biography of Marx; other insightful studies include J. Seigel, *Marx's Fate: The Shape of a Life* (1978); I. Berlin, *Karl Marx: His Life and Environment* (1939, 1966); S. K. Padover, *Karl Marx: An Intimate Biography* (1978); and B. Mazlish, *The Meaning of Karl Marx* (1984). Important for understanding the life and thought of Engels are studies by G. Mayer (1920, 1936), older but still useful; S. Marcus (1974); D. McLellan* (1978); T. Carver, (1990); and J. D. Hunley (1990).

On the theoretical foundations and concrete manifestations of socialism, there is, of course, an enormous and highly controversial literature, to which the books cited for the beginnings of socialism in Chapter XI and for the years after 1870 in Chapter XIV may offer some guidance. Much discussion stresses the relationship between Marx's early writings and his mature thought. A perceptive analysis for the general reader is J. Elster, *An Introduction to Karl Marx** (1986), while the same author's *Making Sense of Marx** (1985), a much longer book, subjects Marx's theories to critical but respectful analysis. Other informative interpretive accounts are E. Fromm, *Marx's Concept of Man* (1969), which reprints and comments on the 1844 manuscripts; R. N. Hunt, *The Political Ideas of Marx and Engels* (2 vols., 1976–1984); R. Tucker's two books: *The Marxian Revolutionary Idea** (1969) and *Philosophy and Myth in Karl Marx* (rev., 1972); A. G. Meyer, *Marxism: Unity of Theory and Practice** (1957); G. Lichtheim, *Marxism: An Historical and Critical Study** (1961); S. Avineri, *The Social and Political Thought of Karl Marx* (1971); and A. H. Wood, *Karl Marx* (1981), less impressed than others by the importance of the early manuscripts.

A large-scale, critical analysis by a distinguished Polish scholar is L. Kolakowski, *Main Currents of Marxism: Its Rise, Growth, and Dissolution** (3 vols.; trans. 1978). E. Wilson, *To the Finland Station: A Study in the Writing and Acting of History** (1940), is an imaginative discussion of the use of history by socialists and non-socialists. Insights into the Marxist interpretation of history are provided in G. A. Cohen, *Karl Marx's Theory of History: A Defense* (1978), an especially cogent analysis: W. H. Shaw, *Marx's Theory of History* (1978); and M. Rader, *Marx's Interpretation of History** (1979).

F. Furet, *Marx and the French Revolution* (trans. 1988), brings together and critically assesses Marx's fragmentary writings on that event, and R. Williams, *Marxism and Literature* (1977), demonstrates one aspect of the wider applicability of Marx's theories.

For Comte and positivism, W. M. Simon, *European Positivism in the Nineteenth Century* (1963), may be supplemented by D. G. Charlton, *Positivist Thought in France During the Second Empire* (1959), and T. R. Wright, *The Religion of Humanity:* *The Impact of Comtean Positivism on Victorian Britain* (1986). G. Lenzer has edited *Auguste Comte and Positivism: The Essential Writings** (1975).

Napoleon III and Bonapartism

The best overview for these years, thoughtfully assessing the progress toward modernization, is A. Plessis, *The Rise and Fall of the Second Empire, 1852–1871** (trans. 1985), Vol. III of the Cambridge History of Modern France. Other informative accounts are J. M. Thompson, *Louis Napoleon and the Second Empire** (1954); B. D. Gooch, *The Second Empire: The Reign of Napoleon III** (1969); and W. H. C. Smith, *Second Empire and Commune: France, 1848–1871** (1985), which focuses on the regime's disastrous foreign policy and collapse. A valuable reference tool is W. E. Echard (ed.), *Historical Dictionary of the French Second Empire* (1985).

Two biographical treatments are T. A. B. Corley, *Democratic Despot: A Life of Napoleon III* (1961); and W. H. C. Smith, *Napoleon III* (1973). Other studies include T. Zeldin, *The Political System of Napoleon III* (1958); G. P. Gooch, *The Second Empire* (1960), a series of judicious essays; H. C. Payne, *The Police State of Louis Napoleon Bonaparte, 1851–1860* (1966); and D. Kulstein, *Napoleon III and the Working Class* (1969). There are three evocative explorations of the age by R. L. Williams: *The World of Napoleon III** (1957, 1965), *The Mortal Napoleon III* (1971), and *Manners and Murders in the World of Louis Napoleon* (1975). On education and social mobility there are available R. D. Anderson, *Education in France, 1848–1870* (1975), and P. J. Harrigan, *Mobility, Elites, and Education in French Society of the Second Empire* (1980), which finds more mobility than other accounts. On the rebuilding of Paris, one may read D. H. Pinkney, *Napoleon III and the Rebuilding of Paris** (1958), and J. M. Chapman and B. Chapman, *The Life and Times of Baron Haussmann* (1957). A scholarly effort to rehabilitate the empress is H. Kurtz, *The Empress Eugénie, 1826–1920* (1964), which may be supplemented by N. N. Barker, *Distaff Diplomacy: The Empress Eugénie and the Foreign Policy of the Second Empire* (1967). Tendencies in recent years to praise Napoleon III for presiding over political stability and material progress are explored in S. L. Campbell, *The Second Empire Revisited: A Study in French Historiography* (1978).

Problems and Readings*

Three booklets are useful: M. Kranzberg (ed.), *1848: A Turning Point?* (1959); S. M. Osgood (ed.), *Napoleon III and the Second Empire* (1973); and D. B. Gooch (ed.), *Napoleon III, Man of Destiny: Enlightened Statesman or Proto-Fascist?* (1963). In the Anvil series, there are G. Bruun, *Revolution and Reaction, 1848–1852: A Midcentury Watershed* (1958), and S. Hook, *Marx and the Marxists: The Ambiguous Legacy* (1955). R. Tucker has edited *The Marx-Engels Reader** (rev., 1978), an anthology with thoughtful introductions, while J. Elster (ed.), *Karl Marx: A Reader** (1986), another helpful anthology, is organized thematically.

XIII. The Consolidation of Large Nation-States, 1859–1871

J. P. T. Bury (ed.), *The Zenith of European Power, 1830–1871* (1966), cited in Chapter XI, offers many informative chapters and N. Rich, *The Age of Nationalism and Reform, 1850–1890** (1970), provides a balanced synthesis. R. C. Binkley, *Realism and Nationalism, 1852–1871** (1935), in the Langer series, is an older effort to clarify the era that followed the revolutions of 1848.

The Crimean War

The larger context of the Crimean War and its implications for the Middle East are treated in detail in the volumes on the "Eastern question" by M. S. Anderson (1966) and M. E. Yapp (1988) cited in Chapter XI. Other useful books are G. B. Henderson, *Crimean War Diplomacy, and Other Historical Essays* (1947); W. Baumgart, *The Peace of Paris, 1856: Studies in War, Diplomacy, and Peacemaking* (1981); and N. Rich, *Why the Crimean War? A Cautionary Tale** (1985), which is of special interest. An impressive account rehabilitating Austrian policy is P. W. Schroeder, *Austria, Great Britain, and the Crimean War: The Destruction of the European Concert* (1972), while J. S. Curtiss, *Russia's Crimean War* (1979), sees the Western pow-

ers more responsible than Russia for the outbreak. The military aspects are treated in L. F. V. Blake, *The Crimean War* (1972); P. Warner, *The Crimean War: A Reappraisal* (1973); A. D. Lambert, *The Crimean War: British Grand Strategy 1853–56* (1990); and H. Strachan, *From Waterloo to Balaclava: Tactics, Technology, and the British Army, 1815–1854* (1985), rejecting the older picture of British unpreparedness. The famous "Charge of the Light Brigade" is skillfully recounted in C. B. Woodham-Smith, *The Reason Why** (1953), and the same author has written a biography of Florence Nightingale (1951), as has F. B. Smith (1982). The impact on England is discussed in O. Anderson, *A Liberal State at War: English Politics and Economics During the Crimean War* (1967), and in J. B. Conacher, *Britain and the Crimea, 1855–56: Problems of War and Peace* (1988), a sympathetic account of Palmerston's direction of the war and the diplomatic negotiations. On the changing nature of warfare emerging in this era, one may read C. B. Falls, *A Hundred Years of War** (1954).

Unification of Italy

General Accounts of the Risorgimento, the unification movement, and the events of 1848 have already appeared in Chapters XI and XII. The most informative studies of the leaders of unification and their interaction are D. Mack Smith, *Cavour and Garibaldi in 1860: A Study in Political Conflict** (1954; reissued 1985); *Giuseppe Garibaldi: A Brief Life* (1956); and *Cavour* (1985), the latter a critical assessment of the Piedmontese statesman's opportunism. For the soldier-hero, one may also read C. Hibbert, *Garibaldi and His Enemies* (1966), a vivid popular account, and J. Ridley, *Garibaldi* (1975), a detailed, authoritative study. For Mazzini there are G. O. Griffith, *Mazzini: Prophet of Modern Europe* (1932), and G. Salvemini, *Mazzini* (1957). The best study of Italy after unification is D. Mack Smith, *Italy: A Modern History* (1959), while the same author's *Italy and Its Monarchy* (1990) portrays the House of Savoy in unflattering terms.

Bismarck and the Founding of the Second Reich

G. A. Craig, *Germany, 1866–1945** (Oxford History of Modern Europe, 1978), is a masterful account covering the years from Bismarck to Hitler, with many insights into German society and culture and a companion volume, *The Germans* (1982), equally perceptive, is a series of essays on selected themes in German history; the same author's *The Politics of the Prussian Army, 1640–1945** (1956, 1964) cited in Chapter V, is also useful for the nineteenth and twentieth centuries.

For Bismarck there are available two large-scale biographical accounts focusing on the Prussian statesman and his significance for Germany and Europe: L. Gall, *Bismarck: The White Revolutionary* (2 vols.; trans. 1986–1987), and O. Pflanze, *Bismarck and the Development of Germany* (3 vols., 1963–1990). E. Eyck, *Bismarck and the German Empire** (1950; reissued 1964), summarizes a German historian's larger critical work. Other biographical accounts include A. Palmer, *Bismarck** (1976), a judicious, well-balanced account; A. J. P. Taylor, *Bismarck: The Man and the Statesman** (1955), less judicious but provocative; and E. Crankshaw, *Bismarck** (1981), which carries his career down to 1871. W. N. Medlicott, *Bismarck and Modern Germany** (Teach Yourself History series, 1965), is an excellent brief introduction, and B. Waller, *Bismarck** (1985), an informative essay. G. O. Kent, *Bismarck and His Times** (1978), is especially useful for the historiographical debate on questions relating to Bismarck.

T. S. Hamerow, *The Social Foundations of German Unification, 1858–1871* (2 vols., 1969–1972), is a solid, rewarding study. A remarkable account of Bismarck's Jewish financial adviser, illuminating much of German history during these years, is F. Stern, *Gold and Iron: Bismarck, Bleichröder, and the Building of the German Empire* (1977). The customs union and its contribution to unification is described in W. D. Henderson, *The Zollverein* (1939), and A. H. Price, *The Evolution of the Zollverein* (1949), while the broad aspects of economic development are examined in W. O. Henderson's larger work, *The Rise of German Industrial Power, 1834–1914** (1976).

For the events of 1870, recommended studies include L. D. Steefel, *Bismarck, the Hohenzollern Candidacy, and the Origins of the Franco-German War of 1870* (1962); W. E. Mosse, *The European Powers and the German Question* (1958); and R. Millman,

British Foreign Policy and the Coming of the Franco-Prussian War (1965). M. Howard, *The Franco-Prussian War: The German Invasion of France, 1870–1871* (1967; reissued 1981), is a major study of the war and related events.

Austria-Hungary

For the Compromise of 1867 that created the Dual Monarchy, the volumes by C. A. Macartney and others, cited for Chapter XI, will be helpful here. W. S. Johnston, *The Austrian Mind: An Intellectual and Social History** (1976), covers broad aspects of Austrian life, while the contributions of a special group are sympathetically assessed in R. S. Wistrich, *The Jews of Vienna in the Age of Franz Joseph* (1989), an impressive study. For the military there are G. E. Rothenberg, *The Army of Francis Joseph* (1976), and I. Deak, *Beyond Nationalism: A Social and Political History of the Habsburg Officer Corps, 1848–1918* (1990), which illuminates the Dual Monarchy in other ways as well. For Hungary, G. Szabod, *Hungarian Political Trends Between the Revolution and the Compromise, 1849–1867* (1977), provides insights into Magyar politics and society, while J. K. Hoensch, *A History of Modern Hungary, 1867–1986** (1988), carries the story forward in time.

The Russia of Alexander II

An authoritative treatment of nineteenth-century Russia is provided in H. Seton-Watson, *The Russian Empire, 1801–1917* (1967), cited in Chapter XI; and in R. Pipes, *Russia Under the Old Regime* (1975). On the reign of the five rulers from Alexander I to Nicholas II, S. Harcave has written *Years of the Golden Cockerel: The Last Romanov Tsars, 1814–1917* (1968), a subject covered also in the latter portions of W. B. Lincoln, *The Romanovs: Autocrats of All the Russias* (1981), cited in Chapter V. B. H. Sumner, *Russia and the Balkans, 1870–1880* (1974), offers more than the title suggests.

On the reforms of Alexander II, one may turn to W. E. Mosse, *Alexander II and the Modernization of Russia** (1958), and to S. Graham, *Tsar of Freedom: The Life and Reign of Alexander II* (1935), a sympathetic biography. The place of the peasant emancipation in Russian history may be studied in two books by J. Blum: *Lord and Peasant in Russia from the Ninth to the Nineteenth Century** (1961) and *The End of the Old Order in Rural Europe** (1978), both cited in earlier chapters; in G. T. Robinson, *Rural Russia Under the Old Regime** (1930, 1980); and in T. Emmons, *The Russian Landed Gentry and the Peasant Emancipation of 1861* (1968). A remarkable comparative study is P. Kolchin, *Unfree Labor: American Slavery and Russian Serfdom* (1987).

For the activist world of nineteenth-century Russia and the world of the Russian exiles there is a helpful synthesis, F. Venturi, *A History of the Populist and Socialist Movements in Nineteenth-Century Russia** (trans. 1983); and many special studies, among them: E. H. Carr, *The Romantic Exiles: A Nineteenth Century Portrait Gallery** (1933, 1949), and *Michael Bakunin* (1937); M. A. Miller, *The Russian Revolutionary Emigrés 1825–1870* (1986); A. P. Mendel, *Michael Bakunin: Roots of Apocalypse* (1982); M. E. Malia, *Alexander Herzen and the Birth of Russian Socialism** (1961); E. Acton, *Alexander Herzen and the Role of the Intellectual Revolutionary* (1979); and V. Broido, *Apostles into Terrorists: Women and the Revolutionary Movement in the Russia of Alexander II* (1977). Special subjects are explored in R. F. Leslie, *Reform and Insurrection in Russian Poland, 1856–1865* (1963), and in J. Frankel, *Prophecy and Politics: Socialism, Nationalism, and the Russian Jews, 1862–1917* (1981). Other books on prerevolutionary Russia will be described in Chapter XVII.

United States

Books on slavery and the slave trade as a Western institution have been described in Chapters III, IX, and XI. To them may be added O. Patterson, *Slavery and Social Death: A Comparative Study* (1982), which examines the institution and practice in various cultures and eras. A large literature has developed on the slave experience and slave culture in America, of which two examples are E. D. Genovese, *Roll, Jordan, Roll: The World the Slaves Made* (1974), and H. G. Gutman, *The Black Family in Slavery and Freedom, 1750–1925* (1976). The controversial R. W. Fogel and S. L. Engerman, *Time on the Cross** (2 vols., 1974), which demonstrated the economic profitability of slavery, despite its immoral-

ity, has been questioned by many historians. Two informative surveys of African-American history are J. H. Franklin, *From Slavery to Freedom: A History of Negro Americans* (rev., 1988), and M. F. Berry and J. Blassingame, *Long Memory: The Black Experience in America* (1982).

The mid-century Civil War and its aftermath of Reconstruction have been the subject of many histories, but two recent books present each with remarkable narrative skill and analytical insight: J. M. McPherson, *Battle Cry of Freedom: The Civil War Era* (1988), and E. Foner, *Reconstruction: America's Unfinished Revolution, 1863–1877** (1988).

Canada

A useful introduction to all subjects relating to Canada is G. M. Craig, *The United States and Canada* (American Foreign Policy Library series, 1968). The growth of Canadian self-government within an imperial framework is described in J. M. Ward, *Colonial Self-Government: The British Experience, 1759–1856* (1976), and the emergence of the dominion idea, beginning in these years, is comprehensively treated in W. D. McIntyre, *The Commonwealth of Nations: Origins and Impact, 1869–1971* (1977). J. B. Brebner, *North Atlantic Triangle: The Interplay of Canada, the United States and Great Britain* (1945), is a rewarding study. The Australian story is ably recounted in the collaborative F. K. Crowley (ed.), *A New History of Australia* (1975), and in J. Rickard, *Australia: A Cultural History** (1988).

Japan and the West

A concise overview of the earlier centuries is C. Totman, *Japan Before Perry: A Short History** (1981). M. Cooper (ed.), *They Came to Japan** (1981) is an absorbing compilation of reports on Japan from 1543 to 1640 by traders and others. G. B. Sansom, *Japan: A Short Cultural History* (1931; rev., 1962), and *The Western World and Japan* (1950), describe Japan before and during the nineteenth century. Three books by E. O. Reischauer: *Japan: The Story of a Nation** (rev., 1989) *The United States and Japan** (rev., 1965), and *The Japanese** (1977), are highly recommended, as are H. Borton, *Japan's Modern Century* (rev., 1970), and

W. G. Beasley, *The Rise of Modern Japan** (1990).

The best account of the Meiji era is W. G. Beasley, *The Meiji Restoration* (1972), but it may be supplemented by P. Duus, *The Rise of Modern Japan* (1976); T. Nejita, *Japan* (1973); and K. B. Pyle, *The Making of Modern Japan* (1986). Two especially illuminating books are C. Gluck, *Japan's Modern Myths: Ideology in the Late Meiji Period* (1985), and D. E. Westney, *Imitation and Innovation: The Transfer of Western Organizational Patterns to Meiji Japan* (1987).

Problems and Readings*

A number of booklets will be useful. On the Crimean War: B. D. Gooch (ed.), *The Origins of the Crimean War* (1969). On Italy: C. F. Delzell (ed.), *The Unification of Italy, 1859–1861* (1965); M. Walker (ed.), *Plombières: Secret Diplomacy and the Rebirth of Italy* (1968); and D. Mack Smith (ed.), *The Making of Italy, 1796–1870* (1968). On Germany: T. S. Hamerow (ed.), *Otto von Bismarck: A Historical Assessment* (rev., 1972); O. Pflanze (ed.), *The Unification of Germany, 1848–1871* (1979); and F. B. M. Hollyday, *Bismarck* (Great Lives Observed series, 1970). On Austria-Hungary: H. J. and N. M. Gordon, *The Austrian Empire: Abortive Federation?* (1975). On Japan: A. Tiedemann, *Modern Japan: A Brief History* (Anvil series, rev., 1962).

XIV. European Civilization, 1871–1914

Two volumes in the Langer series provide coverage for this period: C. J. H. Hayes, *A Generation of Materialism, 1871–1900** (1941; reissued 1983), portraying the dual nature of the age as climax of enlightenment and seedtime of future trouble; and O. J. Hale, *The Great Illusion, 1900–1914** (1971), exploring the many accomplishments of the early twentieth-century years and the widespread belief in continuing peace and progress. E. J. Hobsbawm follows his two earlier books, *The Age of Revolution** (1962), and *The Age of Capital** (1975), both cited earlier, with *The Age of Empire, 1875–1914* (1988) to complete a thoughtful trilogy, valuable for this and the following chapter. G. Barraclough, *An Introduction to Contemporary History** (1964), is a provocative essay, calling for a global approach to the years since 1890, a theme developed at length in

J. Romein, *The Watershed of Two Eras: Europe in 1900* (trans. 1978). Of special interest also is N. Stone, *Europe Transformed, 1878–1919* (1984).

In the New Cambridge Modern History these years are studied in F. H. Hinsley (ed.), *Material Progress and Worldwide Problems, 1870–1898* (1962), and in C. L. Mowat (ed.), *The Shifting Balance of World Forces, 1898–1945* (rev., 1968). There are numerous general surveys of twentieth-century history that begin with these years. Two rewarding collaborative volumes are C. Nicholls (ed.), *Power: A Political History of the Twentieth Century* (1990) and S. Pollard (ed.), *An Economic History of the Twentieth Century* (1990). For Europe economic and social development is studied in F. B. Tipton and R. Aldrich, *An Economic and Social History of Europe, 1890–1939** (1987), with a sequel volume for later years.

A few special books deserve mention. R. Wohl, *The Generation of 1914* (1979), relates the restlessness of the postwar generation to the pre-1914 ferment; B. W. Tuchman, *The Proud Tower: A Portrait of the World Before the War, 1890–1914** (1966), provides selected vignettes for these years; and E. R. Tannenbaum, *1900: The Generation Before the Great War* (1976), offers a potpourri of insights into the social history of the times. A. J. Mayer, *The Persistence of the Old Regime: Europe to the Great War* (1981), contends that aristocratic and not democratic values dominated European society down to 1914.

Women's lives and activities are documented in E. O. Hellerstein, L. P. Hume, and K. M. Offen (eds.), *Victorian Women: A Documentary Account of Women's Lives in Nineteenth Century England, France, and the United States** (1981), and R. J. Evans provides another comparative study in *The Feminists: Women's Emancipation Movements in Europe, America, and Australia, 1840–1920* (1977).

The European and World Economy

For industrial growth on the Continent, in addition to economic histories described in Chapter XI, one may turn to A. S. Milward and S. B. Saul, *The Development of the Economies of Continental Europe, 1850–1914* (1977), a comprehensive treatment for these years. Economic growth in two major European countries is studied comparatively in C. P. Kindleberger, *Economic*

Growth in France and Britain, 1851–1950 (1963). For Germany, one may read G. Stolper and others, The German Economy, 1870 to the Present (1940; trans. 1967), and W. O. Henderson, The Rise of German Industrial Power, 1834–1914* (1976), cited in Chapter XIII. For the global economy there are W. Ashworth, A Short History of the International Economy Since 1850 (rev., 1963); two studies by W. Woodruff: The Impact of Western Man: A Study of Europe's Role in the World Economy, 1750–1960 (1966) and Emergence of an International Economy (1970); and A. G. Kenwood and A. L. Longheed, The Growth of the International Economy, 1820–1980 (1983). W. W. Rostow, The World Economy: History and Prospect (1978), is an ambitious effort to study industrial growth from its origins in eighteenth-century Britain to its global diffusion.

International finance is explored in two older studies: L. H. Jenks, The Migration of British Capital to 1875 (1927, 1938), and H. Feis, Europe, the World's Banker, 1870–1914* (1930). To these should be added C. P. Kindleberger, A Financial History of Western Europe (1984), already cited; M. DeCecco, Money and Empire: The International Gold Standard, 1890–1914 (1974); R. S. Sayers, The Bank of England, 1891–1944 (2 vols., 1985); and R. C. Michie, Capitals of Finance: The London and New York Stock Exchanges, 1850–1914 (1987). The role of foreign capital in the economy of the United States, which made it the world's largest debtor nation in 1914, is clarified in M. Wilkins, The History of Foreign Investment in the United States to 1914 (1989).

Demography and Migration

An introduction to historical demography is provided in C. M. Cipolla, The Economic History of World Populations (1962), and the sources for demographic studies are described in T. H. Hollingsworth, Historical Demography (1969). Other books on earlier population growth have already been mentioned, including the pioneer work on English demography by E. A. Wrigley and R. S. Schonfield cited in the Introduction.

T. McKeown, The Modern Rise of Population (1977), stresses the importance of food availability in the nineteenth century rather than medical advances for population growth. Other aspects are discussed in E. A.

Wrigley, Industrial Growth and Population Change (1961); D. Grigg, Population Growth and Agrarian Change: An Historical Perspective (1980); and in the essays in C. Tilly (ed.), Historical Studies of Changing Fertility* (1978). Population statistics for the contemporary era of expansion may be brought up to date by consulting the United Nations Statistical Yearbook (1948 ff.), and Demographic Yearbook (1948 ff.).

For the movement of peoples, two collections of essays are helpful: W. H. McNeill and R. S. Adams (eds.), Human Migration: Patterns and Politics (1978), and I. Glazier and L. deRosa (eds.), Migration Across Time and Nations: Population Mobility in Historical Contexts (1986). Also available are the earlier volumes by W. F. Willcox and others, International Migrations (2 vols., 1929–1931), and D. R. Taft and R. Robbins, International Migrations: The Immigrant in the Modern World (1955). Focusing on the United States experience are M. L. Hansen, The Atlantic Migration, 1607–1860: A History of the Continuing Settlement of the United States (1940), and P. Taylor, The Distant Magnet: European Migration to the United States (1971). A sampling of other migration studies would include M. Walker, Germany and the Emigration, 1816–1885 (1964); W. Adams, Ireland and the Irish Emigration to the New World (reissued 1967); and K. A. Miller, Emigrants and Exiles: Ireland and the Irish Exodus to North America* (1985). On the absorption of America's immigrants, S. Thernstrom and others (eds.), Harvard Encyclopedia of American Ethnic Groups (1980), is a valuable work of reference.

France, 1870–1914

For all aspects of France in this era the reader might turn first to J. M. Mayeur and M. Rebérioux, The Third Republic from Its Origins to the Great War, 1871–1914* (trans. 1984), Vol. IV of the Cambridge History of Modern France. A concise synthesis with a positive assessment of these years is R. D. Anderson, France, 1870–1914: Politics and Society (1977). A provocative Marxist analysis of these years is provided in S. Elwitt's two-volume study: The Making of the Third Republic: Class and Politics in France, 1865–1884 (1975) and The Third Republic Defended: Bourgeois Reform in France, 1880–1914 (1988). Two older accounts remain valuable: D. Brogan, The Development *of Modern France, 1870–1939* (rev., 1967), and D. Thomson, *Democracy in France* (rev., 1969). An unorthodox history with many absorbing details and insights is T. Zeldin, *France, 1848–1945* (2 vols., 1973): Vol. I, *Ambition, Love, and Politics* and Vol. II, *Intellect, Taste and Anxiety*, available also in five paperback volumes with variants of these titles.

An important study arguing that French national unity was accomplished only belatedly by such agencies as the schools and army, with much detail on rural life in France, is E. Weber, *Peasants into Frenchmen: The Modernization of Rural France, 1870–1914* (1976). The same author's *France, Fin de Siecle** (1986), offers fascinating vignettes and anecdotal insights into French society and life. The arts and cultural life are opened up in R. Shattuck, *The Banquet Years: The Arts in France, 1885–1918* (1958); T. J. Clark, *Image of the People* (1973); and J. Seigel, *Bohemian Paris: Culture, Politics, and the Boundaries of Bourgeois Life, 1830–1930* (1986). A helpful guide to major themes in French history and to writings on France beginning with these years is J. F. McMillan, *Dreyfus to de Gaulle: Politics and Society in France, 1898–1969** (1985), while two works of reference are P. Hutton (ed.), *Encyclopedia of the French Third Republic* (2 vols., 1986), and D. Bell and others (eds.), *A Biographical Dictionary of French Political Leaders since 1870 (1990).*

Outstanding biographies include J. P. T. Bury's three-volume study (1936–1981) of the republican leader Gambetta; D. R. Watson, Georges Clemenceau: A Political Biography (1974), on the Radical statesman; and H. Goldberg, *The Life of Jean Jaurès* (1962), on the Socialist tribune. The two best studies of the Dreyfus Affair of the many available are D. Johnson, *France and the Dreyfus Affair* (1967), and J.-D. Bredin, *The Affair: the Case of Alfred Dreyfus* (trans. 1986). The first serious history of women in the Third Republic is J. F. McMillan, *Housewife or Harlot: The Place of Women in French Society, 1870–1940* (1981), the title derived from a remark by Proudhon; while S. C. Hause with A. R. Kenney, *Women's Suffrage and Social Politics in the French Third Republic* (1984), explores the failed movement to extend the suffrage to women. Some additional works on events, institutions, and personalities relating to France

in these years will be cited later in the chapter.

Great Britain, 1871–1914

E. J. Feuchtwanger, *Democracy and Empire: Britain, 1865–1914** (1985), places the period in broad context, as does a much older but still informative survey, R. C. K. Ensor, *England, 1870–1914** (1936; reissued 1986). The economy is studied in F. Crouzet, *The Victorian Economy** (trans. 1982), and special economic insights are added in A. L. Friedberg, *The Weary Titan: Britain and the Experience of Relative Decline, 1895–1905** (1989), and in S. Pollard, *Britain's Prime and Britain's Decline: The British Economy, 1870–1914* (1989). Syntheses moving well into the twentieth century are K. Robbins, *The Eclipse of a Great Power: Modern Britain, 1870–1975** (1983); A. Havighurst, *Britain in Transition: The Twentieth Century** (rev., 1985); T. O. Lloyd, *Empire to Welfare State: English History, 1906–1985* (rev., 1986); M. Pugh, *The Making of Modern British Politics, 1867–1939* (1982); and B. Porter, *Britain, Europe, and the World, 1850–1986: Delusions of Grandeur** (rev., 1987). Two valuable bibliographical guides are H. J. Hanham (ed.), *Bibliography of British History, 1851–1914* (1977), and A. F. Havighurst, *Modern England, 1901–1984* (rev., 1988).

The patterns of urban and rural life are examined in two outstanding collaborative histories: H. J. Dyos and M. Wolff (eds.), *The Victorian City* (2 vols., 1973), and G. E. Mingay (ed.), *The Victorian Countryside* (2 vols., 1981), and the shift to an urban society in G. E. Mingay, *The Transformation of Britain, 1830–1939* (1986). The changing fortunes of the landed aristocracy are studied in F. M. L. Thompson, *English Landed Society in the Nineteenth Century* (1963), and in a far-reaching, impressive book, D. Cannadine, *The Decline and Fall of the British Aristocracy* (1990), which focuses with telling detail on the years 1880–1980.

For the Victorian era G. M. Young, *Portrait of an Age: Victorian England* (2 vols., 1934; enlarged new edition, 1977), brilliantly evokes the period, while three volumes by A. Briggs are indispensable: *Victorian People* (1954), *Victorian Cities* (1963), and *Victorian Things* (1989). G. S. R. Kitson Clark, *The Making of*

Victorian England (1967), is also highly recommended. For the early twentieth century these books may be supplemented by S. Hynes, The Edwardian Turn of Mind (1968), and P. Thompson, The Edwardians: The Remaking of British Society (1975). Of the many biographies of the queen, one may still turn to L. Strachey's adulatory Queen Victoria* (1921), but one should also read E. Longford, Queen Victoria* (1965), a sympathetic yet balanced account, and S. Weintraub, Victoria: An Intimate Biography (1987), a critical reappraisal.

Of the many studies of Gladstone, including J. Morley's three-volume account (1903), one should read E. J. Feuchtwanger, Gladstone (1975), and P. Stansky, Gladstone* (1979). Two studies that capture in detail the complexities of Gladstone's private and public life are R. Shannon, Gladstone, Vol. I, 1809–1865 (1986), to be followed by a sequel volume; and H. C. G. Matthew, Gladstone, 1809–1874* (1987), which carries the biography through his first ministry. For Disraeli, W. F. Monypenny and G. E. Buckle (6 vols., 1913–1920), has been superseded by R. Blake, Disraeli* (1967), a biography of distinction; there are other studies by G. Bradford (1983) and J. Vincent (1990). Joseph Chamberlain is the subject of an exhaustive six-volume biography, The Life of Joseph Chamberlain (1932–1969), the first four volumes by J. L. Garvin and the final two by J. Amery. Two briefer accounts are R. Jay, Joseph Chamberlain: A Political Study (1981) and M. Balfour, Britain and Joseph Chamberlain (1985). Three volumes of a projected four-volume definitive biography of David Lloyd George have been completed: J. Grigg, The Young Lloyd George (1973), Lloyd George: The People's Champion, 1902–1911 (1978), and Lloyd George: From Peace to War, 1912–1916 (1985); also available are accounts by B. B. Gilbert (1987) and M. Pugh (1988). For Asquith one may read S. Koss, Asquith (1976), and for Balfour, R. F. Mackay, Balfour: Intellectual Statesman (1983).

Political and party issues are examined in depth in M. Cowling, 1867: Disraeli, Gladstone, and Revolution: The Passing of the Second Reform Bill (1967); F. B. Smith, The Making of the Second Reform Bill (1966); and P. Smith, Disraelian Conservatism and Social Reform (1967). The transformation of the Liberals in the era after

Gladstone is studied in P. Stansky, Ambitions and Strategies: The Struggle for the Leadership of the Liberal Party in the 1890's (1964); M. Richter, The Politics of Conscience (1964); C. Cross, The Liberals in Power, 1905–1914 (1963); and G. L. Bernstein, Liberalism and Liberal Politics in Edwardian England (1986). Especially insightful is G. R. Searle, The Quest for National Efficiency: A Study in British Politics and British Political Thought, 1899–1914 (1971). An important account of a critical event is B. K. Murray, The People's Budget, 1909–1910: Lloyd George and Liberal Politics (1980). The emergence of the "new liberalism" is clarified in D. Roberts, Origins of the British Welfare State (1960); P. Clarke, Liberals and Social Democrats (1978); and M. Freeden, The New Liberalism: An Ideology of Social Reform* (1978).

The women's rights movement in this era is studied in J. Kamm, Rapiers and Battleaxes: The Women's Movement and Its Aftermath (1966); C. Rover, Women's Suffrage and Party Politics in Britain, 1866–1914 (1967); D. Morgan, Suffragists and Liberals: The Politics of Woman Suffrage in England (1975); A. Rosen, Rise Up, Women!: The Women's Social and Political Union, 1903–1914 (1974); and J. Luddington and J. Norris, One Hand Tied Behind Us: The Rise of the Women's Suffrage Movement (1978); D. Mitchell's popular account, The Fighting Pankhursts: A Study in Tenacity (1967), may be supplemented by P. W. Romero, E. Sylvia Pankhurst: Portrait of a Radical (1987). S. Holton, Feminism and Democracy: Women's Suffrage and Reform Politics in Britain, 1900–1918 (1986), focuses on less known provincial suffragists, and S. K. Kent, Sex and Suffrage in Britain, 1860–1914* (1990), sees the campaign as part of a broader movement for a reformed society. Of special interest is L. Tickner, The Spectacle of Women: Imagery of the Suffrage Campaign 1907–1914 (1988). The opposition to the extension of the suffrage is described in B. H. Harrison, Separate Spheres: The Opposition to the Woman's Suffrage Movement in Britain (1978), and on the restrictions on male voting before 1918, one may read M. Pugh, Electoral Reform in War and Peace, 1906–1918 (1978).

Among studies that examine the status and role of women of various backgrounds in this era a sampling would include G. Vicinus, Suffer and Be Still: Women in the

Victorian Age (1973), and the volume she has edited, *A Widening Sphere: Changing Roles of Victorian Women* (1977); P. Branca, *Silent Sisterhood: Middle Class Women in the Victorian Home* (1975), and E. Longworth, *Eminent Victorian Women* (1981). Working-class women are studied in N. C. Solden, *Women in British Trade Unions, 1874–1976* (1978), and in E. Roberts, *A Woman's Place: An Oral History of Working Class Women** (1985). A special subject is examined in J. R. Walkowitz, *Prostitution and Victorian Society: Women, Class and the State* (1980), setting the problem in a broad social context, and in P. McHugh, *Prostitution and Victorian Social Reform* (1980).

The Irish question is discussed in J. C. Beckett, *The Making of Modern Ireland* (1966), cited in Chapter IV; L. J. McCaffrey, *The Irish Question, 1800–1922** (1968); K. T. Hoppen, *Ireland Since 1800: Conflict and Conformity** (1989); and in a remarkable study focusing on the years 1912 to 1921, G. Dangerfield, *The Damnable Question: A Study of Anglo-Irish Relations* (1976). The same author's *The Strange Death of Liberal England** (1935), remains provocative as a searching study of all the tensions in English society between 1910 and 1914.

The German Empire

Several titles for Germany in the nineteenth century have been cited in Chapters XI–XIII. To them should be added: A. Rosenberg, *The Birth of the German Republic, 1871–1918* (1931; reissued 1964), an older but still insightful study; H.-U. Wehler, *The German Empire, 1871–1918** (1973; trans. 1985), an influential work reflecting the thinking of a new generation of German historians; and V. R. Berghahn, *Modern Germany: Society, Economy, and Politics in the Twentieth Century* (1983), an admirable survey. An important larger study, the last three volumes of which cover the years 1890–1914, is G. Ritter *The Sword and the Scepter: The Problem of Militarism in Germany* (4 vols.; trans. 1969–1973). An older book, A. Gerschenkron, *Bread and Democracy in Germany,* (1943; reissued 1989) remains valuable for insights into the pressure from agricultural interests on politics and society.

Examples of newer thinking about the structure of imperial Germany and class relationships include D. Blackbourn and G. Eley, *The Peculiarities of German History: Bourgeois Society and Politics in Nineteenth-Century German History** (1984); G. Eley, *From Unification to Nazism: Reinterpreting the German Past* (1986); D. Blackbourn, *Populists and Patricians: Essays in Modern German History* (1987); R. J. Evans, *Rethinking German History: Nineteenth Century Germany and the Origins of the Third Reich** (1990); and the essays in J. C. Fout (ed.), *Politics, Parties, and the Authoritarian State: Imperial Germany, 1871–1918** (2 vols., 1986).

For developments in the immediate post-Bismarckian years one may read J. A. Nichols, *Germany after Bismarck** (1959), on the Caprivi era; and J. C. G. Rohl, *Germany without Bismarck: The Crisis of Government in the Second Reich, 1890–1900* (1968). The best full biography of William II is M. Balfour, *The Kaiser and His Times* (1964), although L. Cecil, *William II: Prince and Emperor, 1859–1900* (1989) is highly recommended for the earlier years. There are stimulating essays in J. C. G. Rohl and N. Sombart (eds.), *Kaiser Wilhelm II: New Interpretations* (1982). For the universities in this era an illuminating study is K. H. Jarausch, *Students, Society, and Politics in Imperial Germany: The Rise of Academic Illiberalism** (1982).

Books focusing on specific localities and providing broad insights into politics, society, and class include: D. Crew, *Town in the Ruhr: A Social History of Bochum, 1860–1914* (1979); D. Blackbourn, *Class, Religion, and Local Politics in Wilhelmine Germany: The Centre Party in Württemberg Before 1914* (1980); M. Nolan, *Social Democracy and Society: Working Class Radicalism in Düsseldorf, 1890–1920* (1980); and S. H. F. Hickey, *Workers in Imperial Germany: The Miners of the Ruhr* (1985). Women as a pressure group for political change are studied in R. J. Evans, *The Feminist Movement in Germany, 1894–1933** (1976), and in U. Frevert, *Women in German History: From Bourgeois Emancipation to Sexual Liberation* (1989).

Austria-Hungary; Italy

To the books on Austria-Hungary cited in Chapter XIII should be added C. E. Schorske, *Fin de Siècle Vienna: Politics and Culture** (1980), a remarkable study of political and intellectual responses to the failure of bourgeois liberalism in the empire. Important also is A. Janik and S. Toulmin, *Wittgenstein's Vienna* (1973). An evocative portrait of life and creativity in the second city of the empire is J. Lukacs, *Budapest 1900: A Historical Portrait of a City and Its Culture* (1989).

The best narrative accounts of Italy since unification are D. Mack Smith, *Italy: A Modern History* (rev., 1969), and M. Clark, *Modern Italy, 1871–1982** (1984). Economic developments are studied in S. B. Clough, *The Economic History of Modern Italy* (1964). For the years immediately after unification, an illuminating account is C. Seton-Watson, *Italy from Liberalism to Fascism, 1870–1925* (1967), which may be supplemented by J. A. Thayer, *Italy and the Great War: Politics and Culture, 1870–1915* (1964); A. W. Salomone, *Italian Democracy in the Making: The Political Scene in the Giolittian Era, 1900–1914* (1949, 1960); and R. A. Webster, *Industrial Imperialism in Italy, 1908–1915* (1976). S. Saladino, *Italy from Unification to 1919: Growth and Decay of a Liberal Regime** (1970), is a brief introduction.

Socialist and Labor Movements

To the general histories of socialism and works on Marx and Marxism cited in Chapters XI and XII may be added H. Mitchell and P. N. Stearns, *Workers and Protest: The European Labor Movement, the Working Classes, and the Origins of Social Democracy, 1890–1914** (1971), and A. Przeworksi, *Capitalism and Social Democracy** (1985), which explores the strategic choices confronted by socialist movements. There are many specific studies of socialist parties in each country. For Germany, there are C. E. Schorske, *German Social Democracy, 1905–1917** (1955), an especially valuable study; A. J. Berlau, *The German Social Democratic Party, 1914–1921* (1949); P. Gay, *The Dilemma of Democratic Socialism: Eduard Bernstein's Challenge to Marx** (1952), a peceptive examination of revisionism; G. Roth, *The Social Democrats in Imperial Germany* (1963); V. L. Lidtke, *The Outlawed Party: Social Democracy in Germany, 1878–1890* (1966); and W. M. Maehl, *Auguste Bebel: Shadow Emperor of the German Workers* (1980). An outstanding study of the working-class culture that de-

veloped around the German socialist movement transcending doctrine and ideology is V. L. Lidtke, *The Alternative Culture: Socialist Labor in Imperial Germany* (1985), while the German socialist position on colonialism is probed in R. Fletcher, *Revisionism and Empire: Socialist Imperialism in Germany, 1897–1914* (1984).

For Britain, N. and J. MacKenzie, *The Fabians* (1977), successfully combines biography and social intellectual history, while two leading Fabians, Sidney and Beatrice Webb, are studied in M. Cole (ed.), *The Webbs and Their Work* (1949), and in K. Muggeridge and R. Adam, *Beatrice Webb: A Life, 1858–1943* (1948). Of special interest also is E. P. Thompson, *William Morris: Romantic or Revolutionary** (rev., 1976). Two volumes by S. Pierson probe the origins of British socialism: *Marxism and the Origins of British Socialism: The Struggle for a New Consciousness* (1973) and *British Socialists: The Journey from Fantasy to Politics* (1979), which carries the story to 1919. Other recommended books are H. Pelling, *The Origins of the Labour Party, 1880–1900* (1954–1965); T. Forester, *The British Labour Party and the Working Class* (1976); R. Moore, *The Emergence of the Labour Party, 1880–1924* (1978), a fine synthesis; D. Tanner, *Political Change and the Labour Party, 1900–1918* (1990); K. O. Morgan, *Labour People: Leaders and Lieutenants: Hardie to Kinnock** (1987); and K. Laybourn, *The Rise of Labour: The British Labour Party, 1890–1979** (1989).

For France, for an overall view with many interesting insights, one may read T. Judt, *Marxism and the French Left: Studies on Labour and Politics in France, 1830–1981* (1986). The origins of the Socialist party are recounted in A. Noland, *The Founding of the French Socialist Party, 1893–1905* (1956), and there are a number of informative biographical studies on Socialist leaders, among them: H. Goldberg on Jean Jaurès (1962), cited earlier; L. Derfler (1977) and M. M. Farrar (1990) on Alexandre Millerand; L. Derfler on Paul Lafargue (1991); and K. S. Vincent on Pierre-Joseph Proudhon (1984). The spiritual precursor of Christian social democracy is studied in H. A. Schmitt, *Charles Péguy: The Decline of an Idealist* (1967).

On the Socialist international organization, there are J. Joll, *The Second International, 1889–1914* (rev., 1974), a concise survey, and J. Braunthal, *History of the International* (3 vols.; trans. 1961–1980), a detailed study. The breakup of the International is described in G. Haupt, *Socialism and the Great War: The Collapse of the Second International* (1972). The most comprehensive introduction to anarchism is G. Woodcock, *Anarchism: A History of Libertarian Ideas and Movements* (1962), but also useful is J. Joll, *The Anarchists** (2nd ed., 1981).

There has been considerable interest in Rosa Luxemburg, who made significant contributions to international socialism. J. P. Nettl, *Rosa Luxemburg** (2 vols., 1966; abr. 1 vol., 1969), is an admirable biography; other studies include N. Geras, *The Legacy of Rosa Luxemburg* (1976); E. Eltinger, *Rosa Luxemburg: A Life* (1987), with new material on her political and personal life; the concise R. Abraham, *Rosa Luxemburg: A Life for the International** (1989); and S. E. Bronner, *Rosa Luxemburg: A Revolutionary for Our Times** (1990).

On the activist role of women in the socialist movement one may turn to R. J. Evans, *Comrades and Sisters: Feminism, Socialism, and Pacifism in Europe, 1870–1945* (1987), and the essays in M. J. Boxer and J. H. Quataert (eds.), *Socialist Women: European Socialist Feminism in the Nineteenth and Early Twentieth Centuries** (1978), cited earlier. For the German socialists there is J. H. Quataert, *Reluctant Feminists in German Social Democracy, 1865–1917* (1979), and for the French, C. Sowerwine, *Sisters or Citizens: Women and Socialism in France Since 1876* (1982), and P. Hilden, *Working Class Women and Socialist Politics in France: A Regional Study, 1880–1914* (1986).

Labor History

Recent efforts at writing labor history have attempted to convey the experiences of laboring men and women apart from organized labor movements and have integrated labor protest into a broader cultural context. Here E. P. Thompson, whose works have been cited, has been a pioneer. Another exemplar is E. J. Hobsbawm who has written, among other works, *Primitive Rebels** (1959), *Labouring Men** (1964), and *Workers: Worlds of Labour** (1985). A successful effort for the English experience in these years is S. Meacham, *A Life Apart: The English Working Class, 1890–1914* (1977). Other interesting examples for British labor are J. Benson, *British Coalminers in the Nineteenth Century* (1980); P. Joyce, *Work, Society and Politics: The Culture of the Factory in Late Victorian England* (1980); D. Kynaston, *The British Working Class, 1850–1914* (1976); J. Benson, *The Working Class in Britain, 1850–1939* (1989); and R. Price, *Labour in British Society: An Interpretive History** (1990). Traditional trade-union history may be studied in H. Pelling, *A History of Trade Unionism* (1963).

For France, examples of the newer labor history would include J. W. Scott, *The Glassmakers of Carmaux: French Craftsmen and Political Action in a Nineteenth-Century City** (1974); B. H. Moss, *The Origins of the French Labor Movement, 1830–1914: The Socialism of Skilled Workers* (1976); L. R. Berlanstein, *The Working People of Paris, 1871–1914* (1984); two books by M. P. Hanagan: *The Logic of Solidarity: Artisans and Workers in Three French Towns, 1871–1914* (1980) and *Nascent Proletarians: Class Formation in Post-Revolutionary France* (1990); and D. Reid, *The Miners of Decazeville: A Genealogy of Deindustrialization* (1986). A comprehensive study is G. Noiriel, *Workers in French Society in the 19th and 20th Centuries* (trans. 1990); and the strike as a social phenomenon in these years is studied in M. Perrot, *Workers on Strike: France, 1871–1890* (trans. 1987). The importance of syndicalism is examined in S. Milner, *French Syndicalism and the International Labor Movement, 1900–1914* (1990).

The New Movement in Science

Several histories of science are cited in Chapter VII. Science in the nineteenth and early twentieth centuries is studied in W. P. D. Wightman, *The Growth of Scientific Ideas* (1951, and D. Knight, *The Age of Science* (1986), which captures the impact of science on the age.

On biology, evolution, and Darwinism one may turn to P. B. Sears, *Charles Darwin: The Naturalist as a Cultural Force* (1950); G. Himmelfarb, *Darwin and the Darwinian Revolution** (1959); R. W. Clark, *The Survival of Charles Darwin: A Biography of a Man and an Idea* (1985), by a popular biographer; L. Eiseley, *Darwin's Century* (1961); and M. Ruse, *The Darwinian*

Revolution (1979). The several books of P. J. Bowler, especially *Evolution: The History of an Idea* (rev., 1989), deserve attention, while brief biographical accounts of two other contributors to evolutionary theory and biological sciences in this era are L. J. Jordanova, *Lamarck** (1985), and V. Orel, *Mendel** (1985), both in a British Past Masters series. The breakthrough in geology and its cultural impact may be studied in C. C. Gillispie, *Genesis and Geology* (1951), and S. J. Gould, *Time's Arrow, Time's Cycle: Myth and Metaphor in the Discovery of Geological Time** (1987).

For the impact of these scientific developments on religion, the classic account is A. D. White, *A History of the Warfare of Science and Theology** (1896, many eds.); more recent studies include W. Irvine, *Apes, Angels, and Victorians* (1955; reissued 1983); J. R. Moore, *The Post-Darwinian Controversies: A Study of the Protestant Struggle to Come to Terms with Darwin in Great Britain and America, 1870–1900** (1979); and the essays in D. C. Lindberg and R. L. Numbers (eds.), *Historical Essays on the Encounter between Christianity and Science** (1986).

On the emergence of modern physics and the transformation of Newtonian concepts one may turn to V. F. Weisskopf, *Physics in the Twentieth Century* (1972). The great twentieth-century physicist may best be approached through A. Pais, *'Subtle is the Lord': The Science and the Life of Albert Einstein** (1982), a major work; H. Cuny, *Albert Einstein** (1962), brief and concise; R. W. Clark, *Einstein: The Life and Times** (1971); and J. Bernstein, *Einstein** (1973).

For the theoretical foundations of science and the nature of scientific discovery one may read the books by T. S. Kuhn* (1962) and I. B. Cohen* (1985) cited in Chapter VII, and two studies by G. Holton, *The Scientific Imagination: Case Studies** (1978), and *Thematic Origins of Scientific Thought: Kepler to Einstein** (rev., 1988).

For Freud, there is an older biography by E. Jones (3 vols., 1953–1957; abr. 1 vol., 1961), an English co-worker of Freud; and an impressive study by P. Gay, *Freud: A Life for Our Time* (1988). Because many questions arise on the importance of Freud's background and experiences in turn-of-the-century Vienna, the reader may also wish to consult W. J. McGrath, *Freud's Discovery of Psychoanalysis: The Politics of Hysteria* (1986), and various other studies. A. Storr, *Freud** (1989) is a thoughtful brief assessment.

Social Thought

Outstanding works are H. S. Hughes, *Consciousness and Society: The Reorientation of European Social Thought, 1890–1930** (1958), G. Masur, *Prophets of Yesterday: Studies in European Culture, 1890–1914** (1961); M. Biddis, *Age of the Masses: Ideas and Society Since 1870* (1977); and S. Kern, *The Culture of Time and Space, 1880–1918** (1983). Virtually a history of thought from Herbert Spencer to the present is W. W. Wagar, *Good Tidings: The Belief in Progress from Darwin to Marcuse* (1972); on that theme one may also read M. Ginsberg, *The Idea of Progress* (1953); R. Nisbet, *History of the Idea of Progress* (1980), cited in Chapter VIII; and a thoughtful collaborative volume, G. Almond, M. Chodorow, and R. H. Pierce (eds.), *Progress and Its Discontents* (1982). An informative study of a dominant nineteenth-century thinker is D. Wiltshire, *The Social and Political Thought of Herbert Spencer* (1978).

The best studies of Nietzsche are W. A. Kaufmann, *Nietzsche: Philosopher, Psychologist, Antichrist** (1950); R. Hayman, *Nietzsche: A Critical Life* (1980); and T. B. Strong, *Friedrich Nietzsche and the Politics of Transfiguration** (rev., 1988). Useful anthologies for these years are R. N. Stromberg (ed.), *Realism, Naturalism, and Symbolism: Modes of Thought and Expression in Europe, 1848–1914** (1968), and E. Weber (ed.), *Movements, Currents, Trends: Aspects of European Thought in the Nineteenth and Twentieth Centuries** (1991).

Religion Since 1870

The relationship between secularized European civilization and its Christian origins is ably treated in O. Chadwick, *The Secularization of the European Mind in the Nineteenth Century* (1976), and in H. McLeod, *Religion and the People of Western Europe, 1789–1970** (1981), cited earlier. For religious thought, J. Pelikan, *Christian Doctrine and Modern Culture: Since 1700* (1990), the final volume in his *The Christian Tradition*, may be read along with C. Welch, *Protestant Thought in the Nineteenth Century* (2 vols., 1985), the second volume studying the years

1870–1914. Other books examining the impact of science on the Protestant churches and their response have been mentioned earlier in this chapter. For the Roman Catholic reaction one may read T. M. Loome, *Liberal Catholicism, Reform Catholicism, and Modernism* (1979); and L. R. Kurtz, *The Politics of Heresy: The Modernist Crisis in Roman Catholicism* (1986).

For Judaism, H. M. Sachar, *The Course of Modern Jewish History** (rev., 1977), and *A History of Israel: From the Rise of Zionism to Our Time* (rev., 1979), incorporate the nineteenth-century background. The fullest account of Zionism as an ideology is the impressive study in three volumes by D. Vital (1975–1987)*: *The Origins of Zionism, Zionism: The Formative Years,* and *Zionism: the Crucial Phase,* which carries the story to 1919. Another insightful work is S. Avinieri, *The Making of Modern Zionism: The Intellectual Origins of the Jewish State* (1981).

The Assault on Liberalism: Racism, the Cult of Violence

Many of the books cited above examine the undermining of liberal values in the late nineteenth century, with implications for the twentieth. Two additional studies are H. Arendt, *The Origins of Totalitarianism** (1951), and J. L. Talmon, *The Myth of the Nation and the Vision of Revolution: The Origins of Ideological Polarization in the Twentieth Century* (1980). J. Barzun, *Darwin, Marx, Wagner: Critique of a Heritage** (rev., 1981), stresses similarities, as he sees it, in the way each of these figures undermined classical liberalism.

For racism and anti-Semitism in these years, one may read P. G. J. Pulzer, *The Rise of Political Anti-Semitism in Germany and Austria** (rev., 1988); L. Poliakov, *The Aryan Myth: A History of Racist and Nationalist Ideas in Europe* (trans. 1974); J. Katz, *From Prejudice to Destruction: Anti-Semitism, 1700–1933* (1980); G. L. Mosse, *Toward the Final Solution: A History of European Racism* (1978); and G. G. Field, *Evangelist of Race: The Germanic Vision of Houston Stewart Chamberlain* (1981). Books on anti-Semitism in France relating to the Dreyfus Affair include R. F. Byrnes, *Anti-Semitism in Modern France: Prologue to the Dreyfus Affair* (1950), and S. Wilson, *Ideology and Experience: Anti-Semitism in Modern France at the Time of the Dreyfus*

Affair (1982), especially insightful. J. J. Roth, *The Cult of Violence: Sorel and the Sorelians* (1980), is illuminating on the founder of syndicalism and his followers. The origins of twentieth-century fascist ideology are studied in Z. Sternhell, *Neither Right Nor Left: Fascist Ideology in France* (1986), a much-debated book, which finds many of the roots of fascist thought in the ideas and ideology of the left. A precursor of fascism is studied in C. S. Doty, *From Cultural Rebellion to Counterrevolution: The Politics of Maurice Barrès* (1976), and in R. Soucy, *Fascism in France: The Case of Maurice Barrès* (1972), the first of other studies by the author on the same subject.

Problems and Readings*

Pamphlets relating to this chapter are R. L. Williams (ed.), *The Commune of Paris, 1871* (1969); S. Edwards (ed.), *The Communards of Paris* (1973); L. Derfler (ed.), *The Dreyfus Affair: Tragedy of Errors?* (1964); H. R. Kedward (ed.), *The Dreyfus Affair: Catalyst for Tensions in French Society* (1965); E. C. Helmreich (ed.), *A Free Church in a Free State: The Catholic Church, Italy, Germany, France, 1864–1914* (1964); T. S. Hamerow (ed.), *The Age of Bismarck: Documents and Interpretations* (1974); J. J. Sheehan (ed.), *Imperial Germany* (1976); H. Schultz (ed.), *English Liberalism and the State: Individualism or Collectivism* (1974); E. C. Black (ed.), *Victorian Culture and Society* (1974); and P. Stansky (ed.), *The Victorian Revolution: Government and Society in Victoria's Britain* (1973). Also useful are H. Vanderpool (ed.), *Darwin and Darwinism* (1974); R. S. Levy (ed.), *Antisemitism in Modern Times: An Anthology of Texts** (1991); M. L. McDougall (ed.), *The Working Class in Modern Europe* (1975); and A. and L. Lees (eds.), *The Urbanization of European Society in the Nineteenth Century* (1975). Materials on science and intellectual developments are available in L. P. Williams (ed.), *Relativity Theory: Its Origins and Impact on Modern Thought* (1968), and in W. W. Wagar (ed.), *Science, Faith, and Man: European Thought since 1914* (1968).

XV. Europe's World Supremacy

Many of the general accounts for the years 1871–1914 cited in the previous chapter will also be helpful here. Other informative introductions include H. Gollwitzer, *Europe in the Age of Imperialism, 1848–1917* (1974); R. F. Betts, *The False Dawn: European Imperialism in the Nineteenth Century* (1979); W. D. Smith, *European Imperialism in the Nineteenth and Twentieth Centuries** (1982); and V. G. Kiernan, *From Conquest to Collapse: European Empires from 1815 to 1960* (1982). W. L. Langer, *The Diplomacy of Imperialism, 1890–1902** (2 vols., 1935; rev., 1965), remains valuable for all aspects of imperialism; it may be supplemented by R. Shannon, *The Crisis of Imperialism, 1865–1915* (1974). The role played by Western technology in European expansion and its implications for the colonial world is examined in two volumes by D. R. Headrick: *The Tools of Empire** (1981) and *The Tentacles of Progress** (1988). A. J. H. Latham explores other aspects of development in the non-Western world in *The International Economy and the Undeveloped World, 1865–1914* (1978).

Imperialism in General

Continuing debate about the motives of imperialism has in part been stimulated by the seminal study of R. Robinson and J. Gallagher, *Africa and the Victorians: The Official Mind of Imperialism** (1961), and their other writings. They see no sharp break with the past in the 1870s, stress the importance of economic penetration over annexation, and argue that the European powers were drawn into formal empires by internal power vacuums so that imperialism cannot be understood without a study of the indigenous societies involved. An excellent introduction to the debate is W. R. Louis (ed.), *Imperialism: The Robinson-Gallagher Controversy** (1976). Two books by D. Fieldhouse, *Economics and Empire, 1830–1914* (1973), and *Colonialism, 1870–1945: An Introduction* (1981), also give a higher priority to national prestige and security than to economic factors. Motives and justifications for imperialism are thoroughly analyzed in R. Koebner and H. D. Schmidt, *Imperialism: The Story and Significance of a Political Word 1840–1960* (1964); A. P. Thornton, *Doctrines of Imperialism* (1965); C. Reynolds, *Modes of Imperialism* (1981); T. Smith, *The Pattern of Imperialism* (1982); and W. J. Mommsen, *Theories of Imperialism* (trans. 1980).

Provocative discussions of the confrontations between Europeans and non-Europeans include R. Maunier, *The Sociology of Colonies: An Introduction to the Study of Race Contact* (2 vols., 1949); D. Mannoni, *Prospero and Caliban: The Psychology of Colonization** (1956), stressing the psychological impact on both rulers and governed; T. Geiger, *The Conflicted Relationship: The West and the Transformation of Asia, Africa, and Latin America* (1967); G. W. Goug, *The Standards of "Civilization" in International Society* (1984); and V. G. Kiernan, *The Lords of Human Kind: Black Man, Yellow Man, and White Man in the Age of Empire** (1987).

British and European Imperialism

Two informative accounts of the British experience are B. Porter, *The Lion's Share: A Short History of British Imperialism, 1850–1983** (rev., 1984), an especially lively account; and R. Hyam, *Britain's Imperial Century, 1815–1914: A Study of Empire and Expansion* (1976). L. E. Davis and A. Huttenback, *Mammon and the Pursuit of Empire: The Economics of British Imperialism, 1860–1912** (1980; abr. ed., 1988), an important in-depth inquiry, concludes that the empire was not a profitable enterprise. The opponents of imperialism at the time are described in A. P. Thornton, *The Imperial Idea and Its Enemies* (1959), and in B. Porter, *Critics of Empire: British Radical Attitudes to Colonialism in Africa, 1895–1914* (1968).

The imperial activities of the other European powers are described in W. O. Henderson, *Studies in German Colonial History* (1963); W. D. Smith, *The German Colonial Empire* (1978); H. Brunschwig, *French Colonialism, 1871–1914: Myths and Realities* (1960; trans. 1966); R. A. Webster, *Industrial Imperialism in Italy, 1908–1915* (1975), cited earlier; M. Kuietenbrouwer, *The Netherlands and the Rise of Modern Imperialism* (trans. 1991); and in other books discussed later in this chapter. On both the theory and practice of imperialism an important comparative study is W. Baumgart, *Imperialism: The Idea and Reality of British and French Colonial Expansion, 1880–1914* (trans. 1982).

The Americas

For all aspects of relationships with Latin America the contributed chapters in the first five volumes (1988) of L. Bethell (ed.), The

Cambridge History of Latin America (9 vols. projected) are valuable: Vols. I and II, *Colonial Latin America*; Vol. III, *From Independence to c. 1870*; and Vols. IV–V, *From 1870 to 1930*. D. Bushnell and N. Macaulay, *The Emergence of Latin America in the Nineteenth Century* (1987), is an outstanding survey; it may be supplemented by E. M. Burns, *The Poverty of Progress: Latin America in the Nineteenth Century** (1980).

D. Dawson, *The Mexican Adventure* (1935), is a careful account of Napoleon III's fiasco during the 1860s, and may be read along with N. N. Baker, *The French Experience in Mexico, 1821–1861* (1979). F. Tannenbaum's *Mexico: The Struggle for Peace and Bread* (1950), provides a thoughtful narrative of Mexican history, but should be supplemented by such books as R. E. Ruiz, *The Great Rebellion: Mexico, 1905–1924** (1980); A. Knight, *The Mexican Revolution* (2 vols., 1986); and J. M. Hart, *Revolutionary Mexico* (1987).

For the imperialist activities of the United States in these years, older studies that remain valuable are: J. W. Pratt, *Expansionists of 1898** (1936); the same author's *America's Colonial Empire* (1954); and G. K. Weinberg, *Manifest Destiny: A Study in Nationalist Expansion in American History** (1935). They may be supplemented by W. LaFeber, *The New Empire* (1963); F. Merk, *Manifest Destiny and Mission in American History* (1963); and J. Dobson, *America's Ascent: The United States Becomes a Great Power, 1880–1914* (1978). W. A. Williams, *The Tragedy of American Democracy** (rev., 1972), is highly critical of American imperialism, while a thoughtful assessment of American motives is to be found in E. R. May's two volumes: *Imperial Democracy* (1961) and *American Imperialism: A Speculative Essay* (1968).

For the Spanish American War one may read W. Millis, *The Martial Spirit** (1931), an older account; F. Freidel, *The Splendid Little War* (1958); and D. F. Trask, *The War with Spain in 1898* (1981). Other episodes of American expansion are recounted in P. Stanley, *A Nation in the Making: The Philippines and the United States* (1974); M. Tate, *The United States and the Hawaiian Kingdom* (1965); D. McCullough, *The Path Between the Seas: The Creation of the Panama Canal, 1870–1914*; and W. LaFeber, *The Panama Canal* (rev., 1989).

The Ottoman Empire, the Middle East, and the Balkans

An informative synthesis for the years from the founding of Islam to the present is S. N. Fisher and W. Ochsenwald, *The Middle East: A History** (rev., 1990), cited earlier, while nineteenth-century economic developments are examined in R. Owen, *The Middle East and the World Economy, 1800–1914* (1981), and in two books by C. Issawi: *The Economic History of the Middle East, 1800–1914* (1966), and *The Fertile Crescent, 1800–1914: A Documentary Economic History* (1988). For the role of the Ottoman Empire in European diplomacy and for national stirrings in the empire, two books cited in Chapter XI by M. S. Anderson (1966) and M. E. Yapp (1988)* are instructive for these years. Older but valuable diplomatic studies include R. W. Seton-Watson, *Disraeli, Gladstone, and the Eastern Question* (1935); W. N. Medlicott, *The Congress of Berlin and After: A Diplomatic History of the Near Eastern Settlement, 1878–1880* (1938, 1963); E. M. Earle, *Turkey, the Great Powers, and the Bagdad Railway* (1923); and M. K. Chapman, *Great Britain and the Bagdad Railway* (1948).

Other recommended books are J. Haslip, *The Sultan: The Life of Abdul Hamid II* (1958), a vivid scholarly account with insight into the empire; R. H. Davison, *Reform in the Ottoman Empire, 1856–1876* (1963); and D. Kushner, *The Rise of Turkish Nationalism, 1876–1908* (1977). For Egypt, there are available H. Dodwell, *The Founder of Modern Egypt: A Study of Muhammad Ali [Mehemet Ali]* (1931); D. S. Landes, *Bankers and Pashas: International Finance and Economic Imperialism in Egypt** (1958); P. Grau, *Islamic Roots of Capitalism: Egypt, 1760–1840* (1979); and R. L. Tignor, *Modernization and British Colonial Rule in Egypt, 1882–1914* (1966). The diplomacy surrounding the construction of the Suez Canal may be studied in J. Marlowe, *World Ditch: The Making of the Suez Canal* (1964); J. Pudney, *Suez: De Lesseps' Canal* (1969); and P. Balfour, *Between Two Seas* (1969). The French experience in Lebanon is examined in J. F. Spagnolo, *French and Ottoman Lebanon, 1861–1914* (1977), which may be supplemented by C. M. Andrew and A. S. Kanya-Forstner, *The Climax of French Imperial Expansion, 1914–1924* (1981); and the Italian experience in Libya is studied in C. G. Segré, *Fourth Shore: The Italian Colonization of Libya* (1975).

For the rivalries in the Balkans and the emergent nationalist movements there, in addition to books cited earlier in Chapter XI, one may turn to B. H. Sumner, *Russia and the Balkans, 1870–1880* (1937); C. Jelavich, *Tsarist Russia and Balkan Nationalism* (1958); G. J. Bobango, *The Emergence of the Romanian National State* (1979); and W. C. Vucinich, *Serbia Between East and West: The Events of 1903–1908* (1954).

Africa

Introductions to African history include J. D. Fage, *A History of Africa** (rev., 1989); B. Davidson, *Africa in History** (rev., 1974); P. D. Curtin, S. Feierman, L. Thompson, and J. Vansina, *African History** (1978); and R. W. July, *A History of the African People** (rev., 1980). A. E. Afigbo, E. A. Ayandele, and other African historians study the continent over the past two centuries in *The Making of Modern Africa* (2 vols.; rev., 1986). In the Cambridge History of Africa Vol. V (1977) and Vol. VI (1985) cover the years of colonial domination and the African response, while these years are also studied in J. F. Ade Ajayi (ed.), *Africa in the Nineteenth Century until the 1880s* (1989), and A. Adu Boahen (ed.), *Africa under Colonial Domination, 1880–1935** (1985; abr. ed. 1990), Vols. VI and VII respectively of the UNESCO General History of Africa.

Vivid accounts on a grand scale are R. Hallett, *Africa to 1875* (1970) and *Africa Since 1875* (1974); in these books and in *The Penetration of Africa: European Exploration in North and West Africa to 1815* (1965), the author seeks to examine the inner workings of African society as well as the European impact. Many insights are also provided in C. Coquery-Vidrovitch, *Africa: Endurance and Change South of the Sahara* (1989), and in D. Lamb, *The Africans** (1983). The use of "oral tradition" in the reconstruction of African history is explained in J. Vansina, *Oral Tradition: A Study of Historical Methodology* (1963), and demonstrated by the same author in *Kingdoms of the Savanna** (1966).

P. Duignan and L. H. Gann, *Burden of Empire: An Appraisal of Western Colonialism South of the Sahara* (1967), and their other writings emphasize a "benevolent imperialism" and attempt to demonstrate that the benefits of European expansion outweighed the debits. The same writers have co-edited a five-volume collaborative history, *Colonialism in Africa, 1870–1960* (1969–1973). In three additional books they focus on colonial administration: *The Rulers of German Africa, 1884–1914* (1977); *The Rulers of British Africa, 1870–1914* (1978); and *The Rulers of Belgian Africa, 1884–1914* (1979); and they have co-edited *African Proconsuls: European Governors in Africa* (1978). For a contrasting point of view, many of the books cited earlier and A. Adu Boahen, *African Perspectives on Colonialism** (1989), should be read.

A well-balanced synthesis is H. S. Wilson, *The Imperial Experience in Sub-Saharan Africa Since 1870* (1977), and two books by W. B. Cohen are also recommended: *Rulers of Empire: The French Colonial Service in Africa* (1971), and *The French Encounter with Africans: White Response to Blacks, 1530–1880* (1981). On the slave trade and its abolition, in addition to works cited in Chapter XI and earlier, one may read B. Davidson, *Black Mother: The Years of the African Slave Trade* (1961), and on the Brussels conference of 1889, S. Miers, *Britain and the Ending of the Slave Trade* (1975).

There are biographical studies of Livingstone by J. Simmons (1955), G. Seaver (1957), F. Debenham (1953), and O. Ransford (1978); the last is psychologically oriented. Other leading figures are examined in R. Hall, *Stanley: An Adventurer Explored* (1976), highly informative; R. Oliver, *Sir Harry Johnston and the Scramble for Africa* (1957); G. Elton, *Gordon of Khartoum* (1954); J. Marlowe, *Mission to Khartoum* (1969); and M. F. Perham, *Lugard: The Years of Adventure, 1858–1898* (1936), an impressive work. For Kitchener, the somewhat adulatory P. Warner, *Kitchener: The Man Behind the Legend* (1986), may be compared with the more critical T. Royle, *The Kitchener Enigma* (1986). The good, brief biography of Cecil Rhodes by J. Flint (1976) may still be read, but R. I. Rotberg, *The Founder: Cecil Rhodes and the Pursuit of Power** (1988), is an outstanding study enriched by psychological insights. For a biography of the African leader who defeated the Italians at Adowa, one may read H. G. Marcus, *The Life and Times of Menelik II: Ethiopia, 1844–1913* (1975).

The best study of the Congo to 1908 is R. Slade, *King Leopold's Congo* (1962), on which one may also read N. Ascherson, *The King Incorporated* (1963), and R. Anstey, *King Leopold's Legacy* (1966); Anstey has also written *Britain and the Congo in the Nineteenth Century* (1962).

For Southern Africa and the emergence of the Union of South Africa L. Thompson, *A History of South Africa* (1990), is a superb synthesis. Two other general accounts are D. Denoon and B. Nyeko, *Southern Africa Since 1800** (rev., 1984), and K. Shillington, *History of Southern Africa** (1987). For the late nineteenth century one may also read D. M. Schreuder, *The Scramble for Southern Africa, 1877–1895* (1981), and on an episode of the Anglo-Zulu war, R. B. Edgerton, *Like Lions They Fought: The Zulu War and the Last Black Empire in South Africa* (1988).

The South African War of 1899–1902 is recounted in B. Farwell, *The Great Anglo-Boer War* (1976), and T. Pakenham, *The Boer War* (1979). Two interesting biographical accounts relating to these years are B. Williams, *Botha, Smuts, and South Africa* (Teach Yourself History series, 1948), and K. Ingham, *Jan Christian Smuts: The Conscience of a South African* (1986).

Asia

Among informative general surveys of the European impact on Asia are J. Pratt, *The Expansion of Europe in the Far East* (1947); K. M. Pannikar, *Asia and Western Dominance: The Vasco da Gama Epoch of Asian History, 1498–1945** (rev., 1950), cited in Chapter VI; P. H. Clyde and B. F. Beers, *The Far East: A History of Western Impacts and Eastern Responses, 1830–1974* (rev., 1975); E. S. Dodge, *Islands and Empires: Western Impact on the Pacific and East Asia* (1976); and R. Murphey, *The Outsiders: The Western Experience in India and China* (1977), a challenging book which disputes some of Pannikar's conclusions.

For nineteenth-century developments in India, in addition to books described in Chapter VI, one may read P. J. Griffiths, *The British Impact on India* (1952); M. Edwardes, *British India, 1772–1947* (1968); W. Golant, *The Long Afternoon: British India, 1601–1947* (1975); and M. E. Chamberlain, *Britain and India: The Interactions of the Peoples* (1974), which shows how little control the British had over forces shaping Indian society. On the revolt of 1857 and its consequences one may read S. Sen, *Eighteen Fifty Seven* (1957); C. Hibbert, *The Great Mutiny: India 1857** (1980); E. Stokes and C. A. Bayly, *The Peasant Armed: The Indian Rebellion of 1857* (1986); and T. R. Metcalf, *The Aftermath of Revolt: India, 1857–1870* (1964).

The best introduction to East Asia is J. K. Fairbank, E. O. Reischauer, and A. M. Craig, *East Asia: Tradition and Transformation** (rev., 1989). Good overviews of Chinese history include C. P. Fitzgerald, *China: A Short Cultural History* (rev., 1961); L. C. Goodrich, *A Short History of the Chinese People* (rev., 1959); C. O. Hucker, *China's Imperial Past: An Introduction to Chinese History and Culture** (1975); N. F. Sizer, *China: A Brief History** (1981); and I. C. Y. Hsu, *The Rise of Modern China* (rev., 1989). The first volumes (1979) of the collaborative Cambridge History of China (D. Twitchett and J. K. Fairbank, gen. eds.), cover the late Ch'ing (or Manchu) period, 1800–1911. The decay of the Ming dynasty, the Manchu conquest, and the consolidation of Manchu rule are recounted in F. Wakeman, Jr., *The Great Enterprise: The Manchu Reconstruction of Imperial Order in Seventeenth Century China* (2 vols., 1985). J. Spence, *The Search for Modern China* (1990), is a masterful study going back over four centuries with perceptive insights into China's relations with the West. The same author's *The Gate of Heavenly Peace: The Chinese and Their Revolution, 1895–1980** (1981) links earlier history to twentieth-century revolution. This link is the subject also of J. K. Fairbank, *The Great Chinese Revolution, 1800–1985** (1986), the distillation of many years of reflection by a distinguished scholar; and of R. A. Scalopino and G. T. Yu, *Modern China and Its Revolutionary Process: Recurrent Challenges to the Traditional Order, 1850–1920* (1988).

A massive, authoritative study of the mid-nineteenth century Taiping upheaval is Jen Yu-wen, *The Taiping Revolutionary Movement* (1973), but one may also read S. Y. Teng, *The Taiping Rebellion and the Western Powers* (rev., 1977). European relations with China, including the Opium Wars, are studied in J. K. Fairbank, *Trade and Diplomacy on the China Coast: The Opening of the Treaty Ports, 1842–1854** (2 vols., 1953); Ssu-yu Teng and J. K. Fairbank, *China's Response to the West: A Documentary Survey, 1839–1923** (1954–1963); and in other books on the Opium Wars by J. Beeching (1976), P. W. Fay

(1975), and B. Ingles (1976). The anti-foreign upheaval of 1898–1900 is examined in V. Purcell, *The Boxer Uprising* (1963), and J. W. Esherick, *The Origins of the Boxer Uprising** (1987).

On the United States role in the Far East and the Open Door policy one may read M. H. Hunt, *Frontier Defense and the Open Door: Manchuria in Chinese American Relations, 1895–1911* (1973); W. Cohen, *America's Response to China* (rev., 1980); and J. C. Thomsen, Jr., P. W. Stanley, and J. C. Perry, *Sentimental Imperialists: The American Experience in East Asia* (1981). For the confrontation between Russia and Japan, one may read I. Nish, *The Origins of the Russo-Japanese War** (1985), while Russian foreign policy in broader scope is studied in B. H. Sumner, *Tsardom and Imperialism in the Far East and the Middle East, 1880–1914* (1942). For the story of the Russian fleet that was defeated at Tsushima by the Japanese, one may read A. Nobikov-Privoy, *Tsushima* (trans. 1944); F. Theiss, *The Voyage of Forgotten Men* (1947); and R. Hough, *The Fleet That Had To Die* (1958). The diplomatic history of the war is recounted in J. A. White, *The Diplomacy of the Russo-Japanese War* (1964), and an admirable general narrative is D. Walder, *The Short Victorious War: The Russo-Japanese Conflict, 1904–1905* (1975).

Problems and Readings*

Relevant titles include H. M. Wright (ed.), *The "New Imperialism": An Analysis of the Late Nineteenth Century Expansion* (rev., 1975); R. Owen and B. Sutcliffe (eds.), *Studies in the Theory of Imperialism* (1972); R. W. Winks (ed.), *British Imperialism: Gold, God, Glory* (1963); W. R. Louis (ed.), *Imperialism: The Robinson-Gallagher Controversy* (1976), cited earlier in this chapter; R. F. Betts (ed.), *The Scramble for Africa: Causes and Dimensions of Empire* (1966); R. I. Rotberg (ed.), *Africa and Its Explorers* (1970); T. C. Caldwell (ed.), *The Anglo-Boer War* (1965); and R. A. Austen (ed.), *Modern Imperialism: Western Overseas Expansion in the Age of Industrialization* (1969). On India, there are M. D. Lewis (ed.), *The British in India* (1962); P. J. Marshall (ed.), *Problems of Empire: Britain and India, 1757–1813* (1968); and A. T. Embree (ed.), *1857 in India: Mutiny or War of Independence?* (1963). A helpful anthology is G. Nadel and P. Curtis (eds.), *Imperialism and Colonialism* (1964).

XVI. The First World War

Diplomatic Background, Origins, Responsibilities

The most judicious account of the war's origins, assessing both the evidence and divergent interpretations, is J. Joll, *The Origins of the First World War** (1984). Two attempts to synthesize the protracted debate over war responsibility are J. W. Langdon, *July 1914: The long Debate: 1918–1990* (1991), and R. J. W. Evans and H. P. van Strandmann (eds.), *The Coming of the First World War* * (1989).

The war-guilt controversy was reopened after 1945 by the West German scholar Fritz Fischer, who on the basis of new archival materials reaffirmed German culpability in *Germany's Aims in the First World War** (1961; trans. 1967). Fischer also presents his interpretations in *War of Illusions: Germany's Policies, 1911–1914* (1969; trans. 1975); the brief *World Power or Decline: The Controversy over Germany's Aims in the First World War* (1965; trans. 1974); and *From Kaiserreich to Third Reich** (trans. 1986). His argument that Germany had to grasp for "world power" or would decline, and that domestic elite groups pressed this objective to thwart democratization, is reinforced by I. Geiss, *German Foreign Policy, 1871–1914* (1976).

Among older works of continuing value are S. B. Fay, *The Origins of the World War** (1928, 1930); B. E. Schmitt, *The Coming of the War, 1914* (2 vols., 1930); P. Renouvin, *The Immediate Origins of the War* (1928); N. Mansergh, *The Coming of the First World War: A Study in the European Balance, 1878–1914* (1949); and L. Albertini, *The Origins of the War of 1914* (3 vols., 1942–1943; trans. 1952–1957), an exhaustive account. A. J. P. Taylor, *The Struggle for Mastery in Europe, 1914–1918* (1954), cited in Chapter XIII, is invaluable. To it may be added Taylor's brief *War by Timetable: How the First World War Began* (1969).

On diplomacy in the decades after 1870, there are the older important studies by W. L. Langer: *European Alliances and Alignments, 1871–1890** (1931, 1950); *The Franco-Russian Alliance, 1880–1894* (1929); and *The Diplomacy of Imperialism, 1890–1902* (2 vols., 1935), the last cited in the previous chapter. A masterful diplomatic account with added insights is in two volumes by the diplomat-historian G. F. Kennan, *The Decline of Bismarck's European Order: Franco-Russian Relations, 1875–1890** (1979), and *The Fateful Alliance: France, Russia, and the Coming of the First World War** (1984).

D. E. Lee's careful study, *Europe's Crucial Years: The Diplomatic Background of World War I, 1902–1914* (1974), reaffirms the argument that each state acted out of desperation in defense of its own presumed interests. Successful efforts in a British series to study domestic and foreign considerations together, in keeping with the newer emphases of diplomatic historians, are V. R. Berghahn, *Germany and the Approach of War in 1914* (1973); Z. S. Steiner, *Britain and the Origins of the First World War* (1977); R. J. B. Bosworth, *Italy, the Least of the Great Powers: Italian Foreign Policy Before the First World War* (1980); J. F. V. Krieger, *France and the Origins of the First World War* (1984); and D. C. B. Lieven, *Russia and the Origins of the First World War* (1984). Three volumes in another British series on foreign policy are also valuable for these years: J. Néré, *The Foreign Policy of France from 1914 to 1945* (trans. 1975); F. R. Bridge, *From Sadowa to Sarajevo: The Foreign Policy of Austria-Hungary, 1866–1914* (1972); and C. J. Lowe and F. Marzari, *Italian Foreign Policy, 1870–1940* (1975). S. R. Williamson, Jr., *Austria-Hungary and the Origins of the First World War** (1991), assesses Austro-Hungarian responsibilities.

Among many specialized assessments of prewar diplomacy and strategic planning, a few stand out: J. A. S. Grenville, *Lord Salisbury and Foreign Policy: The Close of the Nineteenth Century, 1899–1914* (1964); G. Monger, *The End of Isolation: British Foreign Policy, 1900–1907* (1963); C. Andrew, *Théophile Delcassé and the Making of the Entente Cordiale: A Reappraisal of French Foreign Policy, 1898–1905* (1968); S. R. Williamson Jr., *The Politics of Grand Strategy: Britain and France Prepare for War, 1904–1914* (1969); P. M. Kennedy, *The Rise of the Anglo-German Antagonism, 1860–1914** (1980); the same author's *Strategy and Diplomacy, 1870–1945** (1984); and a collaborative volume he has edited, *War Plans of the Great Powers, 1880–1914** (1979). The Balkan antecedents of the war are examined in V. Dedijer, *The Road to Sarajevo* (1966); and two books that capture the mood of 1914 are J. Remak, *Sarajevo: The Story of a Political Murder* (1959), and J. Cameron, *1914* (1959).

On the United States involvement in the war, one may consult E. F. May, *The World War and American Isolation, 1914–1917** (1959), an outstanding study; R. Gregory, *The Origins of American Intervention in the First World War* (1971); P. Devlin, *Too Proud to Fight: Woodrow Wilson's Neutrality* (1974); J. J. Sanford, *Wilsonian Maritime Diplomacy* (1978); and R. H. Ferrell, *Woodrow Wilson and World War I* (1985). On a special subject, there is B. W. Tuchman, *The Zimmermann Telegram** (1985), while T. A. Bailey and P. B. Ryan, *The Lusitania Disaster: An Episode in Modern Warfare and Diplomacy* (1975), makes a case for the German legal position.

The War

For the war there are good narrative accounts by, among others, B. H. Liddell Hart* (1934), C. R. M. Cruttwell, (1934, (1990), C. B. Falls* (1959), and H. Baldwin* (1962). Recommended also is the *American Heritage History of World War I* (1964), superbly illustrated, with the narrative by S. L. A. Marshall; and A. J. P. Taylor, *An Illustrated History of the First World War** (1964). More recent accounts examining both military aspects and the social impact of the war include: M. Ferro, *The Great War, 1914–1918** (trans. 1973); K. Robbins, *The First World War** (1984); B. E. Schmitt and H. C. Vedeler, *The World in the Crucible, 1914–1919** (1984), in the Langer series; and J. M. Winter, *The Experience of World War I* (1989). On the opening phase of the war, B. W. Tuchman, *The Guns of August* (1962), is a gripping account. G. Ritter, *The Schlieffen Plan* (trans. 1958), is a valuable analysis, but L. L. Farrar, *The Short-War Illusion** (1973), also should be consulted. A small sampling of literature on various episodes of the war would include: R. Rhodes James, *Gallipoli* (1965); A. Horne, *The Price of Glory: Verdun, 1916** (1963); R. M. Watt, *Dare Call it Treason* (1963), on the French army mutinies of 1917; and J. Terraine, *To Win a War: 1918, The Year of Victory* (1981). The war in eastern Europe is graphically described in N. Stone, *The Eastern Front, 1914–1917* (1976), and the naval war in R. Hough, *The Great War at Sea, 1914–1918** (1984). Strategy and decision-making are studied in F. Maurice, *Lessons of Allied Co-operation: Naval, Military and Air, 1914–1918* (1942); M. Hankey, *The Supreme Command, 1914–1918* (2 vols., 1961); and C. Barnett, *The Swordbearers: The Supreme Command in the First World War* (1963).

Books that seek to convey the ordeal of trench warfare on the Western Front include: E. J. Leed, *No Man's Land: Combat and Identity in World War I* (1979); T. Ashworth, *Trench Warfare, 1914–1918: The Live and Let-Live System* (1980); and J. Ellis, *Eye-Deep in Hell: Trench Warfare in World War I** (1989). Ellis has also written *The Social History of the Machine Gun** (1986). J. Keegan, *The Face of Battle* (1976), in one memorable chapter evokes the horrors of the Somme. For the American military experience one may read E. M. Coffman, *The War to End All Wars* (1969). A special subject is examined in L. F. Haber, *The Poisonous Cloud: Chemical Warfare in the First World War* (1980), and E. M. Spiers, *Chemical Warfare* (1986).

P. Fussell, *The Great War and Modern Memory** (1975), is a moving account of how the miseries of the war became part of contemporary literature and culture. Two other studies of the intellectual impact of the war are R. N. Stromberg, *Redemption by War: The Intellectuals and 1914* (1982), and M. Ecksteins, *The Rites of Spring: The Great War and the Birth of the Modern Age* (1989), an ambitious inquiry into the war's effect on the shaping of a new cultural consciousness.

The Home Front: Social and Economic Impact of the War

For the impact of war and preparations for war on European society from the late nineteenth century on, one should read B. Bond, *War and Society in Europe, 1870–1970** (1986). The significance of war for social change is also examined in A. Marwick, *War and Social Change in the Twentieth Century: A Comparative Study of Britain, France, Germany, Russia, and the United States* (1975). G. Hardach, *The First World War, 1914–1918* (History of the World Economy in the Twentieth Century series, 1977), is a valuable study focusing on all economic aspects of the war and its consequences. There are many informative studies hidden away in the older multivolume Carnegie Endowment *Economic and Social*

History of the World War (J. T. Shotwell, gen. ed., 1924–1940), of which over one hundred volumes were published.

For the war on the home front one may turn to F. Chambers, *The War Behind the War, 1914–1918* (1939), an older but still valuable account; J. Williams, *The Other Battleground: The Home Fronts—Britain, France and Germany, 1914–1918* (1972); and the essays in R. Wall and J. Winter (eds.), *The Upheaval of War: Family, Work, and Welfare in Europe, 1914–1918* (1989). For Britain, one may read J. M. Winter, *The Great War and the British People* (1986), an outstanding study; A. Marwick, *The Deluge: British Society and the First World War* (1965); T. Wilson, *The Myriad Faces of War: Britain and the Great War, 1914–1918* (1986); B. Waites, *A Class Society at War: England, 1914–1918* (1988); and J. Bourne, *Britain and the Great War, 1914–1918** (1989). The domestic front in other countries is studied in J. Kocka, *Facing Total War: German Society, 1914–1918* (trans. 1984); J.-J. Becker, *The Great War and the French People** (trans. 1986), P. J. Flood, *France, 1914–1918; Public Opinion and the War Effort* (1989); D. M. Kennedy, *Over Here: The First World War and American Society* (1980).

The contributions of women to the war effort are examined in A. Marwick, *Women at War, 1914–1918* (1977); G. Braybon, *Women Workers in the First World War: The British Experience** (1981); and M. W. Greenwald, *Women, War, and Work: The Impact of World War I on Women Workers in the United States* (1980).

Political developments affecting the conduct of the war are examined in E. L. Woodward, *Great Britain and the War of 1914–1918* (1967); P. Guinn, *British Strategy and Policies, 1914–1918* (1965); J. C. King, *Generals and Politicians: Conflict Between France's High Command, Parliament, and Government, 1914–1918* (1951); G. D. Feldman, *Army, Industry, and Labor in Germany, 1914–1918* (1986); and R. B. Armeson, *Total Warfare and Compulsory Labor* (1964), also on Germany. The final volume of G. Ritter, *The Sword and the Scepter: The Problem of Militarism in Germany*, Vol. IV, *The Reign of German Militarism and the Disaster of 1918* (trans. 1973), describes the misuse of the power that the German generals preempted. The dictatorship of the military leaders is examined with telling detail in M. Kitchen, *The Silent Dictator-*

ship: *The Politics of the German High Command under Hindenburg and Ludendorff, 1916–1918* (1976).

The growth of socialist and radical movements opposing the war as it went on may be studied in M. Fainsod, *International Socialism and the World War* (1935), and in F. L. Carsten, *War Against War: British and German Radical Movements in the First World War* (1982).

On the human costs of the war, one may consult T. J. Mitchell and G. M. Smith, *Medical Services: Casualties and Medical Statistics of the Great War* (1931); and for the devastating worldwide influenza epidemic that doubled the combat toll, A. W. Crosby, *America's'Forgotten Pandemic: The Influenza of 1918** (1976, 1990).

One of the less-known tragedies of war, the forced deportation of the Armenians by the Turkish authorities, is recounted in D. H. Boyajian, *Armenia: The Case for a Forgotten Genocide* (1972); C. J. Walker, *Armenia: The Survival of a Nation* (rev. 1990); and D. M. Lang, *The Armenians: A People in Exile** (1989).

Wartime Diplomacy

For wartime diplomacy one will profit from D. Stevenson, *The First World War and International Politics* (1988), and Z. A. B. Zeman, *The Gentlemen Negotiators: A Diplomatic History of the First World War* (1971). The evolution of Allied war objectives is examined in D. Stevenson, *French War Aims Against Germany* (1982), and in V. H. Rothwell, *British War Aims and Peace Diplomacy, 1914–1918* (1971). Two provocative studies focusing on the diplomatic duel between the United States and Russia are V. S. Mamatey, *The United States and East Central Europe, 1914–1918* (1957), and A. J. Mayer, *Political Origins of the New Diplomacy, 1917–1918* (1959). The fate of the German colonial empire is explored in W. R. Louis, *Great Britain and Germany's Lost Colonies, 1914–1919* (1967).

For Allied activities in the Middle East, T. E. Lawrence, *Seven Pillars of Wisdom: A Triumph** (1926, 1935), on the revolt of the Arabs against the Turks, is a fascinating account but must be read with caution, and should be supplemented by C. E. Dawn, *From Ottomanism to Arabism* (1973), and other studies on the twentieth-century origins of Arab nationalism. Also focusing on the Middle East and the end of the

Ottoman Empire are E. Kedourie, *England and the Middle East* (1956), on the years 1914–1921; H. M. Sachar, *The Emergence of the Middle East, 1914–1924* (1969); E. Monroe, *Britain's Moment in the Middle East 1914–1971* (rev., 1981); and P. C. Helmreich, *From Paris to Sèvres: The Partition of the Ottoman Empire at the Peace Conference of 1919–1920* (1974).

The Balfour Declaration of 1917 and the emergence of the British mandate for Palestine are studied in impressive detail in four books: L. Stein, *The Balfour Declaration* (1961); two volumes by I. Friedman: *The Question of Palestine, 1914–1918: British, Jewish, Arab Relations* (1973) and *Germany, Turkey, and Zionism, 1897–1918* (1977); and R. Sanders, *The High Walls of Jerusalem: A History of the Balfour Declaration and the Birth of the British Mandate* (1984).

The Peace

For the armistice, one may turn to F. Maurice, *The Armistice of 1918* (1943); H. R. Rudin, *Armistice, 1918* (1944); and S. Weintraub, *A Stillness Heard Round the World: The End of the Great War, November 1918** (1987), a colorful evocation of the war's end. The revolutionary mood of the early postwar era is described in G. Schulz, *Revolution and Peace Treaties, 1917–1920* (trans. 1972); in F. L. Carsten, *Revolution in Central Europe, 1918–1919* (1972); and in the essays in C. L. Bertrand (ed.), *Revolutionary Situations in Europe, 1917–1922* (1977). The end of the Habsburg empire is studied in A. J. May, *The Passing of the Hapsburg Monarchy, 1914–1918* (2 vols., 1966), and Z. A. B. Zeman, *The Breakup of the Habsburg Empire, 1914–1918* (1961). The British policy toward the independence movements in central and eastern Europe is explored in K. J. Calder, *Britain and the Origins of the New Europe, 1914–1918* (1976).

On the Paris peace conference, the best brief account remains P. Birdsall, *Versailles Twenty Years After* (1941), sympathetic to Wilson. C. L. Mee, *The End of Order: Versailles, 1919* (1980) is a popular, oversimplified account. H. Nicholson, *Peacemaking, 1919* (1933, 1939), and G. B. Noble, *Policies and Opinions at Paris, 1919* (1935), describe the climate in which the momentous decisions were reached, and the decision-making process itself is studied in H. Elcock, *Portrait of a Decision: The Council of Four and the Treaty of Versailles* (1972). The debates were later made available in P. Mantoux (ed.), *The Paris Peace Conference, 1919: Proceedings of the Council of Four* (1955; trans. 1964).

British policy is explored with insight in M. L. Dockrill and J. E. Goold, *Peace Without Promise: Britain and the Peace Conferences, 1919–1923* (1981). On Wilson's role, the best study is A. Walworth, *Wilson and His Peacemakers: American Diplomacy at the Paris Peace Conference, 1919* (1987); one should also read two studies by Wilson's biographer, A. S. Link: *Wilson the Diplomatist* (1957), and *Woodrow Wilson: War, Revolution, and Peace* (1979). Biographies of Clemenceau by D. R. Watson, and of David Lloyd George by Grigg and others have been cited in Chapter XIV. For Orlando and the Italian role one may read R. Albrecht-Carrie, *Italy at the Paris Peace Conference* (1938), older but still helpful.

A brilliant although not entirely convincing study arguing that the major preoccupation underlying decisions at Versailles was the threat of Bolshevism and domestic radicalism is A. J. Mayer, *Politics and Diplomacy of Peacemaking: Containment and Counter-Revolution at Versailles, 1918–1919* (1967); it may be compared with J. M. Thompson, *Russia, Bolshevism, and the Versailles Peace* (1966), which views the revolutionary threat as important but not dominating.

In addition to S. Bonsal, *Suitors and Suppliants: The Little Nations at Versailles* (1946), there are also monographs on many of the smaller countries: F. Deak on Hungary (1942), D. Perman on Czechoslovakia (1962), D. Spector on Romania (1962), T. Komarnicki on Poland (1957), I. J. Lederer on Yugoslavia (1963), and S. Marks on Belgium (1981). The Polish question is carefully examined by a Danish historian, K. Lundrgreen-Nielsen, *The Polish Problem at the Paris Peace Conference* (trans. 1979). J. C. King explores a special subject in *Foch versus Clemenceau: France and German Dismemberment, 1918–1919* (1960), which may be supplemented by W. A. McDougall, *France's Rhineland Diplomacy, 1914–1924: The Last Bid for a Balance of Power in Europe* (1978), a study equally valuable for postwar developments. One of the most hotly disputed issues was reparations, on which J. M. Keynes, *The Economic Consequences of the Peace* (1920), became the most influential single book, vehemently

critical of the entire peace settlement. E. Mantoux, *The Carthaginian Peace—or the Economic Consequences of Mr. Keynes* (1946), is a vigorous reply to Keynes written many years later. The first volume of what promises to be an outstanding study, R. Skidelsky, *John Maynard Keynes: A Biography,* Vol. I, *Hopes Betrayed, 1883–1920** (1986), carries Keynes through the peace conference.

The creation of the League of Nations is explored in H. R. Winkler, *The League of Nations Movement in Great Britain, 1914–1919* (1952), and in G. W. Egerton, *Great Britain and the Creation of the League of Nations: Strategy, Politics, and International Organization, 1914–1919* (1978). A useful reference work for this and subsequent chapters is J. A. S. Grenville (ed.), *The Major International Treaties, 1914–1945: A History and Guide with Texts* (1988), and its sequel volume for the years after 1945, edited by J. A. S. Grenville and B. Wasserstein (1988).

*Problems and Readings**

Pamphlets relating to the war include D. E. Lee (ed.), *The Outbreak of the First World War* (rev., 1976); J. Remak (ed.), *The First World War: Causes, Conduct, Consequences* (1971); H. W. Koch (ed.), *The Origins of the First World War* (1972); I. Geiss (ed.), *July 1914* (1969); and H. H. Herwig (ed.), *The Outbreak of World War I* (1990). For the peace settlement there are I. J. Lederer (ed.), *The Versailles Settlement: Was It Foredoomed to Failure?* (1960); and T. P. Greene (ed.), *Wilson at Versailles* (1957). The war as a whole may be assessed in R. Albrecht-Carrié (ed.), *The Meaning of the First World War* (1965), and J. J. Roth (ed.), *World War I: A Turning Point in Modern History* (1967). Useful for one category of published sources on diplomacy is F. M. Messick (ed.), *Primary Sources in European Diplomacy: A Bibliography of Published Memoirs and Diaries* (1987).

XVII. The Russian Revolution and the Soviet Union

Russia Before 1917: Late Tsarist Russia

For the situation in nineteenth-century Russia the reader should also consult the books cited in Chapter XIII. For late tsarist Russia specifically, one may read H. Rogger, *Russia in the Age of Modernization and Revolution, 1881–1917** (1983), and L. Kochan, *Russia in Revolution, 1890–1918* (1966). Economic change and modernization are also discussed in T. H. Von Laue, *Sergei Witte and the Industrialization of Russia** (1963).

Political thought and ferment may be studied in F. Venturi, *Roots of Revolution** (trans. 1983), cited earlier; A. P. Mendel, *Dilemmas of Progress in Tsarist Russia* (1961); and A. Vucinich, *Social Thought in Tsarist Russia: The Quest for a General Science of Society, 1861–1917* (1976). The world of labor is examined in V. E. Bonnell, *Roots of Rebellion: Workers' Politics and Organizations in St. Petersburg and Moscow, 1900–1914* (1983), and in the volume she has edited of workers' autobiographical accounts, *The Russian Worker: Life and Labor Under the Tsarist Regime** (1983). For the rural world G. T. Robinson, *Rural Russia Under the Old Regime** (1930, 1980), also cited earlier, remains valuable.

Political leaders who served the tsar are studied in R. F. Byrnes, *Pobedonostsev: His Life and Thought* (1968), an exemplar of tsarist obscurantism; and R. Pipes, *Struve* (2 vols., 1970–1980), informative on the sad fate of liberalism. For the emergent revolutionary leaders, in addition to biographies cited later, one may read D. W. Treadgold, *Lenin and His Rivals: The Struggle for Russia's Future, 1898–1906* (1950); L. Haimson, *The Russian Marxists and the Origins of Bolshevism* (1955); I. Getzler, *Martov* (1967); S. H. Baron, *Plekhanov: The Father of Russian Marxism** (1963); and A. Ascher, *Pavel Axelrod and the Development of Menshevism* (1972). On the anarchists, there is P. Avrich, *The Russian Anarchists* (1967); and on a leading exemplar: G. Woodcock and I. Avukamovic, *The Anarchist Prince* (1950); M. A. Miller, *Kropotkin* (1976); and C. Cahm, *Peter Kropotkin and the Rise of Revolutionary Anarchism* (1989).

The events of 1905 are narrated and analyzed in S. Harcave, *First Blood: The Russian Revolution of 1905* (1964); W. Sablinsky, *The Road to Bloody Sunday: Father Gapon and the St. Petersburg Massacre of 1905* (1976); A. Ascher, *The Revolution of 1905: Russia in Disarray* (1988), an outstanding account; and A. M. Verner, *The Crisis of Russian Autocracy: Nicholas II and the 1905 Revolution* (1990). A key insti-

tution originating in the 1905 revolution is studied in O. Anweiler, *The Soviets: The Russian Workers, Peasants, and Soldiers Councils, 1905–1921* (trans. 1975).

Explorations of the ill-fated effort to establish a constitutional monarchy after the 1905 upheaval include A. E. Healy, *The Russian Autocracy in Crisis, 1905–1907* (1976); A. Levin's two studies: *The Second Duma* (1940, 1966) and its sequel, *The Third Duma: Election and Profile* (1973); and G. A. Hosking, *The Russian Constitutional Experiment: Government and Duma, 1906–1914* (1973). The prewar years and the wartime experience are vividly described in W. B. Lincoln, *In War's Dark Shadow* (1983) and *Passage Through Armageddon* (1986), while the confusion at the court graphically emerges from R. K. Massie, *Nicholas and Alexandra* (1967).

The Revolutions of 1917

The best account of the February revolution is T. Hasegawa, *The February Revolution: Petrograd, 1917* (1981); other informative studies are G. Katkov, *Russia 1917: The February Revolution* (1967); M. Ferro, *The Russian Revolution of February 1917* (1971); and E. N. Burdzhalov, *Russia's Second Revolution: The February 1917 Uprising in Petrograd** (1987). The ill-fated Kerensky is studied on R. Abraham, *Alexander Kerensky: The First Love of the Revolution* (1987).

For the Bolshevik revolution one may turn to J. M. Thompson, *Revolutionary Russia, 1917** (1981); R. V. Daniels, *Red October: The Bolshevik Revolution of 1917** (rev., 1984); R. Medvedev, *The October Revolution** (trans. 1985); and the fullest and most comprehensive account, R. Pipes, *The Russian Revolution* (1990). Focusing on the social breadth and depth of the revolution are two books by M. Ferro: *The Fall of Tsarism and the Origins of Bolshevik Power* (trans. 1967) and *October 1917: A Social History of the Russian Revolution* (trans. 1980). Other informative studies on the social dimensions of the upheaval include J. L. H. Keep, *The Russian Revolution: A Study in Mass Mobilization* (1977); A. Rabinowitch, *The Bolsheviks Come to Power: The Revolution of 1917 in Petrograd* (1977); D. Koenker, *Moscow Workers and the 1917 Revolution* (1981); and T. McDaniel, *Autocracy, Capitalism, and Revolution in Russia** (1988). The dissolution of the army and much else is covered in A. K.

Wildman, *The End of the Russian Imperial Army* (2 vols., 1980–1987), and the peasants' role is studied in G. J. Gill, *Peasants and Government in the Russian Revolution* (1979).

The best introductions to the civil war, the formation of the Soviet state, and foreign intervention are E. Mawdsley, *The Russian Civil War** (1987), and W. B. Lincoln, *Red Victory: A History of the Russian Civil War* (1990). The reconquest of the Ukraine and of other parts of the tsarist empire that for a time became independent is described in R. Pipes, *The Formation of the Soviet Union: Communism and Nationalism, 1917–1923** (rev., 1964). For the withdrawal from the war and the subsequent Allied intervention there are available G. F. Kennan's admirable *Soviet-American Relations, 1917–1920* (2 vols., 1956–1958), Vol. I, *Russia Leaves the War** and Vol. II, *The Decision to Intervene**. R. H. Ullman, *Anglo-Soviet Relations, 1917–1921* (3 vols., 1961–1972), is a masterful account of the British role in the intervention. The best study of the peace imposed by Germany is J. W. Wheeler-Bennett, *The Forgotten Peace: Brest-Litovsk, March 1918* (1939), and the stormy relations of the Soviets with newly independent Poland are described in P. S. Wandycz, *Soviet-Polish Relations, 1917–1921* (1969). An authoritative reference guide for all these events is H. Shukman (ed.), *The Blackwell Encyclopedia of the Russian Revolution* (1988).

The U.S.S.R.

For the early years important monographs include: L. Schapiro, *The Origins of the Communist Autocracy: Political Opposition in the Soviet State, 1917–1922* (1955), especially insightful; the same author's *1917: The Russian Revolutions and the Origins of Present-Day Communism* (1984); W. G. Rosenberg, *Liberals in the Russian Revolution: The Constitutional Democratic Party, 1917–1921* (1974); and P. Avrich, *Kronstadt, 1921** (1970, 1991), on the leftist uprising and its suppression by the Bolsheviks. An institution that was destined to endure is studied in L. D. Gerson, *The Secret Police in Lenin's Russia* (1976), and G. Leggett, *The Cheka: Lenin's Political Police** (1981).

For the years under Lenin and the early years of Stalin's rule the most comprehensive account in any language is E. H. Carr's massive *A History of Soviet Russia* (14

vols., 1950–1979), with a one-volume synthesis, *The Russian Revolution from Lenin to Stalin* (1979), in which Carr seeks to make the best possible case for the reconstruction of Soviet society in the years 1917 to 1929. Focusing on sociological and cultural change in this period are S. Fitzpatrick, *The Russian Revolution, 1917–1932** (1982), and R. Stites, *Revolutionary Dreams: Utopian Vision and Experimental Life in the Russian Revolution* (1989), while G. Hosking, *The First Socialist Society: A History of the Soviet Union from Within** (1985) carries his comprehensive social history toward the present. For all aspects of economic developments from 1917 on, one must turn to A. Nove, *An Economic History of the U.S.S.R.** (rev., 1989). For Lenin's New Economic Policy, one may also read A. M. Ball, *Russia's Last Capitalists: The Nepmen, 1921–1929* (1988). Soviet society and the economy before Stalin's tightened grip on the country are described in M. Reiman, *The Birth of Stalinism: The U.S.S.R. on the Eve of the "Second Revolution"* (trans. 1987).

Russian agriculture is examined in perspective in L. Volin, *A Century of Russian Agriculture: From Alexander II to Khrushchev* (1970). Collectivization as a prelude to the First Five-Year Plan is studied in great detail in the first three volumes of R. W. Davies, *The Industrialization of Soviet Russia:* Vol. I, *The Socialist Offensive: The Collectivization of Soviet Agriculture, 1929–1930* (1980); Vol. II, *The Soviet Collective Farm, 1929–1930* (1980); and Vol. III, *The Soviet Economy in Turmoil, 1929–1930* (1989). Especially insightful is M. Lewin, *Russian Peasants and Soviet Power: A Study of Collectivization* (trans. 1975), while R. Conquest, *The Harvest of Sorrow: Soviet Collectivization and the Terror-Famine** (1987) graphically reconstructs the ruthlessness of collectivization and the accompanying famine of 1932 which, the author insists, Stalin encouraged in order to curb nationalist unrest in the Ukraine and elsewhere.

For the political terror in the Stalin era the most revealing studies are R. Medvedev, *Let History Judge: The Origins and Consequences of Stalinism* (1971; expanded and trans. 1989), by a Soviet dissident historian; and for the party purges and terror of 1936–1938, stressing the enormity of the blood bath, now officially conceded, R. Conquest, *The Great Terror: A Reassessment* (1968;

rev., 1990). Some of the corroborative new evidence surfacing in the years after 1985 is discussed in W. Laqueur, *Stalin: The Glasnost Revelations* (1990). The origins of the party purges are examined in R. Conquest, *Stalin and the Kirov Murder** (1988), and in J. A. Getty, *Origins of the Great Purges: The Soviet Communist Party Reconsidered, 1933–1938** (1986), a somewhat revisionist account. Three older studies may also be consulted: L. Schapiro, *The Communist Party of the Soviet Union** (1960); J. A. Armstrong, *The Politics of Totalitarianism: The Communist Party of the Soviet Union* (1961); and Z. B. Brzezinski, *The Permanent Purge: Politics in Soviet Totalitarianism* (1956). An insightful general account of the years from the Revolution to Stalin's death is H. Carrère d'Encausse, *A History of the Soviet Union, 1917–1953** (2 vols.; trans. 1982), Vol. I, *Lenin: Revolution and Power,* Vol. II, *Stalin: Order Through Terror.*

Biographical Accounts

Some excellent biographical accounts further illuminate these years. For the revolution and the early era there are B. D. Wolfe, *Three Who Made a Revolution: A Biographical History* [Lenin, Trotsky, Stalin]* (1948, 1964); C. Hill, *Lenin and the Russian Revolution** (Teach Yourself History series, 1947); H. Shukman, *Lenin and the Russian Revolution** (1987); and an informative study focusing on Lenin, A. B. Ulam, *The Bolsheviks: The Intellectual and Political History of the Triumph of Communism in Russia** (1965), reissued as *Lenin and the Bolsheviks** (1969). There are balanced lives of Lenin by D. Shub* (1948; reissued 1966); L. F. Fischer* (1964); M. C. Morgan (1971); and R. H. W. Theen (1973). The biographies by R. Payne* (1964) and by R. Conquest (1972) are highly critical. Lenin's wife and her fate in the Stalin years are ably studied in R. H. McNeal, *Bride of the Revolution: Krupskaya and Lenin* (1972). Of special interest is M. Lewin, *Lenin's Last Struggle** (1978).

I. Deutscher has written a vivid, although overly sympathetic, three-volume life of Trotsky (1954–1963); equally sympathetic is R. Segal, *Leon Trotsky* (1979). Two balanced appraisals are R. Wistrich, *Trotsky: Fate of a Revolutionary* (1979), and I. Howe, *Leon Trotsky* (1979).

An impressive study of Stalin in the years before the Second World War is R. C. Tucker, *Stalin as Revolutionary, 1879–1929* (1973), and *Stalin in Power: The Revolution from Above, 1928–1941* (1990). Another important study, A. B. Ulam, *Stalin: The Man and His Era** (1973), may be compared with the insightful but overly sympathetic I. Deutscher, *Stalin: A Political Biography** (1949, 1967). One may also read R. H. McNeal, *Stalin: Man and Ruler** (1988), and R. M. Slusser, *Stalin in October: The Man Who Missed the Revolution* (1987), arguing that the dictator compensated in later years for his lesser role in 1917. S. F. Cohen, *Bukharin and the Bolshevik Revolution: A Political Biography, 1888–1938** (1973), is an outstanding study of a leading Old Bolshevik who helped shape Lenin's New Economic Policy and had he prevailed might have steered Russia away from the Stalinist dictatorship. The career of another Old Bolshevik, a victim also of Stalin's terror, is recounted in W. Lerner, *Karl Radek: The Last Internationalist* (1970). An illuminating study of the opposition within the party is R. V. Daniels, *The Conscience of the Revolution** (1960).

Among thoughtful efforts to assess the Russian experience from the Revolution on into the interwar years and beyond are: T. H. Von Laue, *Why Lenin? Why Stalin? A Reappraisal of the Russian Revolution, 1900–1930** (1964); E. Acton, *Rethinking the Russian Revolution** (1990); A. Nove, *Was Stalin Really Necessary?* (1965); S. F. Cohen, *Rethinking the Soviet Experience: Politics and History Since 1917** (1985); and two books by M. Lewin: *The Making of the Soviet System: Essays in the Social History of Interwar Russia** (1985) and *The Gorbachev Phenomenon: A Historical Interpretation* (1988). Other such books will be described in later chapters.

Other Themes and Institutions

On other subjects and institutions one may read R. Kolkowitz, *The Soviet Military and the Communist Party* (1967); J. S. Curtiss, *The Russian Church and the Soviet State (1917–1941)* (1953); L. R. Graham, *Science and Philosophy in the Soviet Union* (1972); and C. V. James, *Soviet Socialist Realism* (1973), on the arts and literature. The historical background to the Jewish question is explored in S. W. Baron, *The Russian Jew under Tsars and Soviets* (1964), and examined in detail in two comprehensive studies: B. Pinkus, *The Jews of the Soviet Union: A History of a National Minority** (1988), and N. Levin, *The Jews in the Soviet Union: Paradox of Survival* (2 vols., 1988).

The role of women in the pre- and post-revolutionary years may be studied in R. Stites, *The Women's Liberation Movement in Russia: Feminism, Nihilism, and Bolshevism, 1860–1930** (rev., 1991); H. T. Dodge, *Women in the Soviet Economy* (1966); K. Geiger, *The Family in Soviet Russia* (1968); G. W. Lapidus, *Women in Soviet Society: Equality, Development, and Social Change** (1978); and B. E. Clements and others (eds.), *Russia's Women: Accommodation, Resistance, Transformation* (1990).

Soviet Foreign Relations and World Communism

The best introduction to Soviet foreign policy is A. B. Ulam, *Expansion and Coexistence: The History of Soviet Foreign Policy, 1917–1973** (rev., 1974), and other writings by the same author. Good older surveys are M. Beloff, *The Foreign Policy of Soviet Russia, 1929–1941* (2 vols., 1947–1949), and two books by L. F. Fischer: *The Soviets in World Affairs, 1917–1929* (2 vols., 1930; 1 vol., 1960) and *Russia's Road from Peace to War: Soviet Foreign Relations, 1917–1941* (1969). B. Jelavich, *St. Petersburg and Moscow: Tsarist and Soviet Foreign Policy, 1814–1974** (1974), effectively notes patterns of continuity.

On the transformation of earlier socialism and Marxism into communism, a number of studies have been described in Chapters XI, XII, and XIV. Recommended also are A. B. Ulam, *The Unfinished Revolution: An Essay on the Sources of Marxism and Communism** (1960); two books by A. G. Meyer: *Leninism* (1957), and *Communism** (1960); and O. A. Narkiewicz, *Marxism and the Reality of Power* (1981). An influential Italian Marxist theoretician is studied in C. Boggs, *Gramsci's Marxism* (1976), and J. Joll, *Antonio Gramsci** (1978); an equally important Hungarian theoretician in G. Lichtheim, *George Lukács* (1970), and M. Gluck, *George Lukács and His Generation, 1900–1918* (1987).

Personal testimonies about the impact of communism may be found in A. Balabanoff, *My Life as a Rebel* (1938), and in R. H. Crossman (ed.), *The God That Failed** (1950), an insightful series of essays on faith and disillusionment. Two biographies of an American participant-observer in Russia in 1917, the author of *Ten Days that Shook the World** (1919), are R. Rosenstone, *Romantic Revolutionary: A Biography of John Reed** (1975), and E. Hornberger, *John Reed* (1991).

On the Comintern, one may turn to H. Seton-Watson, *From Lenin to Khrushchev: The History of World Communism** (1953, 1960); F. Borkenau, *The Communist International* (1938), as seen by a participant; the same author's *World Communism** (1953); and G. Nollan, *International Communism and World Revolution* (1961). Special studies include J. W. Hulse, *The Forming of the Communist International* (1964); R. Fischer, *Stalin and German Communism* (1948); K. E. McKenzie, *Comintern and World Revolution, 1928–1943* (1964); B. Lazitch and M. M. Drachkovitch, *Lenin and the Comintern* (1972), a detailed account to 1921; and E. H. Carr, *Twilight of the Comintern, 1930–1935* (1982). The impact of bolshevism on French, Italian, and German socialism is ably explored in A. S. Lindemann, *The "Red Years": European Socialism vs. Bolshevism, 1918–1920* (1974), while R. Wohl examines the French experience with insight and depth in *French Communism in the Making, 1919–1924* (1966).

Problems and Readings*

Available are R. H. McNeal (ed.), *Russia in Transition, 1905–1914: Evolution or Revolution?* (1969); M. McCauley (ed.), *Octobrists to Bolsheviks: Imperial Russia, 1905–1917* (1984); A. E. Adams (ed.), *Imperial Russia after 1861: Peaceful Modernization or Revolution?* (1965); R. G. Suny and A. F. Adams (eds.), *The Russian Revolution and Bolshevik Victory* (rev., 1990); B. M. Unterberger (ed.), *American Intervention in the Russian Civil War* (1969); S. W. Page (ed.), *Lenin: Dedicated Marxist or Pragmatic Revolutionary?* (1969); R. V. Daniels (ed.), *The Stalin Revolution: Foundations of the Totalitarian Era* (1990); and R. C. Tucker and S. F. Cohen (eds.), *The Great Purge Trials* (1965).

XVIII. The Apparent Victory of Democracy

General accounts of international relations emphasizing the shift from a European to a global balance of power are G. Ross, *The Great Powers and the Decline of the European States System, 1914–1945** (1983); C. J. Bartlett, *The Global Conflict, 1880–1970: The International Rivalry of the Great Powers** (1984); J. Joll, *Europe Since 1870: An International History** (1973); and W. R. Keylor, *The Twentieth-Century World: An International History** (1984).

The attempt in the interwar years to put together a shattered polity in Europe is described in R. J. Sontag, *A Broken World, 1919–1939** (1971), a volume in the Langer series helpful for this and the chapter that follows, while two efforts to examine the pattern of reconstruction in Europe after the war are C. S. Maier, *Recasting Bourgeois Europe: Stabilization in France, Germany and Italy in the Decade After World War I** (1975), stressing the link between interest groups and conservative government, and D. P. Silverman, *Reconstructing Europe After the Great War* (1982).

International Relations in the 1920s

Introductions to international affairs in this era focusing on Europe are P. Renouvin, *War and Aftermath, 1914–1929* (1968), and S. Marks, *The Illusion of Peace: International Relations in Europe, 1918–1933** (1976). The high point of reconciliation is ably treated in J. Jacobson, *Locarno Diplomacy: Germany and the West, 1925–1929* (1972). A thoughtful synthesis for Weimar Germany is M. M. Lee and W. Michalka, *German Foreign Policy, 1917–1933: Continuity or Break?* (1987).

B. Kent, *The Spoils of War: The Politics, Economics, and Diplomacy of Reparations, 1918–1932* (1989), synthesizes the considerable literature on the complex reparations question and related matters, on which recommended studies include M. Trachtenberg, *Reparations in World Politics: France and European Economic Diplomacy, 1916–1923* (1980); S. A. Schuker, *The End of French Predominance in Europe: The Financial Crisis of 1924 and the Adoption of the Dawes Plan* (1976); and M. J. Hogan, *Informal Entente: The Private Structure of Cooperation in Anglo-American Economic Diplomacy, 1918–1928* (1977). The American role in these years in relation to Europe is studied in M. P. Leffler, *The Elusive Quest: America's Pursuit of European Stability and French Security* (1979), and on a broader scale in F. Costigliola, *Awkward Dominion: American Political, Economic, and Cultural Relations with Europe, 1919–1933* (1984); on the British role one may read A. Orde, *British Policy and European Reconstruction After the First World War* (1990). The response of the United States and Britain to the revolutionary events of the era, and not only to the revolution in Russia, is examined in L. C. Gardner, *Safe for Democracy: The Anglo-American Response to Revolution, 1913–1923** (1984).

The cooperation between the Soviet Union and Weimar Germany is studied in G. Freund, *Unholy Alliance* (1957); K. Rosenbaum, *Community of Fate: German-Soviet Diplomatic Relations, 1922–1928* (1965); and H. L. Dyck, *Weimar Germany and Soviet Russia, 1926–1933* (1966).

For the League of Nations one may read F. P. Walters, *A History of the League of Nations* (2 vols., 1952), and F. S. Northedge, *The League of Nations: Its Life and Times, 1920–1946* (1986), which notes that despite its shortcomings it helped to transform the older diplomacy. Other studies include B. Dexter, *The Years of Opportunity: The League of Nations, 1920–1926* (1967), and C. M. Kimmich, *Germany and the League of Nations* (1976). A special problem in which the League played a role is discussed in a wide-ranging study, M. R. Marrus, *The Unwanted: European Refugees in the Twentieth Century** (1985). Books on efforts at disarmament include J. M. Wheeler-Bennett, *Disarmament and Security Since Locarno, 1925–1931* (1932), and *The Pipe Dream of Peace: The Collapse of Disarmament* (1935); R. H. Ferrell, *Peace in Their Time: The Origins of the Kellogg-Briand Pact** (1952); and R. Dingman, *Power in the Pacific: The Origins of Naval Arms Limitation, 1914–1922* (1976). Of special interest on a related question is E. W. Bennett, *German Rearmament and the West, 1932–1933* (1979).

The Revolt of Asia: East Asia

For China in the early part of the twentieth century, the best introductions are H. Z. Schiffrin, *Sun Yat-sen and the Origins of the 1911 Revolution* (1969); F. Wakeman, *The Fall of Imperial China* (1975); and the essays in M. C. Wright (ed.), *China in Revolution: The First Phase, 1900–1913* (1968). The story of the last Manchu ruler (later appointed by the Japanese to rule in conquered Manchuria) is recounted in B. Power, *The Puppet Emperor: The Life of Pu Yi, Last Emperor of China* (1988).

Biographical studies for Sun include L. Sharman, *Sun Yat-sen and Communism* (1961), and C. M. Wilbur, *Sun Yat-sen: Frustrated Patriot* (1976); his successor is studied in E. P. Young, *The Presidency of Yuan Shih-kai: Liberalism and Dictatorship in Early Republican China* (1978). On the resentments stirred up by the Chinese treatment at Versailles, one should read V. Schwarcz, *The Chinese Enlightenment: Intellectuals and the Legacy of the May Fourth Movement of 1919** (1986). The era of Chiang Kai-shek and Kuomintang rule is studied in H. R. Isaacs, *The Tragedy of the Chinese Revolution** (1961), and L. Eastman, *The Abortive Revolution: China under Nationalist Rule, 1927–1937* (1974). Although books on Communist China will be described in later chapters, there should be mentioned here A. Dirlik, *The Origins of Chinese Communism** (1988), and three impressive books on the Long March of 1934–1935 by D. Wilson (1972), H. Salisbury (1984), and B. Yang (1990).

On the rise of militarism in Japan one should read J. B. Crowley, *Japan's Quest for Autonomy: National Security and Foreign Policy, 1930–1938* (1966), an outstanding account; and two books by A. Iriye: *Pacific Estrangement: Japanese and American Expansion, 1897–1911* (1972), and *After Imperialism: The Search for a New Order in the Far East, 1921–1931* (1965). S. R. Smith, *The Manchurian Crisis, 1931–1932: A Tragedy in International Relations* (1948), recounts the first important break in the League's collective security system.

The Revolt of Asia: The Middle East and South Asia

An introduction to the ferment in Asia is provided in J. and J. E. Romein, *The Asian Century: A History of Modern Nationalism in Asia* (trans. 1962), and a good introduction to modern developments in the Middle East is A. Hourani, *The Emergence of the Modern Middle East* (1981). For the Turkish Revolution, B. Lewis, *The Emergence of Modern Turkey* (rev., 1969), and S. J. and E. K. Shaw, *History of the Ottoman Empire and Modern Turkey,* Vol. II (1977), a detailed account, are invaluable; they may be supplemented by R. D. Robinson, *The First Turkish Republic* (1963), and W. F. Weiker, *The Modernization of Turkey: From Ataturk to the Present Day* (1981). Informative biographical accounts of the Turkish statesman-reformer are P. Balfour, *Ataturk: A Biography of Mustafa Kemal* (1965), and V. E. Volkan and N. Itzkowitz, *The Immortal Ataturk: A Psychobiography** (1986).

Arab stirrings in the Middle East are discussed in G. Antonius, *The Arab Awakening** (1965); Z. B. Zeine, *Struggle for Arab Independence* (1960); H. A. R. Gibb, *Modern Trends in Islam* (1947); and E. Kedouri, *Islam and the Modern World* (1980). The response of the European powers is described in A. Williams, *Britain and France in the Middle East and North Africa, 1914–1967* (1969).

For the Indian subcontinent, two histories that try to understand developments in Indian terms and not as reactions to the West are P. Spear, *India: A Modern History* (rev., 1972), and S. Wolpert, *A New History of India** (rev., 1982), cited earlier. The origins of Indian nationalism are discussed in A. Seal, *The Emergence of Indian Nationalism* (1968); R. J. Moore, *The Crisis of Indian Unity, 1917–1940* (1974); A. T. Embree, *India's Search for National Identity** (1972); and S. Sarker, *Modern India, 1885–1947* (1989). The tragedy at Amritsar in 1919 is examined in H. Fein, *Imperial Crime and Punishment: The Massacre at Jallianwala Bagh and British Judgment, 1919–1920* (1977).

There is a large literature on Gandhi. To an older biography by B. R. Nanda (1959), one may add G. Ashe, *Gandhi: A Study in Revolution** (1968); E. H. Erikson, *Gandhi's Truth: On the Origins of Militant Nonviolence** (1969), with interesting psychoanalytical insights; R. N. Iyer, *The Moral and Political Thought of Mahatma Gandhi** (1973), perhaps the best book for grasping the mind of Gandhi; and J. M. Brown's impressive volumes: *Gandhi's Rise to Power in Indian Politics, 1915–1922* (1972), *Gandhi and Civil Disobedience: The Mahatma in Indian Politics, 1928–1934* (1977), and *Gandhi: Prisoner of Hope* (1990). A. Copley, *Gandhi** (1987), is a good brief account. For Nehru there are available S. Gopal, *Jawaharlal Nehru: A Biography* (3 vols., 1976–1984), highly informative on the country as well as the man, and biographies by F. Moraes (1957), M. Brecher* (1959), and E. N. Pandy (1976). Nehru's autobiography, *Toward Freedom* * (1941), and his other writings are rewarding.

The Depression: Collapse of the World Economy

Books on the impact of the depression on politics and society in various countries will appear in the following chapter.

The economy in the framework of the post-1919 world may be studied in D. N. Aldcroft, *From Versailles to Wall Street: The International Economy in the 1920s* * (1977), a volume in the History of the World Economy in the Twentieth Century series; and in G. Ziebura, *World Economy and World Politics, 1924–1931: From Reconstruction to Collapse* (trans. 1990). For the stock market collapse, J. K. Galbraith, *The Great Crash, 1929* (1955), is unsurpassed, while a comprehensive account of the worldwide depression is C. P. Kindleberger, *The World in Depression, 1929–1939* * (rev., 1986), also in the series cited above. Interesting for its comparative insights is J. A. Garraty, *The Great Depression* (1986), and the same author's *Unemployment in History: Economic Thought and Public Policy* (1978). G. Rees, *The Great Slump: Capitalism in Crisis, 1929–1933* (1972), is also informative, while J. M. Laux, *The Great Depression in Europe* (1974), is a brief introduction in the Forums in History series.

Older, still useful surveys include H. V. Hodson, *Slump and Recovery, 1929–1937* (1938); H. W. Arndt, *The Economic Lessons of the Nineteen Thirties* (1944), especially insightful; G. Haberler, *Prosperity and Depression* (3rd ed., 1941); and W. A. Lewis, *Economic Survey, 1919–1939* (1948). There are helpful essays in W. Laqueur and G. L. Mosse (eds.), *The Great Depression* * (1970), originally a volume of the *Journal of Contemporary History,* and in K. Brunner (ed.), *The Great Depression Revisited* (1981), the latter somewhat technical. A neglected subject is examined in A. J. H. Latham, *The Depression and the Developing World, 1914–1939* (1981), and of special interest for international economic relations is E. W. Bennett, *Germany and the Diplomacy of the Financial Crisis, 1931* (1962).

M. Friedman and A. J. Schwartz, *The Great Contraction, 1929–1933* (1965), abstracted from a larger study, argues the monetary causes of the depression; it should be read with P. Temin, *Did Monetary Forces Cause the Great Depression?* (1976); P. Fearon, *The Origins and Nature of the Great Slump, 1929–1932* (1979); and C. P. Kindleberger, *Keynesianism vs. Monetarism and Other Essays in Financial History* * (1985). An important subject is examined in M. Palyi, *The Twilight of Gold, 1914–1936: Myths and Realities* (1972).

For Keynes, whose influence on economic thinking was less important during the depression than in later years, there is the multivolume biography in progress by R. Skidelsky, (Vol. I, 1986), and R. F. Harrod's older account (1951). For Keynes' ideas one turns also to C. Hession, *John Maynard Keynes, A Personalized Biography of the Man Who Revolutionized Capitalism and the Way We Live* (1984), informative despite its inflated title; D. E. Moggridge, *John Maynard Keynes* * (1976); and P. Clarke, *The Keynesian Revolution in the Making, 1924–1936* * (1989). R. Lekachman, *The Age of Keynes* * (1960) focuses on the post-1945 years when Keynesian influence took hold.

Problems and Readings*

For twentieth-century history in general, two anthologies of interpretive readings on controversial topics are G. Wright and A. Mejia, Jr., *An Age of Controversy* * (rev., 1973), and L. Derfler, *An Age of Conflict* * (1990). Two titles in the Heath problems series are relevant for this chapter: M. D. Lewis (ed.), *Gandhi: Maker of Modern India?* (1965), and R. F. Himmelberg (ed.), *The Great Depression and American Capitalism* (1968).

XIX. Democracy and Dictatorship

General accounts for the interwar years and the Great Depression have been described in the previous chapter, and books on the international crises of the 1930s will appear in the chapter that follows. Informative volumes that focus on the democracies and dictatorships in this era are E. Wiskemann, *Europe of the Dictators, 1919–1945* (1960); D. C. Large, *Between Two Fires: Europe's Path in the 1930s* (1990); and M. Kitchen, *Europe Between the Wars* * (1988). Helpful as an introduction to the varieties of European dictatorship is S. J. Lee, *The European Dictatorships, 1918–1945* * (1987).

The United States and the New Deal

Many of the volumes on the Great Depression cited earlier offer insights into the American experience. The interwar years, the impact of the depression, and the New Deal may best be approached through two volumes by W. E. Leuchtenburg: *The Perils of Prosperity** (1958) and *Franklin D. Roosevelt and the New Deal** (1961). Informative also are D. A. Shannon, *Between the Wars: America, 1919–1941** (1965); J. J. Hutmacher, *Trial by War and Depression, 1919–1941** (1973); R. S. McElvaine, *The Great Depression* (1984); P. Conkin, *The New Deal* (1967); and A. Romasco, *The Politics of Recovery* (1983).

Several biographical accounts of Roosevelt offer insights into the bold but pragmatic efforts to cope with the depression and shape the New Deal. Among the most illuminating are the three volumes by A. M. Schlesinger, Jr., *The Age of Roosevelt* (3 vols. to date, 1957–); J. M. Burns, *Roosevelt: The Lion and the Fox** (1956); and F. Freidel's multivolume biography (4 vols. to date, 1952–), which has reached the New Deal era; and the same author's synthesis, *A Rendezvous With Destiny* (1990). The effect on those who lived through the economic crisis is vividly portrayed in C. Bird, *The Invisible Scar** (1966); S. Terkel, *Hard Times: An Oral History of the Great Depression* (1970); R. J. Simon (ed.), *As We Saw the Thirties* (1967); and R. S. McElvaine (ed.), *Down and Out in the Great Depression* (1983). The growth of the labor movement in these years may be studied in I. Bernstein, *The Turbulent Years* (1970), and the impact on women in W. D. Wandersee, *Women's Work and Family Values, 1920–1940* (1981).

Britain Between the Wars

General accounts for Britain, some extending beyond the interwar years, are C. L. Mowat, *Britain Between the Wars, 1918–1940* (1955), an older but still valuable synthesis; A. J. P. Taylor, *English History, 1914–1945** (1965), written with the author's usual verve; A. Marwick, *Britain in the Century of Total War: War, Peace, and Social Change, 1900–1967* (1968); W. N. Medlicott, *Contemporary England, 1914–1964* (1967); and M. Beloff, *Wars and Welfare: Britain, 1914–1945** (1984). An overview of the British economic scene is provided in S. Pollard, *The Development of the British Economy, 1914–1980* (rev., 1983). The British return to protectionism and its consequences are explored in F. Capie, *Depression and Protectionism: Britain Between the Wars** (1984).

An outstanding account of changes in British life for all classes, and much else, is provided in J. Stevenson, *British Society, 1914–1945* (1984). Other suggested studies include W. McElwee, *Britain's Locust Years, 1918–1940* (1962); S. Glynn and J. Oxborrow, *Interwar Britain: Social and Economic History* (1976); N. Branson and M. Heinemann, *Britain in the Nineteen Thirties* (1971); J. Stevenson and C. Cook, *The Slump: Society and Politics During the Depression* (1978); S. Hynes, *The Auden Generation: Literature and Politics in the 1930s* (1977); and R. Blythe, *The Age of Illusion: Some Glimpses of Britain Between the Wars, 1919–1940** (rev., 1984). The gap between popular hopes at the end of the war and postwar realities is highlighted in P. B. Johnson, *Land Fit for Heroes: The Planning of British Reconstruction, 1916–1919* (1968), and in B. B. Gilbert, *British Social Policy, 1914–1939* (1970). The economic lot of the wartime women workers is portrayed in D. Beddoe, *Back to Home and Duty: Women Between the Wars, 1919–1939** (1990), and activist efforts by the first generation of British women to vote are described in B. Harrison, *Prudent Revolutionaries: Portraits of British Feminists Between the Wars* (1987).

On the decline of the Liberal party and the rise of Labour, one may consult W. Wilson, *The Downfall of the Liberal Party, 1914–1935* (1966); M. Freeden, *Liberalism Divided: British Political Thought, 1914–1939* (1986); and R. McKibbin, *The Evolution of the Labour Party, 1910–1924* (1974). Two thoughtful accounts of the general strike are P. Renshaw, *Nine Days That Shook Britain: The 1926 General Strike** (1976), and G. A. Phillips, *The General Strike: The Politics of Industrial Conflict* (1976). The 1931 crisis is explored in R. S. Bassett, *1931: Political Crisis* (1958); R. Skidelsky, *Politicians and the Slump: The Labour Government of 1929–1931* (1967); and H. Berkeley, *The Myth That Will Not Die: The Formation of the National Government, 1931* (1978). The divisions within the left emerge from B. Pimlott, *Labour and the Left in the 1930s** (rev., 1986). The threat of fascism is examined in R. Skidelsky, *Oswald Mosley* (1976), on a Labour leader who became Britain's leading fascist of the era, and on a broader scale in R. Thurlow, *Fascism in Britain: A History, 1918–1985* (1987), and D. S. Lewis, *Illusions of Grandeur: Mosley, Fascism and British Society, 1931–1981* (1990).

There are many biographical studies, among them, biographies of Ramsay MacDonald by D. Marquand (1977) and A. Morgan (1987); of Arthur Henderson, MacDonald's rival for Labour party leadership, by F. M. Leventhal* (1989); of Lloyd George in the years 1922–1931 by J. Campbell (1977) and by J. Grigg in the multivolume work cited earlier; and of Stanley Baldwin written jointly by K. Middlemas and J. Barnes (1969). For Neville Chamberlain, the first volume of a large-scale, highly detailed biography has appeared: D. Dilks, *Neville Chamberlain: Pioneering and Reform, 1870–1929* (1989); books relating to his role in foreign policy will be mentioned in the next chapter, as will a number of other biographical studies. K. Rose, *King George V* (1984), a scholarly biography of the monarch, supersedes all earlier accounts.

On British relations with the dominions one may turn to D. Hall, *Commonwealth: History of the British Commonwealth of Nations* (1971), a detailed account, and N. Mansergh, *The Commonwealth Experience* (1969). An outstanding study of Ireland in this era is J. M. Curran, *The Birth of the Irish Free State, 1921–1923* (1980), and an impressive account on a broader time scale is J. J. Lee, *Ireland, 1912–1985: Politics and Society* (1990).

France Between the Wars

Two volumes in the Cambridge History of Modern France are informative: P. Bernard and H. Dubief, *The Decline of the Third Republic, 1914–1938* (trans. 1985), and J. P. Azéma, *From Munich to the Liberation, 1938–1944* (trans. 1985), the latter somewhat more probing; and there are incisive essays in S. Hoffmann and others, *In Search of France: The Economy, Society, and Political System in the Twentieth Century* (1963). Two helpful studies are T. Kemp, *The French Economy, 1913–1939: The History of a Decline* (1972), and C. Dyer, *Population and Society in Twentieth Century France* (1978). An illuminating study of government planning and economic management, which were less successful in the interwar years than later, is R. F. Kuisel, *Capital and the State in Modern France:* *Renovation and Economic Management in the Twentieth Century* (1981). Two special subjects are examined in M. Wolfe, *The French Franc Between the Wars, 1919–39* (1961), and in G. Wright, *Rural Revolution in France: The Peasantry in the Twentieth Century* (1964). For labor there are available H. W. Ehrmann, *French Labor: From Popular Front to Liberation* (1947), and the relevant chapters in T. Judt, *Marxism and the French Left* (1986), cited earlier.

The response to the depression and the threat to the Third Republic are explored in two books by J. Jackson: *The Politics of Depression in France, 1932–1936* (1985), and *The Popular Front in France: Defending Democracy, 1934–1938* (1988). For the Socialist leader of the Popular Front one may read J. Colton, *Léon Blum: Humanist in Politics* (1966; reissued 1987), and J. Lacouture, *Léon Blum* (1977; trans. 1982). Other studies of the political left in the Popular Front era include P. J. Larmour, *The French Radical Party in the 1930s* (1964); J. T. Marcus, *French Socialism in the Crisis Years, 1933–36* (1958); N. Greene, *Crisis and Decline: The French Socialist Party in the Popular Front Era* (1969); H. Gruber, *Léon Blum, French Socialism, and the Popular Front* (1986); D. Caute, *Communism and the French Intellectuals, 1914–1960* (1965); and D. R. Brower, *The New Jacobins: The French Communist Party and the Popular Front* (1968). The right and extreme right are studied in several of the books cited for the pre-1914 years; to them should be added R. Soucy, *French Fascism: The First Wave, 1924–1933* (1985).

Still valuable for the 1930s are the perceptive journalistic accounts of A. Werth, of which *The Twilight of France, 1933–1940* (1942), is a condensation of his earlier volumes.

Italy: The Fascist Experience

Introductions to the Italian experience include A. Cassels, *Fascist Italy* (1968); E. Wiskemann, *Fascism in Italy: Its Development and Influence* (1969); F. Chabod, *A History of Italian Fascism* (1963), concise but perceptive; and an impressive book on the early years, A. Lyttelton, *The Seizure of Power: Fascism in Italy, 1919–1929* (1973). The relevant chapters in C. Seton-Watson, *Italy from Liberalism to Fascism, 1870–1925* (1967), cited earlier, are valuable as are those in H. S. Hughes, *The United States and Italy* (rev., 1979).

On the nature of the fascist state, H. Finer, *Mussolini's Italy** (1933; reissued 1965), and G. Salvemini, *Under the Axe of Fascism* (1936; reissued 1970), remain informative but should be supplemented by R. Sarti, *Fascism and the Industrial Leadership in Italy, 1919–1940* (1971); and M. Gallo, *Mussolini's Italy: Twenty Years of the Fascist Era* (1973). A. J. Gregor, *Italian Fascism and Developmental Dictatorship** (1979), somewhat reductively tends to equate Italian fascism with forced modernization. The impact on Italian society is comprehensively examined in E. R. Tannenbaum, *The Fascist Experience: Italian Society and Culture, 1922–1945* (1972); and a special area in V. de Grazia, *The Culture of Consent: Mass Organization of Leisure in Fascist Italy* (1981).

The compromise with the church is explored in D. A. Binchy, *Church and State in Fascist Italy* (1942), older but still informative; R. A. Webster, *The Cross and the Fasces: Christian Democracy in Italy* (1960); and J. F. Pollard, *The Vatican and Italian Fascism, 1929–1932: A Study in Conflict* (1985). The emergence of Mussolini's racial policy is studied in M. Michaelis, *Mussolini and the Jews: German-Italian Relations and the Jewish Question in Italy, 1922–1945* (1978), and in S. Zucotti, *The Italians and the Holocaust: Persecution, Rescue, and Survival* (1988).

On *Il Duce* himself, the best biography is D. Mack Smith, *Mussolini* (1982), straightforward and comprehensive, but there is also an informative biography by I. Kirkpatrick, *Mussolini: Study of a Demagogue** (1964). The older G. Megaro, *Mussolini in the Making* (1938), remains useful for the early years but should be supplemented by A. J. Gregor, *Young Mussolini and the Intellectual Origins of Fascism* (1979). There are accounts by L. Fermi* (1961); C. Hibbert (1962), mostly on the latter phases of the dictator's career; and R. H. Collier (1971). An outstanding study of the underground struggle against fascism from 1924 to 1943 is C. F. Delzell, *Mussolini's Enemies: The Italian Anti-Fascist Resistance* (1961). The last phase of the dictator's career is narrated in great detail in F. W. Deakin, *The Brutal Friendship: Mussolini, Hitler, and the Fall of Italian Fascism** (1962), the final portion of which is available as *The Six Hundred Days of Mussolini* (1966). C. G.

Segrè, *Italo Balbo: A Fascist Life* (1987), studies Mussolini's one-time heir apparent.

Foreign policy is examined in G. Barclay, *The Rise and Fall of the New Roman Empire: Italy's Bid for World Power, 1890–1943* (1973), emphasizing pre-Fascist expansionism; A. Cassels, *Mussolini's Early Diplomacy* (1970); and D. Mack Smith, *Mussolini's Roman Empire* (1976). Mussolini as a failed military leader is ably explored in M. Knox, *Mussolini Unleashed, 1939–1941: Politics and Strategy in Fascist Italy's Last War** (1982).

Germany, 1919–1933: The Weimar Republic

Scholars will continue to debate the reasons for the collapse of the Weimar Republic and the triumph of Hitler. Several of the longer-range histories of Germany cited in Chapter XIV will also be helpful here.

Narrative accounts of Weimar include A. J. Nicholls, *Weimar and the Rise of Hitler** (rev., 1991); D. Childs, *Germany Since 1918* (rev., 1980); S. Taylor, *Revolution and Counter-Revolution in Germany, 1918–1933* (1984); and E. Kolb, *The Weimar Republic* (trans. 1988). Two older detailed political histories: A Rosenberg, *A History of the German Republic** (1936), and E. Eyck, *A History of the Weimar Republic* (2 vols., 1954–1956; trans. 1962–1965), and a briefer account, S. W. Halperin, *Germany Tried Democracy: A Political History of the Reich from 1918 to 1933** (1946), remain instructive on parties and personalities. Works on the uneasy early years include R. Watts, *The Kings Depart* (1968); A. J. Ryder, *The German Revolution of 1918: A Study of German Socialism in War and Revolt* (1967); and S. Haffner, *Failure of a Revolution: Germany, 1918–1919* (trans. 1973). The inflation of 1923 is studied in S. B. Webb, *Hyperinflation and Stabilization in Weimar Germany* (1989).

The most informed inquiry into the economic scene and efforts to cope with the depression is H. James, *The German Slump: Politics and Economics, 1924–1936** (1986). The inability of the political parties and diverse interest groups to cooperate in the face of the economic and other troubles is critically analyzed in D. Abraham, *The Collapse of the Weimar Republic: Political Economy and Crisis** (rev., 1986; an amended edition of an earlier work); and in L. E. Jones, *German Liberalism and the Dissolution of the Weimar Party System,*

1918–1933 (1989), an exhaustive study of its subject. A major party of the left is examined in W. L. Guttman, *The German Social Democratic Party, 1875–1933* (1981), while the resort to extraparliamentary tactics by the right and left receives attention from J. M. Riehl, *Paramilitary Politics in Weimar Germany* (1977); P. Fritzsche, *Rehearsals for Fascism: Populism and Political Mobilization in Weimar Germany* (1990); and E. Rosenhaft, *Beating the Fascists? The German Communists and Political Violence, 1929–1933* (1984). The question of army loyalties to the republic is explored in depth in F. L. Carsten, *The Reichswehr and Politics, 1918 to 1933** (trans. 1966); J. W. Wheeler-Bennett, *The Nemesis of Power: The German Army in Politics, 1918–1945** (rev., 1964); and G. A. Craig, *The Politics of the Prussian Army, 1640–1945** (1956, 1964), cited earlier in Chapter V.

Among thoughtful efforts to explore the ideological roots of Weimar's failure are F. Stern, *The Politics of Cultural Despair: A Study in the Use of the Germanic Ideology** (1961); the same author's *The Failure of Illiberalism: Essays on the Political Culture of Germany* (1972); and G. L. Mosse, *The Crisis of German Ideology: Intellectual Origins of the Third Reich** (1964). Cultural history in these years is examined in W. Laqueur, *Weimar: A Cultural History, 1918–1933* (1974); P. Gay, *Weimar Culture: The Outsider as Insider* (1968); and O. Friedrich, *Before the Deluge: A Portrait of Berlin in the 1920s* (1972). Some political leaders of the republic are studied in H. Kessler, *Walter Rathenau* (1929); K. Epstein, *Matthias Erzberger and the Dilemma of German Democracy* (1959); H. W. Gatzke, *Stresemann and the Rearmament of Germany** (1954); H. A. Turner, *Stresemann and the Politics of the Weimar Republic** (1963); J. W. Wheeler-Bennett, *Wooden Titan: Hindenburg in Twenty Years of German History, 1914–1934* (1936); and A. Dorpalen, *Hindenburg and the Weimar Republic* (1964).

Germany, 1933–1945: The Third Reich

A valuable introduction to the vast literature on the Third Reich is I. Kershaw, *The Nazi Dictatorship: Problems and Perspectives of Interpretation** (1985), while P. Ayçoberry, *The Nazi Question: An Essay on the Interpretation of National Socialism, 1922–1975**

(trans. 1981), is an impressive historiographical study.

On the coming to power of the Nazis one may first turn to M. Broszat, *Hitler and the Collapse of Weimar Germany** (trans. 1987), focusing on the years 1929–1933. There are informative essays in T. Eschenburg and others, *The Path to Dictatorship, 1919–1933* (1966); and P. D. Stachura (ed.), *The Nazi Machtergreifung* (1983). In a carefully researched book H. A. Turner, *German Big Business and the Rise of Hitler* (1985), refutes the thesis that big business and heavy industry brought Hitler to power even if they did lend support to various antirepublican elements. Two important studies illuminate the Nazi appeal to diverse segments of the population: W. S. Allen, *The Nazi Seizure of Power: The Experience of a Single German Town, 1922–1945** (1965; rev., 1984), on Northeim in northern Germany, and J. H. Grill, *The Nazi Movement in Baden, 1920–1945* (1984). Two extraordinary efforts to assess the Nazi appeal at the polls are R. F. Hamilton, *Who Voted for Hitler?** (1982), and T. Childers, *The Nazi Voter: The Social Foundations of Fascism in Germany, 1919–1933* (1983), which both tend to confirm the thesis that Nazi support came from all segments of the population, and not only from the lower middle class.

M. H. Kater, *The Nazi Party: A Social Profile of Members and Leaders, 1919–1945** (1983), is an exhaustive sociological analysis of those who joined and led the party, while D. Orlow, *The History of the Nazi Party* (2 vols., 1969–1973), is a comprehensive organizational history. For the SS one may read G. Reitlinger, *SS: Alibi of a Nation, 1922–1945** (1956); R. L. Koehl, *The Black Corps: The Structure and Power Struggles of the SS* (1983); and H. F. Ziegler, *Nazi Germany's New Aristocracy: The SS Leadership, 1925–1939* (1990). The Brownshirts are studied in C. Fischer, *Stormtroopers: A Social, Economic and Ideological Analysis, 1929–1935* (1983). Other institutions of the Nazi era are discussed in numerous books, among them, R. Gellately, *The Gestapo and German Society* (1990); T. Taylor, *Sword and Swastika: Generals and Nazis in the Third Reich** (1952); P. Seabury, *The Wilhelmstrasse: A Study of German Diplomats Under the Nazi Regime* (1955); O. J. Hale, *The Captive Press in the Third Reich* (1964); Z. A. B. Zeman, *Nazi Propaganda* (1964); and P. Hayes, *Industry and*

Ideology: I. G. Farben in the Nazi Era (1987).

Religion and related matters are examined in E. C. Helmreich, *The German Churches under Hitler: Background, Struggle, and Epilogue* (1979); J. S. Conway, *The Nazi Persecution of the Churches, 1933–1945* (1968); G. Lewy, *The Catholic Church and Nazi Germany* (1964); and S. Friedländer, *Pius XII and the Third Reich: A Documentation* (1966). A far-reaching study of Hitler's war against the Jews is S. Gordon, *Hitler, Germans, and the Jewish Question* (1984). Books on the death camps and the Holocaust will be described in the next chapter.

For all aspects of the Nazi era K. Hildebrand, *The Third Reich** (1984), is valuable, while D. G. Williamson, *The Third Reich** (1982), is a helpful introduction. On the Nazi state two outstanding comprehensive analyses are K. D. Bracher, *The German Dictatorship** (trans. 1970), and M. Broszat, *The Hitler State** (trans. 1981). D. Schoenbaum, *Hitler's Social Revolution: Class and Status in Nazi Germany, 1933–1939** (1966) sees a leveling effect not accomplished by earlier regimes. Two studies exploring new avenues to understanding popular responses are T. Kershaw, *The 'Hitler Myth': Image and Reality in the Third Reich** (1987), and D. J. K. Peukert, *Inside Nazi Germany: Conformity, Opposition, and Racism in Everyday Life* (trans. 1987). There are perceptive insights into life under the Nazis in R. Bessel (ed.), *Life in the Third Reich** (1987), and in G. L. Mosse *Nazi Culture: Intellectual, Cultural, and Social Life in the Third Reich* (1966).

The best study of women in the Third Reich, including those who supported and those who resisted the regime, is C. Koonz, *Mothers in the Fatherland: Women, the Family, and Nazi Politics** (1987). It may be supplemented by J. Stephenson's two books: *Women in Nazi Society* (1976) and *The Nazi Organization of Women* (1981), and the essays in R. Bridenthal, A. Grossman, and M. Kaplan, *When Biology Became Destiny: Women in Weimar and Nazi Germany** (1989).

That there was no mass resistance but only opposition from resolute individuals and small groups emerges from two comprehensive accounts: P. Hoffmann, *German Resistance to Hitler** (rev., 1988), and M. Balfour, *Withstanding Hitler in Germany, 1933–1945* (1989). They may be supplemented by H. Rothfels, *The German Opposition to Hitler: An Assessment** (rev., 1987); T. Prittie, *Germans Against Hitler* (1964); and on the failure of the wartime plot of 1944, the essays in R. Manvell and H. A. Jacobsen (eds.), *July 20, 1944: Germans Against Hitler* (1969).

Of the many biographies of Hitler two stand out: A. Bullock, *Hitler: A Study in Tyranny** (1952; rev., 1964), and J. C. Fest, *Hitler* (trans. 1975, somewhat condensed from the German original). R. Binion, *Hitler Among the Germans* (1976), uses psychoanalytical methods to explain the inner wellsprings of the obsessed leader, while R. L. Waite, *The Psychopathic God: Adolf Hitler** (1977), combines psychoanalytical and more conventional techniques to provide some keen insights. Two analytical interpretive essays that raise pertinent questions are S. Haffner, *The Meaning of Hitler** (trans. 1980), and W. Carr, *Hitler: A Study in Personality and Politics* (1979). N. Stone, *Hitler* (1980) focuses on the war years, while the end of the leader and his regime is vividly recounted in H. R. Trevor-Roper, *The Last Days of Hitler** (rev., 1966).

Some of Hitler's associates are studied in J. C. Fest, *The Face of the Third Reich: Portraits of the Nazi Leadership** (trans. 1977); B. F. Smith, *Heinrich Himmler: A Nazi in the Making, 1900–1926* (1971); R. Smelser, *Robert Ley: Hitler's Labor Front Leader* (1989); and D. Irving, *Göring: A Biography* (1989), which as in other books on the Third Reich by this author makes the best possible case for his subject. Two convenient handbooks on the institutions and personalities of the regime are R. Wistrich, *Who's Who in Nazi Germany* (1982), and C. Zentner and F. Bedürftig, *The Encyclopedia of the Third Reich* (2 vols., 1991).

Defining Totalitarianism and Fascism

The origins and nature of twentieth-century ideologies are explored in many books, notably in K. D. Bracher's comprehensive *A History of Political Thought in the Twentieth Century* (trans. 1984). Among efforts to examine totalitarianism, left and right, are C. J. Friedrich and Z. K. Brzezinski, *Totalitarian Dictatorship and Autocracy** (rev., 1965), H. Bucheim, *Totalitarian Rule: Its Nature and Characteristics* (trans. 1968); and A. Perlmutter, *Modern Authoritarianism: A Comparative Institutional Analysis*

(1981). For efforts to arrive at a generic definition of fascism as a phenomenon of the interwar years the best introduction is F. L. Carsten, *The Rise of Fascism** (rev., 1980). E. Nolte, *Three Faces of Fascism: Action Française, Italian Fascism, National Socialism** (trans. 1966), is provocative but difficult for most readers. Among other thoughtful studies are S. G. Payne, *Fascism: Comparison and Definition* (1980), a critique of the debate engendered on the subject; H. R. Kedward, *Fascism in Western Europe, 1900–1945* (1969); R. De Felice, *Fascism: An Informal Introduction to its Theory and Practice* (1976), by the foremost Italian biographer of Mussolini; J. Weiss, *The Fascist Tradition: Radical Right-Wing Extremism in Modern Europe** (1967); A. Cassels, *Fascism** (1975); and A. J. Gregor, *The Ideology of Fascism: The Rationale of Totalitarianism* (1969). Informative also are H. Rogge and E. Weber (eds), *The European Right: A Historical Profile** (1965), and the essays in S. J. Woolf and others, *European Fascism* (1968), as well as those in W. Laqueur and G. L. Mosse (eds.), *International Fascism, 1920–1945** (1966). The results of a sociological investigation into the class origins of fascist supporters in twenty-one countries are available in S. U. Larsen and others (eds.), *Who Were the Fascists? Social Roots of European Fascism* (1980). A special subject is explored in A. Hamilton, *The Appeal of Fascism: The Intellectuals and Fascism* (1968).

Other European Developments in the Interwar Years

Spain and the Spanish Civil War are discussed in the following chapter. The most informative volumes on central and eastern Europe are H. Seton-Watson, *Eastern Europe Between the Wars, 1918–1941* (rev., 1967), J. Rothschild, *East Central Europe Between the Two World Wars** (1975); and the relevant chapters in A. Palmer, *The Lands Between: A History of East-Central Europe Since the Congress of Vienna* (1970). An incisive inquiry blaming political and economic problems on partial modernization in these years is I. T. Berend, *The Crisis Zone of Europe: An Interpretation of East-Central European History in the First Half of the Twentieth Century* (1986). A special subject is explored in E. Mendelsohn, *The Jews of East Central Europe Between the World Wars** (1983). For the Balkans there are available the relevant chapters in R. L. Wolff, *The Balkans in Our Time* (rev., 1978); L. S. Stavrianos, *The Balkans since 1815** (1965); and B. Jelavich, *History of the Balkans: The Twentieth Century* (1983), all cited earlier.

A few titles might be suggested for some of the successor states. For Austria: C. A. Gulick, *Austria from Habsburg to Hitler* (2 vols., 1948), sympathetic to the Austrian socialists; M. MacDonald, *The Republic of Austria, 1918–1934: A Study in the Failure of Democratic Government* (1946); C. E. Edmondson, *The Heimwehr and Austrian Politics, 1918–1936* (1978); M. Kitchen, *The Coming of Austrian Fascism* (1980); F. L. Carsten, *Fascist Movements in Austria: From Schönerer to Hitler** (1977); and B. F. Pauley, *Hitler and the Forgotten Nazis: A History of Austrian National Socialism* (1981). For Hungary: C. A. Macartney, *October Fifteenth: A History of Modern Hungary, 1929–1945* (2 vols.; rev., 1962), R. L. Tönés, *Béla Kun and the Hungarian Soviet Republic* (1967), on the short-lived Communist regime of 1919. For Czechoslovakia: S. H. Thomson, *Czechoslovakia in European History* (1953); R. W. Seton-Watson, *A History of the Czechs and Slovaks* (1943, 1965); A. H. Hermann, *A History of the Czechs* (1976); E. Wiskemann, *Czechs and Germans* (rev., 1967); Z. A. B. Zeman, *The Masaryks: The Making of Czechoslovakia** (1976, 1991); V. Olivova, *The Doomed Democracy: Czechoslovakia in a Disrupted Europe, 1918–1938* (1972); and V. S. Mamatey and R. Luza (eds.), *A History of the Czechoslovakian Republic, 1918–1948* (1973). For Yugoslavia: R. West, *Black Lamb and Grey Falcon* (2 vols., 1941), an insightful account by a gifted journalist; I. Banac, *The National Question in Jugoslavia* (1985), on the genesis of the multiethnic state; and F. Singleton, *A Short History of the Jugoslav Peoples** (1985). For Poland: M. K. Dziewanowski, *Poland in the Twentieth Century* (1977); A. Polonsky, *Politics in Independent Poland, 1921–1939* (1972); H. Roos, *A History of Modern Poland* (1966); and the volumes of N. Davies cited earlier. For Finland and the Baltic States: J. H. Wuorinen, *A History of Finland* (1965); D. G. Kirby, *Finland in the Twentieth Century* (1979); and G. von Rauch, *The Baltic States—Estonia, Latvia,* *and Lithuania: The Years of Independence, 1917–1940* (1947; reissued 1987).

Problems and Readings*

On the American New Deal, a selection of conflicting interpretations is conveniently presented in E. C. Rozwenc (ed.), *The New Deal: Revolution or Evolution?* (rev., 1959), and in M. Keller (ed.), *The New Deal* (1963). For Britain: J. A. Thompson (ed.), *The Collapse of the British Liberal Party: Fate or Self-Destruction?* (1969). For Italy: S. W. Halperin, *Mussolini and Italian Fascism* (1964), and R. Sarti (ed.), *The Ax Within: Italian Fascism in Action* (1974). For Weimar Germany: R. N. Hunt (ed.), *The Creation of the Weimar Republic: Stillborn Democracy?* (1969); and F. K. Ringer (ed.), *The German Inflation of 1923* (1969); and I. Kershaw (ed.), *Weimar: Why Did German Democracy Fail?* (1990). For the Nazi era: F. Stern (ed.), *The Path to Dictatorship* (1967); H. A. Turner (ed.), *Nazism and the Third Reich* (1972); A. Mitchell (ed.), *Hitler's Dictatorship and the German Nation* (rev., 1990); R. G. L. Waite (ed.), *Hitler and Nazi Germany* (rev., 1969); J. Noakes and G. Pridham (eds.), *Documents of Nazism, 1919–1945* (1975). On fascism and totalitarianism, there are available P. T. Mason, *Totalitarianism: Temporary Madness or Permanent Danger?* (1967); E. Weber, *Varieties of Fascism: Doctrines of Revolution in the Twentieth Century* (1964); N. Greene (ed.), *Fascism: An Anthology* (1968); C. F. Delzell (ed.), *Mediterranean Fascism* (1970); W. Laqueur (ed.), *Fascism: A Reader's Guide* (1976); H. A. Turner, Jr., (ed.), *Reappraisals of Fascism* (1975); R. de Felice (ed.), *Interpretations of Fascism* (trans. 1977); and G. L. Mosse (ed.), *International Fascism: New Thoughts and New Appraisals* (1979).

XX. The Second World War

Spain and the Spanish Civil War as Prelude

The most comprehensive narrative account of the Spanish conflict, taking in all aspects including the international ramifications, is H. Thomas, *The Spanish Civil War** (1961; rev. 1977; reissued 1987), in which Franco's skill as a manipulator and survivor clearly emerges; it includes an extensive bibliography. Other recommended accounts are G.

Jackson, *A Concise History of the Spanish Civil War** (1965; abr., 1974); P. Broué and E. Témime, *The Revolution and the Civil War in Spain* (trans. 1972); P. Wyden, *The Passionate War* (1983); and A. Beevor, *The Spanish Civil War* (1983), strong on the military aspects. H. Browne, *Spain's Civil War** (1983), provides a brief overview, and R. Carr, *The Spanish Tragedy: The Civil War in Perspective* (1977), adds analytical insights based on the author's life-long devotion to the study of Spanish history. The turbulent background is ably conveyed in G. Brenan, *The Spanish Labyrinth** (1943); R. A. H. Robinson, *The Origins of Franco Spain: The Right, the Republic, and the Revolution, 1931–1936* (1971); E. E. Malefakis, *Agrarian Reform and Peasant Revolution in Spain: Origins of the Civil War* (1970), an impressive study; and P. Preston, *The Coming of the Spanish Civil War: Reform, Reaction, and Revolution in the Second Republic, 1931–1936* (1978). There are informative essays in three collaborative volumes: M. S. Alexander and H. Graham (eds.), *The French and Spanish Popular Fronts: Comparative Perspectives* (1989); P. Preston (ed.), *Revolution and War in Spain, 1931–1939** (1985); and M. Blinkhorn (ed.), *Spain in Conflict, 1931–1939* (1986).

Three studies of the American response to the war are F. J. Taylor, *The United States and the Spanish Civil War* (1956); A. Guttmann, *The Wound in the Heart: America and the Spanish Civil War* (1962); and R. P. Traina, *American Diplomacy and the Spanish Civil War* (1968). Other memorable aspects are touched upon in P. Stansky and W. Abrahams, *Journey to the Frontier: Julian Bell and John Cornford: Their Lives and the 1930's** (1966), on two young English poets who fought for the Republic; the same authors' *George Orwell* (2 vols., 1972–1980); Orwell's own *Homage to Catalonia** (1938), by one who became disillusioned; and S. Weintraub, *The Last Great Cause: The Intellectuals and the Spanish Civil War* (1968). The volunteers who out of idealism fought for the Republic are studied in V. Brome, *The International Brigades* (1966), and in R. D. Richardson, *Comintern Army: The International Brigades and the Spanish Civil War* (1982), which stresses the Stalinist discipline imposed. The Communist role and Stalin's support for the Republic are thoroughly explored in B. Bolloten, *The Spanish Revolution and the Struggle for*

Power During the Civil War (1961; rev., 1969), and in the same author's *The Spanish Civil War: Revolution and Counterrevolution* (1990). A balanced study of Franco is J. W. D. Trythall, *El Caudillo* (1970), and S. G. Payne has written a comprehensive monograph, *Falange: A History of Spanish Fascism** (1961), and on Franco's years in power, *The Franco Regime, 1936–1975* (1987).

Background to the Second World War

Although there is no one comprehensive treatment taking into account the sources now available for the diplomacy of the interwar years and the background to the Second World War, there are a number of important books on the subject. An excellent series providing bibliographical and archival guidance was inaugurated with C. M. Kimmich (ed.), *German Foreign Policy, 1918–1945: Guide to Research and Research Materials* (1981), with volumes now available for the foreign policy of the other major powers: R. J. Young (ed.), for France; A. Cassels (ed.), for Italy; S. Aster (ed.), for Britain; and G. W. Baer (ed.), for the League and international organizations. The opening of the British and French archives and the availability of the German archives has made many earlier works obsolete or at least incomplete.

Among the most informative general inquiries into the coming of the Second World War are P. Renouvin, *World War II and Its Origins: International Relations 1929–1945* (trans. 1969); M. Baumont, *The Origins of the Second World War* (trans. 1978); A. Adamthwaite, *The Making of the Second World War** (rev., 1979); and P. M. H. Bell, *The Origins of the Second World War in Europe** (1986). Many of the books on the diplomacy of the interwar years cited at the beginning of Chapter XVIII should also be consulted.

On the eleven months between Munich and the outbreak of the war, D. C. Watt, *How War Came: The Immediate Origins of the Second World War, 1938–1939* (1989), is a masterful study. The conclusions tend to refute A. J. P. Taylor's *The Origins of the Second World War** (1961), which depicts Hitler as one who did not desire war but merely took advantage of the uncertainty of his opponents. On the Taylor thesis one may also read the evaluations in G. Martel (ed.), *"The Origins of the Second World War Reconsidered": The A. J. P. Taylor Debate After Twenty-Five Years** (1986).

A major study of German foreign policy based on exhaustive use of the documents and strongly emphasizing Hitler's responsibilities and initiatives is G. L. Weinberg, *The Foreign Policy of Hitler's Germany:* Vol. I, *Diplomatic Revolution in Europe, 1933–1936* (1970), and Vol. II, *Starting World War II, 1937–1939* (1980). A second study with similar conclusions is N. Rich, *Hitler's War Aims* (2 vols., 1973–1974). For assessments of German foreign policy, one may also read K. Hildebrand: *The Foreign Policy of the Third Reich** (1974); J. Hiden, *Germany and Europe, 1919–1939* (1978); E. Jäckel, *Hitler's World View** (1981); and E. M. Robertson, *Hitler's Pre-War Policies and Military Planning, 1933–1939* (1967). Attempts to examine German foreign policy in broad perspective include A. Hillgruber, *Germany and the Two World Wars** (trans. 1981); W. D. Smith, *The Ideological Origins of Nazi Imperialism** (1986); K. Hildebrand, *German Foreign Policy From Bismarck to Adenauer* (trans. 1989); F. Fischer, *From Kaiserreich to Third Reich** (trans. 1986), cited earlier; and the essays in V. R. Berghahn and M. Kitchen (eds.), *Germany and the Age of Total War* (1981).

British policy in the 1930s, including the economic constraints on a more assertive policy, is examined in M. Cowling, *The Impact of Hitler: British Politics and British Policy, 1933–1940** (1975); R. P. Shay, Jr., *British Rearmament in the Thirties: Politics and Profits* (1977); G. C. Peden, *British Rearmament and the Treasury, 1932–1939* (1979); and R. Douglas, *In the Year of Munich* (1978). Highly critical of appeasement are A. L. Rowse, *Appeasement: A Study in Political Decline, 1933–1939** (1961); M. Gilbert and R. Gott, *The Appeasers* (1963); M. Gilbert, *The Roots of Appeasement* (1966); and M. George, *The Warped Vision: British Foreign Policy, 1933–1939* (1965). The opposition to appeasement is also examined in W. R. Rock, *Appeasement on Trial: British Foreign Policy and Its Critics, 1938–1939* (1966), and N. Thompson, *The Anti-Appeasers* (1971). There are informative essays in W. Mommsen and L. Kettenacker (eds.), *The Fascist Challenge and the Policy of Appeasement* (1983), and K. Robbins, *Appeasement** (1988), provides a brief overview of the issues and consequences in the British Historical Association series.

In connection with the 1930s, W. S. Churchill, *The Gathering Storm** (1948), the first volume of his *The Second World War** (6 vols., 1948–1953), covering his years in the opposition, is indispensable. The fifth volume of M. Gilbert's massive biography of Churchill also deals with these years: *Winston S. Churchill*, Vol. V, *The Prophet of Truth, 1922–1939* (1977); the other volumes of Gilbert's biography will be described shortly.

Biographical studies focusing on British foreign policy include two studies of Anthony Eden, one highly critical by D. Carlton (1981), the second more defensive by R. Rhodes James (1987); and a study of Sir Samuel Hoare by J. A. Cross (1977). For Neville Chamberlain there are studies by K. Feiling (1946) and I. MacLeod (1961), both somewhat defensive, and a balanced assessment by W. R. Rock (1969).

Several impressive studies examine British foreign policy in long-range perspective, among them: F. S. Northedge, *The Troubled Giant: Britain Among the Great Powers, 1916–1939* (1966); W. N. Medlicott, *British Foreign Policy Since Versailles, 1919–1963* (rev., 1968); C. Barnett, *The Collapse of British Power* (1972); P. Kennedy, *The Realities Behind Diplomacy: Background Influences on British External Policy, 1865–1980** (1983); C. B. Bartlett, *British Foreign Policy in the Twentieth Century** (1989); and the essays in D. Dilks (ed.), *Retreat From Power: Studies in Britain's Foreign Policy of the Twentieth Century* (2 vols., 1989), the first volume covering the years 1906–1939.

For French foreign policy in these years the fullest account is A. Adamthwaite, *France and the Coming of the Second World War, 1936–1939* (1977), and *Grandeur and Decline: France, 1914–1940* (1991). They may be supplemented by W. E. Scott, *Alliance Against Hitler: The Origins of the Franco-Soviet Pact* (1962); H. Shamir, *Economic Crises and French Foreign Policy, 1930–1936* (1989); A. H. Furnia, *The Diplomacy of Appeasement* (1966); and J. E. Dreifort, *Yvon Delbos at the Quai d'Orsay: French Foreign Policy During the Popular Front, 1936–1938* (1974).

There are many books on specific episodes and subjects. The Ethiopian conquest is studied in two books by G. W. Baer: *The Coming of the Italo-Ethiopian War* (1967) and *Test Case: Italy, Ethiopia, and the League of Nations* (1976); E. M. Robertson, *Mussolini as Empire-Builder: Europe and Africa, 1932–1936* (1977); F. Hardie, *The Abyssinian Crisis* (1974); and A. del Boca, *The Ethiopian War, 1935–1941* (1969). The Rhineland episode is examined in J. T. Emerson, *The Rhineland Crisis, 7 March 1936: A Study in Multilateral Diplomacy* (1977). On the annexation of Austria, one may read G. Brook-Shepherd, *Anschluss: The Rape of Austria* (1963), and *Dolfuss* (1961); J. Gehl, *Austria, Germany and the Anschluss, 1931–1938* (1963); and D. Wagner and G. Tomkowitz, *Anschluss: The Week Hitler Seized Vienna* (1971). For Munich, the best detailed account is T. Taylor, *Munich: The Price of Peace** (1980), but also informative are J. W. Wheeler-Bennett, *Munich: Prologue to Tragedy** (1948; reissued 1963); K. Eubank, *Munich* (1963); H. Noguères, *Munich: "Peace for Our Time"* (trans. 1963); and K. Robbins, *Munich 1938* (1963). F. Gilbert and G. A. Craig (eds.), *The Diplomats, 1919–1939** (1953), include many valuable chapters on the individuals who made foreign policy in the era.

Studies focusing on eastern Europe include D. E. Kaiser, *Economic Diplomacy and the Origins of the Second World War: Germany, Britain, France, and Eastern Europe, 1930–1939* (1980); A. Cienciala, *Poland and the Western Powers, 1938–1939* (1968); S. Newman, *March 1939: The British Guarantee to Poland: A Study in the Continuity of British Foreign Policy* (1976); and A. J. Prazmowska, *Britain, Poland, and the Eastern Front, 1939* (1987). The most comprehensive study, dramatically told, of the origins and subsequent history of the German-Soviet Pact of August 23, 1939, is A. Read and D. Fisher, *The Deadly Embrace: Hitler, Stalin and the Nazi-Soviet Pact, 1939–1941* (1989); valuable also is J. E. McSherry, *Stalin, Hitler, and Europe* (2 vols., 1968–1972).

The role of the United States in these years is traced in two comprehensive volumes by W. L. Langer and S. E. Gleason, *The Challenge to Isolation, 1937–1940* (1952) and *The Undeclared War, 1940–1941* (1953). Other important studies include R. Ferrell, *American Diplomacy in the Great Depression* (1957); C. A. MacDonald, *The United States, Britain, and Appeasement, 1930–1939* (1981); D. Reynolds, *The Creation of the Anglo-American Alliance, 1937–1941* (1982); W. R. Rock, *Chamberlain and Roosevelt: British Foreign Policy and the United States, 1937–1940* (1989); and J. P. Lash, *Roosevelt and Churchill, 1931–1941:*

The Partnership That Saved the West (1976), also on the months of the "undeclared war." The most informative study of Roosevelt's foreign policy, sympathetic yet critical, for these and the war years is R. Dallek, *Franklin D. Roosevelt and American Foreign Policy, 1932–1945** (1979). For the war years it may be supplemented by J. M. Burns, *Roosevelt: The Soldier of Freedom** (1970), and W. F. Kimball, *The Juggler: Franklin Roosevelt as Wartime Statesman* (1991).

The expansion of the European conflict into a global war is related in W. Carr, *Poland to Pearl Harbor: The Making of the Second World War** (1985); and A. Iriye, *The Origins of the Second World War in Asia and the Pacific** (1987). The events in East Asia may also be studied through D. J. Lu, *From the Marco Polo Bridge to Pearl Harbor: Japan's Entry into World War II* (1961); R. Butow, *Tojo and the Coming of the War* (1961); J. B. Crowley, *Japan's Quest for Autonomy: National Security and Foreign Policy, 1930–1938* (1966), cited earlier; and P. W. Schroeder, *The Axis Alliance and Japanese-American Relations, 1941* (1963). The attack of December 7, 1941, is studied in R. Wohlstetter, *Pearl Harbor: Warning and Decision** (1962), and G. W. Prange, *At Dawn We Slept: The Untold Story of Pearl Harbor* (1981).

Hitler's relations with his two major allies are discussed in F. W. Deakin's detailed *The Brutal Friendship,** cited in Chapter XIX, and in J. Menzel, *Hitler and Japan: The Hollow Alliance* (1966).

The War: Military Aspects

Of the numerous narrative histories of the war, the two most comprehensive and up to date are M. Gilbert, *The Second World War: A Complete History* (1989), and J. Keegan, *The Second World War* (1989). Keegan has also edited *The Times Atlas of the Second World War* (1989), a superb volume. Other newer syntheses are H. P. Willmott, *The Great Crusade* (1990), and R. A. C. Parker, *Struggle for Survival** (1990), while an impressive collaborative volume is J. Campbell (ed.), *The Experience of World War II* (1989). Two outstanding older accounts are P. Calvocoressi and G. Wint, *Total War: Causes and Courses of the Second World War** (1972), and G. Wright, *The Ordeal of Total War, 1939–1945** (1968), focusing on Europe, in the Langer series. There are many narrative histories and accounts of

specific campaigns and battles. W. S. Churchill, *The Second World War** (6 vols., 1948–1953; 1 vol. abr., 1959), already mentioned, is an indispensable, full-dress history by the historian-statesman, written in the grand style, but it should be read in conjunction with other studies now available.

Many volumes of the detailed official histories of the United Kingdom, Canada, and the United States have appeared. Of special note is the official U.S. Navy history in fifteen volumes prepared by S. E. Morison (1947 ff.) and published in a one-volume abridgement as *The Two-Ocean War: A Short History of the United States Navy in the Second World War* (1963). On naval warfare, there also are available R. Hough, *The Longest Battle: The War at Sea, 1939–1945* (1986), and J. Creswell, *Sea Warfare, 1939–1945* (1967). The air war as fought by each of the major powers is examined in R. J. Overy, *The Air War, 1939–1945* (1980), and the great air battle of the war in R. Hough and D. Richards, *The Battle of Britain* (1989). C. K. Webster and N. N. Frankland, *Strategic Air Offensive Against Germany, 1939–1945* (1961), official postwar surveys, and a number of other books demonstrate that strategic bombing was less effective than thought at the time.

The war of intelligence is assessed in detail in F. H. Hinsley and others, *British Intelligence in the Second World War* (5 vols., 1979–1991). The history of the Enigma machine, with which the British broke the highest German code, and its use in Operation Ultra by the Allies, unknown at the time and not revealed (or utilized in writing the history of the war) until many years later, is recounted in P. Calvocoressi, *Top Secret Ultra* (1980), and in R. Lewin, *Ultra Goes to War* (1979). Lewin has also described the American penetration of the Japanese codes in *The American Magic** (1982).

Strategy and high-level decisions, Allied and Axis, are discussed in many books, among them K. R. Greenfield (ed.), *Command Decisions* (1959); B. H. Liddell Hart, *The Other Side of the Hill** (1951; rev. ed. of *The German Generals Talk,* 1948); H.-A. Jacobsen and J. Rohwer (eds.), *Decisive Battles of World War II: The German View* (1965); H. Trevor-Roper (ed.), *From Blitzkrieg to Defeat* (1965); and D. Downing, *The Devil's Virtuosos: German Generals at War, 1940–1945* (1977). Useful also is H.-A. Jacobsen and A. L. Smith, Jr., (eds.), *World*

War II: Policy and Strategy (1979), a selection of documents and commentary.

The military aspects of France's defeat in 1940 may be approached through A. Horne, *To Lose a Battle: France, 1940* (1969), the most detailed account; G. Chapman, *Why France Fell: The Defeat of the French Army in 1940* (1969); A. Beaufre, *1940: The Fall of France* (trans. 1968); and J. A. Gunsberg, *Divided and Conquered: The French High Command and the Defeat of the West, 1940* (1979). The background to the defeat is explored in P. C. F. Bankwitz, *Maxime Weygand and Civil-Military Relations in Modern France* (1967); J. M. Hughes, *To the Maginot Line: The Politics of French Military Preparation in the 1920s* (1971); and R. F. Young, *In Command of France: French Foreign Policy and Military Planning, 1933–1940* (1978). The relationship with Britain is studied in E. M. Gates, *End of the Affair: The Collapse of the Anglo-French Alliance, 1939–1940* (1981), and P. H. M. Bell, *A Certain Eventuality: Britain and the Fall of France* (1975). W. L. Shirer, *The Collapse of the Third Republic: An Inquiry into the Fall of France in 1940** (1969), is a thoughtful account by a reflective journalist, and M. Bloch, *Strange Defeat** (1940), is a moving memoir by the eminent medievalist executed as a member of the Resistance. His biography by C. Fink (1989) has been cited earlier.

The Russo-Finnish conflict of 1939–1940 is well treated in R. W. Condon, *The Winter War* (1972); F. Chew, *The White Death* (1971); and M. Jacobson, *The Diplomacy of the Winter War* (1961). For the war in eastern Europe after the German invasion one may read A. Werth, *Russia at War, 1941–1945** (1964); A. Clark, *Barbarossa: The Russian-German Conflict, 1941–1945* (1965); A. Seaton, *The Russo-German War* (1971); E. F. Ziemke and M. E. Bauer, *Moscow to Stalingrad: Decision in the East* (1987); and two impressive military narratives of Stalin's war with Germany by J. Erickson: *The Road to Stalingrad* (1975; reissued 1984) and *The Road to Berlin* (1984), along with the same author's *The Soviet High Command, 1918–1941* (1962). A. Seaton, *Stalin as Military Commander* (1976), merits attention as a careful study.

The war in the Pacific is ably presented in C. Bateson, *The War with Japan* (1968); S. Ienaga, *The Pacific War: World War II and the Japanese, 1931–1945* (trans. 1978), by a distinguished Japanese historian; and in A. Iriye, *Power and Culture: The Japanese-American War, 1941–1945** (1981), offering some new insights. A far-reaching study examining the impact of the war on Asia is C. Thorne, *The Far Eastern War: States and Societies, 1941–1945** (1985; reissued with this title, 1988), while the same author examines the coalition that fought the war in *Allies of a Kind: The United States, Britain, and the War Against Japan, 1941–1945** (1979). On the last phase in the Pacific, R. Butow, *Japan's Decision to Surrender** (1954), and W. Craig, *The Fall of Japan* (1968), help illuminate controversies over how inevitable or imminent Japan's surrender was.

On the development of the atomic bomb and its first use one may read, among many studies, W. L. Laurence, *Dawn Over Zero* (1946), and R. Rhodes, *The Making of the Atomic Bomb* (1986), a remarkably comprehensive account.

Biographical Accounts

M. Gilbert has completed a monumental official biography, *Winston S. Churchill* (8 vols. 1966–1989), already referred to; the first two volumes, for the years before 1914, were prepared by Churchill's son, Randolph Churchill. Accompanying each volume are companion volumes reproducing the sources. The fifth volume, for the 1930s, has already been mentioned. The war years are studied in Vol. VI, *First Hour, 1939–1941** (1983), and Vol. VII, *Road to Victory, 1941–1945** (1986), and the postwar years in *Never Despair, 1945–1965* (1989). The biography is written with clarity and extraordinary chronological detail but is quite devoid of analysis, comment, or reference to divergent interpretations. Gilbert has also written *Churchill: A Photographic Portrait* (1988). Another large-scale biography in progress, W. Manchester, *The Last Lion: Winston Spencer Churchill*, of which Vol. II is *Alone, 1932–1940* (1989), is excessively adulatory. For the early years, focusing on miscalculations and mistakes not dwelled on in these biographies, R. Rhodes James has written *Churchill: A Study in Failure, 1900–1939* (1970), and Churchill's role as wartime leader is scrutinized in the essays in A. J. P. Taylor and others, *Churchill Revised: A Critical Assessment* (1969). There are briefer studies of Churchill by L. Broad (1956), H. Pelling (1974), and T. Morgan (1982). Although demythologizing Churchill may be necessary, D. Irving, *Churchill's War: The Struggle for Power* (1989), the first volume of a projected larger work, is vehemently hostile. Irving, an Australian historian, often offers new materials or new ways of looking at older materials but strains credulity; in *Hitler's War** (1977), he absolves Hitler of any direct responsibility for the war or for the Nazi atrocities. His biography of Rommel, *The Trail of the Fox* (1977), however, is more balanced. Even a limited listing of studies relating to Allied military leaders would have to include F. C. Pogue on George C. Marshall (4 vols., 1963–1987), and M. Stoler on the same subject (1989); S. E. Ambrose on Dwight D. Eisenhower (2 vols.; 1 vol. abr., 1990); M. Schaller on Douglas MacArthur (1989); A. Bryant on Field Marshal Sir Alan Brooke (2 vols., 1957–1959); R. Lamb (1984) and N. Hamilton (1985) on Montgomery; and P. Ziegler on Mountbatten (1985).

The War: Social and Economic Impact

For the social and economic impact of the war the best one-volume synthesis is A. S. Milward, *War, Economy, and Society, 1939–1945** (History of the World Economy in the Twentieth Century series, 1977). For the British wartime scene A. Calder, *The People's War: Britain, 1939–1945* (1969), is highly informative, and there are excellent volumes in the U.K. official history, among them W. C. Hancock and M. M. Gowing, *British War Economy* (1949); R. M. Titmuss, *Problems of Social Policy* (1950); and M. M. Postan, *British War Production* (1950). A graphic documentary and photographic account is A. Marwick, *The Home Front: The British and the Second World War* (1977). Various phases of the American domestic scene are treated in A. R. Buchanan, *The United States and World War II** (2 vols., 1964), and A. M. Winkler, *Home Front U.S.A.** (1986). In a special category, P. Fussell, *Wartime: Understanding and Behavior in the Second World War* (1989), emphasizes the contrast between wartime rhetoric and the miseries of the common soldier.

The entry of women into the wartime labor force is examined in K. Anderson *Wartime Women: Sex Roles, Family Relations, and the Status of Women During World War II* (1981); L. J. Rupp, *Mobilizing Women for War: German and American Propaganda, 1939–1945* (1978); and in sev-

eral of the essays in M. R. Higonnet and others, *Behind the Lines: Gender and the Two World Wars** (1987).

That Hitler did not prepare for war in depth because he expected a quick victory emerges clearly from B. H. Klein, *Germany's Economic Preparations for War* (1959); B. A. Carroll, *Design for Total War: Arms and Economics in the Third Reich* (1968); and A. S. Milward, *The German Economy at War* (1965). In this connection Albert Speer's memoirs, *Inside the Third Reich* (1974), are revealing if read with caution.

Hitler's New Order: Collaboration and Resistance

The first attempt to study the German occupation of Europe as a whole was a specially prepared volume of the *Survey of International Affairs* covering the years 1939–1946, *Hitler's Europe* (1954). Numerous studies have since appeared on individual countries, many on the French experience.

For Vichy the best study is R. O. Paxton, *Vichy France: Old Guard and New Order, 1940–1944** (1972); the same author also has written *Parades and Politics at Vichy* (1966), and with M. R. Marrus, *Vichy France and the Jews* (1981), which shows French culpability for many acts during the German occupation. A good brief introduction is H. R. Kedward, *Occupied France: Collaboration and Resistance** (1985). On collaboration, one may study B. M. Gordon, *Collaborationism in France During the Second World War* (1980), while J. F. Sweets, *Choices in Vichy France: The French Under Nazi Occupation* (1986), poignantly demonstrates the complexities of collaboration and resistance. A. S. Milward, *The New Order and the French Economy* (1970), surveys the economic aspects of the regime, while cultural aspects may be approached through A. Y. Kaplan, *Fascism, Literature, and French Intellectual Life* (1986), and G. Hirshfeld and P. Marsh (eds.), *Collaboration in France: Politics and Culture During the Nazi Occupation, 1940–1944* (1989).

American relations with Vichy are studied in W. L. Langer, *Our Vichy Gamble** (1947), a somewhat defensive account, and British relations in R. T. Thomas, *Britain and Vichy: The Dilemma of Anglo-French Relations, 1940–1942* (1979). There is a biography of Laval by H. Cole (1963), and a detailed study focusing on diplomatic events by G. Warner, *Pierre Laval and the Eclipse of France, 1931–1945* (1968), while H. R. Lottman, *Pétain, Hero or Traitor* (1985), highlights but does not resolve the ambivalent role played by the Marshal. The Resistance in France may be studied in D. Schoenbrun, *Soldiers of the Night: The Story of the French Resistance* (1980); M. R. D. Foot, *SOE in France* (1966); J. F. Sweets, *The Politics of Resistance in France, 1940–1944* (1976); H. R. Kedward, *Resistance in Vichy France: Ideas and Motivation in the Southern Zone, 1940–1942** (1978); and M. L. Rossiter, *Women in the Resistance** (1985). The liberation is dramatically described in R. Aron, *France Reborn* (trans. 1964), and a related event in P. Novick, *The Resistance Versus Vichy: The Purge of Collaborators in Liberated France* (1969), and in H. R. Lottman, *The Purge* (1986). For the years from the 1930s to liberation, Charles de Gaulle's *War Memoirs** (3 vols.; trans. 1958–1960), are indispensable. Specifically on de Gaulle's unsatisfactory wartime relations with London and Washington, there are available A. L. Funk, *Charles de Gaulle: The Crucial Years, 1943–1944* (1959); M. Viorst, *Hostile Allies: FDR and Charles de Gaulle* (1965); F. Kersaudy, *Churchill and de Gaulle* (1982); and R. Aglion, *Roosevelt and de Gaulle: Allies in Conflict* (trans. 1988), written by one of de Gaulle's diplomats. For de Gaulle, J. Lacouture's two-volume biography (three volumes in the French original) is the outstanding account: Vol. I, *The Rebel* (trans. 1990), covering the war years, and Vol. II, *The Ruler* (trans. 1991).

Studies of other countries under the German occupation include W. Warmbrunn, *The Dutch Under German Occupation, 1940–1945* (1963); G. Hirschfeld, *Nazi Rule and Dutch Collaboration, 1940–1945* (trans. 1988); A. S. Milward, *The Fascist Economy in Norway* (1972); R. L. Braham, *The Hungarian Labor Service System, 1939–1945* (1977); and J. Gillingham, *Belgian Business and the Nazi New Order* (1977). The Polish experience is recounted in J. T. Gross, *Polish Society Under German Occupation: The Generalgouvernement, 1939–1944* (1979), and in R. C. Lukas, *The Forgotten Holocaust: The Poles Under German Occupation, 1939–1944* (1986). In its Norwegian setting, collaborationism is illuminated in detail in O. K. Hoidal, *Quisling: A Study in Treason* (1989). For the Soviet Union two studies demonstrating, among other things,

the ineptitude of the Germans in exploiting existing discontent are A. Dallin, *German Rule in Russia, 1941–1945: A Study of Occupation Policies* (rev., 1981), and T. Schulte, *The German Army and Nazi Policies in Occupied Russia, 1941–1945* (1989). Also illuminating are J. A. Armstrong, *Ukrainian Nationalism, 1939–1945* (1955), and C. Andrew, *Vlasov and the Russian Liberation Movement, 1941–1945* (1986), on the collaborationist general.

For the European-wide Resistance, there is the informative study by H. Michel, *The Shadow War: The European Resistance, 1939–1945* (trans. 1972); the useful though somewhat anecdotal M. R. D. Foot, *Resistance: European Resistance to Nazism, 1940–1945* (1977); and J. Haestrup, *European Resistance Movements, 1939–1945: A Complete History* (rev., and issued with this title, 1981), a comprehensive account. Haestrup has also written a detailed history of the Danish experience in *Secret Alliance: A Study of the Danish Resistance Movement, 1940–1945* (3 vols.; trans. 1965–1966). The renovative spirit of the Resistance and its message for the postwar world are captured in J. D. Wilkinson, *The Intellectual Resistance in Europe* (1981), while D. Stafford, *Britain and European Resistance, 1940–1945* (1980), describes the British role in countering Communist influence in the Resistance movements.

The Holocaust

There is a large literature on the grim subject of the Holocaust, the term adopted to describe the systematic mass slaughter by the Nazis of the European Jews during the war years. The most informative and comprehensive studies are R. Hilberg, *The Destruction of the European Jews** (rev. 3 vols., 1983; 1 vol. abr., 1985); M. Gilbert, *The Holocaust: The History of the Jews of Europe During the Second World War** (1986); L. S. Dawidowicz, *The War Against the Jews, 1933–1945** (1976); Y. Bauer, *A History of the Holocaust** (1982); and L. Yahel, *The Holocaust: The Fate of European Jewry, 1932–1945* (trans. 1989). One may also turn to G. Reitlinger, *The Final Solution: The Attempt to Exterminate the Jews of Europe, 1939–1945* (rev., 1968); and N. Levin, *The Holocaust: The Destruction of European Jewry, 1933–1945* (1968), an early attempt at a synthesis, written for a broad audience. A provocative but not entirely persuasive interpretive account is A. J. Mayer, *Why Did the Heavens Not Darken? The "Final Solution" in History* (1989), which sees the root cause in earlier twentieth-century destructiveness. An exhaustive reference work, with contributions by many scholars and with bibliographies in many languages, is Y. Gutman (ed.), *Encyclopedia of the Holocaust* (4 vols., 1989).

H. Fein, *Accounting for Genocide: National Responses and Jewish Victimization During the Holocaust* (1979), examines the diversity of the experience in different countries, while R. L. Braham, *The Politics of Genocide: The Holocaust in Hungary* (2 vols., 1981), is an outstanding study of one country. A key episode of Jewish resistance is recounted in Y. Gutman, *The Jews of Warsaw, 1939–1943: Ghetto, Underground, Revolt* (trans. 1982).

Among many studies of the concentration and death camps are E. Kogon, *The Theory and Practice of Hell** (1950), one of the earliest books by a survivor; T. Des Pres, *The Survivor: An Anatomy of Life in the Death Camps** (1976); T. Segev, *Soldiers of Evil: The Commandants of the Nazi Concentration Camps* (trans. 1989); and R. J. Lifton, *The Death Doctors: Medical Killing and the Psychology of Genocide* (1987). G. Fleming, *Hitler and the Final Solution** (1984), adduces convincing evidence to refute those who absolve Hitler of direct responsibility; one may also read C. R. Browning, *The Final Solution and the German Foreign Office* (1978), and the same author's *Fateful Months: Essays on the Emergence of the Final Solution, 1941–1942* (1985).

How historians have written about the subject is explored in L. S. Dawidowicz, *The Holocaust and the Historians** (1981), and in M. R. Marrus, *The Holocaust in History* (1957), a highly rewarding study. A much discussed essay on the question of responsibility and guilt was H. Arendt, *Eichmann in Jerusalem: A Report on the Banality of Evil** (1963), written at the time of the trial of the high-ranking bureaucrat who carried out the operation. That many questions remain unresolved emerges from the essays in F. Furet (ed.), *Unanswered Questions: Nazi Germany and the Genocide of the Jews** (1989). Y. Bauer, *The Holocaust in Historical Perspective* (1978), argues the uniqueness of the episode and against later misuses of the word "genocide"; on this, one may also read L. Kuper, *Genocide:*

Its Political Use in the Twentieth Century (1982). The acrimonious debate among German historians, in which some have sought to mitigate the evil of the Holocaust by comparing it to other twentieth-century atrocities such as those of Stalin, is thoughtfully explored in C. S. Maier, *The Unmasterable Past: History, Holocaust, and German National Identity* (1988), and in R. J. Evans, *In Hitler's Shadow: West German Historians and the Attempt to Escape from the Nazi Past* (1989).

There is a large literature on the failure of the authorities in the United States, Britain, and the Vatican to rescue the doomed European Jews; among the more searching inquiries are B. Wasserstein, *Britain and the Jews of Europe, 1939–1945* (1979); M. Gilbert, *Auschwitz and the Allies* (1981); W. Laqueur, *The Terrible Secret** (1980); S. Friedländer, *Pius XII and the Third Reich* (1966); and J. F. Morley, *Vatican Diplomacy and the Jews During the Holocaust, 1939–1945* (1980). For the United States, A. D. Morse, *While Six Million Died* (1968), may be supplemented with books, among others, by D. S. Wyman (1968 and 1984), S. M. Finger (1980), Y. Bauer (1981), and D. E. Lipstadt (1986). For the Nazi atrocities against other ethnic groups in Europe, including Russians, Poles, Gypsies, and others, a brief introduction is available in B. Wytwycky, *The Other Holocaust: Many Circles of Hell* (1986).

The proceedings of the Nuremberg trials have been published as International Military Tribunal, *Trial of the Major War Criminals Before the International Military Tribunal, 1945–1946* (42 vols., 1947–1949), and as *Nazi Conspiracy and Aggression* (8 vols., 2 supplements, 1946–1958). Two informative books on the origin and nature of the trials by B. F. Smith, *Reaching Judgment at Nuremberg* (1977), and *The Road to Nuremberg* (1981), argue that they should not be dismissed as merely "victor's justice" and that they prevented an anarchic bloodbath. Other thoughtful discussions are found in P. Calvocoressi, *Nuremberg: The Facts, the Law, and the Consequences* (1948); E. Davidson, *The Trial of the Germans: Nuremberg, 1945–1946* (1966); and W. Maser, *Nuremberg: A Nation on Trial* (1979). A detailed account of the trials is provided in R. E. Conot, *Justice at Nuremberg** (1983). The lesser-known trials of the Japanese war leaders are critically analyzed in R. Minear, *Victor's Justice: The Tokyo War Crimes*

Trial: (1979), which should be supplemented by P. R. Piccigallo, *The Japanese on Trial: Allied War Crimes Operations in the East, 1945–1951* (1979), and A. C. Brackman, *The Other Nuremberg: The Untold Story of the Tokyo War Crimes Trials** (1987).

Wartime Diplomacy and Origins of the Cold War

A large literature has emerged stressing the origins of the Cold War in Soviet-American relations during the Second World War. These books are for the most part listed in the following chapter. Wartime diplomacy and the successes and failures of the Soviet-Western coalition may first be approached through the latter volumes of Churchill's history and through Vols. VI and VII of Gilbert's biography of Churchill, described earlier. E. L. Woodward, *British Foreign Policy in the Second World War* (5 vols., 1962–1977), is based on the Foreign Office archives, to which the author was given early access. The volumes of H. Feis, sympathetic to the Western leaders, are indispensable as an introduction: *Churchill, Roosevelt, Stalin: The War They Waged and the Peace They Sought** (1957), covering the years from 1941 to the collapse of Germany; *Between War and Peace: The Potsdam Conference** (1960); and on the last phase, *The Atomic Bomb and the End of the War in the Pacific** (1961, 1966). Of special value are G. Smith, *American Diplomacy During the Second World War, 1941–1945** (1965), and the volume on Roosevelt's foreign policy by R. Dallek (1979) cited earlier.

Among other studies are C. Wilmot, *The Struggle for Europe* (1952); W. H. McNeill, *America, Britain, and Russia: Their Cooperation and Conflict, 1941–1946* (1953); V. Mastny, *Russia's Road to the Cold War: Diplomacy, Warfare, and the Politics of Communism, 1941–1945* (1979), projecting a case for the logic of Soviet policy-making; and R. V. Daniels, *Russia: The Roots of Confrontation** (1985). Two key studies are G. C. Herring, *Aid to Russia, 1941–1946: Strategy, Diplomacy and the Origins of the Cold War* (1973), and M. Kitchen, *British Policy Toward the Soviet Union During the Second World War* (1987). The early bond between the U.S.S.R. and Britain after Hitler's invasion of Russia is analyzed in S. M. Miner, *Between Churchill and Stalin: The Soviet Union, Great Britain, and the Origins of the Grand Alliance* (1989), while K.

Saintsbury, *The Turning Point: Roosevelt, Stalin, Churchill, and Chiang Kai-shek, 1943: The Moscow, Cairo, and Teheran Conferences* (1985), sees the earlier wartime conferences and not Yalta as pivotal for future developments. On the latter one may read, among other accounts, R. D. Buhite, *Decision at Yalta* (1986). The rift over the opening of a second front is thoughtfully examined in M. Stoler, *The Politics of the Second Front* (1977).

On the significance of the American use of the atomic bomb for relations with the Soviets, one should compare M. J. Sherwin, *A World Destroyed: The Atomic Bomb and the Grand Alliance* (1975), an impressive and balanced study, and the more vehemently critical G. Alperowitz, *Atomic Diplomacy: Hiroshima and Potsdam** (rev., 1985). The use of the bomb is further discussed in B. J. Bernstein, *The Atomic Bomb: The Critical Issues** (1975).

A useful book on the overall postwar settlement is J. W. Wheeler-Bennett and A. Nicholls, *The Semblance of Peace: The Political Settlement After the Second World War** (1972). On population movements during and following the war there are available J. B. Schechtman, *European Population Transfer, 1939–1945* (1946); E. M. Kulischer, *Europeans on the Move: War and Population Changes, 1917–1947* (1948); M. J. Proudfoot, *European Refugees, 1939–1952* (1957); and M. R. Marrus' outstanding study, *The Unwanted: European Refugees in the Twentieth Century** (1985), cited in Chapter XVIII.

Problems and Readings*

In the various series there are available: H. W. Gatzke (ed.), *European Diplomacy Between Two Wars, 1919–1939* (1972); L. F. Schaefer (ed.), *The Ethiopian Crisis: Touchstone of Appeasement?* (1961); G. Jackson (ed.), *The Spanish Civil War: Domestic Crisis or International Conspiracy?* (1967); A. Guttmann (ed.), *American Neutrality and the Spanish Civil War* (1963); F. L. Loewenheim (ed.), *Peace or Appeasement: Hitler, Chamberlain, and the Munich Crisis* (1965); D. E. Lee (ed.), *Munich: Blunder, Plot, or Tragic Necessity?* (1969); S. M. Osgood (ed.), *The Fall of France, 1940* (rev., 1972); I. Morris (ed.), *Japan, 1931–1945: Militarism, Fascism, Japanism?* (1963); W. K. Eubank (ed.), *World War*

II: Roots and Causes (rev., 1991); L. S. Dawidowicz (ed.), *A Holocaust Reader* (1976); and D. Niewyk (ed.), *The Holocaust* (1991). The debate among German historians over the uniqueness of the Holocaust may be sampled in G. Thomas (ed.), *The Unresolved Past: A Debate in German History* (1991).

XXI. The Postwar Era: The Age of the Superpowers

The Cold War: The Opening Decade

There is a large literature on the origins and nature of the Cold War. Several books on the wartime origins of the Soviet-Western rift, and "atomic bomb diplomacy" in 1945, have been described at the end of the previous chapter. Additional titles on the later stages will be suggested in Chapter XXIII.

Among books that attempt to understand Soviet behavior in the early postwar years along with American perceptions and misperceptions are J. L. Gaddis, *The United States and the Origins of the Cold War, 1941–1947* (1972); D. Yergin, *Shattered Peace: The Origins of the Cold War and the National Security State* (1977); R. B. Woods and H. Jones, *Dawning of the Cold War: The United States' Quest for Order* (1991); and W. LaFeber, *America, Russia, and the Cold War 1945–1990* (rev., 1991). Informative also are D. Rees, *The Age of Containment: The Cold War* (1967); P. Dukes, *The Emergence of the Superpowers* (1970); R. Aron, *The Imperial Republic: The United States and the World, 1945–1973* (trans. 1974); and A. B. Ulam's two books: *The Rivals: America and Russia Since World War II* (1971) and *Dangerous Relations: The Soviet Union in World Politics, 1970–1982* (1983). Two early efforts to examine the tensions in historical perspective, i.e., going back at least to 1917, are L. Halle, *The Cold War as History* (1967), and A. Fontaine, *History of the Cold War* (2 vols.; trans. 1968–1969). H. Feis, *From Trust to Terror: The Onset of the Cold War, 1945–1950* (1970), completes that author's wartime diplomatic histories. A large revisionist literature is available blaming American political and economic postwar ambitions or miscalculations for the Cold War. For guidance to the literature one may turn to J. L. Black, *Origins, Evolution, and Nature of the Cold War: An Annotated Bibliography* (1985).

The transition from war to postwar is explored in R. Douglas, *From War to Cold War, 1942–1948* (1981); T. H. Anderson, *The United States, Great Britain, and the Cold War, 1944–1947* (1981); and J. L. Gormby, *The Collapse of the Grand Alliance, 1945–1948* (1987). An impressive first volume of a projected large-scale history of the early postwar years has appeared, H. Thomas, *The Beginnings of the Cold War, 1945–1946* (1987), with perceptive insights into the protagonists. A second detailed account, somewhat overemphasizing Churchill's role, is F. J. Harbutt, *The Iron Curtain: Churchill, America, and the Origins of the Cold War* (1986). The evolution of the Truman Doctrine is studied in T. A. Couloubis, *The U.S., Greece, and Turkey* (1983). On the diplomat who helped shape the American containment policy and later regretted the military form that it came to assume, one should read G. F. Kennan, *American Diplomacy* (1951; rev. and expanded 1985), and his several other books, along with analyses of his thought and career such as D. Mayers, *George Kennan and the Dilemmas of U.S. Foreign Policy* (1988). Kennan, Acheson and other key American foreign policy figures also are studied in W. Isaacson and E. Thomas, *The Wise Men* (1986). On the "Munich syndrome," or the resolve by Truman and others not to repeat the appeasement of the 1930s, one may read G. Rystad, *Prisoners of the Past* (1982), and E. R. May, *The Lessons of the Past: The Use and Misuse of History in American Foreign Policy* (1973).

The revolutionary implications of nuclear weapons for the post-1945 world are made clear in M. Mandelbaum's two books: *The United States and Nuclear Weapons, 1946–1976* (1979) and *The Nuclear Revolution: International Politics Before and After Hiroshima* (1981). The failure of atomic disarmament in the early years and later efforts at arms control are studied in G. Herken, *The Winning Weapon: The Atomic Bomb in the Cold War, 1945–1950* (1980), and R. E. Powaski, *March to Armageddon: The United States and the Nuclear Arms Race, 1939 to the Present* (1987). Additional books on the nuclear arms build-up will be suggested in Chapter XXIII.

The founding of the United Nations is studied in R. B. Russell, *A History of the United Nations, 1940–1945* (1958); F. P. King, *The New Internationalism: Allied Policy and the European Peace, 1939–1945* (1973); and R. C. Hildebrand, *Dumbarton*

Oaks: The Origins of the United Nations and the Search for Postwar Security (1990). Its subsequent history may be traced in C. M. Eichelberger, The UN: The First Twenty Years (1965); E. Luard, A History of the United Nations, Vol. I, The Years of Western Domination, 1945–1955 (1982), with other volumes projected; and T. M. Franck, Nation Against Nation (1985), a sober assessment. Books that examine Western Europe's role in the postwar setting include A. W. DePorte, Europe Between the Superpowers: The Enduring Alliance (rev., 1986); A. Grosser, The Western Alliance: European-American Relations Since 1945 (trans. 1980); and R. S. Jordan and W. J. Feld, Europe in the Balance: The Changing Context of European International Politics (1986). The origins of the North Atlantic Treaty Organization may be studied in T. P. Ireland, Creating the Entangling Alliance: The Origins of the North Atlantic Treaty Organization (1981).

Economic Reconstruction and the Reshaping of the World Economy

The most informative studies of postwar reconstruction and of the economic growth and full employment that followed for close to three decades before being interrupted by recession are H. Van der Wee, Prosperity and Upheaval: The World Economy, 1945–1980 (History of the World Economy in the Twentieth Century, trans. 1986), and P. Armstrong, A. Glyn, and J. Harrison, Capitalism Since World War II: The Making and Breakup of the Great Boom (1984). They may be supplemented with the essays in S. A. Marglin and J. B. Schor (eds.), The Golden Age of Capitalism: Reinterpreting the Postwar Experience (1990).

The evolution of the Bretton Woods monetary arrangements is examined in R. Triffin, The Evolution of the International Monetary System (1964); A. E. Ecks, Jr., A Search for Solvency: Bretton Woods and the International Monetary System, 1941–1971 (1975); E. J. Mason and R. E. Asher, The World Since Bretton Woods (1973); R. Solomon, The International Monetary System, 1945–1976 (1977); and B. Tew, The Evolution of the International Monetary System, 1945–1981 (1981).

For European economic developments one may turn also to C. M. Cipolla (ed.), The Fontana Economic History of Europe: Vol. V, The Twentieth Century (1976), and

Vol. VI, Contemporary Economies (1976). Thoughtful surveys of Europe in the postwar era include W. Laqueur, Europe Since Hitler: The Rebirth of Europe* (rev., 1982); F. Tipton and R. Aldrich, An Economic and Social History of Europe, 1939 to the Present* (1987), the sequel to an earlier volume; and D. Urwin, Western Europe Since 1945* (rev., 1989). G. Ambrosius and W. H. Hubbard, A Social and Economic History of Twentieth-Century Europe (trans. 1989), provides useful statistical and sociological data.

For the immediate postwar years and the American role in reconstruction two key books are A. S. Milward, The Reconstruction of Western Europe, 1945–1951 (1984), which credits European initiative and skills as much as American aid, and M. J. Hogan, The Marshall Plan: America, Britain, and the Reconstruction of Western Europe, 1947–1952* (1987), the fullest account of the Marshall Plan and the European Recovery Program. Other books that merit attention are J. Gimbel, The Origins of the Marshall Plan (1976); R. A. Pollard, Economic Security and the Origins of the Cold War, 1945–1950 (1987); C. L. Mee, The Marshall Plan and the Launching of the Pax Americana (1989); and C. P. Kindleberger, The Marshall Plan Days (1987), reminiscences and analysis by an economist-participant. R. J. Donovan, The Second Victory: The Marshall Plan and the Postwar Revival of Europe (1987) is a brief celebratory account.

An impressive synthesis on postwar reconstruction in all aspects is P. Duignan and L. H. Gann, The Rebirth of the West: Culture, Politics, and Society, 1945–1958 (1990). It may be read along with N. Rosenberg and L. E. Birdzell, Jr., How the West Grew Rich: The Economic Transformation of the Industrial World* (1987), which emphasizes the importance of pluralism and flexibility as a key to Western economic growth. Other studies of European economic recovery and expansion in the postwar years include A. Maddison, Economic Growth in the West (1964); M. M. Postan, An Economic History of Western Europe, 1945–1964* (1967); C. P. Kindleberger, Europe's Postwar Growth (1967); R. Mayne, The Recovery of Europe, 1945–1973 (rev., 1973); and M. Crouzet, The European Renaissance since 1945* (1971).

The postwar welfare state is carefully examined by the British study group, Political and Economic Planning, in Economic

Planning and Policies in Britain, France, and Germany (1968); D. E. Ashford, *The Emergence of the Welfare States* (1987); and P. Baldwin, *The Politics of Social Solidarity: Class Bases of the European Welfare State, 1875–1975* (1990). Detailed analyses are available in P. Flora (ed.), *Growth to Limits: The Western European Welfare States Since World War II* (5 vols., 1986–1988). On Keynes and Keynesianism, highly influential in the managed economies of the early postwar decades, one may read R. Lekachman, *The Age of Keynes** (1966), and other books mentioned in Chapter XIX. On the role of government one may also read A. Shonfield, *Modern Capitalism: The Changing Balance of Public and Private Power* (1969); S. Lieberman, *The Growth of the European Mixed Economies, 1945–1970* (1977); P. A. Hall, *Governing the Economy: The Politics of State Intervention in Britain and France** (1986); and the essays in A. Graham with A. Seldon (eds.), *Government and Economies in the Postwar World* (1990). Some of the social consequences of the economic changes in Europe are explored in S. Rothman, *European Society and Politics: Britain, France, and Germany** (1976), and A. Sampson, *The New Europeans* (rev., 1971). A special subject is examined in two books by S. Castles: *Here For Good: Western Europe's New Ethnic Minorities* (1984) and *Migrant Workers in European Societies** (1989).

On Western European economic cooperation and integration one may read W. Lipgens, *A History of European Integration, 1945–1947: The Formation of the European Unity Movement* (trans. 1982), and M. Jansen, *A History of European Integration, 1947–1975* (trans. 1975). The historical background to unification is explored in J. Lukacs, *Decline and Rise of Europe** (1965); and the "father of European unity," who early on recognized that the path to political unity lay through economic channels is studied in M. and S. Bromberger, *Jean Monnet and the United States of Europe* (trans. 1969), and in the essays in D. Brinkley and C. Hackett (eds.), *Jean Monnet: The Path to European Unity* (1991). Other studies on economic integration include W. Diebold, Jr., *The Schuman Plan* (1959); H. A. Schmitt, *The Path to European Union: From the Marshall Plan to the Common Market* (1962); W. O. Henderson, *The Genesis of the Common Market* (1963); and J. Gillingham, *Coal, Steel, and the Rebirth of Europe,* *1945–1955: The Germans and the French from Ruhr Conflict to Economic Community* (1990). Books on the later evolution of the European Community will be cited in Chapter XXIII.

The Western Countries (and Japan) Since 1945

For all of the Western countries many of the books cited for Chapter XIX will also be helpful.

BRITAIN. The following titles show clearly the concern with Britain's loss of primacy and world power beginning with its "relative decline" in the late nineteenth century: M. W. Kirby, *The Decline of British Power Since 1870* (1981); R. Blake, *The Decline of Power, 1915–1964** (1985); B. Porter, *Britain, Europe, and the World, 1850–1986: Delusion of Grandeur** (1987); T. O. Lloyd, *Empire to Welfare State: English History, 1906–1985** (rev., 1986); and two incisive studies by C. Barnett: *The Collapse of British Power* (1986) and *The Pride and the Fall: The Dream and Illusion of Britain as a Great Nation* (1988). An influential study tracing the loss of leadership to a social and educational system that failed to prize entrepreneurship is M. Wiener, *English Culture and the Decline of the Industrial Spirit, 1850–1980* (1981). That the reasons for decline remain controversial, however, emerges from the debate and discussion in A. Sked, *Britain's Decline: Problems and Perspectives** (1987), and from the essays in B. Collins and K. Robbins (eds.), *British Culture and Economic Decline* (1990).

The best account of the postwar Labour governments and the emergence of the welfare state is K. O. Morgan, *Labour in Power, 1945–1951** (1984), a balanced study with in-depth portraits of Attlee and other key figures; it may be compared with H. Pelling, *The Labour Governments, 1945–1951* (1984), and P. Weiler, *British Labour and the Cold War* (1988). The creation and consolidation of the welfare state is studied in P. Gregg, *The Welfare State: An Economic and Social History of Great Britain From 1945 to the Present Day* (1969), and in S. H. Beer, *British Politics in the Collectivist Age* (1965). For the social impact one may read A. Marwick, *British Society Since 1945** (1982), and A. Sampson, *The New Anatomy of Britain** (rev., 1983). A biographical study of distinction is A. Bullock,

The Life and Times of Ernest Bevin (3 vols., 1960–1983); Bevin's service as foreign secretary from 1945 to 1951 is studied in the third volume. Two of several good surveys of British history in the postwar decades are A. Sked and C. Cook, *Post-War Britain: A Political History** (rev., 1984), and K. O. Morgan, *The People's Peace: British History, 1945–1989* (1991). A special subject is explored in Z. A. Layton-Henry, *The Politics of Race in Britain* (1984).

To studies of the persistent Irish question cited earlier and the troubles in Northern Ireland may be added T. Brown, *Ireland: A Social and Cultural History, 1922 to the Present** (1985); O. MacDonagh, *States of Mind: A Study of Anglo-Irish Conflict, 1780–1980** (1983); and P. Arthur and K. Jeffery, *Northern Ireland Since 1968** (1988).

FRANCE. Fourth and Fifth Republic. The best synthesis for the short-lived Fourth Republic is J.-P. Rioux, *The Fourth Republic, 1944–1958** (trans. 1987), a volume in the Cambridge History of Modern France. It may be supplemented by P. M. Williams, *Crisis and Compromise: Politics in the Fourth Republic** (1965). The formative early years are studied in H. Footitt and J. Simmonds, *France, 1943–1945: The Politics of Liberation* (1988); A. Shennan, *Rethinking France: Plans for Renewal, 1940–1946* (1989); and R. M. Kuisel, *Capitalism and the State in Modern France: Renovation and Economic Management in the Twentieth Century* (1981), which places governmental direction of the economy in historical perspective. Mendès-France's reform efforts in the early 1950s are sympathetically portrayed in J. Lacouture, *Pierre Mendès-France* (trans. 1984).

The colonial wars helped bring down the Fourth Republic. The war in Indochina is graphically portrayed in B. B. Fall, *Street Without Joy: Indochina at War, 1946–1954* (rev., 1964), and in the same author's *Hell in a Very Small Place: The Siege of Dienbienphu* (1967). The ill-fated effort to retain Algeria is described in A. Horne, *A Savage War of Peace: Algeria, 1954–1962* (1978), a comprehensive account, and J. Talbott, *The War Without a Name: France in Algeria, 1954–1962* (1980).

For the Fifth Republic, and the dwindling importance of older divisive issues, one may read S. Hoffmann, *Decline or Renewal? France Since the 1930s* (1974), and M. Larkin, *France Since the Popular Front:*

Government and People, 1936–1986* (1988). Informative volumes are P. M. Williams and M. Harrison, *Politics and Society in de Gaulle's Republic** (1972); H. W. Ehrmann, *Politics in France** (rev., 1976); R. C. Macridis, *French Politics in Transition* (1975); and W. G. Andrews and S. Hoffmann (eds.), *The Fifth Republic at Twenty* (1981). For social changes, D. L. Hanley and others, *Contemporary France: Politics and Society Since 1945** (1979), and J. Ardagh, *The New France: de Gaulle and After* (rev., 1977) are illuminating. C. Tilley, *The Contentious French** (1986), puts much of contemporary France in perspective. J. Lacouture's biography of de Gaulle (2 vols., trans. 1990–1991) has already been mentioned; there are also biographical accounts among others, by B. Crozier (1973), B. Ledwidge (1983), and D. Cook (1984). Two insightful analyses of de Gaulle's views on foreign policy are L. P. de Ménil, *Who Speaks for Europe? The Vision of Charles de Gaulle* (1977), and P. G. Cerny, *The Politics of Grandeur: Ideological Aspects of de Gaulle's Foreign Policy* (1980).

GERMANY. West and East. For West Germany an impressive, comprehensive narrative is D. L. Bark and D. R. Gress, *A History of West Germany* (2 vols., 1990): Vol. I, *From Shadow to Substance, 1945–1963,* and Vol. II, *Democracy and its Discontents, 1963–1988.* Other thoughtful accounts are A. Grosser, *Germany in Our Time** (1971); M. Balfour, *West Germany: A Contemporary History* (rev., 1982); and L. J. Edinger, *West German Politics** (rev., 1985).

On the occupation, the first postwar decade, and economic recovery, there are E. F. Ziemke, *The United States Army in the Occupation of Germany, 1944–1946* (1977), an outstanding study, one of the final volumes in the 79-volume history of the American army in the Second World War; H. Zink, *The United States and Germany, 1945–1955* (1957); J. Gimbel, *The American Occupation of Germany: Politics and the Military, 1945–1949* (1968); and F. Golay, *The Founding of the Federal Republic of Germany* (1958). For the German "economic miracle" one may read H. C. Wallich, *Mainsprings of the German Revival* (1955), and A. Kramer, *The West German Economy, 1945–1955* (1990); and for the powerful economy that later emerged, E. Hartrich, *The Fourth and Richest Reich* (1980), and E. O.

Smith, *The West German Economy* (1983). Of special interest is V. R. Berghahn, *The Americanisation of West German Industry, 1945–1973* (1986). For the Adenauer years, one may read E. Alexander, *Adenauer and the New Germany* (1957), and R. Hiscocks, *The Adenauer Era** (1966). L. J. Edinger offers a portrait of the Social Democratic leader in *Kurt Schumacher: A Study in Personality and Political Behavior* (1965), and T. Prittie has written a biography of Willy Brandt (1974). The emergence of the environmentalists and other activists of the left is studied in R. Burns and W. Van der Will, *Protest and Democracy in West Germany: Extra-Parliamentary Opposition and the Democratic Agenda* (1988).

For West and East Germany, including the interrelationship of the two states over the four postwar decades, one may read H. A. Turner, Jr., *The Two Germanies Since 1945* (1987). For East Germany one may also read J. P. Nettl, *The Eastern Zone and Soviet Policy in Germany, 1945–1950* (1951); K. Southeimer and W. Bleek, *The Government and Politics of East Germany* (1976); and D. Childs, *The GDR: Moscow's German Ally** (1983). The East German Communist leadership is examined in C. Stern, *Ulbrecht: A Political Biography* (1965), and the effort to prevent the flight of the East Germans in P. Galante and P. Miller, *The Berlin Wall* (1965). Willy Brandt's efforts to improve East-West relations are studied in A. Stent, *From Embargo to Ostpolitik: The Political Economy of West German-Soviet Relations, 1955–1980* (1982). Of special interest for foreign affairs is W. F. Henrieder, *Germany, America, Europe: Forty Years of German Foreign Policy* (1990). There are provocative insights into the German search for self-understanding in R. Dahrendorf, *Society and Democracy in Germany* (1967); G. A. Craig, *The Germans** (1982), cited in Chapter XIII; F. Stern, *Dreams and Delusions: The Drama of German History* (1987); and H. James, *A German Identity, 1770–1990* (1990). The reunification in 1990 of the two Germanies may be expected to bring additional assessments by Germans and others of the "German question."

ITALY. Two insightful studies of Italian political life are F. Spotts and T. Wieser, *Italy: A Difficult Democracy—A Survey of Italian Politics** (1986), and J. LaPalombara, *Democracy, Italian Style* (1987). Both describe the paradox whereby the country has known remarkable social and economic progress despite parliamentary instability. For the postwar years one may read D. W. Ellwood, *Italy, 1943–1945* (1985); H. S. Hughes, *The United States and Italy* (rev., 1979), in the American Foreign Policy Library series; G. Mammanella, *Italy After Fascism: A Political History, 1943–1965* (rev., 1966); N. Kogan, *A Political History of Postwar Italy* (2 vols., 1966–1981); and P. Ginsborg, *A History of Contemporary Italy: Society and Politics, 1943–1988* (1990). The American role in the early years is assessed in J. L. Harper, *America and the Reconstruction of Italy, 1945–1948* (1986), and the special role of the Italian Communist party from liberation to the mid-1980s is examined in J. B. Urban, *Moscow and the Italian Communist Party: From Togliatti to Berlinguer* (1986), and in A. De Grand, *The Italian Left in the Twentieth Century: A History of the Socialist and Communist Parties* (1989).

JAPAN. E. O. Reischauer, *The United States and Japan** (rev., 1965), *Japan: The Story of a Nation** (rev., 1977), and *The Japanese Today: Change and Continuity** (1988), are invaluable introductions. Studies of the occupation include K. Kawai, *Japan's American Interlude* (1960); M. Schaller, *The American Occupation of Japan* (1985); H. B. Schonberger, *Aftermath of War* (1989); and R. E. Ward and Y. Sakamoto (eds.), *Democratizing Japan: The Allied Occupation* (1987). Among studies of the economy are J. B. Cohen, *Japan's Post-War Economy* (1958); G. C. Allen, *Japan's Economic Recovery* (1958); and for its later explosive expansion, H. Patrick and H. Rosovsky (eds.), *Asia's New Giant: How the Japanese Economy Works* (1976). Of special interest are C. Johnson, *MITI and the Japanese Miracle: The Growth of Industrial Policy, 1925–1974* (1982), on the government research and development agency, and W. W. Lockwood, *State and Economic Enterprise in Japan* (1986). There are some remarkable, if controversial, insights into the Japanese political culture in K. van Wolferen, *The Enigma of Japanese Power: People and Politics in a Stateless Nation* (1989), which notes the many differences between Japanese and Western political culture.

THE UNITED STATES. Although no listing on domestic developments in the contemporary United States is possible here, an introduction to the postwar years is provided in

C. N. Degler, *Affluence and Anxiety: The United States Since 1945** (1968); G. Hodgson, *America in Our Time* (1976); W. E. Leuchtenburg, *A Troubled Feast: American Society Since 1945** (rev., 1979); and W. H. Chafe, *The Unfinished Journey: America Since World War II* (rev., 1991). Perspectives on contemporary social and economic problems are offered in M. Harrington, *The Other America* (1962); J. T. Patterson, *America's Struggle Against Poverty, 1900–1980* (1981), and R. Polenberg, *One Nation Divisible: Class, Race, and Ethnicity in the United States Since 1938* (1980). A. Hacker, *The U.S.: A Statistical Portrait* (1983), is an invaluable work of reference and analysis.

The Soviet Union: From Stalin to Brezhnev

There are many volumes on the Stalin years listed in Chapter XVII, which should be consulted. One of the best assessments of the Stalinist era in perspective is A. B. Ulam, *Stalin: The Man and His Era* (1987). The postwar years and the evolution of the Soviet system after 1953 are explored in A. Nove, *Stalinism and After: The Road to Gorbachev** (rev., 1989); R. McNeal, *The Bolshevik Tradition: Lenin, Stalin, Khrushchev, Brezhnev** (rev., 1974); S. Bialer, *Stalin's Successors: Leadership, Stability, and Change in the Soviet Union* (1980); and the same author's *The Domestic Context of Soviet Foreign Policy* (1981). The Soviet economy in the early 1980s is assessed in M. I. Goldman, *The U.S.S.R. in Crisis: The Failure of an Economic System* (1983); S. Bialer, *The Soviet Paradox: External Expansion, Internal Decline* (1986); and A. Nove, *The Soviet Economic System* (rev., 1986). Foreign policy is studied in R. Edmonds, *Soviet Foreign Policy: The Brezhnev Years** (1983); the origins and nature of the involvement in Afghanistan in M. Urban, *War in Afghanistan* (rev., 1991).

For the dissenters one may turn to R. Conquest, *The Politics of Ideas in the U.S.S.R.* (1967); P. Reddaway, *Russia's Underground Intellectuals* (1970); A. Rothberg, *The Heirs of Stalin: Dissidence and the Soviet Regime, 1953–1970* (1972); and R. T. Tökes (ed.), *Dissent in the U.S.S.R.: Politics, Ideology, and People* (1975). M. Scammell, *Solzhenitzyn: A Biography* (1984), provides a balanced assessment of the novelist. A. Knight, *The KGB: Police and Politics in the Soviet Union** (1988), carries the story of the secret police to the mid 1980s, while anti-Semitism from the postwar years on may be studied in L. Rapoport, *Stalin's War Against the Jews: The Doctors' Plot and the Soviet Solution* (1990); B. Pinkus, *The Soviet Government and the Jews, 1948–1967** (1985); and R. O. Freedman (ed.), *Soviet Jewry in the Decisive Decade, 1971–1980* (1987). Books on the Soviet Union in the Gorbachev era will be described in Chapter XXIII.

For the Communist movement as a whole, A. Westoby, *Communism Since World War II* (rev., 1989), provides encyclopedic coverage, while J. Braunthal examines the years after the dissolution of the Comintern in *History of the International*, Vol. III, *World Socialism, 1943–1968* (trans. 1980). The break from Moscow control and the phenomenon of Eurocommunism may be studied in G. R. Urban, *Eurocommunism* (1978); A. Kriegel, *Eurocommunism* (trans. 1978); C. Marzani, *The Promise of Eurocommunism* (1980); R. Kindersley (ed.), *In Search of Eurocommunism* (1981); and C. Boggs, *The Impasse of European Communism* (1982).

Eastern Europe Under Soviet Domination

How communism was imposed on Eastern Europe is explored in H. Seton-Watson, *The East European Revolution* (rev., 1956). The years of Communist domination and the mounting restiveness in Eastern Europe are studied in J. Rothschild, *Return to Diversity: A Political History of East Central Europe Since World War II** (1988). For the party purges in the early postwar years one may read G. H. Hodos, *Show Trials: Stalinist Purges in Eastern Europe, 1948–1954* (1988). Other informative studies include F. Fejtö, *A History of the People's Democracies: Eastern Europe Since Stalin* (trans. 1971); Z. K. Brzezinski, *The Soviet Bloc: Unity and Conflict* (1960; rev., 1967); S. Fischer-Galati, *Eastern Europe in the 1980s* (1981); J. Lovenduski and J. Woodall, *Politics and Society in Eastern Europe** (1987); O. Narkiewicz, *Eastern Europe, 1968 to 1984* (1986); and the same author's *Petrification and Progress: Communist Leaders in Eastern Europe, 1956–1988* (1990). A good introduction to the East European economic systems and to industrialization is A. H. Smith, *The Planned Economies of Eastern Europe* (1983), while a more detailed analysis is provided in M. C. Kaser and E. A. Radice (eds.), *The*

Economic History of Eastern Europe, 1919–1975 (3 vols., 1986–1987). Some of the social implications are studied in W. Connor, *Socialism, Politics, and Equality: Hierarchy and Change in Eastern Europe and the U.S.S.R.* (1979).

For Hungary and the uprising in 1956 one may read P. C. Zinner, *Revolution in Hungary* (1962); B. Kovrig, *Communism in Hungary from Kun to Kadar* (1979); and C. Gati, *Hungary and the Soviet Bloc* (1988), an especially rewarding study. Czechoslovakia as victim, first of Hitler then of Stalin, is examined in E. Toborsky, *President Eduard Beneš: Between East and West, 1938–1948* (1981). The crisis of 1968 is studied in G. Golan, *The Czechoslovak Reform Movement: Communism in Crisis, 1962–1968* (1971); V. Kusin, *Intellectual Origins of the Prague Spring* (1971); Z. Zeman, *Prague Spring* (1969); and K. Dawisha, *The Kremlin and the Prague Spring* (1984). For Poland, the origins and evolution of the Solidarity movement are traced in A. Kemp-Welch, *The Birth of Solidarity* (1991). Informative studies of Yugoslavia are D. Rusinow, *The Yugoslav Experiment, 1948–1974** (1977); D. Wilson, *Tito's Yugoslavia* (1979); and H. Lydall, *Yugoslavia in Crisis* (1989).

China Under Mao

As background to the emergence of communism, and for a sense of the continuing revolution in China in modern times, several books cited in Chapters XV and XVIII, especially those by J. D. Spence and J. K. Fairbanks, should be consulted. For China in the years after 1949 the best overviews are M. Meisner, *Mao's China and After: A History of the People's Republic** (rev., 1986), and L. Dittmer, *China's Continuous Revolution: The Post-Liberation Era, 1949–1981* (1987). The radical phases of Mao Zedong's rule, including the Great Leap Forward and the Cultural Revolution, are examined in E. Brugger, *China: Liberation and Transformation, 1942–1962,* and *China: Radicalism to Revisionism, 1962–1970* (rev., 1981).

On the early years there is a rewarding two-volume study by R. MacFarquhar, *The Origins of the Cultural Revolution: Vol. I, Contradictions Among the People 1956–1957** (1974), and Vol. II, *The Great Leap Forward, 1958–1960** (1984). Books that explore the origins and nature of the Communist regime include C. P. Fitzgerald, *The Birth of Communist China** (rev., 1966), and *Mao Tse-tung and China* (1976); B. Schwartz, *Chinese Communism and the Rise of Mao** (1951); C. A. Johnson, *Peasant Nationalism and Communist Power, 1937–1945** (1962); and J. P. Harrison, *The Long March to Power: A History of the Chinese Communist Party, 1921–1972* (1972). An informative study is S. Schram, *The Political Thought of Mao Tse-Tung* (rev., 1969), and an assessment by leading scholars shortly after Mao's death is provided in D. Wilson (ed.), *Mao Tse-tung on the Scales of History** (1977).

The Korean War

The first decade of the Cold War saw a hot war in Korea. For background and an introduction to Asia's role in world politics, one may read D. F. Lach and E. S. Wehrle, *International Politics in East Asia Since World War II* (1975). For American relations with the Asian countries in the early postwar years, W. Borden, *The Pacific Alliance . . . 1947–1955* (1984), and J. Matray, *The Reluctant Crusade: American Foreign Policy in Korea, 1941–1950* (1980), are especially helpful. The fullest inquiry into the origins of the Korean War, with sharp insights into the nature of the two regimes, is the two-volume study of B. Cumings, *The Origins of the Korean War: Vol. I, Liberation and the Emergence of Separate Regimes, 1945–1947* (1981), and Vol. II, *The Roaring of the Cataract, 1947–1950* (1990). Other studies of the origins and nature of the war are P. Lowe, *The Origins of the Korean War** (1986), and accounts by R. Foot (1985), B. I. Kaufman (1986), M. Hastings (1987), and J. Merrill (1989). The military aspects are emphasized in A. Bevin, *Korea* (1987), while the long career of the Communist leader is studied in D. S. Suh, *Kim Il Sung: The North Korean Leader* (1988).

Problems and Readings*

The background to the Cold War may be examined in N. A. Graebner (ed.), *The Cold War: A Conflict of Ideology and Power* (rev., 1976); T. G. Paterson and R. J. McMahon (eds.), *The Origins of the Cold War* (rev., 1991); L. C. Gardner (ed.), *Origins of the Cold War* (1970); and C. S. Maier (ed.), *The Cold War in Europe: Its Origins and Consequences** (rev., 1990). The movement toward European unity is examined in F. R. Willis (ed.), *European Integration* (1975). For the Communist triumph in China there is P. P. Y. Loh, *The Kuomintang Debacle of 1949: Conquest or Collapse?* (1965).

XXII. Empires into Nations: Asia, Africa, the Middle East

End of the European Empires

Many of the books mentioned in Chapters XV and XVIII also should be consulted. For the background to the post-1945 colonial revolutions, one of the best introductions is R. Emerson, *From Empire to Nation: The Rise to Self-Assertion of Asian and African Peoples** (1960). A comprehensive account of the end of empire is offered in F. Ansprenger, *The Dissolution of Colonial Empires** (1989), while M. E. Chamberlain, *Decolonization: The Fall of the European Empires** (1985) is an informative brief synthesis. Books that examine colonial administration in the final phases before independence include M. Perham, *Colonial Sequence, 1930–1949* (1976); R. F. Betts, *Uncertain Dimensions: Western Overseas Empires in the Twentieth Century** (1985), R. von Albertini, *Decolonization: The Administration and Future of the Colonies, 1919–1960** (rev., 1982); and R. F. Holland, *European Decolonization, 1918–1981* (1985). There are interesting vignettes of selected Asian and African nationalist leaders in H. Tinker, *Men Who Overturned Empires: Fighters, Dreamers, and Schemers* (1987).

On nationalism and the emergent nations, many of the books cited in Chapter XI on the older nationalism will also be helpful. Especially informative are E. Kedourie, *Nationalism in Asia and Africa* (1971); two books by A. D. S. Smith: *Nationalism in the Twentieth Century* (1979) and *The Ethnic Origins of Nations* (1986); and E. J. Hobsbawm, *Nations and Nationalism Since 1780: Programme, Myth, Reality* (1990). For understanding the postwar experience one should also read S. P. Huntington, *Political Order in Changing Societies* (1968), and for a comprehensive study of ethnic tensions and rivalries in the contemporary world,

D. L. Horowitz, *Ethnic Groups in Conflict** (1985). A Norwegian historian gives special attention to the Third World in G. Lundestad, *East, West, North, South: Major Developments in International Politics, 1945–1986* (1986).

End of the British Empire

The disintegration of the British empire in Asia, Africa, and the Middle East is thoroughly studied in J. Darwin, *Britain and Decolonisation: The Retreat from Empire in the Post-War World* (1988); the same author has also written *End of Empire** (1990), a briefer account. Wartime controversies between Churchill and Roosevelt over the future of the colonial world are skillfully analyzed in W. R. Louis, *Imperialism at Bay: The United States and the Decolonization of the British Empire 1941–1945** (1978), while the same author examines the largely unsuccessful British effort to hold onto its influence in the Middle East in *The British Empire in the Middle East, 1945–1951: Arab Nationalism, the United States, and Postwar Imperialism** (1984). A comparative study of British and French reactions to the loss of empire is M. Kahler, *Decolonization in Britain and France: The Domestic Consequences of International Relations* (1984).

The British withdrawal from the Indian subcontinent and the early years of independence are examined in H. V. Hodson, *The Great Divide: Britain-India-Pakistan* (rev., 1985), and in W. N. Brown, *The United States and India, Pakistan, and Bangladesh* (rev., 1972), in the American Foreign Policy Library series. For all aspects of India, historical and contemporary, and the politics and culture of all of South Asia, one may turn for guidance to S. Wolpert, *A New History of India** (rev., 1989), cited earlier, and to the same author's *India* (1991), which is thematically organized. The Indian experiment in economic planning and parliamentary democracy is assessed in many books, among them L. I. and S. H. Rudolph, *In Pursuit of Lakshmi* [the Indian Goddess of Fortune]: *The Political Economy of the Indian State* (1987); other studies of development will be cited later in the chapter. The several excellent biographies of Nehru have been mentioned in Chapter XVIII. For the Congress party, Nehru's leadership, and that of Indira Gandhi, one may turn to P. Brass, *The Politics of India Since Independence** (1990). A thoughtful assessment of key forces at work in India is A. T. Embree, *Utopias in Conflict: Religion and Nationalism in Modern India* (1990). The inability of Pakistan to integrate East Pakistan and the emergence of Bangladesh is studied in R. Jahan, *Pakistan: Failure in National Integration* (1972). On the founder of the Muslim state, S. Wolpert has written *Jinnah of Pakistan* (1984).

For developments in Southeast Asia including Burma, Malaysia, Singapore, Indonesia, the Philippines and the countries that emerged out of French Indochina, two good introductions are D. R. Sar Desai, *Southeast Asia: Past and Present** (1988), and J. Pluvier, *Southeast Asia: From Colonialism to Independence* (1974). The war fought by the British in Malaya is most fully described in R. Jackson, *The Malayan Emergency: The Commonwealth Wars, 1948–1966* (1990). For the British success in attracting the newly independent states in Asia, Africa, and elsewhere to membership in the transformed Commonwealth of Nations one may read R. J. Moore, *Making the New Commonwealth* (1987).

The struggle against the Dutch in Indonesia and Indonesian leadership in the years of independence may be approached through two biographical accounts: J. D. Legge, *Sukarno: A Political Biography* (1972), and D. Jenkins, *Suharto and His Generals* (1984).

For Africa, two indispensable volumes are P. Gifford and W. R. Louis (eds.), *The Transfer of Power in Africa: Decolonization, 1940–1960* (1982), and *Decolonization and African Independence: The Transfers of Power, 1960–1980* (1988). The most populous country is studied in L. J. Diamond, *Class, Ethnicity, and Democracy in Nigeria: The Failure of the First Republic* (1988); A. Kirk-Greene, H. Millard, and D. Rimmer, *Nigeria Since 1970* (1981); and the international dimensions of the Ibo attempt at secession in J. J. Stremlau, *The International Politics of the Nigerian Civil War, 1967–1970** (1977).

For West Africa there is A. R. Zolberg, *Creating Political Order: The Party States of West Africa* (1966), and for Ghana one may add D. Rooney, *Kwame Nkrumah: The Political Kingdom in the Third World* (1988). For East Africa the ordeal of Uganda, with

insights into civil-military relationships elsewhere in Africa, is studied in A. Omara-Otunnu, *Politics and the Military in Uganda 1890–1985* (1957). Introductions to two other East African states are N. N. Miller, *Kenya: The Quest for Prosperity** (1984), and R. Yeager, *Tanzania: An African Experiment** (1983).

The stormy beginnings of Zaire and the dictatorship of Mobutu are studied in J. Gérard-Libois, *Katanga Secession* (1960); C. Young, *Politics in the Congo: Decolonization and Independence* (1965); and C. Young and T. Turner, *The Rise and Decline of the Zairian State* (1985). For the north-south civil war in the Sudan there are informative essays in F. M. Deng and P. Gifford (eds.), *The Search for Peace and Unity in the Sudan* (1987). Zimbabwe's struggle against South Africa and the ensuing civil wars are recounted in L. H. Gann and T. H. Henricksen, *The Struggle for Zimbabwe: The Battle in the Bush* (1981). The Portuguese colonies, the war for independence, and the years of civil strife may be approached through G. J. Bender, *Angola Under the Portuguese: The Myth and the Reality** (1978), and A. and B. Isaacman, *Mozambique: From Colonialism to Revolution, 1900–1982** (1983). An introduction to francophone Africa is provided in E. Mortimer, *France and the Africans, 1944–1960* (1969). The appeal of Marxism and the headway it made on the continent is studied in M. Ottaway, *Afrocommunism* (1983).

The best historical introduction to South Africa and its peoples is L. Thompson, *A History of South Africa* (1990). On postwar events one may also read M. Meredith, *In the Name of Apartheid: South Africa in the Postwar Period* (1989). There are many assessments of the country's contemporary difficulties, among them: A. Sparks, *The Mind of South Africa* (1990); J. Brewer (ed.), *Can South Africa Survive?* (1989); S. Johnson (ed.), *South Africa: No Turning Back* (1989); and D. L. Horowitz, *A Democratic South Africa? Constitutional Engineering in a Divided Society* (1990). Two illuminating comparative studies are G. M. Fredrickson, *White Supremacy: A Comparative Study in American and South African History* (1981), and J. W. Cell, *The Highest Stage of White Supremacy: The Origins of Segregation in South Africa and the American South* (1982). The Western role in economic exploitation over the years is studied in W. Minter, *King Solomon's Mines Revisited: Western Intervention and the Burdened History of South Africa* (1987).

The Middle East

For the Middle East, balanced overviews for the postwar years include L. A. Aroian and R. P. Mitchell, *The Modern Middle East and North Africa* (1984); A. Goldschmidt, Jr., *A Concise History of the Middle East** (rev., 1987); and G. Corm, *Fragmentation in the Middle East: The Last 30 Years** (1988).

Books that thoughtfully examine the significance of the Islamic legacy for the contemporary era are J. O. Voll, *Islam: Continuity and Change in the Modern World** (1982); H. Munson, Jr., *Islam and Revolution in the Middle East* (1988); E. Swan's two books: *Radical Islam: Medieval Theology and Modern Politics* (1985) and *Interpretations of Islam: Past and Present* (1988); B. Lewis, *The Political Language of Islam* (1988); and A. S. Ahmed, *Discovering Islam: Making Sense of Muslim History and Society** (1989). Both pan-Arabism and obstacles to Arab unity are explored in the essays in T. E. Farah (ed.), *Pan-Arabism and Arab Nationalism: The Continuing Debate** (1987).

Books that examine the Western involvement are A. Williams, *Britain and France in the Middle East and North Africa, 1914–1967* (1969), cited in Chapter XV; A. Roshwald, *Estranged Bedfellows: Britain and France in the Middle East During World War II* (1990); and H. M. Sachar, *Europe Leaves the Middle East, 1936–1954* (1976). An indispensable study of America's involvement is S. P. Tillman, *The U.S. and the Middle East* (1982).

A few selected titles for the Middle Eastern Arab States may be cited. North Africa: J. M. Abun-Nasir, *A History of the Maghrib* [Maghreb] (rev., 1975), on the Arab states in northwestern Africa; P. J. Vatikiotis, *The History of Egypt** (1986), from 1805 to the present, an impressive history; G. Keppel, *Muslim Extremism in Egypt: The Prophet and the Pharaoh* (trans. 1988); and A. Mc-Dermott, *Egypt from Nasser to Mubarek: A Flawed Revolution* (1988). Syria and Jordan: D. Hopwood, *Syria, 1945–1986: Politics and Society** (1988); M. C. Wilson, *King Abdullah, Britain, and the Making of Jordan* (1988); and P. Gubser, *Jordan: Crossroads*

*of Middle Eastern Events** (1984). Lebanon: A few books that illuminate the tragedy of Lebanon are W. Khalidi, *Conflict and Violence in Lebanon: Confrontation in the Middle East** (1983); I. Rabinovich, *The War for Lebanon, 1970–1983* (1984); S. Khalaf, *Lebanon's Predicament** (1988); S. Mackey, *Lebanon* (1989); and K. Salibi, *A House of Many Mansions: The History of Lebanon Reconsidered* (1989). Other states: N. Safran, *Saudi Arabia: The Ceaseless Quest for Security** (1985), on Saudi Arabia's foreign policy; and R. S. Zahlan, *The Making of the Modern Gulf States: Kuwait, Bahrain, Qatar, United Arab Emirates, Oman** (1989).

For internal developments in Iraq two informative studies are M. F. and P. Sluglett, *Iraq Since 1958: From Revolution to Dictatorship** (1991), and S. al-Khalil, *Republic of Fear: The Politics of Modern Iraq* (1989). The dictator and the Baath party dictatorship are also studied in E. Karsh and I. Rautsi, *Saddam Hussein: A Political Biography* (1991).

The best introduction to the history of modern Israel is H. M. Sachar, *A History of Israel:* Vol. I, *From the Rise of Zionism to Our Time* (rev., 1979), and Vol. II, *From the Aftermath of the Yom Kippur War* (1987); the same author has also written *Diaspora: An Inquiry Into the Contemporary Jewish World* (1984). For the clash of Arab and Jewish interests from 1920 to 1948, the years of the British mandate, and for the recognition of Israel in 1948, one may read M. J. Cohen, *The Origins and Evolution of the Arab-Zionist Conflict** (1987), and the same author's *Truman and Israel* (1990). An overview of the four Arab-Israeli wars from 1948 to 1973 and the later entanglement in Lebanon is provided in R. Ovendale, *The Origins of the Arab-Israeli Wars** (1984), and S. D. Bailey, *Four Arab-Israeli Wars and the Peace Process* (1990). J. N. Moore has been editing extensive readings and documents on the conflict, *The Arab-Israeli Conflict* (4 vols., to date, 1974–1991).

The international crisis in 1956 over Egypt's closing of the Suez Canal is examined in H. Thomas, *The Suez Affair* (1966); D. Carlton, *Britain and the Suez Crisis* (1988); and W. R. Louis and R. Owen (eds.), *Suez 1956: The Crisis and its Consequences* (1989). P. Buckland, *The Arab-Israeli Conflict: The Palestinian Question* (1988), focuses on the territories occupied since 1967.

Two biographies that help understand the early idealism of Zionism are J. Reinharz, *Chaim Weizmann: The Making of a Zionist Leader** (1985), and S. Teveth, *Ben-Gurion: The Burning Ground, 1866–1948* (1987), while M. Cohen, *Zion and State: Nation, Class, and the Shaping of Modern Israel* (1987), explores the divisions between labor Zionism and the conservative nationalism that later came to dominate.

The Revolution in Iran

The background and course of the revolutionary events in Iran may be studied in N. R. Keddie, *Roots of Revolution: An Interpretive History of Modern Iran** (1981); D. Wilber, *Iran Past and Present: From Monarchy to Islamic Republic* (1982); S. Bakhash, *The Reign of the Ayotollahs: Iran and the Islamic Revolution** (1983); and S. A. Arjomand, *The Turban for the Crown: The Islamic Revolution in Iran** (1989). The link between ideology and foreign policy is examined in R. K. Ramazani, *Revolutionary Iran: Challenge and Response in the Middle East* (1987), while special insights are provided in R. Mottahedeh, *The Mantle of the Prophet: Religion and Politics in Iran* (1986). On Islamic fundamentalism one may also read D. Hiro, *Holy Wars: The Rise of Islamic Fundamentalism** (1990). American and British relationships to Iran in the war and postwar years are studied in F. Azimi, *Iran: The Crisis of Democracy, 1941–1953* (1989); M. Lytle, *Origins of the Iranian-American Alliance, 1941–1953* (1987); J. F. Goode, *The United States and Iran, 1946–1951: The Diplomacy of Neglect* (1989); R. Engler, *The Politics of Oil* (1961); and K. Roosevelt, *Countercoup: The Struggle for the Control of Iran* (1979). For the ties with the shah, the impact of the revolution, and the hostage crisis, one may read J. A. Bill, *The Eagle and the Lion: The Tragedy of American-Iranian Relations* (1988), the fullest account. Preliminary assessments of the eight-year war of Iran and Iraq are D. Hiro, *The Longest War: The Iran-Iraq Military Conflict** (1991), and the essays in E. Karsh (ed.), *Iran-Iraq War: Impact and Implications* (1990).

Modernization and Development in the Third World

The impact of modernization is examined historically and comparatively in C. E. Black, *The Dynamics of Modernization: A Study in Comparative History** (1966); I. R. Sinai's two books, *The Challenge of Modernization** (1964) and *In Search of the Modern World* (1968); and D. A. Rustow, *A World of Nations: Problems of Political Modernization** (1967). Of special interest are L. S. Stavrianos, *Global Rift: The Third World Comes of Age* (1981); T. H. Von Laue, *The World Revolution of Modernization: The Twentieth Century in Global Perspective** (1987), which stresses the destabilizing effects of modernization; and M. Adas, *Machines the Measure of Men: Science, Technology and Ideologies of Western Dominance* (1988). P. Bairoch, *The Economic Development of the Third World Since 1900* (trans. 1975) provides useful economic data and analysis on population and resources.

For the economics of development, the different development models followed in the post-1945 years, and theories of growth one may read H. W. Arndt, *Economic Development: The History of an Idea** (1987); I. M. D. Little, *Economic Development: Theory, Policy, and International Relations* (1984), somewhat unsympathetic to planned development; W. W. Rostow, *Theorists of Economic Growth from David Hume to the Present* (1990); and L. E. Harrison, *Underdevelopment Is a State of Mind** (1985).

For the post-1945 development experience in various parts of the world one may turn to C. Young, *Ideology and Development in Africa* (1982); D. K. Fieldhouse, *Black Africa, 1945–1980: Economic Decolonization and Arrested Development** (1986), which studies both British and French former colonies; L. Cockcroft, *Africa's Way: A Journey From the Past* (1990); J. Iliffe, *The African Poor: A History** (1987); R. A. Scalapino, *The Politics of Development: Perspectives on Twentieth-Century Asia* (1989), an insightful small book; A. Richards and J. Waterbury, *A Political Economy of the Middle East: State, Class, and Economic Development** (1988); J. Mayall and A. Payne (eds.), *The Fallacies of Hope: The Post-Colonial Record of the Commonwealth Third World* (1991); and T. Kemp, *Industrialization in the Non-Western World** (1989), with special studies of India, Brazil, and Nigeria. For an introduction to all aspects of change in Latin America in the postwar years one may turn to T. E. Skidmore and P. H. Smith, *Modern Latin America** (rev.,

1988). A knowledgeable, if overdrawn, indictment of the international aid bureaucracy is to be found in G. Hancock, *Lords of Poverty: The Power, Prestige, and Corruption of the International Aid Business* (1989).

The best introduction to the north-south debate over a new international economic order is the special report by the Independent Commission on International Development, chaired by Willy Brandt: *North-South: A Program for Survival* (1980). It may be supplemented by W. A. Lewis, *The Evolution of the International Economic Order** (1978); A. Fishlow and others, *Rich and Poor Nations in the World Economy* (1978); and B. Nossiter, *The Global Struggle for More: Third World Conflicts with the Rich Nations** (1986). The burden of debt in the Third World is explored in J. D. Sachs (ed.), *Developing Country Debt and the World Economy** (1989). Of special interest is J. W. Warnock, *Politics of Hunger: The Global Food System** (1987).

XXIII. The Contemporary Age: A World Transformed

It is difficult to assess the durable value of the literature dealing with the events and developments of recent years. The listings for these sections therefore have been kept brief. For new books the reviews and bibliographies published quarterly in *Foreign Affairs* and in the professional journals should be consulted.

The World Economy

Informative introductions to the global economy as it developed in the post-1945 years are W. W. Rostow, *The World Economy: History and Prospect* (1977); W. M. Scammell, *The International Economy Since 1945* (1980); and A. G. Kenwood and A. I. Lougheed, *The Growth of the International Economy, 1820–1980* (1983). I. Wallerstein's two volumes, *The Capitalist World Economy* (1979) and *The Politics of the World Economy: The States, the Movements, and the Civilisations* (1984), following upon his earlier studies, provide provocative economic and historical analysis. Global economic interdependence emerges clearly from F. L. Block, *The Origins of International Economic Disorders* (1977), and J. E. Spero, *The Politics of International Economic Relations* (1981). The role of oil

in the economy and in global politics is admirably described in D. Yergin, *The Prize: The Epic Quest for Oil, Money, and Power* (1990), and in P. R. Odell, *Oil and World Power** (rev., 1987). The impact of the oil embargo of 1973–1974 on Europe is studied in R. Lieber, *Oil and the Middle East: Europe in the Energy Crisis* (1976). For the multinational corporations one may turn to M. Wilkin, *The Maturing of Multinational Enterprise* (1974); R. J. Barnet and R. E. Muller, *Global Reach* (1974); R. Vernon, *Storm Over the Multinationals: The Real Issues* (1977); and L. Franko, *The European Multinationals* (1976).

There are many jeremiads about the threatened loss of American economic primacy. The Japanese challenge, in particular, is described in E. F. Vogel, *Japan as Number One: Lessons for America** (1979); C. V. Prestowitz, Jr., *Trading Places: How We Allowed Japan to Take the Lead* (1988); and E. L. Frost, *For Richer, For Poorer: The New U.S.-Japan Relationship* (1987). The decline of older American industry is described in B. Bluestone and B. Harrison, *The Deindustrialization of America* (1982), but the continuing importance of the American economy emerges from J. Agnew, *The United States in the World Economy: A Regional Geography** (1987); D. P. Calleo, *The Imperious Economy* (1982); and the essays in M. Feldstein (ed.), *The United States in the World Economy** (1988).

The impact of the global recession that began in 1974 and the dilemmas it posed for policy makers are studied in several of the books on the global economy cited in Chapter XXI; to them should be added L. Anel, *Recession, the Western Economies, and the Changing World Order* (1981); E. S. Einhorn and J. Logue, *Welfare States in Hard Times* (1982); R. Skidelsky (ed.), *The End of the Keynesian Era: Essays on the Disintegration of the Keynesian Political Economy* (1977); and A. Cox (ed.), *Politics, Policy, and the European Recession* (1982). To books already cited on the international monetary system one may add D. C. Kruse, *Monetary Integration in Western Europe* (1980), and P. Ludlow, *The Making of the European Monetary System* (1982).

The operations, accomplishments, and ongoing problems of the European Community may be studied in D. Swann, *The Economics of the Common Market* (rev., 1984); B. C. Hill, *The Common Agricultural Policy: Past, Present and Future* (1984); E.

Neville-Rolf, *The Politics of Agriculture in the European Community* (1984); S. Bulmer and W. E. Paterson, *The Federal Republic of Germany and the European Community* (1987); and S. George, *An Awkward Partner: Britain in the European Community** (1990). There are thoughtful essays assessing the first thirty years of the Rome treaties and plans for closer economic integration in H. Brugmans (ed.), *Europe: Dream, Adventure, Reality* (1987).

On progress toward political unity good guides are D. Marquand, *Parliament for Europe* (1979); P. Scalingi, *The European Parliament: The Three-Decade Search for a United Europe* (1980); D. Lodge (ed.), *European Union* (1986); and R. Pryce (ed.), *The Dynamics of European Union* (1987).

Western Europe: Politics and Society

The books on Britain, France, West Germany, and Italy described in Chapter XXI are almost all relevant here. To them one may add D. W. Urwin and W. E. Paterson (eds.), *Politics in Western Europe Today: Perspectives, Policies, and Issues Since 1980** (1991).

BRITAIN. For Britain, Margaret Thatcher's conservative impact and the British turnaround in the decade after 1979 are assessed in P. Jenkins, *Mrs. Thatcher's Revolution: The Ending of the Socialist Era* (1988), a comprehensive, perceptive account; P. Riddell, *The Thatcher Decade* (1989); D. A. Kavanagh, *Thatcherism and British Politics: The End of Consensus** (rev., 1990); and I. Bradley, *The Strange Rebirth of Liberal England* (1985). One may also wish to read L. Freedman, *Britain and the Falklands War** (1988), and an informative biographical account, H. Young, *The Iron Lady: A Biography of Margaret Thatcher* (1989).

Two comparative studies of the conservative efforts in the United States and Britain in the 1980s to curb the welfare state, encourage the entrepreneurial spirit, and revive national pride are J. Krieger, *Reagan, Thatcher, and the Politics of Decline** (1986), and A. Gamble, *The Free Economy and the Strong State* (1988). Other viewpoints are provided in R. Skidelsky (ed.), *Thatcherism* (1987).

FRANCE. For France the Gaullist and conservative tenure under the Fifth Republic ended with the election in 1981 of a Socialist president, François Mitterrand, and a Socialist legislative majority, but the Socialists in office soon followed a moderate program. The Mitterrand experience is examined in D. S. Bell and B. Criddle, *The French Socialist Party: The Emergence of a Party of Government** (rev., 1988); G. Ross, S. Hoffmann, and S. Malzacher, *The Mitterrand Experiment: Continuity and Change in Modern France** (1987); J. W. Friend, *Seven Years in France: François Mitterrand and the Unintended Revolution, 1981–1988* (1989); and D. Singer, *Is Socialism Doomed? The Meaning of Mitterrand* (1988). These last two volumes may be read in conjunction with M. Harrington, *Socialism Past and Future* (1989), and the essays in W. E. Paterson and A. H. Thomas (eds.), *The Future of Social Democracy* (1986), which probe in a more general way the transformation of once Marxist-oriented parties into social democratic parties. The French Communist loss of leadership of the left, in part because of disillusionment with Moscow, is studied in G. Ross, *Workers and Communists in France: From Popular Front to Eurocommunism* (1982), and in J. Jenson and G. Ross, *The View From Inside: A French Communist Cell in Crisis* (1984).

SPAIN AND PORTUGAL. Profound changes took place in the Iberian peninsula in these years. In Spain, modernization was already underway in the later Franco years, and after Franco's death the country was transformed politically into a progressive constitutional monarchy. On these developments one may read M. Gallo, *Spain Under Franco* (1976); P. Preston (ed.), *Spain in Crisis: The Evolution and Decline of the Franco Regime* (1976); R. Carr and J. P. Fusi-Azpurúa, *Spain: Dictatorship to Democracy* (rev., 1981); and P. Preston, *The Triumph of Democracy in Spain** (1986). The Spanish Socialist party, which came to be the governing party, is studied in R. Gillespie, *The Spanish Socialist Party: A History of Factionalism* (1989).

For Portugal, the long dictatorship, the wars to hold onto the African colonies that led to the revolution of 1974, and the gradual emergence of political stability are studied in H. Kay, *Salazar and Modern Portugal* (1970); A. DeFigueredo, *Portugal: Fifty Years of Dictatorship* (1976); H. G. Ferreira and M. W. Marshall, *Portugal's Revolution: Ten Years On* (1986); and T. Gallagher,

Portugal: A Twentieth Century Interpretation (1983).

The Communist World: China Under Deng

Several of the volumes cited in Chapter XXI for the Mao Zedong era also describe Deng's program of modernization and liberalization. Informative for the Deng reforms are R. P. Suttmeier, *Science, Technology, and China's Drive for Modernization* (1980); R. Garside, *Coming Alive: China After the Cultural Revolution* (1981); H. Harding, *China's Second Revolution: Reformation After Mao* (1987); and D. W.-W. Chang, *China Under Deng Xiaoping: Political and Economic Reform* (1991), optimistic about economic reform despite political repression and party factional struggles. On the population question, one may read J. Banister, *China's Changing Population* (1987).

Change in the Soviet Union: The Gorbachev Reforms

The era that opened with Gorbachev's coming to power in 1985 may be approached through the Soviet leader's own book M. Gorbachev, *Perestroika: New Thinking for Our Country and the World* (trans. 1987), and through Z. A. Medvedev, *Gorbachev** (1986). Studies that attempt to assess the Gorbachev reforms in the perspective of the seventy years since the Revolution include A. Nove, *Glasnost in Action: Cultural Renaissance in Russia** (1989); W. Laqueur, *The Long Road to Freedom: Russia and Glasnost* (1989); M. Lewin, *The Gorbachev Phenomenon: A Historical Interpretation** (rev., 1991), cited earlier; B. Kerblay, *Gorbachev's Russia* (1989); and R. C. Tucker, *Political Culture and Leadership: Soviet Russia from Lenin to Gorbachev* (1987). Specifically on the economy, one may read E. A. Hewett, *Reforming the Soviet Economy: Equality Versus Efficiency** (1988), and A. Aslund, *Gorbachev's Struggle for Economic Reform* (1989). For the ferment among the nationalities, two informative studies are J. E. Mace, *Communism and the Dilemmas of National Liberation* (1983), and B. Nahaylo and V. Swoboda, *Soviet Disunion: A History of the Nationalities Problem in the Soviet Union* (1990), detailed and comprehensive.

International Relations: Confrontation and Détente

Books described in Chapter XXI generally focus on the first decade of Soviet-American relations; to them may be added: R. L. Garthoff, *Détente and Confrontation* (1985); R. W. Stevenson, *The Rise and Fall of Détente* (1985); R. Levering, *The Cold War, 1945–1987** (rev., 1988); and S. R. Ashton, *In Search of Détente: The Politics of East-West Relations Since 1945* (1989). The actions and reactions of the Soviets in these years are best approached through A. B. Ulam, *Dangerous Relations: The Soviet Union and World Politics, 1970–1982* (1983), cited earlier. For the renewed conflict over Berlin one may read J. M. Schick, *The Berlin Crisis, 1958–1962* (1971), and R. M. Slusser, *The Berlin Crisis of 1961* (1973).

How the Third World, including Latin America, became involved in the Soviet-Western confrontation is explored in S. L. Bills, *Empire and Cold War: The Roots of the U.S.-Third World Antagonism, 1945–1947* (1990); R. J. Barnet, *Intervention and Revolution: The United States in the Third World* (1968); G. Kolko, *Confronting the Third World: U.S. Foreign Policy, 1945–1980* (1988), critical of U.S. policies; and B. D. Porter, *The U.S.S.R. in Third World Conflicts: Soviet Arms and Diplomacy in Local Wars, 1945–1980** (1984), which focuses on the Middle East and Africa.

For Latin America two books are especially informative: W. LaFeber, *Inevitable Revolutions: The United States in Central America** (1983), and L. Langley, *America and the Americas* (1989). For U.S.-Cuban relations in historical perspective and for the background and nature of Castro's revolution one may read J. R. Benjamin, *The United States and the Origins of the Cuban Revolution* (1990); L. A. Perez, Jr., *Between Reform and Revolution** (1989); and J. M. del Aquila, *Cuba: Dilemmas of a Revolution** (1988), which also describes Cuba's military activities in Africa. The Bay of Pigs episode is described in T. Higgins, *The Perfect Failure* (1987), and the missile crisis of 1962 is studied in perspective in L. Brune, *The Missile Crisis* (1985), and R. A. Divine (ed.), *The Cuban Missile Crisis** (rev., 1990).

On the United States relationship with its NATO allies one may read R. Barnet, *The Alliance* (1983); D. P. Calleo, *Beyond American Hegemony* (1987); L. S. Kaplan, *NATO and the United States* (1988); J. H.

Wyllie, *European Security in the Nuclear Age* (1986); and the essays in L. S. Kaplan and R. W. Clawson (eds.), *NATO After Thirty Years* (1985).

The Vietnam War

On Vietnam, among efforts to explore Vietnamese history and to place events in historical perspective are J. T. McAlister, *Vietnam: The Origins of Revolution* (1969); D. G. Mair, *Vietnamese Anticolonialism* (1971); A. B. Woodside, *Community and Revolution in Modern Vietnam* (1976); W. J. Duiker, *The Rise of Nationalism in Vietnam, 1900–1941* (1976); T. Hodgkin, *Vietnam: The Revolutionary Path* (1981); and J. P. Harrison, *The Endless War: Vietnam's Struggle for Independence** (1989).

The American involvement is best explained in G. T. McT. Kahin, *Intervention: How America became Involved in Vietnam* (1986), which perceives the United States as ignoring the nationalist aspects of the war and seeing it as Communist aggression only. American miscalculations are heavily emphasized in G. Kolko, *Anatomy of a War: Vietnam, the United States, and the Modern Historical Experience* (1985), while G. Lewy, *America in Vietnam** (1978), is defensive of the morality and legality of United States conduct.

The war itself is studied in G. Herring, *America's Longest War: The United States and Vietnam, 1950–1975** (1979), an outstanding account; S. Karnow, *Vietnam: A History** (1984); B. Palmer, Jr., *The 25-Year War: America's Military Role in Vietnam** (1985), helpful on decision making and strategy; L. Berman, *Lyndon Johnson's War* (1989); and S. Hersh, *The Price of Power* (1983), on the extension of the war under Nixon and Kissinger. A widely read book at the time of the war, critical of the American intrusion in southeast Asia, was F. Fitzgerald, *Fire in the Lake* (1972), while D. Halberstam, *The Best and the Brightest** (1972), demonstrated that American involvement, as in earlier Cold War episodes, stemmed from the desire to avoid a repetition of the appeasement of the 1930s. The Soviet role emerges from D. Pike, *Vietnam and the Soviet Union: Anatomy of an Alliance* (1987).

The aftermath of the war receives a grim assessment in N. Van Canh with E. Cooper, *Vietnam Under Communism, 1975–1982* (1983); the essays in K. D. Jackson (ed.), *Cambodia, 1975–1978: Rendezvous With Death* (1989), on Pol Pot and the Khmer Rouge; and in G. Evans and K. Rowley, *Red Brotherhood at War: Vietnam, Cambodia, and Laos Since 1975** (rev., 1990). On guerrilla warfare in Vietnam and elsewhere, informative books are W. Laqueur, *Guerrilla: A Historical and Critical Study* (1977); R. Asprey, *War in the Shadows: The Guerrilla in History* (1976); E. E. Rice, *Wars of the Third Kind: Conflict in the Underdeveloped Countries* (1988); and M. van Creveld, *The Transformation of War* (1991), a searching reassessment of the pattern of modern conflict.

The Nuclear Arms Build-Up

There are numerous books on the nuclear arms build-up, the apocalyptic dangers the world has learned to live with, and the contributions of strategic deterrence to the armed peace. An outstanding exhaustive study is M. Bundy, *Danger and Survival: Choices About the Bomb in the First Fifty Years* (1988); only gradually, it turns out, did the recognition emerge that the bomb could not be thought of as an instrument of war like other weapons. Other studies, counsels of strategy accepting deterrence but calling for continuing efforts at nuclear arms control, are R. McNamara, *Blundering Into Disaster: Surviving the First Century of the Nuclear Age* (1987); G. F. Kennan, *The Nuclear Delusion: Soviet-American Relations in the Atomic Age** (1983); S. Zuckerman, *Nuclear Illusion and Reality* (1982); and C. Gasteyer, *Searching for World Security: Understanding Global Armament and Disarmament* (1987). Another kind of literature, rejecting deterrence, calls for a fundamental rethinking about nuclear arms even, if necessary, for "the need to reinvent politics." Representative are J. Schell's two books: *The Fate of the Earth* (1982) and *The Abolition* (1984); and F. Dyson, *Weapons and Hope* (1984), by an eminent physicist. An important contribution to the discussion is J. Finnis, J. M. Boyle, Jr., and G. Grisez, *Nuclear Deterrence, Morality, and Realism* (1987), by three Roman Catholic professional philosophers.

Other stimulating books with insights into the nuclear arms race are L. Freedman, *Evolution of Nuclear Strategy* (1983); F. Kaplan, *The Wizards of Armageddon* (1983); G. Herken, *Counsels of War* (1985); and J. Newhouse, *War and Peace in the Nuclear*

Age (1989). Assessments of American foreign policy and the search for security in the perspective of over four decades include J. L. Gaddis: *The Long Peace: Inquiries into the History of the Cold War* (1987); the same author's *Strategies of Containment: A Critical Appraisal of Postwar American National Security Policy* (1982); T. G. Paterson, *Meeting the Communist Threat: Truman to Reagan** (1989); T. J. McCormick, *America's Half-Century: United States Foreign Policy in the Cold War** (1989); J. Chace and C. Carr, *America Invulnerable* (1988); P. Dukes, *The Last Great Game: U.S.A. Versus U.S.S.R.* (1989); and G. Lundestad, *The American Empire and Other Studies of U.S. Foreign Policy in a Comparative Perspective** (1990).

Culture, Science, and Thought

The books described in Chapter XIV should be consulted. An intriguing introduction to contemporary intellectual trends is R. N. Stromberg, *After Everything: Western Intellectual History Since 1945** (1975); the same author has written *Makers of Modern Culture: Five Twentieth-Century Thinkers** (1991), exploring Freud, Einstein, Wittgenstein, Joyce, and Sartre. N. Cantor, *Twentieth-Century Culture: Modernism to Deconstruction* (1988), is a wide-ranging personalized assessment of major artistic and cultural movements. Two books cited earlier deserve mention: W. W. Wagar, *Good Tidings: The Belief in Progress from Darwin to Marcuse* (1972), which reassesses the idea of progress in the contemporary era, and H. S. Hughes, *Consciousness and Society: The Reorientation of European Social Thought, 1890–1930* (1958), which examines post-Enlightenment ways of looking at rationalism, science, and the social sciences; Hughes' volume may be supplemented by his *Sophisticated Rebels: The Political Culture of European Dissent, 1968–1987* (1988). For distinctions between "modern" and "postmodern" in various contexts one may read S. Toulmin, *Cosmopolis: The Hidden Agenda of Modernity* (1989).

Books on Einstein and the new physics have been cited in Chapter XIV. For insights into later developments one may read the dialogues with selected contemporary physicists in J. Bernstein, *Quantum Profiles* (1991). On the biological revolution, one may turn to R. Clowes, *The Structure of Life* (1967); R. Olby, *The Path to the Double Helix* (1974); P. B. and J. S. Medawar, *The Life Science: Current Ideas of Biology* (1977); G. Allen, *Life Science in the Twentieth Century* (1975); J. Goodfield, *Playing God: Genetic Engineering and the Manipulation of Life* (1977); and H. F. Judson, *The Eighth Day of Creation: The Makers of the Revolution in Biology* (1979). In J. Watson, *The Double Helix: A Personal Account of the Discovery of the Structure of DNA* (rev., 1979), a scientist describes himself and other biologists at work. On the need for communication between scientists and nonscientists, an indispensable book with additional reflections in the revised version is C. P. Snow, *The Two Cultures and the Scientific Revolution** (rev., 1965).

The setback to medical science and the challenges to society posed by the sudden appearance of AIDS are studied in M. D. Grmek, *History of AIDS: Emergence and Origin of a Modern Pandemic* (trans. 1990), and in the essays in E. Fee and D. Fox, *AIDS: The Burdens of History** (1988).

For space exploration one should read W. A. McDougall, *. . . the Heavens and the Earth: A Political History of the Space Age** (1985), comprehensive and stimulating; special dimensions are added in V. Cronin, *The View from Planet Earth: Man Looks at the Cosmos* (1981), and J. S. and R. A. Lewis, *Space Resources: Breaking the Bonds of Earth* (1987).

Useful introductions to the activities of the professional philosophers are provided in J. Passmore, *A Hundred Years of Philosophy* (1968); J. O. Urmson, *Philosophical Analysis: Its Development Between the Two World Wars* (1956); O. Hanfling, *Logical Positivism* (1981); and A. J. Ayer, *Philosophy in the Twentieth Century* (1982). The messages of existentialism and of some of its exemplars may be studied in M. Warnock, *Existentialism* (1970); G. Brée, *Camus and Sartre* (1972); and I. Meszaros, *The Work of Sartre* (1979). The life and contributions of a key twentieth-century philosopher are examined in R. Monk, *Ludwig Wittgenstein: the Duty of Genius* (1990).

For the reorientation in contemporary literature, philosophy, and other disciplines one may begin with E. Kurweil, *The Age of Structuralism: Lévi-Strauss to Foucault* (1980), and continue with F. Jameson, *The Prison House of Language: A Critical History of Structuralism and Formalism* (1972); G. H. Hartman, *Saving the Text: Literature, Derrida, Philosophy* (1981); J. Culler, *On*

Deconstruction: Theory and Criticism After Structuralism (1983); and E. Said, *The World, the Text, and the Critic* (1983). Books on the *Annales* school and newer approaches to history have been described in the introductory section of this bibliography. The reorientation of Marxism may be examined in R. S. Gottlieb (ed.), *An Anthology of Western Marxism: From Lukacs and Gramsci to Socialist Feminism* (1988). Introductions to the complexities of contemporary art are provided in A. Neumeyer, *The Search for Meaning in Modern Art* (trans. 1964); H. Rosenberg, *The Anxious Object: Art Today and Its Audience* (1964); G. Woods, *Art Without Boundaries, 1950–1970* (1972); and S. Hunter, *Modern Art from Post-Impressionism to the Present* (rev., 1985).

Western religious thought is explored in J. Macquarrie, *Twentieth-Century Religious Thought: The Frontiers of Philosophy and Theology, 1900–1960* (1963); S. P. Schilling, *Contemporary Continental Theologians* (1966); and J. C. Livingston, *Modern Christian Thought: From the Enlightenment to Vatican II* (1971). R. N. Bellah, *Beyond Belief: Essays on Religion in a Post-Traditional World** (1991), explores religion and society in diverse cultural contexts. The continuing debate between science and religion is studied in E. L. Mascall, *Christian Theology and Natural Science* (1965), and S. L. Jaki, *The Road of Science and the Ways to God* (1978). For the profound doctrinal and social changes in contemporary Roman Catholicism one may turn to L. Gilkey, *Catholicism Confronts Modernity* (1975); J. D. Holmes, *The Papacy in the Modern World, 1914–1978* (1981); and E. O. Hanson, *The Catholic Church in World Politics* (1987).

Activist Movements: 1968

The most complete account of the student upheaval of 1968 as a worldwide phenomenon is D. Caute, *The Year of the Barricades: A Journey Through 1968** (1989); it may be supplemented by G. Katsiafacis, *The Imagination of the New Left: A Global Analysis of 1968** (1987). One may also read L. S. Feuer, *The Conflict of Generations* (1969); S. Spender, *The Year of the Young Rebels* (1969); G. Paloczi-Horvath, *Youth Up in Arms* (1971); A. J. Esler, *Bombs, Beards, and Barricades* (1971); and G. Stotera, *Death of a Utopia: The Development*

and Decline of Student Movements in Europe (1975). The turbulent French scene is studied in R. Aron, *The Elusive Revolution* (trans. 1969); B. E. Brown, *Protest in Paris: Anatomy of a Revolt** (1974); and A. Touraine, *The May Movement: Revolt and Reform** (trans. 1979).

For insight into the emergence of youth and youth culture as a contemporary phenomenon one should read J. R. Gillis, *Youth and History: Tradition and Change in European Age Relations: 1770 to the Present* (rev., 1981), cited earlier, and the essays in A. J. Esler (ed.), *The Youth Revolution: The Conflict of Generations in Modern History* (1974). For the "new left" in the United States and elsewhere one may read J. P. Diggins, *The American Left in the Twentieth Century* (1973); I. Unger, *The Movement: A History of the American New Left, 1959–1972* (1974); T. Gitlin, *The Sixties: Years of Hope, Days of Rage* (1987), mostly a personal testament; M. Cranston (ed.), *The New Left* (1971); and K. Mehnert, *Moscow and the New Left* (1976).

The Women's Liberation Movement

For the background to the women's liberation movement, many of the books on the history of women described in the introductory section will also serve as a guide. A good introduction is O. Banks, *Faces of Feminism: A Study of Feminism as a Social Movement** (1981; reissued 1986), which shows the link between the women's movements of 1840 in the United States and England to the present. One may also read W. O'Neill, *The Woman's Movement: Feminism in the United States and England* (1969); J. S. Chafetz and A. G. Dworkin, *Female Revolt: The Rise of Women's Movements in World and Historical Perspective** (1986); and E. Sullerot, *Women, Society, and Change* (1971). There are informative essays in C. R. Berkin and M. Lovett (eds.), *Women, War, and Revolution* (1980). An anthology of emergent feminism is A. S. Rossi (ed.), *The Feminist Papers: From [Abigail] Adams to [Simone] de Beauvoir** (1974). The link in the United States between feminism and the civil rights movement and other aspects of the changing role of American women are studied in W. R. Chafe, *The Paradox of Change: American Women in the 20th Century* (rev., 1991). For contemporary Europe a good introduction is J. Lovenduski, *Women and European*

Dates given after names of rulers and popes are the years of reigns or pontificates; those given for all others are the years of birth and death.

Pronunciation is indicated where it is not obvious. With foreign words the purpose is not to show their exact pronunciation in their own language but to suggest how they may be acceptably pronounced in English. Fully Anglicized pronunciations are indicated by the abbreviation *Angl.* Pronunciation is shown by respelling, not by symbols, except that the following symbols are used for vowel sounds not found in English:

ø   indicates the sound of ö as in Göttingen. To form this sound, purse the lips as if to say *o*, and then say *ay* as in *ate*.
U   indicates the sound of the French *u,* or of German *ü.* To form this sound, purse the lips as if to say *oo*, and then say *ee* as in *eat*.
aN, oN, uN, iN indicate the sounds of the French nasal vowels. Once learned, these are easily pronounced, roughly as follows: For aN, begin to pronounce the English word *on,* but avoid saying the consonant *n* and "nasalize" the *ah* sound instead. For oN do the same with the English *own;* for uN, with the English prefix *un-;* for iN, with the English word *an.*

The sound of *s* as in the word *treasure* is indicated by *zh.* This sound is common in English, though never found at the beginning or end of a word. *igh* always indicates the so-called long *i* as in *high.* The vowel sound of *hoot* is indicated by *oo,* that of *hood* by *o͝o.*

Compared with English, the European languages are highly regular in their spelling, in that the same letters or combinations of letters are generally pronounced in the same way.

Lantern: The Revolution of '89 Witnessed in Warsaw, Budapest, Berlin, and Prague (1990). The growing restiveness in the years of Soviet domination also emerges from M. Charlton, *The Eagle and the Small Birds: Crisis in the Soviet Union from Yalta to Solidarity* (1987); G. Schöpflin and N. Woods (eds.), *In Search of Central Europe* (1989); and G. Stokes (ed.), *From Stalinism to Pluralism: A Documentary History of Eastern Europe Since 1945** (1991). Prospects for the future are tentatively assessed in E. Hankiss, *East European Alternatives* (1990); V. Tismaneanu, *Eastern Europe After Communism: Reinventing Politics* (1991); R. Dahrendorf, *Reflections on the Revolution in Europe** (1991); and L. F. Freedman (ed.), *Europe Transformed* (1990), an admirable collection of documents.

Past, Present, and Future

The changes in the Soviet Union, the end of the Communist regimes in Eastern Europe, the reunification of Germany, and the fading of the Cold War herald the beginning of a new era in international relations. Whether the United States will retain its economic and political primacy is a question raised in P. F. Kennedy's provocative account of the powers that enjoyed and lost hegemony in the modern centuries, *The Rise and Fall of the Great Powers: Economic Change and Military Conflict from 1500 to 2000** (1987). It may be read along with the historically-oriented collaborative study edited by Kennedy, *Grand Strategies in War and Peace* (1991), and with M. Olson, *The Rise and Decline of Nations* (1982).

Of the many books that explore contemporary international relations in historical perspective and the world's continuing human and social dilemmas, the following represent only a brief but thought-provoking sample. A few have been cited earlier.

THE SEARCH FOR PEACE. G. A. Craig and A. L. George, *Force and Statecraft: Diplomatic Problems of Our Time** (rev., 1990); R. C. Neustadt and E. R. May, *Thinking in Time: The Uses of History for Decision Makers* (1986); W. G. Hyland, *The Cold War Is Over** (1991); R. S. McNamara *Out of the Cold: New Thinking for American Foreign and Defense Policy in the 21st Century* (1989); H. [Helmut] Schmidt, *A Grand Strategy for the West: The Anachronism of National Strategies in an Interdependent World** (1987); M. Mandelbaum, *The Fate of Nations: The Search for National Security in the Nineteenth and Twentieth Centuries** (1988); D. M. Abshire, *Preventing World War III: A Realistic Grand Strategy* (1989); G. Gasteyer, *Searching for World Security: Understanding Global Armament and Disarmament* (1987); M. Walzer, *Just and Unjust Wars* (1977); J. Newhouse, *War and Peace in the Nuclear Age* (1989); and M. Howard, *The Lessons of History* (1991).

THE HUMAN CONDITION. R. Dahrendorf, *The Modern Social Conflict: An Essay on the Politics of Liberty** (1990); J. Feinberg, *Rights, Justice, and the Bounds of Liberty* (1980); J. K. Galbraith, *The Voice of the Poor: Essays in Economic and Political Persuasion* (1983); R. W. Tucker, *The Inequality of Nations* (1977); J. Mokyr, *The Lever of Riches: Technological Creativity and Economic Progress* (1990); G. M. Fredrickson, *The Arrogance of Race: Historical Perspectives on Slavery, Racism, and Social Inequality* (1989); and D. W. Treadgold, *Freedom: A History** (1990).

THE FUTURE. R. G. Heilbroner, *An Inquiry into the Human Prospect* (1974); D. B. King, *The Crisis of Our Time: Reflections on the Course of Western Civilization, Past, Present, and Future* (1988); B. R. Finney and E. M. Jones (eds.), *Interstellar Migration and the Human Experience** (1985); and W. W. Wagar, *A Short History of the Future* (1989), but covering only the years 1995 to 2200.

ILLUSTRATION SOURCES

XLVI Lexington Historical Society; XLVII New York Public Library Picture Collection; XLVIII Library of Congress; XLIX New York Public Library Special Collections; L (above) Culver; LI (above, below) Bibliotheque Nationale; LII (above) Historical Pictures Service; LII (below) Library of Congress; LIII Bettmann Archive; LIV Bibliotheque Nationale; LV Giraudon; LVI (above) Culver; LVI (below) Bettmann Archive; LVII Culver; 453 Kunsthistorisches Museum, Vienna; 500 Historiches Museum Frankfurt am Main; 534, 535, 536 (above, below) The Mansell Collection; 537 New York Public Library; 538 (above) Staatsbibliothek Berlin; 538 (below) The Mansell Collection; 539 New York Public Library; 540 (above) Radio Times Hulton Picture Library; 540 (below) © René-Jacques; 541 © H. Roger-Viollet; 542 The American Numismatic Society; 583 Snark International, Art Gallery, Birmingham, England; 642 The American Numismatic Society; 684 The Mansell Collection; 685 New York Public Library; 686 (above, below), 687, 688 The Mansell Collection; 689 New York Public Library; 690, 691, 692 Radio Times Hulton Picture Library; 693 (left, right) Photoworld, Inc.; 695 Popperfoto; 732 Sovfoto from USSR Magazine; 777 The American Numismatic Society; 834 © Fred Ward/Black Star; 867 United Nations; 919 United Nations; 956 IBM; 957 © Abbas/Gamma/Liaison Agency; 958 © Camera Tres/Black Star; 959 (below) © Gamma/Liaison Agency; 959 (above) © Alain Nogues/Sygma; 960–961 © Sanford H. Roth/Rapho/Photo Researchers; 962 © Francois Lochon/Gamma/Liaison Agency; 963 © C. Spengler/Sygma; 964 © Andanson/Sygma; 965 © Marc & Evelyne Bernheim/Woodfin Camp & Associates; 966 © Georg Gerster/Rapho/Photo Researchers; 967 (above) © Sepp Seitz, 1978/Woodfin Camp & Associates; 967 (below) © Richard Nowitz/Black Star; 968 NASA.

INDEX

Walesa, Lech (1943–   ) (lek vuh-lenss-uh), 1009
Wallachia (wa-lake'i-uh), 485, 545. *See also* Romania
Wannsee, 859
"War communism," 751, 760
"War guilt" clause (1919), 726, 785
Warhol, Andy, 1028
War Industries Board (1918), 721
Warsaw Pact, 877, 911, 982, 1014, 1036
Watergate, 982
Watt, James (1736–1819), 458
Webb, Sidney (1859–1947) and Beatrice (1858–1943), 623
Webster-Ashburton Treaty (1842), 575
Wei-hai-wei (way-high-way), 680
Weimar Republic (vigh-mar), 784–787
Welfare state (after World War II), 886, 887, 888, 985–986, 987. *See also* Social welfare state
Wellington, Duke of (1769–1852), 477, 490, 504
Wells, H. G. (1866–1946), 623
West Bank, 943, 945, 946
Westernization: in Russia, 564–565, 734–735, 746; in Japan, 577–582; in Turkey, 655–656, 791–793; in Africa, 664–666; in India, 672, 721; in Persia (Iran), 673, 792–793; in China, 674
Westminster, Statute of, 814
West Wall (World War II), 843
Whigs, 490–492, 494, 495, 575
Whitehead, Alfred North, 1025
White Lotus Society, 674
White Man's Burden, 650
Whitney, Eli (1765–1835), 458
William I, King of Prussia (1861–1888), German Emperor (1871–1888), 558, 614, 616
William II, German Emperor (1888–1918), 615, 616, 718, 722, 723
Wilson, Harold (1916–   ), 888n
Wilson, Woodrow (1856–1924): and neutrality, 709, 712; enters World War I, 714–715; and Armistice, 716, 717; Fourteen Points and Paris Peace Conference, 722–726, 730, 778, 785, 790
Windischgrätz (1787–1862) (vin'-dish-grets), 512
Witte, Count (1849–1915) (vit'-te), 735
Wittgenstein, Ludwig (1889–1951), 1025–1026
Women: in 19th century, 460, 539, 590; English, in India, 690–691; in World Wars, 719, 852; in Turkey (1920s), 792; under Nazis, 832, 852; suffrage in Europe, 887; equality in China, 915; history, 1026; women's liberation movement, 1034–1035
Woolen industry, 457
World Bank, 899
World economy. *See* Global economy
World War I, 599, 608, 649, 672; diplomatic sit-

uation leading to, 695–706; military events, 706–722; armies in, 706–707, 711, 714–716; naval aspects of, 708–709, 714–715; diplomacy during, 709–712, 714, 716; social and economic impact of, 718–722; Peace of Paris, 722–731
World War II, 775–776, 787, 788, 794, 799; diplomacy preceding, 835–842; military events, 843–860; aftermath, 868, 870–878; casualties, 860; conferences, 860–866; peace treaties, 865–866
Wrangel, General (1887–1928) (*Angl.* wrang'-gl), 752
Wrundt, Wilhelm (1832–1920) (voont), 628

Yalta conference, 862–865, 871, 910, 917
Yalu River, 880
Yangtse River, 675
Yedo (Tokyo), 578, 579, 580
Yellow press, 591
Yiddish, 470
Yom Kippur War, 942, 944
Young Turks, 661, 700–701, 789
Youth rebellion (1960s), 1033–1034
Ypres (eepr), 715
Ypsilanti (1792–1828) (ip-si-lan-tee), 480, 483
Yuan Shih-kai (1859–1916) (shee-kigh), 794
Yugoslavia, 472, 709, 726, 727, 779, 782, 1019; in Little Entente, 788; in World War II, 847, 863; after World War II, 877

Zaibatsu (zigh-bat'soo), 798
Zaire (zah-eer'), 934–935. *See also* Belgian Congo; Congo
Zaire River (Congo River), 662–665
Zambesi River (zamm-bee'-zee), 663
Zambia, 931, 937–938
Zanzibar, 663, 930
Zemstvos (zemst'-voze), 568, 569, 734, 736, 745, 747
Zhao Ziyang, 999
Zhou Enlai (1898–1976), 917
Zhukov, Georgi (1896–1974) (zhoo'-koff), 853
Zia, General Muhammed (1924–1988), 922
Zimbabwe (zim-ba'-bway), 662, 931
Zimmerman, Arthur (1859–1940), telegram from, 710, 714
Zimmerwald program (1915), 772–773
Zinoviev, Gregory (1883–1936), 750, 771, 1002
Zinoviev letter (England), 775, 812
Zionism, 637, 710, 941–946, 1032
Zola, Emile (1840–1902), 630
Zollverein (tsoll'-fe-rine, or *Angl.* zoll'-ve-rine), 515, 530
"Zones" of civilization, 586–587, 643. *See also* Third World

ABOUT THE
AUTHORS

ROBERT ROSWELL PALMER was born in Chicago. After graduating from the University of Chicago he received his doctorate from Cornell University in 1934. From 1936 to 1963 he taught at Princeton University, was then at Washington University in St. Louis from 1963 to 1966, and at Yale from 1969 until his retirement in 1977. He now resides in Princeton, where he is affiliated with the Institute for Advanced Study. His books include *Twelve Who Ruled: The Year of the Terror in the French Revolution* (1941, 1989), and the two-volume *Age of the Democratic Revolution* (1959 and 1964), both volumes of which were History Book Club selections, and the first of which won the Bancroft Prize in 1960. He has likewise written *The World of the French Revolution* (1970) and *The Improvement of Humanity: Education and the French Revolution* (1985), and has edited the *Rand McNally Atlas of World History* (1957). He is the translator of Georges Lefebvre's *Coming of the French Revolution* (1947, 1989), Louis Bergeron's *France under Napoleon* (1981), and Jean-Paul Bertaud's *Army of the French Revolution: From Citizen-Soldiers to Instrument of Power* (1988). He was president of the American Historical Association in 1970. He has received honorary degrees from the Universities of Uppsala, Sweden, and Toulouse, France, and was awarded the Antonio Feltrinelli International Prize for History at Rome, Italy, in 1990.

JOEL COLTON was born in New York City. He graduated from the City College of New York, served as a military intelligence officer in Europe in World War II, and received his Ph.D. from Columbia University in 1950. He joined the Department of History at Duke University in 1947, chaired the department from 1967 to 1974, received a Distinguished Teaching Award in 1986, and became emeritus professor in 1989. From 1974 to 1981, on leave from Duke University, he served with the Rockefeller Foundation in New York as director of its research and fellowship program in the humanities. In 1979 he was elected a Fellow of the American Academy of Arts and Sciences and was named a national Phi Beta Kappa lecturer in 1983–1984. He has received Guggenheim, Rockefeller Foundation, and National Endowment for the Humanities fellowships. He has served on the editorial board of the *Journal of Modern History* and of *French Historical Studies,* and on the advisory board of *Historical Abstracts*. He has been vice-president of the Society of French Historical Studies and co-president of the International Commission on the History of Social Movements and Social Structures. His writings include *Compulsory Labor Arbitration in France, 1936–1939* (1951); *Leon Blum: Humanist in Politics* (1966, 1987), for which he received a Mayflower Award; *Twentieth Century* (1968, 1980), in the *Time-Life Great Ages of Man* series; and numerous contributions to journals, encyclopedias, and collaborative volumes.

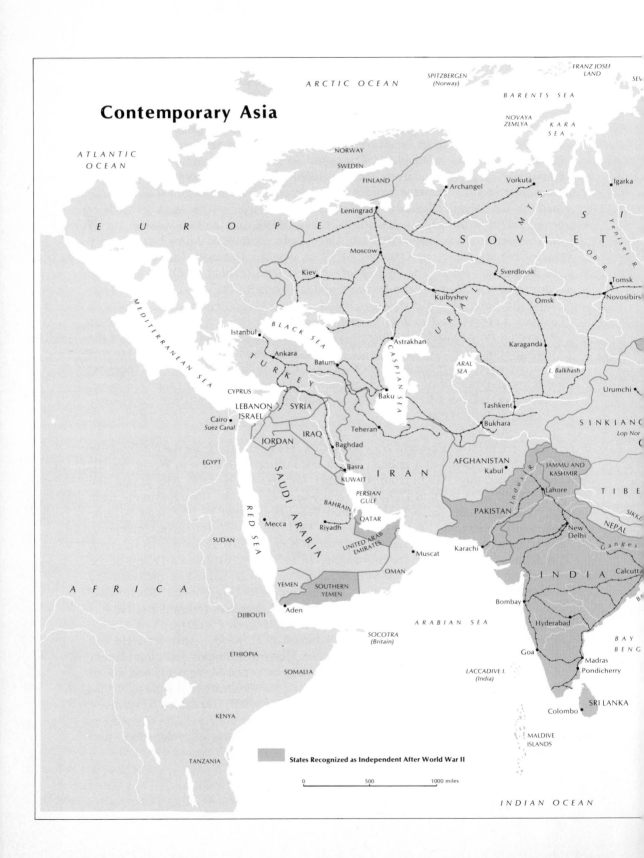

Contemporary Asia

ARCTIC OCEAN

SPITZBERGEN
(Norway)

FRANZ JOSEF
LAND

SEV

BARENTS SEA

NOVAYA
ZEMLYA

KARA
SEA

Vorkuta

Igarka

Archangel

NORWAY

SWEDEN

FINLAND

ATLANTIC
OCEAN

Leningrad

Moscow

Kiev

SOVIET

Sverdlovsk

Kuibyshev

Omsk

Tomsk

Novosibirs

Karaganda

L. Balkhash

Urumchi

MEDITERRANEAN SEA

Istanbul

BLACK SEA

Ankara

Batum

TURKEY

CYPRUS

LEBANON
ISRAEL

Cairo
Suez Canal

SYRIA

JORDAN

IRAQ

Baghdad

Basra

KUWAIT

Astrakhan

CASPIAN SEA

Baku

Teheran

IRAN

ARAL
SEA

Tashkent

Bukhara

AFGHANISTAN

Kabul

SINKIANG

Lop Nor

JAMMU AND
KASHMIR

TIBE

Lahore

EGYPT

SAUDI ARABIA

RED SEA

Mecca

Riyadh

PERSIAN
GULF

BAHRAIN

QATAR

UNITED ARAB
EMIRATES

PAKISTAN

Karachi

New
Delhi

NEPAL

SIKKI

Ganges

Muscat

OMAN

INDIA

Calcutta

SUDAN

Bombay

Hyderabad

AFRICA

YEMEN

SOUTHERN
YEMEN

Aden

ARABIAN SEA

BAY
OF
BENG

DJIBOUTI

SOCOTRA
(Britain)

Goa

Madras

Pondicherry

ETHIOPIA

SOMALIA

LACCADIVE I.
(India)

SRI LANKA

Colombo

KENYA

MALDIVE
ISLANDS

TANZANIA

■ States Recognized as Independent After World War II

0   500   1000 miles

INDIAN OCEAN

ARCTIC OCEAN

WRANGEL I.

NOVO SIBIRSK I.

Bering Strait

ALASKA (U.S.A.)

ALEUTIAN I.

Anadyr

BERING SEA

KOLYMA R.

Lena R.

Yakutsk

Okhotsk

SEA OF OKHOTSK

KAMCHATKA

SAKHALIN

KURILE I.

S I B E R I A

S O V I E T   U N I O N

L. Baikal

Irkutsk

Chita

Amur R.

Sovetskaya Gavan

Khabarovsk

HOKKAIDO

Ulan Bator

MONGOLIAN REPUBLIC

INNER MONGOLIA

MANCHURIA

Harbin

Vladivostok

SEA OF JAPAN

JAPAN

Tokyo

HONSHU

JEHOL

Mukden

NORTH KOREA

SOUTH KOREA

Peking

Tientsin

Lü-Ta

Seoul

Huang Ho

C H I N A

Sian

Tsingtao

SHIKOKU

KYUSHU

Nanking

Shanghai

EAST CHINA SEA

Wuhan

Yangtse Kiang

Chungking

RYUKYU I.

OKINAWA

PACIFIC OCEA'N

WAKE

IWO JIMA

Kunming

Canton

Amoy

Swatow

Taipei

TAIWAN
(Nationalist China)

MARIANA I.

MARSHALL I.

Mekong R.

KWANGSI

Macao
(Portugal)

Hong Kong
(Britain)

MYANMAR
(Burma)

Hanoi

HAINAN

LUZON

U.N. TRUSTEESHIP
U.S.A. ADMINISTRATION

Vientiane

L A O S

VIETNAM

Manila

PHILIPPINE
REPUBLIC

GUAM

YAP

CAROLINE I.

NAURU

Rangoon

THAILAND

Bangkok

CAMBODIA

Phnom Penh

Ho Chi Minh
City

SOUTH CHINA SEA

MINDANAO

PALAU

ANDAMAN I.
(India)

NICOBAR I.
(India)

BRUNEI
(Britain)

NORTH
BORNEO
(SABA)

BISMARCK
ARCHIPELAGO

SOLOMON I.
(Britain)

FEDERATION OF MALAYSIA

SARAWAK

MOLUCCAS

WEST IRIAN

PAPUA-NEW GUINEA

GUADALCANAL

SINGAPORE

Singapore

BORNEO

CELEBES

CERAM

NEW   GUINEA

SUMATRA

I N D O N E S I A

CORAL SEA

Djakarta

JAVA

FLORES

(Portugal)
TIMOR
(Indonesia)

AUSTRALIA

Population Density
Persons per Square Mile

Under 5
5 to 100
101 to 250
Over 250